Legacy of Violence

LEGACY OF VIOLENCE

· A HISTORY OF THE BRITISH EMPIRE ·

Caroline Elkins

Alfred A. Knopf

NEW YORK   2022

Grateful acknowledgment is made to the following for permission to reprint
previously published materials:

HarperCollins Publishers LLC: Excerpts from *Nineteen Eighty-Four* by George
Orwell, copyright © 1949 by HarperCollins Publishers LLC, copyright renewed
1977 by Sonia Brownell Orwell. Reprinted by permission of Mariner Books, an
imprint of HarperCollins Publishers LLC. All rights reserved.

The Times / News Licensing: Excerpt from "Malayan Emergency, II—
Discontents in a Plural Society," Issue 52388 (August 12, 1952).
Reprinted by permission of The Times / News Licensing.

Library of Congress Cataloging-in-Publication Data
Names: Elkins, Caroline, author.
Title: Legacy of violence : a history of the British empire / Caroline Elkins.
Description: First edition. | New York : Alfred A. Knopf, 2022. | "This is
a Borzoi Book published by Alfred A. Knopf." | Includes bibliographical
references and index.
Identifiers: LCCN 2021018550 (print) | LCCN 2021018551 (ebook) |
ISBN 9780307272423 (hardcover) | ISBN 9780593320082 (ebook)
Subjects: LCSH: State-sponsored terrorism—Great Britain—History—
20th century. | Punishment—Great Britain—History—20th century. | Liberalism—
Great Britain—History—20th century. | Imperialism. | Great Britain—Colonies—
Administration—History—20th century. | Great Britain—Colonies—Social
conditions. | Great Britain—Politics and government—20th century.
Classification: LCC JV1062 .E55 2022 (print) | LCC JV1062 (ebook) |
DDC 909/.0971241082—dc23
LC record available at https://lccn.loc.gov/2021018550
LC ebook record available at https://lccn.loc.gov/2021018551

Jacket image: Highlanders during the Indian Mutiny of 1857.
Lebrecht Music & Arts / Alamy
Jacket design by Chip Kidd

Manufactured in the United States of America
1st Printing

For Jake, Andy, and Ingrid

I learned to recognise the thorough and primitive duality of man; I saw that, of the two natures that contended in the field of my consciousness, even if I could rightly be said to be either, it was only because I was radically both.

ROBERT LOUIS STEVENSON,
The Strange Case of Dr. Jekyll and Mr. Hyde

Contents

Author's Note

This book contains derogatory words and phrases, quoted from historical actors, that refer to racial, ethnic, and religious groups. They are offensive. I have chosen to use these words and phrases, in their original forms, because this language represents the attitudes of some historical actors during this period and encodes much of the state-directed violence that I discuss and analyze.

Legacy of Violence

Introduction

Demanding yet denying the human condition makes for an explosive contradiction.

Jean-Paul Sartre
Preface to *The Wretched of the Earth*, 1961

On the overcast afternoon of June 7, 2020, thousands of protesters flooded London's streets where their presence threw into relief an emptiness that the global pandemic had brought to Britain's capital. The void of pedestrian and traffic hum amplified the demonstrators' voices as they reverberated through the city's edifices dedicated to the empire. Indeed, it was the empire and its conflicted past that fueled the crowd's demands. They marched to Westminster, where an oversize statue of Winston Churchill beckoned Parliament to take care of the liberal order that he had so valiantly championed and protected during the high noon of Britain's empire. In death as in life, Churchill was a figure of outsize proportions, and his often-repeated quotes have stood the test of time. "Never give in, never give in, never, never, never," he famously intoned in 1941 to a cadre of impressionable young men at his exclusive alma mater, Harrow School.[1] Yet on that spring day in 2020, the inspired crowd delivered a new message. Clad largely in black with accompanying face masks, the masses gathered around Churchill's statue with fists raised as they chorused, over and again, "Churchill was a racist." A protester with spray paint in hand soon struck out the former prime min-

Statue of Winston Churchill, Parliament Square, London, June 7, 2020

ister's name on the monument's pedestal. The damning words being chanted became the statue's new epitaph.[2]

Demands for racial justice swept through Britain at a time when COVID-19 struck its Black population with the same disproportion already evident in prison populations and police violence. Churchill was not the only historic figure now held to account. Around the time his statue was defaced, another physical testament to empire also went the way of history. In Bristol, a city built on profits gained from the trade and labor of enslaved people, Black Lives Matter demonstrations ignited from backdrafts across the Atlantic. Edward Colston's statue became the target of protesters' fury, and it's not difficult to understand why. Colston was director of the Royal African Company when it forcibly transported around eighty-five thousand African men, women, and children, in conditions so inhumane that nearly a quarter of them perished before they reached the Americas. For over a century, his statue was a monument, for some, to the extraordinary beneficence that Colston bestowed on the city. For others, it represented a nation that still boasted an imperial pride built not only on shameless racial assumptions but also on the backs of countless enslaved and colonized peoples across Britain's empire—an empire that, in its heyday, covered over a quarter of the world's landmass and claimed 700 million people as its subjects. The protesters rendered their judgment when they toppled Colston's statue and launched it into the River Avon.[3]

The silence of Colston's final resting place stood in stark contrast to the debates over the past that haunted and divided the nation. In the eyes of many, Britain had been the purveyor of a benign imperialism that was the standard-bearer for all other empires. For certain, there were blots, like the trade in enslaved peoples, but on history's balance

THE RHODES COLOSSUS
STRIDING FROM CAPE TOWN TO CAIRO.

Cecil Rhodes, "The Rhodes Collosus," *Punch Magazine,* 1892

sheet, any ill-begotten wealth had been more than atoned for through Britain's largesse. When empire's aperture widened to the postemancipation nineteenth and twentieth centuries, the narrative persisted and produced imperial icons like Cecil John Rhodes. Founder of the British South African Company, Rhodes enacted a grandiose "Cape to Cairo" vision with an oppressive hand of economic extraction. He was, according to Oxford's Oriel College, "a businessman and a political deal-maker who prosecuted wars in pursuit of his goals."[4] Rhodes was also a great "race patriot" who had amassed a fortune, in his own words, "exploit[ing] the cheap slave labour that is available from the natives of the colonies."[5] Upon his death in 1902, he bequeathed £100,000 to Oriel College, though the bulk of his money went to the Rhodes Trust and its scholarships for students from the British colonies, the United States, and Germany. For more than a century, Rhodes's statue has gazed at Oxford students—a select few of whom hold the mineral magnate's prestigious fellowship—as they walk past Oriel's north side. This, despite vehement calls for its removal.

Questions over whether "Rhodes must fall" are, of course, proxies for much larger battles over how we in the present remember the past. Debates about the meanings and legacies of Britain's empire are not new. Recent crises, however, spotlight persistent injustices and demand reassessments of how Britain became what it is today. But there are powerful countervailing forces in these "imperial history wars."[6] At Oxford, Regius Professor of Moral and Pastoral Theology Nigel Biggar launched his "Ethics and Empire" project in 2017.[7] The theologian admonishes those who are "wont to assume that domination is an intrinsically bad thing."[8] "Sometimes the imposition of imperial rule," he emphasizes, "can have the salutary effect of imposing a unifying, pacific, and law-abiding order on peoples otherwise inclined to war among themselves."[9] Looking "to develop a nuanced and historically intelligent Christian ethic of empire," Biggar points to real-world implications at stake. "Not allowing our imperial history to be rubbished is important," he emphasizes, "because if indeed our imperial history was all that they say it was, namely a litany of atrocity, then the moral authority of the West is eroded."[10]

In contrast to Biggar's concern with morality, Niall Ferguson's focus is on imperialism's systems and structures. In his blockbuster book *Empire: How Britain Made the Modern World*, the prolific historian champions Britons' noble and triumphant character by stressing their concrete legacies around the globe. "The British Empire," he proclaims, "acted as an agency for imposing free markets, the rule of law, investor protection and relatively incorrupt government on roughly a quarter of the world." Ferguson invites his readers to consider an alternative history. "The imagination reels from the counterfactual of modern history without the British Empire," he insists. "There would be no Calcutta; no Bombay; no Madras. Indians may rename them as many times as they like, but these vast metropoles remain cities founded and built by the British." British ideals and institutions drove unprecedented socioeconomic, legal, and political transformations ushering much of the world into the modern era, Ferguson concludes. "There therefore seems to be a plausible case that the Empire enhanced global welfare—in other words, was a Good Thing."[11]

Biggar and Ferguson are not alone in their views. Nearly 60 percent of the nation, when polled in 2014, believed that "the British Empire was something to be proud of"; more recently, over a quarter of Britons say they want empire back.[12] In June 2016, Britain voted on whether to leave the European Union. Brexit, the portmanteau of *British* and *exit*, won narrowly and memories of empire played no small role. "We have spent 500 years trying to stop continental European powers uniting against us," Boris Johnson reminded his nation in the run-up to the Brexit vote.[13] Such sentiment reflected Britain's long-standing embrace of empire and its ambivalence toward the continent. After the nation entered World War II in September 1939, its vast overseas possessions arguably tipped the scales toward Allied victory. Having imperial winds at its back, the postwar Labour government claimed Big Three status alongside the United States and the Soviet Union. Continental nations laid the foundations for the European Union in 1952, but Britain didn't join until 1973, after it had lost most of its colonies.

"I cannot help remembering," Prime Minister Johnson recently declared, "that this country over the last two hundred years has directed the invasion or conquest of 178 countries—that is most of the members of the UN."[14] The Conservative Party's Brexit campaign touted a "Global Britain" vision, an Empire 2.0. Pushing back his mop of hair and stammering with pride, Johnson reminded his nation that "Churchill was right when he said that the empires of the future will be empires of the mind and in expressing our values I believe that Global Britain is a soft power superpower and that we can be immensely proud of what we are achieving."[15] He urged voters to enact their historically informed destiny. As the influential journalist and author Neal Ascherson observed on the eve of Britain's decision to go it alone: "Behind Brexit stalks the ghost of imperial exception, the feeling that Great Britain can never be just another nation. There's still a providential feeling about Shakespeare's 'sceptred isle' as 'this fortress built by Nature.' "[16]

The British Empire was born from conflict, and coming to terms with its history is no different. To study it is to unlock memory's gate using the key of historical inquiry. But once inside, history's fortress is bewildering. Chimeras abound, spawned hundreds of years ago when Britain began its march toward amassing the largest empire that the world has ever known. Unlike mythical fire-breathing monsters, however, the creatures inhabiting the annals of Britain's imperial past are not illusions. By the nineteenth century, they took fresh breath from a potent ideology of liberal imperialism and from new forms in the British Empire's structures and practices. These monstrosities inflicted untold suffering, though with a deftness that obscured their corrosive effects in images, real and imagined, of imperial reform. The question is, how and why did these enigmatic creatures emerge, develop, and endure? It is also the question behind this book, an account of violence in the British Empire, its origins, institutions, practices, and effects on hundreds of millions of people in the nineteenth and twentieth centuries. The story that unfolds is not the whole story of violence in the empire. This would be impossible to tell in a single account. Instead, my interest lies in British imperialism's entanglement of liberalism, violence, the law, and historical claim making and the ways in which state-directed violence in the British Empire have shaped large parts of the contemporary world.

The arguments that I make unfold in the telling of this lengthy and troublesome story, though setting the broader scene and explaining recurring terms are essential for understanding what follows. The oldest stories of the British Empire read like memorials to a preordained expansion that was various parts secular and religious depending on where one stood. Sprawling across vast territories and bringing order to "savage" landscapes and populations, Britain was to the modern world what the Romans and Greeks were to the ancient one. As with all memorializing, such histories were not pure fiction. In the seventeenth and eighteenth centuries, multimasted ships set sail from a craggy island speck in the North Atlantic. Their knee-breeched crews and motley collection of passengers voyaged across treacherous seas to seek fortune and trade and to claim new territories.

Britain's first empire, as it is often called, was largely a Western one, comprised mostly of free whites, enslaved Black laborers, and indigenous populations dispossessed of land. When the American colonies revolted, Britain suffered a humiliating loss, though it found redemption in a turn to the East. There, in Britain's second empire, imperial ambitions were grandiose. By the nineteenth century, British global expansion and imperialism—or the extension of economic and political control over foreign lands through either informal or formal means—was a defining feature. In search of markets for its goods and capital, Britain preferred to keep the doors of free trade and investment open through informal mechanisms like treaties and the sheer force of its economic dominance. When necessary, however, it would annex a territory and exert formal political control, achieving economic supremacy through protectionist policies, which included tariffs, monopolies, and an accumulation of sterling reserves through a positive trade balance. Whether through informal or formal means, imperialism was a difference of degree, not of kind. Britain exported its investments, manufactured goods, people, language, and culture to the far reaches of the globe while importing raw materials for its factories, food for the nation, and profits for its "gentlemanly capitalists," or financiers, rentiers, and insurance agents who amassed invisible earnings. Through British loans, infrastructure investments, and predatory banking, laissez-faire imperialism rendered places in Latin America as much a sphere of influence as South Africa's Cape of Good Hope or India—where, after 1857, formal annexation and protectionist policies consolidated political control, extortive taxation, and a host of monopolies that included opium and salt.[17]

As the nineteenth century progressed, however, Britain's ability to maintain its empire through informal means diminished. Foreign competition forced British occupations and formal rule in far-flung territories like the Gold Coast, Hong Kong, New Zealand, Kowloon, Sierra Leone, Basutoland, Lagos, and Natal. Some British statesmen balked at further territorial acquisitions. Annexations, though deemed necessary to safeguard the nation's commercial and strategic interests, were expensive. Part of this expense lay in the violence necessary to wrest and maintain control. In the nineteenth century, there were over 250 separate armed conflicts in the British Empire, with at least one in any given year. Among them were revolts in Barbados, Demerara (British Guiana), Ceylon, St. Vincent, and Jamaica. They also included sustained efforts to conquer and dominate—or "pacify" as Britain termed it—the Ashante in the Gold Coast; the Mahdists in Sudan; the Xhosa, Zulu, and Afrikaners in South Africa; the Afghans in Central Asia; and the Burmese in South Asia. Rudyard Kipling called these conflicts the "savage wars of peace": some were short, others protracted and recurring. They became part of imperial life, consuming British manpower, lives, and taxpayer funds while devastating local populations.[18]

Ruling over hundreds of millions of conquered subjects, most of whom were Black or brown, and neither enslaved nor free, presented new challenges. How could Britain justify and maintain its domination of conquered peoples at a time when liberal ideals were rendering its own nation-state increasingly democratic?[19] Before turning to this question, I need to offer some general points about nation-states, as their emergence and peculiarities have implications for our story.[20] Nation-states are a fusion of tangible and subjective realities. The state is largely a political and geographical entity, whereas a nation is a cultural construction comprised of ideas and sentiments. Today, the modern state is the bedrock of our international order. It maintains and defends its own sovereignty, or exclusive and complete control over the people and territory within its borders, and this sovereignty is recognized legally and diplomatically by other states. It also gives rise to complex bureaucracies, including systems of law, taxation, and education. Nations are groups of people who see themselves as sharing a common language, religion, set of traditions, and history—or an identity—that binds them together into an "imagined community," as the political scientist Benedict Anderson once called it.[21] An ideal nation-state is a sovereign state governing a culturally unique nation, and its government is a collection of people through which the state's power is deployed.

The making of the United Kingdom of Great Britain and Northern Ireland—or the modern nation-state called Britain—is often told as a founding story awash with calamity and faith, toil and carnage. After surviving civil wars, a Glorious Revolution giving rise to a constitutional monarchy, and acts of union yoking the United Kingdom together, in the nineteenth century Britain engaged in a bloodless battle. Armed with quills, inkwells, and thoughts scratched onto parchment, towering political philosophers like Adam Smith, Thomas Carlyle, John Stuart Mill, and James Fitzjames Stephen debated liberalism and its political, economic, and legal meanings. This universal philosophy contained the promise of a more inclusive nation-state through the extension of the franchise and protection of property rights, free trade, and equality before the law. It was a bold vision of human progress and inevitable improvement where Britain—with its sovereignty, bureaucracy, rule of law, and peaceful free trade and capitalist exchanges—would vanquish old forms of despotism. No longer would a monarch hold absolute power, nor would justice be arbitrary and displayed with severed heads of alleged criminals stuck onto stakes to deter others from defying local authorities.

Nineteenth-century philosophers drew on earlier foundational works including those of Thomas Hobbes and John Locke, whose ideas would impact domestic and imperial ideas of the state, sovereignty, and law. Often seen as the founder of the modern theory of state formation and sovereignty, Hobbes produced his canonical book *Leviathan* in 1651. Writing during the English Civil War, he pointed to man's predisposition to live by the "laws of nature" with its savagery and argued for replacing such anarchy with highly centralized state authority. "During the time men live without a common power to keep them all in awe, they are in that condition which is called war; and such a war as is of every man against every man," Hobbes famously wrote. During man's natural anarchical state, there was "no account of time; no arts; no letters; no society; and which is worst of all, continual fear, and danger of violent death; and the life of man, solitary, poor, nasty, brutish, and short."[22] For Hobbes a "social contract," whereby free and rational individuals would give up self-interested rights and submit to an absolute sovereign, was the basis for a civil society. He believed no reasonable person would prefer the "State of Nature" over mediating violence through the state.

Whereas *Leviathan* argued for absolute government, Locke rejected undivided and unlimited sovereign power. In *Two Treatises of Government*, he offered a less nihilistic notion of "nasty, brutish, and short."[23] For Locke, the State of Nature had no government, though it was not lacking morality. War occurred when property disputes erupted in the absence of civil authority to mediate them. "Conjugal society," or nuclear families, could create political societies when their male leaders came together and agreed to hand over their power to an executive who kept the peace and exacted punishments. Creating and consenting to a political society and government, men created a new compact, or social contract, with its benefits of laws, judges to adjudicate these laws, and an executive power to enforce the laws. United into "commonwealths," men thus preserved their liberty, lives, property, and general well-being, and laws tamed violence by displacing it from the right of the individual, or natural man, to the right of the state. Indeed, the social contract became foundational for Western liberal societies and nineteenth-century conceptions of a more inclusive nation-state.

Hobbes did not directly address the question of race and empire, though Locke's important interventions on the question of property rights defended his nation's claims to colonial settlements in its first empire.[24] When nineteenth-century liberalism confronted distant places and "backward" people bound by strange religions, hierarchies, and sentimental and dependent relationships, its universalistic claims withered.[25] Britons viewed their imperial center, or metropole, as culturally distinct from their empire, or colonial periphery. Skin color became *the* mark of difference. Whites were at one end of civilization's spectrum, Blacks at the other. All other shades of humanity fell somewhere between, and skin pigment was the visible brand of cultural difference. Race set the terms of rationality and irrationality, civilized and uncivilized.[26]

White settler colonies, which included Canada, New Zealand, and Australia, also adopted such attitudes toward local indigenous populations. The nineteenth-century historian John Seeley, considered the founder of British imperial history, called the polity of settler colonies, separated by oceans and spanning continents, "Greater Britain." Together they preserved British geopolitical, economic, and cultural strength in a world of increasing competition, particularly from Germany and the United States.[27] These "Greater Britain" territories, while they inflicted violent damage on local populations, are not the focus of our story. Rather, the second empire, with colonial governing structures linked directly to London, will be, including Ireland and the two Afrikaner republics of South Africa. In both of these instances, physical skin color was not the marker of local populations' differences; instead, it was a constructed skin color. In effect, Britain "racialized" the Irish and Afrikaners, equating their cultures to those of brown and Black subjects, sometimes using dehumanizing language to describe their physical appearances and living conditions, and believing that, just like the Xhosa of South Africa or the Chinese in Malaya, the Irish and Afrikaners were "backward" populations that needed to be civilized.

A contested though coherent ideology of liberal imperialism emerged that integrated Britain's sovereign claims to empire with a massive undertaking to reform imperial subjects and shepherd them into the modern world. In the mid-nineteenth century, liberal imperialism found further expression in scientific racism's evolutionary model. Developmentalism cleaved to racial hierarchies that likened colonial subjects to children who needed paternalistic guidance to reach full maturity. Like children, empire's "barbarians," as John Stuart Mill called them, were malleable, and British rule would eventually render them rational, respectful of law and order, and prepared to participate in the inviolable social contract that bound modern people and states together in the international world order. The "civilizing mission," as it was known, would take decades if not centuries to carry out this noble enterprise. In the meantime, Britain would shoulder its responsibility for humanity's sake. It had a moral duty to do so. It was, to borrow Rudyard Kipling's famous phrase, the "White Man's Burden."[28]

This is part of our story. If Britain's civilizing mission was reformist in its claims, it was brutal nonetheless. Violence was not just the British Empire's midwife, it was endemic to the structures and systems of British rule. It was not just an occasional means to liberal imperialism's end; it was a means and an end for as long as the British Empire remained alive. Without it, Britain could not have maintained its sovereign claims to its colonies. Indeed, how could it have been otherwise? Much as Hobbes had suggested, the sociologist Max Weber explained in "Politics as a Vocation" that a monopoly over the means of legitimate violence is a necessary condition for a state's existence—a monopoly divested to police forces who enforced the law and the military who waged war.[29] This was as true with the formation of Britain's modern state as it was for its colonies. States-in-the-making always flex their coercive powers while laying claim to sovereignty. In Britain's case, despotism gave way to newfound processes, none more sacrosanct than the rule of law. By the nineteenth century, legal codes and procedures replaced arbitrary justice and publicly inflicted pain, defined sanctioned violence, and became the state's crucial legitimating instrument. From it emerged a bureaucratic web of officials and institutions that, however haltingly, administered a more inclusive body politic.

Turning to the empire, political philosophers like Mill and James Fitzjames Stephen insisted that "good government" would reform backward populations.[30] For them, imposing the rule of law was Pax Britannica's most potent elixir. Stephen was a deep admirer of Hobbes and believed in a kind of imperial *Leviathan*, where liberal lawfulness and the colonial state's monopoly of violence would mediate peace and civilize society. Stephen was unequivocal on this point: "the establishment of a system of law which regulates the most important part of the daily life of a people constitutes in itself a moral conquest, more striking, more durable, and far more solid than the physical conquest renders it possible. It exercises an influence over the minds of the people in many ways comparable to that of a new religion. . . . Our law is, in fact, the sum and substance of what we have to teach them. It is, so to speak, the gospel of the English, and it is a compulsory gospel which admits of no dissent and of no disobedience."[31]

British colonial officials were obsessed with this "compulsory gospel," particularly the legitimation that law bestowed on violence. But good government in empire was liberalism's fever dream. Its rule of law codified difference, curtailed freedoms, expropriated land and property, and ensured a steady stream of labor for the mines and plantations that fed Britain's domestic economy. A state's claim to legitimacy is always open to dispute, but such contestations were rampant in the empire where Britain imposed sovereignty over populations who ostensibly never had it. The developmentalist approach to their reform was pregnant with conflict not least because liberal imperialism contained within it seeds for the colonial state's own unmaking. Britain would eventually have to concede its sovereign claims to empire, though only when its discerning eye judged the once uncivilized to be fully evolved. This *when* was always elusive, however. If subject populations demanded basic rights over their own bodies and freedoms, the colonial state often criminalized them, cast their actions—including vandalism, labor strikes, and riots—as political threats, and invested police forces with legally conferred powers for suppression.[32] It was a developmentalist panopticon in which Britain used its subjects' criminality, or illegitimate violence, as further justification for the civilizing mission's boundless time horizon.

Indigenous populations did not passively accept their fates. Violence was not rolled out onto supine bodies; rather resistance and protest came in many forms, from subversive labor activities like foot dragging, crop destruction, and strikes to deploying the civilizing mission's own logic to demand freedom and equal rights. Across the empire, twentieth-century nationalists decried Britain's unfulfilled liberal promises, as did their supporters in Britain and the United States. These demands crested after the Second World War, when it became clear that the Atlantic Charter's assurance of self-determination didn't apply to British colonial subjects. Instead, in return for their extraordinary wartime contributions and sufferings, hundreds of millions of subjects remained unfree and were subjected to more intensive and systematized forms of colonial control.

British rule was most strained when these demands for liberalism's universalist ideals whiffed of insurrections-in-the-making or blew up into full-scale rebellions.[33] These were crises of legitimacy. Britain feared they would plunge the empire into a Hobbesian world of anarchical violence and incivility. With centuries to go before imperial subjects matured into rational beings, disciplinary crackdowns were needed to pull them out of their moral backsliding. The military was often called in to aid colonial police forces struggling to regain order. Together they were known as security forces, and they didn't just enforce colonial laws to crush these existential threats to the state; they also made them.

Ordinary codes and regulations proved insufficient in quelling empire's rebellions and Britain's spectral fears, so colonial officials turned to legal exceptionalism in the form of martial law and states of emergency, or statutory martial law.[34] While lawful, these states of exception granted extraordinary power to the military and to the government's executive branch. Decision making was left to the men on the spot, and their discretionary authority was staggering. They interpreted when violence was necessary, and at what intensity level, to protect the state and preserve its laws. When security forces needed more discretion, or when their actions constituted unsanctioned violence, the state often rendered their lawless behavior legal by amending old regulations and creating new ones. This tautological process of law creation—of incrementally legalizing, bureaucratizing, and legitimating exceptional state-directed violence when ordinary laws proved insufficient for maintaining order and control—is something I term "legalized lawlessness."[35] As the twentieth century progressed, legalized lawlessness was a recurring phenomenon, and the exception became the norm as British security forces deployed ever-intensifying forms of systematic violence that made empire look like a recurring conquest state.

Repression was about much more than reestablishing British authority. Violence enacted on bodies, minds, souls, cultures, landscapes, communities, and histories was intimately connected to the civilizing mission's developmentalist dogma.[36] In other words, it wasn't just the structures of colonial rule that shaped coercive systems and practices, it was liberal imperialism's ideology as well. It oftentimes cast nationalists and freedom fighters—however complicated their demands—not just as criminals but as terrorists barely clinging to the lowest rung of humanity. Sometimes they would lose their grip and slide into the dehumanizing ether. Coercion would subdue and domesticate them. As Victorian-era parents disciplined their progeny, recalcitrant childlike natives in the empire had to be punished. In a perversion of Proverbs 13:24, "Whoever spares the rod hates his son, but he who loves him is diligent to discipline him," colonial officials and security forces wanted their infantilized subjects to see and feel their own suffering.[37] They wanted them to know it was deliberate and purposeful. Britain had a term for this: the "moral effect" of violence.[38]

Those writing about colonial capitalism read violence in Britain's empire not as a consequence of reform's morality but as the result of brute economic extraction. For writers like Vladimir Lenin and Walter Rodney, the history of the British Empire was inseparable from Britain's economy.[39] With the onset of the industrial revolution, demands for raw materials and for cheap labor to extract them were voracious. The rise of the new global industrial order brought harsh labor regimes to colonial plantations and mines. This unremitting extraction of economic and social value from nonwhite workers is something political scientist Cedric J. Robinson called "racial capitalism." "The development, organization, and expansion of capitalist society pursued essentially racial directions, so too did social ideology," Robinson wrote. "As a material force, then, it could be expected that racialism would inevitably permeate the social structures emergent from capitalism."[40] Histories of racial capitalism and other theories of economic imperialism are abundant, and while I agree that economic extraction is a cornerstone of any story of Britain's empire, it is not my primary focus. Instead, colonial economies and disciplinary labor violence are always there in the background and will enter center stage of our story when ordinary colonial laws and policing could not control labor unrest in the empire.

Violence, the law, and the state congealed during Britain's recurring crises of imperial legitimacy, and these crises often had many dimensions beyond economic ones. By moving ourselves away from arguments only about capitalism's unremitting brutality, we see that violence was inherent to liberalism. It resided in liberalism's reformism, its claims to modernity, its promises of freedom, and its notion of the law—exactly the opposite places where one normally associates violence. If we think about violence in the British Empire as only about brute economic extraction, then our story doesn't tell us much about why liberalism's paradoxical qualities of coercion and reform accreted over time throughout Britain's empire. In fact, the perennial problem of liberalism and violence underwrites many of Britain's current imperial history wars and is also embedded in the nation's contemporary racial issues as well as those of other Western liberal democracies.

In the pages that follow, my concern is less with prosaic forms of coercion, as insidious as they were, than with the "exceptional" and dramatic moments of physical and epistemological violence that accompanied legitimacy crises and required the replacement of ordinary laws and policing with martial or statutory martial law and the deployment of security forces. Such violence included corporal punishments, deportations, detentions without trial, forced migrations, killings, sexual assaults, tortures, and accompanying psychological terror, humiliation, and loss. I'm seeking to explain why and how Britain enacted these large-scale measures and the ways in which Britons understood, legitimated, and re-legitimated them.

Some of the historical events I investigate may be familiar to readers: the Indian Mutiny, the Morant Bay Rebellion, the South African War, the Irish War of Independence, the Arab Revolt, Caribbean strikes, the Zionist Uprising, and states of emergency in Malaya, Kenya, and Cyprus. These moments, which often lasted years and were interconnected through the transference of laws, practices, and personnel around the empire, render most visible and vivid Britain's regimes of colonial oppression, hierarchies of racialized power and difference, systems for deploying legalized lawlessness, and the legitimations that accompanied them. In these episodes, the quotidian coercion punctuating British rule gave way to unimaginable extremes that Britons had to disavow, excise, or somehow accommodate within liberal imperialism's narrative of reform and progress.

Everyone would have a role to play in imagining an exceptionalism that transcended empire's underbelly. "I declare before you all that my whole life whether it be long or short," a youthful Elizabeth proclaimed in her famous 1947 radio address, "shall be devoted to your service and the service of our great imperial family to which we all belong."[41] It is said that the princess wept when first reading this speech. Broadcasting it on her twenty-first birthday from a bougainvillea-studded garden in Cape Town, she marked her destiny using time-worn images and

H.R.H. Princess Elizabeth, Twenty-first Birthday Speech, Cape Town, South Africa, April 19, 1947

inventing new ones. The future Queen Elizabeth II would become the embodiment of Britain and its Commonwealth and empire. This she knew. "If we all go forward together with an unwavering faith, a high courage, and a quiet heart," she beseeched, "we shall be able to make of this ancient commonwealth, which we all love so dearly, an even grander thing—more free, more prosperous, more happy and a more powerful influence for good in the world—than it has been in the greatest days of our forefathers."[42]

Empire was not just a few threads in Britain's national cloth. It was the fabric from which the modern British nation was made, and monarchy was the weft to its warp, from the time Queen Victoria ascended as Empress of India in 1877.[43] Beyond the iron gates of Buckingham Palace was a compelling gestalt, an imperial nationalism that conveyed a deeply essentialist and self-centered view of the world. For many Britons, the empire conferred gravitas and rendered their nation-state a singular giant in the international global order. When whispering her birthday missive into the BBC's microphone, Princess Elizabeth affirmed this: "We must not be daunted by the anxieties and hardships that the war has left behind for every nation of our commonwealth. We know that these things are the price we cheerfully undertook to pay for the high honour of standing alone, seven years ago, in defence of the liberty of the world."[44] A stroke of cultural genius, the message did not easily betray the ways in which British national identity was constantly adapting to changes in the empire and the broader global system of which it was a part. In fact, the empire's heroes, symbols, and rituals, nationalism's lifeblood, endured because of Britain's ability over the turbulent nineteenth and twentieth centuries to develop and work out in ever more complex ways liberal imperialism's meanings, policies, and practices.

Some may say that I'm using the term *liberal imperialism* anachronistically, that it was specific to late Victorian debates over empire, or that liberal imperialism, with its explicit moral purpose, waned and transformed in the aftermath of two explosive nineteenth-century events: the Indian Mutiny and Jamaica's Morant Bay Rebellion.[45] At the time, liberal imperialism's critics cast doubt on Britain's ability to improve inscrutable indigenous societies that were resistant to or addled by modernizing demands. Hard-nosed men like Stephen called for unapologetic authoritarian rule. Others took a more sociological approach to jettisoning reform. Rather than administering developmentalist policies, colonial officials would rule through invigorated native systems of authority and "customary laws" that regulated traditional societies. It was a strategic move to protect against instability and unrest in the Asian and African colonies. This new British governing structure was called "indirect rule."[46]

But liberal imperialism was not time-bound; nor was indirect rule paradigmatic of Britain's approach to empire after the late Victorian era. Dual systems of authority and legitimation coexisted in the British Empire. Customary laws and local leaders who upheld them were one part of it. Parallel legal regimes that protected the state and its colonial economy were the other, and they are the focus of this story. In fact, British colonial rule did not divest its monopoly over violence to pashas and princes and chiefs; rather, Britain legitimated state violence by bringing it into the colonial Leviathan. Customary systems often left indigenous leaders at the bottom of the colonial hierarchy, and they were not adjudicating crimes that violated the social contract. Nor were they calling the shots when it came to suspending ordinary laws and deploying security forces.[47]

We will explore, in the telling of this story, how nineteenth-century events signaled the birth of liberal imperialism and the ways in which deeply contentious and recurring debates were most revealing during violent ruptures in empire. There was no retrenchment from the ideology's saliency, however. Liberal imperialism's capaciousness evolved over time and accommodated a constellation of political philosophers, British statesmen, and agents of empire. They repeatedly debated imperial policies and practices, always tethering them to the civilizing mission's progressive and coercive assumptions in one form or another. Liberal imperialism endured because reform and repression were *both* inherent to its idiom and systems. Its perennial play of universality against racial difference also rippled through the global imperial order. Britain may have been a purveyor of liberal imperial ideals, but it existed in a competitive global system that also sought to dominate non-Western populations.

"I think there is only one ideal that the British Empire can set before itself in this regard," Winston Churchill declared to the 1921 Imperial Conference, "and that is there should be no barriers of race, colour, or creed which should prevent any man by merit from reaching any station if he is fitted for it. . . . But such a principle has to be very carefully and gradually applied because intense local feelings are excited."[48] Empire's top-hatted and self-assured white representatives had gathered behind heavy wooden doors and undrawn draperies in London to deliberate the empire's policies. At the table were two brown-skinned and turbaned delegates, Sir Khengarji III, King of India's Princely State of Kutch and former aide-de-camp to Queen-Empress Victoria, and V. S. Srinivasa Sastri, an Indian statesman. They were shining examples of native potential in an empire tormented by violence.

The conference's summer swelter of imperial debate turned to "trusteeship," the sacred trust between paternalistic rulers and their subjects.[49] It was a topic that would bedevil other imperial conferences in the years ahead as trusteeship expanded beyond its eighteenth-century British origin. It had informed policy for Africa when European delegates met in Berlin in 1884 and 1885 to divvy up the continent. They agreed "to regulate the conditions most favourable to the development of trade and civilization . . . [and] to watch over the preservation of the native tribes, and to care for the improvement of the conditions of their moral and material well-being."[50] After the Great War, League of Nations members divided up the former German and Ottoman empires. The Treaty of Versailles called the war's territorial spoils "mandates" that were "inhabited by peoples *not yet* able to stand by themselves under the strenuous conditions of the modern world," and it consecrated "the principle that the well-being and development of such peoples form a sacred trust of civilisation."[51]

The Second World War signaled the mandate system's demise, though the Versailles Treaty's emphasis on "peoples *not yet* able to stand by themselves" survived. To secure an Anglo-American alliance, Britain maneuvered through American anti-imperialist demands by replacing outdated ideas with new reform efforts. Trusteeship became "partnership," and Britain granted more local political participation in the empire. Churchill's wartime government announced the Colonial Development and Welfare Act, committing £55 million in grants and loans for its subjects' material improvements. But universal rights and self-rule were still not in the offing to an empire that had carried Britain through the war and guaranteed the tiny island nation's claims to Big Three status when the fighting was over. Churchill met Franklin Roosevelt and Joseph Stalin in the winter of 1945 on Crimea's frigid shores, where peacetime talks veered away from Britain's empire. A few months later delegates from fifty Allied nations gathered in San Francisco to hash out the UN charter. Despite vociferous protests from non-Western nations and interest groups, the international organization's founding document affirmed imperialism's place in the new world order. The charter referred to Europe's colonies as "non-self-governing territories" and outlined the "progressive development" of their "peoples and their varying stages of advancement." Colonizing powers also guaranteed "just treatment" and "protection against abuses," pledging to maintain a "sacred trust" that recognized "the interests of the inhabitants of these territories are paramount . . . within the system of international peace and security."[52]

Words on paper were hollow, particularly when they collided with the postwar Labour government's imperial resurgence strategy. In theory, closer partnership with the empire would rescue Britain's embattled economy and ensure its superpower status, even if it meant boots on the ground. Abiding tensions between universal rights and racial differences exploded. The empire began to unravel, but the practice and language of liberal reform was always part of imperial conflicts. Britain even cast the postwar empire's most draconian system of violence—the detention camps and villages of Malaya and Kenya—as redemptive. States of emergency were not wars but campaigns for British subjects' "hearts and minds." So-called terrorists and their supporters could be reformed. Behind barbed wires of detention, civics and home craft lessons would liberate them, as would forced labor's sweat and toil and torture's unfathomable pain. Britain had a new name for this, too. No longer called the "moral effect," it was now "rehabilitation." The empire's lexicon also had other expressions for it. "*Mwiteithia Niateithagio*"—"Abandon hope all ye who enter here"—hung over the entrance to one of Kenya's most notorious detention camps.[53]

By the late 1950s, atrocities in Kenya exposed liberalism's perfidiousness, and Britain had to publicly account for itself to the empire's critics at home and abroad. This twentieth-century scandal was not the first one. There had been others, including those in South Africa, India, Ireland, Palestine, Malaya, and Cyprus. Each instance brought new debates, and somehow Britain always managed to reconcile the logic of necessary violence with its civilizing mission. But the accretion of these scandals eroded Britain's defenses and legitimacy. They also raised questions about the empire's economic toll. Was Britain's postwar imperial resurgence strategy a wise one? Had nationalism gotten in the way of fiscal logic? Recurring and drawn-out empire wars cost taxpayers millions of pounds sterling. There were also opportunity costs. Soldiers were economically productive at home, and perhaps Britain would be better off with an informal empire, much like that of the nineteenth century? Retooled as the British Commonwealth of Nations, white dominions like Canada and Australia, together with colonies ready to stand on their own, formed a political and cultural community that owed allegiance to the queen. The Commonwealth would be the triumphant coda to the greatest empire in world history.

"*Ne vous inquiétez pas.* Compared to the French in Algeria, you are angels of mercy," Henri Junod told a British colonial officer when touring Kenya's detention system in 1957.[54] A delegate of the International Committee of the Red Cross, Junod was not alone in rendering such a comparison. A few years earlier, the world-renowned political theorist Hannah Arendt had published *The Origins of Totalitarianism*, a treatise built on the works of Hobbes and other philosophers. Arendt was quick to point out that *Leviathan*'s author had said "nothing of modern race doctrines. . . . But Hobbes at least provided political thought with the prerequisite for all race doctrines, that is, the exclusion in principle of the idea of humanity which constitutes the sole regulating idea of international law. . . . Racism may indeed carry out the doom of the Western world and, for that matter, of the whole of human civilization."[55] While Arendt believed that in empire "Frenchmen have assumed the role of commanders of a *force noire*, when Englishmen have turned into 'white men,'" she also cleaved to British exceptionalism.[56] "The [French] enterprise was a particularly brutal exploitation of overseas possessions for the sake of the nation," she wrote. "Compared with this blind desperate nationalism, British imperialists . . . looked like guardians of the self-determination of peoples."[57] Some historians contributing to the recent imperial history wars concur: "French wars were always bloodier than those of the British."[58] "Just as the scale of France's wars of decolonisation was far larger than Britain's, so abuses by security forces were also more numerous and perhaps more systematic."[59] The French Empire is not their only reference point: "Faced with similar disturbances [to those Britain encountered], other imperial powers responded much more harshly than the British did. . . . This does not excuse British abuses . . . but it provides some comparative context."[60] In the twentieth century, Germany, Spain, Portugal, Italy, and Belgium all ruled over colonized populations, though when held up against these other European nations, France has always been Britain's bête noire.

Turning to history's balance sheet to determine which European empire was more or less brutal than others can be an invidious exercise. Historians usher objective data to make their case: body counts, number of soldiers on the ground, official reports. But all evidence is subjective, particularly that which is mediated through state bureaucracies. Junod is a case in point. He privately told Kenya's governor that detainees needed a "violent shock"—it "was the price to be paid for" their acquiescence and reform. This "violent shock" was called the "dilution technique," though Junod made no mention of it in his final report, which is catalogued in an official archive.[61] Truth telling can't be found in numbers either. Governments routinely massaged them, under- or overreporting their counts to suit political needs.

What we do know is that all empires were violent. Coercion was central to initial acts of conquest and to the maintenance of rule over nonconsenting populations. How this violence was systematized, enacted, and understood varied. For instance, there was nothing reformist about Belgian king Leopold II's bloody rule in the Congo. He took control of a massive swath of Africa's interior in 1885 and for two decades enabled concession companies to force Africans to labor, using horrific methods, in order to extract rubber.[62] In South West Africa, Germany's military descended into "dysfunctional extremes of violence," nearly wiping out the Herero and Nama peoples, as the historian Isabel V. Hull tells us. Chancellor Otto von Bismarck's constitution isolated the army from external oversight and critique, and its militarism snowballed in Germany's empire and informed fascism's advance.[63] Arendt called this the "boomerang effect," and it was not isolated to Hitler's rise. She looked at Europe's race thinking and "wild murdering" and "terrible massacres" in the colonies and saw in them the origins of European totalitarianism. "When the European mob discovered what a 'lovely virtue' a white skin could be in Africa, when the English conqueror in India became an administrator," Arendt wrote, "convinced of his own innate capacity to rule and dominate, when the dragon-slayers turned into either 'white men' of 'higher breeds' or into bureaucrats and spies . . . the stage seemed to be set for all possible horrors. Lying under anybody's nose were many of the elements which gathered together could create a totalitarian government on the basis of racism."[64]

The British Empire and totalitarian regimes were not the same thing, even if some eyewitnesses reported striking similarities.[65] In fact, Britain's empire looked most like France's. They both wrestled with liberal ideals and racial difference, and their reformism included an end to empire even if their ruling structures and colonial cultures differed. "France is not a country of forty millions; she is a country of one hundred millions," Prime Minister Raymond Poincaré famously announced in 1923.[66] The French Empire was incorporated into the nation's political structure, as dark-skinned delegates from the colonies took seats in the French parliament and Algeria became a department of France. Yet *fraternité* and ideas of a common French civilization rested uncomfortably with race, subjecthood, and French demands for empire's economic and military manpower.[67] In Britain's case, colonial subjects wouldn't have representation in London, except the Irish for a time. No matter how rational and civilized subjects became, they would never *be* British. Violence was endemic in both empires, yet it was Britain's that became metonymic with imperial exception. This was no accident. "The legend of the British Empire," Arendt tells us, "has little to do with the realities of British imperialism. . . . No political structure could have been more evocative of legendary tales and justifications than the British Empire."[68]

My interest resides with the British Empire because it took on a particular configuration that became increasingly violent over time while extolling liberalism's virtues in such a way that it could legitimate episodes of extreme coercion as unfortunate exceptions to modernity's evolutionary triumph. It was not, of course, the only nation that spoke of a civilizing mission and rule of law's virtues. France in particular did this too. But Britain was the nation boasting history's largest empire, whose heroes and justifications led many astray. The legacies Britain's empire left behind have had significant bearings on a quarter of the world's landmass where nations were born out of a cauldron of violence. It is a world where the colonial state rarely had the recognition of legitimate sovereignty from its subjects. Instead, the social contract was forced upon them, and the nationalism and independent states that colonial subjects created would go on to include many of liberalism's contradictions. Delivering a potent colonial critique in *The Wretched of the Earth*, the French West Indian political philosopher Frantz Fanon insisted that formerly colonized people would never free themselves until they moved beyond the liberal nation-state and its paradoxes.[69] This question is also percolating in contemporary Britain and other Western democracies. At a time when some Britons are demanding an imperial reckoning, however, the nation's majority is embracing Prime Minister Boris Johnson's Empire 2.0. Britain's imperial nationalism has endured and is underwriting Britain's belief that the tiny island nation is a giant ready to stake its historically informed claim to the world. In no other contemporary nation-state does imperial nationalism endure with such explicit social, political, and economic consequences. This endurance begs explanation.

I wrote this book because my previous work, *Imperial Reckoning: The Untold Story of Britain's Gulag in Kenya*, raised unanswered questions about violence in the British Empire. It documented the systematic violence that took place in Kenya's detention camps during the Mau Mau Emergency (1952–60). *Imperial Reckoning*'s research was arduous because countless documents were missing from the official archives in

London and Nairobi. I spent years sifting through remaining fragments of evidence and also amassed other historical sources from private document collections, newspaper archives, and hundreds of interviews that I undertook with former colonial officials and survivors of the detention system. During the course of this research, I recognized that for many British officials and security force members Kenya was not their first colonial war, and for others it would not be their last. Some suggested that Kenya's settler community and its virulent racism rendered the colony unique. But perhaps Kenya wasn't so exceptional? I felt I had stepped into a historical moment that was part of a bigger connective story about imperial violence after the Second World War that began in Palestine and moved to Malaya, Kenya, Cyprus, and Aden. It was this story that I set out to investigate over a decade ago.

Imperial Reckoning's afterlife also raised new challenges and questions. In 2009 five survivors of Kenya's detention system sued the British government in London's Royal Courts of Justice for the systematic violence and torture they had endured in the 1950s.[70] My research provided evidence for their unprecedented legal claim, and I served as an expert witness on the claimants' behalf. The case lasted four years, and as part of legal discovery, the British Foreign and Commonwealth Office (FCO), the named defendant in the suit, made a stunning announcement. It "discovered" three hundred boxes of previously unreleased files at Hanslope Park, the highly secure government facility known as "spook central" because it also contained top secret MI5 and MI6 files. At the time of decolonization, colonial officials had packed up these newly discovered Kenyan files and spirited them away from Africa. Alongside these boxes, the FCO found 8,800 files from thirty-six other colonies that had similarly been removed and brought to London at the end of empire. The newly released Kenya files were of great importance to the claimants' case. They also had enormous bearing on my research for this book, particularly the new evidence illuminating the document destruction process. This evidence revealed how British officials had culled and burned files on the eve of decolonization. Similar to the violence they inflicted on subject populations, their document destruction methods became more systematic and intense over time. The archives emerged as part of the bigger story I was seeking to tell about the postwar British Empire.[71]

They also prompted a rethinking of this book's time horizon. I expanded my historical inquiry to include the decades preceding World War II, thinking it would supplement archival gaps and illuminate my sought-after answers. This shift revealed the ways in which the Second

World War is a somewhat arbitrary dividing line in the British Empire's *longue durée* of ideas, policies, and practices. What was to be an introductory chapter morphed into nearly half this book's length as I stretched its time frame back into the nineteenth century and even to eighteenth-century moments that set the stage for the logics of violence that would underwrite much of Britain's twentieth-century empire. These logics, entrenched as they were in liberal imperialism, would evolve over time and were often transferred from one part of the empire to another through the movement of people—whether they were low-level police officers and colonial administrators or other illustrious heroes of the empire's past like Field Marshals Herbert Kitchener and Bernard Montgomery. The legal codes that underwrote the empire moved through transference as well. One governor or high commissioner borrowed from another as he sought to quash insurgent demands and the will of their civilian supporters by enabling security measures through lawful exceptionalism. Intelligence operatives also crisscrossed the globe and brought with them time-honed techniques for getting colonial subjects to cooperate.

But liberal imperialism was never just about those who wielded political power. It was also a story of demands from below—demands for dignity and rights that, in the aftermath of Allied victory over the forces of fascism and incipient cries of "never again," were encoded in universal human rights declarations and conventions as well as in updated humanitarian laws. This human rights regime, however, was not a given for those in empire. "The war, notwithstanding the professions of statesmen," George Padmore wrote, his indignation burning, "is certainly not one for Democracy."[72] At the center of Britain's Black radical thought, Padmore was part of a global network of anti-imperialist writers and activists calling for racial justice and an end to empire. "We have conquered Germany . . . but not their ideas," W. E. B. Du Bois fumed during the UN Charter negotiations. "We still believe in white supremacy, keeping Negroes in their place and lying about democracy when we mean imperial control of 750 millions of human beings in colonies."[73] The Black diaspora gathered in Manchester for the Pan-African Congress in 1945 and presciently warned that "as a last resort, [Africans] may have to appeal to force in an effort to achieve Freedom, even if force destroys them and the world."[74]

Across the empire, the language of freedom included universal rights. The UN Declaration on Human Rights with its talk of "inherent dignity" and "inalienable rights" was deeply aspirational, though it was just a declaration.[75] Once signed and ratified, however, postwar human rights conventions were enforceable, and imperial regimes knew it. Before signing the European Convention on Human Rights, British officials scrupulously edited and amended its drafts to withhold rights guarantees from rebellious populations. Events in the empire would challenge British efforts to ensure its legal exceptionalism in international law as colonies erupted in protests and full-blown independence wars. As tempting as it might be to romanticize universal and nationalist struggles, however, they were rarely unified. Britain not only created civil conflicts through its divide-and-rule policies throughout the empire but also left such conflicts in its wake.

With this book, I am telling *a* history of the British Empire. It is not one of constitutional reform, political economy, military policy, or comparative empires, even though these stories will make appearances from time to time. It is not one of colonial capitalism, though the empire's racialized economy is always present and at times will drive parts of my narrative. This book, rather, is a history of how and why exceptional state-directed violence unfolded across the second empire and in what ways its systems were conceived, enacted, experienced, understood, and exonerated both in the colonies and in Britain. Two trials bookend this story: the eighteenth-century impeachment trial of Warren Hastings that put corruption and accountability in India to the test in Britain's Parliament, and the recent Mau Mau case in London's Royal Courts of Justice. During the intervening two hundred years, recurring questions about imperial violence and accountability dogged successive British governments.

I couldn't possibly address them all. Instead, I have followed the extant historical evidence documenting crises of legitimacy, real and perceived, in Britain's empire. Even then, I've had to make choices to demonstrate how and why violence was not particular to any one location or time period but was rather intrinsic to Britain's civilizing mission. These choices were also guided by the people who circulated through the empire, bringing with them violent methods and the laws enabling them. I chose particular locations because they demonstrate clearly how the circulation of the empire's peripatetic agents as well as nationalists' ideas and practices for demanding liberalism's promises connected South Africa to India, Palestine to Bengal, Ireland to Cyprus, and so forth. If imagined visually, the movement of people, ideas, practices, and legal systems around Britain's empire conjures the silks of a spider's web whose final massive form can be discerned only by stepping back to take in its entirety. As our story unfolds, the places, events, and processes that made it into these pages, when integrated into a single narrative, reveal this web's image. It is one that unmasks the scale and scope of coercion in the British Empire, colonial subjects' responses to these coercive systems, and the tissues connecting violence and its legacies together.

At their core, these sinews of empire are about people, their actions, and the choices they made under the conditions in which they lived and operated. Whether they were towering figures like Churchill and Rhodes or lesser-known actors like the high commissioner of Malaya Henry Gurney and the Kenyan colonial officer Terence Gavaghan, the empire's servants carried forth their civilizing mission in a manner that also shaped and defined Britons at home. Popular culture and consumer goods reinforced a collective sense of imperial greatness and power, and hagiographies of empire—whether in the form of children's books, missionary accounts, or histories scripted by Oxford and Cambridge dons— reminded young and old of their nation's inexorable march toward progress. Citizens of all stripes, including highbrow Tories in Belgravia and miners in Durham, shared the "White Man's Burden" that was subsumed under the monarchy and, together, framed British identity. Indeed, nothing stoked the flames of their national pride like royal pageantry on full display with its literal and symbolic reminders of empire. Such rituals also unfolded on distant shores where, time and again, they reminded British subjects of the benevolent hand that ruled over them. But there was a dissonance in such projections. For hundreds of millions who lived in Britain's imperial expanse, the empire's velvet glove concealed an all-too familiar iron fist.

This book will open up the empire's iron fist and examine closely the permanent scars it left on subjects' bodies and minds. The violence it inflicted was not abstract. It took the form of electric shock, fecal, and water torture; castration; forced hard labor; sodomy with broken bottles and vermin; forced marches through landmines; shin screwing; fingernail extraction; and public execution. Failure to confront these practices diminishes the raw lived experiences in the empire and the legacy they left behind. At times I will recount violent episodes in detail so readers can see and feel their effects and cumulative intensity. Only then is coercion's normalization within Britain's nationalist narrative of progress fully understood. The historical record will also show that not everyone fell in line with Britain's claims to exceptionalism. Jewish and nonconformist Christian dissidents, peace activists, immigrants from the empire and Europe, and the Labour Party's far left members could not reconcile the logic of necessary violence. They demanded official inquiries, undertook their own investigations, kept diaries, wrote scathing letters to the press, and scripted others for private audiences. The most wrenching indictments came from colonial subjects. Together they did little to alter coercion's grip on the empire, but they left behind a trail of evidence that today challenges the official narrative contained in Britain's carefully constructed national archive.

Reflecting back on the Mau Mau case, I remember the shock I felt when I first learned of the scale and intentionality of document destruction and removal in the empire. Today I'm left wondering how many Britons really know about the burning and laundering of their nation's past. How many of them realize the role their heroes and expert civil servants played in trying to manipulate how history would be written? We must reassemble the ashes and fragments that empire left behind to write histories that not only recount liberalism's perfidiousness but also explain it. The story that follows is one attempt at this. My hope is that it will inform today's imperial history wars and struggles for racial equality, pushing debates over whether or not the British Empire was a good or a bad thing, or better or worse than other imperial ventures, toward asking how and why the empire's past continues to shape the present.

I am not the first to raise some of these issues. A new generation of historians has shed light on Britain's archival double-bookkeeping and the ways it distorted earlier accounts of the empire. I am indebted to all of them as they have offered fresh ways of understanding long-tilled and newly released evidence—evidence that I have read together with a vast array of my own original research. Collected across a dozen countries on four continents in nearly two dozen archives, and in hundreds of interviews with those on many sides of the colonial divide, this research further illuminated the answers I was seeking. When my research laid bare the limitations of end-of-empire archives, I turned to broader fields of inquiry, including political theory and social histories of metropolitan culture as well as the economics of empire and postcolonialism. I also looked to past canons of imperial, British, and international history, even if this story moves quickly through some of the events and world systems that they recount in detail. While my own thinking does not always accord with their conclusions, I am nevertheless indebted to these works just as I am to those of the poets, novelists, and playwrights who so often capture the present as it passes with an unvarnished truth telling that eludes so many others. This book, therefore, is as much a result of my own archival research as it is an engagement with wide-ranging ideas about empire often siloed from each other. Integrating these disparate approaches and sources allows a more complete under-standing of Britain's imperial past to emerge. My hope is that in the pages that unfold, this history of British colonial violence will illuminate structures, systems, and lived experiences at the time of empire and the reasons they continue to be contested today.

PART I

AN IMPERIAL NATION

As thunderous applause and cheers drowned out the final words of his maiden public speech, a young Winston Churchill reminded his nation of its uniquely bequeathed past and its duty to uphold the civilizing mission's divinely inspired future. Waving off wisps of unruly hair that animated his oratory, Churchill laid waste to radical Liberals and other critics on the country's political fringe, declaring:

> There are not wanting those who say that in this Jubilee year our Empire has reached the heights of its glory and power, and that now we shall begin to decline, as Babylon, Carthage, Rome declined. Do not believe these croakers but give the lie to their dismal croaking by showing by our actions that the vigour and vitality of our race is unimpaired and that our determination is to uphold the Empire that we have inherited from our fathers as Englishmen [*cheers*], that our flag shall fly high upon the sea, our voice be heard in the councils of Europe, our Sovereign supported by the love of her subjects, then shall we continue to pursue that course marked out for us by an all-wise hand and carry out our mission of bearing peace, civilization and good government to the uttermost ends of the earth.[1]

It was a speech that gestured to the impassioned defenses of Britain's imperial destiny and reflected the Victorian era in which Churchill had come of age. Over a century had passed since Robert Clive and Warren Hastings, two iconic British rulers in Bengal, were seen as the nation's respective founder and consolidator of empire. In the late 1800s, and in the years that followed, few in the island nation rejected out of hand

Britain's rightful claim to empire or its claims to racial superiority, embedded as they were in a broader framework of liberal imperialism that had evolved more fully during the Victorian era. Rather, on that sun-splashed summer afternoon in Bath in 1897, the twenty-two-year-old Churchill, resolute in his convictions, articulated a powerful conception of the British Empire whose legitimacy was rarely questioned, even if its particular interests, as well as its policies and practices, were vigorously contested and debated.[2]

In many ways, Churchill epitomized the imperial soldier-cum-politician. He was steeped in empire from his time at Harrow to his training as a cadet at the Royal Military College at Sandhurst. While Oxford and Cambridge were natural codas for British ruling-class education, Sandhurst would also take its place as an incubator of the empire's future leaders both on and off the battlefields. Churchill was a rather lackluster student, and after passing through Britain's elite military academy, he joined the youthful ranks of those seeking imperial adventures. In 1895 he began his career as a war journalist and traveled to the Americas, where he reported on Spain's efforts to suppress the Cuban war for independence. After a baptism by fire in which he witnessed bloodshed firsthand, he left the island with a lifelong penchant for Havana cigars and his first medal, for having survived an enemy attack.[3] He then embarked on an itinerant several years, launching his nascent political career at home and also serving as a journalist, soldier, and sometimes both, in India's North-West Frontier, where the Malakand region was under attack by a local religious leader whom the British called the "Mad Mullah," and his forces.

For Churchill and thousands of other imperial agents, the journey to the empire's battlefronts was, in and of itself, an education. To reach the North-West Frontier, the future prime minister traveled thousands of miles by rail, then took a horse-drawn tonga another fifty miles to the Malakand Pass. To break the journey's monotony, Churchill stopped at various military outposts, dining with the troops and joining in for evening imperial sing-a-longs, including his personal favorite:

> *Great White Mother, far across the sea,*
> *Ruler of the Empire may she ever be.*
> *Long may she reign, glorious and free,*
> *In the Great White Motherland.*[4]

Churchill's "thinking imperially," a phrase he would famously embody, was incubated during these boisterous episodes of comradery as well as during his solitary hours of voracious reading. In many respects an autodidact, Churchill consumed canonical books on nation, race, and empire—including Thomas Macaulay's *History of England*, Winwood Reade's *The Martyrdom of Man*, and Edward Gibbon's *History of the Decline and Fall of the Roman Empire*—during his weeks of travel and while whittling away endless days of boredom awaiting action.[5]

In the years ahead, Churchill's imperial outlook crystallized further, though his opinions on racial hierarchy, civilization, and the deployment of coercive measures were not antediluvian relative to many of his peers. Like Churchill, a panoply of high-ranking decision makers—in political, military, and colonial administrative orbits—would spend formative years deployed in imperial skirmishes, big and small.[6] Later in their careers, these individuals and their subordinates would play crucial roles in transferring liberal imperialism's ideas and practices to other parts of the colonial world, then back to Britain. To understand the creation of coercive forms in twentieth-century empire, it is important to not only examine the paradoxes of liberalism and the culture from which they sprang but also interrogate how ideas about liberalism's underbelly traveled, who carried them between colonies and in and out of the metropole, and in what ways they were modified and institutionalized on arrival in different locations around the globe.[7]

CHAPTER I

Liberal Imperialism

Forgetting, I would even say historical error, is an essential factor in the creation of a nation and it is for this reason that the progress of historical studies often poses a threat to nationality. Historical inquiry, in effect, throws light on the violent acts that have taken place at the origin of every political formation.

Ernest Renan
What Is a Nation?, 1882[1]

On board the *Syren*, en route from Calcutta to London, John Holwell choked down waves of seasickness, put pen to paper, and wrote to his friend William Davis. He described the night of June 20, 1756, when the English fort in Calcutta fell to the Mughal forces. According to Holwell, he and 145 other prisoners found themselves at club and scimitar point "next to the door of the Black Hole prison . . . [where] we should at all events have rushed upon the guard, and been, as the lesser evil, by our own choice cut to pieces." Instead, the sultry night morphed into one of horror as the men, "exhausted by continual fatigue and action," were crammed into a mere eighteen-by-fourteen-foot space with two tiny windows and "scarce any the least circulation of fresh air." In acts of desperation, prisoners climbed over corpses to gasp between the heavy window bars, and others drank their own sweat. All the while the guards, by Holwell's account, delighted in the suffering that unfolded within the sweltering cubicle of death. "Can it gain belief," Holwell later lamented incredulously, "that this scene of misery proved entertainment to the brutal wretches without? But so it was; and they took care to keep us supplied with water, that they might have the satisfaction of seeing us fight for it . . . and held up lights to the bars that they might lose no part of the inhuman diversion."[2] By daybreak, only twenty-three prisoners drew breath. The rest had perished in the Black Hole of Calcutta.[3]

No single phrase has brought empire, and the savagery that imperiled His Majesty's forces, into the everyday language and culture of Britain with such ominous effect. Yet Holwell's narrative is suspect at best. His is the only eyewitness account of the events in Calcutta on that fateful night in 1756. All subsequent recounting of events, save for one other written sixteen years after the fact, are derivative of Holwell's. More recently, some have questioned the deaths of the Black Hole prisoners, which Holwell unquestionably embellished in scale and circumstance. Estimates based on careful reconstructions suggest that nowhere near 146 prisoners met Holwell's described fate. Instead, informed approximations suggest there were thirty-nine prisoners, and some eighteen perished, largely from the effects of preexisting battle-inflicted wounds. The infamous Black Hole of Calcutta in Bengal, while not entirely made up, was at the very least exaggerated and then internalized in a nationalist narrative.[4]

The Black Hole's significance extends well beyond rhetorical power in Britain's language and culture. The cascading effects of this mythologized event would help shape the course of the British Empire for centuries to come. Britain's checkered history in Bengal began with the East India Company's royal charter in 1600, though it wasn't until the Black Hole that imperial ventures in the East led to the eventual consolidation of British power throughout India. The company, an arm's-length proxy for British political interests and a cash cow for the private economic gain of its shareholders, many of whom were MPs in London, was responsible for forging treaties, negotiating trading rights, levying taxes, and deploying a standing army. In the early 1700s, the Mughal ruler granted the company lucrative customs-free trading rights for a host of items. When war broke out between France and Britain in 1756, the company ignored the orders issued by the ruler of Bengal, the nawab, Siraj-ud-daula, and fortified its trading post in Calcutta for fear of French attack. In response, the nawab sought to drive the British out of Bengal by extending his reach to Calcutta, taking the British fort, and imprisoning all remaining Europeans.

What happened next became not only the stuff of future nationalist legend but also evidence of purported native savagery. The Black Hole of Calcutta was the justification needed for Britain's conquest of Bengal. The Battle of Plassey in 1757 reversed Britain's defeat and avenged the prisoners' fates. Though less a military victory than a negotiated settlement, it firmly placed Britain's imperial stake into the ground. It also buttressed the future reputation of then Lieutenant Colonel Robert Clive as a military genius and the founder of empire. In the battle's aftermath, Clive ensured that Bengal was beholden to the company, and massive profits continued to flow to it.[5]

The company's gains came at great expense to Bengal's population. Clive bequeathed to Britain's expanding empire a future source of revenue when he negotiated the company's right to collect taxes, or *diwani*, from the Mughal *nawab*. The company soon earned a whopping £1.65 million in annual tax revenue. Shares boomed in London, and the government collected £400,000 in an annual payment, which was nothing short of a massive bribe that facilitated the company's corruption.[6] Tax revenue dried up within five years, but shareholder expectations remained high, so the company turned toward oppressive methods of tax collection.[7] The company had cornered the local grain market, in part to feed its army, and contributed to an inflationary spiral and a drying up of local credit lending to starving consumers. Hunger haunted the population and famine soon spread. According to one nineteenth-century historian, "the husbandmen sold their cattle; they sold their implements of agriculture; they devoured their seed-grain; they sold their sons and daughters, till at length no buyer of children could be found; they ate leaves of trees and the grass of the field; and in June 1770 the Resident at [Murshidabad] affirmed that the living were feeding on the dead."[8] Remarkably, the company continued to profit, posting an £8,000 increase in revenue as the famine raged. "It was," as the historian Sugata Bose tells us, "the role of the state and the economically powerful in effecting declines in entitlements to food of vulnerable social groups that turned the 'dearth into a famine.'"[9] An estimated one-third of Bengal's thirty million people died.

Depopulation led to a precipitous decline in tax revenues and, along with Clive's wildly exaggerated claims of the company's future earnings, burst the speculative bubble of share prices. With the company near bankruptcy—which precipitated a worldwide credit crash—a parliamentary inquiry soon followed, as did Lord North's India Bill of 1773, or the Regulating Act. Meant to herald a new era of control over the company in India, the act was in reality a justificatory fig leaf for a large-scale bailout. North facilitated a £1.4 million government loan to the company, not only to rescue it from impending bankruptcy but also to avert possible financial ruin for heavily invested MPs.[10]

Clive had much to answer for. Thought to be among the richest men in Britain, he withstood charges of corruption and went on an offensive of his own. He pointed to the sovereignty he established in Bengal and

shifted blame to his junior colleagues in the company. He further chastened Parliament for not acting swiftly or strongly enough to consolidate his hard-won political and economic gains in the region. Given the
near-catastrophic collapse of the company, Clive's self-serving protests
fell on deaf ears; his personal gains were undeniable, as were many of the
shady dealings that happened on his watch. Yet Clive's image in Britain
was still one of an audacious visionary. He was the man, regardless of his
questionable moral standards, who singularly established Britain's foot-
hold in Bengal. Cleared of all blame in Parliament, Clive never returned
to India, committing suicide in 1774. In the decades ahead, his legacy as
the founder of empire was immortalized in portraits and busts that grace
the halls of Britain's public buildings to this day.[11]

Assuming Clive's mantle was Warren Hastings who, in 1772, was
selected governor of Bengal and a year later was elevated to the position
of governor-general. Hastings had joined the East India Company as a
clerk at the age of seventeen and quickly moved up the ladder. He had
the unenviable charge of taking financial and judicial control of Bengal,
keeping the peace, and instituting administrative improvements, while
also ensuring company profits and extending its operations more generally. Scandal and corruption were to be minimized, and it's here that
Hastings, despite his valuable contributions to streamlining British rule,
went the way of Clive. His vices, and those of the company, were soon
laid bare in a public trial that had implications not only for the East but
also for Britain's future empire.

London recalled Hastings to face impeachment charges a little over
a decade after he assumed the position of governor-general. An epic
seven-year drama unfolded that was putatively about his misdeeds. In
reality, it was the empire's past, as well as future, that were in the dock.[12]
Leading the charge against Hastings in what would become the nation's
longest and most prescient imperial proceedings was Edmund Burke.
The Whig politician had for years been outspoken against the East India
Company's excesses and championed the dire need for reform.[13] For
Burke, the question of the empire's legitimacy was paramount; Britain's
error was not its claim to sovereign power over the region but rather
in its failure to establish stable governance and rule of law.[14] "There
is nothing in the boys we send to India worse than in the boys whom
we are whipping at school, or that we see trailing a pike or bending
over a desk at home," he observed. "But as English youth in India drink
the intoxicating draught of authority and dominion before their heads
are able to bear it, and as they are full grown in fortune long before
they are ripe in principle, neither nature nor reason have any opportu-

nity to exert themselves for remedy of the excesses of their premature power. . . . [They possess] all the avarice of age, and all the impetuosity of youth."[15]

Burke's opening speech to Parliament in 1788 was nothing short of sensational. He stood before the seated Lords, some of whom were cloaked in red robes and others in gray ones. They all sported white wigs, fashioned largely from human hair, that peered out from beneath their black tricorn hats. Together they gathered under Parliament's buttressed rafters, which offered a cavernous atmosphere to the packed gallery that came to witness the moment. Segregated by gender, hundreds of men and women bedecked in the period's finest dress only added to the human aroma in the airless hall. It was a convivial affair until the day's sociability ended, when Burke rose in front of Parliament's half-moon, stained-glass window, declaring to the packed hall, and to the nation, "We have brought before your Lordships the first man in rank, authority and station; . . . one in whom all the frauds, all the peculations, all the violence, all the tyranny in India are embodied, disciplined and arrayed."[16]

Burke was on a crusade to paint Hastings as the villain, even though Clive was far more culpable of excesses than his successor. Few denied Britain's behavior in India or the extraordinary wealth and corrupt practices of the legendary nabobs. These men made vast fortunes in the East

The Trial of Warren Hastings in Westminster Hall, drawn by E. Dayes, engraved by R. Pollard, aquatint by F. Jukes, assembled February 13, 1788.

and returned home to Britain where they married into the landed elite, bought seats in Parliament, and according to Burke, destabilized not only the economy but also the very political system upon which Britain was constituted.[17] The reforms that Burke sought had as much to do with the future of Britain, and Europe, as they did Hastings's treaty violations, widespread corruption, and arbitrary imperial governance. When immigrating to the metropole vis-à-vis the nabobs, imperial despotism was dangerously subversive.[18]

Burke deftly established the moral terms of the trial and with them the terrain on which the empire would be debated, contested, and justified for decades to come. He expounded on the methods of tax collection in India: defaulters were publicly flogged, and their virginal daughters were dragged into public view, where they "were cruelly violated by the basest and wickedest of mankind." "It did not end there," Burke insisted. "The wives of the people of the country only differed in this; that they lost their honour in the bottom of the most cruel dungeons. . . . But they were dragged out, naked and exposed to the public view, and scourged before all the people. . . . They put the nipples of the women into the sharp edges of split bamboos and tore them from their bodies."[19] Such horrors were partly due to the noxious effects of youthful power marring company rule:

> Another circumstance which distinguishes the East-India Company is the youth of the persons who are employed in the system of that service. The servants have almost universally been sent out to begin their progress and careers in active occupation, and in the exercise of high authority, at that period of life which in all other places has been employed in the course of a rigid education. To put the matter in a few words, they are transferred from slippery youth to perilous independence, from perilous independence to inordinate expectations, from inordinate expectations to boundless power. School-boys without tutors, minors without guardians, the world is let loose upon them, with all its temptations; and they are let loose upon the world, with all the powers that despotism involves.[20]

Issues of accountability, good governance, and the interpretation of Oriental despotism drew a bright line under the question of Britain's moral basis in India.[21] Burke saw Hastings's failure to establish stable and lawful governance in Bengal, and to facilitate the continued prosperity of a once-flourishing society, as stains on Britain's historical record, threatening stability in India and at home.[22] Accountability, in his view, was the foundation on which to establish government as a sacred trust—a trust that was aligned with the welfare of its subjects rather than with the abuse and exploitation of their bodies and liberties.[23]

There was an explicit cultural and historical dimension to Burke's argument.[24] In direct contrast to the company's apologists, Burke did not cast "oriental despotism" as a malignancy afflicting the Indian population as a whole or its rich past. Rather, Burke urged his nation to understand India's social, political, religious, and legal structures and share his awe for the customs, institutions, and ancient texts that defined the East. The civilization emerging from India's antiquity was essential to Burke's attempts to transcend growing British prejudices toward Indian difference.[25] He never questioned Britain's rightful claim to India; nor did he condemn empire as a dishonorable enterprise. Rather, he sought to cleanse the company, and Britain's reputation, of its venality and excesses and to establish lawful governance.

After years of public debate and drama, Hastings's impeachment trial ended in acquittal in 1795. Nonetheless the proceedings brought to the fore Burke's calls for genuine change, setting the stage for imperial expansion and future debates over the empire's purpose and legitimacy. For the first time, Burke persuasively introduced into the national imagination Britain's sacred responsibility for subject populations and territories. Empire transformed into a national project that could no longer be entrusted to "school-boys without tutors." Instead, it became for Burke "a natural extension of British sovereign and commercial rights and interests . . . [and] an affair of state answerable to the nation."[26]

As for Hastings, he offered a coercive logic to Pax Britannica, galvanizing support for his imperial methods and escaping from Parliament's scrutiny with his annual £4,000 pension. As the trial stretched on, and parliamentary and public opinion increasingly understood empire within a nationalist agenda, many Britons considered Hastings's infelicities an unfortunate but necessary consequence of empire's consolidation. The man who sat in the dock for 148 days over the course of seven years would soon earn his rightful place next to Clive as a national hero.[27]

A rewriting of the historical record soon followed. Indian society was recast as the antithesis of civilization. James Mill was among the first to produce a reinterpretation of the past. In 1817 he penned *The History of British India*, a historical and cultural onslaught on Indian society. Mill attacked nearly every aspect of India, including its government, arts, religion, and philosophy. He concluded the Hindus did not possess, nor had they ever possessed, "a high state of civilisation."[28] By portraying Indian society as morally degraded, Mill was formulating a different justification for British rule. Replacing Oriental despotism with good governance, or instituting political and legal reform, would transform so-called natives, ridding them of their superstitious and torpid character.

For others, religion was the source of India's corrupt and corrupting society, and they regarded Christianity as essential to British good governance in the East. The late eighteenth century witnessed an evangelical revival, and the Clapham Sect—a group of prominent evangelical Anglicans dedicated to the abolition of enslaved labor, the end of the trade in enslaved people, and penal reform—turned its attention to India. We often associate renowned abolitionists like William Wilberforce and Granville Sharp with the Clapham Sect, but it was another member, Charles Grant, who spoke most forcefully about missionary benefits for India. For Grant, "the true cure of darkness, is the introduction of light," particularly through missionary education, which would "silently undermine, and at length subvert, the fabric of [Hindu] error." Like Burke and Mill, Grant condemned Britain's crimes of conquest and sought absolution through reform. Britain had to establish a "grand moral and political principle, by which we shall henceforth, and in all future generations, govern and deal with our Asiatic subjects," he insisted. "Whether we shall make it our duty to impart to them knowledge, light, and happiness; or under the notion of holding them more quietly in subjection, shall seek to keep them ignorant, corrupt, and mutually injurious, as they are now?" Whether secular or religious, Mill and Grant shared a similar vision: a morally defensible empire aimed at improving British subjects until they were ready to take on the responsibility of self-government. As the political theorist Karuna Mantena reminds us, such transformative ideas were the first of their kind; once Britain's paternalistic responsibility was accepted, "any argument for the continuation of rule merely for the benefit of English prestige, wealth, or honor would be in principle unjustifiable."[29]

Thomas Macaulay soon followed Mill and rescued Clive from the company's tarnishing and Burke's perorations about moral failures in the empire.[30] In Macaulay's view, "Clive, like most men who are born with strong passions and tried by strong temptations, committed great faults. But every person who takes a fair and enlightened view of his whole career must admit that our island, so fertile in heroes and statesmen, has scarcely ever produced a man more truly great either in arms or in council."[31] His invective also discarded Burke's sympathetic view of the Indian population and depicted it as neither victim nor noble. "The path of duty is plain before us: and it is also the path of wisdom, of national prosperity, of national honour," Macaulay later wrote. He underscored that the successes in India were "pacific triumphs of reason over barbarism; that empire is the imperishable empire of our arts and our morals, our literature and our laws."[32]

That Macaulay had served in India and produced influential policy treatises on Indian education and penal codes offered validation to his erasures and distortions. Hastings, according to Macaulay, had been the architect of India's future and that of the entire British Empire. Hastings had asserted British sovereignty over Bengal, brought crucial elements such as taxation under British purview, and made significant efforts to expand formal British influence beyond Bengal in the subcontinent. He was, in Macaulay's words, to be admired for "the amplitude and fertility of his intellect, his rare talents for command, for administration, and for controversy, his dauntless courage, his honourable poverty, his fervent zeal for the interests of state, [and] his noble equanimity."[33]

There emerged in Macaulay's lionization of Hastings a justificatory narrative contextualized in the greater burdens and vicissitudes of empire that were unlike any that statesmen faced at home. "No complication of perils and embarrassments could perplex him," Macaulay insisted. "For every difficulty he had a contrivance ready; and, whatever may be thought of the justice and humanity of some of his contrivances, it is certain that they seldom failed to serve the purpose for which they were designed."[34] An ends-justifies-the-means argument emerged that would be deployed repeatedly in the empire's future. As historians recast Clive and Hastings as the heroic founder and consolidator of empire, respectively, Burke was castigated for the "violence" he perpetrated against Hastings and the entire imperial project. When H. H. Dodwell later declared in the first *Cambridge History of India*, a six-volume collection published between 1922 and 1937, that Burke had behaved with "violent animosity" and that Hastings's impeachment "was a calamitous mistake and before it had gone very far it developed into something like a cruel wrong," few Britons would disagree.[35]

Britain would not witness another trial quite like Hastings's for another two centuries. Burke, with his flair for dramatic and uncensored oratories detailing the colonized's sufferings and arguing for the inherent value in Indian ways of being, demanded public accountability for the East India Company's actions in the name of Britain. But Burke, for all his concessions to the value of life and culture in the East, also sought to protect and perpetuate forms of privilege and domination that would become the hallmarks of British imperial rule. Embedded in debates about accountability and legitimacy, particularly in the after-math of the impeachment trial, were the beginnings of a consolidated liberal imperialism, with all its paternalistic foundations. The anxieties that it created would repeatedly emerge, particularly when Britain had to reconcile coercion in the empire as an unfortunate, though necessary, consequence of governing "backward" peoples who resisted its civilizing beneficence.

Hastings's impeachment proceedings secured Britain's claims to empire and transformed an economy of avarice and rogue traders into a network that integrated British capitalism with nationalistic policies and practices in India and elsewhere. As the empire marched ahead, and a liberal imperialism explicitly emerged in the nineteenth century with its paradoxical qualities of domestic reform and imperial violence, its ultimate goal and, indeed, its perpetuation depended on avoiding the disruptive effects of accountability in the empire whenever possible. Putative acts of transparency would, over time, become increasingly opaque as tools of the emerging liberal imperialism would work in con-cert to immortalize heroes of the empire like Clive and Hastings while denying, justifying, or forgetting open secrets of imperial transgressions.

In little over a hundred years, Britain's imperial bricolage moved from eighteenth-century claims in Bengal to nearly a quarter of the globe, or roughly 14 million square miles. By the end of her reign, Queen Victoria would preside over 450 million subjects around the world. Britain laid claim to a bewildering number of political entities that included colo-nies, protectorates, paramountcies, spheres of influence, treaty ports, consulates, military bases, and princely states.[36] The British Empire of the Victorian era was enormous and diverse. At one end of the political spectrum was India, where Britain ruled as heir to the Mughals. On the other end was Pitcairn, a dot of an island in the southern Pacific Ocean of less than two square miles whose population, descendants of muti-neers and their Tahitian companions, peaked at around two hundred. In between were constellations of red swaths, blotches, and dots on global maps that represented British possessions on every continent save Ant-arctica. From Cape Town to Bombay, Victorian architecture took form in courthouses and railway stations and lent a distinctly British facade to the preexisting cosmopolitanism of the empire's urban centers, whereas other commercial hubs on centuries-old trading routes persisted with little more than a few mud and wattle huts.[37] Some protectorates, like Bechuanaland, were relatively homogenous; other colonies, like Nige-

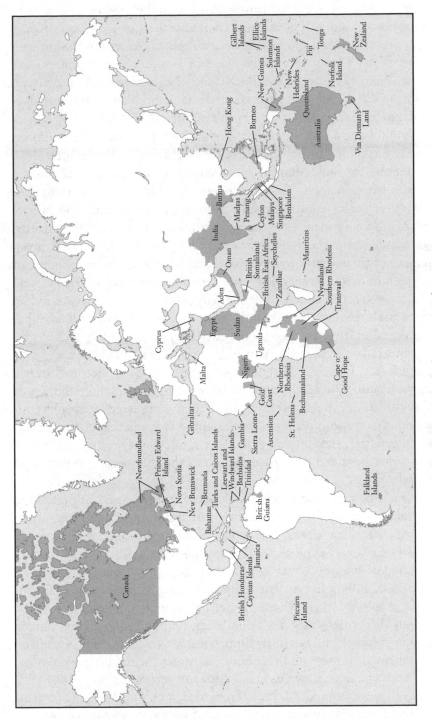

British Empire in the late nineteenth century

ria, counted scores of ethnic groups, many with their own languages and indigenous religions. There were commercial cities like Hong Kong, on the one hand, and the tumbleweed streets of Maseru in Basutoland, on the other. The geographical range of Britain's empire was no less diverse. Natural wonders like the Nile and Niger rivers, Mount Kenya, the Great Rift Valley, and parts of the Sahara and Namib deserts galvanized imperial pride and spurred exploration and tourism.

Technological and scientific innovations abounded when Queen Victoria was on the throne, and they expanded in the decades afterward. Revolutions in transportation and communication systems connected the island nation to its far-flung territories with new steam engines, underwater cables, and telegraphs. Other areas, including the hinterlands of Gambia and many of the 840 islands that made up Fiji, remained disconnected from the greater imperial whole for decades. British steam engines cut their way through remote landscapes and were a source of glory at home. Railways crisscrossed some colonies, and India and Australia boasted formidable lines while outposts like British Honduras had nary a track. On balance, though, engineering feats tamed landscapes and opened up the vast interiors of Africa and Asia. British technicians brought gradated roads all the way into the Great Rift Valley and railways into the Burmese hill country. Just after Queen Victoria's death, engineers and a dizzying array of laborers began building the iconic railway bridge across Victoria Falls. When completed, it would connect Southern and Northern Rhodesia, the two adjacent African colonies named for Cecil Rhodes, and offer countless images for colonial-era posters that heralded Britain's conquest of the thunderous waterfalls in Central Africa.[38]

Plantations sprawled across Ceylonese hillsides, and minerals and gemstones were unearthed in southern African mines. By the twentieth century, coffee, cocoa, tea, and rubber accounted for countless acres of cash crops. At the same time, Britain's position as the world's banker continued with a steady flow of gold that came from South Africa's Witwatersrand. Tilling Britain's fields and servicing its mines was a kaleidoscopic array of workers whose gender, generational, ethnic, racial, and religious diversities knew few boundaries. Some of these cash-strapped migrants came from relatively unproductive colonies like Nyasaland and remained in mine and plantation barracks for months, even years. Across the empire's labor market, British subjects spoke hundreds of different languages; practiced various religions, including Islam, Christianity, Hinduism, Buddhism, and a range of indigenous systems; and had

histories that stretched back to caliphates like that of Sokoto and trading entrepots such as Zanzibar, as well as to more modest villages and
small-scale exchange networks. Kikuyu tea pickers, Chinese tin miners, Indian rubber tappers, Zulu gold miners, Lebanese shopkeepers,
and Malay fishermen were among millions who would experience the
impact of British rule. Agents of the empire were, themselves, scarcely
homogenous. White settlers, earnest Christian missionaries, adventurers, flotsam and jetsam, high-level diplomats, baby-faced colonial officers, commanders, enlisted men, capitalized entrepreneurs, prostitutes,
and convicted felons circulated in the British Empire and made it their
home.

Unifying this empire was an emerging ideological coherence rooted
in a liberal imperial ideal and in the nation's self-imagination more
broadly. The extension of Britain's global power and domination in the
nineteenth century brought with it history-defining debates about universal principles, free markets, the protection of property and, importantly, rule of law. Beginning in the early nineteenth century, and dating
from long before the Hastings trial, liberal thought evolved in Europe
and intersected with the rise of empires. The mutually constitutive relationship between liberalism and imperialism would have profound consequences for British conceptions of liberty, progress, and governance
both at home and abroad.[39]

Liberalism as a doctrine was highly contested and immensely heterogeneous and incremental in its formation and spread. It was a universalist project whereby individuals and societies could be reformed
and transformed through such measures as free trade, education, and
law. Self-reliant, rights-bearing individuals were fundamental to classic
liberalism. These individuals collectively comprised society through the
sum total of their actions. To realize their full potential as character-
driven, rational, and autonomous beings, individuals had to be freed of
anachronistic bonds with despots, feudal aristocrats, and overbearing
priests. The pace and scope of the reforms needed to transform Britain's patronage-driven hierarchies were highly contested. Nonetheless,
in the age of revolutions, liberalism's reformist impulse at home would
make inroads. Its stress on individualism, the virtues of self-fashioning
through discipline, and suffering for one's failures were its hallmarks. It
regarded private property as an indicator of success, the free market as
a vehicle for the common good, and science and technology, and with
them reason and method, as fundamental to human progress.[40] When
looked at historically, imperialist expansion, as witnessed in the vast

empire under Queen Victoria's domain, was inherent to liberalism's ideology of universalistic notions of progress, the extension of capitalism, and moral claims.[41]

These universalistic claims, however, withered when confronted with images of India and other parts of the empire that emerged in the wake of the Hastings trial. Civilization was a priori Western, and race became *the* physical marker of difference. Liberal imperialism would be the mechanism for imposing Western values on peculiar populations with their strange cultures and different skin colors. Detached from the fractious political landscape at home, liberalism developed coherence in an empire that would endure under the banner of the "civilizing mission," which was both reformist and activist.[42] In places like India, reform would take multiple designs, as institutions and practices that defined British civilization were transplanted into Eastern soil. Foremost among them was the rule of law, and with it the legitimate violence needed to protect the state from threats and to ensure the preservation of private property, a steady flow of labor, and the expansion of welfare and development projects. While shaped and reshaped in the century ahead, Britain's reformist impulse would be the dominant ideological framework in which imperial policies would be understood and projected. Coercion's necessity and legality inhered to liberalism, however, and British philosophers and statesmen continued to wrestle with this fact as they worked out what good governance meant for Britain's empire.

"Despotism is a legitimate mode of government in dealing with barbarians provided the end be their improvement, and the means justified by actually effecting that end," John Stuart Mill, son of the legendary father, wrote in 1859.[43] In two canonical texts, *On Liberty* (1859) and *Considerations on Representative Government* (1861), he juxtaposed civilization and barbarism to create new ideological idioms advocating for a narrative of human development that was intimately bound with Britain's civilizing mission.[44] Britons, having already climbed the arduous civilizing scale, sat secure in their position atop the hierarchy of civilizations and in their role as self-appointed shepherds of reform. In contrast, Mill endowed the non-Europeans of the empire with childlike qualities and juxtaposed them with progressive images of the British. Like children, non-Western populations were not yet ready for liberty, which "is meant to apply only to human beings in the maturity of their faculties. . . . We may leave out of consideration those backward states of society in which the race itself may be considered as in its nonage."[45] In the nineteenth century, the analogy of India toddling along toward civilization was the dominant discourse, and Mill imagined the British imposing a "government of leading-strings . . . to carry such a people the most rapidly through the next necessary steps in social progress." To this end, good government in the empire had to be adjusted to local "stages of civilization," so Mill advocated for a "paternal despotism" to tutor the empire's children. "A civilized government, to be really advantageous to [subject populations], will require to be in a considerable degree despotic," he wrote, "and to be one over which they do not themselves exercise con trol, and which imposes a great amount of forcible restraint upon their actions."[46]

Universalist ideas gave way to culture and history conditioning human character. Arguments soon emerged over who was capable of embracing notions of rationality and social and economic progress.[47] In an emerging global citizenry, inclusivity would come in stages, if ever. "To suppose that the same international customs, and the same rules of international morality, can obtain between one civilized nation and another, and between civilized nations and barbarians," Mill wrote, "is a grave error, and one which no statesman can fall into, however it may with those who, from a safe and unresponsible position, criticise statesmen."[48] While written in the mid-Victorian era, echoes of Mill's exclusion of "barbarians" from the "international morality" of the "civilized nations" would resonate in twentieth-century denials of humanitarian and human rights laws to imperial subjects.[49]

Mill was both a product and a shaper of his imperial times. With his formulations, he offered future imperialists on both ends of the political spectrum—ranging from Conservatives like Benjamin Disraeli and Joseph Chamberlain in the nineteenth century to Labour leaders like Clement Attlee and Ernest Bevin in the twentieth—a conception of paternal despotism. As the empire expanded and subject populations refused to conform to British conceptions of progress and civilizing largesse, Mill's liberal imperialism, which denied sovereignty to brown and Black peoples around the world, while holding out the promise of reform, opened the justificatory door to coercion as an instrument of colonial rule.[50]

Britain's second empire repeatedly confronted state violence and attempted to incorporate it within the rule of law that lay at the heart of imperial good governance. In the decades prior to Mill's writings, Britain had declared martial law in Ireland (1798 and 1803), Barbados (1805 and 1816), Ceylon (1817 and 1848), Demerara (1823), Jamaica

(1823–24 and 1831–32), Cape Colony (1835, 1846, 1850–53), and Canada (1837–38).[51] The question of legalized lawlessness—or the colonial violence that produced laws that, in turn, legalized extraordinary acts of coercion and suspensions of due process—weighed heavily and was the fulcrum of disputes back in London. Two questions animated debates: when was state-directed violence a necessity, and was this violence legitimate or lawful?

"It would be the worst of all conceivable grievances—it would be a calamity unspeakable—if the whole law and constitution of England were suspended one hour longer than the most imperious necessity demanded," Lord Brougham insisted during parliamentary debate on martial law in Demerara, a tiny British sugar-producing colony on the northeastern shores of South America.[52] On August 17, 1823, ten to twelve thousand enslaved people launched a rebellion against their impoverished and unfree conditions.[53] "The consequence of the misconduct of those Slaves, is, that they are at this moment suffering all the horrors attendant on the existence of Martial-Law," Demerara's governor John Murray proclaimed, "which I have been compelled to put in force in that part of the Colony, with all its accompanying severity. . . . God Save the King." Order was restored within forty-eight hours, though martial law remained in effect during the governor-ordered trial of dozens of the rebellion's alleged ringleaders. Some were publicly lashed, others were executed and their severed heads nailed to posts, and some were hung by chains outside plantations where their corpses remained suspended for months so that they "might produce salutary effects."[54] Brougham's concern, however, was not for the spectacle's legality but for the unlawful treatment of a Methodist missionary, John Smith, who had been implicated in inciting the insurrection and was subsequently court-martialed, found guilty, and died in prison while awaiting execution.[55] Had the governor maintained martial law for longer than necessary, affording extrajudicial means for trying the accused? This was the crux of parliamentary concern. "If [martial law] survives the necessity on which alone it rests for a single minute, it becomes a mere exercise of lawless violence," the Whig politician James MacKintosh presciently asserted.[56]

In Demerara as elsewhere in the empire, the doctrine of necessity suggested a breakdown in the legal system's ordinary functioning, an incapability of dealing with an existential threat to the state. Regular criminal laws in Britain aspired to define offenses precisely, provide fair trials, assume innocence, avoid double jeopardy, and adhere to the liberal ideal of individual responsibility for everyone, including government officials. While the state maintained its monopoly on the legitimate use of violence, this violence was increasingly limited by common law requirements. In the colonies, evolving criminal codes were unlike those in Britain, providing the colonial state with much greater access to the use of coercion. An expanding list of laws reflected the racialized assumptions and economic needs of the empire, so regulations like master and servants ordinances, which criminalized labor offenses, remained in place well beyond their disuse in Britain. In the case of a rebellion, these laws were often insufficient to thwart threats to the state, whether real or perceived. A different set of laws or regulations, in the form of martial law, statutory martial law, or some combination of both, had to be deployed. It was in these moments of necessity that exceptions from ordinary legal systems were made and the state's power to preserve itself spoke most clearly through its colonial agents and their extraordinary acts of violence.

Political philosophers, jurists, and statesmen searched British precedents at home to define necessity's boundaries, but what they found was a lot of gray area. Even martial law had an ambiguous place in Britain's legal history.[57] When narrowly defined, it existed during a state of war when the military took over for an inoperative civilian government. In such times of necessity, the military's powers were wide ranging. In the case of an internal rebellion, martial law often operated differently. A still-functioning civil government called in the military to assist police forces in restoring order and authority. This is what typically happened in the empire, as in Demerara. Either way, once martial law was over, regular courts would return and could theoretically hold the military accountable for any of its martial law activities that violated ordinary laws. In practice, this rarely happened, and to ensure that it didn't, ex post facto indemnity acts were often passed. Nonetheless, there was precedent for prosecution. In 1812 Lord Mansfield ruled that a soldier had no special exemption and was legally bound by the same rules as any other ordinary citizen, even if he was following a superior's orders. General Sir Charles Napier was furious, querying, "Shall I be shot for forbearance by a Court-Marital, or hanged for over-zeal by a jury?"[58]

There were also British precedents for statutory acts that circumvented ordinary rule of law. Habeas corpus was suspended often in Britain, particularly for those suspected of treason. Suspension acts could delay a person's speedy trial, and once legal proceedings took place, protections were granted to the British government through an indemnity act.[59] There was also the Riot Act, a statutory response to illegal assemblies. Once the Riot Act was read to an unlawfully assembled crowd, it had an hour to disperse before the military seized control. Failing to read the act aloud to the crowd was a criminal neglect of duty; but if the crowd became unmanageable before the hour was up, the military could intervene. Questions remained. When was it necessary to invoke the Riot Act? How much force was too much or too little? "Now a person, whether a magistrate, or peace officer, who has the duty of suppressing a riot, is placed in a very difficult position," one British justice concluded when pondering these queries in 1831. "For if, by his acts, he causes death, he is liable to be indicted for murder or manslaughter, and if he does not act, he is liable to an indictment on an information for neglect; he is therefore, bound to hit the precise line of his duty. . . . I ought to remark, that a mere good feeling, or upright intentions, are not sufficient to discharge a man, if he has not done his duty."[60]

Necessity. Legitimate violence. Unsanctioned violence. Intensity of force. These issues percolated for years and set up epic confrontations between some of Britain's most revered figures. Eruptions in India and Jamaica brought these tense debates to a head and also called into question the ability of so-called native populations to improve along Western lines. Expected to use cartridges rumored to be greased with beef and pork fat, the sepoys of the company army took up arms in May 1857. Widespread revolt ensued, and men and women across India's varied cultural and socioeconomic landscape sought to end British rule.[61] Large swaths of the region remained uncontrollable for over a year, and only suppression restored colonial order. Lurid and often embellished tales of Indian acts perpetrated against Europeans, particularly the rape of white women and girls, fueled Britain's take-no-prisoners response.[62] British forces tied suspected Indian rebels to the mouths of cannons, lit the fuse, and blew them to pieces.[63] They leveled villages and towns as their murderous campaigns against the local population spread. As one British officer recalled, "The orders went out to shoot every soul. . . . It was literally murder. . . . I have seen many bloody and awful sights lately but such a one as I witnessed yesterday I pray I never see again. The women were all spared but their screams on seeing their husbands and sons butchered, were most painful."[64] In Britain, atrocities perpetrated against white civilians shocked the public, and hyperbolic media coverage incited popular opinion during what was called the "Red Year" of 1857.[65] A grim national mood of despair and retribution supported British repressive measures in India. When Britain finally quelled the rebellion at the end of 1858, hardened racial attitudes at home remained and would impact the nation's future imperial rule.[66]

The revolt also signaled legal issues that needed to be addressed. "A reign of lawlessness had commenced, but for a while the avenging hand of the English Government had been restrained by the trammels of the law," officials in India declared. "It was time now to cease from the unequal conflict. . . . A terrible necessity had forced itself upon the rulers of the land. . . . So the law makers stood up and shook themselves loose from the trammels of the law. On the 30 May [1857] the Legislative Council passed an Act which swept away the time honoured seats of justice, wheresoever rebellion was disporting itself." Breathtaking in its scope, this new act, the State Offences Act, targeted anyone who rebelled against the Crown or the East India Company and legally enabled their execution, banishment for life, or imprisonment with hard labor. It permitted local civilian officials to declare a "state of rebellion" in their districts and conduct trials without law officers or rights of appeal. Other acts followed, including the Heinous Offences Act and a Military and State Offences Act, which further circumscribed rights of the accused. There was also legislation for press censorship and suppression. "So under this system various forms of summary justice and emergency action were given legislative authorization," the legal historian A. W. Brian Simpson concludes, "thus making reliance upon martial law in a strict sense unnecessary, though what was involved was a form of statutory martial law."[67]

Eight years after the outbreak of the Indian rebellion, a gentle warm breeze licked the palm trees outside a whitewashed courthouse in Morant Bay, Jamaica. Inside, two colonial magistrates, Francis Bowen and John Walton, were presiding over petty criminal cases. During the week they ran large plantations, and on Saturdays they adjudicated Black-on-Black crimes, including that of a young boy whom they found guilty of a minor assault.[68] He was among hundreds of thousands of laborers whose bodies Britain had abused in pursuit of enormous sugar profits for plantation owners like Bowen and Walton and for traders and financiers in Britain.[69] Prior to the boy's October 7, 1865, trial, events had been tense in Jamaica. Emancipation nearly thirty years earlier was supposed to unburden enslaved people from their past and render them free laborers who would model their lives on Britain's middle class. This was the expectation, at least, of radical evangelicals and abolitionists like William Wilberforce. The realities of postemancipation Jamaica, however, were much different. Many Blacks refused to embrace British social virtues or humbly bow to the island's white population, preferring, as the historian Catherine Hall emphasizes, "their own culture, shaped by slavery, the middle passage, and the plantation . . . [that molded] their own syncretic forms of religion, their own rituals, their own practices, their own African-Jamaican way of life."[70]

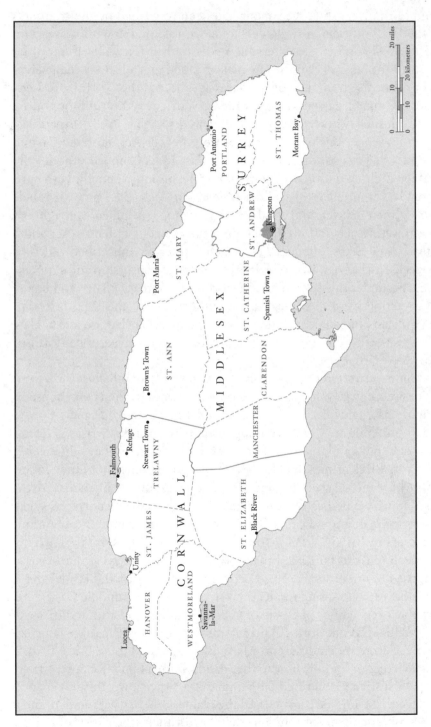

Nineteenth-century Jamaica

Beneath it all was a tension that ran through much of the British Empire. Liberal imperialism's aspirations for accretive liberties and equalities could not be severed from a colonial capitalism built on racialized economic inequality, regardless of whether labor was free or unfree. In the empire, these issues were deeply intertwined, impossible to reconcile, and the source of repeated protests, strikes, riots, and full-scale rebellions. The insurrection brewing in Jamaica, which once had the largest population of enslaved people and still rested alongside India as a jewel in the imperial crown, was poised to test Britain's confused conceptions of freedom and challenge Mill's benevolent despotism.[71]

Disputes between the island's Black and white populations over arbitrary justice, like the rulings Bowen and Walton handed down, as well as draconian labor regimes and property laws ignited a violent protest outside the Morant Bay courthouse on that October afternoon in 1865, leaving several people dead. Forty-two kilometers away in Kingston, news quickly reached Governor Edward John Eyre, sparking his fears

Morant Bay Rebellion, attack on the Court House, St. Thomas-in-the-East, Jamaica, October 11, 1865.

that Blacks were conspiring to overthrow the government and expel all whites from the island. Paul Bogle, a Black man who owned land not far from Morant Bay, had been spreading these revolutionary ideas for months. Eyre convened his council of war and declared martial law for all of Surrey County except Kingston. Unlike those in India, protesters in the Morant Bay rebellion were few in number, with little armed force. Suppression nevertheless ensued. One British commanding officer offered an eyewitness account:

> This morning we made raid with thirty men, all mounted, and got back to head-quarters . . . bringing in a few prisoners, and having flogged nine men, and burned three negro houses, and then had a court-martial on the prisoners, who amounted to about fifty or sixty. Several were flogged without court-martial, from a simple examination; nine were convicted by court-martial: one of them to a hundred lashes, which he got at once, the other eight to be hanged or shot. We quarter on the enemy as much as possible. . . . This is a picture of martial law. The soldiers enjoy it—the inhabitants have to dread it.[72]

Bogle was captured, court-martialed, and executed, as was George William Gordon, a prominent mixed-raced member of the Jamaican House of Assembly. Eyre had taken the extraordinary measure of arresting Gordon, a dissident politician who had made several inflammatory remarks before the rebellion, in Kingston, where martial law was not in effect, and transporting him to Morant Bay so that he could be tried by a military tribunal. Adding to procedural irregularity were the charges levied against Gordon: high treason and complicity with rebels. The only evidence was circumstantial; nonetheless Gordon was tried, found guilty, and executed for a crime in which he had no direct involvement.[73]

When news of the Jamaican events filtered back to Britain, controversy erupted. Eyre went on the offensive and published his account of the events in the November 18 supplement to the *London Gazette*. "The most frightful atrocities were perpetrated," he fervently wrote:

> The Island curate of Bath . . . is said to have had his tongue cut out whilst still alive, and an attempt is said to have been made to skin him alive. One person . . . was ripped open, and his entrails taken out. One gentlemen . . . is said to have been pushed into an outbuilding, which was then set on fire, and kept there until he was literally roasted alive. Many are said to have had their

eyes scooped out; heads were cleft open, and the brains taken out. The baron's fingers were cut off and carried away as trophies by the murderers. Some bodies were half burnt, others horribly battered. Indeed, the whole outrage could only be paralleled by the atrocities of the Indian mutiny.[74]

Eyre boasted that "the retribution has been so prompt and so terrible that it is likely never to be forgotten."[75] A royal commission of inquiry investigated the events in Jamaica and published its findings in April 1866; there appeared to be little evidence to support the governor's lurid justifications for martial law's necessity. The commission did call the rebellion an "apparently formidable insurrection" and enumerated state-directed punishments: 439 Blacks died, many summarily executed; one thousand dwellings were burned; and no fewer than six hundred Blacks were flogged, with suffering particularly cruel in Bath. "At first an ordinary cat was used [for flogging]," the commission reported, "but afterwards, for the punishment of men, wires were twisted round the cords, and the different tails so constructed were knotted. Some of these were produced before us, and it was painful to think that any man should have used such an instrument for the torturing of his fellow creatures."[76] Nonetheless, the report largely excused Eyre's draconian actions and those of Britain's troops as excesses of power that, while unfortunate, were necessary in colonial circumstances.

The same year as the Morant Bay rebellion, John Stuart Mill was elected as a Liberal MP, putting his political theories on liberty and good governance to the empirical test. "My eyes were first opened to the moral condition of the English nation . . . by the atrocities perpetrated in the Indian Mutiny," he observed, and then "came this Jamaica business."[77] Far from the empire's front lines, Mill sat quill in hand, to write *Considerations on Representative Government*. Publishing it four years after the Indian Mutiny, he insisted:

> I am far from condemning, in cases of extreme exigency, the assumption of absolute power in the form of a temporary dictatorship. Free nations have, in times of old, conferred such power by their own choice, as necessary medicine for diseases of the body politic which could not be got rid of by less violent means. But its acceptance, even for a time strictly limited, can only be excused, if, like Solon or Pittacus, the dictator employs the power he assumes in removing the obstacles which debar the nation from the enjoyment of freedom.[78]

Jamaica's Black population, however, did not enjoy freedom. It was something that would come, according to Mill, only after arduous British tutelage. "To determine the form of government most suited to any particular people, we must be able, among the defects and shortcomings which belong to that people, to distinguish those that are the immediate impediment to progress," he concluded. "A people of savages should be taught obedience . . . for carrying [them] through the next stage of progress."[79] This, for Mill, was part of "their object improvement, or Progress."[80] In the aftermath of events in Jamaica, he was at pains to distinguish his "despotism [as] a legitimate mode of government" in empire from Eyre's "crimes of violence & cruelty," which had violated "law & justice as the foundation of order & civilisation . . . [and] lower[ed] the character of England in the eyes of all foreign lovers of liberty."[81]

"I am almost ashamed to speak of such acts with the calmness and in the moderate language which the circumstances require," Mill sputtered across Parliament's packed benches in the summer heat of 1866. "The lives of subjects of her Majesty have been wrongfully taken, and the persons of others wrongfully maltreated; and I maintain that when such things have been done, there is a *prima facie* demand for legal punishment, and that a court of criminal justice can alone determine whether such punishment has been merited, and if merited, what [ought] to be its amount." When *On Liberty*'s theoretical "extreme exigency" played out with barbaric consequences first in India and then in Jamaica, Mill was incredulous, demanding that the law parse legitimate violence from the illegitimate "barbarous" floggings and "burnings . . . wanton and cruel" contained in "the dry facts of the commissioners' summary." Without such distinctions, he told his fellow MPs, Britain's empire was no different from the Oriental despotism it was seeking to reform:

> If men are let loose from all law, from all precedents, from all forms—are left to try people for their lives in any way they please, take evidence as they please, refuse evidence as they please, give facilities to the defence or withhold those facilities as they think fit, and after that pass any sentences they please, and irrevocably execute those sentences, with no bounds to their discretion but their own judgment of what is necessary for the suppression of a rebellion—a judgment which not only may be, but in a vast proportion of cases is sure to be, an exasperate man's judgment, or a frightened man's judgment of necessity [*hear, hear*]; when there is absolutely no guarantee against any extremity of tyrannical violence, but the responsibility which can be afterwards exacted

from the tyrant—then, sir, it is indeed indispensable that he who takes the lives of others under this discretion should know that he risks his own.[82]

For months, the case of Governor Eyre had deeply divided the nation. The Jamaica Committee, comprised of Mill and others including Charles Darwin, Herbert Spencer, Charles Lyell, and John Bright, lobbied first for a commission of inquiry. Unsatisfied with the commission's final 1866 report, the Jamaica Committee demanded that Eyre and his deputies be brought up on criminal charges. The committee members were particularly incensed with the hasty trial and execution of George Gordon, who was not an imminent threat to the state and had been transported into an area under martial law for the purpose of executing him without restraint from ordinary legal procedure. "You see that I am not on this occasion standing up for the negroes," Mill confided in private correspondence, "or for liberty, deeply as both are interested in the subject—but for the first necessity of human society, law."[83] It was the abuse of martial law, as opposed to "human sympathies," that was the crux of the Jamaica Committee's concern.[84] "[If] the civil and military authorities and their agents may run amuck, if such is their pleasure—[they] may do, as far as any legal restraint is concerned, anything they please. . . . We have gained little by our historical struggles, and the blood that has been shed for English liberties has been shed to little purpose," Mill intoned. He reminded his fellow parliamentarians that martial law was not "the negation of all law . . . the negation of all responsibility. . . . [It was] another word for the law of necessity," and "we have the right to dispute the necessity."[85]

Squaring off against the Jamaica Committee were equally vocal supporters of Eyre. They included Charles Dickens, Matthew Arnold, John Ruskin, and Thomas Carlyle, whose publication of "Occasional Discourse on the Negro Question" in 1849 offered a bleak prediction of the postemancipation future, in which Blacks would slide into what was supposed to be their natural state of idleness, if not savagery, and needing the strong hand of white rule. Humanitarian reformers and those advocating for democratic principles were grossly misguided, according to Carlyle, and what was needed was the reintroduction of enslavement and indentured servitude.[86] "Here, sure enough, are peculiar views of the Rights of Negroes," he wrote, pen burning, "involving, it is probable, peculiar ditto of innumerable other rights, duties, expectations, wrongs and disappointments, much argued of by logic and by grapeshot, in these emancipated epochs of the human mind! . . . I feel there is an immense fund of Human Stupidity circulating among us, and much clogging of our affairs for some time past!"[87]

When rushing to Eyre's defense, Carlyle and others extended their harsh views by applying cultural and racial critiques to the law and insisting that Blacks did not have the same legal protections as did whites. A contemporary jurist, William Francis Finlason, wrote prolifically in support of Eyre, arguing that English common law applied only to British-born subjects and their descendants in Jamaica, not to Blacks. In other words, race placed conquered populations into a different legal category, reflecting their stage of development. Moreover, a white minority of 13,000 living amid 350,000 Blacks in Jamaica created "the necessity for deterrent measures," according to Finlason. In effect, when applied to the colonies, the state of legal exception had to account for necessary *preemptive* measures.[88] This was a monumental shift in English common law's understanding of necessity. "What Finlason discloses," Nasser Hussain concludes in *Jurisprudence of Emergency*, "is the fact that the authority for martial law would have to be found not in the self-regulating discourses of legality but in the unspoken [racial] and violent origin of the state."[89]

The events in Jamaica represented the crucial moment in Britain's second empire when the scope of martial law's necessity and the permissibility of violence widened. The Jamaica Committee's repeated failures to bring Eyre up on charges in London confirmed this development. In fact, the committee couldn't even get a grand jury to indict Eyre. "It was clear that to bring English functionaries to the bar of a criminal court for abuses of power committed against Negroes and mulattoes," Mill lamented, "was not a popular proceeding with the English middle classes."[90] It was a far cry from the moral triumph that had accompanied abolitionism at the turn of the nineteenth century. In the American Revolution's aftermath, Britain had grappled with its imperial role and anxieties over its power in the world. The rise of Protestant evangelicalism had pushed the nation to claim a new moral position in the face of its weakening authority overseas. The blow that America's independence induced softened when, in 1807, a refashioning of British imperial sensibilities in the form of abolition brought about the end of trade in enslaved peoples. When Britain ended the use of enslaved labor in most of its empire in 1838, the nation boasted a newfound moral high ground.[91] In the years ahead, the question of whether Britain had abandoned enslaved labor because it was less economically efficient than free labor would be a matter of considerable debate.[92] What is inarguable, however, is the fact that whatever moral currents had given rise to abolitionism were changing by the mid-Victorian era. Coming on the heels of the Indian Mutiny, the Jamaican events legitimized Carlyle's extreme position and breathed oxygen into conservative and racialized fires.

After the Jamaica Committee spent three years unsuccessfully chasing Eyre through the courts, the British government paid all his legal fees and granted him a pension before he retired to bucolic Walreddon Manor in Devon. The debates he sparked, however, were not over. James Fitzjames Stephen had been the Jamaica Committee's lead counsel, though he abandoned his role and the committee to take a hardline stand on coercion. The son of prominent abolitionist parents—his father was an MP and a member of the Clapham Sect, and his mother the daughter of Clapham's rector—Stephen was no jingoistic imperialist. He believed in the law's ability to impose authority and morality in the empire, though force would always mediate its civilizing effects. His formative years at Eton, one of Britain's most exclusive schools, had shaped some of his views. "The process taught me for life," he later reflected, "the lesson that to be weak is to be wretched, that the state of nature is a state of war, and *Vae Victis* [woe to the vanquished] the great law of nature."[93]

Stephen joined forces with Carlyle to criticize Mill's "sentimental liberalism" as undermining political stability in the empire and at home.[94] Mill's "extreme exigency," according to Stephen, was "*the common law right* of the Crown and its representatives to repel force by force in the case of invasion or insurrection, and to act against rebels as it might against invaders."[95] Moreover "commands of this sovereign may be equitable or inequitable—that is, they may, or may not, tend to promote the welfare of the governed; but they cannot be unlawful, for they are themselves the law, and the only laws, of the subject society."[96] For Stephen, law reflected the necessary power of the state to protect itself, and British rule differed from Oriental despotism because it rejected "personal intrigue" and embraced law's codification and procedure, which were inherently moral and just.[97] Without this moral force of the law, society would descend into anarchy. "Disguise it how you will," Stephen wrote, "it is force in one shape or another which determines relations between human beings. . . . Society rests ultimately upon force in these days, just as much as it did in the wildest and most stormy periods of history."[98]

In 1869, Stephen traveled to India, where he served as the legal member for the Imperial Legislative Council. It was "the best corrective in existence to the fundamental fallacies of Liberalism," he later recalled. Out there, "you see real government."[99] Three years later, en route home from Calcutta, he whiled away his hours at sea writing a seething critique of Mill's liberalism. Published in 1873, *Liberty, Equality, and Fraternity*, Stephen's canonical work, insisted, "Force is an absolutely essential element of all law whatever. Indeed law is nothing but regulated force subjected to particular conditions and directed towards particular objects. The abolition of the law of force cannot therefore mean the withdrawal of the element of force from law, for that would be the destruction of law altogether."[100] Ten years later another row over liberalism in empire erupted, and Stephen was uncompromising. As far as he was concerned, Britain had to recognize imperialism for what it was:

> If the Government of India have decided on removing all [legal] anomalies from India, they ought to remove themselves and their countrymen. . . . It is essentially an absolute government, founded, not on consent, but on conquest. It does not represent the native principles of life or of government, and it can never do so until it represents heathenism and barbarism. It represents a belligerent civilization, and no anomaly can be so striking and so dangerous as its administration by men who, being at the head of a Government founded on conquest, implying at every point the superiority of the conquering race, of their ideas, their institutions, their opinions and their principles, and having no justification for its existence except that superiority, shrink from the open, uncompromising, straight forward assertion of it, seek to apologize for their own position, and refuse, from whatever cause, to uphold and support it.[101]

These raging battles between towering philosophers, statesmen, and jurists over liberal imperialism's meanings and practices made one point abundantly clear: the Victorian-era philosophy was a paradox. Liberal imperialism was an oxymoron, rendering it agonizing for thinkers like Mill to reconcile. Liberal imperialism was reformist and coercive, and Victorian-era humanists like Robert Louis Stevenson captured this dialectic in ways that politicians and legal thinkers could not. "All human beings as we meet them are commingled out of good and evil," Stevenson wrote. His novella, *The Strange Case of Dr. Jekyll and Mr. Hyde*, published in 1886, explored these opposites residing in one man's tortured consciousness, capturing through Jekyll's ruminations on the complexities and contradictions that riddled the late nineteenth century:

> With every day, and from both sides of my intelligence, the moral and the intellectual, I thus drew steadily nearer to that

truth by whose partial discovery I have been doomed to such a dreadful shipwreck: that man is not truly one, but truly two. I say two, because the state of my own knowledge does not pass beyond that point. Others will follow, others will outstrip me on the same lines; and I hazard to guess that man will ultimately be known for a mere polity of multifarious, incongruous, and independent denizens. . . . It was on the moral side, and in my own person, that I learned to recognise the thorough and primitive duality of man; I saw that, of the two natures that contended in my field of consciousness, even if I could rightly be said to be either, it was only because I was radically both.[102]

Liberal imperialism was also "radically both." Arguments for coercion and reform were on either end of its spectrum—a spectrum that contained a wide range of viewpoints contingent on empire's time, place, and circumstance. Indeed, if the British Empire were just about unbridled violence justified through the mere rhetoric of reform, then we could hardly explain liberal imperialism's multiple fault lines exposed in the wake of the Indian Mutiny and the Morant Bay Rebellion, or the ways they would repeatedly reveal themselves in the future. When was violence necessary? When was it legal? Could martial law cancel ordinary law and establish new rules of legality to reflect the empire's racialized order? Did this order call for different intensities of violence and reform? And in what ways did colonial violence not only reestablish state authority but also serve a reformist function, teaching natives a biblically inspired moral lesson?

These were some of the questions that lay at the heart of disputes over liberal imperialism, and neither Mill nor Stephen resolved them. For more than a century, liberal imperialism's contradictions would drive ever more complex arguments over the empire's purpose in the face of major global changes; the paradox of coercion and reform would be revealed most vividly when state-directed violence was deployed during exceptional moments. These moments, the Italian philosopher Giorgio Agamben suggests, show us that "exceptional measures are the result of periods of political crisis and, as such, must be understood on political [grounds]. . . . [The state of exception] is this no-man's-land between public law and political fact, and between the juridical order and life."[103]

Victorian-era responses to what was transpiring in India and Jamaica betrayed the state of exception's intrinsic and contested anxieties. While still clinging to the universalisms at liberalism's core, a swath of British public opinion and policy makers condemned their non-European subjects as not only resistant to reform but also historically and culturally unprepared for its transformations.[104] When progressive measures were offered to culturally different and "inferior" populations in the empire, they spawned enigmatic and unfathomable violence that threatened the civilizing hand that shaped them. Britain needed to take a step back and reassess. Politically, it ended elected representation in Jamaica's House of Assembly and brought the island under direct crown colony governance. In India, the mutiny heralded the end of the East India Company's rule and the creation of the British Raj under direct imperial rule in 1858. Culturally, many Britons rejected the idea that Indians or Africans could ever become brown or Black Englishmen.

The fear of too much too soon also ascended in liberal imperial thought. For mid- and late Victorians, convulsions in the empire were the result of British reform efforts rather than the injustices of British rule. Traditional societies had dissolved in the face of a too-rapid civilizing mission and created massive disorder. Going forward, as Karuna Mantena elaborates in *Alibis of Empire*, indigenous political and social forms would be rehabilitated, and often invented, to stabilize indigenous populations.[105] Britain would rule indirectly through local systems and their pashas, princes, and chiefs whose power was directly contingent on British support and the execution of imperial policies on the ground. Alongside Britain's evolving policy of indirect rule was a paternalistic ethos. Imperial actors, such as frontline administrators and missionaries, implemented reform measures with the anticipation that it would now take generations, if not more, for these measures to yield results. At the same time, a parallel legal system evolved that Britain did not entrust to local rulers. Comprised of penal codes, restrictive regulations, and the ability to declare martial law or a state of emergency (statutory martial law), this system suppressed challenges to British rule.

These processes unfolded against a backdrop of unprecedented, and potentially destabilizing, reform in Britain. Conservative critiques of sentimental liberalism were as much about a series of acts that extended the franchise to the working class at home as they were a response to the perceived failures of abolition and programs for reform in the empire. Stephen and others represented a conservative backlash against the dissolution of the old social order. Their anxieties over mass democracy transcended home and empire and conflated threats in India with those from Britain's working class that exploded in Hyde Park in 1866, when demonstrators demanded one man, one vote. In *Liberty, Equality, Fraternity*, Stephen made clear that power and coercion were necessary and legitimate forms of imperial *and* domestic rule. Unlike in Jamaica, however, the tide of transformation in Britain could no longer be held back. Working-class ambitions became acceptable, in part, because white domestic civility stood in relative contrast to the perceived savagery of imperial subjects in the empire. Liberalism at home and its manifestations in the empire were interconnected, and as another political theorist, Jennifer Pitts, has suggested, "Ideas of freedom and despotism, self-government, and the autonomous individual—were imagined and articulated in light of, and in response to, and sometimes in justification of, imperial and commercial expansion beyond Europe."[106]

As social structures underwent unprecedented changes in the late Victorian era, so too did Britain witness an efflorescence of newfound traditions and a mass media culture that were inextricably linked to empire. Even if classical liberalism was not extended to imperial subjects, the extension of suffrage, the sanctity of market transactions, and the rising dominance of class as a substitute for rank hierarchy led to the emergence of mass politics and a weakening of old social bonds at home. In Britain, and indeed in most of Europe, the state played an increasingly decisive role in the day-to-day lives of its domestic population. It became progressively inseparable from civil society, while its national economy, partly rooted in the empire, became an engine of domestic economic development. At the same time, tensions within the ranks of the once secure ruling elite persisted. The question of how to maintain legitimacy, order, and cooperation with the nation's new, expansive body politic created a set of conditions ripe for a patriotism that integrated the old order with the new through the language, ideals, and representations of empire.[107]

In the late nineteenth century, according to the historian Eric Hobsbawm, "an alternative 'civic religion' had to be constructed . . . [and] state, nation and society converged."[108] Within the orbit of the state, practical politicians took center stage to construct the nation's identity. In unofficial channels, the media through which liberalism would do its work—particularly the press, popular culture, and education—played crucial roles in reinforcing a nationalist narrative grounded in a liberal imperialism that was, at once, confident and forgetful. Political and social forces coalesced not only to assuage the potentially undermining effects of rapid social transformation at home but also to forge a nationalist identity that had popular resonance with the expanding electorate. The past, meanwhile, was mined for heroic figures and symbolic meanings.

That British patriotism became bound with the empire was due in no small part to politicians' deliberate entwining of national interest, monarchy, Greater Britain, and the working class.[109] In his Crystal Palace speech of 1872, Prime Minister Benjamin Disraeli chided the sentimental liberalism that threatened "the disintegration of the empire of England" and put a defining question to Britons that would shape their nation's future:

> When you return to your homes, when you return to your counties and your cities, you must tell to all those whom you can influence that the time is at hand, that, at least, it cannot be far distant when England will have to decide between national and cosmopolitan principles. The issue is not a mean one. It is whether you will be content to be a comfortable England, modelled and moulded upon continental principles and meeting in due course an inevitable fate, or whether you will be a great country,—an imperial country—a country where your sons, when they rise, rise to paramount positions, and obtain not merely the esteem of their countrymen, but command the respect of the world.[110]

For Conservatives like Disraeli, and for disaffected Liberal Unionists like Stephen, the empire was an all-encompassing patriotic enterprise, one that located Britain's unique history and national interests in imperial terms.[111] Appealing to the working class, Disraeli linked Conservative concerns for their plight with pride in "belonging to an Imperial country."[112] In so doing, he sought to co-opt the working class that Stephen and others so feared and enlist it behind broader national and imperial agendas.

Resuscitating a beleaguered monarchy was the first order of business. Throughout much of the nineteenth century, the public viewed the British monarchy critically. The adulterous King George IV barred his wife, Queen Caroline, from his 1821 coronation. After a succession crisis marred by illegitimate children and the premature deaths of legitimate heirs to the throne, Princess Victoria ascended to become queen in 1837. When she married her cousin, Prince Albert of Saxe-Coburg and Gotha, the British public disliked his German heritage, and Parliament objected to him becoming a British peer. Following Prince Albert's untimely death in 1861, the queen's personal depression and self-imposed cloistering only added to the monarchy's woes. In 1864 an unsigned notice was affixed to the gates of Buckingham Palace declaring, "These commanding premises to be let or sold, in consequence of the late occupant's declining business." Over the next two decades, Queen Victoria opened Parliament just six times, and as one observer noted, "from causes which it is not difficult to define, the Queen has done almost as much to injure the popularity of the monarchy by her long retirement from public life as the most unworthy of her predecessors did by his profligacy and frivolity."[113]

The 1870s, however, heralded the monarchy's transformation, coinciding with liberal imperialism's violent ruptures. Queen Victoria's longevity, her sense of duty, morality, and virtue, and most of all, her place as the regal matriarch of Europe suddenly endeared her to her subjects. The advent of mass-circulation national dailies that displaced the old Liberal provincial press would hone and perpetuate this image of the queen, and later of her successors, as symbolic figures who towered above politics. The first, crucial stroke to this fashioning was Disraeli's

"NEW CROWNS FOR OLD ONES!"

"New Crowns for Old Ones," Benjamin Disraeli offers the crown of India to Queen Victoria, *Punch Magazine*, April 15, 1876.

push for the enactment of the Royal Titles Bill in 1876. With it, Queen Victoria emerged from her near-twenty-year-long hiatus of mourning to assume the title Empress of India. In a time of cataclysmic change, the queen and the monarchy symbolized unity, permanence, and the resurgence of a nostalgia that politicians like Disraeli ably captured and translated into an imperial-based patriotism for a more inclusive nation. During the first three-quarters of the century, no coronation or other royal ritual had included much of the empire; after 1877 every occasion marking the grandeur of the monarchy, and the nation, was an imperial occasion. A fleet of savvy politicians and courtiers from Disraeli and Joseph Chamberlain to the meticulous Viscount Esher and the royal maestro Edward Elgar updated old ceremonies and invented new ones for the imperial times in which they lived. In the decades ahead, at home and in the empire, such pageantry would leave a deep impression on the British psyche.[114]

It was the Diamond Jubilee, the 1897 capstone to Victoria's reign and celebration of her place as Britain's longest-reigning monarch, that fully enacted empire's importance to Britain's past, present, and future. Esher, known as "the *éminence grise* in British governing circles at the turn of the century," introduced to the occasion a precision, splendor, and public ceremonial efficiency that were soon understood as time-honored traditions. For his part, Elgar composed the first of his many empire-inspired ceremonial scores—his "Imperial March" was a defining, and wildly popular, feature of the queen's anniversary event.[115] Doubling as the "Festival of the British Empire," the Diamond Jubilee's only foreign guests were heads of state and representatives of British colonies and territories from around the world. Britons traveled for days to witness the colors of empire parading through London's streets on June 22, 1897. The nation's capital had emerged in the late nineteenth century as the epicenter of the country and would, in the years ahead, be transformed from the dankness of Dickens's novels into an imperial city. Grand memorials and statues of the empire's heroes would proliferate. The erection of Admiralty Arch, the widening of the Mall, and the refronting of Buckingham Palace, complete with a monument to Queen Victoria, would ensure a commemorative parade ground suitable for the magnificence of Britain's royal and imperial nation.[116]

As night fell the evening before the Diamond Jubilee, London hosted thousands who slept *en plein air* to secure a coveted space along their monarch's route. The next day, as the capital was festooned in Union Jacks and the "Imperial March" filled the air, Victoria had one last act to complete before her seventeen-carriage convoy carrying the royal family and leaders of Britain's imperial corps departed Buckingham Palace. To her 450 million British subjects in the empire, she sent a telegraph message: "From my heart I thank my beloved people. May God bless them. V. R. & I."[117] With that, the cannon fired at a quarter past eleven in the morning, and the monarch and her convoy wound its way through the joyous streets of London, where Britons celebrated God, queen, and empire.

Royally embodied and embedded into a nationalist narrative, the empire appealed to all levels of British society. A late Victorian mentality, grounded in notions of British superiority, Christian ethics, industrial and cultural achievements, and hardened racist attitudes, evolved into a unifying moral and racial authority that would be bequeathed to future generations.[118] By the end of Victoria's reign, a pervasive vision of a Greater Britain emerged, constituted not only through royal ritual and symbolism but also through the language and representations of empire at home. From Birmingham to Liverpool, Britons fashioned themselves in the context of their country's colonial project: the Aborigines of Australia and the Blacks of Jamaica offered living examples of cultural and racial difference that separated the civilized British from those who existed on distant shores.[119] A wide range of responses to empire cleaved along class, religious, gender, generational, and regional lines, but a national identity rooted in empire transcended many of Britain's diversities, uniting an ever more inclusive domestic sphere around racist conceptions of subject populations and the need to mitigate their presumed civilized deficiencies through the heavy hand of British imperial benevolence.[120]

Literature, education, and the media reaffirmed concepts of inclusion and exclusion. They all had an integral role to play in shaping Britain's civilizing mission and representations of it at home, and various genres further shaped the public's understanding of imperial subjects.[121] Children's literature in the Victorian and Edwardian periods, and beyond, was very important. Childhood stories extolled the virtues of Britain and the differences of "backward" subject peoples while at the same time acculturating young Britons into the duties that lay ahead of them.[122] One need only recall Lewis Carroll's "avatar of empire," Alice—who engages with the strangeness of Wonderland and its creatures, while at the same time maintaining a sense of bounded order—to imagine the ways literature played on the imperial imaginations of Britain's youth.[123] More explicitly imperial forms of children's literature also abounded.

The Boy's Own Paper, Victoria Cross,
"Medals Awarded for Valour" issue

Magazines and comics such as *The Boy's Own Paper, Magnet*, and *Union Jack* all extolled British virtue through adventure stories set in imperial contexts.

The works of George Alfred Henty had a widespread influence on the minds of Britain's youth, not only in the Victorian era but also well into the twentieth century. Henty began his career as a journalist, touring the world and reporting on various wars of conquest in the empire. According to one noted literary critic, the authoritarianism of Thomas Carlyle and others deeply influenced Henty, who "exemplified the ethos of the new imperialism, and glorified in its successes."[124] Many of Henty's books mined the British imperial past for heroes and villainous events that included the resurrected founder of empire, Clive, and the epochal Black Hole of Calcutta. By the time he died at the turn of the century, Henty had produced over one hundred books with titles such as *With Clive and India: The Beginning of an Empire; The Young Colonists: A Story of the Zulu and Boer Wars;* and *Maori and Settler: A Tale of the New Zealand War*. In tale after tale, "native savagery" was juxtaposed with British civility, and violence leveled against racially inferior populations went hand in hand with extending British virtues and progress. Most impressive was the circulation of Henty's works. In the 1950s, the family's publishing house estimated that up to 25 million copies of his titles were in circulation, shaping the worldview of some of Britain's most powerful politicians, historians, military leaders, religious figures, and industrialists. From Prime Minister Harold Macmillan and Field Marshal Bernard Montgomery to the historian A. J. P. Taylor and the Bishop of London, Britain's patriarchy, alongside the nation's working and middle classes, waxed lyrical about Henty and his stories of imperial heroism and its accompanying violence.[125]

The heroic proselytizing of the missionary David Livingstone was also legendary in Britain, as were the travails of the adventurers Richard Burton and John Hanning Speke in their quest to secure the headwaters of the Nile for the queen.[126] Livingstone, the most prominent of evangelical adventurers, embodied the Christian ethics that drove industriousness and virtue at home and that took form in the empire through the work of missionaries. Livingstone's famous rallying cry—"Christianity, commerce, and civilization"—not only reflected the sentiments of the men of God but also the self-fashioning of a devout British nation for whom racial superiority, capitalism, and religious virtue were inextricably linked. Sunday schools, religious youth organizations, newspapers, and magazines embraced the adventure tradition of Christian heroes like Livingstone, whose unparalleled moral character and personal sacrifice in the service of empire were examples to which the entire nation should aspire.[127] School textbook publishers similarly peddled a civic pride in the empire and provided teachers with history and geography texts that extolled Britain's civilizing mission and reminded Britain's youth of "native savagery." Whether in or out of the classroom, generations of British schoolchildren were weaned on a triumphant imperial narrative that depicted their nation as waging a moral battle to defend civilization while also bringing light to the world's so-called savages.

A new generation of scholars crafted a history of unbroken British progress. Foremost among them was John Robert Seeley, the founder of British imperial history.[128] In the late nineteenth century, Seeley joined the ranks of a modern historical profession that drew its inspiration from Leopold von Ranke. Ranke, a German scholar and arguably the most influential nineteenth-century historian, revolutionized the practice of historical writing through an emphasis on empiricism. For him, written historical documents and the historian's neutral detachment would produce factual truth telling. Seeley took up Ranke's method, though neither he nor his successors questioned the sanctity of the state archive at the Public Record Office; nor did they challenge Britain's self-representations as liberal imperialists, or the alleged civilizing superiority of the nation's past and its people.[129]

Seeley and the emerging historical profession played an important role in how the nation and the world understood Britain's imperial project. In his lectures on "The Expansion of England," published as a landmark book in 1883, Seeley hitched the Whig narrative of the nation, the idea that British history was a linear story of liberty and progress, to imperial expansion. The work also made interventions into several imperial debates, including those about Ireland and the white dominions, and it addressed the question of British legitimacy in India that stretched back to the Hastings trial. The abiding issue for Seeley was Britain's original conquest of India. Burke had set the moral terms of the debate, critiquing the East India Company's methods; then Stephen

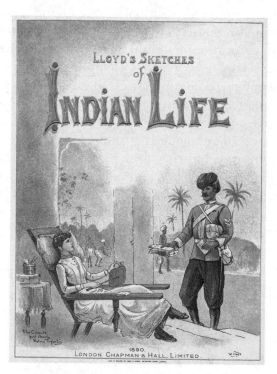

An Indian infantry corporal delivers mail to an English woman in this cover image for *Lloyd's Sketches of Indian Life*, 1890. The original caption read, "The Colonels post orderly. Native infantry."

reappraised the Hastings trial, insisting that the crimes of conquest were wildly exaggerated and possibly contrived. "In this way, conquest," as Mantena tells us, "now devoid of criminality, could emerge as legitimate on its own terms."[130] Seeley, however, suggested that the notion of conquest was misplaced. India was not a nation with a political community; rather, with the fall of the Mughal Empire, the subcontinent was home to a Hobbesian state of anarchy. "It remains entirely incorrect to speak of the English nation as having conquered the nations of India. . . . India can hardly be said to have been conquered at all by foreigners," Seeley insisted, "she has rather conquered herself." In effect, if Britain hadn't conquered India, then it had nothing to atone for; instead, Pax Britannica was necessary because it prevented further disintegration in the East. "There need be no question," Seeley concluded, "about the general fact that the ruling race in British India has a higher and more vigorous civilisation than the native races."[131]

This "general fact" was largely uncontested in Britain. Like Ranke, Seeley assumed that "the way things really were was the way that men of power and influence judged them to be; and to this extent he was a prisoner of his sources as well as of language and religious and philosophical heritage," according to the historian Donald Kelley.[132] Devoid of the explicit moralism infusing the speeches and writings of Victorian-era political philosophers, Seeley deployed embedded argument in his narrative. He also laid claim to Ranke's professional neutrality—which would serve as a justificatory pretext for British imperial historians in the decades to come. Cloaked in neutrality, Whig narratives would combine acts of omission and sleights of hand to create histories that became hagiographies of Britain's civilizing mission. Throughout the twentieth century, historians produced authoritative evidence for Britain's imperial identity and claims to sovereignty in the empire, in the realm of politics, the media, the creation of textbooks, and the shaping of future leaders at Oxford and Cambridge.[133]

As the century turned, Rudyard Kipling breathed poetic life into the empire and endowed it with a function and purpose that reflected its civilizing mission. In his epic work "Regulus," Britain took its place among the great ancient empires. At one point, Kipling quoted Virgil and likened all the purposes and virtues of the Roman Empire to those of Britain's imperial expansion: "Roman! Let this be your care, this your art / To rule over the nations and impose the ways of peace / To spare the underdog, and pull down the proud."[134] By bringing and maintaining order and stability throughout the world, abolishing enslaved labor, alleviating famine, improving education and health care, and construct-

ing the literal and metaphorical groundwork for civilization, Britain
was a modern-day Imperium Romanum. Then, in arguably his most
famous work, "The White Man's Burden," Kipling ensured his legacy as
empire's poet by introducing a phrase into the English language that has
endured to the present day. Written in response to America's takeover
of the Philippines after the Spanish American War, "The White Man's
Burden" soon became synonymous with the imperialist endeavors of all
Western nations, most especially those of Britain. In the poem's opening
stanza, Kipling did not equivocate:

> *Take up the White Man's burden—*
> *Send forth the best ye breed—*
> *Go bind your sons to exile*
> *To serve your captives' need;*
> *To wait in heavy harness,*
> *On fluttered folk and wild—*
> *Your new-caught, sullen peoples,*
> *Half-devil and half-child.*[135]

The British viceroy of India, Lord Curzon, on an elephant with Lady Curzon,
enters Delhi and passes the Red Fort, 1902.

The "half-devil and half-child" colonial subject in the white settler territories, however, did not inhabit the same British Empire. The future of Canada, Australia, and New Zealand was imagined in the ancient Greek tradition of colonization. Greek forms of democracy would unite Britain with its white settlement colonies to create, in the words of British statesman William Gladstone, "so many happy Englands."[136] In 1931 these "happy Englands" were formalized as the British Commonwealth of Nations, which was comprised entirely of the so-called white dominions, or settlement colonies, until after the Second World War. By contrast, the "half-devil and half-child" non-Europeans constituted Britain's dependent empire, to be ruled in the Roman tradition. This tradition would be rendered British through the nation's liberal self-fashioning as the standard-bearer of progress, whose duty it was to spread the gospel of liberty, good government, the rule of law, and free trade and labor throughout the world. Indeed, Britons condemned late-nineteenth-century European empires absent a reformist impulse, like King Leopold's Congo. As liberal imperialism matured in Africa and Asia, British colonial regimes constructed racial difference and defined categories such as tribe and caste in ways that created a praxis through which liberalism could increasingly deploy repressive policies to reform the devil children of empire and protect Western civilization from potential ruinous decline.[137]

A year after Queen Victoria's Diamond Jubilee, Lord George Nathaniel Curzon, the governor-general and viceroy of India, said, "Imperialism is becoming everyday less and less the creed of a party and more and more the faith of a nation."[138] Only a handful of political and social critics disagreed.[139] Not surprisingly, in the aftermath of Britons celebrating their then-longest reigning monarch, the countless subjects who lost their lives and livelihoods to Britain's global rapacity, however ideologically understood and justified their deaths were, would receive no imperial requiem. The British Empire was not carved from *terra nullius* with a minimum degree of force and, over time, a maximum amount of cooperation from gratefully indebted local populations. Instead, in India, West Africa, the Caribbean, Australia, and elsewhere, colonized populations harnessed their agency in the face of an increasingly more sophisticated British imperial regime.[140] Initial acts of conquest gave way in the twentieth century to elaborate legal codes, the proliferation of police and security forces, free market and labor controls for the colonized, and administrative apparatuses that marginalized and oppressed entire populations while fueling racial and ethnic divisions within and between them. The lived realities of Britain's burden in the empire would be vastly different from the nation's self-representations, grounded as they were in a historical consciousness that was as deft at collective erasure and creating approbatory versions of the nation's past as it was in disseminating these ideas through liberalism's official and unofficial channels. From the political and social crucible of monarchy, empire, and nation emerged a powerful identity that would persist throughout the twentieth century and gain renewed saliency with the Conservative Party's recent push for Brexit and Empire 2.0.

The paradox between the lived imperial experiences of the colonized and the laudatory claims of Britain's civilizing mission can be traced to the conjoined nineteenth-century birth of modern liberalism and imperialism. They shaped an era in which national interests were inextricable from the growth and spread of capitalism, and in which a dominant narrative of universal human emancipation, equality, rights, and the civilizing mission materialized simultaneously with an underside of repression as expressed in evolutionary thought. The media through which liberalism did its work—which included bureaucracy, mass media, law, literacy, and the scholarly academy—became means of emancipation and inclusion as well as tools of repression and obfuscation.

In the decades ahead, these paradoxes would be thrown into relief time and again through eruptions of large-scale violence in the empire. The South African War ushered in the twentieth century, soon followed by the events at Amritsar, the Irish War of Independence, the Iraqi Revolt, and the Arab Revolt in Palestine. Each successive imperial drama brought with it measures and practices that were honed and exported from one hot spot to the next. Britain's political and military leaders would cut their teeth on empire and, together with a fleet of lower-level administrators, policemen, security forces, and intelligence operatives, circulate through Britain's colonial possessions bringing learned policies and practices of suppression with them. At home their actions were often understood through the lens of exceptionalism, though as imperial criticism and human rights norms emerged and consolidated in the twentieth century, colonial violence unfolding in plain view relied increasingly on liberalism's justificatory powers of paternal beneficence as well as its twinned abilities to obfuscate and illuminate its behavior in the empire.

CHAPTER 2

Wars Small and Great

In September 1897 Winston Churchill had both pen and rifle in hand as British forces launched a punitive raid in the Mamund Valley of India's North-West Frontier. Observers were stunned when the Pathans—who Churchill's dispatches described as "vermin," possessed with a "strong aboriginal propensity to kill," and "a wild and merciless fanaticism"— delivered "an awful rout," a point the young reporter saved for a private letter to his mother rather than the press.[1] Major General Sir Bindon Blood later restored Britain's honor when he ordered the complete destruction of the Mamund Valley. Churchill dutifully recorded what unfolded before him:

> We proceeded systematically, village by village, and we destroyed the houses, filled up the wells, blew down the towers, cut down the great shady trees, burned the crops and broke the reservoirs in punitive devastation. So long as the villages were in the plain, this was quite easy. The tribesmen sat on the mountains and sullenly watched the destruction of their homes and means of livelihood. . . . At the end of a fortnight the valley was a desert, and honour was satisfied.[2]

The burgeoning statesman defended the scene and wrote that "of course, it is cruel and barbarous, as is everything else in war, but it is only an unphilosophic mind that will hold it legitimate to take a man's life, and illegitimate to destroy his property."[3] Privately, Churchill described his nation's methods, which included the refusal to take any prisoners, including those wounded. An ends-justifies-the-means sub-text typified Churchill's writings, from his immediate dispatches to his prolific, book-length publications, which totaled more than forty works in seventy-two volumes over the course of his life. Much like many of his contemporaries, he cast the struggle in India as one where "civilisation is face to face with militant Mohammedanism." Such good-versus-evil dichotomies would underscore Churchill's writings and his ideological bent for decades to come. His rhetoric that juxtaposed the two sides of liberalism's coin was not unique. Nonetheless, he carefully positioned himself in relation to empire's underbelly, even at his young age, writing to his mother, "I have not soiled my hands with any dirty work, though I recognise the necessity of some things."[4]

The young soldier-reporter later moved to the Sudan and then South Africa, where the discovery of gold in 1886 would have expansive global effects. Reputed to be the single largest find in history, the ore was not

Winston Churchill as a war correspondent in South Africa, 1899. Birth
centenary postage stamp, 1974

alluvial, like that in Australia or California, but rather low grade. That meant, in practical terms, that considerable amounts of capital and labor were required to transform the discovery into massive profits for speculators like Cecil Rhodes, who was making his fortune in Kimberley's diamond mines. Individual capitalists, however, were not the only ones who stood to gain. Britain's economic power, already under threat with the rise of Germany and the United States during the second industrial revolution of the late nineteenth century, was as embedded in invisible earnings as it was in the tangible production and trade of manufactured goods. To maintain its position as the world's banker and, with it, global economic dominance, Britain had to ensure the steady flow of gold.[5]

Standing in the way of British interests were the intransigent Afrikaners. Descendants of early Dutch settlers dating back to the late 1600s, the Afrikaners (or Boers) had fought for decades to sever themselves from British rule and its direct assaults on their way of life in the Cape of Good Hope, or Cape Colony. Britain took control of the colony from the Dutch in 1806, and its administrators and missionaries imagined themselves civilizing not only the Black Africans but also the white ones, whose Afrikaans language, Calvinist-inspired Dutch Reformed Church, and conceptions of race and labor that contested emancipation, were, in the eyes of the mid-Victorian imperialists, anachronistic. In the 1830s, Afrikaners began trekking into the barren and tumbleweed plains of South Africa's vast interior where they staked ethnic territorial claims in two independent republics, the Orange Free State and the Transvaal. The gold discovery on the Witwatersrand, deep in the heart of the Transvaal, upended Afrikaner isolationism. Thousands of Uitlanders— foreigners, primarily British—descended on the Afrikaner nation but found its president, Paul Kruger, along with his fellow Afrikaner republicans, to be inhospitable. The Afrikaner government imposed a series of policies, tariffs, and monopolies that prevented the well-funded Uitlander capitalists from translating the vast gold supply into profit. While the Afrikaners lacked the funds to exploit the gold supply for themselves, they were determined to prevent British capitalists and workers from encroaching on their ethnic enclave.

When the South African War broke out in October 1899, the British government justified it not in self-interested economic terms but rather as a conflict against a xenophobic and racist Boer Republic that deployed illiberal principles and denied Uitlanders their basic rights. Britain's war effort also had an overtly paternalistic dimension. Publicly, British high commissioner Alfred Milner emphasized that the "*ultimate end is a self-governing white community supported by *well-treated* and *justly governed* black labour from Cape Town to Zambesi."[6] In fact, Milner firmly believed in racial hierarchy.

British political and military leaders convinced themselves, and the public, that their initial seventy-five thousand troops would be home by Christmas. Instead, the conflict stretched on for nearly three years, and its sheer scale and repercussions would render it the most costly British conflict waged between 1815 and 1914, while deeply dividing the nation, including its Liberal Party, which splintered on imperial issues as the war dragged on. Nearly 450,000 British and colonial troops were needed to bring the Afrikaners to a negotiated settlement, together with £230 million. Casualty figures exceeded anything the British public had previously witnessed during imperial conflicts. At least 22,000 of its men perished in South Africa's hinterlands and over 75,000 British soldiers and officers returned home invalided from battle wounds and diseases.[7]

High Commissioner Milner, devoted to empire, was a golden child of the British government and colonial administration. A Balliol man, he had carried off an armful of Oxford prizes. This was no small feat considering the company he kept, which included future prime minister H. H. Asquith; St. John Brodrick, the soon-to-be secretary for war; and George Curzon, a rising star of the Conservative Party and future viceroy of India. Milner's meteoric rise as a barrister, journalist, and fiscally brilliant civil servant took him to Egypt as a financial secretary and back to London as chairman of the Inland Revenue, Britain's tax department. In 1897 he was selected to take on the role of governor of Cape Colony and high commissioner for South Africa, which included the Cape Colony and the Colony of Natal, which Britain had annexed in 1843.[8] It was, though, his publication of *England in Egypt* in 1892 that catapulted Milner from a gifted though largely unacknowledged civil servant into an imperial figure of considerable power. The book shaped Milner's popular brand of imperialism that embraced British superiority and state-directed engineering in order to create an imperial race that was as much social and technocratic as it was biological and demographic. Moreover, *England in Egypt* laid out Milner's belief in the state's power to shape colonial economies through direct intervention and reforms. So influential was his intellectual and political clout—the book was in its sixth printing by 1895—that the leader of the Liberal opposition referred to it as *religio Milneriana*.[9]

At a time when British economic and imperial dominance hung in the balance on South Africa's veld, Milner was christened at London's Café Monico as the unassuming second coming of the empire's future. There, on March 27, 1897, his Balliol cadre, together with anyone who was anyone on Britain's political A-list, feted the proconsul and toasted his imminent departure to the Cape Colony.[10] Thin-framed, with hawkish gray eyes and a moustache that partly compensated for his premature hair loss, Milner was more likely to be taken for a detached professor or vicar than for one of the world's most famous imperialists. A gentle and reassuring smile enveloped the self-described "British race patriot" when the conversation turned to imperial ambitions. He harbored grand dreams of a global imperial parliament and wrote a eulogy for himself summarizing the period's zeitgeist (published after his 1925 death in *The Times*): "I am a Nationalist and not a cosmopolitan. . . . I am a British (indeed primarily an English) Nationalist," it began. "If I am also an Imperialist, it is because the destiny of the English race, owing to its insular position and long supremacy at sea, has been to strike roots in different parts of the world. . . . I am an imperialist and not a Little Englander because I am a British Race Patriot."[11]

For Milner, no great principles were involved in so-called native protections. The question was one of national self-interest, and coercion had to be deployed when necessary in order to achieve a racially defined British Empire whose economy was tethered to imperial state power. On these points, Milner never wavered. Just after his arrival in South Africa, he wrote to his Oxford friend Asquith, and reflected on the enormous task facing him as high commissioner. He then turned to the economic and political future of South Africa. "You have only to sacrifice 'the nigger' absolutely," Milner said, "and the game is easy."[12]

As the war dragged on, the media through which liberalism did its work rationalized British policies and maintained the public's morale. The British press dispatched around two hundred correspondents to South Africa, including the now-seasoned Churchill. Founded in 1896, the *Daily Mail* led the charge, and its owner, Alfred Harmsworth, declared that the raison d'être of his newspaper was to stand "for the power, the supremacy and the greatness of the British Empire."[13] With the *Daily Mail*'s masthead later emblazed with "For King and Empire," Harmsworth combined his imperial patriotism with an equal devotion to profit and philanthropy. At the time of the South African War, his news stories and commentaries presented a debased and primitive Boer Republic allegedly murdering wounded British soldiers and innocent civilians. They reflected Kipling's notion that the Afrikaners were a "half caste race" who epitomized "the vices of both the black and white races"; so too could one read between the *Daily Mail*'s lines Milner's negative views of the "medieval race oligarchy" of the Afrikaners, whom his administration considered "semi-civilized," a "dirty, careless lazy lot," and "primitive in the extreme."[14] Less than a year after the war's start, the *Daily Mail*, appealing to the fervent nationalism of a new mass readership, reached a daily circulation of more than 1 million copies.[15]

Opportunities to commoditize and market imperial warfare extended well beyond the press. South African War board games, illustrated magazines, and toy soldiers proliferated, while Christmas catalogues offered Khaki crackers, a holiday party favor. Patriotic hymns, songs, and ballads abounded, but no ode to empire and the war had as much reach and impact as Kipling's "The Absent-Minded Beggar," a contribution to charitable fundraising efforts for the war. Kipling sent the poem to the jingoistic *Daily Mail* with a personal note to Harmsworth to "turn [the proceeds] over to any one of the regularly ordained relief-funds."[16] The four-stanza work was an unprecedented plaiting of empire, patriotism, and charity, with opening lines beseeching:

When you've shouted "Rule Britannia," when you've sung "God Save the
  Queen,"
When you've finished killing Kruger with your mouth,
Will you kindly drop a shilling in my little tambourine
For a gentleman in khaki ordered South?[17]

Harmsworth enlisted Britain's top composer, Sir Arthur Sullivan, to set the poem and its catchy refrain—"Pass the hat for your credit's sake, and pay—pay—pay!"—to music. Soon afterward the artist Richard Caton Woodville drafted an illustration titled "A Gentleman in Khaki," which depicted a wounded British Tommy in battle. Neither the poet, nor the composer, nor the artist drew profit from their work that, within a matter of weeks, became wildly popular. For the duration of the war, theaters and musical halls in Britain and around the world chorused "The Absent-Minded Beggar," and profit makers stuffed its accompanying illustration into cigarette packets and printed it on postcards and other memorabilia. The result was an unprecedented sum of £250,000 raised for soldiers and their bereaved and impoverished families.[18]

News filtering back from South Africa's battlegrounds tested the British public's acceptance of the empire's protracted war and the methods deployed to bring it to an end. The conflict's initial months witnessed the Afrikaner commando forces, comprised of thirty thousand farmers and hunters, tactically outmaneuvering the British and overwhelming them with stalking and marksmanship skills. In early 1900 Field Marshal Lord Frederick Roberts took over as Britain's commander in chief and brought with him several senior officers whose experiences spanned the empire.[19] Among them was Horatio Herbert Kitchener, Roberts's chief of staff, who would leave the greatest mark on South Africa's interior. Kitchener was already legendary for his heroic victories elsewhere in the empire and had been duly rewarded for them. His most famous success came in 1898 at the Battle of Omdurman in the Sudan, where he avenged General Charles George Gordon's death at the hands of the Mahdists, the Sudanese followers of Muslim leader Muhammad Ahmad (al-Mahdī). Equipped with machine guns and modern rifles, Kitchener's troops faced an enemy force nearly twice their size. With Churchill there to bear witness, British forces killed at least ten thousand and wounded over thirteen thousand. The general lost only forty-seven British soldiers, with another 382 wounded. One eyewitness observed: "It was the last day of Mahdism and the greatest. They never get [*sic*] near and they refused to hold back. . . . It was not a battle but an execution. . . . The bodies were not in heaps—bodies hardly ever are; but they spread evenly over acres and acres. Some lay very composedly with their slippers placed under their heads for a last pillow; some knelt, cut short in the middle of a last prayer. Others were torn to pieces."[20]

British media publicized widely the details of Omdurman, and Kitchener became an imperial legend, earning the title "Lord Kitchener of Khartoum." He went on to have an illustrious military career and eventually rose to the rank of secretary of state for war. Holding this cabinet position during the First World War, Kitchener became the commanding face of Britain's famous army recruitment poster. His steady gaze and unwavering pointed index finger were galvanizing forces behind the nation's largest volunteer army. While his glory was cut short—he drowned on the sunken HMS *Hampshire*, off the Orkney Islands, in 1916—he would cast a long shadow across battlefields in the decades to come.

By the fall of 1900, the British, under Roberts's command, had taken nominal control of the Boer Republic. Now the war moved into its final phase as Afrikaners adopted a highly effective guerrilla strategy. To close the war, Kitchener took full charge of the army as commander in chief and launched an all-out assault on an entire ethnic population: or as Kipling termed it, a "dress-parade for Armageddon."[21] The British Army introduced a new blockhouse strategy that, combined with barbed-wire fences, divided the massive interior into smaller areas. Kitchener then deployed a scorched earth policy and systematically burned crops and dumped salt to prevent future cultivation. Sweeper columns mopped up any residual Afrikaner forces. Kitchener eventually deported thirty thousand prisoners of war to remote corners of the empire.[22] British troops also razed homesteads, poisoned wells, and corralled into concentration camps Afrikaner women and children as well as African laborers.

Kitchener was drawing on imperial precedents: this was not the first time the British Empire had sought to solve a crisis through mass encampment. Since 1857 officials in India had experimented with a series of confinement measures that were as much about reform as they were about security and punishment. The Indian Mutiny had spawned the mass incarceration of twenty thousand rebellious subjects whom British officials exiled to the Andaman Islands. There, sparse tented conditions and forced labor were to impart a sense of Victorian-era rehabilitation. Indeed, temporarily separating "degenerate" and "dangerous" segments of the population from the body politic was a hallmark of nineteenth-century Britain. The Poor Law of 1834 and the Habitual Criminals Act of 1869 created social categories of Britons who, like the empire's subjects, were part of liberalism's underbelly. It wasn't just a matter of incarcerating these threats to society; it was also to be an exercise in reforming them through hard physical labor, thus rendering them more rational and civilized. The Raj imported these ideas through legal mechanisms—it translated Britain's Habitual Criminals Act into India's Criminal Tribes Act—as well as through camp systems that reflected the metaphorical language of contagion. Worried that habitual criminal tribes would "infect the social body," colonial officials segregated them into camps where "starvation [would] induce [inmates] to undertake labor of an arduous nature."[23] Such logic was counterintuitive. How could undernourished bodies perform hard labor? It was a perverted concept of reform that would endure. When plague and famine later swept through India in the 1870s and 1890s, new camps sprang up. As a matter of public health, Raj officials detained and segregated colonial subjects and also forced them to labor. Their concern was as much for those outside the camps whom the dirty and parasitical camp populations could infect.[24]

Concepts about mass confinement and reform of refugees in India, along with Victorian-inspired ideals regarding rations and labor, traveled to South Africa during the war. With Kitchener's scorched earth tactics, however, the so-called refugee sites swelled with civilians. Noncombatants comprised the crucial passive wing that offered supplies and informal intelligence to the commandos, and Kitchener was determined to control the Afrikaner and Black "undesirable" populations and, with it, deny the guerrillas their much-needed supply lines. Yet the commander in chief's tactics went beyond dismantling guerrilla resources. He designed concentration camps, about one hundred in all, as punitive hostage sites. Women and children of active guerrillas endured harsher treatment with smaller rations as Kitchener sought to "work on the feelings of the men." Moreover, he targeted the Afrikaner women who were "more bitter than the men"; according to him, the one way to "bring them to their senses" was to weaken them in the camps.[25] The war transformed these women and their children into "legitimate targets of violence," as the historian Aidan Forth suggests.[26] As far as Milner and Kitchener were concerned, the Afrikaners in the camps were "verminous," no doubt emaciated from meager rations and poor sanitation's effects. Kitchener's forces had to either capture the "infested" Afrikaner population or kill them.[27]

British forces herded into the camps more than one hundred thousand Afrikaners who died at alarming rates. Malnutrition, starvation, and outbreaks of endemic diseases wiped out approximately thirty thousand, the disproportionate number of whom were children.[28] Whether the civilian deaths were a deliberate or an unintended consequence of Kitchener's war plans, the establishment of the British concentration camps in South Africa represented the first time a single ethnic group had been targeted en masse for detention or deportation. Reports of camp conditions and death tolls began filtering to Britain in the spring of 1901. The public's response ranged from indifference to outrage. Little more than six months earlier, the nation's general election—popularly known as the "Khaki election" because of its implicit referendum on the South African War—returned to power Prime Minister Robert Cecil, Lord Salisbury's Conservative government and its Liberal Unionist allies. At the time, Britain's electorate believed the war was all but won. Instead, the conflict raged on, and the underside of Britain's liberal imperialism was exposed for the world to see.

The peace activist and British welfare campaigner Emily Hobhouse led the investigatory charge. She arrived in South Africa in late 1900, where she met the full force of High Commissioner Milner, who duly labeled her a "trouble maker" and did everything in his power to obstruct her efforts. Hobhouse returned to publish her *Report of a Visit to the Camps of Women and Children in the Cape and Orange River Colonies* to an increasingly divided British public.[29] A broad pro-Boer coalition had emerged in Britain, which included some Liberal politicians and socialists as well as leading intellectuals like J. A. Hobson, whose economic critique of imperialism was also a South African War product. The future prime minister David Lloyd George brought the matter to the House of Commons, where Milner's Balliol pal and now secretary of state for war St. John Brodrick defended Britain's policies. He claimed the camps, though a "military necessity," were "voluntary," and that the Afrikaners interned there were "contented and comfortable."[30]

Many Britons unfailingly supported the empire, the nation, and the monarchy and embraced the government's defense. They berated Hobhouse as the epitome of pro-Boer sentiment—a sentiment that undermined the war and treasonously affronted Britain's imperial patriotism. The pro-Boers became scapegoats for the war's slow progress, and the press impugned Hobhouse as "hysterical," a "political agitator," and a "disseminator of inaccurate and blood-curdling stories."[31] Still, her report fueled vociferous debates. In Parliament, Lloyd George openly accused the British government of pursuing "a policy of extermination," while MP John Ellis likened the camps to "the Black Hole of Calcutta." The Liberal Party leader Henry Campbell-Bannerman answered his own rhetorical question of "When is a war not a war?" with the answer, "When it is carried on by methods of barbarism in South Africa."[32]

South Africa's concentration camps were headline news around the world. The British government deployed various methods of deflection. It created an internal investigatory commission and appointed Millicent Fawcett, a staunch Hobhouse critic, as its chair. Hobhouse attempted to return to South Africa, but when her steamer docked in Cape Town,

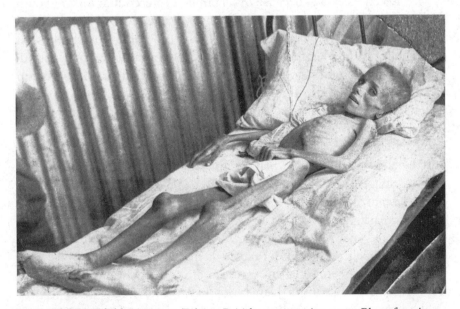

An Afrikaner child, Lizzie van Zyl, in a British concentration camp, Bloemfontein, South Africa

Kitchener took it upon himself to ensure that martial law—newly insti-tuted in the colony, in the military commander's words, for the specific purpose of "prevent[ing] the influx of dangerous persons, war matérial, and to suppress seditious publication"—sent Hobhouse packing. After a few days of drama that included soldiers tying Hobhouse up in her own shawl and physically carrying her onto a ship going to Europe, the activist was deported. Critics at home questioned the legality, not to mention the ethics, of such a maneuver. But Brodrick, defending Brit-ain's actions in Parliament, brushed aside the debate taking place there and in the media and stated matter-of-factly that, under martial law, the British government had the legal right to deport any seditious actor in the South African territory.[33]

While believing the camps were a military necessity, neither civilian nor military leaders wanted to claim responsibility for them. "The black spot—the one very black spot—in the picture is the frightful mortal-ity in the Concentration Camps," Milner admitted. "While a hundred explanations may be offered and a hundred excuses made, they do not really amount to any adequate defence. . . . At the same time a sudden reversal of policy would only make matters worse. . . . I believe we shall mitigate the evil, but we shall never get rid of it."[34] Eventually Kitchener succeeded in foisting the camps' administrative oversight onto Milner and the Colonial Office, though not before the Fawcett commission filed its report confirming all of Hobhouse's allegations.[35] Rather than seeing anything sinister or deliberate, the report pointed to basic issues of hygiene.

Here the tension between the camps as a punitive site and their use as putative locations for relief and reform were made manifest. With Indian Famine Commission reports coming across his desk, Colonial Secretary Joseph Chamberlain was well aware of the Raj's purported suc-cess at containing disease and improving unsanitary conditions behind barbed-wire structures that were actually makeshift work camps. He called in the experts, Colonels Samuel Thomson and James Wilkins of the Indian Medical Service, who had devised bureaucracies of sanitation and control that kept famine refugees and plague victims separated from the Raj's mainstream population and those healthy enough to labor. In South Africa, Thomson and Wilkins introduced systems of spatial design, hygiene, and discipline, leveraging the sanitary measures that the Ladies Concentration Camp Committee recommended and that Britain's War Office had already put in place. These efforts did witness a reduction of mortality rates, even if considerable damage had already been done.[36]

Thomson would leave the government of South Africa with a vision of its relationship to India and the rest of the empire insofar as confinement's future was concerned. For him, the concentration camps offered "an unusual opportunity of determining whether it [was] possible to maintain a large body of men, women and children in large camps, in good health." "The fact was established," he said, that with proper sanitary precautions and firm enforcement of hygiene measures, vast numbers of His Majesty's subjects could be held behind barbed wire. As far as Thomson was concerned, "the lessons learnt in the present instance may . . . prove of interest and utility should more or less similar circumstances arise in the future."[37] Such lessons of segregating, categorizing, and rationalizing large, yet presumed dangerous, populations on a mass scale were now widely known. South Africa had, in historian Aidan Forth's words, "showcased the idea of mass internment to the world," along with its coercive and reformist principles, even if the latter were sometimes difficult to discern.[38]

Despite, or because of, the "methods of barbarism," Kitchener's war of attrition brought the Afrikaners to the bargaining table. It had far-reaching implications for the empire and the region's African population. Both during and after the war, Britain sacrificed its paternalistic protection of South Africa's Blacks on the altar of economic expediency and racial prejudice. In the debates over Afrikaner suffering few voiced concern for the hundred thousand Black Africans held in British concentration camps. While thousands of Blacks supported Britain's war effort on the front lines, some sought military protection and were instead interned. Kitchener's forces indiscriminately rounded up others during punitive raids. The conditions in the sixty-four Black concentration camps were, by most accounts, worse than in those of the Afrikaners. Emaciated and disease-ridden, Blacks undertook forced labor for reduced rations, and their death rates climbed, conservatively, to over 10 percent of the camp populations.[39] With the negotiated Treaty of Vereeniging signed at the end of May 1902, the Boer republics ceded their independence, though with the promise of self-government within the British Empire. Along with a variety of concessions, including postwar reconstruction funds of £3 million, the British eventually bequeathed to the Afrikaners the Black population's political future in South Africa, thus ensuring their subjugation for nearly another century to come. Eight years later the four British colonies of the Cape, Natal, Transvaal, and Orange River would combine into the Union of South Africa, an independent dominion within the empire.

Representing the Afrikaners in negotiations was Jan Smuts, who had been reared in the Cape Colony. In an imperial, Horatio Alger story, at least insofar as political and international influence were concerned, the shy and introspective Smuts was said to have pulled himself out of a backwater through hard work and genius, eventually landing a scholarship to Christ's College, Cambridge, where he read law. Perpetually impoverished there, he survived his homesickness and social stigmatization thanks to a handout from one of his professors who, like many others, recognized his intellectual gifts. By the time he graduated in 1894, Smuts had written a book on Walt Whitman that laid the foundation for his later theory of holism, and he had also taken a double first, an extraordinary honor much like Phi Beta Kappa. He walked away with countless prizes, including the George Long Prize in Roman Law and Jurisprudence. What Smuts lacked in gregariousness he more than made up for in brilliance, as the master of Christ's College declared in 1970, "in 500 years of the College's history, of all its members, past and present, three have been truly outstanding: John Milton, Charles Darwin, and Jan Smuts."[40] After Cambridge, Smuts rejected what would assuredly have been a promising and lucrative legal future in London and returned to South Africa, where he joined the Afrikaner Bond, a hardline ethnic and anti-imperialist party. When war broke out with Britain in 1899, he became President Kruger's right-hand man and dealt with logistics, propaganda, and strategy before he stepped onto the front lines of the empire's battlefields. There the Afrikaner commando leader became renowned for his prowess at hit-and-run tactics and his penchant for pulling from his rucksack a tattered copy of Kant's *Critique of Pure Reason*, which he read under the cover of darkness before launching crack-of-dawn raids.[41]

That this ardent defender of the Afrikaner ethnic enclave was to become one of Britain's most loyal and influential protagonists of the empire may seem, at first glance, rather puzzling. Yet for nearly five decades, Smuts would prove a pivotal figure in shaping not only a nationalist agenda in South Africa but also an international framework that reflected and supported notions of white rule so dear to the maintenance of power in Pretoria, western Europe, and the United States. In the years between the war and the creation of the Union of South Africa, the constitution of which he greatly shaped, Smuts emerged a major figure and assumed various political offices, including the premiership. From the birth of the union through two world wars, the onetime commando knew his nation had little choice but to remain in the empire along with other white dominions, including Australia, New Zealand, and Canada. It was a matter of protecting national sovereignty through the collective white interests of the imperial whole. Or as the historian Mark Mazower points out in his influential work *No Enchanted Palace*: "In [Smuts's] view, South Africa needed to remain within the empire, not only for its own safety but in order to carry out its mission as bearer of civilization on the Dark Continent. The commonwealth idea offered not only a template for this but a way for imagining a new world organization. . . . Smuts naturally aligned himself with those who promoted internationalism *because* they were nationalists."[42] In fact, embedded in Smuts's logic and evolving ideology were the notions of an "imperial internationalism" that would gain considerable currency from Britain's left and right as well as the empire's white settlers after the Great War. This "imperial internationalism" reflected a racially ordered view and would later take form in the League of Nations.[43]

As Smuts was building his nationalist South African order, High Commissioner Milner wasted little time in constructing a postwar colonial capitalist state. Its primary functions were to address the demands of the mining industry and ensure the encoding of racial and cultural differences in the structures, institutions, and practices of rule. While emerging from opposite sides of the war, Milner and Smuts shared a crucial understanding of the future of South Africa and the British Empire. The high commissioner had grandiose ideas of white rule comprising "a great and progressive community, one from Cape Town to Zambezi."[44] Moreover, Milner's postwar racial vision executed through a "conquest state" was not the product of one man, regardless of his power, profile, and self-described sense of isolated burden—a burden that he felt deeply, as if "the whole weight of the Imperial cause in this part of the world rests on me, that I am bearing it alone."[45]

In the context of his imperialist age, Milner epitomized and consolidated the willingness "to sacrifice 'the nigger' absolutely."[46] The high commissioner and his reconstruction regime of like-minded Oxford graduates—known as Milner's Kindergarten—systematically put in place all of Britain's prewar conditions for optimal gold production. They also expended considerable effort in prioritizing white interests and healing the war-scarred divisions between the Afrikaans- and English-speaking communities. These twinned priorities generated a host of social engineering measures that shaped civil society, separated races, ensured massive amounts of cheap Black labor, protected poor whites, and intervened on land and agricultural measures. These state-directed systematic policies laid the foundation for capitalist development in South Africa, the wholesale exploitation of Black labor in the white-owned mines, and the rise of the apartheid regime that, decades later, would come to power on the racist coattails of Milner's Oxford coterie and Smuts's white nationalist constituency.[47]

At home, Britain's collective attention turned toward commemoration. Local communities memorialized the patriotism, glory, and honor of the British men and women who had lost their lives in the war through the creation and funding of nearly nine hundred memorials throughout the nation. Private philanthropy, which individuals like Harmsworth and Kipling had spearheaded, drew contributions of over £6 million into soldier relief funds. It was a staggering amount, equivalent to nearly 4 percent of the British government's total revenue in 1900. In comparison, contributions to Emily Hobhouse's relief fund for Afrikaner women and children totaled around £6,500.[48] If civic pride and philanthropic measures are reflections of public sentiment, then the British public's cultivation of memory and its collective sense of responsibility for imperial soldiers and their families betrayed a nation loyal to the ideals of monarchy and empire, regardless of how damning the evidence of its corroding effects. Such sentiments would pervade the twentieth century. So, too, would commemorative acts, which included the enshrinement of Kitchener after his death in London's St. Paul's Cathedral. There a life-size marble statue of the general, in full repose, graces the northwest corner of the cathedral's All Soul's Chapel. It is a permanent testament not only to his military service but also to a nation's ability to forget the methods of barbarism he introduced and consolidated in Britain's empire.

With British targeting of civilian populations, the South African conflict ushered in new forms of twentieth-century warfare. They would have great bearing on the future of the empire, as well as civil liberties at home. At the same time, Britain's repressive hand began to encounter more sustained challenges not only from burgeoning international accords regulating warfare but also from a growing domestic minority, like that which had been mobilized to protest Afrikaner concentration camps. The critiques were often directed not at the nation's right and duty to maintain the empire; nor were they directed at the evolving political structures that would enable uses of coercion. Rather, they would largely concentrate on specific acts of British imperial repression. This singular focus would dominate critiques going forward while often segregating the act from the conditions in which repression was deployed for the maintenance of British sovereignty and authority in the empire. In the process, critics laid bare some of the most egregious manifestations of violence, while unintentionally prompting a government response:

harsher legal and administrative apparatuses. Over time such apparatuses became acceptable methods of governance as their perceived indispensability often trumped any ambivalence over their justification.[49] Echoes of Kipling's White Man's Burden could be heard in the government's defense of policies and practices in South Africa. Such notions perpetuated old forms of colonial control and gave rise to new ones at the turn of the century. When the "prophet of British imperialism," as George Orwell would christen Kipling, became the first English-language writer to receive the Nobel Prize in Literature in 1907, his international recognition conferred status on the empire's project.

The Nobel laureate's writings also countenanced methods of governance that inscribed racial and cultural differences. These differences became institutionalized at every level of executive, legislative, and judicial rule.[50] As British imperial claims transformed into formal colonial rule, the colonial state—whether early on in India with the emergence of the Raj in 1858, or later with the acquisitions of colonies and territories in Africa and the Middle East—was a far cry from the emerging modern nation-states of Europe. Empires did not rule their subjects through consent. Instead, in the case of Britain, officials' overriding presumption was that indigenous populations were neither capable of ruling themselves, nor effective at tilling their own land, nor respectful or comprehending of the authority of the colonial state without it having recourse to exceptional powers. If forms of colonial rule on the ground were intimately tied to forms of racial and cultural difference, so too were they bound to the realpolitik of Britain's economic landscape.[51] As far as the British were concerned, an unwritten rule of empire, that colonies should be fiscally self-sufficient, was inviolable. Indeed, formal imperialism was expensive, and not all colonies were profitable. Like the rest of the empire, they had to generate revenue for local governing expenses, and colonial subjects paid for their repression in the form of taxes, cheap labor, and in some cases, land expropriation.[52]

Britain's Parliament had ultimate authority over the empire, and Britain, as a constitutional monarchy, had a king or queen who was a ceremonial head of state and therefore constitutionally the symbolic imperial ruler, as we saw confirmed when Queen Victoria was anointed Empress of India in 1877. In terms of running the empire, Parliament claimed absolute sovereignty, and nineteenth-century scholars and philosophers used Britain's constitution as the starting point from which they traced the legal connections between Britain and its colonies. In the words of Albert Venn Dicey, Vinerian Professor of English Law at Oxford and arguably the most towering constitutional scholar in British history (1835–1922), Britain had an "Imperial Constitution." To this day, Dicey's 1885 landmark book, *Introduction to the Study of the Law of the Constitution*, together with his broader corpus of work, remain the departure point for any study on British "rule of law," past or present. According to Dicey, Parliament, unrestrained by a rigid written constitution, had extraordinary powers to make law. When its powers extended to the empire, Parliament in London was an Imperial Parliament that, in Dicey's words, "could make or unmake any law whatever," and constitutionally, local courts and populations in the empire had to accept this principle. In practice, Dicey was aware of the tension between Parliament's unbridled sovereignty and the possibility that imperial unity could be undermined by imperial misrule, which in turn could lead to colonial rebellion.[53]

Before turning to this tension, it's important to recognize that Dicey was a product of the times in which he lived, as were John Stuart Mill and James Fitzjames Stephen, who was Dicey's cousin. In fact, Dicey provided legal advice to Mill, Stephen, and other members of the Jamaica Committee, which had sought to prosecute Governor Eyre for his abuse of martial law during Jamaica's Morant Bay Rebellion, as we have seen. In advising the committee, he derived his position on martial law from the narrow common law position on use of force and public accountability for it, a position he spelled out in his later writings.

> Officers, magistrates, soldiers, policemen, ordinary citizens, all occupy in the eye of the law the same position; they are, each and all of them, bound to withstand and put down breaches of the peace, such as riots and other disturbances; they are, each and all of them authorised to employ so much force, even to the taking of life, as may be necessary for that purpose, and they are none of them entitled to use more; they are, each and all of them, liable to be called to account before a jury for the use of excessive, that is, of unnecessary force.[54]

Dicey compared French law, which permitted exceptional peacetime powers through the declaration of a "state of siege," to that of the British, believing that "this kind of martial law [French state of siege] is in England utterly unknown to the constitution." Instead, under common law:

> Soldiers may suppress a riot as they may resist an invasion, they may fight rebels just as they may fight foreign enemies, but they

have no right under the law to inflict punishment for riot or rebellion. During the effort to restore peace, rebels may be lawfully killed just as enemies may be lawfully slaughtered in battle, or prisoners may be shot to prevent their escape, but any execution (independently of military law) inflicted by a Court-martial is illegal, and technically murder.[55]

In effect, Britain did not need any extraordinary right to proclaim a "state of siege" because ordinary common law accommodated any potential existential threat to the British state. This Diceyan interpretation is important for us to know, as it was often the starting point for future deliberations over necessity and legality in various imperial theaters of British state-directed violence where officials often wanted, and would get, extraordinary powers to suppress riots, strikes, and insurrections while avoiding legal accountability.

A "self-described 'sane Imperialist,'" Dicey also believed that "the maintenance of the British Empire makes it possible, at a cost which is relatively small, compared with the whole number of British subjects, to secure peace, good order, and personal freedom throughout a large part of the world." "Imperialism is to all who share it a form of passionate feeling," he wrote; it was "a political religion . . . a form of patriotism which has a high absolute worth of its own, and is both excited and justified by the lessons of history." He also cleaved to evolutionary ideas of civilization, believing that society's law was fundamentally bound to developmentalism and that the British constitution and its legal regime were the epitome of progress and the bedrock of Pax Britannica. Like Mill and other political philosophers and statesmen, he suggested that "nations, which have not reached a certain stage of development, are unfit for democratic institutions." According to recent work of the legal scholar Dylan Lino, constitutional flexibility meant that Britain could deploy "different forms of rule suited for different peoples of the Empire: 'virtual independence' for the white settler colonies and despotic government by administrators for the uncivilized peoples of India. . . . The fact that the Empire was governed differently to the United Kingdom . . . was the perfect exemplification of Britain's flexible constitutional order."[56]

There were no representatives from the empire sitting in Britain's Parliament, save for Ireland's for a near one-hundred-year period.[57] Dicey felt geographical distance rendered this impossible, and even if there had been colonial representation in Parliament, it would never adequately represent the empire's population the way Britain's parliamentary body represented Britons. Some colonies did have their own colonial legislatures and could pass their own laws, including regulations that surpassed local ordinary laws when existential threats to the state arose in the form of riots or insurrections. Colonial legislatures, however, were subordinate to Britain's Parliament, which could override any local colonial law or regulation, particularly if it conflicted with British legislation; indeed, the very existence of local legislatures in the empire depended on the British Parliament's authorizing statutes. The abolition of enslaved labor and the use of judicial torture are two examples by which Britain's Parliament legislated on behalf of the empire. It could also repeal or alter colonial constitutions. As we've seen, after questions arose over the legality of Governor Eyre's suppression of the Morant Bay Rebellion in Jamaica and the execution of George Gordon, Britain abolished the colony's "ancient constitution" and took away its local representative government.[58]

Dicey was well aware that unrestrained power from Parliament could destabilize the empire. Discontented local populations could revolt, as they did when King George III's imperial overreach introduced taxation policies to the American colonies, forcing "a peaceful population to take up arms and [driving] loyal subjects into rebellion," according to Dicey.[59] After the American Revolution, the empire continued to have responsibility for its own fiscal upkeep and was responsible for contributing to imperial defense, though another unwritten constitutional rule was a prohibition on imperial taxation that funded metropolitan needs, as when George III taxed the American colonies to pay for British war debts.

Other risks of colonial rebellion were inherent to Britain's imperial constitutional system. The empire's civilizational diversity meant it had no uniform common set of institutions. The limits of colonial representation in Britain suggested that Parliament had to act with "a relatively light touch," particularly in the dominions, or self-governing colonies, which had the "moral right to as much independence . . . [that can] be conceded to any country which still forms part of the British Empire," according to Dicey. Turning to the dependent empire, colonies like India, Dicey knew that the despotic nature of the British Parliament's sovereign power courted rebellion. Reflecting the empire's alleged different stages of civilization, there was no standard approach to local colonial governance, which could therefore veer toward misrule if it fell into the wrong hands. Dicey's solution to this problem resided in imperial "experts." But nothing in the British constitution guaranteed the presence of such expertise, so Dicey, and by extension successive

British governments, put an enormous amount of trust in local admin-istrators to execute a benevolent despotism through the rule of law that would develop the empire's "childlike" subjects into rational and civi-lized beings who would eventually have a constitutional independence perhaps similar to that of the white dominions.[60]

What unfolded was a governing structure that differed from Britain's state, which possessed its own sovereignty, defended its own borders, and established a social contract with a population that, beginning with the nineteenth-century reform acts, was represented by a government that increasingly expressed popular will. In contrast, the colonial state was a state within a state. That is, the colonial state was semiautono-mous because it had its own governance structure *and* was governed by Britain. There were also other tensions. "Within Dicey's thought," Lino tells us, "the rule of law and the rule of empire were in a complex and unstable relationship." Like other great thinkers of his era, Dicey had to wrestle with liberal imperialism's paradoxes and the empire's potential for subverting "rule of law," the bedrock of British claims to civiliza-tional superiority. Lino tells us how:

> On the one hand, Dicey believed British imperialism to be jus-tified by Britain's possession of rule of law—the pinnacle of civilisational achievement—and by Britain's capacity to spread that achievement abroad. Dicey's masterwork [*Introduction to the Study of the Law of the Constitution*] was on this score an apology for a liberal version of the British Empire. On the other hand, Dicey was forced to recognise at various points that sustaining the Empire's hierarchical relations could necessitate oppressive departures from the rule of law—in deference to the some-times lawless and frequently discriminatory settler-colonial self-government and to the exigencies of governing rebellious colonial subjects. These departures from the rule of law in turn undercut the Empire's very reason for existence. More funda-mentally, Dicey recognised on occasion that the rule of law could itself be arbitrary and oppressive when imposed on Empire's 'uncivilised' peoples, for whom he believed it was foreign and too advanced. . . . Dicey's thought demonstrates . . . the difficul-ties in sustaining the rule of law and the rule of empire simul-taneously, as well as the potential for the rule of law to collapse into its own form of arbitrary domination when imposed by one society on others.[61]

Despite abiding British views on the colonies' various stages of development, we can see broad continuities in colonial governance throughout the empire. A hallmark was its prefectural style of administration, which incorporated particularities rooted in the unique features of each colony or territory. Some colonies were administratively divided into smaller parts, such as provinces, which were then divided into smaller units called districts. Given the sheer size of Britain's far-flung empire, it was impossible to micromanage day-to-day rule in these areas. Instead, the prevailing ethos was to "trust the man on the spot," which officials in London did with great regularity. In practice, this meant a very small cadre of recruits joined the empire's civil service, though there was a pecking order. The most prestigious administrative positions were in the foreign service, then the Indian civil service, and finally the colonial service. In all these administrative roles, many recruits went to public schools such as Eton and Harrow and continued on to Oxford or Cambridge, where they were steeped in ideals of honor, duty, and discretion. Diffuse and decentralized, colonial rule would be strengthened, it was thought, by tapping men who conformed instinctively to the ethos of liberal imperialism. With little training, they would establish and maintain control over local populations, promote fiscal self-sufficiency and profitability, and maintain the rule of law.[62]

Many administrators were barely out of their teens when they headed off to empire. One lone baby-faced white officer, often hunkered down in an office that was little more than a lean-to or a tin-roofed shack, was typically responsible for approximately one hundred thousand colonial subjects who became, in the minds of colonial administrators, "their natives." This cadre of provincial and district administrators and officers, known as the "thin white line," had a "cultlike" culture, often steadfastly believing in their "real civilising and selfless mission," and were answerable to higher-ups of a colony or territory.[63] They included, for example, High Commissioner Alfred Milner and others with titles like *governor*, *viceroy*, and *lord lieutenant*. These imperial leaders who operated on the spot were the men who Dicey felt had to be particularly "expert" if empire was to run smoothly without insurrection. Above them, in London, were various civil servants in the Foreign, India, and Colonial offices who, in turn, answered to British cabinet ministers, including the foreign secretary, the secretary of state for India, and the secretary of state for the colonies who, in turn, were answerable to Parliament. The idea, of course, was that with a shared pedigree and common liberal imperialist ethos, officials in London would not need to supervise daily the viceroys, governors, and district officers at the bottom of the administrative pyramid, instead trusting "the man on the spot."

In practice, this meant that variations of a colonial state unfolded across the empire that imposed control over local populations first by conquest, then by establishing rule of law and a monopoly over legitimate violence. The law was "the cutting edge of colonialism, an instrument of power of an alien state and part of the process of coercion" that pacified and governed the empire, as the legal scholar John Comaroff writes. "The effort to conquer and control indigenous peoples by the coercive use of legal means" reflected the British assumption that non-Western peoples were mired in custom, lacking "anything approaching 'civilized' judicial procedures. It was appropriate, therefore, that in the name of universal 'progress,' they be subordinated to a superior European legal order."[64] Sometimes indigenous customs were codified and brought into the lowest levels of the colonial legal system for the adjudication of matters such as local property relations and marital practices. Called "customary law," such "traditional" legal practices were often twisted or invented wholesale by colonial administrators and anthropologists, thus bearing little resemblance to the actual customs and practices of local populations. Other times, local practices that were deemed "uncivilized," like *sati*, the rare Hindu practice of a widow burning herself atop her deceased husband's funeral pyre, were statutorily criminalized.[65] A parallel legal regime also emerged that protected the state and its economy and were adjudicated mostly by British judges stationed in the empire. When the ordinary colonial legal regime was insufficient in stamping out riots, strikes, or full-blown rebellions, martial law, as in Jamaica's Morant Bay Rebellion, or legal regulations that created statutory martial law, as for the Indian Mutiny, were introduced to maintain the state and its domination.

The colonial state also co-opted local elites into various levels of the colonial bureaucracy through a system called "indirect rule." These elites, whether they were princes and pashas or chiefs and headmen, represented a dual system of authority that complemented that of the British administrators. Indigenous elites sometimes enforced customary laws in local tribunals or courts and other times became the faces of British imperialism for colonial subjects. Some of these colonial agents had traditional standing in local societies, while others were in positions of power because they chose to align themselves with the interests and patronage benefits of the colonial state.

Regardless, co-opted local elites who, in the words of historian Frederick Cooper, facilitated Britain's "dirty work," were crucial to the empire's functioning, as they were front and center in tax collecting, compelling subject populations into the labor market for pittance wages, and imposing communal forced labor projects, among other measures.[66] Incorporated into the colonial bureaucracy, they became part of the colonial project that institutionalized difference not only between colonizer and colonized but also between and among subject populations, sowing discord and civil conflict by accentuating ethnic and religious differences and rendering them politically and economically salient. This method of colonial governance—divide and rule—fed Britain's need for on-the-ground indigenous agents. There was much about colonial rule, however, that was not indirect. The state, for instance, did not divest to these indigenous agents its monopoly over violence; nor did it divest the adjudication of crimes that violated the colonial-imposed social contract or decision making when it came to the colonial economy or suspending ordinary law and deploying security forces to quash dissent.

British power in the empire was limited in certain respects. Liberal imperialism did not translate into all-out repression at all times in all places. Nor did it fully penetrate indigenous social and cultural forms, creativity, responses to markets, or political activities—something the British would learn all too well in the twentieth century, as local populations continued to mount armed responses, big and small, to imperial rule. However, the empire's capacity to destroy while ostensibly reforming was extraordinary. Economic and political self-interests combined with Kipling-esque concepts of civilization to drive British imperial decision making, ushering in forced economic dependencies, rural immiseration, urban disorder, famine, civil conflict, and unaccountability to subjects. At the same time, reform efforts, including the introduction of new education systems and public health measures, initially through missionary efforts and later through state-sponsored welfare departments and programs, were enacted side by side with policies, like forced labor, that through their harshness were supposed to reform "backward natives," much as stern measures were supposed to advance children to adulthood.

These liberal imperial measures would evolve in the twentieth century and draw on moral conceptions of British rule and so-called native deficiencies. So, too, would they become legally and administratively embedded in Britain's imperial bureaucracy. In other words, the deployment of violence was not the preserve of isolated individuals in the British Empire, important as they were in transferring ideas and techniques from one part of the empire to another. Instead, it reflected the ideological and political will of, and choices made by, the purveyors of institutions that included Downing Street and Whitehall as well as central and district administrations in Ireland, India, Kenya, and elsewhere. As the philosopher and political theorist Judith Shklar reminds us, repression is "always part of a judicial and political system. To ignore that is to falsify its character and to make any effort to halt or impede it impossible."[67]

Military doctrine also reflected the "rule of colonial difference" pervading British discourse, practices, and institutions.[68] As Britain kept ticking off small wars in its empire, its military increasingly theorized best practices for dealing with recalcitrant natives, becoming part of the broader institutionalization of repression that was best captured in the work of Colonel Charles Callwell. A graduate of the Royal Military Academy and a veteran of several nineteenth-century imperial wars, Callwell was a major figure in the study of counterinsurgency practices throughout the twentieth century. His *Small Wars: Their Principles and Practices*, originally written in 1896 and updated after he served as a staff officer and commander in the South African War, would become the starting point for nearly all counterinsurgency theorists and practitioners.[69] Callwell's expansive work not only synthesized Britain's military engagements throughout the empire but also drew lessons from French, Spanish, American, and Russian campaigns. Together these reference points provided him with historical examples that demonstrated the short-term effectiveness of the use of force while constructing an ideological framework that understood such repressive measures to be a necessary aspect of liberal imperialism.

For Callwell, when European troops engaged in wars against the "uncivilised" and "savage" populations of the world, as opposed to civilized armies, they needed a different set of rules.[70] With the heft of numerous examples to support his claims, Callwell pointed to the "moral force of civilisation" that underwrote European superiority and the need to teach "savage" peoples "a lesson which they will not forget."[71] For Callwell, waging total destruction against an enemy brought more than just strategic advantages; brutality wrought on "uncivilised" populations, he emphasized, also had a "moral effect."[72] The tactics' purposes were as clear to Callwell as they were to Kitchener in South Africa: "[The] object is not only to prove to the opposing force unmistakably which is the stronger, but also to inflict punishment on those who have taken up arms." He wrote that the "enemy must be made to feel a moral inferiority throughout. . . . [Fanatics and savages] must be thoroughly brought to book and cowed or they will rise again."[73] Callwell drew inspiration from British military commanders as well as from Thomas-Robert Bugeaud, who had deployed maximum violence in Algeria in the 1830s and 1840s. He also pointed to the famous "White General," Russia's Mikhail Skobelev, who, according to Callwell, "is the master who seizes the people pitilessly by the throat and imposes upon their imagination."[74]

Callwell's "moral effect" reflected the military's ease with fusing the White Man's Burden with battlefield strategies to produce a morality of violence that defined imperial confrontations around the globe and reproduced Victorian-era norms of liberalism in the empire. Repressive measures were a necessary part of ensuring order and civilizing the "backward" races of the world.[75] With its binaries of good versus evil framing justifications of violence in the empire, liberal imperialism both shaped and reflected national opinions in parliamentary and legal debates, media outlets, popular culture, and commemorative acts. It also shaped military thinking and practices for Callwell and many of his successors—from the highest-ranking officials to the ordinary soldiers—in future colonial conflicts.[76] In the years ahead, at question would not be the continued transference of the counterinsurgency practices and conceptual frameworks to other parts of the British Empire from one generation of soldiers to the next. Rather, the dominant issues would be political and legal. As Callwell highlights, once conventional warfare methods are jettisoned, "it is then that the regular troops are forced to resort to cattle lifting and village burning and that the war assumes an aspect which may shock the humanitarian."[77] Successive British governments would need to mollify a vocal minority, both at home and abroad, that was increasingly concerned with the brutality of the liberal imperial project.

As a defensive strategy crystallized, British officials sought to discredit whistleblowers like Hobhouse, deploying terms similar to those found in *Small Wars*. Many also read international conventions and laws regulating warfare—most notably those at Geneva and the Hague—in a liberal imperial frame. They were not alone. For centuries, warfare had been subject to limitations based on customary practices, agreements between adversaries, religious beliefs, and codes of honor. Resuscitating centuries-old conceptions of "just war" stretching back to ancient Egypt, China, Greece, Rome, and India, and addressing the morality of war, nineteenth-century international laws regulating war, and European politicians and international jurists interpreting them, were products of their times.[78]

The birth of modern international humanitarian law, rules that seek, for humanitarian reasons, to minimize the effects of armed conflict, is often associated with Swiss merchant Henri Dunant. In 1859, en route to see French emperor Napoleon III about business concessions in Algeria, Durant witnessed a battle between French and Austrian forces in northern Italy. Three years later, he published *A Memory of Solferino*, recounting his experiences picking through the pockmarked terrain of forty thousand dead and neglected wounded; it galvanized the founding of a small committee, the International Committee of the Red Cross's precursor, in 1863, and the signing of the 1864 Geneva Convention for the Amelioration of the Conditions of the Wounded in Armies in the Field, the first international treaty of its kind. Thirty-five years later the Russian tsar Nicholas II convened an international peace conference in the Hague, where European states adopted their first convention there for governing rules of war. Two separate, though related, initiatives thus emerged: the Geneva Conventions regulating conduct in war, mainly by protecting combatants, and the Hague Conventions, regulating the conduct of war by banning certain weapons and military practices. The combined core aims were not to outlaw war or to protect rights but to implement universal and humane norms of conduct.[79]

Once a state signed and ratified a convention, it was self-regulating, free to decipher how to apply and enforce the convention. There was no independent legal process to curb such self-judgment. Instead, it was international jurists' decentralized duty to give meaning and interpretation to treaties governing the global order, even if they had no institutionalized role in their enforcement.[80] With the establishment of the Institut de droit international in 1873, these international jurists formally recognized one another and their international law profession at a profoundly important time. Indeed, just as Europe was codifying laws regulating armed conflict within Western borders, it was engaged in one of imperial history's most violent periods outside of them. Nonetheless, many international jurists believed nineteenth-century empires differed from those that preceeded them. In fact, some international jurists helped to set rules for Europe's formal carving up of Africa in the late 1880s, contrasting what they believed were the reformist benefits of nineteenth-century imperialism with Spain's draconian sixteenth-century ruling practices in the Americas. They also turned to the teachings of sixteenth-century Dominican theologians, such as Francisco de Vitoria and Bartolomé de Las Casas, who had criticized Spanish conduct in the "new world," insisting on the indigenous population's humanity. Vitoria and Las Casas were among many historical actors celebrated as precursors to modern international law when it emerged in the last third of the nineteenth century during Europe's turn toward acquiring formal empires and formulating a civilizing mission.[81]

When focusing their attention on colonial subjects, nineteenth-century jurists, affirming Europe's legal pedigree as a product of the West's superior history and culture, hewed to developmentalist ideas of their time. "International law has to treat natives as uncivilised," John Westlake, the most prominent nineteenth-century British international lawyer and co-founder of the Institute, wrote. "It regulates, for the mutual benefit of the civilised states, the claims which they make to sovereignty over the region and leaves the treatment of the natives to the conscience of the state of which sovereignty is awarded." He voiced the dominant view of international jurists that a "native" chief, for instance, couldn't transfer sovereignty, because that was purely a European concept of which "natives" had no understanding. Relations between colonial ruler and ruled didn't come under international law. Instead, as was the case with India, they were governed by British constitutional law, which a priori regulated individual rights in relationship to the state—a relationship, as we saw earlier, known as the social contract and grounded in a secular humanism.[82]

Jurists wrestled with distinctions between civilized and uncivilized. Some went so far as to create categories of civilized, barbarian (half-civilized), and savage (uncivilized). Others, like the Swiss lawyer Joseph Hornung, thought a global federation should oversee empires, but he never wavered in his paternalism. "Those who know [the natives] well are able to say that with good treatment, much will be received from them," he wrote. "They are children, of course, but then, let us treat them as one treats children, through gentleness and persuasion. . . . We accept the hegemony and trusteeship of the strong but only in the interests of the weak and in view of their full future emancipation."[83]

Despite criticizing earlier empires, international jurists thought sovereignty had no particular definition beyond its basic claim to the right to rule, protect borders, and enjoy noninterference in matters internal to the state. European colonizers, if they chose, could run roughshod over their colonies with tyrannical states. They could delegate authority to private actors, or pursue variations of indirect rule or assimilation. They could also undertake some combination of all of these. "The sovereignty which they offered to the colonies," as international law expert Martti Koskenniemi tells us, "merely created a right of exclusivity in its European holder. It was their failure to spell out the meaning of sovereignty in social and political terms, as applied to non-European territory, that in retrospect made international lawyers seem such hopeless apologists of empire."[84]

Such hopelessness had consequences, and international jurists' sensibilities cascaded into their reading of international laws governing wars. While these jurists would critique sovereignty in Europe, arguing for more integration, free trade, and international regulations, including in the realm of war, these were ways of reforming a state-based global order, not changing it. Importantly for empires, many jurists believed that "native" populations, uncivilized, were excluded from international law's protection. Moreover, although nineteenth-century laws of war did internationalize a set of rules, war was still understood to be between states, and any internal armed conflict—a civil war or rebellion, for instance—was considered an internal state matter, including those conflicts arising in empires, such as wars of conquest as well as the South African War.

By the turn of the twentieth century, the various codifications of international law sought to balance Western military aims with eliminating unnecessary violence and destruction. Wounded soldiers were no longer considered combatants, and along with medical personnel, they could not be targeted. Prisoners of war were to be granted humane treatment similar to that offered to one's own military. Signatories to the 1899 Hague Convention were to refrain from deploying various techniques and weapons that caused undue suffering such as using civilians as hostages or war workers in occupied territories. They were also prohibited from pillaging and imposing collective punishments and fines on innocent civilians, bombing undefended cities, and deploying poison gas and "arms, projectiles, or material of a nature to cause superfluous injury," including dumdum bullets.[85]

When covering the 1897 Tirah Campaign in India as a correspondent for *The Daily Telegraph*, Churchill had described dumdum bullets' effects:

> The power of the new Lee-Metford rifle with the new Dum-Dum bullet—it is now called, though not officially, the "*ek-dum*" [Hindustani for "at once"] bullet—is tremendous. . . . Of the bullet it may be said, that its stopping power is all that could be desired. The Dum-Dum bullet, though not explosive, is expansive. . . . The result is a wonderful and from the technical point of view a beautiful machine. On striking a bone this causes the bullet to "set up" or spread out, and it then tears and splinters everything before it, causing wounds which in the body must be generally mortal and in any limb necessitate amputation.

Dumdum bullets had also been used by Kitchener's troops at the Battle of Omdurman in 1898, where Churchill was again present to record their effects: "Battalion by battalion . . . the British division began to fire. . . . The empty cartridge-cases, tinkling to the ground, formed small but growing heaps beside each man. And all the time out on the plain on the other side bullets were shearing through flesh, smashing and splintering bone; blood spouted from terrible wounds; valiant men struggling on through a hell of whistling metal, exploding shells, and spurting dust—suffering, despairing, dying."[86]

Despite Western jurists' views on international law and European empires, Britain was sufficiently concerned about the convention's jurisdiction that it refused to adopt the ban on dumdum bullets at the Hague Conference of 1899. It was the only state, aside from Luxembourg, that did not sign the prohibition. Conceptions of "civilized" and "uncivilized" informed British logic: one senior army medical officer emphasized how conventional bullets often passed through the body. "As a rule when a 'white man' is wounded [by such a conventional bullet] he has had enough, and is quite ready to drop out of the ranks and go to the rear; but the savage, like the tiger, is not so impressionable, and will go on fighting even when desperately wounded."[87] Variations on dumdum bullets had been used for big game hunting, and "savages" in the empire were taken down much like rhinos and elephants. International backlash against Britain's rejection of the dumdum ban was severe, and Britain eventually agreed in 1902 to stop using the bullets, though colonial forces continued to use them unofficially in the empire through at least the 1930s. As some military historians observe, "Even after the expanding bullets were universally withdrawn from use, British officers were likelier to order their subordinates to file hard-nosed bullets, turning them into expanding bullets, when confronted with adversaries that [*sic*] did not subscribe to the norm that combatants should fall out of action once wounded."[88] Subscribing to the norm was crucial to British battlefield logic. "Civilized" soldiers understood the rules of warfare; "savages" did not, and therefore different standards applied.

During the South African War, H. H. Asquith—Liberal Party member, ardent imperialist, and part of Milner's Balliol gang—said in Parliament that the Hague Convention did not apply in the South African context:

> These laws were framed not with a view to any such contest as now going on. They were in the main, and in their normal operation adapted to a state of things where you have a considerable number of men . . . arrayed against each other, acting upon some definite plan of campaign, moving in more or less

organised bodies, and subject in greater or less degree to some kind of central control. That description does not in the least correspond with what is now going on in South Africa.[89]

Arguments over traditional forms of warfare gave way to questions of jurisdiction. With regard to the initial Geneva and Hague conventions and subsequent international laws, many British officials, like other European colonizers, refused to acknowledge publicly that their armed conflicts through the empire were wars, a pattern that would repeat in the decades ahead. Instead, they cast them as internal revolts, police actions, or states of emergency and, as such, largely outside the scope of the conventions.

This is not to suggest, however, that in the aftermath of the South African War, questions were not raised about what constituted legal actions in the empire's conflicts. Necessity, intensity of force, legitimate violence—the same concerns that had vexed British jurists in the early nineteenth-century empire were again raised, this time in the context of modern international law. During the South African War, for instance, racializing the enemy had its own confusing logic. British troops did not use dumdum bullets against Afrikaner forces because they were white, though they waged a vicious campaign against the Afrikaner civilian population. "Once the war was over," the historian Isabel V. Hull points out, "the British government continued to believe that military reform was too important to be left to the military."[90] Viscount Esher led a commission that heard from 144 witnesses detailing the army's administrative deficiencies. While it did not investigate several of the military's most brutal methods, including concentration camps, it did examine, and criticize, the military's failure to maintain supply lines of clothing and medicines and to execute strategies. It also pointed to the incompetence of senior and inexperienced staff officers. Colonial Secretary Joseph Chamberlain pressed the issue of international law and whether British actions during the war were in violation of the Hague rules.

Questions of whether the conventions applied to nonsignatories, like the Afrikaners, were also debated. When the fighting was over, some critics insisted that Britain's methods of warfare in South Africa were often in violation of international law's intent to establish humane norms of conduct that were universal. Pressure from outside government (as with Hobhouse) and from within it (as with Chamberlain) forced internal investigations into international legal standards and their applicability to empire. Indeed, Hobhouse was not the only source of public outcry. The South African War was incredibly divisive for the Liberal

Party, as it split between those who considered themselves "liberal imperialists" and those anti-imperialists who "upheld the party's image of resistance to the worst aspects of imperialism," in the historian John W. Auld's words, and who served as a precursor to more radical British anti-imperialist thought that would emerge later in the twentieth century.[91]

Questions over whether international laws were applicable to the "backward" societies of the world were widely contested outside Britain as well, as international jurists would renew deliberations on the issue.[92] Implicit in these debates—debates that became more robust and contested after both world wars—was the question of sovereignty and the ways it intersected with liberal imperialism's hierarchy of civilizations and international law's jurisdiction. These debates were the riptide in modern international law's seas, prompting some British officials to deny publicly protections under international law to those they deemed uncivilized and therefore unprepared for sovereignty. Debates over whether protections and rights were universal, free of contingency, or were conferred when empire's "children," in international jurist Hornung's words, had reached maturity and were therefore prepared for statehood would become more contested in the decades to come. This was particularly the case when internationalism appeared to be the antidote to the fervent nationalism and racist nation-states that would twice cannibalize war-torn Europe and threaten freedoms in ways reminiscent of earlier anxieties, such as those that animated Britain in the era of Warren Hastings.[93]

The First World War was pivotal to the institutionalization of coercion and reform. Very much an imperial conflict, the Great War and its impact stretched from the remotest corners of northern Nigeria and British Guiana to the bustling urban centers of Delhi and Hong Kong. Loyalty, a common enemy, and universal duty to the Crown and the empire were the watchwords transmitted from London to subjects around the globe. Further down the chain of command, colonial troops had been the mainstay of Britain's imperial defense for decades, though the Great War would witness an unprecedented imperial mobilization effort. Millions of men from the British Empire cast their fates with Lord Kitchener, the face of Britain's wartime recruitment drive. These imperial troops fought and perished in well-known battles in France and Gallipoli, while others gave their limbs and lives in remote theaters in Jordan, Palestine, Kenya, Tanganyika, Mesopotamia, Northern Rhodesia, and the Sinai Desert.[94]

Lord Kitchener World War I recruitment poster: "Britons, your
King wants you. Join your country's army! God save the King."

Still, racial categorizations persisted. In British thought, some races,
like those hailing from Nepal and the North Indian provinces, were
more manly and martial and thus were entrusted to take up arms against
white enemies. Others, however, were judged to be at the bottom of
humanity's spectrum and could do little more than labor during the war.
Hundreds of thousands of imperial subjects, particularly those from
Africa, formed the backbone of Britain's military carrier corps (or labor
corps), and their death rates from malnutrition and disease were excep-
tionally high, often nearing 20 percent. The war's toll on the empire had
an economic dimension as well. The contributions of colonial revenues
to Britain's war effort were substantial: India forsook nearly 15 percent
of its revenues by 1918. At the same time, in South Asia some indigenous businessmen profited from the wartime boom, though the population's vast majority suffered from skyrocketing food and import prices,
the effects of which the worldwide influenza pandemic in the war's final
year exacerbated.[95]

At home, Prime Minister David Lloyd George's coalition government was a collection of men reared in the empire. Forged after Prime Minister Asquith resigned in December 1916, this government was a coalition of political views held together with a decades-old imperial tether. Though he famously decried the "policies of extermination" leveled against the Afrikaners, Lloyd George became bedfellows with a host of arch-imperialist veterans from the South African War as well as some of their former adversaries. Among them were Alfred Milner and Leopold "Leo" Amery, as well as Jan Smuts, a mainstay in the prime minister's newly formed imperial war cabinet. As Lloyd George drew substantial financial and manpower support from the white dominions, coordination was crucial and, for men like Smuts, so too was the explicit recognition of dominion autonomy within the empire. Whitehall had already been gesturing toward this in the years leading up to the war: Canada and Australia were the first to shed "colony" status—which connoted the rule over brown and Black peoples in Britain's "dependent" empire—and became dominions in 1867 and 1901, respectively. In 1910, South Africa also became a dominion.

Together these settler-based territories, ensconced in racial privilege and hierarchy, understood the common cause of their collective future. They knew they could not succeed individually, but nor could Britain face the Great War without them. More than any other dominion, South Africa understood that its greatest threat came not from the Black majority but rather from an erosion of the tenuous white alliance between the Afrikaner and British minority populations. It was an alliance whose fragility teetered on the memories Kitchener had left behind. Smuts cast his eye over the unraveling of European alliances that punctuated the Great War and saw in it the greatest threat to the civilizing mission. A divided Europe could not rule over the world's brown and Black majorities, and this realization not only drove Smuts's morally charged rhetoric that brought his new nation into the Great War but also underwrote his vision for the international order that would follow.[96]

To hold the wartime center, Lloyd George's alliances also extended at home. The *Daily Mail*'s jingoistic Harmsworth had been instrumental in the prime minister's ascent—so much so that Lloyd George offered the newspaper magnate a cabinet position. Harmsworth declined and instead took up the post of director of propaganda in 1917, a position for which he was most well suited. The sociologist Max Weber had fretted, with good reason, over the rise of press barons like Harmsworth and the unlimited power they appeared to have over what headlines were splashed across their papers and the content contained therein. "The journalist worker gains less and less," Weber wrote, "as the capitalist lord of the press, of the sort of 'Lord' Northcliffe [Harmsworth], for instance, gains more and more political influence."[97] The First World War would confirm such fears. The politics of an expanding British electorate became entwined with the rise of the press as the fourth estate. As the historian Niall Ferguson points out, broadsheets like Harmsworth's were deployed as "a weapon of warfare" to maintain public morale; moreover, propaganda, together with censorship, emerged as crucial tools to control opinion.[98] Lloyd George understood the importance of shielding his nation from the realities unfolding on Europe's battlefields. He acknowledged during the final throes of the conflict that "if people really knew [what was going on in the trenches,] the war would be stopped tomorrow. But of course they don't and can't know. The correspondents don't write and the censorship would not pass the truth."[99] Government approval extended to a handful of journalists who became official war correspondents in return for their careful adherence to frontline news choreography. Those reporters with an independent streak were arrested and deported from the war zones.

Britain's newfound "weapon of warfare" would be tested, however, and never more so than at the very moment when the nation was secretly preparing for the Battle of the Somme. In April 1916 the cumulative effects of over seven hundred years of British domination in Ireland were poised to erupt under the Great War's pressures and politics. After Britain formally annexed its island neighbor with the Act of Union in 1801, successive waves of Irish nationalists demanded "Home Rule," while a minority of Ulster unionists in northern Ireland resisted any measure of devolution, at least in their Protestant-dominated territories. In 1914 Britain was poised to implement the Third Home Rule Act, which would grant self-government to Ireland and reverse parts of the Act of Union, but it put the measure on hold with the outbreak of the war. The Irish Parliamentary Party and its leader, John Redmond, called for Irish wartime support and sent regiments to fight alongside the Allies with the hope that Home Rule would be a long-overdue reward for loyalty. At the same time, anti-Redmond Irish Volunteers emerged, and the separatist Irish Republican Brotherhood and Sinn Féin prepared for armed resistance against British rule and the establishment of an independent Irish republic.

The lingering Ulster issue, too, partly prompted the delay of Home Rule, and an imagined partition deepened long-standing divisions across Britain, which were about xenophobia and imperial norms as much as anything else. Irish discrimination, rooted in anti-Catholicism, stretched back to the Norman era, when Gerald of Wales's widely circulated texts condemned the Irish as "a truly barbarous people" who "live like animals."[100] Such claims proliferated for centuries and justified exploitation and Ireland's eventual annexation to Britain in 1801. British overlords further consolidated territorial rights, which included vast absentee landlord estates; instituted policies of taxation and economic exploitation; and disregarded human hardship, such as that which unfolded in the mid-nineteenth century with the Great Famine. This disaster claimed the lives of up to 1 million of the poorest of Europe's poor and forced an estimated 3 million to emigrate from Ireland, leading to an overall Irish population decline of nearly 25 percent—a decline that continued such that Ireland's population dropped from 8.1 million in 1841 to 4.5 million in 1901. Such a dramatic emptying out of Ireland left permanent political, cultural, and economic scars, including in Britain, where one-third of its subjects were Irish in the early nineteenth century, though they constituted 10 percent of the nation's subject population by the end of the century.[101]

In Victorian Britain, whiteness did not bestow, a priori, civilization. As with the Afrikaners, Britain's racially ordered world not only depicted the Irish as inferior but at times dehumanized them with ape-like images.[102] Such vitriol transcended political affiliation. On one end of the spectrum, Friedrich Engels both admired Irish resistance and chided the immigrant Irish for "having grown up almost without civilisation" and for infecting the industrial revolution's working class. On the other end, Benjamin Disraeli declared that the Irish "hate our free and fertile isle. They hate our order, our civilisation, our enterprising industry . . . our pure religion. This wild, reckless, indolent, uncertain and superstitious race have no sympathy with the English character. . . . Their history describes an unbroken circle of bigotry and blood."[103]

Few imperial issues sparked such intense bitterness as the Irish question. It splintered populations, due in part to Ireland's ambiguous status. As the historian Stephen Howe notes, Ireland was "neither clearly colonial nor fully integrated into the United Kingdom." It was the only colonial territory that, after the Act of Union, had any kind of representation in Parliament; Irish voters elected their own members to sit in Westminster. Yet historically embedded animosities continued to take form in racial and cultural differences, and in a lack of full Irish integration into Britain's political decision-making structures as well as the creation of a British government located in Ireland's Dublin Castle. Opponents of Irish nationalism and Home Rule during the Great War feared not just imperial decline and its domino effect, whereby devolution of sovereignty in Ireland would lead to the loss of other colonial possessions.

Rather, as Howe tells us, they also feared for "the integrity of the British state itself . . . that breaking the Union with Ireland would destroy the entire state and social order."[104] While Britain wrung its hands over the exigencies of Home Rule, divisions between and among Ulster Unionists, moderate Home Rulers, and more radical Irish nationalists intensified and ensured that any kind of peaceful consensus would be out of reach.

Insofar as Ireland's ambiguous status was concerned, it had none when it came to the question of rule of law and civil liberties. Imperial statesmen thought it essential to have recourse to extraordinary legal measures. Ireland confirmed this pattern. Sir Robert Peel, who laid the groundwork for the Royal Irish Constabulary—Britain's paramilitary police force in Ireland—offered no illusions that liberalism would wash up on Irish shores. He declared, "for scarcely a year during the period that has elapsed since the Union, has Ireland been governed by the ordinary course of law."[105] Whereas in the nineteenth century government by consent increasingly defined England, Scotland, and Wales, officials imposed order on Ireland through a series of insurrection acts, habeas corpus suspension acts, and deployments of martial law. When these were not sufficient, the colonial legislature in Ireland introduced coercion acts, with measures to control arms, provide special systems of trial, and criminalize political and paramilitary oath taking. The Act for the More Effective Suppression of Local Disturbances and Dangerous Associations of 1833 was the precursor for Britain's twentieth-century code of emergency law. It granted Ireland's lord lieutenant power to declare a county incapable of controlling subversive organizations, thus permitting security forces free rein in suppressing these existential threats to the state. "This is the first instance of what came to be called 'declaring a state of emergency,' the English equivalent of declaring a state of siege, as distinct from a military declaration of martial law," the legal historian Simpson points out. It was distinct because "offenses under the Act were not bailable, and became triable by courts-martial. And, very significantly for later developments, nothing done under the act could be questioned in any court of law." In 1871 Ireland's legislature granted the government's executive branch detention powers. Enabled through the Protection of Life and Property Act, the lord lieutenant could detain any person suspected of treasonable offenses or interfering with Ireland's law and order, and as Simpson tells us, "a warrant was conclusive evidence of its own legitimacy. . . . [And] when the Act lapsed what had been done under it could not be subjected to any retrospective legal challenge."[106]

At the time, Britain's leading constitutional authority, Dicey, made clear that the coercion acts were fully incompatible with the rule of law and the ideals of liberties. "In principle [they are] thoroughly vicious," Dicey said. They "in effect gave the Irish executive an unlimited power of arrest; it established in them a despotic government. . . . [They] could not be made permanent, and applied to the whole United Kingdom, without depriving every citizen of security for his personal freedom."[107] Dicey's issue with how the rule of law was being administered in Ireland was partly due to his broader sentiments about the Irish and empire. He repeatedly repudiated Home Rule, which, in his view, would diminish the empire and therefore was "a deliberate and complete surrender of the objects at which English statesmanship has, under one form or another, aimed for centuries." Moreover, Dicey thought Britain and Ireland had "from the beginning of their ill-starred connection been countries standing at a different level, or a different stage, of civilization," and that Irish Catholics "had not reached the stage of development which was absolutely essential for even the understanding of Protestant doctrine."[108] The coercion acts were introduced because Irish juries were failing to convict and therefore nullifying law, according to Dicey, whereas British juries could be entrusted to follow judicial instructions and therefore uphold law. To solve the Irish problem, Dicey wanted special courts that had three judges, with no right to a jury trial, something that was eventually instituted in Ireland and other parts of the empire. Moreover, he had broader objections to special codes like the coercion acts because he believed that "the executive and military could rely upon the common law's recognition of necessity, and take action under martial law."[109]

Dicey's fears that imperial despotism would possibly impact Britain were realized when, during the First World War, Parliament passed the Defence of the Realm Act (DORA), giving the executive branch of government extraordinary power. While martial law was an option during wartime, it had not been used at home since the eighteenth century. There were also perennial questions of necessity, precision, and legality. After the Morant Bay Rebellion in Jamaica and the subsequent Governor Eyre controversy called into question the legality of security force powers, the military had introduced the idea of a comprehensive British code of emergency powers in 1888. Again, while Dicey believed emergency powers were unnecessary because English common law's recognition of necessity was all that the executive and the military needed in order to declare martial law, and because an indemnity act could provide ex post facto legal protection, he lost a crucial battle over the British constitution's powers. For many statesmen, ambiguity remained over the lawfulness of extraordinary measures, and they believed the answer to necessity and the scope of state power resided in DORA. Modeled on Ireland's coercion acts, DORA permitted the executive—through executive decree, or Orders in Council, which bypassed Parliament—to enact regulations "for securing the public safety and the defence of the realm," thereby radically altering the British constitution during an emergency.[110]

During World War I, Britain's executive branch introduced several regulations—including Regulation 14B, which legalized detention without trial—after Parliament had passed the original, basic DORA. Now the civil liberties that British liberalism held so dear were threatened as the executive became the legislature and Parliament an arena only for expressions of public opinion. British officials justified the regulations due to exceptional security circumstances and lifted them soon after the war ended.[111] "In a perverted sense the DORA code, and its successors, respected the ideal of the rule of law," Simpson tells us. "The practical effect of such a code is to introduce what has been called 'a form of statutory martial law.' And whereas under martial law there was . . . the possibility after the emergency ended of challenging what had been done, emergency codes made this impossible by superseding the regular law entirely."[112]

Ireland felt the impact of Britain's wartime state on Easter Monday in 1916, after Patrick Pearse and some 150 Irish Volunteers abandoned constitutional nationalism and seized the general post office in Dublin. Pearse emerged outside the post office with the Proclamation of the Irish Republic in hand. "Irishmen and Irishwomen: In the name of God and of the dead generations from which she receives her old tradition of nationhood, Ireland, through us, summons her children to her flag and strikes for her freedom," he announced to a somewhat bewildered crowd.[113] As these words of defiance spilled from Pearse's lips, Britain's military bigwigs were gathered at the Fairyhouse Racecourse to watch the Grand National. They were well aware that Sinn Féin harbored pro-German sentiments and was pushing antirecruitment campaigns against the war, a conflict that would see over 200,000 Irishmen volunteer and 35,000 lose their lives. Nevertheless, the uprising surprised nearly everyone except the conspirators themselves. Even then the Easter Rising was, by Pearse's calculus, "a blood sacrifice that would revive the spirit of the Irish nation" rather than a realistic attempt to overthrow British rule during wartime.[114]

Ireland's Lord Lieutenant Ivor Churchill Guest, known as Lord Wimborne, a decorated soldier in the South African War and cousin of

POBLACHT NA H EIREANN.

THE PROVISIONAL GOVERNMENT

OF THE

IRISH REPUBLIC

TO THE PEOPLE OF IRELAND.

IRISHMEN AND IRISHWOMEN In the name of God and of the dead generations from which she receives her old tradition of nationhood, Ireland, through us summons her children to her flag and strikes for her freedom.

Having organised and trained her manhood through her secret revolutionary organisation, the Irish Republican Brotherhood, and through her open military organisations, the Irish Volunteers and the Irish Citizen Army, having patiently perfected her discipline, having resolutely waited for the right moment to reveal itself, she now seizes that moment, and, supported by her exiled children in America and by gallant allies in Europe, but relying in the first on her own strength, she strikes in full confidence of victory.

We declare the right of the people of Ireland to the ownership of Ireland, and to the unfettered control of Irish destinies, to be sovereign and indefeasible. The long usurpation of that right by a foreign people and government has not extinguished the right, nor can it ever be extinguished except by the destruction of the Irish people. In every generation the Irish people have asserted their right to national freedom and sovereignty, six times during the past three hundred years they have asserted it in arms. Standing on that fundamental right and again asserting it in arms in the face of the world, we hereby proclaim the Irish Republic as a Sovereign Independent State, and we pledge our lives and the lives of our comrades-in-arms to the cause of its freedom, of its welfare, and of its exaltation among the nations.

The Irish Republic is entitled to, and hereby claims, the allegiance of every Irishman and Irishwoman. The Republic guarantees religious and civil liberty, equal rights and equal opportunities to all its citizens, and declares its resolve to pursue the happiness and prosperity of the whole nation and of all its parts, cherishing all the children of the nation equally, and oblivious of the differences carefully fostered by an alien government, which have divided a minority from the majority in the past.

Until our arms have brought the opportune moment for the establishment of a permanent National Government, representative of the whole people of Ireland and elected by the suffrages of all her men and women, the Provisional Government, hereby constituted, will administer the civil and military affairs of the Republic in trust for the people.

We place the cause of the Irish Republic under the protection of the Most High God, Whose blessing we invoke upon our arms, and we pray that no one who serves that cause will dishonour it by cowardice, inhumanity, or rapine. In this supreme hour the Irish nation must, by its valour and discipline and by the readiness of its children to sacrifice themselves for the common good, prove itself worthy of the august destiny to which it is called.

Signed on Behalf of the Provisional Government,

THOMAS J. CLARKE.

SEAN Mac DIARMADA.   THOMAS MacDONAGH.

P. H. PEARSE.   EAMONN CEANNT.

JAMES CONNOLLY.   JOSEPH PLUNKETT.

Proclamation of the Irish Republic 1916, issued during the Easter Rising

Winston Churchill's, was out of his depth as he managed Ireland's complexities. He had worked assiduously with the War Office to push Irish recruitment and was largely ineffective in establishing law and order. As Irish radicals spread seditious propaganda, deportation proved ineffective, and he demanded more effective security measures and alternatives. The flow of information from the police to Dublin Castle was alarmingly inadequate. "I can't understand how the night manoeuvres in Dublin were omitted from the police report summary," the exasperated lord lieutenant said a month before the uprising. "Why it is that we are left to learn from the press this morning of the arms seizure in Cork? Surely we should have daily reports from the police of any Sinn Féin activities, and action of this kind should not be undertaken without the cognizance of the Executive."[115]

In the weeks leading up to Pearse's proclamation, Wimborne's frustrations mounted. When the Irish Volunteers stormed the post office, cut government communication wires, and killed three police constables, it was clear that Dublin Castle was paralyzed. Panicked and pacing the oriental carpets of the sumptuous Viceregal Lodge, Wimborne "*swilled* brandy the whole time," according to his private secretary.[116] Without consulting his law officers and ignoring the panoply of DORA options, the lord lieutenant declared martial law first in Dublin and then in the whole of Ireland. It was time to call in the military to stamp out the rebellion using any means necessary.

Kitchener, the secretary for war, appointed as military governor for Ireland General John Maxwell, one of his many protégés who had seen action both in the Sudan and in South Africa, instructing him "to take such measures as may in your opinion be necessary for the prompt suppression of the insurrection."[117] When Maxwell arrived in Dublin, the place

British security forces inside the General Post Office in Sackville Street, Dublin, during the Easter Rising of 1916

was a "blazing furnace" and looked eerily like an "après-bombardment European city."[118] The military governor declared he would "not hesitate to destroy all buildings within any area occupied by rebels."[119] He also demanded unconditional surrender. With the aid of another Kitchener disciple, Brigadier General William Lowe, the military governor and his troops repressed the twelve hundred Irish republicans who had taken up arms, along with the entire city of Dublin. Streets became war zones, and shops, hotels, and homes went up in flames of white heat that spewed hundreds of feet into the air as explosions muffled the perpetual gunfire.[120] Within six days, Maxwell and his men quashed the uprising, and in the process they destroyed countless buildings, including the general post office, taking the lives of 500 and wounding another 2,600, most of whom were civilians. Suspensions of due process enabled the arrests of 3,500 incipient leaders and their suspected supporters. Hasty courts-martial then condemned ninety people to death. Within less than ten days, firing squads executed fifteen of them.

At the start of the Easter Uprising, wartime loyalties divided Ireland, and republicans lacked widespread popular support.[121] Opposition to the nationalist cause, however, began to evaporate in the face of wanton British repression. It was not only the Portobello Barracks murders, in which the British military summarily executed the pacifist Francis Sheehy-Skeffington and two others, or the North King Street Massacre, in which British soldiers burst into houses and randomly shot and bayoneted civilians, that so shocked and turned Irish public opinion. It was also the British Army and government's refusal to either accept or apportion accountability. In the case of the North King Street Massacre, for instance, the city coroner's inquest condemned the soldiers for killing "unarmed and unoffending" civilians.[122] Maxwell, however, claimed the civilians were republican sympathizers, and a military court of inquiry ruled that no specific member of the British Army could be held responsible and therefore no one was accountable. Tellingly, Maxwell candidly admitted to his troops' lack of judgment:

> The rebels wore no uniform, and the man who was shooting at a soldier one minute might, for all he knew, be walking quietly beside him in the street at another. . . . Nearly everything had to be left to the troops on the spot. Possibly unfortunate incidents, which we should regret, may have occurred . . . but how were the soldiers to discriminate? They saw their comrades killed beside them by hidden and treacherous assailants, and it is even possible that under the horrors of this peculiar attack some of

them "saw red." That is the inevitable consequence of a rebellion of this kind.[123]

With wartime censorship and press statements like Maxwell's supporting the troops, the British government explained away events unfolding in Ireland.

The Irish republicans understood well the combined power of communication and British repression. At the time of the Easter Rising, Pearse's men commandeered a radio transmitter and broadcast their proclamation of the Irish Republic.[124] The Easter Rising was on the front page of most major American and British newspapers every day for over a fortnight, though news coming out of Ireland was filtered through the lens of information control and obfuscation as much as possible. Against the backdrop of the war, the initial coverage, while urging restraint on both sides, framed the events as Irish folly. Papers like *The New York Times* offered tautological analyses—one editorial stated, "Ireland in a state of rebellion is Irish. Never was it otherwise. . . . Rebellion has been the chronic, almost to say the natural, condition of Ireland, being now and then only a little more acute than usual."[125]

All this changed with the executions of Pearse and fourteen other uprising leaders. Press coverage and public opinion turned. In theory, the Allies were engaged in total war against a German enemy associated with such despotic and cruel measures. *The Times* of London chided the British government on its own moral terms, declared that the firing squads were "unworthy" of their nation, and urged it to "leave that sort of thing to Germany." Appealing to the emerging anti-imperialist sentiments in the United States, *The Washington Post* wrote, "History is too full of instances of brutal and excessive measures by England in dealing with Ireland, and it ought to serve as a warning against such a policy now."[126]

The executions' effects were not lost on John Redmond and his moderate nationalists, who thought the government's response to the rising undermined the legitimacy of British rule. On May 11, 1916, Redmond's deputy, John Dillon, rose in the House of Commons and spoke of the disastrous consequences of Britain's actions in Ireland, and its efforts to cover up and justify the suspension of civil liberties:

> The primary object of my Motion is to put an absolute and a final stop to these executions. You are letting loose a river of blood, and, make no mistake about it, between two races who, after three hundred years of hatred and of strife, we had nearly

succeeded in bringing together. . . . It is no use indulging in smooth words to cloak over the truth of the situation. We have a great deal of well-founded criticism in this House, and still more in the Press, as to the practice of the Government throwing a heavy cloak over the truth, and trying to get along with—optimistic statements blinding the public to the realities of the situation.[127]

Such passion, even in the context of increasing public outrage, failed to stop the executions. For his part, Lloyd George was sanguine. Poised to take over for Kitchener as secretary of state for war before climbing his way to Downing Street, the future prime minister adopted relativistic logic: "People are getting accustomed to scenes of blood. Their own sons are falling by the hundred-thousand and the nation is harder and more ruthless than it has ever been." Lloyd George's reasoning, however, was no match for Dillon's foreboding retort. "Since the executions," he emphasized, "we have a *new* Ireland to deal with—seething with discontent and rage against the government. Old historic passions have been aroused to a *terrible* extent."[128]

Other measures further stoked nationalist flames. In the wake of the Easter Rising, the British government detained fifteen hundred men without trial under Regulation 14B. Largely held in the Frongoch internment camp, a crude conglomeration of huts and an abandoned distillery on the Welsh coast, detainees like Michael Collins took the lead in transforming their incarceration into a recruitment opportunity. Frongoch became known as *ollscoil na reabhbhloide*, the university of revolution, and Collins and others gave lessons in revolutionary ideology and guerrilla tactics, which included those deployed in South Africa.[129] In fact, two Irish brigades, including that of recently executed John MacBride, had fought alongside the Afrikaners, picking up guerrilla maneuvers and inspiration.[130] Afrikaner backdraft informed Irish radicalism and would be felt from the very top of its emerging organization down to its lower-level recruits.

Collins, arguably the most famous and influential Irish republican leader, had been reared in the nationalism of County Cork. There his father was a member of the Irish Republican Brotherhood, an organization the young Collins would eventually lead. Like countless others, the future republican leader's influences also originated farther from home. He spent his youth idolizing the famed Afrikaner general Christiaan de Wet and his commando tactics and eventually assumed the moniker "the Irish de Wet." Sinn Féin traced part of its origins back to the pro-Boer movement and the Irish Transvaal Committee, which actively raised funds and enlisted men to fight alongside Afrikaner forces. Further down the chain of command, one of Collins's foot soldiers from a remote village in Cork recalled a shared history of racialized white suffering under British rule:

> The stories of, and the discussions on, the Boer War never ended without reference to Ireland. Small wonder. The handful of farmers who stood up against an empire and humiliated it set an example for the oppressed and downtrodden of the world. The example was not lost on the militant-minded in our own country. My uncle was one of these and it was from him that I first heard of the only sure way to shake off the foreign oppressor.[131]

Britain's internment response to the Easter Rising opened ideological and physical spaces for Irish radicals to process their own histories of hardship as well as their strategic future in confronting British liberal imperialism. So, too, did it stoke the nationalism of their countrymen and the creative imaginations of Ireland's humanists, who fashioned literary works, songs, and elaborate funeral processionals from the ashes of imperial destruction and nationalist longings.[132] Just as Britain had Rudyard Kipling, so too did colonies have their own decorated bards of imperialism. William Butler Yeats emerged foremost among republican literary geniuses and gave expression to the unspeakable and to visions of freedom. The poet for the masses stood with international giants and became the first from Ireland to win the Nobel Prize in Literature in 1923. The lyricism of his poem "The Rose Tree" betrayed a republican self-understanding in the wake of the Easter Rising, as his last stanza intoned:

> *"But where can we draw water,"*
> *Said Pearse to Connolly,*
> *"When all the wells are parched away?*
> *O plain as plain can be*
> *There's nothing but our own red blood*
> *Can make a right Rose Tree."*[133]

Yeats's popular "Easter, 1916" offered a eulogistic lamentation for those executed as well as a coming-to-terms for the poet, and countless other moderates, with the rising's impact on republican nationalism. In the final lines of his poem, Yeats looks to the martyring of those executed:

Now and in time to be,
Wherever green is worn,
Are changed, changed utterly:
A terrible beauty is born.[134]

With the Great War's end, Lloyd George's popularity helped assuage a shocked nation that was reeling from the loss of nearly a million lives and the wounding of 3 million soldiers. Disarmament and pacifism became watchwords for a generation that sought to redefine a global order in the wake of unimaginable suffering. Strikingly, multiple sets of actors, including radical peace activists and postwar statesmen deeply invested in reaffirming the British Empire, increasingly found their concerns located in an emerging internationalism centered on the imperial framework as a model for federation. Smuts's belief that the empire's white dominions could not be safeguarded in a narrow collectivity, but rather needed a broader international organization, gained traction.[135] Having spent years pondering the ways in which nationalism, or more specifically, white nationalism, was compatible with the broader international interests and loyalties of Europe and the United States, Smuts imagined not only a "British Commonwealth of Nations" but also something much grander in its reach. For him, Britain's imperial architecture would be a model for what, at that juncture, was a Wilsonian vision without a substantive form. Marshaling Kipling's earlier poetic parallels, Smuts said that "the elements of the future World Government, which will no longer rest on the Imperial ideas adopted from Roman law, are already in operation in our Commonwealth of Nations. . . . As the Roman ideas guided European civilisation for almost two thousand years, so the newer ideas embedded in the British constitutional and Colonial system may, when carried to their full development, guide the future civilisation for ages to come."[136] Yet when Smuts and Lord Robert Cecil packed their bags in January 1919 and traveled to the Palace of Versailles, where the Paris Peace Conference was to take place, Smuts's blueprint for the League of Nations scarcely had cabinet approval. While the notion of imperial integrity went down well, few of Lloyd George's men wanted any oversight of their empire or any imperial entanglements in European affairs. Smuts, though, had one last card to play: an appeal to closer cooperation with the Americans, something upon which most everyone could agree.

President Woodrow Wilson's name was initially associated with the idea of the League of Nations. Prior to entering the global conflict, he was outspoken over the need for "an organized common peace" and a "community of power" as opposed to "a balance of power." Wilson saw in the United States a model for federalism that could be translated into a peacetime organization that would be an international force for good. When the time came to articulate his vision into a concrete plan in Paris, however, he didn't have one, or at least not one that was fully conceived. Instead, it was Smuts who had his ear and offered up not only a sympathetic articulation of communal interests and ethics as opposed to individual state interests, but also an out for the American president, who was encumbered with anti-imperialism at home.[137]

Wilson's future imagined the backward races of the world under the "tutelage" not of individual imperial nations but rather of an internationalist organization that would be held accountable for purveying and maintaining new norms, including those that pertained to rules of warfare.[138] How then to reconcile a Wilsonian moment that would usher in a new era, one that would eschew further territorial annexation and fulfill Smuts's desire and that of Britain and other European nations to absorb the former Ottoman and German colonial territories and to have the League serve as a mechanism for the defense of empires? Here Smuts's genius was on full display. Making what would be a relatively minor concession in return for American sign-off, Smuts pushed for international trusteeships, as did others in Britain's Paris Peace Conference delegation. To consolidate support of the British cabinet and the dominions, they gutted most of the future League's oversight clauses. In the end, the League of Nations was a product of empire and condoned annexation in everything but name. The League was "an eminently Victorian institution, based on the notional superiority of the great powers, an instrument for a global civilizing mission through the use of international law and simultaneously a means of undergirding British imperial world leadership and cementing its partnership with the United States," as Mark Mazower recently emphasized.[139]

Some jurists hoped the League would strengthen international law. The war had proved the Hague system a failure, though some international jurists thought the system failed because it had not gone far enough. "It had left wide gaps through which states could evade the judicial or arbitral settlement of disputes," the historian Stephen Wertheim points out. "Politicians had too much free play, and their publics proved startlingly bellicose. Only when lawyers and judges supplanted politicians as the protagonists of world affairs would principle trump 'expediency' and peace replace war." Law had to reign over politics in a kind of utopia that, jurists knew, would take time to implement, as such an arrangement would be deeply unpopular, not least because it would require states to give up some of their sovereignty to a higher international order. Such designs for an international order rested on the development of legal codes so that future disputes would fall under an international rule of law, enforced by expert judges. During the Great War, jurists had spent years reviewing the precise arrangements that an international league of nations should adopt, but as Wertheim tells us, when British and American leaders met at Versailles in 1919, they "demoted legalism" and "privileged politicians' judgment above judicial settlement, and 'public opinion' above armed enforcement. . . . Seamless legal codes and judicial procedures would, they thought, trample society underfoot. Lawyers had to get out of the way of politicians attuned to popular sentiment, the true agent of historical progress."[140]

The Americans, mired in postwar isolationism, exited negotiations and the incipient League, though the spurning of proposals to take the League in a more formal juridical direction remained. Then a Russia consumed with revolution and a disgraced Germany shackled with wartime reparations left the League fully to the world's colonizing powers and their "imperial internationalism." Britain and France dominated the remaining proceedings in 1919, and Lloyd George handed over the final divvying up of German and Ottoman territories to his colonial secretary, Alfred Milner. In some ways, the moment reflected a passage of the South African baton between Smuts and his long-ago adversary. However, when it came time for Milner to run his internationalist leg, he proclaimed, "I am very doubtful myself about the success of the League of Nations." Nonetheless, he shared fully in Smuts's imperial ethos, saying, "We must try to extend the *pax Britannica* into *a pax mundi*." The scuttled Americans would have agreed "to generalize the British Empire's excellent practices," as the League of Nations authority Susan Pedersen has suggested, even though its track record of repression in South Africa, Ireland, and elsewhere was well known.[141]

Milner wheeled and dealt on Britain's behalf according to the principles soon captured in Article 22 of the League's covenant. Replete with lofty, imperial rhetoric, Article 22 spoke of "those colonies and territories . . . which are inhabited by peoples *not yet* able to stand by themselves under the strenuous condition of the modern world."[142] From this principle, the League created a system that categorized former German and Ottoman territories based on their perceived levels of civilization and preparedness for self-government. It put into international practice the bureaucratized coding of racial and cultural differences inherent to the British Empire. Such differences were explicitly inscribed into class

A, B, and C mandates, with class A mandates such as Palestine and Syria furthest along in their preparedness to "stand alone." As for the class B mandates, Milner and others could scarcely contain their racial condescension for these largely African territories like Tanganyika and Togo. At the bottom of the mandate hierarchy sat places like Western Samoa and South West Africa. Europeans conceived of them as so backward and childlike that any kind of self-government for them lay in the very distant future.[143]

In the aftermath of World War I, the British Empire doubled down on its commitments. By assuming administrative responsibilities for the League mandates of Tanganyika, Palestine, Mesopotamia (later Iraq), and parts of Samoa, Cameroon, and Togo, the British Empire was at its largest size. Britain and its allies had to deflect the charge that the war had been fought to facilitate greater territorial annexation. On this point, the League's mandate system legitimated the war's territorial settlement in the language of internationalism. Moreover, it asserted the principle that sovereignty did not reside with the individual mandatory powers; rather, the League's future Permanent Mandates Commission would have oversight of the trust territories, even if it lacked any legal powers of enforcement. That the commission even had oversight was due to the League's smaller states pushing for such powers—an indication that larger states couldn't always get their way. Indeed, the commission was originally supposed to be, not an oversight regime, but merely a vehicle for consultation among European colonial secretaries.[144] Nevertheless, the implications of its enforcement impotence would soon bear out in complicated and sometimes unanticipated ways, particularly on the eve of the Second World War, when the atmosphere in Geneva became "toxic," and Britain found itself perpetually mired in Middle Eastern mandatory conflicts.[145]

A barometer of the broad grassroots support for the League's ideals in Britain was the vigor and scale of the League of Nations Union. One of Britain's largest voluntary associations during the interwar period, the union at its peak in 1931 had nearly three thousand local branches that boasted more than 400,000 members. Together they produced streams of pamphlets, educational outreach initiatives, and radio broadcasts from a wide swath of notables, including those who haggled over the mandates. Rivaling both major political parties, churches, and other voluntary organizations, the union counted over a million Britons who, at some point, would sign up for membership. While it was left leaning, the union presented itself as apolitical, and its strength lay in the premise of the League of Nations: it was a fair-minded and civic-oriented collection of individuals who were determined to keep the peace through internationalism. Like the League, the union embraced an "imperial internationalism" that presupposed, at least outwardly, the empire as a collective civilizing force that would usher in global peace and progress not only for the less-developed brown and Black peoples of the world but also for other empires that were not nearly as advanced as Britain's. While the union was concerned with internationalism, this concern was a priori a domestic reflection of a particular kind of internationalism self-fashioned in Britain's imperial image. It was an image that reflected the myths of empire's civilizing benevolence and humanity as symbolized in its statues and legacies, its bipartisan imperial rhetoric, and the union's diverse scope and size.[146]

Britain and her victorious imperial allies were more than happy to sacrifice the much-needed wartime goodwill of their colonized populations to further their own territorial claims, regardless of how enshrined they were in the rhetoric of peaceful and harmonious internationalism. The deception for imperial subjects was far-reaching. As Pedersen concludes in her magisterial *The Guardians:*

> For a politicized minority in those territories to which it was applied the mandates system was something simpler: a shameless betrayal of the promises of self-determination the allies had made in 1918 with their backs to the wall. Britain and France hadn't just called on indigenous voices and troops in their campaigns; they had also promised that any new dispensation—in Africa as well as the Middle East, if Lloyd George was to be believed—would be crafted in consultation with the populations themselves. Yet, once they had secured their conquests—and, of course, once the United States exited the room—those promises had been pushed aside.[147]

The broken trust threw into relief the moral bankruptcy of a capitalist, industrialized Europe that had mechanized the slaughter of millions of its young men while it asserted racial birthrights to progress, rationality, scientific innovation, and industriousness. The primitivism and savagery so long contained in empire's racial order had been inverted in the fetid trenches of Europe. To many colonized eyes, the white man no longer appeared invincible, and the civilizing mission's potency was eroding, both in its progressive concepts of humanity and in its legal and institutional claims. In the Americas, Africa, and Asia, a generation of humanists and activists began to script critiques of European superiority, often challenging the West on its own terms. They produced a cross-cultural discourse that would threaten European imperial dominance and gain traction with ordinary peasants and laborers in the decades ahead.[148]

The Great War changed irrevocably the perspectives and perceptions of subject populations around the world. Within the empire itself, changes were afoot. Different cultural forms and burgeoning political movements debated fundamental issues like rights, ethics, sovereignty, legality, and dignity. Many political movements were transimperial in nature: Irish republicanism spread across the Atlantic to the United States, and W. E. B. Du Bois's Pan-Africanist movement made inroads in Europe that would animate the years ahead. Meanwhile, imperial actors continued to circulate between Britain and the empire and, in the process, internalize and reflect liberalism's coercive and reformist ethos. Their deployment of repressive measures hardened nationalist sentiments regardless of how divided subject populations were. Indeed, European empires, while fundamental to the Allied powers' victory, also "committed suicide during the 1914–18 war by fomenting nationalism as a form of political warfare against their opponents," as Mazower reminds us.[149]

During the interwar years, war weary and economically crippled, Britain's empire faced a series of crises. No sooner had Milner signed on to the League of Nations than he cast his gaze across Britain's imperial expanse and observed, "The whole world is rocking . . . in a state of raging chaos."[150] Still, British officials would not substantively rethink coercive measures such as those that they had unleashed in South Africa and subsequently in Ireland. Their successive governments would defend imperial interests and the nation's body politic so closely linked with the empire. They would do so partly by continuing to expand legal frameworks, both within the empire and at home, that enabled the use of force and the subversion of civil liberties with little or no accountability. In essence, Callwell's "moral effect"—meant to pull along fair-minded public opinion, as embodied in organizations like the League of Nations Union, as well as to silence the critical minority at home—would lead to the further legal enablement of repressive measures. Events unfolding most notably in India, Ireland, and Palestine would catalyze the convergence of repressive military and policing tactics with restrictive laws and ordinances from Britain and throughout the empire to create highly coercive systems enabled through a veneer of legal permissibility.

CHAPTER 3

Legalized Lawlessness

On April 13, 1919, in the northern reaches of India's Punjab region, a radiant sun beat down on the seven-acre park known as Jallianwala Bagh. It was the Sunday of Vaisakhi, a day of profound significance in the region. It was the solar new year, the Punjab's spring harvest festival, and, for Sikhs, the marking of Guru Gobind Singh's proclamation of the Khalsa order in 1699 as well as the later coronation of Ranjit Singh as their *maharaja* (great ruler). Thousands of Muslims, Hindus, and Sikhs thus congregated in the city of Amritsar, some to worship at the Golden Temple and bathe in its sacred pools. Thousands of others from surrounding towns and villages also flooded in to attend the cattle and horse fair. By late afternoon, the park held fifteen thousand people. Religious pilgrims and livestock traders intermingled with city residents, some of whom were there for a peaceful political debate about the current situation in India. By all accounts, it was a massive but sociable affair as the crowds listened to political speakers in between card games, rounds of gossip, and afternoon dozes in the shade of trees growing out of the courtyard's baked earth.[1]

Underneath Jallianwala Bagh's Sunday afternoon conviviality, however, bitterness seethed. With nearly 1.5 million of its own people fighting in support of Britain and her allies in the Great War, India faced ever-increasing economic and personal hardships. Significant revolutionary attacks and intercommunal disorder in Punjab and farther east in Bengal made parts of India virtually ungovernable. Then in February

1915, the British government narrowly averted a full-scale army mutiny. It then exported Defence of the Realm Act regulations to India and that same year passed the Defence of India Act, which enabled India's executive to pass any regulation to secure the public safety and defense of the British Raj. In Bengal alone eight hundred orders were put into force that eviscerated civil and political liberties, such as they existed.[2]

The global cultural discourse that drove resistance and liberation movements within and across colonies and empires was, arguably, the most historically rooted in India.[3] There educated figures including Swami Vivekananda, Aurobindo Ghose, and Rabindranath Tagore drew upon rich precolonial intellectual legacies, spiritual beliefs, civilizational discourses, and Western and local conceptions of a nation to imagine alternative frameworks for India's future that differed from Britain's liberal imperial plans for the region. In 1908 Ghose and nearly three dozen others were arrested, charged with "waging war against the King" for their roles in what was known as the Alipore conspiracy case: running a massive bomb-making workshop and collecting arms and ammunition at the Ghoses' family home, and unsuccessfully attempting to assassinate the governor of Bengal and a district judge. The judge's bridge partners, two European women, were mistakenly killed by a bomb intended for him. The 1908 to 1909 trial was considered the "first state trial of any magnitude in India." Several of the defendants were convicted, though Ghose was acquitted. During the months he had spent in jail awaiting trial, however, he underwent a life-changing spiritual experience. After his acquittal, he departed for the nearby French enclave of Pondicherry, where he wrote prolifically and became a spiritual leader in the Indian independence movement.[4]

Tagore took a different path. The son of an intellectually distinguished Bengali family, he became the most celebrated humanist in India, sometimes called the "Bard of Bengal," and in 1913 was the first Asian to win the Nobel Prize for Literature. He emerged as one of the era's greatest Western critics and espoused Eastern alternatives to Europe's excesses; like Yeats and other towering literary figures from the empire, he beckoned colonized populations of the world to forge their own culturally informed destinies. Still, despite having taken part in the anti-British movement in 1905, he remained loyal to Britain during the war, unlike the Cambridge-educated Ghose.[5]

Concepts like Ghose's and Tagore's infused Indian politics, and by the First World War, they circulated widely in the Indian National Congress. Founded in 1885 as a platform for civil and political dialogue, the Congress, though perpetually divided on questions of radicalism and moderation, was the colony's predominant nationalist party. Political flashpoints, however, created moments of unity, and the Defence of India Act provided just such an occasion as India's elites negotiated the Lucknow Pact of 1916. The landmark agreement between the Congress and the All-India Muslim League pledged solidarity, albeit tenuously, and made a series of demands of the British Raj that included a broad expansion of the franchise for nearly all provincial and central legislative elections.[6]

In the middle of the negotiations was Mohandas Gandhi, who had recently returned home after twenty years in South Africa. Born in Gujarat in 1869, Gandhi was educated in India, then left for London to read law at the Inner Temple. While there, he did his best to adopt English customs and habits, though homesickness and the need for proper vegetarian food eventually led him to the Theosophical Society, which was devoted to the study of Buddhist and Hindu literature; it brought him into the world of Victorian countercultures and radicals, including suffragettes, socialists, pacifists, and anti-imperialists.[7] Returning to India as a barrister in 1891, he brought with him a newfound interest in religious thought. Two years later his Bombay law practice failed, and Gandhi took what was to be a one-year post in South Africa's Natal Colony. During the South African War, he eventually supported the British, raising an ambulance corps of 1,100 volunteers, though he later emerged as one of the foremost organizers against colonial injustice and repression, both as a barrister and as a purveyor of emergent Indian nationalism. For over two decades, Gandhi defied Milner's reconstruction regime's institutionalized racism, together with that of Smuts's Afrikaner government. After burning pass registration cards and ignoring registration laws, he and his thousands of followers endured public floggings, open gunfire on their strikes, and revolving jail time. Throughout, Gandhi advocated his evolving satyagraha movement of truth and nonviolent protest.[8]

Gandhi returned to India, where he acquired the moniker "Mahatma," or "Great Soul," for having defended the rights of the poor.[9] India quickly tested his two decades of honed political and spiritual skills. There the British Raj's half-hearted attempts at reform, followed by further legalized repression, catalyzed the spread of postwar anticolonial and intercommunal disorder. In 1918 the Montagu-Chelmsford reforms—eponymously named after its protagonists, Secretary of State for India Edwin Montagu and Viceroy of India Lord Chelmsford—offered limited Indian political participation. Swift, widespread protest erupted, and the draconian Rowlatt Act of 1919 soon followed. It extended wartime emergency powers that included the right to search without a warrant and to detain without trial for up to a year. The act also allowed for a bench of three judges to try political offenders, who had no right to an appeal.[10]

The Congress responded immediately, and Gandhi took his satyagraha movement to Bombay. In Amritsar, he called for a *hartal*, a closing down of shops. While some peaceful demonstrations ensued, so did violence in Delhi, Ahmedabad, and Lahore.[11] Governing the Punjab was the notoriously heavy-handed Sir Michael O'Dwyer, who as lieutenant governor had crushed wartime dissent with press controls and movement restrictions. The Rowlatt Act further emboldened him legally to stymie protests with repressive measures. On April 9, 1919, when reports noted "fraternization" between Muslims and Hindus during the religious festival Ram Naumi, O'Dwyer sensed a dangerous transcendence of Britain's divide-and-rule policy was under way. He arrested two local leaders, Dr. Saif-ud-Din Kitchlew and Dr. Satyapal; mass protests in Amritsar followed. British colonial troops opened fire and killed twenty-five people. In the counterviolence, Indian protesters looted and burned shops, cut telegraph and telephone wires, damaged railway tracks, and killed five Europeans and attacked others, including a white missionary named Miss Sherwood who had been left for dead.[12]

By the time thousands gathered in Jallianwala Bagh on April 13, the situation in Amritsar had calmed down. Brigadier General Reginald Dyer arrived on the scene and reinforced the local garrison to ensure that no additional violence erupted. Dyer took a hardline approach, announcing on the morning of the Jallianwala Bagh gathering that all meetings and processions were forbidden and that any such "unlawful assembly" would be "dispersed by force if necessary."[13] He then proceeded to put on a full display of military might. With two armored cars affixed with machine guns and fifty Gurkha and Sikh riflemen, he made his way to the Jallianwala Bagh park, which was smaller than Trafalgar Square and walled off on all sides save for one common entrance and egress. He gave no notice to the fifteen thousand or so unarmed civilians there, nor any order to disperse. Instead, he commanded his men to fire. Within ten minutes they discharged about 1,650 rounds and left nearly four hundred dead. At least twelve hundred civilians lay wounded in the blood-soaked earth, where they remained as Dyer and his men retreated, making no attempt to assist those who survived the massacre.[14]

The violence was the start of several days of widespread British-led reprisals. On April 15 the Raj imposed martial law on Amritsar and several other Punjabi districts and, at Lieutenant Governor O'Dwyer's request, backdated it to March 30. The military and O'Dwyer's men had ex post facto coverage for their actions over the previous two weeks, which included the arrests of Drs. Kitchlew and Satyapal, who now stood trial under a summary court, with no recording of evidence and limited cross-examination. Along with the two doctors, martial law commissioners tried another 852 suspects in camera, convicted 581, sentenced to death 108, and sentenced to "transportation for life," or banishment to a remote penal facility, another 264, including Kitchlew and Satyapal. By the time massive public protest led to a reintroduction of the right of appeal, eighteen men had already been publicly hanged.[15]

Collective punishments unfolded throughout the region. Raj agents confiscated personal property for the troops, cut off electricity and water supplies, expelled students from schools via a quota system, and prevented peasants at gunpoint from harvesting their crops. Public floggings, a routine punishment in India, South Africa, and elsewhere in the empire, skyrocketed. Europeans gathered round for the spectacles and urged cane wielders to inflict harsher punishments. Indeed, Raj forces flogged an entire wedding party for being part of an illegal gathering, and throughout the region they physically and mentally coerced Indian eyewitnesses into giving false evidence that, in turn, legally exonerated ritualized European repression.[16]

Reprisals extended to what Captain A. C. Doveton in Kasur called "fancy punishments."[17] Security forces compelled men and women to skip, touch their noses to the ground, and recite poetry; they literally whitewashed local peasants; and they made men undertake the work of untouchables, which the Hindu population considered a religious pollution. In neighboring Gujranwala, the district commissioner, Lieutenant Colonel Aubrey John "A. J." O'Brien, issued orders that required salaaming: "persons riding on animals or on or in wheeled conveyances will alight, persons carrying opened and raised umbrellas shall lower them, and all persons shall salute or 'salaam' with the hand."[18] Security forces made those who failed to comply with the order lick officers' boots as punishment. General Dyer's "flogging lane" typified in hyperbolic fashion the ritualized humiliation unfolding throughout the Punjab. Particularly incensed by the attack on Miss Sherwood, Dyer vowed to find a "suitable punishment." He looked no further than the street on which she was assaulted, where he set up a flogging booth at one end.[19]

Soon after the Jallianwala Bagh Massacre and subsequent reprisals, the civil and military command condoned Dyer's actions. In early May, lauded as the "Saviour of the Punjab," the lieutenant general headed off to defend Britain's empire on the Afghan border. Not until three

Flogging booth erected by General Dyer in the middle of the lane where
Miss Sherwood was assaulted in the wake of Amritsar Massacre, April 1919

months later did he file his official report on the Amritsar events. In
a striking repetition of Callwell's *Small Wars* treatise, his succinct and
justificatory narrative was steeped in language that encoded racial and
cultural difference. For him, as for Callwell, Kitchener, and other British military leaders and foot soldiers, the very moral fiber of Britain's
empire was under threat. Only through harsh, legally enabled methods
could they restore the natural order of things by teaching the so-called
natives a moral lesson. Without inhibition, Dyer laid out the reasons for
his measures:

> I fired and continued to fire until the crowd dispersed and I con-
> sider this the least amount of firing which would produce the
> necessary *moral and widespread effect* it was my duty to produce,
> if I was to justify my action. If more troops had been at hand the
> casualties would have been greater in proportion. It was no lon-
> ger a question of merely dispersing the crowd, but one of pro-
> ducing a sufficient *moral effect*, from a military point of view, not
> only on those who were present but more specifically through-
> out the Punjab. There could be no question of undue severity.[20]

Just as Dyer's "moral effect" was a verbatim repetition of Callwell's mantra, so too did Dyer's later insistence on "punish[ing] the naughty boy" for "salutary effect" harken back to Victorian-era ideas that equated "natives" with children, as well as to Kipling's "new-caught, sullen peoples, half-devil and half-child."[21] The White Man's Burden still required a peculiar paternalistic blend of moral uplift and repression—repression that served both as punishment and as deterrent for future challenges to British rule and order. In effect, Dyer was a product of Britain and the empire, and both refracted his tactics, and O'Dwyer's complicity, in myriad ways once news of events reached the halls of Westminster and Fleet Street in London.

The events in Amritsar quickly became a referendum on violence and empire. Questions of morality and the use of force, the roots of which stretched back to the Victorian debates over liberal imperialism, reemerged in the post–World War I context. Britons were war-weary and brutalized from the "war to end all wars" though also deeply loyal to

India during the interwar period

their troops that had given life and limb to protect their liberties and the ideals of empire. There were familiar defenses of empire, though anger also accreted in Britain, India, Ireland, and elsewhere in the colonies, as well as in conversations that increasingly crossed empires and oceans. Novelists such as the Martinican René Maran, for instance, railed against colonialism's empty promises. In time his work, and that of George Padmore, C. L. R. James, and W. E. B. Du Bois, would influence a generation of African and African American intellectuals. Black radical ideas would converge in the Pan-African Congresses, five in total between 1919 and 1945, and eventually the Négritude movement of the 1930s. Just as being Protestant or Catholic, or Hindu or Muslim, could unite as much as divide, race did not universally bond those whose experiences of exploitation under Western regimes varied as much as their solutions to subverting European dominance. When Black thinkers and writers arrived at the Pan-African Congress in 1919, for instance, they were deeply divided over whether to challenge European colonialism directly and violently, or to pursue more moderate and conciliatory approaches in the world's colonized regions.[22]

The pressures mounting from the empire itself influenced the growing minority of imperial critics in Britain who continued to challenge the policies and practices of British rule. In opposition to Lloyd George's coalition government, independent Liberals and members of the emerging Labour Party collectively sustained the criticism of Dyer and the imperial system more generally.[23] "At the beginning of the War we were profoundly moved by the wickedness of military terrorism," Norman Angell, Labour Party politician and recipient of the Nobel Peace Prize in 1933, wrote in one of his many condemnations of the conflict's irrationality. "At its close we employ it—whether by means of starvation, blockade, armed Negro savages in German cities, reprisals in Ireland, or the ruthless slaughter of unarmed civilians in India—without creating any strong revulsion of feeling at home."

> At the beginning of the War we realised that the governmental organisation of hatred with the prostitution of art to "hymns of hate" was vile and despicable. We copied that governmental organisation of hatred, and famous English authors duly produce *our* hymns of hate. We felt at the beginning that all human freedom was menaced by the German theory of the State as the master of man and not as his instrument, with all that that means of political inquisition and repression. When some of its worst features are applied at home, we are so indifferent to the fact

that we do not even recognize that the thing against which we fought has been imposed upon ourselves.[24]

For Angell, civilization was receding as the war had unleashed a collective madness, corrupting Britons and their state: "We [must] face squarely the fact that the voice of the people is usually the voice of Satan." Others were more optimistic. "The 'war to end war' has been succeeded by a chain of wars," Holford Knight lamented in September 1928. A radical lawyer, Knight upended the claims of Britain's wartime leaders, who had contrasted their idealized rule over colonial subjects with German militarism: the fight to defeat "Prussian" militarism, he said, had brought "Prussianism" to the British state and exposed its hold on colonial states in the empire as well. "All this is intensely alien to the British temperament," Knight insisted, and was unacceptable to "public opinion." While his view was more sanguine than Angell's, it was still radical. Knight pressed ahead, thinking that war fatigue and concerns over the war's cultural legacy in Britain had engendered a "friendlier spirit between man and man."[25]

On the issue of Amritsar, however, the relentless voice of critique coming from the prime minister's own secretary of state for India, Edwin Montagu, was the most difficult to dismiss and, ultimately, the most revealing about liberal imperialism's twinned ability to repress and reform. Montagu, a prematurely balding Cambridge man who sported a handlebar moustache, was a lightning rod for antagonism. He first took his seat in Parliament with his party's 1906 election sweep. He harbored a deep commitment to the empire, though he was a widely unpopular choice to head the India Office under Lloyd George. He was Jewish, in fact one of the few Jewish members to serve in a British cabinet. Conservative opposition to his appointment, not to mention his long-standing rivalry with Churchill, who was five years his senior, tormented him almost as much as his unhappy marriage. Montagu was disgusted by the events at Amritsar, and his bull-in-a-china-shop approach to condemnation was scarcely politic in the context of the times.[26]

Labour Party and Indian nationalist pressures emboldened Montagu to support an inquiry, and the former Scottish judge Lord Hunter was appointed to chair an investigation into "the recent disturbances in Bombay, Delhi and Punjab, about their causes, and the measures taken to cope with them."[27] The Hunter Commission took some four months to do its work, and when its members interviewed Dyer, he was his own worst enemy. He refused legal counsel and was wholly unrepentant for his enforcement of the "moral effect." He declared that he had made up his mind to open fire on the courtyard prior to his arrival, and he affirmed the conviction, expressed by the senior commanding officer in Delhi, Brigadier-General D. H. Drake-Brockman, that the crowd were "the scum of Delhi."[28] "I am of opinion that if they had got a bit more firing given them it would have done them a world of good," Drake-Brockman told the Hunter Commission. "Their attitude would be much more amenable and respectful, as force is the only thing that an Asiatic has any respect for."[29] Dyer's responses and demeanor, and those of officers like Drake-Brockman, reflected the ethos in which they had been steeped, which for Dyer was first at Sandhurst and then as a peripatetic army officer on the Raj's frontier and in Persia and Burma. A combination of imperial zealotry, reckless courage, and steadfast protection of racial hierarchies and social norms—particularly imagined European female purity—fueled his responses to real and perceived threats to the empire. The cold-blooded shootings in Jallianwala Bagh were one of the most spectacular examples of this widespread ethos, though by no means an exception.[30]

The Hunter Commission's report, submitted in March 1920, helped frame the British government's official narrative. Dyer was responsible for the massacre at Jallianwala Bagh, and his justifications vis-à-vis the "moral effect" were, in the commission's view, "a mistaken conception of his duty."[31] The commission unanimously condemned Dyer's response, though it stopped short of imposing any penal or disciplinary penalties on him because his superiors had condoned his actions at the time. The viceroy's executive council in India subsequently accepted the commission's recommendations and was near unanimous in its conclusion that Dyer should be retired without prosecution.[32] As for the other officers and Raj officials who had been involved, the executive council said no one should be held accountable.

Montagu and the incensed Indian nationalists, among others, thought the Hunter Commission and the viceroy's executive council had not gone far enough.[33] Yet an equally strong, if not stronger, countervailing sentiment came from the British Indian establishment, Conservative MPs, the army, large swaths of the British public, and factions of the press, all of whom offered Dyer massive support. As Parliament geared up for a debate in the summer of 1920, events around the empire—which included unrest in Egypt, the continued collapse of British authority in Ireland, and the Bolshevik threat that seemed to lurk everywhere—meant Dyer would become symbolic of the bigger issues that threatened the fraying Lloyd George coalition. Ultimately, the whole matter became a referendum on the treacheries that imperiled the empire.[34]

The British government could not contain the public exposure of Dyer's measures and sought to separate him from the colonial state in India and from imperial policies and practices more generally. It did its best to choreograph the pending parliamentary proceedings, which were delayed awaiting the independent Army Council report into Dyer's actions. As the days ticked by, Montagu became more undone. Having suffered a nervous breakdown a few months earlier, he was aware of the revulsion he evinced from the opposition. One of his confidants, Viceroy Secretary J. L. Maffey, noted at the time, "The Hunter Debate hangs over [Montagu] as a nightmare, and he evidently feels most keenly the bitter personal attacks to which he has been subjected. [He] wants to refute Sir Michael O'Dwyer and to attack his administration. I persuaded him to drop it. . . . He had prepared a good deal of rather violent stuff and did not care much for my line."[35]

Montagu's moral revulsion trumped Maffey's counsel, particularly when press editorials, like that in *The Morning Post*, reflected an outspoken portion of public opinion: "We do not wonder that the name of General Dyer is universally held in honour at the present moment by Englishwomen in Northern India. . . . He may not be excused in the eyes of the law, but posterity will say that he saved a situation the possible, if not probable, horrors of which cannot be exaggerated."[36] Harmsworth's *Daily Mail* gave voice to an honorable and victimized Dyer who, in his words, had performed "my duty—my horrible, dirty duty."[37]

On July 8 the Army Council issued its decision: it denied Dyer a future post, but it offered him half-pay and the maintenance of his rank and status.[38] Raucous MPs and gallery members filed into Westminster, and an infuriated Montagu marched straight into the electrified House of Commons ready for a barefisted fight. In front of a packed gallery that included Dyer and his entourage, Montagu denounced the entire Punjab affair as "a doctrine of terrorism."[39] Rather than articulating the facts, which many in the crowd actually had little grasp of, Montagu demanded Dyer be censured. He asked his peers, "Are you going to keep your hold upon India by terrorism, racial humiliation and subordination, and frightfulness, or are you going to rest it upon the goodwill, and the growing goodwill, of the people of your Indian Empire?"[40] Conservative MPs interrupted his repetitive moralizing and accusations of "frightfulness" with insults and cries of "It saved a mutiny," "Bolshevism!," and "You are making an incendiary speech."[41] Montagu soldiered on. The shouting match verged on physical assault as Montagu impugned Dyer's liberal imperial character, and by extension, the very foundations of the British Empire and the nation. The opposition was having none of it.

Austen Chamberlain, the soon-to-be leader of the Conservative Party, summed up his acolytes' sentiments when he noted, "A Jew, a foreigner, rounding on an Englishman and throwing him to the wolves—that was the feeling."[42]

In contrast to Montagu's morally instigated meltdown, Churchill offered a master class in parliamentary politics. Rising to his feet, the secretary of state for war understood the merits of calculation and of creating political fact through historical fiction. At once, he assuaged opposition outrage and offered a long-view lesson on how to sacrifice one army general as an anomalous renegade rather than engage in questions over the state's extraordinary powers in India or the empire's ruling ethos. Throughout, he stuck to the facts of the case and pointed to "the slaughter of nearly 400 persons and the wounding of probably three or four times as many, at the Jallian Wallah Bagh," as "an event of an entirely different order from any of those tragical occurrences which take place when troops are brought into collision with the civil population. It is an extraordinary event, a monstrous event, an event which stands in singular and sinister isolation."[43] Amnesiac of the thousands of Africans and Afrikaners who perished in South Africa's concentration camps, not to mention the deaths of poorly armed populations in the North-West Frontier and the Sudan, which he had seen with his own eyes, Churchill painted Amritsar as a horrific one-off.[44] In so doing, he publicly distanced himself from the extreme views of some MPs, while at the same time mollifying others, at least in part, by reminding them that the government sought not to punish Dyer but rather to censure him.

Churchill's historical rescripting omitted from his condemnations of Dyer any mention of Britain's widespread "legalized lawlessness," a term I use to describe the incremental legalizing, bureaucratizing, and legitimating of exceptional state-directed violence when ordinary laws proved insufficient for maintaining order and control. This instance of legalized lawlessness had enveloped the Punjab—of which Dyer's was the most extreme—in the aftermath of the Montagu-Chelmsford announcement. Instead, Churchill used his performative political moment to remind his nation of liberal imperialism's fictions, then wrapped his condemnation of Dyer in the sheep's clothing of one of the biggest: "Governments who have seized upon power by violence and by usurpation have often resorted to terrorism in their desperate efforts to keep what they have stolen, but the august and venerable structure of the British Empire, where lawful authority descends from hand to hand and generation after generation, does not need such aid. Such ideas are absolutely foreign to the British way of doing things."[45] The combined effect of scapegoating, historical forgetting, and social fact creation allowed Churchill to excise the Jallianwala Bagh Massacre as a gross aberration, thus leaving the empire's civilizing narrative relatively unscathed.

Both the far left and right decried his logic, albeit for very different reasons. In the aftermath of the events in the Punjab, Gandhi had focused on the institutionalized racism, violence, and cultural difference that produced individuals like Dyer instead of the other way around. "We do not want to punish Dyer," he asserted. "We have no desire for revenge. We want to change the system that produced Dyer."[46] The Labour MP Ben Spoor echoed Indian nationalist outrage and its exposure of the empire's legalized lawlessness, insisting "that Amritsar is not an isolated event any more than General Dyer is an isolated officer."[47] Moreover, he reminded his fellow ministers that a fortnight earlier the Labour Party had passed a resolution demanding the recall of the viceroy and the impeachment of O'Dwyer. It had also called for the full trials of other junior-ranking officers and an immediate repeal "of all that repressive and coercive legislation which more than anything else has contributed to the present unhappy state of affairs in India."[48]

Conservative MPs likewise argued that Dyer was hardly an aberration, but for them, he had performed his moral duty to save India and the empire from the clutches of tyranny. For Brigadier-General Herbert Surtees and his brethren, empire was a confidence trick, and that confidence was now under reckless parliamentary threat. "Once you destroy that British prestige," he concluded, "then the Empire will collapse like a house of cards, and with it all the trade which feeds, clothes, and gives employment to our people."[49] The Conservative die-hards could scarcely contain their anger. Rupert Gwynne closed out their defense of Dyer with a full-on lambasting of Churchill and Montagu. How was it, he questioned, that the government rewarded Churchill for his colossal failure at Gallipoli, a failure that had risked thousands of lives, with an appointment as secretary for war, whereas Dyer had "committed an error of judgment . . . but there is no pity for him?" As for Montagu, Gwynne stated for the record what many in the boisterous backbenches were murmuring and shouting: "As regards the Secretary of State for India . . . [he] is a very much greater danger to that country [than Dyer]."[50]

When the censure of Dyer finally came to a vote, the House of Commons passed the government's measure by 101 votes. Nonetheless, 119 of the 129 voting in opposition were Unionists in the Lloyd George coalition, or MPs who saw the government's India policies and the censure of Dyer as a slippery slope on which Ireland would soon tumble. The court of public opinion, along with the House of Lords, were poised to resuscitate and finance Dyer. Parliament's upper chamber condemned the House of Commons measure, and Lord Lamington summed up in a single line what others waxed on about at considerable animated length: "I deplore what I consider to be the grave mismanagement and bungling by the Government in this case."[51] Without equivocating, the lords pointed to the "mob" in the Punjab and juxtaposed it with the gallantry of Britain's troops upon whom the empire and the nation relied. In condemning what he considered the scapegoating of Dyer, Viscount Finlay spoke for many and previewed future justifications of unaccountability in the empire:

> One of the main stays of our Empire has been the feeling that every officer whose duty it was to take action in times of difficulty, might rely, so long as he acted honestly, and in the discharge of his duty, upon his superiors standing by him. If once the suspicion were created that for any reason, political or otherwise, an officer who had done what he believed to be his duty was to be thrown over, no-one can exaggerate the mischievous effect such a feeling might have upon our public service.[52]

The Morning Post's editorial column asked for financial contributions, big and small, to assure "General Dyer [who] saved India, [that] the politicians are saving themselves at his expense. It is a burning reproach to the British nation that such a thing could be possible."[53] The Appeal to Patriots fund reached a staggering £26,317. Contributions came from dukes and earls, dock and railway workers, schoolchildren and their teachers, countesses and ladies' organizations, Anglo-Indian newspapers and clubs, and countless army officers and Indian government civil servants—despite prohibitions against such donations. Kipling sent in ten pounds along with his imperial two cents: "He did his duty, as he saw it."[54] Not only did violence in the empire become more and more business as usual, but it was also further entrenched in notions of duty, honor, defense of the empire, and with it, defense of the nation.

Montagu's fate was an ominous coda to the tragedies of Jallianwala Bagh and the empire's future. His unceremonious exit from the House—as a cacophony of "Montagu, Resign! Resign!" echoed off its medieval walls—was a harbinger of the secretary's spiraling decline.[55] The press followed up with anti-Semitic and xenophobic charges that included *The Times*'s comment that "Mr Montagu, patriotic and sincere English Liberal as he is, is also a Jew, and in excitement has the mental idiom of the East."[56] A year later he had yet another dust-up with

Churchill, who was by then the colonial secretary. The issue this time was Indian rights in Kenya: Montagu supported ending Indians' legally enabled segregation from European spaces. For his part, Churchill not only outmaneuvered his ailing foe but also declared his unyielding support for the rich and fertile White Highlands, located in central Kenya, to remain exclusively white-owned in perpetuity. A few weeks later, after a ministerial faux pas that would normally have gone unchecked, Montagu resigned from the cabinet. He lost his parliamentary seat in the next general election. Within two years, tarred for his moralizing and relentless demands for widespread accountability in the empire, Montagu was dead at forty-five.[57]

In India, Jallianwala Bagh and the institutionalized racism and state-sanctioned violence that it threw into relief unleashed nationalist fury. The Indian literary genius Tagore wrote a historic letter to Viceroy Chelmsford, in which he renounced his knighthood and other British honors:

> The enormity of the measures taken by the Government in the Punjab for quelling some local disturbances has, with a rude shock, revealed to our minds the helplessness of our position as British subjects in India. . . . The time has come when badges of honour make our shame glaring in the incongruous context of humiliation, and I for my part wish to stand, shorn, of all special distinctions, by the side of those of my countrymen who, for their so-called insignificance, are liable to suffer degradation not fit for human beings.[58]

Meanwhile Gandhi focused on *swaraj*—or complete individual, spiritual, and political independence—through noncooperation and *swadeshi*, or the boycott of foreign-made goods, particularly British ones. In symbolic and practical terms, noncooperation meant a rejection of the Raj and constituted a bid to take control of India's future. In December 1921, Gandhi's popularity among Hindus and Muslims catapulted him to the Indian National Congress's helm. He led the party's reorganization and the creation of a constitution that transformed it from an elite organization to one with mass national appeal, even though protests continued to take violent turns. After fifty-eight died in Bombay riots and protesters killed twenty-three Indian police officers in Chauri Chaura, Gandhi called off his noncooperation movement. In the spring of 1922, the British government deployed its exceptional legal measures: it convicted Gandhi of sedition and sentenced him to six years in prison.[59]

In Whitehall, Churchill concluded that any further political concessions would lead only to more violence, and he was self-assured of the colonial state's legitimate use of force and its civilizing effects. Lloyd George readily agreed when Churchill announced that his nation needed to "keep the Flag flying" in India and preserve "the prestige & authority of the white man undiminished." "Our true duty in India lies," said Churchill, "to those 300 millions whose lives & means of existence wd [*sic*] be squandered if entrusted to the chatterboxes who are supposed to speak for India today."[60] In the end, he played his political cards well. While the British government may have strategically sacrificed Dyer, its liberal imperialism continued under a rule-of-law fig leaf that justified continued political imprisonments, harsh crackdowns, and minimal accountability in the years to come in India and beyond.

The explosion of anticolonial protest, violence, and counterviolence was not unique to India. Crises in the empire erupted in Africa, Asia, Europe, and Latin America, where nationalist elites, often feeding off each other, harnessed the anger and bewildered letdown that accompanied Wilson's failed rhetoric and the unfulfilled expectations of political rewards in return for wartime cooperation. Propelling them forward was also the success of the Bolshevik revolution and, with it, the imagined possibilities for the disempowered around the world. There were riots in Jamaica, Trinidad, and British Honduras as well as in Somaliland, South Darfur, and Kenya.[61] It was, however, events in the Middle East and Ireland that, together with those in India, stretched the Lloyd George coalition and its intransigent members of Parliament who were, according to the imperial historian John Gallagher, "hard-faced men who had little sympathy with lesser breeds without the vote."[62]

The Dyer affair unfolded in the context of interlocking crises. Those wielding power in Britain viewed anticolonial demands and ready deployments of repression in one hotspot as a referendum on the specter of imperial defeat that loomed elsewhere. In retrospect, Montagu hardly stood a chance against the hardening huge commitment to Britain's brand of liberal imperialism. Still, he articulated clearly the entangled imperial factors that undermined any real hope of sustained reformist inroads into the policies and practices of imperial governance. "The concessions which look likely to be necessary in Ireland harden public opinion against any new concessions in Egypt," Montagu had lamented. "Anything that is done as to complete independence of Egypt might appear to encourage Indian extremists."[63]

Like their Indian counterparts, Egyptians reeled from the war's effects. One and a half million of their men had served, primarily in the Labour Corps that largely undertook the war's manual labor needs, and the British Army had requisitioned buildings, food supplies, and animals. In the war's aftermath, an Egyptian delegation, led by Saad Zaghlul, sought an audience at the Paris Peace Conference and demanded independence and unity with Sudan. Zaghlul was unsuccessful, but he used his bureaucratic skills to harness mass discontent through widespread grassroots support of the Wafd Party. He soon launched a civil disobedience campaign—modeled on Gandhi's—to overthrow the British protectorate of Egypt and the Sudan.[64]

When indigenous populations rebelled against the paternalistic hand that ostensibly fed them, British officials were indignant. In postwar Egypt, they underestimated the widespread support for Zaghlul and the ideas he and others espoused, so they fell back on familiar tactics. They summarily arrested and deported the Egyptian leader and "some of his associates" to Malta and then to the Seychelles. They believed that decapitating the extremist leadership of the movement would calm things down.[65] Instead, violence erupted. With martial law in force, British security forces razed villages and imposed collective punishments while the targets of their repression destroyed buildings and railways. At the end of March 1919, Britain reversed its position and released Zaghlul and his fellow exiles. Its forces needed another four months to quell the demonstrations and strikes across the region that had halted business and daily life. By the time Britain wrested control, nearly three thousand Egyptians were dead and thousands more wounded, with both pro-Wafd Muslims and Christians comprising the casualties.[66]

In December, Alfred Milner arrived on the scene. Fresh off his stint of divvying up the colonial spoils of Germany and the former Ottoman Empire, he chaired an internal commission of inquiry into the Egyptian events. At this point in his career, the decades of outmaneuvering colonial subjects and European rivals to the empire had cumulatively shaped the arch-imperialist. When faced with the Egyptian challenge, Milner blithely repeated a refrain heard elsewhere in Whitehall and around the empire: "Anti-British feeling is practically confined to the upper class and *intelligentzia*. . . . Actual rebellion is less to be apprehended than the progressive weakening of authority and respect for Government."[67] In fact, the situation was dire. Nationalists with their broad support boycotted the commission. According to government reports, "Indian affairs" unduly influenced the rebels, as did "Russian Bolsheviks [who] . . . plan to undermine British power by rousing the East to rebellion." Milner was incensed by the Wafd leadership's affront to authority, not to mention its presumed manipulation of the masses, whose demand for "complete independence" was "passed from mouth to mouth throughout the country." Milner remarked that complete independence "is a sort of spell or charm which everybody shouts, chants, sings, mutters, writes, telegraphs. . . . [Even] responsible men, the most influential in the country, have let themselves be carried away into joining the outcry."[68]

Such "spells" and "charms," however, would prove no match for Milner and his men, whose years of dealings routinely ensured the preservation of British imperial interests and ideals. Delicate negotiations could effectively give away little. Milner's Foreign Office counterpart, Lord Curzon, agreed in the most revealing of analogies: "these eastern peoples with whom we have to ride pillion have different seats from Europeans and it does not seem to me to matter much whether we put them on the saddle in front of us or whether they cling on behind and hold us round the waist. The great thing is that the firm seat in the saddle shall be ours."[69] Curzon's imperial saddle seat was bound with political, economic, and strategic interests, foremost among them the protection of the Suez Canal. Moreover, British officials were keenly aware as well that any concessions to Zaghlul and his followers would strengthen or help create political and intellectual leaders elsewhere in the empire. Concessions could also open doors to potential European rivals in the region and close others to trade and communications. With Britain facing postwar economic troubles, such possibilities had to be avoided. At the same time, the coalition government, already stretched to its limits, could ill afford multiple costly conflicts in the empire and needed to negotiate its way toward stability rather than relying entirely on costly sustained repression.[70]

For three years, Britain dangled the carrot of sovereignty before a settlement was reached. While London and Cairo continued their collective repressive ways under martial law, the British press—which now featured about 2,200 newspapers—urged its government to find a middle ground.[71] Indeed, in the aftermath of a negotiated memorandum that Milner and the Egyptian delegation had drawn up, *The Times* declared a British moral victory: "In spite of occasional mistakes in more recent years, Great Britain has never done a nobler or more successful piece of work in the cause of civilisation."[72] The memorandum soon proved a false start, however, and Britain again deported the intransigent Zaghlul, this time to the Seychelles. Here again the fourth estate, including *The Daily Chronicle*, echoed the government's right to repression as well as its nationalist demonizings and ever-elusive search for moderates who understood the civilizing, if forceful, ways of their colonizer:

> In the last resort, no doubt, all Government depends on physical force, but in Egypt of all places, where our legal position is so anomalous and difficult, it is most important that whatever measures of coercion are necessary should have behind them the authority of an Egyptian Government and . . . the public opinion that it can command. Zaghlul Pasha is an extremist, and the measures that have been taken against him are very probably no more than are necessary in the interests of peace. But the danger of these measures is that they may force moderate men into unwilling alliance with the extremists.[73]

In the end, Milner and his successors—including the sympathetic Egyptian high commissioner Lord Allenby, a veteran of the South African War and British wartime campaigns in Palestine—played an independence smoke-and-mirrors game. The "Declaration to Egypt by his Britannic Majesty's Government" issued in February 1922 "recognise[d] Egypt as an independent sovereign State," without actually granting Egyptians full sovereignty.[74] Effectively, until further notice, Britain claimed the right to maintain its communications facilities, its standing army to defend "against all foreign aggression or interference, direct or indirect" as well as foreign interests, and its protectorate over the Sudan. Furthermore, Britain's self-granting act of indemnification for past misdeeds would be subject to no future renegotiation.[75] "His Britannic Majesty's" men secured their nation's immediate interests and kicked the can of full sovereignty down a decades-long imperial road. Negotiations, violence, and intrigue would shape and define high politics and lived experiences in Egypt before the semiautonomous nation fully freed itself from British influence.

Linked by empire, postwar negotiations with Egypt were intimately bound to the centuries-old Irish question.[76] At the same time as Zaghlul was launching his initial demands for independence, simmering hostilities erupted again in Ireland. The imposition of wartime conscription with explicit links to Home Rule precipitated Irish anger and propelled the Irish republican party, Sinn Féin, to a landslide general election victory in late 1918. The Sinn Féin MPs refused to take up their seats in

Westminster and instead issued a declaration of independence, formed a breakaway Irish parliament known as the Dáil, and constituted the Irish Republican Army, or IRA. Then on January 21, the day of the Dáil's first convening, the IRA shot and killed two members of the Royal Irish Constabulary, Britain's police force in Ireland. Widely regarded as the start of the Irish War of Independence, the police officers' deaths triggered Ireland's assistant undersecretary Mark Sturgis and others to demand martial law. Sturgis believed that "if hard hitting is the policy it is the soldier's job and is done by him more efficiently and more cleanly than can be the case under the cloak of so called Civil Government."[77] Along with the assistant undersecretary, an imperial chorus called for official coercion and its anticipated moral effects. The incoming lord lieutenant, Sir John French, telegrammed Churchill and echoed the war secretary's own sentiments: "In my mind I am convinced that 'force' is the only power that will ever solve the Irish question; and I am equally convinced that if applied at once and efficiently it would solve the question in a very short space of time."[78]

As Amritsar's contemporaneous cloud gathered over martial law, the long-held belief in the moral effect of violence remained largely unquestioned. The problem became one of legalizing state-directed violence in the postwar period's realpolitik.[79] In Ireland, the British government initially eschewed an Egyptian-style independence negotiation and instead armed the civilian state with a host of highly authoritarian regulations similar to those in India and derived from the metropolitan Defence of the Realm Act (DORA). Among other measures, Lloyd George's men outlawed the Dáil and Sinn Féin and made another lackluster run at Home Rule. They also believed the republicans were a renegade "murder gang" rather than a legitimate nationalist force with widespread support.[80] The British government failed with appeasement and instead sublimated conceptions of subject populations into the paradigm of moral effect. Wielding DORA-enabled strategies of coercion, Whitehall and its Dublin Castle counterpart fueled a war that spiraled with killings, reprisals, and counterreprisals. Still, South African War veteran and Chief of the Imperial General Staff Sir Henry Wilson was unconvinced of the totality of Britain's coercive arsenal and made the point to Churchill: "I told him that the present policy was suicidal, that it would lead to our being put out of Ireland, that we must take strong measures or retire, that if we retired we lost our Empire, that before taking strong measures we must convince England that they are necessary."[81]

For the Dáil, sovereignty was everything. Ignoring the ban and going underground, its members understood the combined effect of political organization and unconventional warfare. The Irish nationalists fashioned themselves into a republic, collected taxes, enforced their own laws, and maintained armed forces. It also took the propaganda war to the British with remarkable success, despite censorship acts that saw the closing down of seventeen Irish newspapers. Circumventing such strict measures, Sinn Féin created an elaborate public opinion machine. It churned out its *Irish Bulletin* with notable regularity and distributed it to local presses. It also targeted foreign news outlets with a particular eye to the United States and its Irish diaspora, which included many immigrants who had escaped the 1840s famine.[82] Not only did Sinn Féin master the art of disinformation, when necessary, but it also laid claim to self-determination by turning Wilsonian language and the ideals of World War I into referenda on imperial decay. Sinn Féin bristled at its "murder gang" label and sought legitimacy, in part, by hitching its declaration of independence to other nascent nationalist movements in the British Empire.[83] A master narrative evolved that framed violence and the Dail's sovereignty as representing, in the words of one Sinn Féin politician, "democratic principles, against Imperialism and upon the side of liberty throughout the world."[84]

Michael Collins emerged as the Dáil's de facto political and military leader. While the self-declared republic's president, Eamon de Valera, canvassed the United States for political and financial support during the first eighteen months of the war, Collins stayed put in Ireland. He ensured the Dáil's fiscal solvency, organized the IRA, managed arms smuggling, and targeted assaults. In total, the IRA had over one hundred thousand members, with fifteen thousand active during the war. Collins and the IRA's national and regional commanders oversaw tactics and general strategy, which included a vast intelligence network that infiltrated the British administration. The IRA, often replicating successful Afrikaner insurgent tactics, jettisoned uniforms and deployed quick raids against British military and civilian targets. It also made use of Collins's intelligence and special assassination unit—known as "The Squad"—to target British officials and informers, as well as the Royal Irish Constabulary (RIC).[85] Indeed, for decades, the RIC was soldier-like in its practices and served as the British government's "eyes and ears" and strong right arm. For the IRA, the colonial police force represented not only British repression but also a healthy source of armaments and supplies. Countless raids on isolated constabulary barracks as well as a targeted campaign to ostracize police officers—particularly those who were Irish Catholic—punctuated the IRA's unfolding strategy.[86]

Unable to gain the upper hand and responding to on-the-spot

reports that "the police and military forces are too small to cope," the Lloyd George government took the fateful decision to augment the constabulary's dwindling ranks.[87] It imported a staggering ten thousand men from Britain, most of whom were unemployed ex-soldiers from the Great War.[88] In short order, the Black and Tans—so known because of their irregular khaki and very dark green or blue uniforms—integrated into the Royal Irish Constabulary and became infamous for terrorizing Ireland's civilian population, particularly the Catholic majority, under the banner of restoring British law and order. Many longtime members of Ireland's constabulary, while already anesthetized to the use of force, marveled at their new brethren. "They were very rough," recalled one constable, "f—ing and blinding and drinking and booze and all. They'd have shot their mother, oh desperate altogether."[89] Another constable reflected a common refrain when he referred to the Black and Tans as "a low-down lot of scoundrels, and it was believed that they were mostly jail-birds and men of bad repute."[90] Such finger-pointing deflected responsibility from the constabulary's old-timers, though few would disagree over the Black and Tans' pernicious reputation.

The term *Black and Tans* became synonymous with British imperial brutality, though violence was sometimes misattributed to their ranks. Many acts were, in fact, the handiwork of Churchill's Auxiliaries. Around the time he was sacrificing Dyer on the altar of imperial expediency, Churchill was creating a "special corps of Gendarmerie" known as the Auxiliary Division of the Royal Irish Constabulary, which consisted of fifteen hundred ex-officers with wartime and imperial experience.[91] Better paid and equipped, the Auxiliaries were one of many sources of discontent within British policing ranks. IRA members considered them the most ruthless of Britain's security forces: one of Collins's intelligence operators characterized them as "far more dangerous and intelligent than the Tans [and] they, too, created a reign of terror."[92] The two new policing units were fully armed and legally licensed paramilitary forces.

As in future conflicts in the empire, what happened in Ireland was as much a colonial policing operation as it was a military one. Coordination was crucial though often elusive, and Lloyd George's government sought a "special officer" who would oversee all intelligence and policing. In May 1920, Churchill handpicked Major-General Henry Tudor for the role. The men's friendship stretched back to their rough-and-ready, sing-along days in India where they witnessed liberal imperialism in action before they went on to suppress subject populations in other parts of the empire. Tudor was fully prepared to deploy systematic force in Ireland and believed that "given the proper support, it would be possible to crush the present campaign of outrage."[93] He quickly enlisted a lineup of imperial veterans, nearly all of whom had seen action against the Afrikaners. Top among them was General Frank Percy Crozier, who took command of the Auxiliaries, and his successor, Brigadier General Edward Allan Wood.

Legalizing the paramilitary police force were nearly seventy regulations passed with the Restoration of Order in Ireland Act in August 1920. A necessary extension of the Defence of the Realm Act as it neared its postwar expiration, the act was reminiscent of legislation in India, and variations of it would be exported to other parts of the empire. Among other subversions of civil liberties, the act enabled continued executive detention, allowing the lord lieutenant to incarcerate suspected subversives without trial. It also thwarted due process and British accountability when regulations replaced all jury trials with courts-martial and scrapped coroners' inquests for military courts of inquiry.[94]

"They did not take everybody," John Derham, a Sinn Féin town commissioner in Balbriggan recalled. "They picked them out like they did me."[95] On the night of September 20, 1920, Black and Tan forces clubbed Derham in the head with a rifle butt and beat his son, Michael, unconscious, while ransacking and burning their pub. His Majesty's forces were on a rampage, seeking vengeance for the IRA's killing of a head constable and wounding of a sergeant. Many British reprisals were clumsy and senseless, destroying property and attacking civilians, but the one targeted at Balbriggan was viciously directed. By the time the paramilitary's rampage was over, more than fifty homes and establishments were razed, countless were wounded, two Republicans were summarily executed, and hundreds of locals were left homeless and jobless.[96] "Just twenty miles north of Dublin, Balbriggan was unusually accessible to British newspaper correspondents," the historian Jon Lawrence points out. "Murder for murder" themes dominated horrified press accounts. But the public mood in Britain was "strangely indifferent" to the Irish atrocities' "indelible stain," one Labour publication observed.[97]

Britain's coercive measures soon proved counterproductive, and their cumulative effects ignited public outrage in Ireland and tested a war-weary British public that was still imagining itself as civilization's "peaceable" people. Interned IRA members began to hunger strike. Terence MacSwiney, the lord mayor of Cork, was among them. A playwright and novelist, MacSwiney began his prison fast after a hasty court-martial declared him guilty of possessing seditious materials. At the end of August 1920, just weeks into the fast, George V received hundreds of telegrams and letters from Britain and Ireland that implored him to exercise his royal prerogative of pardon. Protests took place in Germany and France, Americans threatened to boycott British goods, and the pope received direct global appeals. Britain's monarch wrote to the Home Office and advocated for clemency, but not even His Royal Highness could sway Lloyd George's government, which was steadfast in holding the authoritarian line. The monarch received official word from Downing Street that "release of [the] Lord Mayor would have disastrous results in Ireland and probably lead to mutiny of both police and military in Ireland." George V, privately vocal over his discontent with Lloyd George's handling of the war, had earlier written to the prime minister querying "if this policy of reprisals is to be continued and if so where it will lead?"[98] Official evasiveness met royal concerns, and the king soon found briefings on MacSwiney few and far between. Like his subjects, he relied instead on the daily papers for updates. The lord mayor died on October 25 after seventy-four days without food. Tens of thousands flocked to his viewing at St. George's Cathedral in London. The impact of his sacrifice spread across the empire. In 1921 a collection of MacSwiney's writings, *Principles of Freedom*, was published, and his political ideas, expounded through a harrowing form of protest, inspired nationalist counterparts, including Mahatma Gandhi, Jawaharlal Nehru, and Bhagat Singh.

The lord mayor was no sooner interred in Cork than public sentiment reached a fevered pitch with the British government's execution of Kevin Barry. A teenage medical student, Barry had joined members of the IRA's C Company when it ambushed a British Army truck on Bolton Street in Dublin. The raid turned lethal as trigger-happy IRA members opened fire and killed three British soldiers, all of whom, like Barry, were little more than children. A court-martial tried Barry a month after his capture, even though its evidence was questionable. The lethal bullets had come from a .45 caliber pistol, whereas Barry carried a .38 when arrested on the spot. With nine officers presiding over the case, Barry declared his loyalty to the Irish Republic and refused to recognize the court. He learned his fate later that evening while in his cell: guilty, death by hanging.[99] Demands for clemency and castigations of Britain's abuse of power were widespread. The novelist and onetime supporter of the British Empire turned Irish nationalist Erskine Childers published a scathing letter in the press that captured the sentiments of many:

> This lad Barry was doing precisely what Englishmen would be doing under the same circumstances and with the same bitter and intolerable provocation—the suppression by military force

of their country's liberty. To hang him for murder is an insulting outrage, and it is more: it is an abuse of power; an unworthy act of vengeance. . . . To hang Barry is to push to its logical extreme the hypocritical pretense that the national movement in Ireland[,] unflinchingly supported by the great mass of the Irish people, is a squalid conspiracy of a "murder gang." That is false; it is a natural uprising: a collision between two Governments, one resting on consent, the other on force. The Irish are struggling against overwhelming odds to defend their own elected institutions against extinction.[100]

Such politicized diatribes, a blend of nationalist romanticism and justified furor over legalized British repression, fell on deaf ears. Barry refused to turn informant, and on November 1 he was hanged. It was the first execution in Ireland since the Easter Uprising. For many, his arrest, torture, and hanging were symbolic of Britain's moral bankruptcy, and sentiments like Childers's were soon immortalized in Irish cultural nationalism. "Kevin Barry," one of many popular folk songs, captured in its most famous verse the impact of Britain's reprisals on Irish republican consciousness:

> *Another martyr for old Ireland,*
> *Another murder for the crown,*
> *Whose brutal laws may kill the Irish,*
> *But won't keep their spirit down.*
> *Lads like Barry are no cowards.*
> *From the foe they will not fly.*
> *Lads like Barry will free Ireland,*
> *For her sake they'll live and die.*[101]

By the fall of 1920, local streets, churches, and parks became battlefronts where murders that British government and republican forces perpetrated were far more prevalent than conventional engagements. Boundaries separating home fronts from battlefields blurred. Other times paramilitary forces disappeared suspected troublemakers, or randomly fired off rounds that took the lives of or wounded countless civilians. Ellen Quinn was minding her children in their Galway home garden when passing police discharged rounds from their vehicle. They killed the seven-months-pregnant mother, though miraculously missed the infant in her arms. Days later a hasty military court of inquiry issued a verdict: "death by misadventure."[102] Father John Considine led demands for justice and highlighted the lack of material witnesses called. The British government's response was a variation on its standard answer: "The case was very sad & most regrettable, but while [the] present state of affairs continues such cases are liable to occur. The police must take precautions to protect their lives & if [the] innocent accidentally suffer at times those who ambush & murder policemen are to blame."[103]

When convenient legal processes failed to apportion account-ability, the British government sidestepped them altogether and took cover under its rhetoric of law and order. Such was the case with Father Michael Griffin, a republican Catholic priest who disappeared from his residence at St. Joseph's Church in Galway after he answered the door to a late-night visitor. With the British security forces accused of kid-napping him, Chief Secretary Hamar Greenwood, who was second-in-command of British administration in Ireland after the lord lieutenant, responded defiantly to queries in the House of Commons: "I do not believe for a moment that this priest has been kidnapped by any armed forces of the Crown. It is obviously such a stupid thing that no mem-bers of the forces of the Crown would do it."[104] In fact, Father Griffin's fate was similar to many others whom British security forces had disap-peared: they shot him, execution style, through the head and buried him in a shallow grave. It wasn't until several months later that the truth of his fate would emerge.

By November 21, 1920, the deaths of MacSwiney and Barry, along with hundreds of less high-profile murders like those of Quinn and Grif-fin, combined with the effects of widespread repression, mass intern-ment, and multiple hunger strikes to feed public opinion and embolden Collins and his men. In the wake of improved British intelligence mea-sures, they regrouped with Afrikaner-inspired guerrilla flying columns. From the start of the conflict, British efforts were mired in relentless rivalries among its different security forces, not to mention a thorough breakdown in information gathering and assessment. To streamline efforts and infiltrate Collins's operations, several intelligence officers came in from Bengal and other parts of the empire. The IRA quickly sniffed them out. Calling the empire's imports the "Cairo Gang," Col-lins's men turned their attention to one operative code-named "O" and the others joining him. The IRA soon shook the intelligence agents from their sleep in Dublin's early-morning hours and shot fourteen of them in cold blood.[105] Later that day, in what would become one of the most spectacular reprisals, Tudor's paramilitary squads drove into a Dublin Gaelic football match and opened fire into the crowd. They killed at least fourteen unarmed civilians and wounded scores of others. A few hours later three Irish Republican prisoners died in Dublin Castle. The IRA believed Britain's "law and order" forces had tortured and murdered them, whereas the official account claimed the prisoners were shot "while trying to escape."[106] A few days later, eighteen Auxiliaries were killed in an ambush.[107]

In response to Bloody Sunday, Prime Minister Lloyd George turned up the repressive heat, authorizing official reprisals for all members of the British security forces. This, despite the fact that Churchill had informed him and the cabinet a month earlier that "the troops are getting out of control, taking the law into their own hands, and that besides clumsy and indiscriminate destruction, actual thieving and looting as well as drunkenness and gross disorder are occurring."[108] Now "the troops" had legal license to carry out often deadly reprisals. Throughout the uprising, the British government deflected criticism, remaining publicly steadfast in its defense of coercion, even if internally it debated the methods. Tudor summed up widespread sentiment when he declared "the whole country was intimidated and would thank God for stern measures"; meanwhile, Churchill publicly lauded the Black and Tans and the Auxiliaries as "loyal and gallant."[109] Lloyd George was unequivocal in support of repression: "There is no doubt that at last [the police force's] patience has given way and there has been some severe hitting back. . . . Let us be fair to these gallant men who are doing their duty in Ireland. . . . It is no use talking about this being war and these being reprisals when these things are being done [by the IRA] with impunity in Ireland."[110]

The cabinet recognized that the civil authorities were increasingly impotent, which made the legalization of official reprisals all the more alarming. It soon yielded, in part, on the issue of martial law and authorized it in four of Munster's counties on December 10, 1920.[111] Now that the military command was calling the shots in these hotly contested areas, the British Army could impose curfews, ban markets, control movements, and expand the use of internment and executions.

No sooner had the government officially endorsed reprisals and declared martial law than parts of the city of Cork went up in flames. Infuriated by an IRA ambush close to their Victoria Barracks, the Auxiliaries, together with a group of British soldiers, rampaged their way through the city. They bashed in doors, pulled civilians into the street, and dragged others from their cars. In public view, British security forces meted out thrashings while forcing Cork's citizens to sing "God Save the King." They also razed houses and buildings, exploded bombs, beat residents who tried to intervene, and actively prevented firefighters from dousing the blazes. Just before daybreak, fires engulfed City Hall and the nearby Carnegie Library with its vast collection of city records.[112] One member of the Auxiliaries recalled that many "who witnessed similar scenes in France and Flanders say, that nothing they had experienced was comparable to the punishment meted out to Cork."[113] Britain's forces caused £3 million in damage there, £140 million in today's currency.

Public outcry over the conflict's most spectacular reprisal was immediate and widespread. Corners of the popular press that had once been in the pocket of the Lloyd George government were swift in their denunciations and apportion of blame. *The Manchester Guardian*, an emerging voice for anticolonial critique, called the Burning of Cork "the crowning wickedness of the reprisals campaign," while the Labour Party's *Daily Herald* claimed there was "abundant evidence that the fires were started by the forces of the Crown."[114] On the other hand, London's *Morning Post* and other outlets were steadfastly pro-government and suggested the Sinn Féin "murder gangs," masquerading as British security forces, were responsible for burning down the city.[115]

"You will have murders, and more murders, on either side," the Conservative MP William Ormsby-Gore told Parliament. Attitudes were

The Burning of Cork, St. Patrick's Street, photograph taken c. December 14, 1920

hardening over Ireland, and British paramilitary forces, once defended by MPs as having "precisely the same as the character of the average soldier who fought in the war," were now the target of criticism. Distinctions were being made between "the ordinary British Tommy"—who, "of all the heroic figures the world has ever seen," was "the most chivalrous, the most honourable," according to the MP John Ward—and paramilitary recruits, who were men of "very evil character," "degenerates," and "victims of war . . . suffering from nerve strain," as far as the Labour Party was concerned. Its voice piece, *The Daily Herald* wrote that "no ordinary English soldier would have done such work," when discussing the sack of Balbriggan, and this sentiment carried forward in the aftermaths of Bloody Sunday and Cork, as few were willing to accept that, other than a few anomalies, the "British Tommy" was anything but "honourable," "gentlemanly," "kind" to prisoners, and restrained "in the face of frightful difficulties." Instead, it was the British state, and its semiautonomous colonial state stationed in Ireland's Dublin Castle, that created laws and systems of "brutalization." "It is the Germans who have won the War," Commander Kenworthy told Parliament, "because the spirit of frightfulness and Prussianism has been transplanted in Ireland."[116]

"Unprecedented in English history," *The Liberal Magazine* concluded in July 1921, perpetuating a myth of exceptionalism reminiscent of Churchill's claims during the Amritsar debates.[117] Dyer had been an aberration to "the British way of doing things," according to Churchill. Now Ireland was another exception, and this time the main target of criticism was the state and its policies. Legalized lawlessness, however, had been evolving in the empire for decades, and with each conflict—Jamaica, India, the South African War—state power accreted as administrators, police officers, and military forces consolidated Britain's civilizing mission. Ireland and the men who enforced Britain's rule of law were no exceptions to what their counterparts had been doing in the empire for years. Instead, critiques of government policies during the Irish War of Independence reflected Britain's larger mood. The nation was war-weary from a global conflict that had forced it to suspend its peaceful character, sending its men into the trenches to defeat German militarism. Ordinarily, Britain was "a peaceable kingdom." It was another myth that Britons told themselves, this time to make sense of the aftermath of the Great War's horrors.[118]

In the aftermath of Cork's burning, the military convened an internal inquiry that Major General Sir E. P. Strickland chaired. It submitted its findings, known as the Strickland Report, to the cabinet in late

December 1920, though not before it warned Lloyd George's inner circle of the damning conclusions. According to the confidential inquiry, the ill-disciplined and inexperienced men in the paramilitary police were to blame, specifically the Auxiliaries' K Company and other members of the Royal Irish Constabulary. The military brass, not surprisingly, found its authorities in Cork beyond reproach, despite the fact that they were technically in charge, and failed to account for eyewitnesses who placed army soldiers at the scene.[119]

Faced with mounting pressure and incontrovertible evidence, the British government once again fell back on obfuscation, stonewalling, and outright denial. At a decisive cabinet meeting, those officially overseeing policies and practices in Ireland—including Lloyd George, Churchill, Chief Secretary Greenwood, Tudor, and the commander in charge of Britain's military forces in Ireland, General Nevil Macready—agreed that "the effect of publishing the Report if Parliament was sitting would be disastrous to the Government's whole policy in Ireland."[120] Greenwood, finding himself on the front lines, defended the government's position and lied repeatedly in the House of Commons and to the press not only about Cork but also about the government's handling of Ireland more generally. Giving voice to the cabinet's collective view, he disavowed British security forces' role in the burnings and fed the press the position that Sinn Féin was to blame.[121] Greenwood had a track record of defending and denying reprisal arsons and murders while also supporting policies of "legitimate burnings and shootings by forces of the Crown."[122] The government refused to publish the Strickland Report, claiming such inquiries were confidential, and refused any further official investigation into the Cork matter. The press was outraged. In an editorial, *The Times* condemned the government in terms that dealt with the officially orchestrated violence and secrecy that would shape and define government policies in the empire for decades to come:

> While the Government have already said enough about events at Cork to confirm the worst suspicions, they have failed signally to show the candour which could alone have disposed of the charge that they dare not publish the full truth. From the first there could be little doubt that the burnings at Cork were among the "many wild deeds" done by the Forces of the CROWN. . . . Now, however, there is no longer room for doubt that the Irish administration must bear the stain of a lasting disgree [*sic*], which cannot fail to react upon the good repute of England. The authors of the present policy of Irish administration are

directly to blame for connivance which rendered the burnings at Cork possible, and their offence is morally no less grave than that of the criminals who actually perpetrated the arson.[123]

No one was held accountable for the razing of Cork. Throughout the war, few were brought up on charges for the "many wild deeds" undertaken in the name of the Crown, despite the fact that internally a handful drew a line in the sand and sought to rein in the legalized lawlessness of their subordinates. One such high-ranking official was General Frank Crozier, the officer in charge of the Auxiliaries, who was by no means a boy scout. Major-General Tudor had handpicked the stocky and seasoned Crozier to oversee Churchill's personal police force. But then the general dismissed nearly two dozen Auxiliaries for their involvement in the "notorious looting of Trim," as the IRA branded the British security forces' ransacking of a Unionist-owned grocery store in February 1921, whereupon the major general refused to back his man. While conspiring with Lloyd George and others in London on how to handle the Strickland Report, Tudor stopped Crozier from taking any action on the Trim issue until his return. Crozier fired off his resignation letter in response and wrote to his superior that he could not "honestly associate myself with a force in which such acts are condoned."[124]

Overnight official wagons circled. Dublin Castle labeled the former head of the Auxiliaries a "worthless fellow" and questioned his war record. It also launched a full-scale investigation into newfound accounting issues during Crozier's period of command.[125] Crozier in turn took his uncensored critique of Britain's security forces to the press. His long piece in *The Manchester Guardian*, "The RIC and the Auxiliaries: Their Organisation and Discipline," provided further grist to the outrage mill over the Strickland Report.[126] In it and other public declarations, Crozier accused the British government of suborning witnesses, routinely lying about abuses, and covering up dozens of murders, including that of Father Michael Griffin, the priest whose death at the hands of British security forces had made for Greenwood's very public denial, and derision, months earlier.[127]

Little came of Crozier's efforts. While a few Auxiliaries at the bottom of the ladder were wrist-slapped for their roles in Trim, most were let off and restored to duty. Crozier later stood unsuccessfully as a Labour MP and, disillusioned, became a committed pacifist before he died at fifty-eight in 1937. In its obituary, *The Times* glossed over Crozier's resignation and his explanation for it. To the daily's credit, however, it published a subsequent letter from Crozier's widow who reminded the forgetful paper, and public, that her late husband "could not condone the murder of Irishmen by Irishmen instigated . . . by Government emissaries to justify what they called the 'Black and Tan operations' in Ireland."[128]

Clearly not everyone shared the abiding belief, held in many circles, that "reprisals do good of a sort."[129] Despite evidence to the contrary, and outcries condemning Britain's use of them, Lloyd George's cabinet was self-assured and noted in private discussion that "reprisals had unquestionably had a visible effect both in enabling the executive to obtain information about ambushes and plots, and in driving a wedge between the moderates and the extremists in the Sinn Fein."[130] If their forces applied enough pressure, so it was thought, the civilian population would cower and support the empire or, at a minimum, further fracture among themselves. Instead, the effects of reprisals and martial law only exacerbated the spiraling situation. Further empowered and indemnified, the British security forces continued to raze the homes of hundreds of IRA suspects and their supporters in the aftermath of Cork. Coupled with the effects of the estimated fifty thousand home raids since the start of the conflict, this widespread domestic destruction further terrorized the civilian population, which was precisely the point.

In the face of legalized British repression, the IRA's civilian recruitment campaign was a snowballing product of the insurgency as much as it had been its precipitating cause, if not more so.[131] At once beleaguered and galvanized, local communities offered further sustenance, gun running, courier services, intelligence, and safe houses for the IRA. Like other conflicts that had kaleidoscopic anticolonial and civil dimensions, Ireland's, too, witnessed what one historian has called "total war at the grassroots level," and its all-encompassing dimensions transcended age and gender.[132]

Many women participated in the war, while others sat on the fence or switched sides.[133] Thousands joined the republican women's organization, Cumann na mBan, which boasted over six hundred branches. As the war escalated and its polarization hardened the battle lines, both republicans and British security forces singled out women. The latter suspected some women of actively supporting the republicans, and as in South Africa, they also targeted family members of known IRA men. Seldom interning women, paramilitary forces instead staged night raids, bursting into homes and dragging women from their beds. Children, paralyzed with fear, looked on as British forces beat and harassed their mothers, sisters, and grandmothers, sometimes forcibly shaving their hair. The IRA was equally vengeful. Collins's men staged reprisals against suspected British loyalists and punished them for acts real and perceived, like informing or consorting with the police. The IRA similarly humiliated women of all ages and also shaved their hair or tied them to lampposts with affixed placards that read, "Long tongues beware."[134]

With neither side able to gain the upper hand, a truce was declared in July 1921. Like many other colonial conflicts, this one became one of attrition, in which Britain underestimated the resilience and resourcefulness, both military and political, of their opponents and those who supported them. Much more than a "murder gang," the so-called IRA extremists effectively capitalized not only on the multiple layers of Irish discontent but also on the British government's racial and cultural hierarchies that militated against any substantive understanding of subject populations and the complexities of their resentment. Lloyd George's men misunderstood Irish nationalism and overestimated their own security force's power to establish hegemony through legalized lawlessness in the face of the IRA's strategic and brazen tactics.

Even after the appointment of Tudor and the military's command over parts of Ireland, centralized control remained elusive. Nevertheless, regardless of some in the military who rebuked the Royal Irish Constabulary and its Black and Tan and Auxiliary appendages, the paramilitary forces, with official backing from Downing Street, adopted an unapologetic commitment to the moral effect of repression that characterized the British Army's approach to Ireland and the empire.[135] Until the bitter end, the military commander General Macready clung to the widespread belief that Britain's repressive measures worked—even as those measures drove Irish moderates into the arms of the nationalists, pitted Unionists against nationalists both in Ireland and at home, left countless civilians playing both sides, and precipitated critiques of Britain's moral failures in the empire. In his weekly cabinet briefing, just days after the truce signing, Macready remarked, "In my own mind I am quite clear that the present negotiations have only been made possible by the fact that the unceasing efforts of troops and police together with the arrival of reinforcing units from England have brought home to the Sinn Fein leaders the advisability of coming to some terms before the rebellion is openly and obviously crushed."[136]

Negotiating a settlement that balanced Sinn Féin's demand for full independence with the continued support for the Protestant Unionists at home, and the British government's overarching goal of offering Ireland dominion status within the empire, were challenging tasks.[137] Among those squaring off during eight weeks of negotiations were Churchill and Collins. Also involved was Erskine Childers, whose " 'chief recollection of these inexpressibly miserable hours' was of Churchill in his evening dress walking up and down 'with his loping stoop and long strides and a huge cigar like a bowsprit.' "[138] In December 1921, the British government's final offer was rife with foreboding: Ireland could undergo partition and take an oath of allegiance to the Crown, or it could return to more repression. The Irish Free State chose to become a self-governing dominion, while the six counties that comprised Northern Ireland exercised their right to opt out forthwith. All remaining MPs in the new Free State had to swear their fidelity to King George V.

When his delegation signed the Anglo-Irish Treaty, Collins believed it gave Ireland wide berth to determine its future, much like South Africa and other dominions, yet he understood well Ireland's lethal fractiousness. By signing the treaty, he knew, in his own words, that he had signed his own "death warrant." Seasoned veterans like Constance Markievicz, who had narrowly escaped a death sentence during the Easter Rising, felt Collins and his team had sold out the nationalist cause in Ireland and beyond. I "would sooner die than give a declaration of fidelity to King George or the British Empire," she sputtered, barely containing her outrage. "If we pledge ourselves to this oath we pledge our allegiance to this thing, whether you call it Empire or Commonwealth of Nations, that is treading down the people of Egypt and of India. . . . And mind you, England wants peace in Ireland to bring her troops over to India and Egypt."[139] In the end, the Dáil narrowly approved the treaty by 64 votes to 57, while De Valera, Markievicz, and others denounced the terms, and the country descended again into civil war.

Collins, however, did not live to fight another day. True to his prediction, De Valera's supporters cornered him in an unplanned ambush in Cork. There men who had for years pledged their loyalty to Collins turned against him and without compunction shot him in the head. Offering a poetic device for future Irish bards, Collins drew his last breath in his beloved home county. His funeral in Dublin drew over half a million Irish men and women, or nearly 20 percent of the new nation's population.[140] It was, though, Collins's cryptic last telegram to Whitehall that suggested Churchill's outsize place in shaping Ireland's complex nationalist imagination: "Tell Winston we could never have done anything without him."[141]

CHAPTER 4

"I'm merely pro-British"

As night fell over the Mesopotamian desert one evening in the summer of 1923, one can imagine Britain's maverick Royal Air Force pilot Arthur "Bomber" Harris fending off the disorienting effects of the distant horizon that melded with the sea of sand below. The hum of his plane's engines echoed through the surrounding windswept silence, even as the expanse rendered him a speck on the empire's landscape. In the desolate frontier beneath him, a village soon emerged with shadowy figures scurrying across it frantically in search of temporary shelter. These so-called recalcitrant men, women, and children, not to mention their homes and livestock, were Bomber's targets. Perhaps the derided tribespeople had refused to acquiesce to British control, or perhaps they had harbored rebel leaders or actively resisted themselves. Perhaps they were innocent of any subterfuge, and the intelligence guiding Harris's plane, like many that flew before and after him, was wrong. Faulty guesswork, however, deterred neither the pilot nor the military men and politicians who called the shots. In their minds, the moral effect of immediate mass destruction was the same. With Bomber's go-ahead, the plane released its deadly cargo, and flames erupting from below soon pierced the evening sky. As the plane disappeared, the pilot, deafened by engine noise, scarcely heard the secondary explosions from the delayed-action bombs or the screams of pain and loss that accompanied them.[1]

Harris arrived in Mesopotamia—or Iraq, as it would come to be known after the Great War—as one of the new wunderkinder of the skies. The youngest son of a cash-strapped British civil servant in India, Harris spent twelve self-described miserable years in second-rate English boarding schools, where he was often cold and hungry and lonely for his family. At eighteen, he bade farewell to Allhallows School and sought fortune and adventure in Southern Rhodesia, then enlisted in the war effort. After fighting alongside South African imperial forces to conquer and occupy the nearby German colony South West Africa, the ginger-haired Harris with his signature Hitler-esque moustache, signed up for Britain's Royal Flying Corps. By the end of the war, he had risen to the rank of commanding officer for the No. 31 Squadron.[2] From early on, Harris always sported his RHODESIA shoulder flash and "was very keen on bombing and he was good," according to one of his peers. Indeed, Harris's initiatives heralded the conversion of transport planes into heavy bombers with capacities for larger loads and bigger bombs.[3] Eventually he was a force behind the creation of small incendiary bombs as well as the delayed-action bombs that, pending their detonation times, became embedded land mines in civilian areas. Bomber Harris was poised to become a decorated soldier of the empire in the postwar years.[4]

The spoils that occupied Harris had brought more imperial burdens at a time when Britain could barely keep its fiscal head above the water. On the immediate chopping block after the Great War were excessive military expenditures. Churchill, now secretary for war and air, scrambled to find ways to defend and administer the vast swaths of former Ottoman territory—including Mesopotamia, Transjordan, and Palestine—that had become part of the British Empire as League of Nations mandated territories. British officials believed Middle Eastern expanses were like other massive tracts that they considered boundary-less territories, including those in the Sudan and the North-West Frontier, where pacification efforts drained manpower and material resources due to the perpetual states of conflict. In the case of Iraq, colonial policies drove resistance, starting with Britain's vague idea of creating an Arab state without having any idea what this meant. Nearly half of Iraq's population was Shi'ite Arabs whose religious traditions were similar to those in neighboring Persia; Kurds in the north and Sunni Arabs comprised another fifth of the population; and a combination of Jews, Christians, Yezidis, and Turks made up most of the rest. The Iraqi Revolt of 1920, the mopping up of which had brought Harris to the region, saw Shi'ite and Sunni Arabs cooperating along with embittered officers from the old Ottoman army against British occupation and its imposition of direct administration using civil servants from India. Meanwhile in the north, Kurds took up arms in a drive for an independent Kurdistan. Many local leaders had fought in the Ottoman and Arab-backed British armies, knew modern warfare tactics, and had a stockpile of weapons from the collapsed Ottoman Empire. To suppress the revolts and retake control, Britain saw £40 million evaporate in Mesopotamia's desert sands (more than it had spent backing the Arabs when they revolted against the Turks during the Great War), at a time when conflict costs in Ireland, Egypt, and India were accruing.[5] Necessity proved the handmaiden of innovation, and Churchill, well aware of the infant air service that had become the Royal Air Force (RAF), had already been making the fateful connection between the empire's newly acquired deserts and the possibilities of air control, when the revolts in Iraq erupted.[6]

Thunderously prodding the secretary along was the influential voice of Sir Hugh Trenchard.[7] Remarkably loud for a man who had lost a lung on South Africa's battlefield, Trenchard later served on punitive expeditions in Nigeria before he squeaked in under the age limitation for military pilot training. He turned to the skies in the Great War, took command of the military wing of the Royal Flying Corps, and mentored young hotshots like Harris. He soon gained renown as the "Father of the Royal Air Force."[8] For Trenchard, the superiority of the airplane as a weapon of attack that could replace vast numbers of conventional troops—particularly in wide-open spaces, like deserts—was an article of faith. So, too, was his steadfast belief in the effects of aerial bombing. Trenchard elided matters of economy with the "civilizing" imperatives that underwrote liberal imperialism. He summed up his views in early 1919: "At present the moral effect of bombing stands undoubtedly to the material effect in a proportion of 20 to 1."[9]

Another cadre of advisers professed to have a unique understanding of the desert population marked for destruction. Possessed of Oxford degrees and desert-honed credentials, Gertrude Bell, Thomas Edward Lawrence, and others fashioned themselves as part omniscient intellectuals, part mystical spies. As the historian Priya Satia has pointed out in her path-breaking research, their work provided the on-the-ground know-how to guide men like Harris, and to justify the devastating effects of air control and other evolving forms of colonial pacification and punishment.[10]

In the postwar era, a mélange of self-proclaimed experts—including scholars, former diplomats, peripatetic journalists, and career military officers—constituted the empire's hydra-headed intelligence beast.[11] Political dissent throughout the empire, often fractious, gained momentum, and the British government needed intelligence officers to figure out what its colonial subjects were up to by gathering information and translating what appeared to be an inscrutable web of demands and conditions. Such needs were scarcely new. Stretching back to the days of the East India Company, British officials recruited local informants to pass on knowledge. Intelligence gathering required not only direct surveillance but also an infiltration into local social and communication networks. The East India Company, the subsequent Raj, and multiple other local colonial and military administrations in the empire struggled endlessly with such efforts.

In addition, the widespread practice of co-opting local ruling elites was a fraught enterprise when it came to the intelligence phalanx and information collection. Not only did these elites represent a narrow window into communities over which Britain imposed its authority, but they were also in a structurally inferior position within the colonial hierarchy. It was one that left them struggling for their own legitimacy as they mediated between a colonial regime and local populations while at the same time often challenging the colonial power structures themselves and vying for self-interested opportunities. These asymmetric conditions were scarcely conducive to fostering accurate clandestine information flows back to colonial and military authorities.[12] The empire's "information order" encompassed a wide swath of colonial-generated knowledge, and monitoring it ranged from population, economic, and environmental statistics and regulatory measures, to the state's attempt to influence and control local autonomous spaces like markets, social gatherings, vernacular media, and religious rituals and places of worship.[13]

While Rudyard Kipling rendered the North-West Frontier legendary for intelligence operations with his espionage novel *Kim*, in reality early British agents were an amateurish lot who bore little resemblance to Kipling's fictionalized Great Game of spies and informants. France, Russia, and Germany had developed coordinated and increasingly technical systems of agents and code breaking, but Victorian and Edwardian Britain sniffed its nose at such pursuits because they were unbecoming of an English gentleman.[14] Any pretext of honor, however, evaporated with the acquisition of new colonial territories—first at the end of the nineteenth century in Africa and Asia, then with the new League of Nations mandated territories—not to mention the exigencies of long-held places like India, because more and better information was needed.

On the front lines of such knowledge acquisition were colonial police departments and their burgeoning criminal investigation departments. There were also less apparent colonial actors, like tax collectors, local district administrators, and agricultural and welfare officers. Their numbers were comparatively meager due in no small part to Britain's empty pocketbook. A common scrutinizing lens, though, assessed much of the decentralized information gathering, a lens that was, in itself, a product of the colonial project. At once racially exclusionary and fearful of its own ignorance—or at best rooted in superficial knowledge of local cultures—intelligence assessments failed to break free of the liberal imperialism that underwrote British rule in the first place. If increasing reliance on state-directed repression was a barometer of Britain's intelligence capabilities in the empire, then crises that stretched from as far back as the 1857 Indian Mutiny to the repeated interwar uprisings would prove them, over and again, to be spectacular failures.[15]

Lessons of failure also brought with them little ideological self-reflection but rather a greater proliferation of intelligence experts, organizations, and new techniques for monitoring the empire and extracting information. A key turning point came with the intelligence humiliations of the South African War, along with the convergence of a rising German threat. In the fall of 1909, the Committee on Imperial Defence created Britain's first peacetime intelligence department, the "Secret Service Bureau," which was split into domestic and foreign branches. During the Great War each branch took on names that are recognizable today: Military Intelligence 5, or MI5, which was also called the Security Service after the war, oversaw domestic intelligence that included counterespionage, countersabotage, and countersubversion; Military Intelligence 6, or MI6, which postwar was also called Secret Intelligence Service, was responsible for all things foreign within the Secret Service Bureau. By war's end, the gathering and assessment of intelligence expanded, and there were greater efforts at coordination among the intelligence branches of Britain's three military units (RAF, army, and Royal Navy) and, to a lesser extent, its counterparts in colonial policing. Signals intelligence and cryptography, which the Indian Army pioneered in 1844, was undoubtedly the area of Britain's greatest wartime intelligence advancement, and even human intelligence made some strides, particularly with the capture of prisoners of war.[16]

Collective learning experiences brought with them card catalog index registries and a passing on of trial-and-error methods of intelligence gathering and collation. Such processes had been emerging prior to the Great War and included the nineteenth-century use of fingerprinting techniques that India's police force had pioneered, and surveillance techniques deployed in Ireland. Nonetheless, the most enduring feature of Britain's emerging intelligence hydra was its turf wars and rivalries. During the interwar period MI5, under the watchful eye of its first director, Sir Vernon Kell, took full responsibility for the empire and Commonwealth, whereas MI6 was confined to a three-mile demarcation line outside all British territories. MI5's ascendancy, however, was largely aborted until the Second World War, as budget cuts left the Security Service with just fifteen operatives in the empire by 1935. Other parts of the intelligence hydra lived on, as many of those who had staffed India's Civil Service, the Sudan Political Service, and the Egyptian High Commission and its appendage, the Arab Bureau, brought with them accumulated experiences and shared knowledge as they increasingly circulated within and between imperial locations.[17]

Failed experimental efforts were the norm, often serving to alienate the same subject populations that the "intelligence order" sought to comprehend.[18] In the Middle East, the epicenter for such methods was the Arab Bureau. Established in January 1916 and housed in a warren of three rooms at Cairo's Savoy Hotel, the Arab Bureau was a coordinating body for wartime political and military intelligence in the face of Ottoman intransigence, not to mention that of Arab public opinion. Growing incrementally out of wartime necessity, the intelligence den answered to multiple superiors—including the Foreign Office, the Cairo Residency (Britain's administrative hub in Egypt), and intelligence for the Egyptian Expeditionary Force, Britain's imperial military formation in the Middle East. But in the end, it was largely a force unto itself. Despite routine cock-ups, the bureau became, after the war, a crucial precedent for Britain's intelligence gathering in the empire.[19] Above all else, intelligence experts often displayed an arresting level of self-importance, convinced as they were of their unique abilities to read indigenous social and political structures, understand colonial governance, and pinpoint sites of disorder and dissent. Intelligence produced in this cauldron of misplaced conviction would guide RAF planes, military troops, and colonial policing operations as they attempted to root out suspected dissent and suppress uprisings across the empire.[20]

Few agents of empire would claim the legendary status of T. E. Lawrence, otherwise known as Lawrence of Arabia. While he took his degree in history with first class honors, Lawrence's education extended well beyond Oxford's Jesus College. For three months, he undertook a tour through Ottoman Syria and wandered over a thousand miles alone through the arid landscape. When the war broke out, his intellectual prowess soon found him assigned to Britain's Middle East Intelligence Staff based in Cairo, where he became one of the Arab Bureau's fixtures. Naturally rancorous toward military authority—toward any authority, for that matter—Lawrence earned the title "the untidiest officer in Egypt." When not unkempt, he bedecked his five-foot-five frame in traditional flowing robes complete with headgear and a bejeweled knife sheath cinched to his waist.[21] For some of the war he was embedded with Arab regulars behind Ottoman enemy lines where he fought in desert raids and large-scale battles—with assistance from the emerging signals and image intelligence, which provided intercepted and decoded enemy communications and aerial photography. In fact, the Arab Bureau's few successes—which included the British-backed Arab Revolt of 1916–17, a military uprising of Arab forces against the Ottoman Empire—were due largely to technological advances guiding ground troops as opposed to instinctive British know-how. Nonetheless, Lawrence's cultivated legend earned him enough notoriety that the Turks put a £15,000 price on his head. Even with such a bounty, no one betrayed him, not least because the sharif of Mecca bestowed on him the status of fictive son.[22]

Lawrence's knowledge and that of his fellow agents shaped Churchill's evolving plan for Iraq and the Middle East generally. Guided by such experts, Whitehall constructed an alternative moral universe for populations it perceived to be off civilization's scale of humanity, in an otherworldly order distinctly their own. In the colonial imagination, Arabia was a biblical anachronism, absent of Western sensibilities like reason and feeling, according to Priya Satia's detailed historical account, *Spies in Arabia*.[23] For Lawrence, Arabs thought the bombs raining down upon them to be the "will of God" and "a misfortune from heaven striking the community." He felt the Arab was unknowable to any imperial mind, only to gurus like himself. Other self-professed experts joined Lawrence's chorus of romantic perversion, including the RAF intelligence officer John Glubb, who insisted the "world of violence, bloodshed and war" that defined Arabia also embraced a "hatred, reckless bloodshed . . . lust of plunder of which our lukewarm natures seem no longer capable."[24]

Whatever moral universe they imagined for the Arab population, it paled in comparison to the beliefs of Churchill and his fleet of intelligence and RAF experts, and their evolving air control theology. Moving from the War Office, which oversaw the British military, to head the Colonial Office overseeing administration for much of the British Empire in early 1921, Churchill formally inducted his advisers—including Lawrence, Reader Bullard, and Richard Meinertzhagen—as part of the new Middle East department. These field-tested experts had a form of paternalism that blended a professed love for the Arab with an ethno-psychobabble that branded the Oriental world as astonishingly devoid of emotional and physical pain. Like other agents of empire, Lawrence and his cabal refused to concede that local populations had any legitimate grievances, even in the face of British occupation and crippling tax burdens imposed on them.[25] The "backward" Arabs were, in the experts' eyes, the misguided victims of faceless global forces that were sweeping through the eastern Empire more generally. Based on these supposed gurus' unchallenged expertise, and on the relentless Trenchard's advocacy of air control and a place for his beloved RAF in the postwar world, Churchill found a way to police and subdue the empire on the cheap while also inaugurating an early-twentieth-century version of shock and awe. Behind closed doors and in secret memoranda, officials enthused over the "'frightfulness' in a more or less severe form" and the "real casualties and material damage" being inflicted.[26]

As untold suffering unfolded in the desert, far from the media's reach and prying liberal eyes, Iraq became a playground for weapons testing. In late 1922, London's Air Ministry circulated a "Forms of Frightfulness" memo in which it considered smoke bombs, aerial darts, tear gas, phosphorus bombs, war rockets, long-delay "action" bombs, tracer ammunition, man-killing shrapnel bombs, "liquid" fire (the precursor to napalm), and crude oil to pollute water supplies. The ministry deployed some of these options.[27] At the time, officials knew mustard gas caused, at the very least, "very painful sores" and other physical problems. Such consequences mattered little to the Air Ministry's brigadier general: "I am of the opinion that for a given carrying weight of aeroplane high explosive bombs or shrapnel bombs are superior to any other firm [*sic*] of frightfulness, except gas. If mustard gas can be accepted for this type of savage warfare, it should prove more efficient than any other known form of frightfulness."[28] A year earlier, Churchill had said that he was "ready to authorize the construction of [gas] bombs at once."[29]

British officials thought better of gas, though the RAF logged over four thousand hours of missions, dropped nearly one hundred tons of bombs, and fired some two hundred thousand rounds.[30] By the end of 1924, Air Marshal John Salmond, the commanding officer in Iraq, enthused "that aircraft achieve their result by their effect on morale, and by the material damage they do, and by the interference they cause to the daily routine of life and not through the infliction of casualties."[31] The long-term effects, as Salmond's report suggested, of damaging crops, poisoning wells, and destroying fuel supplies and livestock meant that populations were starving from lack of food and dying from exposure.[32] Harris and his comrades executed the operations. One British wing commander, J. A. Chamier, later described that "the attack with

bombs and machine-guns must be relentless and unremitting and carried on continuously by day and night, on houses, inhabitants, crops and
cattle."[33] In 1924, though, Harris was the most articulate in painting a
portrait of the scenes unfolding beneath British aircraft:

> Where the Arab and Kurd had just begun to realise that if they
> could stand a little noise, they could stand bombing. . . . They
> now know what real bombing means, in casualties and damage;
> they now know that within forty-five minutes a full-sized village
> (vide attached photos of Kushan-Al-Ajaza) can be practically
> wiped out and a third of its inhabitants killed or injured by four
> or five machines which offer them no real target, no opportunity
> for glory as warriors, no effective means of escape.[34]

Bomber's description and photos evaded the public eye. They had
been part of a larger report to Parliament in 1924, when Britain's first
Labour government came to power and wanted some form of RAF
assessment on "heavy casualties caused by air policing."[35] The realities
of air control were swept under the rug, thanks in no small part to calculated maneuverings and larger, looming Middle Eastern imperatives.
On the heels of Churchill denouncing the "frightfulness" of Amritsar
and Dyer's "moral effect" on the floor of Parliament, British officials
were massaging the air control body count. Moreover, reports like those
from Salmond repeatedly emphasized bombing as a "merciful act," and
Trenchard would later defend air control theology to the House of
Lords while reminding its members of the alternative moral universe
of their Arab subjects. "The native of a lot of these tribes love fighting
for fighting's sake," Trenchard said. "They have no objection to being
killed."[36] "No mention should be made of the other theatres in which
resort has been had to air action in the course of the last year or two,"
the Air Ministry emphasized when preparing to speak to the House of
Commons about the report.[37]

While minimizing air control's realities, British officials were also busy
engineering the coronation of Faysal bin Husayn, the recently deposed
monarch of French-controlled Syria, as king of Iraq. Prompted by the
Mesopotamian occupation's skyrocketing military and financial costs,
even with the alleged promises of air control, the British installed Faysal
as part of a larger plan to engineer a loyal Arab government in Baghdad—a plan hammered out as the 1920 revolt was unfolding and final-

ized at the Cairo Conference of March 1921. "Faysal alone of all Arabian potentates has any idea of [the] practical difficulties of running a civilized government," officer and acting civil commissioner in the region Sir Arnold Wilson commented, even though Britain had to strong-arm local leaders into accepting Faysal's authority—no easy task.[38] Wearing a full-dress military uniform rather than traditional Arab robes, Faysal was crowned king of Iraq in August 1921, ensuring institutionalized British support in the region for over a quarter-century.[39]

How did Britain manage to install Faysal and ensure its interests by ruling through a client state in the Middle East for decades? It's a story that, as we've seen, began in the aftermath of the Great War, though its details offer insights into the enormity and deftness of British skills marshaled to ensure national self-interest. As early as 1918, Britain was preparing to grant Iraq self-government, a bold move, particularly as it later confirmed to the League of Nations a commitment to maintaining Iraq's Class A Mandate status. The League "very strongly resented" Britain's maneuvers to affirm a bilateral treaty with Iraq, claiming it would upend other Western powers from imperial internationalism's benefits, like access to Iraq's oil supply and airspace, which Britain was clearly planning to claim for itself by rendering Iraq a client state outside the League's international reach.[40]

Britain forged ahead anyway, drafting a treaty that promised Faysal and other Iraqi collaborators "national sovereignty" in return for staggering concessions that rendered Iraq an informal British colony. For the Iraqis, however, the treaty was the lesser of two evils, guaranteeing sovereignty such as it was, and ensuring local elites their power in an "independent" state. As Susan Pedersen underscores in *The Guardians:*

> If Faysal's rule rested on British support and the collaboration of much the same Sunni elite that had been the backbone of the Ottoman state, he was aware of the tenuous nature of his legitimacy. His governments thus spoke the language of Arab nation-building, sought to disguise the extent of their dependence on the British, built up an army and bureaucracy capable of uniting (and dominating) this disparate population, and cultivated the loyalty of largely Shi'i rural sheikhs by strengthening their near-feudal hold on their impoverished tenant-cultivators.[41]

To gain international approval for Iraq's emancipation, Britain invested nearly six years seeking support for the Anglo-Iraq Treaty of 1930 and obtained it by ensuring that the Middle Eastern pot was sweetened for other League nations. Germany got trade concessions, while Italy received a share of Iraqi oil, or the "veritable 'lake of petroleum' of almost inexhaustible supply," as one observer called it; the French got a nod for their own clientelist domination in Syria. Faysal assured the League's Permanent Mandates Commission that he would protect minorities, including the Kurds and Assyrians who had been anxiously petitioning the commission, fearing a continued erosion of their rights and further RAF aerial bombings meant to quash their protests.[42]

In October 1932, Iraq gained formal Independence and joined the League of Nations, even though one PMC official had given Faysal's new regime "a very grudging 'pass degree,'" and for good reason. Within a year, Faysal's troops gunned down Assyrians, who were viewed as British collaborators. Iraq's oil supply, despite earlier concessions, remained in the hands of the Iraq Petroleum Company, a subsidiary of Anglo-Persian oil, which had exclusive exploration rights. The company had a disincentive, however, to drill in Iraq, given its oil interests elsewhere in the world. By delaying Iraqi oil production, it could boost world oil prices, though such delays cost Faysal's government much-needed royalty payments. Britain also gained in other ways, maintaining its RAF presence in Iraq and securing the right to move troops over Iraqi soil, owning two air bases, training and equipping Faysal's army, installing British judges, and guaranteeing a slow wind-down of British administrative staff. Member of the Permanent Mandates Commission, the Swiss professor William Rappard, thought Britain had compelled Iraq "to accept conditions contrary to its interests," and he was right.[43]

As the local population continued to live in poverty and Faysal's British-backed troops took aim at Iraq's minority populations after 1932, Rappard could only lament that "[even] though at the time I did everything I could to prevent the premature emancipation of Iraq, I am not yet at peace about the blood spilt as an immediate consequence of the decision I opposed." Consequences of the Iraq deal had cascading effects for the League and the Middle East as a whole. Iraqi independence was held up as a shining example of what happened when self-government was granted too quickly. Now openly hostile to Arab nationalism, members of the Permanent Mandates Commission actively thwarted independence demands from other Middle Eastern territories, including those of the Arabs in Palestine.[44]

As for air control, its fate had also been sealed. The RAF's 1924 report, "Note on the Method of Employment of the Air Arm in Iraq," had been a whitewash. It had expunged Harris's account of wiping out Arabs and Kurds and omitted any mention of one British staff officer's denunciation of the RAF's bomb-induced deaths of nearly two dozen women and children in a crowded bazaar as "the nearest thing to wanton slaughter."[45] Instead, the report was a compendium of air control's virtues as a modern-day method of containing ungovernable populations. Churchill's earlier promise to Lloyd George that air control would "save millions" in expenditures proved hollow; operation costs in Iraq soared to over £40 million, or twice the budget allotted.[46] Still the bombings continued, not only in the Middle East but elsewhere in Britain's empire, despite ongoing criticism. When Britain targeted the North-West Frontier and other parts of the region, the army's commander in chief in India, Philip Chetwode, wrote a memo to the viceroy—a memo that he was later forced to retract—stating, "I loathe bombing and never agree to it without a guilty conscience. . . . [It] is to me a revolting method of making war, especially by a great power against tribesmen."[47]

The most trenchant critique, though, came from subjects of empire. While British airmen bombed the Mahsud villages in Afghanistan's borderland region where resistance to colonial rule persisted, one plane crash-landed, and several old women brandishing knives confronted the airmen. Instead of harming them, however, the elderly villagers led the fliers to a cave's safety where, together, they rode out another twenty-four hours of bombing. The villagers then escorted the airmen out of harm's way. The contrast between East and West, humanity and inhumanity, became fodder for India's cultural icon and imperial critic Rabindranath Tagore. In reflecting on this moment and countless others that brought destruction from above onto the empire's subjects, he wrote:

> The West has made wonderful progress. She has opened her path across the ethereal region of the earth; the explosive force of the bomb has developed its mechanical power of wholesale destruction to a degree that could be represented in the past only by the personal valour of a large number of men. But such enormous progress has made Man diminutive. He proudly imagines that he expresses himself when he displays the things that he produces and the power that he holds in his hands. The bigness of the results and the mechanical perfection of the apparatus hide from him the fact that the Man in him has been smothered.[48]

On June 22, 1922, as British operatives in the Middle East were leaving their combined imprints on the empire, Henry Tudor stood in the late afternoon shadow of London's Victoria Station a marked man. He waved goodbye to his wife and eldest daughter, Elizabeth, knowing he was only one step ahead of the Irish republicans. The IRA had not forgotten the brutality that Tudor and his band of paramilitaries had meted out during the long struggle for independence. The former commander of Britain's multiheaded police force in Ireland received threatening handwritten letter after letter, like the one scribbled out in poorly formed block capitals. It read: "YOUR DAYS ARE NUMBERED. DO NOT THINK THAT BY LEAVING THE COUNTRY OR REMAINING IN THE CASTLE YOU WILL ESCAPE THE HAND OF JUSTICE. YOUR DEATH WARRANT IS SIGNED. I.R.A."[49] Tudor was number two on the IRA's "death list." Field Marshal Sir Henry Wilson, who had been the chief of the Imperial General Staff during the Irish War of Independence and also shepherded the postwar crises in Egypt and Mesopotamia, was the IRA's number-one marked man.[50]

Around the same time that Tudor was settling into his train carriage, Wilson returned to his Eaton Place home in London's old-moneyed enclave of Belgravia where, on his front doorstep, two IRA assassins gunned him down.[51] Tudor spent the remainder of his life looking over his Black and Tanned shoulder. He might well have shared Wilson's fate had he not been one of Churchill's most trusted confidants. Their Great War friendship had been forged at Ploegsteert, Belgium, where, while charting war maneuvers in 1916, Churchill confided his planned political future to Tudor. He addressed him as "my dear friend" in dozens of handwritten correspondences. And in the spring of 1922, Churchill handpicked him to take on the roles of general officer commanding Palestine and director of Palestine security.[52] This, despite the torrent of criticism heaped on Tudor when he spearheaded British repression in Ireland.

Churchill had multiple pretexts for shipping Tudor to Palestine at a most precarious and necessary time. Riots and bloodshed had punctuated 1920 in Jerusalem, and a cyclical violence enveloped the Arab and Jewish divide as much as it did British imperial forces. The largely urban disorder, however, was not conducive to the new air control methods, or so it was thought. Instead, the colonial secretary needed someone from his inner circle who could brandish British power and organize a paramilitary police force on the cheap. The force would re-create Churchill's Irish Auxiliaries and would be to Palestine what aerial bombing was to Iraq. Hundreds of ex-Auxiliaries, along with Black and Tans and other members of the former Royal Irish Constabulary, were also poised to depart to the Middle East. Their brand of Irish-honed colonial policing would leave an indelible mark on the Mandate's future.

Much as in Ireland, the political scene in the Middle East was largely set before Tudor and his men arrived there. In 1915 the British high commissioner in Egypt, Sir Henry McMahon, had shored up wartime support against the Ottomans and assured Sharif Husayn of Mecca that after the war, in return for Arab allegiance, Britain would support an independent "Arab Khalifate of Islam."[53] The agreement's terms, later known as the Husayn-McMahon Correspondence, were negotiated through ten letters between McMahon and Husayn. Husayn laid out in his correspondence that Palestine was to be included in the territorial deal. "I have . . . lost no time in informing the Government of Great Britain of the contents of your [third] letter," McMahon assured Husayn. With the exception of a few exclusions, and one final clause stating that the agreement would pertain to "those regions . . . wherein Great Britain is free to act without detriment to the interest of her ally, France," McMahon wrote, "Great Britain is prepared to recognize and support the independence of the Arabs in all the regions within the limits demanded by the Sherif of Mecca."[54] Britain's intentions, however, soon proved less clear.

When Lloyd George came to power in December 1916, he approached the region with a biblical frame of mind. It was anchored in a long British tradition of Christian Zionism, as well as a personal fascination with Palestine, or as he referred to it, "Canaan." He believed the "Jewish race" had the financial wherewithal to direct the outcome of the war and was available to the highest bidder, which included Germany and Russia. That transformed Lloyd George's religious romanticism into a political priority.[55] Britain, according to Lloyd George, had no option but "to make a contract with Jewry."[56]

The perceived link between the Zionist movement and the global Jewish community was due in no small part to the work of Belarus-born Chaim Weizmann. Upon arriving at the University of Manchester as a lecturer in chemistry in 1904, Weizmann took charge of the Zionist movement in Britain, even though at the time he held no official office in the World Zionist Organization (WZO). Charismatic and politically shrewd, he convincingly presented the fragmented Zionist movement as a unified endeavor with significant international influence, particularly on matters pertaining to Germany and Russia. In a few short years, Weizmann leveraged his networks to become a British citizen and managed to gain an audience with key officials of the Foreign Office, members of Parliament, and eventually ministers in Lloyd George's cabinet.[57]

Among them was the foreign secretary, Arthur James Balfour, who had been prime minister in 1903 when East Africa was proposed as a

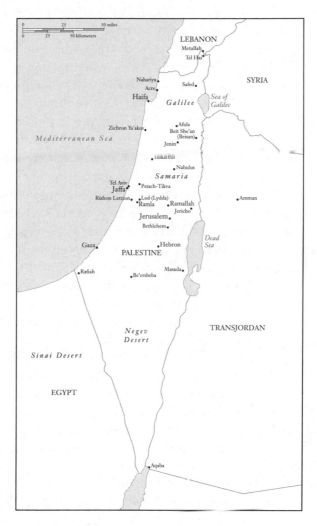

Palestine Mandate, 1922–1948

solution to "the Jewish Question."[58] The WZO had rejected the offer and stood firm to its Basel Program of 1897, which stated: "Zionism seeks to establish a home for the Jewish people in Palestine, secured under public law."[59] Weizmann persuaded Balfour, Lloyd George, and others that their Christian faith led them to take a position that aligned with British and Zionist interests. It was the interplay between biblical romanticism and broader geopolitical and imperial considerations that shaped policy making in London. Moreover, the Great War witnessed British leaders rethinking their positions in the context of shifting concerns over ally support. "Zionism, be it right or wrong, good or bad," Balfour later wrote, is "of far more profounder import than the desire and prejudices of the 700,000 Arabs who now inhabit that ancient land."[60] The foreign secretary was poised to sign a declaration that established Palestine as "a national home for the Jewish people."[61]

Not everyone, however, shared Balfour's sentiments. Lord Curzon delivered a scathing rebuke of what he viewed as his government's double-dealing with the Arabs as well as its unrealistic assurances to the Jews.[62] For starters, Palestine was not an empty land; 700,000 Arabs—compared to 60,000 Jews—lived there with legitimate territorial claims. Clearly the small arid territory could not absorb a large portion of the world's 12 million Jews. Finally, the declaration referred to an entity called the Jewish "national home," language that came directly from the WZO. Curzon argued that it was purposely ambiguous so as to mask Zionism's true intention: the creation of an independent state rather than a Jewish spiritual center. For Curzon, the ambiguous term *national home* was no basis for a British commitment. Finally, there was McMahon's agreement with Husayn. Curzon believed "Palestine was included in the areas as to which Great Britain pledged itself that they should be Arab and independent in the future," arguing along with numerous high-ranking British officials in Cairo that a pro-Zionist proclamation would anger the Arabs who were holding Britain to its word. He urged that the Balfour Declaration not be issued.[63]

In this game of political chess, Weizmann was a master, even toward those within the Jewish community who challenged him. In the face of wide-ranging critiques, his behind-the-scenes negotiations with Washington were arguably what tipped the scales.[64] He turned to his friend the Supreme Court justice Louis Brandeis who, in turn, lobbied the American president. Wilson offered no objections to the Zionist cause, convincing Lloyd George that Jewish influence extended all the way to the Oval Office. The Balfour Declaration of 1917 was approved a few weeks later.[65]

Above all, it emphasized the creation of a Jewish "national home" and also safeguarded the rights of Palestine's indigenous populations. Still, the vagueness of the term *national home*, as Curzon had warned, opened the way to a multiplicity of readings. Ultimately, the declaration was an attempt at appeasement, in which Britain sought to safeguard, first and foremost, its own self-interests, which would require shifting degrees of support for Arabs and Zionists in the years ahead.[66] Indeed, Britain's self-interest wasn't always clear, particularly in its early days in Palestine. In fact, Lloyd George had originally wanted the United States to take the mandated territory, but Wilson refused. Unlike Iraq, Palestine was not awash in oil, though the Iraq Petroleum Company would build a pipeline in the early 1930s from Mosul in northern Iraq to Palestine's coastal port, Haifa. Some Britons had an emotional attachment to the "holy land," which was no small matter, while others were enamored of the Zionist project, either because they disliked the Jews and wanted to ship them off to an arid wasteland or because they supported Jewish desires for their own state.[67]

Such support was shrewdly cultivated, as we have seen with Weizmann's efforts, and Zionist lobbying extended beyond his one-man crusade. During the Balfour negotiations, its reach was both real and perceived, though its impact on crucial Anglo-American relations and Palestine's future in the decades to come would be very real indeed. With the WZO, Palestine's Jewish community, or Yishuv, had global support from which it could draw substantial political and financial strength. Such support set it apart from other nationalist-based movements, including that of the Irish. Nonetheless, Britain read the Zionist movement in its developmentalist register. Lloyd George, Balfour, Curzon, and others regularly deployed the term "Jewish race," and were it not for an edit in one of the Balfour Declaration's final drafts, the document would have referred to the "Jewish race" instead of the "Jewish people." Despite this change, historical circumstances were shaping the British view of the Jews as a separate racial category. "There has been," Arnold Toynbee later wrote, "a 'racialization' of the division between those inside and those outside the civilised pale," and many Britons still considered the Jews to be on the outside.[68]

British officials also excluded Arabs—arguably more than Jews—from the category of civilized. Britain's self-proclaimed experts failed to acknowledge the Arabs' rich history in Palestine of elaborate legal, cultural, political, and economic systems.[69] Throughout the Arab countryside, patron-client relations between the *a'yan*—notable leaders, whose authority rested on claims of religious or genealogical status—and the vast peasantry stretched back centuries. Above all else, these relations rested on a moral and religious economy that ensured a variety of exchanges, including commodities, and most crucially access to land. Ottoman rule, however, had further integrated the region into capitalist markets, and patron-client relations—often understood in overlapping and competing notions of kinship, village, region, and tribe—began to transform. The Ottomans also ushered in new land codes in the 1850s, with the result that wealthy Arabs from outside Palestine embarked on unprecedented land purchases. Still, not until twenty years later did the

greatest threat to *a'yan* hegemony emerge when European Jewish settlers with substantial capital entered the land grab in Palestine. Unable
to till crops or pasture their herds on lands they believed rightfully their
own, the fellaheen, or Arab peasants, raided and harassed Jewish settlements. They also questioned long-standing patron-client relations.
An increasingly politicized consciousness rooted in personal grievances
emerged, one that many future British colonizers would scarcely consider plausible.

Vehement opposition to Zionism became the unifying theme, and
it was espoused in vernacular newspapers, poems, proverbs, and other
cultural forms, particularly in the wake of the Balfour Declaration. Britain's new policy also drove popular radicalism into the arms of a growing
nationalist movement that tapped into the burgeoning mass of landless and land-poor peasants, further challenging *a'yan* hegemony. Locals
expressed this propensity toward unity and division through proverbs
such as "I and my brother unite to fight against my cousin, but I and my
cousin unite to fight against a stranger." They wanted to toss out Palestine's strangers, be they Jewish or British.

Not surprisingly, paroxysms of strife soon unfolded. Vladimir Jabotinsky, a Russian-born Jew and decorated soldier who had fought for
Britain in the Jewish Legion during the Great War, was, by March 1920,
openly training scores of volunteers in vigilantism, or self-defense,
depending on one's perspective. "The pogrom is now liable to break
out any day," he warned Weizmann in his stream of alarming letters.[70]
His extremism differed from that of the Zionist Commission, which the
WZO had established under Weizmann's leadership. Through the commission, and its successor, the Jewish Agency, Britain aided Zionist colonization in Palestine, which included the construction of settlements,
further Arab land sales, and immigration. In time, the Jewish Agency
found itself under increasing fire from extremist groups, Jabotinsky's
among them, that deployed vigilante violence.

Less than a month after Jabotinsky raised the alarm in early 1920,
and Britain's head-in-the-sand response to Weizmann, who had traveled
to Palestine to warn British officials of the incipient violence, conflict
erupted in Jerusalem. At the start of the Muslim Nebi Musa celebrations, nearly seventy thousand Arabs, many from rural areas, congregated in the city square. Multiple injustices overshadowed the annual
religious celebration. Rates of Zionist immigration, land purchases, and
peasant evictions were skyrocketing, and British policies ranging from
crippling local tax rates to the abandonment of Faysal in Syria pushed
local Arabs, inclined toward measured resistance, to the brink. Decades

The Nebi Musa gathering prior to the riots, Jerusalem, April 1920

of peaceful coexistence in Palestine were shattered when Arabs attacked Jews in the Old City's labyrinth of alleyways, from which escape was nearly impossible. From the balcony of the Arab Club, an offshoot of the Damascus-based Arab nationalist organization, leaders delivered anti-Zionist rhetoric, and large crowds shouted "Independence, Independence!"[71] Some Arab police joined in the applause. Lootings, burglaries, rapes, and murders ensued, and rioters set homes alight and shattered tombstones. The British government called in the army, declared martial law, and sealed off the Old City. It also evacuated local garrisons from the riot's front lines, and the Old City Jews were left to fend for themselves. Jabotinsky and his volunteers were virtually powerless. The three-day riot left five Jews and twenty-eight Arabs dead, and two hundred Jews and scores of Arabs wounded.[72]

The British colonel and member of Churchill's Arabian spy posse Richard Meinertzhagen, who had spent the early part of the century crushing resistance to imperial rule in East Africa, soon intervened. He accused several members of the military and civil administration—nearly all of whom were opposed to the establishment of a Palestinian Jewish national home—not only of harboring anti-Semitic and anti-Zionist sentiments but also of inciting the riots and providing the Arab leadership with specific instructions. The Zionist Commission supported Meinertzhagen's claims, though a British commission of inquiry thought its men-on-the-spot were guilty of "overconfidence" and largely blamed the Zionists "whose impatience to achieve their ultimate goal and indiscretion are largely responsible for this unhappy state of feeling."[73] It also considered Arab motivations, conceding that the British "faced with a native population thoroughly exaperated [sic] by a sense of injustice and disappointed hopes, panic stricken as to their future and as to ninety per cent of their numbers in consequence bitterly hostile to the British."[74] British officials ignored their government's role in the events, singling out Jabotinsky in particular and sentencing him to fifteen years in prison. Scores of other Jews whose sentences were harsher than those of the Arabs joined him. The commander of the British forces in Egypt and Palestine, General Sir Walter Norris Congreve, eventually scuttled Meinertzhagen and released Jabotinsky and his compatriots. Congreve was hardly a Zionist ally, however. "I dislike them all equally," he wrote. "Arabs and Jews and Christians, in Syria and Palestine, they are all alike, a beastly people. The whole lot of them is not worth a single Englishman!"[75]

"This regime has declared open war on the Jews of Palestine," one Zionist periodical announced, as the Nebi Musa dust was settling. "There had been no clashes like these for a hundred years," Moshe Smilansky wrote in *Ha'aretz*, pointing to Britain's role in redefining and deepening the divides between the Arab and Jewish communities in Palestine.[76] In the coming years, British officials made new self-interested proclamations, often adjusted Jewish immigration quotas, and reassured Arabs that Palestine was not to be a Jewish "national home" but rather there would be a Jewish "national home" in Palestine. In September 1923, Britain's assumption of mandatory power and responsibility in Palestine under the League of Nations institutionalized a never-ending balancing act. Regardless of whatever pro-Arab and anti-Zionist sentiments had spurred the Nebi Musa riots, Britain was, under the terms of the mandate system, charged with forming a "sacred trust of civilisation" with those "peoples not yet able to stand by themselves under the strenuous conditions of the modern world." It was also "responsible for putting into effect the declaration originally made on November 2, 1917, by the Government of His Britannic Majesty," and for recognizing "the historical connection of the Jewish people with Palestine and to the grounds for reconstituting their national home in that country."[77]

Britain's ability to maneuver politically around a "Jewish national home" in Palestine was therefore greatly diminished as the League of Nations held British officials to the original Mandate terms, particularly after Britain began its questionable bilateral negotiations with Iraq. Instead, British officials, when it suited their nation's interests, sought to reassure Palestine's Arab population by taking diplomatic measures and by issuing various mandatory-power white papers that introduced Jewish immigration quotas based on the "economic capacity of the country to absorb new arrivals."[78]

As Britain worked toward anointing Faysal king of Iraq, it likewise sought and created allies in Palestine, as in other parts of the empire, to serve its interests and facilitate local subjugation and control. As British officials worked with the Jewish Agency they also created the Supreme Muslim Council and appointed Al-Hajj Amin al-Husayni, a member of the powerful al-Husayni aristocracy, as its president. Al-Husayni, also appointed the grand mufti of Jerusalem, faced the impossible task of containing anti-British and anti-Zionist sentiment among the Arab population. At the same time, alternative sources of Arab power included rival *a'yan* who reasserted their hegemony in the face of continued rioting and British counterviolence. Much like the splintering of the Zionists with the more radical followers of Jabotinsky, the *a'yan* constituted a locus of power, meeting in Palestine Arab Congresses and creating an Arab Executive. This organization operated separately from, though sometimes in concert with, the grand mufti.[79] These cleavages, tinged as they were with local politics, power, and opportunism, would become crucial to British interests in the years ahead as local officials exploited them to further divide the Arab population and reward those Arabs who were willing to use violence against their own people if it meant furthering Britain's agenda in the Mandate.

It was into this divisive and charged political atmosphere that Henry Tudor's band of Auxiliaries and Black and Tans stepped when they disembarked at the ancient port city of Jaffa. The men landed in mandate territory beleaguered but battle ready. Their first opponent was the sweltering heat. Kitted out in khaki uniforms and Stetson hats, complete with a thin green band that tipped to their Irish heritage, the new arrivals marched through the streets of Jaffa and paused only for an occasional vomit from the effects of dust and humidity.[80]

Tudor soon had unrivaled policing power in Palestine. He took charge of the new seven-hundred-member, Irish-tested British gendarmerie; the Palestine gendarmerie that consisted of British officers who oversaw Arab and Jewish members; and a small British garrison. Joining the fresh recruits from Ireland were others from Malta, Sudan, Southern Rhodesia, Mauritius, and Cyprus, and they all came with their own ideas, prejudices, and learned experiences, which extended into Palestine's broader colonial administration. Yet none of the new arrivals had any local knowledge, few spoke even rudimentary Arabic, and only a handful had experience outside Ireland. Palestine's first high commissioner, a British Jew and ardent Zionist, Herbert Samuel, was skeptical, as were Congreve and Wilson, before the IRA took Wilson out in Belgravia. Congreve sarcastically chided Churchill for his plan to govern the region with "hot air, aeroplanes [and] Jews," along with a band of former Black and Tans, which together would "no doubt" bring "profound peace in that somewhat uncertain country."[81] "The real fact," he said, was that "Winston is between a cheap and fatal tenure of Mesopotamia and Palestine and a *real* occupation with security and peace which he can't pay for."[82] That the British Empire operated on a shoestring budget was a common theme.[83] In Palestine, prior to the arrival of Tudor and his men, there had been fewer than twenty British police officers for a population of over 600,000.

The influx of the Irish-trained forces quickly changed the Mandate's policing tenor and would have long-term effects on other parts of the empire as well. Tudor's men spread paramilitary tactics and training and included former Royal Irish Constabulary officers like James Munro, Raymond Cafferata, and Douglas Duff. Within two years, Tudor, a half-step ahead of the IRA, left for the coast of Newfoundland, where he lived incognito for the rest of his life. Prior to his departure, his units became a full-fledged police force, and Munro served as the first commandant of the British Police Training School in Palestine. By the early 1930s, the Mandate replaced Ireland as the official and unofficial training ground for colonial police indoctrination, and it produced scores of senior police officers and future paramilitary counterinsurgents for the entire empire.[84]

In the late 1920s, as the Palestine police force militarized, a relative period of calm was shattered. Commandeering accommodations along the coastal roads to Tiberias and Haifa and making a destructive mess of things, the police had already established a poor local reputation. British police detachments tossed a resistant Arab clerk—along with his filing cabinet, desk, and chair—out a window, though much darker images emerged. According to Douglas Duff, hanging on the wall in Nablus was "an old cigarette-tin containing the brains of a man whose skull [one policeman] had splintered with his rifle-butt."[85] He reflected on the *mentalité* that underwrote such collective behavior: "We regarded 'the lesser breeds without the law' far differently than is the case today. Mentally, I suppose, we were still living in the great days of Empire; our attitude was that of Britons of the Diamond Jubilee era, to us all non-Europeans were 'wogs,' and Western non-Britons only slightly more worthy." Duff said that seeing the can of brains "altered something deep inside of me; people who owned skins other than pink Western ones became human beings."[86] The future police inspector for Jerusalem, however, scarcely enacted his self-described transformation. By his own, conflicted account, Duff believed in liberal imperialism's firm hand.

Duff's proclivities, and those of his subordinates, were soon on full display as the clash between Arab and Jewish claims to Jerusalem's Western Wall came to a head. Both Muslims and Jews regarded the wall as a sacred place. Muslims called it al-Buraq, named for the site where the Prophet Muhammad reportedly tied his mythical steed, al-Buraq, before ascending to paradise. They also considered it the western border of al-Haram al-Sharif, or Temple Mount, located on a hill in Jerusalem's Old City. It was one of the most venerated holy sites for Muslims,

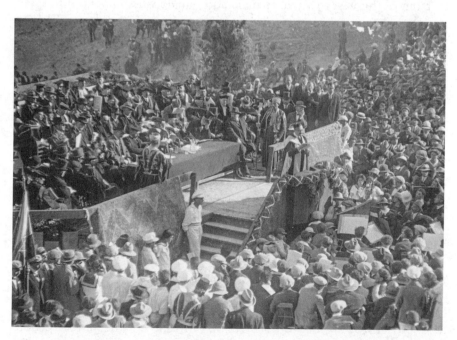

Chaim Weizmann speaking at Hebrew University, Jerusalem, 1925

Jews, and Christians. Jews, for their part, thought the Western or "Wailing" Wall was the last remnant of Jerusalem's Jewish Temple that the Romans destroyed in the first century. For hundreds of years, a flexible understanding had evolved whereby Muslims had legal claim to the wall, though each religious group accessed it and prohibitions, in practice, were overlooked. That is, until the Balfour Declaration.

In early 1918, Weizmann was already complaining to Balfour about the "miserable dirty cottages and derelict buildings" near the wall, assuring him that the Zionists would liberally compensate for the "handing over of the Wailing Wall [which was] in the hands of some doubtful Moghreb religious community."[87] "A Jew of prominence approached certain of the Muslims interested with a pecuniary offer," the Colonial Office soon reported, and "Muslim opinion thereupon became seriously agitated."[88] As tensions mounted, Jabotinsky saw the wall as *the* issue for galvanizing mass support for Zionist nationalism in the Mandate, staging public marches and facilitating religious intrusions into the long-standing status quo regulating the wall's access. Jews set up benches and chairs on the pavement abutting the wall during worship, contravening long-standing practices, and they objected to Muslim clearing of weeds growing in the interstices of the wall's stones. On the eve of Yom Kippur services in 1928, Jewish acolytes affixed a large screen to the pavement in front of the wall to separate male and female worshippers. Infuriated by another transgression of past practices, Muslim officials appealed to the British deputy district commissioner for Jerusalem Edward Keith-Roach, who ordered the police to remove the screen.

Duff and several former Black and Tan reinforcements soon arrived from Mount Scopus wearing steel helmets and marching as Arab residents cheered their arrival. The paramilitaries tore down the makeshift screen and threw it, along with a Jew who refused to let go, into the Kidron Valley. Days of unrest followed, and Duff's own xenophobia washed over him. He described cracking the whip he carried and indiscriminately kicking crowds: "Once again I experienced that strange and utterly sublime ecstasy of 'going berserk,' as my barbarian forefathers had done. I had no consciousness of what I was doing as I sprang at that crowd."[89] A "mob of police . . . a mob of gang leaders made a sudden swoop upon the assembly, took the place by storm as though it were a besieged fortress held by the enemy or a den of armed robbers, and made liberal use of their fists and elbows, scattering the worshippers in all directions," Weizmann's deputy Nahum Sokolow wrote. There was also "throwing of stones by Arab riff-raff. . . . The Jewish people must husband their resources and watch for an opportune moment."[90]

"If Jews cannot be guaranteed unrestricted rights of public worship . . . in their own National Home, of what value is the Palestine Mandate?," another Zionist supporter queried.[91]

British officials had little to say other than that they were fulfilling the Mandate's terms "for protecting what it has deemed to be 'existing rights' in the Holy Places . . . by seeking to maintain the *status quo*."[92] In November 1928, Britain issued a White Paper in which it stated:

> The Western or Wailing Wall formed part of the western exterior of the ancient Jewish Temple; as such it is holy to the Jewish community and their custom of praying there extends back to the Middle Ages and possibly further. The Wall is also part of the Haram-al-Sharif; as such it is holy to Moslems. Moreover, it is legally the absolute property of the Moslem community and the strip of pavement facing it is Waqf property, as is shown by documents preserved by the Guardian of the Waqf. The Jewish community have established an undoubted right of access to the pavement for the purposes of their devotions but, whenever protests were made by the Moslem authorities, the Turkish authorities repeatedly ruled that they would not permit such departures from the existing practice as the bringing of chairs and benches to the pavement. It is understood that a ruling prohibiting the bringing of screens to the pavement was given in 1912.[93]

Weizmann and other Zionist leaders publicly backed down in their attempts to upend the status quo, releasing a statement, at Britain's urging, recognizing "the inviolability of the Muslim Holy places." Jabotinsky, however, did not. He and his followers demanded outright possession of the wall, thereby splintering the Zionist community. "You [Jabotinsky] prepare the way for killing Jews," Itamar Ben-Avi, founder of the Hebrew newspaper *Doar HaYom* (*The Daily Mail*), wrote in January 1929. "You will be responsible for Jews' deaths and will be judged."[94] Despite such dire predictions, WZO leadership followed Jabotinsky's aggressive demands, using his outrageous claims to bargain for more moderate conciliations and to push Britain "toward a negotiated *modus vivendi* in which Zionist rights would be enlarged," as the historian Mary Ellen Lundsten points out.[95]

"Although the mandate entrusted to [us] did not explicitly refer to conciliation," British officials acknowledged, "[we] thought it a duty incumbent upon [us] to try to bring about a friendly settlement between the Parties."[96] This was a stunning admission of British naïveté. A "friendly settlement" was well out of reach, as al-Husayni strained to control Arab militants, who were incensed that Jabotinsky's followers vowed bloodshed if their demands were not met. A symbolic flashpoint, the wall represented competing claims to Palestine's past and future as well as real socioeconomic hardships disproportionately felt by Arab peasants who bore the brunt of British taxation and increased land sales.[97]

The Western Wall dispute sparked months of simmering tensions that erupted again in 1929, the consequences of which dwarfed the events from the previous year. In the early morning light of August 23, thousands of Arab peasants, whose socioeconomic grievances were ignited by the ongoing Western Wall disputes, streamed into Jerusalem from surrounding rural areas. At midday, chaos broke out among Arabs, Jews, and Mandate authorities. An understaffed British police force, which had been reduced during the ostensibly peaceful period, was incapable of controlling the mayhem. Reinforcements were brought in from Transjordan and Egypt. The mufti tried to restore calm, though his speech to the angry crowd appeared only to make matters worse. Disorder shook the city and spread throughout the Mandate. Some of the most alarming scenes unfolded in Hebron, thirty kilometers south of Jerusalem. There Raymond Cafferata, who had previously served in Ireland, had just assumed command of a twenty-three-man police force that was responsible for forty villages and twenty thousand people, most of whom were Arabs. A small Jewish population of eight hundred also resided in Hebron and had done so for generations until peaceful relations began to fray with the Zionist push for increased immigration. Arab nationalist responses came partly from their resentment of old Jewish merchant families to whom they were often indebted, as well as from their anger at foreigners who dispossessed them of their land and violated the sanctity of Islam.[98]

Patrolling Hebron and its rural areas in a five-horsepower Citroën that was scarcely desert ready, let alone riot proof, Cafferata abandoned his vehicle for horseback when the riot was no longer controllable. Firing rounds into crowds, he and his men narrowly cleared a path through the hordes in an effort to rescue Jews trapped in their own homes. Cafferata entered a house and later described the scene: "An Arab [was] in the act of cutting off a child's head with a sword. . . . I shot him low in the groin. Behind him was a Jewish woman smothered in blood with a man I recognized as [an Arab] police constable, named Issa Sherrif from Jaffa. . . . He was standing over the woman with a dagger in his hand. He saw me and bolted into another room, shouting in Arabic, 'Your honor, I am a policeman.' I got into the room and shot him."[99] The sight of an

Arab policeman perpetrating such an act was not an anomaly. Gaining the consistent loyalties of local police—both Arabs and Jews—would forever elude British forces in Palestine, and elsewhere in the empire.

The bright lines of divide blurred over and over again. In Hebron nearly two-thirds of the Jewish community took refuge in the homes of their Arab neighbors. Some of those providing safe havens were seriously injured as a result, while others actively cared for the wounded. In the end, over sixty Jews died, some tortured and mutilated. David Ben Gurion, the head of the Jewish Agency, likened the massacre to a pogrom. This was the most gruesome attack and part of an unprecedented week in the Mandate: 133 Jews were dead and another 339 wounded; at least 116 Arabs were killed with 232 wounded, though the Arab casualties were probably underreported.[100]

Cafferata received the King's Police Medal and became a local cult hero back home in Liverpool for his rescue of the Jews and his defense of British honor. "I am not anti-Semitic nor anti-Arab, I'm merely pro-British," he reflected. It was a facile though revealing sentiment as Pax Britannica in Palestine was creating conflict under the auspices of rule of law. Britain's complicity in the events leading up to the massacre was unquestionable. Some in the local colonial administration, steeped in the precedent of Ireland, were thinking, as Cafferata did, that Palestine was a "repetition of the Irish show," and unless Britain made some concessions to Arab demands, like limiting Jewish immigration and land sales as well as claims to Muslim holy places, there was going to be an explosion on a greater scale.[101]

Political vicissitudes were not the only threats to stability in the Mandate. Black and Tan culture was washing away whatever goodwill remained between Britain and Palestine's local population. After Duff and his men went "berserk" at the Western Wall, they threaded their way through the Mandate's countryside subduing Arab unrest that was erupting beyond Jerusalem. He later wrote that he "personally, saw a deal of the beating and 'third degree' that was endured by many dozens of people in the hill village . . . and [there were] many scores of cases where the 'Hoist,' or the 'water-can,' was employed." He continued:

> The victim was held down, flat on his back, while a thin-spouted coffee-pot poured a trickle of water up his nose, while his head was clamped immovably between cushions that left no marks of bruising. It is not pleasant to talk about and even unpleasanter to admit having witnessed. Usually, we British officers remained discreetly in the background, not wishing to have the skirts of

our garments soiled, but we were ready to benefit by information wrung by our subordinates from the wretched suspects or
criminals.[102]

Later written off by senior officials as a bad apple, Duff located his own
behavior within the broader, permissible norms of the time. In fact, he
would be defended, and commended, for his actions during the Western Wall tensions. Only in 1931 did the high commissioner review a
criminal court case against Duff in which he stood accused of ordering
the "bodily distress" of one Farid Muhammad Sheik Ibrahim. The case
gave the higher-ups a reason to scuttle him, not necessarily because of
any outrage over his use of torture, but rather because of his publicly
foolish ways, which included the Western Wall incident, not to mention
his difficult personality.[103]

The impact of Duff's handiwork and that of his brethren was irre-
versible. A university student, Chaim Shalom Halevi, wrote to his family
in Europe, who were still awaiting immigration to Palestine, of Duff's
"horrible acts" at the Western Wall. Halevi considered these acts intrinsic to Britain's police forces and administration, which included District
Commissioner Keith-Roach. "My heart hurts too much and the wound
has not yet healed so it is still impossible for me to evaluate the matter,"
Halevi wrote. He later reflected on the antipathy that emerged between
two populations that sought sovereignty on the same land: "They hate
us and they are right, because we hate them too." The only way to realize the Zionist dream was to rid the country of Arabs, he wrote.[104]

The newly elected and untested British Labour government, led by
Ramsay MacDonald, sent out a commission of inquiry, this one under
the direction of Sir Walter Shaw. Like Cafferata, Palestine's new high
commissioner, Sir John Chancellor, endorsed making some concessions
to the Arabs, if only to establish some kind of stability in the best interests of the British administration. In Palestine's countryside, the Shaw
Commission collected Arab testimonies, chronicling bitter resentment
and opposition to British policies. In the village of Qabab, local resident
shaykh Sa'id Abu Ghosh told the commission:

> Contrary to what you've been told, we understand well what is
> intended for us by the Balfour declaration [wa'd], and we realize
> the dangers and catastrophes which have befallen us and which
> will eliminate us. Even if the city-dwellers are silent, we the peas-
> ants will resist it with all of our power and we will not be silent.
> If a peasant sells his land to the Jews, he does so because of the

abundance of taxes which are imposed upon him by the government in support of the Balfour declaration and on account of the
poor economic condition to which this cursed declaration has
given birth. Verily, we have come to reckon our presence [*dhill*]
an apparition of the Balfour declaration and to fear it for the
great multitude of things which with it has pained us.[105]

The Shaw Commission's final report took a conciliatory position
and became a lightning rod for the ongoing question of whether Arab
demands for self-government could be reconciled with the terms of the
Balfour Declaration. Published in March 1930, the report refused to concede any premeditation for the recent violence or apportion any blame
to the mufti or other Arab leaders for incitement. Instead, the larger
issues of continued Jewish immigration and land sales, together with the
Mandate's dual obligation, were said to be at the heart of things.[106]

The League of Nations Permanent Mandates Commission (PMC)
scheduled a special session in June on the matter. Weizmann led the
Zionist lobbying effort, as he had done during the Western Wall riots
in 1929, when he effectively leveraged the PMC's Zionist sympathies
and rising anti-Arab sentiments, which were no doubt tied to the PMC's
misgivings over the ongoing Iraqi deal. Leading the charge against the
Shaw Commission report, Weizmann was whispering into the ears of
PMC members. The special session quickly descended into a near full-
frontal assault on the Shaw Report, along with an attack on Britain's lack
of political and coercive will. Why hadn't British officials used more of
an iron fist? members of the PMC queried. Why weren't there tougher
censorship laws and harsher interventions at the start of the rioting? And
why suspend Jewish immigration, which was nothing short of a concession to Arab violence? There was some dissent among the commission,
but as far as the PMC was concerned, Arab demands were irreconcilable
with Balfour's promises. Its task was to carry out the terms of the Mandate, not change them, even if these terms were increasingly telescoped
around the single issue of Jewish immigration as opposed to the "dual
obligation."[107]

Weizmann galvanized support against the government's freshly
minted Passfield White Paper, which sought to turn the recommendations of the Shaw Report, together with the subsequent Hope Simpson Report, into a policy of limiting Jewish immigration.[108] Churchill,
Lloyd George, former colonial secretary Leopold Amery, and former
foreign secretary Austen Chamberlain were all in Weizmann's corner.
MacDonald sent a letter to Weizmann a few months later that effec-

tively relegated the White Paper to the empire's dustbin. The Balfour Declaration, codified into the Palestine Mandate, contained, as Lloyd George reminded the prime minister, "the ruling words."[109] Moreover, the PMC's calls for more British repression reflected the League's liberal imperial, or "imperial international," ethos. This, together with Weizmann's astuteness in lobbying every corner for Zionist support and tapping into the growing demands for self-determination sweeping the colonized world, meant the Mandate was on a collision course.

State-directed violence was reaching a crucial maturation point in Palestine and elsewhere in the empire. This violence, with all its evolving logic, would soon be deployed in unprecedented forms and scope when Palestinian Arabs again took up arms and directed their anger squarely at His Majesty's foot soldiers. It would be there, in the Mandate, that the likes of Harris and his air control underlings, together with methods of intelligence gathering and interrogation, and a deliberate perpetuation and institutionalization of the empire's Black and Tan methods, would coalesce. This convergence was not planned; rather, it unfolded in response to escalating events in the Mandate, as did the extraordinary regulatory measures, accreting in the empire for decades, needed to legalize British lawlessness.

CHAPTER 5

Imperial Convergence

In June 1939, as war clouds gathered over Europe and countless Jews continued desperately to seek safe passage from the continent's eastern reaches to Palestine's promised land, Jamal al-Husayni, the president of the Palestine Arab Delegation to the League of Nations, was cloistered within Geneva's once elegant, now shabby lakeside Hotel Victoria. Putting pen to paper, he begged the League's Permanent Mandates Commission to investigate the horrors unfolding not in the Third Reich but rather in Britain's liberal imperialist regime in Palestine.[1]

In this sliver of a mandated territory, no bigger than Belgium or Wales, the League, under Article 22 of its Covenant, had bestowed on Britain a "sacred trust of civilisation" to promote the "well-being and development" of Palestine's inhabitants.[2] Al-Husayni saw little that was sacred or trustworthy about British rule. Born into one of Jerusalem's most influential and political families, the middle-aged, moustached Arab diplomat with piercingly alert eyes had spent nearly his entire adult life under British shadows. During the interwar years, he became a quietly important player in the debacle unfolding in Palestine. He crisscrossed the mandated territory and the broader Middle East, the United States, and Europe and was known, even in British circles, for his pragmatism and conciliatory approach. Time and again he addressed Palestine's spiraling civil and colonial disorder and the triangulated intractability of Anglo, Arab, and Jewish relations, particularly around the question of expanding Jewish immigration and land purchases.[3]

By the time al-Husayni found himself in the Hotel Victoria's tired grandeur, the situation in his homeland had been dire for three years. The Arab Revolt, as it was known, had ignited as a general strike in April 1936 and then spread throughout much of the territory's rural areas. Palestine's Arab population was demanding the end of open-ended Jewish immigration and land sales, a repeal of the Balfour Declaration and its promise of a Jewish "national home," and independence. Britain's response was draconian. Arab politicians, as well as European missionaries, local colonial officials, residents of Palestine, and military and police personnel, documented those repressive measures targeted primarily at the Palestinian Arab population.[4] Some of these accounts were brought to Britain's successive high commissioners in Palestine, as well as to the archbishop of the Anglican Church and Britain's War and Colonial offices.[5]

The official responses were denials that had been well rehearsed in previous imperial dramas. In this instance, according to British officials, the accounts contained lies and exaggerations that were the handiwork of Arab propagandists, fueled in no small way by the opportunistic inveigling of Europe's rising fascist tide that sought to discredit the good name of Britain and its empire.[6] Neville Chamberlain, who had become prime minister in May 1937, and his cabinet dismissed the flow of allegations coming from Palestine as "absolutely baseless" and declared "the character of the British soldier is too well known to require vindication."[7]

Drawing on his international reputation and mindful of the flow of accusations piling up on his desk, al-Husayni went above Britain's imperial head to the League of Nations. "Your Excellency," he demurred to the "President" of the PMC, "British troops . . . have adopted increasing measures of repression and terrorisation against the Arabs of Palestine who stand to defend their country." Gesturing to the situation's gravity through historical analogy, he continued:

> Such atrocities of the dark ages, to which the human race, nowadays, look back with disgust and horror, of torturing men during criminal investigation and assaulting peaceful people and destroying their properties wholesale when peacefully lying within their homes are actions that have daily been perpetrated in the Holy Land during the greater part of the last three years.

Among other excesses, al-Husayni described the "scorching" of body parts with "hot iron rods," "severe beating with lashes," the "pulling out [of] nails and scorching the skin under them by special appliances," and the "pulling of the sexual organs." He detailed the British forces' widespread ransacking and looting of homes, summary executions, disappearances, denial of food and water to innocent civilians, rapes of women and girls, and destruction of livestock. The diplomat closed his appeal with a reasonable request: "If the Mandatory [power of Britain] is innocent of these excesses then our demand for a neutral enquiry should be welcomed by all concerned."[8]

The outcome of al-Husayni's appeal hung in an international balance that weighed the realpolitik of fascism's advances. It was also calibrated within a framework of permissible norms. These norms were deeply rooted in the *longue durée* of liberal imperialism's spread, particularly in Britain and its empire. There, stretching back before the Victorian era, conceptions of brown and Black subjects, justifications for, if not the necessity of, violence, and moral claims to a superior civilization created a tapestry of ideas that found expression in colonial administrations and imperial security forces, enabling legal scaffoldings, and nationalist conceptions of Britain. So, too, did they sometimes find expression in the League's Permanent Mandates Commission, which was as much a reflection of liberal imperialism's agenda as it was an oversight agent for its alleged transgressions.

Given the rising global anticolonial discourse and condemnations of British-directed repression that infused protests, political tracts, and literary works in the empire, al-Husayni surely had some knowledge of the ways interwar Palestine was a convergence site of ideas, institutions, and personalities that had been incubated elsewhere in the imperial world. In this world, violence had evolved into a framework that was not simply justificatory but was also internalized as de rigueur by many of those wielding power, from the highest reaches of British decision making to the lowest levels of execution. On the eve of the Second World War, it was in mandatory Palestine where decades of liberal imperialist ideas and practices that had matured across vast swaths of the British Empire would consolidate in the most dramatic and consequential of ways. The reach and impact of these ideas and practices, as well as of the individuals executing them, would extend well beyond Palestine, where Britain would systematically deploy violence in its effort to hang on to the empire and secure a place in the new world order.

Three years before Jamal al-Husayni issued his dramatic appeal to the PMC, the Right Reverend Weston Henry Stewart had embarked on

similar, albeit lower-level, entreaties. In early June 1936, reports from
his flock of missionaries and other God-fearing Christians in Palestine
suggested that British forces were unleashing terror on innocent Arabs.
Ensconced in his Jerusalem rectory, the bespectacled Anglican archdeacon scrutinized details of wanton killing of innocent civilians, senseless
damage to property, blowing up of villages, and widespread looting,
among other disturbing incidents. He had already paid a call to the Mandate's chief secretary, John Hathorn Hall, to raise the alarm; nothing
changed and the time had come to put his concerns in writing. "From
every side complaints are reaching me daily of the unnecessary and quite
indiscriminate roughness which is being displayed by the British Police
in their handling of the native, and particularly the Arab, population,"
he relayed to Hall. In the case of Arab suspects, "the British Police" had
"definitely ordered to 'Duff them up' "—a phrase that referred, according to the archdeacon, to the infamous Douglas Duff and his band of
former Black and Tans who introduced the term "Duffing up" into common parlance in Palestine and later to the global discourse on prisoner
abuse. Stewart stated that the police "are endeavoring to take the law
into their own hands. . . . And it is certainly my business, as representing
for the time being the Anglican Church, to speak out when fundamental

Palestine Police Force, armored car in Nazareth, Arab Revolt, 1936–39

principles of justice are being overridden and basic Christian standards are being ignored."[9]

A week after the archdeacon's letter, another landed on the chief secretary's desk, this one from his own government welfare inspector, Margaret Dixon, who had ventured into the Mandate's northern region. According to the inspector, she "heard such constant rumours of atrocities" in the area that she undertook a full inspection of five villages, as was her duty. She confirmed to the chief secretary that British military troops were, in fact, blazing through villages, where they beat local men, broke apart doors and windows, and "smashed to atoms . . . furniture, crockery, sewing machines, gramophones, [and] radios." The troops were "ordered even to grind [the Bedouin] tents to pieces under their tanks. . . . I beg to state that I consider these bullying terrorising methods are such that no decent fair-minded person can hear of them without shame and disgust."[10]

Chief Secretary Hall, who was the high commissioner's right-hand man, responded immediately both to the archdeacon and to his own welfare inspector. He reassured Stewart that "after more than six weeks of incessant, harassing and frequently dangerous duty, the strain was beginning to tell on some of the men . . . but, in any event, [the police inspector] has, I am sure, now succeeded in steadying the unsteady ones." Moreover, he underscored the likelihood that such allegations were "exaggeration due to political motives."[11] A few days after Dixon filed her report, she was summoned in front of a Mr. Moody, one of the chief secretary's minions who, according to Dixon, "had the unpleasant task of censuring me for going to make certain investigations without the authority of the Government." When Dixon threatened resignation, she was informed that it "would considerably embarrass the Government at this time." She was "to make no further enquiries of this sort without first referring to the Government." Dixon stayed on for another couple of years, though she refocused her energies on benign women and children's issues, which was her original mandate.[12] As for the archdeacon, his sense of foreboding mounted. He privately wrote that above all else, "the general situation . . . is getting steadily worse."[13]

In the weeks and months ahead, Stewart and his coterie of missionaries filled their files with reports of continuing abuses. The early 1930s had witnessed mounting Arab attacks against Jewish settlers and colonial authorities. In 1933 the Nazis seized power, Hitler became chancellor, the Reichstag went up in flames, and Nazi mobs marched through Munich and Vienna, all of which transformed the plight of European Jews and, with it, the volatile situation in Palestine. League of Nations

British security forces during blasting operations of Arab houses, Arab Revolt in Palestine, 1936–39

members pressed Britain, for different reasons, to accept more Jews into Palestine. Some states, including Poland, Romania, and Hungary, were eager to rid themselves of Jews residing in their countries, while others wanted to save them.[14] Regardless of competing European logic, the result was the same: between 1933 and 1936, the Mandate swelled with some four hundred thousand refugees, an 85 percent increase of Jewish immigrants over the three-year period. Constituting around 30 percent of Palestine's population, Jewish settlers continued purchasing land, largely from Arab peasants, thanks in part to the World Zionist Organization's agreement with the Nazis that allowed Jews to import capital to Palestine. Crippled by colonial tax burdens, limited access to credit, a series of bad harvests, and effects of the global depression, nearly one-third of the impoverished fellaheen were already landless in 1930, and another 75 percent had insufficient land to eke out a subsistence livelihood. An Arab peasant described his dire circumstances to *Falastin*, Palestine's leading Arabic-language newspaper:

> I sell my land and property because the Government compels
> me to pay taxes and tithes at a time when I do not possess the

necessary means of subsistence for myself and my family. In the circumstances I am forced to appeal to a rich person for a loan which I undertake to refund together with an interest of 50% after a month or two. I keep renewing the bill and doubling the debt . . . which eventually forces me to sell my land in order to refund my debt out of which I took only a meager sum.[15]

Such indebtedness skyrocketed, and together with growing land-lessness, Arab peasants began permanently emigrating to Haifa, Jaffa, and Jerusalem, where they worked mainly as casual laborers. Moreover, while Jewish capital led to a unique industrial expansion during the Great Depression that created new urban employment in Palestine, most jobs went to Jewish workers, which generated further Arab resentment.[16]

Young educated men from the villages found fertile ground for radical nationalist ideas, and the rural countryside, particularly in the Triangle—the northern regions of Nablus, Jenin, and Tulkarm—became a hotbed of dissent. Much like revolutionary Ireland, songs and poems deployed evocative language through simple form and verse to reach not only the rural areas but urban markets and coffee shops as well. Locals read aloud and sang works by artists including Ibrahim Tuqan and 'Abd al-Rahim Mahmud. By many accounts, these works were crucial to the spread of more radical ideas.[17] Among Arab youth, for instance, one song in particular circulated widely:

> *Swords renew the youth of age*
> *and blood erase the life of disgrace.*
> *Students of Palestine it is now time,*
> *Wake up and die to redeem your fatherland. . . .*
>
> *Walk on the edges of swords*
> *and sell your blood in the way of your country*
> *Swords shall judge*
> *Palestine never give up*
> *We shall all die for your prosperity.*[18]

During the late 1920s and early '30s, multiple populist Arab political parties materialized in Palestine. It was, however, the radical Islamic reformist Shaykh 'Izz al-Din al-Qassam who zeroed in on the rapidly expanding dispossessed and casual laborers in the urban slums at a time when cheap agricultural imports and a series of crop failures worsened the economic situation of those remaining in the countryside. He offered them all a Janus-faced message that drew on traditional notions of Arab yesteryear and on newer ideas that centered on democracy, the nation, and reformist Islam. Al-Qassam's message effectively created a direct challenge not only to the Zionists and British rule but also to the *a'yan*, through whom British authorities had hoped to wield influence and maintain some modicum of peace.[19]

A rapidly growing peasant consciousness had caught the attention of the Shaw Commission, which underscored how the "Arab fellaheen and villagers are . . . probably more politically minded than many of the people of Europe."[20] In practical terms, this meant the colonial-appointed mufti al-Hajj Amin al-Husayni—Jamal al-Husayni's cousin—found himself in an increasingly untenable position as he sought to maintain credibility with the British as well as with an increasingly radical and militant population, while also satisfying his self-interest. Al-Qassam's followers, meanwhile, began mounting small armed attacks on Zionist villages in the early 1930s, and in November 1935 al-Qassam readied for a full-scale revolt. British forces killed him before a widespread uprising could take root. His death left peasants and populist organizations with a martyr, a legacy of militant nationalism, and a model for armed bands.

Characteristically, the British dismissed al-Qassam as a charlatan and his followers as fanatics. Blinded by their warped understanding of Arabs that stretched back to Lawrence of Arabia and other self-professed experts, British officials misjudged the grassroots level of discontent into which al-Qassam had tapped. Instead, they located the roots of Arab dissent in the notables' struggle for power: the mufti's al-Husayni family was on one side of the divide, and their rivals, the Nashashibis, were on the other. In contrast, Ben-Gurion was far more prescient in his assessment. He realized that al-Qassam's death at the hands of the British "was a watershed in the development of Arab consciousness."[21]

The Mandate was on the precipice of a massive revolt. All that was needed was a spark, which came on April 15, 1936, at a checkpoint on the Nablus-to-Tulkarm road, when assailants, most likely Qassamites, shot two Jewish passengers. That touched off a series of reprisals and counterreprisals between Arab and Jewish organizations. On April 19, various Arab militant organizations, backed by a "new grassroots political infrastructure," called for a general strike. "Alongside the national committees," as the historian Charles Anderson points out, "there were committees for strike supervision, medical relief, financial support, provisioning, legal services, and the boycott of Jewish and British goods, as well as arbitration and conflict resolution bodies and a host of women's and students' groups." A "process of rebel state formation" was under

Arab Higher Committee, April 1936. Jamal al-Husayni is in the back row, far left; Mufti al-Hajj Amin al-Husayni is in the front row, second from left.

way, organized around the principle of popular sovereignty.[22] High-ranking *a'yan*—including the al-Husayni and Nashashibi families—fell in line in an effort to retake control. Less than a week later, the mufti, together with a range of Arab parties, set up the Arab Higher Committee, a clear indication of militant nationalists entering into Palestinian politics. It declared that the general strike would continue until British officials ended Jewish immigration, banned land sales, and met a host of other demands.

The British government then undertook a series of steps that consolidated decades of legalized lawlessness into a set of emergency powers that would become the model for future counterinsurgency campaigns. In 1931, in the wake of the Western Wall violence and the League's chastening of Britain's lack of coercive will, the mandatory government passed the Palestine (Defence) Order in Council. It conferred on the high commissioner a set of powers that exceeded any similar legislation to date. Based on earlier codes in Ireland and India, it had lain unpublished in the proverbial drawer until the general strike and, with it, the start of the Arab Revolt. Arthur Wauchope, a wounded veteran of the South African War and career military man who became Palestine's high commissioner in 1931, was thus enabled to declare a state of emergency in the Mandate on April 19, 1936. The new regulations included authorization to take possession of buildings and essential items; control of transport, firearms, telecommunications, and shipping; press regulation and censorship; arrests without warrants; detention without trial; deportation; the power to demolish buildings, including villages and homes; and the imposition of the death penalty for discharging firearms and sabotaging phone and rail lines.[23]

Air Vice Marshal Richard Peirse, the military man in charge of Palestine and Transjordan since 1933, and his successor, Lieutenant General John Greer Dill, who took charge in September 1936, believed the emergency regulations were inadequate, particularly when it came to the punitive destruction of property and the unleashing of reprisals, which had been permissible in Ireland. That the Collective Responsibility and Punishment Ordinances had been on the books in Palestine since the mid-1920s seemed to matter little; nor did the recently enacted Collective Fines Ordinance. Peirse wanted martial law. Officials from the Colonial and War offices met in London with Attorney General Donald Somervell, a former commissioned officer in India and Mesopotamia, and Solicitor General Terence O'Connor, who had served in West Africa, and the military was furious with their determination. "Even at the time of the Jacobite risings in 1715 and 1745 no such powers were ever claimed by the armed forces of the Crown as are now claimed or recommended by the military authorities," Somervell and O'Connor said. They also insisted martial law wouldn't bestow on the military the powers it wanted, determining it to be, in fact, too restrictive. For instance, civil courts in Palestine could well challenge repressive military actions and could also decide that a state of war didn't exist. "This meeting effectively signed the death warrant of martial law," the legal historian Simpson underscores. "Martial law was just too restrictive of the powers of the soldiers."[24]

It was a crucial moment in the evolution of legalized lawlessness in the empire, as Britain's attorney general and solicitor general, along with others in the meeting, recommended a new code of regulations that conferred and spelled out the military's draconian power. In martial law's place came the Palestine Martial Law (Defence) Order in Council of September 26, 1936. It was so named because, as Simpson reminds us, "the cabinet decision to introduce martial law was known, and the title was intended to show no weakening in government resolution, and to give the impression to the Arab rebels, who would not be familiar with the technicalities of the subject, that martial law, with its overtones of ruthless military action, was being introduced." Subsequently a new Palestine (Defence) Order in Council on March 18, 1937, gave even more power to the executive. Section 6(1) of the new order stated that the high commissioner might "make such Regulations . . . as appear to him in his unfettered discretion to be necessary or expedient for securing the public safety, the defence of Palestine, the maintenance of public order and the suppression of mutiny, rebellion and riot, and for maintaining supplies and services essential to the life of the community."[25]

Shades of the empire's Victorian past were cast into the Mandate's present when the nineteenth-century political philosopher James Fitzjames Stephen's avowal that "law is nothing but regulated force" was taken to its logical conclusion in Palestine. Necessity and legitimate violence—issues that had animated legal debates over state-directed violence in colonies like Demerara, Jamaica, Ireland, and India—would be resolved through an extraordinary regulatory measure in Palestine, where the high commissioner, and with him, all security forces, including the police and military, could do whatever they liked, which included punitive destruction of property and trial by military courts without right to appeal.[26] Legalized lawlessness—ideologically rooted in the birthing of liberal imperialism, and having evolved over decades in various empire theaters and courtrooms, and at home under the Defence of the Realm Act—was now fully matured.[27]

Insofar as the military had its own rules, the War Office ensured its field officers and soldiers had a wide berth in defining and implementing the use of force. Building on Charles Callwell's earlier and highly influential work that spoke of violence's "moral effect" on "uncivilized" populations, Major General Sir Charles Gwynn's book *Imperial Policing* helped to shape how British soldiers conducted themselves "in aid of the civil power" when fighting colonial wars, which Gwynn and many others understood to be policing operations as much as military ones, if not more so.[28] The military norms had been codified under the *Manual of Military Law* in 1929, and the relevant portions—"Notes on Imperial Policing and Duties in the Aid of the Civil Power"—were reproduced for the troops in pocket form for easy reference while on the front lines in Palestine and elsewhere.[29] The 1929 military manual was a rewrite that offered little alteration to the army's methods in contending with riots or in aid of the civil power, despite the Amritsar Massacre. When lecturing to the empire's future leaders, some of the military's teaching staff, including Colonel John George Smyth, condemned the Hunter Commission and explained away Dyer's actions in Amritsar in justificatory terms. Such sentiments stretched from the highest ranks of the military to the lowest rung in the chain of command.[30]

Ultimately, the new pages of military legalspeak in 1929 reminded the troops that a soldier "is not only a soldier but a citizen also, and as such is subject to the civil as well as to the military law." The manual said "the existence of an armed insurrection would justify the use of any degree of force necessary effectually to meet and cope with the insurrection," all of which could well "inflict suffering upon innocent individuals . . . [and was] indispensable as a last resource."[31] Between the military's own code of conduct and the civil emergency measures that offered legal coverage, Britain's troops, along with the local police force, operated virtually without restraint or fear of prosecution. When the steady stream of complaints and accounts of abuses piled up on Archdeacon Stewart's desk, along with those of Palestine's chief secretary and officials in London's Colonial and War offices, almost nothing, legally, had to be done. In the few cases where prosecutions eventually took place, acquittals were more the norm than the exception. The issue of public opinion would be left to the British government and its obfuscating skills, as well as the broader international landscape, which included the Permanent Mandates Commission.

The League of Nations had a role to play in translating liberal imperialism into a twentieth-century framework of permissible norms in Palestine and beyond. The PMC again entered the fray after the first phase of the Arab Revolt, which stretched from April through a ceasefire in October 1936. During this six-month period, as the archdeacon and others documented, British forces had unleashed all too familiar "Black and Tan" tactics as well as extraordinary acts of military repression. "It was quickly evident that the only way to regain the initiative from the rebels was by initiating measures against the villagers from which the rebels and saboteurs came," Air Vice Marshal Peirse noted. "I therefore initiated, in co-operation with the Inspector General of Police R. G. B. Spicer, village searches. Ostensibly, these searches were undertaken to find arms and wanted persons, actually the measures adopted by the police on the lines of similar Turkish methods, were punitive and effective."[32]

What constituted "punitive" under the military's culture of permissible norms, even before the introduction of statutory martial law, was open to broad interpretation. The linchpin to connecting cause and effect of Peirse's "punitive" and "effective" was cruelty, which was on full display in the old city of Jaffa in June 1936. There, allegedly for the health and sanitation of the residents but in reality for the facilitation of military access to the rebel-held area, the British Army used gelignite charges to blow up some 250 multiresident houses, which left as many as six thousand Arabs homeless. In a half-hearted gesture, the army had air-dropped warning leaflets the morning of the destructions that gave residents a few hours to vacate and find new homes. A homeless crisis ensued—something that would grow to epic proportions in the years ahead—as countless families escaped with nothing but the clothes on their backs.[33] The sympathy for Arabs that many British soldiers and police officers harbored prior to the revolt began to evaporate.

A handful of administrators, however, were horrified, including Chief Justice Sir Michael McDonnell. "The petitioner has done a public service in exposing a singularly disingenuous lack of moral courage," McDonnell said in hearing one of the few Arab cases that made it to a courtroom. "It would have been more creditable, if the Government, instead of endeavouring to throw dust in people's eyes by professing to be inspired with aesthetic or other quasi-philanthropic motives, [if those responsible], had said frankly and truthfully, that it was primarily for defensive purposes."[34] The government sacked the chief justice for his condemnation, sending a strong message to the Mandate's judiciary about its ostensible independence from the state's military and administrative complexes that were working in ever-increasing concert. Still, McDonnell's condemnation electrified the Arab community, which printed up copies of the chief justice's judgment by the thousands and distributed them as pamphlets. To evade press censorship, Arab papers reported on the Jaffa events under the cover of satire. Headlines blazed with "Goodbye, goodbye, old Jaffa, the army has exploded you," and articles chided the army for rendering the city "more beautiful" through the detonation of His Majesty's "boxes of dynamite."[35]

The destruction of property continued through the summer. In September 1936, the Colonial Office stated the obvious: the revolt was "a direct challenge to the authority of the British government in Palestine."[36] The alienation of indigenous populations only galvanized recruits and support for the Qassamites and other armed urban and rural commandos, many of whom were operating independently from the Arab Higher Committee leadership. This included Fawzi al-Qawuqji, a military legend first in Syria and then in Iraq, who took his fighting skills, along with an armed detachment of pan-Arab volunteers, to Palestine and declared himself commander in chief of the uprising. Al-Qawuqji oversaw the division of commandos into four fronts, each of which had a district commander, as well as individual platoon leaders who oversaw two hundred armed insurgents.[37] Other leaders emerged and together with their followers rendered the triangle of Nablus, Jenin, and Tulkarm into the "Triangle of Terror." By the end of September, when Lieutenant General John Dill took over the military, Britain had deployed twenty thousand troops "with a view to rounding up the Arab bands."[38]

The mufti and other *a'yan* in the Arab Higher Committee tenuously maintained an upper hand and negotiated a temporary truce with British authorities with the help of Arab diplomatic conduits throughout the Middle East. Yet another royal commission of inquiry, this one headed by Lord Peel, soon made its way to the scene to determine Palestine's future. Nine months later the Peel Report, over four hundred pages, affirmed that "the longer the Mandate operated, the stronger and more bitter Arab antagonism to it became," and it gestured, perhaps unwittingly, to Britain's role in feeding local resentment, stating that "peace, order and good government can only be maintained in Palestine for any length of time by a rigorous system of repression." The Peel Commission lamented, "It is not easy to pursue the dark path of repression without seeing daylight at the end of it."[39] The only way to reach this light was to roll back the Balfour Declaration and, as with Ireland, slice up the Mandate.

The Peel Report's explosive recommendation to partition Palestine came with a stiff rebuke for the local colonial administration and its apparent lack of will in deploying coercive measures. Martial law should have been declared, according to the report, and in the case of any future revolts, "the country [should be placed] under undivided military control."[40] It would seem that the commission was unaware of the recommendation of Britain's attorney general and solicitor general that extraordinary emergency regulations were more permissive than martial law in legalizing state-directed violence and in preventing potential prosecutions for the security forces' brutal methods.

When the League's Permanent Mandates Commission met in July 1937, its pro-Zionist members questioned Britain's will to enforce the Mandate and, with it, the need for partition. Jamal al-Husayni, Weizmann, and others seeking to lobby the PMC all descended on Geneva, as did the international press corps. Al-Husayni, along with the League's Iraqi member, represented Arab adamant opposition, while Weizmann was more open to divvying up Palestine than were other Zionist leaders. Unabashedly pro-Zionist, the PMC was less concerned with the dual obligation than with the failures of Britain's custodianship, by which it meant failing to support Jewish immigration with force.[41] Its members took the Peel Report's censure several steps further. They decried the "perfervid nationalism" of the Arabs, and shared Colonial Secretary William Ormsby-Gore's belief that the Arabs were a "backward race," particularly when "compared with the Jews and with European standards."[42]

A civilizational discourse reminiscent of nineteenth-century ideas about racialized stages of development and the broader liberal imperialist agenda—an agenda that underwrote the League's conceptualization in the first place—framed the weeks of relentless PMC questioning and answering that Ormsby Gore and his entourage, including Palestine's chief secretary, John Hathorn Hall, withstood in Geneva. Britain should have deployed more violence against the Arabs; imposed martial law; exercised stricter censorship; locked up those Arabs petitioning the British government, presumably Jamal al-Husayni among them; and threatened to bomb villages. "For better or worse, the people of Great Britain were a liberal and democratic people," Ormsby-Gore insisted. They would not "for long be persuaded to use military force to settle a conflict between right and right."[43]

Colonial Secretary Ormsby-Gore was correct about one thing: no amount of the PMC's parsing legalistic interpretation of decades-old texts was going to settle the matter. Depending on where one stood, both the Arabs and the Jews had legitimate claims. On the issue of a British liberal democracy deploying "military force," however, Ormsby-Gore was lying, and truth be told, it was his own government's state-directed violence in Palestine that helped land him in Geneva in 1937 defending an indefensible mess largely of Britain's own making. Above his lofty though hollow protests, the PMC advocated, yet again, more repressive measures.[44] British officials, with Hall on Palestine's front line, in fact had been masterful at denying their extreme methods and at stifling those who had raised concerns. The degree to which, in 1937, the PMC had full knowledge of events in the Mandate is uncertain, though given the pressing urgency for more Jewish immigration to Palestine, its advocacy of repression would likely have remained unchanged regardless.

In London, imperial pride and Weizmann's interventions directed concerns away from repressive measures, save for the government's repeated denials. Its members searched for their moral purpose, and in one of several heated House of Commons debates, MP Archibald Sinclair declared he could not "read [the Peel Report] without a sense of humiliation, for it makes it clear that since 1929 the record of British administration in Palestine has been one of irresolution and that we are now faced with the bankruptcy of one of the most imaginative enterprises British statesmanship has ever undertaken." He underscored a sentiment that others in the chamber echoed: "let us be clear about the pledge which was given to the Jews."[45] Another member of Parliament summed up the views of many when he said that "the proposals [for partition] are ill-considered, hopelessly inconclusive, tremendously speculative and hazardous, and may well even create less peace in the future than there has been during the past 15 years."[46]

As Parliament licked its imperial wounds and reaffirmed assurances to Weizmann and others, the impact of the discourse in London and Geneva around governance and authority would be far-reaching. Britain's duty to maintain its governing imperatives through the monopoly over physical and symbolic violence vis-à-vis the efflorescence of legalized lawlessness would soon take priority over all other measures, including diplomatic. In Palestine as elsewhere in the British Empire, the semiautonomous colonial state that had little to no consent from local societies only appeared to stand above the vicissitudes of coercion and reform that gave life to the liberal imperial project. In reality, the state was an epiphenomenon of these long-rooted ideas. Moreover, as the different registers of mandatory governance and state-sponsored violence so starkly reveal, the civilizing mission's ideals, particularly in times of crisis, gave rise to liberal imperialism's potent military and administrative complexes. The effects, in real time, would be devastating for the ordinary fellaheen in Palestine and countless other indigenous populations under British rule throughout the empire.[47]

Partition sparked universal Arab opposition, and the mufti, along with his cousin, Jamal, and other family members were soon on the run. The Arab Higher Committee denounced the Peel Report's recommendation, and the mufti convened a pan-Arab conference of four hundred delegates in Syria. He vehemently denounced the British and renewed calls that demanded, among other things, an un-partitioned Palestine and repeal of the Mandate and Balfour Declaration. A recrudescence of disorder in Palestine soon witnessed the assassination of Lewis Andrews, the district commissioner of Galilee, on September 26, 1937, and with it, the second phase of the Arab Revolt began.

The colonial government sought to decapitate the movement, misguidedly thinking it would collapse without its elite leadership. The Arab Higher Committee and the Supreme Muslim Council were forcibly disbanded, and Britain swiftly deported several Arab leaders to the Seychelles. After a cat-and-mouse game that took the mufti in disguise and under the cover of darkness to Jaffa, Haifa, and eventually to Lebanon, he eluded arrest, as did Jamal, who made his way to Syria.

Together they rallied support in various corners of the Arab world for the Palestinian cause. Crucially, Jamal, the internationally seasoned and respected diplomat, established the Information Office in Damascus in 1938. From there, he and his colleagues gathered and disseminated news and manifestos and were also in direct contact with the Arab Bureau in London as well as various sympathetic parties in Palestine, including those in the missionary community. Al-Husayni and his information nerve center also received some assistance from the Italian and German consulates, which gave a whiff of credence to Britain's claims of fascist collaboration with the Arabs.[48]

With the al-Husayni leadership either locked up or in exile, some members of the Nashashibi family seized the moment to challenge their rivals once and for all. To do so, they cooperated with the British to serve their own ends. Fakhri Nashashibi and his uncle and family head, Ragheb Nashashibi, led the charge. They formed the al-Mua'rada, the Opposition or "Defence" party, working with British officials and the Zionist leadership. The unholy alliance took its most far-reaching form in what were euphemistically called "peace bands," or in certain British circles, "peace gangs."[49] In a move that harkened back to precedents in Ireland and elsewhere, and that would further spread in the empire's postwar years, the peace bands reflected Britain's deliberate exploitation of cleavages within indigenous populations for its own ends. Civil and military officials armed seemingly cooperative segments of local societies and demanded in return public displays of loyalty. At home, Colonial Secretary Malcolm MacDonald, who would succeed the beleaguered Ormsby-Gore in May 1938, described the peace band policy to the rest of Chamberlain's cabinet with laconic flair: "the policy which we were pursuing was affording encouragement to [the Nashashibi] faction."[50] In practice, as a local doctor, H. D. Forster, noted, this meant that "every mukhtar [village chief] was told that he was expected to sign a declaration, on behalf of his quarter, of loyalty to the Government, and abhorrence of the rebellion. Otherwise the quarter is to be treated as the professed enemy of the Government, and they all realise what that means in these civilised days."[51]

The government-sponsored bands grew in size and impact as the second phase of the Arab Revolt unfolded. This phase witnessed further devastation of the countryside and its fellaheen, many of whom found themselves caught between warring factions. On this point, Forster observed that "each mukhtar has also received a personal letter from the oozles [Arab rebels], saying that if he does sign [the British loyalty pledge], he will be bumped off. . . . The army frankly admit that they can offer no protection to those that sign."[52] This mattered little to those calling the shots, and British forces bombed, picked off, ground down, and tortured those who refused to cooperate and side with them and their chosen Arab conduits, the Nashashibis, and their peace bands. The British government knew full well that those who demonstrated imperial loyalty through actions—whether mukhtars signing declarations or war-weary villagers informing or delivering intelligence—affirmed their own death warrants with the rebel forces.

Ultimately, the peace bands and their leader, Fakhri 'Abd al-Hadi—whom locals nicknamed "the butcher"—were interested in lining their own pockets, settling local scores, and pursuing family vendettas.[53] They used British-supplied weaponry and support to do so. The peace bands were just as likely to play both sides to achieve these ends, something British authorities knew well. Still, they would play an integral role in rendering Palestine's Arab villagers more fearful of the British government and its security forces than the insurgent bands. Indeed, these insurgent bands looked to usurp rural authority, setting up governing structures in their respective locales, including systems for tax collection, labor conscription, intelligence, and justice. "The rebels," as the historian Anderson tells us, "moved not only to expel the colonial sovereign but to establish themselves as a ruling regime."[54] Looking to crush this regime-in-the-making and the peasants supporting it, the government continued deploying peace bands, despite the fact that, at times, local officials had difficulty telling who was on what side of the Arab divide. In many ways, the peace bands were the final coup de grâce in Britain's repressive policies. The government's opportunities to exploit internal Arab divisions fully emerged only once British forces had so crushed the fellaheen, physically and psychologically, that they were willing to do just about anything to survive.[55] Descending to this lowest denominator of British rule was a process that worsened over the second phase of the Arab Revolt.

The Nashashibi and al-Husayni reversal of fortunes was paired with Britain's full-scale purging of high-ranking administrators who were considered too soft and ill equipped to dole out full-scale repression to the rebels and the broader Arab population. Palestine historically had a higher turnover of high commissioners, and Wauchope, derisively known as "The Washout" for his feckless and dithering ways, was the first to go.[56] Like so many of his predecessors, he had arrived hopeful, even ebullient, about his prospects. In the end, he wrote to his new chief secretary, William Battershill, "You can imagine how I hate retiring, especially at this juncture, when Palestine is in so bad a way. If Weizmann had not so constantly used the word, I'd say I was heartbroken." The Colonial Office replaced him with the more bellicose Harold MacMichael, from whom the powers of legalized lawlessness would be liberally, if at times begrudgingly, conferred on the Mandate's security forces. The Zionists were at the very least suspicious of the cold-blooded bureaucrat. Ben-Gurion thought him a snob, neither pro-Arab nor pro-Zionist. Like so many colonial actors at various ranks, MacMichael "was British," Ben-Gurion wrote, "and acted in accordance with the interests of his administration."[57] A who's who of the empire's dark arts of colonial policing, military repression, aerial bombing, and interrogation and intelligence gathering quickly descended on Palestine, where they continued to embrace Jewish and Arab cooperation when it suited their twin objectives of crushing the revolt and defending Britain's interests, such as they were.

Among the first on the scene was the legendary Calcutta commissioner of police, Charles Tegart. An Irishman who joined the Indian Police Service in 1901, he rapidly rose through the ranks of command. Known by all as the "Man of Iron," Tegart was synonymous with suppressing "terrorism" in Bengal and elsewhere in the empire.[58] Bengal had a history of armed protest, which is hardly surprising given the imperial-inflicted wounds of famine, violence, and corruption it suffered over the previous decades. Locals understood that their present-day injustices were rooted in Britain's historical deceptions: Clive and Hastings, lionized at home, were castigated in the land they had once pillaged.

The Raj's divide and rule partition of Bengal in 1905 into two separate entities—one predominantly Hindu, the other Muslim—had sparked the *swadeshi* movement calling for one's own country, or self-rule, and a boycotting of foreign goods. So, too, emerged a well-organized movement of the *bhadralok*, or educated Hindu "respectables," that was committed to armed insurrection, bombings, and targeted assassinations aimed at the British Raj.[59] Even within the Congress's mainstream *swadeshi* movement calling for nonviolence, extremists like Bepin Chandra Pal and Aurobindo Ghose, who, as we saw, famously stood trial (and was exonerated) in the 1908-9 Alipore conspiracy case before becoming a spiritual leader, demanded militant action. Their informed and fiery rhetoric had a wide circulation in the mainstream press, which included the English paper that Ghose edited, *Bande Mataram*, and Bengali weeklies such as *Yugantar* and *Sandhya*.[60] Early on these widely circulated papers critiqued British liberal imperialism, as in this 1907 *Bande Mataram* article, "Shall India be Free?"

> The idea that despotism of any kind was an offence against humanity, had crystallised into an instinctive feeling, and modern morality and sentiment revolted against the enslavement of nation by nation, of class by class or of man by man. Imperialism had to justify itself to this modern sentiment and could only do so by pretending to be a trustee of liberty, commissioned from on high to civilise the uncivilised and train the untrained until the time had come when the benevolent conqueror had done his work and could unselfishly retire. . . . These Pharisaic pretensions were especially necessary to British Imperialism because in England the Puritanic middle class had risen to power and imparted to the English temperament a sanctimonious self-righteousness which refused to indulge in injustice and selfish spoliation except under a cloak of virtue, benevolence and unselfish altruism.[61]

Bengali nationalists knew they were not alone in their views.[62] The movement's leadership and its rank and file turned to other parts of the empire, particularly Ireland, for inspiration and strategies.[63] Debates over rival forms of action spread through the region. Gandhi decried "the Sinn Feiners [who] resort to violence in every shape and form, [with a] 'frightfulness' not unlike General Dyer's."[64] In contrast, his counterparts in Bengal mined Ireland, and to a lesser degree South Africa, for martyrs and heroes. Bengalis consciously assumed the moniker of the Indian Republican Army, or IRA. They demanded a fully sovereign India as opposed to a half-baked promise of self-government in the British Empire. Michael Collins and Eamon de Valera were natural heroes as guerrilla strategist par excellence and nation builder, respectively.[65] But it was Patrick Pearse and his martyrdom during the Easter Rising of 1916 that emerged as iconic: revolutionary pamphlets urged Bengalis to "read and learn the history of Pearse—the gem of young Ireland and you will find how noble is his sacrifice. . . . Pearse died and by so dying he roused in the heart of the nation an indomitable desire for armed revolution. Who will deny this truth?" Lord Mayor of Cork Terence MacSwiney's self-sacrifice inspired the Bengali revolutionary Jatindranath Das, in 1929, to go on a hunger strike in a Lahore jail. Das "was almost worshipped by politically conscious Bengalis," according to one local observer. After his death, Calcutta's mayor wrote to MacSwiney's widow telling her that her husband "showed the way to Ireland's freedom [and] Jatin Das has followed him."[66]

As in Ireland, funerals and folksongs became the nationalist fabric, which in this case knitted bereaved Bengali communities together toward a common imagined tomorrow.[67] When the Raj tried, found guilty, and executed eighteen-year-old Khudiram Bose in August 1908 for attempting to assassinate the district magistrate, and instead killing two women, it rendered Bose, according to *The Times* of London, "a martyr and a hero."[68] One of the most widely sung nationalist songs in Bengal paid tribute to Bose's sacrifice. It captured *Yugantar's* urging of all Bengalis to "give up your lives by first taking lives. Sacrifice your life at the altar of liberty" and the revolutionary narrative of an imagined maternal nation:

Bid me farewell, mother, just once; I'm off on a trip.
With a smile on my face, I'll wear the noose; all of India will watch.
Saturday at ten: the judge's court was bursting with people.
For Abhiram it was transportation, for Khudiram death by hanging.
After ten months and ten days, I'll be born again at my aunt's.
If you don't recognize me then, mother, look for the noose around my neck.[69]

Arguably, it was Dan Breen's *My Fight for Irish Freedom* that had the greatest impact on Bengali revolutionary activity. Published in 1924 and translated into Hindu, Punjabi, and Tamil, the book was the first memoir by an Irish Republican Army member. It quickly became a how-to manual for rebellion and outlined the necessity of taking out "Irish 'traitors,' police, informants, and high government officials." Bengali revolutionaries referred to the text as "one of our bibles," and it inspired, among other acts, the Chittagong Armory Raid of April 1930, when nearly sixty revolutionaries occupied the police armory and seized weapons and ammunition; other rebel forces destroyed rail and telegraph lines.[70] One government official called the raid, which self-consciously drew on the Irish War of Independence and the Easter Rising of 1916, "the biggest coup the terrorist party in Bengal ever brought off."[71] While Chittagong was the most spectacular act, it was scarcely the only one. Between 1906 and 1935, the Bengal Police Intelligence Branch logged over five hundred "revolutionary crimes," and another two hundred cases of arms and ammunition theft. By the late 1920s, assassinations were widespread; between 1930 and 1934, Bengali revolutionaries took out local informers and police officers as well as nine British officials, including the inspector general of police. They were, according to one critic, the "Sinn Fein of India," and by 1932, King George V, exasperated by the unabated reports of terror and marked men declared, "What is *wrong* with Bengal?"[72]

Ireland's significance was not confined to those advocating revolutionary change through violent measures. Within the policing ranks, Tegart was the empire's quintessential Irish officer, and his legendary work represented one of Britain's policing and intelligence models in Bengal (and elsewhere). He was not alone. From the rank and file to the highest positions of command, men such as Alfred O'Sullivan, the inspector general of the Bengal police, and Philip Vickery, a member of the Indian Imperial Police and the head of Indian Political Intelligence (the top-secret Indian intelligence office), were of Irish blood and had little sympathy toward revolutionaries. Their unique heritage spanned lived colonial experiences and the divisiveness they wrought, as well as an imperial present that deployed these men as hardened and battle-tested agents of empire. As one Bengali commentator observed, "Many Anglo-Indian officers have tried to understand the Hindu mind, but there is no denying the fact that the most successful attempts at comprehension have generally been made by Irishmen" who leveraged their insights to clamp down on Bengali resistance to British rule.[73]

Ireland's repressive hands also found new homes in local administrations.[74] The Indian civil service's ranks, for instance, included the infamous Sir Michael O'Dwyer, the Punjab's lieutenant governor during the Amritsar Massacre. There was also Sir John Anderson, who had been undersecretary of state at Dublin Castle during the Irish War of Independence and administratively oversaw the Black and Tans and Auxiliaries as well as the exhaustive legalization of mass arrests and detentions without trial under the Restoration of Ireland Act. A decade later Anderson was appointed to what one high-ranking observer called the "dirty job" of governor of Bengal, where the Irish precedent of harsh repression would be crucial to carrying out similar measures in southern India.[75]

During his tenure, Anderson ruled with an iron fist and introduced Irish-inspired legal measures that would expand the colonial state's already repressive capacities in Bengal. Administering what became known as "ordinance raj," he passed a series of new executive orders in Bengal; India's viceroy called this approach to suppressing political violence "efficient despotism."[76] Anderson also put a heavy premium on increasing military action with both British and Indian army units, along with their intelligence officers, called in for the job. Their tactics—

not unlike those in Ireland, the North-West Frontier, Palestine, and elsewhere—included indiscriminate village searches for suspects, contraband, and information. In the words of one officer, the combined armies' method "of countering violence with violence [was crude]," and homesteads were "ransacked in a search—often fruitless—for arms."[77] By the time Anderson departed Bengal in 1937, locals reviled him. The *Ananda Bazar Patrika* wrote that his "painful memory" would not be forgotten, "just as Ireland has not as yet been able to forget the story of the Andersonian era in that country."[78]

Insofar as Anderson had a counterpart in Bengal's police force, Tegart was the man. A native of Ulster, though raised in the south of Ireland, he spent his entire career suppressing the so-called terrorists of the empire. After ascending to deputy police commissioner in Calcutta in 1906, Tegart took over as chief of the newly created intelligence branch of the India colonial police seven years later. In 1917 he was appointed to the Rowlatt Commission, which was charged with investigating "terrorism" or revolutionary activity in India, particularly in Bengal and the Punjab.[79] Officials across the empire considered Tegart a renowned expert in counterterrorism, and he played no small role in the commission's highly influential findings that, as a leading scholar of India, Partha Chatterjee, notes, "concluded that the only effective method was the use of punitive and preventative administrative powers against those most likely to conspire to commit violent acts against the state."[80]

Tegart's peers knew him for introducing a more systematic approach to intelligence gathering as much as for being "imperturbable in the face of danger," according to one India colonial officer.[81] He was also a master of disguise and could pass as a Sikh taxi driver, a Bengali gentleman picking up prostitutes in the red-light district, or an ordinary Kabuli or Pathan. When he was not undercover, he was often side by side with his men leading raids against the Bengali revolutionaries, whom he held in the utmost contempt.[82] They were, in Tegart's words, an "inferior" and effeminate lot who were "intensely sensitive and emotional being[s]."[83] Above all else, theirs was a "misdirected patriotism." When Tegart could not get the results he wanted, he deployed, according to his fellow officers, "unconventional and daredevil" methods and was "not above the circumvention of law . . . to achieve results."[84] He used heavy-handed tactics during interrogations, both in Calcutta and within the confines of a prison located on the Andaman Islands, a Bay of Bengal archipelago situated 130 kilometers off the coast of Burma.[85] One of the British Empire's most notorious penal institutions, the Cellular Jail, as it was also known, was built in the late nineteenth century as a "matter of great urgency."[86] At considerable cost, the British government transformed the tropical island from a site of exile into a notorious prison, which further entailed a waterborne journey across the Kala Pani ("Death Water" or "Black Water"). The island's panopticon spread out like a seven-petal flower, and it became home to countless political prisoners, many of whom were from Bengal: their large-scale detentions and deportations took off with the Defence of India Act in 1915. Subjected to a punishing labor regime, starved, tossed into solitary for months at a time, deprived of the most basic sanitation and hygiene, and tortured with mechanical devices, among other persecutions, these men were well known to Tegart and vice versa.[87]

As much as his colonial brethren revered the "legendary figure" who "radiate[d] confidence," the locals detested him.[88] Under constant threat of assassination, having survived at least six near misses, he remained brazenly undeterred. Tegart was often seen driving in his open-top car through the streets of Calcutta with his ever-present Staffordshire bull terrier perched on the hood.[89] In 1918 one of Britain's relentless advocates for Indian self-rule, Annie Besant, was at the center of Britain's radical counterculture and had Tegart in her sights. Founder of the pan-Indian Home Rule League, one of earliest organizations calling for self-rule, and member of the Theosophical Society and the Indian National Congress, serving as its president in 1917, Besant had lived in India for forty years. She was clearly no stranger to dissent and had been locked up in one of India's prisons until the Congress and Muslim League threatened full-scale protest unless Besant was released. Local colonial authorities loathed her, in no small part because she publicly accused Tegart and his men of beating up prisoners and threatening to kill them. A dog-and-pony internal investigation ensued, and Tegart was cleared of all charges.[90]

Nevertheless, a scandalous scent lingered, and Tegart took a leave of absence from his post. Prime Minister Lloyd George hand-selected him to return to England, where Tegart undertook counterespionage work as part of Britain's Security Service. From there, he was off to his native Ireland, having again been recruited from the top, this time by Churchill. Tegart's stay was short-lived, however, in part because of his frustration with Ireland's intelligence morass. Within months he and a handful of other intelligence officers exited Ireland, narrowly missing the IRA's nighttime massacre of British spies. Tegart returned to Bengal—collecting a knighthood along the way—to do what he did best: root out terrorism. After a Bengali nationalist threw a bomb at his feet in the summer of 1930, and Tegart narrowly escaped death, he soon retired, though not before becoming an imperial paragon to aspiring heavy-hands.[91] Tegart's "name is permanently imprinted on the mind of every individual who served in the India Civil Service or the Indian Police in Bengal at that time," Sir Percival Griffiths, a prominent businessman and member of the Indian administration, later commented. "He was in fact a model which many of us would have wished to follow had we been capable of doing so."[92]

When Palestine came calling a few years later, Tegart was poised to leave a similar signature on the annals of the Mandate's history and, with it, the future of repression in the empire. The Arab Revolt's second phase had just begun when Colonial Secretary Ormsby-Gore personally tapped Tegart to serve as an adviser for a full-scale reorganization of Palestine's police force.[93] Tegart landed in Palestine in December 1937, along with his handpicked assistant, David Petrie. The former director of the Intelligence Bureau in India and a longtime admirer of Tegart's methods, Petrie was the yin to Tegart's yang. "I'm impulsive and inclined to rush to get things done and impatient if I don't see immediate action," Tegart recalled. "Petrie's hard headed and arrives at his judgments by slow, logical reasoning. Between us we ought to be able to get a good line on the situation [in Palestine]."[94] Together they provided a blueprint for further toughening the Black and Tan police, as well as a thoroughgoing dismantling and re-membering of the Mandate's lackluster intelligence operations.

"The tough type of man, not necessarily literate, who knows as much of the game as the other side," was what was needed to root out the Arab "gangs of banditry," according to Tegart and Petrie. They called for a British "striking force" similar to Bengal's. Civilians would not be spared. Tegart and Petrie wanted registers that identified "bad" villages for punishments and "good" villages for rewards like tax remissions, as had been done in India.[95] They also liaised with Lieutenant Colonel Gilbert MacKereth, Britain's consul and a highly respected intelligence officer in the French Mandate of Syria, a hotbed of Arab Palestinian support. Pan-Arab networks across the Middle East were funding and providing logistics for their brethren in the Mandate, and the al-Husaynis were bunkered down in Damascus and Beirut, where they coordinated these support efforts. Some rebels crossed the Syrian border seeking safe harbor and became easy prey for MacKereth, who targeted them, turning some into British spies. In fact, the peace bands' leader, Fakhri 'Abd al-Hadi, was one of MacKereth's protégés—so much so that the British consul sent him back to Palestine, along with other collaborators, in an effort to splinter the revolt and ultimately undermine it. By the time Tegart and Petrie visited Damascus and MacKereth in early 1938, 'Abd al-Hadi had already teamed up with Fakhri Nashashibi in Palestine to launch the peace bands. Not surprisingly, for his freewheeling efforts, MacKereth found himself atop the Black Hand Gang's assassination list, which prompted him to cable London asking for a bulletproof waistcoat. He would survive the Qassamite gang's death warrant, though many of the Nashashibis weren't so lucky—the mufti's gunmen picked off several family members, including Fakhri, though not until 1941.[96]

Tegart and Petrie also imported to Palestine interrogation tactics and training from elsewhere in the empire.[97] They dismissed the Mandate's existing criminal investigation department, or CID, as disastrous with its poor training, virtual absence of any Arabic-speaking officers, inadequate staffing, and bordering-on-incompetent command structure. Tegart's aged figure, with locks of white hair and lines etched in his grizzled face, did not impede his launch of "Arab investigation centres." Modeled on his Bengal interrogation cells and the Cellular Jail on Andaman Island, Tegart's centers, according to one Mandate official, had "'selected' police officers [who] were to be trained in the gentle art of 'third degree,' for use on Arabs until they 'spilled the beans,' as it is termed in criminal circles."[98] These interrogation tactics spread across Palestine and were deployed routinely in police forts known as "Tegarts." Built in phases, Tegart's brainchildren, seventy in all, strategically dotted Palestine's landscape. During the Arab Revolt, those thrown up along the border of Syria and Lebanon—the largest of which was the behemoth at Nebi Yusha, which overlooked the Hula Valley—were intended for joint police-military operational use. When complete, the reinforced concrete Tegarts, inspired by similar police forts in India, were self-contained units with interrogation rooms and detention cells, recreational spaces for the joint security forces, and multiple amenities that included a laundry, mess hall, kitchen, and living quarters for singles and married couples.[99]

Tegart's mark on Palestine's physical landscape did not stop there. The eponymous "Tegart Wall" was an infamous barbed-wire fence that stretched eighty kilometers from the Mediterranean to Lake Huleh, with concrete guard posts, or "pillboxes," interspersed at strategic points.[100] According to the Palestine Post, the fence was actually "two parallel barbed wire fences some 6 feet high and 5 feet apart . . . the space between the two fences not only criss-crossed with barbed wire but also filled with loose masses of tangled wire below."[101] The wall was meant to keep the gunrunners, insurgents, and rebel intelligence flow from crossing the northern border. Costing nearly £100,000, its effectiveness scarcely measured up to its costs. At night Arabs cut through its wires or attached several ropes to camels and pulled down large sections, which they then flattened with trucks and sold for bed frames.[102]

Still, Tegart's impact was without question. Nine months after his initial fact-finding and report, he returned to Palestine at the Colonial Office's pleading.[103] In the intervening period, the Arab rebels had steadily gained control of the rural areas, particularly in Palestine's northern district; most roads and many towns, including Jaffa and Jerusalem, were besieged; railway stations and tracks were destroyed to the point of being unusable; police stations, post offices, banks, and other government installations were routinely attacked and robbed; landmines threatened virtually all road travel; and assassinations of British colonial officials, policemen, and suspected informers continued unabated. While intercommunal violence was rife among Arabs and between Arabs and Jews, insurgents targeted their activities largely at the British. His Majesty's forces had lost control. "The situation was such that civil administration and control of the country was, to all practical purposes, non-existent," General Robert Haining, the new military commander in charge of operations, wrote in September 1938.[104] That same month the Zionist-sympathizing Tegart assumed a sweeping liaison role between the Mandate's police force and the military, making clear to Whitehall that he did not "want further definition as regards the intention" of his role.[105]

Haining's military men had little regard for the police, and even less for its new inspector general, Alan Saunders, whom they viewed as impotent, yet coordination was crucial. Tegart was there to smooth the rough edges and facilitate the extraction of intelligence and its dissemination between the various units of the security forces—particularly between the RAF's intelligence organization, the police department's criminal investigation department, and MacKereth's operation in Damascus. He also had every intention of cooperating with Ben-Gurion and the Jewish Agency. In London, the Colonial Office and its surrogates, including Lewis Namier, a close friend of Weizmann's, kept the ever-present Zionist leader apprised of Tegart's work and that of the Mandate's administration's efforts more generally. Tegart assisted in tripling the number of British police officers in Palestine to some three thousand; expanding the use of Jewish supernumerary forces to nearly twelve thousand men, in part, to replace Arab policemen who had been relieved of active duty;

and quadrupling the Mandate's internal security budget from £842,000 to £3.5 million, at a time when Britain's meager war chest was poised to finance a much bigger war in Europe and beyond.[106]

Yet Tegart's dramatic initiatives and the ramping up of personnel and spending were not enough to win the day. As the new liaison officer was returning to Palestine, High Commissioner MacMichael telegraphed Whitehall to send as many warm bodies as possible to fill the ranks of the police forces. The Shaw Commission's warning of a heavily politicized Arab population was very real, indeed, and the high commissioner observed with grave alarm that the revolt "has unquestionably become a national revolt involving all classes of the Arab community in Palestine and enjoying considerable support from the Arabs outside. While there are still a number of foreign volunteers it is no longer the fact that the majority of the armed men are foreigners; on the contrary they are 'locals' and moreover there have been several instances of villages turning out en masse to assist a gang which is engaged with Government forces."[107] General Haining urgently appealed to London to dispatch military reinforcements in the form of a second division. The War Office initially balked, considering the imminent threat of war in Europe, but the Munich Agreement in September 1938 averted immediate conflict with Nazi Germany, and the military mandarins granted Haining's request. Two full divisions, twenty thousand soldiers, were soon stationed in Palestine, supported by a sizable RAF deployment. Haining also took over total operational control of all British security forces—including the police—who, despite the military's castigation of their second-rate abilities and loose lips, continued to be integrated in various operations, particularly the punitive actions directed at Arab villages.[108]

In effect, High Commissioner MacMichael had been brushed aside, and Haining and his men—who included the divisional commander Bernard Montgomery, along with Tegart and his cadre of intelligence officers—took over for the duration of the revolt. Together they took to heart the military's general staff report on the first phase of the Arab Revolt: "In the long run the adoption of repressive measures from the very start will probably be both the most expedient and the most humane way of restoring peace"; moreover, it warned of the consequences of the "failure to carry repression to its logical conclusion."[109] In no uncertain terms, the Arab Revolt had to be crushed. Now that the empire's military and administrative complex was in the driver's seat—albeit one upholstered in unending disagreements and friction with Palestine's administration, MacMichael included—all that was left was for it to unleash its normatively permissible and legally enabled powers of repression.

It was the summer of 1938, and the Arab Revolt in Mandatory Palestine had been raging for two years. All sides of the revolt's divide terrorized Arab villagers. The rebels dominated the countryside, destroyed vast swaths of Palestine's infrastructure, and dug up the precious oil pipeline, blowing holes in it, then setting the pulsing fuel ablaze. As Britain scrambled to reassemble a new leadership cadre to take charge and crush the rebellion once and for all, a lone intelligence officer stepped forward with a plan, according to one corporal, to "terrorize the terrorists . . . [to] catch them and just wipe them out."[110]

The intelligence officer, Captain Orde Wingate, would soon become the stuff of legend, so much so that he referred to himself, even to superiors, by the single moniker: "Wingate." In appearance and comportment, the army captain was unconventional. He careened about the mine-filled roads of Palestine in a shabby open-air 1937 Studebaker, carelessly taunting the Arab assassins who had been picking off colonial administrators, suspected informers, and police officers at will. A veritable arsenal of weapons and assorted paraphernalia was strewn across the car's seats and floors: a handful of grenades, a bandolier of rifle ammunition, an SMLE rifle, and various maps and papers encrusted with the territory's ever-present dust.[111]

In many ways, the car, a deceptive cockpit of ingenuity, if not audacity, reflected its driver. Bedecked in a Palm Beach suit with one sock often slouched about his ankle and two six-shooters at his hips, the scruffy man with a bushy black beard, steely eyes, and an ever-present panama hat looked anything but soldierly. He often strung raw onions and garlic around his neck and took a bite from time to time—to ward off mosquitoes, as he liked to say. He strained tea through his dirty socks and had a penchant for wearing an alarm clock around his wrist. Once the bell screamed, he terminated any meeting, even in midsentence. He also eschewed the formalities of clothing in the oddest of circumstances, sometimes stepping out of the shower with nothing on but a bathing cap to give an impromptu order to his troops. During Wingate's formal briefings, he occasionally pontificated before his men, stark naked, while combing his pubic hair with his toothbrush, an apparently effective means of delousing.[112] But his will of steel and his fire-breathing zealotry for the British Empire and for Zionism more than compensated for his diminutive frame and lack of Anglo-manliness as measured in athleticism. Wingate was renowned for outpacing his troops in the field through sheer determination. He slept little, ate little, and demanded a similar mental and physical fortitude from his men.

It was Wingate's creation of the Special Night Squads, combined with his devotion to the Zionist cause and his utter contempt for Arabs, that left his mark on Palestine and eventually on other parts of the violence-wracked British Empire during and after the Second World War. Arriving in the Mandate in 1936, the newly appointed captain and intelligence officer was already fluent in Arabic. He had served, among other postings, in the Sudan Defence Force, where he introduced ambushing as part of his patrol operations. A linguistic master, Wingate was fluent in Hebrew within six months of his arrival in Palestine. Having been reared in a conservative, evangelical home in colonial India, he could also quote lengthy and obscure verses of the Bible at will.

Wingate was renowned for his networking, and he gained the trust and protection, at least for a period of time, of powerful military and political figures. They included three successive general officers commanding British forces in Palestine: Lieutenant General John Dill, General Sir Archibald Wavell, and General Sir Robert Haining.[113] Their support stood him in good stead when, by the spring of 1938, Britain had to wrest nighttime control of Palestine from the Arabs, and Haining officially endorsed Wingate's well-thought-out plan "to set up a system [of] undetected movement of troops and police by night, across country and into villages, surprising gangs, restoring confidence to peasants, and gaining government control of rural areas." Wingate had every intention of translating Britain's superior "national character" and prowess in training and natural aggression into a highly disciplined counterterror operation with the single goal of wiping out Arab rebels and anyone else who stood in his way.[114] At first, he wanted to name his private army "Night Squads Gideon Force" to pay homage to his Old Testament hero. Wingate's superiors nixed the partisan idea.[115]

Organizationally, the Special Night Squads were made up of a hand-selected group of British soldiers as well as Jewish recruits. This flew in the face of publicly agreed-on policy between the army, the Colonial Office, and Palestine High Commissioner Wauchope. Wauchope had blanched at the idea of arming the Jewish community, or Yishuv, and warned officials in London that "if Jewish units are allowed to act offensively against Arabs in Palestine, I fear the chances of the two people ever living together amicably will vanish for generations."[116] Still, during the Arab Revolt, successive military commanders unofficially drew on organized Jewish support. By 1938, Wauchope's hawkish successor, Harold MacMichael, informed the colonial secretary that he and his administration had been willing to "turn a blind eye" to enlisting Jews in the police and other operations.[117] On this point, Wingate minced no words:

> The Jews are loyal to the empire. The Jews are men of their word. . . . You can have no idea what they have already done here. You would be amazed to see the desert blossom like a rose; intensive horticulture everywhere—such energy, faith, ability and inventiveness as the world has not seen. . . . The Jews will provide better soldiery than ours. We have only to train it. They will equip it. Palestine is essential to our Empire—our Empire is essential to England—England is essential to world peace. Islam is out of it.[118]

Many of Wingate's contemporaries harbored anti-Semitism against the "incomprehensible" Jew and a romantic admiration for Arabic cul-

Special Night Squad training, late 1930s, Palestine

ture. Wingate, however, thought there was nothing noble about the Arab, particularly on the battlefield: Arabs were "quite unable to face any sort of change or surprise onslaught. This is their character and they are quite unable to change it. In person they are feeble and their whole theory of war is cut and run. Like all ignorant and primitive people they are especially liable to panic."[119] Wingate's worldview combined his religious beliefs with military strategy to produce an unyielding commitment to the Zionist cause. It also fueled his anti-Arabism, as did his personal loathing of his famed cousin, Lawrence of Arabia.[120]

The antipodal cousins shared one common cause, however, and that was their commitment to Britain's empire and interests, regardless of how widely they diverged in interpreting them. Wingate and his Special Night Squads seized on the alleged Arab propensity to "panic" in the face of "surprise onslaught" and took their brand of counterterrorism straight to the heart of the Arab villages and other suspected rebel lairs. The night raid that witnessed the oil pipeline's destruction ended like several others. Once there, Wingate's men interrogated the local villagers, none of whom confessed to having heard or seen a thing. At this point, according to Corporal Frank Howbrook, who took part in the operation, Wingate said, " 'We'll teach these so-and-sos a lesson.' So we got all the men in the village. Outside . . . there's a big pool of black oil burned. And we got all the men by the side of this and then we took an arm and leg each and flung them into the middle of it."[121]

Humiliations gave way to more lethal forms of counterterrorism. The Special Night Squads soon earned legendary status, at a time when body counts and repression were the metrics for success. Engendering jealousy among the army's rank and file for their autonomy and renown, the Special Night Squads preferred inflicting bodily harm, on their captain's orders, with bayonets and bombs rather than bullets. Their leader's "morality of punishment" inspired them.[122] Reprisals became part of the squads' repertoire: they stuffed oil-soaked sand into the mouths of uncooperative Arabs, particularly those who had launched attacks on Jewish settlements. Wingate boasted that "anyone hanging about the [pipe]line for an unlawful purpose was liable swiftly and silently to vanish away."[123] He trained his Jewish subordinates ruthlessly, treating them "like dirt" and physically abusing those who in his mind needed toughening up. Still, respect for Wingate was legion: Tzion Cohen recalled that "Wingate taught us to be good soldiers with values."[124] Cohen and other Jewish "supernumeraries," as they were called, worked side by side with their British counterparts and forced Arab villagers to defile their faces in oil and mud. At other times during village raids, Arabs were counted off, and every fifteenth man was shot dead; women and children were killed in their sleep. Like Wauchope, some among the Jewish leadership bristled at Wingate's tactics. Moshe Shertok, head of the Jewish Agency's political department, wrote that the methods were anathema to the "innate inhibitions of the best of our people."[125] Nonetheless, in the deadly game of loyalty to Britain and the empire, as one report stated, "It has been proven to the British army that the young Jew can be a good soldier and good comrade and that the Hebrew Yishuv is not made up only of money-grubbing storekeepers."[126]

The Special Night Squads became a training ground for future Jewish insurgents, first against Britain and eventually against the Arab population. So, too, did they embrace a wide swath of British security forces, some of whom, like Howbrook, were professional soldiers trained to kill. When the Special Night Squads expanded, others, like Sydney Burr, were inexperienced. On a policing contract in Palestine, Burr knew Arabs only as "wogs" and casually recounted that "most of the information we get is extracted by third degree methods, it is the only way with these people."[127] The Palestine police force steeped such young, rough-and-ready recruits in Black and Tan traditions. Hugh Foot, who later became governor of Cyprus and ascended as Lord Caradon, joined in the nighttime expeditions when he was a young colonial officer. Raised on British boyhood mythologies of the empire's good-versus-evil simplicities, and hankering for adventure, Lord Caradon later recounted:

Of course [during the Arab Revolt] it got pretty rough. But I am ashamed to say that at that age and in that time we enjoyed it, we enjoyed the rebellion. Tremendous fun it was. Sort of boy scout stuff it was. Leading all night, on foot a company of troops to surround a village on the highland of Tulkarm. Dropping off just at dusk at Jenin and going straight across country so that they wouldn't have any idea you were coming. Surrounding the village if you could that you wouldn't make the dogs bark. And then going in and trying to find some desperate character. The British police were magnificent working with us all the time and the troops I knew very well. . . . There is of course bound to be a good deal of roughness and indeed worse on some occasions.[128]

Perched in his top-floor office in Jerusalem's famed King David Hotel, Arthur "Bomber" Harris looked out over his half-moon glasses and across his oversize desk to size up the young flying officer, James Pelly-

Fry, who sat before him. Bedecked in countless medals, Harris, with his broad shoulders and unflinching gaze, stared straight through "Pelly," as Harris had christened him. The flying ace's thoughts wandered to Palestine's war-torn landscape and the skies above it. Like Tegart and Wingate's hard-earned stripes of empire, Harris's had garnered him a similar stellar and hard-nosed reputation when it came to achieving results. Youngsters feared and respected him, and some, like Pelly-Fry, effused of the boss, "I have never known any other man who was so quick to appreciate, so accurate in his judgement and so swift to take action."[129]

The RAF's wunderkind was a long way from his desert days in Iraq, having ascended to air officer commanding Palestine and Transjordan. In the summer of 1938, he and his bride, Jill, arrived in Jerusalem where the new Mrs. Harris tended to the couple's stunningly beautiful villa with its rolling olive groves and hosted scores of dinner parties that were among the hottest tickets in town. When British security forces weren't wiping out Arab rebels and repressing civilians—or recovering from local hazards like sand fly fever, malaria, and typhoid—social life and leisure were top priorities. Men of all ranks coveted the territory's unrivaled duck hunting and its endless supply of Arab beaters. Pedestrian pursuits included football matches and billiards, as well as novelties like table tennis and the Brits' locally invented death game of tarantula versus scorpion, which generally saw the scorpion living to see another day. Heavy drinking was another favorite pastime, sometimes followed with a good dust-up in a local souk or café, where Arabs were beaten and killed for sport.[130]

Harris threw back his beloved whiskey and sodas, mentored his fleet of young officers, and did what he did best. His renowned "judgment" translated into tactical ruthlessness. He believed "the only thing the Arab understands is a heavy hand," and he waxed on about the value of bombing: "We must (and under such circumstances can) make up for a lack of numbers by using rougher methods with the rebels than we dare do in peace. One 250lb or 500lb in each village that speaks out of turn within a few minutes or hours of having so spoken; or the complete blotting out of a few selected haunts, *pour encourager les autres*."[131] During the Arab Revolt's first phase, the prime minister's cabinet ministers had been clear on bombing limitations: they "should not include any bombing of the civil population."[132] But they soon gave the RAF the nod to take "air action by machine-gun first . . . against a house or those houses in villages" that fired against His Majesty's forces.[133] The RAF dropped 112-pound-delayed-action bombs; dive-bombed with regularity, front guns blazing; and shook villages to their core with a series of twenty-pound bombs that were, according to the rules of the game, permissible within five hundred yards of dwellings. The RAF was responsible for nearly half the official enemy kills during the Arab Revolt: one reconnaissance alone wiped out nearly 130 Arab rebels; on other occasions, bagging a score or more was typical. That there was collateral damage was unquestionable.[134] At the time, the local doctor H. D. Forster recorded in his diary that he "watched [airplanes] rise and dive, as they machine-gunned the ground beneath them—an unpleasant sight."[135] Forster would tend to the wounded in his clinic. Among them was a shepherd who had been tending his flock "when he had been hit from the air"; his abdomen had been "severely wounded," and despite surgery, he died from "internal injuries."[136]

Harris and his men also provided crucial coverage for the on-the-ground troops through an "XX call system," which was a call for immediate assistance that took priority over all other radio requests.[137] Harris's pilots, on the spot in a matter of minutes by following visual ground-to-air signals like smoke grenades, provided aerial reinforcement. Other tactics were also used, like "pinning action," or "a system of cordoning villages from the air pending the arrival [of] ground forces." Harris made clear that his men above would "shoot anyone escaping with multi-gun Gladiators." The Sixth Squadron's operational record book routinely logged that it had taken out "cordon breakers," some of whom were rebels, others surely civilians who had been fleeing the pending army and police onslaught.[138]

As Harris unleashed his forces from above, he was well aware of the operations unfolding by night on the ground. There, he knew, the best rebel takedowns were being "done by 'special' night squads (very secret) composed of a select officer and up to say thirty mixed volunteer soldiers and sworn in local (mostly Jew) toughs." Harris thought Wingate's brainchild made up for "what is really lacking in the internal security provisions locally." By the summer of 1938, the Special Night Squads were fully deployed. General Haining lauded their cover-of-darkness subterfuge and brute tactics:

> I cannot speak too highly . . . of the Special Night Squads . . . organized and trained by Captain OC WINGATE, Royal Artillery, from my Staff, who has shown great resource, enterprise and courage in leading and controlling their activities. These Squads have been supplemented by Jewish supernumeraries who have done excellent work in combination with the British personnel. The story of the inception and gradual development of this form

of activity, and its successful results, provide a great tribute to the initiative and ingenuity of all concerned.[139]

The British military high command was not alone in championing Wingate. So did Chaim Weizmann. In Palestine, he befriended Wingate. Weizmann and Wingate shared many beliefs, some of which were rooted in British military doctrine. Just as Callwell's *Small Wars* influenced countless politicians and colonial agents, so did Wingate's purpose and language animate Weizmann's views on violence. When reflecting on the ongoing Arab repression, the Zionist leader was heartened to know that "it has produced a salutary moral effect."[140] Wingate gave Weizmann firsthand reports of the "effect" and its civilizing impact on the ground.[141]

Other ideas of Wingate's were embedded in the British military's long history of empire wars. He zeroed in on Britain's "national character" and the "primitive" nature of the Arabs in much the way Callwell did in *Small Wars*. So, too, did he gesture to the military's subsequent *Field Service Regulations*. In its post–World War I revised editions, the regulations reflected an institutional focus on the "real soldiering" taking place in the empire.[142] Within this context, multiple "irregular forces" emerged with their roots found in Callwell's work as well as from ideas and practices in India, Ireland, and Palestine, including Tegart's. Wingate, as innovative as he was, did not produce his June 1938 memorandum, "Principles Governing the Employment of Special Night Squads," in a historical or military vacuum; nor did his men's brutal tactics—which one of his officers euphemistically termed " 'Wild West, six-shooter' exuberance"—come out of nowhere.[143]

Neither did the military's redoubled mercilessness appear out of thin air. Bernard "Monty" Montgomery, who arrived in Palestine in November 1938, was every bit a counterpart to Harris in his disdain for Arab "gangs of professional bandits." They had, according to Montgomery, besmirched Britain's good name through a "campaign [that] was *not* a national movement."[144] Politics mattered little, if at all, to the ambitious Anglo-Irishman, who had taken it to Sinn Féin in the Irish War of Independence. He was clear in his approach: "I think I regarded all civilians as 'Shinners' [Sein Féin supporters], and I never had any dealings with any of them. . . . My own view is that to win a war of this sort, you must be ruthless."[145] Bringing this ethos to Palestine, Montgomery commanded his own division, using the Mandate as a testing ground for the show that was poised to unfold in Europe.

Riot at Jaffa Gate, Jerusalem, January 1938

Like Harris, Montgomery ascended in rank with his move to Palestine where, in the words of one junior second lieutenant, "he was like God."[146] The newly minted Major-General Montgomery arrived on the scene like "a new star [that] has burst into our firmament," according to the Mandate's chief secretary, William Battershill. The administration feared he'd take over, which he and his coterie effectively did.[147] Montgomery immediately declared "we are definitely at war" and was single-minded in his approach: his troops had "to hunt down and destroy the rebel armed gangs. . . . [Furthermore] they must be hunted relentlessly; when engaged in battle with them we must shoot to kill."[148]

Such tactics incorporated Wingate's Special Night Squads. Wingate received a Distinguished Service Order, one of the military's highest awards. But shortly thereafter, in the fall of 1938, while he was on leave in London, he approached Churchill and other government officials, lobbying for the Zionist cause and detailing the extensive use of Jewish supernumeraries in his night raids. Wingate broke rank, so higher command unceremoniously relieved him of his Palestine duties. As far as General Haining was concerned, Wingate's direct appeals "render[ed] his services in the Intelligence Branch nugatory and embarrassing."[149] Nevertheless, Wingate's Special Night Squads continued in earnest, and military intelligence summaries underscored in 1939 that "a few highly trained night squads and ambush patrols can have greater moral and material effect than columns."[150]

In practice, Montgomery and others green-lighted "the use of any degree of force necessary effectually to meet and cope with the insurrection," in the words of the military's manual. With sweeping emergency powers in effect, few legal measures existed to curtail the security force's measures.[151] By many accounts, military and police handiwork were indistinguishable. As the revolt progressed through its second phase, the army, the RAF, the police, and various intelligence gatherers worked hand in glove, particularly in village raids.

Missionaries and administrators weren't the only ones taking note of these domestic assaults. Soldiers and police officers also recounted at the time, and in later memoirs and interviews, their punitive destruction of villages, though often left out their looting, which other observers, like Dr. Forster, recorded in detail.[152] The police officer Sydney Burr, writing home, blithely recounted that after a certain "gang" eluded capture, he and others in his patrol "had orders to decimate the whole [nearby village,] which we did, all animals & grain & food were destroyed & the sheik & all his hangers on beaten up with rifle butts. There will be quite a number of funerals their [sic] I should imagine. . . . When you get shot here it is a nasty business as they are using Dum Dum bullets, but so are we unofficially."[153]

Burr cautioned his family "for heaven's sake don't get the impression that we are dealing with the noble Arab." He noted that "no news of course is given in the newspapers so what you read in the papers is just enough to allay public uneasiness in England."[154] Press control was crucial to Britain for managing the flow of damaging information that was circulating within Palestine and for preventing it from migrating to the metropole as well as to other parts of the empire, where nationalists voraciously followed the pursuits of their counterparts. In New Delhi, for instance, the Indian grand mufti declared "the Jihad in Palestine as both national and religious" and "British oppression as barbaric"; British officials in Palestine shut down three Arab newspapers for reproducing the text. Censorship was an emergency regulation cornerstone, drawing precedent from Britain's Great War Press Bureau, nicknamed the "Suppress Bureau" at the time. Information management had precedents in the empire: in 1930s India, nationalist violence and Gandhi's civil disobedience prompted the government to redeploy the Press Act of 1910 in even stricter and more punitive forms. Under Montgomery, press censorship was exercised with particular zeal in Palestine. Among other moves, the reproduction of all "unauthorised" photography was banned, and the major general instituted a virtual media blackout in the Haifa region when he packed the remaining press corps into three trucks and, according to one eyewitness, "kicked them out, took them to Jerusalem."[155]

Punitive raids like those that British Army officer John Grafton led, therefore, rarely made it into the official news. Like so many of his counterparts, the young Grafton had deep family connections to the British Army of India; he was groomed at Sandhurst and arrived in Palestine in 1936. Once there he was reminded of his imperial birthplace where, "when you had terrorists, or frontiersmen in India, doing something they shouldn't ought to do," he recalled, "you went in and knocked the living daylights out of the place. . . . The RAF used to bomb the villages." He would exercise the same brand of Britain's civilizing mission in the village of Safad, where he and others learned, in situ, the art of "a punitive raid." At first, leveling a village by smashing everything in sight, mixing the detritus with olive oil from broken pots, and terrifying villagers didn't come easily to Grafton's men. In fact, their commanding officer had to teach them the art of punitive roughness. But according to Grafton, "once they started you couldn't stop them, and you've never seen such devastation. . . . It's quite enlightening, this day when you can't be beastly to anybody, to tell you what happened because this is what we did. And I may say, that we never heard another peep out of Safad, that, really, they understood the lesson."[156]

There were countless documented instances like that of Safad, including the "punitive measures" that Desmond Woods and others in the Royal Ulster Rifles undertook at al-Bassa.[157] In a reprisal act after a rebel landmine blew up several of their men, the Ulsters took aim at the nearest village, al-Bassa. There, according to Woods, numerous "Rolls-Royce armoured cars" arrived on the scene, and the soldiers began "peppering Bassa with machine gun fire . . . [before] we burnt the village to the ground." As Montgomery stood on his Haifa balcony and watched the distant black smoke rising from the village inferno, his men executed further retribution using previously honed tactics. According to Woods, his men put "Arabs from the cage [a temporary holding pen]" in commandeered taxis to lead army patrols, which was a form of human mine sweeping that left Arabs blown to bits. When taxis filled "with Arabs, the naughty boys," weren't heavy enough to detonate the mines, the Ulster officer recalled that "we got hold of buses and we used to fill them with Arabs and send them down the road in front of our patrols and that did the trick."[158]

Later, as the al-Bassa reprisal continued, police officer Harry Arrigonie's eyewitness account of events was not dissimilar from Woods's memory of earlier maneuvers: "The soldiers collected approximately 50 men [from al-Bassa], herding about 20 of them onto a bus. Villagers who panicked were shot. The driver of the bus was forced to drive along the road, over a land mine buried by the soldiers. [A] second mine was much more powerful than the first and it completely destroyed the bus, scattering the maimed and mutilated bodies of the men on board everywhere. The villagers were then forced to dig a pit, collect the bodies, and throw them unceremoniously into it."[159]

Arrigonie took photographs, which he published in 1998, but at the time official reporting scarcely betrayed the realities of al-Bassa or nearby Zib. The government's mouthpiece, the *Palestine Post*, stated, "Punitive action is being taken against Bassa and Zib village, which are near the scene of the crime."[160] Montgomery called in the Ulsters' commanding officer, Gerald Whitfield, for a debrief; Whitfield defended his actions and claimed, "I would have lost control of the frontier if I hadn't" taken "punitive measures." After ruminating momentarily, Monty replied, "Well, all right, just go a wee bit easier in the future." As for Woods, he later recalled that "the Royal Ulster Rifles treated the Arabs very firmly indeed, but by Jove it paid dividends, but of course, you can't do those sort of things today."[161]

There was also the matter of torture and interrogation. In early 1938 the Anglican bishop of Jerusalem paid a call to Chief Secretary Battershill. The bishop had files full of brutal interrogation reports that had left many innocent suspects either dead or with broken limbs and teeth, skin scorched, and eyes swollen shut. He raised the alarm again over what "were in effect the use of Third Degree methods including physical torture." He underscored that "evidence which I saw myself . . . seemed to substantiate the possibility of some truth in the worst rumours regarding the exaggerated acts of terrorism attributed to the Military and to the Government."[162] The bishop's concerns had plenty of eyewitness corroboration from within the ranks of the military and police. According to one British soldier, David Smiley, when Arab suspects refused to talk, the police turned one of them upside down and beat the soles of his feet "with a leather belt"; another applied "a lighted cigarette to his

British security force mobile column, Tiberias, Palestine, July 1938

testicles" before they got him to spill the proverbial beans. At the time, Smiley observed that "this sort of thing savours of the Gestapo," and his likening of British tactics to those of Europe's rising fascist regimes was not isolated.[163] Such comparisons were also based on visual images of the police force who, according to Burr, "stuck large Swasticas [*sic*]" on the "fronts of [their] shields," and when "passing one another in the street" gave the "Nazi salute," a practice that even their superiors admonished them not to use.[164]

The political profaneness of liberal imperialism's repackaged symbols was surpassed only by the horror of its practices as the Arab Revolt continued. These practices combined empire-tested forms of punishment with new methods of destruction. Arthur Lane, who joined the Manchester Regiment when he was fifteen, recalled that when he and his comrades were holding captured rebels in the back of their military wagon, or tied to a post, they used "anything, anything [we] could find— rifle butts, bayonets, scabbard bayonets, fists, boots, whatever" when they "knocked [them] about." On one such occasion, Lane recalled:

There was one poor sod there and he was, I would imagine he was my age, actually. And, I'd heard people say in the past that

you can take your eye out, have it cleaned, and put it back, and
I always believed it. But it's not so, because this lad's eye was
hanging down on his lip, on his cheek. The whole eye had been
knocked out and it was hanging down, and there was blood dripping on his face. . . . And you know he was in a state, but he
wasn't crying and he wasn't pleading or anything like that. The
lot of them, they just sat there, talking between themselves, even
though they'd been knocked about.

Later, Lane's cadre held seven rebel prisoners who were slated to stand
trial at Acre Prison. Their next move showed that General Dyer's practices were alive and well in Palestine. Lane later described how he and
the other soldiers

took [the prisoners] around the back and any lads who were
doing nothing at the time, they were all, we all gathered around,
and we stood [and formed] two lines of men, some with pick
axes, like pick awls, some with bayonet scabbards with a bayonet
inside, some with rifles, whatever was there, tent mallets, tent
pegs, and the rebels were sent one at a time through this, what do
you call it, gauntlet, and they were belted and bashed until they
got to the other end. Now, anyone could run when they got to
the other end, run straight into the police meat wagon, and they
were sent down to Acre. Any that died, they went into the other
meat wagon and they were dumped at one of the villages on the
outside. Now when they was taken to Acre, they usually lasted
two days, a day, for all of them, and then they were hung.[165]

Swift death sentences like these were often carried out based on minimal
evidence, much of which was amassed from suspects under torture. False
evidence, however, mattered little to the empire's hand of justice or to
its gallows at Acre.

Arab prisoners had little protection from the likes of Lane and his
buddies. Acre was their favored pick-up point, from where, according to
the soldier, they would

borrow say five rebels, three rebels, and you'd sit him on the
bonnet so the guy up in the hill could see an Arab on the truck
so he wouldn't blow it. . . . [Then] when you'd finished your
duty . . . the driver would do this with his wagon, he'd switch
his wheel, he'd switch his wheel back and forth . . . to make the

truck waver, and the poor wog on the front would roll off on the deck. Well if he was lucky he'd get away with a broken leg. But if he was unlucky, the truck behind, coming up behind him, would hit him. But nobody bothered to pick the bits up, they were left.

Lane and his counterparts also blew up villages, burned down houses when their occupants couldn't pay taxes or collective fines, and participated in reprisals. When recollecting why he and others did what they did, Lane gestured to the cascading effects of an imperial despotism that Edmund Burke had cautioned against over a century earlier: "In those days, I don't know, you was a young warrior and it was excitement. And you was, I don't know, you was supreme, you was in charge, you was in control, you had the power. And this is what it was all about, you know, being the soldier, you had the power to do things, and you did it."[166]

By the time Jamal al-Husayni's plea for a "neutral enquiry" into British "excesses" landed on the desk of the Permanent Mandates Commission, the Arab Revolt, while nearly over, was as brutal as ever. In May 1939 the Black Watch Regiment surrounded the village of Halhul and corralled all its men into "good" and "bad" cages. They gave those in the "good" cages food, water, and shelter, and left those in the "bad" cages in the scorching sun with minimal water. If a villager in a "bad" cage cooperated by providing information, he would be relabeled "good" and moved accordingly. By the end of the ordeal, those imprisoned in the "bad" cages were drinking their own urine to survive; a dozen of them perished. Locally, the incident was well known, and Dr. Forster noted, "We may yet teach Hitler something new about the conduct of concentration camps." According to Forster, a "strictly hush-hush" military court of inquiry went nowhere, and colonial administrator Edward Keith-Roach later confirmed that High Commissioner MacMichael had stepped in to ensure that no further investigations followed.[167] Officials in London were also aware of the incident, though they fretted far more over the details reaching Indian nationalists than they did the fate of the fellaheen who suffered.

The final mop-up in the rural areas continued in earnest, and the so-called Arab peace bands helped execute the empire's remaining dirty work with particular zeal. The civilian population, all but decimated, were willing to do just about anything to survive and began to fall into line with the divisive "good" and "bad" village policy.[168] By July 1939, Montgomery boasted to the War Office that "the rebellion is definitely and finally smashed," and he along with his military comrades began looking to the more ominous European horizons.[169]

In the meantime, the League of Nations and the British government were well aware of the brutalities that had befallen the Arab population in Palestine long before al-Husayni's letter reached Geneva. Frances Newton's publications made public what others privately and repeatedly conveyed to officials in Palestine and Britain, as well as in Switzerland. A member of the Church Missionary Society, Newton had been living and working in Palestine for forty years when the Arab Revolt erupted. She translated her horror at British actions into a painstaking collection of evidence that included not only her own eyewitness accounts but also scores of others from the local population as well as other European missionaries, business people, and colonial officials, most of whom refused to lend their names for fear of retribution.[170]

Such concerns were hardly unfounded. In 1937 Newton had published a pamphlet entitled "Punitive Methods in Palestine," which London's Arab Center circulated widely. The pamphlet soon made its way to Parliament, where the Labour Party's Reginald Sorenson took up the cause. Sorenson was no stranger to imperial critique, having leveled charges at the Labour Party Congress in 1933 that "the operation of Imperialism in India is in essence no different from the operations of Hitlerism. . . . We are appalled by what is happening to the Jews in Germany, but what has been happening in India is just as bad."[171] In March 1938 Sorenson turned his spotlight on Palestine and, with Newton's work in hand, asked Colonial Secretary Ormsby-Gore "whether his attention has been drawn to the continuing Arab propaganda alleging ruthless and lawless behavior of troops and police in Palestine and cruelty and misconduct; what steps he has taken to counteract this propaganda and, in particular, whether he will have these charges investigated with a view to publishing the result of such investigations?"[172]

Ormsby-Gore's reply was part of the broader, effective campaign to stifle the empire's critics. "I consider that such propaganda is sufficiently discredited by its own obvious falsity and extravagance," the colonial secretary said, despite shuttling back and forth to Geneva, where British representatives spoke of "slay[ing] large numbers of Arabs" and members of the Permanent Mandates Commission demanded more coercion.[173] Continuing his imperial opprobrium to Parliament, he maintained, "I do not propose to add to the many burdens of the Palestine Administration that of investigating each reckless and unsupported charge against British forces who are endeavouring to combat a campaign of murder and outrage."[174] As far as the British government was concerned, Newton's well-researched charges were "all lies," as were any other allegations emanating from Palestine—a point that Ormsby-Gore, after his House of Commons denials, made in a terse, personal letter to the bishop of Jerusalem. The bishop had been poking his Anglican nose where it didn't belong, including into a lengthy conversation with Montgomery, who the bishop considered "blood mad" in the wake of al-Bassa.[175] The bishop had also privately defended Newton to the colonial secretary, writing, "I do know that there is sufficient truth in, for instance, the publication entitled 'Punitive Measures in Palestine.'"[176] Ormsby-Gore's message could not have been clearer: the bishop was to pipe down and stay out of politics.

For Newton's efforts, the British government gave her the imperial boot. High Commissioner MacMichael invoked his emergency powers and issued her deportation order, which sent a strong message to others contemplating a similar public path. So as to ensure that there was no ambiguity on this score, General Haining wrote to Archdeacon Stewart in Palestine and informed him, "It is so easy, in this credulous country, to start a campaign of misrepresentation . . . [and the] effective work carried out by the Army, in such circumstances, is the real reason for the propaganda against it."[177] From then on, the archdeacon kept mum and comforted himself with the Almighty's imagined workings. "If I didn't believe that out of the hateful sufferings of the innocent God somehow works redemption," Stewart wrote, "I should want to throw in my hand."[178] Having been exiled from the territory to which she had given decades of service, Newton refused any such vow of silence and continued her this-worldly pursuits. She obsessively continued her information gathering in London and Geneva, providing Jamal al-Husayni with additional evidence of British repression in Palestine, which was contained in his final plea for an independent inquiry.[179]

Regardless of the extensive evidence he provided, al-Husayni was no match either for Weizmann and his uncanny political skills, or for the liberal imperial ethos. He also faced the understandably obsessive desire for unrestricted Jewish immigration to Palestine that infused the League of Nations on the eve of the Second World War. Perhaps even al-Husayni knew his letter was more a symbolic gesture, written as much for the historical record as it was for effecting change within the League's chambers and in war-torn Palestine. The PMC had already dismissed similar petitions that other concerned Arabs had filed, some of which included allegations of the use of poison gas and of British forces behaving "in a manner inconsistent with their duty to maintain public security and protect life and property."[180] The Zionist lobby, together with the commission's unwavering position that Britain had failed to uphold the original terms of the Mandate, particularly on the issue of Jewish immigration, and had not been repressive enough, meant any further appeal for a "neutral enquiry," even from the likes of Jamal al-Husayni, would fall on deaf ears.

Al-Husayni never received a response. Germany invaded Poland on September 1, 1939, and the world war that had been looming erupted. Britain, so long beholden to the League's inflexible policies, embedded as they were in the Balfour Declaration, shifted course as the Permanent Mandates Commission met its wartime demise. Politics would trump the League's legalistic readings of the Mandate's founding documents, and for the time being, British officials jettisoned what they self-servingly called "Lord Balfour's error of judgment."[181]

As the dust settled over the corpses and broken bodies of Palestine's fellaheen population, Britain announced policies in favor of Arab demands that, in the context of September 1939, aligned with British interests, as we shall see. London issued the White Paper of 1939, declaring that seventy-five thousand more Jewish immigrants would be allowed during the following five years into Palestine, after which all entries were subject to Arab consent. In effect, while hundreds of thousands of Jews desperately sought passage out of Europe, Britain closed down their Palestine escape option. Such a move was extraordinary, not least because Britain had withstood years of immense pressure from the PMC to open fully Palestine's borders to Jewish immigration. Weizmann had pleaded for "elementary justice and political decency."[182] British representatives refused. Its "dual obligation" to both Jews *and* Arabs militated against an open-ended immigration policy, Britain claimed. Yet by the time of the White Paper, British security forces had ground the Arabs into submission, leaving them incapable of resisting increases in Jewish immigrants. Britain's self-interests, however, were changing. Wielding their newfound, imperial free agency in Palestine, British officials sacrificed their onetime Zionist allies for strategic necessity. Britain needed wartime support from its Arab client states and a reduction in troop commitments to Palestine. As far as London was concerned, the Jews could hardly jettison Britain in the face of Nazi anti-Semitic policies.

The White Paper also imagined the creation of a unitary state in Palestine within a decade. It would not be a Jewish state, or binational state, according to the White Paper, but an Arab state with protections for a Jewish minority. Such imperial maneuvering scarcely considered the unintended consequences of cultivating the Jews as situational allies in the context of the Arab Revolt. Its three years had witnessed the efflo-rescence of legalized lawlessness and the consolidation of norms and logics that various British actors had honed elsewhere in the empire, whether in the air, on unconventional battlefields and interrogation sites, in domestic spheres, or on the floor of Parliament and in the cabi-net's smoke-filled rooms. The Arab Revolt was a crucial turning point in imperial convergences, but it also had a political coda that ensured another Palestine conflict in the years to come. This time Weizmann, the well-trained Jewish supernumeraries, and the Zionist network of support and intelligence gathering would not be on Britain's side. But first, the island nation had an even bigger conflict to fight, one in which empire-tested forms of warfare would be brought home to Britain and to the battlefields and interrogation centers of Europe and beyond.

PART II

EMPIRE AT WAR

After the Japanese bombing of Pearl Harbor, as its forces moved up the Malay Peninsula, Anthony Daniels and countless others manned Britain's "Fortress Singapore" with little idea of the fate that awaited them. A young Eurasian living with his extended family amid the rows of multiethnic shop houses on Singapore's Balestier Road, Daniels embodied a cosmopolitanism that punctuated Britain's gateway to the East. Educated at St. James School by day and returning to the Asian pluralism of Balestier Road in the evenings, he answered an interview call with the British Army in 1937 and landed a post in the Royal Army Medical Corps as a nursing orderly.[1] At the time, Singapore was the bastion of the empire. Since announcing its plans for Sembawang in 1923, Britain had sunk over £25 million into the naval base on the island's north side. A symbol of strength and commitment to the empire east of Suez, Sembawang was synonymous with British impregnability in Southeast Asia and beyond. That nearly 25 percent of the empire's trade passed through the southern tip of the Malay Peninsula and on to the Indian Ocean added economic purchase to the island's value. By the Second World War, the defense of the entire region and a substantial portion of the British economy rested on the empire's most expensive piece of real estate.[2]

Yet shortly after the attack on Pearl Harbor, millions watched in disbelief as the Japanese commander Tomoyuki Yamashita called Britain's greatest wartime bluff. He entered the Malay Peninsula from the northern border of Thailand and swiftly brought destruction throughout the region. Just weeks after Britons consumed government-produced newsreels like "Imperial Forces for Malaya's Defence"—complete with footage of friendly Australians waving as they embarked for Singapore, and

Indian soldiers drilling with hyperefficiency—Japanese troops clad in matching gossamer-like jungle outfits gutted areas like Penang.[3]

Aerial bombings soon set ablaze one of Britain's oldest footholds in Southeast Asia. Relentless attacks followed, and hospitals quickly overflowed with limbless victims and their collective gangrenous stench. Japanese propaganda baited Britain's complacent superiority with radio broadcasts that queried, "You English gentlemen: How do you like our bombing? Isn't it a better tonic than your whisky soda?" Near the end of December, Alfred Duff Cooper, Britain's highest-ranking civilian official in the region, reassured the public that "the majority of the population had been evacuated."[4] By this he meant the white population of planters, merchants, civil servants, and their families. For those who remained, internment camps, typhoid, and cholera soon followed, as millions of subjects were left to face the consequences of British imperial hubris.

From Penang, the Japanese cut their way down the peninsula on bicycles. British strategists thought the dense jungles were the key line of defense against a potential Japanese onslaught, but their own engineers and the colony's vast labor pool had constructed the empire's most extensive road network from Malaya's northern border with Thailand to the southern shores of Johor. Japan's "bicycle Blitzkrieg" was brilliant in its efficiency: as tens of thousands of Hirohito's soldiers pedaled

Imperial Japanese Army bicycle force, Malaya, moving toward Singapore, 1942

furiously southward, British forces mistook the din for enemy tanks rumbling through the colony's arteries.[5] By the time the Japanese were within striking distance of Singapore, the conquered territory behind them was ravaged, first by their onslaught, and then at the hands of British forces who unleashed scorched-earth tactics to destroy the region's natural and manmade resources. The colony's European society also raced southward to hunker down in Singapore's presumed safety, though one British woman who looked back at Malaya's shores and saw the faces of those she was leaving behind later wrote that it was "a thing which I am sure will never be forgotten or forgiven."[6] The Malayan Raj had crumbled and, with it, over a century and a half of British rule and pretense of paternalistic authority and protection.[7]

Some five years earlier Britain's military leader on the scene, Lieutenant-General Arthur Percival, had warned of Japan's ability to "burgle Malaya by the back door."[8] By the spring of 1941, when Percival took on his appointment as general officer in charge of the Malaya command, wartime Britain was stretched globally, and Churchill was prioritizing other theaters—including the Middle East, with its coveted Suez Canal, and Russia—over possible attacks in Southeast Asia. Moreover, Churchill believed his own hype and the army's "invention of the imaginary fortress of Singapore."[9]

Compounding Britain's self-deceptions were the racist notions that underpinned its own sense of nationhood and purpose in the empire. From Percival across the chain of command, most British officials believed the Japanese were tiny, weak men, on a par with Italians at best, in their opinion, and hardly a worthy enemy for their military. Britain's humiliating defeat in Malaya laid waste to such assumptions. Even greater ignominy befell the empire in early February 1942, when the Japanese overran Singapore and so handed Britain its worst imperial defeat since the Battle of Yorktown. It was a loss that Churchill called the "the worst disaster and largest capitulation in British History."[10]

With the Battle of Singapore all but over, Anthony Daniels stood, blood soaked, in Tanglin Hospital, having triaged hundreds of casualties.[11] The rapid carnage afforded Percival little time to train impressed recruits in the black arts of guerrilla warfare that he had helped to pioneer in Britain's war against Sinn Féin. Instead, British forces scrambled for nearly a week with defensive maneuvers, all of which merely staved off the inevitable. As defeat loomed on the horizon, soldiers and civilians alike took to drink. They wiped out the bar at the legendary Raffles Hotel, dutifully signing chits as if a familiar Anglo tomorrow would still break at dawn.[12]

Fall of Singapore, February 1942

In London, Churchill desperately cabled Archibald Wavell, Britain's commander in chief for India who oversaw the region's wartime operations, and demanded a sacrificial last stand for empire and nation. "There must at this stage be no thought of saving the troops or sparing the population," Churchill wrote. "The battle must be fought to the bitter end and at all costs. . . . Commanders and senior officers should die with their troops. The honour of the British Empire and the British Army is at stake."[13] The honor of the British Empire, however, was already on the sacrificial altar of Japan's superior military strength and Britain's false claims of imperial fortitude. By the time Percival surrendered to Yamashita, the prime minister's Armageddon orders had played out in effect, if not in practice.

On February 15, 1942, the Rising Sun flew over Singapore's highest building. The entire region was decimated. British casualty figures neared ten thousand, and an untold number of British subjects and migrants had met their fates at the hands of the Japanese. Hirohito's forces captured over 130,000 British personnel, many of whom were sent to the notorious prisoner-of-war camps. By the end of the war, over 100,000 British subjects in Malaya and Singapore would perish from Japanese brutality, disease, and starvation. Others, like Anthony Daniels, survived Singapore's fall and then Japanese interrogation and forced labor on the Siam-Burma Death Railway, only to escape captivity and join Britain's secret Force 136, also known as the Special Operations Executive, or SOE.[14] While the British Empire in Southeast Asia was shaken to its core, unbeknownst to many, Daniels and countless other British soldiers and subjects remained there, embedded behind enemy lines. Together they were legacies of the nation's imperial past as well as its hope for the future.

It would be three years before Daniels and Force 136 emerged to rekindle British imperial hopes in Southeast Asia. Until then Britain depended on its remaining empire to defeat fascism, deploying not only personnel and supplies from around its imperial globe but also wartime tactics and methods that His Majesty's men had honed in the air and on the ground in interwar Ireland, Palestine, Bengal, and elsewhere. For Britain, the empire came home during the war, and so too was it poised to save a nation, and its allies, from the precipice of defeat.

CHAPTER 6

An Imperial War

When Britain entered the war on September 3, 1939, it did so as arguably the world's leading global superpower. Only the Americans came close with their economic prowess, though in many respects—from imperial expanse and influence to military strength and reputation—Britain still towered over her colonial progeny. The empire was the backbone of British dominance, and the Second World War threw into relief its importance not only to Britain but also to a world fighting fascism.

Britain's empire shaped and reflected the nation's war efforts. Its reach stretched to every continent save for Antarctica and encompassed some of the world's most vital ports and sea routes, air bases and landing strips, and mineral and agricultural resources, not to mention sources of labor and military manpower. When Prime Minister Chamberlain's ultimatum to Hitler expired on the morning of September 3, over fifty of Britain's territories threw their weight behind the declaration of war. After 1941 they collectively fought a European and Asian conflict, unlike any of Britain's enemies. The fascists took out the only other major imperial power, France, just nine months into the fighting. The psychological consequences for Britain were profound, and so were those that unfolded on the ground. France's rapid demise rendered vulnerable the British Empire in Asia where, according to one senior official, the Vichy government in Indochina had "opened the door"—even if it was already ajar—for the Japanese invasions of Malaya, Singapore, Siam, Burma, and elsewhere.[1]

Hours before Germany's advance through France, Chamberlain resigned as Britain's prime minister, and Churchill assumed the premiership with unmatched imperial bona fides, stretching from the North-West Frontier, Omdurman, and the South African War to parliamentary undersecretary of state for the colonies, first lord of the admiralty, secretary of state for war and minister of air, and secretary of state for the colonies. In his maiden speech to Parliament as prime minister on May 13, 1940, Churchill spoke not to the British nation but to the British imperial nation: "We have before us an ordeal of the most grievous kind. . . . You ask, what is our aim? I can answer in one word: It is victory, victory at all costs, victory in spite of all terror, victory, however long and hard the road may be; for without victory, there is no survival. Let that be realised; no survival for the British Empire, no survival for all that the British Empire has stood for, no survival for the urge and impulse of the ages, that mankind will move forward towards its goal."[2]

At the nation's symbolic head, King George VI took to his diary in September 1939, writing that Hitler had gone to war "with the knowledge that the whole might of the British Empire would be against him."[3] Across imperial expanses, many men and women pledged their loyalty to Britain at the war's outset, even if only the simple nod from a British colonial overlord committed them. The governor-general and viceroy of India, Lord Linlithgow, did this for the Raj's 400 million people. Before this fiat, however, Gandhi had told Linlithgow that he had contemplated the global conflict "with an English heart," and he began to weep when he conjured the image of a destroyed London. It was a thought, he said, that "stirred [him] to the very depths."[4] Churchill reflected on the role of the nation's white dominions when he wrote wistfully that "in that dark, terrific, and also glorious hour we received from all parts of His Majesty's Dominions, from the greatest to the smallest . . . the assurance that we would all go down or come through together."[5]

The full weight of Britain's imperial past and present, however, would not be enough for the nation to win on the European and Asian fronts. It also needed help from its onetime colony across the Atlantic, though negotiations for dollars and manpower brought ideological debates on both sides that were the harbinger of a new world order. Until the summer of 1940, Britain's coalition government "consistently deprecated," in Churchill's words, "the formulation of peace aims or war aims."[6] No one wanted to offer up specifics. Anything other than rousing yet vague statements could lead to later demands for commitments that Britain could not, or would not, uphold. In November 1939, Chamberlain had summed up the war aim succinctly. His nation had to defeat "that aggressive, bullying mentality which seeks continually to dominate other peoples by force, which finds a brutal satisfaction in the persecution and torture of inoffensive citizens and, in the name of interests of the state, justifies the repudiation of its own pledged word whenever it finds it convenient."[7] A few months later Churchill was more to the point in declaring that Britain's aim was "victory"[8]

Britain's leaders wanted to rebuild Europe, negotiate boundaries, and reduce arms, all under the rubric of goodwill. They paid scant attention to the imperial question or to international rights and their protections. One notable exception was Chamberlain's aristocratic, High Anglican foreign secretary, Lord Halifax, who openly justified the war in evangelizing terms. "The rhetoric of the time," as the legal historian Simpson reminds us, was one of "Christianity, Western Civilization, Democracy, and the Rule of Law [which] featured as a seamless whole." Halifax embodied this ethos, which had endured from the Victorian era to the Second World War. His high-minded sensibilities, however, propelled him one step further. He spoke of the war as "a crusade for Christianity," emphasizing the concept of "human rights." "In general it is no business of one nation to interfere with the internal administration of another," he stressed.

> But when the challenge in the sphere of international relations is sharpened, as today in Germany, by the denial to men and women of elementary human rights, that challenge is at once extended to something instinctive and profound in the universal conscience of mankind. We are, therefore, fighting to maintain the rule of law and the quality of mercy in dealings between man and man and in the great society of civilised states.[9]

Outside government, Halifax was a relative anomaly—few in Britain wrote about "human rights" as the brick, let alone the foundation, of the peacetime edifice. H. G. Wells was an exception. He insisted that his *The Rights of Man* was a crucial part of war aims. Wells wrote prolifically about the need to protect rights—such as the right to education, religion, work, and protection of property and personhood—as well as freedoms, such as freedoms from torture, involuntary medical treatment, and forcible feeding. He published his declaration, in early 1940, in multiple outlets, including *The Times* and the *Daily Herald*, which would be sites for a "Great Debate," Wells hoped. The declaration, which some thought stressed a Bolshevik-inspired socialist utopia, circulated around the world in multiple languages. The degree to which Wells influenced future discussions over international protection of individual rights is a matter of debate. What is clear, however, is that he and his movement alone did not move the dial in the corridors of Whitehall. Instead, that push was going to come from across the Atlantic.[10]

When Americans reelected Franklin Delano Roosevelt president in November 1940 for an unprecedented third term, he offered both hope and concern for Britain. Negotiations were under way to move the Americans from any pretense of wartime neutrality to outright support for the Allies with economic and military aid. Roosevelt had first to sell the deal to Congress, and he was poised to do so with his State of the Union address. Out of concern that FDR would gain the ideological upper hand, Britain's wartime coalition finally established the War Aims Committee to develop some sort of vision for a postwar future. When it came to rights, Churchill's men, and jurists more generally, cleaved to the renowned constitutional authority Albert Venn Dicey's belief that a civilized government did not need to make any declarations about rights as they were, a priori, part of that sovereign polity.[11] With the exception of a few murmurings from the famed historian Arnold Toynbee about "maintaining a measure of individual liberty," only Halifax had much to say about the preservation and protection of liberties, which, for him, were enshrined in the "Christian belief in the brotherhood of man." He also wrote of "the right to live without fear either of injustice or want," though Churchill never uttered these notions nor any support for the committee's other considerations. Instead, the committee's final statement of war aims remained in the prime minister's inbox, partly because Churchill disliked its main protagonist, Halifax, and partly because the Americans, who had had a pass at the draft statement, seemed to offer it little support.[12]

A few weeks later, on January 6, 1941, echoes of Halifax's affirmation of freedoms could be heard reverberating off Congress's walls and over America's airwaves. FDR pitched his Lend-Lease policy to Congress and to the American public within an ideological framework that spoke to isolationists and played to an American electorate that needed both rhetorical and practical reasons to support the Allied war effort. Roosevelt spoke of "a world founded upon four essential freedoms": freedom of speech and expression, freedom to worship God as each person saw fit, freedom from want, and freedom from fear. He continued, rousing a nation and the world:

That is no vision of a distant millennium. It is a definite basis for a kind of world attainable in our own time and generation.

That kind of world is the very antithesis of the so-called new order of tyranny. . . . Since the beginning of our American history, we have been engaged in change—in a perpetual peaceful revolution—a revolution which goes on steadily, quietly adjusting itself to changing conditions—without the concentration camp or the quick-lime in the ditch. The world order which we seek is the cooperation of free countries, working together in a friendly, civilized society. . . . Freedom means the supremacy of *human rights* everywhere. Our support goes to those who struggle to gain those rights or keep them. Our strength is our unity of purpose.[13]

Roosevelt inserted "human rights" into the national and diplomatic discourses on war aims at a profoundly important historical moment. Lord Halifax, who had become Britain's ambassador to the United States a few weeks before Roosevelt's speech, was ebullient. Others, like Anthony Eden, were more measured. He said he would not discuss "the political questions involved giving real effect to President Roosevelt's 'freedom from fear'" or "elaborate our views about the President's first and second freedoms."[14] Eden and others also left the question of "human rights" untouched. Regardless, Roosevelt's triumph pulled the British government along on the human rights cause, at least insofar as it was a war aim. What that meant—indeed, neither FDR nor Halifax defined *human rights*—or how their protections would be implemented was anyone's guess.[15]

Still, with his "four freedoms" oratory, Roosevelt drove the ideological stake into the ground for the establishment of a new "kind of world . . . the very antithesis of the so-called new order of tyranny."[16] Practically speaking, the formation of a new world order hinged on the United States delivering Allied support. By March, the president had secured congressional approval to supply Britain with planes, warships, food, oil, and weaponry. This approval soon applied to other American allies in the war and was eventually worth $50 billion, over $30 billion of which was directed to Britain. In return, the Allied powers leased various army and naval bases to the United States for the duration of the war. For the Americans, the payoff was clear: Lend-Lease, by keeping Britain and the Allies in the war, would keep the Americans out of it.

Months later Roosevelt, Churchill, and high-ranking staff members found themselves floating in Placentia Bay, Newfoundland. There aboard the USS *Augusta*, the president and prime minister met for the first time since a brief encounter in 1918. It was the start of a friend-

Franklin Roosevelt and Winston Churchill, Newfoundland, 1941

ship of sorts. "Just to hear the President shout 'Hello' is like drinking a bottle of champagne," Churchill later effused. By war's end, the two men would communicate more than two thousand times. Churchill wrote elegant prose that spoke of "our friendship [being] my greatest standby" to a reserved Roosevelt, who privately described his British counterpart as "a real old Tory of the old school."[17] They undoubtedly shared mutual respect and a clear understanding that Britain and the United States were natural allies whose cooperation was imperative during wartime. Nevertheless, antagonisms punctuated the Anglo-American relationship, particularly when it came to Britain's empire. Roosevelt privately disliked Churchill's "eighteenth-century methods" of ruling over 700 million subjects around the globe, just as the prime minister needled America's "sentimental" attitude toward the world's lesser races, which included, in his words, the "pigtails" and "Chinks."[18]

At home, the president fought a bitter battle with isolationists and was determined not to make the same mistakes as Woodrow Wilson. Along with misreading the isolationist landscape after the First World War, Wilson had believed in colonial reform rather than immediate liberation, though on this score he was not terribly far from broader

American sentiment. Insofar as self-determination was concerned, "he envisioned [non-European peoples] achieving it through an evolutionary process under the benevolent tutelage of a 'civilized' power that would prepare them for self-government," according to the Wilson expert Erez Manela.[19] Such a process would take time and require the oversight of an international institution. Some two decades later, when Roosevelt cast his view across America, it was clear that imperialism was hardly in vogue. Neither isolationists nor the broader electorate were going to risk life and limb to defend Britain's maintenance of empire. Influential British writer and colonial expert Margery Perham, in a *Foreign Affairs* article, summed up the issues at hand:

> The American view which reaches us through war's interruptions and by way of our shrunken newspapers may be put in the following brief and therefore blunt terms: "The British are guilty of a sin called Empire. They committed it against the American people until these broke clear of British control to become a nation. The Americans are innocent of any such guilt. They thus are in a moral position to condemn Britain as they watch her continuing in her way of sin against other people. The situation is the more distressing to Americans as they are being asked, in this war, to defend and support the British Empire."[20]

By the time Roosevelt and Churchill met in Placentia Bay in August 1941, both mutual cooperation and suspicion infused their discussions. In the run-up to the meeting, the empire was certainly on Roosevelt's mind as he ruminated over possible postwar scenarios. While British officials focused on the pressing issues of winning the war, which included appealing to the American electorate, FDR and his entourage sought to extract British concessions with an eye to the postwar settlement. The Americans wanted to scrap imperial preferences, which the 1932 Ottawa Agreement had outlined, creating a zone of limited tariffs within the empire and high tariffs for countries outside it, and to stymie any British hopes for postwar expansion. Their British counterparts were equally as determined to prevent the Americans from creating a new empire out of the possible ashes of their own. Churchill had no doubt that, as the historian William Roger Louis suggests, "the future world order would be based in large measure on the power, prosperity, and prestige of the British Empire, as it had in the nineteenth century."[21] In the postwar era, the empire would be, at best, a conglomeration of self-governing entities within the British Commonwealth; still, British officials thought some colonies far too small and backward to ever have an independent seat at the table. As for Roosevelt, his thinking on the empire was evolving, though it would soon be clear that, for him, independence was the uncompromising objective, as was a kind of guardianship that would ensure imperial accountability. FDR wanted timetables to independence—sometimes twenty to thirty years, but timetables nonetheless—that an international guardianship would oversee to hold imperial feet to the fire over questions of economic and social development as well as devolution of colonial power.[22]

Roosevelt had a few tricks up his sleeve: he unexpectedly offered up to Churchill the idea of issuing a joint press statement on their agreed-on war and peacetime aims. The president's coterie showed up with a draft ready to go, which set their British counterparts scrambling. Nevertheless, Churchill would not miss the opportunity to shore up American solidarity. After a few rounds of concessions and edits, Roosevelt and Churchill offered the world "The Anglo-American Eight Point Plan." The press christened it the Atlantic Charter, while Churchill called it "a united Declaration [that] sets up a milestone or monument which needs only the stroke of victory to become a permanent part of the history of human progress."[23] Press release, declaration, plan, or charter, it would have far-reaching wartime effects with its aspirational preamble that proclaimed Anglo-American solidarity in making "known certain common principles in the national policies of their respective countries on which they base their hopes for a better future for the world."[24]

In London, the Foreign Office was beside itself. While Churchill had not given away the system of imperial preference, nor mentioned "human rights," he had still signed off on a document that, depending on one's political register, could be understood as having anticolonial undercurrents at the very least. One Foreign Office official described it as "a terrible woolly document full of old clichés of the League of Nations period." He continued, "there is obviously no alternative but to accept it, woolly though it is. . . . A.E. [Anthony Eden] feels that F.D.R. has bowled the P.M. a very quick one—such a document should have been communicated in advance."[25] The chief woolliness concern centered on the charter's third point, in which the president and the prime minister declared: "They respect the right of all peoples to choose the form of government under which they will live; and they wish to see *sovereign rights* and *self government* restored to those who have been forcibly deprived of them."[26]

At Placentia Bay, there had been no controversy about this issue. Once the two world leaders parted ways, however, it became clear that countless colonized peoples and their supporters around the globe would read the charter's third point as a signal, unambiguous call for freedom. Colonial governors quickly got word to London that their subjects would seize on it in bids for independence after the war. Roosevelt didn't waver, believing that "self government" applied to everyone around the world, which included Black and brown colonial subjects, particularly those in India, which was at the top of the president's agenda. He believed Britain needed to apply the lessons of American independence. Perhaps an interim measure, like the Articles of Confederation, would provide a transition toward India's independence, FDR would later suggest.

So, too, did domestic pressure mount in Britain. The *Daily Herald*, Labour's newspaper, seized on the Atlantic Charter as a liberation manifesto for the colonies. Its headline proclaimed, "The Atlantic Charter . . . IT MEANS DARK RACES AS WELL," and the article continued: "Coloured peoples, as well as white, will share the benefits of the Churchill-Roosevelt Atlantic Charter." Speaking to a West African student group days after the joint press release, Clement Attlee reassured his audience that Britain had "nobler ideas" contrasted with those of the Nazis, and he let loose the word "freedom." The independence genie was out of her bottle, and it was the Atlantic Charter that had set her free.[27]

Churchill had to defend a statement that, at the time of its writing, had seemed innocuous enough, at least to him. The prime minister thought the charter's third point clearly referred to the return of sovereignty to European peoples who were currently under Nazi rule. British colonies had never had "sovereign rights," and hence there was no self-government to restore. Churchill's war cabinet backed him and pointed out, for the Americans, the implications were the text read as any kind of liberation doctrine. The charter, in the words of the cabinet, "was not intended to deal with the internal affairs of the British Empire, or with relations between the United States and, for example, the Philippines."[28]

Colonial Secretary Lord Moyne was particularly animated, given the implications of the charter to his corner of government. No sooner had it hit the papers than he and his office undertook a massive campaign to stamp out the rising flames of public doubt. In his perorations to the cabinet, he hit every reactionary note. "In the Colonies we cannot admit a right of unfettered choice to those who, in the words of the League of Nations Covenant, are 'not yet able to stand by themselves under the strenuous conditions of the modern world.'" He maintained that "the development of institutions to the fullest practicable extent has been and is our policy.

But I am certain that it would be premature to commit ourselves to the belief that this will eventually lead to fully responsible government for every unit within the Empire. There are at least fifty governmental units in the Colonial Empire and, although the number might be reduced by federation, many would still remain too small, while others are strategically too important, for them ever to be completely masters of their destiny.

Ultimately, Moyne's Colonial Office was emphatic that the colonies' "evolution must continue on lines that accord with British conceptions of freedom and justice."[29]

A month after the meeting in Placentia Bay, Churchill took to the floor of Parliament to admonish his American counterpart and also make clear his imperial intentions: "It is a wise rule that when two parties have agreed a statement one of them shall not, thereafter, without consultation with the other, seek to put special or strained interpretations upon this or that passage. I propose, therefore, to speak to-day only in one exclusive sense." Turning to the question of the "Joint Declaration," he insisted that it "does not qualify in any way the various statements of policy which have been made from time to time about the development of constitutional government in India, Burma or other parts of the British Empire." He stressed that the charter's third point pertained only to "the restoration of the sovereignty, self-government and national life of the States and nations of Europe now under the Nazi yoke." Churchill regarded it as self-evident that European liberation

> is quite a separate problem from the progressive evolution of self-governing institutions in the regions and peoples which owe allegiance to the British Crown. We have made declarations on these matters which are complete in themselves, free from abiguity [sic] and related to the conditions and circumstances of the territories and peoples affected. They will be found to be entirely in harmony with the high conception of freedom and justice which inspired the Joint Declaration.[30]

So entered into Churchill's annals of wartime history "the high conception of freedom and justice" that was, in the minds of most Britons, at the heart of their nation's colonial enterprise. So, too, did the prime minister's insistence that Britain's declarations about colonial "self-governing institutions" were "free from ambiguity." In fact, ambiguity riddled the Colonial Office files. Moyne's men scrambled to compile anything that resembled a thoroughgoing list of declarations, partly because for many colonies none existed other than fuzzy memories and uneven records of political participation in the empire. Moreover, this participation, at least at levels of significant decision making, was, more often than not, largely a preserve of the white settlers and planters who dotted Britain's imperial map.[31]

Ultimately, it was neither the concept of "human rights" nor the debates over "self-government" and "freedom and justice" that moved the Americans closer to war. It was the Japanese bombs that fell on Pearl Harbor. Less than twenty-four hours after receiving news of the attack, a somber Roosevelt stood before Congress and announced: "December 7, 1941—a date which will live in infamy—the United States of America was suddenly and deliberately attacked by naval and air forces of the Empire of Japan." He grimly underscored Japan's audacity, both for his nation and for the world. Hirohito had not only rejected American attempts at the "maintenance of peace in the Pacific" but also launched simultaneous strikes against the Philippines and other Pacific territories as well as Malaya and Hong Kong.[32] The United States declared war on Japan, and with Italy and Germany's declaration of war against the United States three days later, the earlier Anglo-American gestures of support quickly morphed into a wartime alliance that witnessed Britain's anemia in the face of Japanese power in Asia. Less than two months after Pearl Harbor, Hong Kong fell, and Japanese forces pedaled their bicycles down the Malay Peninsula, all the way to Singapore, leaving devastation in their wake.

As wartime prime minister, Churchill formed a coalition government that incorporated a wide swath of men who, complementing his own unrivaled credentials, had had significant experiences in the empire or had previously held positions within government that conditioned them to maintaining Britain's imperial possessions and the ethos that underwrote them.[33] Chamberlain stayed on in Churchill's initial war cabinet as lord president of the council, until his death in November 1940, and brought with him a deep imperial legacy. Among other influences, he had come of age as a personal steward of his father's West Indies plantation, which was a physical testament to Joseph Chamberlain's imperial devotion as a cabinet minister in the late Victorian era. John Anderson would succeed the younger Chamberlain and eventually took Chamberlain's seat in Churchill's war cabinet. It was Anderson who had undertaken the "dirty job," first in Ireland as undersecretary and then in

Bengal as governor, where he and Charles Tegart had combined forces to produce a brand of British imperial repression, the "painful memory" of which locals had not forgotten. In fact, when George V had quipped about what was wrong with Bengal, it was Anderson who had shot back, "The most conspicuous and the most urgent of our problems is without question the suppression of terrorism."[34]

So, too, had the arch-imperialist Leo Amery been weaned in Britain's geographical expanse. Born in India, he had served alongside Churchill as a correspondent during the South African War, when he and the future prime minister narrowly escaped capture. Amery had helped draft the Balfour Declaration and later derided Woodrow Wilson's "facile slogan of self-determination" along with the League of Nations' notion that all states in the world were equal, with equal voting rights.[35] During the interwar years, he had served as colonial secretary during some of the empire's most tumultuous events, and in Churchill's wartime government, he was secretary for India and Burma. The position often saw him at loggerheads with his boss, and he later recorded in his memoirs that Churchill knew "as much of the Indian problem as George III did of the American colonies."[36]

The cabinet included other veterans of the empire, such as Churchill's heir apparent, Anthony Eden, who had served during the interwar years in the Foreign Office and was minister for the League of Nations, a post created just for him. He was also foreign minister under Chamberlain, a position from which he resigned in protest over appeasement with Italy. The move, at the time, had left Churchill in "dark waters of despair." "There seemed one strong young figure up against long, dismal, drawling tides of drift and surrender, of wrong measurements and

Britain's wartime cabinet, 1941

feeble impulse," Churchill recalled. "He seemed to me at this moment to embody the life-hope of the British nation, the grand old British race that had done so much for men, and had yet some more to give."[37]

Racial segregationists from the empire also saw action in Churchill's circles. After the Great War, Jan Smuts had turned down the post of high commissioner of Palestine, though he continued to push South Africa as a model for other colonies. Throughout Smuts's career, "the visionary, globe-trotting statesman-philosopher, [was] committed to his evolutionist paradigm of cosmic harmony under beneficent white guidance," as the historian Mark Mazower reminds us. Smuts's wartime support for Britain would prove his final clutch on power in South Africa before he was washed away with the 1948 rise of arch-nationalist D. F. Malan and the apartheid regime.[38]

There was also Lord Moyne, who had chaired the West Indies Royal Commission before the war and later held various posts in Churchill's war ministry, which included colonial secretary, as we have seen in his maneuvering through the Atlantic Charter fallout. Having come of age as a member of the Imperial Yeomanry in the South African War, Moyne—or Walter Guinness, as he had originally been known in his Irish

Winston Churchill and Jan Smuts, British Embassy garden, Cairo, August 8, 1942

homeland—was both a Conservative politician and scion of the legendary beer brewing family. Like his pal Churchill, Moyne did not hold back in expressing his opinions or his love for the high seas, where he cruised often on one of his many yachts. Renowned for his harsh Conservative line, Moyne did not equivocate when he ruminated over Woodrow Wilson's new world vision. "Since the days of Mahomet," he declared, "no prophet has been listened to with more superstitious respect."[39]

The fourth estate had a seat in Churchill's government as well. The prime minister's close confidant Lord Beaverbrook held various positions in the cabinet throughout the war. Owner of the *Daily Express*, the Conservative MP had been the minister for information in Lloyd George's Great War government. The position complemented that of his *Daily Mail* rival, Harmsworth, who had been director of propaganda. Beaverbrook understood the power of the press and called it a "flaming sword which will cut through any political armour"; he symbolically crafted a crusader as his paper's symbol.[40] He was also a shrewd businessman who appealed to, and reflected, the sentiments of the masses. By 1936 Beaverbrook had taken the *Daily Express* into broadsheet history with a daily circulation of 2.25 million, the largest of any newspaper in the world. (It would peak at 4 million in 1949.) The fourth estate's titan was also unabashed in his imperial views. Just as the *Daily Mail* was emblazoned with "For King and Empire" across its front page, the *Daily Express* was a voice for its owner's view of Britain and its place in the world. "In the Empire, and not in Europe, our future lies, and the Daily Express has never failed to preach the Imperial doctrine in good or in bad times," Beaverbrook boasted. "The Daily Express believes that the British Empire is the greatest instrument for good that the world has ever seen."[41]

On the war's front lines, nearly all of Britain's chiefs of staff had significant experience in the empire, as had the majority of senior theater commanders as well as their generals. Montgomery was fresh off dusting the Arabs in Palestine. Archibald Wavell, who had joined in the action there as the general officer commanding Middle East, would remain in this post before moving on to Southeast Asia. William Slim, commander of the Fourteenth Army in Burma, and Claude Auchinleck, who commanded troops in the Middle East and later India, had both been militarily reared in India, where they rose through the ranks. Scores of other empire-tested officers also took their orders, including Orde Wingate. Wavell was a personal admirer of Wingate's unorthodox tactics and had green-lighted them during the Arab Revolt (1936–39); a few years later, he tapped Wingate to launch a Special Operations Executive (SOE) force in Ethiopia.

In the years ahead, SOE would operate first in occupied Europe and later in Southeast Asia and in West and East Africa. Early in the war, the minister of economic warfare and Labour member of Churchill's cabinet Hugh Dalton had formed the SOE, also known as the "Baker Street Irregulars," after the organization's secret London headquarters. The SOE had other sobriquets such as "Churchill's Secret Army" and "the Ministry of Ungentlemanly Warfare." With espionage, sabotage, and reconnaissance as its top priorities, the SOE operated under the public radar, which continued when the organization expanded into the empire. It was, though, the empire that helped to drive the SOE's conceptualization as a state-sponsored guerrilla organization. In fact, in June 1940, when the war cabinet gave the SOE its official blessing, Churchill's first directive was for Dalton to "now go and set Europe ablaze."[42] To do so, the new political head of the SOE turned to the Irish Republican Army as a model, as well as to T. E. Lawrence's activities during World War I.[43]

Orde Wingate and the Chindits, Burma, 1944

In East Africa, Wingate's new Gideon force—comprised of numerous Zionist veterans of the Special Night Squads, as well as Sudanese and Ethiopian soldiers—would lead a successful, behind-the-lines offensive to retake Ethiopia from the Italians. Afterward Wavell gave Wingate a free hand at organizing long-range penetration units behind Japanese lines. Despite an uneven record, at best, Wingate's SOE forces, now known as the Chindits, were a personal favorite of Churchill's, a ray of wartime sunshine. By September 1943, Wingate—together with his brigadier, the empire-reared Michael "Mad Mike" Calvert—would lead a series of jungle force units in the risky task of attacking Japanese troops and installations, particularly in Burma. There and elsewhere throughout South Asia, Chindit and SOE operations combined forces with local, indigenous resistance units, which included those in rural Malaya, where imperial subjects like Anthony Daniels had eventually made their way after Singapore's fall.[44]

In the skies, Arthur Harris returned to Europe from his Palestine command center and rose to the rank of commander in chief of the RAF Bomber Command. Serving under Chief of the Air Staff Charles Portal, who himself had earned his interwar imperial stripes as commander of the British forces in Aden, Harris was Churchill's man when it came to the bombardment of German cities. While the prime minister had shown no mercy in using aerial destruction on subjects in the empire, he fretted endlessly over unleashing similar tactics on European civilians. In the summer of 1943, the RAF leveled Hamburg—an assault that took the lives of forty-five thousand people, who perished largely in a two-day firestorm, and left a million people homeless—and Harris grew frustrated with Britain's public insistence that the planes were bombing industrial and economic targets, not human ones. Civilian destruction was in Harris's imperial blood, and he had witnessed, firsthand, its lethal consequences in Iraq and Palestine. After a smaller attack on Kassel produced another firestorm that killed at least 5,500 people, Harris wrote to London, "The aim of the Combined Bomber Offensive, and the part which Bomber Command is required by agreed British–United States strategy to play in it, should be unambiguously and publicly stated. That aim is the destruction of German cities, the killing of German workers, and the disruption of civilised community life throughout Germany."[45] The bombing offensive continued, as Britain's imperial-tested air forces reduced Dresden and other German cities to rubble, even if the horrendous civilian suffering did not break Nazi morale.[46]

The legalized lawlessness that underwrote the work of Harris and his counterparts in Palestine and elsewhere in the empire came home to Britain in 1939 with the emergency codes, which also evolved from the Great War's Defence of the Realm Acts. In August 1939, with war imminent, an accommodating Parliament passed the Emergency Powers (Defence) Act, which gave the executive authority to create and implement defense regulations. As war clouds were breaking, the act was ready for legislative approval because of the Committee on Imperial Defence's painstaking behind-the-scenes work. For two years, the committee had been considering what laws and regulations would be needed should war erupt, and when it did, its recommendations resulted in wartime legislation such as Regulation 39A, preventing acts that could incite disaffection in the military; Regulation 39B, outlawing the creation of alarm or despondency over Britain's participation in the war; and Regulation 2C and 2D, regulating the publication of offensive material.[47]

The most significant and controversial regulation addressed executive detention, or detention without trial, which was meant for British subjects. Whereas the powers of royal prerogative could be exercised to detain "noncitizen enemy aliens," or any foreigner living in Britain, they could not be used for British subjects. Such prerogative, originating from the era of monarchical rule, enabled British ministers to undertake a range of responsibilities, from deploying armed forces to making international treaties and to interning foreigners. For British subjects, a new regulation was issued, Regulation 18B, an extraordinary curtailment of civil liberties. Modeled on Regulation 14B used during World War I, it drew on evolving executive detention policies in the empire and looked to interwar imperial detention policies for legal precedent. Ultimately, the regulations enabled the government to detain any British subject who posed a threat to national security, and to do so without charge, trial, or indicated length of term. Wartime power of detention would rest with the home secretary and an advisory committee, chaired by the well-known barrister Norman Birkett, who was also a Methodist minister and would later be an alternate judge in the Nuremberg trials. The committee would oversee the bureaucratic process of issuing detention orders before the home secretary approved them, and of hearing appeals, which would be few in number, and even fewer successful. Such "oversight" assuaged the concerns of some members of Parliament, who were outraged at the prospect of wartime infringement of British civil liberties.[48]

It's important, however, to put this detailed though important legal and bureaucratic history in context. When Churchill took office in May 1940, an invasion scare was gripping the nation. Hitler's forces were rolling through Europe, and nation after nation was falling: Denmark,

Norway, Belgium, the Netherlands, Luxemburg, and most astonishingly, France. By late May, Churchill was evacuating his troops from the beaches of Dunkirk, while the Nazis were preparing to invade Britain. Throughout the nation, spy fever spiked, and everyone from shopkeepers in remote Yorkshire villages to the prime minister in Downing Street was convinced that a fifth column of spies and collaborators had bolstered Nazi success on the continent, and some of them were poised to subvert Britain's war effort from within. With the Battle of Britain looming on the horizon, in which the RAF would defend the nation against relentless aerial attacks from the Luftwaffe, and as Britain faced a possible Nazi invasion by sea after the fall of Belgium and France, Britons were panicked. It was against this backdrop that the prime minister endorsed a wholesale policy of rounding up and detaining enemy aliens, most of whom were European Jews who had managed to find refuge in Britain. Some were sent to squalid internment camps across the country, some to rat-infested factories, others merely to tents on water-soaked grounds. These sites were not in compliance with international conventions, one MP charged; another MP wanted disciplinary action taken against government officials overseeing the operation. Nearly thirty thousand aliens were interned in wartime Britain, a harrowing experience made worse by detainees' interrogation and categorization as A, B, or C, denoting their descending threat levels. Others were deported to Canada for internment there, though nearly twelve hundred didn't make it, drowning when their ship was torpedoed off the coast of Ireland.[49]

"This malignancy in our midst has been effectively stamped out," Churchill declared, after aliens were interned and he'd turned his attention to British subjects suspected of treasonous or politically threatening activities.[50] MI5 had been ruthlessly compiling files on possible suspects, which the advisory committee reviewed, a process that was described "as combining elements of a court martial with an ecclesiastical tea party."[51] By June, the home secretary had 826 detention orders on his desk, which he was to review, amounting to 138 hours of work if he'd given just ten minutes to review each file. Instead, the eye-raising omnibus order was introduced, consolidating dozens of names into a single order that was approved with one stroke of the home secretary's pen, often sending innocent British subjects to detention. The British government rationalized it as a preventative measure, one that justified keeping two thousand of its subjects detained during the war to preempt any crimes they *might* have committed had they remained free.[52]

It wasn't just the wartime emergency powers that brought detention without trial from the empire back to Britain. Initially overseeing the whole operation was John Anderson, Churchill's first home secretary. His aristocratic arrogance earned him the nickname "God's Butler." Emboldened by his earned reputation in Ireland and Bengal, Anderson asked for authority to take drastic action against anyone who impinged on the war effort. The cabinet agreed and stated that the way forward was through the "entrusting [of] the Home Secretary with wide powers and leaving it to his discretion to decide in what cases these powers should be exercised." As in South Asia, Anderson showed little mercy, an observer later writing that Anderson "took a broad general view of the information put before him. . . . He did not hold an enquiry going meticulously into every detail. He decided from his knowledge of the case and his perusal of the dossier that detention was necessary." He made snap judgments, which prompted the Labour MP Edith Summerskill to ask, "Is it in order for the Home Secretary to treat this as if we were natives of Bengal?" Another Labour member, Herbert Morrison, decried the "really extraordinary sweeping powers under which, it seems to me, anybody whom the home secretary did not like could be hanged, drawn or quartered almost without any reasonable or proper means of defending himself."[53] In October 1940 Anderson ascended to become lord president of the council and a full member of the war cabinet, while his onetime critic, Morrison, replaced him as home secretary. So highly did Churchill value Anderson's brand of liberal imperialism that he wrote to George VI informing him that "in this case there can be no doubt that it is the Prime Minister's duty to advise Your Majesty to send for Sir John Anderson in the event of the Prime Minister and the Foreign Secretary [Eden] being killed."[54]

Churchill took particular interest in intelligence gathering, so much so that he created the secretive Whitehall committee known as the Home Defence (Security) Executive, immediately after he assumed the premiership. The Conservative stalwart Philip Cunliffe-Lister, first Earl of Swinton, chaired the Security Executive, packing it with a roster of future counterinsurgency and secret service notables. Among them was the young Oxford-educated barrister Kenneth Diplock, who was being groomed for his future legal role in defending Britain's counterinsurgency methods and suspensions of due process, which later resulted in the eponymous Diplock Courts of Northern Ireland. Some thought the Security Executive smacked of a "Conservative front organization" of the worst kind.[55]

During the course of the war, Britain opened several interrogation centers that were the direct responsibility of the Security Executive as well as MI5.[56] Camp 020, located near the pastoral London suburb of

Ham Common, was housed in a Victorian mansion called Latchmere House. The British government created another interrogation center in Kensington Palace Gardens, the posh section of the nation's capital renowned today for its stately mansions and billionaire owners. Between the summer of 1940 and September 1945, Kensington Gardens nos. 7, 8, and 9 were combined into one of Britain's most secret military sites, the London Cage. Run by the War Office, the London Cage, like Camp 020, was staffed with interrogators and clerks drawn from the military and MI5. Many had experience in the empire, while others were German and Austrian nationals who worked on behalf of the British Army.[57]

Two MI5 recruits with extensive imperial histories oversaw day-to-day operations of the London interrogation centers. Camp 020 was home to Lieutenant-Colonel Robin "Tin Eye" Stephens, so-called because of the monocle affixed to his face that created an exaggerated, steely-eyed glare. With his hair meticulously combed back, starched uniform, and military awards and ribbons framing his left shoulder, Stephens epitomized menacing comportment. Born and raised in Alexandria, he came of age in the North-West Frontier and later spent time in various other parts of the empire, which included twenty more years of active duty in India. This, together with his fluency in German, Italian, and French, and varying degrees of proficiency in Urdu, Arabic, Somali, and Amharic, made him the ideal MI5 recruit. Part of the old-boy network, from a relatively privileged family, and above all else, a product of the empire, Stephens was a spy among peers when he joined Britain's Security Service (MI5).[58]

The first director general of MI5, Vernon Kell, recruited Stephens and other MI5 candidates exclusively from a circle of friends and family. The majority of his recruits had held posts in India and other British colonies. Kell's successors followed a similar course. First up was David Petrie, who had served in Bengal and also with Charles Tegart in Palestine, overhauling policing during the Arab Revolt. Thereafter Percy Sillitoe, head of the intelligence branch in the British South Africa Police Force, continued the colonial old-boy recruiting practices for Britain's Security Service, as did several of the director generals who followed him. In fact, when Anderson took over as lord president of the council, he tapped his imperial pal Petrie, with whom he had spent time repressing so-called terrorists in Bengal, to undertake a full review of MI5.[59] In April 1941, Petrie became MI5's head, to carry out the service's reorganization based on his extensive work in the empire. After helping to create the Arab Investigation Centre in Palestine as well as other imperial interrogation sites, he oversaw interrogations at the highest levels in

Britain. It was hardly surprising, then, that Stephens and his colleagues were connected not only through sensibilities and shared experiences of colonial rule and pastimes but also through a culture of empire that reflected liberalism's underbelly. This was the culture that migrated home during wartime.[60]

The commandant of the London Cage, however, had an imperial heritage that was as expansive as his propensity to write down his wartime interrogation experiences. Alexander Scotland, a onetime military intelligence officer, came out of retirement to run the cage at Kensington Palace Gardens. Having picked up an Order of the British Empire (OBE) for his success in interrogating German prisoners of war during World War I, Scotland had battle scars that extended back to the turn-of-the-century empire in Africa. Looking for adventure, he had moved to German South West Africa, where he joined the German Army, changed his last name to Schottland, and fought in the genocidal wars against the Herero and Namaqua populations who resisted colonial rule. The Germans suspected him of being a British spy and incarcerated Scotland in Windhoek, the colony's capital, for over a year. German interrogation techniques left a deep impression on him. "During the long, arduous questioning I was given by the staff officer attached to the German colonial troops, I learned perhaps the most valuable lesson of my career in South Africa," Scotland recalled. "I acquired some of the techniques of interrogating an enemy subject."[61]

In wartime London, the War Office stressed the importance of its interrogation and intelligence operations. "The Combined Services Detailed Interrogation Centre (C.S.D.I.C.) is administered by the War Office (M.I.9.) on behalf of all three Services and has the duty of extracting all forms of information from enemy [prisoners of war] by special methods of interrogation," War Office officials stressed. "It is no exaggeration to say that the results achieved are of the greatest operational importance."[62] In the case of one CSDIC (pronounced *sizdik*), Camp 020, Tin Eye Stephens personally oversaw all the detainees and the "special methods of interrogation."[63] These methods drew on past imperial experiences and also evolved through trial and error. Stephens recruited interrogators whom he defined as either "breakers" or "investigators." Breakers softened detainees up and established their guilt, while investigators fleshed out the details and relevant intelligence.[64]

Stephens was accountable to Guy Liddell and Dick White, the first and second in command of MI5's B-Division, as well as Churchill's Security Executive. More than anyone else, White was in the trenches, overseeing the wartime interrogation system. He worked closely with the War

Office to establish nine "cages," or interrogation centers, around Britain. Interrogation teams screened enemy suspects to determine whether to dispatch them to one of the country's POW centers, or to London for further interrogation. These wartime experiences would have a bearing on Britain's secret state more broadly—as well as on the multiple end-of-empire wars on the horizon—as White went on to head MI5 and MI6, a unique achievement in the history of Britain's intelligence services.

It wasn't just those leading and staffing the interrogation sites who had imperial connections: so did some of the prisoners. It's unclear from the historical record how many prisoners were held in the CSDICs, or the final fate of many who underwent interrogation. What we do know is that some of these men were held under Regulation 18B and were therefore British subjects, whereas others were aliens detained under royal prerogative. Still others were picked up outside Britain, including in the empire. In 1942 intelligence decryptions revealed several high-level Nazi agents operating incognito in far-flung imperial corners like the steamy coastal city of Mombasa, Kenya. Without legal oversight, Camp 020 was ideal for interrogating these operatives, as well as fascist spies ensconced in European colonies like Portuguese Mozambique. There, in one case, MI5 paid a prostitute to lure a German, known for his sexual dalliances, across the border into Swaziland, a British territory, where he was picked up and sent to London's Camp 020. Obsessed with rule of law, MI5 felt it might have more legal coverage for seizing an operative in British rather than foreign territory, which was astonishing given that the operations effectively kidnapped foreign spies for rendition to Britain, where they were interrogated in a black spot. Concerns for legal protection went to the top brass when Dick White asked MI5's chief legal counsels whether the rendition operations were legally justifiable:

> We shall find ourselves in a particularly serious position if it is ruled that the legal machinery for detaining an enemy agent in a Colony and subsequently bringing him to the U.K. is found to be faulty in law. . . . I am afraid that this is a case in which we cannot leave the matter in doubt, for were the detention of an enemy agent brought here under this proposal to be tested by Habeas Corpus [the legal process by which a prisoner can demand to be brought before a court], in all probability it would be a moment when he was already installed in Camp 020. Subsequent publicity attendant upon a test of Habeas Corpus would be extremely detrimental to Camp 020 and might jeopardise our whole position with regard to it.[65]

Detention of these alleged Nazi agents was questionable under Britain's wartime emergency regulations, as was MI5's kidnapping of these suspects from British colonial territories, many of which had no equivalent of Regulation 18B, meaning it would be legally permissible for aliens detained in these colonies to bring habeas corpus proceedings. Hidebound to the rule of law, however perverted it was, Dick White huddled with MI5 and Colonial Office legal advisers who agreed to " 'ad hoc' legislation" that empowered a colonial governor "to remove a suspect alien from a ship or aircraft visiting the colony, and to detain him pending his removal from the colony." Without this ad hoc measure, some of Britain's greatest legal minds could find no legal justification for detaining and transporting a foreign national without due process.[66] Their solution was a clear example of how legalized lawlessness worked.

Some historians deny that any violence or torture took place in London's interrogation sites.[67] Historical evidence, however, suggests otherwise. Stephens and Scotland's cages became subjects of scrutiny when several prisoners alleged torture and other cruelties. In the case of Camp 020, the Security Executive had handpicked Harold Dearden as the camp's chief medical officer. He, working alongside Stephens and the other interrogators, devised torture techniques that were conducive to plausible deniability defenses and that included starvation tactics, sleep deprivation, and threats of hanging and death by firing squads. One former prisoner recalled being treated by Dearden at Camp 020: "it was not long before my memory began to deteriorate. Certain periods of my life completely disappeared from my mind. . . . [The resident doctor] stated to me plainly that the treatment was intended to produce a state of 'mental atrophy and unreserved loquacity.' "[68]

Several former prisoners alleged mistreatment at the London Cage. In 1943 Otto Witt lodged a formal protest with Britain's war secretary over torture. A few years later torture allegations surfaced in Hamburg, when a court tried Gestapo members for the murder of fifty RAF officers who had been shot after tunneling their way out of Stalag Luft III. Many of the German defendants claimed they had been systematically beaten and tortured in the London Cage and only then signed confessions; they all gave detailed descriptions of their ordeals under Scotland's watch. Fourteen of the fifty defendants were hanged, and nothing came of their accusations of abuse in the cage.[69]

Later, Fritz Knöchlein leveled allegations of systematic ill-treatment meted out to him and other prisoners. They had been humiliated, starved, water tortured, worked without respite, and sleep deprived, according to Knöchlein.[70] At the time, he faced the death penalty for the murder of 124

British soldiers. Still, the British government took his allegations seriously enough—given their lengthy and detailed nature—to consider an inquiry, though it ultimately decided to pass. Given Knöchlein's crimes, officials noted that "any court of inquiry into these allegations would be futile."[71] Knöchlein was eventually executed, though not before the local London police, according to Scotland, were "called in to enquire why such a din was emanating from sedate Kensington Palace Gardens." It turned out that the neighbors had heard Knöchlein's screams.[72] In 1954 Scotland wrote a manuscript describing activities at the London Cage. Prior to the government's heavy censoring, it contained descriptions of methods of interrogation that would cause "considerable embarrassment to HMG [Her Majesty's government]," according to the Foreign Office. MI5's legal adviser was adamant that if the manuscript was published without serious redaction, Britain would be "guilty of a 'clear breach' of the Geneva Convention and had employed methods that were 'completely contrary to the express terms' of international law." A watered-down version was published several years later.[73]

British officials thought imperial techniques developed in their wartime interrogation centers were of enormous value not only to the collection of intelligence but also to the creation of the counterintelligence and espionage operation known as the Double Cross System. Churchill's fifth column scare was not unjustified. Germany's intelligence service, the Abwehr, did send hundreds of spies into Britain via parachute, submarine, and travel through neutral countries. MI5 and military intelligence were effective in capturing and then, during interrogation, turning them into double agents. They deployed classic wartime techniques, like "M cover," or the extensive use of hidden microphones, and stool pigeons, and used them alongside a host of other interrogation techniques in order to render German spies amenable to Double Cross participation. Behind the scenes, the entire double agent enterprise was the brainchild of MI5 and its Twenty Committee of intelligence officers and academics. Chaired by John Masterman, an Oxford University professor and mentor of MI5's Dick White from his Oxford days at Christ Church, the Twenty Committee oversaw the large-scale deception system and lent its name to the operation: the name Double Cross was derived from the Roman numerals XX. Masterman, who wrote the official history of the Double Cross System, proudly boasted that under his leadership, *"we actively ran and controlled the German espionage system in this country."*[74]

Interrogation teams used unorthodox methods to convince the Nazi spies to switch sides, just as they deployed such methods to gather intelligence more broadly. Guy Liddell, head of MI5's B-Division, noted in his diaries that Scotland, while interrogating a prisoner, would rough him up and punch him in the jaw. For round two, Scotland used a "syringe containing some drug or other, which it was thought would induce the prisoner to speak."[75] In the end, Scotland turned the prisoner, Wulf Schmidt. Under the code-name "Tate," Schmidt successfully operated as a double agent against the Germans. While MI5 created an effective system for turning Hitler's men, its wartime triumphs in the realm of intelligence and counterintelligence came at an enormous cost to civil liberties, despite Churchill's claims to the contrary.

In one particularly fraught moment when the cages were in full operation, the prime minister backed his beleaguered home secretary, Morrison, who, at the start of the war, had condemned the government's use of emergency powers. The high-profile case of Oswald Mosley, leader of the British Union of Fascists, and his release from detention played out in the press and Parliament, which vigorously debated the issue before voting in favor of Morrison's decision to release Mosley. Still, according to one legal historian, before the debate "there was the risk that Morrison would be forced to resign, or even that the coalition might collapse." It was at this moment in November 1943 that Churchill cabled his home secretary from Cairo and wrote, "I highly approve your action." The prime minister cabled again three days later, and famously stated:

> The power of the Executive to cast a man into prison without formulating any charge known to the law, and particularly to deny him the judgment of his peers, is in the highest degree odious and is the foundation of all totalitarian government whether Nazi or Communist. . . . *Nothing is more abhorrent than to imprison a person or keep him in prison because he is unpopular. This is really the test of civilization.*[76]

Although civil liberties had narrowly been vindicated at home with Mosley's case, they were still widely trammeled in others: the empire continued to leave an indelible imprint on Britain's war efforts across the globe. Not only had imperial landscapes consolidated wartime psychologies and tactics, but they also provided fresh recruits as well as training grounds and bases. Together they were essential to Allied victory. Nearly half of Bomber Command's wartime airmen, for instance, had learned the ropes in the British Empire and Commonwealth. Australia, South Africa, Southern Rhodesia, and Canada produced 150,000 airmen through the British Empire Training Scheme. Supposed backwaters like

Gold Coast and Assam emerged as crucial air bases for the Middle East and Asia. Airstrips, aerodromes, and flying boat anchorages spanned the imperial world and gave relative geographical specks like Bahrain, Mauritius, the Maldives and Cocos Islands, and Ceylon new strategic importance. On the seas, the empire continued to be the backbone for a global network of ports and bases that served as home for fleets of boats that patrolled and traded with the world. Now that the "imaginary fortress of Singapore" was a painful memory, Britain expanded other facilities and created others anew, in the Maldives, Freetown, Halifax, and Durban. The world's sea lanes were vital to British wartime survival, ferrying men and resources between North America, Britain, and disparate corners of the world.[77]

The empire's manpower strength was likewise staggering. Over 5.5 million imperial combatants and noncombatants served in the war and comprised nearly half of Britain's overall forces. For six years, there was scarcely a campaign or battle in which British soldiers weren't fighting alongside their imperial brethren to defeat Germany, Japan, Italy, and their allies. The Eighth Army, for example, was but a quarter British in late 1941. The rest of its members hailed from an empire and Commonwealth roll call: India, New Zealand, South Africa, Southern Rhodesia, Australia, Basutoland, Bechuanaland, Ceylon, Cyprus, the Gambia, the Gold Coast, Kenya, Mauritius, Nigeria, Palestine, Sierra Leone, the Seychelles, Swaziland, Tanganyika, and Uganda. Admiral Lord Louis Mountbatten's South East Asia Command's personnel was 25 percent African and nearly 60 percent Indian by the summer of 1945. In fact, India contributed more to the war effort than any other imperial possession; the size of its army increased from 205,058 in October 1939 to 2,251,050 in July 1945.[78] The empire's soldiers fought on the front lines in campaigns in Iran, Iraq, Borneo, Kenya, Madagascar, Somaliland, the Sudan, Syria, and Sumatra, among other locations. Less obscure battlefronts for such soldiers ran across North Africa and other parts of Asia and the Pacific; the Indian Ocean, much like the Atlantic and Mediterranean, was the site of major naval operations and engagements due in no small part to its vital sea routes.

Without question, two imperial locations took precedence over all others in their importance: Singapore and Suez. While much of Southeast Asia fell, the Middle East did not. Tiny Malta withstood relentless Axis attacks for three years and held Britain's Mediterranean position and, with it, Suez. The imperial-heavy Eighth Army then inflicted defeats on the enemy beginning in 1942. Later, with the help of British and American forces entering from North Africa, it drove the Axis pow-

British World War II "Unity of Strength" poster

ers out of the region. When the war broke out, Chief of the Imperial General Staff Sir Edmund Ironside had declared that the Suez Canal was "the center of the British Empire." By the end of 1943, the Middle East had more than proved its significance, both on its own terms and certainly in the wake of Singapore's fall. Its importance as a communication conduit vis-à-vis Suez was unquestionable, as was its oil, to Britain's war efforts. In defense of the region, His Majesty's troops occupied Iraq, Iran, and Syria in 1941, and Cairo—despite its nominal independence—was the British Empire's military capital for much of the war.[79]

The Middle East was not alone in its resource contributions to Britain's bottomless pit of wartime needs. India contributed over £2 billion in goods and services, and the war catalyzed India's industrialization with long-term economic benefits in the realm of self-sufficiency. As India scholar Madhusree Mukerjee points out:

The colony's entire commercial production of timber, woolen textiles, and leather goods, and three-quarters of its steel and cement production, would be required for the war. Factories near Calcutta were soon turning out ammunition, grenades, bombs, guns, and other weaponry; Bombay's mills were producing uniforms and parachutes, while plants all over the country were contributing boots, jeep bodies and chassis, machine parts, and hundreds of ancillary items such as binoculars for which the need had suddenly swelled. Apart for the United Kingdom itself, India would become the largest contributor to the empire's war.

Ordinary Indians felt the full weight of the emergency-empowered state coming down on them: widespread requisitioning and rationing, not to mention recruitment and provisioning of the armed forces, entered the day-to-day lives of countless subjects. Wartime grain exports to feed hungry troops further decimated a starving population, nearly 60 percent of whom, according to a 1933 survey, were "poorly nourished" or "very badly nourished."[80]

Elsewhere, tropical resources were crucial to the war effort. Britain exploited them fully through an increasingly intrusive state that deployed harsh methods of control to feed the war machine. It instituted bulk-purchasing schemes for major exports like Northern Rhodesian copper, Ceylonese tea, East African cotton and sisal, and Caribbean bananas. Local labor was forced, when necessary, to toil in the empire's mines, fields, and factories. After the fall of Malaya, and with it one of Britain's major tin sources, Nigeria's colonial administration impressed nearly 100,000 Africans into open-cast mines on the Jos Plateau. Tanganyika saw 85,000 Africans conscripted into farms and plantations that yielded sisal and other products. When workers went on strike on the Northern Rhodesia copper belt in 1940, and in the Bahamas in 1942, the police and military opened fire on them. Force as an instrument of control proliferated during wartime, as the survival of the British nation was at stake.[81]

Such wartime tactics were thrown into relief in India. Continued nationalist demands once again revealed Britain's slow-going measures of political inclusion. Divide and rule strategies ascended, and repressive measures accompanied them in new and foreboding ways. When Viceroy Linlithgow unilaterally brought India into war, he did not consult Indian nationalist leaders, who afterward universally pushed back. The Government of India Act of 1935 had instituted some reform measures, which included "responsible government" at the provincial level, though it stopped short of significant Indian representation at the federal level. As far as the Raj was concerned, Indians lived in these prov-

"Dig for Victory," propaganda wartime poster
for Britain's African colonies, c. 1940

inces and voted according to their various identitics, religion foremost
among them. Of course, that the British created separate electorates in
1909 based on religion played no small part in Indians voting according to their religious identities.[82] After the viceroy's war declaration, the
Indian National Congress demanded immediate transfer of power and
resigned en masse from their provincial posts. The Muslim League,
however, threw its support behind Britain and the war effort, which
only strengthened its hand, particularly in the wake of Congress's self-
induced political vacuum.

After France fell in June 1940, shoring up Congress's support had
become urgent. Britain needed to mitigate any further political instability in a colony whose support was crucial to the war effort. Underscoring
the immediate need for "unity of national purpose in India," Linlithgow
delivered the wartime coalition's "August Offer." India secretary Leo

Amery conveyed it to Parliament, highlighting the government's conditions: the viceroy would invite "a certain number of representative Indians to join [his] Executive Council" and would establish a War Advisory Council "which would meet at regular intervals and which would contain representatives of the Indian States and of other interests in the national life of India as a whole." His Majesty's government, however, "could not contemplate transfer of their present responsibilities for the peace and welfare of India to any system of Government whose authority is directly denied by large and powerful elements in India's national life." Ultimately, he and the viceroy would oversee a process that "pave[ed] the way toward the attainment by India of that free and equal partnership in the British Commonwealth which remains the proclaimed and accepted goal of the Imperial Crown and of the British Parliament."[83]

Britain's deal was largely a repackaged version of previous offers of self-government within the Commonwealth, offers that the Congress and Muslim League had declined in the 1930s. Moreover Britain inserted new conditions. For the first time, it insisted on an internal consensus that included minority interests. Here Britain dangerously pandered to the Muslim League and revealed its misjudgments in the region. Muhammad Ali Jinnah's League had adopted the Lahore Resolution in March 1940, demanding the creation of a Pakistani state, or set of states. The viceroy thought Jinnah and his followers feared a "Hindu Raj" and were therefore looking for minority protections as opposed to any kind of breakaway from a federated India.[84] Both the Congress and the Muslim League rejected the August Offer. Outraged, some Congress members called for immediate civil disobedience, and Gandhi's targeted satyagraha prevailed. Individual Congress members made antiwar speeches with the aim of getting arrested; twenty thousand people were locked up.

In 1942 wartime events brought Britain back for another round of negotiations with Congress and the Muslim League. Singapore's fall, followed by a rapid British retreat from Rangoon, had made fears that Japan would overrun India immediate and real. Earlier, FDR had exerted pressure on Churchill to introduce a transitional government. "I reacted so strongly and at such length that he never raised it verbally again," Churchill recalled.

> The President's mind was back in the American War of Independence, and he thought of the Indian problem in terms of thirteen colonies fighting George III at the end of the eighteen century. . . . This was no time for a constitutional experiment with a "period of trial and error" to determine the "future rela-

tionship" of India to the British Empire. Nor was the issue one upon which the satisfying of public opinion in the United States could be a determining factor. We could not desert the Indian peoples by abandoning our responsibility and leaving them to anarchy or subjugation.[85]

Leading with his paternalistic claims, albeit chastened somewhat by the war, Churchill dispatched Labour MP Stafford Cripps to India to make a deal with the deeply divided Congress and Muslim League. Hostility and religious fervor greeted him. Some League members called for an all-out revolt against Britain, while thousands of Jinnah's followers paraded in the streets and waved green flags in honor of the Lahore Resolution's second anniversary. Cripps offered both parties full dominion status at the end of the war with the option of leaving the Commonwealth at some unspecified future point.

Jinnah demanded clearer concessions for his Muslim constituents, who comprised around 35 percent of the population, even though he admitted to being "rather surprised" to see how far Cripps was willing to go "to meeting the Pakistan case."[86] Still, Jinnah rejected the offer, though he and the League remained in Britain's camp for the remainder of the war. The Congress leadership felt minority protections had gone too far. Moreover, Britain's half-hearted power sharing during wartime, not to mention the continued notion of self-government within the Commonwealth, was unacceptable. By August 1942, it rejected Cripps's offer and demanded immediate self-government in return for war support.

Nehru, Gandhi, and others opposed the Axis powers, though the allegiances of some within the Congress leaned toward Berlin and Tokyo. In fact, since the turn of the century, the Japanese had pursued a pan-Asian imperialist agenda complete with military academies—known as "language" and "foreign affairs" schools—that prepared young army and intelligence officers for Japan's imperialist destiny throughout Asia. Japan would be modern once it had an empire, so it was thought, and imperialist projections were not just about force and subterfuge. Japanese trade and investment permeated the entire region and integrated Japan into the broader Southeast Asian economies. Japanese goods—bicycles, toys, clothing, milk, and more—flooded Malaya and other British colonial markets, while Japanese boats, prostitutes, chemists, tourists, and financiers of all types were ever present. They served the local economies as well as the Japanese state as spies who, not surprisingly, targeted the discontent within the Indian National Congress as well as other Southeast nationalist movements, including those in Burma and Malaya.[87]

In the 1930s Tokyo had been a haven for radical Asian nationalists who joined study groups, went to universities, and participated in anticolonial societies. Some could not square the circle of Japan's pan-Asianist visions with its ruthless aggression in China. But by wartime, Axis allegiance offered an alternative to intransigent British rule, with its repressive policies and half-baked promises of social and political inclusion. When the Raj entered the conflict by fiat and drafted troops, a window for the Japanese opened. Disaffected members of the Indian Army and Bengali radicals offered fertile recruitment ground. Among those listening to the Japanese call was Rash Behari Bose, an early Bengali revolutionary who had escaped British detention, fleeing to Tokyo. He stood alongside Japanese lecturers and tutored younger radicals in anti-British lessons. Bose also founded the Indian Independence League, which organized Indians who lived anywhere in Asia "to eliminate," in the words of Pritam Singham, the league's leader in Bangkok, "the Anglo-Saxon from the whole of Asia."[88]

Subhas Chandra Bose, no relation to Rash Behari Bose, would go on to find other reasons to ally his cause with Japan. One of fourteen children born into a wealthy Bengali family, he was incensed by the Raj's version of the White Man's Burden. His early brushes with civil disobedience included an expulsion from school for retaliating against a teacher. Still, his intellect and family connections propelled him to Cambridge, and afterward he sat for the India Civil Services examination. He finished fourth on the exam and assured his father that his revolutionary ways were behind him. Not so. Bose returned to India in 1921, where he rose through the ranks of the Congress and became leader of the Forward Bloc, the party's most radical faction aside from the Communists. He spent as much of the next two decades in jail as out of it. When he was free to maneuver, he circulated through Europe, where he exchanged notes and ideas with other anticolonial revolutionaries, Eamon de Valera from Ireland among them.

Bose, along with Nehru, was Gandhi's heir apparent, though their paths to liberation diverged widely. In 1938 Bose became Congress president, but the coming war further revealed the deep cleavages within the Indian nationalist movement. While Gandhi and Nehru cautioned moderation, Bose openly demanded a mass civil disobedience campaign protesting British rule. Such radicalism pushed the moderate Congress to the brink. Bose was forced to resign, and from his leadership ashes, the radical nationalist rose to create a full-on revolutionary movement. His first agenda item was deeply symbolic. He attacked Britain's Black Hole of Calcutta myth by demanding that the Raj remove the Holwell Monument, an obelisk in the heart of Calcutta that commemorated the soldiers and residents who died in the so-called Black Hole in 1756. Moreover, he asked, where was the monument to the countless Bengalis who had lost their lives to British colonial repression and neglect? Bose organized demonstrations and soon found himself back behind bars. More protests ensued, Bose went on a hunger strike, and not long after his release from prison for medical reasons, he slipped out of Bengal and made his way to Kabul, then Moscow, and finally to Berlin.[89]

In the wake of the failed Cripps mission, the legend of Bose's radicalism reflected and, in some cases, galvanized widespread discontent, particularly among the colony's youth. Gandhi called for a civil disobedience campaign, known as Quit India, which soon took on a life of its own. In early August 1942, widespread demonstrations broke out against the Raj, and protesters attacked police stations and government and public buildings. As the historians Christopher Bayly and Tim Harper point out, "The most important point about the Quit India movement was not the way in which it drew on the disgruntled and resentful across

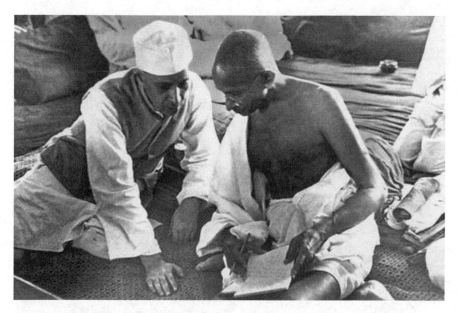

Jawaharlal Nehru and Mahatma Gandhi, adoption of the Quit India resolution, August 8, 1942

India but that, at root, it was an unorganized, popular movement."[90] Any reverence for British colonial strength disappeared. Indians of all religions, races, and castes saw defeated white troops making their way back from Singapore, Malaya, and Burma to Calcutta via Assam. Disease-ridden and demoralized members of the Indian Army shared stories of the heroic and disciplined Japanese who defeated imperialist Britain in battle after battle. Massive sit-ins dotted the Raj's landscape, and old disputes over land came to the fore, as did anger at recent expropriations for Britain's war effort. Grassroots protesters directed their activities toward the Raj's wartime centers of communication, transportation, and factory production: they ripped up railway tracks, cut telegraph lines, and blew up bridges.[91]

The legalized lawlessness that had evolved in the empire, and matured in Palestine during the Arab Revolt, had further proliferated in India with the 1939 Defence of India Act, which enabled the arrest of twenty thousand disciples of Gandhi's satyagraha. Quit India, however, was of a completely different order. Britain introduced a series of emergency regulations, known as the Defence of India rules, which gave the colonial government widespread repressive powers to stamp out the movement, which further spiraled thanks to Britain's draconian responses. The colonial government's swift detention of Gandhi,

Tear gas at Gowalia Tank Maidan, Quit India, Bombay, August 9, 1942

Nehru, and scores of other Congress leaders ensured that grassroots Congress nationalism would spread, its limited direction in the hands of low-level leaders. Many of these leaders had previously exited the Congress because of their factional loyalties and had incited local communal violence. From where he sat in Berlin, Bose knew it was time to return home, confiding to one of his brothers that "machine gunning, aerial bombardment, tear gas, bayonet charges, capital punishment—none of these ruthless measures has succeeded in cowing down the unarmed masses of Indians."[92]

For the British Raj, Quit India was the most damaging uprising since 1857. This time, however, war imperatives, more robust legal codes, and military manpower meant government forces quashed it within a matter of weeks, leaving 2,500 people dead. The Raj used aerial strafing honed in the North-West Frontier and carried out whipping sentences on another 2,500 subjects with alacrity. All the while, it deployed wartime emergency powers to contain public knowledge of its repressive measures. Britain's well-planned strike detained Congress's leadership, including Gandhi, for much of the war. For many detainees, prison conditions were unbearable. Some disowned the Congress in exchange for early release; others, like Nehru, who spent nearly three years behind bars, refused to barter for privileges. Writing to his sister, Vijayalakshmi Pandit, who was also swept up in the Raj's mass arrests and incarcerations, Nehru made clear his unwillingness to bend to British authority: "I do not fancy being treated like a wild beast in a cage with occasional rope allowed so that I can move a few feet if I behave myself. . . . Where force prevents me from acting as I wish, I have to accept it, but I prefer to retain such freedom of mind and action as I possess."[93]

Behind bars, the Mahatma's health declined. He was dismayed by Linlithgow's refusal to believe he was committed to nonviolence, particularly in the context of Quit India. As the historian Judith Brown points out, "Gandhi was still utterly convinced of the rightness of his own case, and argued that violence was in fact the government's fault because by repression it had goaded people into violence."[94] He soon announced he would fast for three weeks in protest. So concerned were officials about his weakened state that they offered him temporary release during his fast. Gandhi refused, and preventive measures went into effect. One Raj governor wrote acerbically that "it is a mad feature of the present situation in India that because of the 'Mahatmic superstition' we have to employ police and troops all over the country in case the old zealot should die."[95] Throughout his detention, Gandhi could not reconcile the government's views of him with the realities fueling Quit India. By the time of his release in the spring of 1944, the Congress's spiritual leader had severe malaria, hookworm, and amoebic dysentery, all of which exacerbated his kidney and heart problems. Fourteen thousand of the one hundred thousand arrested demonstrators and political activists also endured horrendous treatment as they remained locked up for much of the war.[96]

Totally prepared to dispense with nonviolence, Bose cared only about India's liberation. He was willing, after meeting with Nazi high commanders, to put fascism's policies aside if it meant breaking free of British colonial rule once and for all. He took a German U-boat to Tokyo where he became the obvious choice to head Major Iwaichi Fujiwara's brainchild, the Indian National Army (INA), a pro-Axis force comprised of disaffected British subjects who were willing to fight the Allies, including the British Empire. Fujiwara's position within Japanese intelligence reflected his self-professed understanding of Asian nationalist cultures. The INA first took life in Singapore, and its initial manpower came from the sixty thousand Indian prisoners of war held in Japanese camps. Its leadership, however, struggled. POWs and rank-and-file INA members wanted a Japanese-backed Indian leader who would take them to the promised land of independence. Bose was their choice.[97]

Having earned his revolutionary credibility behind bars and in the streets, Bose soon took control not only of the INA but also of the Indian Independence League, which had gained considerable strength with the Japanese occupation. In fact, the league's first major conference was in Tokyo just months after Singapore's fall. A year later it held its second conference in Bangkok, where delegates represented chapters from Malaya, Thailand, India, Burma, Hong Kong, Singapore, Manila, and Java. Together they pledged themselves to liberation. With Bose in charge, the league swelled to 350,000 members across the Greater Asian region, and nearly 100,000 INA volunteers came from the ranks of not only Japanese POWs but also peasants, plantation workers, traders, businessmen, and barristers. Moreover, some Indian Army members defected to Bose's INA. While the Raj's repressive measures may have reasserted British control during and after Quit India, they also betrayed its anxieties that had been ubiquitous since 1857. The INA passed around a message that reached beleaguered forces fighting to save Britain and her empire: "Dear Indian Brothers, The Japanese forces do not wish to fight against their Asiatic brothers, therefore you should not fight against us. It will be foolish to lose your lives by fighting for Britain who has been keeping you in slavery for years and has been ill treating you."[98]

With its broad-based composition, the INA actively fought Allied

Subhas Chandra Bose swearing in former prisoners to the Indian National Army

forces. Many of its members were more than willing volunteers and committed themselves to Bose's ethos of "Give me blood and I promise you freedom!"[99] In October 1943 he proclaimed the Arzi Hukumat-e-Azad Hind (Azad Hind), or provisional government of Free India. At the end of the month, he declared war on Britain and the United States in return for liberation after Axis victory. Despite the free in "Free India," however, Bose's provisional government remained a Japanese append-age. It was the Japanese who located the Azad Hind's government on the Andaman and Nicobar islands. Bose's nationalists renamed Britain's onetime interrogation islands Shaheed (Martyr) and Swaraj (Independence). The Japanese tortured suspected Indian traitors in the Cellular Jail. Administrators and propagandists from the Indian Independence League remained influential, populating the Free India government and creating provisional institutions and symbols, which included postage stamps, currency, courts, and civil codes. The Axis powers recognized the newly formed government and the INA's right to defend it. For much of the war, Bose remained stationed in Singapore, where he broadcast messages through Azad Hind Radio and directed the INA's multiple engagements against British forces, particularly in Burma.[100]

Azad Hind stamp, produced in Germany
though never issued, 1943

The cracks in Britain's imperial armor were evident to anyone willing to look: the fall of Singapore, the massive Quit India protests, and Bose's renegade and impressive INA, as well as the empire-wide crackdowns, Ireland's neutrality throughout the war, and South Africa's entrance only after a bitter parliamentary fight. For Britain, however, these were relative footnotes to its wartime belief in imperial strength and unity. Widespread and demonstrative gestures of support for Britain's war effort offset acts of imperial aggression or the empire's fraught relationships to it. In the end, nearly forty-five thousand Irishmen, including Catholics, volunteered to fight. South Africans sent two divisions to the front and offered up ports like Durban to the cause. The Australian prime minister Robert Menzies had declared on September 3, 1939, there was "unity in the Empire ranks—one King, one flag, one cause." "We range ourselves without fear beside Britain. Where she goes, we go, where she stands, we stand," New Zealand prime minister Michael Savage reassured his nation via radio address.[101]

Other colonial elites made their sentiments known as well. A member of Nigeria's legislative council, the Honourable Adeyemo Alakija, for instance, introduced a motion to pledge the support of his colony's Black subjects in a "war which this time is not going to be a war to end all wars, but a war which will ensure to the human race perpetual peace and freedom."[102] Wartime gifts of various sorts poured in, and the northern Nigerian city of Kano raised £10 million for a Spitfire fighter. Sierra Leone, a colony whose history stretched back to Britain's resettlement of former enslaved people, attached a nostalgic poesy to its cash gift: "In grateful recognition of the great benefits which Sierra Leone has received during the last 135 years under the British flag."[103] In India, despite or because of, the Quit India crackdown, the colony produced the largest volunteer army in history, as many of its soldiers joined its ranks as much for the rations as for imperial duty. The Indian Army's contributions to Allied successes were massive, a point that Field Marshal Claude Auchinleck, commander in chief of the Middle East and then India, made when he asserted that Britain "couldn't have come through [World War I and World War II] if they hadn't had the Indian Army."[104]

Such contributions fed Britain's wartime propaganda machine, which spread its message across the world like a thick blanket woven from patriotism's yarns. It was carefully loomed by historians and statesmen who selected threads that, when carefully arranged, created a tapestry that wrapped the nation and its loyal subjects in myths of Britain's imperial past. History. Heroes. Symbols. During the war's grinding years of uncertainty, hardship, and loss, they were crucial to British survival. Churchill's government knew this, packaging Britain's imperial nationalism for subjects at home and around the globe. Crises, however, also bring ruptures, offering those willing to look closely enough a chance to question the past and imagine the world anew. Colonial subjects were well conditioned for the war and the fault lines it exposed. Often deprived of basic needs and coerced within the empire's rapacious economic system, they experienced Britain's developmentalist logic and its hollowing out of sovereignty's promises. Their pens aflame, some of these subjects put to words what others were experiencing: Britain's empire was the devil's kitchen. It was a system of violence. It was a fascist-imperial project. Different histories, heroes, and symbols would prove their case, as would data and facts. A war of ideas between Black radicals and British historians and statesmen would reveal how deeply rooted contemporary imperial history wars are.

CHAPTER 7

A War of Ideas

The war, notwithstanding the professions of statesmen, is certainly not one for Democracy.

George Padmore, Pan-Africanist leader
November 1939[1]

That wartime loyalties ran high in the face of fascism's abyss was undoubtedly true. For many colonial subjects, however, there was also the issue of the lesser of two evils, combined with the hope of a new moral contract for wartime support.[2] In Nigeria, an editorial in the *West African Pilot* underscored local understandings insofar as wartime contributions were concerned. As Britain's appeasement negotiations unfolded in 1938, the paper declared "confidence begets confidence," and "the ideals of democracy which is the bedrock of the British constitution" must be given life in the form of political and socioeconomic equalities. The paper insisted:

> Men have the right to say under what form of Government they wish to live, and where nationality is concerned they have the right to determine their own allegiance. . . . It is an elaboration of the principle of self-determination for minorities who find themselves unable to enjoy political autonomy. Even though this principle is generally applied to Europeans, we see no reason why it should not be applied to Africans. . . . This is the voice of the Renascent African challenging international morality.[3]

The *West African Pilot* was the brainchild of Nnamdi Azikiwe, who had founded the newspaper in 1937 as an outlet for grievances, nationalist demands, and the public imaginings of a future different from its colonial present. The Nigerian paper was part of a larger revolution in local presses and pamphlets that gave life to alternative discourses that circulated not only in individual colonies but also in transregional and global networks. What appeared in the *West African Pilot* later appeared in Jamaica's *Public Opinion* or Trinidad's the *Vanguard;* Bengal headlined news of Ireland's struggles; India reprinted newspaper columnists in the Gold Coast, and vice versa; and London-based articles found their way into the NAACP's *The Crisis* and more mainstream American presses; the Communist Party's *The Negro Worker* and the Independent Labour Party's *New Leader* disseminated news from around the world.[4]

Anticolonialists of many stripes, including nationalists and those who pressed for international visions, wrote books and treatises that spoke to the empire's intellectual elite and reached colonial subjects in the streets, fields, and labor lines through local newspapers and vernacular presses. Azikiwe, for instance, scripted a treatise on "Renascent Africa" in 1937 that ran over three hundred pages and laid out a binary option to the continent's colonized: "It is either Freedom or Servitude." He urged them to "let Renascent Africans usher in a New Africa, and Africans of to-morrow need not continue to be in political servitude." Instead, he argued, "forces of nationalism" would bring the "right of self-determination." Quoting from Liberia's 1847 Declaration of Independence, he reminded all Africans that they "recognized in all men certain inalienable rights; among these are life, liberty, and the right to acquire, possess, enjoy, and defend property."[5]

Azikiwe was scarcely alone. As fascism advanced through Europe, Black writers from Britain's empire published books at a prolific pace. They disseminated ideas about enslavement, repression, forced labor, the color bar, freedom, and justice. These ideas intersected with those of Azikiwe and other Black intellectuals, journalists, nationalists, Communists, and Pan-Africanists who, together, fed a collective consciousness among many of the empire's subjects. It was in this context that the Trinidad-born Eric Williams, while a student at Oxford, worked on a thesis that eventually became *Capitalism and Slavery.* Williams's book questioned Britain's lofty notion that it had abolished the trade of enslaved peoples and enslaved labor due to an attack of conscience as opposed to hard economic calculations. At the same time, Jomo Kenyatta, who hailed from Kenya's Central Province, produced his defense of Kikuyu culture, later published as *Facing Mount Kenya,* while a student at the

London School of Economics (LSE). And the St. Lucian W. Arthur Lewis, also a student at the LSE, incubated his "Lewis Thesis" on labor and capitalist growth, which was the basis for his Nobel Prize in Economics in 1979—the only time the prize went to a Black man.[6]

C. L. R. James, too, was part of this Black diasporic tradition forged during the interwar period in colonial conditions that were, by any measure, unbearable. The descendant of enslaved people, James was born at the turn of the century in Tunapuna, Trinidad, where the postemancipation world that he inhabited had changed little from that of his forebears. There were, though, interstices in which he could move, and James earned a secondary school scholarship to Queen's Royal College in Port of Spain, then went on to teach English to up-and-comers like Williams. A gifted writer and emerging activist, James was a member of the anticolonial Beacon Group, a collection of local writers who published in *The Beacon* and whose literary work influenced, and was influenced by, a global Black community with roots in Marcus Garvey's Harlem, W. E. B. Du Bois's writings, and the confluence of European intellectual thought and interwar socialist ideas that spread throughout Britain's empire in the wake of the Bolshevik Revolution.[7]

By any measure, the itinerant West Indies community emerged as a locus of transnationalist, anticolonial thought. "I do not think there has been anything in human history," the Barbadian author George Lamming emphasized, "quite like the meeting of Africa, Asia, and Europe in this American archipelago we call the Caribbean."[8] These islands and their diaspora produced not only James, Lewis, and Williams but also Marcus Garvey, René Maran, Aimé Césaire, Frantz Fanon, and Stokely Carmichael. Here too, in his Tunapuna boyhood days, James forged a lifelong friendship with Malcolm Nurse. Sharing a family history of enslavement, they grew up in the extraordinary library of Nurse's father, where they consumed the writings of Black intellectuals alongside the canons of European thought. The distinctly imperial world in which they came of age steeped them in British thought and habit and imparted to them a fluency in language that reflected, at once, their understandings of colonial power and subjecthood.

In the early 1930s, these men, having mastered their own versions of colonial Britishness, went their own ways. James headed east, or in the Trinidadian's words, "the British intellectual was going to Britain," where he embraced his love for *Vanity Fair* and cricket.[9] His first job was with *The Manchester Guardian*. He wrote about his favored sport, though it wasn't long before James made his way to a Trotskyist study group in London. Even Trotsky, however, thought his "cast of mind all too typically English."[10] In the years ahead, the evolution of James's work reflected his coming to terms with rapidly unfolding events in the empire, events that contoured his own British colonial identity, which he in turn projected into his writing. "About Britain I was a strange compound of knowledge and ignorance," he professed. "Luckily, I knew it. . . . For a non-white colonial to adjust his sights to England and not to lose focus is the devil's own job and the devil pays great attention to it."[11] A fiery pathos emerged in James's work. On the one hand, it reflected the British values espoused in his beloved literature and encapsulated in the progressive nature of British liberalism. On the other hand, it revealed the realities of lived experiences in the empire and in Britain.[12] Indeed, for James, the transformation of his very ability to write and speak his mind when he left the imperial frontier for Britain was evidence of liberalism's capacity to repress when it extended beyond British shores:

> It is not surprising that the famous English tolerance leaves [an Englishman] almost entirely [in the colonies]. At home he was distinguished for the liberality and freedom of his views. . . . But in the colonies any man who speaks for his country, who tries to do for his own people what Englishmen are so proud that other Englishmen have done for theirs, immediately becomes in the eyes of the colonial Englishman a dangerous person, a wild revolutionary. . . . What at home is the greatest virtue becomes in the colonies the greatest crime.[13]

Nurse, for his part, headed to the United States. He first studied medicine at Fisk University, then abandoned it for New York City and the Communist Party. With his growing radicalism, he acquired a new name, George Padmore. Like many Black intellectuals from Britain's empire, emigration fed Padmore's consciousness. His entrance into the London scene in 1933 followed a circuitous route that, after New York, took him to Washington, D.C., the American South, Moscow, and Germany. Along the way he befriended Du Bois, Kenyatta, Azikiwe, Ralph Bunche, Alain Locke, and Sierra Leonean activist and politician Isaac Wallace-Johnson, as well as white allies largely from the fringe left. During his peripatetic years, Padmore became a die-hard Comintern member and organizer across the United States and Europe, and he copiously disseminated his ideas through various media, which included *The Negro Worker*. With a reach that spanned across the British Empire and much of the world—London, Paris, New York, Cape Town, Nairobi, and Cardiff—*The Negro Worker*, under Padmore's editorial direction, was revolutionary for its time. The paper challenged those, particularly within Black and intellectual circles, who sought reform of a system that was, for its editor, the source of the problem.[14]

When the Nazis ascended to power in early 1933, Padmore was in Hamburg. Crackdowns led to his arrest and deportation to Britain, where his colonial subjecthood entitled him to safe passage. There he spent five weeks looking for housing, despite his ever-polished appearance that included a meticulously pressed suit, tie, shined shoes, pocket square, and neatly combed hair. Like James, he embodied the civilizing mission's original, progressive aspiration: the creation of a Black Englishman, at least in comportment if not in ideology. That mattered little in interwar London, where few wanted to let a flat to a Black man, even one who wore tweed and smoked a pipe. At the time, only twenty to thirty thousand people of color—including Blacks, those from the subcontinent, and Middle Easterners—were living in a Britain that, in 1930, had a population of 45 million. Britain's whiteness was decidedly Anglo-Saxon. Jews—or the "Jewish race," as Britons commonly called them—comprised less than 1 percent of the population, around three hundred thousand people, while the predominantly Catholic Irish population numbers were higher, around five hundred thousand.[15] When reflecting on this time, Padmore later wrote in *The Crisis:*

> Towards all peoples of whatever race the British have built up a characteristic attitude of cultivated aloofness, but most Britons, irrespective of social status, display an added aversion to peoples of darker skin. It is this racial egotism and national arrogance which has created a conflict between the British and coloured peoples of the Empire, which will render a social reconciliation between them extremely difficult even after a political and economic adjustment has been effected.

He then described the realities of a non-white immigrant living in Britain:

> Most coloured students coming to England politically unconscious and with great illusions about British democracy and hospitality, drummed into them by their missionary teachers at home, soon have all this nonsense knocked out of them by boarding house and hotel keepers. The Colour Bar in Britain is certainly creating much anti-British feeling among colonial intellectuals and students. It has helped to mould many a future

George Padmore

anti-imperialist leader of the coloured peoples. The British people are creating their own grave-diggers![16]

It was in London that Padmore and James reunited and found themselves in a locus of African diasporic thought and political action that focused its attention on Black workers. It also questioned the colonial-inspired world that had given rise to their sufferings. Padmore's living room on Cranleigh Street became a salon for the emergent Black radicalism that spoke a shared—though constantly contested and evolving—language of liberation, justice, and dignity. It was in London that Du Bois's "double consciousness" melded and fused with contestations of the very system that was colonialism. Echoes of *The Souls of Black Folk* and its wish "to make it possible for a man to be both a Negro and an American without being cursed and spit upon by his fellows, without having the doors of Opportunity closed roughly in his face," could be heard in the work of Padmore, James, and other intellectuals from the

Caribbean and Africa who wrote against the racialized premise at the heart of Britain's liberal imperialism.[17] So, too, their questionings of the very system that gave rise to oppression could later be found in Du Bois's autobiographical reflections. In the meantime, other Black writers and activists, like Harold Moody, who spearheaded the politically moderate League of Coloured Peoples in Britain, were far less radical in their conceptions of the larger structural issues at play.[18]

Even before his arrival in London, Padmore interrogated the white world's system and zeroed in on European imperialism and the labor question. He spoke a language of racial capitalism and in 1931 published his first tour de force, *The Life and Struggles of Negro Toilers*. In it, he offered example after example of the unholy alliance between capitalism, racism, and colonialism. For him, it was a trinity bound together through repression. Partly driven by Padmore's own eyewitness accounts of liberal imperialism at work, *Life and Struggles* moved from Kenya—where the King's African Rifles opened fire on demonstrators, most of whom were women protesting the arrest of Harry Thuku, a Kenyan politician—to Nigeria, where typical government responses to protests included burning huts and crops and conducting mass arrests of over thirty thousand women. He offered up examples from Basutoland, the Gambia, Gold Coast, Sierra Leone, and the West Indies, where colonial regimes deployed legalized lawlessness, local police, and when necessary, troops, to suppress local protests against the effects of racial capitalism and the colonial repression that accompanied it throughout Britain's empire.[19]

Life and Struggles eviscerated the colonial "system"—whether it be the "system of forced labour" or the "plantation system" or the "system of government"—that allowed for slavelike conditions complete with collective punishments, appropriation of land, the perpetuation of the color bar, and denial of free speech and assembly.[20] Padmore also directed his ire toward bankrupt petit-bourgeois reformists—who, for him, included South African trade union leader Clements Kadalie and Garvey whose methods would not deliver the "freedom and emancipation" that his black transnationalism envisaged.[21] *Life and Struggles* was immediately banned in parts of Britain's empire, which only added to its popularity and clandestine circulation. As for its impact, Ras Makonnen recalled his old friend, Malcolm Nurse, as someone with a "magic weapon in his hands." In Makonnen's mind, *Life and Struggles* heralded a new era. Padmore's "language was entirely different," he wrote, "and a revelation to me with its new approach. It was almost as if he had invented a new dictionary of terms."[22]

Padmore's prodigious writing offered a singular clarity of language that gave life to thousands of fractured voices in Britain's empire. The forcefulness and sheer volume of his prose were not mere rhetorical postures. Rather, facts infused his counterdiscourse. He analyzed copious public data that he culled from government publications, parliamentary debates, and politicians' speeches. His skills reflected a mastery not only of the colonizer's language but also of the documentation needed to turn this language against the colonial project itself. His vision moved much closer to a Pan-Africanist one, with a distinctive practical bent.[23] This trend was most apparent after the Nazi seizure of power, when Moscow edged closer to Britain and other Western nations, and the clear enemy was now fascism. The Comintern put European imperialism on the back burner. With that, Padmore resigned. In turn, the Comintern blackballed him. Padmore would always consider Lenin to be history's most important thinker, and materialism's framework would be ever present in his future writings, though race and colonialism—which the Comintern so readily jettisoned—would be the enduring epicenter of his consciousness.[24]

Two sets of events galvanized Padmore and the London-based Black intellectuals and marked fundamental moments in their thinking and writing. The first was the Italian invasion of Abyssinia in October 1935. When Haile Selassie's nation—the only African territory, along with Liberia, that had been free of European imperial rule—fell to Mussolini's troops, the League of Nations response was ineffective. Padmore pilloried the League, calling it the "Thieves' Kitchen," a term he borrowed from Lenin's playbook. He found it, and the Western democracies that sat at its table, complicit in allowing fascist "aggressive nationalism" and "territorial expansion" to march forward under the banner of "the white race."[25] Outrage rebounding in his London living room spilled over into Ras Makonnen's Afro-Caribbean café, the Independent Labour Party (ILP), and the city's protest corners and theater stages. James, Kenyatta, Williams, and others from the Black intellectual community joined forces with Sylvia Pankhurst, Nancy Cunard, the novelist Ethel Mannin and her future husband, Reginald Reynolds, and Fenner Brockway, the ILP's leader.

The Independent Labour Party had been opposed to the First World War, and with fascist advances, a growing alliance between Britain's political parties was again on display. Founded in 1893, the ILP was a group of individual socialists and radicals who became part of Labour in 1906. At its beginning, Labour was a coalition of preexisting trade unions and socialist societies; when Labour changed to individual membership in 1918, the ILP members moved further left, breaking away in 1932. While relatively small and heterogeneous, the ILP had a disproportionate influence on far-left discourse by the end of the interwar period. Its high-profile members—including George Orwell and Kingsley Martin, the *New Statesman and Nation*'s editor—accounted for some of this influence, but so did London's Black radicals writing on imperial issues. Many notable left-wing imperial critics had been associated with the ILP at various points, including J. A. Hobson, whose economic critique of imperialism and theory of underconsumption (inadequate consumer demand) were groundbreaking, and Leonard Woolf, a writer and political theorist as well as husband to Virginia Woolf. Brockway had a close personal friendship with Jawaharlal Nehru that dated back to the 1920s, as did Reginald Reynolds, and Nehru wrote on occasion for the party's *New Leader*. So, too, had ILP members expressed concerns about Palestine and demonstrated a deeper involvement in Indian politics: on the floor of Parliament, Brockway and others protested liberal imperialism and imprisonment in India while also working closely at various points with the London-based Indian League.[26]

George Padmore, ILP Summer School, 1938

During the interwar years, however, the ILP made only small inroads into Labour's approach to the empire, which was largely gradualist and focused on economic issues. There were outbursts over spectacular occasions of repression, such as in Ireland during the war of independence or in Amritsar. Other dramatic events, however, like the quotidian cycles of violence in Palestine, captivated little sustained attention. Differences between Conservatives and Labour were often a matter of degree rather than kind when it came to imperial issues. Debates that took place were typically within parties, particularly between Labour's mainstream and the socialists and radicals who constituted the ILP.[27] Even then, these debates were rather lopsided, particularly as the ILP's numbers dwindled once the party disaffiliated from the larger Labour Party. Instead, throughout the 1930s, there was an "apparent consensus on the Labour benches," as the historian Stephen Howe reminds us. It was "developmentalist, paternalist, emphasising economic rather than political change and firmly excluding talk of decolonization.... The doctrine of colonial trusteeship ... was an article of faith for Labour orthodoxy."[28]

Abyssinia's fall to Mussolini was a turning point in Black radical thought and the counterdiscourse it brought to bear on British imperial consensus. Padmore and James found allies within and outside the ILP—allies with money and connections. Together, they catalyzed a shift in the ILP's imperial focus and, for some of its members, a radicalization in its language and critique of Britain's imperial project. Indeed, when some ILP members balked at sanctioning Italy for its imperial aggression, Padmore drew a bright line between right and wrong on the Abyssinian issue. Writing in the *New Leader*, James was clear: "British imperialism will not fight Italy either for Abyssinia or for collective security. It will fight for British Imperialist interests and nothing else."[29]

Those who had experienced the empire as brown and Black subjects saw but shades of difference between fascism and imperialism. This equation emerged most forcefully in Padmore's 1936 publication *How Britain Rules Africa*. "Everywhere we shall see stark imperialist oppression and exploitation, allied with racial ignorance and arrogance, swaggering about without the least sign of shame," he wrote in his opening salvo.

This is especially so in countries like South Africa, Southern Rhodesia, South-West Africa and Kenya. Such brutality and barbarity remind us of conditions in Germany to-day. It is therefore

no accident that General Goering [*sic*], the leader of the notorious Nazi Secret Police, addressing his own men at a meeting
of ex-colonials in Berlin, "solemnly declared them heirs to the
traditions of the former German-East African armed colonial
force."[30]

Padmore was not alone in his thinking. Kenyatta wrote a piece in
the *New Leader* with the headline "Hitler could not improve on Kenya."
He lambasted "British Labour organisations" for being unable "to
distinguish the difference between the imperialist forces and the anti-
imperialists," and pointed to the detention camps in Kenya as "similar to concentration or labour camps in fascist countries."[31] The Sierra
Leonean Isaac Wallace-Johnson also adopted a radicalized discourse and
reminded his audience, "When the British people talk of Fascism they
should look not to Germany and Italy, but within their own Empire,
where their ruling classes have filched the lands from the natives whom
they have forced to work for them in wretched conditions and for less
than starvation wages; where they have turned the whole land into one
large concentration camp."[32]

Padmore coined new phrases for the times: "fascist-imperialism"
and "colonial fascism."[33] This message spread across the Black world,
as Trinidad's *The People* and the NAACP's *The Crisis* published extracts
from Padmore and Wallace-Johnson's writings and speeches. There was
nothing subtle about these critiques, which would, as the historian Susan
Pennybacker points out, challenge "liberal, radical, and imperial reform
currents among white activists."[34] Some in the ILP countenanced more
measured language and rejected Abyssinia as a defining issue for the
party. Brockway, like others, was fully radicalized by the eve of the war:

> Under Imperialism the native peoples are denied democratic
> rights. In that it is similar to Nazism. . . . There is no personal
> freedom in Germany. Anyone can be put in prison or concen-
> tration camp for an indefinite period without trial. This is also
> commonplace in India and the Crown Colonies. . . . The Nazis
> in Germany regard themselves as a superior race and treat the
> Jews particularly as though they were sub-human animals. This
> is also the attitude of the white "Sahibs" towards the coloured
> peoples.[35]

It was not only far-left whites who either got on board or were on the
receiving end of radical criticism. Even those whom Padmore had

pegged as the Black intellectual bourgeoisie—or, in the parlance of the time, "respectable" leaders—were relentlessly challenged. When Harold Moody spoke of moderation, for example, Padmore shot back:

> What is imperialism but a political and economic system of violence? How do you think these hypocritical psalm singing rascals like that high churchman Lord Halifax and his non-conformist chief Chamberlain acquired their empire? Was it not violence? How is it being maintained? Is it not by violence? When Jamaican Negroes ask their white masters for a few coppers are they not met by violence? Why, *it seems to me that violence is the high priest of imperialism.*[36]

The Abyssinian crisis galvanized political organization beyond Moody's moderate League of Coloured Peoples. Other associations included the West African Student Union and the broader League Against Imperialism that, while well intentioned and broad-based, was largely ineffective. James, along with Amy Ashwood Garvey, formed the International African Friends of Ethiopia (IAFE). In May 1937, Padmore had pushed for a more inclusive International African Service Bureau (IASB) to replace it. The new bureau looked to unify various constituencies in Britain's Black diasporic community around a pan-Africanism that critiqued race, capitalism, and imperialism. It also wanted to translate such ideas in a way that would impact British public opinion. The bureau included many ILP members and other white champions of the cause. The future colonial secretary Arthur Creech Jones worked alongside Sylvia Pankhurst, founder of a pro-Ethiopian publication, and Nancy Cunard; Fenner Brockway was primed to offer the *New Leader* as an outlet for IASB ideas.[37] All the while, the Black intellectuals kept writing in extraordinary volume. Padmore's 1937 *Africa and World Peace* pointed to imperialism as the source of Western statesmen's "Armageddon." Stafford Cripps penned its foreword, something that made him no friends among imperialist die-hards. "George Padmore has performed another great service of enlightenment in this book," he began.

> The facts he discloses so ruthlessly are undoubtedly unpleasant facts, the story which he tells of the colonization of Africa is sordid in the extreme, but both the facts and the story are true. We have, so many of us, been brought up in the atmosphere of "the white man's burden," and have had our minds clouded and confused by the continued propaganda for imperialism that we

may be almost shocked by this bare and courageous exposure of the great myth of the civilizing mission of western democracies in Africa.[38]

A year later the ILP fully interrogated "the way to fight War, Fascism and Imperialism" when Brockway devoted a special supplement of the *New Leader*'s May Day edition to "Empire."[39] Its editors intended the supplement as an informed wake-up call for Britain's working class:

> We have done this because there is a great danger at present time that our hatred of the tyranny of Fascism may cause us to forget the tyranny of imperialism. Our pages show that the barbarities which Mussolini and Hitler practice in Italy and Germany are being practiced constantly within the British Empire. . . . The truth is that four-fifths of the British Empire is as much a dictatorship as the Fascist countries. . . . The democratic rights which we enjoy in the British Isles are due only to the oppression which is practiced within the British Empire.[40]

While many pieces were variations on this theme—Reginald Reynolds offered one on India, Kenyatta on Kenya, and Padmore on Trinidad—it was the firsthand evidence and data that were most noteworthy about the *New Leader*'s supplement. One article, "Tribes Terrorised by Aerial Bombing," quoted a Tory MP commending Britain's forces in India's North-West Frontier; another article ventriloquized the Colonial Office and its lauding of Arthur Harris's aerial bombing missions over the Middle East.[41] Forced labor, the color bar, and the use of live ammunition against striking women in Nigeria all had eyewitness documentation and were headlined in the *New Leader* with dramatic flair: "Africa Empire Is Slave Colony: Revolting Workers Shot Down," "Colonial Fascism in the West Indies," and "British Imperialism in Ireland: A Hundred Years of Terror." All were meant to draw readers into the articles' data-driven methods of persuasion.[42]

Radicalism reached Britain's public in dramatic fashion when it found its way to London's Westminster Theatre. There James's production of *Toussaint Louverture: The Story of the Only Successful Slave Revolt in History*, with its broad message of imperialism's brutal conditions and revolution's solution for freedom, spoke to an anticolonial crowd.[43] Indeed, of all the Black radicals who converged in London during this period, it was James whose sheer literary genius and eloquence moved audiences to imagine hitherto unthought-of connections. Two years

C. L. R. James, Trafalgar Square, London, 1935

after his sold-out performances, James published his book *The Black Jacobins*, in which Toussaint L'Ouverture's past was understood in the imperial present. For his readers, the message remained a timeless one. "When history is written as it ought to be written," James said, "it is the moderation and long patience of the masses at which men will wonder, not their ferocity."[44]

On the eve of the Second World War, it was the very system under which Blacks lived that radicals called into question. Padmore laid bare what he termed the "system of imperialism" in ways reminiscent of Gandhi's words in the wake of Amritsar, when he said he wanted not to punish Dyer but rather to change the system that had produced him.[45] More than thirty years after *Souls of Black Folk*, Du Bois also bore witness to the unholy trinity of racism, capitalism, and imperialism, conceding how he failed to fully grasp these interlocking structures in his early years. He reflected in *Dusk of Dawn* that, in his original writings, "my criticism was confined to the relation of my people to the world movement. I was not questioning the world movement in itself. What the white world was doing, its goals and ideals, I had not doubted were quite right."[46] The renowned American historian Robin D. G. Kelley reminds us that by the Second World War this changed, and Du Bois, along with James, Padmore, and other Black radicals, "understood fascism not as some aberration from the march of progress, an unexpected right-wing turn, but a logical development of Western Civilization itself. They viewed fascism as a blood relative of slavery and imperialism, global systems rooted not only in capitalist political economy but racist ideologies that were already in place at the dawn of modernity."[47]

These men were not alone. From his perch at Howard University, Ralph Bunche also promulgated the "fascist-imperialism" concept and the empire's "comic-opera glorification of race."[48] As Britain and the United States were both on the cusp of world war, the Black diaspora on both sides of the Atlantic fully critiqued the systems that liberal imperialism created, whether the British variant or that which gave rise to Jim Crow in the United States. Transnational linkages, despite the persistent differences in methods and aims, were forged in systems that were distinctly similar and would transcend any imperial color bar. That was, at least, the hope of the IASB's intellectuals, activists, and politicians. "We preach no narrow race doctrine," the organization declared. "It is the business of the Intellectuals of African descent to work in the closest harmony with the East Indians."[49]

Such sentiments were expressed in the context of events in the Caribbean. Protests and riots erupted one after the other, and sometimes simultaneously, in Jamaica, Barbados, British Honduras, British Guiana, Saint Kitts, Saint Vincent, Saint Lucia, and Trinidad, among other locations. In the late 1930s, individual and collective demands reflected an economic and social system that had changed little since the abolition of enslaved labor a century earlier.[50] Access to the means of production was still largely the privilege of a white landholding class, and coercion remained the common denominator of social control across the region. Commissions, like that which Sir Henry Norman chaired in 1897, recommended diversifying local economies and moving away from plantation systems. Local colonial governments ignored such suggestions and, with the support of London, ensured the perpetuation of British interests at home and in the empire as well as local living standards that were appalling by any measure.[51]

After the Italian invasion of Abyssinia, the sequence of riots throughout the Caribbean—and indeed, in some parts of Africa, including Northern Rhodesia and Nigeria—was the second major event, or set of events, that galvanized Black radical thought. That the location of violent discontent was buried in their own colonial roots was no small matter for the Black intellectuals and activists. They took to their pens and to the streets of London where protests at Speakers' Corner in Hyde Park reflected the shifting terms of debate that the diasporic radicals had ignited. Of all of them, it was Padmore who cut to the heart of liberalism's twinned ability to emancipate and repress, and to illuminate and obfuscate. He, like those from the colonies with whom he debated and organized, had experienced liberal imperialism's overarching system, in which liberalism's underbelly framed colonial lived experiences of racism, xenophobia, and exploitation. In many ways, the protests over the West Indies shared a similar language to that of the Abyssinia crisis. Just as the League of Nations was a handmaiden of European imperialism for the Black radicals, the riots erupting around the empire were a long-burning consequence of liberal imperialism's misplaced juxtaposition of savagery and civilization. The repressive glue holding racism, capitalism, and the empire together threw into relief liberal imperialism's moth-eaten promises of redemption at some unspecified future time. From where they sat in time and space, Padmore, James, Du Bois, Bunche, and others saw little difference between British imperialism and fascism. It was a view that Hitler shared.

The Führer and other German imperialists had long admired the British Empire as the wellspring for the island nation's disproportionate world power. Britain had ridden the "Great Divergence's" wave on the back of brown and Black peoples around the world, with land, energy, markets, and a population outlet that fueled the industrial revolution and ensured Anglo-Saxon greatness. Their admiration did not stop there. "No people has ever with greater brutality better prepared its economic conquests with the sword, and later ruthlessly defended them, than the English nation," Hitler effused in *Mein Kampf*.[52] Britain's imperial past was replete with examples that supported the Nazis' inclination. In India, according to Hitler, the British wielded the "whip," while other examples of *terra nullius* policies involved the wiping out of local populations, something Victorian anthropologists recorded and, in some cases, encouraged. There were also the South African concentration camps, the aerial bombings in Iraq and the North-West Frontier, and the grinding destruction of the Arab Revolt.[53]

In the mid-nineteenth century, the Indian Mutiny had exposed liberal imperialism's propensity toward and, indeed, justifications of violence. In its wake, as we have seen, James Fitzjames Stephen had insisted that "law is nothing but regulated force," and he upped the ante when he declared in 1883 that "'an absolute government, founded not on consent but on conquest'—such as that in India—represented 'a belligerent civilisation' that should not 'shrink from the open, uncompromising, straightforward assertion of [its own] superiority.'"[54] British imperial governance had not shrunk from this ethos in its African colonies, Palestine, India, Ireland, Bengal, the Middle East, or the Caribbean. Repression took many forms and included the day-to-day principles of labor organization. For decades, Britain deployed master and servants contracts, which criminalized labor contract violations, and repressed incipient trade unions. Ultimately, the rule of law that Britons held so dear was, in fact, an enabling and legitimating instrument in its liberal imperial tool kit. One had just to look at the unfolding legalized lawlessness across the empire to understand that colonial legal regimes reflected the ideological and political frameworks from which they had sprung.

That the civilizing mission had a reformist impulse was still undoubtedly true, however. There were, among other things, attempts like those in India at constitutional reforms, however divisive and attuned they were to the maintenance of British interests. Importantly, from Britain's standpoint, and indeed for most of Europe's nineteenth-century colonizing powers, the nation had not taken sovereignty from its imperial subjects in India or elsewhere, because they never had it, even though India and all other parts of the world had various political formations prior to colonization. Rather, Britain would bequeath sovereignty to colonized peoples in a progressive fashion that cleaved to conceptions of race and progress. Such a view was reflected in international law, which, according to one Indian civil servant, regulated "the relations of independent and co-equal European states" while it also legitimated, and reflected, the premise of European colonial rule.[55]

In contrast, there was nothing reformist about Nazi imperial ambitions.[56] In Hitler's regime, racial differences were immutable, and the empire was to last in perpetuity. If laws were legitimating instruments in Britain's empire, so too were they in Hitler's, though the system that law legitimated, and from which it sprang, was of a different ilk than that of the liberal imperialists. Progressive notions of reform were anathema to Nazi ideology, as were any future imperial divestments. Nazi extremism, rooted in racial purity, led to the creation of a regime that bureaucratized and systematized exterminations on a mass scale. In Germany's empire, racial domination was an end unto itself. Hitler turned international law on its head when his troops rolled through eastern Europe—the heartland of Nazi imperial ambitions—and claimed once-sovereign territories, much as Britain and France had claimed large swaths of Africa. "Wiping out the independent states of Czechoslovakia and Poland, the Nazis reversed the progressivist assumption that sovereignty, once gained, could not as an aspect of civilized life, be abolished or whittled down," as Mazower reminds us.[57]

Questions of international law and sovereignty exposed the weakness of the League of Nations, and its European constituents, insofar as Padmore and others were concerned. The League had done little, if anything, when Mussolini reversed Ethiopian sovereignty, but when the Nazis conquered eastern Europe, the principle that imperialism was confined to a non-European world evaporated. This very issue—"the rule of colonial difference" and the laws that reflected and legitimated such polices—came home to Europe and terrified British statesmen, regardless of where they fell on the political divide.[58] They spent much of the war under a shadow where legalized lawlessness made its appearance again, as with the Defence of the Realm Act. Under John Anderson's direction, these laws, deemed a temporary necessity, legitimized the erosion of civil liberties in wartime Britain just as Hitler's reverse engineering of eastern European sovereignty shattered the myth that the empire was something over there, where brown and Black peoples lived.

Back in the empire and in London's radical circles, a counterdiscourse emerged, encoded in a language that reflected the context of the time. It spoke of a liberal imperial system embedded in racialized difference, exploitation, and injustice. It was a system that, at times, led to massive colonial acts of violence, nearly all of which were legitimized to varying degrees within the confines of law. When compared to fascism, however, British imperialism showed itself to be both repressive and emancipatory. As much as it obfuscated colonial violence and exploitation within the civilizing mission's discourse, it did, at times, illuminate injustice, even if accountability was hard to come by. For colonized populations in Britain's empire, such differences may have felt academic relative to their lived experiences, which looked and felt like the fascism that German imperialists incubated in their African empire and brought home to their rapidly expanding European one in the 1930s. Such differences were real, however, and they made allegations of systematized colonial violence, racism, and exploitation—supported by data-driven evidence and eyewitness accounts, or not—difficult to make stick in any way that fundamentally transformed the British colonial system. Moreover, in the crucible of the coming war, these differences influenced how Britain responded to imperial crises. Turning its attention to the riots and protests erupting throughout the Caribbean, the British government's ability to reshape its own discourse to appeal to a wide range of imperial supporters reflected an ideological elasticity that was absent in Nazi fascism. This elasticity was crucial to liberal imperialism's survival.

In the midst of the Hyde Park protests, and less than a year before Britain entered the war, Lord Moyne headed a commission to investigate the Caribbean's widespread unrest. As far as the British government was concerned, Moyne was to allay any imperial concerns and shore up the continued flow of raw materials from the region, including Trinidadian oil, before Britain turned her full attention to the fascist war on the horizon. Still, body counts, casualties, and arrests in the British West Indies mounted. In 1938 in Jamaica alone a series of strikes resulted in eight deaths as well as two hundred casualties and seven hundred people jailed.

The commission's scope was massive and covered issues like housing, prisons, docks, schools, land settlement, political and constitutional matters, asylums for the mentally ill, and factories. It collected evidence from nearly four hundred witnesses or witness groups across twenty-six centers. So too did it amass evidence from Britain: the IASB, Moody's League of Coloured Peoples, and the Negro Welfare Association offered recommendations; Creech Jones and the Labour peer Sydney Olivier, whose Caribbean credentials stretched back to his time as governor of Jamaica, also offered opinions that pushed back on the security forces' repressive measures and the government's racialized discourse that justified them. Olivier pointed to colonial officials, many of whom rotated between colonies and commissions, as "mostly third-rate products of the educational system of our capitalistic society . . . incapable of taking a socialist point of view, or of regarding black people as commensurable human beings."[59]

By the time the report was finished, nearly five hundred pages in all, even hard-liners like Moyne had been moved.[60] The rioters conjured images of "a canary in the imperial coal mine"—a coal mine that was, according to London, "the British show-window for the USA" and its ever-prying critical eyes.[61] There was also the issue of the broader empire, where ideas circulated at greater and ever-widening clips, despite best efforts at censorship and suppression. "There was," as the historian Thomas Holt points out, "also concern that events in the West Indies prefigured the future of the entire colonial empire, especially the vast, important colonies of Africa. Indeed, for key British policymakers, the violence and protest in the West Indies brought into question the future of the entire colonial empire."[62]

The Moyne Commission also reflected a significant divergence point between American and British consensus. It emphasized economic as opposed to political reform, as if the two sides of the same coin could be separated. Going forward, the White Man's Burden would accommodate welfare measures to assuage fears of future uprisings and bring colonial policy in line with evolving ideas of colonial trusteeship. In the meantime, the iron fist was strengthened by deploying the regional British commander who sought to expand the "inadequate" police force and "if necessary by provision of military forces from the UK or elsewhere."[63]

This iron fist was velvet gloved when it came time to release the Moyne Report to the public. The commission's findings were too explosive for wartime publication. On the one hand, Goebbels's Nazi propaganda machine hammered away at Britain for "living in luxury on the wealth collected from 66,000,000 poverty-stricken native serfs" in her empire, and feature films like *Ohm Krüger*—widely considered to be one of the most successful Nazi propaganda efforts—portrayed the suffering of Afrikaner women and children in British concentration camps during the South African War. On the other hand, many Americans were hostile toward the idea of supporting a British war effort if it meant donating cash and lives for the perpetuation of an anachronistic empire.[64] At the same time, some Labour MPs threw their weight behind Creech Jones and others who pressed for a debate over the report. The government blocked these demands, and in the face of Britain's wartime machine, the extraparliamentary work of Padmore and others was withering, as we shall see.

It was Britain's Ministry of Information (MOI), formally established at the war's outbreak, that stepped in. At its helm was a succession of formidable imperial enthusiasts who included Harry Hodson, Alfred Duff-Cooper, and Brendan Bracken. Its empire division traced its genealogical roots back to the days of Alfred Milner and the South African War. The legendary imperialist and several of his "kindergarteners" had founded the Round Table movement in 1909, which was part Anglo-Saxon boys' club and part think tank for the future closer union between Britain and her self-governing colonies. Steeped in "Milnerism," the movement was, according to one historian, "so conceived—better still, so experienced—[and was] properly understood as a vision of Empire, rooted in a particular supposition about Britain's greatness. It presumed a civilised superiority that made a worldwide mission both necessary and possible."[65] A year later Milner, Lionel Curtis, Philip Kerr, and Geoffrey Dawson established a journal—*The Round Table: A Quarterly Review of the Politics of the British Empire*—that, among other things, incubated and further promoted their ideas, which included imperial federation. While its members disagreed on various points, the Round Table steadfastly believed the British Empire and Commonwealth needed to be preserved.[66]

When the MOI officially launched, Milner's cohort found itself imbricated in wartime propaganda. *The Round Table*'s editor, Harry Hodson, seamlessly moved from one imperial voice piece to another when he became the head of the ministry's empire division. He brought with him the gravitas of being not only the official pen wielder for his elite coterie's journal but also a fellow at All Souls. He, along with several other Milnerites, had landed at this Oxford college thanks in part to Geoffrey Dawson. In 1912 Dawson became editor of *The Times* and, a few months later, a distinguished fellow of All Souls. The value of Dawson's editorship was not lost on his fellow Round Table members, one of whom candidly made the connection between the fourth estate and *religio Milneriana*: "Imperial Union . . . is safe now the Round Table has so potent an ally."[67]

By the eve of the Second World War, Dawson had become synonymous with *The Times*. However, he had been out in the cold between 1919 and 1923 after Harmsworth—owner of not only the *Daily Mail* but also *The Times*, among other outlets—showed him an unceremonious, if temporary, exit from the paper. Dawson's wilderness years from the paper were hardly idle ones. Instead, Dawson and his Round Table posse looked at the crises of empire sweeping through Ireland, Egypt, India, and elsewhere and concluded that solutions to Britain's imperial malaise needed new and interconnected ideas. They promulgated imperial visions through *The Round Table*, referring to John Seeley's earlier historical groundwork for imperial thinking and rationale in his late-nineteenth-century landmark book *The Expansion of England*. Nevertheless, Milnerites believed the empire lacked political theories. Deliberate studying, planning, and dissemination of ideas were also absent, as was any institutionalized academic and administrative cooperation.[68] Cooling his heels during the interwar years, Dawson turned to All Souls and zeroed in on the seven "research fellowships" that had remained unfilled for decades. It became clear to him that "All Souls might in future best contribute both to the practical amelioration of Britain's most pressing political problem and to the intellectual fertilisation of Oxford's emerging research ambitions not by becoming just another teaching college but rather by appointing a number of self-styled 'students of Empire' to its academic ranks."[69]

The first such appointment was Lawrence of Arabia, whom Dawson believed would serve as a conduit for British domination in the Middle East. Disappointingly, Lawrence's only major output at All Souls was his *Seven Pillars of Wisdom*, though others soon joined him who were also imperially minded but more productive. Among them was Lionel Curtis, co-founder of *The Round Table* and Beit Lecturer in Colonial History at Oxford in 1912. It was South Africa that had made Curtis's career; he had served there in the war and later as Milner's right-hand man. Curtis helped reconstruct the region and rationalize its urban spaces and labor supplies along racial lines; he also laid the groundwork for one of his major contributions to the future of the empire. He imagined a British Commonwealth modeled on South Africa's successful confederation. Curtis emphasized the phrase "British Commonwealth of Nations," which often graced *The Round Table*'s pages. His selection to All Souls in 1921 marked the start of imperial history as a major enterprise, with seminars and visitors, and further institutionalized the relationship between Oxford and Whitehall's corridors of power.[70] Curtis embraced the empire with a fervency that bordered on religious. He once posed the question, "If Christ came back to earth, where, in the present day world, would he find that his precepts were best being practised?" To which he responded, "The British Commonwealth."[71]

Arguably the most important of Dawson's recruits to his All Souls project and to the future of British imperial history was Reginald Coupland. Coupland was originally a historian of distinction focused on the ancient world before Curtis helped convert him to imperial studies and wooed him to All Souls. Coupland soon took over the editorship of *The Round Table* and then, in 1920, at the age of thirty-five, assumed the Beit Chair in Colonial History. More than anyone, Coupland brought academic prestige to the All Souls enterprise, which handed down key ideas on the empire and world affairs. Over the span of thirty years, Coupland published a dozen books that embraced the ethos of "the history of the Empire as the story of unfolding liberty."[72] He also served in several influential positions that took his ideas straight back to the empire. Among them was a membership in the Peel Commission on Palestine, for which he drafted the report, as well as a staff position with the Cripps Mission to India. Moreover, through the Raleigh Club—an undergraduate society that met on Sunday evenings at Rhodes House to debate colonial issues—Coupland recruited scores of promising young, like-minded men to serve in and for the British Empire. As this imperial heyday at Oxford and beyond gained momentum, other historians and thinkers joined the Round Table movement. Together they embraced similar sentiments about the empire's past, present, and future, albeit with disagreements over what imperial federation would look like going forward. Still, the basic mindset was the same.[73]

While All Souls had a powerful role to play, it was by no means alone in the enterprise of empire. British imperial historians, particularly those at Oxford, Cambridge, and Kings College London, ordered their narratives to conform to a dominant worldview and offered explicit ideological defenses of the ongoing British endeavors throughout the colonized world. For decades, Anglo-Saxon trusteeship, and the supposed fairness if not humility with which the White Man's Burden brought humanity and civilization to the lesser races of the world, breathed life into the pages of Britain's imperial past. The jingoistic roots of such histories were located in the imperial project itself. In fact, the Beit Chair in Colonial History was the first imperial professorship, endowed by the South African War's beneficiaries. A few years later other endowments similarly rooted in imperial patriotism created the Rhodes Chair of Imperial History at Kings College London and the Vere Harmsworth Chair of Imperial and Naval History at Cambridge. Towering figures like the first two occupiers of the Beit Chair—Egerton and Coupland—picked up Macaulay and Seeley's earlier mantles. They hooked the wagon of empire to the Whig narrative of the nation, or the idea that British history writ large was a story of progress. This triumphant forward march spread liberty throughout Britain and eventually the world. Ultimately, for these historians, the essence of British imperial rule was the extension of constitutional freedom and, with it, the deployment of power using free labor instead of enslaved labor, free trade, and a system of governance and law absent the despotism and barbarism that allegedly plagued the lesser races of the world. Such ideals were soon entombed in massive, multivolume bodies of work, including *The Cambridge History of the British Empire*.[74]

These teleological histories of the empire denied the role of violence in imperial expansion. Coercion and terror were either absent or minimized and explained away. That crises of the empire, and overt British repression, were playing out in Ireland, Egypt, India, and Palestine mattered little to Coupland when he delivered his inaugural Beit Chair lecture in 1921. Instead, he lauded the virtues of "the growth of the doctrine of trusteeship."[75] In an earlier pamphlet entitled "Is the British Empire the Result of Wholesale Robbery?," Coupland's Beit Chair predecessor,

Egerton, answered with an emphatic no and claimed that "it is equally false to suggest that our empire took its rise in violence. What happened was peaceful occupation of, apparently, vacant lands, though afterwards, no doubt, trouble sometimes arose from the neighbourhood of aboriginal Indians."[76] In Asia and Africa, according to Egerton, Britain was left with no choice but to wield paternalistic power to fill moral and political lacunas because "the effect of contact with European civilisation is to undermine the foundations of the native system of government, and to produce a state of anarchy which necessitates further intervention."[77]

Coupland took such sentiments directly to the British public, holding forth on BBC Radio in 1933. At the same time that an estimated twenty thousand Indian National Congress members and supporters were languishing in prison, the Beit Chair lectured Britons that save for a brief decade in the eighteenth century, there had been no "indubitably black years in the long record of the British connection with India." Likewise, his counterpart at Kings College London and fellow Round Table member Vincent Harlow was, according to the historian Richard Drayton, a "professional apostle of this Anglican Liberal Imperialist school of imperial history." Harlow spearheaded an industry that focused on Britain's imperial "humanitarianism," especially the abolition of trade in enslaved people and enslaved labor, as well as missionary activities.[78]

Not surprisingly, when it came time for the Ministry of Information to round out Harry Hodson's work as the head of the empire division, the government enlisted Harlow to head its colonial section with the explicit purpose of generating wartime propaganda. Historians' production of knowledge fueled and reflected defenses of Britain's liberal imperialism that soon flowed from the MOI's airwaves, films, press releases, and newsreels. A myriad of Colonial Office information officers joined the ministry's campaign. They followed its lead as well as that of Noel Sabine, the first public relations officer for the colonies. Turf wars were rampant, though the ultimate goal was the same: a considered empire publicity campaign that was as much for an American audience as it was for buoying the home front in the face of Goebbels's propaganda machine. To a lesser extent, it also sought to dispatch the Independent Labour Party's troublemakers, together with their cries of "fascist imperialism."

The campaign's semiofficial kickoff was the suppression of the Moyne Report, the contents of which wouldn't see the light of day until 1945. In February 1940 the war cabinet approved the commission's release only of recommendations that deliberately veered away from the political lightning rod of empire. The British government sought to sidestep damning critiques that came from allies and enemies. At the same time, it carefully navigated its imperial sticky wicket when it recast the political economy of exploitation in the colonies into a progressive policy of "social and economic development."[79] There were few regions like the Caribbean, where British colonial violence was so closely linked to economic inequalities and also deeply rooted in social and racial divisions stretching to a pre-emancipation past that had witnessed little change by the 1930s. Instead, the Depression era with its declining profit margins for sugar and with competition from beet sugar saw workers' wages squeezed well below the poverty line, while countless others suffered layoffs with no access to smallholdings or sharecropping for the most basic of foodstuffs. In Jamaica's capital alone, unemployment hovered around 50 percent while British imperialism's broader governing structure routinely denied the right to assembly. Various forms of repression were often closely linked to extreme poverty in the Caribbean as elsewhere in Britain's empire.[80]

In the case of Jamaica and surrounding colonies, local police, with their paramilitary training and recourse to army and navy reinforcements, depended on the use of violence or its threat to maintain a racial hierarchy that reflected and refracted the region's political economy. Ellen Wilkinson, left-leaning Labour MP, drove this point home when she asked whether the omnipresence of British troops "is not being used to overawe people who are making a perfectly legitimate protest against low wages?"[81] Moreover, labor dissent and police crackdowns, with subsequent government inquiries, were defining features not only in Jamaica but also in other parts of the empire. When massive riots broke out in Ceylon in the spring of 1915, for example, the British government created a routine investigative committee—a time-honored strategy that provided political cover and gestured toward reform, yet committed the government to taking little if any action.[82]

In so far as the Moyne Report differed, it was because the near simultaneous publication of the Colonial Development and Welfare Act in 1940 deflected attention away from the suppression of everything but the report's recommendations and focused attention on Britain's imperial benevolence, even in its "darkest hour." In place of the old Lugardian "Dual Mandate," responsibility for "native" uplift and economic and political benefits for Britain, a more progressive form of trusteeship would shape British policies in its empire. In a magnanimous gesture, Britain announced:

The time has come to announce the Government's policy on the broad questions of development and welfare in the Colonial Empire. Though the unhappy intervention of war may inevitably affect the rate of advance, the Government propose to proceed with their policy of development as far and as fast as the exigencies of the times permit. . . . The whole effort will be one of collaboration between the authorities in the Colonies and those at home.[83]

Denying any economic exploitation in Britain's imperial endeavors, the government assured its colonial subjects, and the world, that British taxpayers would contribute up to £55 million in grants and loans over the next ten years for colonial development projects. Colonial Secretary Malcolm MacDonald was on point to manage the announcement. He was an old imperial hand, having worked in Palestine during the Arab Revolt. He positioned the government's new commitment to "social and economic development" so that it was not construed "as a new departure which might betoken an attack of conscience on our part, but as the logical and normal development of our whole policy towards dependent people."[84]

When the time came to peddle the Colonial Development and Welfare Act, the Ministry of Information's publicity campaign of 1940 reflected the sentiments of the Colonial Office's apostle, as well as those of Hodson, Harlow, and their imperialist Round Table brethren. His Majesty's subjects in the empire, according to the MOI report, were "loyal and happy under our rule and helping us to the limit of their resources" and their policy "was enlightened, humane and reasonably progressive." The Milnerite crowd and the broader world of officialdom were quite confident in their abilities to convey and persuade. Fifty-five million pounds of economic purchase underwrote their commitment to imperial loyalty and progressive development, and they brushed aside homegrown critiques as "merely ripples in the pool."[85]

CHAPTER 8

"Partnership"

The disaster of Singapore shook the Ministry of Information's faith in the empire as it strengthened American anti-imperialist views. Just months after Percival's surrender, Sumner Welles, Roosevelt's highly influential undersecretary of state, publicly reaffirmed his government's position: "The principles of the Atlantic Charter must be guaranteed to the world as a whole—in all oceans and in all continents." He then pointed to Singapore's collapse as symbolic: "If this war is in fact a war for the liberation of peoples it must assure the sovereign equality of peoples throughout the world, as well as in the world of the Americas. Our victory must bring in its train the liberation of all peoples. Discrimination between peoples because of their race, creed or color must be abolished. The age of imperialism is dead."[1]

Mainstream public intellectuals and journalists joined the chorus. In his influential *Washington Post* column, Walter Lippmann reflected pervasive American sentiments when he called out what the MOI sought to sidestep ever since it helped bury the Moyne Report: that is, that imperial progressivism, however window-dressed in a new rhetoric about development and welfare, was a 2.0 version of Kipling. With "the fall of Shanghai, Hongkong, Singapore, and the prospective fall of Rangoon," Lippmann wrote, ". . . the western nations must now do what hitherto they lacked the will and the imagination to do: they must identify their cause with the freedom and the security of the peoples of the East, putting away the 'white man's burden' and purging themselves of the taint of an obsolete and obviously unworkable white man's imperialism."[2]

In Britain, George Padmore teamed up with Nancy Cunard to publish the pamphlet "White Man's Duty: An Analysis of the Colonial Question in Light of the Atlantic Charter." Since the start of the war, Padmore and his Cranleigh Street collaborators had been relatively quiet. The Defence of the Realm Act that allowed John Anderson and MI5 to do their work in Britain's cages also suppressed other civil liberties, as discussed in chapter 6. Regulation 39B, recall, made it a crime to "endeavor to influence, orally or otherwise, public opinion in a manner likely to be prejudicial to the efficient prosecution of the war or the defence of the realm."[3] Other regulations banned political rallies, effectively ensuring silence at Hyde Park's Speaker's Corner. The International African Service Bureau was a shell of its former self during the war due to Britain's suspension of civil liberties. James departed for the United States in late 1938; Kenyatta decamped to Sussex, where he remained politically quiescent; Makonnen ran a few small businesses in Manchester; and Wallace-Johnson went home to Sierra Leone, where he was promptly imprisoned and later held under house arrest.[4]

Well aware of the wartime regulations that hung over Britain's far left and right, Padmore toned down his earlier "fascist-imperialism" language and, together with Cunard, played up a "sincerity of purpose." Still, as Padmore's biographer Leslie James points out, the "White Man's Duty" pamphlet was vintage Padmore, "taking the words of the colonizer, of making visible government pronouncements regarding colonial governance, and holding them to account."[5] It opened by questioning imperial loyalties, reiterating a point that Cunard and Padmore had made for their American audience in *The Crisis*:

> The Singapore natives, like those on the mainland, had no voice in their own affairs. Surely it is not really surprising that when the crisis came, the Governor, Sir Shenton Thomas, was unable to mobilize the common people—Malayan, Chinese, Indian—to withstand the Japanese onslaught. How could a people, whose existence has been entirely ignored, presumably because they were considered unfit to participate in the government of the country, suddenly resuscitate themselves, as it were, and assume responsibility in the defence of the system which had until then failed to recognise their existence?[6]

While some of these "Singapore natives" proved eager recruits for Bose and the Japanese-sponsored Indian National Army, Padmore and Cunard saw Britain's humiliations in the East as rooted in colonialism's failures. These failures were as much about liberalism's deficiencies in the empire—something that Bose tapped into with great effect—as they were about imperial overreach and military hubris. Padmore and Cunard spoke the language of rights, freedom, and the removal of the color bar throughout the empire and in the metropole. So, too, did they address the abiding issue of accountability. Citing his exchange with Lord Moyne, who was colonial secretary at the time of Singapore's fall, Padmore recalled the aristocrat's business-as-usual response: "The supreme authority of the governor must be preserved, and it is essential that he should have the necessary powers of 'certificate' and 'veto.'" Here the catastrophe in the East intersected with the Moyne Report and Churchill's full-throated defense of the empire despite, or because, of the Atlantic Charter. The debate's fulcrum was self-determination. On this score, Padmore would not waver: "*politically* self-government is the necessary pre-requisite for bringing about *social* and *economic* amelioration."[7]

Events in the East invigorated the post–Atlantic Charter calls for self-determination and had cascading effects in Britain. "The Malayan disaster," in the words of quintessential liberal paternalist Margery Perham, "shocked [Britons] into sudden attention to the structure of our Colonial Empire."[8] A prolific writer and lecturer, the grande dame Perham, with her encyclopedic knowledge of the empire and its administration, was arguably one of the most influential colonial stalwarts of the time. She had vast African experience that the Rhodes trustees partly funded. She was also the first female fellow of Nuffield College, Oxford, and a reader in colonial administration. When she was not writing for the press, publishing books, or rubbing shoulders with parliamentarians and government officials, she offered courses for colonial administrators, training young men in the ways of civil service. With these courses, she etched her signature on many colonial servants before they shipped off to the empire.[9] In the wake of "the Malayan disaster," Perham observed in *The Times*:

> Events such as we have known in the last few weeks are rough teachers, but our survival as a Great Power may depend upon our being able to learn their lesson. . . . Most people in this country have been startled into a sudden questioning, or rather into an intuitive certainty that our colonial administration needs adjustment to the new conditions of our world. This is the more

required since our allies are turning anxious and critical eyes upon the Empire they are helping us to defend.[10]

Perham's idea of colonial "adjustment" was not a clarion call for self-determination. Her twists and turns reflected a new desire to meet the demands of World War II, a people's war across the empire, and perpetuate the empire in a new and more progressive way. Indeed, at this moment, the empire didn't need Churchill; it needed Perham and her crafting of new ideas and language. She ruminated in the press that a Victorian-inspired empire needed changing and a picked-up pace of "native" progress:

> We [have] regarded Empire as part of the order of things, at once beneficent and enduring. We developed towards our backward charges a paternalism that could hardly conceive their coming of age. We established standards of administrative purity that we could not bear to see diluted by too much possibly clumsy and corrupt native participation. With our cult of "thorough" and our belief that human institutions are not made but grow, we set ourselves to bring change by gradual development from the old order rather than through the rapid imposition of the new. Some of these were merits of their day, and have not become defects overnight. But since modern inventions and administrative methods have changed the whole tempo of human affairs, they, too, need some revision.

It was a moment when liberal imperialism's elasticity, its ability to recast itself, would be on full display. Perham believed the idea of trusteeship in wartime's context was outdated. "Differences of race, colour, language and customs are barriers; backwardness is a dividing fact," she wrote. "But there is a level of education and of potential common interests upon which we are held back only by our prejudices from cooperation and friendship. Yet, without these, imperial rule cannot change into the working partnership which the coming age demands."[11]

Indeed, "partnership" became liberal imperialism's new catch-phrase.[12] In theory, Britain would redouble her civilizing efforts by partnering with colonized peoples throughout the empire to address the social and economic inequalities that had been on display in the West Indies, for example, and which the Japanese assault on the Malay Peninsula had exposed. Perham was not alone as *The Times*'s editorial headlines interrogated "The Colonial Future." It was a future soon subject to debate in Parliament and the corridors of Whitehall. Any reevaluation was safely in the hands of Lord Hailey, whose many admirers included not only Perham but also Moyne and Colonial Office bureaucrats, not to mention his peers in the House of Lords. It was Hailey who—as chairman of the Colonial Office's postwar problems committee, former governor of India's Punjab and United Provinces, and author of the mammoth-sized *African Survey*—incubated the idea of "partnership" in the face of post-Singaporean critiques leveled at Britain's civilizing mission and, in particular, the effectiveness of colonial servants.[13] It was not a moment, as *The Times* reminded its readers, to cast aspersions on empire's loyal foot soldiers, who have "performed great services in the past . . . and [the colonial government] has constituted a remarkable stage in the expansion of European civilization all over the world." Rather, the paper betrayed its anxieties and called on readers to reimagine an empire that "has been too long and too deeply rooted in the traditions of a bygone era . . . [riddled with] misguided conceptions of racial prestige and narrow and obsolete interpretations of economic interest."[14]

This reimagining played out in parliamentary debates, none more revealing than those in the House of Lords, where Hailey offered a roadmap for postwar liberal imperialism. His peers paid homage to Lord Milner, who had fulfilled "*in loco parentis*" duties, and they underscored that he and others like him "were to give up everything, not for their own careers, but for the people among whom they worked."[15] For his part, Lord Moyne imagined a colonial service future that the war's lessons strengthened. It would be infused with modern technical know-how, expanded recruitment measures, and streamlined knowledge sharing. Still, neither he nor Hailey believed that "what we have suffered in the way of military disaster in the East has conveyed any clear lesson of the failure of our civil administration."[16] For Hailey in particular, at issue was reform, albeit one that hewed to British priorities. "I can say with conviction," he asserted, "that recent years have shown, whether the administration has been Conservative or Liberal or under other auspices, no departure from the principle of trusteeship [has occurred]." He carried on, signaling the civilizing mission's capaciousness in the context of the war and beyond:

It is true that we now have a new interpretation of [trusteeship]. Instead of the old interpretation, based on ideas which fundamentally looked to the State as the protector of rights, as providing a safeguard against abuses, political or otherwise, but otherwise regarded the State largely from a *laissez faire* point of view, we have now everywhere, as a part of the background of all of our domestic thought, the conception of the State as the chief agency for social welfare. It is that conception which is now forcing its way from domestic into Colonial politics, and which is giving us a new and, as I hold, a more constructive and more beneficial interpretation of trusteeship.[17]

Reminding his audience of the Colonial Development and Welfare Act, Hailey believed "trusteeship has to-day a new and more positive meaning for us." Moreover, the demands for self-determination and critiques that included "false analogies" showed "the term [*trusteeship*] is irritating to Colonial people."[18] "If we need to express ourselves in a formula at all," he suggested, "let our relations be of those of senior and junior partners in the same enterprise, and let it be said that our contract of partnership involves the progressive increase of the share which the junior partners have in the conduct of that undertaking."[19]

While reform was in the air, this was not a moment of dramatic turnaround. At Hailey's urging, the House rebranded the parent-child relationship as one of junior-senior partner, while some of its members referred to the empire's "nigger" and stressed the wartime need for continued "compulsory forced labour" and "penal sanctions" in the colonies.[20] So, too, did it reject any call for a "Colonial Charter" that would, in the wake of the Atlantic Charter debate, lay out a self-determination timetable. The Colonial Office was still scrambling to document Churchill's claims that individual schedules existed, though neither the House of Lords, nor the Commons, for that matter, was going to offer a lifeline. Instead, as Hailey stressed, and Lord Cranborne—who had replaced the empire-bound Moyne as colonial secretary—concurred, the empire was just too heterogeneous to allow for any kind of universal charter. Besides, the "Atlantic Charter was drawn up to deal with a completely new situation . . . created by Hitler," Cranborne reminded the House, whereas "the position in the Colonial Empire is quite different. It is not a new situation; it is what I may call a continuing Situation." As often happened in colonial debates, the language of nineteenth-century philosophers and statesmen also crept in. "There is also a danger," the colonial secretary continued, "that, if one made such a general declaration, certain of the less developed peoples might wish to run before they could walk; and, if they were not really fit to run, and we did not think that they were, they might charge us with a breach of faith."[21]

Fear of the empire's subjects who were considered to be "not really fit to run" was at an all-time high. In Kenya, the governor banned Perham's 1941 book, *Africans and British Rule*, because of its "anti-settler bias," which was "likely to stir up racial feelings to an extent that does no one any good."[22] Arthur Lewis penned a lengthy takedown of it in the League of Coloured People's *Newsletter* and remarked that "from the prosperous seclusion of Oxford it is easy to ride the high horse of cultural superiority." With its implicit justification of the "colour bar" and de rigueur tropes of "backward" and "savage" natives, *Africans and British Rule* was nothing short of an "apology for imperialism," according to Lewis.[23] Padmore considered Perham the colonial administration's "official apologist, who is always extolling it as democracy's gift to backward Africans."[24] Indeed, Perham was a liberal paternalist, and her putting to words liberal imperialism's dynamism incensed Padmore as much as it did the racist settlers in Kenya.

Africa and British Rule inflamed the empire's extremes, but it hardly ruffled the feathers of mainstream Labour. Up until the eruption of violence in the West Indies and the Moyne Report, Labour issued no party policy document on the empire of any significance during the interwar years. In the wake of the Moyne Commission, it proved anemic in pressing for a full debate of the report's issues, and even then its focus was on economic reform as opposed to any kind of sweeping change. Such sentiments were institutionalized in the Fabian Colonial Bureau, which Arthur Creech Jones and Rita Hinden founded in 1940. Occasionally sympathetic to anticolonial critics such as Padmore and Lewis, the bureau was an engine for colonial research but not a cockpit for self-determination demands. Instead, it made clear its gradualist claims, which were easily located on a spectrum of "partnership" support:

> We feel they [the anticolonial groups in and around Labour's left wing] are unrealistic in demanding independence for all territories under colonial rule now. We agree with the policy of the Government which seeks to lead the Colonies towards self-government within the Commonwealth, and appreciate that whereas some Colonies . . . are almost ready for self-government other Colonies, such as the East and Central African territories, are not.[25]

Even Creech Jones, one of Labour's more enlightened members on imperial matters, offered critiques of "partnership" that were matters of degree rather than of kind. While debating the issue in the House of Commons, he agreed that "trusteeship" was outdated and emphasized that "some of us want a new relationship with the Colonial peoples which conveys the idea of equality and fellowship, the idea of service and practical assistance and which expresses it in dynamic and constructive terms." Creech Jones found Hailey's version of "partnership" lacking in even the most basic political and social rights, with the "colour bar" the most glaring example. He issued another call for a "supplementary charter" that would provide "assurance . . . in real and convincing terms of periodic programmes so that the Colonial peoples may know how they may advance to a realization of the principles embodied in such Charter."[26] Beyond that, Creech Jones, in the context of wartime bipartisanship, did not offer much "partnership" pushback.

A few Labour backbenchers like Leslie Haden-Guest were more strident, however. Haden-Guest called "partnership" as he saw it: "just another form of words to delude people. I had no doubt heard of partners and junior partners. . . . Is it now the policy of the Government . . . that the Colonies are in fact to be taken in equal partnership, or is it just a form of words, soft soap and soothing syrup, which means nothing? What does 'partnership' mean?"[27] Indeed, it was the very ambiguity of "partnership"—with its inherent flexibility to include Hailey's junior and senior status, Perham's liberal paternalism, mainstream Labour's focus on economic improvements, and Creech Jones's hope for a move toward greater equality at some point in the future—that made it such a genius stroke in wartime thought.

The Ministry of Information quickly seized on the dynamic "partnership" and packaged it for consumption at home and around the world. It recruited new spin doctors and brought in Gervas Huxley, who had served at the Empire Marketing Board, another government propaganda machine. Huxley eschewed "trusteeship" and instead declared the empire a "dynamic partnership between Great Britain and the Colonial peoples in progress toward the development of self-governing institutions in the political sphere and toward a better and fuller life in the social sphere."[28] When it came time to convince critics, the ministry undertook an impressive, multipronged effort. Well aware of its own misdeeds in the empire, the Colonial Office initially balked at leading with anti-German propaganda, lest it be "hoisted by [its] own petard," while the long-term effects of portraying Nazi evil could well have unintended consequences.[29] "Once an appetite for hatred is created, it is not so easily allayed," one Colonial Office memorandum warned. "When the excuse for hating the Germans has been removed the sentiment may be transferred to what is uppermost in the minds of all Africans as they attain political and social consciousness. . . . Having been encouraged to hate one branch of the white race, they may extend that feeling to oth-

"The Empire's Strength," British wartime propaganda poster

ers."[30] Despite such fears, the MOI ran with an "Evil Things" theme, and it peddled, in Harry Hodson's words, "Nazi destruction of freedom, law, religion, the home, militarism and cruelty." Pamphlets such as "Germans Would Make West Africans into Slaves" gained considerable traction across British Africa. Hitler's declaration in *Mein Kampf* that "it is criminal lunacy to keep on drilling a born half-ape until people think they have made a lawyer out of him" was the stuff of propagandists' dreams, and the MOI used it to great effect.[31]

So, too, did a concerted effort at encouraging "an appreciation and understanding" of Britain's imperial objectives occupy much of the propagandists' time. Themes of gratitude and, with it, interdependence, dominated airwaves, pamphlets, posters, pictures, articles, government newspapers and newssheets, leaflets, newsreels, and films—some of which roved around remote countrysides in mobile cinema vans to reach His Majesty's distant imperial subjects. The ministry's pamphlets, including "Sixty Million of Us," reminded African subjects that they were part of a greater imperial whole. Films like *Katsina Tank*, shot in Nigeria, and *Soldier Comforts from Uganda* showed locals that their financial contributions and personal sacrifices were being used to protect them from fascism.

The Crown was front and center in the Ministry of Information's loyalty campaign. Images of the royal family in full regalia were plastered in colonial offices, thatched roof huts, and in the alleyways of the empire, where the monarchy's symbolism was meant to project the awe and strength of future victors in the global conflict.[32] Disraeli-era conceptions of filial loyalty to the Crown endured. Churchill's colonial-tested ministers offered nostalgic fillips to the ministry's campaign. They waxed on about the potent union of nation, empire, and monarchy and its combined strength to overcome the wartime challenges throughout Britain's imperial world. Ultimately, for ministers like Secretary of State for India Amery, there was no question that the empire was

> one single, indissoluble body corporate composed of the King and his subjects. . . . As subjects of the King all inhabitants of the Empire owe loyalty not only to the King, but in virtue of their loyalty to him, to each other. . . . [There is] a common tradition interwoven with each local tradition, a common patriotism of Empire not excluding but embracing and enlarging the narrower patriotism of nation or community.[33]

At home, the MOI foregrounded colonial knowledge, facts, and histories as well as Victorian-era ideas about nation, empire, and monarchy. Harlow and his Round Table crowd were crucial in these endeavors.[34] Insisting that "existing commercial and private channels of distributions should be used as far as possible," Hodson and the ministry bankrolled various books and pamphlets. Together with the Colonial Office, they chose topics and selected historians to script homages to the empire under the guise of academic impartiality.[35] Harlow produced *The British Colonies* in 1944, and Keith Hancock wrote *Argument of Empire* as a Penguin Special in 1943. The first Australian to be elected a fellow of All Souls in 1924, Hancock attempted to accommodate both "*imperium et libertas*" and believed Australians could "be in love with two soils." By many accounts, he would end his career as "far and away the greatest historian of the Empire and Commonwealth."[36]

In *Argument of Empire*, Hancock opened with John Bull waking up to read the morning headlines, "which give him the impression the Americans are making the liquidation of the British Empire one of their war aims."[37] He then offered an apologia for the empire, which included a full-dress parade of the Colonial Development and Welfare Act, passed six weeks after Dunkirk. The act was a clear commitment, according to the historian, to the same principles of development and progress that Americans held so dear. While the book was written as much, if not more, for Americans as for the audience at home, sales figures in the United States betrayed a decided lack of interest. Britons, however, consumed the book rapaciously, and its impressive first printing of seventy-five thousand copies quickly sold out.[38] This pattern continued. As one Colonial Office official noted, it would "be optimistic to hope that the malicious ill-will which characterises so much of American criticism of the British Empire . . . would be dissipated by promulgating the scholarship of Hancock, Harlow and Coupland."[39]

Argument of Empire self-consciously reminded His Majesty's subjects of Churchill's oration in June 1940. In perhaps his most famous wartime speech, the prime minister had tapped into his nation's heroic past and entwined its wartime identity, and future, with its vast imperial landscape. "Let us therefore brace ourselves to our duty," he declared, "and so bear ourselves that if the British Commonwealth and Empire lasts for a thousand years men will still say, 'This was their finest hour.' "[40] The MOI executed an all-out campaign to influence Britons' imperial sentiments, producing basic documents like "Fifty Facts about the Colonies," "Britain Overseas," "The British Colonial Empire and the British Public," "Pioneers Who Served," "Wars Not Yet Won," and the Commonwealth of Nations' map, which outlined various forms of government; it offered newspapers feature articles, and distributed to schools, youth groups, factory lines, voluntary associations, trade schools, academic institutions, and the Army Bureau of Current Affairs countless documents, glossy pictures and pamphlets, maps, books, leaflets, and speakers' notes. It also took the show on the road. Traveling exhibitions dotted Britain's cities and villages, while special conferences gathered teachers, ministers, missionaries, and leaders of voluntary societies. The BBC oversaw radio and television, and in conjunction with the ministry, it gave massive publicity to the empire, which included films that projected a romantic view of imperial rule and partnership.[41]

Less than a year before peace returned to Britain, Noel Sabine surveyed his efforts and that of the Colonial Office and the MOI with conflicted satisfaction. While the empire was front and center in the media, and the population at home embraced its imperial past, present, and future, the question of partnership still hung in the balance. For Sabine, the notion generated lackluster enthusiasm in his decidedly white nation and was unsustainable in the long term. Instead, as the war was coming to an end, Britain needed reminding that it had no future as a global power without the empire. It was a view that reflected the sentiments of many in Britain's wartime coalition. Going forward, policies and propaganda would have to focus on national self-interest, and the role of the empire in postwar recovery, because as far as this seasoned veteran and others in government were concerned, "the future of Great Britain depends on its future as an Empire and Commonwealth and not as a small island in the North Sea with a population of 46,000,000."[42]

On a mid-September afternoon in 1944, in what is today Tahrir Square, Eliahu Hakim and four others blended in with the crowd as they chatted intently over their drinks in Cairo's Astra Café. They were a few blocks from the Nile River and not far from Giza's pyramids. It was a fashionable gathering spot that gave life to an imperial cosmopolitanism absent in the Round Table's tracts or the Ministry of Information's propaganda stream. Absent, too, were the sources of Hakim's angst and those of his compatriots for whom "partnership" was scarcely top of mind.

With all the MOI's self-congratulatory propaganda, few in Britain had paid much attention when, seven months earlier, Menachem Begin declared war on Britain. Begin was the leader of the Irgun Zvai Leumi (National Military Organization), a Revisionist group, fixated on controlling all of Eretz Israel, that broke away from Palestine's Jewish Agency. He was, however, not out of the Zionist mainstream when it came to his outrage over Britain's 1939 White Paper. In the Yishuv's collective view—that is, the view of most pre-independence Jews in the Mandate—the policy sacrificed countless lives for Britain's wartime policy of Arab appeasement.[43] With a quota of ten thousand Jews permitted to immigrate to the Mandate annually, the White Paper was, for all of Palestine's Jewish community, an act of betrayal. "Satan himself could not have created a more distressing and horrible nightmare," Ben-Gurion later wrote.[44] His longtime personal and political friend Malcolm MacDonald, colonial secretary when the 1939 White Paper was issued, was now one of the "greatest crooks" in Britain. MacDonald's actions undermined Ben-Gurion's moderate position against the rising tide of Revisionism, which rejected mainstream Zionist policies, in the Yishuv.[45] Moreover, as MacDonald had declared a few years earlier, so too did his Colonial Office successors agree: they would not succumb to "an attack of conscience" on any imperial issue that jettisoned their nation's basic principle of Britain first.[46] Moreover, to protect this dogma, they were prepared to deploy repressive measures when necessary, as Britain had done with Quit India.

For all sides of the Zionist divide, immigration was still a nonnegotiable issue. While Ben-Gurion, head of Palestine's Jewish Agency, pledged his community's support for Britain's war effort, he vowed that the Yishuv would "fight the White Paper as if there were no war" through a combination of diplomatic, economic, and military means.[47] His program was a twofold offensive: first, a policy of noncooperation with British authorities in Palestine and a disregard of White Paper–enabled laws, particularly those that limited immigration; second, the creation of a state within a state—or an expansion of the Jewish Agency's shadow government powers by vitalizing its own military forces and strengthening its worldwide network of support. On the latter, Ben-Gurion and Weizmann worked closely with allies in the United States to form the American Emergency Committee for Zionist Affairs, with the objective of galvanizing American Zionists. Spearheaded by the formidable Rabbi Abba Hillel Silver and later reorganized as the American Zionist Emergency Council, the organization was several hundred thousand strong by the early 1940s.[48]

Much like Gandhi and Nehru, neither Ben-Gurion, nor Weizmann, nor the mainstream Zionist lobby outside Palestine wanted a direct military confrontation with the British. During wartime, the Jewish Agency's survival depended on Britain's victory, and Ben-Gurion marshaled his forces to support the empire in the Middle East and Europe. So, too, did Britain depend on its loyal subjects. As in the Arab Revolt, colonial officials turned to the Haganah and its recent elite formation, the Palmach, as well as its intelligence wing, the Shai. Absorbed within the ranks of Britain's Special Operations Executive, some Palmach members were embedded in Orde Wingate's Gideon force in Ethiopia. Others worked undercover against the Axis and would provide the backbone of resistance should the German Afrika Korps overrun Palestine. Ben-Gurion, however, regarded the Zionist brigade within the British Army in September 1944 as the Jewish Agency's biggest diplomatic triumph. With five thousand Jewish volunteers from Palestine organized into three infantry battalions fighting for the Allied cause, the Zionist leader and his counterparts outside the Mandate gained more confidence that Britain would reverse the White Paper after the war.[49]

But splits within the Yishuv were poised to undermine the Jewish Agency's optimism. In 1943 Menachem Begin had assumed the Irgun's leadership and urged not a return to the Balfour Declaration but direct military confrontation to drive Britain out of Palestine. Under Begin, the Irgun's political objectives included the incorporation of Palestine and Transjordan into an independent Jewish state and the creation of a Jewish-majority population through large-scale immigration as a precondition to independence. Begin was calling for a war for liberation, and on February 1, 1944, the Irgun proclaimed an armed revolt against Britain.[50] Its declaration addressed the Yishuv and its imperial overlords:

> Four years have passed since the war began, and all the hopes that beat in your hearts then have evaporated without a trace. We have not been accorded international status, no Jewish Army has been set up, the gates of the country have not been opened. The British regime has sealed its shameful betrayal of the Jewish people and there is no moral basis whatsoever for its presence in Eretz Israel.
>
> We shall fearlessly draw conclusions. There is no longer any armistice between the Jewish people and the British Administration in Eretz Israel which hands our brothers over to Hitler. Our people is at war with this regime—war to the end. . . . We shall fight, every Jew in the Homeland will fight. The God of Israel, the Lord of Hosts will aid us. There will be no retreat. Freedom— or death.[51]

The radicalism of the Irgun was surpassed only by that of Lohamei Herut Israel (Fighters for the Freedom of Israel), or Lehi. Its founder, Abraham Stern, advocated indiscriminate terrorist tactics that helped distinguish this small breakaway group of a few hundred members. Sometimes referred to as the "Stern Gang," this organization tarred the British Empire as the main enemy of Zionism and unleashed a violent campaign that targeted British policemen, administrators, and imperial installations. Ideologically, Lehi espoused a peculiar mix of anti-imperialism and fascism. It went so far as to offer support for a Nazi conquest of Palestine if, in return, Germany would back mass resettlement of Jews in the Mandate. The writings and actions of European anarchist movements influenced Stern, who advocated "individual terrorism" and believed assassinations of key figures had the potential to change entirely the course of political events. In February 1942, Stern died under suspicious circumstances while in police custody. His followers, however, stepped up their efforts, particularly against British policemen, in obsessive attempts to avenge their leader's death.[52]

Among these followers was Eliahu Hakim who, on that September afternoon in 1944, sat in the Astra Café. As a teenager, he had emigrated to the Mandate from Beirut. He detested the British occupation of Palestine and refusal to grant Jews a national home. He joined the Irgun in 1941 but soon defected to Lehi. With his upper-class background and Sephardic heritage, Hakim was unlike his Lehi counterparts, most of whom were lower- and middle-class Ashkenazi Jews from Central or Eastern Europe. When Hakim's parents begged him to leave his extremist ways behind, he seemingly complied, joining the British Army. When he reached Cairo, however, he quickly rejoined Lehi, became an arms smuggler, and loaded suitcases full of weapons that were then ferried across the Sinai Desert. In time, he abandoned the British Army and returned to Palestine, where he became one of the chief operatives in Lehi's ongoing attacks against all things British.[53]

As the year 1944 unfolded, operatives like Hakim rendered the Mandate increasingly ungovernable. A series of attacks left nearly a score of policemen dead and their stations in Jerusalem, Tel Aviv, Jaffa, and Haifa destroyed. "The security position may be deteriorating, and the outlook is not encouraging," a panicked High Commissioner MacMichael wrote to London.[54] The terrorist attacks continued, and 150 Irgun members blew up four heavily armored police posts. For his part, Hakim participated in two unsuccessful attempts on MacMichael's life. The assistant superintendent of the criminal investigation department, Tom Wilkin, was not as fortunate: in Jerusalem's broad daylight, he died at the hands of a Lehi gunman.

Churchill viewed radicals like Hakim as inconveniences and softened on Palestine even as extremists picked off his men in the Mandate. Above all else, he considered himself a Zionist and did not, according to one of his biographers, think the movement "a corrective for current societal ills or an existential necessity for Jews but a rectification of a historical injury and a positive force for the present and future."[55] Churchill considered the White Paper of 1939 a "breach of faith" and a "repudiation" of the Balfour Declaration; he insisted the 1917 proclamation had made a commitment to Jews both within and outside Palestine. "This pledge of a home of refuge, of an asylum," he argued, "was not made to the Jews in Palestine but to the Jews outside Palestine, to that vast, unhappy mass of scattered, persecuted, wandering Jews whose intense, unchanging unconquerable desire has been for a National Home."[56]

Like Lloyd George, Churchill believed the Jewish lobby in America had been highly influential on U.S. policy during the First World War and that it had only grown in strength. "What will be the opinion of the United States of America?" he queried. "Shall we not lose more [with the White Paper]—and this is a question to be considered maturely—in the growing support and sympathy of the United States than we shall gain in local administrative convenience, if gain at all indeed we do?"[57] Roosevelt asked his secretary of state why the British were "reneging" on their "promise" to give Palestine to the Jews. Urged on by American domestic protests, Roosevelt refused support for the White Paper on the grounds that it contravened the terms of the original Mandate.[58]

When Begin announced "there is no moral basis whatsoever for [Britain's] presence in Eretz Israel," several of Churchill's ministers, and many members of the British administration and military in the Mandate, expressed sympathy for the Arabs. They vehemently warned against any repudiation of the White Paper. But with the German threat in the Middle East receding, belief that the Arabs had been of little use during the war, and Churchill's own strongly held position on the White Paper—along with mounting Zionist protest in Palestine and U.S. opposition to existing policy—there would be another British reversal, this time in the direction of partition. In early November 1944, the prime minister confided to Weizmann that he supported partition and calendared the topic for a cabinet meeting in the near future. In turn, the head of the World Zionist Organization declared his faith that the prime minister and Roosevelt would work together to resolve the Palestine question and so create a home for the refugees that Hitler's policies had displaced.[59]

While Churchill considered carving up the Mandate, the Yishuv's Revisionists had different plans. With false papers in his pocket, Hakim arrived in Egypt in September 1944 to join Lehi's seventeen-person conspiracy cell. The cell's leader, Raphael Sadovsky, met Hakim and the three other operatives at the Astra Café, where they began to lay the groundwork for the assassination of the British minister resident in the Middle East— Lord Moyne. By this point in his career, the Guinness heir was not only one of Churchill's oldest establishment pals but also one of the empire's more peripatetic administrators. In the years following his Caribbean, fact-finding venture—the full details of which were still under official wraps—and a stint as junior minister and then colonial secretary in the wartime government, Moyne moved to Cairo, where he soon ascended to the Middle East's top post.

Hakim was joined by Eliahu Bet-Zuri, a member of Lehi and Yitzhak Shamir's protégé. The two had an indelible bond due to a bomb that had detonated too soon, leaving Shamir with unsightly burns and Bet-Zuri with disfigured legs. Shamir was a pivotal figure in Lehi and the unfolding plot. Along with countless other British subjects, he incubated ideas and earned grassroots credibility behind bars. The British government had detained Shamir and scores of Stern's followers at the start of the Second World War. Shamir managed to free himself and several other Lehi detainees. Those left behind were soon confined to Latrun Prison, where Bet-Zuri spearheaded another mass escape. In November 1943 Lehi was reconstituted, and Shamir was directing operations. It was he who chose Hakim and Bet-Zuri for the Cairo mission—a mission that he conceived as "an act to shock the world."[60]

In fact, Stern had hatched the plan prior to his untimely death. Murdering the British minister in the Middle East, he wrote, "would be a lesson to the world and to the Yishuv that our fight is not one against the British Administration in Palestine but against Britain herself. It would be an example and model to enslaved peoples that here we rise in revolt against this mighty empire, and we shall not stop until we achieve independence."[61] When Moyne assumed Cairo's top post in January 1944, Shamir reactivated Stern's assassination plan. Moyne's position of office made him a target, as had his zealous enforcement of the immigration policies, which resulted in the *Struma* incident of February 1942. As colonial secretary, Moyne refused to allow the ship's Jewish passengers to disembark in Palestine; more than one hundred of them later drowned at sea after a Soviet torpedo hit their boat.[62]

"Gunmen Murder Lord Moyne on Doorstep," *Daily Express*, November 7, 1944

By the time Moyne's chauffeur made his way to the front of the minister's stately residence on November 6, 1944, Shamir's men had spent countless hours watching, waiting, and plotting. Their reconnaissance wasn't difficult. Although colonial administrators had been murdered throughout the empire, Moyne rarely varied his lunchtime routine. On that November afternoon, he sat in his limo's back seat as he did on any other day. When his aide-de-camp, Captain A. G. Hughes-Onslow, moved to open the residence's front door, Moyne waited in the vehicle—and heard Hakim's slow, calm voice: "Don't move. Stay where you are. Don't move." The limo's driver sprang at Bet-Zuri, who gunned him down. Hakim then leaned into the car and shot the minister three times at point-blank range. Empire's servant, who had survived Gallipoli and heavy battles in France and Flanders, succumbed a few hours later.[63]

Hakim and Bet-Zuri were apprehended after a brief but dramatic foot chase.[64] A few months later the assassins were tried in Cairo, where they turned the proceedings into an anti-imperialist campaign. Hakim made clear the purpose of their "propaganda of the deed":

We are accused of the murder of Lord Moyne. We did it intentionally and with full premeditation. But we accuse the British Government of having killed intentionally and with full premeditation hundreds and hundreds of our brothers and sisters. Lord Moyne was representing this criminal policy in the Middle East. We are coming from people educated on a book, the Bible, where it is written: Thou shalt not kill. But if we took a gun to shoot, it is because we knew we were doing an act of justice.

Bet-Zuri deployed literary analogies to convey on-the-ground realities of Britain's liberal imperialism. "Great Britain is the country of Dr. Jekyll and Mr. Hyde," Bet-Zuri claimed. "In England they are all Dr. Jekylls, but when they take the boat for the colonies they all become Mr. Hydes."[65] Three months later Bet-Zuri and Hakim were executed as the Lehi propaganda machine publicized their courtroom speeches around the globe.

Churchill was visibly moved over the loss of his dear friend. Another imperial official was dead at the hands of subjects who demanded liberation. Addressing Parliament, he condemned Lehi's violence and walked back his earlier promises to Weizmann:

This shameful crime has shocked the world. It has affected none more strongly than those, like myself, who, in the past, have been consistent friends of the Jews and constant architects of their future. If our dreams for Zionism are to end in the smoke of assassins' pistols and our labours for its future to produce only a new set of gangsters worthy of Nazi Germany, many like myself will have to reconsider the position we have maintained so consistently and so long in the past. If there is to be any hope of a peaceful and successful future for Zionism, these wicked activities must cease, and those responsible for them must be destroyed root and branch.[66]

Before stepping down as high commissioner in the summer of 1944, he and his wife having narrowly escaped one last attempt on their lives, MacMichael made clear that extremism was "an effective method of drawing attention to Zionist demands." Begin and his followers felt that the Revisionist movement could "intimidate HMG into further measures of appeasement and to stimulate their official leaders [the Jewish Agency] into decisive action," according to MacMichael. For its part, though, the Ministry of Information inveigled to keep Revisionist strikes and assassination attempts out of the public eye. It worked closely with the Mandate administration to "purposely not [hasten] a climax by disclosing to the people of Palestine that [we] know of the danger, or to the rest of the world that the danger exists."[67] Moreover, with the war still ongoing, Palestine was not a priority. In the years ahead, Labour MP Richard Crossman reflected that, for members of Parliament, "Palestine was just something extra on an overcrowded plate"; he further emphasized that "no British election would ever be decided on the merits of the Government's handling of Palestine."[68] Instead, between government censorship and the ongoing war in Europe, relatively small eruptions of terrorism in the Middle East were not headline grabbing.

Moyne's assassination, however, was a bridge too far. Newspapers splashed his death, and Hakim and Bet-Zuri's subsequent trial, across their covers. The moderate Zionist community was horrified.[69] "The harm done to our cause by the assassination of Lord Moyne and by the whole terror," Weizmann lamented, ". . . was not in changing the intentions of the British Government, but rather in providing our enemies with a convenient excuse and in helping to justify their course before the bar of public opinion."[70] Ben-Gurion was similarly outraged. The fault lines between the Jewish Agency and the Revisionists ran along issues of methods and legitimacy. They were also about personality and power. Ben-Gurion despised Begin and believed the deployment of terrorist tactics was targeted, in part, to seize control of the Yishuv and the Zionist movement as a whole. He compared his rival to the Führer and called the Irgun a "Nazi gang" and "Jewish Nazis."[71]

Overnight, British officials in Palestine and London felt enormous pressure to respond with swift, punitive action. They considered the suspension of Jewish immigration to the Mandate and a massive operation to seize all illegal Jewish arms. Colonial Secretary Oliver Stanley concluded that any measures undertaken "should be immediate and that every effort should be made to dramatise them in the public eye. We have to consider the effect not merely upon Palestine but upon the Middle East and the world in general. Some striking display will be required in the interests of British prestige. Troop movements on an impressive scale would clearly be one of the best measures to achieve this end."[72]

Guided partly by Churchill's hard-earned wisdom in the empire, the war cabinet had other ideas. According to the prime minister, suspending Jewish immigration would "play into the hands of the extremists," and he took it off the table.[73] Insofar as arms searches were concerned, the cabinet determined that wartime Britain did not have the manpower for the two battalions needed to execute the operation. The British government also lacked the necessary political will. Cabinet members raised concerns that operations similar to those undertaken during the Arab Revolt would worsen the situation and compel the more moderate Jewish Agency and its Haganah forces to rebel. There were also, of course, the Americans to consider.

Instead, Churchill's government made one unwavering demand. The Jewish Agency had to choose sides. Simply put, in a high-stakes game of divide and rule, if the Yishuv did not actively cooperate with Britain to stamp out the terrorists, then Britain would bring the full force of its punitive measures to bear against the Jewish community in Palestine. Ben-Gurion had to wrest control not only to placate the British but also to ensure his own place atop the Yishuv's leadership structure. He unleashed the Haganah to curb the extremists and used whatever means necessary. The resulting power struggle was known as the Saison, short for "hunting season." The Jewish Agency cooperated with British authorities to provide copious amounts of intelligence on the whereabouts and activities of the Revisionist movement's members. Ben-Gurion's organization also aided in their arrests, interrogations, and assassinations.

With the Saison under way, Shamir and his fellow Lehi members suspended operations and went underground. Begin refused to hide, and his followers felt the full force of Ben-Gurion's fury. Within a few months, the British realized that the Jewish Agency was using the

November 1944 cooperation agreement to move beyond the rooting out of terrorists. Its members were settling old political scores and diverting suspects from the police to secret Haganah detention facilities. British policies fueled an escalating civil war and, as elsewhere in the empire, struggled to rein in the spiraling situation. The colonial state, while projecting power with its get-tough policies, had a tenuous hold on the monopoly of violence.

Haganah agents scoffed at local authorities' demands that they release their prisoners. Instead, kidnapping, detention, and harsh interrogations continued on the Jewish Agency's watch. On November 13, 1944, Begin had handed down an edict: "Do not raise a hand and do not use a weapon. . . . [The Saison operatives] are not guilty. They are our brothers. . . . There will not be a civil war, but [we] will approach the big day, in which the nation will rise up—despite the will of those obstructing the way—as one fighting camp." Begin managed to keep a lid on counterreprisals while Ben-Gurion delivered on his promises. As of January 1945, there was not a single terrorist incident in Palestine. Nevertheless, regardless of how actively the Jewish Agency and Haganah contributed manpower and provided the Palestine police force with intelligence, it was never enough to dampen British calls for punitive action. That view was fiercest among the prime minister's officials in the Middle East. Moyne's adviser on Arab affairs, Brigadier Sir Iltyd Clayton, wrote a single-spaced, four-page letter that ripped the British government for its spinelessness.

> All well-informed authorities in the Middle East agree that the murder of Lord Moyne is not the end of the terrorist campaign but only a stage in its development. . . . There are some grounds for believing that a "black list" of British officials and personalities marked down for assassination is in existence. . . . Already the Arabs in Palestine are reported to be saying that . . . when the District Commissioner of Galilee was shot by Arab gangsters in 1937, the British rounded up and deported to the Seychelles every important Arab leader in Palestine; but when the Jews shoot a member of the British Cabinet, nothing happens.

Lord Killearn, Britain's long-serving ambassador to Egypt and high commissioner of Sudan, summed up the sentiments of Britain's imperial foot soldiers: "Poor Walter's murder is surely a pretty high price to have had to pay for our previous inaction. Do I really understand that the CO [Colonial Office] are deliberately prepared to await another outrage (they in fact say so) before having the guts to do the needful. If so, one really begins to feel ashamed that one is an Englishman!"[74]

Churchill believed the Yishuv's shock at Moyne's assassination to be genuine, as well as Weizmann's frantic attempts at "counsels of moderation." Weizmann's bereavement surpassed even that which he felt for his twenty-five-year-old son Michael, who died during a Royal Air Force mission two years earlier. "When my son was killed it was my personal tragedy," he said. "*Hasem natan, Hashem lackah* [God gives, God takes]—but here [Moyne's murder] is the tragedy of the entire nation."[75] Anti-British violence, on the one hand, and rooting out extremists, on the other, revealed the struggle within the Jewish community. Caught between these two extremes, the Yishuv stood on the brink of civil war.

Ultimately, it was the Zionists' relationship with Britain that Weizmann mourned. His earlier confidence that Lord Moyne's death would not change "the intentions of the British Government" evaporated, as any talk of partition was over. Churchill had put the topic back on the shelf, which was abundantly apparent at Yalta in 1945. Just days before Moyne's assassination, Churchill floated the idea of hosting the Big Three conference in Jerusalem. Instead, when Britain's prime minister arrived on the shores of the Black Sea to discuss the postwar future, Palestine was nowhere on his agenda. In fact, Churchill had no plan to offer, and when Roosevelt and Stalin raised the topic, he said not a word.[76]

In the wake of Lord Moyne's death, Churchill's war cabinet demanded "carefully picked expert personnel" to straighten things out in the Mandate.[77] MI5's Director General Petrie, who had had firsthand experience battling terrorists in Bengal and Palestine alongside Charles Tegart, selected London-based Alex Kellar as the man for the job. Already a legend among spies with his flamboyant personality and utter genius when it came to international cat and mouse games, Kellar was the ideal choice. His knowledge of Zionist organizations and the intricacies of the Yishuv's politics were also unmatched, as was his access to the intelligence community's secret intercepts between Jewish Agency officials in London and Jerusalem. He also had vast knowledge of the empire's broader intelligence and counterinsurgency hydra. Looking at the web of operations across the empire influencing Kellar's course of action in Palestine offers us a tangled image of harsh bureaucratized systems that consolidated at war's end and that would have direct bearing on how Britain would conceive and implement its postwar imperial strategies.

It took little time for Kellar to zero in on the Mandate's lackluster intelligence and policing operations. For one thing, there weren't enough bodies to fill the ranks of the Palestine Police Force, given the level of terrorist activities. Local intelligence was so poor that the criminal investigation department had failed to interrogate key Zionist suspects before shipping them off to an Eritrean detention camp. Kellar personally saw to it that several of these detainees were sent from Eritrea to a Combined Services Detailed Interrogation Center (CSDIC, recall, pronounced *sizdik*) in Maadi, Egypt, just outside Cairo. Established in the early years of the war, this interrogation site initially processed sixty prisoners a day using London-based CSDIC techniques of direct questioning, "M" cover (hidden microphones), and stool pigeons, as well as turned prisoners or undercover agents whom camp officials deployed as spies within interrogation holding cells. As the Allies scored successive victories in North Africa, more interrogators from London arrived not only to break prisoners down in Maadi but also to staff five mobile CSDIC units that operated throughout the Middle East. These units screened prisoners on the spot and sent valuable intelligence on to the troops before suspects went to the CSDIC outside Cairo for further interrogation.[78] Even with these seasoned interrogators, however, "the [detained Zionist] men concerned are cast in the fanatical mould," Kellar observed, "and, like the I.R.A. during the 'Black and Tan' period, they will probably prove difficult or perhaps impossible to break."[79]

The Middle East was part of a larger imperial problem. As Allied victories accrued, establishing bureaucratized systems for processing, interrogating, and turning prisoners of war overwhelmed British officials. Casting about the empire, they decided to concentrate Britain's "experimental campaign of propaganda" at several newly created CSDICs located in the Himalayan foothills. The Raj had a history of contending with large populations of prisoners, as well as famine and plague refugees, and perhaps, officials thought, it offered solutions to their massive wartime confinement and interrogation issues. As we saw in chapter 2, India had offered South Africa one blueprint for refugee camps, which, by the end of the turn-of-the-century war on the veld, Kitchener had turned into the twentieth century's model for concentration camps. Decades later in wartime India, the Raj threw up several detention camps, or black spots, where British officials sent over one-quarter of its 275,000 Italian POWs. The Ministry of Information, which was simultaneously working on its empire information campaign on both sides of the Atlantic, was responsible for the camps' propaganda, while veterans from the London Cage oversaw POW interrogations.

Despite wartime success in Britain's CSDICs, India proved another matter. Camp officials could not screen, classify, and segregate fast enough the devout fascists from those who were willing to cooperate. In fact, British personnel spent much of the first two years of the CSDIC experiment screening and re-screening prisoners as either "white," "grey," or "black," denoting a POW's ascending fascist support. "Firm discipline" was meant as a reform measure, according to one camp official; in practice, it only hardened POWs, 20 percent of whom were "black." Soon detainees were fashioning fascist membership cards from old cigarette packets. Prisoners were "more in awe of the secret Fascist cells than of the British authorities," one interrogation officer reported. "Collective bravado and love of heroics without danger is a contributory factor to this state of mind. Men who in Italy joined with everyone else in feeling bored when *Giovanezza* [sic; the official hymn of the Italian National Fascist Party] was sung now join in its choral chanting with the utmost fervor. Fascism has become identified in their minds with patriotism."[80]

British officials had imagined a "re-education" program, changing hearts and minds, in its Indian CSDICs. They would lure "white" POWs, once segregated, toward a "Fifth Column" allegiance with better rations, English-language classes, newspapers, antifascist propaganda, and a personal copy of Kipling's *Kim*. When Britain gave up on creating a Free Italy movement in 1943, it needed labor more than prisoner loyalty. POWs were sent en masse to various parts of India, Australia, the Middle East, and Britain, where Allied forces made them work.[81] The interrogators left behind soon joined wartime veterans across the intelligence community, as well as in the colonial administration and military, bringing repressive tactics and hard-earned knowledge to the empire's interrogation centers, detention camps, urban streets, and rural villages in the postwar years.

As with India's nineteenth-century refugee camps and South Africa's concentration camps, crises spawned new forms of control, relief, and coercion. In the case of wartime India, those interrogators who remained fanned out across the region particularly in the Raj's eastern frontiers, where thousands of refugees crossed the border. There interrogation teams and scores of supporting personnel from the army, police, and welfare ranks guarded, escorted, and oversaw the day-to-day operations of the network of advance camps, collection centers, and base camps. Much as they had done for Italian POWs, British officials categorized those considered loyal to the empire as whites. Greys were those "subject to Japanese INA/IIL propaganda" but were not considered dangerous. Blacks, however, were those "whose loyalty was definitely in question and who were regarded as a potential danger to security." Specially trained MI5 and military operatives interrogated some of them at Attock Fort, a secret detention camp, or black spot, near the Afghan border, whereas the rest were locked up, screened, and disciplined at the new Central Examination Center, located in Delhi's famous Mughal Red Fort—the same Red Fort that had been at the center of the 1857 Mutiny.[82]

Equally vexing were the number of grey detainees filling the Raj's detention sites. To run down the numbers, the government tried its hand at "reconditioning" them and established "Holiday Rest Camps" in the Himalayan foothills much as it had for the Italian prisoners. There greys were called "patients," because CSDIC personnel considered them "infected" with treasonous ideas and anti-British sentiments. With proper rest and food, together with sport and reeducation programs, it was thought they would come around in their loyalties. The "Holiday Rest Camps," however, had limited space, and the sheer volume of Indian National Army personnel to be processed, let alone interrogated and reconditioned, or "rehabilitated," was overwhelming. The whole operation became a color-coding nightmare, with new definitions and destinations for whites and greys, and the invention of a new category: "dark greys," who weren't quite hardened blacks but weren't entirely ready for a Himalayan holiday, either.[83]

The final, operational coup de grâce came near war's end when Europe and Britain launched operation "Green Service," a mass "evacuation, hospitalization and disposal of British, Indian, Dominion, Colonial and Allied [POWs], including civilian internees." Officials obsessed over a clandestine Indian regiment in Europe, known as the Free Indian Legion, infiltrating the Raj. Bose had formed the regiment with the Nazi high command early in the war with the idea that it would invade India from the western front, liberating it from British rule. The invasion never happened, and by 1945 Free Indian Legion members were slipping back into India along with the Green Service's crushing sea of prisoners, refugees, and other displaced populations. Military and colonial officials worked in haste interrogating suspects at Green Service reception ports in Madras, Calcutta, and Bangalore, and looking for others on the "black list" who had yet to surface in Green Service dragnets.[84] Some of those apprehended were sent to Attock Fort, whereas others met their fates through courts of inquiry held in Bengal detention sites. Officials transferred hundreds more remaining prisoners to Delhi's Red Fort where they awaited the Raj's next move.

· · ·

With victory over the Axis within reach, the British government subordinated state-directed violence in Palestine and the locking up of colonial subjects in India to its narrative of imperial loyalty during the war, and the empire's durability thereafter. The official line fueled the translation of lofty statements about peacetime into hard, complex policies that reflected the dawning new world order. As with all conflicts, the war had been as much about words as it had been about destruction and death. Just as Churchill and his propaganda machine hammered away at the empire's endurance under the new "partnership" banner, Roosevelt too had continued to proselytize his anti-imperialist sentiments. More often than not, his "four freedoms," the Atlantic Charter, and human rights were conflated into a language that aspired to a new form of postwar "civilization."[85] Such sentiments were on full display when he and Churchill, along with twenty-four other nations, had affirmed the Atlantic Charter and pledged full support to the war and an agreed, collective peace. When released from the White House on January 1, 1942, "The Declaration by United Nations," with its short preamble, inspired a world deep in the war's trenches. Its signatories were "convinced that complete victory over their enemies is essential to defend life, liberty, independence and religious freedom, and to preserve human rights and justice in their own lands as well as in other lands, and that they are now engaged in a common struggle against savage and brutal forces seeking to subjugate the world."[86]

Each of the leading wartime allies had its own audience. If Britons were roused with reminders of nation, empire, and monarchy, Americans were reminded that their sacrifices would be the handmaiden to future global liberties. Roosevelt missed few opportunities to "fireside chat" his message. "We of the United Nations are agreed on certain broad principles in the kind of peace we seek," he affirmed on the heels of the declaration's signing. "The Atlantic Charter applies not only to the parts of the world that border the Atlantic but also to the whole world; disarmament of aggressors, self-determination of nations and peoples, and the four freedoms—freedom of speech, freedom of religion, freedom from want, and freedom from fear."[87] A few months later the president broadcast his message once again and this time targeted an assembly of international students. "Today the embattled youth of Russia and China are realizing a new individual dignity, casting off the last links of the ancient chains of imperial despotism which had bound them so long," Roosevelt insisted. "The old term 'Western Civilization,' no longer applies. World events and the common needs of all humanity are joining the culture of Asia with the culture of Europe and the Americas to form, for the first time, a real world civilization." He then offered his ubiquitous coda: "In the concept of our Four Freedoms, in the basic principles of the Atlantic Charter, we have set for ourselves high goals, unlimited objectives."[88]

That the U.S. president spoke repeatedly and forcefully of human rights and self-determination was no small matter. He added undeniable heft to such calls coming from Britain's empire. Rights talk had infused anticolonial discourse and demands for self-determination since the nineteenth century in Africa and elsewhere across the empire, even if it did, to varying degrees, draw on European legal and declaratory frameworks.[89] In the run-up to the Second World War, this entwined discourse of rights and liberation became increasingly international in scope. Churchill signed off on the Declaration of United Nations, when for some it seemed anathema to Britain's business of imperial rule, because he saw little, if any, contradiction between the language of the declaration and liberal imperialism. Churchill processed the language of rights in a different register than Roosevelt did. Britain and its empire—and all modern European nations and their empires—did not regard rights as universal. Rather, they were something that a state created and bequeathed to its citizens. With the nineteenth-century rise of nationalism, natural rights had become an Enlightenment vestige. In the twentieth century, the state would control who did and did not enjoy certain rights. Moreover, as the historian of political thought Andrew Fitzmaurice points out, the emergence of positivism meant "that peoples outside the nation could possess rights only by virtue of possessing sovereignty."[90]

If the Atlantic Charter returned sovereignty only to conquered peoples—to the nations that Hitler had invaded—then, in the context of twentieth-century rights, Britain's imperial subjects were in a double bind, as sovereignty and rights went hand in hand. When taken to its logical conclusion, for the 700 million people around the world who had no sovereignty, it meant that Britain would decide when to grant it, based on its gradualist approach that reflected race-based, civilizational stages. In the meantime, insofar as human rights were concerned—or any rights, for that matter—colonial subjects were effectively stateless people who would, someday, progress toward statehood, and it would be that state that would confer its own conceptions of rights on its newly endowed citizens.[91]

If, as the historian and political theorist Anthony Pagden suggests, "it was an article of faith among nineteenth-century nationalists that a person without a nation was barely a person at all," then in what ways, if at all, did the lofty wartime statements about freedoms and rights apply to Britain's colonial subjects if their personhood barely existed, at least in the eyes of the state?[92] Insofar as it did, or would, exist, Britain held the interlocking keys to sovereignty. This sovereignty would come in gradualist stages of progressive self-government and, with it, accompanying rights. Only then would colonial subjects be recognized fully as people, at least in positivist law, which was in the twentieth century the law of nations.

As colonial subjects moved toward sovereignty, however, they were not entirely devoid of rights, even though at many times, in many places, those rights were difficult to discern. What made liberal empires unique was their gradual doling out of progressive self-government and, with it, progressive rights. Britain held the enduring belief that, even in the face of self-determination demands that were fractured and increasingly violent, it could control the pace of change. In collaboration with London, local colonial governments carefully populated their lower ranks with indigenous representatives. They also bequeathed certain rights to Britain's subjects, provided that these people passed developmentalist benchmarks that, in turn, earned them limited franchise rights, freedom of movement, and other benefits.

The Second World War was a watershed moment, though the pace and form of change were not guaranteed. Debates about the universality of rights were not going away, and at war's end and in the years ahead, British officials were well aware of this. Nor would concerns for protecting nation-states in the shifting sands of world power disappear. By the summer of 1944, when Roosevelt and Churchill were at the Dumbarton Oaks table with Stalin and a representative from China, the issues that mattered most were largely the same as those at the end of the Great War: the balance of power and sovereignty or, more specifically, national and imperial jurisdiction. To ensure the former, Roosevelt gave up on the latter, at least for the peoples of the empire. Not long after the Washington talks, he publicly endorsed a view that could have easily flowed from Churchill's lips:

> There are certain . . . "pronouncements," call it that, that in all history have been made. Some of them are of a good deal of importance, some of them do have an effect on the thinking of a public towards objectives, and for a better world.
>
> And the Atlantic Charter stands as an objective. A great many of the previous pronouncements that go back many centuries have not been attained yet, and yet the objective is still

just as good as it was when it was announced several thousand years ago.[93]

For all the president's wartime statements about freedoms, accountability, and timetables for self-determination in the empire, he stopped pressing for any kind of immediate liberation. At the end of it all, the arguable leader of the free world would trade 700 million subject peoples to ensure freedom and security in the United States and western Europe.

While Roosevelt's abandonment of his anti-imperialist verve may have surprised some, for Jan Smuts, Britain's longtime imperial warhorse, it was predictable. A year before Dumbarton Oaks, he had forecast a new world order that rested on a Big Three balance of power; and, as Britain's power lay in its empire, there was no question that it would endure, as would American support for it. From where Smuts sat, the empire had to evolve—there were future visions of federations that rationalized the bits and pieces of the empire in places like Africa—though its premise would remain the same.[94] At Dumbarton Oaks, the main details of a great power framework that shaped postwar internationalism and, with it, the United Nations were worked out. "Formally, the plans moved away from both regionalism and trusteeship," the legal scholar Samuel Moyn tells us. "Informally, their goal remained in effect to embed great power 'dictatorship' (as some critics put it) as the kernel of international governance."[95]

The United Nations Charter was more or less a done deal before any of the delegates arrived in San Francisco in the spring of 1945. Roosevelt's death and Truman's ascent into the Oval Office less than two weeks before the conference suggested that anti-imperialist sentiment was passing, but such nostalgia does not betray the new world order that the Americans, at Roosevelt's direction, drove from the time of Dumbarton Oaks through San Francisco and beyond. As had not been the case in the negotiations for the League of Nations, this time the United States sat in the driver's seat, and isolationism, particularly with memories of Pearl Harbor still fresh and Wilson's failures not far behind, was no longer an option. There would be no postwar utopia based on universal ideals and a capitulation of national sovereignty for some kind of international greater good. Instead, any kind of moral accountability was scrapped in favor of great power balance, as reflected in the Security Council's voting mechanisms. Despite recent claims that San Francisco was the harbinger of "A New Deal for the World," it certainly was anything but that for imperial subjects around the globe.[96]

United Nations Conference, San Francisco, 1945

Western statesmen, however, were not at the table through fiat. Public sentiment mattered, and convincing beleaguered voters on either side of the Atlantic that the net result of their sufferings was a reconstituted global balance of power was scarcely the stuff that put politicians into office. Jan Smuts thought that nothing at Dumbarton Oaks militated against his vision of a federated empire in Africa with white spheres of power, even if his vision was radically different from the pan-African one that Padmore and others imagined. Yet for this dressed-up League of Nations to fly, it had to have public support. Smuts's preamble to the UN Charter was lofty and aspirational—and committed its signatories to absolutely nothing.[97] Nor did it undermine the British Empire's

Christian morality and progressive development that could include Lord Halifax, on the one hand, and Creech Jones, on the other. Smuts praised Britain as the "greatest colonial power" and traced its arc from the nineteenth century through the League's imperial internationalism and into the postwar era. It was an empire where "men and women everywhere, including dependent peoples, still unable to look after themselves, are thus drawn into the vast plan to prevent war."[98]

Insofar as these "dependent people"—hundreds of millions in all—were concerned, the empire, from Britain's vantage point, would carry on much as it had prior to the war. At Yalta in February 1945, Churchill insisted he would "never consent to the fumbling fingers of forty or fifty nations prying into the life's existence of the British Empire." Even with events in Palestine and Lord Moyne's death fresh in everyone's mind, not to mention the abiding concerns that Americans had with India, where thousands remained locked up, Roosevelt had given up the anti-imperialist ghost for the more important matters at hand.[99] Sir Hilton Poynton, permanent undersecretary to the Colonial Office and its lead protagonist in San Francisco, carried forward Churchill's demand. He made it clear to the other delegates that "I do not accept that the United Nations should have the right to meddle in our Colonial Affairs."[100] When two months of charter negotiations ended, Article 73 spoke the Victorian language of "a sacred trust" that would promote the well-being of the world's colonized populations. In discourse taken straight from British parliamentary debates, European empires were to assist "in the progressive development of their free political institutions, according to the particular circumstances in each territory and its peoples and their varying stages of advancement."[101] Under the charter, League mandates would become Trust Territories, and the new International Trusteeship System—as opposed to an International "Partnership" System—differed little from the former Permanent Mandates Commission except for the fact that it was even more attuned to issues of sovereignty and was explicitly aligned with great power interests.

As for Europe's other colonial possessions, they were now called "non-self-governing territories," and the UN had no right under the charter to interfere with them. Each administering power, or empire, had only to submit updates on a territory's economic, social, and educational conditions. For the seventy-one non-self-governing territories, forty-one of which were British, politics of any kind were off the regulatory table, as was the right to petition the UN.[102] Charles Webster, another member of Britain's delegation, remarked at the time how his nation had "allowed our mandates to go under the new control [of the

UN's Trusteeship Commission], but for the rest [of the empire,] the matter remains exactly as before [the war]."[103] When all was said and done, *Time* magazine took a hard look at what transpired in San Francisco and declared the "charter [was] written for a world of power, tempered by a little reason. It was a document produced by and designed for great concentrations of force, somewhat restrained by a great distrust of force."[104]

Many in the colonized world, along with their supporters, looked on in disbelief. In the Atlantic Charter fallout, the leading Nigerian nationalist, Nnamdi Azikiwe, queried Britain's prime minister in the pages of his newspaper, *West African Pilot*. "Are we fighting for the security of Europe," he asked, "whilst Africans continue to live under pre-war status?"[105] After San Francisco, the answer was clear. It's not to suggest that scores of the 282 official delegates who represented fifty nations, not to mention the countless lobbyists who descended on the scene, didn't put up a fight. Ethiopian, Filipino, Egyptian, and Ecuadorian representatives, among others, vocally dissented, as did W. E. B. Du Bois, who was a consultant representative for the United States. Yet just as *The Washington Post* dismissed those who sought to influence events from the outside as a "little army of independistas lobbying the press and delegates," so were token U.S. representatives and peripheral nations dismissed by the great powers as powerless to change the UN outcome.[106] Some representatives were relentless, however, and Lord Cranborne needed to call in the Americans to silence Filipino representative General Carlos Romulo when he wouldn't let the question of colonial independence go. In his inimical fashion, the former colonial secretary spelled out clearly the way of the so-called new world to the rest of the anti-imperialist dissenters:

> At the bottom rung of the ladder there are the most primitive peoples capable at present of taking only a limited part in the administration of their own affairs. . . . We are all of us in favour of freedom, but freedom for many of these territories means assistance and guidance and protection. . . . Colonial empires were welded into one vast machine for the defence of liberty. Could we really contemplate the destruction of this machine?[107]

Partway through the San Francisco conference, Du Bois recognized that his bearing witness to Smuts on the international stage was more than symbolic. Smuts's racist policies were given fresh life in San Francisco. In May, Du Bois understood the deal was largely done: "We have conquered Germany . . . but not their ideas. We still believe in white supremacy, keeping Negroes in their place and lying about democracy when we mean imperial control of 750 millions of human beings in colonies." Others from the Black radical diaspora, including Azikiwe, also lambasted the UN negotiations. In Lagos, he realized it would be status quo at best, and wrote that "there is no New Deal for the black man. . . . Colonialism and economic enslavement of the Negro are to be maintained."[108] Five months later, in October 1945, Du Bois, Padmore, and scores of other leaders from the Black diaspora gathered in Manchester for the Pan-African Congress. There they spoke of the Charter's moral bankruptcy and the empty promises of sovereignty that the Allies had held out to colonial subjects around the world. "The claims of 'partnership,' 'trusteeship,' 'guardianship,' and the 'mandate system,' do not serve the political wishes of the people," the Manchester delegates insisted. "The democratic nature of the indigenous institutions of the peoples . . . has been crushed by obnoxious and oppressive laws and regulations, and replaced by autocratic systems of Government which are inimical to the political wishes of the people."[109] Going forward, the delegates embraced a radical internationalism that vowed to "fight in every way we can for freedom, democracy and social betterment . . . [and] as a last resort, [Africans] may have to appeal to force in the effort to achieve Freedom, even if force destroys them and the world."[110]

Turning to human rights, those in Manchester and beyond knew self-determination would beget them. While demands for independence were the first priority, this did not mean that the concept of universal rights—rights that ensured human dignity, free from repression—evaporated. For countries like Britain, unmoored ideas about such rights created anxieties insofar as they challenged the state and its relationship to its subjects. For colonized peoples throughout the world, human rights offered a broadly recognized ideal and language that demanded a level of basic dignity so long denied.[111] Even if Britain and Europe's other empires won the battle in San Francisco, there was still the larger war to fight. All sides were emboldened, though one thing was for certain. As Nigeria's *Daily Service* observed, "San Francisco and the world has once more returned to [a] terrific scramble for colonial territories and spheres of influence. . . . New life has been infused into predatory imperialism."[112]

CHAPTER 9

Imperial Resurgence

On the morning of July 5, 1945, the polls opened for Britain's first general election in nearly a decade. During the wartime years, the partners in Britain's coalition government, with Churchill holding the premiership and Clement Attlee serving as deputy prime minister, had put their electoral differences aside to fight forces greater than their own. With V-E Day came a new political dawn, and Churchill's number two refused to wait for Japan's last wartime gasp to hold a general election. The results, announced three weeks later, were stunning. The Labour Party won with a 12 percent voter swing away from Churchill's Conservative Party—the largest in any British postwar national election—and ensured a parliamentary majority of 146 seats.

That most Britons revered Churchill was beyond question. Many considered him to have been the right man at the right time to lead the nation through the war. Postwar recovery was another matter, however, and Labour beckoned Britons down a less trodden path. "Let us Face the Future," the party declared with its 1945 election manifesto, pointing to the nation's failures after the First World War and assuring Britons that past need not be prologue. "The 'hard-faced men who had done well out of the war' were able to get the kind of peace that suited themselves," the manifesto warned. "The people lost that peace. And when we say 'peace' we mean not only the Treaty, but the social and economic policy which followed the fighting." Alluding to the Conservative coterie that sat alongside them in Churchill's coalition government, and others who

V-E Day, London, 1945

had made their fortunes off the backs of Britain's working class, Labour took aim at the "hard-faced men":

> They controlled the banks, the mines, the big industries, largely the press and the cinema. They controlled the means by which the people got their living. They controlled the ways by which most of the people learned about the world outside. . . . The great inter-war slumps were not acts of God or of blind forces. They were the sure and certain result of the concentration of too much economic power in the hands of too few men. These men had only learned how to act in the interest of their own bureaucratically-run private monopolies which may be likened to totalitarian oligarchies within our democratic State. They had and they felt no responsibility to the nation.[1]

In its place, Labour offered "the nation a plan which will win the Peace for the People."[2] It focused on rebuilding a nation that remembered the high unemployment rates that had accompanied the Conservative government before the war. Labour capitalized on the widespread electoral support for the 1942 Beveridge Report, which outlined a social welfare system that addressed the "five giants" of idleness, ignorance, disease, squalor, and want.[3] The party promised full employment in the postwar years and a welfare state that attended to health care, social security, and education. There was a clear call for economic planning, which included the nationalization of certain areas of industry. In contrast, some Conservatives mistakenly believed they would ride back into power on Churchill's wartime coattails of continued international security. As for a real postwar recovery plan, they offered vague promises on social issues and economic controls. Churchill's own tone deafness was a measure of his party's overconfidence. Labour's agenda was nothing short of socialism, as far as Churchill and other Conservatives were concerned, and the campaigning prime minister said that implementing it would require "some form of a Gestapo."[4]

Labour's victory was not an accident. In hindsight, the party's landslide reflected an evolution in its national appeal and embrace of the media.[5] For certain, Labour's meteoric rise between the turn of the century and 1945 had its roots in a host of interwar phenomena that included the introduction of mass democracy. In the decade after 1918, Britain's electorate expanded fourfold, and working-class men and trade unionists, together with millions of women, entered polling stations for the first time. The heterogeneity of Britain's growing democracy was reflected in the Labour Party's wide-ranging membership: trade unionists; socialists who ranged from Marxists to Fabians; and disgruntled Liberals, among others. Unlike the Conservatives, whose rank and file were exceptional at cleaving to the party line, Labour contended early and often with dissent from within. Only rarely, as when the handful of Independent Labour Party members defected, was the party insufficiently capacious to embrace a wide ideological swath of members.[6]

During the interwar years, the Conservatives were geniuses at swaddling "national" interests with a blanket of "class-stereotypes" and "conventional wisdoms," as the historian Ross McKibbin reminds us.[7] Their leadership capitalized on the fact that some Britons preferred the idea of voting against their economic best interests. The realpolitik of Britain's staggering unemployment rates in the run-up to the Second World War soon found many voters putting self-interest before prejudice or, at the very least, rendered them receptive to Labour's ideas about socioeconomic regeneration. So, too, did a concerted Labour media campaign. Labour's media blitz reshaped understandings of "the nation" and its age-old "constitutional classes" into one that embraced broader conceptions of "the people" and their interests. The Labour Party leadership needed a broad-based electorate that cut across class and gender lines, transforming its narrow popularity to one that would seize control of Westminster and, with it, Downing Street. As the Second World War came to a close, the party capitalized on years of reframing and selling its socialist policies in an accessible language that shifted fears away from an Anglo-Bolshevik revolution and toward a future of social democratic reform.[8]

It was no coincidence that alongside Labour's rise was a democratization of British culture that permeated nearly all aspects of the nation's day-to-day life. Owing to revolutions in advertising and cinema, as well as in radio and print media, Britons consumed ideas and images at a rapidly expanding clip. In 1939 nearly half of the nation's 50 million people were weekly moviegoers; over 70 percent owned a radio, up from barely 1 percent in 1922; and the daily sales of London's main newspapers had more than doubled since 1921, to around 11 million. During wartime, the Ministry of Information tapped straight into this with its successful empire campaign.[9]

During the interwar years, few Labour leaders were as adept at articulating the party's evolving message and leveraging media's power as Herbert Morrison. Educated on London's streets as an errand boy, Morrison connected with Britons who were far removed from the Oxford Union and Boodles. He spoke a language that fused the "nation" and "patriotism" with the "modern." Morrison and Labour imagined a deeply progressive future that aligned with socialist policies, particularly around issues of employment, welfare, and education. As the historian Laura Beers points out, Morrison "instinctively conceptualized the British public in terms of demographics—trade unionists, clerks, secretaries and other 'black-coated' workers, housewives, middle-class suburbanites. . . . His political appeals were constructed to reach across social and cultural divides and unite these disparate interests."[10]

Morrison's know-how percolated through his party, and in 1945 the pro-Labour *Daily Herald* competed with the Conservative stalwart dailies, the *Daily Mail*, *The Daily Mirror*, and the *Daily Express*. Though accounting for less than 20 percent of daily sales, Labour's newspaper still distributed over 1.8 million copies a day. This was no small figure considering the money and machinery behind Lord Northcliffe and his successor, Lord Rothermere, as well as Lord Beaverbrook's privately held Conservative machines. The *Daily Mail*, *The Daily Mirror*, and *Daily Express* did the Conservative Party's work even as they shamelessly advocated their owners' self-interests, as was the case with Beaverbrook and imperial preference. Still, Morrison was not alone, and by the time Labour proclaimed victory in 1945 with Attlee at the helm, the party had proved itself modern in adapting and appealing to a broad electorate.[11]

Absent from this message was any major Labour pronouncement on the empire, let alone any call to separate the nation from the empire and the Commonwealth. Labour's only clear statement about Britain's place in the postwar world was its position vis-à-vis the Soviets. According to the manifesto, the principle that "left can speak to left" would be a bellwether for future negotiations.[12] Otherwise, the party went all in for a domestic welfare state, drawing on Labour economist William Beveridge's highly influential 1942 report. With the exception of the far left, anticolonial radicals did not move Labour members in any meaningful way. The *New Leader*'s special empire edition was hardly material for an election campaign in a nation that rarely questioned its right to maintain the empire. While the landslide victory swept in MPs like Harold Wilson and Hugh Gaitskell, who would go on to become major Labour leaders, they were not activists when it came to the empire. Nor would Labour's imperial critique come from mainstream channels like Creech Jones's Fabian Colonial Bureau, which continued to preach the gospel of economic reform and partnership. Rather, it would come from the Movement for Colonial Freedom, whose launch was still nearly a decade away. Sustained parliamentary questioning of the "system" of liberal imperialism and, with it, Padmore's emphatic charge that "violence is the high priest of imperialism" remained in the distant future. Until then, the question in front of Attlee's government was what role the empire would play in Britain's recovery and in the nation's self-imagination.

Labour's victory celebrations gave way to peacetime's grinding devastation. As the nation welcomed shell-shocked and limbless heroes home from battlefronts around the world and mourned the four hundred thousand soldiers and civilians who had perished, a cloud hung over victory's dystopia. It was a cloud that reflected the interior space of many Britons and the socioeconomic realities that enveloped them. Even as recovery was inching along, children still scavenged for food and for hope, some clinging to ration books as they navigated through piles of Blitz-induced rubble. When wages began to increase, the nation's poor still worked relatively low-paying jobs in shipyards, factories, and iron and steel plants. Rationing continued through the early 1950s, and the dawning postwar boom did not betray the scars of suffering. "This was essentially a nineteenth-century world, not a brave new post-war dispensation," the cultural historian John MacKenzie reminds us. "It is not surprising that in those conditions, the thoughts of the British should once again turn to empire as a solution to their social and economic problems."[13]

From the time Disraeli conspired to reintroduce Queen Victoria as Empress of India in 1877 and so consciously craft a national identity, the empire's durable place in the psyche of Britons was as noteworthy for its breadth as for its persistence. It was an imperial nationalism that encompassed monarchy, permissible coercion, and social Darwinism to create a unique view of the world that was embedded at every level of popular culture. For certain, the Ministry of Information and the historians who shaped imperial knowledge during wartime promoted and sustained the empire, but they did not prey on a false consciousness of the masses. Rather, they reflected dominant understandings of self and Britain. Moralistic claims further charged patriotism at home. The White Man's Burden created a national sense of purpose, while at the same time, it reminded Britain's beleaguered working class that they, too, ruled over others, either through consumption and cultural patterns or on the front lines of the empire as soldiers, police officers, settlers, and administrators.[14]

At the moment when the Great War ended some twenty-five years earlier, pacifism at home rested, for the most part, comfortably with imperial patriotism and violence on the empire's frontiers, as well as with its many cultural and political forms. During the interwar years, marketing, propaganda, and public relations emerged and coalesced, never more so than around the theme of empire. There were critics and public condemnations of Britain's use of coercion in some imperial locations. Labour Party's report on Ireland in 1921, for example, called "the situation . . . nothing short of a tragedy . . . [and the] recourse to methods of violence as a confession of bankruptcy of statesmanship and the desperate expedient of men lost to all sense of humanity."[15] Ireland was not alone, and extraordinary moments of violence did give rise to anxieties over British benevolence, particularly when turn-of-the-century images of dying Afrikaner women and children reached the metropole.

Some of the nation's intelligentsia offered scathing critiques of this imperial ethos. George Orwell's were based on his firsthand experiences. As a police officer in Burma from 1922 to 1927, he was, according to one biographer, "responsible for the kicking, flogging, torturing and hanging of men. . . . He saw the dirty work of Empire at close quarters."[16] When he returned home, Orwell wrote that "the landscapes of

Burma . . . so appalled me as to assume the qualities of a nightmare, [and] afterwards stayed so hauntingly in my mind that I was obliged to write a novel about them to get rid of them."[17] So he did with his publication of *Burmese Days* in 1934. Through his semiautobiographical character, James Flory, Orwell ventriloquized his own feelings of guilt as well as his belief in the degenerating capacities of imperialism. But on the eve of the war, Orwell needed no Flory-esque mouthpiece to condemn left-wing politics as "humbug" when it came to the empire. In his "Not Counting Niggers," the former imperial servant saw but "a few tiny germs lying here and there in unwatered soil" that might rise up "to right imperial justice."[18] As for Kipling, Orwell published a personal takedown in 1942, calling him the "prophet of British imperialism . . . a jingo imperialist, he is morally insensitive and aesthetically disgusting."[19]

The concerns of many other critics, however, were situational and fleeting and also revealed the nation's equal, and arguably more potent, support for imperial purveyors of violence in the empire like Hastings

Imperial Airways poster

and Dyer. At a minimum, once temperatures cooled, colonial violence was routinely brushed aside, explained away, or buried in unpublished reports both before and during the war. In the end, there was no serious domestic challenge to Britain's right to rule over 700 million subjects, even if it meant deploying repressive measures to do so.

Both before and after the Second World War, the British nation was more Kipling than Orwell. In 1942 Orwell lamented in *The Lion and the Unicorn* that "the really important fact about so many of the English intelligentsia [is] their severance from the common culture of the country. . . . In the general patriotism of the country they form a sort of island of dissident thought. England is perhaps the only great country whose intellectuals are ashamed of their own nationality."[20] In retrospect, if Kipling was a prophet, so were historians like Coupland, Harlow, and their Round Table compatriots, not only in the academy but also in government, finance, media, and elsewhere. The trickle-down effect of knowledge production reached schoolchildren around the nation. Robert Roberts in *The Classic Slum* recalled the mindset of Edwardian Britons who would continue to influence the postwar generation: "Teachers,

Empire Youth Annual, cover

fed on Seeley's imperialistic work *The Expansion of England*, and often
great readers of Kipling, spelled out patriotism among us with a fervor
that with some edged on the religious."[21]

In the postwar era, the moralism and triumphs of liberal imperialism
along with monarchy, hierarchy, and racial exclusion not only littered
classrooms but also persisted in children's books like those of George
Henty, Henry Rider Haggard, and R. M. Ballantyne. The *Empire Youth
Annual* continued to be published through the 1950s, and nearly every
major publisher had a series on the empire ranging from imperial lives
to heroes, like Kitchener and Robert Baden-Powell. So influential were
Baden-Powell's Boy Scouts—inspired by its founder's fighting in various imperial campaigns, particularly the South African War—that they,
along with similar youth movements such as the Boys' Brigade, boasted
a membership of 40 percent of Britain's youth population. When looked
at as a whole, the twentieth century saw three out of five Britons, male
and female, belonging to one of the imperial-inspired youth groups.[22]
For adult men, there was, among other organizations, the Overseas
Club. Founded in 1910, it was "a kind of 'Grown-up Boy Scouts.'"[23]
These organizations often embraced internationalism, but it was a
decidedly white internationalism that could easily accommodate itself to
the hierarchy of races.[24]

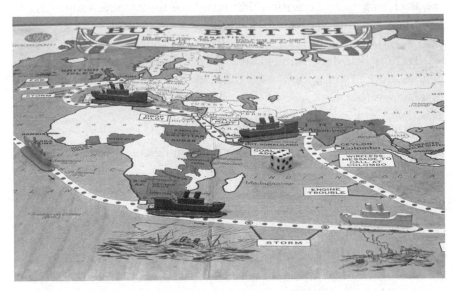

Buy British board game, described as "an exciting world race, and one which will
teach the players Trade within the Empire"

The new media of film and broadcasting reflected such trends. There was a massive boom in feature films, newsreels, and documentaries that depicted Britain's role, and control, in the empire. Romantic biopics breathed life into literature's hagiographies, like *Clive of India* (1935), *Rhodes of Africa* (1936), and *Stanley and Livingstone* (1939). Alexander Korda and Michael Balcon's great imperial epics routinely drew some of the largest box office in the 1930s and well into the 1940s. During the war, the Ministry of Information produced films like *Men of Two Worlds*, which featured a British colonial officer and an African concert pianist. After 1945, films that highlighted British colonial insurrections and heroic pioneers who defended the empire lit up the big screen. They included feature films set amid empire battles such as the Malayan Emergency's *The Planter's Wife* (1952); the Mau Mau Insurgency's *Simba* (1955); and the Cypriot conflict's *The High Bright Sun* (1965). The BBC, an imperial warhorse, continued, among other broadcasts, its Christmas Day flagship program. A national favorite, the program toured the empire through the 1950s, and Laurence Olivier and John Gielgud gave the images life with their mesmerizing voiceovers. As postwar rationing abated, listeners drank their "cuppa" Ceylonese tea, sometimes with a spoon or two of sugar, thanks to Britain's Caribbean colonies, and opened biscuits wrapped in imperial-adorned packaging— packaging that was ubiquitous not only on food items and beverages but also on advertising landscapes that included textiles, cars, and other items. There was no question that images of the empire—appealing to a national sensibility, particularly in the postwar years of recovery—sold goods, and these goods reflected the empire's abundances.[25]

In 1953 British consumers, like their late nineteenth-century predecessors, flocked to London to see the empire and Commonwealth on full display, this time for Queen Elizabeth II's coronation. As with Victoria's Diamond Jubilee, bedecked in imperial uniforms and costumes, representatives from Britain's expanse around the world, together with politicians, diplomats, and swaths of Britain's middle and working classes, came to see the parade of the empire's majesty. Soon thereafter, the young queen and her duke boarded the royal yacht for the most extensive tour of the British Empire and Commonwealth that the monarchy has ever taken. Back home, the press, radio, television, and countless newsreels chronicled the tour. Moreover, royalty was scarcely alone in its imperial travels. Passengers departed weekly to the empire and Commonwealth from Southampton, Liverpool, Glasgow, and Tilbury, and imperial shipping lines plied back and forth between the far reaches of British influence and these principal ports. Among those boarding ships of the P&O, Cunard, and Union-Castle were Britons who emigrated to the empire. Some of them were disillusioned, demobilized soldiers who joined their Great War counterparts in places like Kenya, where the 1919 Soldier Settlement Scheme had helped swell settler ranks with ex-military men. The vast majority, however, flocked to the white dominions of Canada, Australia, and New Zealand—nearly 1.8 million in the two decades after 1945.[26]

Britain was not Britain without her empire, a point that "appeared particularly obvious to the British," according to the late Tony Judt. In his magisterial *Postwar*, Judt reflected on his own imperial sensibilities and those of his nation:

> To anyone raised (like the present author) in post-war Britain, "England," "Britain," and "British Empire" were near-synonymous terms. Elementary school maps showed a world heavily daubed in imperial red; history textbooks paid close attention to the history of British conquests in India and Africa especially; cinema newsreels, radio news bulletins, newspapers, illustrated magazines, children's stories, comics, sporting contests, biscuit tins, canned fruit labels, butcher shop windows: everything was a reminder of England's pivotal presence at the historical and geographical heart of an international sea-borne empire.[27]

It was something that all major political parties understood at the time. Decade after decade, support for maintaining the empire transcended political affiliation. It was one of the few issues that most Labour, Conservatives, Liberals, and Unionists agreed upon, even though a late 1940s Colonial Office survey revealed stunning public ignorance when it came to the geography and constitutional composition of Britain's imperial expanse. But how much did the particulars really matter, as opposed to a broad consensus that, as one historian has suggested, was a "generalised imperial vision rather than any sophisticated concept of Empire"?[28] Indeed, a particular British worldview, a sensibility, rendered the nation and the empire synonymous, and the sense of moral and cultural superiority and self-satisfaction that they generated spanned the late Victorian era through the aftermath of the Second World War.

A sense of control, albeit an ephemeral if not an illusory one, punctuated imperial understandings. The underbelly of the empire was at times erased from the picture. In his 1933 BBC radio address, the historian Reginald Coupland claimed there were no "black years" of British rule in nineteenth- and twentieth-century India. When violence did appear, most Britons justified and normalized it, in rhetoric that harkened back to Victorian-era beliefs. These beliefs transcended class and region when the British nation was held against the alleged substandards of brown and Black subjects around the world. Such normalization often gave way to glorification, as witnessed in the continued defense of General Dyer, the lionization of the empire's heroes like Kitchener, and the indoctrination of Britain's youth into the trappings of liberal imperialism with the mass circulation of books like Henty's and organizations like Baden-Powell's.[29] The empire's significance, with its racialized violence and heroism infusing cultural forms, was not to be underestimated. As Orwell observed:

> Personally I believe that most people are influenced far more than they would care to admit by novels, serial stories, films and so forth, and that from this point the worst books are often the most important, because they are usually the ones read earliest in life. It is probable that many people who would consider themselves extremely sophisticated and "advanced" are actually carrying through life an imaginative background which they acquired in childhood.[30]

Officials and civilians on all sides of the political divide played active roles in cultivating Britain's narrative of imperial triumph, not only for the immediate postwar period but also for generations to come. When colonial violence was too public to deny—whether in Jamaica, Ireland, India, or elsewhere—it did not subvert support for Britain's civilizing mission. Rather, imperial contingencies, which invariably included subjects' purported savagery that needed to be tamed and reformed using violence, the White Man's Burden of ruling, and occasional bad apples were not mere window dressing but rather inherent to a liberal imperialism that shaped not only Britain's rule in the empire but also national imaginations at home.

The war's destruction, to be sure, exposed cracks in the imperial armor. Having raised the Rising Sun over Singapore, Japan marched on to take Burma and made it to the threshold of India. There its sweep ended, though not because of British strength alone. A monsoon deluged supply lines; without that and other accidental factors, India might have fallen to the Japanese, and the region's history would have gone in a very different direction. Devastation was ubiquitous, nonetheless. In 1943 Bengal suffered one of the world's worst famines: some 3 million people died due to British wartime requisitioning policies, diverting resources away from Bengal's crisis and laying bare the hollowness of Britain's claim to be running an efficient and benevolent empire. As commentators on all sides of the political divide suggested, events in Southeast Asia suggested Britain's political and moral weaknesses.[31]

Elsewhere around the world, Britain had struck wartime compromises, the effects of which would be felt in the years to come. The Middle East, with its vast oil supply and wartime importance, was paramount to British interests. London had ensured Arab support, though the cost of this deal to the future of the British Empire, not to mention to Middle Eastern stability, would extend well beyond the war.[32] As peace returned to Europe, Menachem Begin's declaration of revolt remained salient. Britain had recruited four hundred thousand of its African subjects to serve in the Middle East, North Africa, and Southeast Asia. On those battlefields, African soldiers who were far from home for the first time in their lives witnessed the vulnerabilities of their white colonizers at the hands of Asians. These colonial subjects also became literate—nearly 70 percent of them—and engaged in self-determination's global discourse. They returned home at war's end infused with knowledge of the Atlantic Charter, South Asian nationalism, and Communism. For the first time, a widespread anticolonial ethos percolated down to the grassroots level of African society, where it often intersected with civil conflicts and local conceptions of freedom and authority.[33]

On the empire's frontiers, the ushering in of Attlee's government was legitimate cause for optimism. During the war the new prime minister had gone on record in support of the Atlantic Charter's applicability to the empire. In the war's aftermath, his cabinet ministers who potentially held the greatest sway over colonial policy—including Foreign Secretary Ernest Bevin and Colonial Undersecretary Arthur Creech Jones, who stepped into the secretary's shoes in the fall of 1946—made grand statements that suggested a break from imperialism's past. In Parliament's first colonial policy debate in July 1946, Creech Jones dutifully listened to all sides of the political aisle, then jettisoned the idea that "for all practical purposes, there is no difference between the policy of the Coalition Government, and the policy of the present Labour Administration." He went on to gently disabuse his fellow party members and point a moral finger at their Conservative counterparts: "When Labour Members of Parliament endorse this sentiment that there is a close familiarity between Conservative politics in the Colonial field, and Labour policy in the same field, let me remind them of the strong advocacy by Socialists, by humanitarians, in regard to the treatment of Colonial peoples, of fierce attack and continual analysis of the nature of imperialism, and of the economic criticism which we have continuously applied." He took a deep breath and continued:

> We have witnessed a much more liberal attitude on the part of the British public, a desire to get the content of Imperialism changed, and the application to the Colonial peoples of *a progressive policy which recognises their inherent rights as human beings and their claims to freedom, liberty and economic justice.* Therefore, instead of Labour Members endorsing the sentiment that the policy of the Labour Government is just the continuity of previous policies, they should rejoice that, at last, our propaganda has succeeded in converting the Tory Benches to a much more human and liberal approach to the problems with which this Government have now to contend.[34]

Two years later Ernest Bevin, arguably the most influential Labour figure in postwar international affairs, declared that "we have ceased to be an imperialist race; we dominate nobody."[35]

How to reconcile such statements with hindsight's prevailing sentiment that Labour scarcely moved the dial on imperial policy after the war? Creech Jones, though earnestly well intentioned, certainly exaggerated when he suggested that Brockway, Padmore, Orwell, and others had made any serious dent in Labour's position on the empire. Instead, the cross-party consensus that had emerged after Ramsey MacDonald's 1907 publication of *Labour and Empire* was alive and well when the party came to power under Attlee. This is not to suggest, however, that Labour's first prime minister did not have his misgivings. "So long as we regard the native as some one whom *we* must rule," MacDonald wrote, "we are attempting the palpable impossibility of ruling democratically at home and despotically abroad." He warned, much as Burke had over a century earlier, "The result will be that our own democracy will be tainted, and our democratic systems will crumble, eaten to the heart of their supports by the autocracy of our dependency rule."[36]

While such anxieties over the empire's corrosive effects at home would continue in the decades ahead, Labour's approach was consistently reactive. The party did not offer a strategy and philosophy that, when put into practice, differed in any substantive way from that of the Conservatives. Insofar as Labour sought to self-fashion a different imperial persona, it was one of "constructive imperialists" who were, in the words of the postwar colonial secretary George Hall, opposed to "dominating or exploiting." Of course, Hall forgot to mention that his party's consent had helped lock up Gandhi, Nehru, and thousands of Congress members during the war and that it had also supported other repressive measures, such as forced labor, as wartime necessities.[37] Yet even here, as Hall put forward "the first peacetime statement on Colonial policy since the Election," he peddled bipartisan language that reminded his peers and the nation that "to us the Colonies are a great trust . . . and they shall go as fast as they show themselves capable of going [toward self-government]." His biggest concern was the empire's postwar image. If only Britain's approach toward the empire, so rooted now in partnership and socioeconomic progress, were "better known and better understood," the colonial secretary lamented, perhaps "we would then hear much less criticism at home and abroad of what, in some quarters, is still stigmatised as British Imperialism."[38]

Some members of Labour advocated a kind of socialist paternalism rooted in the rule of difference that had infused Britain's liberal imperialism since the Victorian era, while the new prime minister casually spoke of "backward peoples," as did Creech Jones and Bevin.[39] When the American press asked Herbert Morrison if his party was to "preside over the liquidation of the Empire," the image merchant dismissed such absurdity. He effused that Labour was "great friends of the jolly old Empire." Morrison, who, according to his biographers, had "an almost Kiplingesque reverence for empire," later dismissed any notion of present-day freedoms in Africa and much of Southeast Asia.[40] As with previous administrations, the issue of race shaped liberalism not only in the empire but also at home. Attlee and his men represented a predominantly white nation whose sense of purpose and self-interest were located on an island nearly devoid of browns and Blacks. It was against these colonial subjects that Britons measured their own Anglo-Saxon civility, updated for postwar times.[41] The empire was still "over there," and when it did come home, as it did for the young queen's coronation, just as it had for her father's, the de facto color bar kept some of it at a respectable distance.[42] It was one thing to rule over others; it was quite another to have them sleeping in your hotel rooms and eating off your establishment's china.

It was the principles of scientific socialism and the alleviation of poverty that had drawn politicians like Attlee into the Labour Party. He could square the circle of his Atlantic Charter interpretation using a gradualist pen filled with a nineteenth-century cartridge, albeit one with a few splashes of socialist ink. In the end, he was not a foreordained liberator, even in India, for which he supported dominion status as part of the British Commonwealth with continued military ties. At the other end of the political spectrum, Churchill believed the Raj would simply carry on, and he was no anachronistic anomaly among the MPs. As for African colonies and other darker-skinned territories, any move toward self-government in the near future would be, in Morrison's words, like "giving a child of ten a latch-key, a bank account and a shotgun."[43] Few in Parliament disagreed, at least in principle.

Practically speaking, Labour was unprepared and ill-equipped to take on the empire. The Conservatives who had packed Churchill's wartime cabinet brought with them a wealth of firsthand experience. In the empire, most senior colonial administrators were card-carrying Conservatives, and when they returned home, they formed a network of expert advisers to the party. In comparison, Labour, while it boasted a deep bench of technocrats on domestic policies, was largely devoid of seasoned expertise on colonial matters. So, too, was this the case with military and intelligence, both of which overlapped with the Foreign, India, and Colonial Offices' work, particularly when issues of repression were front and center in the empire.[44]

Some Labour members did have colonial and foreign experience, but it was surprising that, in the words of the historian Stephen Howe, "the awarding of cabinet posts had little to do with expertise, experience and interest."[45] In 1945 Hugh Dalton was the clear choice for foreign secretary. He had bitterly opposed Chamberlain's appeasement policies and later formed and helped direct the Special Operations Executive that employed Orde Wingate and others. However, he took on the role of chancellor of the exchequer, and Ernest Bevin stepped in to lead the Foreign Office. Morrison, a brilliant domestic strategist, later succeeded Bevin even though he knew dangerously little about foreign matters. As for the Colonial Office, the ex-miner George Hall, who fretted about Britain's imperial image and dutifully rolled off wish lists of imperial development programs, had only a fraction of the bona fides of his predecessors. Within a year, Creech Jones, arguably the one Labour member with significant colonial experience and interest, took the Colonial Office's reins, though the politics of personality and Britain's place in the emerging new world order would undermine his influence on the empire's future direction.[46]

. . .

The costs of victory in the war were staggering, and Attlee's new government stared down what John Maynard Keynes declared a "Financial Dunkirk."[47] Yet in mid-August 1945, after the celebratory frenzy of V-J Day quieted down in London's streets, Britons weren't thinking about selling off the empire to pay for domestic recovery. Lord Cranborne captured the mood when he declared that for Britons, "In this moment of victory, their first thoughts would go to God, who had brought them through this great danger; and next to their King, the corner stone of that great Empire of which they were proud to be citizens." Across the pond, victory dances had a different step. Despite the deals done at Dumbarton Oaks, Yalta, and San Francisco, many Americans were happily issuing imperial sell-date reminders to Britain. That British troops had reclaimed Singapore and Hong Kong in the wake of Japanese retreat, and self-determination had receded into the empire's rearview mirror with the UN Charter, lent credence to American fears that lives had been lost to sustain Britain's thousand-year fantasies. The *Chicago Tribune* issued a warning shared by others: "We have no interest in maintaining [Britain's] oppressive empire, and we are certainly not going to allow her domination of our foreign policy to continue, which is the only way in which that empire can be maintained."[48] When Gallup polled Americans, it found that nearly 60 percent disapproved of giving any further loans to their onetime colonizers.[49]

At higher levels of government, the United States reminded Britain about who controlled the purse strings and, with them, the empire's fate. With the war over the United States ended Lend-Lease, and Keynes played the crucial role in negotiations with the Americans over Britain's financial future. Five years earlier the most influential economist of the twentieth century had scripted *How to Pay for the War*. In it, Keynes had counseled Britain to avoid deficit spending, and with it inflation, by financing the global conflict through higher taxes and forced savings, which workers would be able to draw on for spending once peace returned.[50] In July 1944, as the war came to a close, the Cambridge don, despite a series of heart attacks and general ill health, led the British delegation at Bretton Woods. There at the Mount Washington Hotel nestled in New Hampshire's White Mountains, the United States launched its first shot over the bow, wanting to translate its economic strength into negotiating power.

Keynes believed that to avoid a financial Armageddon, Britain had to slash defense spending, ramp up exports, and, crucially, secure a loan from the United States. The economic guru set aside his disgust for the

John Maynard Keynes, Bretton Woods Conference, 1944

Americans and their attempts to capitalize on Britain's financial weakness by "pick[ing] out the eyes of the British Empire," as he so vividly put it. Weeks after Hirohito's surrender, Keynes traveled to Washington and, together with Lord Halifax, desperately negotiated a lending deal. Another member of the British entourage captured the mood that hung over the Washington negotiations when he said: "A visitor from Mars might well be pardoned for thinking that we were the representatives of a vanquished people discussing the economic penalties of defeat."[51]

The British press decried American avarice and short-term memory when it came to wartime victory. Hadn't it been Britain that, in the darkest hours, stood alone as the United States dithered? Hadn't British soldiers given life and limb to defend the world against fascism? Wasn't it Britain whose home front stepped up with France's early demise, then endured the Blitz? Shouldn't the Americans, as *The Times* headlined, offer a "Retrospective Lend-Lease" that compensated Britain for purchases it made after the fall of France and "before lend-lease supplies began to come in an appreciable flow on the American entry into the war"?[52] Washington scoffed at such ideas and instead held Halifax and Keynes to the letter of Article VII of Lend-Lease, which pledged Anglo-American support for tariff reductions. With Britain over the financial barrel, the Americans used Article VII to bludgeon imperial preference, which discriminated against those countries, including the United States, who were outside Britain's imperial system of trade by hitting their goods with tariffs while lowering or eliminating tariffs for those countries and colonies within the system. Its eradication was a wartime issue from the time of the Atlantic Charter, with American postwar visions for a global free-trade economy at the heart of the matter. As far as the United States was concerned, Britain's protectionist policies, dependent as they were on imperialism, tariffs, and subsidies for traded goods, were anachronistic. The Americans wanted to force the doors of free trade open, much like the British had done in the early and mid-nineteenth century, through the strength of its economy, and they were willing to go to great lengths to make that happen.

Standing in their way was not just imperial preference's trade agreements but also Britain's imperial monetary cooperation. Briefly, let's take a look at what this meant and why the complex story of Britain's monetary and trade policies mattered to postwar recovery and the empire. Close British monetary links with the empire stretched back to the nineteenth century, and while there was no formal monetary union for many years, monetary dependence became another feature of British hegemony. The empire did not have a single currency, though monetary policy was controlled through colonial currency boards and the Bank of England. Because of sterling's dominance as the currency for international transactions, it also made sense for territories within the empire, as well as for those outside the empire, to fix their exchange rates to sterling and to use sterling to denominate their international transactions. Sterling became the unrivaled means for exchange and reserves, and the City of London was the place for commercial and financial services. This system worked because British manufactured goods and raw materials from the empire dominated world markets, and transactions for these goods and materials were done in sterling.[53]

The interwar period, however, saw a weakening of Britain's economic position. The global demand for American goods, which had to be purchased in dollars, was increasing, thus setting off international currency issues for Britain. The 1932 Imperial Economic Conference responded with its famous Empire Trade Preference system, known as imperial preference. In terms of monetary policy, the empire and Commonwealth agreed to the sterling bloc, an informal association, that fixed their exchange rates to the pound, which Britain floated against gold and other currencies. During this period, many of the dominions and India created their own central banks that worked closely with the Bank of England, or Britain's central bank, which held most of the sterling bloc's reserves, or sterling balances. When the Second World War broke out, Britain passed legislation that formalized these sterling bloc nations into a closely integrated monetary association called the sterling area. Sterling convertibility, or the exchange of the pound for other currencies, like the U.S. dollar, was suspended, and the empire's monetary relations were worked out through a series of Emergency Defence Finance Regulations, which included Britain borrowing from sterling members' reserves held in London.[54]

When the war ended, half of global trade was denominated in sterling, which also constituted 80 percent of global foreign exchange reserves. The entire international monetary system depended on the pound, and many of the deals struck at Bretton Woods in 1944 proved unworkable. Bretton Woods had created mechanisms intended to liberalize international payments by facilitating convertibility of the pound to the dollar, for example, but demands for capital for postwar reconstruction and recovery were just too high. "As the peacetime reconstruction began," the economist Catherine Schenk reminds us, "the global demand for American goods and investment far outstripped the dollar resources to buy them, so if European currencies were convertible to the dollar they would quickly exhaust the meager supply of dollars held in European central banks," Britain's included. Yet the war had greatly diminished Europe's productive power. For Britain and its Commonwealth and empire, the sterling area offered a less ambitious but self-serving and workable solution for postwar recovery. As Schenk points out:

> Members of the sterling area agreed to maintain fixed exchange rates with sterling, to hold the bulk of their foreign exchange reserves in sterling, and to impose exchange control in common with Britain to protect against possible flight from sterling to other currencies (in particular the $US). In return, members enjoyed freer trade with Britain and freer access to British capital than other countries. Access to the London capital market had particular importance in the 1950s because other markets were heavily restricted by capital controls under the Bretton Woods system.

Crucially, if a country left the sterling area, there were harsh penalties. Outside the sterling area's exchange controls, the country's sterling assets "would no longer be convertible to other currencies." This is precisely what would happen to a few members, like Egypt, who eventually left the sterling area and had its assets "blocked."[55]

For the colonies, however, the system was ripe for exploitation. They had been brought into the sterling area by fiat, and like other members, their local currency was backed by sterling assets. However, as Schenk points out, since the colonies' primary economic activity was foreign trade, "the money supply moved directly with the balance of payments. In order to ensure the convertibility of the local currency to a fixed exchange rate, local currency was backed 100 to 110 percent by sterling assets."[56] Britain's empire was exposed to fluctuations in balance of payments and the reserve policy enforced by the Bank of England—100 to 110 percent backing by sterling assets—meant that Britain deprived the empire of much-needed development capital, instead drawing on it for domestic needs. In effect, Britain was using its monetary policies to profit from the empire. This is the point we must keep in mind when considering the Attlee government's postwar decision making.

Britain's exploitative monetary policies had another dimension. Because all sterling area members collectively held their foreign exchange reserves, they pooled and sold all their currency earnings, including those in U.S. dollars, in London. After the war, there was a scarcity of U.S. dollars to buy consumer goods, so annual import targets were set from the dollar area. However, as Schenk tells us, since Britain "usually ran a trade surplus with other members of the sterling area, who in turn usually ran a surplus with the rest of the world, this meant that Britain had access to the foreign currency earnings of the Empire and Commonwealth through pooled foreign reserves in London." This meant that raw materials from the empire, in particular, could be exceedingly important to Britain in the years ahead because they generated surpluses that would offset Britain's massive deficits. In addition, the United States was a major purchaser of these raw materials, which meant foreign exchange in the form of U.S. dollars could flow into London, which could, in turn, be used to service British debts and purchase U.S. goods, provided that the colonies didn't use these dollars locally for their own needs.[57]

Clearly imperial preference, with its favorable tariffs and exchanges in sterling, was, for many British observers, crucial to postwar recovery, as was American forgiveness of wartime debt and the issuance of new loans. Keynes's protracted negotiations in Washington in 1945 therefore had London on tenterhooks. The question of how to pay for the peace hung in the balance, as Britain, once the world's banker, was also in debt to its own empire and Commonwealth. Britain owed £1.3 billion to India alone. The Lend-Lease tab proved American wartime largesse had not been a freebie, even though Churchill had peddled it as the panacea for his nation's financial straits. Instead, the fiscal can had been kicked down the road, and Labour inherited a postwar financial crisis that included a $27 billion Lend-Lease bill.[58]

Taken together, the size of Britain's postwar debt was staggering. Between the wartime loss of assets abroad and accumulated liabilities, the country's total wealth had plummeted by 28 percent. By concluding the Anglo-American Loan Agreement, Keynes and Halifax bought Britain more time. Washington wrote down the Lend-Lease debt to $650 million, Britain walked away with a $3.75 billion loan, and the Americans set up a lengthy repayment schedule, with the clock starting in 1951 and ending in 2006. The price to Britain, if the dominions also agreed, was to abandon imperial preference's 1932 Ottawa terms. The question of protective tariffs, and Britain's exports and imports to and from its empire and Commonwealth as well as the sterling area, would be a major source of Anglo-American friction in the years of postwar recovery.[59]

The issue of sterling balances, and the sterling area as a whole, were recurring sources of postwar British angst. Reflecting on wartime fiscal decision making, Britain had not followed Keynes's earlier advice. Instead, in the economic maestro's words, the country had thrown "the principles of good housekeeping . . . to the winds" and financed much of its wartime spending on credit.[60] British officials hoped the dominions and India would negotiate their sterling balances. If ever there was a hint of a power shift between Britain and its imperial relations, it was on this issue. Prior to the war, most colonial territories were indebted to Britain. After the war, many of these same territories were Britain's creditors due to wartime loans. In India's case, it held the metropole to the 1939 Defence Expenditure Agreement. The £1.3 billion that it charged to Britain for wartime contributions remained on the books. Initially, Australia and New Zealand both wrote off 1 percent of Britain's debt, and Canada offered up a $1.25 billion loan that was as much about keeping British markets afloat as it was for loyalty.[61]

When Keynes stepped off the boat from Washington and made his way to the House of Lords, there was nothing to cheer about, even if most lauded the economist for his efforts. For now, he had saved Britain from "Financial Dunkirk," but the country's fiscal future was still grim. Its new loans totaled $5 billion and its sterling balances were £3.6 billion. *The Economist* wrote that "our reward for losing a quarter of our national wealth in the common cause is to pay tribute for half a century to those who have been enriched by the war. . . . Beggars cannot be choosers. But they can by long tradition put a curse on the ambitious and the rich."[62] The issue was not just money. American economic power and the will to deploy it had relegated Britain to a humiliating junior partner status, first on display at Bretton Woods and far more blatant in the 1945 Lend-Lease and loan negotiations. These key moments signaled the Americans' willingness to pursue economic strategies that were clearly marked by a continued dislike for the British Empire and the protectionist policies that kept it, and Britain, afloat.

Attlee's cabinet confronted a series of interrelated decisions. Here the sheer force of personality filled the vacuum of the Labour government's relative lack of international and colonial experience. Stepping into the void was Attlee's boorish and irascible foreign secretary, Ernest Bevin. Bespectacled in lenses that enlarged his fleshy features, he was the furthest thing from the suave Lord Moyne or Anderson of the Churchill era. Prone to bouts of room-clearing flatulence, Bevin was renowned for reducing his boss to junior-like ministerial status on all matters foreign and colonial; he was the epitome of an imperial hawk in a Labour suit. With little formal education, he had risen through the ranks of his party through the Transport and General Workers Union. Indeed, he was deeply respected for his complex union negotiations and was one of the few trade unionists to understand Keynesianism. Insofar as his ascent to foreign secretary was a measure of the common man's support for the empire's power and purpose, he was, in the words of Churchill, "a working class John Bull"—no doubt a backhanded compliment, but a compliment nonetheless.[63]

During the war, Bevin had proved his mettle as a member of Churchill's war cabinet, and in the summer of 1945, he had put his international skills on display in Potsdam while meeting with the Russians and the Americans. Lord Listowel, the former Labour whip in the House of Lords and itinerant colonial official under the Attlee administration, considered Foreign Secretary Bevin "at heart an old fashioned imperialist, keener to expand than contract the Empire." The trait rendered Bevin beloved among the Oxbridge civil servants who sustained the postwar Foreign and Colonial offices.[64] Such affection and loyalty were noteworthy given the clear culture clash between the secretary and his underlings and the fact that the Colonial Office was theoretically outside his purview. Bevin's sheer force of will subordinated Creech Jones and extended his own influence over all empire matters. The prime minister was willing to let this slide, believing Creech Jones "had not appeared to have a real grip of administration in the Colonial Office. He was bad in the House and contributed nothing in Cabinet."[65] In contrast, Dalton, a high-minded patrician figure known for his bullying tactics, who had been the most obvious choice for foreign secretary, bristled against Bevin's heavy-handedness. He called for a rapid reduction in Britain's military overreach that the beleaguered Treasury could not, in his opinion, withstand. It was an opinion that Attlee, ever conscious of his party's ambitious domestic agenda, shared, at least in the early days of his administration.[66]

Foreign Secretary Bevin had no rival in shaping and defining Britain's postwar imperial policies. Other nations, as his biographer Alan Bullock observed, "were not slow to read the signs [of Britain's economic weakness] and also treat Britain as a once great empire in decline. . . . It fell to Bevin . . . to make clear to those who presumed too far that while Britain might no longer be as powerful as she had been, she was still a nation to be reckoned with and had no intentions of being pushed around or left out of account."[67] When he addressed the Labour Party's annual conference in 1945, his position was unequivocal: "You will have to form a Government which is at the centre of a great Empire and Commonwealth of Nations, which touches all parts of the world. . . . Revolutions do not change geography, and revolutions do not change geographical need."[68]

Maintaining Britain's great power status and its place in the Big Three with the incipient Cold War was a top priority for the foreign secretary as well as the chiefs of staff. Casting his eye across the globe in 1945, Bevin saw Britain's future refracted in his imperial nation's past glories and its recent collective mobilization to defeat fascism. From his vantage point, Britain's postwar empire looked remarkably similar to that over which Queen Victoria had presided at the end of the nineteenth century. India, the jewel of the imperial crown, was still under British rule; so too was much of Southeast Asia, which included Burma, Malaya, and Singapore. Britain still had vast colonial possessions in Africa, like Kenya, the Rhodesias, Nigeria, and the Gold Coast; various islands in the Caribbean and South Pacific; and Palestine, Aden, Hong Kong, and other territories that claimed dominion status like Australia, New Zealand, and Canada. The British Empire still encompassed nearly 25 percent of the world's landmass, and as the Japanese surrendered and the devastating war ended, George VI ruled over 700 million subjects around the globe. The Colonial Office was poised to expand at home, and there were no timetables for independence in British Asia, Africa, or elsewhere, save for vague notions wrapped in national self-interest.[69]

For Bevin, Britain's role in the new world order, its ability to maneuver out from under America's thumb, and its postwar economic recovery all converged with the empire. Reasserting imperial strength, especially in the Middle East with its combined geopolitical importance and sources of oil, framed Bevin's strategy. The staggering costs of the war, and the Americans' role in bailing Britain out in humiliating fashion, provided little deterrent and, in fact, only galvanized Bevin's unwavering belief that the empire would redeem Britain.

Such imperial calculations, however, gave scant attention to the empire's postwar conditions. India and Palestine were both poised to erupt in more anticolonial and civil violence. Unlike Europe, there was no Marshall Plan for His Majesty's colonial subjects. Southeast Asia, in particular, was utterly devastated from its years of Japanese occupation. It's not difficult to understand why some in Attlee's government pressed for a major rethinking of Britain's overseas possessions and the troops needed to maintain them. Just when the nation needed its men home and working in the factories, whose export earnings, it was thought, would pull Britain out of the fiscal hole, they were still deployed in Germany's occupied zone and parts of the empire. In fact, despite expectations of a rapid postwar demobilization, 3.5 million men were still stationed throughout the world.[70]

A bipartisan consensus supported the maintenance, if not resurgence, of Britain's imperial power. The prime minister and Dalton were the only major dissenting voices. Bevin wanted British autonomy, and as the historian Philip Murphy suggests, "cooperation with the US was initially viewed as a temporary expedient while the essential task was undertaken of reconstructing the British empire–Commonwealth."[71] Bevin's determination to "pull our weight in foreign affairs" and operate in the postwar world free of American interference stood in tension with the nation's ability to keep its head above fiscal waters.[72] Imposing additional military spending burdens on the Treasury would only exacerbate the mounting crisis in Dalton's portfolio. At the end of 1946, the chancellor of the exchequer confided to his diary, "as I constantly tell my colleagues, we shall be on the rocks in two years' time, if we have exhausted the Canadian and U.S. Loans, unless we have severely cut down our overseas expenditures (military and other) and built up our exports to a much higher level than now."[73] Dalton understood that while Britain might not have been Britain without her empire, with it she was heading toward financial wreckage.

Ultimately in the postwar era, the "special relationship" between Britain and the United States evolved, as London constantly pushed back on Washington, though it was undeniably tethered to it. The relationship, however, was far from one-sided. The hardening of East-

West relations complicated America's position on European empires, Britain's included. In the immediate postwar years, Communism rapidly marched forward, starting with the Moscow-backed coup d'état in Czechoslovakia. The Berlin blockade followed, in which the Soviets cut off transportation access to Western-controlled areas of Berlin. Then came Soviet advances in the eastern Mediterranean and the Middle East, as well as the later Maoist takeover of China and the Korean War. With these developments, the British Empire was both a source of concern and advantage to the Americans. As the Cold War historian Odd Arne Westad suggests, "Any attempts to defy local nationalism by bankrupt, inefficient European governments under threat from Communism at home (and therefore dependent on American aid there) simply did not make sense to Washington."[74] Yet the strategic value of Britain's empire was undeniable.

The Cold War confirmed Roosevelt's reimagining of the new world order and the place of Britain's empire within it. American policy, once so decidedly anti-imperialist, was more willing to support the British Empire in the face of Communism's spread. After the president's death in April 1945, Keynes was clear that "America . . . was underwriting British policy in other parts of the world."[75] As the new world order came into sharper view, the Truman Doctrine, dependent as it was on Europe, continued to underwrite the sterling area and trod lightly on Britain's imperial consensus and policies of resurgence. Anti-Communism trumped anti-imperialism, and the United States threw its weight behind bolstering its allies, which included Britain and France, in defense of Western Europe and its need for reconstruction. As the historian William Roger Louis points out, Britain's empire was so important to the fight against Communism that "the Americans subsidized the imperial system generously in one way or another as a measure of national defense . . . [while] the British voter could have his imperial cake and eat at the same time."[76]

Successive American statements, both internal and public, supported this view. In June 1948 a State Department memo unequivocally translated into policy the U.S. practice of bolstering Britain's Empire: "The United Kingdom, the Dominions, Colonies and Dependencies, form a world-wide network of strategically located territories of great military value, which have served as defensive outposts and as bridgeheads for operations. Subject to our general policy of favoring eventual self-determination of people, it is our objective that the integrity of this area be maintained."[77] Later, when testifying to the Senate on the North Atlantic Treaty, Senator Henry Cabot Lodge Jr. emphasized that "we need . . . these countries to be strong, and they cannot be strong without their colonies."[78] In 1950 George F. Kennan, the renowned Cold War diplomat and historian, confirmed America's position, writing, "the dissolution of the [British] empire was not in our interest as there were many things the Commonwealth could do which we could not do and which we wished them to continue doing."[79]

Nonetheless, in London, imperial stalwarts continued to bristle at the American hand that fed them. They believed Britain would emerge an independent operator on the global scene through the strength of its empire. It was here that Bevin and others connected Britain's role in the new world order with its fiscal crisis, using the glue of empire to bind the two together. In his memo "The Threat to Western Civilization," the foreign secretary captured prevailing sentiments: "It should be possible to develop our own power and influence equal to that of the United States of America and the USSR. We have the material resources in the Colonial Empire, if we develop them, and by giving a spiritual lead now, we should be able to carry out our task in a way which will show clearly that we are not subservient to the United States of America or to the Soviet Union."[80]

Bevin preached the liberal imperial gospel that elevated Britain above all other nations and placed development in the empire as part of the larger attempt to "organize and consolidate the ethical and spiritual forces inherent in this Western civilization of which we are the chief protagonists."[81] The empire offered Britain a panacea for not only its international standing but also for its financial crisis. Bevin made explicit the postwar meaning of imperial "partnership" when he declared that "the colonial empire could make a major contribution towards the solution of our present economic difficulties."[82] He and other ministers believed the solution to Britain's financial crisis and immiseration at home, not to mention its increasing dependence on the United States, rested in the oil fields of the Middle East, the rubber plantations of Malaya, and other commodity-producing colonies scattered throughout the world. After 1945, "the growth of the sterling balances and the contribution which the colonies made to the overall deficit of the Sterling Area with the USA and other countries in the dollar area" became exceedingly important as the economic historian Charles H. Feinstein reminds us.[83] Exports from the empire of rubber, cocoa, copper, and other raw materials to the dollar area generated significant revenue, and Britain leaned heavily on its colonial administrators to minimize spending these dollar accumulations on imports from the United States. This led to a large dollar surplus that other sterling area members used for their benefit, particularly Britain and the white dominions. With Britain poised to accumulate a $9.85 billion deficit in gold and dollars by 1952, the empire's contributions of hundreds of millions of annual dollar surpluses was significant to servicing Britain's debts.[84]

In 1948 Malaya alone brought in $120 million—it was considered the "dollar arsenal of the sterling area."[85] Commodity exports became an obsession in London, particularly those destined for the United States like rubber, cocoa, sisal, and minerals. These were, however, not the only items that Britain ramped up for worldwide export. Rice from Sierra Leone and Borneo, tobacco from Southern Rhodesia, coffee from Kenya, and groundnuts, soya bean, linseed, tea, and timber from various colonies in the far reaches of the empire were but a few of the raw materials that Britain targeted for expanded export, particularly to the world's dollar zones. The 1940 Colonial Development and Welfare Act, packaged in its "partnership" language, was crucial to Britain's financial recovery. By recrafting old promises into a new and improved series of development projects, the act committed funds from the metropole— which increased substantially after 1945—toward programs specifically geared toward long-term economic development and increased revenue for Britain's use. We can think of this in historic terms by way of George III's taxation policies on the American colonies, which was a much cruder way of squeezing the empire to service Britain's eighteenth-century war debts. These policies ignited the American Revolution. Indeed, recall that the influential jurist Albert Venn Dicey concluded that the consequences of such British "misrule," American insurrection and independence, rendered the future prohibition of imperial taxation for British domestic needs an unwritten constitutional rule. Through Britain's monetary policies, the Colonial Development and Welfare Act would be a more sophisticated mechanism for using the empire to service Britain's twentieth-century war debts.

Britain launched its Colonial Development Corporation in 1948. According to Creech Jones, its primary purpose was to produce raw materials and foodstuffs "where supply to the U.K. or sale overseas will assist our balance of payments."[86] With Britain raiding export earnings on reserve in London to meet metropolitan needs, the empire and Commonwealth sterling area, together with continued imperial preferences discriminating against American goods, helped underwrite Britain's fiscal recovery. Grants for ramping up imperial production were tied directly to projects that might yield rapid returns: enormous capital investments went to large-scale schemes such as gold dredging in Guiana, egg farming in the Gambia, and sealing in the Falklands.[87] In the short term, such broader measures that protected sterling area markets and, with them,

Britain's place in the international monetary system while also pumping cash into select colonial economies for the expansion of oil, rubber, and other cash crop production—even if some schemes were complete busts—meant that the real and perceived economic value of the empire and the Commonwealth was arguably at its highest during the Attlee years.[88]

In the long term, such measures had the effect of stifling British industrial competitiveness and innovation, draining investments away from domestic growth, and creating artificially high interest rates to support sterling. Moreover, there were opportunity costs insofar as Europe was concerned. Immediate possibilities for closer integration with the continent existed, but Britain rarely entered the game.[89] Labour made interwar overtures toward a "united socialist states of Europe," but these were mostly "rhetorical flourishes," according to the historian Stephen Howe, and "neither Bevin nor Dalton were really a European at heart." Meanwhile broad swaths of the party supported Morrison's view of European integration: "'the Durham miners won't wear it.'"[90] The heartbeat of British national identity was not Europe but the empire, and its effect on economic decision making was undeniable. This had been true in the Hastings and East India Company era, and it remained so after World War II, when nearly everything economic was tied to the empire, including sterling.

Britain routinely faced dramatic proof of its own financial weakness, and each time it called on the United States for a bailout in one form or another. When sterling-dollar convertibility was introduced in July 1947, a provision of the U.S. loan that Keynes had negotiated, the run on Britain's dollar reserves was so extreme that it had to be shut down. "Whereas the collapse of the sterling might have been expected to force Britain to bow to the growing US pressure to revise the international role of the currency in association with a changed relationship with Europe," the economic historian Bernard Alford points out, "the growing threat of Communism from the East intervened and caused a rapid volte face in US foreign policy. . . . Sterling was patched up and allowed to soldier on."[91] Two years later, in September 1949, Britain devaluated its currency from $4.03 to $2.80 to the pound, a result of the financial markets undervaluing the dollar as much as of overvaluing the pound. Nonetheless, the pound fell by 30 percent in parity to the dollar. The ripple effects stretched across Britain and its empire and Commonwealth, where import costs rose and international confidence in sterling reached new lows.[92]

In hindsight, the economic practices of imperial resurgence were acts of nationalist desperation if not folly. Moreover, while anticolonial anger metastasized all over the empire, legitimate charges of exploitation dogged the Colonial Development Corporation and Britain's other fiscal measures and only added to British woes. Accusations were coming partly from the imperial frontiers where men and women who lived in remote villages felt the full weight of British economic and technical interference together with newly introduced labor requirements such as agricultural terracing projects to combat the severe soil erosion brought on by colonial cash crop overproduction. During this period, Attlee's cabinet calculated that "any suggestions that colonial territories were to be exploited for the benefit of Europe should be avoided."[93] The government's primary concern was not the voices from the imperial periphery but those from the Soviet Union. As Attlee emphasized, there was "considerable talk in the colonies of 'exploitation' of the Colonial peoples in order to help Britain out of her difficulties," and the Soviets leveraged it to some effect.[94] Still, no matter how much they tried to sidestep the matter, Attlee and his men presided over an era that has come to be known by historians as the second colonial occupation. It was one of the most economically exploitative periods in the empire's history.

Implementing Labour's new imperial resurgence polices invariably led to ramping up repression in the empire. Palestine remained a tinderbox, hundreds of INA members were locked up in India's Red Fort, and calls for anticolonial violence, such as those at the 1945 Pan-African Conference, all pointed to a postwar imperial collision course. As some of Attlee's ministers negotiated their way through fiscal disaster, others turned to the business of state-directed violence. Liberal imperialism came home during the war, bringing harsh practices and legalized lawlessness in the form of various interrogation centers and the regulations needed to make them legally permissible, including those that made them rendition sites for suspected Nazis picked up in the empire. When peace returned, some of the interrogation practices migrated to postwar Europe and the empire, carried by many of the operatives who had worked in Camp 020 and the London Cage. The circulation of ideas in and out of Britain continued, and interrogation centers in Germany and the empire offer examples of this phenomenon.

Around the time Attlee moved into Downing Street, the empire-seasoned head of MI5, David Petrie, and Dick White of B-Division, deployed a select group of interrogators, guards, and other personnel to Germany. They were to collect information for the upcoming Nurem-

Lieutenant-Colonel Robin "Tin Eye"
Stephens

berg trials. Overseeing the operation on the ground was Lieutenant-Colonel Robin "Tin Eye" Stephens, the officer in charge of Camp 020 who was now to establish a new interrogation center at Bad Nenndorf, where a onetime spa's private bathing rooms made for ideal interrogation and isolation cells.[95] Interrogators brought with them the wartime tactics of starvation and water torture, as well as various other forms of physical and mental pressure to bring about, in Stephens's words, "truth in the shortest possible time."[96]

Bad Nenndorf was not a lone operation. Rather, it was one of several Combined Services Detailed Interrogation Centers that formed a much larger system of interrogation and intelligence gathering across the empire and other spheres of British influence. Scores of CSDICs had mushroomed in India, while others had sprung up in Palestine, Syria, Iraq, Greece, Southeast Asia, and various parts of North and East Africa. They all became sites for intelligence gathering where, according to a War Office report, the continuity of personnel and the wartime "lessons learned have obvious value."[97] From the use of water and sewage torture and the experimentation with drugs such as amphetamines and thyroxine to the deployment of starvation methods and hallucinogenic experiments with visual and audio stimulation, CSDIC tactics and personnel became increasingly recognizable from place to place.[98]

The British government made every effort to keep these tactics, individual interrogators, and even the existence of the interrogation centers under wraps. In the case of Bad Nenndorf, however, locals heard screams coming from the reconstituted spa house, and the nearby hospital reported that detainees were dumped at its doorstep in various stages of starvation and "dangerously ill."[99] Desperate, one swallowed a spoon, others lost limbs to amputations, and some were so emaciated that observers called them a "horrifying spectacle"; several died from their ordeals.[100] The army could not keep the abuses hidden, and as German public pressure mounted, it labeled Stephens and his underlings bad apples. Britain's Security Service asserted that it had "no responsibility in the matter, and the only link which this organisation has with the case is the fact that Lt. Colonel Stephens, the Camp Commandant, has . . . applied for employment in M.I.5."[101] There were also mitigating factors. An internal report of the case stated that "the existence of [CSDIC 74] was essential in the interests of security and that the methods of interrogation had of necessity to be more drastic than those permitted in the ordinary detection of crime. . . . The interrogations in [CSDIC 74] had produced information of the utmost value."[102]

On paper, interrogation orders were ambiguous at best. Interrogators undertook their work in "a humane fashion," though they also knew not to "[unduly impair] the physical and mental health of the internees"; moreover, the "methods of interrogation" were "of a very top-secret nature."[103] Stephens verbally translated these instructions for his Bad Nenndorf interrogators, and told them what techniques to deploy on particular prisoners and what techniques to avoid. He noted that "each case has its special orders [from Intelligence Division,] and these are carried out." According to Stephens, the head of Intelligence Division inspected Bad Nenndorf on numerous occasions and provided verbal instructions during such visits; Stephens's underlings backed him on this.[104] Since little was written down, attributing blame for inflicting "physical assaults on certain prisoners with the object of reducing them to a state of physical collapse and of making them more amenable to interrogation" beyond a few renegades in charge of the interrogation camp was impossible.[105] On this point, Attlee's government did not equivocate:

> The Camp Commandant, Colonel Stephens, must bear overriding responsibility for the system of committal to punishment

cells and the harsh treatment which prisoners received there and for the grossly negligent medical treatment of sick prisoners. In addition, Colonel Stephens' failure to cause a full and proper investigation into the death of a prisoner who was alleged to have committed suicide justified a disciplinary charge of neglect of duty.[106]

The Control Commission soon investigated and uncovered scores of credible reports from detainees of physical and mental torture, as well as deaths. It stated that "it is the opinion of the Court that the Intelligence Division [Dick White and commanding officer Major-General Lethbridge] must themselves bear the major share in the ultimate responsibility for the treatment meted out at Bad Nenndorf."[107] Officials in London did their best to make the problem go away. Unfortunately for the Foreign and War offices as well as MI5, however, the Control Commission answered to none of them and took it upon itself to request a full court of inquiry with Tom Hayward in charge. In the end, Hayward left no stone unturned. His 130-page report reviewed nearly every scrap of medical reports. He interviewed Stephens and nearly all the guards, medical officers, orderlies, and interrogators in his charge, several of whom had honed their craft in Camp 020. Along with the interrogators, Hayward also interviewed fifty guards and orderlies who received immunity in return for their testimonies. Nearly all gave detailed accounts of horrific abuse in Bad Nenndorf. With several detainees dead, and the overwhelming corroborating evidence of physical and psychological torture, malnutrition, humiliation of various kinds, the use of Nazi-era instruments such as shin screws, and routine use of prolonged solitary confinement, Hayward's report made for disturbing reading. Within days of its submission, Commander in Chief of British Land Forces General Sir Brian Robertson ordered Stephens's arrest, along with several of his underlings, and their courts-martial.[108]

The impending military trial presented several problems. First, the question of publicity loomed large. Bevin's Foreign Office recognized that not only was the evidence of abuse widespread and damning, but also some of the tortured detainees had, in fact, been Soviets who were trying to defect. As one official told Bevin, "There are two main points on which publicity could fasten in this case: the fact that Bad Nenndorf was used inter alia for obtaining intelligence on the Russian Zone and that Russian as well as German nationals were held there; the fact that *we are alleged to have treated internees in a manner reminiscent of the German Concentration Camps.*" Another issue was that other CSDICs dotted

Germany and various parts of the British Empire. Many of them operated under the radar; the Red Cross and other organizations had no knowledge of their existence. The Stephens case, in particular, threatened to expose Britain's operations. "They may wish to call evidence . . . that other similar centres still exist in the British Zone," one Foreign Office official warned. He then mused that there were, of course, mitigating circumstances insofar as the "brutality [was] designed to extract information from people sent there for the specific purpose of interrogation."[109]

For his part, Stephens never denied that abuses and torture had taken place at Bad Nenndorf. Instead, he claimed that he had no knowledge of them.[110] Lord Swinton, who testified in Stephens's defense, calling him the model commandant, conceded not an inch on the endorsement of violence or other cruelties used to break down prisoners during interrogation.[111] Much was at stake, and should Stephens go down, few up the ladder could claim plausible deniability, including Attlee. This Stephens knew and used to his advantage. Before the start of his court-martial, he wrote to the War Office multiple times and threatened to spill the beans on Camp 020 among other operations. Not long thereafter Attorney General Hartley Shawcross wrote to the prime minister, informing him of Stephens's threat and his plan to assert "that if cruelties did occur at Bad Nenndorf they were of the kind systematically adopted as the practice at MI5 Interrogation Centres during the war, and at Camps in Germany subsequently authorized by Ministers through Sir David Petrie." Moreover, Stephens's defense team made clear they planned to roll-call nearly the entire British Security Service—including David Petrie, who oversaw the operation from the top, Dick White, and Lord Swinton, the head of the Security Executive—to confirm that ministers at the highest level of government had authorized MI5 to "systematically" adopt torture and other abuses at Camp 020 and elsewhere.[112] If Petrie, White, Swinton, and others were put on the stand and were uncooperative in Stephens's defense, they could be asked if they knew of, or gave the orders to have, prisoners whipped, beaten, frozen, humiliated, sleep deprived, starved, and sometimes worked to death not only at Bad Nenndorf but also at Camp 020 and in other CSDICs mushrooming in the empire.

In the end, there was no accountability. The British government thought the techniques honed at Camp 020 and Bad Nenndorf were too good to give up and too dangerous politically to reveal. The director of Military Intelligence Major-General Douglas Packard testified privately to the court about the role of CSDICs and their importance to both past and future military practices. "So far as is known," Packard stated, "our results were superior to anything obtained by the interrogation procedures of our enemies," and neither postwar CSDICs nor the existence of Camp 020 could be made public during the court-martial proceedings.[113] In fact, the British government kept all details of wrongdoing from the public for decades. The absence of some of Britain's most notable spies and powerful members of government from the dock suggests that the court decided the case on evidence that was not brought before it, and on that which it heard behind closed doors. Despite medical evidence and testimonies from former guards and inmates to various forms of torture, Stephens exited the courtroom a free man.

He would soon reemerge in the empire as part of MI5's operations clamping down on nationalists who threatened Britain's imperial resurgence efforts. Stripped of its propaganda, Labour's postwar strategy invariably thrust operatives like Stephens, together with expanding security forces, onto the empire's front lines, where legal exceptions became the rule. Indeed, the empire's economic benefits, however real or perceived, were inseparable from the legalized lawlessness and systems of bureaucratized control that were needed to enforce "civilizing" discipline and push British colonial subjects into labor markets to aid domestic recovery. More than ever, the British government needed to resort to violence if it was to render the empire a panacea for the nation's economic troubles and to ensure its place in the new world order. The levers of power embedded in legal exceptionalism, long tested and evolved in the empire and at home, were at Attlee's fingertips. How and where he chose to pull them would shape his Labour government and define its imperial legacy.

PART III

TRYSTS WITH DESTINY

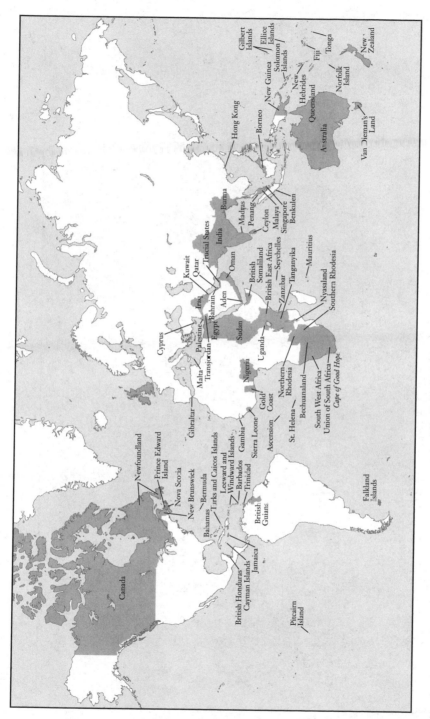

The British Empire in 1945

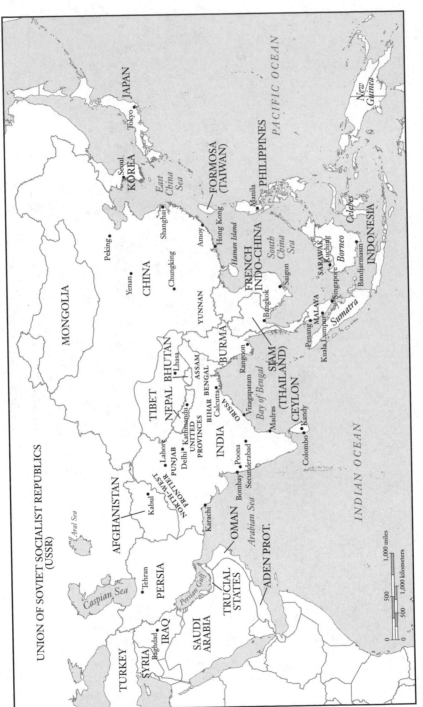

UNION OF SOVIET SOCIALIST REPUBLICS
(USSR)

Aral Sea

TURKEY
SYRIA
IRAQ
Baghdad

SAUDI
ARABIA

PERSIA
Tehran

Caspian Sea

AFGHANISTAN
Kabul

TRUCIAL
STATES

Persian Gulf

OMAN

ADEN PROT.

Arabian Sea

NORTH-WEST FRONTIER
PUNJAB
Lahore
Delhi
Karachi

Kathmandu
UNITED
PROVINCES

NEPAL
TIBET
Lhasa

BHUTAN
ASSAM

MONGOLIA

BIHAR BENGAL
Calcutta

INDIA
Secunderabad
Poona
Bombay

ORISSA
Vizagapatam

Bay of Bengal

Madras

CEYLON
Kandy
Colombo

INDIAN OCEAN

CHINA
Yenan
Peking

Chungking

YUNNAN

BURMA
Rangoon

SIAM
(THAILAND)
Bangkok

Shanghai

Amoy

East China Sea

KOREA
Seoul

Tokyo
JAPAN

FORMOSA
(TAIWAN)

Hong Kong
Hainan Island

FRENCH
INDO-CHINA
Saigon

*South
China
Sea*

Manila
PHILIPPINES

PACIFIC OCEAN

MALAYA
Penang
Kuala Lumpur
Singapore

Sumatra

SARAWAK
Kuching
Borneo
Bandjarmasin

Celebes

INDONESIA

*New
Guinea*

0   500   1,000 miles
0   500   1,000 kilometers

Asia in 1945

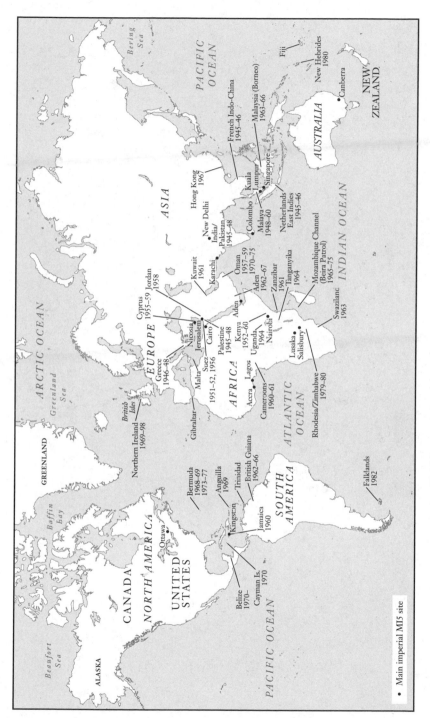

Bering
Sea

PACIFIC
OCEAN

Fiji

New Hebrides
1980

French Indo-China
1945–46

Malaysia (Borneo)
1963–66

Canberra

ASIA

Hong Kong
1967

Kuala
Lumpur

Singapore

AUSTRALIA

NEW
ZEALAND

New Delhi
India/
Pakistan
1945–48

Colombo

Malaya
1948–60

Netherlands
East Indies
1945–46

INDIAN OCEAN

ARCTIC OCEAN

Kuwait
1961

Karachi

Oman
1957–59

Aden
1962–67

Zanzibar
1961

Mozambique Channel
(Beira Patrol)
1965–75

Greenland
Sea

Cyprus
1955–59

Jordan
1958

Tanganyika
1964

EUROPE

Nicosia

Jerusalem

Cairo

Palestine
1945–48

Kenya
1952–60

Uganda
1964

Nairobi

Swaziland
1963

Malta

Suez
1951–52, 1956

AFRICA

Accra

Lagos

Lusaka

Salisbury

GREENLAND

Gibraltar

Cameroons
1960–61

ATLANTIC
OCEAN

Rhodesia/Zimbabwe
1979–80

British
Isles

Northern Ireland
1969–98

Baffin
Bay

Beaufort
Sea

CANADA

NORTH AMERICA

Ottawa

Bermuda
1968–69
1973–77

Anguilla
1969

Trinidad

British Guiana
1962–66

SOUTH
AMERICA

Falklands
1982

ALASKA

UNITED
STATES

Kingston

Jamaica
1960

Belize
1970–

Cayman Is.
1970

PACIFIC OCEAN

• Main imperial MI5 site

British states of emergency and main MI5 posts

On the evening of August 14, 1947, Jawaharlal Nehru mesmerized India's Constituent Assembly with a speech that beckoned a future of hope and opportunity not only for India but for the entire colonized world. With his nation's independence hours away, Nehru appealed to the local and worldly sensibilities of the assembly members and reminded them that their collective dreams for the future transcended both time and place. "Long years ago," he proclaimed, "we made a

Jawaharlal Nehru delivering his "tryst with destiny" speech, August 14, 1947

tryst with destiny, and now the time comes when we shall redeem our pledge, not wholly or in full measure, but very substantially." As the soon-to-be prime minister continued with his historic speech, he exhorted his colleagues that "a moment comes, which comes but rarely in history, when we step out from the old to the new, when an age ends, and when the soul of a nation, long suppressed, finds utterance. It is fitting that at this solemn moment we take the pledge of dedication to the service of India and her people and to the still larger cause of humanity."[1]

India was not the only nation facing a "tryst with destiny" in August 1947. Few were as keenly aware of Britain's imperial legacy, and its priorities, as Prime Minister Attlee and his cabinet. The nation's future economic and political standing in the new world order hinged on a postwar empire that refused to knuckle under to Britain's repressive tactics and its expanding policies of economic exploitation. Fueling the Labour government's discontent was the relentless criticism coming from the nation's wartime leader. Still bruised by his eviction from Downing Street two years earlier, Churchill hammered Attlee on India, calling the Labour Party's colonial policies Operation Scuttle.[2]

For Churchill, India was a deeply personal issue and one that stirred his emotions like no other part of the empire. His sing-along days in the North-West Frontier colored his recent memories of overseeing Cripps's failed mission to secure India's full cooperation and wartime support, endorsing violence to quell the Quit India movement, and refusing to send relief to millions of Bengalis hit by the region's worst famine since the eighteenth century. Thanks to Churchill's policies and practices and those of countless British governments before him, Attlee's government inherited a giant Southeast Asian tinderbox. It had worked desperately with the Indian National Congress and the Muslim League, as thousands of soldiers from both the Indian Army and Bose's renegade Indian National Army (INA) were returning, to broker a deal to keep India within the Commonwealth.

Until the final months and weeks before Indian independence, much was still uncertain, except for Churchill's bombastic behavior. During Commons debates, he liberally berated Foreign Secretary Bevin and gutted the Labour Party for its imperial policies. "It is with deep grief I watch the clattering down of the British Empire, with all its glories and all the services it has rendered to mankind," Churchill bemoaned to his fellow members of Parliament. He issued orders reminiscent of his last-stand commands for the troops defending Singapore:

We must face the evils that are coming upon us, and that we are powerless to avert. We must do our best in all these circumstances, and not exclude any expedient that may help to mitigate the ruin and disaster that will follow the disappearance of Britain from the East. But, at least, let us not add—by shameful flight, by a premature, hurried scuttle—at least, let us not add, to the pangs of sorrow so many of us feel, the taint and smear of shame.[3]

In the pages ahead, we will turn to Churchill's "smear of shame," picking up our story in World War II's immediate aftermath. That was when Viceroy Archibald Wavell, leading a decimated Raj, faced the trials of "traitorous" INA detainees as well as the return of Britain's Indian Army and millions of refugees picking their way through the subcontinent's ruins. Enervating Wavell were the festering Hindu and Muslim divisions that had deepened during the war's chaos. Recall the fate of the Quit India movement: the colonial state had snuffed out the Congress's civil disobedience campaign, locking up Nehru and Gandhi for much of the war. The Muslim League's Muhammad Ali Jinnah, however, did not join the protest and remained a steadfast British ally during wartime, convincing both the Raj and Muslim opinion that Hindu dominance was the real threat. Jinnah, like Nehru, was an Anglicized product of empire, disarming Raj officials with his Saville Row suits and silk ties, barrister credentials, clean-shaven look, and secular practices—he drank whiskey and rarely went to mosque. With the Lucknow Pact in 1916, he had been declared "the Ambassador of Hindu-Muslim Unity," though his relationship with Gandhi, who was committed to a unified India, was a complex one. Gandhi's spiritualism irked him because it fed religious chauvinism, including Jinnah's own. During the Second World War, Jinnah had demanded that Muslims have their own state, even though it was unclear, even to him, what that meant.[4]

In Jinnah's address to the Constituent Assembly of Pakistan, delivered around the same time as Nehru's "tryst with destiny" speech, he likened his new nation's religious tolerance to that of Britain's. "Roman Catholics and Protestants persecuted each other," he noted. But "what exists now is that every man is a citizen, an equal citizen of Great Britain, and they are all members of the Nation." Even as sectarian blood was spilling across newly created Pakistan and India, he continued without pause: "Thank God, we are not starting in those days [of persecutions]. . . . We are starting in the days where there is no discrimination,

Lord Louis Mountbatten handing over power to Muhammed Ali Jinnah, August
1947

no distinction between one community and another, no discrimination
between one caste or creed and another. We are starting with this fundamental principle: that we are all citizens, and equal citizens, of one
State."[5] Gandhi called him "an evil genius."[6]

Britain had its own postwar designs. Despite Churchill's invectives
to the contrary, India's pending freedom did not portend a sweeping
moment of liberation for the rest of the empire, or so the Labour government repeated often and forcefully. On this point, Attlee's cabinet
was unequivocal: "withdrawal from India need not appear to be forced
upon us by our weakness nor to be the first step in the dissolution of
the Empire."[7] Instead, for Bevin and others, imperial priorities were in
the Middle East and other parts of the empire equally coveted for their
commodity production and geopolitical advantages. The foreign secretary and his successors, both Labour and Conservative, often promoted
Churchill's policies of partnering with "suggestible princes and pashas,"
as opposed to the younger nationalist elements that the United States
promoted in the oil-rich countries of the Gulf, Africa, and Southeast
Asia.[8] Such continuities, however, betrayed a tone deafness to the post-

war era and rested on the false assumption that wartime loyalties, as concocted as they were real, would carry on unaffected by the experiences of the war itself.

Just as Labour inherited an imperial ethos and framework from its predecessors, it was also poised to deploy the tools of repression that had evolved for decades across the empire. In some ways, British responses to local demands for freedom and authority scarcely deviated from those unleashed in Palestine's Arab Revolt. The Emergency Powers Order In Council of 1939 enabled colonial officials to deploy a legalized lawlessness similar to the policies and practices that had unfolded in the late 1930s Mandate. "The Emergency Regulations were continually being added to and tightened up," Palestine's postwar chief secretary Henry Gurney wrote, "so that in the end it might almost have been said that the whole book of regulations could have been expressed in a simple provision empowering the High Commissioner to take any action he wished."[9]

Britain also had new arrows in its quiver of imperial repression and destruction. Mass movements of prisoners of war—which included screening, categorizing, and implementing policies of reward and punishment—had evolved during the war and were poised to transform imperial battlefronts. The empire would soon witness the largest mass movement of civilians since the era of the transatlantic trade in enslaved peoples, as Britain introduced draconian methods of population control, surveillance, and interrogation to suppress revolts in such colonies as Malaya and Kenya. Its officials also enacted extraordinary measures to sidestep evolving human rights norms while attempting to reconcile the logics of violence that had animated liberal imperialism since the nineteenth century.

British practices of systematized violence were to be expunged from the imperial record. Plumes of document ashes littered India's independence day ceremonies, but they would recede in future end-of-empire exits. It was not that British agents of empire disengaged from widescale document destruction; rather, like the violence they inflicted on local populations, they became better at covering them up. As their nation faced its own "tryst with destiny" in the postwar years, British officials around the globe embarked on processes of document removal and destruction that reflected an increasingly secret Cold War government and further shaped the myths of British imperial benevolence and triumph.

CHAPTER 10

Glass Houses

To use the past to justify the present is bad enough—but it's just as bad to use the present to justify the past. And you can be sure that there are plenty of people to do that too: it's just that we don't have to put up with them.

Amitav Ghosh, *The Glass Palace*[1]

After enduring days of interrogation in New Delhi's Red Fort, Dharam Chand Bhandari offered little to those who sought answers from him. Interrogators demanded to know why he had defected from His Majesty's troops, and what exactly he had undertaken during his four years as a member of Subhas Bose's renegade army that the British had dubbed the "Jiffs," a term synonymous with "traitors."[2] Tight-lipped on most questions, Bhandari conceded that events he had witnessed in Singapore ignited his commitment to the Indian National Army and the future Azad Hind, the provisional government of Free India that had allied itself with the Axis. When the Malay Peninsula fell, Bhandari had joined the INA and directed propaganda at the Japanese prisoner of war camp, just north of Singapore. His job: to write and stage plays for prisoners that encouraged their "National Spirit." Dramas such as *Ek Hi Rasta* (*The Only Way*), *Milap* (*Unity*), and *Balidan* (*Sacrifice*) were "popular and effective at winning new recruits for the INA," according to Bhandari. Under British interrogation, another INA detainee recalled *Ek Hi Rasta*'s message of "how Indians were treated with torture and brutality under the British yoke through the Indian Police" as particularly compelling.[3]

But it was a tattered copy of Bhandari's most coveted, and confiscated, document—*The Rani of Zanshi: A Play in Three Acts*—that
revealed the depths to which Bose's followers had deployed Britain's past
to recruit soldiers. Set in 1857, the play gave life to the queen (*rani*) of
the princely state of Jhansi, a leading figure in the Mutiny. The rani of
Jhansi also lent her title to an eponymous regiment, an all-female unit
that was "a feat unique and unparalleled in world history," according to
the play. In its opening act, an illiterate weaver defines the Raj's arc of
repression and uses a historical counternarrative that dispelled any ideas
of future partnership:

> You came as petty hawkers and now you pose yourself to be a
> Government? What kind of Government? Which Government?
> An impertinent vagabond called Clive came here a hundred
> years ago to work on a job of two hundred rupees a month, and
> he treacherously ruined Sirajuddaula. Warren Hastings forged a
> document himself and hanged Nandkumar a wealthy citizen of
> Bengal for it. He starved the Begums of Oudh in a locked room
> and extorted all their wealth from them. . . . Is this what you call
> your Government? Speak out . . . speak out![4]

INA propagandists, literary and otherwise, were well aware of their
army's significance. Since the uprising against the Raj in 1857, the INA
spearheaded the only other mass armed rebellion against British imperial rule.

By the time of his interrogation in August 1946, Bhandari was one
of eighteen thousand surrendered or captured INA members whom Raj
officials transported back to India and locked up.[5] For many detainees
like Bhandari, interrogations continued for months after Japan's surrender in August 1945, which coincided with Bose's death in a plane crash
on the Japanese-held island of Formosa (today Taiwan). The plane's
impact had created a firestorm, and Bose stumbled out of the aircraft
in a ball of flames. With third-degree burns covering much of his body,
the forty-eight-year-old "Revered Leader" reportedly spoke of India's
independence until he succumbed to his injuries several hours later. The
Japanese soon cremated his charred remains, which they sent back to
Tokyo for interment.[6]

When news of Bose's death spread, shock and sorrow overcame his
war-weary and traumatized supporters. The "Nightingale of India,"
Sarojini Naidu—who had been imprisoned with thousands of other Quit
India protesters—wrote movingly of Bose's contributions to India. An

esteemed Congress leader and poet, Naidu had opposed Bose's chosen path to freedom. Nevertheless, she emoted a "deep personal bereavement" that she shared with "myriads of men and women." "His proud, importunate and violent spirit was a flaming sword forever unsheathed in defense of the land he worshiped with such surpassing devotion," she wrote in a form of public eulogy. "A greater love hath not man than this, that he lay down his life for his country and his people."[7] Naidu's stirring words for the "Revered Leader" transcended wartime loyalties for countless Raj subjects. Bose was now a martyr.

That some within Britain's military establishment were disconnected from their Indian troops and the toll that the war had taken on them was thrown into relief as INA detainees awaited prosecution. Military brass seemed impervious to the Indian Army's hardships and the war's impact on their nationalist sentiments. The troops had endured the conflict's strain and deprivations without respite. Most of the Indian Army's 2.5 million men were deployed for over three years, and few had had any leave for two. An estimated ninety thousand were killed or wounded. At fifty psychiatric centers in India, Burma, and Ceylon, mental health professionals chronicled "massive psychological dysfunction."[8] For Britain's loyal Indian soldiers, the war did not end with Japan's surrender. Some were deployed to Indonesia and Indochina to help Britain's Dutch and French allies restore order. In November 1945 Britain deployed the Indian Army for the last time in combat: it launched twenty-four thousand troops and two dozen tanks and aircrafts to carry out a massive assault on the Indonesian city of Surabaya. Yet rapid demobilization did not follow. As of the spring of 1946, the army still had two brigades in the Middle East and Japan, and one brigade in Hong Kong, as well as four divisions in Burma and Indonesia, three divisions in Malaya, and one division in Borneo and Siam. Only 20 percent of its forces were demobilized, and it would take until April 1947 to run its numbers down to half a million.[9]

Wartime had taken an incalculable toll. Across the "Great Crescent" of Southeast Asia that stretched from Calcutta in the north to Singapore in the south, soldiers had borne witness to liberal imperialism's weaknesses and been subsumed in its physical and mental destructions.[10] In Burma and Malaya, hundreds of thousands of refugees staggered home to a postwar landscape riddled with hunger, cholera, and tuberculosis. Sardar Vallabhbhai Patel, the Congress's general secretary, observed that "entire cities, children, the old, animals and all have been wiped out. What a demonstration of the limitless cruelty of Western civilization."[11] The Indian Army experienced such cruelties firsthand, and they did not abate in the postwar years. In Malaya, a rapacious British Military Administration impressed local laborers to rebuild infrastructure and what was left of "Fortress Singapore." British officials threatened half-starved workers with force and enticed them with illegally trafficked opium. Widespread addiction resulted. Every six months, the British government went through 50 million opium grains, which were recognizable because of their uniquely colored hue. Inflation on a scale rivaling that of Weimar Germany crushed already decimated local economies, and basic staples like rice sold for thirty to forty times their prewar prices. British and Commonwealth troops controlled local black markets and openly flaunted their profits and corrupt practices. Local populations that had been left behind during Britain's 1942 evacuation were again treated as the empire's castaways. "The army," in the words of one European observer, "behaved as if they were in conquered territory," and any British moral authority that remained in the region evaporated.[12] Britain's empire in Southeast Asia, the one that was to serve as a springboard for the nation's domestic economic recovery, not to mention the maintenance of its Big Three status alongside the United States and Soviet Union, looked nothing like the empire of British nationalist imaginations.

When demobilized soldiers finally reached India, their pay was a pittance, in the face of skyrocketing prices. The Raj instituted rationing, and black marketers peddled basic necessities. Starvation conditions continued to haunt populations, particularly in Bengal, where survivors of the famine still littered the streets and scavenged for food, wearing nothing but rags. Memories of bloated and rotten corpses scarred cities and villages. While many in the army were Punjabi, Britain's callousness had grossly contributed to the deaths of 3 million Bengalis in 1943–44, as was widely known, as were the Raj's racialized views of India's population. At the time, Secretary for India Amery accused Churchill of having a "Hitler-like attitude" toward the entire lot, though he himself insisted that the famine was the result of some kind of Malthusian dilemma and refused to send relief.[13] Nehru's sister, Vijayalakshmi Pandit, toured the famine-stricken region and observed "rickety babies with arms and legs like sticks; nursing mothers with wrinkled faces; children with swollen faces and hollow-eyes through lack of food and sleep; [and the] men exhausted and weary, walking skeletons."[14] Much of the Indian Army refused to kowtow to British officers, who continued their paternalistic ways and whose sacrifices were scarcely on par with their own. That the war's damage transformed hundreds of millions of lives, and with them nationalist sentiments, should have come as no surprise, and yet for many Britons, it did.

In this postwar context, the question of what to do with the INA detainees was a loaded one. Some Indians denounced Bose as "selfish, vain, [and] ruthless" and thought his followers should be sent to the gallows. Commander in Chief in India Claude Auchinleck thought the INA's alleged use of torture, and the brutal treatment it reportedly meted out to those who refused to join its ranks, were bridges too far. They were, but such allegations were mired in Britain's version of events: only harsh measures could have compelled Indian Army members to redirect their loyalties away from the empire toward Bose's traitorous regime. Indian grassroots support and that of the demobilized Indian Army, which was 2 million strong, were undeniable, however, and transcended sectarian divisions. Ultimately, the Raj asserted itself as the arbiter of what constituted legitimate violence. The irony of Britain claiming legal authority to parse differences between legitimate and illegitimate violence was not lost on its colonial subjects.[15]

In November 1945 Raj officials decided, after much deliberation, to release INA detainees who had only violated their oath and rebelled against His Majesty's government. They focused, instead, on prosecuting the seven thousand "black" detainees who had allegedly committed illegal acts of violence, which included flogging, torture, and murder. INA officers were the first in the dock. Recently released Congress leaders denounced Britain for contemplating such a move, though not necessarily because of their full-throttled support for Bose's officers. Nehru thought they were "misguided," though "patriots" nonetheless. His bigger concern, and one that other Congress leaders shared, was losing control of a population that had ignited "mass glorification" campaigns of INA support across the Raj, particularly in Bengal. To maintain authority and capitalize on the moment, Congress leaders rode the detainees' popular support wave, turning unified anticolonial outrage into an electoral advantage.[16]

It was in Bengal, the site of quotidian violence for decades, that postwar tensions manifested in anti-British protests. "Long live the revolution!" could be heard as locals sought to avenge over two centuries of rapes, village burnings, crowd shootings, and widespread famine, for which the British were responsible. Hadn't the British in Bengal been as bad as the Nazis? locals queried. The press demanded to know: "Will the UN have the courage and the fairness to hold trials in India?" When INA detainees were released, crowds across India exuberantly welcomed them as heroes. These moments of celebration often gave way to more anti-British protests and more violence and deaths at the hands of local police, who desperately tried to maintain some sense of order.[17]

During the war, Bose had cultivated broad-based religious support in his ranks, bringing together Hindus, Muslims, and Sikhs in opposition to British rule. The Raj's INA show trials were poised to ignite such unity, albeit temporarily, across India's postwar masses. As Japanese war criminals awaited their fates and Nazi officials were set for trial in Nuremberg, the Raj planned to make an example of Captain Shahnawaz Khan, Captain Prem Kumar Sehgal, and Lieutenant Gurbaksh Dhillon, putting them on trial for treason and for the execution and torture of INA soldiers trying to defect. The selection of these defendants— a Muslim, a Hindu, and a Sikh, respectively—was a British judgment error, feeding grassroots support that transcended religious differences. On November 5, 1945, the Raj prosecution opened its case against the accused INA officers at Red Fort in Delhi. The site of the trial, where the British had tried the last Mughal emperor after the 1857 Mutiny, was another miscalculation, sending the country into a memory-induced frenzy.[18] The officers soon amassed a sizable defense fund thanks to the Congress's organizing efforts. The fund only grew when Indians in Delhi and across the Raj—and indeed throughout Southeast Asia—celebrated INA Week, honoring Bose and his followers for their defiance of British imperialism, which coincided with the start of the trial. The week culminated with INA Day, when locals closed shops and protests again turned violent. Nearly three days of protests left thirty people dead in Calcutta, and widespread disorder also erupted elsewhere across India.[19]

The Red Fort trial became a referendum on British rule and the international order enabling and legitimating it. Congress vigorously defended the accused, while its leadership, including Nehru, sat at the defense table. Indians outside the courtroom and across the subcontinent were mesmerized. Newspapers published the daily court transcripts, and the Raj's intelligence services reported widespread sympathy for the defendants, which seemed to grow by the day if the protests and violence were any measure of support. Defense tactics inside the courtroom zeroed in on liberal imperialism's moral and legal deficiencies and exposed further the folly of the prosecutions.

The defendants' lead counsel, Bhulabhai Desai, crafted a masterful argument, turning international law on its head by insisting it was not the preserve of European states. European empires were running roughshod over hundreds of millions of subjects, he said in his opening statement, while hiding behind their self-proclaimed role as the arbiter of civilization and, with it, sovereignty. Why were "just wars" only those waged between sovereign European states? he asked. While the prosecution claimed that the British king-emporer's sovereign rule over India was unconditional, Desai demanded a full accounting of Western claims that denied subjugated populations the right to wage war. "International law in the question of war is not static," he insisted, and Europe's gatekeeping membership to the "law of nations" had "created a vicious circle, that [ensured] a subject race will remain in perpetuity a subject race. It can never make a legitimate war for the purpose of liberating itself."[20]

Britain's moral failures and criminal deeds should be subject to legal scrutiny, Desai insisted. Shouldn't Lord Linlithgow also stand trial for the empire's famine-induced deaths of some 3 million Bengalis in 1943? Hadn't Percival handed over the Indians, and all His Majesty's subjects, to Yamashita when Singapore fell, and commanded them to "obey the orders of the Japanese in the way that you obeyed the British government. Otherwise you will be punished"? Hadn't foreign powers recognized the Azad Hind, much as some had recognized the United States of America in its infancy? Therefore, based upon Western precedent, the Azad Hind was an independent government with "recognition a proof . . . of statehood," and the INA was an independent army with the right to make war "for the liberation of its own countrymen."[21] The British court ultimately rejected Desai's revisionist reading of international law and his challenge to Britain's unfettered sovereignty claims. It convicted the accused of rebellion against the king-emperor, though British officials never imposed the sentences of transportation for life, instead dishonorably discharging the officers from the Indian Army.[22] "Any attempt to enforce the sentence," Auchinleck later confided, "would have led to chaos in the country at large and probably to mutiny and dissension in the Army, culminating in its dissolution."[23]

Such dissension, however, was well under way. For all to see, the Red Fort trial exposed the Raj's inability to define what was and was not legitimate violence in the aftermath of the war, and its ripple effects betrayed Britain's inability to maintain repressive control. Quotidian civilian unrest was bad enough, but the military's breakdown of command revealed Britain's irreparable weakness. During the INA trials, members of the Royal Indian Air Force and Indian Army openly donated to the officers' defense fund and attended support rallies in full uniform. In early 1946 such support gave way to protests, if not outright mutinies, in the Royal Indian Air Force and the Royal Indian Navy. In January, an estimated fifty thousand men at fourteen air force stations across Southeast Asia protested their pitiable conditions and continued deployment in Indonesia and throughout India; their call to arms soon spread across the empire, fueled in no small way by local presses, and strikes hit Royal Air Force bases as far afield as Gibraltar, Cairo, and Singapore.[24]

Inspired by their air force counterparts, the Royal Indian Navy sailors on HMIS *Talwar* in Bombay launched their own massive protest against poor rations and continued racial discrimination. They marched through Bombay's streets holding aloft posters of Bose, demanding the release of the remaining INA detainees. Their ships flew Congress flags, as well as those of the Muslim League and the Communist Party. Demonstrations quickly spread across other vessels in Bombay's harbor and eventually to four hundred others in the subcontinent's seas. In total, thirty thousand men issued demands for demobilization, increases in pay, and the release of INA detainees. The massive outpouring of public support for the cause—which sparked further unrest—arguably had more to do with individual and communal anger over postwar conditions than with solidarity for the sailors' complaints. Protesters in Bombay and Karachi halted all commerce, burned trains and automobiles, and blocked streets. Were it not for the intervention of the Congress and the Muslim League, both of which feared a full-blown uprising that lacked direction and control, Raj officials would have needed to make good on their threats of force to quash the demonstrations, though whether they could have successfully snuffed them out was anyone's guess.[25]

With some of its armed forces openly rebelling and protesting, and deeply unsure of the Indian Army's loyalty if it were asked to suppress the incipient mutinies, the Raj was done. Even if Attlee's government hadn't yet come to terms with this fact, local British officials saw the writing on the wall. Corresponding with his sister back home, one British observer remarked that he felt, while navigating through the streets of Calcutta, "rather like a Nazi officer must have felt walking along a Paris boulevard."[26] Ongoing British policies only exacerbated local anger and the communal tensions that were erupting alongside shows of INA solidarity. Lacking recourse to what sociologist Max Weber called a "monopoly of the legitimate use of physical force," however legitimized through legalized lawlessness, the Raj could not carry on.[27]

In the spring of 1945, Viceroy Archibald Wavell held a political conference in Simla to reconstitute his executive council; it collapsed when Jinnah insisted on having the Muslim League appoint Muslim representatives. The viceroy called for elections to form provincial governments and a central legislature that would restructure the constitution. The results, announced in 1946, reflected a divided India where, for decades, political categories, a function of both British social engineering and indigenous responses to colonial rule, had arisen out of local religious affiliations and fed into the particularities of Indian society and politics. Congress won most of the non-Muslim seats, and the Muslim League took Punjab and Bengal and performed well with the Muslim populations in Bombay and Madras. Jinnah sold the election as a referendum on Pakistan, even if few had any idea of what that exactly meant territorially. The clear religious divisions between the parties brought a British delegation to India, hoping to negotiate a workable constitution and ultimately a transfer of power.[28]

Again, Stafford Cripps arrived on the scene, recycling the distrust between British officials, the Congress, and the Muslim League. Nehru had not forgotten Cripps's failed wartime mission, or the years he and his fellow congressmen had spent locked up. Neither Congress nor the League could agree on major points of power sharing. Jinnah was "an obvious example of the utter lack of the civilised mind," Nehru thought. "What I am afraid of is . . . Gandhi," Jinnah confided to a friend. "He has brains and always [tries] to put me in the wrong. I have to be on guard and alert all the time."[29] Once more Cripps's mission was a failure.

No sooner had Britain's delegation exited than Jinnah called a Direct Action Day for August 16, demanding an "end [of] British slavery" and committing to "fight the contemplated caste-Hindu domination."[30] What began as a mass Muslim protest against the British in Calcutta quickly morphed into one of India's worst rounds of sectarian violence. Known as the "Great Calcutta Killings," the massacres left at least six thousand Hindus and Muslims dead and another twelve thousand wounded. It took the government nearly three days to suppress the disorder, which never fully abated. Corpses littered the streets, and cholera soon claimed as many lives as the fratricidal violence. Beyond Bengal, over sixteen hundred industrial actions brought commerce in the Raj to a virtual standstill. In the countryside, peasants were armed and mobilized against the landowners and usurers who demanded forced labor in return for rents and loans. Protests over the 5,500 remaining INA detainees continued into early 1947. In the end, Viceroy Wavell and Commander in Chief Auchinleck had no choice but to concede. All but twenty INA detainees were released; only twelve were convicted.[31]

The viceroy knew the imperial project in India was over, imagining a rapid "breakdown plan" in the hope of getting British residents and the army out alive. That clear concession of British powerlessness got the "martial paternalist" recalled, though it was the pace of power's devolution, not the transition itself, that was at issue. Bevin wrote to the prime minister that the Raj government was "trying nothing except to scuttle out of it, without dignity or plan," and he was opposed to setting a fixed date for Britain's departure. "A scuttle it will be if things are allowed to drift," Attlee replied, chastening his foreign secretary for having no alternative plan. If the prime minister was going to salvage something of Britain's "good governance" record, then an orderly political handover had to be fashioned. On February 20, 1947, Attlee announced to Parliament a timetable for retreat, scheduling Britain's exit from India for June 1948. "It is quite clear we can't go on holding people down against their will, however incompetent they are to govern themselves," Chancellor of the Exchequer Hugh Dalton confided in his diary a few days after the announcement. "For the whole pace, as determined in the East, has quickened over the war years, and it would be a waste of both British men and money to try to hold down any of this crowd against their will. They must be allowed to find their own way, even blood and corruption and incompetence of all kinds, to what they regard as 'freedom.'"[32]

As the Raj's last viceroy, Attlee appointed George VI's cousin, Admiral Lord Louis "Dickie" Mountbatten, who demanded "plenipotentiary powers," which he got. Mountbatten was a statesman, administrator, and military commander whose "irresistible charm" and dashing good looks gave physical expression to the Raj's idealized images back home. The high aristocrat was as comfortable with celebrities as he was with nationalists, and Attlee gave him until June 1948 to do what others couldn't: bring Gandhi, Nehru, and Jinnah to the bargaining table and maintain Britain's legacy with "some form of central Government for British India."[33] Mountbatten was known for his military style and swift judgments, attributes that some saw as both a strength and a weakness. "No man could get us out of a mess more quickly, or into one, than Mountbatten," one of his men recalled.[34]

Mountbatten was no less impulsive as India's viceroy, quickly sizing Jinnah up as "a psychopathic case" and declaring there was no reconciling the Congress and the Muslim League. Shocking everyone, he announced August 15, 1947, as the date for the power transfer—a full ten months earlier than Attlee's deadline. Debate remains over why Mountbatten moved with unrepentant haste, but the author of *Midnight's Furies* Nisid Hajari's explanation is convincing: "Most raj officials were burned-out and cynical, and they had no interest in refereeing a civil war."[35] Partition had to happen, and happen quickly, before India's sectarian violence brought Britain down with it. Years later Attlee would offer his own views on Britain's accelerated departure, principal among them, according to one interviewer, "the erosion of loyalty to the British crown among the Indian army and Navy personnel as a result of the military activities of Netaji [Bose]."[36]

Lacking coercive means to maintain power, Britain stumbled forward with its partition plan to create two new independent dominions within the Commonwealth. While British officials in London quibbled over George VI's future signature—would he sign as king-emperor, "George Rex Imperator," or merely as "George Rex"—Attlee pushed through legislation in Parliament that outlined provisional boundaries separating Pakistan from India until a boundary commission could determine which "Muslim majority . . . and non-Muslim majority districts" in the territory's northwestern Punjab and southeastern Bengal would be permanently part of the two new nations.[37]

Mountbatten drafted Sir Cyril Radcliffe, who had never before set foot in India, as the commission's chair. Radcliffe's commission set to work, first carving up the Punjab and then twisting its bureaucratic knife through Bengal. Sequestered in Calcutta's Belvedere House, the draftsmen, beads of sweat dripping down their brows, endured the swelter of India's summer moisture that wept from Belvedere's impossibly tall ceilings, chandeliers, oil paintings, and gargantuan arched-window panes.

Belvedere House, Alipur, Calcutta (Kolkata), painting by William Prinsep, c. 1838

Everything about their work was imposing and historic. Even Belvedere, a whitewashed eighteenth-century palace built in Italian Renaissance style and set on thirty acres of tropical gardens, had reputedly been gifted by Mir Jafar, *nawab* of Bengal, to Warren Hastings, the mythologized consolidator of the British Empire, who had lived there until he was recalled to London in 1785 for his misconduct and eventual impeachment trial.

Sitting in Belvedere's Metcalfe Hall amid its massive Corinthian pillars supporting the room's wraparound interior balcony, the commission pored over maps and documents and heard testimonies from local political parties desperately trying to influence Radcliffe's decision making. His commission remarkably wrapped up its work ahead of schedule, and Radcliffe quickly slipped out of India while Mountbatten waited to release Pakistan and India's official boundaries until two days after independence, thinking it would slow down the massive population movements that were gaining chaotic momentum in anticipation of partition's official borders, which created, in Jinnah's words, "a mutilated and moth-eaten" nation-state pastiche.[38]

Mountbatten's hubris and cold efficiency were staggering. In late July, Punjab's governor had reported to him that "feeling in Lahore is perhaps worse than it has ever been . . . daily fires, stabbings and bomb explosions." However, he insisted that "I think it will be wise to avoid postponing the relief of British troops for too long. It would be awkward if trouble on a large scale started while the relief was in progress." Mountbatten visited Lahore, where he would not permit British troops to help protect local populations, instead expediting the army's "relief."[39] By August, with sectarian violence poised to reach epic proportions, His Majesty's army in full retreat, and civilians evacuated, Britain prepared for its ceremonial transfer of power. On August 14 thousands flooded into New Delhi, where their new nation's tricolor flag would soon rise. There, too, were Mountbatten and his staff of colonial-clad officers. Having carefully choreographed their departure ceremony, Mountbatten and his men were a study in contrast with the exuberance that surrounded them. In physical comportment, they projected what their government at home sought to convey: that Britain was managing events not only in India but in the remaining empire as well.

Across radio waves in August 1947, Mountbatten could be heard reading George VI's message to India, Pakistan, his nation, and its vast, remaining empire: "Freedom loving people everywhere will wish to share in your celebrations, for with this transfer of power by consent comes the fulfillment of a great democratic ideal to which the British and Indian peoples alike are firmly dedicated. It is inspiring to think that all this has been achieved by means of a peaceful change."[40] Britons also heard Jinnah's assurances of religious tolerance as well as the Cambridge-educated Nehru's eloquently clipped Edwardian words and were reassured that their nation's civilizing mission had been a resounding success.

After two hundred years of British rule, an orderly transfer of power was the coda to what Britain saw as the carefully tended record of civilizing triumph. Clearly colonial officials went to great lengths to shore up their nation's legacy, presenting evidence for it in the words of lofty speeches, in the reflection of Mountbatten's gilded epaulets, and in the jubilance of the independence day crowd in New Delhi, the force of

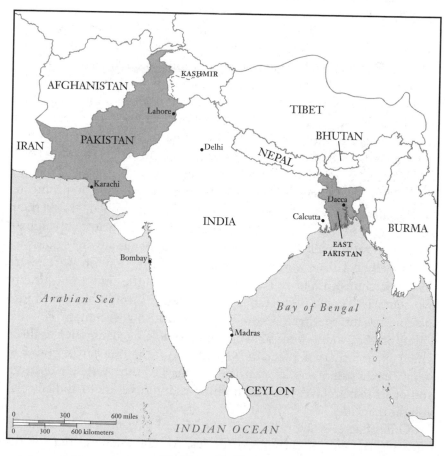

Partition of India, 1947

which broke through the specially cordoned area for colonial officials and subverted for one last time the pomp and circumstance of the British Raj.[41] But in reality, one must imagine the lingering smell of char that infused the Indian summer air in 1947, the ash scattered along New Delhi's distant footpaths, and the weight of the smoke-filled sky that hung over India's independence day drama.

In the final days of the Raj, document pyres were the repositories of the British Empire's smoldering remains in India. In the infamous Red Fort's main courtyard, British agents dumped wheelbarrows full of files into bonfires that lit up New Delhi's skies for weeks. They culled, purged, and reduced to ash documents that, if they fell into the wrong hands, would embarrass His Majesty's government and undermine Britain's past, present, and future claims as the purveyor of moral authority throughout the world.[42] Among these documents were untold numbers of intelligence files chronicling British interrogation systems and methods as well as surveillance operations across India.

The interrogator Hugh Toye, who had once been charged with prying intelligence from "black" detainees, sorted and destroyed documents as one of the Raj's final archivists. Toye would go on to memorialize his heroics of chasing down Bose and his supporters when he published *The Springing Tiger* in 1959. His book, however, makes no mention of his arsonist activities in New Delhi's Red Fort.[43] Twenty-five years later, Toye privately recollected the document destruction process. Wavell had directed some of it prior to his unceremonious departure. According to the viceroy's diary, he had an exchange with Nehru about the files. "They [Intelligence Bureau] have destroyed all the compromising papers," Nehru reportedly observed. "Yes," Wavell replied, "I told them to make sure of that."[44] According to the viceroy, Nehru then laughed, but whether it was a knowing one or a nervous one is anyone's guess.

Wavell and Toye were not alone. Officials in London were aware that their clumsy, rapid retreat from India left little time to dispose of two centuries' worth of documents. Such lessons would be carried into the empire's future where, according to the British government, colonial agents on the ground were to avoid "undesirable incidents such as those which apparently took place in New Delhi on the transfer of power in 1947 when a pall of smoke over the city marked the wholesale destruction of British archives and did nothing to improve Anglo-Indian relations at that time."[45]

Other flames rose on the eve of India and Pakistan's independence. After his last day of ceremonial duties, Mountbatten retired for the evening with his wife, turning on Bob Hope's new romantic comedy,

My Favorite Brunette, to pass the time. As the final hours of British rule ticked away, terrifying scenes unfolded outside their well-guarded comfort at Viceroy House. In the months leading up to Partition, sectarian violence had spread, particularly in Punjab and Bengal, the two provinces vivisected by Britain's mapmaking. While Mountbatten settled into watching his televised comedy, he whispered to himself "for still a few minutes I am the most powerful man on earth."[46] Meanwhile, his remaining officials in Lahore—Punjab's capital, situated just over the new Pakastani border with northern India—scurried to catch the Bombay Express, navigating around dead bodies littering the streets before reaching the train station and its blood-soaked platform. They watched as their southbound train, an enduring symbol of British technological progress, carried them past village after village, ablaze.[47]

The sectarian violence that had been building for years engulfed the Raj's last days, shattering the king's message of "peaceful change." A refugee wave of historic proportions swept across the subcontinent as Hindus and Sikhs desperately fled the newly created Pakistan for India, while panic-stricken Muslims left generations-old homes in India for safety across the Pakistani border.[48] En route, refugees were slaughtered, as were those who risked staying put. "Gangs of killers set whole

A refugee special train at Ambala Station, 1947

villages aflame, hacking to death men and children and the aged while carrying off young women to be raped," Nisid Hajari recounts in *Midnight's Furies*.

> British soldiers and journalists who had witnessed the Nazi death camps claimed Partition's brutalities were worse: pregnant women had their breasts cut off and babies hacked out of their bellies; infants were found literally roasted on spits. Foot caravans of destitute refugees fleeing the violence stretched for 50 miles and more. As the peasants trudged along wearily, mounted guerrillas charged out of the tall crops that lined the road and culled them like sheep. Special refugee trains, filled to bursting when they set out, suffered repeated ambushes along the way. All too often they crossed the border in funereal silence, blood seeping from under their carriage doors.[49]

While the communal cleansing was most pronounced in Punjab, much of India was subsumed in it. In 1948 the great migration ended after displacing more than 15 million people. In her magisterial book *The Great Partition*, Yasmin Khan offers a sobering conclusion:

> The Partition of 1947 is also a loud reminder, should we care to listen, of the dangers of colonial interventions and the profound difficulties that dog regime change. It stands testament to the follies of empire, which ruptures community evolution, distorts historical trajectories and forces violent state formation from societies that would otherwise have taken different—and unknowable—paths. Partition is a lasting lesson of both the dangers of imperial hubris and the reactions of extreme nationalism. For better or worse, two nations continue to live alongside each other in South Asia and continue to live with these legacies.[50]

For nearly a thousand years, communities on the Indian subcontinent had coexisted in a cultural melting where religious identity was less salient than ethnic or linguistic identity. "A hybrid Indo-Islamic civilization emerged," according to the historian of India William Dalrymple. "In the nineteenth century, India was still a place where traditions, languages, and cultures cut across religious groupings, and where people did not define themselves primarily through their religious faith."[51] Much as communities had negotiated means of coexistence in pre-Mandate Palestine only to see them unravel during British rule, the

Refugee camp in Delhi during Partition, 1947

subcontinent's communal arrangements corroded when the full weight of Britain's colonial state bore down on them. The Raj's divide and rule policies produced a chemical-like reaction, shattering long-standing traditions of coexistence and interacting with local personalities who had their own ambitions, passions, and allegiances. It was another liberal experiment in empire gone horribly wrong, and on a scale so epic that once history's chain of contingent events combusted, no one could contain it.

Estimates place Partition's death toll at 1 million to 2 million people. Those who survived faced cholera and typhoid epidemics in refugee centers that were "human dumps," in the words of one doctor. Gandhi predicted that "the peace of the grave" would come with Mountbatten's Partition deal, while Nehru responded in horror as post-Partition events unfolded. He confided to a fellow congressman that "I could not conceive of the gross brutality and sadistic cruelty that people have indulged in. . . . Little children are butchered in the streets. The houses in many parts of Delhi are still full of corpses. . . . I am fairly thick-skinned but I find this kind of thing more than I can bear." Mountbatten seemed rather nonplussed by the mounting deaths. When he paid a visit to Nehru, he invited him to London to attend Princess Elizabeth's wedding to his beloved nephew, Philip Mountbatten.[52]

A few months later, with war-fueled tensions over Kashmir mounting and India refusing to pay Pakistan 550 million rupees, Pakistan's share of Britain's outstanding war debt, Gandhi began to fast. "This time my fast is not only against Hindus and Muslims," the Mahatma said, "but also against the Judases who put on false appearances and betray themselves, myself and society."[53] The elderly and frail man who was India's symbolic political and spiritual leader went three days without food before India's cabinet agreed to pay Pakistan, something Nehru had long promised Jinnah he would do. The move was a Pyrrhic victory for Gandhi. Radical Hindu organizations had already labeled him "Jinnah's stooge" and "Mohammad Gandhi."[54] They saw Gandhi's calls for peace as acts of disloyalty, and his fasting over payments to Pakistan offered further grist for their mill.

On January 30, 1948, two weeks after his fast, the Mahatma was still recovering in New Delhi. At Birla House he made his way through the gardens to lead the evening's prayer meetings, his grandniece Manuben and adopted daughter Abha steadying him on either side. As they made their way past the gathered crowd, a radical Hindu nationalist, Nathuram Godse, stepped forward and at close range fired three shots into Gandhi. The Mahatma collapsed into his daughter's lap as the sun was beginning to set. Amid a din of cries, his robes soaked with blood, Gandhi reportedly uttered the words, "*Hé Ra . . . ma! Hé Ra . . . !* [Oh . . . God! Oh . . . !]"[55] A few hours later Nehru addressed the new nation, first in Hindi and then in English: "The light has gone out of our lives and there is darkness everywhere. I do not know what to tell you or how to say it. Our beloved leader, Bapu as we called him, the Father of our Nation, is no more."[56]

Gandhi was another casualty of empire's aftermath. So was his assassin, who, along with one of his accomplices, was sentenced to death. "In every one of his speeches is a drop of poison," Jinnah had said a few weeks before Gandhi's assassination. He was notably partisan in his eulogizing of Mahatma. "Whatever our political differences, he was one of the greatest men produced by the Hindu community, and a leader who commanded their universal confidence and respect. I wish to express my deep sorrow, and sincerely sympathise with the great Hindu community and his family in their bereavement at this momentous, historical and critical juncture so soon after the birth of freedom and freedom for Hindustan and Pakistan."[57] Around the world, however, an outpouring of grief and eulogies followed, universalizing Gandhi's character. In

Britain, left and right came together. Attlee spoke to Britons of his "profound horror" when he learned the news of the murder of "one of the outstanding figures in the world today [who] strove for peace and condemned the resort to violence."[58] Jan Smuts exclaimed, "A prince among men has passed away and we grieve with India in her irreparable loss."[59] Leo Amery, the arch-imperialist and secretary for India in Churchill's cabinet, revealed a deeper bitterness:

> His part in the history of India and Anglo-Indian relations in the last generation can only be assessed by history. At any rate, it can be said that no one contributed more to the particular way in which the charter of British rule in India has ended than Mahatma Gandhi himself. His death comes at the close of a great chapter in world history. In the mind of India, at least, he will always be identified with the opening of the new chapter which, however troubled at the outset, we should all hope, will develop in peace, concord and prosperity for India.[60]

As liberal imperialism's partnership motif was unraveling in postwar India, thousands of miles away in Jerusalem, on July 22, 1946, Richard Catling picked his way through roadblocked and barbed-wired streets en route to the King David Hotel. Over a decade earlier, the Suffolk-born Catling had had a chance encounter on the Ipswich train platform with a schoolboy friend who told him he had just signed up for the Palestine Police Force. Looking to leave behind the Depression-era hopelessness of his farming family, seek his fortune, and "see some other life and lives," an inspired Catling hurried to the Crown Agents office, empire's centralized finance and recruitment unit, at Millbank in central London. After a brief interview, he got a job in the Palestine Police Force. He saw considerable action in the Arab Revolt, which he recalled as "all good clean fun," and thereafter the wiry and often pursed-lipped Catling quickly rose through the ranks. By the time he strode up the front steps of the King David Hotel to see Roderick Musgrave, his old pal from the police special branch, he had reason to be proud. He was now assistant inspector general of the criminal investigation department and in charge of its Jewish affairs section.[61]

The circumstances in Palestine would have taxed any colonial police officer. Since Labour's election victory, Palestine was reminiscent of 1920s Ireland with its reprisals and counterreprisals. In July 1945 much of the Zionist community celebrated Attlee's rise to power. A Labour resolution had called for an abrogation of the despised 1939 White Paper and, with it, allowance for unlimited Jewish immigration to the Mandate. Britain's move toward imperial resurgence rested squarely on the Middle East. Ernest Bevin was convinced that the oil-rich region was vital to Britain's economic recovery and crucial to the maintenance of Britain's Great Power status.[62] But Anglo-Arab relations would have to be strengthened, a goal that ran counter to Labour's pre-election position on Palestine. Bevin, with the support of a pro-Arab Foreign Office and cabinet, nonetheless accomplished it.

Anglo-American cooperation over Palestine, however, proved to be one of the most contentious and frustrating issues in the Labour government's broader imperial agenda. It was arguably at the heart of Bevin's dogged determination to get out from under Washington's thumb. Truman, an unelected and relatively unpopular American leader, relied heavily on the advice of his pro-Zionist White House advisers, who urged him not to antagonize the American Jewish vote. "I have to answer to hundreds of thousands who are anxious for the success of Zionism; I do not have hundreds of thousands of Arabs in my constituents," Truman said.[63] It wasn't all about politics, however: the images of post-Holocaust Europe were unshakable for the president. "In my own mind," he later wrote, "the aims and goals of the Zionists at this stage to set up a Jewish state were secondary to the more immediate problem of finding means to relieve the human misery of the displaced persons."[64] This was no fine point of distinction. Immigration was the most salient issue in the Anglo-American dispute over Palestine, as it would be in much of the controversy between Britain and the Yishuv. Even before Labour took office, Truman had asked Churchill at Potsdam to lift the restrictions on immigration.[65] Soon thereafter the president received U.S. representative of the Intergovernmental Commission Earl G. Harrison's report on displaced persons in Europe, which detailed the horrific conditions of the refugee camps. "We appear to be treating the Jews as the Nazis treated them," the report stated, "except that we do not exterminate them. They are in concentration camps in large numbers under our military guard instead of S.S. troops."[66] Harrison recommended the British grant an additional one hundred thousand immigration certificates for displaced Jews to enter Palestine. Truman fixated on that number and refused to budge in any future negotiations.

Whitehall took a different view. It could not risk alienating Arab support in the region or, worse, inciting Arab anger over the specter of large-scale Jewish immigration to Palestine. Instead, the Jews had to be reintegrated back into Europe. Bevin's callousness regarding the plight of Holocaust survivors hardly endeared him either to Truman or to the Zionist movement. Moreover, the foreign secretary's odd humor and general insensitivity regarding wartime Jewish suffering led to a series of missteps that opened him to repeated charges of anti-Semitism. At the very least, Bevin harbored stereotypical views of "international Jewry" and believed a Zionist-Soviet conspiracy was brewing. "I am sure," the foreign secretary later wrote, that the Russians "are convinced that by immigration they can pour in sufficient indoctrinated Jews to turn it into a Communist state in a very short time. The New York Jews have been doing their work for them."[67]

The challenges Bevin faced were daunting by any standard. They included Britain's fiscal insolvency; its strategic overextension and perceived dependence on the Middle East; and rising Zionist violence and accompanying Arab intransigence. American involvement and the saliency of its domestic policies were also constant factors. Bevin believed he could bring Truman around by appealing to reason. He endorsed the creation of a joint committee to study the problem of displaced persons in Europe and immigration into Palestine. Under the rubric of the Anglo-American Committee of Inquiry on Palestine, the two governments agreed to consult all parties concerned, and Bevin stated he would abide by the recommendations of a unanimous report. In presenting the commission's mandate to the House of Commons in November 1945, he assured his peers that he had Palestine in hand and declared, "I will stake my political future on solving this problem."[68]

Bevin's refusal to repudiate the 1939 White Paper and his broader support for the creation of a binational state in Palestine rather than an independent Jewish one outraged the Jewish Agency, which forged a truce with the Irgun and Lehi. Together they entered into a tenuous alliance to extract concessions from Britain and ensure the terms set forth in the Balfour Declaration. In effect, just weeks before Bevin staked his political future on Palestine, the Yishuv established the Jewish Resistance Movement, and with that, the entire Jewish community declared war on Britain.[69]

In fact, just days before the INA trials opened in Delhi, the Yishuv's paramilitary forces launched their first major combined strike on British installations in Palestine. On November 1, 1945, fifty Palmach sections sabotaged the Mandate's railway networks in over 150 different locations, while Irgun forces blew up train junctions, railway shunting points, and small bridges. Known as "The Night of the Trains," the spectacular display of coordinated force extended to the Haifa oil refineries, which Lehi members bombed relentlessly. It also included the police patrol stations in Haifa and Jaffa, where Palmach operatives attacked and sank three boats that had been used to hunt down illegal Jewish immigration ships. As the smoke from the raging Haifa oil fires cast a dark cloud over Palestine's coastline, Bevin and the British government had not yet faced the realities of the Mandate's postwar landscape. Although the strength of the Yishuv's united militia was undeniable, Bevin was unmoved. He said as much when, around the time of the attacks, he challenged Weizmann in London: "If you want a fight, you can have it."[70]

These were strong words coming from a foreign secretary poised to wage a war against a formidable opponent, from a position of economic and diplomatic weakness. In the fall of 1945, the Yishuv had a population of over 550,000, the result of 25 percent growth during the interwar years, and it had established 350 settlements in Palestine. The Zionist project was surging economically, industrial output increasing fivefold from 1937 to 1943, reaching P£37.5 million. Such a growth rate, and the realities of Palestine's Jewish-led industrialization, rendered the high commissioner's postwar economic plans, focusing on the Mandate's agricultural potential, stunningly out of touch. Militarily, the Jewish Agency's Haganah was nearly 45,000 strong, and its highly trained elite Palmach numbered close to 9,000. While the Irgun and Lehi were comparatively small in size—with approximately 1,500 and 400 members, respectively—the Revisionist militia with its proclaimed willingness to deploy violence played a major role in the campaign. Together the armed insurgents comprised nearly 10 percent of the Jewish population in Palestine, a staggeringly high insurgent-to-civilian ratio compared to that of other imperial conflicts.[71]

Politically, the Jewish Agency was well organized and disciplined within Palestine, and its networks beyond the Mandate's borders were equally as strong. The World Zionist Organization's objectives framed much of the Jewish Agency's agenda as well as the Haganah's strategy. The Zionist Organization of America (ZOA) and Rabbi Abba Hillel Silver's broader umbrella organization, the American Zionist Emergency Council, boasted a membership of 1 million people. The ZOA alone distributed more than a million leaflets and pamphlets to media outlets, and newspapers reprinted more than four thousand of its news releases in 1945. The Revisionists were similarly well organized. Under Begin's direction, the Irgun drew its foreign support primarily from the largest of American-based Revisionist leader Hillel Kook's organizations, the

American League for a Free Palestine, while Lehi drew its American support from the Political Action Committee for Palestine.[72]

The rising strength of Zionism contrasted with Britain's growing infirmity. From the time Labour took office in 1945 until his death in the spring of 1951, Bevin pursued a grand imperial strategy and demonstrated no lack of will in the Middle East. Like his predecessors, his doctrine was above all pro-British, even if Britain's changing alliances undermined Middle Eastern stability, thwarting British interests, which were, at times, unclear. Indeed, if "war is a continuation of state policy by other means"—as the Prussian general and military theorist Carl von Clausewitz famously said—then a succession of Mandate high commissioners experienced great frustrations. For over twenty years, London oscillated in different directions depending on which way the winds of perceived British interests blew. There were changing policies from on high, countless interpretations and commissions, and multiple, contradictory white papers. As the historian Tom Segev points out, for a man like High Commissioner MacMichael, "everything was possible, if someone would only tell him what to do. If they wanted partition, there would be partition. If they wanted a state, there would be a state. It was all the same to him. MacMichael had no interest in politics; he did not understand it. That was not his business, and it was not his job. His job was to keep order."[73]

To do his job, MacMichael and others fell back on coercion, which the British military supported when necessary. This included punitive expeditions into insurgent territories, the destruction of villages and ethnic urban quarters, the humiliation and torture of civilian populations, heavy deployments of artillery and aerial bombing, and the hanging of suspects for even the most minor of infractions. In the end, coercion was not only inherent to British liberal imperialism but also a necessary tactic to maintain an upper hand over the cyclical Arab and Jewish violence that followed every bend in London's high-policy road.

When confronted with the Zionist insurgency, London once again changed personnel, believing that would solve the problem. In November 1945, Alan Cunningham lumbered in as the new high commissioner. The fifty-eight-year-old bachelor and career soldier brought lessons of his own personal failures during the Second World War. As a lieutenant general on the North African front, Cunningham had suffered early losses in an offensive in Libya, after which he recommended a curtailment of the operation. Instead, his superiors relieved him of his command and shipped him back to Britain, where he remained at a desk job for the rest of the war. His later promotion to general and his assignment to a civilian posting in Palestine presented Cunningham with an opportunity for redemption.

Cunningham quickly grasped the conflict's nuances and the imperial constraints unique to Palestine. In the face of daily Zionist attacks, he had the power of unbridled force at his fingertips. Unleashing it, however, would potentially undermine the fading credibility of the moderate Jewish Agency and drive defectors into the camp of the Revisionists, who showed no mercy in their willingness to take out human targets. Moreover, international scrutiny filtered through the lens of Zionist propaganda proved to be a powerful and unprecedented check on British force.[74] As the high commissioner repeatedly pointed out, "military means had to be dovetailed into political requirements."[75]

The escalating conflict, however, demanded some kind of immediate action. Cunningham turned to Defence (Emergency) Regulations and the legalized measures consolidated and deployed during the Arab Revolt. The wartime Defence of the Realm Act in Britain and the Emergency Powers (Defence) Act of 1939 informed the empire's 1939 Emergency Powers Order in Council, which empowered a colonial governor or high commissioner to declare a state of emergency when ordinary laws were insufficient for suppressing disorder and to make "such Regulations as appear to him to be necessary or expedient for securing the public safety, the defence of the territory, the maintenance of public order and the suppression of mutiny, rebellion and riot, and for maintaining supplies and services essential to the life of the community."[76] When the time came, Palestine's new high commissioner relied on fifty printed paragraphs of emergency regulations that enabled security forces to enforce curfews, confiscations, collective fines, arrests, and detentions. The new regulations reintroduced the death penalty for a range of offenses, including the carrying of firearms or explosives, and it reinstated military tribunals that had wide-ranging powers to enter summary judgments without pretrial inquiries, or furnishing evidence to the accused, or the right of appeal except to the general officer commanding (GOC) the British forces in Palestine, who had the sole authority to pardon, confirm, or dismiss a conviction.

The emergency regulations did little to quell the Jewish Resistance Movement's coordinated attacks, daily booby traps, destruction of government property, and assassinations of British officials. Moshe Shertok, head of the Jewish Agency's political department, gave voice to moderate Jewish sentiment, saying the emergency regulations were "murderous and atrocious laws, which threaten the public as a whole."[77] The

Revisionists devised strategies that attacked Britain's repressive measures head-on. "History and our observation persuaded us that if we could succeed in destroying the government's prestige in Eretz Israel, the removal of its rule would follow automatically," Menachem Begin recalled. "Thenceforward we gave no peace to this weak spot. Throughout all the years of our uprising, we hit at the British Government's prestige deliberately, tirelessly, unceasingly."[78]

British officials on the ground knew exactly what this meant. The Irgun leaders "believe in the efficacy of their present tactics . . . that violence is the only means of inducing the British Government to make political concessions," one intelligence report noted.[79] Samuel Katz, a member of the Irgun's high command and "one of the wisest of men," according to Begin, understood the relationship between violence and Britain's political weaknesses in the postwar context:

> There were limits of oppression beyond which the British government dared not go. She could not apply the full force of her power against us. Palestine was not a remote hill village in Afghanistan which could be bombed into submission. Palestine was a glass house watched with intent interest by the rest of the world. The British had discovered in 1945 that their behavior towards the Jews was an important factor in American attitudes and policies.[80]

Begin's "Logic of the Revolt" underscored Katz's point. "Eretz Israel . . . resembled a glass house." Begin extended the analogy, noting that "arms were our weapons of attacks; the transparency of the 'glass' was our shield of defence."[81] Underlying all this strategy was a broader Revisionist ethos—"We fight, therefore we are"—that was at once emancipatory in its logic as well as grounded in the realpolitik of British rule.[82] "Josiah Wedgwood used to say that the British would not listen to anybody, or take a political movement seriously, until they had broken the windows of a few British embassies," recalled Benjamin Akzin, a Revisionist member and later a law professor at Hebrew University.[83]

Neither British officers nor the rank and file sympathized with Cunningham's broader concerns over moderate Zionist support and international scrutiny. Nor did Britain's security forces care greatly about the political circumstances fueling the Zionist uprising. For many, the issue was the reestablishment of control using well-tested methods of repression. The high commissioner had to temper demands for unbridled coercion coming from successive GOCs as well as from Field Marshal Bernard Montgomery in his role as chief of the Imperial General Staff. Montgomery saw no difference between the Haganah, the Irgun, and Lehi. With each assault, he further castigated Cunningham for his failure to stamp out the terrorists. In 1945 the entire Sixth Airborne Division of 20,000 men arrived in Palestine; troop strength would swell to over 100,000 at the height of the insurgency. By the historian John Bowyer Bell's count:

> There were [also] two cruisers, three destroyers, other naval units off the coast, and naval radar and communication bases on the shore. The ratio of British security forces to the Jewish population was approximately one to five. . . . The Mandate was an armed camp, the countryside studded with the huge, concrete Tegart fortresses, British army camps, reinforced roadblocks, and observation points. The cities were constantly patrolled, and all government buildings protected by concertinas of barbed wire and sentry blocks. There were armed guards on the trains. For safety's sake, the British withdrew into wired and sandbagged compounds, self-imposed ghettos.[84]

Cunningham refused to mount an Arab Revolt–like offensive because no green light had come from Attlee's cabinet, at least not yet.

Meanwhile, the Palestine Police Force remained the first line of defense, much as it had been during earlier outbreaks of Arab and Jewish dissent. Its reputation for paramilitary training, using coercive tactics, and increasing indiscipline was widespread and not without merit. The Second World War had witnessed a marked increase in tensions between the force's British section and the Revisionist militia. Raymond "Caff" Cafferata, the Citroën-driving police officer who over a decade earlier had tackled the Hebron riots and was now the district commander of Haifa, was in the middle of the action. He oversaw police raids on Zionist settlements in search of arms and ammunition. In one instance, he commanded forty vehicle-loads of police who, together with nearly eight hundred soldiers who had aerial cover, raided the kibbutz of Ramat HaKovesh in 1943. The police herded Jewish men into cages similar to those used in the Arab Revolt, ransacked the kibbutz, wounded twenty-four settlers, and left another dead. One policeman claimed that he and others had been provoked into beating women and children who had formed human shields; these Jewish civilians had "behaved like demented wild beasts" and engaged in "vicious attacks" against the police and army, according to official reports.[85] Hebrew-language newspapers voiced outrage, and the mandatory government summarily shut them down, which only incited more violence, this time in Tel Aviv. In the years ahead, the raids would continue, and Cafferata would lead an operation in the kibbutz of Givat Haim that included tank-supported security forces in full battle armor who left scores of settlers wounded, seven dead, and a trail of self-defense claims.[86]

In some ways, as we saw in chapter 4, Cafferata was a typical police officer in Palestine. A former member of the Royal Irish Constabulary before his transfer to the Mandate, he rose to the top of the force, where his facile ethos—the familiar "I'm merely pro-British"—informed his actions. Suffering from a manpower shortage during World War II, the Palestine administration, backed by parliamentary legislation, placed its police force under military command, thus ensuring a retention of men when their three-year contracts ran out. It also meant that the Palestine Police Force, according to an internal report, was "a military force, subject to military law."[87] This move only reinforced the force's Black and Tan–inspired paramilitary culture. In 1943 five out of the eight district police commanders in Palestine had formerly been of the Black and Tans; together, they helped shape the force's actions and had little fear of discipline from above.[88]

Manpower issues dogged Palestine's colonial administration in the postwar years. Despite recruitment campaigns, its police force was routinely and alarmingly under strength. At the end of 1945, nearly three thousand policemen departed at the end of their contracts, which prompted Chief Secretary John Shaw to plead desperately with the Colonial Office that reinforcements were a *vital necessity.*[89] The Palestine Mobile Force, an elite, paramilitary force, was also grossly understaffed, with only half of the two thousand men needed in its ranks. In 1946 the British government lowered the mobile force's age requirement. Nearly 75 percent of its new recruits were eighteen or nineteen. In a few short weeks, these youngsters became quasi-soldiers through "square-bashing" (marching drill) exercises, weapons drills, and the bare minimum of language training. (Less than 4 percent of the total force spoke Hebrew.) The mobile force was outfitted and trained on military lines. Its members wore battle dress uniforms and were equipped with mortars, Brownings, machine guns, and smoke dischargers. They patrolled the Mandate in armored cars that could have passed for light tanks.[90] In effect, teenagers with an intense incubation in paramilitary culture but with no combat experience were placed into heavily armed mobile units that were often poorly organized and inadequately officered, then dispatched into high-risk and immensely stressful situations.

It's no wonder Montgomery thought the Palestine Mobile Force "could never be any better than third class soldiers."[91]

These youngsters confronted escalating attacks on a daily basis. During the first six months of the insurgency, the Jewish Resistance Movement launched nearly fifty strikes. On February 25, 1946, a combined Irgun and Lehi attack on the RAF airfields at Lydda, Qastina, and Kfar Sirkin dealt the British a most humiliating blow. The Zionist militia destroyed three Halifaxes and crippled eight others, while it exploded seven Spitfires, two Ansons, and three other small aircraft. Commando-style raids, sneak attacks, and remote destruction using mines and explosives were not limited to Britain's imperial infrastructure. Human targets were increasingly fair game. Relentless raids against the police ensued, as the Revisionists targeted the criminal investigation department, whose agents tried, often unsuccessfully, to infiltrate insurgent networks. The British deemed Zionist tactics "dishonorable" and "despicable."[92] The insurgents, many of whom had cut their teeth during the Arab Revolt and later as Special Operations Executive operatives during the Second World War, had fought shoulder to shoulder with the British and had learned not only British tactics but their weaknesses as well.

Britain was fighting the entire Yishuv, which refused to share information. "The truth is that no Jew will ever inform to a Gentile on another Jew," Palestine's new chief secretary, Henry Gurney, wrote.[93] His predecessor had left because of death threats; not surprisingly, fear had a chilling effect on potential Jewish informants. Palestine's criminal investigation department remained ill-equipped to run its own intelligence operations. Even Catling, the head of its Jewish section, didn't understand Hebrew. "Throughout that time I was in Special branch in Jerusalem, Police HQ—there was no more than two British officers who could speak Hebrew with reasonable fluency," he recalled. "This was disastrous. It meant that we were limited in our means of interrogation; in our ability to translate confiscated documents in Hebrew; and our ability to conduct operations—to overhear conversations, for example, between two Jewish suspects put in the same cell."[94]

Despite attempts to reorganize the Mandate's intelligence units, complete with MI5 operatives dropping in to offer advice, there was too much ground to cover. Decades of poor organization, underfunding, and an overall lack of interest in learning local languages and cultures—the crucial gateways to understanding subject populations—hamstrung British efforts. As the situation worsened, the criminal investigation department focused as much on keeping its members alive as it did on gathering intelligence. Moreover, successive military leaders gave intelligence a low priority relative to the perceived value of brute force. MI5's best inroads came with the handful of career intelligence agents who were brought in for the job. Major Desmond Doran was one such operative. Having been stationed in Cairo with Security Intelligence Middle East during the war, Doran transferred to Palestine, where his impeccable Hebrew, textbook knowledge of Lehi, and renowned interrogation skills also made him a prime target for the Revisionists. He was gunned down in his Tel Aviv home, which Irgun assassins then blew up, in September 1946.[95]

In contrast, the British could take few initiatives without the Zionists having at least some forewarning. Those in the police force who were from the Yishuv masterfully spied on their British colleagues. One police officer later recollected that they were, "I think . . . if not a fifth column, then certainly a fourth column."[96] Many Jewish members of the police force were sympathetic to the Haganah, while others were active in its underground.[97] Still others worked in various lower-level ranks within the colonial administration. Cafferata's secretary, for example, dutifully typed out his letters—and then made a copy for the Haganah. Lehi, whose members hadn't forgotten what Cafferata had done in Ramat HaKovesh and Givat Haim, had him on its hit list. On a rainy spring day in 1946, he narrowly managed to escape gunfire sprayed across the back window of his car. He was soon shipped home.[98]

In the wake of an April parking lot attack that took out several members of the Sixth Airborne, Lieutenant General D'Arcy strained to keep his troops under control. According to D'Arcy, who had led the retaking of Dublin's post office during Ireland's Easter Rising, his men in Palestine "took the law into their own hands for a short time" and were primed for a retributive rampage for the "mass murder" of their comrades.[99] He met with Cunningham, demanding collective punishment and the forcible disarming of all Jews in Tel Aviv. To his disgust, the high commissioner agreed only to an extended curfew. Cunningham's hands were in fact tied. On April 30, 1946, he received notice that any serious reprisals against the Yishuv would need cabinet authorization from London. Not coincidentally, on the same day the Anglo-American Committee report was published, and much to the outrage of Attlee and Bevin, Truman endorsed its recommendation that one hundred thousand more Jews be allowed into Palestine. Britain continued to view any increase in Jewish immigration as a potential source of Arab incitement, and Attlee's government would not allow more Jewish refugees into the Mandate.[100]

The Haganah, incensed by Britain's rejection of the Anglo-American Committee's recommendation, blew up ten train and road bridges, mostly along the Transjordan border. The Irgun followed this June 16, 1946, "Night of the Bridges" with a brazen kidnapping of five British officers while they lunched at the Tel Aviv Officers' Club. Begin's men chained the officers in a cellar hideout, then released two of them with a message. They would execute the other three British officers if the Mandate government did not release two Irgun members it had condemned to hang.

The time had come for British forces to claim the initiative, and Field Marshal Montgomery took the lead. Having toured Palestine earlier in June, he was "much perturbed by what [he] heard and saw" and noted that "British rule existed only in name; the true rulers seemed to me to be the Jews."[101] He placed blame not only at the feet of Cunningham but also at the hapless decision making in London that had rendered Britain's security forces impotent. In a heated cabinet meeting, Montgomery wrested Bevin's support to launch an offensive, and on June 29, D'Arcy's replacement, Evelyn Barker, ordered Operation Agatha.

The military imposed a curfew throughout the country, and nearly the entire strength of the British security forces—one hundred thousand men—surrounded scores of Zionist settlements. One of Barker's staff officers, Peter Martin, said that settlers at Mishek Yergoa stared down Agatha's security forces and tanks, blocking the gate of their kibbutz with a human shield of women and children. Martin's men threw gas grenades into the settlement, which children quickly covered with a "wet sandbag . . . and then a woman scooped it up, and tossed it in the back into water." What was to be an orderly search quickly descended into mayhem as the acting brigadier shouted, "Shoot them, Shoot them." "But [at] that moment," according to Martin, a soldier who was building barbed-wire cages for interrogations

> came up with two wasp flamethrowers, but these flamethrowers, instead of having flame fuel had been filled with crude oil from oil changers on the vehicles. So they were absolutely full with thick dirty frisky, dirty black oil. So I addressed [the settlers] and I said that if they did not move out of the way that we would open fire with these wasp flamethrowers. . . . I can remember them now quite clearly. One woman in particular in a white cotton dress with big red flowers on it . . . was absolutely in the center of the target area. . . . I gave note to fire and out shot a

solid jet of thick black crude oil and it struck the women on their hairs and faces and cotton frocks.[102]

Security forces raided the Jewish Agency's offices and removed tons of documents as evidence, including some of those that Cafferata's secretary had dutifully copied. Their widespread searches uncovered over thirty arms caches containing a half-million rounds of ammunition, more than five hundred weapons, and a quarter-ton of explosives. Mass arrests ensued; by the end of the day, security forces had picked up over one thousand suspects. They included four Jewish Agency executive members, Moshe Shertok among them. All prisoners were immediately shipped to the Latrun Detention Camp, and hundreds eventually went to camps in East Africa where they were detained without trial for the duration of the insurgency. Operation Agatha, or the "Black Sabbath," as locals called it, weakened the Haganah, but it barely touched the Irgun or Lehi, despite continued curfews, roadblocks, and interrogations. Still, Britain's show of strength gave its forces a renewed sense of control. Those at the top commuted the sentences of the two Irgun prisoners who were set to hang. The next day the Irgun chloroformed and boxed into a crate the three British officers it had kidnapped, then unceremoniously dumped them onto Rothschild Avenue in downtown Tel Aviv.

Even in the midst of the insurgency, there was nothing like Jerusalem's elegant King David Hotel in the rest of Palestine or, arguably, Britain's empire. For military officers, administrators, and high-end civilians, it was a four-and-a-half-acre slice of heaven perched above the Old City, surrounded by a cordon of barbed wire, antigrenade netting, state-of-the-art alarm controls, machine gun pits, and countless security force members. Gentlemen in dark suits and tuxedos, ladies in evening dresses, and Sudanese waiters plying aperitifs mingled there after a day of tennis or swimming and before a night of recitals, literary events, or some other form of cultural incongruity relative to the conflict that raged outside the hotel's artillery and bombproof walls. The British Army had requisitioned part of the hotel ever since the Arab Revolt, and the Mandate's secretariat had moved most administrative functions to its upper three floors in the south wing.[103] It was there that the senior police officer Richard Catling was chatting with his friend Roderick Musgrave on July 22, 1946, when an explosion sent them both racing to the balcony for a closer look through the midday sun. Catling hustled down the steps to ask his driver idling outside what had happened. The event was dismissed as a minor explosion.[104]

As Catling made his way back through the hotel lobby, seven large milk churns filled with explosives detonated and shredded the military and secretariat offices. Catling survived with only minor injuries, which was miraculous given the carnage. "You could see the bodies of people trapped by the rubble," one police officer recalled.[105] The Irgun's strike, which had entailed weeks of planning and subterfuge, had used force the size of a thousand-pound aerial bomb. The south wing of the hotel collapsed, one story crashing into the next from the detonation's force. By the time the smoke finally receded, the so-called bombproof build-

British security forces search for survivors after the King David Hotel bomb explosion, July 28, 1946.

ing had been reduced to piles of mangled concrete and shattered glass. Various government departments had lost nearly a quarter of their staff to injury or death. The secretariat's staff, with whom Catling had been chatting moments before the blast, was the hardest hit. Musgrave was killed. "So you see, these are the reasons why I think this stays with me as the worst atrocity," Catling recalled, assessing the impact of the day's events. "The size of the death toll—innocent people—absolutely innocent—most of them Palestinian—and the fact that I only just got away. And when you come close to death the circumstances at the time do remain in your mind. . . . If you were implicated at all in the particular incident, you would never forget it."[106]

Personal loss touched nearly everyone in the Mandate's administration and security forces. Demands for retribution ran all the way up to Montgomery, who wrote, "We shall show the world and the Jews that we are not going to submit tamely to violence."[107] This was the Irgun's most spectacular hit. The Jewish Agency and Lehi knew who was responsible for the attack, and British intelligence had "theories . . . but we in the investigation that followed this attack on the King David Hotel did not identify, arrest, and take to court those responsible," said Catling.[108]

In the wake of the King David Hotel's destruction, British forces launched Operation Shark, sealed off Tel Aviv, and conducted house-to-house searches and interrogations of the entire adult population. A thousand suspects were detained. Police Sergeant T. G. Martin picked out Yitzhak Shamir, the mastermind of the Lord Moyne assassination and the Lehi leader, in a lineup, even though he was disguised as a rabbi. Shamir was deported to an East African detention camp for interrogation. Martin was gunned down on a tennis court in Haifa two months later.

The Jewish Agency could not stomach the levels of violence and withdrew from the Jewish Resistance Movement, even though it continued its illegal immigration operations. As far as Ben-Gurion was concerned, "the Irgun is the enemy of the Jewish people," and Begin was as much a threat to the Yishuv as the British.[109] The head of the Jewish Agency tried to walk the line between London's unacceptable policies and the Revisionist ascent within the Mandate. Cunningham hoped Ben-Gurion's men would carry out a "Little Saison," releasing some of their detainees as a good faith gesture. But with no immigration concessions, that wouldn't come to pass.

Irgun and Lehi violence continued "deliberately, tirelessly, [and] unceasingly," making a mockery of British rule. "In the development of certain British Colonies the whip has been made to serve an educational purpose," Begin wrote. "It is applied, of course, not to recalcitrant boys but to adults who are treated like disorderly children."[110] The Irgun zeroed in on this loathed symbol of imperial paternalism, a method of "civilizing" reform, and turned it against British soldiers with startling effect. At the end of 1946, Begin declared through the Irgun's underground publication, *Herut*:

> For hundreds of years you have been whipping "natives" in your colonies—without retaliation. In your foolish pride you regard the Jews of Eretz Israel as natives too. You are mistaken. Zion is not exile. Jews are not Zulus. You will not whip Jews in their Homeland. And if the British Authorities whip them—British officers will be whipped publicly in return.[111]

True to his threat, and in retaliation for British security forces caning two young Irgun members, Begin had several of his men abduct Major Paddy Brett while he dined with his wife at a waterfront hotel in Netanya. Shortly thereafter armed Irgun fighters took three more British officers hostage. They whipped the captured men severely, binding them to a tree in a public garden, where a search patrol later found them.[112]

Britain's security forces felt that the entire Yishuv was culpable for the violence, deaths, and humiliations. It was no longer possible, according to one high-ranking officer, "to differentiate between passive onlookers and active armed members of the Jewish population, and the word 'terrorist' is no longer being applied to differentiate one from the other. All suffer from the martyrdom complex and instability of temperament, which makes their reactions in circumstances of any political stress both violent and unpredictable."[113] After the King David Hotel attack, General Barker issued a nonfraternization edict and ordered all security forces to stay away from Jewish establishments. It "will be punishing the Jews in a way the race dislikes as much as any," he announced, "by striking at their pockets and showing our contempt for them."[114] An uproar from international Zionist organizations followed, and Barker backpedaled publicly. Privately, however, he confided to his affluent Arab lover, "Yes I loathe the lot—whether they be Zionists or not. Why should we be afraid of saying we hate them—it's time this damned race knew what we think of them—loathsome people."[115]

Mounting security force frustration and its plummeting morale translated into open hostility. The Jewish Agency routinely filed complaints against soldiers and policemen who used anti-Semitic slurs. Security force members shouted "Bloody Jew," "pigs," and *"Heil Hit-*

ler," promising to finish off what Hitler began.[116] Members of the police force derided the Jews as "dirty" and "filthy." "You could have kicked the Arab up the bottom and nothing would have been said, but if you put a little finger on a Jew-boy Westminster would have gone crazy. . . . When I came out of the force, I thought, well, I wouldn't urinate on a Jew if he was on fire," one of its officers scoffed.[117] Others in the police force were more measured, and their sentiments shifted as British policies oscillated between Arab and Zionist support. "I suppose it's the way the pendulum swings," one officer recalled. "In the first years, the Jews were our friends and the Arabs our enemies. . . . The Jews became more aggressive," at which point police force sentiment swung the other way.[118]

Montgomery was furious not at his troops but at the British government. He had returned to Palestine to repress Zionist insurgents with the same force that he had used to quash Arabs a decade earlier. Instead, the situation had gone from bad to worse. Britain's casualty rate was up to two a day. "If we are not prepared to maintain law and order in Palestine," Montgomery told Attlee, "then it would be better to get out."[119] He went on to eviscerate Cunningham, calling his policies "gutless and spineless"; the high commissioner had "failed to produce law and order in Palestine . . . and [he needed to adopt] a more robust mentality in his methods to keep the King's peace."[120] Moreover, Cunningham was damaged goods as far as Montgomery was concerned. "You will remember," the commanding officer said, "he gave in at Sidi Rezihg in December 1941 forty-eight hours too soon."[121]

Cunningham continued to push for a political solution with the Jewish Agency, but by the end of 1946, support for this was greatly diminished. Churchill in Parliament made a laughingstock of Bevin's policies, deriding him that Britain was on "the road of abject defeat."[122] A widely circulated War Office memo made clear the military's position: "Viewed from a military standpoint the policy of appeasement has failed. . . . The restoration of law and order can depend only on the adoption of a consistent and vigorous policy in dealing with disturbers of the peace. Such a policy is not in force. If we are to prevent the present situation in Palestine from getting out of hand, strong military preventive action must be taken in Palestine at once."[123] After the flogging incident, and at Montgomery's urging, Bevin and the Labour government finally gave him the go-ahead following a New Year's Day cabinet meeting. He was informed that a new policy would be implemented "firmly and relentlessly and despite world opinion or Jewish reaction in America."[124] Cunningham soon received new orders: "All possible steps will be taken at once to restore law and order. . . . The police and troops should be designed to take the offensive against breakers of the law and to ensure that the initiative lies with the forces of the Crown."[125] A cabinet directive, which Montgomery drafted, followed that offered "the full support of His Majesty's Government . . . [for] such action as you may take to implement the policy outline," with "such action" enabled through statutory martial law.[126] In January 1947 the field marshal expected to regain an initiative that his hundred-thousand-strong force had never had and to win the conflict through Britain's repressive strength alone.

CHAPTER II

Exit Palestine, Enter Malaya

Political language—and with variations this is true of all political parties, from Conservatives to Anarchists—is designed to make lies sound truthful and murder respectable, and to give an appearance of solidity to pure wind. One cannot change this all in a moment, but one can at least change one's own habits, and from time to time one can even, if one jeers loudly enough, send some worn-out and useless phrase . . . into the dustbin where it belongs.

George Orwell, 1946[1]

In December 1947, George Orwell ruminated over these words while living on the island of Jura, just off Scotland's west coast. He'd rented Barnhill, a farmhouse on Jura's desolate northern tip, using the proceeds from *Animal Farm* to buy tranquility away from London's postwar gloom and the melancholy that had haunted him ever since his wife's untimely death. Nature did not cooperate, nor did his worsening health. Temperatures plummeted, snow drifted against Barnhill's shingles, and frost crept inside, crocheting across the windows, down tattered draperies, and onto the plank floors. Orwell abandoned drafting his new manuscript and sought medical attention in Glasgow, where he was diagnosed with tuberculosis. Nurses temporarily confiscated his typewriter, but not his cigarettes, and he endured painful procedures, including having his lung collapsed. None of it did much to ease his infection's ravaging effects.[2]

Orwell needed the new "miracle drug" streptomycin, an antibiotic that was widely available in the United States but years away from production in Britain. With limited dollar reserves, the British government spat in the ocean of need, buying just fifty kilograms of the drug from the United States and setting up randomized allocations to study its effects. The BBC broadcast emergency appeals for more doses, and a black market for the drug mushroomed. With death stalking him, Orwell inveigled a way to buy the antibiotic directly from the United States and finally did, though he was unusually affected by it. "My face became noticeably redder & the skin had a tendency to flake off," he wrote. "It was very painful to swallow. . . . There was now ulceration with blisters in my throat & in the insides of my cheeks." His hair fell out and his infected blisters burst. He discontinued the drug and picked up his writing.[3]

"*Doublethink* means the power of holding two contradictory beliefs in one's mind simultaneously, and accepting them both. The Party intellectual knows in which direction memories must be altered; he therefore knows that he is playing tricks with reality; but by the exercise of *doublethink* he also satisfies himself that reality is not violated."[4] Orwell pecked out *1984*'s dystopian universe while battling his infection in various hospitals, sanatoria, and Barnhill, to which he was able to return for a time. He finished "that bloody book," a masterpiece illustrating deceit's ominous effects, in 1948, allegedly twisting the year's numbers to create one of the twentieth century's most famous titles.[5] *1984* is about totalitarianism's consequences, but it also speaks to those of liberal imperialism whose evolutionary framing could adapt under duress, as we've seen with the postwar partnership motif. Yet liberal imperialism's reforms became harder to discern, save for triumphant rhetoric and independence day ceremonies obfuscating the repression needed to hang on to the empire's most coveted jewels until the bitter end. How much the public knew about the violence, and what knowing meant, impacted the state's response, and it was here that Orwell's fictive Oceania, where "War is Peace" and "Freedom is Slavery," reflected Britain and its empire. One of imperialism's staunchest critics, Orwell knew the state was masterful at speaking with a forked tongue and at choreographing internal investigations that played to good governance and rule of law while avoiding accountability.

There were other forms of knowing, however, that state-directed practices, including bonfires, could not erase entirely. Recall the Black radicals like George Padmore who wrote prolifically about "fascist-imperialism" and marshaled firsthand evidence; the soldiers who sent home letters recounting the empire's coercive front lines; the missionaries who went public with eyewitness accounts; the newspaper articles and editorials, some hard-hitting, recounting the empire's conflicts in South Africa, India, and Palestine; and the fictionalized versions of abuse, like those in Orwell's *Burmese Days*, which were widely read. These sources of knowledge mattered, raising public consciousness of events in the empire. They also prodded Britain's official doublethink, which pointed to Pax Britannica's successes and denied violence, or rationalized its purpose of reforming "backward" subjects who, like children, needed to be brought along with a firm hand. "Things like the continuance of British rule in India," Orwell wrote in 1946, ". . . can indeed be defended, but only by arguments which are too brutal for most people to face, and which do not square with the professed aims of political parties."[6]

After World War II, many Britons were exhausted and desperately trying to rebuild. Indifference toward the empire's violent methods was its own scourge, as was the bellicose imperial nationalism that endured in many British circles. Cultural conditions were ripe for an Orwellian universe, but one rooted in liberalism, not in fascism. With other forms of knowing threatening to erode state secrecy, doublethink doubled down, protecting the British state and the nation's future. Orwell's own experiences with empire informed his thinking on how this duplicity worked:

> The process has to be conscious, or it would not be carried out with sufficient precision, but it also has to be unconscious, or it would bring with it a feeling of falsity and hence of guilt. . . . To tell deliberate lies while genuinely believing in them, to forget any fact that has become inconvenient, and then, when it becomes necessary again, to draw it back from oblivion for just so long as it is needed, to deny the existence of objective reality and all the while to take account of the reality which one denies—all this is indispensably necessary.[7]

1984's publisher rushed the novel's release in June 1949. In one of the final scenes, the novel's protagonist, Winston, is sitting beside a chessboard, drinking gin, in the Chestnut Tree café. "Winston's heart stirred," Orwell began.

> All day, with little spurts of excitement, the thought of a smashing defeat in Africa had been in and out of his mind. He seemed actually to see the Eurasian army swarming across the never-broken frontier pouring down into the tip of Africa like a column of ants. Why had it not been possible to outflank them in some way? The outline of the West African coast stood out vividly in his mind. He picked up the white knight and moved it across the [chess] board. *There* was the proper spot. Even while

he saw the black horde racing southward he saw another force, mysteriously assembled, suddenly planted in their rear, cutting their communications by land and sea. . . . But it was necessary to act quickly. If they could get control of the whole of Africa, if they had airfields and submarine bases at the Cape, it would cut Oceania in two. It might mean anything: defeat, breakdown, the redivision of the world, the destruction of the Party! He drew a deep breath. . . . He put the white knight back in its place. . . . His thoughts wandered again. Almost unconsciously he traced with his finger in the dust on the table:

$$2 + 2 = 5.^8$$

Seven months after *1984*'s publication, Britain's truth teller was dead at the age of forty-six. The empire's doublethink lived on.

. . .

Prisoners clearing snow on Fairfield Common, Buxton, Derbyshire, 1947

The winter of 1947, the harshest in sixty years, took other tolls. The shortening days were frigid, January reaching record low temperatures and bringing blizzards and snowdrifts that blocked roads and railways, cutting off dangerously low coal stocks from reaching electric power stations. Energy disruptions left homes unbearably cold and shut down industries, leaving as many as 4 million Britons unemployed. Animals froze in the fields or starved, and vegetables froze in the ground. Television was suspended, radio broadcasts were limited, and newspapers were reduced in size. Minister of Fuel and Power Emanuel Shinwell, having received multiple death threats, was under police guard. Labour's polling numbers, already eroding, had the party three to four points ahead of the Conservatives; by spring it was an even split. In the midst of the freeze, Shinwell admitted to shockingly low coal stocks, and the government tried to feed its people *snoek*, an inexpensive South African fish that was so unpalatable, it was eventually ground into cat food.[9] The crisis was not "an act of God, but the inactivity of Emmanuel [*sic*] [Shinwell]," Conservative stalwart Lord Swinton proclaimed.[10] Swinton's party didn't need the empire to hammer at Labour's incompetence, but India and Palestine left the government's flanks exposed, which Conservatives ruthlessly exploited.

On February 14, 1947, the sun hadn't shone on Britain for nearly two weeks. Attlee's cabinet bundled up and trudged through snowdrifts to convene at 10 Downing Street. They had already decided, but not yet announced, Britain's retreat from the Raj by June 1948. But Palestine's future remained unresolved. From his seat, Attlee looked across the colossal Gladstone-era table at the ice-covered windows blocking his view of London's suffering. Behind him, the room's only fireplace struggled against the chill, while the portrait of Sir Robert Walpole, Britain's powerful eighteenth-century prime minister, hung above its mantle, staring down on Attlee's ministers, hunched and crooked from the winter's freeze and nourished by their country's despair.

Foreign Secretary Bevin remained mired in an Arab-Zionist impasse, having convened another set of negotiations in London earlier in the year in the hope of finding some resolution. Bevin was balancing an immensely complicated set of plans and issues, as were the Arabs, Zionists, and with greater intensity and intrigue in the postwar years, the Americans. British statesmen agreed that Palestine's future could not be solved without Truman's input, the American Zionist lobby was thought too influential, and Britain needed continuing American financial support to recover from the war. The earlier Anglo-American Committee, which in 1946 had announced its recommendation of admitting an additional hundred thousand Jewish immigrants into Palestine, already conceded American influence. At the time, one might have thought the United States was finally doing its share to address the human tragedy of Jewish refugees. "The period from 1933 to 1944 had been one of continuous persecution in Europe in which hundreds of thousands of innocent persons had become refugees," British delegate on the committee Richard Crossman reminded his fellow members. He compared Britain's admission of two hundred thousand Jewish refugees before and during the war to that of the Americans:

> In this period of appalling suffering the American [immigration] quota had been so administered as to cut down the number of immigrants. . . . In this period, three hundred sixty-five thousand immigrants had been permitted to enter the country— roughly two hundred fifty thousand of them refugees, *the lowest immigration figures for a hundred years*. Despite the Nazi persecution the number of Jewish immigrants was only one hundred sixty thousand in these eleven years, about half the number of Jews who entered America in the twenties. The records of Canada and Australia were no better.[11]

After the war, Jewish refugees lived in squalid European displaced persons camps. Few countries wanted to take responsibility for them. The British were allowing fifteen hundred Jews into Palestine per month, whereas the Americans let in less than six thousand between May 1945 and September 1946, an average of 350 per month. "By shouting for a Jewish state, Americans satisfy many motives," Crossman complained. "They are attacking the Empire and British imperialism, they are espousing a moral cause, for whose fulfilment they will take no responsibility, and most important of all, they are diverting attention from the fact that their own immigration laws are the basic cause of the problem." The American Zionists, he said, were "passionately anti-British and have organized nearly all the American Jews and all the Press."[12] They also, according to Crossman, had the direct ear of Truman through his special adviser, David Niles, whose job was to keep the Zionists happy. Of the Americans, Bevin said "they don't want too many Jews in New York," another poorly judged remark, offending both Truman and the Zionists in a single statement.[13]

In light of Anglo-American friction, it was miraculous that a proposal, called the Morrison-Grady plan, was agreed on and ready for a

The American Zionist Emergency Council organized a protest against British policy in Palestine, Madison Square Park, July 1946.

series of Arab-Zionist meetings in London during the fall of 1946. "The central element of the Morrison-Grady plan was ambiguity," the historian William Roger Louis points out:

> It could be read as a step towards partition or a binational state. . . . There would be provisional autonomy with certain powers reserved to the central administering authority (Britain as the trusteeship power would be the 'administering authority' for an indefinite period). . . . There would be a Jewish province and an Arab province, together with a district of Jerusalem and a district of the largely uninhabited desert territory of the Negev. The central government would have reserved powers over foreign relations, defence, justice, and taxation. . . . Final control over immigration would rest with the central government which would authorize provincial requests for immigrants up to absorptive economic capacity.[14]

The Americans refused to commit to boots on the ground to enforce the plan and rejected joint trusteeship with Britain. By the end of negotiations over the Morrison-Grady plan, even Truman was exhausted by the Zionist lobby, who berated him for co-creating a "ghetto" in Palestine, an insult he took seriously given Jewish voting power, real and perceived. "Jesus Christ couldn't please them when he was here on earth," he told his cabinet, "so how could anyone expect I would have any luck?"[15]

Truman thought, as did Chaim Weizmann, that the plan was a precursor to a Jewish state in Palestine. When the Zionist Congress met in Basel in December 1946, its delegates disagreed, voting 171 to 154 to boycott the next round of negotiations in London, which was a clear rejection of the Morrison-Grady plan and Bevin's latest revision of it, the allowance of one hundred thousand Jewish immigrants to Palestine over two years. Blanche Dugdale, Weizmann's long-serving assistant and a niece of Arthur Balfour, who had spearheaded Palestine's fateful 1917 Balfour Declaration, recorded events in her diary. Having for years used her establishment connections to further Weizmann's agenda, Dugdale couldn't bear the Basel vote. It crushed Weizmann, she lamented. Delegates dismissed him as "too flippant—too pro-British." Rabbi Silver "threw down the gauntlet—against partition and in favour of 'resistance'—but not one word to distinguish it from terrorism." Having to choose loyalty, Dugdale resigned after supporting Weizmann and the World Zionist Organization for decades. "I cannot work for or with any Executive that is pursuing a policy of non-cooperation with Britain."[16]

That Bevin thought he could quixotically broker a deal in London against a backdrop of reprisals and counterreprisals in Palestine and the cabinet's January 1947 green-lighting of full military force to suppress the Zionist insurgency is eyebrow raising. The London conference was a bust, confirming Arab and Zionist entrenched positions and Bevin's diplomatic paralysis. The Arabs were resolutely opposed to partition and a continuation of Jewish immigration, while the Zionists were equally insistent on the creation of a Jewish state. "It has been assumed hitherto that the maintenance of influence in the Middle East should be a major objective of British policy," Bevin's Foreign Office told him, "both because of our interest in the strategic importance of the Area and because of our interest in its increasingly important oil production. . . . In considering our policy there, we must take account of this general background and of the specifically British interests which are involved."[17]

On that frigid February 14 day in Downing Street's cabinet room, Bevin and Colonial Secretary Creech Jones made the case for going to the United Nations. They advised Attlee and other British ministers that the Arabs and Jews were opposed to UN interference, and if Britain "now announced our firm intention" to do so, "this might bring [the Arabs and Jews] to a more reasonable frame of mind," according to Bevin. The General Assembly wouldn't sit for another seven months, so there was plenty of time to let the weight of Britain's threat take effect. The cabinet had previously considered such a move but dismissed it as "extremely embarrassing." Bevin assured his fellow ministers that Britain was not legally required to "enforce whatever solution the United Nations might approve."[18]

Conflicted hope raised the cabinet's despairing mood. Bevin's recommendation was approved, and on February 18, two days before Attlee announced to Parliament Britain's timetable for leaving India, Bevin delivered the news about Palestine:

> His Majesty's Government have of themselves no power, under the terms of the Mandate, to award the country either to the Arabs or to the Jews, or even to partition it between them. It is in these circumstances that we have decided that we are unable to accept the scheme put forward either by the Arabs or by the Jews, or to impose ourselves a solution of our own. We have, therefore, reached the conclusion that the only course now open to us is to submit the problem to the judgment of the United Nations. . . . Though we shall give immediate notice of our intentions, we see great difficulty in having this matter considered by the United Nations before the next regular session of the General Assembly in September. We regret that the final settlement should be subject to this further delay, particularly in view of the continuing strain on the British Administration and Services during this further period. We trust, however, that as the question is now to be referred to the United Nations all concerned will exercise restraint until their judgment is known.[19]

Churchill was incredulous. Ever since Zionist assassins had murdered Lord Moyne in Cairo, he had modified his previous position on Palestine, never again meeting with Weizmann. Of the original Balfour Declaration, Churchill said, "Promises were made far beyond those to which responsible Governments should have committed themselves."[20] It was time for the UN to step in, the sooner the better. Instead, Labour, according to Churchill, was protracting a crisis made catastrophic by its feckless policies:

Are we to understand that we are to go on bearing the whole of
this burden, with no solution to offer, no guidance to give—the
whole of this burden of maintaining law and order in Palestine,
and carrying on the administration, not only until September,
which is a long way from February, not only until then, when
the United Nations are to have it laid before them, but until
those United Nations have solved the problem, to which the
right hon. Gentleman has declared himself, after 18 months of
protracted delay, incapable of offering any solution? How does
he justify keeping 100,000 British soldiers in Palestine, who are
needed here, and spending £30 million to £40 million a year
from our diminishing resources upon this vast apparatus of pro-
traction and delay?[21]

"I very much regret this rhetorical display about protracted delay,"
Bevin shot back; it "is totally unjust."[22] There was no placating Churchill,
however. It was his imperial playbook guiding Attlee's government,
which belatedly discharged the full weight of state-directed violence.
In fact, as we have seen, the cabinet had authorized a full "offensive" in
January, more than a month before Bevin announced plans to appeal to
the UN to broker a diplomatic solution. The foreign secretary disingenuously bought more time to subdue the Zionist insurgents, forcing
them to offer additional concessions to the Arabs, whose interests now
aligned most closely with Britain's.

In the winter of 1947, Montgomery wasn't the only one unleashing state-
directed coercion on Palestine's Yishuv. As far back as March 1946, High
Commissioner Cunningham had been beefing up his approach to counterinsurgency, bringing in former Royal Marine Commando Colonel
William Nicol Gray, who had no policing experience but had seen years
of war-tested combat, to take over as police commissioner. Gray, Scottish and well over six feet tall, had stormed the beaches of Normandy and
launched a textbook assault on the Rhine. His war-hero legend entered
the pages of masculine glorification in *The Boy's Own Paper*, a standard
read for countless British adolescents coming of age. He was known
as a "man of action" with "little time for subtle intelligence work"; he
was also notorious for his discipline and imperious brusqueness that dis-
comforted some and alienated others.[23] The Colonial Office and Cunningham handpicked the marine commando after considerable debate.

Ten most wanted men in Palestine, including "Menahem Beigin," Menachem Begin (top left), 1947

While routine policing duties could potentially yield more intelligence from a placated population, that ship had long sailed if it had ever been hitched to an imperial mooring in the first place. First and foremost, the insurgency had to be defeated. The dwindling ranks of policemen who "are hated like poison out here and any chance of shooting them is welcomed," according to one police officer, had to be protected while the Mandate's leadership devised new strategies.[24]

Commando experiences and covert operations in the empire and wartime Europe were Gray's forte. Visiting London in October 1946, when the cabinet was considering multiple diplomatic solutions for Palestine, Gray consulted closely with the Colonial Office, MI5 and MI6, the network of Special Operations Executive and Special Air Service operatives, and Attlee himself.[25] Together, they formulated plans for undercover units that were nothing short of hit squads.

Gray first tapped Bernard Fergusson to take charge of the Mandate's clandestine "anti-terrorist activities." Fergusson's pedigree for such a task was beyond question. The thirty-five-year-old Scotsman had a long imperial lineage. His father and grandfather were military men who had served as governors in the empire, and the latter was a former undersecretary for India. A graduate of Sandhurst, Fergusson was an intelligence officer and General Archibald Wavell's protégé. Together, they had taken it to the Arabs in the late 1930s, with Fergusson traversing the Mandate's terrain in an old Austin Seven and liaising with Orde Wingate, who offered him lessons in how to hunt down and eliminate Arab suspects. This was Fergusson's first tutorial from the Special Night Squads' mastermind; a few years later he joined Wingate's Chindit operations in Burma. After that, Fergusson returned to Britain where he, in turn, schooled the next generation of covert operatives at the Combined Operations Headquarters.[26] By the time Fergusson returned to Palestine in late 1946, as the historian Charles Townshend remarked, "Orde Wingate was dead, but his Chindit right-hand man, Bernard Fergusson, came to Palestine as Assistant Inspector General."[27]

In fact, Fergusson was the Colonial Office's first choice for Gray's job, but it wasn't until the Palestine crisis reached alarming proportions in the fall of 1946 that the War Office was willing to second him to the Mandate's police force. Fergusson quietly amassed a new fleet of covert operatives, calling them "special squads" and informing the Colonial Office that he would recruit members from the army's "small number of officers who have both technical and psychological knowledge of terrorism." Once in Palestine, he would dress them as civilians, hoping they would pass for members of the Yishuv.[28] His top recruit was Roy Farran. Short yet chiseled, with sandy blond hair and arresting blue eyes, Farran was the stuff of legend. Reared in India, where his father was an RAF officer, and later trained at Sandhurst, he had shipped out in 1940 to fight alongside imperial forces in Egypt, Libya, and Crete. His heroics earned him an astonishing breast full of medals—the military cross with two bars, the Croix de Guerre, and the Distinguished Service Order among them. He served in the Special Air Service, a behind-the-lines commando operation that fanned out across European theaters. By the time Fergusson returned to London in early 1947 to recruit covert operatives, the twenty-six-year-old Farran, a self-described "relic of Kiplingesque times," was renowned for his courage. He was also ruthless in taking out enemies and oozed a charismatic, imperial masculinity that captivated the rank and file as well as the ladies.[29] Farran was precisely the kind of operative Fergusson needed.[30]

In March 1947, a month after Britain referred Palestine to the UN, Farran landed at Lydda airport together with Alistair McGregor, both resplendent in their new Palestine police uniforms. They had once sat in Fergusson's Sandhurst classroom. Like Farran, McGregor had extensive wartime covert experience in the Special Air Service as well as the Special Operations Executive and MI6. As for their mission, Farran recalled, "We would each have full power to operate as we pleased within our own specific areas. We were to advise on defence against terror and to take an active part in hunting down dissidents. It was to all intents and purposes a *carte blanche* and the original conception of our part filled me with excitement. A free hand for us against terror when all others were so closely hobbled."[31]

He and McGregor staffed their special squads with men from the Palestine Police Force, several of whom had also served in wartime special forces. For two weeks, they trained their recruits in the fine art of close-range killing. The "Fergusson Force" then suited up to look like kibbutzniks, though few spoke any Hebrew, and the government issued them battered civilian cars and trucks loaded with weapons and ammunition. It also assigned them urban safe houses stocked with supplies. Fergusson's entire operation rested on making targeted strikes with little or no intelligence to go on. Commando hubris riddled the whole operation. "The circumstances were not right," Richard Catling recalled. "The scene of operations was not right, the enemy was not right, the population was hostile, everything was against its success."[32] Farran later insisted that his operation bagged quick victories, but there's little other than his word for it.

In Britain in the immediate postwar years, MI5 considered the Zionists the nation's greatest security threat, for good reason.[33] On October 31, 1946, months after the King David Hotel attack, the Irgun had struck the British embassy in Rome, shearing off its ornate exterior wall from roof to ground with the explosive force of a thousand-pound bomb. Eliyahu Tavin, the Irgun's point person in Italy, found ready recruits among those who had survived Hitler's concentration camps only to languish in the displaced persons camps that swelled with refugees whom Britain had captured when they tried to enter Palestine. In all, MI5 estimated there were 350,000 displaced persons across Europe whose desperate fates were hanging in the international negotiating balance. Ya'acov Eliav, better known as "Dynamite Man," was similarly recruited for Lehi in Europe, from where he targeted Britain. Both Revisionist cells received support and training from the Irish Republican Army, which, in the words of one of its members, "would do business with Hitler if it was in Ireland's good."[34]

MI5 worked around the clock from its Cairo nerve center to stymie the Irgun not only in Palestine but also in Europe. The empire-bred MI5 directors-general David Petrie and Percy Sillitoe in London read hair-raising reports. According to one, the Revisionists were "training members for the purpose of sending them to the United Kingdom to assassinate members of Her Majesty's Government, Mr Bevin being especially mentioned. . . . Irgun Zvai Leumi and Stern Gang have decided to send five cells to London to operate in a manner similar to the IRA."[35]

MI5 knew attacks were coming, but it couldn't infiltrate the Revisionist organizations; nor could it crack the Revisionists' vertically organized cell structures with members of one cell being purposefully unaware of members in another cell. In March 1947 British intelligence failed to stop Lehi from blowing up the Colonial Club in central London. Nor, a month later, did it stop Betty Knout from walking straight through the Colonial Office's front door with a coat-concealed bomb, wrapped in copies of *The Daily Telegraph* and the *Evening Standard*, under her arm. She left the package on a toilet seat in the building's downstairs cloakroom. Had it not been for the bomb's detonation wire failing, the Colonial Office would have gone the way of the King David Hotel. Meanwhile letter and package bombs arrived on the doorsteps of VIPs across the country, though most failed to explode.[36]

On May 4, 1947, Menachem Begin's men launched another brazen strike in Palestine, this one on Acre prison, another symbol of Britain's imagined impregnability.[37] Irgun insurgents managed to overcome seventy-foot-high walls that were three feet thick, medieval-like iron gates and portcullises, and a gargantuan moat to liberate nearly 250 Acre prisoners. Begin called the operation "amongst the most daring attacks of the Hebrew underground and possibly of any underground."[38] Such bravado came at a price, however. The Irgun's casualties were substantial, and British forces captured five insurgents—three of whom, Avshalom Habib, Meir Nakar, and Ya'acov Weiss—would be tried by a British military court.

"The attack on Acre jail has been seen here as a serious blow to British prestige," London's *Haaretz* correspondent wrote the day after the raid. Foreign journalists called it "the greatest jail break in history" and "an ambitious mission, [the Irgun's] most challenging so far, in perfect fashion." What was His Majesty's government planning to do, former colonial secretary Oliver Stanley asked Parliament, "in light of the events at Acre prison which had reduced British prestige to a nadir"?[39] In Palestine, the pending trial of Habib, Nakar, and Weiss was not enough. Humiliated, British security forces wanted counterreprisals, and they quickly got one from the newly formed hit squads.

On the evening of May 6, Farran and his men were trolling the tree-lined Jerusalem suburb of Rehavia when they spotted sixteen-year-old Alexander Rubowitz. Rubowitz had joined the Jewish underground at a young age and was a courier who moved guns around the city and also hung Revisionist posters in streets and alleyways. Sometime around eight p.m. an eyewitness saw a "burly, fair-haired man" chasing Rubowitz down Haran Street. Two other boys nearby saw a six-seater sedan pull up, and after a violent struggle, the men inside forced Rubowitz into the back seat. Before the car sped off, the boys heard a scream: "I'm from the Rubowitz family." Next morning, Rubowitz's brothers inquired about Alexander's whereabouts at the local police station; coming up empty-handed, the family went to the Hebrew press. *Haaretz* published a brief account of the incident under the headline "Abducted or Arrested?" The search continued, with the *Palestine Post* picking up the story. Many of the tips that came in pointed directly to Farran. They included a physical description and a felt hat found at the abduction scene with the letters "FAR-AN" or "FARSAN" smudged on its leather headband.[40]

Farran and his men had driven twenty-five kilometers to Jericho where, in a remote olive grove, they tied Rubowitz to a tree "for further questioning." Farran recalled that he "had gone further than he should in trying to make the youth talk," during which time he "had killed the youth by bashing his head in with a stone and that knife wounds had been added to the body after death. [He also said that] the dead youth's clothing had been removed and burned and that the body had been left unburied somewhere in the open country off the Jericho road."[41]

The morning after, Farran confessed these events to Fergusson, who then went to great lengths—along with many higher-ups in Palestine and members of the Colonial Office—to cover up the crime. The local press exposed more and more pieces of evidence pointing to Farran's guilt, which included the damning felt hat. At the end of May, Inspector General Gray had to launch an official investigation. Farran fled to Syria, where he hoped to parlay a deal within the old boy channels. In mid-June his luck seemed to run out when he was apprehended and brought back to Jerusalem, where he awaited his trial in a heavily guarded military court. For months, newspapers in Palestine and the

United States splashed outrage in their headlines. They decried Britain's "'infiltration squads' . . . using unorthodox methods against terrorists" and accused Whitehall of a "private war of gangs of English-speaking men against Jews." The courtroom drama was poised to expose not just the inner workings of Gray and Fergusson's hit squads but also the lengths to which officials all the way up the chain of command went to cover them up, along with Farran's murderous deed.[42]

In the pared-down, two-day trial that opened on October 1, 1947, Farran refused to testify in the face of possible self-incrimination. The court ruled his confession inadmissible due to an exaggerated interpretation of attorney-client privilege. Without a body, the eyewitness accounts of the abduction were circumstantial. According to Farran's counsel, English law was clear: given the evidence, or lack thereof, the defendant could not be charged with murder. After fifteen minutes of deliberation, the military panel agreed. It acquitted Farran, and cheers of "jolly good show" filled the courtroom packed with British officers. Farran quickly left Palestine for Liverpool where, according to the press, he was greeted with "rounds of cheers from the troops." Hebrew-signed death threats from "The Avenger" and others piled up in Farran's mailbox. Nonetheless, he made his way to London to shake hands with a beaming U.S. general who pinned him with the American Legion of Merit medal for his bravery and leadership during World War II. A few months later Farran was back at Buckingham Palace where George VI decorated him with a Distinguished Service Order medal and whispered to Roy that "he was very glad the whole business was over." The Revisionists, however, were still targeting Roy, leaving a package bomb on his doorstep. It detonated, killing Roy's brother, Rex. The pillar of empire Roy Farran eventually made his way to Canada, where he took his place alongside earlier IRA targets pensioning in the Commonwealth's tundra.[43]

On June 16, as the Farran scandal was unfolding, a British military court found the three Acre prison defendants—Habib, Nakar, and Weiss—guilty, sentencing them to the gallows. Habib addressed the court, paying homage to "the sons of Ireland":

> You [British tyrants] set up gallows, you murdered in the streets, you exiled, you ran amok and stupidly believed that by dint of persecution you would break the spirit of resistance of free Irishmen. . . . If you were wise, British tyrants, and would learn from history, the example of Ireland or of America would be enough to convince you that you ought to hurry out of our country,

which is enveloped in the flames of holy revolt, flames which are not extinguished but only flare up the more with every drop of blood shed by you or in the fight against you.[44]

Britain's commanding military officer refused to commute the execution orders. The Irgun was poised to reciprocate.

Weeks later, on the evening of July 11, 1947, Sergeants Clifford Martin and Mervyn Paice, members of British Army Intelligence, made their way to the Gan Vered Café, a small coffee shop not far from their military camp in north Netanya, where they met with Aharon Weinberg, one of the handful of Haganah intelligence officers who was willing to do business in the aftermath of the King David Hotel bombing and myriad other Revisionist strikes. As they strolled home afterward, a large black sedan pulled up beside them, and five masked men wielding machine guns jumped out, clubbed, chloroformed, and bound and gagged all three, then shoved them into the vehicle and sped off. Martin and Paice were taken to an abandoned diamond factory on the outskirts of the city, where the Irgun held them captive in a specially prepared pitch-black, soundproof, and airless three-cubic-meter underground cell complete with oxygen tanks, food, and a toilet bucket. Begin's men then dumped Weinberg, bound but alive, in a nearby orange grove, where he eventually wrestled his feet free and spread word of the kidnappings. A massive search ensued. Over five thousand soldiers combed a thirty-square-mile cordoned area, and police and army units together with members of the Haganah frantically swept through settlements, businesses, homes, groves, and fields to no avail. The unsuccessful searches and harsh crackdown measures accompanying them triggered seventy separate Revisionist incidents in less than two weeks after the sergeants' abductions, which was more than in the prior three months combined.[45]

On July 29, two weeks after the sergeants' kidnapping, Habib, Nakar, and Weiss sang "Ha-Tikva" as they made their way to the hangman. Hours after their executions, Begin instructed his men to carry out a death sentence on Martin and Paice. Earlier, an Irgun court had found the British sergeants guilty of a host of Revisionist-defined crimes that included "illegal entry into our homeland" and "membership in the British criminal-terrorist organization." Irgun operatives summarily removed the two men from below the diamond factory floor and hung them. For deliberate effect, Begin's men blindfolded the baby-faced soldiers in their khaki shirts, stuffed the sergeants' legs into their original khaki trousers, and bound their hands and bare feet. They also pinned straight through the sergeants' flesh and bloodied undershirts the

Irgun's execution orders. The Zionist insurgents then evaded swarms of security force patrols and, in a nearby eucalyptus grove, hung the bound corpses from a pair of trees. Two days later an army patrol discovered the bodies. The press corps was called to witness the scene. An army captain cut Martin down, and the corpse fell onto an undetected mine below. The blast shredded what was left of the sergeant, hurdled Paice's corpse across the grove, and seriously injured the captain.[46]

The following morning photographs of the mutilated British soldiers, juxtaposed with earlier pictures capturing their schoolboy youth,

"HANGED BRITONS: Picture that will shock the world,"
Daily Express, August 1, 1947

were on the front pages of British newspapers. Responses to the sergeants' deaths were dramatic and defining. "The feeling of revulsion which affected every member of the Government and Security Forces in Palestine cannot be adequately described. . . . Those on the spot were most deeply affected," one member of the Sixth Airborne recalled.[47] For him, the sergeants' deaths changed everything, and the sentiment was widely shared across Britain's security forces.[48] In Tel Aviv, police went on a rampage. They burned buses and homes and tossed grenades into cafés and other civilian establishments. Britain witnessed five days of unprecedented anti-Semitic riots, which broke out first in Liverpool, then spread throughout the country. Rioters burned synagogues and ransacked shops; in all, they destroyed over three hundred Jewish establishments and defaced others with graffiti and signs reading "Hang all Jews," "Hitler was right," and "Destroy Judah."[49] The press fueled public anger. Newspapers printed the mutilated images of the sergeants day after day and often refused to run Jewish condemnations of Revisionist terrorism.

The Zionists weren't alone in deploying brutal tactics and being scorned for them. From the insurgency's inception, the British government had fended off attacks for its counterinsurgency methods, many leveled by the Jewish Agency's information office in coordination with the American press. Some of the charges were wholly justified, the British government knowing well that anti-Semitism was spreading among its security forces. One British officer warned Bevin's office that "Goebbels has many apt pupils wearing British uniform in Palestine" and "suspicion and hatred of the Jews is being widely voiced with the bitterest venom." Whitehall routinely brushed off such concerns. So did High Commissioner Cunningham, who fell back on the standard line: "The British public may be aware of the type of propaganda which is being disseminated about their army which is carrying out in Palestine, with characteristic patience, restraint and good humour, a difficult and distasteful job." To get ahead of the conversation, the British government embedded its own press officers within the security forces, hoping to publish propaganda before real newsmen published their accounts. When this proved inadequate, Cunningham deployed censorship measures similar to those that had shut down the information flow during the Arab Revolt. The network of Hebrew presses and watchful international eyes, however, made a complete clampdown on information impossible.[50]

In Britain, anti-Semitism's rise corresponded with the Revisionists' relentless attacks against "British prestige." As far as Bevin was concerned, the Jews had themselves to thank for this outcome. "I've always been of the opinion that Hitler's treatment of the Jewish people was the right one," a middle-aged Briton declared. "The only thing I disapprove of with regard to Hitler's gas chambers was that there were not enough and that they were not efficiently run." The Conservative dailies, in particular, zeroed in on Revisionist violence relative to that of Britain's security forces. *The Daily Mirror* routinely referred to "Jew terror," and only *The Daily Herald* and a handful of other left-wing presses gave any attention to those in the Jewish community who emphatically stood "against any form of terrorism." By the time the *Daily Express* plastered Martin's and Paice's corpses on its front page, declaring it a "picture that will shock the world," press demand for more British repression was rising. The public shared this sentiment, particularly "amongst the working classes," as Bevin was quick to point out.[51] As far as many Britons were concerned, liberal imperialism was literally being blown to smithereens and its entrails scattered across the Holy Land for all to see. Either Attlee's men had to crush the Zionists using every means necessary, or Britain had to get out of Palestine.

British imperial pride and calls for vengeance were not the only salient issues. There were also matters of economy. While many in Attlee's government saw the empire as a potential postwar treasure chest, others like Chancellor of the Exchequer Dalton looked at the money pit that was Palestine with alarm. With nearly one-tenth of the army deployed there, the war was costing British taxpayers £40 million a year in military expenses alone. "The time has come not to examine international or Arab or Jewish or even American interests in Palestine, but to write the British balance sheet," *The Economist* said in August 1947. "Why should the British community bear the cost? For one thing is certain. The cost of Palestine to Britain is incalculable."[52] Britain's civilizing mission was now bankrupt in more ways than one. Jettisoning the Balfour Declaration and instituting partition were the only solutions, as far as *The Economist* was concerned, "not primarily because it is in the best interests of the Jews or the Arabs, or of the international community in general, it is simply because it is in the best interests of the long-suffering British."[53]

Once again the repressive center could not hold, and Begin was promising to finish Britain off in Palestine. "You did not expect it—dirty oppressors? But we warned you," the Irgun's underground radio, Voice of Fighting Zion, announced in August, days before *The Economist* voiced its concerns. "We warned you day in and day out, that just as we smashed your whips we would uproot your gallows—or, if we did not succeed in uprooting them, we would set up next to your gallows, gallows for you. . . . And we have not yet settled our hanging accounts with you, Nazi-British enslavers."[54] The Labour MP Harold Lever castigated his government for "two years of planless, gutless and witless behavior which has not only cost us treasure in terms of money but uncountable treasure in manpower and loss of life . . . [and was] polluting English public-life with anti-Semitism." He also inveighed on behalf of "the sanctity of human life." Colonial Secretary Creech Jones's "unflinching determination" in Palestine was nothing more than a repeat of the Irish show where, according to Lever, "we went too late. . . . We stayed on in Ireland until we were virtually driven out."[55] Churchill urged his fellow members in the House to "take stock round the world at the present moment":

> We declare ourselves ready to abandon the mighty Empire and Continent of India with all the work we have done in the last 200 years, territory over which we possess unimpeachable sovereignty. The Government are, apparently, ready to leave 400 million Indians to fall into all the horrors of sanguinary civil war—civil war compared to which anything that could happen in Palestine would be microscopic; wars of elephants compared with wars of mice.[56]

Churchill's prescience would play out in India on a tragically epic scale, as we've seen, though not because civil war was inevitable without British rule. Rather, it was Britain's method of rule in India, dividing populations and hastily abdicating responsibility in the face of incipient violence, that helped define the Raj's legacy. Events were poised to obliterate the remaining luster on British imperial resurgence in Palestine.

The UN Special Committee on Palestine hastened Britain's exit terms. In the summer of 1947, its delegation undertook a probing fact-finding mission, and two of its members were on hand to witness yet another British public relations disaster. The Royal Navy had been intercepting Jewish immigrants en route to Palestine, who were then deported to European displaced persons camps. For many observers, these operations were the hallmark of British callousness. Behind the scenes, MI6 worked clandestinely to stymie the flow of Jewish refugees to Palestine. Its "Embarrass" operation targeted passenger-less, docked refugee boats, either sabotaging or blowing them up. The British government then blamed the Defenders of Arab Palestine, a fictive organization of Britain's own making, and also spread lies that the Soviets, too, were involved.[57]

That Britain had thought it a good idea to intercept the *Exodus* on July 18, 1947, while the UN's special committee was undertaking its work in Palestine, was sheer folly. Bevin's Foreign Office took charge of the operation. Having set sail from France, the boat carried 4,500 Holocaust survivors. As it neared Palestine, British troops boarded it, and after a fierce hand-to-hand struggle, three Jews were dead and scores of others injured. Security forces awaited the seized vessel at Haifa, where its men forced the remaining refugees onto three British boats primed to carry their human cargo back to Europe. Nearly all the Holocaust survivors aboard were deposited in Hamburg, from where they were taken by rail to either Poppendorf or Am Stau, two displaced persons camps. Three members of the UN's special committee witnessed the events play out in Palestine.[58] Bevin's attempt to "teach the Jews a lesson" backfired, and even Weizmann, the staunchest of Anglophiles, thought him "brutal, vulgar and anti-Semitic."[59]

In September 1947, the UN Special Committee on Palestine released a hundred-plus-page report. Its eleven members unanimously recommended ending the British mandate in Palestine, and the majority supported partition. Two months later, the UN general assembly overwhelmingly supported the adoption of Resolution 181: Palestine, after a period of British mandatory trusteeship to end no later than August 1, 1948, would be carved into two independent states, one Arab the other Jewish, linked by a joint economic oversight board, as well as a "special international regime" for the City of Jerusalem administered by the UN. The Zionists accepted the partition plan, while Arabs in Palestine and in the surrounding states unanimously rejected it.[60]

Bevin and other British officials had miscalculated UN sentiment and underestimated Sumner Welles's organizing ability in support of the Zionist cause. A seasoned veteran in international affairs as the former United States undersecretary of state (1936–1943), Welles thought Bevin a "dangerous perpetuator of Churchill's 'imperialist' policies," so much so that he had a name for the foreign secretary's brand of postwar British imperialism: "Bevin-pox." Welles was "one of the masterminds behind the Zionist United Nations strategy," according to the historian William Roger Louis, working his contacts and lobbying tirelessly for pro-Zionist votes on the partition plan, particularly among the UN's Latin American representatives. When news broke on the UN's approval, Weizmann's first celebratory call was to Welles, who gained some satisfaction knowing the UN proved a vital venue in his broader efforts to bring down the British Empire.[61]

A sick child is removed from the *Exodus*, 1947

Clearly Bevin's gambit for greater Zionist concessions to the Arabs had failed. Rather than caving at the threat of Britain going to the UN, the Zionists ratcheted up their attacks, and the colonial state lost its monopoly on legitimate violence. Still, Britain remained focused on the Middle East and the "retention of Arab good will."[62] That British forces had blown up Jewish refugee boats and blamed the Arabs and Soviets for their handiwork mattered little in Bevin's calculus of fairness. As far as he was concerned, the UN recommendation was "so manifestly unjust to the Arabs that it is difficult to see how . . . we could reconcile it with our conscience."[63] In his mind and that of the collective cabinet, the only option was immediate withdrawal. "British lives," he reasoned, "would not be lost, nor British forces expended, in suppressing one Palestinian community to the advantage of the other, and we should not be pursuing a policy destructive of our own interests in the Middle East."[64] By the end of September, prior to the general assembly vote, Creech Jones had already informed the United Nations of his government's "plan for an early withdrawal of British forces and of the British administration from Palestine."[65]

Hemorrhaging money and men, with the Mandate poised to descend into civil war, Britain moved its exit date forward. In their final months, Palestine's administrators, confined largely to their security zones, which the locals derisively called "Bevingrads," destroyed docu-

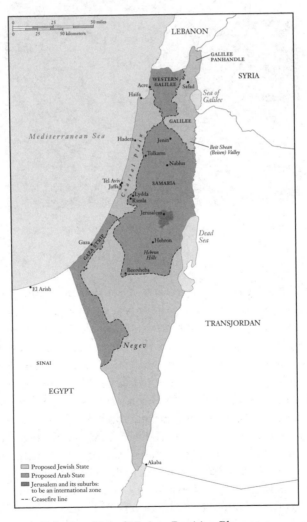

Palestine, United Nations Partition Plan, 1947

ments. James Pollock, the Irish pro-Unionist and former district commissioner of Jerusalem, justified the destruction as a "usual practice" for British imperial retreat.[66] Other officials divvied up horses and the ever-present South African Dobermans. Meanwhile the security forces were subsumed in a civil war that escalated as the date of their withdrawal drew near. Some of their members openly participated in anti-Zionist attacks, while others deserted to assist the Arabs in preparations for their coming war against the Yishuv. "The last three months in Palestine were quite horrific," police officer John Sankey recalled. "We no longer had authority in fact. The two communities were then establishing themselves within their enclaves, and we were driving through, sort of Jewish road blocks and Arab road blocks, and having to submit to being stopped. . . . Clearly we had no more authority, and we were no longer a police force. Just in name."[67] The Zionist War of Independence was already well under way. For the Arabs, it was the start of the Nakba, or the Catastrophe. The British presence quickly became a sideshow to the civil struggle for Palestine's future, and High Commissioner Cunningham, secretly a Zionist, felt he had to remain neutral; it was therefore his duty "to allow both sides to defend themselves."[68]

On May 14, 1948, at Government House on Jerusalem's Mount Zion, Cunningham struck the Union Jack, while a lone officer's bagpipe wept the Highland Lament. Cunningham then flew to Haifa, where magnesium-fueled tracers were streaking red across the port city's blinding blue sky, a sign of the civil conflict at hand. He inspected an honor guard for the last time, then climbed into the back seat of his armor-plated car with one-inch-thick windows, built during the Blitz for George VI. The vehicle wove through what remained of Haifa's streets, stopping twice at Jewish and Arab checkpoints, and deposited Palestine's last high commissioner at the dock, where he boarded his cruiser, HMS *Euryalus*.[69]

With His Majesty's last ship sailing out of Haifa and thirty years of tumultuous British rule in Palestine over, the Zionists declared the establishment of the State of Israel, and the territory descended into a brutal war. Nearby Arab countries sent troops, and the Zionists organized the new Israeli Defense Force (IDF), deriving tactics and strategies from years of British training during the Arab Revolt and the Second World War.[70] By the time the fighting paused, the Zionists had ground down Arab homes, villages, and communities in ways reminiscent of Britain's 1930s tactics. "More than half of Palestine's native population, close to 800,000 people, had been uprooted," according to the historian Ilan Pappe. "531 villages had been destroyed, and eleven urban neighbour-

Chaim Weizmann, president of the State of Israel, February 20, 1949

hoods emptied of their inhabitants."[71] The massive dislocated population sought refuge in nearby Arab states or in the Palestinian territories
that Egypt and Jordan had captured. The 1948 war proved to be the first
of many conflicts, all sides of the Arab-Zionist divide having historically
rooted claims to Palestine. It was the gift that the Balfour Declaration
and Britain's vacillating, self-interested policies bequeathed to them.
The use of state-directed violence to enforce British policies and interests created a culture of violence, the legacy of which fueled sensibilities,
tactics, and strategies in the Mandate's aftermath. "I would go so far as
to say, after this period of time, that the whole of the troubles in the
Middle East which have affected the world since 1948, can be laid fairly
and squarely at Britain's door," John Beard, who served in the Palestine
Police Force for nearly thirty years, recalled.[72]

In Britain, exit from the Mandate was another clumsy and humiliating sign of imperial decline. "What I cannot respect is our simply throwing over the work of 30 years to destruction and washing our hands of
all responsibility for either Jews or Arabs," said Leo Amery, a onetime
member of Alfred Milner's "kindergarten" and a bellicose imperialist.

"It looks as if our whole moral, as well as material position in the Middle East has been disastrously weakened. We shall not win any favour from the Arabs over this."[73] Such concerns would recede as Britain eventually recognized the State of Israel with Ben-Gurion and Weizmann serving as its first prime minister and president, respectively. It also crafted a triumphant narrative, entwining the heroics of Orde Wingate with the history of Israel. In 1990 in the Victoria Embankment Gardens, not far from London's Ministry of Defence, Prince Philip unveiled a monument to Wingate, whose untimely demise at forty-one in a plane crash over northern India during World War II, his body and those of the other men in his Chindit force charred beyond recognition, only added to his legend. Beneath the memorial's life-size profile of Wingate is etched: "A man of genius who might well have become a

Chindit war memorial in Victoria Embankment Gardens, London

man of destiny." This epitaph, bestowed by Churchill, is accompanied by a second one: "An Important Influence in the Creation of the Israel Defence Force and the Foundation of the State of Israel."[74]

Such sentiments are not solely British. "Wingate was the father of the IDF," Israeli Knesset member Michael Oren recently said. "The IDF today remains Wingatean in terms of its tactics." On the seventy-fifth anniversary of Wingate's death in March 2019, *The Times of Israel* offered a lengthy tribute to the man who "might have become the Israel Defence Force's first chief of staff" had he lived. "Few non-Jews and even fewer British soldiers are regarded as highly in Israel as Orde Charles Wingate, a senior officer who became a legend here by shaping Israel's prestate military," the article effused. "Many Israeli towns have a Wingate street or square, and relatives and others who share his name are often reminded of Israel's debt to him."[75]

At the time of Britain's ignominious retreat from Palestine, other legacies of British rule there rippled through the empire. The Palestine Police Force would have a vastly disproportionate influence over colonial policing tactics and personnel. In the 1930s, the Mandate was the empire's chief training ground not only for the rank and file but also for those destined to lead. Between 1926 and 1947, around ten thousand men passed through either the police training depot at Jenin or the potential officers training unit outside Ramallah. Over these decades, Palestine's police force developed a culture all its own. The early years of Irish influence mattered greatly, but so did the acculturating effects of British rule in Palestine. It had developed its own ethos, training methods, and traditions. Indeed, just as events in Palestine were crucial to the convergence and consolidation of colonial-era legalized lawlessness during the Arab Revolt, they were also pivotal in the evolution of paramilitary mindsets, tactics, and equipment that undulated through the empire with the circulation of thousands of men trained and combat-tested in Palestine.[76]

Two months after Britain's retreat from the Mandate, Inspector General Nicol Gray stood one last time before his Palestine policemen adorned in their full-dress uniforms, hundreds of them assembled in perfectly aligned rows, eyes forward. Their steely upright postures betrayed a sense of unmitigated pride as George VI, clad in full military dress, surveyed them. There, at Buckingham Palace, they took their final stand down in a ceremony loaded with imperial ritual. With cameras on hand to capture images for the next day's dailies, His Majesty put a final discursive imprint on the Mandate's narrative when he declared to Gray and his force, "You can look back on a job well done."[77]

Richard Catling was among those in attendance. He was still reeling from "the shock" of Britain's retreat and from the anger, humiliation, anxiety, and frustration that had accompanied Britain's final years in Palestine.[78] He was not alone. General Evelyn Barker remained furious that "our officers in Palestine were kidnapped, killed and even flogged," and Chief Secretary Henry Gurney chalked the whole debacle up to "stupidity" that "the American press and American Zionists" only hastened.[79] As far as the former Inspector General Gray was concerned:

> An empire can permit itself to be unjust, even tyrannical and terrifying. It can permit itself defeats on the battlefield or in the diplomatic arena; but it cannot allow itself one thing: to lose prestige and become a laughingstock. When the underground killed our men, we could treat it as murder; but when they erected gallows and executed our men, it was as if they were saying, "We rule here as much as you do," and that no administration can bear. Our choice was obvious. Either total suppression or get out, and we chose the second.[80]

When George VI congratulated those assembled in July 1948 for "a job well done," he also emboldened them for their next imperial mission. Nearly fourteen hundred disbanded Palestine policemen soon fanned out across the empire and the Commonwealth. One of them was John Coles, who developed a strike force in the Gold Coast similar to the Mandate's. There, in Britain's West African colony, dozens of other former Palestine policemen joined him. The Gold Coast's force expanded to eight thousand, suppressing local rioting and nationalist demands emerging from Kwame Nkrumah and his supporters, some of whom had incubated ideas alongside George Padmore in London. Other agents of empire who had learned ideas and techniques in Britain also made their way to the Gold Coast. Among them was Robin "Tin Eye" Stephens, fresh from his acquittal on charges of torture in the postwar interrogation cells in Bad Nenndorf.

Appointed as a special liaison officer between MI5 and the local colonial government, Stephens had a direct pipeline to Governor Charles Arden-Clarke. The relationship reflected Stephens's track record and skills. For years, he routinely oversaw torture techniques to get suspects to talk. He also tapped into British operations in London, where agents ran extensive surveillance on the West African National Secretariat.

Indeed, Home Office warrants kept MI5 abreast of the West African organization's activities. Nkrumah was the West African National Secretariat's general secretary, and he considered the organization crucial. Its hub in London was a "rendezvous" location, according to Nkrumah, "of all African and West Indian students and their friends. It was there that we used to assemble to discuss our plans, to voice our opinions and air our grievances." As the direct conduit to the Gold Coast after 1948, Stephens passed the Home Office's surveillance of Nkrumah's London operations on to the colony's governor. Stephens sent back to London intelligence that he and his men pried loose in the Gold Coast.[81]

The Gold Coast was one of several locations around the empire beset with possible Communist threats. In February 1948, in the face of local riots, colonial authorities arrested and locked up Nkrumah. They had discovered on him an unsigned Communist Party of Great Britain membership card, along with notes on something called the "Circle," an organization about which local intelligence knew nothing. While Coles, Stephens, and others on the ground investigated, in London top security officials such as Guy Liddell retained their liberal imperial views:

> In so far as West and East Africa were concerned, there was no evidence of Communism as it was understood in Europe, there was no local Communist Party. There was, however, a lot of nationalism, which received considerable encouragement from all sorts of people who went out to preach British democracy. It was true that niggers coming here often went to the C.P. This did not mean that they were Communists or that they understood anything about Karl Marx or dialectical materialism: it merely meant that they found the Communists sympathetic because they had no racial discrimination and were all in favour of the niggers running their own show.[82]

Thousands of miles away in Malaya, another rebellion was brewing. There the disastrous legacies of the war, together with Britain's self-interested recovery efforts, witnessed rising levels of civil and labor conflict. Communism also spread among parts of the colony's Chinese population. On June 16, 1948, three young Chinese, aggrieved by their exploitative conditions, pedaled to the Elphil estate in Sungai Siput, in the colony's northern region, and shot its manager dead. The same day a dozen other similarly aggrieved Chinese surrounded two European planters on the Phin Soon estate and executed them on their veranda chairs. Two days later Britain declared a circumscribed state of emergency.[83] Attlee's government turned to those who had just exited Palestine to enforce it. One of Britain's top choices to lead the way in Malaya was Nicol Gray. Palestine's former inspector general of police took to Kuala Lumpur his paramilitary training and his particular brand of leadership, along with nearly five hundred of his policemen, many of them self-described as disgraced, angry, and demoralized over the Mandate's loss. Initially, Richard Catling was not among them. Had he not caught Gray's eye at Buckingham Palace, he would have gone to Greece. But Gray needed Catling's help in Malaya's intelligence unit and wouldn't take no for an answer. "You're coming with me!" Gray barked to his old comrade, and by August 1948, the two men and scores of others fresh out of the crucible that was Palestine's final months were on planes to the Malay Peninsula where familiar tactics and heated emotions would be redeployed against a new enemy.[84]

To understand why Gray, Catling, and hundreds of former Palestine policemen were en route to Kuala Lumpur, we need to return to Southeast Asia in the aftermath of the Second World War. A chain of events, each one contingent on the one before, fueled Chinese anger that had been building around British economic policies and concerted attempts to engineer a postwar multiracial society. Colonial administrators, however, underestimated local ways of configuring society and of ensuring long-held ethnic power. These struggles coalesced, and as often happened, isolated events, in this case the murders of Malaya's European planters in June 1948, trigged the empire's defenses.

The British designed passing-out rituals, elaborate ceremonies marking the completion of military or policing service, to confirm imperial narratives and reaffirm power. Such rites, however, were not restricted to parades on Pall Mall and the grandeur of Buckingham Palace. In Malaya, nearly three years before the Palestine veterans boarded their planes for Kuala Lumpur, Ho Thean Fook stood in Alor Star, a city near Malaya's west coast, among spectators jostling to catch a glimpse of the dignitaries who stood on the dais. Countless others crammed the streets outside to take in the moment as neighboring locals leaned out their windows overlooking the spectacle. It was mid-November 1945, and the city was host to members of the Malayan Peoples' Anti-Japanese Army, Ho among them, who paraded through the town before they assembled in front of Britain's highest-ranking officer. General Frank Messervy promised them land for cultivation, hawkers' licenses, and mechanical training, together with $350 to "tide [them] over until [they] were settled in civil life."[85]

For British officials, the day was a symbolic end to the humbling and disgraceful necessities that Singapore's fall engendered, and a return to Malaya's status quo. Yet as army members like Ho took in the RAF aircraft "flying demonstration sorties" and listened to "God Save the King," they were reminded of their subjecthood. Ho and his compatriots wondered what their three years of grueling jungle life and resistance to Japan's occupation had done for them. Returning to the barracks, he recalled that the former guerrillas "surrendered their weapons by throwing them into a heap as if they were old brooms," after which they burned their copies of Messervy's speech along with the empire's other parting gifts. "Of what use were the showy flashes, ribbons and campaign medals to us now that the war was over?" Ho brooded. "We could not buy a cup of coffee or exchange them for a plate of *mee rebus* [a noodle dish], could we?" He spent $150 from his pay to purchase some waxed duck, a salty preserved meat. It was an indulgence that drowned his thoughts as he contemplated what next to do with his life.[86]

At first glance, Ho did not look like a guerrilla fighter. An ethnic Chinese born and raised in Ipoh, Ho was a well-educated English teacher with a bespectacled, studious face. He harbored little Communist sympathies either before or after the war. Instead, he was an aspiring middle-class young man who wanted to teach his students and "get married and raise a family like any other ordinary human being."[87] The global conflict, however, put such youthful dreams on hold. He recalled the disbelief that washed over him and his educated Chinese friends as the "short, puny Japanese soldiers" beat "the tall, big white men" all the way down Malaya's spine to Singapore.[88] After relentless aerial assaults decimated Ipoh, Japanese trucks rambled through its streets, and Ho remembered that "fear and anxiety" were rampant, but they didn't paralyze him.[89] As the Japanese put to death his countrymen or marched them off to prison camps, he and six friends heard the Communists' resistance message, spreading in cover-of-darkness meetings, and decided to join the movement. In the face of looming Japanese oppression, the Communists' message transcended ideology and spoke to Ho. He and his friends soon entered the underground, having gathered tommy guns and cartridges from Australian soldiers killed in action, and bicycled their way by night toward the jungle's edge. With the support of other civilians who fed and protected them, Ho and his companions reached the guerrilla camp of the incipient Malayan People's Anti-Japanese Army.[90]

Behind enemy lines in Malaya's dense jungles, a disparate group converged. Among the four thousand men and women were Chinese Communists, townsfolk, and triage nurse Anthony Daniels, who had survived the last-stand effort against Yamashita's army in Singapore. Together with men and women like Ho, they comprised eight regionally divided regiments, spearheaded and controlled by the Malayan Communist Party. British officials had a long-standing relationship with the party's general secretary, Lai Teck, also known as "Mr. Wright," who was Britain's most valuable double agent in Malaya. Chin Peng, the party's second-in-command, was not in Britain's hip pocket, but the war created allies overnight, and Chin proved himself "Britain's most trusted guerrilla fighter," according to one of his British colleagues in the unit.[91] In fact, Britain's special ops Force 136 provided training for him and over 150 members of Malaya's resistance army at its special training school. There another British officer declared these men "probably the best material we had ever had at the School" and lauded "the rank and file" with whom he fought alongside in the jungles as "absolutely magnificent." "I can hardly find words to express my admiration for their courage, fortitude, and consistent cheerfulness in adversity," he later effused.[92]

Force 136 also offered the guerrillas logistical support in their hit-and-run efforts against the Japanese. But it was the Chinese civilian resistance that proffered some of the most crucial aid. The Japanese Army dealt swiftly and harshly with them. The Sook Ching (purification by elimination) Operation that took place after Singapore's fall offered a preview of what was to come for those whom the British had left behind in the region. It claimed the lives of 25,000 to 50,000 Chinese whom the Japanese first indiscriminately screened for antifascist sentiments before killing them, often in the most brutal of ways.[93] The Malayan People's Anti-Japanese Army worked assiduously to cultivate ideological and material support from the hundreds of thousands of ethnic Chinese who had fled the urban areas and lived as squatters in the relative safety of the jungle's edges. This squatter population had been accordion-like in size since the First World War. Many ethnic Chinese moved in and out of marginal land for subsistence with the rise and fall of employment opportunities in the territory's tin mines and rubber plantations. With Japanese occupation, the mass exodus to the jungle's periphery saw squatter numbers reach four hundred thousand.[94] Many of them constituted a front organization known as the Malayan People's Anti-Japanese Union. It provided Chin Peng's men with an extensive underground network of supporters who offered food, clothing, funds, weapons, intelligence, and dozens of new recruits.[95]

Admiral Lord Louis Mountbatten congratulating Chin Peng, Singapore, 1945

Chin Peng's followers were anti-imperialist, whether the foreign rule be Asian or European. After the Second World War, the British military high command initially brushed aside the Malayan army's vital contributions to Allied victory in the East. The guerrillas, for their part, emerged from their encampments and unleashed a new form of terror on suspected Japanese collaborators—or "running dogs," as the Communists termed them. Kangaroo courts tried them, and angry mobs took over the region with vigilante justice. Distinctions between criminality and ideology blurred. The civil conflict was precisely the pretext that the British Military Administration needed to reassert colonial control in Malaya with its own form of liberal imperial harshness.[96]

On January 6, 1946, two months after Ho's passing-out ritual in Alor Star, Supreme Allied Commander Louis Mountbatten—who, as we've seen, would oversee India during the Raj's final days—held another ceremony in Singapore. It marked an end, as well as an ill-fated beginning. Shifting from their earlier dismissive course, British officials put Chin Peng and seven other Malayan People's Anti-Japanese Army leaders up

Malaya in 1945

in Singapore's Raffles Hotel. They wined and dined the wartime guerrillas before the supremo himself awarded each of them with the Burma Star and the 1939/45 Star. With crowds and photographers there to bear witness, the event was a resplendent affair. Its meticulous choreography projected a Britain that was now firmly in control as Mountbatten, clad in white military dress, represented the king and the empire. But rather than symbolically kissing the imperial ring with a formal salute, all eight men stood before Mountbatten with their clenched fists straight in the air. Whatever goodwill might have remained between the onetime allies was evaporating.[97]

Two and a half years later, when the Chinese Communists took out the three European planters in cold blood, it took many by surprise, including Chin Peng and High Commissioner Edward Gent. In the intervening years, Britain had sought to establish greater political control and a new inclusive citizenship status across Malaya. The territory was 465 miles long, about the size of England, and geographically, politically, and ethnically divided. Separating the South China Sea from the Bay of Bengal, the Malay Peninsula was home to mountains covered in a sweltering jungle that cut through the territory's middle from north to south, blanketing nearly 75 percent of it. Along the coastline, plains were home to vast estates, mines, and semihabitable jungle fringes. British rule was a hodgepodge of political units. Malay sultans governed nine protectorates and Britain directly ruled Singapore as well as Penang and Malacca, which were crown colonies and collectively known as the Straits Settlements.

In April 1946, Britain combined the nine Malayan protectorates and the Straits Settlements into a single political entity, the Malayan Union, while leaving Singapore as a separate crown colony. It was a British attempt to impose political order under a banner of multiracialism. In real time, partnership meant aggressive attempts to engineer postwar Malayan nationalism and identity. It also sought to circumscribe the sultans' influence by centralizing the power of the Malay states and Malacca and Penang into a single, directly ruled British entity. Britain also sought to confer "Malayan Union Citizenship," a distinct common citizenship status, on all locally born Chinese and Indians, who would join the Malay population already holding citizenship claims bestowed by the sultans. The newly formed United Malays National Organisation, comprised almost entirely of Malays, rebuffed British plans. For the organization's members, Britain was violating the inviolable: the nominal sovereignty of Malay rulers and the privileges of their constituents that extended back to the eighteenth century.[98]

Of the 5 million people who inhabited Malaya and Singapore after the Second World War, Malays comprised 50 percent of the population, Chinese made up 38 percent, and a religiously diverse mix of Indians 11 percent; several smaller groups comprised the remaining 1 percent.[99] In the postwar years, all three communities felt the full weight of Britain's imperial resurgence as fleets of technocrats, welfare officers, and social science researchers bore down on the peninsula as never before. Britain expected Malaya's indigenous communities, still reeling from the war's effects, to lift themselves out of traumatized poverty largely through self-help. Communism found further traction, and by 1947 the Malayan Communist Party boasted twelve thousand members, nearly all of whom were Chinese, though by no means were all Chinese Communists. Chinese of many political persuasions joined Indian and other laborers in the broad-based Pan-Malayan Federation of Trade Unions, boasting over a quarter-million members. Countless strikes—some three hundred in 1947 alone that led to a loss of well over a million man-days of work—rocked the Malay Peninsula, in an escalating cycle of violence and government crackdowns that witnessed British troops opening fire on civilian hunger marches.[100] Malays were staging bitter protests under the United Malays National Organisation banner, and the sultans boycotted the Malayan Union altogether. Sparked by layers of local conflicts, communal violence wracked the rural areas,

Rubber production in Malaya

compounding Britain's problems. One British Military Administration officer described a postmassacre scene along the Perak River, recalling that "we poled down the river in sampans. . . . There were dead men, women and children, all Malay, lying everywhere for about a mile and a half along the riverside . . . the total was 56."[101]

Britain wanted political and civil order to facilitate economic control. Most workers across the region, some of whom were demobilized members of the Malayan People's Anti-Japanese Army, survived the war only to inhabit a world riddled with social crises, homelessness, disease, and semistarvation. Into this world, Britain introduced its second colonial occupation, resulting in high unemployment, inflation, and increased taxes. To satisfy domestic economic needs, colonial officials sacrificed those of their subjects, while rescuing Malaya's planters and miners to bring crucial dollars from the lucrative rubber and tin industries into the sterling area. After the war, 30 percent of Malaya's exports went to the United States. British exchange controls, which reduced American imports thus conserving dollars, meant that Malaya had a trade surplus with the United States that surpassed the empire's top four dollar-earning colonies combined. In 1948, while Britain suffered from an overall $1.8 billion deficit, Malaya brought in $170 million, followed by the Gold Coast at $47.5 million, the Gambia at $24.5 million, and Ceylon at $23 million.[102] Malaya was the empire's cash cow, and worker protest and local communal violence threatened it.

The death knell to the supposed era of multiracial liberalization was rung when the Federation of Malaya replaced the contentious Union in February 1948. This new political entity turned the imperial clock back to the pre-1941 era. The sultans maintained their nominal sovereignty, the Malay elites kept their positions within federal bureaucracies, and Britain ensured that their Malay constituents would have certain citizenship rights while denying them to much of the Chinese and Indian populations. Some Chinese families had resided in Malacca since Portuguese rule centuries earlier, but under the new Federation, the citizenship bar was set incredibly high for them. A non-Malay had to have lived in the Federation for fifteen years, with both parents born in the Federation. While most non-Malays born in Malacca and Penang (the Settlements) were British subjects, the vast majority of those born in any one of the nine Malay states were considered "aliens." In contemporary terms, they were stateless.[103]

Nonetheless, the colonial state managed to strengthen its centralized hand. Under a high commissioner, a strong bureaucracy and laws ensured the local European planter class its much-needed labor by reducing wages, limiting trade union activities, and cracking down on trade union recruitment.[104] Long-cultivated cultural norms guaranteed the European population its position atop Malayan society. Indeed, nothing proclaimed exclusive British "civility" like Kuala Lumpur's Lake Club, where the colony's privileged whites found their enclave. Overseeing it all was the governor-general of Malaya and Singapore, Malcolm Mac-Donald, an Attlee appointee and the son of Labour's first prime minister, Ramsay MacDonald. The Oxford-educated younger MacDonald brought with him a wide range of imperial experience. He had served as colonial secretary twice and had been secretary of the dominion office. In fact, Malcolm MacDonald had been colonial secretary during Palestine's Arab Revolt and had prepared the White Paper that limited Jewish immigration to the Mandate both during and after the Second World War. Prior to taking up his post in Southeast Asia, the itinerant imperial standby had been high commissioner to Canada. Arriving in Kuala Lumpur with his young Canadian wife in 1946, MacDonald, much like the flying ace Arthur Harris in 1930s Palestine, was at the center of the local social scene. While the Lake Club remained a sort of British Eden, the governor-general did undertake to integrate local elites in the hotels, dance halls, and golf courses before the whole multiracial enterprise plummeted. Even then, many Chinese and Indian businessmen, some of whom had vast holdings throughout the peninsula, had far more in common with the European company directors and plantation and mine owners than they did with ordinary laborers. Men and women like Ho found themselves somewhere in between these extremes.[105]

Despite the peninsula's enduring conflicts, the local Malayan Security Service gave MacDonald and Malaya's High Commissioner Gent a measure of assurance. On June 14, 1948, it issued a report insisting there was "no immediate threat to internal security in Malaya," though offering the obvious caution that "the position is constantly changing and is potentially dangerous."[106] Meanwhile in 1947 Chin Peng ascended to general secretary of the Malayan Communist Party, after its members had finally uncovered his predecessor's double dealings and, according to reports, assassinated him across the border in Thailand. The upheaval within the party and Chin Peng's regrouping hardly spelled the moment for a major strike against imperial rule. Instead, the movement's radicalism surged on its own. Chinese grassroots demands for change, a better life without discrimination, were behind the planters' murders. These assassinations took place just two days after the Malayan Security Service issued its "no immediate threat report." Chinese vigilantes were also responsible for the elimination of Chinese labor contractors, who were as much their targets as the European planters because of their association with exploitative wage and labor regulations.[107] There was no top-down Chinese Communist plot to overthrow British rule in mid-June 1948, though Britain's immediate state-of-emergency response raised tensions.

It was into this uncertainty that Gray, Catling, and other Palestine Police Force veterans arrived in Singapore in August 1948. So swift was their dispatch that men like James Niven arrived fully kitted out in "Palestine Police uniforms and caps and PP badges." Still embittered from having "no more authority" as a force in the Mandate, they were ready to reclaim their imperially prescribed manhood.[108] In short order, *Palestinian* replaced *Black and Tan* as the empire's new watchword for legalized lawlessness. The "Old Malayans," as the existing force was known, chafed against Gray's appointment because it bucked internal promotion expectations. When several of Gray's Palestinians, like Catling, assumed leadership positions within the force, animosities ran even higher. It was a move the Old Malayans described as the "promotion of Palestinian henchmen." When Gray packed the upper ranks of police with his Palestinian men, the locals called them the "Praetorian Guard."[109] Several Old Malayans petitioned the Colonial Office, reminding its officials that "economic considerations" took priority over security in the war's aftermath. Moreover, only they understood the "ordinary illiterate or semi literate classes which make up the great body of the Malayan public." As far as the Old Malayans were concerned, locally honed paternalism rendered them omniscient on when "to be tough" with their "natives" and "just how 'tough' to be" without engendering "bitterness." However, under Gray and his "totalitarian police state," the old force, according to some of its members, became "a bunch of school prefects" who could only say yes to Gray and his "commando tactics in the suppression of terrorism."[110]

In the summer of 1948, the Old Malayan police force was still recovering from the years of Japanese occupation. Some of the men had barely survived Japan's prisoner of war camps. Eleven thousand were left to patrol a population of 5 million people. Only twelve British officers spoke Chinese, and there were only 228 Chinese police force members. The heterogeneity of the Chinese community—which included groups speaking Hokkien, Mandarin, and Cantonese dialects—further exacerbated the forces' limited language and cultural skills.[111] The government's immediate dispatching of the so-called Palestinians was not just about much-needed manpower, however. Their arrival witnessed the reinvention of Palestine's ill-fated covert squads as "Ferret Forces," which included several of Orde Wingate's protégés.[112] It wasn't long before government reports noted local complaints: "the Force is ceasing to be a Police Force and is becoming a paramilitary organisation."[113] The British government, however, had selected Gray and his men for their jobs in 1948 Malaya precisely to create a coercive police force. As one of Gray's biographers points out, he "was not appointed as a diplomat, nor even as a policeman, but as a soldier taking command of a gendarmerie that was in grave danger of losing control."[114] This point was further driven home when a police mission sent to investigate Gray dismissed the "Old Malayans'" claims that a dysfunctional "totalitarian" regime had sidelined them.[115]

Even before the "Palestinians" arrived on the scene, planters and mine owners called for more draconian methods. The local *Straits Times* had summed up demands that harkened back to Britain's humiliations in the Mandate: "Govern or get out."[116] Many planters were also wartime veterans, and some had served in Force 136. They quickly hunkered down behind self-fashioned fortresses of barbed wire, spotlights, trenches, and booby traps filled with broken glass and other shrapnel. They amassed their own private armies, complete with American-funded ammunition to protect rubber destined for U.S. markets, and bullet-proof vehicles jerry-rigged from rusted-out Japanese tanks.[117]

At the start of the emergency, looking to arrest and detain the Federation's Communist leadership and any local leader who defied Britain's attempts to control the political and economic future of the region, security forces launched Operation Frustration, a clamp-down on all forms of democratic activity. It effectively decapitated political organizations, except for the United Malays National Organisation. It also gave Chin Peng, who managed to evade the operation, a recruiting bonanza. Former members of the Malayan Peoples' Anti-Japanese Army fled to the jungles in fear of arrest. The Malayan Communist Party reconstituted between two and three thousand of them, eventually calling the new insurgent group the Malayan National Liberation Army.[118] The Chinese civilian population that had been a backbone of guerrilla support during the war emerged as a crucial passive wing offering information and supplies from the little it had. Known as the Min Yuen, or "People's Movement," the civilian supporters—some enthusiastic and others coerced into supplying Chin Peng's forces—were drawn largely from the five hundred thousand squatters who lived on the jungle's edges.[119]

The British government at home reckoned there were between 2,200 and 6,100 armed insurgents in the jungles. Britain's mission was to "destroy the Communist Party organisation in Malaya" and to guarantee

that "the economic life of the country continues." Such a move, according to British internal reports, "entails the protection of the rubber and
tin industries, of the personnel employed by them, and the maintenance
of the confidence of the people in the ability of Government to protect
them."[120] But with the police force grossly under strength and military
reinforcements delayed until December, the situation rapidly deteriorated. Chin Peng's men and women staged ambushes, slashed precious
rubber trees, and sent shock waves through the local European population, many of whom were rightly terrified as they hunkered into their
isolated locations across the Federation.

Less than two weeks after Gent declared a special emergency,
Creech Jones recalled him. As the Colonial Office mulled over the high
commissioner's replacement, one dissenting administrator noted that
they were headed down a familiar path "allowing our regime to become
purely one of repression. This was, after all, the final tragedy of our rule
in Palestine."[121] But Creech Jones's mind was soon made up. Just as Gray
and his men had been hand-selected for their liberal imperial methods,
so too did the Colonial Office make a deliberate choice in appointing Sir
Henry "Jimmy" Gurney, Palestine's last chief secretary, to take charge as
Malaya's high commissioner, despite the failures riddling the Mandate
during Gurney's time.[122]

This was a battle not only to control crucial imperial resources but
also to contain Communism in the early years of the Cold War. Gurney had cultivated his craft for nearly three decades, making his way
up the colonial career ladder, first in one of Kenya's district outposts,
then in Jamaica, then in the Gold Coast, and eventually in Palestine.
By the time Gurney landed in Kuala Lumpur, he had picked up the
Knight Commander of the Order of St. Michael and St. George from
His Majesty and had self-fashioned into a battle-tested and stern leader
whose trademark moustache punctuated his ever-present scowl. Gurney knew there were rules to the game that had evolved over decades
in the empire, and he transplanted Palestine's legalized lawlessness into
Malaya through 149 pages of emergency regulations, empowering him,
in his words, "to take any action he wished."[123] He continually added to
them as the months ticked by. Like the Mandate, the high commissioner's evolving police state included the civilian administration's power to
search and seize as well as to censor. It could impose bans, curfews, and
collective punishments together with the death sentence for a range of
offenses, which included the possession of firearms and consorting with
terrorists.[124] Locally, the *Straits Times* editors questioned the appointment of yet "another Palestinian," with the "Colonial Office . . . falling

into the fallacy of supposing that Malaya is a second Palestine"—which, of course, was precisely the mindset that drove Gurney's appointment and the personnel, tactics, and regulations that came with it.[125]

Malaya and Palestine were similar in other ways, not least in the complete breakdown in intelligence: the Federation was unable to collect and analyze local information. As elsewhere in the empire, economy dictated some of this problem. Britain's imperial overstretch consistently required cutting fiscal corners, and its effects were thrown into relief with one end-of-empire crisis after another in the postwar era. In Malaya as in Palestine, most British police officers and members of the special branch, dedicated to political security and intelligence, did not understand the local languages. Literally unable to speak to subject populations or to translate documents, British officials refracted the little information they did obtain through the civilizing mission's prism. Many British officials still cast ordinary peasants and townspeople across

Cathay Theatre and Cathay Building, Singapore, 1941

the imperial globe in childlike images, albeit ones that were increasingly petulant if not criminal. For them, any popular demands for freedom and human dignity, no matter how fractured, were the result of Machiavellian leaders like Gandhi, Jinnah, al-Husayni, Begin, and Chin Peng, who exploited their followers. According to liberal imperialism's logic, these acolytes had not yet developed sufficient skills and sensibilities to distinguish between self-interested nationalism, or terrorism, and Britain's paternalistic benevolence. That British colonial officials like those in Malaya were routinely and astonishingly caught off guard when populist demands gave rise to violent insurrections was a reflection of the liberal imperial ethos that shaped and defined Britain's empire and those who served it.

In spite, or because, of these limitations, as we've seen, MI5's systems and tactics for intelligence collection expanded in the postwar era. In the case of Malaya, MI5 director-general Percy Sillitoe looked to augment and systematize the colony's intelligence operations. In August 1948 he made a personal visit to Kuala Lumpur, where he declared the Malayan Security Service an unmitigated disaster. It was soon disbanded. He then transferred his Middle East go-to operative, Alex Kellar, who was by then head of the Security Intelligence Middle East station in Cairo, to take charge of its sister operation in Southeast Asia. Based in Singapore, Security Intelligence Far East was a clearinghouse for the collation and assessment of all intelligence that security liaison officers, or local MI5 operatives, accumulated together with the region's special branch officers. Headquartered alongside Malcolm MacDonald's offices in Singapore's Cathay Building, the combined operations were known locally as the "tropical duplication of Whitehall."[126] The Cathay Building was a cultural landmark, the first skyscraper in all Southeast Asia. It had a famed restaurant, a dance hall, a rooftop garden, and a thirteen-hundred-person, air-conditioned cinema, where moviegoers could relax in armchairs while local waitresses served them aperitifs and lit their cigarettes.

Kellar's arrival did not go unnoticed. He strode through the Cathay Building's corridors wearing Palm Beach and Saigon linen suits, white Egyptian-cotton shirts, and sharkskin dinner jackets.[127] He billed headquarters for his tropical getups, which hardly endeared him to MacDonald; neither did his rumored homosexuality. Indeed, Malaya's administration became a toxic cesspool of personality clashes. MacDonald and Kellar were a disastrous combination from day one, which led to Kellar's eventual ouster and replacement with Jack Morton, a long-time veteran of the Indian Special Branch. Gurney, Gray, Catling, and

William Jenkins—the initial director of intelligence in Malaya—were constantly at odds as they struggled for control over the police and intelligence gathering. Even the police rank and file couldn't get along, generally cleaving along Palestinian and Old Malayan lines. Gray's rapid expansion of the police force from 11,000 to 73,000 members further exacerbated local clashes as new recruits were often young or subpar or both. Included in the expanding police rank were 41,000 men, mostly Malay, who enlisted into the special constabulary, and 1,000 planters, who were "seconded" to the force, a typical move in Britain's empire where local Europeans were often co-opted into the colonial service to help suppress insurgencies. More than 250,000 Malays also joined the part-time auxiliaries and Kampong Guards. In addition, three battalions of British Army personnel, many of whom were National Servicemen barely out of their teens, would arrive to track down terrorists in the jungle and also contend with the Min Yuen.[128] If numbers are a measure, Britain was throwing massive weight behind the forces of law and order suppressing the insurgency and restoring colonial control.

In the early years, British officials danced around what to call the Communist insurgents, partly because of economic considerations. Insurance companies covered Malayan estates and mines for "riot and civil commotion" but not for "rebellion" or "insurrection." The Rubber Growers' Association, powerful London lobbyists, implored the Colonial Office to stop using terms like *rebellion* and *insurrection* lest the Malayan planters be uninsured, forcing them to turn to Attlee's financially strapped government to cover losses.[129] Malaya was no exception to the empire's long-standing practice of criminalizing political dissent, and as in previous colonial conflicts, British officials concluded that insurgents were infected with mysterious pathologies.

At first, Colonial Secretary Creech Jones blamed the violence on "gangsters" who were "Communist-instigated," but this soon gave way to a general belief that a "secret society complex" infused the Chinese, who were an evil people and, according to Gurney, "accustomed to acquiesce to pressure."[130] The colonial secretary made clear that Britain was launching a "vigorous counter-attack on Communist propaganda both at home and abroad" to counter any notion that the "present troubles in Malaya arise from a genuine nationalist movement of the people of the country."[131] Such representations shaped broader understandings of Communist aims, providing whatever legitimation Britain needed to unleash legalized lawlessness in the extreme. The new high commissioner took this one step further, making snap judgments about Malaya's Chinese community and the Communism that spread rapidly through its population. The emerging Min Yuen and particularly the squatters "have no part whatsoever in the community life of Malaya," Gurney declared. "They do not speak the Malay language and remain completely Chinese in outlook. By no stretch of the imagination can they lay claim at present to belong to the country."[132] As for Communism, in the words of the new high commissioner, it was "not a political doctrine; it is banditry and lawlessness."[133]

Not only were Chinese civilians criminals and their ethnically based movement unrepresentative of a Malayan nationalism, they were also illegal residents of the Federation. Simply put, the Chinese minority were held to be "aliens" in Malaya, despite their climbing demographics and socioeconomic participation in the territory since the turn of the century. At the eve of the Second World War, "Malaya had been transformed from a collection of Malay states into a politically significant 'plural society,'" according to the historian Albert Lau. Together, the Chinese and Indian "immigrant races" outnumbered the indigenous Malays, prompting colonial officials in London to imagine various ways in which non-Malays, as we've seen, could be granted a kind of citizenship status. During the war, tens of thousands of people in the Malay Peninsula who had managed to survive Japanese purges and labor camps were internally displaced. This created a massive problem that only fueled the ongoing civil conflict during Britain's reoccupation. Part of the struggle for survival was laying claim to the colonial state. Ethnic Malays, demanding that the British put a stop to their expanded citizenship schemes, which they did by abandoning the Malayan Union for the Federation, pointed to their historically embedded rights as located within a Malayan ancien régime that British colonial rule had historically leveraged and protected. In spite of such claims, however, by 1947 over 60 percent of the so-called immigrant population had, in fact, been born in Malaya, and as the historian Tim Harper points out, "disease and disorder shaped the world-view of [this] generation."[134]

It was the Communist insurgents in this generation populating Malaya, along with others born outside the territory, whom British officials now labeled "thugs," "terrorists," and "bandits." For years, British orthodoxy held firm: the Malayan Communist Party was inspired by the Zhdanov Doctrine, a cultural doctrine developed by Soviet Central Committee secretary Andrei Zhdanov dividing the world into Western "imperialistic" regimes and Soviet "democratic" ones; and Calcutta and Peking regionally orchestrated the insurgency. London looked to cast Malayan Communism as "part of the Kremlin's worldwide campaign against western powers." This view squared with the Colonial Office's broader 1950 report, written as much for the Americans as for White-hall, reappraising the British Empire in the context of the Cold War and pushing an alleged Moscow conspiracy to launch a global attack on the colonies.[135] Some officials in London and Malaya were more convinced of China's influence, though the best anyone could show were government messages of support for the Malayan "liberation movement" that came from the soon-to-be People's Republic of China.[136] Whether it was the Soviet Union or China wielding influence, the underlying British point was that the local population, so uneducated and devoid of sophistication, could never have spawned its own Communist movement. In reality, Chin Peng and his followers were waging a war for national liberation that received little outside material support.[137]

In the struggle over ideas, the Malayan Communist Party had the early upper hand. The party was a propaganda machine, and its distribution network of leaflets spread the message of British "white terrorism." The party had a newspaper, *Freedom News*, but the Communists' direct messaging to the Federation's beleaguered population was what swelled its ranks. Much like Ho's recruitment during the Japanese occupation, those joining the Communist insurgency attended late-night lectures; and like Indian National Army recruits, would-be Chin Peng supporters visualized and heard the Communist message in dramatic plays and readings. This message was anti-imperialism as much as it was doctrinaire Communism. Such rhetoric had a broad appeal to the largely illiterate rural population who had been the casualties of war since the Japanese invasion over six years earlier.[138]

That colonial officials dismissed the Chinese population as misguided criminals at best and alien subjects at worst did nothing to help the empire's cause. Major-General Charles Boucher, a former officer in India, arrived in late June 1948 to direct the military campaign. His troops were headed toward a straight-on battle against some of Britain's best Special Operations Executive–trained guerrillas who had operated behind enemy lines in Force 136 during World War II, a point Boucher failed to grasp. "I can tell you this is by far the easiest problem I have ever tackled," he announced. "In spite of the appalling country, and ease with which he can hide, the enemy is far weaker in technique and courage than either the Greek or Indian reds."[139] As in the North-West Frontier, the plan was for the British forces to restore order by making a show of force of bombs and other aerial assaults, smoking the rebels out of the jungles, then eliminating them. Such assumptions would soon give way to the realities of Malaya, its impenetrable jungle terrain, and its Chinese population, about whom colonial officials knew very little.[140]

As local papers chronicled more ambushes, gruesome murders of Europeans as well as locals, and the destruction of hundreds of thousands of rubber trees, it became clear that the stiffening emergency regulations and the combined tactics of Gray and Boucher were not working.[141]

The local mouthpiece of Malaya's planters and other economic interests, *The Straits Times*, relentlessly berated the colonial government. "Malaya Tougher Than Palestine," it headlined just before Gurney's arrival. "Malaya's Security Forces Are Not Enough," it complained once Gurney was installed, demanding more repression.[142] In London, undersecretary of state for the colonies David Rees-Williams made clear that the Attlee government was giving Malaya the full panoply of powers needed to suppress the Communist uprising:

> We will do all we can to protect the lives of innocent and law-abiding citizens. All the necessary powers for which we have been asked have been given to the Government of Malaya. If they need any more which can be given them, we shall give them those powers and take all steps possible to support them. In fact, we will not engage in what was described by one hon. Member opposite as a cat-and-mouse act. We are going right through with it, and we are going to stamp the disorder out. On our part and on the part of the Government of Malaya there will be no sheathing of the sword until we have completed our task.[143]

A handful of British officers in Malaya knew they were in for a protracted struggle. Among them was Robert Thompson, the son of a vicar who had studied at Cambridge and was fluent in Cantonese and several other Chinese dialects. Thompson joined the Malayan civil service in 1938 and was "a dashing, handsome, highly intelligent bachelor, with a ready chuckle, [and] far removed from the generally accepted image of the stuffy Colonial administrator," according to one observer.[144] During the war, Thompson emerged as another Orde Wingate protégé in the famed Chindits, fighting alongside several of the men who later comprised Palestine's covert forces. He returned to Malaya after Japan's surrender, where he became a permanent fixture in the Chinese affairs department in Perak and an indispensable colonial servant to British military leaders. His language and cultural skills, together with his Special Operations Executive training, made Thompson unique among colonial and military officials in the Federation. At the start of the emergency, he was among the few who warned that Malaya was no "Empire skirmish."[145]

It wasn't until late 1948 that Gurney came around to the same conclusion. In his opening remarks to the Federation's Legislative Council, he reversed his October announcement that "it is only a matter of time before the Communists are destroyed."[146] He slowly walked back his optimism, acknowledging that "terrorism is the most expensive form of illness from which any community can suffer and becomes more so the longer it is permitted to drag on."[147] He recognized the toll that the emergency was inflicting on Malaya, the dangers of a protracted conflict, and Britain's role in its intractability. Yet the impact of Palestine continued to loom large not only in Malaya but also back home. There *The Times* correspondent Louis Heren drew on his wartime coverage during the final years of the Mandate, capturing prevailing sentiment in a two-part series titled "Malayan Emergency." "There is no evidence to show that Malaya's Communists are incapable of intensifying and extending their campaign of terrorism," Heren wrote.

> Fifty ex-members of the *Irgun Zvei Leumi*, whom your Correspondent knew in Palestine, could, if it were possible to disguise them as Asians, bring the country to a standstill and drive the administration to the safety and impotence of barbed-wire enclosures as they did in Jerusalem. Efficiency in terrorism is not a Jewish monopoly. . . . The Malayan terrorists are learning; they have their own efficiency campaign. Their ambuscades, for instance, are now almost text-book demonstrations, whereas previously they were ragged, ill-planned affrays. Their gun positions are sited to bring fire to bear simultaneously on all vehicles of the usual military three-vehicle convoy. . . . They have learned to construct landmines and detonate them electrically.[148]

"It is very doubtful that [the Communists'] expansion can be checked with the present tactics and methods," Heren wrote. He concluded "the end is still not in sight and war weariness is increasing dangerously."[149] Heren wrote this piece in August 1952, when for four years Britain had been waging a costly and brutal battle largely for economic resources in a territory where Palestine continued to cast a shadow over emotions and events, however much liberal imperial strategies in Malaya began to expand beyond those deployed in the Mandate.

CHAPTER 12

Small Places, Close to Home

It was a dirty war, I mean all guerilla warfares are a dirty war. It can't be otherwise. . . . In war as in love, all is fair.[1]

Arthur Humphrey,
secretary for internal security and defense,
Federation of Malaya

On December 10, 1948, in the *grande salle* of Paris's Palais de Chaillot, forty-eight of the United Nations' fifty-eight members, Britain among them, voted in favor of Resolution 217A. With it, newspapers around the world heralded the newly adopted Universal Declaration of Human Rights (UDHR) as a turning point in history. For its protagonists, like the UN's chair of the Committee on Human Rights, Eleanor Roosevelt, the declaration's preamble and thirty articles were the culmination of her husband's Four Freedoms. They enshrined the universal beliefs in the basic rights of individuals that President Roosevelt had championed in Congress before America's entry into the Second World War. In addressing the General Assembly on the eve of the UDHR's adoption, the former first lady spoke to the promises of universal rights, suggesting that the declaration "may well become the international Magna Carta of all men everywhere. We hope its proclamation by the General Assembly will be an event comparable to the proclamation of the Declaration of Rights of Man . . . [and] the Bill of Rights by the people of the United States."[2] While she carried the human rights torch for her late husband, his presidential legacy was compromised insofar as self-determination was concerned. Still, few at the time underestimated her role in navigating postwar international politics while also being attuned to the meaning of universal rights to the world's population. "Where, after all, do universal human rights begin?" Roosevelt would later ask. Her reply:

> In small places, close to home—so close and so small that they cannot be seen on any maps of the world. . . . Such are the places where every man, woman, and child seeks equal justice, equal opportunity, equal dignity without discrimination. Unless these rights have meaning there, they have little meaning anywhere.[3]

December 10 is still celebrated as Human Rights Day, as it ushered in a new article of faith in basic humanity and the need, above all else, to protect inalienable rights that are intrinsically possessed, not conferred.

At the time, the mood in Whitehall was somber, though not defeatist. Many in its halls still believed in the civilizing mission's role in bestow-

Eleanor Roosevelt displays the Spanish-language version of the Universal Declaration of Human Rights, 1949.

ing rights incrementally on the empire's subjects. Such ideas endured, even though the global esprit de corps was shifting as a result of the war and its devastation. In the months leading up to the December 10 vote, British officials had maneuvered between the UDHR, which like the UN Charter's preamble was not legally enforceable against its signatories because of its purely declarative status, and its covenants, which would be enforceable as binding agreements in states that signed and ratified them. Fortunately for Britain, the covenants were taking significant negotiation time and were ultimately decoupled from the declaration. This change rendered one Labour MP, Eric Fletcher, incredulous:

> The [UN] charter contemplated that following the last war, some international machinery would be set up to define and protect human rights—the four freedoms, in the classic phrase of President Roosevelt. . . . It was felt, in the light of the experience of Fascism and Nazism, that there was an intimate link between the recognition of human rights and the preservation of the peace of the world.

Fletcher punctuated his concerns with an abiding point: "I should regard it as a mere mockery and a sham to proceed with a pious declaration which would not be binding and enforceable."[4] In the end, however, that was precisely what happened, at least in the near term. The Colonial Office was therefore sanguine about the turn of events: Creech Jones wrote that "the conclusion of a Covenant and proposals for [its] implementation . . . may drag on for some time. From the colonial point of view this possibility would not appear to be particularly disadvantageous."[5]

It would take another three decades for the covenants to be drafted, signed, ratified, and entered into force, though the aspirational UDHR still caused British officials concern. In the words of the Colonial Office, Articles 13, 21, and 25 of the declaration—freedom of movement, right to participation in government, and right to basic standards of living—"may be extremely difficult to reconcile" in the empire.[6] Creech Jones said the UDHR was potentially "a source of embarrassment" as far as the empire was concerned.[7] Many governors and high commissioners refused to publish its contents, or even refer to its existence, in their *Official Gazettes*, and they certainly had no intention of disseminating such seditious thoughts to their subjects. "It is felt . . . that [the UDHR's] terms are not easily comprehensible, and that there is a likelihood of it being regarded by pupils as a form of lay catechism," the

Colonial Office told its governors and high commissioners around the empire. "There is also a danger that politically inclined school teachers would be placed in a position to use the Declaration to confuse pupils on current political issues."[8]

Regardless, for some, the lack of legally enforceable mechanisms for the declaration gutted it of much moral purpose. A year after the celebrations, Hersch Lauterpacht, Whewell Professor of International Law at Cambridge and renowned international lawyer advocating for the human rights of all, said as much. "At the time of the adoption of the Declaration there was no feeling of embarrassment at the incongruity between the enthusiastic acknowledgment of the fundamental character of the human rights proclaimed in the Declaration," he wrote, "and the refusal to recognize them as a source of legal obligation binding in the sphere of conduct—a fact which in itself raises a cardinal issue of international morality."[9]

Lauterpacht's solution to the "sphere of conduct" was to hand over interpretations of human rights, and accountability for them, to competent international bodies, particularly courts, as international law expert Martti Koskenniemi tells us in his landmark book, *The Gentle Civilizer of Nations*.[10] The tragic events of World War II reinforced Lauterpacht's belief in international law and institutions that had been percolating for years, reflecting his own life's journey through the tumultuous early twentieth century. Born in 1897 in a tiny Galician village (formerly part of the Austro-Hungarian Empire, today Galicia straddles southeastern Poland and eastern Ukraine), he left home to study in Vienna after the First World War, part of a Jewish exodus fleeing persecutions that resulted in a 20 percent decrease in Galicia's Jewish population in 1919–20.[11]

At the University of Vienna, Lauterpacht studied international law, though discrimination undermined his future in Austria. With two doctoral degrees in hand, he left continental Europe's anti-Semitism for that of Britain, where he let his Jewish identity fade into the background as he assimilated into the British legal community's interwar liberal internationalism. He became part of a global Eurocentric culture and practice of international law that, as we saw in chapter 2, had been affirmed in 1873 with the founding of an international association of jurists, the influential Institut de droit international.

While earlier jurists were steeped in developmentalist ideas of "civilized" Europe and "uncivilized" empire, Lauterpacht was ambivalent toward the colonial enterprise. He found the Spinoza Doctrine, which espoused law as a form of social control that ordered human behavior through coercion, to be insufficient, believing there were coercive and reformist impulses in the empire.[12] Nationalistic imperialism was "the most ruthless economic exploitation of native peoples, maintained by the despotic rule of military administration," he said, while admiring the "liberal tradition in British foreign policy" that abolished the trade in enslaved peoples. He saw the latter as part of international law's natural progress, a Victorian-era idea of improvement's march forward toward a world ordered by rational liberal ideals.[13]

By the interwar years, disillusioned by world events, jurists increasingly advocated international solutions not only for Europe but also for its empires. Lauterpacht called the League of Nations Covenant, the topic of his Viennese doctoral dissertation, a "fundamental charter of the international society."[14] Its deficiency was its procedural framework, which allocated interpretation to the members. That was why the League's intervention during the Abyssinian crisis was undercut by Great Power collusion, prompting George Padmore to call it "Thieves' Kitchen," as we've seen.[15] Nevertheless, for Lauterpacht, the Mandate system, which categorized territories held in "sacred trust" as A, B, and C based on a civilizational scale, contained processes for protecting indigenous rights, even if League member states policed their enforcement. Some international jurists pushed for an extension of universal human rights law, successfully pressing the Institut de droit international to adopt a "Declaration of the International Rights of Man" in 1929. Aimed as much at minority protections in Europe as to "uncivilized" populations in the empire, the declaration was nonetheless grounded in a universal secular humanism that the war's fervent nationalism had trampled. The declaration was clear: "The juridical conscience of the civilized world demands the recognition for the individual of rights preserved from all infringement on the part of the State," whose duty it was to recognize for all individuals "without distinction as to nationality, sex, race, language, or religion" the right to life, liberty, property, free exercise of religion, and use of language.[16]

Formative wartime experiences prompted other internationalists, like Swiss doctor and one of the International Committee of the Red Cross's (ICRC) leading figures, Frédéric Ferrière, to advocate for a major revision in international laws of war to protect civilians from state terror. The 1919 Allied Commission Report highlighted what he and others had witnessed firsthand: deportations, collective punishments, hostage killing, torture, and sexual violence. The ICRC spearheaded incremental changes, including a nonbinding resolution declaring that all victims of European wartime violence had a right to help, meaning the ICRC could access and aid victims of war. However, the wide-ranging civilian protections that Ferrière was calling for were shelved, thanks largely to the French, who argued that such protections fell within the domain of state sovereignty.[17] The ICRC backed down on comprehensive civilian protections: at its Tokyo conference in 1934, it offered up a proposal with humanitarian impulses that were once again severely narrowed by state claims to sovereignty rather than expanded by any kind of universal human right regulating warfare. Undeterred, a group of international jurists gathered in Monaco, where they drafted a comprehensive proposal, including sanctions, to protect *"des droits de l'humanité en temps de guerre,"* linking their 1929 declaration of individual human rights to the regulation of warfare. Neither the ICRC nor the world's powers had any enthusiasm for the Monaco Draft, rejecting it. With the Spanish Civil War and the Sino-Japanese War ongoing, and some of the parties to the negotiations also deporting unwanted populations and imprisoning political dissidents, the ICRC-sponsored Tokyo Draft was also scrapped by 1937.[18]

The important point is that human rights thinking—whether about humanitarian or human rights law, which clearly were intersecting before and after the Second World War—was not new when Eleanor Roosevelt worked with countless nations and representatives, many from the non-Western world, to draft the UDHR.[19] But it remained on the periphery until Germany brought colonial counterinsurgency methods to Europe, upending, as we've seen, the Western natural order of things by gobbling up sovereign states into the Nazi empire and unleashing genocidal practices whose impact rippled through the international community. Lauterpacht's entire family, with the exception of one niece, were murdered along with 6 million other Jews, while the ICRC, refusing to violate its neutrality and nondenunciation policies, did little to condemn the unprecedented atrocities. Jean Simon Pictet, a Swiss international humanitarian lawyer, led the reinvention of the ICRC in the wake of its disastrous wartime decisions and, together with Frede Castberg, a highly influential Norwegian human rights lawyer, headed a group of jurists whose stated goal was to protect human dignity in armed conflicts, including the elimination of collective penalties and torture, and whose reach, some jurists argued, should extend to civil and colonial wars. This was a striking and major change, breaking from the civilizational hierarchy that condemned colonized peoples to imperial rule and denied them sovereignty and the protections of international law.

In the summer of 1948, fifty governments and fifty-two national

Red Cross societies gathered in Stockholm to revise and update earlier treaties regulating conduct in war. Together, four new conventions, later known as the Geneva Conventions of 1949, comprising 429 articles of law were being drafted. Each convention addressed the protection of a particular category of persons during armed conflicts: the First and Second Geneva Conventions covered the wounded, sick, and shipwrecked; the Third Geneva Convention prisoners of war; and the Fourth Geneva Convention civilians. There were also articles common to all four conventions, with Common Article 3 arguably the most contentious of them all. Often referred to as a "mini-convention," this common article rendered the conventions applicable to noninternational armed conflicts. Its initial draft reached not only into domestic state matters but into imperial ones as well, stating: "In all cases of armed conflict which are not of an international character, especially cases of civil war, colonial conflicts, or wars of religion, which may occur in the territory of one or more of the High Contracting Parties, the implementing of the principles of the present Convention shall be obligatory on each of the adversaries."[20]

The ICRC, however, was divided over "confronting absolute colonial sovereignty head-on." The British and French clearly wouldn't agree to Common Article 3's initial draft, potentially thwarting progress toward more extensive protections for the free world, so the former ICRC president Max Huber, "aware of the sensitive link between the entangled questions of colonial sovereignty, belligerency, and partisans, opted for a far more cautious path," according to the legal historian Boyd van Dijk.[21] References to "cases of civil war, colonial conflicts, or wars of religion" were removed and replaced with the phrase "cases of armed conflict not of an international character," with the meaning of *conflict* undefined. In later negotiations, the French delegation introduced a preamble for the Fourth Geneva Convention (Protection of Civilian Persons in Time of War), stating that the signatories would be "conscious of their obligation . . . in order to protect civilian populations from the horrors of war, [to] undertake to respect the principles of human rights which constitute the safeguard of civilization and, in particular, to apply, at any time and in all places," even if they had no intention of extending such protections to partisans in occupied territory or to Viet Minh fighters.[22] Jurists nevertheless merged this preamble with several draft articles that legislated individual criminal responsibilities and fair trials. Britain's Colonial and Foreign offices were furious, as was the War Office, its officials raging against such a "blanket" that would "safeguard the 'principles of human rights'" and refusing any connection between the revised and expanded

Geneva Conventions, human rights law, criminal law, and attempts to regulate colonial conflicts.[23] The preamble was eventually scrapped altogether and, with it, any mention of "human rights," leaving this subject to the parallel drafting of the UDHR.

What's clear is that British and French officials, with ongoing conflicts in Malaya and Indochina, wanted to protect their sovereign free hand in their empires, while Cold War concerns consumed the Americans, who undermined protections for victims of air bombing along with the British. So, too, did European powers narrow the rights of "partisans": British officials feared they could include "hostile . . . armed underground movements . . . such movements as the 'Stern Gang' in Palestine," while France's "experience of being occupied during the second world war" fueled its own protection concerns. The "crucial test," according to British negotiators, was to craft "a definition [of *partisan*] wide enough to include such people [as the French sought domestically, but] avoid admitting the existing 'terrorist' elements in Palestine, when captured, to the rights of prisoners of war."[24] This was achieved.

On August 12, 1949, seventeen delegates, including Britain, signed the four Geneva Conventions, including the new fourth convention that, for the first time in international humanitarian law, protected civilians during wartime from "violence to life and person," hostage taking, "outrages upon personal dignity, in particular humiliating and degrading treatment," and "executions without previous judgment pronounced by a regularly constituted court . . . which are recognized as indispensable by civilized peoples."[25] By the end of 1950, sixty-one states had signed the conventions, and while many did not ratify them until several years later (Britain ratified in 1957), signing created an obligation to refrain, in good faith, from acts that would undermine the treaty's purpose. To this day, the Geneva Conventions of 1864, 1906, 1929, and 1949, together with later Additional Protocols in 1977 and 2005 and the Hague Conventions (1899 and 1907), comprise part of the corpus of international humanitarian law known as the "laws and customs of war."[26]

In 1949 Lauterpacht saw the Geneva Conventions as the dawn of a new era not just in international law but in human rights as well. "In fact it might be said that this [convention], in its limited sphere, is a veritable universal declaration of human rights," he effused. "Unlike the Declaration adopted by the General Assembly in December 1948, it is an instrument laying down legal rights and obligations as distinguished from a mere pronouncement of moral principles and ideal standards of conduct."[27] But the conventions weren't enforceable, at least not by any international court. State courts were to enforce "grave breaches" of the conventions by their own agents. In other words, individual states were to try their own soldiers or citizens for "grave breaches"—a highly unlikely occurrence, as it turned out. There was, however, an important caveat, which was remarkable in its intent if inconsistently put into practice. State courts were given "power to try foreigners as well as the persons normally within their jurisdiction," as the military and legal historian Geoffrey Best underscores in his classic book *War and Law Since 1945*. "High Contracting Parties were committed to making sure that 'persons alleged to have committed such grave breaches' were brought to justice; if not in their own courts, then by process of extradition to another's."[28]

The conventions, however, were not comprehensive, despite Lauterpacht's crowd-pleasing applause. "What was an 'armed conflict not of an international character'?" Best also asked:

> The question remained unanswered. Everyone agreed that it could not mean "the exploits of bandits or riots of any kind," just as everyone agreed that it must mean "civil war" and (although admittedly imperial powers would not admit this publicly) colonial rebellion. But where the one sort of conflict began and the other ended, no one sought to enquire. It seemed to satisfy delegates to observe that the question hardly mattered, since no more was being asked of governments than elementary decencies they would (supposedly) be observing anyway. Henceforth, the argument ran, all States were going to respect basic human rights; no State would contemplate the torture or serious maltreatment or execution without fair trial even of criminals, bandits, and so on. Why then fuss about whether a non-international armed conflict existed or not?[29]

As we've seen, however, Britain and France put up all sorts of fuss, and they were either individually or collectively behind the removal from the conventions of any reference to "colonial wars" and the elimination of the preamble with a "blanket" mention of "human rights." In practice, imperial powers routinely claimed Common Article 3 did not apply to conflicts within their empires because these were internal security matters, with "criminals," "bandits," and "thugs" threatening the state and lawful order, which did not rise to the level of "armed conflict."

This was, of course, preposterous. The ICRC, however, couldn't compel these imperial powers to comply with the Geneva Conventions and, being a neutral party, was forced to engage in delicate negotiations just to deliver humanitarian assistance to conflict victims and civilian populations in European empires. In Britain's case, it was left to anti-colonial insurgents and their international supporters, often spear-headed in the United Nations by India and in Britain by the far left, to turn the "laws and customs" of war against the state, shaming the government for its humanitarian duplicity by using postwar international conventions and their powerful rights discourse. Indeed, demands for basic rights during wartime, and human rights more generally, were also linked to demands for self-determination. From within and outside the empire, non-Western actors would use international institutions like the UN as a platform for challenging the British state's doublethink and to demand accountability, and ultimately independence, for the remaining colonized world.

Another avenue for holding empires accountable also emerged in the postwar years when Europe moved toward drafting and adopting its own set of human rights laws, known as the European Convention on Human Rights (ECHR), which would prove to be one of the world's most progressive and enforceable conventions. Much like international humanitarian law, Europe's postwar human rights laws were a product

Signing of the European Convention on Human Rights, November 4, 1950

of the totalitarian crisis that had befallen the continent and the world. In 1948, seven hundred and fifty delegates from eighteen European nations gathered for the Congress of Europe in the Hague. With Winston Churchill as honorary chairman, they worked toward a new political order, rooted in ideas of international law that had been percolating and evolving since the nineteenth century, and that would "define a specifically European concept of human rights and of the relationship between citizens and the State in order to differentiate from the Universal Declaration of Human Rights that was being drawn up."[30] There was a call for the creation of a European Court of Human Rights. These initiatives led to the formation of the Council of Europe, supported by ten European governments, Britain's among them, and, greatly influenced by the European Movement, a nongovernmental association calling for greater postwar unity in Europe.

Britain played a leading role in the Council of Europe and its drafting of the European Convention on Human Rights in Strasbourg, France, during the summer of 1949, partly to counter charges that it was isolated from the continent, which had increased in the wake of the country's imperial-oriented economic policies and its lack of interest in integration. It would be an easy win for Bevin's beleaguered Foreign Office, which was concerned with European security matters. The British government concentrated its efforts to ensure European liberties, banding together with its continental counterparts to stave off Communist subversion whose potential seemed limitless. Or as Britain's representative to the Council of Europe's negotiations, Lord Layton, stressed, the convention was "a means of strengthening the resistance in all our countries against insidious attempts to undermine our democratic way of life from within or without, and thus to give to Western Europe as a whole greater political stability."[31]

On November 4, 1950, representatives of member states from the Council of Europe gathered in one of Rome's most opulent papal palaces, Palazzo Barberini. There, under Pietro da Cortona's *Triumph of Divine Providence*, they signed the European Convention for the Protection of Human Rights and Fundamental Freedoms. Britain was the first to ratify the convention in March 1951, and while it did not come into force until September 1953, when Luxembourg offered the tenth ratification, there was reason to celebrate. Paul Henri-Spaak, one of the continent's most ardent champions of integration and human rights, captured the convention's historic significance in his speech "From the Europe of Dachau to the Europe of Strasbourg," in which he provided a symbolic coda to the council's efforts.[32] Despite such celebrations, British officials harbored deep concerns that the convention, so necessary for the preservation of Western liberties particularly as the Cold War advanced, as Britain agreed, could easily undermine use of the repressive measures necessary to snuff out rebellion or subversion elsewhere.[33] The day after Britain ratified the convention, as it happened, Labour's media-savvy Herbert Morrison replaced the ailing Bevin as foreign secretary. Morrison gave away just enough to placate the human rights faithful while, at the same time, ensuring an international legal structure that not only facilitated but also legitimated the legalized lawlessness on which many parts of Britain's empire depended.

Even as Britain negotiated the European Convention on Human Rights, it was mired in multiple states of emergency, which included the one in Malaya. The convention's Article 63, the "colonial clause," waived its a priori application in Europe's empires. As far as the British government was concerned, the ECHR was the lesser of two human rights evils when it came to its colonial subjects. Officials presumed its European allies would be far more predictable than the United Nations, which was negotiating its own covenants. Morrison's Foreign Office was clear in its position: "the sooner we disengage from an exercise [with the UN] which can only be embarrassing from the Colonial point of view the better."[34] It's not surprising, therefore, that the Foreign Office extended the ECHR to forty-five of its colonies and territories, not because it wanted "to improve the lot of colonial subjects," as one historian has observed, but rather "to present British colonial policy and practice in a favourable light, by publicly committing colonial governments to respect . . . human rights and to furnish an argument for not accepting a UN Covenant if one was ever adopted."[35]

Moreover, Britain thought it had given up very little by extending the European convention to its empire. First, the convention permitted, though did not require, the right of individual petition. Britain rejected individual petition until 1966, and until that time only accepted the right of other member states to lodge a petition to the European Commission of Human Rights, the body that received complaints. British officials argued that international law applied only to states, not to individuals. However, as the legal historian Simpson points out, "the United Kingdom's real reason was fear of repercussions in colonies and protectorates."[36] Second, in early ECHR drafts, the British government introduced, and insisted on, a derogation article that allowed a contracting party relief from the convention in "time of war or other public emergency threatening the interests of the people."[37] It was eventually enshrined as Article 15, which permitted the derogation of much of the convention during wartime, including a state of emergency. Even if a signatory derogated the convention under Article 15, however, a handful of articles remained in place. The most notable was Article 3, the "Prohibition on Torture," which stated, "No one shall be subjected to torture or to inhuman or degrading treatment or punishment."[38] Nevertheless, with the stroke of a pen, the derogation article allowed contingent "necessity" to undermine universal rights. In the years ahead, the two UN covenants would adopt similar derogations and contingencies, much to Britain's approval. As for the ECHR, France didn't ratify the convention until 1974, so it was not applied to Algeria or any other major French overseas territory, whereas Britain maintained its historic ability to dominate, coerce, and exclude even under the convention's rubric.

Throughout their humanitarian law and human rights negotiations, British officials were obviously well aware of the policies and practices unfolding in Malaya. In fact, in December 1949, Attlee's cabinet discussed the matter of Common Article 3: "the present provision would make it more difficult to deal promptly and effectively with rebellion, and that some of the provisions could not be carried out in practice. It was to be hoped, for example, that no endeavor would be made to argue that the Convention should apply to the operations now in progress in Malaya."[39] The convention's undefined "armed conflict not of an international character," clearly an intentional imperial stroke, assuaged some of the cabinet's concerns. Indeed, the cabinet had more than a vague sense of what counterinsurgency meant in Malaya. In a January 1949 memorandum to the Colonial Office, High Commissioner Gurney had been unequivocal. "At present time the police and army are breaking the law every day," he wrote. It was "most important that police and soldiers, who are not saints, should not get the impression that every small mistake is going to be the subject of a public enquiry or that it is better to do nothing at all than to do the wrong thing quickly."[40]

The legalized lawlessness that Gurney enabled through emergency regulations was in fact not enough to encompass the security force's actions. So he took further action, creating another legally enabled process that directly targeted the Federation's Chinese population. Drawing on the empire's lessons, Malayan officials introduced a combined set of new policies. Their first line of defense was deportation: they sent as much of the suspect population as possible back to China. Gurney's men then detained without trial some of those who remained. The rest they gathered up and resettled into confined spaces across the Federation. The system became rife with corruption and suffering. The measures were in and of themselves coercive, and so was the high commissioner's message. The Chinese "are as you know notoriously inclined to lean towards whichever side frightens them more," Gurney wrote to the colonial secretary, "and at the moment this seems to be the Government."[41]

Nonetheless, the high commissioner wanted more government-sponsored terror. He told Creech Jones that Malaya needed measures that were "stronger than the bandits and at the same time inspiring greater fear."[42] Throughout his correspondence with the colonial secretary, Gurney's reference point was the Mandate and the lessons that came from a delayed police state. In May 1949 he foreshadowed what was on Malaya's horizon:

> In Palestine the Emergency Regulations were continually being added to and tightened up, so that at the end it might almost have been said that the whole book of Regulations could have been expressed in a single provision empowering the High Commissioner to take any action he wished. If all these powers had been taken and exercised immediately at the beginning, perhaps the outcome might have been different. Similarly, in Malaya, the same process has developed and powers for the more drastic and indeed ruthless measures were not provided or exercised until six months after the outbreak.[43]

Before Gurney was installed as high commissioner in October 1948, Federation officials had created a national registration system that included everyone in Malaya over the age of twelve.[44] This was not the first time British officials issued identity cards in the empire to surveil and control subject populations. In Palestine, they had introduced them during the Arab Revolt, when security forces used identity checks to round up suspects. "National registration [in Malaya] was . . . a way of distinguishing the law-breaking from the law-abiding—in principle a separation of the carded from the uncarded," according to the historian Anthony Short.[45] The Malayan Communist Party and its supporters knew this, tearing up cards and threatening photographers and finger-printing registration teams who had been co-opted into the process. It was also a way of identifying the hundreds of thousands of Chinese who, based upon the Federation's citizenship laws, were considered "alien Chinese squatters" and therefore were subject to deportation.[46]

Registration was largely completed by the end of 1948, whereupon the government began detaining and deporting in earnest, insisting "the interests of national safety must remain paramount."[47] Defending the measures, Creech Jones emphasized that every effort was being taken to ensure that the innocent were not being punished and that the guilty were treated fairly. Privately, however, his office would concede that "the needs of security must, in present circumstances, come first and it might be necessary sometimes to put aside fundamental human rights."[48] New emergency regulations enabled the parsing of humanity, a heavy-handed and bureaucratized process demanding more of Malaya's dwindling resources. Taken together, Emergency Regulations 17B, 17C, and 17D allowed for sweeping arrests and detention of all Chinese "bandits" and those suspected of abetting them, together with their dependents. Gray's paramilitary forces stepped up their work, sending fifty or more to the detention camps daily, quickly exceeding their six-thousand-person capacity until the detainees were deported to China, clearing the way for more.[49] Entire villages were collectively arrested and detained for the smallest infractions, including providing food and intelligence to the Malayan National Liberation Army. Friction soon emerged, between the police commissioner and General Officer Commanding Malaya Charles Boucher, over who had the upper hand in the village sweeps, including screening and wanton destruction reminiscent of the Arab Revolt. "I am afraid we shall have a lot of trouble regarding this question of burning down buildings by the military," one police officer reported. He noted that "General Boucher mentioned the fact that it was not proposed to obey this law" and inferred that civilian homestead razing was a policing purview.[50]

Regardless of the bickering, it was clear from the start of the emergency in June 1948 that destroying Chinese villages was a go-to punitive measure. So, too, was Gurney's view that "the day is past in which a clear dividing line could be drawn" between the police and "local military forces"; rather, they collectively comprised Britain's security forces and had to operate in unison if the government was going to effectively use draconian measures to quash Malaya's Communist insurgency.[51] "80 Houses Burned by Police," *The Straits Times* headlined, publishing similar articles chronicling village destruction, of which MPs in London knew.[52] Britain's internal government reports emphasized that such incendiary practices had a "most deterrent effect" on the villagers who were "backing the wrong horse."[53] The present situation could be dealt with only "by fire and slaughter," one colonel said.[54] In the case of Kachau, a Communist stronghold, security forces targeted its four hundred inhabitants after someone murdered a Malay barber in the village center. They gave locals two hours to leave their homes before they burned them to the ground. Gurney claimed the whole operation was, in fact, a "complete and voluntary exodus of the squatters from the surrounding area."[55] The Communist *Freedom News* told a different story: "Such atrocious measures as arson, killing, imprisonment, mopping up and compelling the people to quit their homes by force" were part of Britain's broader "man-slaughtering and bloody war."[56]

The government, frustrated with those still "sitting on the fence," launched a propaganda campaign.[57] It produced 51 million information leaflets with simplistic messages like "Give information to the police. Get Good Rewards" and "Communism is the enemy of the honest worker." Airplanes dumped the leaflets into the jungle canopy, and "public relations officers" distributed them in the villages. Enticement mixed with fear when gruesome photos of dead insurgents were passed around along with the message, "Live happily with your family." The local idiom was unknown to colonial officials, while the Communist Party continued offering straightforward ideas in an argot and form familiar to villagers through storytelling, late-night gatherings, and a robust underground press that included not only *Freedom News* but also *Humanity News*, the *Vanguard Press*, and *Combatant News*.[58]

Chin Peng's forces could be as cold-blooded as government officials, feeding the terror-induced strife pervading Malaya's rural areas. They murdered suspected informers and squeezed locals for food and supplies as well as the protection money that funded their ongoing battle.[59] The Communist Party threatened anyone suspected of disloyalty, often brutally attacking informers, real and perceived, as well as those who worked with the government, including members of the newly constituted Malayan Chinese Association (MCA). Under the leadership of Tan Cheng Lock, considered politically safe by the British and willing to work toward Federation unity, the conservative association comprised some of the peninsula's wealthiest businessmen who were looking to leverage age-old patronage networks in the villages. Gurney was "midwife" to the MCA, believing "the squatters would hitch themselves onto anything with a badge of authority, whether Boy Scouts or Methodists." The association was the target of repeated Communist attacks, including one on its Perak office; Tan narrowly escaped with his life, though never fully recovered from his injuries.[60]

The British government relentlessly tightened its coercive legislation, providing us with repeated examples of legalized lawlessness. After the leveling of Kachau, for instance, Gurney swiftly inaugurated

Emergency Regulations 18A and 18B, which gave the security forces the power to "destroy buildings and structures" as well as retroactive legal coverage for their wiping out of Kachau.[61] British security forces could now collectively march in toto those from "bad areas" like Kachau, to detention camps, which were overflowing because of the indiscriminate sweeps and arrests.[62]

"Without repatriation to China, we cannot win the present conflict in Malaya," Gurney had told the colonial secretary in the spring of 1949.[63] *The Straits Times* agreed. Even prior to Gurney's arrival, it had berated the government for its perceived go-slow deportation policies. Before the emergency, the Federation government had already legalized questionable policies, using its banishment powers to send "alien" convicted criminals back to their countries of origin, which more often than not was China.[64] With the insurgency, locals wanted a rapid scale-up of past practices. Headlining "Undesirables Must Go," the paper reminded its readers that a year earlier it had:

> felt itself compelled to urge the Government to take decisive action and banish the cut-throats, thugs and gangsters who then were terrorizing the country, plundering whole villages and holding them to ransom and murdering police and civilians until lawlessness had become the order of the day. . . . It must be clear to the Government that no real, final and lasting control of the situation can be gained unless the illegal immigrant is apprehended and deported with all possible speed.[65]

Banishment powers were cumbersome, however: a senior judge and executive council had to review each deportation case. Gurney cut through this by early 1949, amending and introducing Emergency Regulations 17C and 17D, respectively, to circumvent the review process, thus enabling his men to legally deport suspects en masse, provided they did not "belong to the territory," the official term for anyone not considered a Federation citizen. "Even the European-owned *Straits Times* found [the new deportation procedures] hard to stomach," the historian Karl Hack points out.[66] Indeed, many suspects had been born in Malaya or had lived in the territory for years, but the government now considered them all "alien Chinese squatters," so it wasn't banishing but rather repatriating them, according to Gurney. Moreover, his government reminded London that "no country is by international law bound to admit foreigners to settle in its territory."[67]

Gurney launched a deportation campaign, the intended scale of which was unprecedented in the empire. In January 1949 he set repatriation quotas of two thousand per month for all inhabitants deemed alien to the Federation, along with their dependents.[68] Malcolm MacDonald, disparaged as "the white monkey leader" in Communist circles, called the new regulation "drastic" but "imperative," in part because it would help solve "the racial problem." Creech Jones was aware of the campaign against so-called "alien Chinese squatters," noting "there is no appeal from an order made under [the new regulations] and no such order can be called in question by any court." The colonial secretary wrote to his Foreign Office counterpart, suggesting the whole operation could lead to "grave injustice" but accepting it as a "fait accompli."[69] Prime Minister Attlee signed off on the policy.[70]

The practices undertaken to execute approximately twenty-five thousand deportations reflected the Malayan government's determination, if not desperation, to gain control. Colonial officials in London noted that "the whole question of the form of procedure to be adopted, and whether it should be publicised, was left to [the high commissioner]. We have heard nothing further to this, and presumably no publicity was given to whatever procedure is employed in banishment cases."[71] While banishment, or repatriation, emerged as a cornerstone of counterinsurgency policy, the entire operation was contingent on momentous events in China, where the Kuomintang and the Communists were fighting a bitter civil war. In October 1949 the People's Republic of China (PRC) seized power, closing all ports and refusing to take those who awaited deportation from Malaya. Protracted negotiations ensued between Gurney, various offices in London, and colonial officials in Hong Kong, North Borneo, Kenya, and elsewhere. The high commissioner looked for somewhere else in the empire, or a neighboring location like Formosa, to "dump" the deportees. All the while, thousands slated for deportation insisted they belonged to Malaya and had no idea where their so-called homes were in China.[72]

A 1950 Commonwealth parliamentary delegation visited Port Swettenham Transit Camp where men, women, and children—some separated from their families—awaited deportation in sweltering conditions beneath the camp's corrugated iron roofs.[73] The colonial secretary was aware that the MPs, led by the future colonial secretary Alan Lennox-Boyd, were "disturbed by the restricted conditions in the camp, [and] the fact that women and children were detained there."[74] Locally, Gurney, Gray, and the attorney general decided whether a village's inhabitants were marked for deportation. Transit camps soon overflowed from the mass purges. In the first three months of 1949 alone, Gray's forces carried out seven operations, with more to come. Deputy Chief Secretary Edgeworth David described the waiting deportees as being "in a condition of complete or semi-destitution," awaiting return to China where they "may be left to starve and not reach their villages at all." He assessed the policy through historical analogy:

> Much has been written about the inhumanity of mass transfer of population during the war in Europe and except for the smaller scale on which we are working it is difficult to distinguish the circumstances which attend the removal of our Chinese repatriates. . . . However strong the conception of collective guilt put forward in justification there is no question that these operations involve a degree of hardship and inhumanity which is very difficult to defend.[75]

Britain's own "rule of law" policies were swallowing what remained of its civilizing mission in Malaya, but necessity prevailed. With China's doors closed and the scale and scope of arrests expanding, Port Swettenham morphed from a transit camp into a longer-term detention site. Malaya's chief secretary David Watherston readily admitted it "is . . . below the standard of the rest as it is intended purely as a staging post." Moreover, the ripple effects of the deportation crisis meant there was "increasing congestion in the other camps," even though the government rapidly threw up more barbed-wire pens in existing detention sites. Still, as Watherston pointed out to the Conservative MP Alan Lennox-Boyd and to Creech Jones, "I cannot end without saying that no thinking person in Malaya can view with satisfaction the continued detention of the large numbers of detainees which we now have but that their presence is an unfortunate necessity under present circumstances."[76] Both Lennox-Boyd and Creech Jones, together with the majority of their respective political parties, agreed.

The Colonial Office cleaved to necessity and batted aside moral and ethical questions as it had to explain how the Federation government eventually restarted the deportations.[77] As Watherston pointed out, the slowdown after the Communist takeover of China was "considered to be one of the most serious aspects of the emergency," and failure to solve the problem was having "grave effects" on those Chinese "who have supported the Government" and who feared reprisals should suspects slated for deportation be released.[78] Officials in Malaya and London knew such fears of reprisal were well founded, not least because some villagers were accusing their neighbors in order to settle local scores. Chinese police officers "were [also] not above reporting people as suspects for personal reasons," according to a House of Commons report.[79] Internal memoranda confirmed what Arthur Humphrey, a Malayan civil servant and its future secretary for internal security and defense, recalled years later. "It was ruthless," he said, and it "led to a great deal of distress . . . you know, women breaking down and children screaming and all this sort of thing."[80] He described his role in the operations:

> I organized a deportation of nearly 40,000 Chinese. They were in fact mostly Chinese because naturally that Communist movement was basically Chinese although they did their best to try to give it a multi-racial appearance. . . . There were some sad cases. . . . One has to admit a lot of families got broken up. And we had considerable problems with the deportation of these people. People were first put into detention camps on the grounds that they had assisted or lended in support of the Communists.

Humphrey also elaborated on the deportation process:

> We had a whole series of ships going from Port Swettenham to [China] carrying these deportees. The whole thing was done hush, hush. It didn't get into the press very much. . . . We were told to keep it very quiet, partly because we were bribing the Communist authorities on the other end. . . . They [the deportees] were carried in ships flying the Norwegian flag from Port Swettenham, and the officers on the ships were Scandinavians. . . . We simply put enough money into the pockets of the Scandinavian master and the crew of the ship to keep them going. But, still, when the integrity and the safety of a country is at stake, you don't begrudge a little bit of bribery to get your ends achieved, do you?[81]

Even with mass deportations, the detention camp population continued to grow. Various departments scrambled to find suitable accommodations, staff, and supplies. They turned former quarantine stations like that at Pulau Jerejak into detention sites and created several new camps, such as those at Tanjong Bruas and Majeedi. In total there were more than a dozen camps, each of which had a particular reformist function— which the government called "a progressive stage system"—in Britain's counterinsurgency strategy. Members of the police special branch drew on previous imperial practices of screening, detention, and refugee processing in places such as wartime India. They eventually comprised police interrogation units that questioned and then classified detainees according to their level of Communist indoctrination. "Blacks" were considered hard-core and irredeemable; and "greys" were of lesser Communist sympathies and therefore slated for rehabilitation. The Federation government hoped it could deport all the "blacks," but hundreds of them "belonged to the territory," and despite trying, officials could not slip them under the radar to China or elsewhere. Instead, they sent these "blacks" to "special detention camps" where they could, according to policy, force the detainees to labor in spite of the fact that such practices contravened International Labour Organisation conventions. The remaining detainees went to one of several camps where they worked voluntarily, at least in theory. Once a detainee was cooperative, he or she was moved to a rehabilitation center for vocational and other skill-building courses; Min Yuen supporters who screening teams initially labeled "grey" often met them there. At its peak in mid-1950, the camp population was over ten thousand, including several hundred Malays and Indians alongside the Chinese majority. The operation's material costs were staggering: by 1952, the Federation government had shelled out nearly $30 million on detention camps alone.[82]

The largest reform center was Taiping Rehabilitation Camp. James Patrick helped oversee its activities as deputy head of rehabilitation. He later described the detainees, guards, and rehabilitation staff as "one big happy family," with "the object of the exercise . . . to try to re-educate them so they were good lads when they went back and read the gospel of the glory of British rule and so on." "Many refused to be re-educated in any way," he also recalled. "The hard core chaps . . . weren't going to give in under any circumstances."[83] Tom Driberg, a Labour MP and an old friend of Mountbatten's, visited Taiping in 1950 and offered a different perspective.[84] He likened the camp to the wartime internment facility at Wilton Park and minced no words when he offered his observations in the *Reynolds News:* it was "a disgrace to the British Commonwealth, to the Federation of Malaya and to the Labour Government."[85] Taken as a whole, the camps were hardly the reform meccas of Patrick's recollection. Instead, they often morphed into sites of Communist indoctrination, and hard-core detainees—who called the camp Taiping University—converted ordinary criminals and innocents who had been swept up in the mass arrests.[86] At Ipoh Camp, among the worst, thirteen hundred detainees resorted to hunger strikes and rioting, demanding the release of all female detainees and better camp conditions. In some instances, guards "lost their heads" and opened fire with live ammunition; in other cases, the situation, according to the deputy commissioner of Malaya's criminal investigation department, "was now worse than that experienced by internees under [the] Jap regime."[87]

"Rehabilitation" was liberal imperialism's counterpart to its innocuous-sounding "repatriation," another in a long line of ever-evolving terms that began with "moral effect." The reformist impulses in Malaya's "progressive stage system" of confinement were less important than the ideologically, structurally, and legally enabled layers of control and coercion. Detainees who returned to China told disturbing stories of abuse to the PRC's Overseas Chinese Relief Committee.[88] One detainee, Chen Yung-liang, recounted to the committee that he had been arrested under suspicion of "being a messenger of the Malayan communists." He described what happened next:

> After taking me to the police station, the detectives stripped me of all my clothes and said to me: "Your body is not made of steel. Now speak and be quick!" When I simply replied that I knew nothing, their fists rained upon my head and body. In the evening they again forced me to take off my clothes, shut me in a bathroom and poured water on me with a hose for several hours. They then dried me with an electric fan. This process was repeated again and again until I was stiffened with cold. Afterwards I was tortured with all sorts of cruel methods, such as forcing sharp bamboo sticks into my finger tips.[89]

Another repatriate, Cheng Chun-yung, told how interrogators tied ropes to one finger on each of his hands as well as to one toe on each of his feet. The British torturers then hoisted him to the ceiling, after which they let go of the ropes. They then starved him for several days. He also recollected a camp riot that "British troops and police" suppressed using live ammunition and "rifle butts and clubs"; the security forces killed three detainees and injured several others. Among the uninjured, Cheng was locked with other detainees in cages beneath the hot sun for several days, after which he went back to "a dark cell" where interrogators "inserted 2½ inch pins under my finger nails and burned these pins with fire." Chen Sze-an, a female repatriate, recounted that camp personnel "took off the clothes of the female prisoners and pricked their breasts with pins." Another former Chinese squatter said he had "soapy water [forced] down his throat."[90]

The committee published the repatriates' accounts, wrote to Britain's Foreign Office on several occasions, and copied the UN Economic and Social Department, among other external bodies. The Chinese government demanded permission to inspect Malaya's detention and transit camps, appealing to the British public writ large: "We believe that every fair-minded Englishman who wishes to live peaceably side by side with the Chinese will hope along with us for the success of this mission of investigation."[91] Authorities in Peking "protested against various cruelties which the British Colonial authorities in Malaya have committed against Chinese," emphasizing that it had received no reply. They targeted the "so-called emergency regulations since 18th June 1948," stating:

> The torture, beatings, swindling and rape which our compatriots have suffered are too numerous to mention. . . . As for the various shocking and bloody incidents, as to the searchings of Chinese schools under various pretexts, the alteration of the visa procedure for the return to Malaya, the bombing of Chinese villages, the application of "collective punishment," the impressment of able-bodied men and the establishment of "ghost areas," they are even more numerous.[92]

Newspapers in Britain and the United States picked up the story. *The Observer* dismissed the alleged "British 'persecution' of the Chinese" as Communist propaganda, saying that "the best thing, evidently, would be to let this delegation in. Its members would quickly find that the preposterous allegations contained in the statement were without foundation."[93]

Within government circles in Kuala Lumpur and London, outrage and obfuscation reigned. Officials in the Foreign Office characterized the Overseas Chinese Relief Committee as "violently attacking British authorities in Malaya," though they were at a loss as to how to respond.[94] Still, deportations had to continue: "We should not let ourselves be deterred by threats when we have a good case for the deportation of undesirables," the Foreign Office said.[95] As for China's demands, internal British memoranda emphasized that "press correspondents have never been permitted to visit detention camps," and the Chinese relief delegation was several rungs below the fourth estate when it came to access to Malaya.[96] Moreover, against the spirit of the Geneva Conventions, which allowed humanitarian organizations like the Red Cross "to offer its services," top British officials overseeing operations in Southeast Asia informed the colonial secretary that "we were not in favour of encouraging inspection by an impartial body such as the International

Red Cross. The detention camps, though extremely good by Asian standards, might bring forth unfavourable comments from anyone unaccustomed to those standards."[97]

While the British government gave some attention to denying MP Driberg's accusations, it dismissed out of hand China's allegations through a litany of condemnations. In a memorandum sent to "His Majesty's Representatives" in just about every country and colony around the world, the Foreign Office reminded its emissaries that the "press and radio propaganda" coming from the Chinese Ministry of Foreign Affairs in no way reflected the British government's repatriation policies or conditions in the detention and transit camps.[98] As far as Foreign Secretary Morrison was concerned, it was the Chinese government that was to blame. He informed Chinese officials that those slated for repatriation "would not be in detention camps now if China had been willing to accept the obligations of a sovereign state to take back its own subjects when they are deported. . . . If the Chinese Government continues to cut itself off from contacts with the outside world, and to muzzle the press in China, it is natural that wholly distorted notions should prevail in China regarding events outside."[99]

In February 1950, eighteen months into the emergency, Malaya's mounting crisis continued. According to Gurney, "security in the Federation has seriously deteriorated as a result of increased Communist activity. This is borne out by a rise in the number of incidents, a decrease in bandit killings and by reports of comparatively large-scale bandit movements and concentrations."[100] Detention camps were full, and even as the "hush hush" deportations continued, colonial officials could not possibly issue detention and deportation orders for the entire population of suspected Communist insurgents and their civilian supporters. The high commissioner made clear to Malcolm MacDonald the crux of the problem: "I have always held and have recently said publicly that upon the solution of this squatter problem depends the ending of the Emergency, because it is this floating, illiterate and mostly alien community that supplies the bandit forces with men, food and shelter. Its existence is a legacy of the Japanese occupation."[101] Gurney said that nothing more could be done from "the civil side to hasten action in this field."[102]

The "squatter problem" had to be solved, and Malaya's first director of operations, Lieutenant-General Harold Briggs, soon came out of retirement to take charge, laying the groundwork for the Federation's future military strategy. Briggs had been selected for the job because of his extensive wartime experience, which included the Burmese refugee crisis. Much like Gray, Briggs was a career military man appointed to a civilian post. Briggs ranked above Gray, coordinated all security forces, and developed an operational strategy that would transform the Federation's rural areas.[103] It was these areas—or Eleanor Roosevelt's "small places, close to home"—where hundreds of thousands of Chinese squatters lived. A new set of emergency regulations and the practices used to carry them out were poised to test Roosevelt's quip that "unless [universal human] rights have meaning there, they have little meaning anywhere."[104]

Prior to Briggs's arrival, colonial officials had experimented with resettlement policies, particularly in areas notorious for aiding insurgents. In late 1948 the Federation created a committee to investigate squatter policy. It recommended the government settle-in-place the vast peasant population rather than move it, though events soon rendered the committee's suggestions unworkable. The area of Pulai was one early hotbed of struggle. Security forces rounded up its inhabitants, dispatched some to camps, and settled-in-place nearly 350 others. The village was surrounded with two layers of barbed wire, and was controlled through curfews, body searches, movement orders, and food distribution policies "in an attempt," according to the historian Tan Tang Phee, "to cut off supplies between the Communists and the villagers."[105] In other cases, colonial officials relocated nearly two thousand villagers from Sungei Siput and another thousand from Sungei Batu to other areas. In the case of Sungei Batu, the government's poor planning found villagers living in dilapidated tents, some desperately trying to escape.

In Titi, locals remembered Japanese massacres, and many who survived remained in the village and became steadfast Communists after the war. The nearby district officer looked to the past for a present-day solution. He suggested, "The Japs put barbed wire around Titi and Pertang, garrisoned these towns with troops and made all Chinese of the locality live within the defended areas. . . . Could we not try the same idea?" A few months later the police and army moved in and forcibly removed six hundred villagers, burning their huts to the ground and rendering Titi a "no human area."[106] Individual state administrations oversaw resettlement processes, which meant they were rife with logistical and bureaucratic challenges when one state sought to resettle "alien squatters" into the territory of another.[107] Then there was the matter of security. Gurney's men could not protect a village that "had declared its loyalty and was under administrative control" from being "a bandit target." According to the high commissioner, one such example was

Simpang Tiga, where the Malayan National Liberation Army evaded "barbed-wire defences and auxiliary police" and burned the village to the ground.[108]

Part of the new Briggs Plan, launched in June 1950, was legally enabled through Emergency Regulation 17E, which created powers to forcibly relocate.[109] Colonial authorities removed squatters from the jungle fringes into "protected areas." Like previous experiments, barbed wire surrounded these areas where police enforced strict control and punishment measures with "domination . . . essentially the police priority task."[110] By cutting the civilian supply lines and shooting to kill any suspected Communist insurgent trying to enter the resettled areas, or any civilian exiting without permission, Briggs planned to win the war by starving Chin Peng's men of material support and much-needed information, while also eliminating them whenever possible. He also directly targeted the Federation's civilian population. According to one top secret report, "successes against bandit gangs, though essential to security, is only in effect a 'rap on the Knuckles.' It is at the 'heart' that we must aim—to dominate the Chinese populated and squatter areas."[111]

To do so, Briggs launched the British Empire's largest forced migration since the era of trade in enslaved people. Five-hundred seventy-three thousand people, nearly 90 percent of whom were Chinese, were relocated into 480 resettlements. It was not only the scale of the forced migration but also its speed that created massive bureaucratic challenges and hardships. The resource-strapped Federation government remarkably guaranteed individual states all the funds, supplies, and manpower necessary to execute the policy. Alongside the resettlement of rural squatters, Briggs also took aim at the rubber plantation and the tin mine laborers. He created "labour lines," which were effectively resettlement areas and labor pools for the Federation's dollar-producing industries, much as the resettlement camps were sources of "casual labour" for the Federation's estate owners. In total, officials displaced and relocated approximately 650,000 workers into the "labour lines," which brought the overall forced migration and resettlement of British subjects and alleged aliens to nearly 1.2 million.[112]

In February 1950 James Griffiths took the helm of the Colonial Office in London, and the Federation government informed him, as it had Creech Jones, that it needed "more ruthless action against those helping the terrorists."[113] As Briggs launched his assault on the rural population, Gurney's government tightened further its "power to detain a suspect on the lines of the United Kingdom Wartime Regulation 18B."[114] Federation officials already used the power of preventive detention much as the metropolitan government had during the Second World War; in the words of one Federation report, "a person is in short tried for what it is believed he has done; he is detained for what it is reasonably thought he is likely to do."[115] A detainee's right of appeal and release was now more stringent.[116] A few months later Malaya's attorney general wrote to Colonial Secretary Griffiths informing him "there is no room for any 'sitting on the fence.' All those who believe in the democratic way of life must join in the fight, and *we must fight with our gloves off*—all of us—Malays, Chinese, Indians, Europeans and Eurasians. . . . Let everyone declare himself now, and give wholehearted support to the men of our Security Forces who are giving such valiant service to our cause."[117]

For those Chinese living in Malaya's rural areas, Britain's "gloves off" policy meant, in many cases, that the government did not warn villagers of their impending removals. This was particularly true in areas branded as "bad" or "black." One colonial official later described that "when resettlement happened, the first thing was that it was like an ambush almost; suddenly the dawn morning, all of the police, all of the soldiers came in and surrounded the village. It was pretty terrifying."[118] With the element of surprise, security forces hoped to prevent anyone from slipping through the cordon and making their way to the Communist insurgent camps. The rapid-paced operations meant villagers often gathered few possessions before they were loaded into trucks awaiting their transfer to resettlement camps. Families were separated in the confusion and villages dispersed. As truckloads of "alien Chinese squatters" were brought to new resettlement sites that dotted the Malayan countryside and urban fringes, security forces torched everything left behind. One Communist insurgent witnessed his village burn to the ground: "I would never forget the scene. The British soldiers set fire and burned down my homeland. For nearly a week, I could not do anything except watch the smoke go up to the sky. The fury only fuelled my hatred and strengthened my will to fight against the British Colonial Government."[119]

According to government reports, "safe and protected" living sites awaited the dislocated masses. Government financial assistance would help with the resettlement process, as would medical services, schools, water supplies, electrification, and cultivatable plots for villagers' crops. In reality, the sites welcoming the internally displaced hordes were inhospitable when not uninhabitable. They included "sandy wasteland[s]," intermittent swamp areas, muddy areas with little to no drainage, and vast tracts piled with lode tin tailings.[120] Occasionally government barracks were hastily erected for habitation, though temporary shelter often consisted of little more than a lean-to. Local officials expected refugees to build their own permanent dwellings with whatever materials they had brought with them, or with items they purchased using the government "upheaval allowance." In a kind of colonial debt peonage, the "allowance" was, in fact, a loan, for those able to get one.

The government fragmented preexisting social networks of support and belonging. Many villagers could not understand their new neighbors. Local officials purposefully settled Hokkien and Cantonese speakers alongside those who spoke Hakkas, Teochius, and Foochow, to prevent solidarity and stymie the flow of information.[121] Some resettlement camps had as many as thirteen thousand people, though on average populations were small, as one hundred to a thousand refugees from disparate parts of the Federation were thrown together in various states of hunger, terror, and confusion.

Few witnesses to the events recall the resettlement amenities touted in government circulars at the time.[122] According to one press report, "None of the squatter resettlement areas in Johore, Kedah, Kelantan, Trengganu and Malacca has piped water or electricity."[123] Villagers navigated putrid conditions just to reach fresh water. In her autobiographical accounts of the period, Han Suyin recalled "a fetid mangrove swamp . . . [and] the jungle rearing its sombre menace behind . . . the barbed wire manned by a police post." According to Han Suyin, there were "four hundred beings, including children, huddled there; foot-deep in brackish mud."

> The families moved to the swamp were without water. The ditches were of earth, shallow and overflowing with dirt within a week. The wells were across the road. . . . To get to the road, and then up to the highground wells, to the shops or out to the rubber estates, the people of the swamp crossed two police posts. Soon it was an unwritten rule that the people of the swamp must pay ten cents each time they crossed [a police post] to collect their water from the wells.[124]

Malaya's vast peasant population scurried just to feed itself. Federation officials had burned their crops and confiscated some of their livestock during the forced removals, yet in the resettlement areas "the huts were squeezed tight together," according to Han Suyin, and there was "no room for poultry runs, no room for pigsties, no room for vegetable plots." In her camp, officials allocated the small plot of vacant land for a "police-playing field." There were few clinics or schools during the early 1950s.[125]

The government did find funds, however, to ensure a twenty-four-hour regime of control, surveillance, and discipline. During the early months of the operation, officials needed 770 tons of barbed wire to secure the "resettlement areas," according to *The Straits Times*. This was hardly surprising since a seven-and-a-half-foot double apron fence surrounded most villages.[126] While electricity was often nonexistent in the refugees' makeshift dwellings, multiple watchtowers with spotlights eventually dotted the resettlement edges, fanning out from the police post located in the area's center. Federation officials painted a number on each household door and listed alongside it the names, ages, and occupations of those who lived inside. The government strictly controlled the villagers' movements with dusk-to-dawn curfews within the settlement's gates. Guards monitored these gates and lined up men and women in gender-divided queues for thorough searches every time villagers entered or exited the barbed-wire compound. In some areas, colonial officials introduced twenty-two-hour house lockdowns as a form of collective punishment for "non-cooperation." They also introduced food control. Rubber tappers who worked in the estates by day recalled the resettlement years as ones of semistarvation.[127] "I was happy to know we were going to have our own farming lot from the government," one refugee recalled. "I thought we could be protected by the government and kept safe from the Communists. . . . I never thought life behind barbed wire could be like that. Like a concentration camp."[128]

These resettlement areas became one of many sites for screening, or interrogation, further exacerbating a problem festering since the emergency's inception in the spring of 1948. Coercive measures were of little use without intelligence and lots of it, something the Colonial Office and MI5 well understood. Malaya's spiraling crisis became another example of intelligence failure. Once again, in still another corner of the empire, the absence of political policing reflected a self-satisfied hubris that had internalized the empire's partnership ethos, at best, and clung to nineteenth-century ideas of toddling children, at worst. The empire needed a massive intelligence overhaul, and MI5 was doing the best it could. Successive directors-general and countless security liaison officers circulated across the empire's hotspots, though their eruptions outpaced MI5's capacity to keep up. In 1949 Creech Jones had wanted to export more wartime intelligence knowledge to the empire, writing to all his governors and high commissioners, "I am aware that in several Colonies progress has been made in strengthening [intelligence and special branches], but it may well be that there is still more to be done in improving their efficiency and in applying the experience of [European] metropolitan countries and the methods which have been developed there."[129]

By "methods," the colonial secretary was referring to those developed in Britain's wartime Combined Services Detailed Interrogation Centres (CSDICs) in London and Bad Nenndorf, Germany, as discussed in earlier chapters. During and after the war, the methods cultivated in these sites devolved to certain colonial locations but by no means all of them. In the case of Malaya, Creech Jones's men had bemoaned to military brass "the shortage of Interrogators" and let it be known that "apart from the shortage of trained staff, we suspect that the Government of the Federation of Malaya is not fully aware of the methods and techniques developed during the war when interrogation on a large scale had to be undertaken."[130] Malaya's hydra-headed intelligence problem had both organizational and human resource dimensions, something the Colonial Office was again quick to point out to its military counterparts: "Our biggest weakness is the lack of full-time interrogation teams, manned by experienced officers and the very necessary interpreters. Until interrogation can be tackled on a large scale, estimates of enemy strength remain largely a matter of 'knocking off noughts' or 'dividing by three' as the occasion appears to warrant it."[131]

In August 1949 officials in London were still looking on in despair at the continued lack of trained interrogators and interpreters, a problem so evident throughout the empire that one wonders, with the benefit of hindsight, how such glaring mistakes kept recurring. A massive colonial bureaucracy operated from London, and reining in decentralized authority in the colonies required an administrative reorganization. The culture of British imperial governance, however, rested on the "trust the man on the spot" ethos, and while the Colonial Office worked to centralize intelligence matters and disseminate knowledge accumulated in one colony to other parts of the empire, its officials could only cajole local governors and high commissioners on matters of day-to-day operations. They continued with their invectives "urging the Government of the Federation of Malaya to agree to set up a translation and interrogation center [CSDIC]. . . . The project is, we consider, essential for the high-grade interrogation of bandit prisoners."[132] Later that year Gurney and Gray finally agreed to bring on "Colonel MacMillan," who had "wide experience of the interrogation of prisoners of war in the Middle East." He would advise them on the establishment of a CSDIC with the understanding that "the Centre will be directly under Commissioner of Police, Federation [i.e., Gray]."[133] The center was modeled on the "CSDIC experience" elsewhere, which included "the methods and organisation employed in Burma . . . for the interrogation of Japanese prisoners of war and the examination of captured documents."[134] Moreover, high-ranking spies in Singapore and in London laid out precisely how Malaya's new intelligence operation should be staffed and organized based on successful interrogation operations in other imperial locales. According to internal reports, there had to be "provision of screening teams to be available for police and military operations at all levels . . . systematic interrogation of important prisoners . . . the examination of captured documents on a co-ordinated basis . . . and a detailed interrogation centre."[135]

Around the time of Briggs's arrival in 1950, the Malayan Combined Services Interrogation Centre was finally semioperational. According to Leon Comber, a Chinese-speaking member of Malaya's special branch, Malaya's CSDIC was located at a top-secret military interrogation site, which had been "cater[ing] for the reception, interrogation and the aftercare of surrendered enemy personnel." Surrounded by a ten-foot-high barbed-wire fence and under 24/7 army patrol, the newly constituted CSDIC was located just outside Kuala Lumpur near the police training depot. The existence of the interrogation center, which the few in the know called the "White House," was kept under wraps. Alongside the center was a landing strip where Auster aircraft deposited captured or surrendered insurgents for interrogation before they were sent to detention or turned and rendered double agents ready for deployment against their former comrades still in the jungle. Its interior was kitted out much like the London Cage and Camp 020. According to Comber, two-way mirrors graced interrogation rooms, and covert listening devices abounded. There was also a special workshop where agents crafted "technical devices," or local versions of James Bond–like "gadgets . . . as the various implements of sabotage and destruction were known."[136]

As for interrogators, Comber remembered that "MI5 and MI6 officers, including a future director, flit[ted] in and out, and the army provided Special Branch with military intelligence officers."[137] The Federation sent locally sourced interrogators "for training at MI5's headquarters," where officers like Gray mingled with other colonial police commissioners; together they had opportunities "to meet senior military intelligence officers, the director-general of MI5, other senior British intelligence officers and senior Colonial officials."[138] Such shared knowledge extended well beyond face-to-face indoctrination and in-person conversations and lectures. In the spring of 1949, at Creech Jones's behest, Gurney had penned a top-secret, eleven-page memorandum "setting out the present operations in Malaya which the Oversea[s] Defence Committee could consider with a view to its use as a basis for general guidance to Colonial Governments." The Colonial Office had already circulated a "Preparation of Defence Schemes" to administrators throughout the empire and threw its full weight behind the high commissioner's detailed, single-spaced document. It drew directly on Gurney's experiences in the Gold Coast, Palestine, and Malaya, and addressed everything from "terrorism" and identity "registration" to "information and intelligence." As with the earlier "Preparation of Defence Schemes," Gurney's memo was secretly circulated to governors and high commissioners across the British Empire.[139]

Chinese interpreters were also imported to Malaya. Successful recruitment drives throughout Asia as well as in London's School of Oriental and African Studies offered "invaluable assistance" to MI5 and Federation officials. These interpreters worked alongside special branch and military intelligence officers based in the White House and in the countryside's mobile interrogation units. The increased intelligence flow was used not only for operational purposes but also for more effective psychological warfare activities. In early 1950, the Joint Information and Propaganda Committee coordinated military and civilian units in Malaya to improve the Federation's previous, lackluster information efforts. Still, so much depended on local knowledge, and British officials struggled to get it. "During the first three years we had no intelligence," one officer recalled, "no material upon which to study the enemy's mentality and to study his future policies and intentions."[140]

Military command stated clearly that "an Interrogation Centre cannot be run as a welfare institution. . . . It is a place where firm discipline needs to be maintained." Questions remained on how effective interrogation teams were in exacting useful, reliable information.[141] For certain, CSDIC interrogators deployed unorthodox and coercive tactics—some horrific—to squeeze information out of suspects, some of whom they turned into double agents. With the Briggs Plan well under way, a panoply of interrogators deployed their crafts in Malaya. They included special branch officers; military intelligence officers, some of whom were attached to special branch units; MI5 operatives, who included security liaison officers; and surrendered enemy personnel, whom interrogators had "turned" much as they had during Britain's wartime Double Cross operations. It wasn't until the signing and ratifying of postwar humanitarian laws—not long after British interrogators were shin-screwing prisoners in Bad Nenndorf, as the British government knew—that Britain was bound by international law not only to condemn such practices but also to enforce their prohibition within British domestic jurisdiction.

Turning to Malaya, the Geneva Conventions of 1949 universally forbade torture, and regardless of whether British officials agreed that an "armed conflict not of an international character," as outlined under Common Article 3, existed in the Federation, the British military would, in 1955, suggest that the thrust of the conventions applied. In its pamphlet "Interrogation in War," the War Office stated:

> Prisoners will be treated according to the Geneva Convention at all times; interrogation by torture or ill-treatment is not, in any circumstances, permitted. Indeed, it is to be doubted whether such methods would prove fruitful as the prisoner might tend to say what he believed the interrogator wanted to hear, whether or not this accorded with the facts. Acts of violence or spite only tend to arouse the prisoner's animosity. Moreover, such an approach really amounts to a confession of failure. The basic aim of the interrogator is to win the willing co-operation of the prisoner since only then is he likely to gain complete, reliable and accurate military information. This co-operation and respect he is likely to gain by a blend of firmness, understanding and sympathy.[142]

It may seem disingenuous that the military would issue such commands demanding compliance with the Geneva Conventions while knowing full well that it had encouraged, as did the British colonial administration and security services, the creation of interrogation systems and the spread of interrogation methods that had been so effective during wartime but that now violated international law, at least in the spirit, if not original intent, of the convention's drafters, as we've seen. Brutal interrogation techniques and the systems enabling them were, indeed, deliberately expanded through the empire both before and after 1955 and quietly condoned because their results were thought similar to those brought about in Bad Nenndorf, which Director of Military Intelligence Major-General Douglas Packard had called "superior to anything obtained by the interrogation procedures of our enemies."[143]

There's much debate about this among historians. Some insist that prisoners in the wartime CSDICs "were fed and clothed, and then questioned in a quiet and sympathetic manner," while others concede that torture unfolded in German interrogation cells and those throughout the empire, though such one-offs occurred because of "Britain's unwillingness to standardise its interrogation practices . . . for a remarkably long time," and "poor discipline among interrogation officials."[144] The latter was true, giving rise to gruesome innovations, which authorities often knew about, doing little to stop them and instead actively covering them up when necessary. Standardization of interrogation had also been ongoing for years, and in the postwar era it was spreading across the empire where, as we shall see, methods to force suspects to talk were increasingly similar from one interrogation center to the next.

Several British officials insisted, however, that little pressure was needed to get Communist insurgents and suspects to cooperate. They suggested this was due to fighting fatigue and the interrogators' powers of restraint and persuasion. Guy Madoc, the head of Malaya's special branch from 1952 to 1954, remembers that he toed this line. "A captured or surrendered terrorist," Madoc insisted, "found that he was quite reasonably treated, kindly treated."[145] Others like John Sankey, who had served in the Palestine Police Force before he spent twelve years in Malaya, recalled that "the main way" of turning a suspect was "psychological, really":

> The techniques of the good man and the bad man, the harsh man and the easy man . . . you continue to bombard the suspect with questions, you keep at it. Tiredness came into it. That was a great weapon. . . . You'd keep suspects awake. You'd make sure that they suffer from fatigue, and by these means you'd break their resistance down. And in the end, I don't know one who didn't in the end give us some information.[146]

Others had different recollections. In 1960 a national serviceman recounted his intelligence corps training over a decade earlier. According to him, this training was at odds with the military guidelines:

> My platoon was taught, among other things, the way in which to interrogate a prisoner and we were told that, in certain cases, it would probably be necessary for us to use various forms of physical torture. The tortures that were described to us had the advantage of leaving none of the visible traces which might be noticed by members of the International Red Cross and included beating the prisoner after his body had been wrapped in a wet blanket, filling his body with water and holding him against a hot stove. Our instructor, a Regular sergeant in the Intelligence

Corps, told us that he had seen these tortures used against Japanese prisoners in Burma.[147]

Another army recruit, who served in Kenya before he arrived in Malaya, had a similar recollection. "Yeah, it [torture in order to get intelligence] was normal," he said. "Oh yeah, beat a guy senseless you know, if necessary. Some of those guys would spill as soon as they saw you," because they knew torture awaited them if they didn't.[148] Deportees returning to China added specificity to such accounts. Their testimonies, as we've seen, suggest methods different from those that were supposed to leave no "visible traces." At the time, British authorities knew that "threats with revolver shots, kickings, punchings, and severe beatings with a rattan cane to the insertion of a needle under the fingernails" took place.[149] According to one special branch officer, Dick Craig, "Officers on the ground were left to collect information in whatever manner they saw fit. The employment of excessive strong-arm measures to extract information was common, and much use was made of the highly vaunted truth drug."[150] Others, like the local journalist Harry Miller, who befriended senior police officials and had a rare inside view of their tactics, wrote:

> To many of these sergeants every Chinese was a bandit or a potential bandit, and there was only one treatment for them, they were to be "bashed around." If they would not talk a sock on the jaw or a kick in the guts might have the desired result. I myself once saw a British sergeant encouraging a heavy-booted policeman to treat a suspect like a football.[151]

The resettlement areas themselves were vast interrogation sites where teams could screen the local population in situ and at will. Alongside special branch, police, MI5, and military officers, local Chinese home guards also had a role to play. They sussed out those who still slipped materials to insurgents and forced others to divulge information. More often than not, frustration prevailed. British information officer John Perry Robinson described how screening teams "infuriated by the squatters' stubborn silence, by their not having seen anything of an incident committed right under their noses, by their not having the least idea who put up the Communist posters plastered on their huts, dismissed them all as 'f-ing Reds' and were liable to knock them about."[152]

Interrogation teams behind the barbed wire were ubiquitous. Some organized screening parades whereby villagers would walk, one at a time, past a small van. Inside were turned insurgents or special branch informers, known locally as "ghost heads." When a suspected sympathizer walked by, they knocked on the van's interior to alert the screening teams, who then pulled aside the suspect for further interrogation. Other times, villagers quietly called out a neighbor, who local officials then picked up for interrogation and possibly detention or deportation, or both.[153]

Few villagers knew who they could and could not trust. They were terrified of British security force members, who they called "red-haired devils."[154] Guan Shui Lian recalled that one of her brothers went to Ipoh Detention Camp before he was deported to China. As for her other brother:

> I heard my mother crying at the door. My brother had led a group of guerrillas to a tin quarry to get food from the villagers. Unfortunately, the authorities had been tipped off and he was shot dead while trying to escape. They then stripped off his clothes and left only his underwear on. They tied his corpse to a truck and dragged him like a dead dog for more than 10 kilometres back to our camp. He was already unrecognisable by the time the truck arrived.[155]

The scale and scope of the Briggs Plan, and the tactics used to implement it, were seemingly successful vis-à-vis the Communists. As the historians Bayly and Harper tell us:

> Chin Peng, for one, had assumed that the forced movement of people by the British would fail, just as similar schemes by the Japanese had failed. The central strategic assumption of the revolution was that the villages would rise in resistance to the British. But the MNLA [Malayan National Liberation Army] could offer them little protection from an equally tenacious and better-equipped regime. Peasant resistance was futile, the Malayan revolution foundered on a false premise.[156]

With dwindling Min Yuen food supplies, the Communists could not hold larger units together. They issued their October Directives in 1951, creating smaller insurgent units, initiating food production in the jungle, deemphasizing sabotage on infrastructure and rubber trees that brought civilian suffering, and focusing on arms raids and attacks on the security forces. While Federation officials may not have felt it in the moment, resettlement forced the Communists to undertake a drastic change in strategy while "avoiding harming the people."[157] The October Directives were partly a recognition that Communist-sponsored terror produced a terrified population. "You just keep silent, away from both sides, the local Min Yuen and government informants, otherwise you will get into trouble one day," one squatter recalled.[158] The Communists pinned future hopes on peasants like this but were slow to recognize how self-defeating their actions had been. For many villagers, just surviving the insurgency was their priority.

Early that month, Gurney climbed into the back of his Rolls-Royce together with his wife and private secretary and settled in for the ride to Fraser's Hill, a resort town nestled in the highlands north of Kuala Lumpur, for a weekend of colonial leisure. His Rolls was fitted out for a man in his position, complete with a crown insignia and a Federation flag, which flapped in the breeze as the vehicle climbed the narrow road that wound through mile after mile of dense thickets. Unbeknownst to Gurney or his single escort vehicle, hidden within the jungle brush was a Communist platoon of thirty insurgents who had been waiting, on and off, for nearly two days for a suitable target. In their most opportunistic strike of the insurgency, Chin Peng's men opened fire with Bren guns as Gurney's vehicle rounded a sharp bend. Within moments, dozens of bullet holes riddled the Rolls-Royce. The high commissioner, hit in the head and body, staggered out of its back seat toward a bank, where he collapsed, dead in one of the empire's remote, roadside gutters. His two companions survived.[159]

While Gurney had no doubt been careless, the ambush was nonetheless another measure of Britain's perceived failure not only to get hold of the Malayan situation but also to protect its own.[160] According to one army officer, the empire for those who lived in it was no longer the "sort of *Boys' Own Paper* stuff."[161] Indeed, Gurney's killing shattered some soldiers' boyhood fantasies. "The effect on British morale in the country was, of course, pronounced," said Richard Catling, who had survived Palestine's King David Hotel bombing and now grappled with Gurney's assassination, which devastated whatever camaraderie still bound Malaya's divided military and civil servants.[162] "I'm sorry to say," Guy Madoc, head of Malaya's special branch, recalled, "that a whole lot of us who thought about this finally reached the conclusion that the dreadful death of Gurney . . . was perhaps the turning point of the whole thing."[163]

CHAPTER 13

Systematized Violence

News of Gurney's assassination reached London just weeks before the 1951 general election. An ailing George VI, poised to undertake a long foreign tour, looked on with grave concern at the whittling away of Labour's majority, which was now only five seats. Such a razor-thin margin was thought to be unsustainable, and the king, who as head of state had to be present to approve a new prime minister, albeit ceremonially, feared he might find himself at a distant imperial outpost when Attlee's government fell. In September, at the king's urging, the prime minister dissolved Parliament and called for a snap election a month later.[1] His party ran on a platform of four main issues: "to secure peace; to maintain full employment and increase production; to bring down the cost of living; [and] to build a just society." The party's election manifesto reminded voters of its basic principles of "welfare at home, peace abroad, with a constant striving for international cooperation." Insofar as the empire was concerned, Labour drew a noteworthy bright line between its liberal imperialism and that of the Conservative Party with its "dark past":

> The Tory still thinks in terms of Victorian imperialism and colonial exploitation. His reaction in a crisis is to threaten force. His narrow outlook is an obstacle to that world-wide co-operation which alone makes peace secure. He would have denied freedom to India, Pakistan, Ceylon and Burma. . . . It is vital to the fate of

civilisation that the voice of Labour should be heard wherever and whenever the issues of war and peace are discussed between the spokesmen of the Great Powers.[2]

Whether voters were buying Labour's distinctions in imperial policies and practices is uncertain. What is clear is that Britons were overwhelmingly in favor of maintaining their nation's empire. In 1951 the Central Office of Information undertook a survey for the Colonial Office on "public knowledge of colonial affairs." While respondents remained woefully short on details—only four out of ten surveyed could name a single colony—nearly 75 percent of them believed Britain would be worse off without her empire. Insofar as partnership was concerned, only 20 percent believed Britain had a welfare role to play in the colonies. One respondent reflected the sentiment of many: "We are all taxed so high now—how can we help them?" One Colonial Office official whined over "the popular press, radio and cinemas . . . [continuing] to reflect public indifference and ignorance."[3] There's no denying the indifference of some Britons still trying to make sense of a costly war and a present and future where the empire was just there, like the tattered but comforting wallpaper in their living rooms. Measuring sentiment is holistic business, irreducible to one civil servant's focus on details and bureaucracy as opposed to an imperial sentiment that abounded in various forms—an imperial sentiment that popular media, the press, and marketers continued to reflect and reinforce. For the many bellicose imperialists in Britain's hardscrabble postwar world, the empire still reflected a greatness that was slipping through voters' fingers as they continued to face economic hardships that often remained on par with wartime conditions.

As far as the Tories were concerned, Labour had led the nation into fiscal ruin and international decline. The Conservatives' 1951 election manifesto played to their long-cultivated public sentiment, reminding Britons of what they once were and what had become of them:

Contrast our position to-day with what it was six years ago. Then all our foes had yielded. We all had a right to believe and hope that the fear of war would not afflict our generation nor our children. We were respected, honoured and admired throughout the world. . . . The attempt to impose a doctrinaire Socialism upon an Island which has grown great and famous by free enterprise has inflicted serious injury upon our strength and prosperity.[4]

Devaluation, nationalization, and the fiscal "reckless manner of our present rulers," the manifesto declared, had brought Britain to the brink. Yet there was hope for renewal for "the only Socialist Government in the Empire and Commonwealth" and its people, a hope that resided in the imperial past, present, and future. Churchill drew directly from his 1945 manifesto in messaging the era before Labour's "scuttling" of the empire:

> In the wider world outside this Island we put first the safety, progress and cohesion of the British Empire and Commonwealth of Nations. We must all stand together and help each other with all our strength both in Defence and Trade. To foster commerce within the Empire we shall maintain Imperial Preference. In our home market the Empire producer will have a place second only to the home producer. Next, there is the unity of the English-speaking peoples who together number hundreds of millions. They have only to act in harmony to preserve their own freedom and the general peace.[5]

For Labour, the 1951 election was an unmitigated disaster. Despite winning the popular vote, it lost twenty seats, which gave the Conservatives the majority and catapulted Churchill back into Downing Street. In a twist of fate, one premise for Attlee calling the election, George VI's trip, never took place. The king was too ill to travel, so Princess Elizabeth and the Duke of Edinburgh had undertaken the royal tour on his behalf. Three months after their departure the royal couple was at Treetops, a game lodge at the edge of Kenya's Aberdares forests, when they learned the news: the king was dead. Britain now had a twenty-five-year-old monarch sitting on its throne. In her first prorogation of Parliament, echoes of Queen Victoria could be heard. The nation's new queen reminded her grieving nation of its imperial greatness and the sacrifices being made to save the empire from encroaching terrorism. "My thoughts turn first to My beloved Father whose death was so deeply mourned throughout the Commonwealth and beyond," she wrote in pursuance of Her Majesty's commands. Elizabeth's attention then turned to Britain's place in the world rather than to the domestic and fiscal issues that continued to cripple a still-rationing nation. "My Ministers," she assured her people, "have continued to give the fullest support to the United Nations Organisation in its effort to promote international co-operation and to maintain peace." She then reminded Britons of the sacrifices being made to save Southeast Asia from further

Colonial troops in Queen Elizabeth II's coronation ceremony, processing from Westminster Abbey to Buckingham Palace, June 2, 1953

ruin: "In Malaya My Forces and the civil administration are carrying out a difficult task with patience and determination. In spite of great loss and suffering all communities are playing an ever more active part in the defence of their freedom."[6]

The queen was over eight months into her reign when she offered this imperial-internationalist fillip. In the intervening period, Churchill's new colonial secretary, Oliver Lyttleton, had undertaken a tour of Malaya—complete with an armored car, a caravan escort of six, and 350 members of the security forces acting as bodyguards. He returned to offer a scathing assessment of the Federation and its conflict-ridden administration. It was time, he asserted, as much of the Chinese population was effectively in lockup, to take firm control. Montgomery, now the deputy commander of the Supreme Headquarters of NATO, also weighed in, informing Churchill that "in all this welter of trouble 'the man' is what counts." He then wrote to Lyttleton in the pithiest of terms:

"We must have a plan, Secondly, we must have a man. When we have a plan and a man, we shall succeed: not otherwise."[7] Rumors abounded that Montgomery himself was going to take the helm, and British ministers gave serious consideration to him and to others like Arthur Harris, who had ascended to marshal of the Royal Air Force for having taken imperial lessons to the sky with his aerial bombardments of Germany.[8]

In the end, they brought in another empire-seasoned Irishman who, by the time he was finished, was synonymous with counterinsurgency success. He earned the sobriquet "Tiger of Malaya," one previously bestowed on Yamashita after he had carved through the Malay Peninsula and raised the Rising Sun over Singapore. The newly anointed tiger was the diminutive General Sir Gerald Templer, whose cocksure grin was perennially framed between a thin moustache and a Sam Browne belt whose narrow upper-body strap passed diagonally across his shoulder and chest, which was accessorized with a hefty amount of symbolic hardware. Templer, a Royal Irish Fusilier, had gone to Sandhurst and seen action on multiple fronts, including Iraq during Churchill's aerial bombing campaigns. While in Palestine during the Arab Revolt's "moral effect" years, according to his biographer, "he personally led patrols and set ambushes and carried out searches."[9] By the time Malaya came calling, Templer had picked up a knighthood, served as director of intelligence at the War Office, and was later vice-chief of the Imperial General Staff as Montgomery's protégé—all of which were crucial in preparing him for his new combined role as high commissioner and director of operations.

Templer "swept through Malaya like a whirlwind" and, according to his intelligence chief, generated "an electric change [that] came over the scene and things literally began to hum."[10] By the time Templer assumed his role in January 1952, the new supremo had more power than any general in British history since Oliver Cromwell. It was "absolute power," in the words of his biographer, and Templer quickly used it along with his charismatic verve to streamline command, stymie residual jealousies and petty squabbles, and further consolidate Malaya's intelligence system.[11] With complete civil and military power at his fingertips, he also benefited from personnel shakeups. After Gurney's death, several resignations were handed in; one departing official left to run the new top-secret intelligence department in the Commonwealth Relations Office. A cancer-ridden Briggs went to Cyprus, where he soon died.

Templer had the backing of Colonial Secretary Lyttleton, who prior to his personal venture through the peninsula lamented that "it is evident that we [are] on the way to losing control of the country, and

Communist attack in Perak, Malaya, c. 1952

soon."[12] Lyttleton wanted more military strength, and he got little push-back from Parliament, which had been notably quiescent throughout the emergency, with the exception of rumblings over government's decision to send eighteen-year-olds, including those conscripted under the National Service Act, into combat. Britain needed boots on the ground, and the Malayan military effort would prove an empire-wide one. Soldiers, pilots, sailors, and auxiliaries from around the world descended on the Federation in the form of ten RAF squadrons, seven British and eight Gurkha battalions, two Royal Armoured Corps regiments, one Royal Marine Commando brigade, a small flotilla from the navy, and three colonial battalions that drew forces from Southern Rhodesia and colonies in East Africa and the South Pacific. There were also the Malayan Regiment battalions. At the end of 1952, there were thirty thousand military personnel in Malaya. Those from the King's African Rifles, however, saw no reprieve from the empire's racialized hierarchy. The military's sliding pay scale and rations reflected liberal imperialism's values, as did the Africans' uniforms: khakis that looked more like inferior public school issue, with no belt loops or pockets. To pee in the jungle, a Black *askari*, or soldier, had to drop his fly-less trou. One said the uniforms "were insulting . . . and brought us no respect."[13]

Special Air Service evacuating an injured soldier from the jungle, Malaya, published 1953

Another military force present was the Malayan Scouts, led for a time by Colonel "Mad Mike" Calvert with rough-and-ready methods reminiscent of Palestine. Second-in-command to Orde Wingate in Burma, Calvert was well pedigreed to lead the covert activities of redeployed, wartime Special Air Service operatives. Joining these covert forces were white recruits from New Zealand, Australia, Southern Rhodesia, and South Africa, where frontier spirits combined with legally enabled systems of racial domination. Around the time Templer arrived, such a noxious combination had led to Calvert's scuttling, as the Malayan Scouts' methods and behavior, from bucking the chain of command to holding wild parties, were noteworthy, even in the context of the times.[14] Nevertheless, in some civil and military circles, the unwavering belief in covert operations persisted. At the start of the Malayan Emergency, and in the aftermath of Palestine's covert operation fiascos, Creech Jones and others were keen to have still another go at hit squads. The Colonial Office had endorsed the recruitment of ex–Force 136 officers—many of whom were found on the barstools of the Special Forces Club in Knightsbridge—to spearhead Gurney's "frontier force" or "jungle force" initiative, otherwise known as the Ferret Force. Joining them were former Special Operations Executive (SOE) pioneers like the Chinese expert and colonial administrator Robert Thompson, and together, they directed the police, who constituted much of the force's rank and file. According to the Colonial Office, these ferretized men were to "locate and destroy insurgent elements who are taking cover in jungle country [and] to drive such elements into open country where they can be dealt with by regular Army and police units."[15]

While the Ferret Force had uneven success in implementing its own form of guerrilla warfare, the idea of covert operations remained alive and well. Lyttleton was obsessed with it and reassured Churchill's new cabinet that "special investigation teams aimed at certain individuals—that is, to hunt down individual men from Communist higher formations through their families, sweethearts, etc. . . . will be undertaken shortly."[16] That Templer was an old hand with the SOE was no small matter in reviving like-minded units in the empire. While invaliding in London during the war—he had fallen victim in Italy to a baby grand piano flying out of a bombed truck—Templer sat on the SOE's executive council. Such a leadership role no doubt fueled his ideas on how to eliminate Communists in Malaya, whom he renamed "communist terrorists," or CTs for short. In fact, it was under his government's order that "the designation 'bandit' will not be used in future official reports and Press releases."[17]

The shift in nomenclature was as much for the outside world, particularly the Americans, as for anyone else. On this score, a British liaison in Washington could not have been clearer:

> As we saw in Greece, when the Greek Government were for long anxious to describe the Communists only as banditry, international public opinion in the United States . . . and elsewhere is inclined to take the line that when wholesale military actions are required to suppress mere internal unrest, it is in some way due to bad government. This is especially so in a colony; and instead of receiving sympathy and support from American public opinion in our praiseworthy struggle to combat the well-known international Communist menace, we shall merely be regarded as a bad colonial power coping with rebellions.[18]

Along with jettisoning the term *bandit*, the British government did not share with the Americans all the unsavory details of its counterinsurgency efforts and other aspects of its colonial rule. According to a secret memorandum "disclosed only to expatriate officers and only then on a very strict 'need-to-know' basis":

> "GUARD" applied to official documents, including signals and reports, means that the particular document is NOT to be shown to the Americans without the prior agreement of the originator. The fact that a document does not bear the word "GUARD" does not necessarily mean that it may be shown to the Americans. In particular, no Foreign Office document may be shown to the Americans, whether marked GUARD or not, without consultation with the Foreign Office. . . . Signals whose contents must never, so far as can be foreseen, be disclosed to the Americans, will be marked "TOP SECRET AND GUARD," regardless of the security classification of their contents.

This applied throughout the empire.[19]

When it came to Templer's reimagining of Wingate's earlier Special Night Squads, he was again in lockstep with the Colonial Office. "I propose to use special squads of experienced jungle fighters," he wrote to Lyttleton. "They will really be 'killer squads' (though I can promise you that I won't call them that, with a view to the questions you might have to answer in the House)." Templer's biggest worry, however, was maintaining order in his troops. "The use of 'killer squads,'" he noted to the colonial secretary, "has a bad effect on the fighting morale of all those who are not in the 'killer squads' since they never get a proper crack."[20]

At the core of Templer's success was his expansion of the CSDICs, which we have seen evolving during the wartime and postwar periods, as well as other interrogation practices. He told Harry Miller of *The Straits Times* that they were his "absolute top priority" and emphasized that "the Emergency will be won by our intelligence system."[21] Here too the Colonial Office agreed that "the importance of intelligence in the Malayan campaign cannot be exaggerated."[22] With Gurney and his bickering cabal gone, Templer's first choice to fill the post of director of intelligence was Dick White, one of the masterminds behind the wartime CSDICs and their expansion to Bad Nenndorf, among other postwar locales. White, however, was on to bigger things, poised as he was to take over MI5. He did visit Malaya in 1954 after he ascended to

MI5's directorship to further shore up colonial relations and to provide additional MI5 officers to tutor recruits at the Malayan Special Branch Training School.[23] Templer ultimately tapped Jack Morton from Security Intelligence Far East in Singapore as director of intelligence. Guy Madoc, a onetime Japanese POW who secretly began his magnus opus on Malayan birds while imprisoned, became head of special branch in 1952 and remained in the post before taking over for Morton two years later. Robert Thompson, who had served under Briggs, stayed on, bringing his own pre-emergency knowledge, as another of Wingate's former right-hand men, to Templer's jungle hunts for terrorists.[24]

This was a major turnaround from the controversial earlier Ferret Force. Wingate's disciples had made good with the men they had, which included 4,500 national servicemen by May 1950. Many of these national servicemen "would have rather been doing something else," as John William Noble recalled. Ambushed on his train ride into the Federation, Noble emphasized that while "our training was done by people who had done it before," little prepared him for hunting down the Communists, or in local parlance, "jungle bashing." "It took so long to get so few bandits" in a jungle that was as feared as the "bandits" who had "terrorized European planters . . . kidnapped and tortured them," according to Noble. Leeches were ever present, and if they were not removed with a cigarette, they would turn a wound septic. Mosquitoes, snakes, fire ants, and centipedes swarmed, and protection had to be constantly self-fashioned to keep not just the leeches away but the skin dry and free of painful rashes that covered backsides and genitalia—an exercise that often proved futile.[25]

Templer, Lyttleton, and others fixated on capturing Chin Peng while also wiping out his embedded insurgents who, for the most part, had eluded Britain's repeated show of force and ferreting since the emergency's inception. Templer was precisely what the demoralized administration and troops needed, while for those on his receiving end, he was, like his predecessor, ruthless. Climbing into Gurney's bullet-ridden Rolls, Templer deployed what was by then a familiar British strategy, divvying up of the Federation into "white," "grey," and "black" areas. In some cases, he personally oversaw collective punishments of "bad" villages, or "black" areas like Tanjong Malim. There Templer heaped opprobrium on locals who refused to give up a Communist platoon that cut off the town's water supply, ambushed a security force patrol sent in to restore order, killed a dozen soldiers, and wounded several others. What followed was a preview of Templer's brisk, take-charge approach that did not refashion the Gurney-and-Briggs-crafted noose but rather tightened it. Templer imposed a twenty-two-hour curfew, replacing the dusk-to-dawn one, and ordered other collective punishments and fines. He began to starve out locals through stringent "food denial" efforts. Abatement came only when locals offered information on anonymous questionnaires, which were placed into a lockbox. So successful was this new strategy with some forty arrests made that Templer extended Operation Letter Box throughout the Federation.[26]

"Stern food control measures" were introduced in the resettlement areas, areas that Templer had renamed "New Villages."[27] Templer continued to squeeze the beleaguered population and soon introduced Operation Sodium to destroy crops, which would starve villagers into submission or, at a minimum, reduce any extra food for insurgents. He also introduced a new "regulation [that authorized] the lethal electrification of a fence declared to be a 'perimeter fence'" and allocated resources for "adequate perimeter lighting at night" to detect any insurgent trying to slip into a village under the cover of darkness.[28]

Letterbox-named peasants were sent elsewhere for further "pumping," in Templer's words. He and his men were after "live" intelligence for "deep penetration of the enemy," as opposed to that which came from "corpses, prisoners of war and captured documents."[29] Within a year the combined intelligence units had an unprecedented road map to Chin Peng's Communist organization both within and outside the jungle, and a relentless pursuit of its members ensued. The tide began to change, and intelligence's virtuous cycle was helped along by CSDIC interrogators who worked to "break" and "turn" "Surrendered Enemy Personnel" at impressive rates. Introduced by Gurney, the lure of handsome cash rewards for information and captures prompted some villagers and enemy personnel to cooperate at a more rapid clip. Setups were not uncommon: special branch planted Communist literature or weapons, arrested the framed offender, then threatened him or her with detention and deportation. As one former information officer noted, "threat of the death penalty was often used to exact information."[30]

There was also the threat of sending surrendered guerrillas back to their platoons, whereupon death at the hands of "traitor-killing camps"—or Chin Peng's internal security units—was all but assured. The Communists enforced brutal discipline over their forces, something the journalist Harry Miller discovered in his review of hundreds of captured documents. "An offender may be tied to a tree and exposed to the sun for hours without water. He can be beaten with a bamboo pole for as much as thirty-six strokes. Men have been executed by being buried alive. Discipline is in accord with the background. It is jungle discipline."[31] Still Her Majesty's interrogators were notably successful in "turning" Communists into covert colonial agents.

Lincolns dropped thousand-pound bombs into the jungle, and Spitfires pierced its canopy with machine-gun fire. Both tactics had more of a "psychological effect" than anything else. Chin Peng retreated to Malaya's northern border with Thailand. He later reported that subterfuge had hobbled such defensive efforts. Local "Grik comrades had recognised there was a traitor in their midst but could not identify him." Eventually, Communist officials sussed out Lian Sung, a local committee official, and found a $50,000 government-issued check in his pocket. They eliminated Lian though not before he inflicted irreparable damage to Chin Peng's supply lines, which forced the Communist leader to set up headquarters in Thailand.[32]

In 1954 the British government proudly pointed to its metrics of progress. The number of Communist kills was on a steady climb, attacks against government security forces were down, and Chin Peng's men were hunkered deep in the jungles. With supply lines compromised, growing food became an insurgent priority, so the government used chemical weapons to destroy crops and deforest undergrowth and jungle fringes.

Before Gurney's death, the colonial government had experimented with sodium arsenate to destroy "large areas of cultivation planted by bandits driven out of populated areas and forced to rely on their own resources." The arsenic-based spray rendered "the whole green field of cultivation [into] a brown shrivelled up mass," though it was so toxic that officials turned to London for help.[33] At Colonial Secretary Lyttleton's behest, Geoffrey Emett Blackman, secretary for Britain's Biological Warfare Committee, advised on using "chemical agents . . . in clearing the undergrowth" in November 1951, and so began a series of trial-and-error experiments with Agent Orange compounds as well as sodium trichloroacetate (STCA) and other chemicals. Federation officials were "apparently very optimistic about the success of the experiments."[34] At issue were the chemicals' poisonous effects. Local officials insisted on taking precautions that, according to one report, "consist of avoiding any contact of the skin, eyes, etc., with the solid STCA or with its solutions, and include the washing down with water of all surfaces, water proof garments, gloves, etc., after contact with the chemical."[35] After local colonial officials tried methods like the "spraying lorry" that shot "a very high volume solution 'through a fire hose,'" aerial spraying of 2,4,5-T (trichlorophenoxyacetic acid, an ingredient in Agent Orange) became the preferred practice.[36] The Federation government had purchased from Britain's largest chemical manufacturer, Imperial Chemical Industries, its entire stockpile of 2,4,5-T, and Templer decided to use what remained in the depths of the jungle to wipe out the Communists' crops. In March 1953 helicopter spraying began in earnest. *The Manchester Guardian* criticized the general's use of "herbicides," which it felt amounted to "chemical warfare." The Colonial Office brushed aside such concerns:

> It has been common knowledge for a long time that experiments aimed at destroying terrorist food crops were being carried out, and the rather ridiculous cry of "chemical warfare" has already been fully exploited in communist propaganda. Whenever it has been raised with us we have been able to give a convincing answer and I do not think there is any need to pursue the point further now.[37]

Few in the opposition or the broader public offered much push-back that threatened operations on the ground or Conservatives' assertion that they had saved civilization from Communism's clutches. In November 1952 Lyttleton took to Parliament's floor and waxed lyrical about Templer: "He has by his unbounded energy, foresight and liberal approach to political problems transformed public morale and given everyone in Malaya something to do now and something to look forward to in the future."[38] A month later Templer's subtle grin graced the cover of *Time*, which was headlined "Templer of Malaya: The jungle has been neutralized." The lengthy article, "Smiling Tiger," was nothing short of a full-throated hagiography rounded out with contextual justifications for "collective punishments" and a lauding of "British boys . . . risking their lives side by side with Malays, Chinese and Indians. . . . These men see their real enemy—Communism." The magazine also took aim at the "Communist Daily Worker," which had published lurid photos of insurgents who British security forces had decapitated. One photo showed a beaming young marine holding up a severed Chinese head. Later, the *Daily Worker* correspondent had asked Templer "if his collective punishment policy was not the same as that used by the Nazis," and *Time* recounted the exchange that followed:

> Templer's lip curled into a smile like a soundless snarl. Grimly he recited the prosaic, ghastly facts & figures he had had to deal with. "I notice you do not deny using the Fascist system," said the Daily Worker reporter. "Didn't bother to," said Templer.

"Templer of Malaya," *Time* cover, December 15, 1952

The Communist reporter asked: "What is the level of anemic malnutrition in Malaya?" Answered Templer: "I haven't the vaguest idea." The reporter: "Why don't you? You're High Commissioner, aren't you?" Templer said quietly: "You sit down. You sit down, or get out." The Communist sat down.[39]

That such hard-hitting reporting existed rarely outside the *Daily Worker*, and occasional pieces in the *Daily Herald, The Manchester Guardian*, and *The Observer*, reflected the fourth estate's rally around imperial governance at this time of crisis.[40] Unlike the daily headlines and images during Britain's exit from Palestine that showed the gruesome photos of the two murdered British sergeants, no paper other than the *Daily Worker* republished the severed head images. An unwavering sense of patriotic duty to support "our boys" fighting a ghastly war against Communist terrorists pervaded. Churchill's government drew on decades of bipartisan sidestepping skills, reminiscent of Orwell's doublethink, with ready-made answers to charges of abuse and state-sponsored terror. Government representatives trumpeted the impossible task facing the Crown's troops, who needed every ounce of government and public support. There were, of course, some outlying critics. Labour MP Tom Driberg, who had earlier offered a scathing indictment after he toured the Federation's detention and transit facilities, pressed the coercion issues with Colonial Under-Secretary Alan Lennox-Boyd. The BBC Home Service illuminated the exchange:

> Mr. Driberg (Labour) asked what enquiries had been made into the methods used by police officers in interrogating suspects in Malaya. Lennox Boyd said there had been many rather wild accusations of ill-treatment and it was clearly in the Communists' interests to propagate those stories. He said any specific allegations had been investigated, and in a few cases where cause had been shown, stern action had been taken. Mr. Driberg said the Colonial Secretary should be asked to investigate this subject. Mr. Lennox Boyd replied that more time and trouble should be devoted to considering the problem of the police officers themselves in their appallingly difficult task. He said much time spent in checking ill-founded allegations could have been better employed in helping to bring the dreadful war to an end.[41]

Driberg and other critics were at government's mercy when it came to investigating charges of abuse. British officials fed the press daily briefings filled with official metrics. These facts, the lifeblood of the journalists' trade, stood in stark contrast to unsubstantiated allegations that came from behind Malaya's wires and jungle thickets. Insofar as there were "a few cases" of abuse, they were isolated and not systematic, according to government statements. The mainstream press cleaved to a positivist reporting style and preferred not to run a story if it meant contravening government-ready facts with the slimmest of suggestive evidence—evidence that the press could rarely verify given its limited access to the camps and villages as well as to security forces, who seldom broke rank. Within military circles, photos of severed heads, which rarely circulated publicly, were barbaric trophies. The Official Secrets Acts—Britain was the world's leader in criminalizing what it believed was improper information flow—went a long way in silencing any would-be whistleblower. As the historian Erik Linstrum points out, some media outlets like the BBC demanded two-source verification, a near-impossible task given government's stranglehold on information and its severe penalties for anyone in the civil administration or military forces who went public. Skeptical reporters like those from the *Daily Worker* and *The Times*'s Louis Heren were given limited or no access to official interviews, and were often victims of government harassment. The British government grandstanded internal fact-finding efforts that upheld the official line and denied charges that abuse was systemic to Britain's defense of civilization.[42]

The insistence that officials investigated "specific allegations" was a kernel of truth wrapped in a husk of lies. Driberg knew this and lambasted the government's "new and more ruthless policy" under Templer. The MP framed collective punishments as "that barbarous and undemocratic method," questioning whether "Her Majesty's Government adhere[d] to the old administrative principles that the end justifies the means?"[43] When another Labour MP asked whether "collective punishment is consistent with the Charter of Human Rights of the United Nations," Lyttleton said collective punishments were "in my opinion not a contravention of that Charter."[44] The issue of collective punish-

Scots Guards on jungle patrol, Malaya, 1950

ments proved a thorn in the Conservative government's side as it was the only one that garnered widespread bipartisan support for discussion. Churchill's Colonial Office deftly sidestepped queries by pointing, over and again, to the bravery of the nation's embattled troops in the face of a vicious Communist enemy. One high-ranking official in Kuala Lumpur confided to the local British adviser, "There are often excellent reasons for limiting the scope of an enquiry (improper as it may be) and it is not for this office to cause embarrassment by pressing for further information."[45]

A most modest mechanism for investigating alleged wrongdoing had emerged in Malaya in the early years of the war and persisted through Templer's time and beyond. The most notorious recorded incident unfolded in mid-December 1948, when a fourteen-man patrol of 2 Battalion Scots Guards seized twenty-six insurgents at a Chinese rubber-tapping settlement in Batang Kali. They shot the captured insurgents who were trying to escape, according to initial reports. *The Straits Times* questioned the incident, and rumors began to swirl "that the Chinese had been murdered in cold blood"—this from a paper that repeatedly prodded the government to take harsher measures.[46] A defiant Major-General Boucher said that "when the [suspects] started running they went into the direction of the sentries, who were in position. There was a terrific amount of firing."[47] Beyond confirming that the Scots Guard platoon killed some two dozen suspects, the major-general refused to offer any further details.

The Communist press had a field day, and a cloud of lingering questions hung over Gurney's government. Malaya's attorney general soon launched an internal investigation that was never made public. Creech Jones rebuffed a House question with ease: "An inquiry into this incident was made by the civil authorities and, after careful consideration of the evidence and a personal visit to the place concerned, the attorney general was satisfied that, had the Security Forces not opened fire, the suspect Chinese would have made good on an attempt at escape which had been obviously pre-arranged."[48] Behind the scenes, however, a different conversation unfolded. Federation communications with the Colonial Office betrayed an evolving pattern of justification and cover-up that persisted and served as another precedent for the empire's other wars. In one secret telegram the prevailing ethos was evident:

> One of the difficulties of the situation is that we have a war of terrorism on our hands and we are at the same time endeavouring to maintain the rule of law. It is an easy matter from

one's office and home to criticize action taken by the security forces in the heat of operations and working under jungle conditions but not so easy to do the job oneself. Rightly or wrongly we feel here that we must be conservative in our criticism of the men who are undoubtedly carrying out a most arduous and dangerous job. . . . We feel it is most damaging to the morale of the security forces to feel that every action of theirs, after the event, is going to be examined with the most meticulous care.[49]

It would take another four decades before more facts emerged about Batang Kali, including those detailed in a 1993 BBC documentary, *In Cold Blood*, suggesting an order had been given for the Batang Kali murders, which was then covered up.[50]

The Conservative government masterfully employed the language of reform, which again contained threads of truth woven into a basket of lies. Templer's "New Villages," which were just harshly run resettlement areas, were the epitome of liberal imperialism's ability to transform subject populations, at least as far as the British government was concerned. Behind the double rows of electrified barbed wire, Communists and their supporters were ostensibly being "rehabilitated" into modern men and women. In the spring of 1953, Lyttleton was effusive on the floor of Parliament when he discussed the New Villages and Templer's far-reaching and unprecedented measures during colonial wartime:

> There have for some time been village committees but these are now being replaced by elected local councils with powers to finance and run local services. Schools and community halls have been provided. Home Guard units are being raised from volunteers in every village. Civics courses are attended by village leaders; sport and other local activities are encouraged. . . . I am glad to say that in the great majority of the new villages community feeling and loyalty are growing and real co-operation with Government is manifest.[51]

Another liberal imperialist watchword gained currency—"community development." According to official reports, Malaya was replete with the institutions and services long absent from the war-torn peninsula.

Colonial officials and their propaganda machines touted the unprecedented expansion of schools and health services across the Federation's New Villages. Officials were said to prepare confined civilians for their enfranchisement and independence through new civics courses reminiscent of those offered to fascists in the Raj's wartime Himalayan "holiday camps." For many colonial officials, harsh discipline remained a cornerstone of reform, civilizing "child-like natives," though how much rehabilitation and social welfare programs were responsible for turning the Communist tide is questionable. For certain, it was only after Britain locked up 1.2 million Chinese "alien squatters" in a detention camp or New Village that social development measures across the Federation's barbed-wired landscape were introduced in small measure. All sides of Malaya's divide terrorized Chinese men, women, and children while British colonial agents starved, punished, interrogated, tortured, and exploited them. The civilian population was shattered and left near penniless when the "New Village" ethos emerged as liberal imperialism's reformist currency. Progress existed in the form of self-help organizations, the establishment of women's institutes, and expanded citizenship status. Community-based policing was introduced and engendered some confidence in public servants. At most, liberal imperialism's lowest denominator was raised a notch. When asked in 1954 what the biggest difference was between the conduct of British forces then compared to five years earlier, a police officer replied, "Less beating up."[52]

In the years ahead, Templer's New Villages—and counterinsurgency methods more generally—would be considered the first successful "hearts and minds" campaign and a model for others, including the Americans. This remarkable achievement was due in no small part to Britain's propaganda machine, both at home and in Malaya. The government spent around $5 million a year on the Federation's "information services," and Templer waged a personal charm offensive with the Americans.[53] After hosting Vice President Richard Nixon and briefing him on Britain's far-reaching counterinsurgency methods, the general received a letter from Dwight Eisenhower. "I wish to congratulate you on the inspiring leadership you have provided," the president wrote, underscoring the basis of Templer's success in "quelling Communist terrorism":

> I should like to reiterate our sympathy with the United Kingdom's far-sighted policy of assisting the diverse peoples of Malaya in forging in due course a united and self-governing Malayan nation. We appreciate the problems involved in achieving this goal and the imaginative leadership you and your Government have provided in the progressive steps being undertaken to this end.[54]

That Templer would later burnish his reformist legacy was no small matter in perpetuating the "hearts and minds" illusion. Over a decade after his departure from Malaya, *The Straits Times* published his reflections on events:

> You cannot win this sort of war with bullets. You can only win the people over in my opinion—to use that nauseating phrase I think I invented—by capturing their hearts and minds. The strategy is to win it by getting people on your side, by getting prosperity, a higher standard of living among the people and so proving that what we call the Western way of life is better than the Communist way of life.[55]

If Gurney's, Briggs's, and Templer's unremitting assaults on Chinese civilians raise questions about "hearts and minds," so do the facts and numbers. No analysis bears out any kind of full-scale socioeconomic reform effort in the midst of government-sponsored terror, intelligence gathering, hit squads, deportations, mass resettlements, and detentions. In the early days of the war, Gurney had presciently warned that "terrorism is the most expensive form of illness from which any community can suffer and becomes more so the longer it is permitted to drag on."[56] When Templer arrived, military expenditures were nearly £50 million, and Malaya's federal government shouldered emergency costs of £29 million, or nearly half its overall £66 million budget. Not surprisingly, some of the first expenditures to go were those crucial to social reform and community development.[57] According to the Federation's 1950 draft development plan, "very little capital will be available for expansion of the social services, unless cuts are made in present recurrent expenditure, or revenue is increased. Indeed, there is not really even this alternative, since if economies of any size were to be effected this could only be done at the cost of existing social services."[58]

Were it not for the Korean War, the Federation would have further sunk fiscally before it seized the counterinsurgency initiative. Tin prices nearly doubled between 1949 and 1951, but it was rubber's spike in demand and price that rescued Malaya's economy. The Federation estimated that it received $274 million in rubber revenues in 1950, while the actual receipts were $443 million; for 1951 the estimate was $410 million and receipts $735 million.[59] Templer did allocate spending increases, as education expenditures went up from $2.7 million in 1949 to $14.2 million in 1951, and health care spending rose from $6.9 million to $13.3 million during the same period. Nonetheless, at the end of 1955, actual overall spending on social development programs was significantly less than what had been budgeted under the draft development plan—a plan that officials had compiled prior to the Korean War boom.[60] This was partly due to the recession that followed the war boom, in which a modest increase in workers' wages was offset by price inflation.

The Colonial Office was well aware tough decisions had to be made, and reform—let alone a complete transformation of Malaya's socioeconomic landscape—was the first to go. The process of creating New Villages had been, according to Templer, "a hurried one, and without the opportunity for careful sociological and economic survey and planning which would normally precede so abrupt a disturbance of a long established pattern of rural life."[61] Plans for transforming rural conditions of Britain's own making were scrapped. In 1953 Malcolm MacDonald wrote to Lyttleton from his desk in Singapore's tropical Whitehall:

> even if the Federation increases its taxation to a considerably higher level, revenue is unlikely to come anywhere near the sum required for expenditure on essential services plus adequate economic, social Welfare, education and other development works. Unless, therefore, we can get aid from elsewhere, it seems that Templer will have no alternative but to cut these development works drastically. He is already having to do this to a most unfortunate extent. . . . Already the economies being made are having a depressing effect on public morale.[62]

In the years ahead, Britain was well aware that Malaya's rural areas were deteriorating; one official noted that "the New Villages at Cameron Highlands are living on a failing economy."[63]

In the end, local elites set the pace and scope of socioeconomic change in Malaya's New Villages. The Korean War boom galvanized Asian businesses, and Chinese profits were increasingly reinvested in local companies and shares in rubber estates. Packed with businessmen whom Gurney had earlier supported, the Malayan Chinese Association took charge in the rural communities, offering funding and manpower to the government, just as Malay officials consolidated their power and influence within their ethnic communities. Templer had seized the war's initiative by the time he left in 1954, but Britain was more or less sidelined insofar as local politics were concerned. "It was a battle to reconstruct communities, and for the elite to restore the networks and patron-client relationships that had been so damaged in the Japanese occupation," Bayly and Harper point out in *Forgotten Wars*. "This was done increasingly on an ethnic basis. Above all, the fate of the rebellion was decided by the continuing rapprochement between Malay administrative power and Chinese economic muscle."[64]

Templer had arrived in February 1952 with a mandate to accelerate self-government—or, in local parlance, to hasten *merdeka*, or freedom. While Malaya looked like a conquest state during the emergency, Britain could not maintain that level of coercion to continue colonial rule in the long term; nor did it have to as long as it cultivated leaders who could fill the colonial government's shoes. Yet defeating the Communists first was crucial not only in the wake of humiliating defeat in the Mandate but also in the eyes of the Americans, who looked to their Anglo counterparts to shine a light on the new counterinsurgency, interrogation, and covert operations that emerged as Cold War imperatives. So too did British officials need to solve the perennial end-of-empire issue of finding a suitable pasha or prince, or some other elite, who would facilitate Britain's economic and geopolitical interests after formal imperial retreat.[65]

At the level of national politics, when Templer departed in 1954, Britain still had its hand on the tiller, though it was unclear who had the nationalist credentials to lead a future independent Malaya and a willingness to maintain British interests in Southeast Asia. A most unlikely candidate, Tunku Abdul Rahman, who had earned kudos during the war as a colonial district officer assisting Malay victims of the Burma-Siam Railway, stepped forward. The *tunku*, or prince of Kedah, was also a Cambridge-educated lawyer with a hard-earned reputation for fast living and faster driving. Single-handedly responsible for Cambridge's ban on undergraduate automobile use, "Prince Bobby," as he was affectionately known, had taken over fifteen years to earn his "third-class degree." What the bon vivant lacked in academic rigor, however, he more than made up for in emotional intelligence and political savvy. The *tunku* understood the labyrinth of late colonial politics and played a genius hand, appealing to Malay ethnic nationalism while brokering deals with the colony's Chinese and Indian elite.[66]

"Who are these 'Malayans'?" he queried in his first address as head of the United Malays National Organisation (UMNO). "This country was received from the Malays and to the Malays it ought to be returned. What is called 'Malayans,' it is not yet certain who they are; therefore let the Malays alone settle who they are."[67] When Malay radicals were released from detention, having been swept up during the emergency for their trade unionism and far left demands, the *tunku*'s appealing message brought them into the UMNO. When Britain dragged its feet toward independence, he had the wind of support at his back, threatening noncooperation if colonial officials didn't hasten the transfer of power process. They conceded, but on condition the *tunku* agreed to forge a united, multiethnic political front. Under his leadership, the UMNO and the Malayan Chinese Association created a well-organized and -financed electoral alliance, which soon included the Malayan Indian Congress as well. Together, they were formidable and conservative ethnic-based parties that swept up seats in the first federal elections, held in 1955, taking 80 percent of the popular vote. It was, nonetheless, a principally Malay election—85 percent of voters were Malay, and of the Federation's six hundred thousand eligible Chinese voters registered to cast a ballot, only one hundred and forty thousand did so, about one-eighth of Malaya's total Chinese population.[68]

"Tunku Abdul Rahman has an overwhelming Parliamentary majority," a top-ranking colonial official cabled to London. "The local forces and police are largely Malay, and for his own ends he will keep legal powers to detain without trial. . . . He gives the impression of aiming at an old-fashioned Muslim dictatorship, with some democratic trappings, ready if need be to deal ruthlessly with Chinese who give trouble."[69] This was a far cry from Britain's vision after the war. Looking to atone for the humiliating Japanese takeover of the Malay Peninsula, British officials had tried to "form a 'Malayan' nationalism that was organic and multiracial," the historians Bayly and Harper tell us.[70] Local Malays were not impressed. Their ancien régime, a formidable force that Britain had further empowered through its own prewar policies, proved its mettle by stymieing British multicultural efforts in the postwar years. Such Malayan ascendency was helped along in no small way by Britain's emergency policies, which questioned Chinese belonging, calling them "alien subjects," and crushing many of the Chinese who had not been deported. By 1955, the colony was ripe for the *tunku*'s ethnic nationalism, supported by elite Chinese and Indian businessmen, to take hold.

In Singapore, David Marshall, son of Sephardic Jews who had immigrated from Baghdad in 1908 to escape Ottoman Empire rule, led the Labour Front to victory in the 1955 federal elections. A British-trained lawyer, he had volunteered for military service after Germany invaded Czechoslovakia in 1939, fought in the Battle of Singapore, been captured by the Japanese, and been interned in Changi Prison. Finally he was shipped to a forced labor camp in Japan. "Of course, I have known cruelty before," he recalled of his POW experience. "But widespread, long-term, cold-blooded, permanent cruelty, I've never experienced before, not even from the British imperialists no matter how arrogant they were."[71] After the war, he returned to Singapore, where he successfully defended locals charged with capital offenses. By the time of his election, Marshall irritated proper colonial officialdom with his bare feet exposed in open sandals and his bush jacket unbuttoned to reveal his hairy barrel chest. As Singapore's chief minister, he led negotiations toward his country's independence.

One detail remained, however, for the *tunku* and Marshall. In 1955 Chin Peng and his beleaguered Malayan Communist Party (MCP) forces were still hunkered in the jungles of Thailand, maintaining their claims to be fighting for independence. Chin Peng emerged in December, hoping to strike a deal with the *tunku* and Marshall, who met him for talks at a remote Baling schoolhouse in Malaya's northern frontier. Cameras whirled, and reporters jockeyed to catch a glimpse of the MCP's guerrilla leader who still had a $250,000 British bounty on his head. Chin Peng was forbidden to speak to the press, but he made his demands clear during the private negotiations: the MCP would lay down its weapons if its insurgents were able to return to Malaya with full amnesty and the party was permitted to operate openly, competing in future elections.[72] The negotiations broke down immediately. "If you demand our surrender," an outraged Chin Peng threatened, "we would prefer to fight to the last man."[73] He returned to Thailand's jungles and eventually went to Beijing. When asked later if he was discouraged over the failed Baling meeting, the *tunku* said, "No, I'm not. I never wanted it to be a success."[74] The Baling talks were a stroke of political genius for the *tunku*, who proved his loyalty to the British by holding the line against Chin Peng and the Communists, while touting negotiation attempts to his constituency as a good faith effort at conciliation. Even as more and more power devolved to him and his political alliance, however, some in Britain, like the Conservative MP Robert Boothby, when asked how long Britain would remain in Malaya, declared, "A thousand years."[75]

Boothby's millennium was short-lived. In early 1956, despite the ongoing emergency, a constitutional conference was held in London where Britain promised the *tunku* independence for the Federation, appointing the Reid Commission to make constitutional recommendations, which it did a year later. Crucial economic and military points were provisionally agreed upon, securing Malaya's place in Britain's monetary and geopolitical future. Indeed, with its massive dollar-earning capacity, Malaya remaining in the sterling area, and adhering to its dollar-spending policies was crucial to the British economy; its agreement to do so after independence, scheduled for August 1957, was a major win for Britain. In return, Malaya was assured that it would have "sympathetic consideration" in its borrowing from London and access to its capital markets. Britain also guaranteed that it would pay ongoing insurgency-related expenses—expenses that would last until 1960, when the independent Malayan government finally lifted the state of emergency.[76]

The maintenance of Britain's relationship with Malaya via the sterling area perpetuated an unequal economic relationship that had evolved throughout the nineteenth and twentieth centuries, supporting the British state and economy, particularly as it teetered after the Second World War. Malayans, however, were not entirely at Britain's mercy: they shrewdly demanded a generous aid package, which London's Treasury initially chafed against. It took colonial officials still in Malaya to spell out what was at stake:

> The main economic argument for financial aid is, quite simply, dollars. On the prosperity of Malaya and on the stability of its economy depends one of the biggest single sources of American dollars at the disposal of the Sterling bloc, if not indeed the biggest individual source. Malaya earns some hundreds of millions of dollars a year, a quarter or more of the total dollars accruing to the whole sterling area. Surely the greater the strain on the sterling, the greater the need to conserve such a vital source of dollars. If that can be done by sterling expenditure, it is cheap at almost any price.[77]

The *tunku's* soon-to-be finance minister, a prominent ethnic Chinese businessman, got Malaya its aid, to the tune of £37 million in grants through 1961, while Britain's sterling area benefited from Malaya's pooled dollars. After independence, the region became the hub for "crony capitalism" with Chinese businessmen, Malay directors, and British investors working in concert to ensure their positions. Nearly a decade later, 65 percent of Malaysia's capital was British in origin while China's Overseas Chinese Banking Corporation held two-thirds of Chinese deposits in Malaysia, which was now a hub of old and new capital flows, and their sources transcending East-West divides.[78]

Fears of Communist influence throughout the region drove the Anglo-Malayan Defence Agreement negotiations, which provided security for the Federation after independence and was another win for Britain. Its military forces remained in Malaya, and Singapore, not yet independent though with limited self-government, also needed British boots on the ground, particularly as social unrest repeatedly erupted. The bush-jacket-wearing Marshall was soon voted out, but his successors were equally mired in conflict with Chinese students and trade unionists. When Lim Yew Hock took over as chief minister, he deployed emergency regulations to arrest and imprison them.

In the end, the emergency laws, policies, and practices systematically destroyed Communist support, brutalizing individuals and communities, and paved the way for decolonization in Southeast Asia. They also ensured British interests and legal continuities between the colonial and postcolonial regimes, a nonnegotiable condition for independence. The *tunku* and Lee Kuan Yew, who became Singapore's first prime minister in 1959, retained the full panoply of Britain's repressive powers, wielding local versions of legalized lawlessness to suppress political opposition and keep Communism at bay, much to the knowledge of officials in London.[79] British influence over Singapore's defense and foreign policies continued, with ten thousand soldiers stationed on the island. A virtual revolving door of spies continued to use tropical Whitehall as their staging post for Southeast Asian operations. MI5 and other London-based officers staffed the Federation's postindependence special branch, and a permanent MI5 agent was posted within the *tunku*'s government. As it prepared for formal retreat, Britain had resurrected a new version of Fortress Singapore from the ashes of 1942's defeat. "Although politically free," a dispirited Movement for Colonial Freedom wrote, "Malaya has yet far to go before she can truly call herself 'independent.' For even in the instrument of independence—the London Agreement—the economic and military interests of Britain still bind Malaya."[80]

Days after the February 1956 constitutional agreement was signed, another state-directed policy secretly took form. In Malaya, colonial officials began sorting, culling, transferring, and burning files. Much like interrogation systems and those created for deportation, resettlement, and detention, those spawned for document sifting and destruction had evolved from haphazard processes, such as those in India and Palestine, to ones that were increasingly bureaucratized. British officials obsessively monitored secret registries, maintained strong rooms, carefully vetted officials, and triple-checked that categorized documents were destroyed, repatriated, or transferred to Malaya's independent government.[81]

It took eighteen months to complete the culling. In the final days of Malaya, one of Britain's MI5 agents responsible for the Federation's systematized destruction could report "with confidence that the risk of compromise or embarrassment arising out of any paper left behind is very slight."[82]

Across Britain's imperial expanse, another kind of systematic destruction was unfolding in Kenya's one hundred detention camps. A state of emergency had been declared in October 1952, and by the spring of 1957 twelve thousand "hard-core" or "black" detainees were refusing to cooperate with colonial authorities, while thousands of other "greys" labored in the "works camps." Detainees rioted and staged hunger strikes. Camp guards and interrogation teams inflicted quotidian punishment and forced labor routines, rendering life behind the wire unbearable, if not lethal. In the summer of 1955, the Colonial Office had already wondered, "How long can we hope to keep 12,000 people locked up?"[83] The British government had planned to sidestep the European Convention on Human Rights, which it had been derogating under Article 15, by sending the "hard-core" to a limited number of permanent "exile camps" within the colony once it lifted the state of emergency. Such a move promised perpetual detention without trial for thousands of subjects in Kenya, a violation of the convention. Once Britain lifted the state of emergency, derogation under Article 15 was no longer an option, or so it appeared. Kenya's governor, Sir Evelyn Baring, and Colonial Secretary Lennox-Boyd were masterminding a way around international human rights law, and scale was the deciding factor. "Her Majesty's Government could in the first instance be expected to justify a breach of the Convention to other signatories if the numbers concerned were not too large," Baring emphasized.[84]

The task for officials in London and Nairobi was clear: empty the camps of most detainees and enter quiet negotiations over the convention's terms that would result in legislation authorizing permanent exile.[85] It was time for Britain's men-on-the-spot to seize the initiative, and Carruthers Johnston, in charge of the ministries for African affairs and community development as well as special commissioner for Kenya's Central Province, took the lead. He needed his own man with a plan, or someone who could break all of Kenya's hard-core detainees, except for the twelve thousand slated for permanent exile, and help move the colony toward a postemergency future.

Kenya's crisis point was nearly five years in the making. When Governor Baring declared a state of emergency on October 20, 1952, he and others assured the public it would all be over by Christmas. Senior

Senior Chief Waruhiu, assassinated in his Hudson sedan, October 1952

Chief Waruhiu, who many locals considered a Black traitor because of his self-serving support for the colonial regime, had just been brazenly assassinated in the back seat of his sedan, prompting Baring's emergency declaration. This was not the first sign of trouble; parts of the colony had been increasingly ungovernable since the Second World War. Kenya, with its European settler population and policies of land appropriation as well as harsh labor and color bar laws, was awash in inequities. The 1.5 million Kikuyu who comprised around 20 percent of the colony's population were the hardest hit. Europeans lived on much of their appropriated land. There settlers grew coffee and tea—lucrative cash crops that only white farmers could legally produce—while the Kikuyu toiled under harsh master and servants laws, a hangover from Britain's Victorian-era domestic labor laws, which criminalized labor offenses.

By the interwar years, the colonial government had undertaken three interrelated measures to control African laborers and push them into the wage economy. First it created ethnically based "native reserves," physically separating the colony's various tribes. Reserve policies contained the Kikuyu in three Central Province districts—Kiambu, Fort Hall, and Nyeri—that fanned out from Nairobi to the north and were purposefully overcrowded and incapable of supporting the population's basic needs. The government also introduced a hut tax and poll tax, which together amounted to twenty-five shillings, or the equivalent of almost two months of a typical African's wages. In response, thousands of Kikuyu migrated out of the reserves to find land and employment on European farms. Colonial officials controlled this movement through the third measure: the requirement that all Africans carry a pass, or *kipande*, that recorded a person's name, fingerprint, ethnic group, past employment history, and current employer's signature; without it, an African could be fined, imprisoned, or both. The *kipande* became one of Kenya's most detested symbols of colonial rule and was an indicator of how far ahead the colony was relative to other parts of the empire in controlling and surveilling its subject population.[86] Indeed, Kenya was a glaring example of what the political scientist Cedric Robinson famously called "racial capitalism," the process of extracting economic and social value from brown and Black populations for the benefit of white ones. When enterprising Africans tried to sidestep this grossly unfair system by circumventing the Euro-controlled labor market, growing and selling maize locally to generate independent income and undercutting inefficient white farmer production, the colonial government eventually shut this down as well, setting up marketing boards that required Africans to sell their grain at a set price, determined by the colonial government.[87]

Up until the Second World War, European farms in the "White Highlands"—so called because of the area's racial exclusivity insofar as landownership was concerned—offered safety valves for many Kikuyus. There they became squatters, or sharecroppers, for the notoriously inefficient white landholders. This feudal-like tenancy option, however, began to close down as the wartime boom fueled demand for Kenya's raw materials and as increasing revenues paid for agricultural mechanization. For many displaced squatters, returning to the overcrowded reserves was not an option, and they instead migrated to the slums of Nairobi. At the same time, thousands of African soldiers returned home from the war, and their eyewitness accounts of white fallibility, as well as ideas of self-determination, circulated alongside the growing nationalist discourse of Jomo Kenyatta's Kenya African Union. For war veterans who anticipated life improving as a reward for their contributions to fascism's demise, liberal imperialism's partnership was a hollow promise filled with the Labour government's exploitative colonial development and welfare schemes aimed at resuscitating Britain's economy on the backs and from the pocketbooks of its subjects around the empire.[88]

Kenyatta, the Kikuyu leader, had come a long way since his prewar

Cranleigh Street days, when George Padmore and others had fueled debates about "systematized violence" in the empire. He had been at the epicenter of Black radical thought, produced articles for the *New Leader* such as "Hitler Could Not Improve on Kenya," and added to his bona fides by taking courses with the famed anthropologist Bronislaw Malinowski at the London School of Economics; publishing a book, *Facing Mount Kenya,* a defense of Kikuyu society; and playing a key organizing role in the Manchester Conference in 1945, which was the Pan-African response to the UN Charter meeting in San Francisco.[89] Kenyatta's pan-African zeal and Communist leanings evolved over the years; by the time he returned to Kenya in 1946, he had fallen out with the Communist Party for reasons not dissimilar to Padmore's. Like the other so-called "anti-British agitators," Kenyatta had been under the watchful eye of Britain's Security Service. They reported his move away from radicalism during his war years spent farming in Sussex, though Kenya authorities still considered the charismatic Kenyatta a Communist who was filling uneducated peasants' heads with wild notions about equality and self-determination.[90]

It was not Kenyatta, however, who mobilized the masses; rather, it was a practice that emerged from a group of Kikuyu squatters whom Europeans had evicted from their Rift Valley farms. Once landless, these squatters radicalized Kikuyu oathing practices that elders traditionally administered to forge solidarity among men during times of war or internal crises. Local Kikuyu leaders now administered this ritualized, moral contract not only to men but also to women and children in a collective effort to fight their evictions from European estates. Mass oathing spread rapidly as African politicians recognized its organizing force. The more conservative Kenya African Union soon lost control to a diffuse collection of militants who spread oathing across settler estates in the White Highlands, the slums of Nairobi, and the Kikuyu reserves.[91] By 1950, oathing's scope and scale led the African affairs department to note with alarm that "secret meetings were being held in which an illegal oath, accompanied by appropriately horrid ritual, was being administered to initiates binding them to treat all Government servants as enemies, to disobey Government orders and eventually to evict all Europeans from the country."[92]

The movement, known as Mau Mau, became synonymous with atavistic savagery in liberal imperialism's lexicon. Not since the "Black Hole of Calcutta" had a phrase from the empire so evoked racialized images of bloodthirsty natives who stoked fear in the hearts of Kenya's European settlers. That the Mau Mau oaths were secretive and often accompanied by multiple rituals, including the slaughtering of a goat and the biting and ingesting of its flesh, only fed European frenzy. The oath had seven gradations, and each successive level represented a greater commitment to the movement. For each oath, initiates repeated various vows, followed by the refrain "May this oath kill me." Two of the most common pledges were "If I know of any enemy of our organization and fail to kill him, may this oath kill me," and "If I reveal this oath to any European, may this oath kill me." The oath created not only a new status for the Kikuyu as reborn members of Mau Mau but also a genuine fear of reprisal. "It was a very strong oath in the Kikuyu belief, just like during the old days," Nelson Macharia Gathigi, a rural peasant from Kenya's Central Province, recalled, believing that he could not elude its power.[93] Like many Mau Mau adherents, Gathigi feared that the Kikuyu creator god, Ngai, would punish him, through injury or death, should he break his pledge. While the colonial government and settlers viewed oathing as barbaric mumbo-jumbo and further evidence of Kikuyu backwardness, the practice had logic and purpose. It was the rational response of a rural people seeking to understand the enormous socioeconomic and political changes taking place around them while attempting to respond collectively to new and unjust realities.[94]

Mau Mau's overarching objective was *ithaka na wiyathi*, land and freedom. For those who pledged themselves to the movement, however, the meanings of the two words were more complex than merely tossing off the British yoke and reclaiming the land of their ancestors. Mau Mau's meanings varied depending on an oath taker's age, gender, and birthplace. For Gathigi, it offered the hope of claiming new land, starting his own family, and breaking away from elders who he thought were holding him back; for others, like Lucy Ngima Mugwe, *wiyathi*, freedom, meant an end to the British government's backbreaking communal labor projects.[95] It was as much the ambiguity as the specificity of Mau Mau's demand for *ithaka na wiyathi* that made it so appealing to the Kikuyu masses and rendered it such a powerful and difficult movement for the British to suppress. The colonial government estimated that nearly 90 percent of the 1.5 million Kikuyu people had taken the first Mau Mau oath, or the oath of unity.

Mau Mau antipathy targeted not only the colony's European population but also the colonial-appointed African chiefs and their followers, who became known broadly as "loyalists." In the context of the incipient war, the government defined a "loyalist" as someone who actively fought on its side against Mau Mau and who, in turn, received a "loyalist certificate" ensuring franchise rights in local elections as well as economic privileges like trading licenses and preferred access to land. Many loyalists accumulated wealth and power at the expense of the broader Kikuyu community, becoming Mau Mau targets; the loyalist Senior Chief Waruhiu was among the first to be killed.

In this regard, Kenya was not unique in that its anticolonial war was also a civil war. Kenya's state of emergency descended into another one of the empire's reprisal and counterreprisal cycles. Emergency policies created laws and structures that drew an unprecedented bright line between those whom the government deemed loyal to the empire and those it decided were not. Many Kikuyus, however, didn't perceive themselves in such stark terms, often cleaving along lines beyond that of the colonial-appointed chiefs and ordinary *wanainchi*, or people. Affinities in Kenya's African societies had ethnic, class, geographical, and gender dimensions, though the government's emergency policies tried to flatten these, even if Britain's binary categories—*you're either with us or against us*—did not play out so neatly on the ground. Much as in Malaya, the civilian population often played both sides to survive. Nonetheless, the Colonial Office approved "the Kenya Government's policy of building on the 'loyalists' to the exclusion of ex–Mau Mau leaders."[96]

Government press releases depicted Mau Mau as criminals and gangsters, at best, who terrorized the local European population. They circulated around the world gruesome images of Mau Mau's method of killing with a *panga*, or machete. According to Granville Roberts, the Kenya public relations officer based in London's Colonial Office, "the horror of Mau Mau" stood in contrast to the "white" and "enlightened" forces of liberal imperialism and its "peaceful and progressive conditions" in Kenya prior to the emergency.[97] But of course, white supremacy had long manifested itself in Kenya through various kinds of rough settler justice, which included public floggings, beating deaths, and summary executions.[98] Most whites in Kenya placed Africans at the very bottom of humanity's hierarchy, but the emergency inflamed the empire's racism. Settlers and colonial administrators described Mau Mau as "vermin," "animals," and "barbarians" who lived in the "untidy, sprawling heaps . . . hovels, with seething mud and animals in the huts," or in the "bush" with other wildlife. Like other predatory animals, they were "cunning," "vicious," and "bloodthirsty."[99] Mau Mau killed thirty-two European settlers during the emergency. A handful of high-profile murders sent over fifteen hundred white colonists into Nairobi's streets, demanding the elimination of Mau Mau by any means necessary. Lynch mob sentiments abounded.

Local demands quickly reverberated back home. Lyttleton ventriloquized the Kiplingesque horror sweeping across Britain. The "half-devil, half-child" of yesteryear had morphed into something sinister and seemingly unredeemable. In the colonial secretary's words, "The Mau Mau oath is the most bestial, filthy and nauseating incantation which perverted minds can ever have brewed. . . . [I have never felt] the forces of evil to be so near and so strong as in Mau Mau. As I wrote memoranda or instruction, I would suddenly see a shadow fall across the page— the horned shadow of the Devil himself."[100]

Colonial officials considered Mau Mau a rejection of all things Western but soon conceded it was homegrown, not Communist. They turned to Malaya as a blueprint for Kenya's state of emergency, much as Malayan officials had turned to Palestine. Governor Baring quickly launched Operation Jock Scott, which like Malaya's Operation Frustration targeted the alleged leaders. Jomo Kenyatta, whom *The Daily Telegraph* had branded "A Small-Scale African Hitler," was chief among them.[101] A show trial in Kapenguria, complete with a corrupt judge and bribed witnesses, ended with the conviction of Kenyatta and five others. They remained incarcerated in the colony's northern wasteland for much of the emergency. Nonetheless, Mau Mau grew in strength. The British government miscalculated the political sophistication of ordinary Kikuyus and their social and economic grievances.[102]

Baring imported the full panoply of Malaya's emergency regulations, based on those in Palestine and elsewhere. Curfews, collective punishments and fines, control of individual and mass movements of people, confiscation of property and land, censorship and banning of publications, disbanding of all African political organizations, control and disposition of labor, suspension of due process, and detention without trial were but some of the weapons in Kenya's police state arsenal. As in Southeast Asia, the government fought a two-pronged battle. Around twenty thousand Mau Mau insurgents fled to the Mount Kenya and Aberdares forests, from where they launched attacks, and the 90 percent of the 1.5 million Kikuyu civilians offered varying amounts of passive support like intelligence and food supplies. British security forces in Kenya called these civilians the "passive wing," as they had in Malaya. Some Kikuyu civilians offered support willingly; others were forced to do so by Mau Mau insurgents, just as Chin Peng's forces had terrorized Chinese peasants into offering intelligence and supplies.

Unlike in Malaya, however, no single person led Britain's counter-insurgency charge. Rather, a bifurcated leadership structure emerged:

successive military commanders were supposed to oversee security force operations, which included the coordination and execution of all military and policing operations, while Governor Baring and his administration of ministers and provincial and district officers were responsible for the civilian side of the war. In practice, operations and personnel often combined, and the colony's War Council—created in early 1954 and comprised of the governor, deputy governor, the military's commander in chief, and Michael Blundell, the settler representative—oversaw it all. That one of War Council's four positions was for a settler indicated the disproportionate influence the community had in Kenya. Indeed, the political power of Kenya's twenty-nine thousand European settlers had been institutionalized for decades. The colony's constitution was oriented around their interests, which were further ensured through their disproportionate number of seats—eleven in all—in Kenya's Legislative Council. Such influence percolated through the colony's emergency operations, together with what Margery Perham, one of Britain's leading postwar "partnership" architects, called a "pathological atmosphere." Settlers, some of whom spoke local languages, comprised the Kenya Regiment, took part in interrogation operations, and joined the ranks of the colonial administration as seconded members.[103] Eventually, Kenyan officials imported Templer's type of integration of decision making and information flow through a series of federal, provincial, and district emergency committees.

The no-nonsense General Sir George Erskine, a personal friend of Churchill's who had led troops in World War II and in colonial operations in India and Egypt, became the first commander in chief of East Africa Command. He was answerable directly to the War Office and had full operational control of "all Colonial, Auxiliary, Police, and Security Forces."[104] He had the power, if needed, to declare martial law, something he never deployed, partly because he didn't need it with emergency powers and partly because he loathed the settler population, its virulent racism, and its decadent lifestyle that persisted in exclusive enclaves like the famed Muthaiga Club. So too was he incensed that Blundell had a privileged place on the War Council and made every effort to snub him whenever possible. "I hate the guts of them all," Erskine wrote to his wife, "they are all middle-class sluts. I never want to see another Kenya man or woman and I dislike them all with few exceptions."[105]

By 1953, a myriad of military personnel descended on the colony. It included three British battalions, four battalions of King's African Rifles (some fresh from their tour in Malaya), the Kenya Regiment with its local volunteers, an artillery battery, and an armored car squadron—all with

British security forces guard Mau Mau suspects, 1954

the support of the Royal Air Force squadrons of Vampire jets and heavy bombers. Their mission was to defeat a Mau Mau force known as the Land and Freedom Army, who were embedded in the Mount Kenya and Aberdares forests and armed largely with homemade weapons, though lacking a single organizational structure. Three leaders emerged—Field Marshal Dedan Kimathi, Waruhiu Itote (self-styled General China), and Stanley Mathenge—though they were woefully inadequate in launching coordinated attacks, and only General China, who commanded insurgents in the Mount Kenya region, effectively managed his guerrillas and communications with the civilian passive wing. General China was a product of the empire's wartime culture, joining Allied troops fighting the Japanese and learning not just military skills and discipline but also revolutionary ideas from the war's global melting pot of brown and

Black soldiers. One African American soldier told him about Haiti's liberation, and an Indian nationalist was astonished by Africa, which he thought lagged in any significant challenge to European colonial rule.[106]

Despite the insurgents' shortcomings and Britain's superior firepower, Erskine's forces took until the end of 1954 to gain the military initiative, partly because of the impenetrable forests and Mau Mau's civilian support. Erskine looked to Palestine and Malaya for guidance. With Kenya's version of covert operations in the works, he coordinated with Baring to target the Kikuyu civilian population in Nairobi, the reserves, and the European farms. By locking down all suspected oath takers and cutting off their supply lines to the insurgents in the forests, security forces planned to starve the guerrillas and take them out using Kenya's version of killer squads.

The all-out civilian assault began with sweeping arrests and detentions without trial combined with the forced removal of Kikuyus who remained in the White Highlands. Colonial officials packed thousands into railcars and lorries and shipped them back to the reserves. In the spring of 1953, the volume of internally displaced people was staggering, and members of Kenya's Legislative Council repeatedly commented that the "trickle [of repatriates] became a stream." In a few months, the government moved over one hundred thousand Kikuyus via transit camps. Many languished with inadequate sanitation, clean water, and rations as officials figured out how to squeeze them back into the overcrowded reserves.[107] Erskine believed "a breakdown of law and order" gripped Nairobi, which "had become the main Mau Mau supply base from which the terrorists obtained recruits, money, supplies and ammunition."[108] In the early morning of April 24, 1954, he launched Operation Anvil, a repeat of similar shows of force in Palestine like Operation Shark. The general deployed twenty-five thousand security force members, who cordoned off the city for a sector-by-sector purge of Africans to rid Nairobi of any suspected Mau Mau sympathizers. Interrogation teams identified those meant for removal. Observers described the operation as "Gestapolike," and by the time Erskine declared it a success, his forces had packed over twenty thousand Mau Mau suspects into caged-in trucks for transit to Langata Camp, where they were classified using the color codes now typical in the empire's counterinsurgency operations. Thirty thousand other Kikuyus, considered less risky, were deported back to the reserves.[109]

Interrogation in Kenya was known as "screening," and security forces were desperate for any information it yielded. Kenya's special branch, responsible for political policing, needed a rapid ramp-up in intelligence much like its counterpart in Malaya. A dizzying array of operatives descended on Kenya, and familiarizing ourselves with them offers another glimpse at the tightly spun web connecting various parts of the empire to each other and to London. John Shaw was the head of MI5's Overseas Section when Kenya came calling for help a month into the insurgency. The former Palestine chief secretary had narrowly escaped death in the King David Hotel bombing, after which he took over the new Overseas Section. He monitored Nkrumah, Padmore, and other Black radicals who migrated in and out of Britain. He made his way multiple times around the Middle East, Africa, and Asia, advising intelligence operations on the ground and dispatching to Kenya Overseas Section officer Alex Kellar, who was fresh off his stint in Malaya, and former India police officer Alex MacDonald. MI5 director-general Sillitoe led the mission. The spies assessed a poorly funded and understaffed special branch that was "grossly overworked, bogged down in paper." MacDonald stayed on for one year as a permanent adviser, training and reorganizing the force and coordinating intelligence activities. By his own account, it was a resounding success. He reported back to headquarters that "Special Branch goes from strength to strength and we now have some excellent sources operating. I have no qualms at leaving this lusty infant to look after itself." MacDonald soon became MI5's first security intelligence adviser seconded to the Colonial Office, a position that signaled the Security Service's primary role in reforming the empire's intelligence systems and transferring its practices from one colony to the next. In time, forty MI5 security liaison officers had permanent posts across Britain's imperial expanse.[110]

Kenya maintained a steady MI5 presence throughout the emergency. The Kenya Intelligence Committee included the governor, along with MI5's security liaison officer, military intelligence, and the police commissioner. It also included the director of intelligence and security, Trevor Jenkins, fresh from his work in the Gold Coast with Colonel Robin "Tin Eye" Stephens, who, recall, prior to his West Africa assignment had run London's wartime Camp 020 and escaped conviction for his role in torturing Nazi suspects in postwar Bad Nenndorf, Germany. John Prendergast, who had similarly served in the Gold Coast after his stint in Palestine at the end of the Mandate, later took over for Jenkins.[111]

Screening teams were "formed as in Malaya," according to official reports, and operated in dozens of gazetted interrogation centers, including the infamous Mau Mau Investigation Center at Embakasi, which appears to have been modeled on the CSDIC in Malaya and elsewhere.[112] Screening teams were ubiquitous as well in military operations, including Operation Anvil, in the transit camps, and in the expanding detention camps system, not to mention in unofficial interrogations that unfolded on European farms and police stations. In some instances, they marshaled Mau Mau suspects through a screening parade where a *gakunia*—a Kikuyu loyalist covered in a hood—determined with a nod whether someone went for more screening and detention or was shipped back to the reserves. The "hooded men" screening technique was the brainchild of Frank Kitson, a young military intelligence officer who would play a key role, along with special branch officer Ian Henderson, in hunting down and interrogating Mau Mau insurgents.

Born in Scotland, Henderson migrated with his parents to Kenya, where he grew up with the children of Kikuyu laborers on his family's farm, so understood local culture and spoke the vernacular with native fluency, skills that served him well in his new role. His work complemented Kitson's, which delivered to Kenya pseudo-gang operations, another variation on the empire's killer squads that saw "turned" Mau Mau insurgents embedded with British security force patrols, who were sometimes "black-faced" while hunting for Mau Mau forest "gangs." Their goal: to use a "turned" operative, threatened with a court-ordered execution if he did not cooperate, to locate the gangs and reengage with them as if he were still a fellow freedom fighter, in order to gather intelligence. In January 1954 a larger security force patrol captured General China, delivering him to Henderson, who interrogated the Mau Mau leader for sixty-eight hours before turning him over to an emergency court, which rendered its sentence: death by hanging. Remarkably, a behind-the-scenes deal was struck, sparing General China's life in return for his cooperation. The high-level agent proved invaluable, negotiating a cease-fire and convincing one thousand Mau Mau fighters to gather to hear surrender terms, until British security forces shattered the delicate negotiations by firing on the gathering. The Mau Mau guerrillas fled to the forests, thinking the negotiations were a setup to kill them. No longer useful, General China was sent to prison at Lokitaung, located in the colony's northern desert wasteland, where Kenyatta was incarcerated. The experience of shared confinement soon found the two men forging a lasting and consequential friendship.[113]

Meanwhile, pseudo-gangs were yielding tremendous results, and of the three insurgent leaders, Dedan Kimathi was the last to be captured. The hunt for him was on, Henderson spearheading the obsessive search.[114] Britain portrayed Kimathi as a ruthless and psychotic rebel; to the Kikuyu, he was a fearless and noble crusader, whose heroic mythol-

Main detention camp locations, Kenya

ogizing continues to this day in Kenya. The truth was somewhere in between, though once Henderson's security force team finally sussed Kimathi out—shooting and capturing him on October 21, 1956, four years to the day since the emergency's inception—the forest war was over, save for shoot-to-kill orders used to eliminate remaining errant insurgents.[115] The civilian war, however, was not. Kimathi was quickly tried and convicted of capital offenses under Kenya's emergency regulations, and as he was marched to gallows located behind the imposing gates and barbed wire of Kamiti Prison, far from any prying eyes or cameramen, Baring's colonial administration had the intractable problem of breaking hundreds of thousands of Kikuyu civilians still committed to "land and freedom."

From the emergency's start, a trickle, then a stream of complaints landed on Baring's desk. One of the first came from Canon T. F. C. Bewes of the Church Missionary Society, who accused Britain's security forces of "third degree" methods that included beating deaths and other forms of torture such as "the police . . . using castrating instruments."[116] Official and unofficial interrogation teams became ubiquitous, and *screening* was the one word in Kikuyu synonymous with British colonial rule during Mau Mau. In fact, no translation in Kikuyu or Kiswahili captures the full meaning of the term. To this day, those Kikuyus who lived through the Mau Mau period deploy the English word *screening* to connote emergency-era coercion and torture. Screening teams, security forces, and detention and village personnel demanded intelligence and oath confessions. Sometimes they deployed horrific measures out of anger, other times for the apparent enjoyment of it all. Insofar as such abuses had a logic, they were epiphenomena of a broader system of permissible norms, conceptions of humanity, and individual beliefs embedded in the culture of Britain's civilizing mission.

White and Black agents of empire perpetrated horrific crimes in defense of British rule in Kenya. They used electric shock and hooked suspects up to car batteries. They tied suspects to vehicle bumpers with just enough rope to drag them to death. They employed burning cigarettes, fire, and hot coals. They thrust bottles (often broken), gun barrels, knives, snakes, vermin, sticks, and hot eggs up men's rectums and into women's vaginas. They crushed bones and teeth; sliced off fingers or their tips; and castrated men with specially designed instruments or by beating a suspect's testicles "till the scrotum burst," according to Anglican church officials. Some used a *kiboko*, or a rhino whip, for beating; others used clubs, fists, and truncheons. "Bucket fatigue" was a routine practice, as were various forms of human excrement torture. Mau Mau suspects and detainees were forced to clean nightsoil buckets barehanded and run for hours around a compound holding a full nightsoil bucket aloft, which then spilled over, encrusting the person holding it with feces and urine.[117] No Kikuyu—man, woman, or child—was safe. Some of the harshest measures were exacted in the Mau Mau Investigation Center. According to one settler who was a member of the Kenya Regiment:

This is where we liked to send the worst gang members when we captured them. . . . We knew the slow method of torture [at the Mau Mau Investigation Center] was worse than anything we could do. Special Branch there had a way of slowly electrocuting a Kuke—they'd rough one up for days. Once I went personally to drop off one gang member who needed special treatment. I stayed for a few hours to help the boys out, softening him up. Things got a little out of hand. By the time I cut his balls off he had no ears, and his eyeball, the right one, I think, was hanging out of its socket. Too bad, he died before we got much out of him.[118]

By the time Erskine was mopping up from Operation Anvil in May 1954, Kenya was well on its way to creating the largest archipelago of detention and prison camps in the history of Britain's empire. As far as Baring was concerned, all Mau Mau suspects "are a type who in another form of action, would become prisoners of war" and thus protected under the recently signed Geneva Conventions. He, together with Carruthers Johnston and head of the prisons department, John Lewis, was responsible for all those held behind the wire.[119] Inspired by Malaya's "progressive stage system" of detention, the Pipeline, as Kenya's string of camps was called, had a logic that began when interrogation teams screened and classified suspects using, by now, a well-known system. "Whites" were considered clean and repatriated back to the Kikuyu reserves, "greys" were more compliant oath takers and were sent down the Pipeline to works camps. In theory, detainees labored voluntarily on one of Kenya's many public works projects, which included the thirty-seven-mile-long irrigation furrow at South Yatta that detainees dug by hand. As for the "blacks," officials labeled them "hard-core" and sent them up the Pipeline to special detention camps where they were forced to labor.[120]

The Pipeline included not only detainees held without trial but also thousands who had been convicted of Mau Mau–related crimes and sent to prison. Most attorneys representing Mau Mau defendants came from a small group of South Asians based in Nairobi, like Fitz de Souza. Prior to Mau Mau, de Souza's South Asian community, nearly one hundred thousand strong, had a conflicted place in Kenya's history. Some members or their forebears arrived as indentured laborers, constructing at the turn of the century Britain's railway, which stretched from Mombasa to Nairobi and eventually into East Africa's interior. Conditions were atrocious, and thousands of these laborers, whom the British called "coolies," died from exhaustion, disease, or all-too-common lion attacks. Other South Asians had arrived separately from the railway's

indentured labor scheme, part of a centuries-long history of migration
bringing them and Middle Easterners to East Africa's coastal region and
eventually to its interior. Many were financiers and traders who some
Africans considered loathsome middlemen; Britain's policies of divide
and rule, placing this nonwhite population between Europeans and
Blacks in colonialism's hierarchy, hardened such sentiments.[121] Often
harassed by the colonial police and risking worse, South Asian attorneys
like de Souza transcended these racial and ethnic stereotypes to defend
Mau Mau suspects going before emergency courts. De Souza recalled
what colonial justice looked like in 1950s Kenya:

> [I had] no time to prepare a defense. These suspects were gen-
> erally brought up on trumped-up charges. Evidence was often
> planted, prosecution witnesses were brought in at the last min-
> ute, and we were not even allowed to cross-examine them when
> they did testify. There was no discovery at all. We just showed up
> to represent our clients, who were not even identified by name,
> but rather by a number. There was little we could do to help
> them, other than argue for lesser sentencing. These men were

Mau Mau suspects about to stand trial, identified by number, April 1953

Mau Mau suspects, Langata Detention Camp, Nairobi, 1954

sentenced to prison—sometimes for a lifetime of hard labor—through a mockery of the legal system.[122]

Some never made it to prison. Emergency courts sent 1,090 Africans to the gallows, surpassing the number of state executions for any other single conflict in the empire's history.[123] At the end of prisoners' sentences, nearly all were "Form C'ed," meaning they immediately became a detainee held without trial and were transferred to one of the Pipeline's camps.[124]

All male detainees officially entered the Pipeline through enormous holding camps at Manyani and Mackinnon Road. The camp populations quickly exceeded their combined capacity of twenty thousand. Subjected to repeated screening, detainees ran a Kenya-style gauntlet when they entered the camps. White officers shouted *"Piga, piga sana"* (Beat them, keep beating them) to camp guards, who also liberally helped themselves to the detainees' possessions. They forced each detainee to strip down and march through a cattle dip of disinfectant, where several drowned. To those who survived, colonial officials issued diaphanous schoolboy uniforms much like those that *askaris* had worn in Malaya. They gave each detainee a unique number, which was stamped onto a crude iron bracelet that officials soldered onto the detainee's wrist. Most of the camps were for men, but one, Kamiti, was all-female and another, at Athi River, held women considered the most hard-core. Initially, six different types of camps comprised the Pipeline—holding camps, works camps, special detention camps, exile camps, women and juvenile camps, and chiefs camps, which were located in a detainee's home district and operated by local loyalists and British administrators, who together had the final say on when a detainee would be released.[125]

The Pipeline was supposed to be the site of unprecedented reform. Baring depicted Kenya as a war for the hearts and minds of the Kikuyu people, as Templer did for Malaya. With the mass screening, forced removals, and detentions under way, Hugh Fraser, parliamentary undersecretary to Lyttleton, traveled to Kenya and reported, "Although there are only . . . about 1,500 detained, the number of detainees may well increase by June next year to some 25,000–40,000. Should such numbers have to be involved I have stressed to HE [His Excellency Governor Baring] the importance of the word Rehabilitation, and machinery for this purpose is being set up."[126]

Baring telegrammed Templer and asked him to send one of his civil servants to Kenya. Templer said he couldn't spare a body, though he agreed to host one of Kenya's colonial officers in order to tutor him in the ways of rehabilitation. Commissioner for community development Thomas Askwith soon undertook a two-week tour of the Federation, after which he reported idealistically that the detention camps and New Villages were not punitive sites but rather opportunities to transform Communist sympathizers and to reinstill confidence in colonial governance. Even Askwith, a reformist whose career embraced a humanity that was forward-reaching for his time, understood that the difficulties that Kenya faced were far greater than those in Malaya. For starters, the Colonial Office ruled that Mau Mau adherents "belonged to the territory" and therefore could not be deported outside Kenya.[127] While officials imagined permanent exile camps for twelve thousand hard-core, the rest had to be cleansed of their "Mau Mau filth" and resettled into the reserves. But over one hundred thousand Kikuyu had already been deported back to the reserves, which were collapsing under the weight of overpopulation. Without jobs or expanded landholdings to keep pace with the release of detainees, Askwith predicted that "rehabilitation [would] be a waste of time, money and effort."[128]

Even for the commissioner, whose liberal sensibilities recognized the socioeconomic dimension of Kikuyu unrest, the "oath represented everything evil in Mau Mau."[129] He soon took the lead in Kenya's "hearts and minds" campaign when Baring created an expanded position for him as commissioner for community development and rehabilitation. Askwith incubated views on reform in the context of Mau Mau and local understandings of the Kikuyu psyche. Here the emerging field of ethno-psychiatry and Dr. J. C. Carothers's report, "The Psychology of Mau Mau," intersected with the ideas of the famed archaeologist Louis Leakey, who had grown up among the Kikuyu and spoke their language. According to Leakey, the power of a traditional Kikuyu oath could be broken only if an initiate confessed to having taken it. Such a concept melded with local missionary thought, as well as Carothers's, which called for a confession and the replacement of Mau Mau devotion with the reformist principles of Christian stewardship that were at the heart of Britain's civilizing mission. Under Askwith, rehabilitation was an integration of these ideas, together with vocational training, civics and homecraft classes, and tutelage in Western education. These were the linchpins to Kenya's "hearts and minds" campaign behind the wires of detention.[130]

Not everyone believed in reform, of course. One visitor described the local attitude toward rehabilitation:

> What do the settlers say? . . . The policy of appeasement over the past few years must be halted. Justice must be done more promptly and effectively—and it must be seen to be done. The slow careful process of British justice, so cherished at home, is neither understood nor appreciated by the African mind moulded by centuries of rough tribal discipline. This outlook is not changed to order by a dose of the three R's, nor yet by what may often be no more than a veneer of Christianity.[131]

If Kenya was short on the will to reform, it was even shorter on funding.[132] In June 1954, with the Pipeline pushed beyond capacity, the War Council decided to introduce a version of Malaya's resettlement policy. The goal was to cut the supply lines between Mau Mau civilians and the guerrillas while also controlling the Kikuyu population and subjecting them to collective punishments and fines as well as forced labor and other ongoing detention camp policies and practices. The Kenya government called it "villagisation." Its officials forced the Kikuyus, who traditionally lived in scattered homesteads, into 804 villages that consisted of 230,000 huts.

Villagization took less than eighteen months. During that time,

Home Guard post, overlooking an emergency village, Central Province, Kenya

Kenyan officials forcibly relocated 1,040,899 Kikuyus within the reserves and corralled an unrecorded number of White Highland squatters into labor lines like those in Malaya. These labor lines were effectively private detention centers, located on European estates, where Kenya's settlers and security forces surveilled, punished, and exacted labor from Kikuyu squatters using methods similar to those being deployed in the new Kikuyu reserve villages.[133] Whereas the labor lines were less tightly controlled, barbed wire, spiked trenches, and twenty-four-hour guards surrounded the "emergency villages" that saw little formal rehabilitation on offer: Askwith had around 250 rehabilitation staff for the entire Kikuyu population, a ratio of 1 to 6,000.

Christian missionaries, however, filled the gap, as they did in the detention camps. In fact, the Pipeline was well known to Kenya's men of God, who visited the detainees regularly, offering spiritual guidance in the hope of enticing them to confess their oaths, and converting them to Christianity once they'd done so. Moral Rearmament, by then a global movement, also played a role in the camps. Its members espoused a kind of ersatz Christian faith, pushing a doctrine of personal justification through works alone and espousing four absolute standards: honesty, purity, unselfishness, and love. Together with the various Christian missionaries, Moral Rearmament evangelists inundated the detainees with lectures, sermons, and nightly public broadcasts blaring the Lord's message.[134] In the Kikuyu reserves, local missionaries and Maendeleo ya Wanawake (Progress Among Women Club), a voluntary self-help organization led by the Anglican archbishop's wife, Mary Beecher, stepped in with home craft classes and concern over village conditions. "[We] deprecate the excessive use of communal labour for women," Beecher told Governor Baring, "as it leaves too little time for the care of homes and children, causes great suffering, creates anti-Government feeling, and makes the teaching given in the Maendeleo Clubs very largely useless."[135]

The villages became detention camps in all but name. When their numbers were combined with the estimated 140,000 to 320,000 detainees who passed through the Pipeline, the British colonial government had managed, by the end of 1955, to detain nearly the entire Kikuyu population—a feat that was unprecedented in the empire save for the Chinese population in Malaya. Officially, the government buried its real detention numbers in statistical sleights of hand. According to press handouts and reports in Parliament, the Kenya government detained 70,000 to 80,000 Mau Mau suspects without trial. These figures, however, were daily average figures that did not reflect the number of detainees who entered and exited the Pipeline. When detainee intake and release rates are taken into account, the overall detention figures go up by two- to fourfold. Moreover, the government never included in its detainee figures those Kikuyus it relocated in villages or held in labor lines.[136]

Life in the Kikuyu reserves became unbearable, and accounts of villagization were reminiscent of security force operations in Malaya. Early morning security force raids and village burnings were widespread in Kenya. Ruth Ndegwa, who, like many women, lived in Kenya's Central Province while her husband was in the Pipeline, remembered:

> We had not been given any warning beforehand that our houses were going to be burned. No one in the whole ridge knew that we were to move. The police just came one day, and drove everybody out of their homes, while the Home Guards burned the houses right behind us. . . . Everything, even our clothes were burned down. . . . During the move I got separated from my

children, and I could not trace them. They had been in front, leading our remaining cattle, but I failed to find them. During the whole night I could hear a lot of shooting and screaming. I cried the whole night, knowing that my children were gone.[137]

Internally, Erskine readily admitted that villagization was "a punitive measure" that produced "valuable results," as some women, starved and traumatized, slowly began to cooperate with security forces by giving them information and refusing to supply insurgents with support.[138] It was also a measure that he incrementally tightened. In his words, the general in charge of all operations "spoke to H. E. [Baring] on the subject . . . and told him that I did not think we were being sufficiently tough and I was convinced that unless we were much more tough we should not break the passive wing. I found H. E. quite sympathetic and ready to lower his standards on collective punishments."[139] In mid-1955, the Kenya government allowed eleven British Red Cross workers into the villages to distribute food alongside missionaries who were also providing such relief. Baring, however, was in lockstep with Erskine and his successor, Lieutenant General Sir Gerald Lathbury, who similarly targeted civilians for punishment. The governor insisted the Red Cross and missionaries distribute food and supplies not to those Kikuyus needing relief but to loyalists who were demanding ever-greater government support.[140] The colony's medical department issued scathing reports highlighting the "alarming number of deaths occurring amongst children in the 'punitive' villages" and the "political considerations" that were blocking the Red Cross relief efforts.[141]

The ICRC received urgent reports from its delegate for British Central Africa, G. C. Senn, that Britain's national Red Cross Society was acting in its government's interest rather than maintaining nonpartisanship. "The British Red Cross does NOT do its duty in the whole matter, has never done it and does not show any intention to change its attitude," Senn wrote.[142] Indeed, the British Red Cross leadership actively opposed any relief intervention coming from ICRC representatives in Geneva. It justified such obstructionism by pointing to its own relief workers who were already providing humanitarian aid thanks to the generosity of the British government, which maintained that Common Article 3 of the Geneva Conventions did not apply to Kenya's state of emergency, and therefore it wasn't required to let in any Red Cross workers but had generously done so. Doublethink shot through humanitarian relief in Kenya, and the British Red Cross played its part in the charade.[143]

By this point in the insurgency, collective punishment was de rigueur in Britain's empire. In Kenya, special branch worked with security forces to use punitive tactics modeled on Malaya's, as detailed in its memorandum "Techniques for Dealing with Known Bad Villages."[144] The War Office's 1949 publication *Imperial Policing and Duties in Aid of the Civil Power* made clear that, in spite of international humanitarian laws, there were different rules for different people. "The degree of force necessary and the methods of applying it will obviously differ very greatly as between the United Kingdom and places overseas," Britain's top military brass emphasized.[145] In deliberations over the revised and expanded Geneva Conventions with the Lord Chancellor's Office, the Colonial Office noted that " 'collective punishment' *has* been used—e.g., the burning of villages, and so on—and may well be used again."[146] The War Office tweaked the principle of "necessity," replacing it in 1949 with the phrase "the minimum use of force," which it reproduced in the army's updated "Imperial Policing" pocket-size pamphlet.[147] However, in 1958, the revised *Manual of Military Law* restated the War Office's previous long-standing position: "The existence of an armed insurrection would justify *the use of any degree of force necessary* effectually to meet and cope with the insurrection."[118]

Necessity. Minimum use of force. Any degree of force necessary. Such excruciating nomenclature exercises didn't change the fact that Britain was violating the ethos of postwar international humanitarian law, which sought to reduce the suffering that British forces were inflicting to defeat colonial insurgencies. That the British government formally sidestepped Common Article 3 of the Geneva Conventions through a definitional loophole was shameful, though, to use the ubiquitous term, necessary, as far as the government and military were concerned. They publicly rationalized Britain's "just war" using variations on a now-familiar argument: the nation's troops were saving civilization from the clutches of savagery, terrorism, and Communism. There was also the issue of military acculturation. The historian Huw Bennett summarizes the situation perfectly:

> Under the Geneva and Hague Conventions, states were required to give instruction during both peace and war, including disseminating the original treaty texts. Even in 1966 it was apparent that instruction on the Geneva Conventions was not being provided at the staff colleges, Imperial Defence College or any other "key Service institutions and unit." The Directorate of

Army Legal Services failed to provide instruction, and even worse, itself needed instruction in the conventions.[149]

Clearly Britain's military wasn't abiding by the conventions at the most basic level of instruction, though it did teach the troops, according to the Army's Staff College syllabus, that an act of indemnity was "a statute intended to make transactions legal which were illegal when they took place, and to free the individuals concerned from legal liability."[150] The concept of legalized lawlessness, which we have seen unfold throughout our story, was officially being taught to young soldiers.

In Malaya and Kenya, collective punishment with its intended devastating effects was both "inevitable" and "a necessity," according to the War Office.[151] According to Erskine, villages were "the key to the whole problem of tighter control. Once villages are established curfew, roll calls, searches, and food control become merely a matter of organisation."[152] "Food control," or "food denial," as we have seen in other parts of the empire, was another form of "punishment of the civil population for lack of co-operation."[153] The point was to starve villagers into submission while working them without respite.[154] Some women reported burying emaciated children in unmarked graves, and local newspapers began to comment on the malnutrition that swept through the Kikuyu reserves.[155]

Kenya's War Council ordered "that publicity for food denial measures should be kept to a minimum," though its starvation policies weren't the only cause for concern.[156] The Kikuyu reserves had become, like the Pipeline, sites of extreme violence, and the loyalists, or Home Guards, were at the center of much of it. Erskine recruited Colonel Philip Morcombe from Malaya to serve as director of the Kikuyu Guard, or Home Guard, and he outfitted his African force with uniforms and easily recognizable silver armbands. Much like their counterparts in Palestine and Malaya, as we've seen, Kenya's Home Guards were known for *fitina*, or intrigue, which included "pay[ing] off old scores against Mau Mau," according to one junior officer who later compiled a history of the force.[157] Colonial officials erected a Home Guard post in each emergency village; inside the posts, rapes and beatings were widespread, as were tortures that included confinement in small cells filled with vermin and excrement. The security forces were implicated in rapes. Twenty-one of the sixty-two allegations filed with the chief secretary's complaint coordinating committee described military members who defiled women and young girls.[158] Christina Wambui offered testimony to the *End of Empire* documentary series:

Home Guards plus army soldiers would come to our village early at 6am. You would hear doors being hit thus (ku ku)—open the doors! "Open up. Open the doors." Once they got in they went straight to beating you. They would beat us and take some to the guard post—in critical condition. Once there she would be beaten further until she was completely dead. Once the police soldiers got in, they would search the house while army soldiers would rape the women. Ten of the army soldiers would rape one woman. In other cases five of them would rape one woman.[159]

"It must be faced up to quite openly and frankly," wrote the assistant commissioner of police K. P. Hadingham, "that Summary Justice has, undoubtedly, been carried out in many instances. . . . Acts of murder, rape, arson, robbery and extortion directed against the local population, even though they may be Mau Mau sympathizers, can never be termed as 'the Administration of Justice.'"[160]

In the conflict's early years, the Colonial Office had amassed a file called "Allegations of atrocities" that enumerated multiple complaints. They included those of Tony Cross, a temporary police officer, who wrote about the "Gestapo stuff" for his friends back home. It also included the case of Elijah Gideon Njeru, who had been beaten to death during interrogation. A local magistrate undertook a preliminary internal investigation and found that the British perpetrators had "quite obviously suffered considerable punishment in the form of worry and remorse. . . . I do not in any case consider that it is in the public interest that such action [prosecutions] should be taken at the present time, when all must unite in the effort to restore this country to a state in which such circumstances as these could not arise."[161] Baring concurred, as did the Colonial Office.

A pattern emerged similar to elsewhere in the empire whereby prosecutions for torture and murder in Kenya's screening operations and detention camps and villages were either buried or, in the rare instance where guilt was assigned, mitigating circumstances often prevailed.[162] It simply was not in the best interest of anyone, so the logic went, to undermine security force morale; moreover, whatever crimes may or may not have been perpetrated were minor in comparison to Mau Mau's savagery. Still, the colony's attorney general couldn't help but observe through analogy that the situation was "distressingly reminiscent of conditions in Nazi Germany or Communist Russia."[163] Even Erskine internally made known the circumstances unfolding in Kenya.

Corresponding directly to the secretary of state for war Antony Head, he wrote:

> There was a great deal of indiscriminate shooting by Army and Police. I am quite certain prisoners were beaten to extract information. It is a short step from beating to torture and I am now sure, although it has taken me some time to realise it, that torture was a feature of many police posts. . . . You ought to know about "screening teams." They work under the Administration and their object is to comb through labour and distinguish Mau Mau from the rest and the degree of Mau Mau. Some of these screening teams have used methods of torture.[164]

In June 1953 the commander in chief said in a widely publicized statement, "I strongly disapprove of 'beating up' the inhabitants of this country just because they are inhabitants." He went on to underscore that there would be "full mutual co-operation between the Police and Army in regard to all such investigations."[165] Such strong words meant nothing, because Erskine was part of a larger culture of complicity that obscured conditions that were worsening. Cases of assaults, torture, rape, and murder accumulated in the chief secretary's office, and Lennox-Boyd found himself repeatedly on the floor of Parliament defending the indefensible through obstructive and obfuscating means, another example of Orwellian doublethink. So, too, were colonial officials well aware of their questionable forced labor practices. At the emergency's start, Lyttleton wrote to Baring, noting that the "proposal [of detainee labor] was contrary to the letter of the International Convention on Forced Labour." The colonial secretary had to "refute any allegations that [the detainees] are being used as 'slave' or 'cheap labour' for the profit of government."[166] Lyttleton urged the governor to introduce "special detention camps" modeled on those Templer had created—the idea again being that Britain would be seen as violating international conventions only some of the time.[167] A year later, however, Kenya's minister for defense assessed the colony's works camps where labor was ostensibly voluntary and paid, remarking, "We are *slave traders* and the employment of our slaves are, in this instance, by the Public Works Department."[168]

Less than a year earlier, in February 1954, Colonel Arthur Young had been brought to Kenya. Commissioner of police of the City of London, Young had been seconded to Malaya in 1952 to establish community-based policing. After a year, his Operation Service, which did not address political policing or intelligence gathering, was declared a huge success, and he was soon sent to Kenya to undertake a similar job. As Kenya's new commissioner of police, Young had a more daunting task: he was to render the force independent and uncorruptible. It wasn't long, however, before he became disgusted with Kenyan officials, particularly the governor. "I found it my unpleasant duty," Young recalled, "to pursue with Baring my apprehensions that members of the civilian security forces were uncontrolled and were committing crimes of violence and brutality upon their alleged enemies, which were unjustified and abhorrent."[169] The governor did nothing to address these crimes. Instead, from Young's perspective, Baring did everything he could to stonewall if not actively stymie independent investigations. "I addressed an official report to H. E. [Baring] expressing my apprehensions in writing, with the belief that supporting evidence would soon be forthcoming," Young recorded in his diary. "I also requested that he should take an initiative in administrative action which would indicate his own repugnance of brutality committed by security forces and do what he could to bring this to an end. I received no acknowledgment of this appreciation, far less an answer to it, in spite of a number of reminders."[170]

By December 1954, Young could not create an "impartial status" for the police and tendered his resignation. "If we have a weak Police force we have a strong Administrative service," Baring insisted to the Colonial Office, "and I am convinced that we cannot and should not weaken the position of our Administrative officers."[171] Baring felt a strong, independent police force might undermine his cadre of colonial officers and their staffs in the reserves and Pipeline; put another way, with someone like Young at the helm, an independent police force would surely have exposed the administration's corruption and its brutal policies and practices.

Baring's fears were well-founded. Young provided him with exhaustive details of the "many serious and revolting crimes [that] were being perpetrated by 'loyal' Africans and by Europeans, not infrequently with the tacit approval of the Administration, concerning which no reports were being received at Police Headquarters."[172] For the first time in our longer story of abuses in the empire, we have a single piece of comprehensive evidence from a top official in the colonial government pointing not only to police-directed abuses but to the colonial administration's firsthand role in them as well, thanks to Young's account—an account he deposited in the private archives at Oxford University in 1971 and, because it was included in his personal collection of papers, had not been part of the state-directed end-of-empire document purges. Young's papers make clear that members of the police force were complicit in these "revolting crimes," and they made his job of creating an impartial investigation unit all the more challenging, if not impossible, without Baring's support.

When Young returned to London in January 1955, his reception at the Colonial Office was decidedly chilly. Lennox-Boyd and Baring had been friends since their Oxford days, and they shared a ruling-class conviction and vision for the empire. In fact, when Lennox-Boyd took over for Lyttleton in July 1954, he considered himself a "brake" on self-government anywhere in the empire, let alone Kenya.[173] This ethos translated into a hands-on approach, and Lennox-Boyd traveled to Kenya on several occasions. His tour of South Nyeri, the northern-most region of the Kikuyu reserves in the colony's Central Province, just four months after he took over the Colonial Office, was particularly noteworthy. Together with the governor, Lennox-Boyd inspected various emergency sites. At the time, both Lennox-Boyd and Baring were well aware of the pending case against Chief Mundia of Nyeri's Mundia District. The chief was charged, along with a handful of his Home Guards, with beating several detainees, one of whom died. Assistant police commissioner Hadingham was the group's police escort, recalling that "HE [the Governor] drew me aside for some ten minutes to discuss the Chief Mundia case. . . . HE said [it] was 'off the record,' and while he would not give me any directions in the matter he considered it would be politically most inexpedient to prosecute a loyal chief who had taken a leading part in the fight against Mau Mau."[174]

Lennox-Boyd had every intention of supporting the governor, which meant silencing Young. Like all those who served in the empire, Young had signed the Official Secrets Act. If Young had published his letter of resignation, its political damage would have been potentially irreparable. "In retrospect," Young wrote, "it is clear that if my report had been published to Parliament, the Governor in the very least would have been recalled and the Colonial Secretary himself would have been in a very hazardous position."[175] Instead, he and Lennox-Boyd drafted a carefully scripted press release that was devoid of any particulars contained in the police commissioner's original resignation letter. For the purposes of public consumption, Young had stepped down due to a "difference of opinion" with the "Kenya Government."[176]

As for any ongoing brutalities, the press release emphasized they were "the activities of the Home Guard whose powers were liable to abuse owing to their lack of discipline," and government was "deter-

mined to eradicate abuses among members of Kikuyu Guard." Blaming
Kenya's "uncivilized" Black population for Britain's legalized lawlessness, there was no mention of the multiple recorded crimes that European members of the security forces, administration, and detention
camp staff had perpetrated. Rather, the Colonial Office doubled down
on the emergency's exigencies when it came to jettisoning out of hand
a 1954 parliamentary delegation's recommendation for an "impartial"
police force.[177] The carefully worded release was just another iteration
of the British government's official line:

> There was . . . a difference of opinion between the Kenya Gov-
> ernment and Colonel Young on the functions of the Police Force
> in the Emergency. . . . The Kenya Government . . . considered
> that for as long as the present violent phase of the Emergency
> lasted it was essential that the Administration, the Police and the
> military should jointly concentrate all their efforts on bringing
> terrorism to an early end and that for all this purpose there must
> be the highest degree of integration and co-ordination between
> the three bodies at all levels.[178]

On the heels of Young's resignation, the British government shipped
several of those who supported his efforts out of Kenya. Chief among
them was the colony's attorney general, who was promoted to chief justice of Singapore; Eric Griffith-Jones, whose attitude toward coercion
and prosecutions mirrored those of the governor, replaced him. Young's
replacement, Richard Catling, who had survived the King David Hotel
bombing and transferred to Malaya where he rose through its policing
ranks, left his high-level post in the Federation to take over as the new
commissioner of police in Kenya. "Mau Mau was a rather easier problem to deal with than the emergencies that I had known before in Palestine and Malaya," as far as Catling was concerned. For the new police
commissioner, there "was no outside influence" and his job was to work
closely with Kenya's combined intelligence units to break and turn those
infected with Mau Mau.[179]

For colonial officials in Kenya and Britain, Young's exit was not
enough. They remained vulnerable. Johnston witnessed the violence
being hushed up across the colony and the anxieties accompanying it.
"What the District Officers fear," he wrote to the attorney general,
"is . . . an atrocities commission intended to show that the Administration have been guilty of innumerable war crimes. I need not stress the
undesirability of a witch hunt of this sort. Would you please consult the

Solicitor General [in London] and ask him what he has in mind by way of a general indemnity ordinance to cover the action taken by the administration and the Security Forces during the Emergency."[180] Churchill and his cabinet collectively approved a blanket amnesty: the security force's white and Black members, along with those in the administration, would remain unaccountable for any crime committed prior to the governor's official declaration of the amnesty on January 18, 1955.[181]

A day after the amnesty's signing, Baring reiterated the colonial administration's policy regarding the hard-core detainees, or "irreconcilables." He publicly reassured a crowd in Nyeri that Lennox-Boyd said "'there is no question whatsoever of irreconcilables being allowed to return to areas where loyal Kikuyu live.'"[182] By the end of 1955, however, he and the colonial secretary were walking back their statements as questions over the European Convention on Human Rights and its Article 15 proved more vexing than originally anticipated. Recall that, once the emergency was lifted, Britain could no longer derogate the convention, which forbade detention without trial. With nearly thirty thousand detainees still in the Pipeline, the governor and colonial secretary demanded a step-up in the rate of release, and Johnston was to solve the problem.

As elsewhere in the empire, the British government's policies created a series of unforeseen, cascading effects, two of which vexed Johnston. First, there was a "blockage" in the Pipeline: camps like Manyani—originally designated a reception center for ten thousand detainees—were created as hubs from which officials dispersed detainees to other camps once screening teams interrogated and categorized them. But detainees up and down the Pipeline were refusing to cooperate, which meant release rates were abysmally low, and there was nowhere to send the detainees held in the vast reception centers. Officials soon redesignated Manyani, which was six thousand detainees over capacity, a "holding camp."

Some of the blockage was also due to Erskine's sweep of Nairobi. The Pipeline had never recovered from Operation Anvil's effects, as the detainee population reached over fifty-two thousand—an increase of 2,500 percent during 1954 alone. Health officials called "holding camps" like Manyani and Mackinnon Road "sanitary menace[s]" and quarantined them at various points because of communicable diseases like typhoid.[183] Moreover, by the time Johnston had to increase the release rates, the bleak and brutal camp conditions hardened many detainees. Some turned the compounds into opportunities for further Mau Mau indoctrination. Educated detainees informed others on the details of international laws that purportedly protected them. Others led discussion groups on Kenya's independent future and what it meant to them. Britain's policies and practices transformed the Kikuyu movement and steeled thousands of detainees, some of whom had been ambivalent about Mau Mau at the time of their arrest but now refused to cooperate.[184]

Johnston also had to solve the "reabsorption problem," or the overcrowded Kikuyu reserves' insufficient carrying capacity to handle the pending detainees' return. This second issue was deeply problematic, in part because it intersected with the government's broader loyalist reward system. Ongoing land consolidation and other agrarian reforms, known as the Swynnerton Plan, were meant to rationalize scattered landholdings and render the Kikuyu countryside more productive. They would also guarantee the long-term socioeconomic and political ascendancy of the government's loyalist supporters who were already exempt from any of the communal punishments or fines meted out in the reserves. As one colonial administrator observed insofar as new settlement schemes were concerned, they were "essentially one of 'reward' for loyal Kikuyu, Meru, and Embu and not for the reclamation of doubtful Mau Mau."[185] As loyalists were given disproportionately large plots of land, to solve the problem of reabsorbing detainees after their release, Johnston asked, "*What standard of living is aimed at?*"[186] By tinkering with the official numbers and readjusting the originally targeted African standard of living downward, he and his resettlement committee were able, with a stroke of the pen, to accommodate an additional 150,000 in the reserves.[187] In effect, just as the Kikuyu majority were starving, the colonial government solved its reabsorption problem by reducing a standard of living that was already woefully inadequate. Such measures, however, began to alleviate the Pipeline's "blockage," once the government introduced new Pipeline policies to "soften" greys who soon confessed their oaths, the first sign, according to the government, of cooperation. In turn, screening teams reclassified them as white, and then shipped them to chiefs camps in their home areas where the chiefs eventually released them into the reserves.

Turning his attention to the reported thirty thousand detainees who remained in the Pipeline, Johnston tried to force their cooperation by tightening the screws further, using amended emergency regulations. In response to detainees who refused to work as required under Emergency (Detained Persons) Regulation 22, Baring amended Emergency (Detained Persons) Regulation 17 to include several minor infractions as "major offenses." Previously "disobedience to a lawful order in such manner as to show wilful defiance of authority" was a minor offense; with the amendment it became a "major offense."[188] Legally, camp authorities could now, for instance, put a detainee in solitary confinement or use corporal punishment. Lennox-Boyd, while supportive, raised bigger picture concerns when he condoned the amendment, which was absent any reform incentives:

> As you are aware, the use of corporal punishment to maintain discipline among convicts is opposed by a large body of vocal opinion which will be reinforced in this instance by the thought that we are concerned with detainees whose responsibility for criminal actions has never been established by the courts. . . . I have noted the character of these detainees . . . and am anxious to afford you every support in dealing with a dangerous and difficult problem. On the other hand, I would be uneasy if the power of the Kenya Government to control large concentrations of the more obdurate detainees were to rest solely on the threat or use of corporal punishment.[189]

Kenya's strike forces were called in to enforce discipline when necessary. Entire camps like that on Mageta Island, whose occupants had been rioting over forced labor requirements—legally enabled under Emergency (Detained Persons) Regulation 22—were beaten and starved into submission. The problem wasn't just forced labor but also the detainees' knowledge of the government's land policies. Despite lockdown conditions, the detainees were hungry for information outside the wire and devised myriad ways, including bribing guards, to receive and send news. A consistent theme in Mau Mau demands was a "return of stolen land," yet Johnston and the governor had no plans for that. Instead, alongside his get-tough policies, the special commissioner attempted to increase the rate of release through the introduction of a new classification system that replaced the color system of "black," "grey," and "white" with a more complex letter-based system. "Blacks" were separated into "Z1s" and "Z2s," "greys" into "Ys," and "whites" became either "Xs" or "Cs." By separating the most recalcitrant "blacks" from those who agreed to work but not to confess, Johnston thought he would have better success at breaking the hard-core. The maneuver, however, was reminiscent of earlier futile attempts, first in India and later in Malaya.

Adding to Johnston's woes, the governor introduced new quotas. In the spring of 1956, Baring demanded a doubling of release rates from 1,000 to 2,000 detainees per month, informing Johnston that he had reduced the 12,000 spots for permanent exile to a few thousand, a reduction, if you recall, prompted by the European Convention on Human Rights' prohibition of detention without trial, which would be salient once the emergency was over and Britain could no longer derogate under the convention's Article 15. The governor and the Colonial Office's legal counsel had discovered that their planned manipulation of international human rights law, using back-channel negotiations with the conventions' other signatories, was more difficult than anticipated. They needed to reduce the long-term detention-without-trial numbers as much as possible. This left the special commissioner with the unenviable task of breaking an additional 8,000 to 9,000 "irreconcilable" detainees. Again, Johnston tried to refine the classification system. He hoped that more discrete categories would separate the waverers from the true hard-core, rendering them more amenable to cooperation and confession. Multiple new classifications included "Zs" and "Y1s," "YYs" and "XRs." The whole exercise became a bureaucratic parody, and Johnston quickly realized the futility of his changes.[190]

Johnston, needing drastic action, did what his imperial predecessors in Kenya had failed to do: he stepped up with his own man with a plan. In the spring of 1957, Kenya's second-most-powerful administrator tapped Terence Gavaghan for the newly created position of district officer in charge of rehabilitation. Gavaghan's portfolio included all five works camps on Kenya's Mwea Plain, and his reporting line went directly to Johnston. An Irishman who stood well over six feet tall, Gavaghan had short-cropped hair, a formidable physique, translucent-like blue eyes, and a bent nose gratis a squash accident and one too many brawls. By all accounts, including his own, he inhabited a self-fashioned masculine toughness. Some of Kenya's public school, Oxbridge-trained officers chafed at his hardscrabble pedigree, not to mention his insatiable sexual appetite. Gavaghan spent his youth in India's middle-class milieu, returned on scholarship to Britain for school, joined the Royal Ulsters, and eventually took a job in Kenya's civil service at the age of twenty-one. He rose quickly through its ranks before the special commissioner came calling. Much like the unorthodox Wingate and the somewhat more doctrinaire Templer, Gavaghan was a product of his times and stood in a long line of results men. He was precisely the person Johnston needed.

Gavaghan turned first to John Cowan. A local prisons staff officer at Gathigiriri, one of the five Mwea camps, Cowan had been experimenting with a new method for breaking the hard-core—something called the "dilution technique." Under Cowan's direction, camp officials took fifty detainees in leg irons from one of the other four Mwea camps and sent them to Gathigiriri. There officers and guards broke the fifty down further into smaller groups, after which they deployed unbridled force to pummel the detainees. They used blows from fists, clubs, truncheons, whips, and any other weapons at their disposal. Such force continued until detainees cooperated by listening to orders, working, and ultimately confessing. Kenya's minister for defense, Jake Cusack, witnessed dilution, and its results so impressed him that he recommended the strategy be exported immediately to other camps. Cowan had finally offered a tangible and proven solution to the cooperation-and-release dilemma.[191] There was, however, one wrinkle. Detainees undergoing dilution were dying. In one instance, Baring informed Lennox-Boyd that Muchiri Githuma, a Gathigiriri detainee, was "severely beaten and died as a result" of the dilution technique.[192] Undeterred, Baring wrote to the colonial secretary summing up the thoughts of all those at the top: "If we abandon the 'dilution' method a severe check would be given to a process which is not only working well but also offers hope of bringing down a 'pipeline' towards release many Mau Mau detainees who a few months ago we all considered would remain irreconcilable for years."[193]

Gavaghan, calling his new mission Operation Progress, resurrected the dilution technique into a systematized and well-executed program of brutality that began with an all-out blitz inside the compounds, together with an overwhelming "show of force." He enlisted the help of prison and rehabilitation officers posted at the Mwea camps and recruited his own "Praetorian Guard" of loyalist Kikuyus. According to Gavaghan, they had "good physique and address . . . [and] were quickly drilled in simple unarmed combat and equipped with short wooden truncheons slung from leather belts binding judo style heavy cotton tunics over calf length trousers." Operation Progress was, in Gavaghan's words, a "kind of rape." Its deployment in the Mwea camps was so successful that he was poised to expand dilution to Manyani Holding Camp to break detainees there.[194] "I should have thought that this was potentially dangerous," one Kenyan minister wrote. "My impression was that the violence used at Gathigiriri [the camp where a detainee was killed in January] was mild compared to that meted out at the present time."[195] The War Council was also concerned, not for the detainees, but for "the officers . . . [who] may well be in danger of prosecution as a result of incidents occurring during the [dilution] process."[196]

In June 1957 Baring and Attorney General Griffith-Jones sent numerous secret memoranda to the Colonial Office outlining their plan for systematic violence and asking for the colonial secretary's official input and approval. "Gavaghan has been perfectly open with us," the governor told Lennox-Boyd. "He has said that he can cope with a regular flow in of Manyani 'Zs' and turn them out later to the district camps. We believe that he will be able to go on doing this a very long way down the list of the worst detainees. But he can only do it if the hard cases are dealt with on their first arrival in a rough way. . . . There must be with some a phase of violent shock."[197] In a separate memorandum sent to the colonial secretary, Griffith-Jones provided extensive details on Mwea, details that he and several other high-level colonial officials witnessed firsthand when they observed Gavaghan's work. Again, the colonial secretary was fully apprised of what transpired:

> Gavaghan explained, however, that there had, in past intakes, been more persistent resistors, who had had to be forcibly changed into camp clothing; that some of them had started the "Mau Mau moan," a familiar cry which was promptly taken up by the rest of the camp, representing a concerted and symbolic defiance of the camp authorities; that in such cases it was essential to prevent the infection of this "moan" spreading through the camp, and that accordingly a resistor who started it was promptly put on the ground, a foot placed on his throat and mud stuffed in his mouth; and that a man whose resistance could not be broken down was in the last resort knocked unconscious.[198]

Lennox-Boyd initially balked not at Gavaghan's methods per se but rather at the request for his official sanctioning of them. The colonial secretary was on the verge of officially adopting systematized violence as a way to break down the thousands of detainees who remained in the Pipeline. Griffith-Jones sensed some concern and drafted a series of codes written in legal doublespeak, which Lennox-Boyd approved.[199] These codes distinguished something Griffith-Jones termed legal *compelling force* from otherwise illegal *punitive force*. Compelling force could be used "when immediately necessary to restrain or overpower a refractory detained person, or to compel compliance with a lawful order to prevent disorder." Punitive force described any kind of unlawful physical punishment.[200] Given that Emergency (Detained Persons) Regulation 17 had already been amended, and given that colonial officials were well aware of the punitive force widely used in the camps and villages with little or no legal recourse, the efforts they undertook to provide legal coverage once violence was systematized and sanctioned is noteworthy. Even so, Kenya's police commissioner insisted the British government had not gone far enough. "It is my firm opinion," he wrote, "that the officers concerned should receive some form of indemnity for there might easily be a fatal accident."[201] Nevertheless, when his name was on the line, not to mention the Conservative government, the colonial secretary inveigled with officials in Kenya and London to render otherwise illegal behavior legal.[202]

"Hell on Earth" is the name detainees gave the Mwea camps and their dilution technique practices.[203] By the time Gavaghan stepped down from his role in March 1958, however, Baring and Lennox-Boyd considered Operation Progress such a success that they redesigned the Pipeline around Gavaghan's version of the dilution technique. Aguthi and Mweru camps in Nyeri District, Mariira Camp in Fort Hall, as well as Athi River Camp were all practicing dilution and had accordingly been renamed "filter camps," which was the government's code name for those camps that deployed officially sanctioned systematized violence.

This episode was the most extreme example of liberal imperialism's capacity to repress and reform. Operation Progress's coercion is impossible not to see, and it was justified by the detainees' alleged Mau Mau savagery as well as the undeniable pressure felt by the Kenya government to reduce the number of detainees slated for exile camps. There was also the perverted logic equating "natives" to children who needed harsh discipline, which was inseparable from reform. Without a "violent shock," intractable detainees would have no hope of moving along the civilizing mission's evolutionary path, with rehabilitation offered to detainees moving down the Pipeline, largely through missionaries who offered Christian tutelage. Members of Kenya's Moral Rearmament organization likewise provided instruction, and a handful of rehabilitation officers organized football matches and civics instruction. Indeed, when Griffith-Jones wrote about overpowering a "refractory detained person," his striking word choice reflected a broader ethos. In the language of the time, a "refractory child" was stubbornly disobedient or impossible to manage, much like a "refractory detained person," at least in the eyes of men providing legal coverage for the detainees' horrific beatings.

Baring and his coterie fired a handful of colonial officers who pushed back on Operation Progress. Among them was Askwith, whose political sensibilities were reminiscent of Margery Perham's postwar paternalism, which advocated for accelerating reformist measures in the empire. He wrote several reports to Johnston as well as Chief Secretary Richard Turnbull, "the gist of which," in Askwith's words, "was I considered that the violent treatment to which the detainees were subjected to obtain their obedience and submission might well by misfortune lead to death or serious injury."[204] He made his appeals all the way up to Lennox-Boyd, to no avail. The governor then transferred all responsibility for the detainees and their "rehabilitation" to Johnston and, through him, to Gavaghan. "Askwith left a disgruntled man—got no honor," Cowan said, summing up the situation. "Most people of his rank get one—he was a nuisance at the end. The government had their hands full with the Emergency, and [Askwith] went on with rehabilitation and the brutal methods at Mwea. Government was hard-pressed and didn't need pressure from within , , , though I admire him for sticking to his guns the way he did."[205]

By "got no honor," Cowan was referring to the coveted "gongs"—the Order of the British Empire (OBE) and Member of the British Empire (MBE)—that the queen bestowed. For colonial officers, such conferred status separated the men from the boys in liberal imperialism's hierarchy. Gavaghan not only was awarded an MBE, but he became the youngest district commissioner in Kenya's history, a role that included responsibility for hundreds of thousands of men and women still behind villagization's wires. Cowan's gong was on the horizon, though not before he finished expanding Kenya's systematized violence across the Pipeline's landscape.

CHAPTER 14

Operation Legacy

Once a colonial war breaks out, we all become its prisoners.

Barbara Castle, member of Parliament, June 1962[1]

Around the time Kenya's Governor Baring declared a state of emergency in October 1952, Winston Churchill's private secretary, John Colville, was fretting that the seventy-seven-year-old prime minister was "getting tired and visibly ageing. He finds it hard to work to compose a speech and ideas no longer flow. He has made two strangely simple errors in the [House of Commons] lately."[2] Such slips paled compared to those after Churchill's stroke in June 1953. The prime minister contemplated stepping aside but instead forged ahead. His agitated distraction betrayed no less determination to back his colonial secretary and minister of defense, Harold Macmillan, who a year earlier had made clear that he felt Britain faced a choice: "the slide into a shoddy and slushy Socialism, or the march to the third British Empire."[3]

As the prime minister declined, few doubted that Anthony Eden was well positioned to take his place. The popular and charming politician who frequently offered up his "Peace comes first, always" credo represented Conservative continuity, embracing Britain's determination to remain an independent operator in an increasingly globalized world. The party's heir apparent was poised to continue the imperial resurgence strategy while navigating American support in the context of the Cold War. For over two decades, Eden had held one ministerial position after another in government, most recently as Churchill's foreign secretary, a position that found him often tangling with President Eisenhower and his secretary of state, John Foster Dulles, over military tactics and priorities.

Churchill shuffled through his last days at Downing Street murmuring variations on the same theme—"We have thrown away our glorious Empire, our wonderful Indian Empire, we have cast it away"—which only emphasized how "inconsequent he seemed," Colville observed.[4] Regardless, his shoes would be difficult to fill. By the time he wrapped up his last cabinet meeting in the spring of 1955 and exited for Chartwell and his beloved fishpond stocked with golden orfe, he was second only to the monarchy in contemporary imperial imaginations. Churchill was, of course, one of history's most prolific authors, and the empire was ever-present in his pages and in speeches. When, in 1953, the Nobel Prize Committee anointed Sir Winston Leonard Spencer Churchill as the laureate in literature, it cited his "brilliant oratory in defending exalted human values."[5] Those values endured in Britain's approach to maintaining its empire. While losses had accrued under Clement Attlee, including India and Pakistan in 1947, and Palestine, Burma, and Ceylon a year later, there were no further retreats for Churchill who, in turn, handed off to Eden an empire whose expanse was held together with the familiar reliance on coercive measures and promises of development. Insofar as adaptations were based on nationalist demands, they were couched in self-interested strategies that deviated little from a mindset of real and imagined control, whether it was in the realm of bending civilian populations to British will or selecting postcolonial leaders who would continue power and profit-sharing with Britain and safeguard its strategic and economic assets. The Conservative MP Leo Amery's wartime refrain—the need for "the continuous creation of new sources of power overseas to readdress the balance of the Old World"—continued to hold sway, as did Britain's methods for crafting and maintaining its influence.[6]

Attlee's government had laid the groundwork for imperial continuity when it came to the postwar human rights movement. Under his stewardship, Britain was, as we saw, among the first to sign the European Convention on Human Rights, with its Article 15—spelling out the right to derogate in times of emergency—an out clause for liberal imperialism's unrestrained use of force. At the time, the Colonial Office agreed to Article 63(3), which enabled Britain to ratify the convention in 1951 "without immediately committing the dependent territories," according to one official.[7] Officials in London undertook widespread consultation with their men in the empire over the question of extending the European convention. That states of emergency were erupting scarcely rendered colonial governors and high commissioners receptive to the idea of international oversight, let alone one that came tethered to universal human rights. The events in Malaya and Kenya grabbed headlines, but police state policies and practices were unfolding in colonies such as Jamaica, Grenada, and British Guiana at the same time. In the end, Article 15 was enough to assuage the concerns of many of those in the Colonial Office, who considered it a gigantic "loop-hole." According to Whitehall, the European convention's extension to the empire was of enormous "propaganda value" while also a bit of a charade, because Britain opted "to send in a list of derogations which virtually nullify the whole thing." When Britain gave notice to the Council of Europe that it would extend the convention to forty-two British territories that encompassed nearly 70 million people, exclusions remained. Hong Kong was among them. Ongoing violence and threats there from presumed Communist agitators led Hong Kong officials to write that "a complete negation of human rights is the order of the day."[8]

As the 1950s progressed, the exceptional and temporary became the rule. Legally enabled emergency conditions beset colony after colony, where statutory martial law created police states aimed at quashing dissent and installing politically acceptable regimes that would facilitate Britain's interests. Moreover, there were no limits on how many derogations a country could file using minimal evidence to support its Article 15 claims. Within six weeks of the European convention coming into force in much of its empire, Britain derogated for Malaya and Singapore, with Kenya, British Guiana, and Uganda's Bugandan Province soon to follow. In fact, nearly thirty British derogations in the European Convention on Human Rights' first decade surpassed the combined total of the other forty-five members of the Council of Europe for the first sixty years of the convention's application. The imbalance was partly due to the long delay of France, Europe's second-largest postwar colonizer, in ratifying the convention. By the time France finally did so in 1974, most of its overseas territories, including Algeria, the site of a brutal and drawn-out counterinsurgency campaign, were independent. It was, therefore, as the legal scholar John Reynolds has pointed out, Britain that became synonymous with a "derogation regime" that not only shaped the lived experiences of millions of colonial subjects around the world but also normalized the exception in international law and practice.[9]

There were important differences between the pre–World War II era and the 1950s. International law now encoded exclusions and inclusions of rights that were conditional, not universal. The derogation article of Europe's postwar human rights convention, for instance, allowed contracting parties to suspend rights to a fair trial, liberty, property protection, and respect for family and private life. It also suspended the prohibition against the death penalty. Derogation, however, did not allow a contracting party the right to torture or use enslaved labor, or to punish someone "for something that wasn't against the law at the time," which, of course, only incentivized colonial states to issue copious pages of emergency regulations to ensure that they covered all possible insurgency-related offenses. International humanitarian laws further excluded a range of protections, as the Geneva Conventions' definition of "armed conflict not of an international character" was left undefined, providing an opening to Britain and France to deny the application of Common Article 3 to their empires' insurgencies, although torture was still prohibited in all circumstances. Together, these exclusions and inclusions were part of a liberal imperialism that had ostensibly reformed itself, that championed human rights and humanitarian laws, but that ultimately bound a nation like Britain to virtually nothing in its empire. The "rule of law," as one historian points out, continued to be a "potent fiction," one that legitimated a range of repressive actions.[10]

In many ways, such abuses of power and the eschewing of human rights and humanitarian principles were intimately tied to a set of abiding beliefs about Britain's hierarchical right to rule in the empire. They were also vital to Britain's continued postwar economic recovery efforts. Ever since the Hastings trial at the turn of the nineteenth century, British capitalism had been explicitly entwined with the empire and national identity. Its economic relations were never about free trade with equal partners. This unequal and coercive through-line in Britain's liberal imperialism endured even after the Second World War.[11] With the onset of the Cold War, Britain framed its empire as a potential subversive hotbed for, and bulwark against, the rising red tide. Successive governments also saw it as the panacea for economic recovery, with such recovery dependent on systems of repression that were increasingly impolitic in the face of human rights demands, however circumscribed through derogations, petitioning processes, and anemic oversight committees. The position that Attlee's government had ushered in witnessed little change under Churchill. For his part, Anthony Eden stayed the course. In the early 1950s, in fact, Labour's lackluster economic recovery efforts began to give way to an inching upward that would continue for nearly two decades.[12] Increases in real GDP and output efficiency rivaled those of any other period of British economic growth since the eighteenth-century industrial revolution. Among other upward trends, the postwar period heralded expanding international trade, and Britain, far more than its European counterparts, capitalized on export demand for basic consumer and capital goods, as its relative productive capacity was far greater than those of war-torn countries across the continent.[13]

There was reason to believe that imperial resurgence was working, but the massive military costs accruing drained the postwar recovery. Military costs were 20 percent of total public expenditure, or nearly 8 percent of GDP, versus the United States's 5 percent, but they could not be cut without imperiling the very policies on which recovery rested. Britain's economic policies depended on expensive coercive measures that at the same time did extensive damage to the hearts, minds, and bodies of countless colonial subjects. That the empire was fundamental to Britain's economy remained an article of faith, despite the fact that, as we saw early in our story, nineteenth-century statesmen much preferred informal empire's cost-effective rewards. "To trade with civilized men is infinitely more profitable than to govern savages," Thomas Macaulay had insisted in 1833.[14] As one of Britain's most influential historians and politicians who served on the governor-general's council in India, he had condemned non-Western cultures, believing "that a single shelf of a good European library was worth the whole native literature of India and Arabia." After the 1857 mutiny, Macaulay helped craft India's penal code, inspiring future legislation throughout the empire.[15] "Those wretched colonies," the future prime minister Benjamin Disraeli declared in 1852, are "a millstone round our necks." He wasn't wrong in his fiscal assessment: British colonial defense amounted to £4 million, while its total export trade was valued at £8 million.[16]

Britain's satisfied place in the world was slipping away, and "action seems to be forced on us," the foreign official Percy Anderson wrote in 1883. "Protectorates are unwelcome burdens, but in this case it is . . . a question between British protectorates, which would be unwelcome, and French protectorates, which would be fatal."[17] In 1884 and 1885, when British statesmen met in Berlin with other European powers to carve up Africa, it was global political and economic competition that drove them there. A liberal-imperial *mentalité* animated European leaders, who committed their nations "to care for the improvement of the conditions of [the native tribes'] moral and material well-being" while also guaranteeing "conditions most favourable to the development of trade and civilization."[18] Disraeli, who had earlier denounced the empire's economic folly, went on to spearhead the creation of a late-nineteenth-century British identity that wove together the nation, the empire, and the monarchy and was on full display when Queen Victoria assumed the title Empress of India in 1877. Britain imagined herself a uniquely imperial nation, the standard-bearer among peers, the purveyor of the world's greatest civilizing mission, delivering Pax Britannica's civilizing rule of law that would transform "native children" who were not yet ready to take their place in the modern world.

By the turn of the twentieth century, Britain's economy was enmeshed in the nation's new religion: imperial nationalism. Cecil Rhodes called the colonies a "bread and butter question," even if some critics, like economist J. A. Hobson, pushed back, saying the empire benefited only Britain's capitalist oligarchy, who overproduced goods and needed the markets of the empire because local consumers at home didn't have the financial wherewithal to purchase them. Radically redistributing resources in Britain, Hobson argued, would render unnecessary the whole costly enterprise of conquering and reconquering foreign territory, and "civilizing" local populations who would, in theory, purchase British goods, because Britons, whose disposable income would no longer be squeezed with wealth distribution, would have the means to purchase the capitalists' consumer products. At the turn of the century, Hobson's economic theories were thought radical, and the academic community largely dismissed them, while most statesmen thought he was a lefty crank questioning Britain's imperial economy, now part of the nationalist fabric.[19]

Nearly fifty years later, Montgomery, as chief of the imperial staff, declared that a postwar empire was crucial "to enable Great Britain to maintain her standard of living, and to survive."[20] If past and present Conservative icons were in agreement, so too were many of the left. When Bevin declared "the possession of an empire has been widely regarded as a condition for the improvement, or even the maintenance, of the standard of life of the British people," few disagreed.[21] Forty years earlier Britain's great "race patriot," Alfred Milner, had been more direct, though the underlying sentiment remained the same, when he said that sacrificing "the nigger" was all that was necessary.[22]

Many intellectuals embraced the empire's material benefits as a given, even while condemning them. In the run-up to the Second World War, Orwell had cast about and observed in *The Road to Wigan Pier*:

Every left-wing "intellectual" is, as a matter of course, an anti-imperialist. He claims to be outside the empire-racket as automatically and self-righteously as he claims to be outside the class-racket. Even the right-wing "intellectual," who is not definitely in revolt against British imperialism, pretends to regard it with a sort of amused attachment. It is so easy to be witty about the British Empire. The White Man's Burden and "Rule, Britannia" and Kipling's novels and Anglo-Indian bores—who could even mention such things without a snigger?[23]

Orwell saw British imperial protests wither when faced with the realities of life without an empire—protests that would change little for much of the 1950s, save for those that came from Fenner Brockway's newly formed Movement for Colonial Freedom. As Orwell had presciently observed:

> Under the capitalist system, in order that England may live in comparative comfort, a hundred million Indians must live on the verge of starvation—an evil state of affairs. . . . The alternative is to throw the Empire overboard and reduce England to a cold and unimportant little island where we should all have to work very hard and live mainly on herrings and potatoes. That is the very last thing that any left-winger wants. Yet the left-winger continues to feel that he has no moral responsibility for imperialism. He is perfectly ready to accept the products of Empire and to save his soul by sneering at the people who hold the Empire together.[24]

By the time Eden became prime minister in April 1955, the empire's economic purchase and the idea of an evolving Greater Britain, or Commonwealth, pervaded. It wasn't only the dependent empire, places such as Kenya and Jamaica, that was part of Britain's view of dominance and belonging, however unequal the latter continued to be. Rather, it was the self-governing dominions of Canada, Australia, New Zealand, and South Africa—largely autonomous operators within the empire—who were the original members of an imagined Greater Britain and that were now at the heart of its 1950s present and future. An imperial invention, the dominions had proved their Anglo-loyalty and mettle during the war. In the decade that followed, they were the cornerstone of an imperial system rooted in hierarchy and economic gain.[25] The Commonwealth's self-governing British subjects distinguished themselves from the lesser breeds in the dependent empire, a distinction that was not lost on most Britons. Between 1948 and 1957, over one million British migrants dispersed to the dominions, a number exceeding all those entering Britain from India, the West Indies, and elsewhere in the empire. While South Africa was extreme in its racial policies, with the Nationalist Party coming to power in 1948, its white supremacist measures had sprung from the same racialized well as had other dominions' treatment of non-European societies. It was for good reason that South Africa's Afrikaner Broederbond looked to the British Empire for cultural inspiration and legal guidance. In the early 1950s, the apartheid state's prime minister, D. F. Malan, praised Kenya for having "given him an example of how to treat discontented Africans."[26] While South Africa pursued a separation of races, Australia and New Zealand imposed assimilationist policies that obliterated local languages and traditional practices and circumscribed land rights. Britain's second colonial occupation was alive and well not only in the dependent empire but also in the self-governing territories that were practicing their own forms of internal colonization and race-based conceptions of belonging.[27]

As Milner's turn-of-the-century "race patriotism" continued to inform the idea of a Greater Britain, it's not surprising that the Round Table survived the war, only to refashion *religio Milneriana*'s "destiny of the English race" to Britain's shifting needs in the increasingly globalized world.[28] After providing historians for Britain's wartime Ministry of Information, the Round Table carried on with a dominion-wide membership much like that of the Milner era. The empire's moral premise bound these diverse members together, much as it had their predecessors.[29] For the Round Table—as for MPs across Britain's political parties—creating a British sphere of power to compete with the Americans and Soviets was an unfolding process whose near term remained aggressively bound to racialized hierarchies that would, in time, give way to a multicultural conception of Britishness. Such multiculturalism was understood as a culmination of generations-long tutelage that remolded indigenous peoples and cultures in the Anglo image. This was how India's independence, with Nehru's perfectly clipped Edwardian English lyricizing his "Tryst with Destiny," could be written into a narrative of evolutionary imperial success. A newfound and uneasy multi-racialism emerged that reflected liberal imperialism's ability to evolve in the face of traumatic rupture. This time its transformation accommodated the fraying of the "crimson thread of kinship" that had bound together notions of a Greater Britain.[30] The civilizing mission was now as much about "race patriotism's" cultural values as it was about skin color, at least in theory; India's and Pakistan's independence within the Commonwealth could be explained as a triumph as opposed to a loss, even if most Conservatives and skeptics on the left hardly saw it as such. Indeed, questions lingered. Could browns and Blacks really *be* British? For most Britons, the answer was no.

A new multicultural Commonwealth had economic analogues, particularly on the question of maintaining the sterling area. Britain's monetary policy was inseparable from the larger geopolitical and military issues at play, much as it had been for decades. As discussed, Britain much preferred the nineteenth-century era of informal imperialism in its approach to finance and trade, which by the 1930s had reversed course. The 1932 Imperial Economic Conference adopted a policy of imperial preference, lowering or eliminating tariffs for those countries and colonies within its system and discriminating against those, like the United States, outside it. In terms of monetary policy, the empire and Commonwealth countries, which had no uniform currency, agreed to a sterling bloc, an informal association that fixed their exchange rates to the pound. Then, with the outbreak of the Second World War, the sterling bloc became a closely integrated monetary association called the sterling area. During wartime, as the economic historian Gerold Krozewski points out:

> The convertibility of sterling was suspended: free movement of goods and payments was confined to the so-called sterling area, and discriminatory measures were implemented against the rest of the world. These allowed the British to manage transactions with the dollar area through a pooling system, and they provided a mechanism whereby other members of the sterling area accumulated sterling balances whenever their exports were not balanced (or requited) by imports. The balances acted as a form of credit that helped Britain to support its balance of payments. However, they also represented claims on Britain that might one day have to be met. Britain had to find ways to limit this risk while enhancing the performance of the sterling area.[31]

After the war, Britain worked tirelessly to keep the Americans from interfering with its sterling-based arrangements for trade and payments, while also worrying about Europe, whose closer cooperation challenged Britain's financial systems by "countering the discriminatory strategies that protected Britain's balance of payments and reserve position."[32]

The empire had to play a major postwar role in helping Britain, vis-à-vis the sterling area, save dollars and accumulate sterling balances. The Colonial Development and Welfare Act, as we've seen, pumped sterling into the colonies to ramp up raw material exports, chiefly to the Americans and other dollar-spending countries. Colonies like Malaya and the Gold Coast were huge dollar earners, and they held their foreign exchange currency in London, much as they did their sterling assets. Therefore, provided the colonies didn't use these dollars for their own local needs, which Britain ensured they didn't by strong-arming local colonial finance ministries, then these foreign exchange reserves could be used to service British debts to the Americans and to purchase U.S. goods for domestic needs. Britain also forced colonies to back their local currencies by 100 to 110 percent with sterling assets, depriving the empire of its much-needed development capital while leaving these sterling assets in London, which Britain could then draw upon.[33]

It's not surprising, therefore, that Britain, having fought the South African War over the Witwatersrand's massive gold deposits while also keeping the Germans at bay, also waged a costly and brutal counterinsurgency in Malaya to buttress its monetary policy while holding back Communism's spread in Southeast Asia. Indeed, postwar imperial resurgence meant keeping Europe at a distance and also preserving the sterling as an international currency, particularly in the face of the almighty dollar, while amassing foreign exchange reserves and sterling balances from the empire. It's here that the Cold War's myriad effects revealed Anglo-American tensions. The reluctant Americans had to underwrite British imperial and currency demands and make concessions to its monetary policies, not only to stymie encroaching Soviet influence in far-flung corners of the world but also in defense of Europe. Washington balanced this against its own undeniable quest for power and, with it, a global economic liberalization that rejected Britain's continued protectionist policies.

For all of Foreign Secretary Bevin's blunders, he played a crucial role in maintaining Britain's distance from the continent while also brokering the North Atlantic Treaty that served as the legal basis for the North Atlantic Treaty Organization (NATO).[34] Throughout the negotiations, the tension with the Americans, much as Keynes had experienced in Bretton Woods and in his subsequent dealings with Washington, was palpable. The United States was inexorably pushing for a liberalization of international trade and strengthening of Europe, even though it was backed into the geopolitical corner of supporting Britain's empire and with it the maintenance of the sterling and imperial preference, at least for the time being.

Over and over Britain was faced with dramatic proof of its own financial weakness, and each time it called on the United States for a bailout in one form or another. When convertibility was introduced in July 1947, the rapid depletion of Britain's dollar reserves was so extreme that convertibility had to be shut down. The United States, facing Communism's growing threat, intervened and "sterling was patched up and allowed to soldier on," as the economic historian Bernard Alford points out.[35] Britain's steadfast commitment to an export drive also fueled such soldiering on, as did its need to grow sterling balances and address the massive deficit to the Americans. Again, one of the Colonial Development and Welfare Act's major features was the ramp-up of current and future raw material production for export to the dollar area. The move proved particularly advantageous with the commodity boom in the early 1950s, as did Britain's persuasive efforts to place limits on the empire's imports from the United States. Wartime sterling balances from the colonies further accumulated and strengthened reserves and the pound. Between 1946 and 1952, the colonies contributed nearly $2 billion in dollar surplus to Britain's $11.2 billion deficit in gold and dollars. Britain pooled surpluses for all sterling area members, though the metropole and the dominions were the prime beneficiaries, not the empire's dependent territories, as we've also seen. While the convertibility crisis militated against arguments for broader multilateral trading, Britain's monetary policies had knock-on effects for Australia, New Zealand, and South Africa in particular. These Commonwealth nations saw in the sterling area advantages that outweighed their writing off of Britain's remaining wartime balances, at least in part, which then alleviated some of the strain on the pound.[36]

These were some of the attractions for dominions like Australia and New Zealand to remain in the sterling area. The maintenance of imperial preference was another net positive for the dominions, and Britain clung to its protectionist policies that had long underwritten the imperial economy since the 1930s. Such a cleaving to old ideas, however, betrayed a massive blind spot to its global position after the war. Perhaps it was partly the empire's invaluable contributions to defeating fascism that made it so appealing for postwar recovery. Even so, the empire had not been strong enough to defeat the Axis without the Americans stepping in and offering a preview to their superpower ascent, which included financial and trade dominance.[37] In the war's aftermath, a Conservative Party resolution affirmed "that the development, prosperity and defence of the British Commonwealth and Empire call for economic unity and, therefore, the principle of Imperial Preference must be maintained."[38]

International trade was evolving at a rapid clip, however, and while Britain realized economic improvements in absolute terms, it soon fell behind on a relative basis.[39] The nation had dusted off its factories and was pumping sterling into, and draining dollars out of, its empire as the rest of Europe pulled itself out of the postwar rubble. In the early 1950s, Britain's competitive weaknesses became apparent. With a head start, Britain supplied once-devasted markets, and her factories didn't need to innovate. Instead, they produced inferior-quality goods at higher prices with long delivery times. Meanwhile, every time the United States came to the sterling's rescue, it came with demands, including a steady push for free multilateral trade and an erosion of imperial preference. Britain was clearly dependent on the United States, not to mention Europe, insofar as its current and future economic well-being were concerned. Year after year British products were destined for these markets, while the dominions and colonies became less and less important. In 1954 even the die-hard Conservatives acquiesced, and Britain finally ended imperial preference, committing itself to the General Agreement on Tariffs and Trade.[40]

Maintaining the sterling area required American underwriting, and as the Cold War intensified, the United States was equally bound to Britain and its empire. The Americans needed to tread lightly on imperial designs lest they antagonize their much-needed NATO partners and jettison imperial territories standing firm against the Soviets. When the Attlee government tripled defense expenditures to bolster NATO, it was President Truman who footed the balance of payment costs; when Britain exercised its coercive prerogative in places like Malaya and Kenya, it was the Americans who looked the other way. The United States was more than willing to have Britain do its bidding, particularly when threats of Communism reared their heads near American shores.

Such was the case with British Guiana, where subjecthood for the empire's laborers had changed little since the Moyne Report. With its sugar plantations, along with its lucrative bauxite deposits that, together with neighboring Surinam, provided the United States with two-thirds of its global supply, British Guiana found itself in the crosshairs of both Washington and London. In 1953 Cheddi Jagan and his People's Progressive Party won 51 percent of the popular vote in the colony's first general election; the Americans cast him as a Communist in their own backyard. British officials fabricated evidence that he was poised to unleash civil disorder "to turn British Guiana into a totalitarian state

British soldiers marching in Georgetown, British Guiana, 1953

subordinate to Moscow." For them, Jagan threatened the "century-old" tradition of British business interests squeezing local labor and so ensuring the flow of dollars into the sterling area from bauxite sales.[41]

British Guiana's edging toward self-government quickly ended. Jagan and his ministers lasted 133 days in office before Churchill sent in the troops. Governor Alfred Savage declared a state of emergency, suspended the constitution, and locked up the People's Progressive Party's leadership. It was the start of protracted Anglo-American connivance—both overt and covert—to manipulate British Guiana's future and install the "anti-Communist" Forbes Burnham as premier.[42] This territory was one of many examples revealing the mutually dependent though uneasy relationship between the United States and Britain over imperial matters. Or as the historical experts on the Anglo-American alliance William Roger Louis and Ronald Robinson highlight, "At metropolitan and international levels British imperial power was substantially an Anglo-American revival. Neither side cared to publish the fact, the one to avoid the taint of imperialism, the other to keep the prestige of Empire untarnished."[43]

This alliance was put to the test in the Middle East when, a little over a year into his premiership, Eden decided to go it alone. Officials in London had a nagging sense that "nationalists [were] sapping at our position of world power" and so threatening global confidence in sterling; that played a role in their decision to invade Egypt, where Cold War imperatives and "the march to the third British Empire" would collide.[44] Trouble had been brewing ever since Churchill assumed office in 1951. Britain's right to the Suez Canal base, a massive conglomeration, the size of Wales, of military installations, railways, and workshops, was due to expire in 1956, and the Conservative government faced the intractable problem of what to do: "a prolonged humiliating scuttle before all the world," in Churchill's words, or a negotiated retreat. British policies had already sparked riots that swept through Cairo, including on "Black Saturday," January 26, 1952, when wealthy parts of the city were aflame, with clouds of smoke darkening their skies as rioters unleashed their anger on British residents and local pashas. "Degraded savages" murdered Britons, Churchill said, insisting that Egyptians "cannot be classed as a civilized power until they have purged themselves."[45] Purge they did, except that the Egyptian revolution that ousted King Farouk six months later brought Colonel Mohammed Neguib to power. He lasted until 1954, when Gamal Abdel Nasser took control of the Egyptian government. Churchill was ready for a fight, though Eden's calls for appeasement won the day. Geopolitical factors, not to mention Britain's need for military boots on the ground in Kenya and Malaya, rendered the Suez base a vestige of the pre-nuclear-weapons era. In the end, Britain withdrew her eighty thousand troops for redeployment elsewhere, on condition that, in case of emergency, British forces could return. The RAF also maintained its air bases and right to Egyptian airspace.[46]

Nasser was hardly an Anglo-American stooge. In late 1955 he accepted Soviet aid via an arms deal with Czechoslovakia, throwing the Middle East region's balance of Cold War power. The Eden-led government reversed its conciliatory course despite, or because of, diplomatic measures, and pushed for an invasion. Nasser and Eden met once, and the prime minister behaved "like a prince dealing with vagabonds," according to his Egyptian counterpart.[47] Then in July 1956, as Britain pulled out its last troops from the Suez base, Nasser nationalized the Suez Canal Company, the last vestige of colonial legacy in Egypt. His move was prompted by the Americans and British, days earlier, withdrawing their promise to fund the Aswan High Dam. With two-thirds of Europe's oil supply at risk, Britain again argued for invasion. "The peoples of the Near East and of North Africa and, to some extent, all of Asia and all of Africa," President Eisenhower wrote, admonishing Eden over any hint of an armed intervention, "would be consolidated against the West to a degree which, I fear, could not be overcome in a generation and, perhaps, not even in a century, particularly having in mind the capacity of the Russians to make mischief."[48]

Eden was now "violently anti-Nasser," comparing him to Mussolini, according to his personal secretary.[49] The Bank of England's George Bolton also raised the alarm.[50] "I feel that the situation created by the Egyptian Government," Bolton wrote, "imperils the survival of the U.K. and the Commonwealth, and represents a very great danger to the sterling."[51] Chancellor of the Exchequer Harold Macmillan thought Nasser would block the canal should Britain invade, but he was sanguine on continued American dollar support for alternative Latin American oil supplies. In the end, Britain colluded with France and Israel to land an

Anglo-French troops occupy Port Said, part of the town burned by fire, November 8, 1956.

expedition and left the Americans out of the loop. "We should let them know at once," Eisenhower fumed when he learned of his allies' subterfuge, "that we recognize that much is on their side in this dispute with the Egyptians, but that nothing justifies double-crossing us."[52]

The Suez invasion quickly turned into the Suez crisis. Confidence in the pound was shaken as Nasser's men blocked the canal and sabotaged crucial pipelines, threatening oil export revenues that brought in much-needed sterling and precipitating a massive run on the pound.[53] With sterling reserves dwindling, Macmillan offered up two scenarios: Britain could float her currency, which would be "a catastrophe affecting not merely the [British] cost of living but also . . . all our external economic relations," or turn to the Americans for another massive bailout.[54] Eisenhower rescued the pound with a billion dollars from the IMF and the Export-Import Bank only after Eden agreed to withdraw from Egypt. Nasser became a pan-Arab hero overnight, while the whole fiasco brought down Eden's premiership.

The events in Suez marked the end of Britain's play for superpower status. For Conservative hardliners, Suez was "Britain's Waterloo," signaling the moment when Britain was no longer one of the postwar Big Three, if it had ever been.[55] The crisis laid bare Britain's dependence on the United States and plummeting international confidence in sterling. Yet Britain didn't have to be a superpower to retain its empire. When Eden's successor, Harold Macmillan, and Eisenhower met in 1957, they pledged themselves to a continued Anglo-American alliance that included a coordinated front against Communism and a closer relationship with Europe vis-à-vis NATO. Macmillan now spoke in terms of Britain's "junior partnership" with the United States, while the Americans wanted cooperative nationalists and would, for the time being, provide sterling area nations and colonies with economic and military aid.[56]

In spite of the yawning weaknesses in British monetary and military policies, Macmillan and his government hadn't lost their will to unleash coercive measures in an empire it still sought to maintain. Indeed, people and nations are as beholden to sentiment as they are to empiricism. With the shocking embarrassment of Suez—much like that in Palestine— some British agents transferred frustration over their country's exposed superpower impotence into colonial possessions. There even the Americans quietly continued to let Britain deal with truculent nationalists, or "terrorists," more or less as it saw fit, provided the end result was the installation of a postcolonial regime that embraced the West.

With Britain's reputation tarnished after Suez, Macmillan, despite his public proclamations, sensibly called for an imperial audit behind the scenes. "I should . . . like to see something like a profit and loss account for each of our Colonial possessions," he told his cabinet, "so that we may be better able to gauge whether, from the financial and economic point of view, we are likely to gain or lose by its departure." This audit was to assess "the political and strategic considerations involved in each case."[57] Macmillan insisted he "had no intention of presiding over the liquidation of the British empire," though he needed to rethink imperial strategy:

> We had chosen instead [after the war] to try to hold on wherever we could—and we were now in a position of a great land-owner who, faced with high taxation and heavy death duties, declined to give up the old house even though he had to close some of the wings and cut down some of the trees. . . . The fact was that we were still trying to do more than we could easily do with the resources at our command. . . . Though we no longer had authority, we still had great influence.[58]

At home, the financial tide had finally turned. "Let us be frank about it—most of our people never had it so good," Macmillan declared. "Go around the country, go to the industrial towns, go to the farms, and you will see a state of prosperity such as we have never had in our lifetime—nor, indeed, in the history of this country."[59] So in 1957 the question was how liberal imperialism might, once again, reimagine itself in the face of change. Macmillan's answer, using now well-known developmentalist language, was that the empire was "not breaking up: it was growing up."[60]

The government's reevaluation exposed the ideological and pragmatic divides in Macmillan's cabinet. The Treasury and the Colonial Office were on either end of the spectrum when it came to assessing the empire's future. The Colonial Policy Committee looked closely at Britain's entwined economic and imperial systems to parse out what parts of the empire best served the nation's interests. Its report reflected Britain's broader historically embedded predicaments. When assessing decolonization, the committee adopted a consistent stand:

> The economic considerations tend to be evenly matched and were unlikely in themselves to be decisive in determining whether or not a territory should become independent. . . . Although damage could certainly be done by the premature grant of independence, the economic dangers to the United

Kingdom of deferring the grant of independence for her own selfish interests after the country is politically and economically ripe for independence would be far greater than any dangers resulting from an act of independence negotiated in an atmosphere of goodwill such as has been the case with Ghana and Malaya. Meanwhile, during the period when we can still exercise control in any territory, it is most important to take every step open to us to ensure, as far as we can, that British standards and methods of business and administration permeate the whole life of the territory.[61]

The committee did not interrogate the "atmosphere of goodwill" it so readily attributed to the moods in Ghana (the former Gold Coast) and Malaya as opposed to Britain's terms for independence, which included colonies remaining in the sterling area and adhering to its foreign exchange rules. The economic global picture was changing rapidly, and it focused on the bottom line. Commodity prices dropped after 1953; the Colonial Development and Welfare Act still cost Britain millions of pounds a year; London's capital markets lacked investor confidence in independent governments and wouldn't meet the £25 million to £30 million in demand for loan finance; and cabinet ministers urged "sharing the burden" of the remaining colonies with Commonwealth nations, particularly Canada.[62] The military costs of propping up the empire and waging costly counterinsurgencies were also factored in. Treasury received a measure of support from the Ministry of Defence, which emphasized in its 1957 review, "Britain's position and influence in the world depend first and foremost upon the health of her internal economy and the success of her export trade."[63] The review recommended Britain should phase out national service, cut its seven hundred thousand troop strength in half by 1962, and thereby "release skilled men, including many badly needed scientists and technicians, for employment in civilian industry. Both exports and capital investment will gain."[64]

The question of sterling loomed largest of all, as did global trade. The expanding international economy—prodded along by the Americans, and by Europe's recovery and integration—was oriented toward the developed world, pushing Britain's decision to move toward full convertibility by 1958. The Colonial Policy Committee partially allayed fears of a sterling run with decolonization when it took a close look at the books and learned that some of the dependent empire's deposits were not readily liquid. Nonetheless Macmillan's economic gurus were making a gamble on the bedrock of future political relationships in the

empire, dressed up as they would be under the umbrella of a multicultural Commonwealth, given that Britain had some £4 billion in liabilities in early 1957 with only £700 million in reserves. It also needed an
annual surplus of £400 million in current accounts in order to maintain
confidence in its currency.[65] Whether Britons "never had it so good" was
still tethered to the vicissitudes of their nation's currency problems and
to postcolonial nations backing British interests.[66] Insofar as the empire
was the political manifestation of the sterling area, one just had to look
around to realize that, while colonies had no choice but to prop up Britain's reserves and hence the pound, violent counterinsurgency operations threatened the kind of postcolonial relationships, the wellspring
of colonial loyalty, that would support the sterling area over the long
term. In the end, the Treasury was no longer pegging Britain's economic
future to the formal empire. Instead, Britain would maintain the sterling
area and the pound's value through free trade and exchange conditions
that looked more like Britain's nineteenth-century "imperialism of free
trade." In that era, Britain hadn't needed a formal empire because, as
we've seen, it kept trade doors open through the unchallenged strength
of its economy. In 1957, however, the global economy and Britain's place
within it looked nothing like the way it had in the nation's bygone era
of dominance.[67]

For some of Macmillan's ministers, particularly Colonial Secretary Lennox-Boyd, divesting the empire, even understood as an imperial coda of triumph, was unacceptable. Lennox-Boyd was adamantly
opposed to any "premature withdrawal" from the empire that, in some
cases, would lead to "anarchy or near-anarchy."[68] His influence was clear
in the committee's final report:

> Successive Governments in the United Kingdom have for many
> years pursued, with a broad measure of public support, a Colo-
> nial policy of assisting dependent peoples towards the greatest
> practicable measure of self-government. . . . The United King-
> dom stands to gain no credit for launching a number of imma-
> ture, unstable and impoverished units whose performances as
> "independent" countries would be an embarrassment and whose
> chaotic existence would be a temptation to our enemies.[69]

The Colonial Policy Committee reflected a persistent tension that
underwrote imperial policy for much of the twentieth century. Britain's
financial overstretch was crippling in the postwar years, and it needed
imperial contributions to its monetary system, though squeezing the

empire economically only sparked more protests and insurgencies in colonies that were already awash in the rising tide of demands for self-determination and universal rights.

As Macmillan pondered the committee's findings, Britain remained mired in colonial insurgencies that spanned four continents. Among them was an ongoing insurgency in Cyprus. The tiny Mediterranean island was a strategic base not only for Britain but also for the United States. Home to future atomic weapons sites, covert facilities, and broadcasting and listening stations, Cyprus was also the most important Anglo-American signals intelligence site. The colony had unrivaled geographic proximity to the Soviet Union's southern reaches, where the Communist nerve center for aircraft and missile testing was located.[70] For years, discord had wracked Cyprus, and the National Organization of Cypriot Fighters—known by its Greek acronym EOKA—was now waging a war for *enosis*, or union, with Greece, and liberation from British rule. With nearly 80 percent of the island's half-million inhabitants identifying as Greek Cypriot, support for the movement's political leader, Archbishop Makarios III, was overwhelming. Much like the Zionists in Palestine, however, Greek Cypriots held divided opinions over EOKA's methods for achieving *enosis*. Still, the island's major civil fault lines were not within its Greek community but between the Greek Cypriots and the local ethnic Turks, who constituted the remaining 20 percent of the island's population and preferred partition to union with Greece.[71]

General Georgios Grivas directed the front lines of EOKA's insurgency. He was known by his nom de guerre Dighenis, a hat tip to a legendary Byzantine hero. Such historic mystique was further embedded in the island itself. An idyll of mythological proportions, its antiquity-era cities of Limassol and Famagusta hugged aquamarine coastlines that gave way to the interior's distant Troodos Mountains, where Greek Orthodox monasteries and their intricate mosaic facades gleamed radiant in the morning and afternoon light. Grivas capitalized on his knowledge of Cyprus's terrain while unleashing strategies drawn from insurgent leaders across the empire. Like Menachem Begin and Michael Collins, he ruthlessly disciplined insurgents and demanded their fealty to Cyprus's liberation. "I issued warnings," Grivas said, "that I alone would give orders and everyone would obey: disobedience would be punished by death."[72] A brazen campaign unfolded, and his small EOKA force picked off British personnel on beaches and blew up military installa-

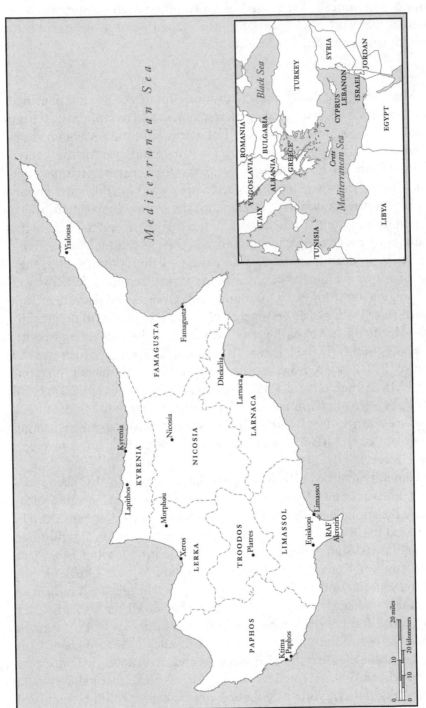

Cyprus in 1956

tions. In late November 1955, Britain declared a state of emergency and soon derogated the European Convention on Human Rights under Article 15.[73]

British colonial officials were remarkably out of touch with local populations, and Cyprus became another intelligence failure.[74] Once again the civilizing mission's inability to understand colonial subjects outside an Anglo register, infused with racialized perceptions of power, meaning, and hierarchy, would cost the British dearly. In 1954 Alex MacDonald, the MI5 officer who became the first security intelligence adviser to the Colonial Office, established a special branch operation in Cyprus that was inept. It took British agents months to figure out that EOKA wasn't Communist but, in fact, a far-right-wing organization.[75]

The Colonial Office soon scrapped Cyprus's governor, Robert Armitage, replacing him with Field Marshal John Harding. Tested in Palestine, Malaya, and Kenya, Harding had full military and political power, much like Templer had in Malaya. In Cyprus he drew on the empire's playbook, notably its emergency regulations, creating nearly eighty new laws, such as the Public Officers' Protection Regulation, that shielded British security forces, which grew to over thirty thousand, from prosecution.[76] Shows of force and cordon-and-sweep operations, together with screening teams and empire-inspired killer squads, could not weed out the one thousand EOKA insurgents and their civilian supporters on the island.

A brief roll call of imperial veterans descending on Cyprus reveals the empire's web of connections from yet another angle. Governor Harding worked closely with Donald Stephens, a highly seasoned MI5 officer who filled the role of intelligence director and was at the "very centre" of the entire EOKA counterinsurgency "and enjoying every minute of it."[77] Benneth Wadeley left his Kenyan post for Cyprus, where he was "now playing a leading part in the reorganisation of our Special Branch," according to the governor.[78] John Prendergast, one of the empire's preeminent MI5 operatives, later arrived and took over as director of intelligence.[79] By 1958 the island's intelligence unit had an impressive cadre of empire-tested agents, which included Hugh Toye, who had interrogated Indian detainees in Delhi's Red Fort, where he also burned documents before Britain's 1947 retreat. Together, their job was to execute in haste what Britain had failed to accomplish during its previous seventy-five years of colonial rule in Cyprus: understand the local population, whose language they did not speak and whose culture they hardly understood and often disdained, while convincing EOKA

captives and suspects, together with a handful of Greek Cypriot informers, to offer up usable information to an illegitimate British regime.[80]

While Colonial Secretary Lennox-Boyd mulled over the use of
"sickening gas"—or "an arsenical material technically classified as a war
gas" that had been tested on colonial subjects in Hong Kong—"white
trackers" came in from the Kenya Regiment to tutor security forces at
Cyprus's Tracker Training School. Harding was crystal-clear about his
strategy: it was time to "take the gloves off."[81] His right-hand man and
chief of staff, Brigadier Geoffrey Baker, spelled out what this meant in
practice. "The CYPRIOT understands and responds to firmness of
treatment and punishment," Baker wrote. The "moral effect" of violence, the phrase Charles Callwell had coined in his late-nineteenth-
century book *Small Wars* and that we've seen repeatedly deployed in the
early twentieth century, was alive and well. "In spite of political outcries
from outside and whines from within," the brigadier insisted, "punishment, whether individual or collective, must be a real deterrent to the
wrong-doer."[82] He and Harding then addressed the issue of intelligence
gathering: it was "unanimous that NO written instructions should be
issued to interrogators."[83]

Reports of colonial abuses came flooding into the British government and were notably similar to those from Malaya and Kenya, as
well as Palestine. Security forces and interrogation teams forced EOKA
suspects and Greek Cypriot civilians to take hallucinogenic drugs, run
the gauntlet, strip naked, undergo water torture while handcuffed to
bed frames, and suffer through genital mutilation and testicle twisting
with torture instruments. They were beaten with various instruments,
suffocated with pillowcases, electrocuted, hung from ceilings and lad-
ders, starved, boxed on the head while wearing metal buckets, tortured
with iron head rings affixed with screws that tightened into the tem-
ples, and forced to lick salt from the ground. Some refused to offer up
information—citing the binding nature of the EOKA oath and their
allegiance to Grivas—and were murdered; others gave false as well as
usable information and managed to live through their ordeals. They
called British interrogators "HMTs," or "Her Majesty's Torturers," and
those who survived their injuries would go on to finger some of them by
name and physical description. Colonial authorities, however, took great
care to redact their operators' identities.[84]

But 1950s Cyprus was not 1930s Palestine. Even with the sustained maneuverings of British officials throughout the human rights
and humanitarian law negotiations and their subsequent adoptions and
enforcements, narrow openings remained in the postwar human rights

minefield where, if navigated properly, Britain's "derogation regime" could be challenged. The Cyprus Bar Council, led by Stelios Pavlides, John Clerides, and Clerides's son, Glafkos, began to register complaint after complaint with the British government. Local Greek mayors, who collectively wrote to the British government, backed them. The emergency regulations were "enacted with utter disregard to the basic principles of Justice and human rights," the mayors fumed. "The ultimate object, as well as the object of their numerous amendments from time to time, has been to grant a deceptive cloak of legality to the virtually criminal excesses of the Security Forces."[85] Much like contemporary human rights organizations, the Cyprus Bar Council documented, named and shamed, and relentlessly challenged Britain on its own legal terms. In the words of John Clerides, they did so "for the purposes of remedying a situation which discredits the prestige of the British Administration."[86] Peter Benenson, the future co-founder of Amnesty International, soon arrived, and Charles Foley, owner of the *Times of Cyprus*, was an ally. Unbound by Fleet Street's conventions, Foley published allegations of torture and abuse. Harding and his men responded with threats of "prosecution for publishing such disturbing reports," and the governor followed up by tightening press censorship regulations.[87] Behind the scenes, his office conceded that a "number of allegations may have at the bottom some germ of truth, and we must be careful not to start a prosecution which provides a propaganda platform for enemies of the Government."[88]

What neither Harding nor British officials in London anticipated, however, was Greece's intervention. In May 1956 Greece submitted an application to the European Commission of Human Rights on behalf of Greek Cypriots alleging Britain had violated the European Convention on Human Rights in Cyprus. It marked the first interstate complaint filed since the convention's ratification. The commission, based in Strasbourg, France, oversaw the ECHR's implementation and mediated Greek and British legal teams at a June meeting. Greece agreed to limit the proceedings to the question of the state of emergency itself and whether it, and its regulations, were a breach of the convention. The commission, however, left the door open for Greece to submit a second application on the question of torture and abuse at a later date.[89]

As the Strasbourg-based commission sent a team to begin its investigatory work, Harding launched a full-on "legal offensive."[90] At precisely the moment when the commission's investigatory team began collecting evidence, he expanded emergency regulations to crack down on local dissent and protect screening teams and interrogators. Francis Vallat, the Foreign Office's legal adviser, recommended a "policy of gentle co-operation and the gradual whittling away of the sting of the Greek application by one means or another."[91] Whether such methods would prove effective remained to be seen as the Conservative government found itself fighting battles over colonial abuses on multiple fronts. The United Nations, increasingly populated by representatives from independent states who joined forces with existing members harboring anti-imperial sentiments, as we saw in the case of Palestine's partition, proved a thorn in Britain's side. Greek Cypriot detainees tapped directly into this anti-imperial support, writing to the UN Human Rights Committee and copying the UN's secretary general as well as Britain's prime minister. In one instance, those held at Kokkinotrimithia Detention Camp wrote that "armed soldiers" had "brutally beaten . . . and tortured [them] in the most barbarous way."[92]

In London, the muted response to charges of abuse in Malaya had given way to the Labour opposition's more sustained critiques, due partly to the Movement for Colonial Freedom (MCF). Founded in 1954, the MCF's origins stretched back to the interwar years when Black activists, particularly George Padmore, schooled Fenner Brockway and others on the importance of rigorously documenting colonial abuses to challenge the system that gave rise to them. The movement, an amalgamation of several anticolonial organizations, proved itself to be one of the postwar period's most significant extraparliamentary pressure groups, boasting a membership of 3 million at its peak. With its own newsletter and *Peace News*, a veteran pacifist publication, as disseminating outlets, it was also a source of evidence to be deployed in parliamentary debates. By 1957, MPs in the movement's ranks, around one hundred in all, raised nearly two thousand colonial-related questions, many of which had to do with the empire's states of emergency. The MCF was a "moral crusade," according to the historian Stephen Howe, castigating colonial abuses in human rights terms and also pointing to Britain's coercive policies and practices as further indications of the immediate need for self-determination. Its broad anticolonial and emancipatory agenda attracted a wide-ranging membership for nearly a decade.[93]

Cyprus's insurgency was not the first colonial conflict to top the movement's agenda. Kenya had occupied some of its parliamentary focus, and Arthur Young's dramatic resignation in December 1954 as well as Kenya's subsequent amnesty were behind many of its investigatory demands. In response after response, the Colonial Office offered its standard answer: "The Governor is investigating the matter."[94] But such investigations amounted to little if anything. In 1955 the Church

Missionary Society's executive committee published its first round of censure in *The Times*, pointing out that the governor's entreaties "not to maltreat people held in captivity . . . have not led to a cessation of malpractices by members of the security forces."[95] It went on to publish "Kenya—Time for Action!"[96] The demands for investigations soon spilled into Parliament, where Lord Jowitt, a former solicitor general and then attorney general in the Labour government, took to the floor:

> We must paint these events in their true colours. There is nothing whatever to be said for massacring disarmed prisoners or for employing torture to exact confessions. These things are repellent to the Christian ideal and repellent to the British system of justice. He who tries to gloss them over as mere excess of loyalty, or to make light of them, is doing no good service to our good name.[97]

In the House of Commons, Labour MPs demanded a full explanation. Barbara Castle led the charge. An MCF member who was swept into office with Labour's 1945 victory, Castle was a rising star in the party and staked much of her political future on exposing colonial injustices and pushing for independence. With her fiery red hair and superb instincts, Castle relentlessly challenged Lennox-Boyd's stonewalling, but he "brushed us aside," she later recalled. "There had been some abuses, he admitted, but the Governor of Kenya was correcting them. We must not forget the horrors of Mau Mau and so on."[98] "You were chasing a sense of complacency and cover up by the government in Kenya and at home that made one realize there was something very wrong," she insisted.[99] After Young's resignation, she traveled to the colony to investigate further the death of Kamau Kichina, which, through her initial research, "revealed a picture of behaviour so horrifying that one could not imagine it happening in a British colony."[100] In Kenya she made the rounds and befriended Young's assistant, Duncan McPherson, who was like-minded in exposing the truth, though equally as cautious. He drove Castle to the middle of Kenya's National Park where only the roaming zebra and wildebeest were privy, then unloaded horrific details, recounting that "the conditions in these camps were worse than he himself had ever experienced in the Japanese prisoner of war camps."[101] As for the rest of the colonial administration, they were tight-lipped, evasive, and dismissive.

When Castle returned to London, *The Daily Mirror*, which had sponsored her tour, published articles such as "The Truth About the Secret

Barbara Castle, London, September 1957

Police," and the *New Statesman and Nation* also ran her piece "Justice in Kenya."[102] Lennox-Boyd offered rebukes in the Commons, accusing her of "monstrous slanders," as did various media outlets.[103] "Defending the rights of the untried against the Fleet Street lynch mob, who were determined that all black Kenyans were implicated in the indiscriminate brutality of the Mau Mau," Castle's biographer points out, "was a course guaranteeing fame and abuse in almost equal measure."[104] In Kenya, there was a crackdown on information leaks. Memoranda like "Security of Information" circulated to all detention camp commandants, reminding them and all their staff that the colony's code of regulations prohibited speaking to the press, publishing information, or circulating photographs, and that "disciplinary action against any officer contravening" would be swiftly enforced.[105]

Still, information kept flowing out of Kenya. As Lennox-Boyd maneuvered through press reports and parliamentary demands for investigations, he also deflected repeated queries and condemnations over Cyprus. In December 1956, nearly thirty Labour and Liberal MPs introduced a motion that denounced the "ruthless severity" of Britain's actions in its war against EOKA, zeroing in on the emergency regulations.[106] In the House of Lords, Lord Strabolgi expressed sentiments that other Labour peers shared:

> What sort of State is this? Is it a police State? Is it a State like that set up by Nazi Germany, or a State which is trying to copy the methods of Soviet Russia? I think that there is a very great need for the Government to investigate these allegations. . . . Surely this kind of Government that we have set up in Cyprus cannot go on indefinitely in this way. There seem to be these beatings of youths, roundings-up, interrogations, brutalities in prison, and the hanging of people for actions which here would not be punishable by death, if we have done anything in Cyprus, we have erected a gallows tree as a symbol—that seems now to be the symbol of that unhappy Island—from which hangs the martyred corpse of Cypriot youth. But as Baudelaire described in his poem *Voyage to Cytherea*, as we approach nearer, we find the corpse that hangs from that gallows is in our own image, the image of our own guilt and shame.[107]

Refractions of guilt and shame, however, were nowhere to be found in Harding's response to either MPs back home or to the European Commission of Human Rights. He telegraphed Lennox-Boyd insisting, "The Cyprus Government is convinced that the smear campaign concerning alleged maltreatment is a deliberate tactic designed to impress public opinion."[108] He took the matter into his own hands with a widely circulated white paper rebutting all charges. The field marshal's "smear campaign" crusade went one step further, calling the allegations part of "a deliberate and organised conspiracy."[109]

Macmillan's government found itself on a razor's edge. In September 1958, the European commission had issued its findings on whether or not the state of emergency in Cyprus was justifiable: an emergency that "threatened the life of the nation" in Cyprus existed, "no substantive violations of the [European Convention on Human Rights] had been established," and the continued use of emergency regulations was permissible. The outcome was, as legal scholars have pointed out, "hardly . . . a triumph for the international protection of human rights."[110] Any relief in London over the commission's determinations, however, was short-lived as other accusations pended. In July 1957, Greece, drawing largely on evidence amassed by the Cyprus Bar Council, had, in fact, filed a second application with the commission charging British officials with the torture of forty-nine individuals. As Prendergast and other operatives

British security forces at barbed-wire barricades in a mountain village, Cyprus, April 1956

were shipped in to tighten the screws on EOKA suspects, Britain had no choice but to allow commission investigators into Cyprus. According to the colony's new governor, Hugh Foot—who had come of age as one of Wingate's men in Palestine and served in multiple posts throughout the empire—they "have been hearing evidence of ill-treatment."[111]

Lennox-Boyd's indefatigable sparring partner, Barbara Castle, also made an appearance. Much as during her trip to Kenya, she spoke with those on the ground willing to offer candid views. This included Governor Foot who, unlike his predecessor, made attempts to curtail the abuses. His efforts atrophied, though, in the face of a long-standing culture of violence that he himself had played a role in cultivating during the Arab Revolt. He recounted to Castle that "the troops [in Cyprus] were permitted and even encouraged to use unnecessarily rough measures after a shooting incident on the grounds that they were engaged in hot pursuit."[112] Behind the scenes, the new governor was also part of the problem. To hold the official line, he created the Special Investigation Group, which scoured the record for exaggerated accounts of abuse and helped cover up those abuses that were, indeed, very real. The group was a mainstay in the crafting of Britain's narrative of events. "The trick [in Cyprus] is to disguise what is propaganda so that it appears to be perfectly ordinary news," one British military officer emphasized.[113]

A referendum on the public's threshold for colonial violence soon emerged when Castle called out the security forces and their "rough measures" in the *Daily Herald*. Overnight, her currency in the Labour Party plummeted. It was one thing to expose abuses in the empire; it was quite another to cross loyalty's line when it came to Britain's troops. Castle's own party labeled her "Makarios's messenger girl," while the right-wing press savaged her.[114] Behind closed doors, Labour leadership, led by Hugh Gaitskell, gave her a full dressing-down and members of the League of Empire Loyalists, dedicated to stopping the empire's dissolution, showed up to an MCF meeting, heckling, "Traitor, traitor."[115] The MCF had momentum but far less than Brockway and others cared to admit: exposing colonial abuses and championing self-determination still remained fringe politics. They were useful bits when drubbing the Conservative government, but Gaitskell and other Labour leaders were not going to rock their party's domestic agenda by going after their nation's troops. To do so would be political suicide. As far as some Tories were concerned, Castle's investigations were a boon. "Public opinion [in Britain]," wrote indomitable Conservative Julian Amery, "could not be sounder about Cyprus. Mrs Castle must have been worth a million votes to us already!"[116] There was sustained support for the security force's coercive measures. Indeed, they were a necessity. "Every soldier in Cyprus knows that whatever action he is called upon to take in aid of the civil power has to be done with the minimum of force," one Conservative MP said, "but we must never forget that the rôle of the security forces in Cyprus is to conquer terrorism, and that there are and will be many instances when the minimum of force necessary is quite a lot of force."[117]

Castle was wounded but not deterred, and neither was the European commission. Its second investigation into torture allegations continued, and internally British officials acknowledged that "it is . . . desirable that as few as possible should see the report" from Greece's first application. While Strasbourg had kept it private, there was no telling what would happen once the commission made its way through Greece's pending application alleging torture.[118] Meanwhile maintaining local morale was vitally important, as accountability, so anathema in the British Empire, acquired new meaning under the commission's scrutiny. "The resentment felt by senior members of the administration cannot be overstressed," noted a member of Cyprus's judiciary when he reflected on the first application's investigation. "On the Security Forces side the feel-

British security forces conducting searches of Milikouri village and nearby Kykko Monastery, Cyprus

ing runs even higher," he continued. "Even allowed for prejudice, our witnesses generally formed a poor impression of the Sub-Commission and . . . respected neither their ability nor their integrity."[119]

More probing was assuredly on the horizon. Strasbourg's commission heard Greece's second application in November 1958 and approved thirteen of the forty-nine torture cases for additional investigation. Britain felt the methods needed to sustain its power—however imbricated it was in the postwar human rights regime—could not be exposed for all to see; nor could it be perceived as conceding to so-called terrorists. The only way out of the impasse was negotiation. So with Britain's go-ahead, the Greek and Turkish governments decided Cyprus's fate in the comforts of Zurich and London. There would be, not *enosis*, but rather Cypriot independence in 1960 as a unified political entity. Britain kept its much-needed military bases and installations, retaining them to the present day. Eisenhower, saying he couldn't have been more pleased, sent Macmillan a personal telegram, while Lennox-Boyd penned a personal note to his boss, lauding him for having "re-stablished the Concert of Europe."[120] As for the ongoing application in Strasbourg, there would be no accountability. As part of the independence deal, Greece and Britain agreed to drop the proceedings, and the Strasbourg commission concurred, saying "the recent unhappy chapter in the history of the island should be brought to a close as speedily and completely as possible."[121]

In February 1959, while the prime minister's government was pirouetting around charges of brutality in Cyprus, its cover-ups played out on other stages of the empire, Kenya among them. The colonial secretary had fought off repeated abuse charges—charges that came in detainee letters, from whistleblowers in his own administration, from church leaders, and in press reports like *The Observer's* article headlined "No More Whitewash."[122] These accusations culminated in a House of Commons motion to authorize an independent inquiry. After a bitter debate in which opposition members demanded "some decent and factual Answers," excoriating the government's policies and practices as "monstrous," the vote split along party lines, with 232 in favor and 288 opposed. It was an outcome *The Daily Telegraph* considered a vindication of government and another failed ploy by the "Socialists."[123] Still, Kenya remained headline news, though the *New Statesman and Nation's* dismantling of Macmillan's "Old Pal Protection Society" was less stinging to Conservatives than was *The Economist's* more measured reflection on the independent inquiry vote: "The one overriding consideration in treating any present-day colonial question must be what last memories of the British way of doing things are to be left behind before the connections with Westminster are severed."[124]

But "the British way of doing things" when confronting rebellion in the empire had metastasized. Just days after the Conservative MPs defeated the independent inquiry, word arrived that ten detainees had died in Hola Camp, and "the deaths occurred after they had drunk water from a cart."[125] The MCF's investigatory networks, with Barbara Castle at the epicenter, soon revealed some of the truth, and the government's standard "death by misadventure" could not stand up to its own internal investigation.[126] It turned out that John Cowan, the right-hand man of Terence Gavaghan, had transplanted the dilution technique to Hola Camp, and for the first time, he had put to paper and circulated the dilution technique's use of systematized violence. The so-called Cowan Plan became the center of senior resident magistrate W. H. Goudie's internal report on Hola, and Macmillan's government had no choice but to release it. While the report was short on details, Goudie's findings clearly exposed the "water cart" incident for the cover-up it was. "In

Hola Detention Camp, June 1959

each case death was found to have been caused by shock and haemor-rhage '*due to multiple bruising caused by violence*,'" the report emphasized, ". . . and there was a very considerable amount of beating by warders with batons solely for the purpose of compelling [the victims] to work or punishing them for refusing to work."[127]

The cover-up of "The Hola Massacre," as the press termed it, was the kind of scandal that could bring down a government. Macmillan knew this, confiding to his diary that he was "in a real jam."[128] He refused to accept Lennox-Boyd's resignation, knowing it could open the door to calls for further accountability. That his own government had approved of the dilution technique had to remain secret. So too must his government's crafting of legal coverage for Gavaghan, Cowan, and oth-ers. Governor Baring, knowing how this story could end, flew to Lon-don to insist that his men not be made into "scape goats."[129] As storm clouds continued to gather, Cowan received his "gong," or Member of the British Empire (MBE). The public relations bungle led Macmillan to rebuke the colonial secretary's shop as "a badly run office."[130] Nevertheless, Cowan's MBE reflected Lennox-Boyd's unremitting belief in the work, however messy, that his men-on-the-spot undertook in the name of Her Majesty's government. On the eve of the parliamentary showdown over Hola, the prime minister and his cabinet retreated to Chequers but agreed to stay the course: yes, some unfortunate incidents had occurred at the hands of a few low-level officers, but Britain's brave and loyal servants of empire were winning the war against Mau Mau savagery in Kenya.

Making matters worse, the Hola debate was scheduled around the same late July date that Britain's use of suppression in Nyasaland, a small central African colony, was also on Parliament's docket for debate. Governor Armitage, the same governor scuttled from Cyprus to make room for Field Marshal Harding, had declared a state of emergency on March 3, 1959, and derogated the European Convention on Human Rights under Article 15. Armitage still felt the sting of his failure to

British security force roadblock search, Mlanje, Nyasaland, March 1959

crush EOKA in the early days of Cyprus's conflict. He believed self-redemption would come if he quashed Nyasaland's leading nationalist party, the African National Congress, and its opposition to the Central African Federation, which, in 1953 had united Nyasaland with Southern and Northern Rhodesia into a single political entity in which white minority settlers held disproportionate power. To "nip trouble in the bud," in Armitage's words, he deployed the now-standard policies and practices of legalized lawlessness.[131] Congress's leadership upbraided liberal imperialism's methods and took its claims that "the British have violated the rights of man" directly to the UN secretary-general Dag Hammarskjöld, and the press.[132] Lennox-Boyd assigned the highly respected judge Lord Devlin to conduct a limited investigation. Despite Lennox-Boyd's close censorship, Devlin slipped into his final report that Armitage was overseeing a "police state" in the heart of British Africa. The prime minister called Devlin's findings "dynamite."[133]

Confidence in Macmillan's government, and with it the empire, hung in the balance. During the Hola debate, Castle was among the first to speak and recalled that she "was trembling so much from anger I could barely get out my facts."[134] She offered a catalogue of atrocities that led up to and included Hola, though it was Enoch Powell, a disaffected member of the Conservative Party, whose words electrified the chamber. Deploying a stance much like Churchill's during the Amritsar debates, Powell admonished Castle for being "a little too kind" to the Kenyan administration and singled out Carruthers Johnston, the tripartite minister with powers second only to Governor Baring, and Kenya defence minister Jake Cusack, for their roles in Kenya's detention camp system.[135] Churchill had called Amritsar "an extraordinary event, a monstrous event, an event which stands in singular and sinister isolation"; now Powell called the Cowan Plan "a serious departure from anything attempted before."[136] Yet for nearly two years the dilution technique had been standard practice in Kenya, to the knowledge and approval of Macmillan's government. Further reminiscent of events surrounding the 1919 massacre in India, Powell made clear that accountability was needed, though in this instance it rested with officials in Kenya. In Powell's words, the colonial secretary was "without any jot or tittle of blame for what happened in Kenya." He underscored that Lennox-Boyd's "administration . . . has been the greatest exercise of the office of Colonial Secretary in modern times. It is in the name of that record, it is in the name of his personal blamelessness, that I beg of him to ensure that the responsibility is recognised and carried where it properly belongs, and is seen to belong."[137] Then, in a final rhetorical gesture, he played to the crowd's enduring belief in the civilizing mission's purpose:

> We cannot say, "We will have African standards in Africa, Asian standards in Asia and perhaps British standards here at home." We have not that choice to make. We must be consistent with ourselves everywhere. All Government, all influence of man upon man, rests upon opinion. What we can do in Africa, where we still govern and where we no longer govern, depends upon the opinion which is entertained of the way in which this country acts and the way in which Englishmen act. We cannot, we dare not, in Africa of all places, fall below our own highest standards in the acceptance of responsibility.[138]

Just days after the Hola debate and the one that followed on Nyasaland, Macmillan wrote to Queen Elizabeth II to reassure her that, while the Hola "incident" was by no means "excused," the colonial secretary and his governor "can hardly be held responsible for the faults of commission or omission of quite minor officials."[139] In his mind, "it would have been an intolerable hardship had [Lennox-Boyd's] fine career been tarnished," though much larger issues were now at play.[140] General Dyer had been held accountable for his actions in 1919 Amritsar, but in 1959 the British government could sacrifice no one of consequence in Kenya because the paper trail of internal correspondence went straight up to the highest levels of Macmillan's government. Such questions of accountability weren't the prime minister's only concerns. Fulfilling the Colonial Policy Committee's optimistic recommendations about future economic buoyancy depended on maintaining "an atmosphere of goodwill" and an "orderly transfer of power" in the empire, which successive insurgencies, investigations, and scandalous cover-ups were undermining.

International humanitarian law also reared its head. Prior to the Hola debate, the British government was under enormous public pressure and thought of publishing an ICRC report that had been undertaken in February 1957. At Governor Baring's urging, Henri Junod, an old friend of his and a well-respected member of Switzerland's missionary and humanitarian Junod family, made a two-month tour of the detention camps and villages with Colonial Office approval.[141] It was clear even before Junod's arrival that the ICRC's neutrality was compromised. "I privately discussed this question [a phase of violent shock] with Dr. Junod of the International Red Cross, who I knew well in South

Africa and who has spent his whole life working with Africans and most of it with African prisoners," Baring told Lennox-Boyd. "He has no doubt in his own mind that if the violent shock is the price to be paid for pushing detainees out . . . we should pay it."[142] After touring the Mwea camps and witnessing the dilution technique firsthand, Junod turned to Gavaghan and said, *"Ne vous inquiétez pas* [Do not distress yourself]. Compared to the French in Algeria, you are angels of mercy."[143] When Junod submitted his report, it made no mention of the dilution technique, nor of the starvation conditions in the eighteen villages he had toured, nor of the forced labor and violence in the fifty-two detention camps he had visited. The only critical note was about whipping, a punishment that was legally permissible in Kenya but that the ICRC wanted stopped. Junod remained a confidant of Baring's: the governor sought his suggestions a few months later for harsher alternatives to the dilution technique, even if they might lead to serious "political difficulties."[144]

When the Colonial Office approached the ICRC in June 1959 about publishing its earlier confidential report, Geneva representatives raised no objections, though said two years had elapsed since Junod's tour of Kenya and recommended a new mission in light of recent events. Baring was enthusiastic, "particularly if Monsieur Junod could again be associated with this work, since he has great experience of prisons and detainee camps and a wide knowledge of Africa."[145] London agreed, and once again Henri Junod toured Kenya, along with Dr. Jean-Maurice Rubli. Their findings were so alarming that the ICRC vice president Marcel Junod and Rubli flew to London to discuss them with the British government before the final report was submitted. Henri Junod did not attend; rather his cousin Marcel, one of the ICRC's highest-ranking, most-decorated officials from his work during the Spanish Civil War and missions in Europe and Japan during World War II, was left to salvage the family's reputation. The ICRC's recent mission, according to Marcel Junod, found the level of violence and use of torture by British colonial servants to break Mau Mau detainees shocking. These practices had to be suspended immediately, he said, and the British government complied, releasing all remaining detainees, a decision that had already been made after the Hola disaster.[146]

One wonders what Marcel had to say to his cousin Henri about his 1957 tour, a missed opportunity to bring Kenya's appalling conditions to the ICRC's attention in Geneva. Instead, two years had lapsed, during which time Britain had made a mockery of international humanitarian law, and countless Africans had been murdered, tortured, and starved to death. Henri tried to mitigate his earlier cover-ups, writing in the final

1959 ICRC report that there had been "a sharp increase in persecution and bad treatment" in Kenya's detention camps since he visited them in 1957.[147] Even some officials in the Colonial Office backpedaled, saying the "problems in Kenya" might well have been mitigated had Britain applied Common Article 3 of the Geneva Conventions to the Mau Mau Insurgency.[148]

Macmillan seized the doublethink narrative once his party had secured a general election victory in October 1959, less than three months after the Hola debate. The Conservative manifesto ushered in its "never had it so good" evidence, using the sterling as "the currency in which nearly half the world's trade is done" as dubious proxy for its imperial success.[149] So, too, did it address the ongoing "smear campaign"—largely at the hands of the socialists—that sullied the good name of Britain and her empire. "Our duty to ourselves and to the cause of freedom everywhere [is] to see that the facts are known, and that misrepresentation about British 'colonialism' does not go unchallenged," was prominently stated in the Conservative platform.[150]

While Macmillan was spinning the public narrative, the combined impact of Kenya, Cyprus, and Nyasaland was *the* tipping point for widespread colonial retreat. The Conservative government was a half-step ahead of the Labour Party, the ICRC, the European Commission on Human Rights, the growing force of former colonies now sitting in the United Nations, the media, and a litany of missionary and humanitarians across the globe. With the legacy of the British Empire at stake, and aligned with the Colonial Policy Committee report's economic optimism, Macmillan moved toward transforming formal rule into informal influence. After the general election, he ousted his embattled colonial secretary, Lennox-Boyd, replacing him with Ian Macleod, who soon became synonymous both with propagating the empire's emancipatory narrative and with shoring up liberal imperialism's obfuscating practices. He and Macmillan knew their nation's decades-old practices were untenable, not only because of the empire's repeated abuse scandals but also because concessions were sweeping across the Anglo-Saxon world. In the Commonwealth, officials rolled back assimilationist policies, and in the United States desegregation in schools, while meeting with fierce resistance, had begun and the passage of the Civil Rights Act was on the horizon. Just as new patterns of regional and global trade replaced liberal imperialism's old ecosystems of exchange, so too did conceptions of human rights, dignity, and equality force the hands of those in favor of the empire to recognize, however grudgingly, that brazen violations of universal norms could not continue without exposing Britain's "derogation regime" in ways that would undermine the triumphant narrative proclaiming the civilizing mission a success.[151]

Macleod understood this well. Just weeks after taking office, he informed the governor of Kenya that he had "decided to draw a veil over the past."[152] Ashes of evidence once again spread through the empire as the colonial secretary issued a sweeping directive that no documents were to be passed on to independent governments that

(a) Might embarrass Her Majesty's Government or other governments;
(b) Might embarrass members of the Police, military forces, public servants or others (such as Police agents or informers);
(c) Might compromise sources of intelligence;
(d) Might be used unethically by Ministers in successor government.[153]

The document-purging process, called Operation Legacy in some parts of the empire, drew on systems of destruction that had unfolded in Malaya and India.[154] In Kenya, officials developed the "Watch" system. With it, every ministry and department divided its documents into two categories: "Watch" and "Legacy." Those they designated "Watch" were destroyed or sent to Britain; those that constituted "Legacy" were eventually handed over to Kenya's independent government.[155]

The "Watch" system was orchestrated directly under Macleod's purview.[156] In total, some three and a half tons of documents were slated for the incinerator.[157] As in Malaya, Kenyan officials, in accordance with Rule 3 (iv) of Colonial Office Secret Circular Dispatch no. 1282/59, filled out a destruction certificate for each document destroyed.[158] Copies of all destruction certificates were sent to the Colonial Office, where they were to constitute a permanent record. A hand-selected group of the government's most trusted officers oversaw operations on the ground, chief among them Gavaghan.[159] The British government's director of torture in Kenya became, in the final days of colonial rule, its trusted archivist.

As variations of Operation Legacy were enacted throughout Britain's remaining empire, Macmillan toured Africa where, in February 1960, he delivered his famous "Winds of Change" speech to both houses of South Africa's parliament.[160] Apartheid leaders looked on as he laid out the realities of the moment:

We have seen the awakening of national consciousness in peoples who have for centuries lived in dependence upon some other power. Fifteen years ago this movement spread through

Asia. Many countries there of different races and civilisations pressed their claim to an independent national life. Today the same thing is happening in Africa. . . . The wind of change is blowing through this continent, and, whether we like it or not, this growth of national consciousness is a political fact. We must all accept it as a fact, and our national policies must take account of it.[161]

Weeks later the apartheid government responded: its security forces opened fire on unarmed Black protesters demonstrating against British-inspired pass laws in Sharpeville, killing or wounding 255 of them. Cameras captured the events of March 21, 1960, known as the Sharpeville Massacre, and the world saw images of the apartheid state's brutality; a week later the South African government, again drawing on laws inspired by those in Britain's empire, declared a state of emergency and arrested two thousand people.

At the United Nations, the changing constitution of its General Assembly, with India often leading the way, catalyzed the passage of Resolution 1514 at the end of the year, proving once again that Britain miscalculated the UN's potential as a locus for anti-imperialism. Known as the "Declaration on the Granting of Independence to Colonial Countries and Peoples," the resolution made clear that the demand for rapid and unconditional decolonization was directly linked to "the determination proclaimed by the peoples of the world in the Charter of

Sharpeville Massacre, Transvaal Province, South Africa, March 21, 1960

the United Nations to reaffirm faith in fundamental human rights, in the dignity and worth of the human person, in the equal rights of men and women."[162] Resolution 1514 achieved what the UN Declaration of Human Rights had failed to do, but what nationalists in Malaya, Kenya, Cyprus, Nyasaland, and elsewhere around the empire had achieved: it linked the demands for human rights and their protections, something even the European Convention on Human Rights had failed to uphold, to self-determination and the creation of states that would, it was hoped, guarantee the legal protections that British colonialism had trammeled.

As the Union Jack was lowered, and the flags of new nations were raised in ceremony after ceremony—in Cyprus (1960), Nigeria (1960), Sierra Leone (1961), Tanganyika (1961), Uganda (1962), Jamaica (1962), Zanzibar (1963), Nyasaland (renamed Malawi, 1964), Northern Rhodesia (renamed Zambia, 1964), Malta (1964), and The Gambia (1965)—the consequences of colonial rule did not recede into the night. Kenya was a case in point. After Britain's 1959 general election, many of the colony's settlers, bunkered in white privilege, were optimistic. The settler leader Michael Blundell, however, knew change was coming. The "prevailing mood" after Hola, he wrote, was best captured by the remarks of one Conservative MP: "What do I care about the f . . . cking settlers, let them bloody well look after themselves."[163]

Events in Kenya's Pipeline had changed everything, or so it seemed. "Jomo Kenyatta was the recognized leader of the non-co-operation movement which organised Mau Mau," Patrick Renison, Kenya's new governor, announced in May 1960. "Mau Mau, with its foul oathing and violent aims, had been declared an unlawful society. [Kenyatta] was convicted of managing that unlawful society and being a member of it. He appealed to the Supreme Court and the Privy Council. In these three courts his guilt was established and confirmed. Here was the African leader to darkness and death."[164] He echoed the sentiments of Britain's official report on Mau Mau, published a few months earlier. When writing the so-called definitive history of the movement, which he called "wholly evil," its author, F. D. Corfield, relied entirely on British and African loyalist sources.[165] Few whites, including Baring before he stepped down, doubted that Kenyatta was Mau Mau's mastermind.[166] Corfield's evidence gave more heft to this view, despite the fact that Kenyatta's trial had been rigged, and the Crown's star witness, Rawson Macharia, had stepped forward in 1958 with a sworn affidavit admitting that he and other witnesses had perjured themselves in return for government bribes. Britain responded by prosecuting Macharia for swearing to a false affidavit.[167]

In May 1960, when African and British officials gathered for their first round of constitutional and independence negotiations in London's Lancaster House, they agreed to move toward a parliamentary democracy with an African majority. Kenya's first colony-wide elections were scheduled for February 1961, and the only outstanding issue was Kenyatta. Renison's public denunciation of him had antagonized Kenya's African nationalists at a time when Macleod was intent on installing moderate Africans in power, including Kikuyu loyalists, who would safeguard Britain's commercial and strategic interests, before handing over the colony to majority rule. As universally enfranchised voters prepared to cast their ballots in 1961, Kenyatta's release was the most consequential issue. The Kenya African National Union (KANU), a coalition party of Kikuyu and Luo, the second largest ethnic group in Kenya, campaigned on the pledge that its candidates would not take their seats in office unless Kenyatta was released. The opposition, the Kenya African Democratic Union (KADU), which the British government secretly supported, championed minority ethnic rights, including those of the European settlers. When the election results came in, KANU won by a landslide, and its members fulfilled the party's campaign promise. For

Jomo Kenyatta after his release from prison, August 14, 1961

the first time the African majority had the upper hand, backing Britain into a corner and leaving Macleod no choice but to set Kenyatta free.

"I have been greatly misrepresented by some of you, but today I hope you will stick to the truth and refrain from writing sensational stories about me," Kenyatta told a scrum of reporters, officials, and curiosity seekers witnessing his first press conference in April 1961. Gaunt, with eyes sunken from over eight years of incarceration, the seventy-year-old Kenyatta stood in front of the cameras wearing his trademark leather jacket and speaking in a voice that was clear and firm, characteristic of his interwar days working with other Black radicals in George Padmore's Cranleigh Street living room. He denounced the Corfield Report as "a pack of lies," then turned to those who had convicted and incarcerated him: "Father forgive them, for they know not what they do." The man schooled by Presbyterian missionaries as a young boy assured the world that he sought no vengeance before offering one enduring message. "*Uhuru*," he declared. "*Uhuru*." The Kiswahili word for freedom became the slogan for Africans in Kenya in the weeks and months ahead. It was the greeting on the streets, the closing word in conversations, and a popular lyric in songs and praise poems: "*Uhuru na Kenyatta*," Freedom and Kenyatta.[168]

"I wept, I wept with joy," one former detainee recalled when learning of Kenyatta's liberation. "Word got around very quickly when he was released, and we danced and celebrated into the morning. Our leader was free, and he was going to save us from the colonial oppressors. Ngai had answered our prayers."[169] Triumphal appearances followed, with Kenyatta touring the colony for the first time in nearly a decade. His image gripped millions of Britons in their living rooms when the BBC broadcast a forty-five-minute, prime-time interview with him. No one quite knew what to make of this enigmatic man who spoke eloquently, wore a Western-style suit, quoted from the Bible, and had no horns sticking out of his forehead. By all appearances he was "civilized," his transformation reflecting Britain's power of reform, even in the darkest, most evil of circumstances.

"This is the greatest day in Kenya's history and the happiest day in my life," Kenyatta told the ecstatic crowd gathered in Nairobi's Uhuru Stadium on December 11, 1963, to witness Britain's final transfer of power in Kenya. Standing beside him were dignitaries from around the world, including the Duke of Edinburgh who represented the queen. He was there to witness the thirty-fourth country in Africa achieve its independence from European rule. At midnight, a spotlight zeroed in on the Union Jack being lowered and Kenya's new flag being raised for

Jomo Kenyatta and the Duke of Edinburgh celebrating Kenya's independence, Nairobi, December 12, 1963

the first time. For a moment, though, it refused to unfurl. The duke leaned over and whispered into the soon-to-be president's ear, "Do you want to change your mind?" Kenyatta grinned and watched as the wind finally picked up his country's flag, and the crowd below him roared.[170]

Kenyatta quickly emerged as a postcolonial leader with whom Britain could do business. "Let this be the day on which all of us commit ourselves to erase from our minds all the hatred and the difficulties of those years which now belong to history," he declared on October 20, 1964, the anniversary of Baring's declaration of emergency in 1952, now celebrated as the new nation's first Kenyatta Day. "Let us agree that we shall never refer to the past. Let us instead, unite, in all our utterances and activities, in concern for the reconstruction of our country and the vitality of Kenya's future."[171] There would be no reckoning for the crimes committed during the Mau Mau era; no memorialization for those who fought for freedom in the forests or in the detention camps or villages; no prosecution of loyalists; no purging of European settlers or British colonial officials who remained in the colony after independence. "We all fought for freedom" framed Kenyatta's new independence narrative as he sought to erase the public memory of Mau Mau, replacing it with a widely embracing message.

Was he the great reconciler or a conservative politician claiming a future that looked similar to Kenya's colonial past? The nation's Central Province, Kikuyu country, was bitterly divided. Former Mau Mau adherents, often impoverished, lived side by side with former loyalists who had perpetrated horrific crimes during the emergency, some owning large parcels of land that the colonial government had confiscated from detainees. Similarly, Mau Mau adherents, though on a diminished relative scale, had also perpetrated crimes against fellow Kikuyu, including the murder of Senior Chief Waruhiu, as we've seen. Calls for vengeance were strong, and only Kenyatta had the moral authority to contain the anger, even if he couldn't eliminate it. Millions of other Africans had been uninvolved with Mau Mau and were now deeply suspicious of a Kikuyu oligarchy taking over the country. If Kenyatta recognized Mau Mau's contributions to accelerating decolonization, where would this leave Kenya's dozens of other ethnic groups in their claims to the fruits of independence?

Nearly thirty years had passed since Kenyatta wrote articles condemning British rule in the *New Leader*. He now had no interest in dismantling the structures and systems of the colonial state. Instead, he adopted them to aggrandize his own so-called democratic power, using the language of law and order to justify his actions. "We shall not allow hooligans to rule Kenya," he insisted publicly. "We must have no hatred towards one another. Mau Mau was a disease which had been eradicated."[172] He locked up those Africans who protested, using the same emergency-era laws the British had enforced, signing detention orders on the same desk that Governor Baring had used to sign his. Other dissidents, like Bildad Kaggia and Paul Ngei, who had been imprisoned with Kenyatta, became MPs in Kenya's government, though their advocating for land and compensation for former Mau Mau detainees and their civilian supporters was repeatedly stonewalled. They were soon pushed aside, eventually to live impoverished lives, while another high-profile detainee who wrote a memoir about his time behind the wire, Josiah Mwangi Kariuki, was assassinated.

The fruits of freedom were being divided up between Kenyatta's emerging oligarchy, loyalists, and those settlers who remained in Kenya. Indeed, Kenyatta did his best to allay white fears. "Let us join hands and work for the benefit of Kenya," he told them. "We want you to stay and farm well in this country: that is the policy of this government."[173] Thousands of settlers were having none of Kenyatta's new credo, *"Harambee,"* or "Let's All Pull Together," and left Kenya. The independent government bought their land at market rates, using £12.5 million in British loans to finance the buyout. Wealthy European investors and well-capitalized African loyalists purchased much of this property. Many settlers stayed in Kenya, however, where they remained, together with their investments, on some of the country's most fertile and productive land. Meanwhile, Kenyatta's embrace of Western capitalism made him a darling of the West in the Cold War scramble for Africa.

Many British administrators also left the colony and contributed to the empire's legacy in one way or another, adding to the web of imperial connections that continued to be spun even as formal British imperialism declined. Of those tied to Hola, Governor Baring settled into the luxury of his family estate at Howick, where he pursued his passion for bird-watching until becoming the head of the Colonial Development Corporation, soon renamed the Commonwealth Development Corporation. A vestige of Attlee's imperial resurgence era, the corporation invested directly in development projects, mostly in Britain's former empire. More recently, the corporation, still wholly owned by the British government, spun out an emerging market, private equity fund manager, Actis, which came under scrutiny for alleged informal imperial practices, reputedly seeking out large self-enriching profits that brought little benefit to developing nations.[174]

The Bank of England also employed former Kenyan officials regardless of their financial skills, including John Cowan, author of the Cowan Plan. Carruthers Johnston, the colonial official whose power had been second only to Baring's, went to work for military intelligence. Ian Henderson, who had worked on the front lines of intelligence gathering, was hailed by one general as having "probably done more than any single individual to bring the Emergency to an end"; he left for the British oil-producing protectorate of Bahrain, where he oversaw the general directorate for state security investigations from 1966 to 1998. Known as the "Butcher of Bahrain" for his use of torture, village burning, and violation of numerous human rights accords, Henderson was never prosecuted. Despite demands from international organizations, Britain refused to release documents pertaining to his Bahraini activities due to "national security" concerns. He did, though, receive a CBE from the queen in 1984 to go with the George Medal he received from her thirty years earlier.[175]

In Kenya as in other former colonies, Britain maintained military bases, and does so to the present day. After independence, MI5 security liaison officers stayed behind to facilitate Britain's geopolitical security operations, as did colonial-era administrators who tutored those who had not yet "grown up" in the ways of governance. Among them was Terence Gavaghan, the architect of one of the empire's most notorious regimes of systematized violence. The man who had crafted the dilution technique and helped to oversee Operation Legacy in the final days of British rule in Kenya was now in charge of the "Africanisation" program for Kenyatta's independent government. That is, he was responsible for training the hundreds of new civil servants populating Kenya's postcolonial bureaucracy. It was "a crash programme under extreme pressure," Gavaghan said, because of the relatively few number of Africans seemingly prepared to take over the day-to-day management of Kenya's new independent state.[176]

"It is a pleasure and a challenge to write this . . . taking up an invitation which Terence Gavaghan threw down in the guise of a gauntlet," the Cambridge historian John Lonsdale reflected in his foreword to Gavaghan's memoir, published in 1999.

> A fine account of a full life, well charged with risk and good companions along the way. . . . Rehabilitation was, in retrospect, the precondition for [Gavaghan's] later role in Africanisation. Approved by the Colonial Office, [rehabilitation] was a programme of political re-education unparalleled in the history of British counter-insurgency. . . . Some readers may nonetheless be shocked by the physical violence used to break the detainees' will to resist. . . . Why should men who in their own lights were freedom fighters, prisoners of war, be forced to conform with what their foreign rulers chose to define as co-operation, even if it was to advance their mutually convergent interest in freedom? It is a hard question, where the pride and pain of [the British colonial] service are most knotted.[177]

Other colonial officers from around the empire also wrote self-serving memoirs, though few had a conferred-status like Gavaghan's. He was among the empire's former servants holding forth in Oxbridge seminars where they schooled imperial historians and eager graduate students on the civilizing mission, joining the sherry hours that followed to offer twilight codas to their day's lessons on colonial rule. The milieu still largely cleaved to what the historian Richard Drayton calls the "anti-ideological turn." In the 1950s this turn replaced some of the empire's hagiographies with narratives that focused on the "official mind" of imperial expansion and retreat as well as Britain's consistent aim of preserving economic interests. Influenced by two towering scholars of British imperialism, Ronald Robinson and John Gallagher, these histories rarely questioned the archive. But "this post-1950 anti-ideological moment was itself a kind of ideological position," as Drayton points out. "For if the story no longer made Britain its hero, it was still sceptical and often mocking of the claims of anti-colonial nationalism, while still evasive of the question of British violence, of economic exploitation, racism and their consequences. It was the perfect form of Imperial history for a British nation no longer so confident of its imperial role."[178] What the empire's former servants offered up by way of memoirs and seminar lectures, along with those documents retained in the archives, shaped the ways in which the next generation understood Britain's imperial past. Narratives of success often glossed over the realities of decolonization, which included liberal imperialism's dependence on coercion.

Around the time of Macmillan's "Winds of Change" speech, there were other indications of the empire's fall. The nation's application to the European Economic Community (the precursor to the European Union) in 1961 was one, though in the eyes of many, it was the almighty sterling's fate that signaled the end of the empire. The sterling area had been hooked to liberal imperialism's broader systems of violence and extraction, and once these went away with independence, the phasing out of postcolonial monetary deals had an inevitable impact on Britain's monetary system. After a series of crises and devaluation in 1967, Britain failed to produce enough of a surplus to retain confidence in the pound, and by 1972 the sterling era was over. Of course, multiple factors were responsible for that, though the end of territorial empire, and the reasons for its demise, were certainly one of them.[179]

How much the Colonial Policy Committee's assumption that colonies would remain loyal in the face of tumultuous ends-of-empire conflicts is up for debate, but Britain's shaping of its triumphant "hearts and minds" narrative is not. Perhaps the committee, like much of the British public, didn't question the civilizing mission's success, even when it was executed during brutal counterinsurgencies. Liberal imperialism's Janus face of reform and coercion was powerful, beckoning Britons to focus on the peace in Pax Britannica while either denying or minimizing its violent means or reconciling them as inherent and necessary features—the "pride and pain" of British colonial servants, as Lonsdale tells us—for transforming "childlike" colonial subjects and shepherding them into the modern world.

That "hearts and minds" influenced future counterinsurgencies is also undebatable. After Britain's campaign in Malaya, the term became shorthand for modern counterinsurgency doctrine, and officials there brought it directly to the South Vietnamese and the Americans during the 1960s. Robert Thompson, one of the Malayan Emergency's key players, introduced the concept of New Villages, or civilian population control, to Vietnam, where it took form in the Strategic Hamlet Program. As head of the British Advisory Mission in South Vietnam (BRIAM, 1961–65), Thompson "was widely regarded on both sides of the Atlantic as the world's leading expert on countering . . . rural guerrilla insurgency," according to *The Times*.[180] He gained the attention of President John F. Kennedy and Defense Secretary Robert McNamara, advocating for the creation of Malaya-inspired villages, or hamlets, "to create the conditions in which the population has the security to exercise the choice between supporting the insurgent forces and supporting the forces of the government. . . . There should be in the whole of the government's approach an adroit and judicious mixture of ruthlessness and sympathy," with the "dividing line" between the two determined by "necessity."[181]

Britain's age-old balance between necessity and ruthlessness was brought to bear on a massive scale when the South Vietnamese proclaimed 1962 the "Year of Strategic Hamlets." Over 4 million people were corralled into 3,225 hamlets, though the operation was disastrously unsuccessful, earning condemnation from General William C. Westmoreland at one extreme and Noam Chomsky—who facetiously called Thompson "one of Britain's gifts to the Vietnamese people"—at the other.[182] The British ambassador in Saigon blamed Ngo Dinh Diem, the president of South Vietnam, and his government for creating hamlets too rapidly and for forcing "its policy down the throats of the people regardless of their convenience or even of their elementary human rights."[183] Of course, this is precisely what the British had done in Malaya, and some likelier sources of failure included the strength of the Viet Cong insurgents relative to Communists in Malaya; American aerial bombing, which incensed Thompson; and the fact that the Americans could not appoint their version of General Templer to enforce and coordinate policy.[184] Vietnam was not an American colony the way Malaya had been for the British; had the United States appointed its own man with a plan, such interference "would have convinced all the less sophisticated parts of the world already that South Vietnam is in the pocket of the Americans," according to military expert Ian F. W. Beckett.[185]

After his departure from BRIAM, Thompson went on to write one of the most influential manuals on counterinsurgencies. Published in 1966, *Defeating Communist Insurgency* codified British counterinsurgency practices by laying out five principles, which included the necessity of adhering to the rule of law and winning the hearts and minds of the civilian population. There was no data, however, to support Thompson's conclusions on hearts and minds, and Templer lacked such information as well; no one gathered information from the Chinese villagers in Malaya to understand why they stopped supporting the colony's Communist insurgents. Moreover, as we have seen in our account of the Malayan insurgency, Thompson's "judicious mixture" approach had much more "ruthlessness" than "sympathy" or reform, and "the rule of law" was a time-honored term in the empire for legalized lawlessness. Nonetheless, Britain's campaign in Malaya emerged as *the* reference point for counterinsurgency success, influencing the American's Petraeus Doctrine in Iraq and shaping Western counterinsurgency operations to this day.[186]

When the Northern Ireland "Troubles" erupted in the 1960s after decades of sectarian violence, Britain's connective web once again expanded. Some of the empire's most seasoned veterans arrived on the scene, including Frank Kitson, who had hopscotched his way through Kenya, Malaya, Cyprus, Oman, and Aden; in Northern Ireland he rose to the rank of general. Geoffrey Baker, who was Harding's number two in Cyprus, was also a general by the time he arrived in Northern Ireland and had written the "Baker Report," in which he called dealing with human rights complaints "a bitter and distasteful experience."[187] Joining them was the "Aden Gang," a group of intelligence agents and covert operatives who had enacted harsh methods during Britain's final years of rule in Aden.

This sliver of territory on the Arabian Peninsula had been the site of another British state of emergency from 1963 to 1967. Richard Turnbull, fresh off his stint as chief secretary in Kenya, served as Aden's governor. John Prendergast, who had directed intelligence in Kenya and Cyprus, executed repressive policies and practices, often in Aden's Fort Morbut Interrogation Center, similar to those he oversaw elsewhere in the empire. Already Prendergast was legendary as "the real life James Bond" with his "Gary Cooper or Cary Grant"–like good looks, according to *The Times*, picking up one of the most coveted gongs, the George Medal, for his work in breaking Mau Mau suspects in Kenya.[188] He lacked not an ounce of hubris when he inveigled with Turnbull, who had a copy of Baker's report from Cyprus, to frustrate the ICRC and Amnesty International's investigations into allegations of torture.[189]

Also circulating to Northern Ireland was MI5 agent Jack Morton, who had been Templer's right-hand intelligence man in Malaya and later seconded to Aden, where he compiled a major intelligence report in 1964. Morton's imperial heritage stretched back to India, where he was a policeman. "It dawned upon me, and became deeply ingrained, that the British were the rulers of India and that the Indians were a sort of immature, backward and needy people whom it was the natural British function to govern and administer," he recalled. "It was inspiring to realise that I was born into this splendid heritage and that to be British was to be a superior sort of person."[190] He brought this ethos and his imperial seasoning to Northern Ireland when, in 1973, he wrote the "ambitious" report on police reform during the Troubles, advocating a "shake-up" of the Royal Ulster Constabulary's Special Branch.[191] While Morton's report remains unpublished despite efforts to force its release, what is widely known are details on Northern Ireland's torture techniques.[192]

Internment and interrogation were two of the most contested issues during the Troubles. Their roots stretched to the former empire, as well as to Western allies. After the Second World War, MI5 and the CIA had experimented with hallucinogenic drugs for enhanced interrogations, and then combined forces with the Canadians to develop "sensory deprivation" and "self-inflicted" pain for interrogation use, techniques that had long evolved in the British Empire.[193] On August 9, 1971, when Britain launched Operation Demetrius—the dawn raid that led to the mass arrest and internment of 342 IRA suspects and sparked three days of violence that left twenty-four people dead—internment began again in Northern Ireland. This time British forces were legally enabled through the Northern Ireland Special Powers Act, rooted in the empire's long history of emergency regulations and introduced at the time of Ireland's 1921 partition. After the operation's roundups, fourteen suspects, soon known as the "Hooded Men" or the "Guinea Pigs," went to a secret interrogation center at Ballykelly airfield, where British security forces subjected them to the "five techniques," which included wall-standing, hooding, subjection to noise, and sleep and food deprivation. During the Troubles, many internees were subjected to such treatment and worse.[194]

Once again, Britain was accused of violating international law, this time in Northern Ireland, when the Irish government, on behalf of those subjected to alleged abuses, filed an application with the European Commission on Human Rights in December 1971.[195] Nothing more than the five techniques were used, British officials said in their defense, claiming these interrogation methods did not amount to "torture" or "inhuman or degrading treatment or punishment." Britain also undertook every effort to render the commission's investigation difficult, much like it had in Cyprus and with the ICRC and Amnesty International's work in Aden. Nonetheless, in the case of Northern Ireland the commission ruled, in 1976, that "the systematic application of the techniques for the purpose of inducing a person to give information shows a clear resemblance to those methods of systematic torture which have been known over the ages."[196] The case was then referred to the European Court on Human Rights, which, in 1978, partially reversed the commission's unanimous decision, calling the five techniques "inhuman and degrading" methods of interrogation, a breach of Article 3, though it said "they did not occasion suffering of the particular intensity and cruelty implied by the word torture as so understood."[197] While the British government reaffirmed during the second proceeding that it would no longer use the five techniques during interrogation—a commitment Prime Minister Edward Heath had already made to Parliament in 1972 with little effect

General Sir Frank Kitson, commander in chief of the UK Land Forces (right), greeted by Queen Elizabeth II (1982), who had earlier knighted Kitson in 1980

on his security forces—it continued to do so for years, including in Iraq during the early 2000s.

Frank Kitson's "we beat terrorists before we negotiate with them" battle cry informed his pseudo-gang operations in Kenya, his squads in Malaya, and eventually his approach to covert penetration and intelligence gathering more generally.[198] In January 1972 he also led his Belfast-based battalions in an attack against a civilian anti-internment march in Londonderry. His paratroopers left fourteen unarmed protesters dead, and wounded more than a dozen more in what is now known as the notorious Bloody Sunday.[199] The queen knighted Kitson eight years later. He was one of the empire's most illustrious veterans, and had also put to paper his hard-earned lessons in a how-to counterinsurgency manual, *Low Intensity Operations*, published in the early 1970s. A follow-up to Thompson's codification of Britain's "hearts and minds" strategy, Kitson's book clearly, if disingenuously, affirmed the military belief that Britain somehow managed to get counterinsurgency right.[200] In due time, these same strategies and tactics played out on the twenty-first-century battlefields of Afghanistan and Iraq.[201]

Bloody Sunday, Londonderry, Ireland, January 30, 1972

The Troubles in Northern Ireland also struck Britain's monarchy. On August 27, 1979, Lord Louis "Dickie" Mountbatten, India's last viceroy and great-grandson of Queen Victoria, second cousin to Queen Elizabeth II, great-uncle to the Duke of Edinburgh, as well as Prince Charles's beloved mentor, was holidaying with his family in their summer castle, called Classiebawn, on Ireland's northwestern coast. The wartime Supreme Allied Commander South East Asia Command and chairman of NATO's military committee had largely retired from his many active duties, spending time socializing with the royal court and its hangers-on, writing military articles, and enjoying the great outdoors. On the morning of August 27, Mountbatten piled his family into *Shadow V,* his twenty-nine-foot fishing boat, and set out to catch lobsters. Fifteen minutes after leaving the dock, the boat exploded, shrieking the sky with deafening noise and throwing thousands of pieces of splintered wood, life vests, shoes, and metal seats into the air. "The boat was there one minute and the next minute it was like a lot of matchsticks floating on the water," a stunned witness recounted. The aftermath was eerily silent, except for the sounds of those who survived struggling for safety under a mushroom cloud of smoke.[202]

"Who the hell would want to kill an old man anyway?" Mountbatten had scoffed when offered a security detail while summering in Ireland.[203] The IRA did. Its members had been threatening him since the 1960s and had already aborted at least one close attempt on Mountbatten's life. Indeed, aside from Queen Elizabeth II, he was arguably the royal who most embodied nation, empire, and monarchy, though unlike the queen, he had been on the empire's front lines where he symbolized in comportment, attitude, and deed liberal imperialism's underbelly. On the night of August 26, two IRA members had planted a remote-controlled, fifty-pound gelignite bomb under *Shadow V,* and its blast killed three of the boaters instantly, Mountbatten included. When rescuers found him, he was facedown in the chilly sea, both legs nearly severed off. Hours later the IRA made a second strike near the Irish border at Warrenpoint, killing eighteen British soldiers in a bombing ambush. "It was the single heaviest death toll for the British Army in the 10 years since it was sent to quell fighting between Roman Catholic and Protestant militants," *The New York Times* reported.[204]

"This operation is one of the discriminate ways we can bring to the attention of the English people the continuing occupation of our country," the IRA proclaimed, taking immediate responsibility for the attacks.[205] Some said Mountbatten's murder was in retaliation for Bloody

Sunday, though Prime Minister Margaret Thatcher, newly elected, was not knuckling under. She withdrew "special category" prisoner status granting certain rights to locked up IRA members, and Bobby Sands, serving fourteen years in Maze Prison, went on a hunger strike, dying on May 5, 1981. Britain and Northern Ireland entered into one of its darkest periods, which largely ended with the Good Friday Agreement in 1998. The effects of Mountbatten's death, however, lingered, perhaps nowhere more poignantly than within the monarchy. After delivering a eulogy for "the grandfather I never had" to two thousand mourners in Westminster Abbey, Prince Charles wept, fully revealing himself only in his private journal:

Lord Louis Mountbatten's funeral procession, Pall Mall, London, September 5, 1979

A mixture of desperate emotions swept over me—agony, disbelief, a kind of wretched numbness, closely followed by fierce and violent determination to see that something was done about the IRA. . . . Life will *never* be the same now that he has gone and I fear it will take me a very long time to forgive those people who today achieved something that two world wars and *thousands* of Germans and Japanese failed to achieve. I only hope I can live up to the expectations he had of me and be able to do *something* to honour the name of Mountbatten.[206]

More than three decades later, Queen Elizabeth II and Prince Charles were ambassadors for reconciliation with Ireland, seeking to achieve for Britain what its politicians could not do: heal imperial wounds. In 2011 the queen, during a four-day visit to Ireland, shook hands with the former IRA commander Martin McGuinness, Sinn Féin's deputy first minister of Northern Ireland. *The Guardian* recently reported that at the time this "was hailed as a highly significant step" toward rapprochement. Four years later Charles made a similar conciliatory gesture, shaking hands with Sinn Féin president Gerry Adams in Galway. After a ten-minute private conversation, Adams emerged saying there had been "a meeting of minds. . . . Both he and we expressed our regret for what had happened from 1968 onwards. We were of a common mind. Thankfully all of that is behind us. The war is over."[207]

One just has to glance at the work of Nobel laureates hailing from the former empire, Tagore and Yeats among them, to read complex accounts of suffering and resilience that challenged the civilizing ideals of Churchill and Kipling, who too had been feted in Stockholm. Memoirs and local histories from those who lived through colonial rule accompanied other literary contributions, while the field of postcolonial studies, initially grounded in works from South Asia, challenged the British imperial narrative that stretched back to the eras of Seeley and Hastings. So did the writings of Stuart Hall, the Jamaican-born scholar-activist who co-founded in 1960 the influential *New Left Review*, as well as the field of British cultural studies, and who, after his death in 2014, was hailed as "one of the most influential intellectuals of the last sixty years."[208] In Africa, Josiah Mwangi Kariuki's memoir, *"Mau Mau" Detainee* (1963) and Ngũgĩ wa Thiong'o's *Weep Not, Child* (1964), the first novel by an East African to be published in English, offered firsthand accounts of suffering during Kenya's state of emergency.[209]

Wole Soyinka receiving the Nobel Prize in Literature, Stockholm, 1986

In North Africa, Frantz Fanon's *The Wretched of the Earth* was a seismic intervention into colonial hagiography when published in 1961. "The colonized must be made to see that colonialism never gives away anything for nothing," he wrote. "Whatever gains the colonized make through armed or political struggle, they are not the result of the colonizer's good will or goodness of heart but to the fact that he can no longer postpone such concessions."[210]

West Africa brought the world Wole Soyinka who, in December 1986, became the first African to receive the Nobel Prize in Literature. Standing before an audience in Stockholm in a stunning beige-and-white-striped dashiki, Soyinka was well aware of the moment's historic meaning. A Yoruba man born at the high noon of Britain's empire, he was free to offer a lecture on any topic of his choosing. His address was titled "This Past Must Address Its Present," signaling he would be dealing with history's injunctions. A shock of gray hair animated his resonant baritone voice as he began with a brief dedication to Nelson Mandela who, for over twenty years, was incarcerated on Robben Island in South

Africa, where he remained. Soyinka knew better than anyone the significance not only of his words but also of where he chose to start his story. After framing his thoughts on the world's most famous prisoner, he could have gestured to his Nigerian homeland or to countless other parts of the continent across the twentieth century. Instead, he turned to Kenya and the Hola Massacre.

For Soyinka, the story was personal. As a young, aspiring writer and actor, he lived in late 1950s London, where he was part of an improvisation group at the Royal Court Theatre. He recounted to his Stockholm audience that after singing some traditional songs, he refused to take the stage—in spite of the efforts of Black South African actor Bloke Modisane to physically pull him into the scene—when the thespians were reenacting the beating deaths that had taken place in Kenya's detention camp. The struggle between the two men had unfolded in plain view of the audience. It was something Africa's first Nobel laureate remembered "vividly," and thirty years later he felt it necessary to explain himself.[211]

Soyinka said the Hola production in front of London's white audience gave off "a strong odour of perenniality, that feeling of 'I have been here before.' 'I have been a witness to this.' 'The past enacts its presence.'" "In such an instance," he told Stockholm's mostly white crowd, "that sense of perenniality can serve . . . that audience, every death of a freedom fighter was a notch on a gun, the death of a fiend, an animal, a bestial mutant, not the martyrdom of a patriot," much as Mandela's passage in apartheid's isolated cell continued to feed the sands of white imperialism's hourglass. He then punctuated his memory's muse—inscribed as it was with Enoch Powell's self-serving calls for accountability, and the "liberals, humanitarians and reformists [who] had taken up the cause of justice for the victims"—with a final exhortation:

> This profound unease, which paralysed my creative will . . . I traced its roots to my own feelings of assaulted humanity, and its clamour for a different form of response. It provoked a feeling of indecency about the presentation, rather like the deformed arm of a leper which is thrust at the healthy to provoke a charitable sentiment. This, I believe, was the cause of that intangible, but totally visceral rejection which thwarted the demand of my calling, rendered it inadequate and mocked the empathy of my colleagues. It was as if the inhuman totality, of which that scene was a mere fragment, was saying to us: Kindly keep your comfortable sentiment to yourselves.[212]

At that moment and in that place, Soyinka reminded the world of liberal imperialism's deftness—of its ability to obliterate with an "inhuman totality" not only the men at Hola but also a young Nigerian man's ability to express the inexpressible.

Literature, though, has always had a way of begetting new narratives that illuminate the past when others choose to cleave to those that they themselves have helped to shape. Whether through prose or visual and performance culture, the creative arts have invariably been several steps ahead of historians in giving voice to silences and reminding the world that alternative narratives lie buried beneath the rubble of power. Soyinka's Nobel speech was a testament to just that as he took aim not only at liberal imperialism's past but also at the ways it continued to shape the present. His 1963 play, *A Dance of the Forests*, is one example of many that expose through allegory the culture of deceit and repression that infused Britain's colonies and carried over into independence. In it the "illustrious ancestor[s]" are called on to celebrate Nigerian independence but "instead of being the idealized figures of the tribal imagination . . . [they] turn out to be full of ancient bitterness and resentment and are shunned by everyone as 'obscenities.'"[213] As the living meet the venerated dead, Soyinka points to the continuities between the past and present as well as to an independence era, where many of the same methods of repression would punctuate postcolonial regimes not only in Nigeria but also throughout the former British Empire.

Such continuities were grounded in law. Colonial independence was enacted through British statutes, and despite the recurring fanfares and dramatic midnight ceremonies, it did not signal a shift in postcolonial states' legal regimes. Indeed, Britain bequeathed its colonial Leviathan—a state with laws, bureaucracies, and institutions—and would continue to shape nearly a quarter of the modern world. This Leviathan, to invoke Thomas Hobbes's iconic seventeenth-century work on the state, had been foisted on colonial populations. Postcolonial states, like their predecessors, continued to protect their sovereignty through a monopoly over the legitimate use of violence, invoking old laws and making new ones in order to defend against existential threats. Such threats often came from the same nationalist movements that had demanded independent state sovereignty—movements that were often fractured because of colonial policies, like divide and rule and loyalist-reward schemes enacted under extreme and often brutal conditions. We have seen this repeatedly in Britain's empire, in India, Ireland, Palestine, Malaya, Kenya, and Cyprus, where subject populations rarely recognized the colonial state's legitimacy, save for a handful of indigenous elites who found opportunities in imperial rule. Postcolonial states struggled to forge national unity, particularly when divisions between and among different ethnic, religious, and cultural groups remained, and fictive narratives like "We all fought for freedom" and *"Harambee"* were used to paper over historically embedded wounds from the colonial era. The historian Basil Davidson has aptly called these legacies "the Curse of the Nation-state."[214]

Such a curse is one reason why Soyinka foresaw postcolonial repression in Nigeria and, as I said, why Jomo Kenyatta was able to deploy many of the same emergency regulations, including the Preservation of the Public Security Act, that were part of Britain's colonial regime. Outside Africa, other new states followed similar patterns. The India Independence Act of 1947, for instance, provided Pakistan and India with the constitutional framework from the Government of India Act of 1935 until each new state created its own constitution. In Pakistan, where no new constitution had been enacted seven years after independence, Iskander Mirza presided as governor-general over a postcolonial state that still looked to the British precedent of "necessity" to guide legal decision making. In 1956 a new constitution rendered Mirza the first Pakistani president ruling over an Islamic Republic that retained the right to detain without trial on a permanent basis. Two years later Pakistan's military staged a coup, declared martial law, and ousted Mirza. General Muhammad Ayub Khan took over, justifying his move using Britain's precedent of the "law of state necessity."[215]

In India's case, Nehru, while conceding to "fundamental constitutional rights," still advocated for emergency provisions like administrative detention in Article 22 of India's constitution. This was later widened in scope through the adoption of the Preventive Detention Act, the Defence of India Act, the Defence of India Rules, and the Maintenance of Internal Security Act, all of which, according to the legal historian Simpson, "reproduced the 1939 Defence of India Act and the wartime British emergency code."[216] Article 352 of India's constitution also permitted a state of emergency, which Prime Minister Indira Gandhi (daughter of Nehru and no relation to Mahatma Gandhi) declared in June 1975, claiming threats to national security coming from internal strikes and protests against her government's economic policies. For two years she ruled by decree, locked up political opponents, suspended civil liberties, and censored the press. Similar constitutional provisions and regulations unfolded throughout Britain's former empire: Israel's Knesset deployed British emergency regulations principally against Arabs under the Law and Administration Ordinance of 1948, Ghana passed the Preventive Detention Act of 1958, Malaysia adopted the Internal Security Act of 1960 and the Emergency (Public Order and Prevention of Crime) Ordinance, and Singaporean officials enacted administrative detention under Part XII of their constitution.[217]

The impact of Pax Britannica's past extends well beyond a cataloguing of draconian regulations and constitutions trumpeting law-and-order regimes. We must "leave the dead some room to dance," as Soyinka suggests, if the complexities of the past are to be fully understood. Glimpses at such a macabre performance, however, are jarring to present-day sensibilities of those reaping the benefits of power that are steeped in such tragic history. We must not turn away from this complicated dance but instead, as I have sought to do, center liberal imperialism's state-directed violence on its stage to see how and why Britain's empire helped shape the modern world.

Empire Comes Home

On a brilliant April morning in 2011, five elderly Kikuyu stood on the front steps of London's Royal Courts of Justice before a phalanx of journalists, cameramen, and photographers jostling for images for the evening news and the next day's dailies. Dressed in their Sunday best with octogenarian faces betraying years of rural labor, the two women and three men—Jane Muthoni Mara, Susan Ngondi, Ndiku Mutua, Paulo Nzili, and Wambugu wa Nyingi—looked nonplussed as a steady, buzzing whirl of camera shutters filled the air. Standing in silence, they held the placards that reflected their interior thoughts and the demands they were bringing to the court and the British public. The messages were carefully spelled out in bold letters and left little doubt as to the issues at stake: PAY UP FOR THE BRITISH GULAG IN KENYA, JUSTICE NOW FOR THE MAU MAU VICTIMS OF TORTURE!, and HUMAN RIGHTS FOR ALL.[1]

It was a scene that surely no one imagined when ground was broken for the Royal Courts in 1873. Over the decade that followed, the architect George Edmund Street's vision of imposing gothic splendor rose from central London's six-acre site, where 450 houses had been leveled to make way for Britain's edifice to justice. When it was completed, breathtaking stained-glass windows framed the courts' towering Central Hall, and its mosaic marble floor reverberated with whispered echoes from the inner chamber. Coats of arms accented its medievally inspired interior, while outer porch carvings paid homage to Jesus and Moses alongside some of Britain's most distinguished arbiters of justice.

Mau Mau claimants outside the Royal Courts of Justice, London, April 7, 2011

Queen Victoria herself had opened the Royal Courts in 1882, where her presence—five years after she ascended as Empress of India—generated much fanfare and put a monarchical imprint on the physical testament to Britain's commitment to the rule of law. Over one hundred years later, this very commitment and Victorian-era principles hung in the balance as the empire's former subjects filed suit against Her Majesty's government. Having submitted their initial pleading in June 2009, Ndiku Mutua and four other claimants alleged systematic torture and abuse at the hands of British colonial agents in the detention camps and villages built during the declared emergency in Kenya from 1952 to 1960; they sought to recover more than £300,000 in damages as well as an amount for "pain, suffering and loss of amenity."[2]

It would be the first time since the late eighteenth century and Warren Hastings's impeachment trial that the British Empire spent years in a metropolitan dock. Much as in the Hastings case, questions about accountability would be front and center, though this time not on Parliament's floor but rather behind the imposing iron gates that separated the Royal Courts from the pedestrian hum outside. Still, histories that chronicled Hastings's acquittal and the dawn of the Victorian era helped frame the legal arguments that propelled the Mau Mau claimants through their case. Just as the White Man's Burden had been a ubiquitous presence in the heyday of the empire and had remained a driving force over Britain's imperial map well into the 1950s, so too did its penumbra linger on that shining April morning in 2011, even if disguised in an updated lexicon.

In Britain's twenty-first-century Royal Courts of Justice, Kipling's now-unfashionable phrase gave way to another, "duty of care." Questions at the center of the case struck at the heart of Britain's colonial legacy: Had the British government upheld its common law "duty of care" in Kenya during the Mau Mau Emergency, or had it failed? And if "duty of care" had been breached, who was to blame? Had it been those "acting in right of Kenya" or those "acting in right of Britain," or both? Britain's usual defenses against abuses in the empire—they were isolated occurrences and entirely due to the rogue behavior of "bad apples"— were also contested. Had officials "acting in right of Britain" been actively complicit in creating and maintaining a "system" and command structure "under which the claimants had been mistreated"?[3] To answer these queries, the Mau Mau case interrogated long-held truths and unveiled new ones over a tumultuous four years of witness statements and testimonies, document requests and discoveries, and countless legal maneuverings. Along the way, the five elderly claimants from Kenya's rural highlands stirred the strategic amnesia of the British government, as well as its archives, rendering the courtroom an arbiter of the past and an uncomfortable Nietzschean "gravedigger of the present."[4]

As the Mau Mau trial was poised to examine liberal imperialism's underbelly, it exposed an aspect of empire forgotten in many British corners. By the time Britain gathered its defenses against the charges of systematized violence in colonial Kenya, the empire no longer existed in its physical state, save for a handful of territories, though its memory remained immortalized in multiple forms, including Britain's urban architecture, the textbooks of its schoolchildren, and the rhetorical gestures of politicians on all sides of the ideological divide. Occasionally after a day's proceedings, the claimants would pass by monuments to, and statues of, the empire's heroes—Clive, Wingate, Montgomery, Kitchener. London's built environment evoked centuries of racialized hierarchies and Britain's alleged benevolent role in governing millions of those who, like the claimants, had ostensibly been unable to govern themselves. Had the five elderly Kikuyus toured south of the Thames, they would have meandered through streets with such names as Cabul and Candahar, the yesteryear spellings and reminders of the Second Afghan War in the nineteenth century. Cities including Liverpool and

Liverpool Town Hall, Water Street, Liverpool

Bristol had been built on the trade of enslaved peoples and the empire's consumable goods. Had the claimants visited Liverpool's Town Hall, its architectural friezes—accented by crocodiles, elephants, and exaggerated African visages—would have gazed down on them as they did on a nation whose queen still symbolically presided over former imperial possessions, Kenya among them, now contained within the Commonwealth.[5]

Queen Elizabeth II held a conflicted place in the hearts and minds of the Mau Mau claimants. Buckingham Palace was their preferred drive-by on their tour of London, as they wanted to pay homage to the silver-haired aged queen, even if they had not been invited to greet her personally. Queen Elizabeth II had first mourned her father on Kenya's sacred soil, and her youthful image had long ago hung in the detention camps of Kenya's colonial Pipeline, where British officials urged detainees to recognize her and the monarchy as their symbolic and benevolent rulers. In the minds of the claimants, it was to this same monarch that they were now appealing for justice long denied—a monarch who had once presided over one of the largest empires in the world's history. Now, the realities of its legalized lawlessness and police states threatened the very myths that perpetuated Britain's imperial ethos and threw into relief the kaleidoscopic changes to the nation's geopolitical, economic, and military realities that unfolded in the 1950s.

For decades after the 1960s sweep of independence washed away much of Britain's remaining empire, the deeds of Terence Gavaghan and others remained under the radar of public scrutiny—that is, until Ndiku Mutua and the four other elderly claimants filed suit against Her Majesty's Government. Some fifty years after the events, and with so many witnesses either deceased or hampered by faulty memories, the case would largely succeed or fail based on the written historical evidence. The claimants' attorneys had had to marshal documents as they attempted through London's High Court to do what the European Court on Human Rights had failed to achieve: hold Britain accountable for torture in the empire.

Unlike the Cypriot and Northern Ireland claims, which were rooted in the European convention and involved one European government bringing an application against another, the High Court case was a common law tort claim, a massive personal injury case that charged Britain with breaching its common law "duty of care" and with creating and maintaining a "system" of abuse. The concept of "duty of care," an unintentional tort or negligence claim, is at the heart of English common law but is not a statute. Its modern formulation dates to 1932 and the case of *Donoghue v. Stevenson*, a liability proceeding over a ginger beer drink in Scotland that established the "neighbor principle": a person, according to the House of Lords' ruling, "must take reasonable care to avoid acts or omissions which [he or she] can reasonably foresee would be likely to injure [his or her] neighbor." This general principle formed the basis for the law of negligence. The *Caparo v. Dickman* case in 1990 updated it when the House of Lords ruled that three principles must be met to establish whether a party—which in the case of the Mau Mau claimants was the British government—had "duty of care": the harm is reasonably foreseeable; the relationship between the parties is "proximate"; and it is fair, just, and reasonable to impose a duty of care. In contrast, the claimants' allegation that the British government was willfully and actively complicit in the creation and maintenance of a "system" of abuse was an intentional tort claim.[6]

That the claimants had been able to file their case in 2009 hinged on changes in the ways history was being written. New interrogations into the ugly business of the empire interrupted the muse of forgetting and asked many once-evasive historians to confront colonial violence in ways that were discomforting. A barometer of that can be found in the

Terence Gavaghan

sometimes-hostile reception of the 2005 publication of two complementary books, my own *Imperial Reckoning*, which was the first full account of the detention camps and emergency villages in Kenya during the Mau Mau Emergency, and David Anderson's *Histories of the Hanged*, which investigated the capital crime cases during the insurgency. In the case of *Imperial Reckoning*, the evidence that eyewitnesses left behind, together with the interrogations in Parliament and the media from Castle and others, offered signposts to fragments in the official archives. I spent over ten years culling this evidence and reading it alongside, and against, memoirs by and interviews with former detainees and colonial officials. A history unfolded that challenged the official narrative, one that had been cultivated and guarded for nearly half a century.

Few purges, however vast, can rid archives of all incriminating evidence. In Kenya's case, two thick files of letters that detainees had written in the 1950s managed to escape the incinerators and landed in the Kenya National Archives. They offered account after account of abuse and begged the governor, the colonial secretary, MP Castle, and even Her Majesty the Queen to intervene.[7] As crucial as these letters were and are to reconstructing Kenya's past, it was a single file remaining in Britain's National Archives that opened the way to connecting the detainees' accounts of torture, rape, and murder to the British government's role in their systematic execution. This file contained the June 1957 correspondence between Governor Baring and Colonial Secretary Lennox-Boyd, which we saw in chapter 13 of this book. Together with accompanying telegrams and memoranda, it laid out the dilution technique, granted approval at the highest levels of governance for its use, and crafted legal coverage. It established a chain of evidence that connected officials in London to Kenya's systematic violence.[8] At the center of the correspondence was the colonial officer who had designed and executed the dilution technique on the ground, Terence Gavaghan, who, up until the time of *Imperial Reckoning*, had not made his way into written historical accounts of Mau Mau, save for his own two memoirs. This absence is also notable considering Gavaghan's participation in Oxbridge seminars and social hours, as well as the foreword to his second memoir written by a Cambridge professor, as we've seen.

Gavaghan, of course, had not acted alone. The usual argument of a few "bad apples" receded under the weight of the historical evidence, which London's High Court was poised to adjudicate.[9] It was a moment when revisionist history and its challenges to liberal imperialism's long-held myths had to withstand the scrutiny of the court's lens. Holding Britain's civilizing mission accountable allowed no room for subjectivity's purveying of doubt. Rather, something was a fact or an act, or it wasn't. Whatever dramas existed around history's crafting and the imperial wars accompanying it had no place in Justice Richard McCombe's courtroom. As the single judge adjudicating the case, he wanted to see and hear for himself the evidence that supported the extraordinary claims of the aged Kenyans who sat before him. To provide it, three historians were called in as experts: first myself, and then nearly two years later, Anderson, whose expertise was extrajudicial hangings during Mau Mau, and Huw Bennett, whose work investigated the British Army in Kenya. Together, our triumvirate had a combined expertise that we brought before the court in the form of written witness statements.

The Foreign and Commonwealth Office (FCO), the named defendant, twice sought to end the proceedings using a strike-out motion, which is similar to a motion for summary judgment in the U.S. legal system. Hiding behind legal procedure, its Queen's Counsel (QC) Robert Jay argued that all liability had transferred to the independent Kenya government in December 1963, and therefore the current British government was not responsible for events that took place during the colonial period and the case should be struck out. If the court did not agree, then, according to Jay, the claimants' case should be dismissed because it long exceeded the three-year statute of limitations, and it would be impossible for the British government to receive a fair trial some fifty years after the events in question. The claimants' legal team at Leigh Day, one of Britain's foremost human rights firms that took the case on a conditional fee basis, had not only to defend against these arguments but also to demonstrate that there was enough evidence for the court to adjudicate the case should McCombe's rulings open the way to a full trial.

The first strike-out hearing was set for April 2011, and prior to it each historian had to submit witness statements based on their research. In submissions to the court, we referenced all the archival documentation that was relevant to the claimants' case, though the witness statements were to be devoid of interpretation.[10] My first witness statement was thus an exercise in embedded argument. It pointed to hundreds of archival documents from Britain and Kenya that I had used in *Imperial Reckoning* and that were relevant for the court, as well as possible witnesses for the claimants. They included documents concerning Gavaghan, who was then living on his government pension in Putney in Southwest London, and retired general Frank Kitson. Both men did not give evidence as the FCO made the general statement that all living witnesses were far too old to provide reliable evidence. My witness statement did not include oral transcripts from my earlier research, though I referenced my work with oral testimonies, including those from Gavaghan, and the role they played in my revisionist reading of long-tilled evidence and new documents, including the June 1957 correspondence and detainee letters.[11]

In his fifty-eight-page "Approved Judgment," McCombe ruled on these findings. His ruling pointed to the fact that "the materials evidencing the continuing abuses in detention camps . . . are substantial, as is the evidence of the knowledge of both governments that they were happening and of the failure to take effective action to stop them."[12] With regard to the British government's claim that legal liability had passed to Kenya at the time of decolonization, the judge agreed that for British personnel, "acting in right of Kenya," liability for their alleged abuses in principle passed to the Kenyan state upon independence. However, the judge opened the door to the possibility of "vicarious liability," or the fact that the British government "holds joint liability" with the former "Colonial administration and individual perpetrators." Also, because the British counterinsurgency's command structure went through the British Army and the War Office, there was an arguable case that the British government, acting in "right of Britain," was also jointly liable for abuses. He further ruled that the British government could be held liable for authorizing the "system," or dilution technique, as outlined in the June 1957 correspondence, and that it could also be held "liable in negligence for breach of a common law duty of care." Justice McCombe ended his ruling with a meditation on the interrelated, civilizing mission themes of "honour" and "duty of care":

> That word honour . . . is what underlies the legal technicalities of this appeal. The use of torture is dishonourable. . . . When judicial torture was routine all over Europe, its rejection by the common law was a source of national pride and the admiration of enlightened foreign writers such as Voltaire and Beccaria. . . . It may well be thought strange, or perhaps even "dishonourable," that a legal system which will not in any circumstances admit into its proceedings evidence obtained by torture should yet refuse to entertain a claim . . . [of] government's allegedly negligent failure to prevent torture which it had the means to prevent, on the basis of a supposed absence of a duty of care.[13]

The production of historical evidence in the Mau Mau case was a two-way street. Just months prior to the 2011 hearing, the Foreign and Commonwealth Office made a stunning announcement. As a result of the claimants' persistent requests for document disclosure, the British government "discovered" an enormous cache of files in Hanslope Park, the fortress-like warehouse for top-secret government files, which included those from MI5 and MI6. Located in bucolic Buckinghamshire, Hanslope Park is also known as "spook central." The cache amounted to three hundred boxes of previously undisclosed documents that contained nearly fifteen hundred files that had been removed from Kenya on the eve of imperial retreat. The FCO also disclosed that, alongside the Kenya boxes, there were around 8,800 files from thirty-six other former British colonies that had been spirited away at the time of decolonization. In effect, these were the documents that had escaped the incinerators in Kenya, Malaya, and elsewhere and had been sent back to London where they were held under lock and key until the Mau Mau case legally forced them into the light.

Why the British government decided to disclose the documents' existence has been cause for much conjecture. There has been some speculation that, in the era of Wikileaks, which launched in 2006, possibly too many people on the inside knew about these files, and there may have been concern that if the FCO did not abide by the court's evidentiary rules, the documents might be leaked, exposing the British government's cover-up. Were that to have happened, the legal and public relations implications would have been enormous. There is another explanation, grounded in the rule of law: the FCO had to comply with their strict disclosure duties and it was pushed to do so by its legal team.

When the archival revelation was announced, it set off a media firestorm. Defending the British government, Jay told the High Court that "the existence of the repository [that] was discovered . . . no doubt caused embarrassment to my clients understandably."[14] He maintained that the handling of the documents was the result of administrative error and cost controls, and "as a result," he concluded, "the files relating to the former colonies have just been sitting in a corner and neglected."[15] In Parliament, Lord Howell of Guildford acknowledged the full extent of the archival find, arguing that "it was . . . general practice for the colonial Administration to transfer to the United Kingdom, in accordance with Colonial Office instructions, shortly before independence, selected documents held by the Governor which were not appropriate to hand on to successor Government." The contents of the repatriated files, Lord Howell promised, would be reviewed, and "those selected for permanent preservation will be transferred to the National Archives for the public to access."[16]

"This process of transparency is overdue, essential to upholding our moral authority as a nation, and in the long term interests of our country," Foreign Secretary William Hague insisted, assuring the public that a full disclosure process was under way and gesturing not only to the historical significance of the Hanslope discovery but also to its ethical meanings. He confirmed that mistakes with the Mau Mau files had been made. These files should have been "properly recorded and made available to the public," he conceded, though he also reiterated that there had been "no deliberate attempt to withhold information." Instead, the foreign secretary sought to capitalize on the moment as best he could, standing on a newfound moral high ground of full disclosure. "We are a government that believes in transparency and openness," he said. "We will release every part of every paper of interest, subject to any legal exemptions. This work will be overseen by a senior and independent figure appointed by me. The willingness to shine a light on our faults and to learn from our mistakes of the past is an enduring strength of British democracy."[17]

True to his word, the foreign secretary appointed Anthony Cary, former British high commissioner to Canada, to undertake an internal review of how and why colonial-era files had been out of public reach for decades, in violation of the Public Records Act of 1958. According to

Cary's final report, the British government was guilty of administrative mismanagement, as opposed to any kind of conspiratorial suppression of historical evidence. Lord Howell took it as nothing short of a vindication for the British government and "fully endorse[d] . . . [the] tribute" that Cary made toward the "professionalism and commitment of current FCO staff."[18] Hague then set his sights on releasing the long-held colonial-era files. He appointed the Cambridge professor of American history Anthony Badger as independent reviewer for the transfer of all end-of-empire documents—over a million pages—found at Hanslope Park to the National Archives at Kew.

The "migrated archives," as the FCO now termed the Hanslope documents, were set to travel to their final destination. Aside from those files exempted under the Freedom of Information Act—that is, those that posed a threat to national security or personal privacy—the government would make public everything it had uncovered at Hanslope Park.[19] In April 2012, the FCO released the first tranche of migrated archives to a media circus of its own making. Cameras zeroed in on the archival behemoth at Kew, reporters clamored to touch the newly released colonial-era documents, and headlines trumpeted the "secrets" emerging from the government's official records.[20] Foreign Secretary Hague's office fed the media frenzy and issued official news statements of its open-book approach to the document transfers; in total there would be six tranches of file releases, with the last making its way to Kew by the end of 2013.[21]

Badger said the discovery of the files in Hanslope Park placed the British government in an "embarrassing, scandalous" position, though he insisted "that the release of the migrated archives is a very conscientious and transparent process and that the Foreign Secretary's goal of releasing every paper of interest will be met."[22] Badger suggested that the documents told the story of the "banality of bureaucracy," or the day-to-day running of the empire, which was of historical value. But when reflecting on the migrated archives as a whole, he wrote, "I am not sure this is going to cast dramatic new light on the messy history of the transition to independence or provide 'smoking guns' on the nature of London's and the colonial governments' responsibilities for the dirty wars fought against nationalist insurgents or nail down government complicity in torture and atrocities."[23] In many ways, Badger's conclusions have since proved largely correct, as the migrated archives, once released in full, did not contain any "smoking guns" comparable to the June 1957 correspondence that had escaped censorship and landed in the National Archives in the 1990s. However, some documents do illuminate further the activities of on-the-ground colonial officials and the knowledge the British government had of them.

Issues surrounding document disclosure and secrecy were scarcely new to the British government. In some ways, the Mau Mau case and the Hanslope Park revelation present a textbook response from Her Majesty's bureaucracy. The first clue is the internal report that Hague commissioned, and Cary executed, to investigate how 8,800 files had gone missing for so long. Cary's findings are reminiscent of countless internal investigations that took place during the era of British imperial rule. Stopping short of being a full whitewash, the Cary Report expends much effort exonerating civil servants, repeatedly referring to lack of funds and understaffing, which doubtless hamstrung recent efforts, much as they did those of yesteryear's colonial servants. Yet the similarities in the processes of internal investigations and their whitewashing outcomes offer a window into the performative practices of British secrecy that continue to the present day.

So, too, does the recruitment of academic experts. The co-optation of official historians for sensitive topics like MI5's activities has a long tradition, and their recruitment was often part of a complicated story.[24] Some historians who were brought into the empire's propaganda fold during World War II were privy to the secrets of Ultra, the code used to crack Hitler's Enigma communications. The government later impressed on these historians not to betray official secrets and to offer up watered-down versions of wartime intelligence and its history. "The story of modern secret service offers us a clear warning," the British intelligence expert Richard Aldrich reminds us. "Governments are not only adept at hiding substantial secrets, they are quick to offer their own carefully packaged versions of the past . . . [creating] a concerted programme for the management of history equivalent to a wartime deception operation itself." Such a program included the indoctrination of official historians and "well-packaged programmes of document release"—programs much like the release of the migrated archives. When the British government occasionally opened select security service files, newspaper headlines proclaimed, "MI5 thrills historians with secret service archives." In reality, these document dumps were a kind of "good faith distraction material" with little real substance.[25]

Issues of document selection and destruction were center stage in Justice McCombe's courtroom. As the migrated archive drama played out in public, the Mau Mau case moved to its next phase: the strike-out hearing on statute of limitations slated for July 2012. To prepare, the claimants' historical experts had privileged access to a searchable database that contained all the Hanslope Disclosure documents that the FCO had released to the court. Along with a team of five Harvard students who collectively worked around the clock for nearly a year, I reviewed around thirty thousand pages, though the British government first culled the entire disclosure for sensitivity and perceived relevancy. The initial release offered thousands of pages of uncatalogued files, among them a treasure trove of documents that chronicled, for the first time, the document destruction process at the time of decolonization.

But there were many files that the FCO did not release, and a struggle ensued. My team and I compiled lists of documents we believed relevant to the case. The claimants' attorneys then pushed for their release in disclosure correspondence with the FCO's legal team, which was slow to respond and often handed the documents over in piecemeal fashion. Final witness statements, though, supported my previous findings with thousands of pages of new evidence. They also interrogated several end-of-empire questions that were relevant to the court and that have also long vexed historians.[26] Justice McCombe wanted further evidence to understand whether the government's "official mind" oversaw the creation and maintenance of systematized violence in Kenya, and to what degree the government was complicit in destroying and removing evidence at the time of decolonization. In its efforts to determine liability, the court, if the case went to full trial, would also have to parse out which colonial government failed in its duty of care—that in London and "acting in right of Britain," or that in Nairobi and "acting in right of Kenya." This was one of the key issues at the heart of the Mau Mau case: to what degree were the abuse and destruction of life and property part of a calculated and systematic British counterinsurgency policy in Kenya, and to what degree were colonial officials in London, "acting in right of Britain," implicated in these acts?

Such questions cut straight to the British colonial state and the ways it functioned. Indeed, as we've seen, the colonial state in Kenya was a state within a state. Its semiautonomous relationship to metropolitan rule created official actors in Nairobi and London whose authority waxed and waned depending on the circumstances. Put another way, London and Nairobi had a relationship of both unity and separation, and both sides strategically played up or down each aspect depending on the context. When the dilution technique was declared a success because Gavaghan broke the bottleneck of recalcitrant detainees in Kenya's Pipeline, for instance, he was awarded an OBE, promoted, and lauded publicly. But when the Hola Massacre became a scandal threatening the

Conservative government, Governor Baring flew to London to protect his men from scapegoating, while MP Enoch Powell sought to distance British officials in London from those in Kenya, whom Powell was more than willing to sacrifice if it meant maintaining what remained of Britain's benevolent image. Unquestionably, London's High Court and its questions reflected the difficulties that historians have encountered in defining the colonial state, its kaleidoscopic processes, and the lines of responsibility during crises.

When Justice McCombe convened his courtroom for the hearing on the statute of limitations, few anticipated the British government's next move. The first claimant to the stand was Jane Muthoni Mara. She recounted in heart-wrenching detail the torture she had endured, which included having a "glass soda bottle" inserted into her vagina, despite her "screaming and resisting and trying to wriggle and free myself from the men who were holding me down."[27] As her testimony concluded, few in the courtroom remained unmoved. Then it was the British government's turn to cross-examine. The government's new QC Guy Mansfield rose to his feet, paused for a moment, then announced—to audible gasps—that the FCO did not dispute her testimony. After each successive claimant gave testimony, Mansfield summarized the FCO's position. "The Government does not dispute that each of the claimants suffered torture and other ill treatment at the hands of the Colonial Administration," he said crisply and clearly to a silent judge and courtroom gallery. "I do not dispute that terrible things happened."[28] By this juncture in the case—a case that many jurists, politicians, and historians had dismissed as a pack of lies at worst and a moon shot at best—the evidence of systematic abuse, layered as it was with thousands of new pages of evidence, was overwhelming. Thus, the FCO concentrated on legal technicalities.

As it had in the eras of Winston Churchill and Enoch Powell, the British government looked to make a distinction between colonial officials who were "acting in right of Britain" from those rogue operators "acting in right of Kenya." According to Mansfield, the officials on the ground, men like Gavaghan, had acted independently not only in the Mau Mau detention camps, screening centers, and emergency villages but also in Nairobi's secret document culling sites on the eve of decolonization. For certain, Colonial Secretary Macleod had issued destruction orders, Mansfield argued. But Gavaghan and others took this operation much farther than officials "acting in right of Britain" had intended. As a result, nearly three and a half tons of documents went up in smoke, and those that couldn't be reduced to ash in the empire's incinerators were dumped into the Indian Ocean. Moreover, thanks to some of my work and that of the attorneys at Leigh Day, the claimants themselves had submitted pages of evidence supporting the British government's case that massive document destruction had taken place. How then, Mansfield asked, could his client be granted a fair trial, when Kenya's rogue operators had destroyed so much of the evidence—evidence that could potentially exonerate Her Majesty's government in this Mau Mau case?

Justice McCombe was visibly moved during the course of the second hearing, and the FCO's argument that it could not receive a fair hearing so long after the events was put to the test. The claimants' central burden in this hearing was to persuade the judge that the evidential picture was so rich that it was possible for a fair trial to take place. Working in the claimants' favor was not just their compelling witness testimonies. There were also the thousands of pages of additional Hanslope documents that had escaped the end-of-empire destruction process. These documents, when read along with evidence in *Imperial Reckoning* and *Histories of the Hanged*, demonstrated how information management had shaped the official files that had long been available to historians. For example, document destruction certificates from around the empire— likely tens of thousands of them, if not more—were sent to London, where they were to constitute part of the official record. Not a single one of these certificates, however, existed in the public domain until the release of the Hanslope documents. This was just one example of many that demonstrated the significance of the Hanslope "discovery" to the claimants' evidentiary needs in the context of the second hearing.

While challenges to the experts' revisionist histories unfolded outside the courtroom, no historian joined the side of the FCO in its defense— a defense that had to prove that historical accounts of *systematic* violence in colonial Kenya had existed prior to *Imperial Reckoning* and *Histories of the Hanged*. Had they existed, then the FCO could argue that knowledge of such systematic abuse was in the public domain prior to *Imperial Reckoning* and *Histories of the Hanged*, therefore compelling Justice McCombe not to waive statute of limitations because the claimants *could* have filed their case earlier. It was incumbent on the claimants to demonstrate that, because of the absence of academic research on the abuses and tortures of Mau Mau prior to *Imperial Reckoning* and *Histories of the Hanged*—an absence related to Britain's destruction and concealment of evidence— they could not have filed their claims until the publication of these works.

After three months of consideration, Justice McCombe rendered his verdict, once again producing a weighty "Approved Judgment." In it, he waived the statute of limitations, and opened the way for a "fair trial" in which the claims of "vicarious liability," negligence, and joint liability would be adjudicated. The British government now faced the possibility of a lengthy full trial over systematic abuses in front of a single judge who had, in the context of the first strike-out hearing, already admonished the FCO for a "dishonourable" defense on the matter of its "duty of care" in colonial Kenya. The FCO vowed to appeal, though behind the scenes it worked toward a settlement that broadened the number of claimants. The attorneys at Leigh Day—as well as those from the Kenya Human Rights Commission, who played a crucial role in liaising with the claimants in Kenya—interviewed around 15,000 individuals alleging abuse in the Mau Mau camps and villages, whereupon another 5,225 individuals joined the case.

When a settlement was reached and with its ink drying, Foreign Secretary Hague slowly rose to his feet in the House of Commons to tell his peers what Barbara Castle might well have thought unfathomable had she lived to witness the moment. "I would like to make a statement on a legal settlement that the Government have reached concerning the claims of Kenyan citizens who lived through the emergency period and the Mau Mau insurgency from October 1952 to December 1963," he began. He went on to cite the honorable sacrifices that "British personnel" had made in "difficult and dangerous circumstances" as a prelude to the admission at hand:

> I would like to make it clear now and for the first time on behalf of Her Majesty's Government that we understand the pain and grievance felt by those who were involved in the events of the emergency in Kenya. The British Government recognise that Kenyans were subject to torture and other forms of ill treatment at the hands of the colonial administration. The British Government sincerely regret that these abuses took place and that they marred Kenya's progress towards independence. Torture and ill treatment are abhorrent violations of human dignity, which we unreservedly condemn.[29]

As the foreign secretary delivered his statement to a muted House of Commons, Britain's high commissioner to Kenya, Christian Turner, sat among a much different sort of crowd. There, in the cavernous ballroom of Nairobi's Hilton Hotel, hundreds of the Mau Mau claimants gathered to celebrate their bittersweet victory. No sooner had Hague taken his seat back in London than Turner rose to read the same statement that his boss had entered into the parliamentary record—a statement that also confirmed Britain's financial payout of nearly £20 million

Christian Turner (right), British high commissioner to Kenya, at the unveiling of the memorial to victims of torture and ill-treatment by the British, Uhuru Park, Nairobi, September 12, 2015

in damages and legal costs and a commitment to build a memorial in Nairobi to commemorate "the victims of torture and ill treatment during the colonial era."[30]

That day in June 2013 brought a form of closure to the thousands of claimants. It also brought one to High Commissioner Turner. For him, the historic moment had a poignancy that transcended his official role:

> My personal part in this story is because my step-grandfather, Colonel Arthur Young, was Commissioner of Police in Kenya in 1954 and resigned over the colonial administration's failure to address brutality committed by the security forces. For him, and all those who suffered in the Emergency Period, I hope that we can ensure the UK-Kenya relationship continues to be based on mutual respect, partnership and shared interests, with links that benefit both our countries in a spirit of understanding, inclusivity and dignity.[31]

For the historians who served in the case, the story was not yet over. Their pending requests for undisclosed Hanslope documents remained unanswered. Historians would demand their release, along with count-less other files that remained hidden from public view, in the years ahead. For the original claimants like Wambugu wa Nyingi, though, such evi-dentiary battles no longer had much meaning. "I have brought this case because I want the world to know about the years I have lost and what was taken from a generation of Kenyans," he had told the court.

> If I could speak to the Queen I would say that Britain did many
> good things in Kenya but that they also did many bad things.
> The settlers took our land, they killed our people and they burnt
> down our houses. In the years before independence people were
> beaten, their land was stolen, women were raped, men were cas-
> trated and their children were killed. I do not hold her person-
> ally responsible but I would like the wrongs which were done to
> me and other Kenyans to be recognized by the British govern-
> ment so that I can die in peace.[32]

"I think we should celebrate much of our past rather than apologise for it," Gordon Brown had announced, "and we should talk, rightly so, about British values."[33] Brown had been Labour prime minister in 2009, when the Mau Mau claimants filed their suit, and his Conservative successor, David Cameron, picked up the age-old mantle of the empire, breath-ing life into Brown's early proclamation about celebrating Britain's past. His government's avowed determination to fight the High Court case to the bitter end wasn't surprising; nor was its broader attempts to shore up Britain's imperial legacy while an independent High Court judge was scrutinizing the empire in Kenya. Cameron's government wanted heroes of the empire stretching back to Clive of India to be secured in the nation's consciousness, and his education secretary, Michael Gove, assembled a committee of historians to ensure just that.

Among those offering input were Niall Ferguson, author of *Empire: How Britain Made the Modern World*. By 2010, Ferguson was a public intellectual of undeniable fame, shooting to prominence with his lec-tures and television appearances, including a widely viewed six-part documentary on the empire in which he pressed his view that "empire is more necessary in the twenty-first century than ever before" and that no nation offered a better model for it than Britain. His follow-up book, *Civilization: The West and the Rest*, provided six reasons why civilization is a Western phenomenon, including its enduring "rule of law."

Joining Ferguson was Andrew Roberts, also an unabashed imperialist whose book *A History of the English Speaking Peoples Since 1900* was a call to arms for white nations like Britain, the United States, and the original Commonwealth members: a "decent, honest, generous, fair-minded and self-sacrificing *imperium*," he argued, was "the last, best hope for Mankind."[34] "Imperialism," he declared, "is an idea whose time has come again."[35] Such affirmations of nationalist mythmaking in Britain's school curriculum met with fierce resistance from British historical organizations, including the Royal Historical Society. "Offensive and insulting," the historian Simon Schama said, and other deeply respected professionals like the Cambridge Regius professor of history Richard Evans concurred.[36] Gove was forced to backtrack, signaling a change in how history was being written in the academy, though questions remained as to whether such change affected schoolchildren. No longer was the government's Ministry of Information handing out patriotic primers and lesson plans for teachers, though the perpetuation of myths, with or without Gove's new curriculum, continued. "Some historians and politicians have criticised schools for failing to teach about the empire and in particular the achievements of empire," *The Guardian* reported in 2016. "Among them is the former education secretary, Michael Gove, who once complained that too much history teaching was informed by post-colonial guilt." In fact, according to the paper, a recent "study does not support the claim that students in English schools are not taught about the British empire. Neither does the testimony from teachers, text books and history education websites support the idea . . . that the British empire is taught in a negative and anti-British way."[37]

The four-year High Court case had received considerable news coverage with its revelations of systematic torture in the empire, the "discovery" of long-held secret files at Hanslope Park, Justice McCombe's rulings, and the British government's apology and £20 million payout. But it did little to change the views of Britons, outside a narrow range of actors. Nor did a successor case on systematic abuses in the empire usher in much change. Filed in 2015 by Cypriot survivors of British torture, the four-year-long case received scant media coverage, and when the British government quietly settled, paying out £1 million in damages, it barely made news.[38] There was a similar reaction in 2013 when journalist Ian Cobain broke the story of secret archival stashes that dwarfed those that had been discovered during the High Court case. The Ministry of Defence was withholding sixty-six thousand files and the FCO an additional 1.2 million files, occupying fifteen miles of floor-to-ceiling shelving, all in breach of the Public Records Act and effectively beyond the reach of the Freedom of Information Act. While such concealment of documents was big news to historians, the public cared little, and without a legal case compelling the British government to release its secret files, historians and journalists could do little to force these documents into public light.[39] What's clear is that government secrecy about the nation's past continued unimpeded, and Ferguson and Roberts were in step with much of popular British sentiment. In 2014, when Britons were asked whether "the British Empire was something to be proud of," nearly 60 percent of respondents agreed it was.[40]

Such sentiments existed long before the Mau Mau case and helped to propel Nigel Farage, leader of the United Kingdom Independent Party, to an influential role in British politics. Farage represents populist views in Britain, including imperial nationalism, Euroskepticism, and opposition to immigration, often taking them to the airwaves. In 2012 he and I debated on Britain's Channel 4 News the significance of the High Court case and the British government's admission of the use of torture during the Mau Mau Emergency. Assuming a Churchill- and Powell-like stance, he acknowledged "we got things wrong, and we did things very badly" in Kenya:

> *but*, the difficulty is, beyond issuing a full apology, the thought that we should launch upon a series of trials that could go on forever, you know, evidence that is given in court six decades after the alleged atrocities is very unreliable. . . . Just look at what the Belgians did in the Congo and every other European power in Africa. We all did things in the past that we now would think were absolutely wrong, we should hold our hands up, say we're sorry, but for the British to have this launch upon a series of legal cases like this, frankly, is a waste of time and money.[41]

It is time to look forward, Farage argued. He then turned to the debate's overarching theme: Were today's Britons responsible for every infraction in the empire, particularly when balanced against all the good their forebears had spread through the world? His answer was no.

Farage's deft defensiveness drew on a much deeper wellspring of populist ideas that had been circulating in Britain for decades. We must look at the connections between liberal imperialism and ideas about race and belonging in Britain to see how and why the empire's legacies have manifested themselves in British conceptions of the nation. Indeed, Farage is a product of history, and we can see him as Britain's contemporary iteration of Enoch Powell, whose 1968 "Rivers of Blood" speech catapulted him into the annals of Britain's racialized history. In 1959 during the Hola debate, Powell had famously spoken of the "way in which Englishmen act" in colonial Kenya; in his "Rivers of Blood" address, he referred casually to the "wide-grinning piccaninnies" who were shading Britain black when they immigrated there after decolonization. He spoke of the "supreme function of statesmanship . . . to provide against preventable evils," then ventriloquized his sentiments through those of his constituents. One of these constituents, Powell recalled, told him, "If I had the money to go, I wouldn't stay in this country. . . . In this country in 15 or 20 years' time the black man will have the whip hand over the white man." Stoking the fires of racist and immigrant fears befalling Britain, the Conservative MP decried the "annual inflow of some 50,000 dependants," which was "like watching a nation busily engaged in heaping up its own funeral pyre." Powell's ominous coda, using an historical analogy drawn from Virgil's *Aeneid*, was what gave the speech its title. "As I look ahead, I am filled with foreboding," he impressed on his audience. "Like the Roman, I seem to see 'the River Tiber foaming with much blood.'"[42] London dockworkers soon took to the streets under banners that made clear where they stood: "Back Britain, Not Black Britain." An opinion poll charting Powell's evisceration of "coloured" immigrants found that nearly 75 percent of Britons supported it. The nation swept the Conservative Party into a general election victory in June 1970.

Powell tapped into a visceral anti-immigrant and racialized culture that had been long metastasizing in Britain. "Most Britons, irrespective of social status, display an added aversion to peoples of darker skin," George Padmore had written, his typewriter steaming, in 1938. "It is this racial egotism and national arrogance which has created a conflict between the British and the coloured peoples of the Empire, which will render a social reconciliation between them extremely difficult even after a political and economic adjustment has been effected." Recall that during the interwar years, leading Black radicals like Padmore and C. L. R. James had lived in Britain, where they experienced the nation's racial climate and color bar laws, which remained in force until the 1960s. "The Colour Bar in Britain is certainly creating much anti-British feeling among colonial intellectuals and students," Padmore warned. "It has helped to mould many a future anti-imperialist leader of the coloured peoples. The British people are creating their own grave-diggers!"[43]

These prophecies would come home to Britain after the Second World War, when end-of-empire conflicts were not the only threats to liberal imperialism's "partnership" claims. Colonialism's reverse migra-

Enoch Powell

tion of brown and Black subjects began in earnest, famously signaled when the *Empire Windrush* docked at Tilbury on June 22, 1948, and deposited its human cargo of at least five hundred Jamaican migrants.[44] The 1948 British Nationality Act, as part of a strategy for maintaining empire, created a single form of citizenship for "the United Kingdom and Colonies," keeping the British immigration door open to people living in the colonies and independent Commonwealth states. As the immigration expert Ian Sanjay Patel tells us, the act was

> an important part of Britain's effort to ensure the Commonwealth remained an imperial project. . . . This was a legal structure that aimed to ensure that the citizenships of Commonwealth states would be forever linked in the imperial heartland of Britain. Despite the fact that Australia, Canada and India, among others, were now sovereign entities, the Act was designed to ensure imperial continuity in the post-war world. . . . The citizenship created in 1948 was the primary and topmost form of British nationality, and was often referred to simply as "British citizen-

Empire Windrush, transporting West Indian immigrants, on its arrival at Port of Tilbury, River Thames, June 22, 1948

ship" by British politicians. After 1948, a non-white person born in colonial Kenya or Jamaica had enjoyed identical citizenship, on equal terms, to Winston Churchill.[45]

The Commonwealth is "an equal partnership of nations and races" Elizabeth II proclaimed in her Christmas message broadcast from Auckland, New Zealand, in 1953.[46] But such royal sentiments and the Nationality Act legally backing them rested uncomfortably with ideas about the Commonwealth, which had always been imagined as a Greater Britain born from white settlement. So when migrants began arriving from the West Indies as well as South Asia and West Africa, politicians panicked over what was now called an "influx" of arrivals from the "New Commonwealth," the term for a postwar Black and brown imperial community as opposed to the white Anglo-Saxon one comprised of Canada, Australia, and New Zealand.[47] Liberal imperialism was now coming home to Britain, and a new White Man's Burden unfolded, marked by spectacular efforts, informal and formal, to maintain a British nation-state, gatekeep immigration, and ensure white citizenship rights in defense of sovereignty.

"Keep Britain White." Churchill considered that slogan for the 1955 general election, while his Labour predecessor, Attlee, had contemplated introducing immigration control for "coloured Commonwealth citizens" as early as 1951.[48] Churchill decided against such overt racism, though his message reflected the realities of London outside Downing Street. "No blacks, no Irish, no dogs" was a typical sign displayed in boardinghouse windows, while "Keep Britain White" was emblazoned on leaflets and plastered on walls across the city.[49] By the end of the 1950s the size of Britain's non-white population was 210,000, according to one study, including 115,000 West Indians and 25,000 West Africans, as well as 55,000 Indians and Pakistanis, and 15,000 from other territories. A chronic housing shortage wracked London, and Black renters were forced into its overcrowded slums, living in filthy and unsanitary conditions. Many of the Afro-Caribbean migrants crammed into tiny single rooms in Shepherd's Bush, Brixton, and Notting Hill, where "a new identity has been forged in the crucible of racist Britain," as the historian Winston James observes.[50]

The crucible's effects spilled into Britain's streets, where young white men, dressed in the Teddy Boy style of postwar poshness and galvanized by the White Defence League and other overtly racist organizations, were openly hostile to Black and brown communities. Simmering racial conflict erupted in late August 1958, when a white mob of three to four hundred descended on Notting Hill, attacked Black homes and persons, and incited two weeks of rioting, the worst racial violence Britain had ever seen on its own soil. The violence mushroomed as far as Paddington and Marylebone, reflecting a growing nationwide sentiment that "pictured [immigrants] as invading hordes who, with their peculiar practices and origins and predilection for crime and moral turpitude, would never be able to assimilate," as the sociologist Adrian Favell points out.[51] The Notting Hill events were a crucial time in Britain's domestic history of race. "Before the riots I was British—I was born under the Union Jack," one Notting Hill resident recalled. "But the race riots made me realise who I am and what I am. They turned me into a staunch Jamaican."[52] In the aftermath of the riots, there were dozens of arrests and prosecutions of both Blacks and whites, but senior police officers assured the govern-

Two boys dressed as characters from *The Black and White Minstrel Show*, Prestwood village, July 28, 1967

ment's home secretary that there had been little or no racial motivation behind the disturbances.[53]

It was into this context of rapidly deepening racial division, opposition to immigration, and open hostility directed at Black communities that news of atrocities in Kenya reached Britain in the 1950s. The street and communal violence reflected broader entwined sentiments about race, belonging, and the British Empire. The Cambridge history professor Richard Evans recalled the atmosphere of the times. As a child, he had learned to read from *Little Black Sambo*, a primer about a Tamil boy and his parents, Black Mumbo and Black Jumbo, and he had played with free miniature "golliwogs," which were given out as part of Robinson's Golden Shred marmalade's marketing campaign. Another racist characterization of Blacks much like pickaninnies and minstrels, golliwogs were rag dolls with jet black skin, exaggerated white eyes, thick red lips, and frizzy, wildlike hair. In the late 1950s, Evans's family bought a television set and tuned into *The Black and White Minstrel Show* weekly when white singers, in blackface, delivered performances with "stereotypical 'black' gestures, body movements and Al Jolson accents." "I listened to my parents arguing with one of their schoolteacher friends," Evans lamented, "over whether black people were further down the scale of evolution than whites, located somewhere in the vicinity of the apes, as their friend maintained, or perhaps a bit higher up."[54]

Were such attitudes typical of postwar Britain? Certainly some felt otherwise, but much like voices protesting abuse in the empire, they were a minority. "Unthinking racism was woven into the fabric of everyday life in Britain through the Fifties," Evans suggests, "accepted as part of the natural order of things for the great majority of white people." *The Black and White Minstrel Show*'s success offers one barometer of such everyday racism. The television program launched as a regular series in 1958 and quickly became one of the BBC's biggest hits. In the 1960s it had weekly audiences nearing 16 million viewers and won the prestigious Golden Rose of Montreux in 1961. The program was on the air for twenty years, despite calls from the Campaign Against Racial Discrimination to terminate it. The head of BBC's publicity routinely turned to the letters page of the *Daily Mail* to gauge public opinion and determined that "the programme was not racially offensive." The BBC's director-general, Hugh Greene, concurred, stating that "no further action was necessary."[55]

It's not at all surprising, therefore, that when news broke over atrocities in Kenya and other parts of the empire, it was met largely with indifference or approval, a necessary part of Pax Britannica. There was plenty of information in news reports and parliamentary debates to suggest these incidents weren't a series of one-offs, even if the full extent of the violence and cover-ups remained hidden. The British government's doublethink was powerful, and its audience was well primed. Nearly a century of liberal imperial ideas reminded Britons, time and again, of their unique place atop civilization's scale and of the empire's need for a heavy hand to execute its civilizing mission. Indeed, as we've seen, insofar as Labour united over state-directed violence in the empire, it was during spectacular moments of exposure, as with Hola and Nyasaland's Devlin Report, when party leaders like Hugh Gaitskell, previously distanced from such matters, rallied around left-wing members like Barbara Castle as a way to bludgeon the Conservatives over their cover-ups. It was a difficult needle to thread, particularly since Labour was undeniably as responsible for the systematic deployment of violence in the empire as it was in its support, albeit less bellicose, for keeping Britain white when postwar migrations brought the empire home.

Immigration law rollbacks began in 1962 with the Commonwealth Immigrants Act, which was obviously intended to restrict "coloured immigration" into Britain.[56] It was spurred by populist racist views, to which successive Conservative and Labour governments responded. "If you want a nigger neighbour, vote Labour," was the campaign slogan that propelled one Conservative MP to a by-election victory in 1959.[57] At the time when Powell spoke of "Rivers of Blood" in 1968, giving voice to the nation's Black and brown spectral fears, Harold Wilson's Labour government was in power and further tightened immigration

Kenyan Asians demonstrating against the Commonwealth Immigrants Act at Nairobi airport, 1968

laws. By this point, Britain had witnessed the number of new non-white arrivals more than doubling between 1960 and 1962 as five hundred thousand migrants arrived in time to beat the 1962 Commonwealth Immigrants Act coming into effect. Despite this surge, which included a spike in South Asian arrivals, the number of non-whites constituted around 1 percent of Britain's overall population when the Commonwealth Immigrants Act of 1968 passed under Wilson's government.[58] This new immigration tightening targeted the Indian population who were fleeing to British safety from violent purges in East Africa, where racial conflict between African and South Asian communities was yet another legacy of British colonial divide and rule policies. Indeed, as Britain's most influential scholar of race, Paul Gilroy, points out, "Patriotism has taken the new racism beyond the grasp of the old distinction between left and right."[59] Such transcendence, however, was not new. As we have seen, party distinctions were often difficult to discern on imperial matters, whether "over there" or at home.

This through-line of racialized hierarchies and images of native savages threatening civilization had infused British culture for over a century; its consequences exploded when those migrating from the empire began disembarking near London in the postwar years. Powell didn't invent popular racism, but he deftly tapped into it with his defense of national sovereignty, opposition to immigration, Euroskepticism, and beliefs in the empire's enduring exceptionalism. When he said to BBC journalist Michael Cockerell "What's wrong with racism? Racism is the basis of nationality," he gave voice to Britain's not-so-silent majority.[60] "What do they know of England who only England know?" Powell queried on St. George's Day in 1961. The quote was from Kipling's poem, "The English Flag," in which the empire's jingoistic bard beckoned his countrymen to wrap themselves in the Union Jack fluttering across the nation and stretching to the shores of Britain's empire. Powell rooted his nationalism in Britain's exceptional past:

> For the unbroken life of the English nation over a thousand years and more is a phenomenon unique in history, the product of a specific set of circumstances like those which in biology are supposed to start by chance a new line of evolution. . . . From this continuous life of a united people in its island home spring, as from the soil of England, all that is peculiar in the gift and the achievements of the English nation. All its impact on the outer world in earlier colonies, in the later Pax Britannica, in government and lawgiving, in commerce and in thought

has flowed from impulses generated here. And this continuing life of England is symbolized and expressed, as by nothing else, by English kingship. . . . The danger is not always violence and force; them we have withstood before and can again. The peril can also be indifference and humbug, which might squander the accumulated wealth of tradition and devalue our sacred symbolism to achieve some cheap compromise or some evanescent purpose.[61]

If we compromise, Powell insisted, we will not "guard, as highly to honour, the parent stem of England." Black migrants threatened such legacy, as did closer union with Europe, which would, for Powell, snatch the nation's sovereignty and deprive the descendants of such imperial greatness of their destiny, a history of British exceptionalism thus far unbroken since time immemorial.

By the time Britain introduced the Immigration Act of 1971, under which Commonwealth citizens lost their automatic right to remain in Britain, the number of Britons born in the Caribbean had grown from 15,000 in 1951 to over 300,000. The act was a clear attempt to institutionalize a "two-tier" race-based immigration and citizenship system, introducing the term *patrial* and tying it to another new phrase, *right to abode*. That is, *patrial*, etymologically akin to *patriot*, denoted a British citizen who had been (or whose parents or grandparents had been) born, adopted, registered, or naturalized in Britain. *Patrial* also applied to anyone from a Commonwealth state with a parent born in Britain. *The Economist* called the patrial concept "a nasty bit of tribal jargon" as it clearly kept the immigration door open for white British "kith and kin" living abroad, while largely closing it to Blacks and browns seeking to reside in Britain. India's press decried the "use of racial criteria in determining [British immigration] priorities," and some British Labour party members were equally outraged, including House of Lords peer Baron (Charles) Royle. "There is the introduction of this word 'patrial,'" he fumed in Parliament. "I had never heard of this word . . . and even the Home Secretary himself said that he was not quite sure how to pronounce it. If the introduction of this word and the principle behind it is not discrimination, what on earth is discrimination?" The 1971 Act did more than discriminate based on lineage. It introduced compulsory police registration for immigrants, and empowered Britain's home secretary with sweeping deportation powers, facilitating the removal, without right to a trial or appeal, of any unwanted immigrant who threatened "national security." While Prime Minister Edward Heath's Conservative government introduced the act, when Labour returned to power in 1974 it did nothing to repeal a law that was the final in a series of acts that are, according to Patel, "the ultimate source of today's 'hostile environment' for immigrants."[62]

Such a move in 1971 was partly a response to the escalating racial violence pockmarking Britain. In Notting Hill, Frank Crichlow's Mangrove Restaurant, much like Padmore's Cranleigh Street living room in the 1930s, was the Black community's beating heart, where intellectuals like C. L. R. James and Lionel Morrison, artists such as Bob Marley and Nina Simone, and locals socialized and debated civil rights activism. Inspired by Malcolm X and Stokley Carmichael, Britain's Black Power movement was also rooted in the nation's past. Padmore died in 1959, but James had returned to Britain in 1953, where he lived on and off for the next thirty years before permanently residing in Brixton. His writings, *The Black Jacobins* included, were among the many that inspired Obi Egbuna, a Nigerian-born novelist, playwright, and activist, to pioneer Black Power in Britain and co-found the Universal Coloured People's Association in the late 1960s, whose cross-Atlantic connections were similar to Padmore's pan-Africanism during the interwar years.[63]

A hub of Black Power dissent and planning, the Mangrove was the

Notting Hill protest march, photograph in evidence for Mangrove Nine trial

target of repeated police raids. In the summer of 1970, locals protested, marching to a police station, where violence erupted, and dozens were arrested. Eventually nine defendants including Crichlow, known as the Mangrove Nine, were tried at the Old Bailey. The British government thought of charging the defendants with "incitement to racial hatred" under the Race Relations Act of 1965. Before it finally passed, the act was introduced multiple times between 1956 and 1964 by MP Fenner Brockway, who, you will recall, had been part of the parliamentary vanguard demanding self-determination, equity, and justice in the empire for decades, now turning its attention to similar issues at home. The act outlawed discrimination in "any place of public resort" and created the "incitement of racial hatred" offense, though it took another three years to outlaw discrimination in shops and boardinghouses, and enforcement was weak.[64]

Rather than charging the Mangrove Nine with inciting white hatred, the government charged them with less spurious offenses, including inciting a riot. The fifty-five-day trial became the "watershed" case, according to Ian Macdonald, who is considered the "Father of immigration law" and "a pioneer of anti-racist legal practice" in Britain.[65] Like Fenner Brockway and Barbara Castle, Macdonald was a Black and brown ally, lobbying for the Race Relations Act and enforcement through the Race Relations Board, while also helping the Mangrove Nine devise a legal strategy. Some of the accused defended themselves, refusing counsel like Macdonald's and turning Britain's cherished "rule of law" on its head. Much as Black Power activists in the United States cited the Fourteenth Amendment guaranteeing equal protection under the law, the Mangrove Nine insisted that such basic rights, including a trial by a jury of one's peers, in this case Black peers, were enshrined in the Magna Carta. The court dismissed their argument, though the Mangrove Nine succeeded, after rejecting sixty-three possible jurors, in empaneling two Black members of the twelve-person jury. The trial became a referendum on racial discrimination in Britain and the Metropolitan Police Force's role in it. The jury exonerated the nine of the main charges. The judge commented that the trial has "shown evidence of racial hatred on both sides," a remarkable statement at the time and the first instance of judicial acknowledgment of racial prejudice among the nation's police force.[66] "We learnt through experience how to confront the power of the court," Macdonald recalled, "because the defendants refused to play the role of 'victim' and rely on the so called 'expertise' of the lawyer. Once you recognise the defendant as a self-assertive human being, everything in the court has to change. The power and role of lawyers—the advocacy and the case preparation. . . . What all radical lawyers have to decide is whether they want to retain their slice of traditional lawyers cake or to participate in a bold new experience."[67]

It was hardly the dawn of a postracial era, however, and in Brixton in April 1981, a three-day riot erupted, another symptom of liberalism's perfidiousness in modern Britain. "It looked like a kind of war," local resident Ros Griffiths recalled. "The Brixton riot was a Brixton uprising. It was a watershed moment for race relations," igniting violent protests in other areas of London and across Britain.[68] In Brixton, the riot's immediate trigger was "Operation Swamp 81," so-named because of Prime Minister Thatcher's earlier comments: if certain immigrants kept coming to Britain "by the end of the century there would be four million people of the new Commonwealth or Pakistan here. . . . I think it means that people are really rather afraid that this country might be rather *swamped* by people with a different culture."[69] Operation Swamp 81 was a ten-day sweep of Brixton during which time 150 plainclothes police officers made over 1,000 stops and 150 arrests, enabled by "sus law," an age-old stop and search law permitting police to arrest suspects and secure their convictions based on suspicion of impending illegality. Lord Scarman, immediately commissioned by the government to investigate the Brixton events, published his report in November. "The evidence which I have received," he wrote,

> leaves no doubt in my mind that racial disadvantage is a fact of current British life. Urgent action is needed if it is not to become an endemic, ineradicable disease threatening the very survival of our society. . . . "Institutional racism" does not exist in Britain: but racial disadvantage and its nasty associate, racial discrimination, have not yet been eliminated. They poison minds and attitudes: they are, and so long as they remain will continue to be, a potent factor of unrest. . . . Good policing will be of no avail, unless we also tackle and eliminate basic flaws in our society.

Scarman offered a series of social welfare and policing recommendations, including making "racially prejudiced or discriminatory behaviour" a disciplinary offense for police officers. He continued to support, however, " 'hard' policing methods," which included "the power of stop and search," and the use of "water canon, CS gas [tear gas] and plastic bullets," which were a "necessity" in Scarman's view.[70]

In the same year as the Brixton Riot and *Scarman Report*, Britain passed a new British Nationality Act, which tethered citizenship to

Britain rather than the Commonwealth. After 1981, a British citizen was defined as "a person born in the United Kingdom" with a parent who was a British citizen. After decades of slowly dismantling the 1948 British Nationality Act through a series of discriminatory immigration acts, Britain finally conceded that British imperial citizenship, which had facilitated the arrival of hundreds of thousands of "coloured immigrants," was over. Addressing fears of the nation being "swamped," new British nationality law now spelled out clearly who "belonged" to Britain, jettisoning any pretense that Blacks and browns from the Commonwealth could really become British.[71]

Continued police profiling and harassment of Blacks throughout the 1980s culminated in the infamous case of Stephen Lawrence, the son of Jamaican parents, who was brutally murdered in April 1993 by white youths in a racially motivated attack. The incident and bungled trial of the offenders led to the MacPherson Inquiry, which produced a scathing report in 1999 pointing to many of Scarman's unimplemented reform suggestions and reciting the litany of police errors, from failing to provide Lawrence with first aid on the scene to failing to investigate suspects. Its most damning finding was that "institutional racism . . . exists both in the Metropolitan Police Service and in other Police Services and other institutions countrywide," and it made seventy recommendations for improvement.[72] While some inroads of change were subsequently made, they proved insufficient. Institutions like the police, as we have seen in case after case in the empire, are not hermetically sealed from the nation's broader racial attitudes and the state's self-protection against perceived existential threats; rather they are epiphenomena of them. Brutal police tactics, including the controversial death of Rashan Charles in 2017, and the routine stopping and searching of Blacks at a rate nineteen times that for whites, have not changed much since Lawrence's murder. "The Met police today looks and feels as racist as it was before Macpherson['s report]," Leroy Logan, former superintendent in the Metropolitan Police and chair of the Britain's Black Police Association, wrote in October 2020.[73]

Fifty years after "Rivers of Blood," Powellism is alive and well today, and his ideas of nation, sovereignty, purity of citizenship, and British exceptionalism underwrite the Conservative Party's platform, tangling Brexit, the empire, migrant workers "stealing" British jobs, and Britain's unique ability to go it alone, though there are changes afoot. Of the 64.6 million people living in Britain as of this writing, 56.2 million, or 87.2 percent, identify as "White." But in London's demographics, a minority 45 percent identify as white.[74] Sadiq Khan, a product of the

#WindrushDayOfAction protest, London, June 22, 2019

empire coming home after the Second World War, now serves as mayor of the nation's capital. Born into a working-class Sunni Muslim family in South London, Khan is the son of Pakistani immigrants. A highly respected attorney, Khan specialized in human rights and discrimination cases before entering Parliament in 2005. He became London's mayor in 2016 with 57 percent of the vote. A volte-face to his predecessor, Boris Johnson, Khan announced in June 2020, in response to Black Lives Matter protesters, a Commission for Diversity in the Public Realm to address statues and street names from a "bygone era." Some Britons were outraged, including the conservative Oxford theologian Nigel Biggar, whose "Ethics and Empire" project advocates for "the salutary effect of imposing a unifying, pacific, and law-abiding order on peoples otherwise inclined to war among themselves."[75] "The historical assumptions of the 'decolonisation' movement are very largely wrong," Biggar insists. "The 'decolonisation' of public statuary, therefore, amounts to the public triumph of a false historical narrative . . . to say that the truth of the narrative that prevails in public does not matter."[76] Removing statues, whether by force or by design, and replacing them with new ones doesn't create "a false historical narrative," however. Burning and concealing documents surely do, as does a turning away from the empire's state-directed violence.[77]

As imperial history wars continue to play out in academic circles, in the press, and in debates over empire's memorialization in public spaces, it's difficult to keep up with the drama. In 2018 Prime Minister Theresa May's Home Office oversaw detention, deprivation of legal rights, passport confiscations, and threats of deportation—making good on at least eighty-three of them—for thousands of British subjects who had arrived in Britain prior to 1973. Known as the Windrush generation, the Home Office had destroyed records of their legal immigration to Britain, leaving them undocumented and thus treating them as aliens who did not "belong to the territory," much as the colonial government had labeled Chinese "aliens" in 1950s Malaya.

The scandal of such blatant discriminatory policies erupted in 2018, followed not by an internal parliamentary inquiry like those for the empire, but by one conducted by an independent reviewer, Wendy Williams, a defense lawyer who also had two decades of experience in the Crown Prosecution Service. "The causes of the Windrush scandal can be traced back through successive rounds of policy and legislation about immigration and nationality from the 1960s onward, the aim of which was to restrict the eligibility of certain groups to live in the UK," she wrote in her March 2020 final report, "Windrush Lessons Learned Review." "Successive governments wanted to demonstrate that they were being tough on immigration by tightening immigration control and passing laws creating, and then expanding the hostile environment, this was done with a complete disregard for the Windrush generation." She then pointed to the Home Office's "operating environment." Offering mismanagement excuses and saying she was "unable to make a definitive finding of institutional racism within the department," she did offer "30 recommendations for change and improvement which can be boiled down to three elements: the Home Office must acknowledge the wrong which has been done; it must open itself up to greater external scrutiny; and it must change its culture to recognise that migration and wider Home Office policy is about people and, whatever its objective, should be rooted in humanity."[78]

The Home Office did offer up apologies but pushed through other immigration restrictions with Britain's exit from the European Union. Then another migrant issue arose, this one in Buckingham Palace. The union of Prince Harry and Meghan Markle in May 2018 was heralded as the start of a postracial era for the monarchy, long imbricated in Britain's imperial nationalist identity. Indeed, as the future Duchess of Sussex walked into Windsor Castle's St. George's Chapel, she carried the empire with her, the flowers from all fifty-three British Commonwealth nations delicately embroidered into her sixteen-foot-long wedding veil. As is well known, it took less than two years for such postracial dreams to shatter: the prince and the duchess broke with their official royal roles and decamped to the United States. When they sat down with Oprah Winfrey in early 2021, they shared painful stories of racism, including royal questioning of their son Archie's skin color before he was born. How would family portraits look, were they to depict little Prince Louis, the namesake of Louis Mountbatten, last viceroy of India and victim of the IRA's brutal assassination, sitting on the queen's one knee, and a potentially dark-skinned Archie, a descendant of Blacks who had possibly labored in the empire's fields and violently risen up against such conditions, balancing on the other? *The Irish Times*, long a thorn in Britain's imperial side, predicted how the whole affair would end: "Despite the tabloid frenzy, this was never the story of an ungrateful pauper being elevated by the monarchy. This was about the potential union of two great houses, the Windsors and Californian Celebrity. Only one of those things has a future, and it's the one with the Netflix deal."[79]

Racial discrimination and the empire's afterlife in Britain transcend the monarchy, as we know well by now. According to Prime Minister Johnson's government, however, Britain is an "open society" and "a model for other White-majority countries." This conclusion was highlighted in the Commission on Race and Ethnic Disparities' 2021 report. Constituted in the wake of Black Lives Matter protests in the spring of 2020, the commission was chaired by Tony Sewell, a British educational consultant and the son of Jamaican immigrants. While the report acknowledged the existence of some overt racism in Britain, and offered "distressing" data including homicide and COVID death rates that reflect a vastly disproportionate number of Blacks dying, it found no evidence "of systemic or institutional racism." Insofar as disparities between whites and members of the Black, Asian, and minority ethnic community exist, the commission was clear in its findings: "Put simply we no longer see a Britain where the system is deliberately rigged against ethnic minorities. The impediments and disparities do exist, they are varied, and ironically very few of them are directly to do with racism. Too often 'racism' is the catch-all explanation, and can be simply implicitly accepted rather than explicitly examined."[80]

How then to explain disparities in contemporary British society? Once again the issue was with those who were *not yet* fully evolved. Culture and religion were some of the scourges holding back Britain's minority communities, and according to the report, "there is much evidence to suggest . . . that different experiences of family life and structure can explain many disparities in education outcomes and crimes." What was needed to close the disparity gap was a "new period, which we [the commission] have described as the era of 'participation.'" Much as past liberal imperial regimes deployed terms like *trusteeship* and *partnership* to accommodate changing political circumstances, Johnson's commission predictably adopted the long-standing practice of drawing from liberalism's lexicon to, in the words of one of the report's many critics, create "government level gaslighting."[81]

"We want to create a teaching resource that looks at the influence of the UK, particularly during the Empire period," Sewell and his fellow commission members proclaimed. "We want to see how Britishness influenced the Commonwealth and local communities, and how the Commonwealth and local communities influenced what we now know as modern Britain." One might imagine the commission would have turned some of its attention to the legacies of the trade and labor of enslaved people, or perhaps of the state-directed violence that unfolded during the era of Pax Britannica. Instead, it continued the story of imperial progress and cleaved to developmentalism, with its myth that Black and brown people could ever *be* British. "There is a new story about the Caribbean experience," the commission tells us, "which speaks to the slave period not only being about profit and suffering but how culturally African people transformed themselves into a re-modelled African/Britain."[82]

Lest we forget, even before the Powellism-fueled rise of Nigel Farage and Boris Johnson, Tony Blair's "New Labour" regime had touted its own "new liberal imperialism" to contend with parts of the world that were *not yet* modern. Despite decades of colonial rule, largely under Pax Britannica, these nations were seemingly unable to stand on their own. At the start of the Iraq War in 2003, liberal imperialism, now an Anglo-American endeavor, had to adapt yet again, using the powers of coercion and reform. According to Blair's foreign policy adviser Robert Cooper:

> The challenge to the postmodern world is to get used to the idea of double standards. Among ourselves, we operate on the basis of laws and open cooperative security. But when dealing with more old-fashioned kinds of states outside the postmodern continent of Europe, we need to revert to the rougher methods of

an earlier era—force, pre-emptive attack, deception, whatever is necessary to deal with those who still live in the nineteenth century world of every state for itself. Among ourselves, we keep the law but when we are operating in the jungle, we must also use the laws of the jungle.[83]

Labour's "new liberal imperialism" was a stunning admission of the civilizing mission's failure to create a modern world, despite the official narrative, peddled for decades, of the empire's success. To square the circle, it framed disorder in the former empire as a result of children being allowed to walk too soon. Black and brown nations around the world had as yet not fully evolved, and so despotic rule, a necessary component of the liberal imperial framework since the nineteenth century, remained alive and well, even if formal empires were now unfashionable. "What form should intervention take?" Cooper asked, to which he replied:

> The most logical way to deal with chaos, and the one most employed in the past is colonisation. But colonisation is unacceptable to postmodern states (and, as it happens, to some modern states too). It is precisely because of the death of imperialism that we are seeing the emergence of the pre-modern world. Empire and imperialism are words that have become a form of abuse in the postmodern world. Today, there are no colonial powers willing to take on the job, though the opportunities, perhaps even the need for colonisation is as great as it ever was in the nineteenth century.

For the Blair administration, the answer was not a return to individual European empires but an embrace of the informal imperialism of the global economy, "operated by an international consortium . . . such as the IMF and World Bank," and the creation of an *über*-imperial structure. Western civilization would take over, as the European Union extended a new collective empire that would rule, police, and reform:

> The lightest of touches will be required from the centre; the "imperial bureaucracy" must be under control, accountable, and the servant, not the master, of the commonwealth. Such an institution must be as dedicated to liberty and democracy as its constituent parts. Like Rome, this commonwealth would provide its citizens with some of its laws, some coins and the occasional road.[84]

Prime Minister Blair urged the Americans to play their part. "[National] values and [national] interests merge," he told the Economic Club of Chicago. "If we can establish and spread the values of liberty, the rule of law, human rights, and an open society then that is in our national interests too. The spread of our values makes us safer."[85] Blair's foreign policy had deep connections to Britain's imperial past and the uneasy though enduring postwar Anglo-American alliance. In fact, he had long admired the Royal Institute of Foreign Affairs, known as Chatham House, which was the successor to the imperialist Round Table movement. Recall that the Round Table was consolidated during the interwar years under Lionel Curtis's leadership, populated by the self-proclaimed "great race patriot" Alfred Milner's "kindergarten" of public intellectuals, statesmen, and historians who helped craft British pro-imperial propaganda during the Second World War and espoused ideas of a British imperial federation, or the commonwealth of white dominions. Important for our story, during the interwar period Curtis also established Chatham House, with the monarch as its patron, and successfully incorporated his Round Table compatriots into it while working with American counterparts to raise the funding to create a sister organization in the United States, the Council on Foreign Relations.[86]

Together, these two organizations were, in the words of international politics expert Inderjeet Parmar, "founded on a racialised world-view based on Anglo-Saxon biological and cultural superiority," and some of their members influenced greatly Anglo-American policy formation in the postwar years.[87] At the start of the war in Iraq in 2003, many marveled that New Labour's Blair and the Republican George W. Bush united for a war where their troops deployed a twenty-first-century version of the British Empire's "hearts and minds" strategy. When looked at through the *longue durée* of liberal imperialism and the web of Anglo-American connections that transcended political affiliation, it should have come as little surprise.

Today liberal imperialism continues to hold sway, though the British government's configuration of white power clearly jettisons prospects for a federation of Western states. With the 2016 Brexit vote, the Conservatives, preferring to go it alone, prevailed by holding up Britain's mythologized past and targeting the forces undermining the nation's unique values and, with them, its glories and identity. "Take Back Control" was Brexit's enduring slogan, a control that Britain ostensibly lost when it integrated with Europe and opened its doors to the continent's immigrants, who further "polluted" the nation. Britain's Foreign and Commonwealth Office peddled "Empire 2.0" alongside Theresa May's delusions of a "Global Britain" conjured from the embers of the empire's postwar demise.[88] But old lessons die hard, if they are ever learned at all. When the international trade minister Liam Fox spoke of the Commonwealth as the panacea for a post-Brexit trade boost, he reflected the nation casting its fate, yet again, in the lair of imperial sentiments and Euroskepticism as opposed to economic empiricism.[89]

The same kind of control, and the dog whistles of populist racialized power that beckon it, have unfolded across the globe in various forms, whether they be in demands to go it alone, to privilege racial, ethnic, and religious majorities, or to Make America Great Again. Indeed, a "rule of law" similar to the one that underwrote events in Hola and elsewhere in the British Empire is clearly being deployed today in the language of "law and order" to justify crackdowns on dissent, be they repeated protests against racial injustice in Britain, or peaceful demonstrations challenging the invocation of colonial-era laws in Modi's India, or the repression of Blacks at the hands of police forces ostensibly there to "protect and serve." That edifices lending glory to liberalism's capacity to repress are being torn down around the world should come as no surprise. Reform is also inherent to the Janus-faced liberal project, though demands for statue removals and the renaming of streets, as important as they are, are but one of the larger issues at play. Those holding the keys to power rarely end systemic discrimination, enforce civil rights laws, or ensure equal opportunities. When these gatekeepers do yield, they dole out reform measures haltingly to those perceived as still "not yet" ready to stand on their own, while deportations, crackdowns, and incarcerations continue to punish society's alleged pollutants who threaten the natural order of things. As history has borne out over and over, those who have lived the experiences of liberalism's "inhuman totality" must demand universal rights and unfettered inclusion, sometimes peacefully and other times forcefully. Even then, that totality's ability to rear its head again, reinvented under another banner of reform, is an enduring feature of liberal states, as are demands for democracy's ever-elusive promise of universal dignity and equality.

Acknowledgments

It feels like a lifetime and then some since I embarked on this project, which grew in scope and complexity with each passing year. I tried, and failed, several times to wrestle it to the ground and to find my way into the narrative. It was after years of returning to more archives, reading within and across fields, amassing a database that required a new hard drive, and writing countless outlines that my friend and colleague Susan Pedersen told me I was falling down the hole of infinite regression. The only way to write this book was to start writing. She was right, and to her and countless others, I owe much gratitude for their input, support, advice, and friendship over the many years that it took to bring this project to press.

I'd like to start with my students. The greatest privilege of being at Harvard is working with, and learning from, incredible young people who are unafraid to ask hard questions. During the course of the High Court case, I put together an incredible research team of Harvard students: Erin Mosely, Will Grogan, Lili Pike, Kristen Roupenian, and Megan Shutzer. Together we had a nearly around-the-clock schedule for a year, and the data we generated were important not only to the case but also to my writing of this book. I am indebted to each of them for their perseverance, belief in the case, and willingness to travel to London, where we excavated the newly released migrated archives at the National Archives, Kew. While we collected enough data for several books, it is our enduring friendships that matter most.

Harvard classrooms have also been a laboratory for my ideas, and countless students have pushed me to examine and reexamine questions of violence and empire, liberalism and reform, and national cultures. I would like to offer particular gratitude to Sreemati Mitter, James Esdaile, Kirin Gupta, Panashe Chigumandzi, Iman Mohammed, Safia

Aidid, Nate Grau, Ariella Kahan, and Kirk McCleod. Both Sreemati and James went above and beyond, chasing down documents for me in foreign archives. Sreemati also led a research team of undergraduates at the Radcliffe Institute, transcribed countless hours of interviews, and never failed to challenge me to be sharper in my thinking and analyses. Special thanks as well to Mircea Raianu and Alissa Costello for their attention to detail and tireless efforts in helping me amass a virtual archive of documents, and to Ariella Kahan for superb work indexing my research on Cyprus and Aden.

My friends and colleagues at Harvard and beyond have equally sustained me and offered critical input and advice on numerous occasions. I am deeply grateful for Jean and John Comaroff's boundless generosity in reading draft chapters. They provided more intellectual sustenance and friendship than I could possibly have hoped for. Susan Pedersen has offered similar advice and constant friendship, reading draft chapters and offering crucial feedback, as have Waël Bayazid, Jacqueline Bhabha, Sugata Bose, Vincent Brown, Ian Cobain, Stephen Howe, Maya Jasanoff, Vikram Jayanti, Tarun Khanna, Liora Lazarus, Daniel Leader, William Roger Louis, Sreemati Mitter, Meg Rithmire, Priya Satia, and Robert Tignor. In the final stages of this book, I had the joy of being part of a writing group that was sustaining beyond measure. Karuna Mantena, Stephanie McCurry, Susan Pedersen, and Camille Robcis read several draft chapters and provided invaluable feedback that saved me from myself on many occasions. It has been a singular gift to be part of this group of fiercely smart and supportive women whose humor and kindness are matched only by their wisdom and generosity.

One of the many privileges of having been at Harvard for over twenty-five years has been forging friendships that both embrace and transcend the exchange of intellectual ideas. Jacqueline and Homi Bhabha, and their little boy, Django, have sustained me with their love, bountiful meals (Homi's curry is a gift from the heavens), and laughter. Larry Bobo and Marcy Morgan have the most extraordinary intellects, devotion to friendships, and side-splitting humor, all of which I can never get enough of. Evelynn Hammonds, my gratitude for your unwavering presence in my life; I will always be your wingman. Evelyn Higginbotham has taught me more about how to integrate scholarship with bravery, kindness, and gentle fierceness than I could ever put into practice. Many other colleagues deserve special thanks: Suzanne Blier, Emma Dench, Drew Faust, Marla Frederick, Henry Louis Gates Jr., Elizabeth Hinton, Jamaica Kincaid, Bill Kirby, Michèle Lamont, Jill Lepore, Mary Lewis, Sarah Lewis, George Mieu, Martha Minow, Diane

Paulus, Lisa Randall, Tommie Shelby, Diana Sorensen, Kirsten Weld, and Cornel West. To Cory Paulsen and Kimberly O'Hagan, my gratitude for your unyielding support in making my work possible, as well as to the formidable team at the Center for African Studies, particularly Margie Jenkins, Maggie Lopes, and Candace Lowe, whose kindness and tireless support have meant more than I can convey.

Over the past several years, I've had the privilege of teaching and working with colleagues at Harvard Business School who have welcomed me with extraordinary warmth and collegial and intellectual generosity. My time at the school has enriched this book immeasurably, pushing me to think about the connections between violence and monetary policy, marketing and imperial nationalism, and economic sentiment and empiricism. I would like to offer particular gratitude to Srikant Datar and Nitin Noria, as well as Juan Alcacar, Laura Alfaro, Jill Avery, Raj Choudhury, Robin Ely, Kristin Fabbe, Matts Fibiger, Frances Frei, Jan Hammond, Reshma Hussam, Tarun Khanna, Karim Lakhani, Kathleen McGinn, Karen Mills, Cynthia Montgomery, David Moss, Kristin Mugford, Tsedal Neeley, Mike Norton, Felix Oberholzer-Gee, Forest Reinhart, Meg Rithmire, Jan Rivkin, Len Schlessinger, Debora Spar, and Sandra Sucher. I would like to extend a special thanks to several other HBS colleagues whose tireless work made my ability to bring this book to completion possible: Jean Cunningham, Valerie Porciello, Rae Mucciarone, Ashley Dreimiller, and Joyce Kim, one of the most skilled researchers with whom I have had the pleasure of working. Joyce helped bring this book across the finish line, fact- and quote-checking, chasing down copyright clearances, and reading countless copy edits.

A special thanks as well to Saskia Pedersen, whose work on compiling this book's bibliography from the works cited was nothing short of heroic, as was Joyce Kim's in the bibliography's final stages. Simone Rivera and Juli Huss offered great assistance with interview transcriptions and indexing. Haya Al-Noaimi and Clara Natividada Martins Pereira kindly scanned documents for me at crucial moments.

I benefited greatly from fellowship years at the Radcliffe Institute for Advanced Study and the Hutchins Center for African and African American Research. At Radcliffe and beyond, Lizabeth Cohen offered her unyielding friendship, advice, and support, as did all my fellow colleagues. So, too, did the late Judith Vichniac and Lindy Hess, as well as Sharon Bromberg-Lin, Rebecca Haley, and Alison Ney. Radcliffe also supported a wonderful team of undergraduate research assistants to whom I am also most grateful: Meredith Baker, Katryna Cadle, Alissa Costello, Matthew Disler, Alyssa Leader, and Sharon Stovesky.

The Hutchins Center for African and African American Research created a home and sense of family as only the Hutchins Center can. My deepest gratitude to its team for their incredible friendship, unremitting humor, and support: Henry Louis Gates Jr., Abby Wolf, and Krishna Lewis. A special thanks to the most incredible fellowship class I could imagine. While my productivity level may have been lackluster at times, and the "busker" took much of the blame, it was really due to building friendships that are enduring, so much so that Steven Nelson has dibs on my shearling coat. To Steven, Franco Barchiesi, Devyn Spence Benson, David Bindman, Damon Burchell-Sajnani, Kerry Chance, Kathleen Cleaver, Gregg Hecimovich, Carrie Lambert-Beatty, Sarah Lewis, Xolela Mangcu, Kate Masur, Maria Carla Sanchez, and Maria Tatar, my affection and gratitude.

I offered various papers and early chapter drafts to colleagues who kindly invited me to their institutions to share ideas and offer feedback or who joined me in panels at various conferences. My sincerest thanks, in particular, to Sunil Amrith, Jordanna Bailkin, Leela Gandhi, Durba Gosh, Richard Hermer, Erik Linstrum, Liora Lazarus, William Roger Louis, Kristen Monroe, Philip Murphy, Susan Pennybacker, Ngũgĩ wa Thiong'o, and Stuart Ward; and to colleagues and participants at Brown University, Boston University, Davis Center (Princeton), Institute of Commonwealth Studies (London), Matrix Chambers (London), University of California (Irvine), University of Copenhagen, University of Nairobi, University of North Carolina (Chapel Hill), University of Texas (Austin), University of Toronto, University of Virginia, and the Wilson Center (Washington, D.C.). I am also grateful to the Radcliffe Institute for Advanced Study, Harvard Law School, and the Center for African Studies for their funding of exploratory seminars on archives, history, and the law, and to fellow participants for their insights, collegiality, and feedback: Jean and John Comaroff, Richard Drayton, Karl Hack, Liora Lazarus, Mahmood Mamdani, Martha Minow, Erin Mosely, and Kirsten Weld. These events were immensely generative for me, and in particular, my gratitude to Martha Minow, whose intervention on "facticity" came at precisely the right time, as did Richard Drayton's thinking about time (and myriad other topics), as have their support and friendship on numerous occasions.

Along with the institutes and organizations already mentioned, my sincerest thanks to the Guggenheim Foundation, the Social Science Research Council (Burkhardt Fellowship), the Weatherhead Center for International Affairs, and Harvard's Asia Center for their financial support, which allowed me to both write and undertake research in multiple geographies. Archivists across the world offered abundant knowledge, generosity, and patience with my many questions and requests, for which I am most grateful. They include those located at the National Archives (Kew), Bodleian Library (Oxford), School of Oriental and African Studies (London), Imperial War Museum (London), Royal Air Force Museum (Hendon), Middle East Center (Oxford), Widener Library (Harvard), Hoover Institution (Stanford), Arkib Negara Malaysia (Kuala Lumpur), National Archives of Singapore, EOKA Museum and Archives (Nicosia), Cyprus State Archives, Kenya National Archives, Macmillan Library (Nairobi), Avraham Harman Institute of Contemporary Jewry (Jerusalem), Haganah Historical Archives (Tel Aviv), and Israel State Archives (Jerusalem). My sincerest gratitude as well to the hundreds of individuals willing to speak with me and offer their testimonies and insights into their lived experiences in the former British Empire. I would also like to thank Ian Cobain, whose many journalistic interventions have been crucial, as have been his books and essays, to moving the field forward, and whose assistance with interview leads was a true gift, as have been his friendship and consummate collegiality. One of these leads was Petros Petrides, whose assistance in Cyprus was extraordinary, as was his kindness to and generosity with me and my family.

The Mau Mau case in London's High Court brought with it a team of human rights lawyers who inspired me beyond words. Their dedication to the claimants and to historical facts were boundless, and the years I spent working with them were transformative both professionally and personally. I offer my unyielding gratitude and admiration to Martyn Day, Richard Hermer, Phillippa Kaufmann, Sapna Malik, George Morara, David Roberts, Muthoni Wanyeki, and last but not least, Daniel Leader, who continues to inspire me with his dedication to the law and human rights, kindness, and friendship. My many social visits on both sides of the pond with Dan and Anneke van Woudenberg, and their daughter Olivia, have been sustaining and a wonderful legacy to our many years of work together on the case. The ultimate success of the case rested on the claimants' courage, which was, and continues to be, awe inspiring, as was John Nottingham's. John was a dear friend, colleague, co-conspirator, and mischief maker, whose impact on the Mau Mau field was immeasurable and whose presence I miss greatly.

Friends across the globe have opened their doors and hearts to me during my many research and lecture trips, as well as during various writing stages, and I offer each of them my gratitude and unyielding affection: Patricia and Nicholas Aherns, Wendy and Hylton Applebaum, Linda and Michael Baden, Myma and Hakeem Belo-Osagie, Chantal and Alex Biner, Michele Bonamy, the late Sylvie and Jonathan Campaigne, Firle Davies, Richard Drayton and Vita Peacock, Janet Heard, Jane Hunter and Mark Walsh, Zainab and Mujtaba Jaffer, Vikram Jayanti, Sandrine Bonamy-Lebia and Ludovic Leiba, James and Mary Mwangi, the late Jennifer and Jonathan Oppenheimer, the late Bettina and Tyrone Pike, and Raenette Taljaard. A special thanks to Waël and Maria Bayazid for inviting me into their home and allowing me to ask myriad questions about Waël's family, including his grandfather (Jamal al-Husayni), and for Waël's careful reading of my chapter on Palestine's Arab Revolt. Ellen Berkman and David Bryant, Diane Borger, Nancy Corkery, Jill Creevy, C. C. Dyer, Margaret Gee, Ifeoma Fafunwa, Betsy Fallon, Uzo Iweala, Allison O'Neil, and Terry Wairimu, my gratitude to you for years of friendship, wisdom, and laughter. And to Anna Deavere Smith, for her sheer genius, love, and support in all things, my unyielding affection and thanks.

This book would not have been possible without the unwavering support and guidance of my agent, Jill Kneerim, and the entire team at Kneerim and Williams. Jill is my trusted confidante and truth teller on all things publishing-related, cheering me on and giving me a gentle nudge (more than once) when I most needed it. My editor, Jon Segal, is without question one of the wisest and most accomplished people I know, and his handwritten notes across hundreds of draft pages, countless suggestions, ample praise, and much-deserved critiques made the final version of this book infinitely better than its first draft. I also offer my deepest gratitude to the entire team at Knopf, particularly Erin Sellers and Sarah Perrin, who helped bring the book across the finish line.

I've left my family for last, not because they don't deserve gratitude in abundance, but because I could never offer them enough of it. It's difficult to put to words the ways in which my life's rhythms for more than a decade have been entwined with this book. It's been a member of my family, one uninvited by everyone except for me. A bit like the houseguest who shows up for a weekend and never leaves despite everyone's best efforts, this book has been hanging around my house for every "official" working day, weekend, special event, and holiday, and eventually my family relented, occasionally embracing it, though mostly putting up with it, and me. It would have never been possible to undertake this project with two young children had my mother, aka Mimi, not only stepped in but insisted that I forge ahead, taking over household operations for months on end with her ever-present love and efficiency. My brother, Chris, is my beacon, a man of true integrity whose support for all things in my life is endless. My deepest gratitude as well to my sister-in-law Lynn, who has offered constant support. My nephews, Tyler and Robbie, have lived with us at various times and brought endless good humor and affection into my life, as has my cousin, Will Burbank, who has taken on his self-appointed role of older brother to my boys in ways for which I could never possibly thank him enough.

My sons, Andy and Jake, are without question my greatest accomplishments and joys. Raising them while writing this book was, however, a harrowing task at times, as they led me on a merry chase on more than one occasion, and I give them a solid A for their boundless ingenuity in trying to outsmart me during their teenage years and a generous gentleman's B for their contrition. They are also two of the kindest, most brilliant, affectionate, hard-working, empathic, ridiculously witty, and devoted sons a mother could possibly hope for. I took the decision early on to bring them with me on research trips, eating buckets of snails in Cyprus and jungle trekking for interviews in Malaysia (both of which they loved), and learning how to excavate archives in places like Singapore (which wasn't such a hit). Having them with me on this book's journey brought a dimension to my thinking and analysis that would have been woefully absent without them, and I am forever grateful for that, and for the fact that they have still yet to beat me in our cumulative long-standing hearts game. My wife, Ingrid Monson, has been my devoted partner in every sense of the word. She has shown me by example what it means to be a rigorous scholar, a humanist, an unconditional friend, and a fun-loving and compassionate companion. Reading countless drafts of this work, she has offered more input than I can possibly thank her for, while also reminding me over and over how much there is to our life beyond our shared love for research, teaching, and writing. It is to Ingrid, Andy, and Jake that I offer my love and this book's dedication, which is but small recompense for all that they have given to me.

Notes

INTRODUCTION

1. Winston Churchill, "Never Give In, Never, Never, Never," October 29, 1941, https://www.nationalchurchillmuseum.org/never-give-in-never-never-never .html.
2. See, for example, "Winston Churchill Memorial Defaced with 'Was a Racist' During London Black Lives Matter Protest," *Evening Standard*, June 7, 2020.
3. See, for example, Gurminder K. Bhambra, "A Statue Was Toppled: Can We Finally Talk About the British Empire?," *New York Times*, June 12, 2020. The toppling of Colston's statue came after two decades of debates over, and demands for, its removal. See Araujo, *Slavery in the Age of Memory*, 70–79.
4. Oriel College, Oxford University, "Cecil John Rhodes (1853–1902)," https:// www.oriel.ox.ac.uk/cecil-john-rhodes-1853-1902#:~:text=By%20the%20 1890s%20Rhodes%20was,in%20his%20will%20%5B7%5D.
5. Bell, *Reordering the World*, 193; and Brown, *Merchant Kings*, 249.
6. For a trenchant engagement with the "imperial history wars," see Maya Jasanoff, "Operation Legacy," *New Yorker*, November 2, 2020. See also Kennedy, *Imperial History Wars*; and Ward and Rasch, *Embers of Empire*, 1–14.
7. For a full account of the Biggar debate, see Drayton, "Biggar vs Little Britain," 143–56.
8. Nigel Biggar, "Less Hegel, More Histories! Christian Ethics and Political Realities," *Providence*, May 18, 2016, https://providencemag.com/2016/05/less -hegel-history-christian-ethics-political-realities/.
9. Biggar, *Between Kin and Cosmopolis*, 91.
10. "Ethics and Empire," McDonald Centre for Ethics, https://www.mcdonald centre.org.uk/ethics-and-empire; and Andrew Gimson, "Interview: Nigel Biggar Says Human Rights Are Not Enough and the British Empire Was Good as Well as Bad," *Conservativehome*, September 16, 2020, https://www.conservative home.com/highlights/2020/09/interview-nigel-biggar-says-human-rights-are -not-enough-and-the-british-empire-was-good-as-well-as-bad.html.
11. Ferguson, *Empire*, xix–xx. For an excellent overview of the broader debate on liberalism and empire, see Sartori, "British Empire and Liberal Mission."
12. Throughout, the opinion polls and accompanying statistics are drawn from

Richard J. Evans, "History Wars," *New Statesman*, June 17, 2020; and Robin Booth, "UK More Nostalgic for Empire than Other Ex-Colonial Powers," *Guardian*, March 11, 2020.

13. "Boris Johnson Exclusive: There Is Only One Way to Get the Change We Want—Vote to Leave the EU," *Telegraph*, March 16, 2016.

14. Ibid.; and "Full Text: Boris Johnson's Conference Speech," *Spectator*, October 1, 2016.

15. "The Rest of the World Believes in Britain. It's Time That We Do Too," *Telegraph*, July 15, 2018; and "Full Text: Boris Johnson's Conference Speech," *Spectator*, October 1, 2016.

16. Neal Ascherson, "From Great Britain to Little England," *New York Times*, June 16, 2016.

17. Gallagher and Robinson, "Imperialism of Free Trade"; and Cain and Hopkins, "Gentlemanly Capitalism."

18. "The White Man's Burden," *McClure's Magazine*, February 12, 1899; Farwell, *Queen Victoria's Little Wars*; and Hensley, *Forms of Empire*, 1–2.

19. The move toward increased democratic participation in Britain was deeply fraught, and in nineteenth-century Britain, the "backwardness" of certain domestic constituencies was as salient an issue as it was with subject populations in the empire. See, for example, Gareth Stedman Jones's work on "outcast London" in Stedman Jones, *Outcast London*. For a foundational text written in the nineteenth century see Mayhew, *London Labour*.

20. The points I am making are very general and not intended to flatten the enormous scholarship and debates about nation-states. Several major comparative-historical works contest the formation of states or political systems, including Anderson, *Lineages of Absolutist State*; Moore, *Social Origins of Dictatorship*; Eisenstadt, *Political Systems of Empires*; and Abrams, *Historical Sociology*.

21. Anderson, *Imagined Communities*.

22. Hobbes, *Leviathan*, 95–96.

23. Locke, *Two Treatises of Government*.

24. There is a substantial literature on John Locke and empire. See, for example, Arneil, *Locke and America*; and Armitage, "Locke: Theorist of Empire?".

25. As previously noted, conceptions of "backward" people also unfolded domestically in Britain, including in Stedman Jones's "outcast London," as well as with laborers in the North and the Irish in factories, mines, and domestic services. The canonical work analyzing domestic and imperial subjecthood, and the relationship between the two, is Hall, *Civilising Subjects*.

26. Chapter 1 will discuss these points in detail, referring to the extensive literature on the topic of liberalism, race, and empire. For an excellent recent account on the empire's subjects reading and debating canonical works on liberalism, see Harper, *Underground Asia*.

27. Seeley, *Expansion of England*; Armitage, "Greater Britain"; and Bell, *Idea of Greater Britain*.

28. "The White Man's Burden," *McClure's Magazine*, February 12, 1899.

29. Weber, "Politics as a Vocation."

30. Comaroff and Comaroff, *Truth About Crime*, 3–22; and Mantena, *Alibis of*

Empire, 22 and passim. For "good government" and its relationship to "rule of law" see Hussain, *Jurisprudence of Emergency.*

31. Stephen, *Life of Stephen*, 286.

32. Stoler, "Perceptions of Protest"; Comaroff and Comaroff, *Truth About Crime*, 3–22.

33. I am drawing on an important body of theoretical work in analyzing states of exception, as well as law-preserving and law-making violence. They include the work of the German jurist Carl Schmitt and the Italian philosopher Giorgio Agamben. See Schmitt, *Political Theology*; and Agamben, *State of Exception.* For law-preserving and law-making violence, see Benjamin, *Essays, Aphorisms*, 277–300.

34. A significant literature on martial law and statutory martial law debates its "legality" and exceptionalism. Three of the most trenchant overviews are Hussain, *Jurisprudence of Emergency*, 99–132; Poole, *Reason of State*, 196–209; and Simpson, *Human Rights*, 1–220. For the pre-1900 period, see Benton, *Search for Sovereignty*, 279–99.

35. This concept draws on numerous works, most directly Walter Benjamin's "Critique of Violence," in which he discusses law-preserving and law-making violence, and Dylan Lino's "Rule of Law and Rule of Empire," 742–43, in which he discusses the "rule of law" and lawless practices. See also Agamben, *State of Exception*; Foucault, *Discipline and Punish*; and Ann Laura Stoler's and Jean and John Comaroff's numerous critiques of Foucault's biopower and modern "capillary" power in the context of race and empires. For example, Stoler, *Race and the Education of Desire*; Stoler, *Imperial Debris*; and Comaroff and Comaroff, *Truth About Crime*, 3–22. For a broader literary, theoretical, and jurisprudential discussion of violence and empire, see Bhabha, "Foreword: Framing Fanon," vii–xli; and Hussain, *Jurisprudence of Emergency.* In the present day, some legal scholars use the term *veneer of legality* to describe thin legal legitimation for things that are not typically legal. My discussion of "legalized lawlessness" can be read as an analysis of the legal precedents in the empire to "veneer of legality." I am grateful to Liora Lazarus for raising these points with me.

36. Bhabha, "Foreword: Framing Fanon."

37. Proverbs 13:24 is quoted here from the English Standard Version. The King James Version reads, "He that spareth his rod hateth his son: but he that loveth him chasteneth him betimes." Several other Proverbs have similar themes of love and discipline, including Proverbs 29:17, 23:13–14, 29:15, and 19:18.

38. Elkins, "'Moral Effect' of Legalized Lawlessness."

39. Lenin, *Imperialism*; Rodney, *How Europe Underdeveloped Africa*; and Luxemburg, *Accumulation of Capital*, 434–47.

40. Robinson, *Black Marxism*, 2.

41. Elizabeth II, "A Speech by the Queen on Her 21st Birthday, 1947," https://www.royal.uk/21st-birthday-speech-21-april-1947#:~:text=I%20declare%20before%20you%20all,to%20which%20we%20all%20belong.

42. Ibid.; and "My Grandfather Wrote the Princess's Speech," *Oldie*, no date, https://www.theoldie.co.uk/article/my-grandfather-wrote-the-princesss-speech.

43. An image that Bhabha elaborates in "Foreword: Framing Fanon."

44. Elizabeth II, "Speech by the Queen on Her 21st Birthday, 1947."

45. Late Victorian debates gave rise to the term *liberal imperialism*, typically associated with Lord Roseberry's efforts to make a liberal argument to counter William Gladstone in favor of expansion and empire. It is then suggested that when the Liberal Party split in 1886, after a dispute about Ireland and whether ideas of democracy and self-government were applicable to the dependent empire, liberal imperialism receded along with moral claims to empire. For a discussion, see Mantena, *Alibis of Empire*.

46. See, for example, Mantena, *Alibis of Empire*; Metcalf, *Ideologies of the Raj*; and Mehta, *Liberalism and Empire*.

47. I am indebted to John and Jean Comaroff for our extensive conversations about the relationship between customary laws and systems, violence, liberalism, and the colonial state.

48. Hansard, "Native Policy in Empire," July 9, 1937, vol. 105, col. 426., HL Deb.

49. Hansard, "Imperial Conference," June 17, 1921, vol. 143, cols. 783–860, HC Deb; "The Imperial Conference," *Round Table: Commonwealth Journal of International Affairs* 11, no. 44 (1921): 735–58; and "The Future of Colonial Trusteeship," *Round Table* 24, no. 96 (1934): 732–45.

50. General Act of the Berlin Conference on West Africa, February 26, 1885, https://loveman.sdsu.edu/docs/1885GeneralActBerlinConference.pdf. Note that the Berlin Conference established the principles of free trade and effective occupation, the notion that European powers could not hold paper claims to African territories but rather had to effectively occupy with administrative presence, which took a variety of forms, including charter companies and officers administrating on behalf of their European governments.

51. League of Nations, Covenant, https://avalon.law.yale.edu/20th_century/leagcov.asp#art22, emphasis added.

52. United Nations, Statute of the International Court of Justice, chap. 11, Article 73, https://www.un.org/en/sections/un-charter/chapter-xi/index.html.

53. Elkins, *Imperial Reckoning*, 190.

54. Gavaghan, *Of Lions and Dung Beetles*, 235.

55. Arendt, *Origins*, 157. Note that Arendt was drawing upon the work of Black radical writers, including Aimé Césaire who published *Discourse on Colonialism* in 1950, which drew upon themes he developed in his 1939 poem "Cahier d'un retour au pays natal." Other Black radicals who predated Arendt's publication of *Origins* will be discussed in chapter 7.

56. Arendt, *Origins*, 157.

57. Ibid., 129–30.

58. Dwyer and Nettelbeck, " 'Savage Wars of Peace.' "

59. Howe, "Colonising and Exterminating?" 8. Note Howe qualifies his opinion, writing that he is rendering it "with all due caution and all possible vigilance for a British author's own potential biases."

60. Hughes, "Banality of Brutality," 354.

61. Elkins, *Imperial Reckoning*, 331.

62. Hochschild, *King Leopold's Ghost.*

63. Hull, *Absolute Destruction*, 2.

64. Arendt, *Origins*, 185, 221. See also Lindquist, *"Exterminate All the Brutes";* and King and Stone, *Arendt and Uses of History*, 1–20.

65. As we shall see, similarities between the British Empire and totalitarian regimes were partly due to Nazi officials borrowing from British imperial laws and practices. While outside the scope of this book, the Nazi regime was also inspired by Jim Crow segregation policies and practices, as were South Africa's apartheid officials.

66. Arendt, *Origins*, 129.

67. See, for example, Conklin, *Mission to Civilize;* Stora, *Histoire de l'Algérie coloniale;* and Aldrich, *Greater France.*

68. Arendt, *Origins*, 209.

69. Fanon, *Wretched of the Earth.*

70. The five original claimants were Ndiku Mutua, Paulo Mzili, Wambugu wa Nyingi, Jane Muthoni Mara, and Susan Ngondi. For the original particulars of the claim, see Richard Hermer and Phillippa Kaufmann, "Particulars of Claim," 2009, *Ndiku Mutua and 4 Others and FCO*, Royal Courts of Justice; and Hon. Mr. Justice McCombe, Approved Judgment, 2011, ibid.

71. Elkins, "Looking Beyond Mau Mau."

72. George Padmore, "The Second World War and the Dark Races," *Crisis*, November 1939, 27.

73. Getachew, *Worldmaking*, 72.

74. Padmore, *History of Pan-African Congress*, 5.

75. United Nations, General Assembly, "Universal Declaration of Human Rights," December 10, 1948.

PART I: AN IMPERIAL NATION

1. Winston Churchill, Primrose League Speech, July 26, 1897, http://www .churchillarchive.com/explore/page?id=CHAR%202%2F21%2F1#image=0.

2. Perry, *Winston Churchill*, 52–53; and Toye, *Churchill's Empire*, 32–33.

3. Jenkins, *Churchill*, 28–29.

4. Toye, *Churchill's Empire*, 39.

5. Later in his life, Churchill said that Nirad C. Chaudhuri's *The Autobiography of an Unknown Indian*, published in 1951, was one of the most influential books he had ever read. My gratitude to William Roger Louis for reminding me of this.

6. Several recent works gesture to the various military, intelligence, and administrative actors whose careers spanned the empire in different capacities, particularly during their formative years of professional training. For a recent discussion of military actors, see French, *British Way;* for intelligence actors, see Walton, *Empire of Secrets;* and for administrative actors, see Grob-Fitzgibbon, *Imperial Endgame.*

7. For a similar point made on the transference and evolution of ideas across time and space, see Armitage, "International Turn in Intellectual History," 241.

CHAPTER 1: LIBERAL IMPERIALISM

1. Renan, *Qu'est-ce qu'une nation?* 7–9.
2. John Zephaniah Holwell to William David, February 28, 1757, in Holwell, *India Tracts*, 257–58, 261.
3. Partha Chatterjee and Nicholas Dirks have both written seminal works that point to, and draw upon, the Black Hole of Calcutta as the precipitating moment in establishing Britain's empire in the East. See Chatterjee, *Black Hole of Empire;* and Dirks, *Scandal of Empire.* For a popular version of the Black Hole of Calcutta perpetuating the myths and images of the event, see Barber, *Black Hole of Calcutta.*
4. See Gupta, *Sirajjuddaullah,* 70–80; and Dirks, *Scandal of Empire,* 3–4.
5. Dirks, *Scandal of Empire,* 11. The scale of company profit was substantial in Bengal. Its profit margins were two to three times that of merchant trade in Britain, and for tobacco and salt, among other select commodities, profits were 75 percent or more. For an account of Britain's conquest of India through the period of the Raj, see Wilson, *Chaos of Empire.*
6. Mukerjee, *Churchill's Secret War,* xiv.
7. Travers, *Ideology and Empire,* chap. 2.
8. As quoted in Mukerjee, *Churchill's Secret War,* xv.
9. Bose, *Peasant Labour,* 18.
10. See Travers, *Ideology and Empire,* 143–46, 181–206; and Dirks, *Scandal of Empire,* 14–18.
11. Travers, *Ideology and Empire,* 217–23; and Dirks, *Scandal of Empire,* 14–18.
12. See Travers, *Ideology and Empire,* 217–21; Dirks, *Scandal of Empire;* Marshall, *Impeachment of Hastings;* Marshall, "Making of an Imperial Icon"; and Warren Hastings, *History of Trial of Hastings.*
13. For a thoroughgoing analysis of Burke's life and engagement with the empire, see Bourke, *Empire and Revolution.*
14. Mantena, *Alibis of Empire,* 24–25; and Travers, *Ideology and Empire,* 217.
15. Edmund Burke, "Fox's India Bill Speech," in Marshall, *Writings and Speeches of Burke,* 5:402–3.
16. Marshall, *Writings and Speeches of Burke,* 6:275–76.
17. Robert Travers elaborates fully on these arguments in *Ideology and Empire.*
18. Ibid., 217–18.
19. Marshall, *Writings and Speeches of Burke,* 6:420–21.
20. Burke, *Speeches of the Right Honourable Edmund Burke,* Vol. I, 28.
21. The violence accompanying Clive's initial conquest of Bengal was, importantly, not a concern of Burke's. He was quite content with bypassing this episode—and presumably later such episodes that would punctuate Britain's imperial future—famously stating, "There is a secret veil to be drawn over the beginnings of all governments. They had their origins, as the beginning of all such things have had, in some matters that had as good be covered in obscurity." See Edmund Burke, "Speech on Opening of Impeachment," February 15, 1778, in Marshall, *Writings and Speeches of Burke,* 6:316.
22. Ibid., 6:317.

23. Mantena, *Alibis of Empire*, 24.

24. Burke, "Fox's India Bill Speech," 5:390.

25. Mantena, *Alibis of Empire*, 25.

26. Dirks, *Scandal of Empire*, xii, 125.

27. Note that it was not only Britons at home, but also those residing in the empire, who voiced their strong support for Hastings. For instance, plantation owners in Jamaica, who shared a political kinship with the *nabobs*, expressed their sympathy for Hastings. Simon Taylor, Jamaica's wealthiest man, stated: "Mr Hastings fate is truly deplorable, to be Sacrificed to the Rumour of a set of Miscreants. . . . If a man in the time of an actual Invasion is to be bound by the Rules of Westminster Hall, I believe the Country would be soon overrun and those men who were ruining the Mother Country at home by their mutinous factions are endeavouring to Ruin the only two Men who Acted with Honour in their Country's Defence." Simon Taylor to Chaloner Arcedeckne, June 3, 1787, Vanneck Papers, Cambridge University Library, Cambridge, United Kingdom. I am grateful to Vincent Brown for sharing this quote and citation with me. For biographical details on Taylor, see Brown, *Reaper's Garden*, 21–22.

28. Mill, *History of British India*, 2:83.

29. Mantena, *Alibis of Empire*, 28, 30.

30. Macaulay's five-volume work, *History of England from the Reign of James III*, was a Victorian best seller that was, according to the historian Catherine Hall, "a story of progress, of the long transition from barbarism, a state in which many peoples of the empire still languished, to one of civilisation. England, he was convinced, was the most civilised nation in the world, suited to its position of global dominance, ready to lead others." Or, in Macaulay's words, "The history of our country during the last hundred and sixty years is eminently the history of physical, of moral, and of intellectual improvement." See Catherine Hall, *Macaulay and Son*, xii.

31. Hudson, *Macaulay's Essays on Clive*, 3.

32. July 10, 1833, vol. 19, col. 536, HC Deb.

33. Tucker, *Macaulay's Essay*, 149.

34. Ibid., 99.

35. Dirks, *Scandal of Empire*, 326–27. For further additional early historical accounts, see Marshall, "Making of an Imperial Icon," 13.

36. The following description of the British Empire is drawn from a variety of sources, particularly Morris, *Farewell the Trumpets*, and Hyam, *Britain's Declining Empire*, 3–12, both of which offer sweeping overviews similar to the one here.

37. See, for example, Metcalf, *An Imperial Vision*; and Metcalf, *Early Nineteenth Century Architecture*.

38. For example, Drayton, "Science, Medicine, and British Empire," 5:264–76; and Davis, Wilburn, and Robinson, *Railway Imperialism*.

39. My analysis here draws on the robust literature on the mutually constitutive relationship between liberalism and imperialism, and the shifts that occurred in the nineteenth century. See Metcalf, *Ideologies of the Raj*; Mehta, *Liberalism and Empire*; Bhabha, "Of Mimicry and Man"; Mantena, *Alibis of Empire*;

Pitts, *Turn to Empire*; Losurdo, *Liberalism*; Sartori, *Liberalism in Empire*; Armitage, "Fifty Years' Rift"; Pitts, "Political Theory of Empire"; and Armitage, "Locke, Carolina, and Two Treatises," 602, where he states, "It is now a commonplace in the history of political thought that there has long been a mutually constitutive relationship between liberalism and colonialism." Armitage also notes (620n1) that *liberalism* and *colonialism* are anachronistic and imprecise terms when applied prior to the nineteenth century, though they do offer a useful shorthand.

40. See the sources referenced above in note 39. For a trenchant overview of liberalism and the individual, see Comaroff, "Images of Empire," 169–72.

41. Mehta, *Liberalism and Empire*, 20.

42. Metcalf, *Ideologies of the Raj*, 29. On the emergence of indigenous meanings of liberalism in India and Cape Town, South Africa, see Bayly, *Recovering Liberties*; and Trapido, "Liberalism in the Cape."

43. Mill, *On Liberty* in *Collected Works*, 18:236–37.

44. For a comprehensive analysis of Mill and imperialism, see Sullivan, "Liberalism and Imperialism." See also Mantena, *Alibis of Empire*, 1–55; Metcalf, *Ideologies of the Raj*, 31–41; and Pitts, *Turn to Empire*, 133–60. For full texts, see Mill, *On Liberty*, in *Collected Works*, 18:231–37; and John Stuart Mill, *Considerations on Representative Government*, in Mill, *Essays on Politics and Society*, pt. 2, 50–210.

45. Mill, *On Liberty* in *Collected Works*, 18:236.

46. Mill, "Considerations," 69, 56, 54.

47. Stoler and Cooper, "Between Metropole and Colony."

48. John Stuart Mill, "A Few Words on Non-Intervention," in Mill, *Dissertations and Discussions*, 171.

49. Mantena makes this point in *Alibis of Empire*, 33.

50. See, for example, Urbinati, "Many Heads of the Hydra," 74–75.

51. For details of these events in the Atlantic World see, for example, Rugemer, *Slave Law*.

52. Hussain, *Jurisprudence of Emergency*, 109.

53. For the authoritative account of the Demerara rebellion, see Viotti da Costa, *Crowns of Glory*.

54. Bryant, *Account of Insurrection*, quote on 44, and 44–88 for narrative details.

55. Viotti da Costa, *Crowns of Glory*, 252–74; and Hochschild, *Bury the Chains*, 328–37.

56. Hussain, *Jurisprudence of Emergency*, 109.

57. For a trenchant review of martial law's history, see ibid., 99–132; Poole, *Reason of State*, 196–209; and Simpson, *Human Rights*, 1–220. For the pre-1900 period, see Benton, *Search for Sovereignty*, 279–99.

58. Hussain, *Jurisprudence of Emergency*, 105.

59. Simpson, *Human Rights*, 57.

60. *Rex v. Pinney, Esq.*, 560–61.

61. Stokes, *Peasant and Raj*, 90–204.

62. See, for example, Chakravarty, *Indian Mutiny*.

63. Holmes, *Sahib*.

64. Dalrymple, *Last Mughul*, 4–5.

65. Herbert, *War of No Pity*, 2.

66. Ibid.; and Judd, *Lion and Tiger*, 70–90.

67. Simpson, *Human Rights*, 77, 78.

68. For a listing of plantation owners and estate managers, among others, serving as magistrates in Jamaica in 1865, see *Report of the Royal Commission, Part II, Minutes of Evidence and Appendix*, 1101.

69. Holt, *Problem of Freedom*, 295.

70. Hall, *Civilizing Subjects*, 138.

71. Holt, *Problem of Freedom*, 6–9.

72. Jamaica Committee, *Jamaica Papers, No. 1*, 21.

73. Holt, *Problem of Freedom*, 295–302.

74. Jamaica Committee, *Jamaica Papers, No. 1*, 86.

75. Gorrie, *Jamaica Papers, No. 6*, 9.

76. *Report of the Jamaica Royal Commission*, 15573, 18, 25–26.

77. John Stuart Mill correspondence with David Urquhart, October 4, 1866, in Mill, *Later Letters of Mill*, 206.

78. Mill, "Considerations," in Mill, *Essays on Politics and Society*, pt. 2, 75.

79. Ibid., 69.

80. Ibid.

81. Mill, *On Liberty* in *Collected Works*, 18:236–37; and John Stuart Mill correspondence with William Sims Pratten, June 9, 1868, in Mill, *Later Letters of Mill*, 393–94.

82. Mill, "Disturbances in Jamaica, July 31, 1866," in *Collected Works*, 28: 107, 157.

83. John Stuart Mill to David Urquhart, October 4, 1866, in Mill, *Later Letters of Mill*, 206.

84. John Stuart Mill to William Sims Pratten, June 9, 1868, ibid., 393.

85. Mill, "Disturbances in Jamaica," 155.

86. Carlyle, "Occasional Discourse." Caryle originally published this essay anonymously in *Fraser's Magazine* in 1849. Four years later he published it under his name as a pamphlet.

87. Ibid., 670, 679.

88. The *preemptive* point is drawn from Poole, *Reason of State*, 200–201; and Hussain, *Jurisprudence of Emergency*, 112–14. For a discussion of a similar legal logic in the French Empire, see Ghachem, *Old Regime and the Haitian Revolution*, chap. 4.

89. Hussain, *Jurisprudence of Emergency*, 113. The passage above is drawn from Hussain's narrative on Finlason (112–14).

90. Ibid., 114.

91. Legislation abolishing the use of enslaved labor in the British Empire was passed in 1833. It established formal emancipation for August 1, 1834, but the use of enslaved labor only ended in 1838 after the apprenticeship period. I am indebted to Vincent Brown for reminding me of these points, as well as of the fact that reactions to the Indian Mutiny and Morant Bay Rebellion were part of a longer process of reactions to uprisings in European empires, particularly the Haitian Revolution (see, for example, Fischer, *Modernity Disavowed*).

92. Brown, *Moral Capital*; and Williams, *Capitalism and Slavery*. Note that Brown

points out the more general moral reform movement and imagined responsibility for subject populations that swept through Britain in the wake of the Seven Years War (1756–63) and the American Revolution. It is within this context that the Warren Hasting trial must also be read. See Brown, "Empire without Slaves."

93. R. J. White, introduction to Stephen, *Liberty, Equality, Fraternity*, 4.

94. For two robust analyses of the Governor Eyre controversy and its impact on liberalism see Mantena, *Alibis of Empire*, 37–39; and Metcalf, *Ideologies of the Raj*, 52–59. Similarly, the impact of the Indian Mutiny on ideological shifts in liberalism began with Stokes, *English Utilitarians in India*.

95. Jamaica Committee, *Jamaica Papers, No. 1*, 70.

96. James Fitzjames Stephen, "Sovereignty," in Stephen, *Horae Sabbaticae*, 55.

97. Hussain, *Jurisprudence of Emergency*, 67–68.

98. Stephen, *Liberty, Equality, Fraternity*, 209, 202.

99. R. J. White, introduction to ibid., 11.

100. Ibid., 200.

101. Mantena, *Alibis of Empire*, 40–41.

102. Stevenson, *Strange Case of Jekyll and Hyde*, 42. For an excellent analysis of Victorian-era literature and violence in empire, see Hensley, *Forms of Empire*.

103. Agamben, *State of Exception*, 1.

104. Mantena, *Alibis of Empire*, 1–55; and Metcalf, *Ideologies of the Raj*, 28–65.

105. This point is expansively argued in Mantena, *Alibis of Empire*.

106. Pitts, "Political Theory of Empire and Imperialism," 215. For early modern roots of the ideologies of empire, and their relationship to the metropole, see Armitage, *Ideological Origins*.

107. Hobsbawm, "Mass-Producing Traditions," 263–69.

108. Ibid., 269, 265.

109. Metcalf, *Ideologies of the Raj*, 59.

110. Benjamin Disraeli, *Speech at the Banquet of the National Union of Conservative and Constitutional Associations at the Crystal Palace, June 24, 1872* (London: R. J. Mitchell & Sons, 1872), 11.

111. Stephen would split from the Liberal Party in 1886 over the question of Irish Home Rule.

112. Metcalf, *Ideologies of the Raj*, 59.

113. Cannadine, "Context, Performance and Meaning," 119.

114. Ibid., 101–64.

115. Ibid., 134–36.

116. Ibid., 127–28.

117. Besant, *Queen's Reign*, 92.

118. For the role of Social Darwinism and race in British ideology and self-representations, see Stocking, *Victorian Anthropology*; Stocking, *Race, Culture, and Evolution*; and Satia, *Time's Monster*, 124–25.

119. See, for example, Hall, *Civilising Subjects*; Thompson, *Empire Strikes Back?*; and Thompson and Kowalsky, "Social Life and Cultural Representation."

120. This point is well made in Thompson and Kowalsky, "Social Life and Cultural Representation," 253–54.

121. In evaluating cultural work and literary forms by "tracing the social energies that circulate very broadly through culture," I am drawing on Gallagher and Greenblatt, *Practicing New Historicism*, 6. There is a robust literature that analyzes the ways in which fiction shaped understandings of the empire. I shall draw on some of these works in the pages ahead. I have had to make choices, however, so there is an abundant amount of writing, including that of Paul Scott, Graham Greene, V. S. Naipaul, and Joseph Conrad, that I do not engage with, though this should not diminish its importance and impact.

122. Edward Said and George Orwell were well aware of the lasting effects of childhood literature on adulthood worldviews, and the connections that they had to the empire. See Said, *Orientalism*, 13; and Orwell, *Collection of Essays* (1981 ed.), 305.

123. For the reference to Alice as a "living avatar of empire," see Griffin, "Tales of Empire" (Ph.D. diss.), 6. See also Bivona, *British Imperial Literature*; and Richards, *Imperialism and Juvenile Literature*. For *Alice and Wonderland*, see Carroll, *Alice's Adventures*.

124. Castle, *Britannia's Children*, 55.

125. MacKenzie, "Popular Culture," 222–23. See also MacKenzie, *Propaganda and Empire*; MacKenzie, *Imperialism and Popular Culture*; and Ward, *British Culture*, 1–20.

126. Tomkins, *David Livingstone*; and Rice, *Captain Sir Burton*.

127. MacKenzie, "Popular Culture," 221.

128. William Roger Louis, introduction to Winks and Low, *Historiography*, 8.

129. For Leopold von Ranke's influence on modern history see Novick, *That Noble Dream*. On Seeley, documents, and the Public Record Office, see Johnson, "Empire," 100.

130. Mantena, *Alibis of Empire*, 45.

131. Seeley, *Expansion of England*, 212, 251.

132. Kelley, *Frontiers of History*, 218.

133. Drayton, "Where Does World Historian Write From?"; and Satia, *Time's Monster*, 119–24.

134. Kipling's "Regulus" was composed in 1908, and first published in *Nash's Magazine*, *Pall Mall*, and *Metropolitan Magazine* in April 1917, and subsequently collected in *A Diversity of Creatures* (1917).

135. Kipling, "The White Man's Burden," was published in *McClure's Magazine*, February 12, 1899.

136. Matthew, *Gladstone*, 74.

137. Cooper and Stoler, *Tensions of Empire*, 4, 11, and 31.

138. Nicolson, *Curzon*, 13, as quoted in Mehta, *Liberalism and Empire*, 5.

139. Porter, *Critical of Empire*; and Matikkala, *Empire and Imperial Ambition*.

140. For example, Gott, *Britain's Empire*; and Kolsky, *Colonial Justice*.

CHAPTER 2: WARS SMALL AND GREAT

1. Toye, *Churchill's Empire*, 40.

2. Churchill, *Early Life*, 146.

3. Jablonsky, *Churchill, the Great Game*, 36.

4. Toye, *Churchill's Empire*, 39–40, 41.

5. Hobsbawm, *Industry and Empire*, 190–91; and Nairn, *Break-Up of Britain*, 23.

6. As quoted in Denoon, "Participation," 110.

7. Royal commission on the war in South Africa, Cd. 1789, 35; Omissi and Thompson, *Impact of South African War*, 8; and Thompson, "Publicity, Philanthropy and Commemoration," 100–101. For important policy surveys and social histories of the war and its camps, see Spies, *Methods of Barbarism?*; and Van Heyningen, *Concentration Camp*.

8. Thompson, *Wider Patriotism*, 1–40; Pakenham, *Boer War*, 11–15; and Brendon, *Decline and Fall*, 220–25.

9. O'Brien, *Milner*, 177; Gollin, *Proconsul in Politics*; Thompson, *Life of Milner*, 87; and Milner, *England in Egypt*.

10. Thompson, *Wider Patriotism*, 38.

11. "Milner's Credo," *Times*, July 27, 1925.

12. Pakenham, *Boer War*, 119–20.

13. Brighton and Foy, *News Values*, 78.

14. Forth, *Barbed-Wire Imperialism*, 137–38; and Forth, "Britain's Archipelago," 669.

15. Thompson, "Publicity, Philanthropy and Commemoration," 100–104.

16. "Poem Fund Now £50,000," *Daily Mail*, December 1899.

17. Kipling, *Absent Minded Beggar*.

18. John Cannon, "The Absent-Minded Beggar," *Gilbert and Sullivan News* 11, no. 8 (1997): 16–17; John Cannon, "A Little-Heralded Sullivan Century," *Gilbert and Sullivan News* 11, no. 16 (1999): 18; and John Cannon, "Following the Absent-Minded Beggar," *Gilbert and Sullivan News* 4, no. 12 (2010): 10–12.

19. Roberts himself had helped quell the Indian Mutiny of 1857, receiving a Victoria Cross for killing two sepoys, one of whom he nearly decapitated "on the spot." Among the seasoned veterans was William Nicholson, who had seen considerable wartime action in Southeast Asia and eventually rose to the positions of chief of the Imperial General Staff and aide-de-camp general to Victoria's successor, Edward VII. See *London Gazette*, December 24, 1858, 5516.

20. As quoted in Ellis, *Social History of Machine Gun*, 86.

21. Carrington, *Rudyard Kipling*, 327.

22. Pakenham, *Boer War*, 493.

23. Forth, "Britain's Archipelago," 655–62; and Anderson, "Politics of Convict Space," 40–55. For Victorian Britain and the segregation of East London from the city's urban areas, see Stedman Jones, *Outcast London*. For Victorian and early twentieth-century British work camps, see Field, *Working Men's Bodies*.

24. Forth, *Barbed-Wire Imperialism*, chaps. 2 and 3.

25. Nasson, *South African War*, 221.

26. Forth, "Britain's Archipelago," 668.

27. Forth, *Barbed-Wire Imperialism*, 138–39.

28. Spies, *Methods of Barbarism?*, 265.

29. Hobhouse, *Report of a Visit*.

30. March 8, 1901, vol. 90, col. 1027, HC Deb; June 17, 1901, vol. 95, col. 592, HC Deb.

31. Seibold, *Emily Hobhouse*, 75.

32. June 17, 1901, vol. 95, cols. 580 and 587, HC Deb. For Campbell-Bannerman's June 1901 speech to the National Reform Union, see Douglas, *Liberals*, 106.

33. Seibold, *Emily Hobhouse*, quote on 88, for narrative details see, 87–98.

34. Ibid., 110–11.

35. *Report on the Concentration Camps in South Africa*, Cd. 893.

36. Forth and Kreienbaum, "Shared Malady," 253–55.

37. Forth, *Barbed-Wire Imperialism*, 212.

38. Forth, "Britain's Archipelago," 653.

39. Given the paucity of records on the African camps and mortality rates, this percentage is likely quite conservative. See Spies, *Methods of Barbarism?*, 265–66. Forth puts the combined total of Afrikaners and Black Africans interned in the concentration camps at 250,000. See Forth, "Britain's Archipelago," 666–67.

40. Spies and Nattrass, *Jan Smuts*, 19.

41. Hancock, *Smuts*, 1:1–35; and Smuts, *Jan Christian Smuts*, 1–24.

42. Mazower, *No Enchanted Palace*, 20, 34.

43. Here I am drawing directly on Mazower's notion of "imperial internationalism," as well as Smuts's role, and that of others, including Milner, in its development in the early twentieth century through the creation of the League of Nations and ultimately the United Nations. See Mazower, *No Enchanted Palace*.

44. Ibid., 33.

45. For "conquest state," see Marks and Trapido, "Lord Milner," 72; and Stokes, "Milnerism," 58.

46. Pakenham, *Boer War*, 119.

47. Marks and Trapido, "Lord Milner," 50–80; and Stokes, "Milnerism," 47–60.

48. Thompson, "Publicity, Philanthropy and Commemoration," 113, 120.

49. Other scholars have made this similar point when examining issues of torture, violence, and states. See, for example, Samuel Moyn, "Torture and Taboo: On Elaine Scarry," *Nation*, February 5, 2013.

50. Hussain, "Towards a Jurisprudence of Emergency," 101–3; and Chatterjee, *Nation and its Fragments*, chap. 2.

51. Hussain, "Towards a Jurisprudence of Emergency," 102.

52. Cooper, "Modernizing Colonialism," 67.

53. Lino, "Dicey and Constitutional Theory" and "Rule of Law." My reading of Dicey and imperialism is greatly indebted to Dylan Lino, whom I consider the foremost authority on the topic. As Lino points out, Dicey, in his introduction to *Introduction to the Study of the Law*, in its eighth edition in 1915, offers a lengthy discussion of imperial constitutional relations. For another analysis of Dicey and parliamentary sovereignty, see Oliver, *Constitution of Independence*, chap. 3. For Dicey and "rule of law," see Waldron, "The Rule of Law."

54. Dicey, *Introduction to Study of Law*, 289.

55. Ibid., 292–3.

56. Lino, "Dicey and Constitutional Theory," quotes on 762–63, 766, 769.

57. I am referring to representatives from the empire sitting in Parliament representing constituents from the empire. By contrast, Dadabhai Naoroji was the first British Indian MP elected to Parliament in 1892, representing the Liberal Party in Finsbury Central. From this position, he did advocate for improvements in India.

58. Lino, "Dicey and Constitutional Theory," 771–72.

59. Ibid., 773.

60. Ibid., 776–78. "Relatively light touch" is quoted on 776.

61. Lino, "Rule of Law," 742–43.

62. Symonds, *Oxford and Empire*; Kirk-Greene, "Thin White Line"; and Berry, "Hegemony on a Shoestring."

63. Kirk-Greene, "Thin White Line." I am grateful to William Roger Louis for emphasizing the "cultlike" culture of the colonial administration, and also pointing me to Harold Nicolson's diary, in which Nicolson, a British foreign service officer and Conservative MP, offered a sentiment shared by many colonial officers: "nobody will persuade me that our work in the Sudan was anything but a real civilising and selfless mission." Nicolson, *The Later Years*, 237.

64. Comaroff, "Colonialism, Culture, and Law," 305–6. Comaroff is also drawing on Chanock, *Law, Custom*, 4.

65. Comaroff, "Colonialism, Culture, and Law," 306; and Benton, *Law and Colonial Cultures*, 127–29.

66. Pitts, "Political Theory of Empire," 220; Cooper, "'Modernizing Colonialism," 66; and Berman, "Perils of Bula Matari."

67. Shklar, "Torturers."

68. Chatterjee, *Nation and Its Fragments*, 10.

69. These future theorists and practitioners include Robert Thompson, who notably left his imprint on Malaya and Vietnam, and Frank Kitson, who saw action in several imperial conflicts before emerging in 1970s Northern Ireland. See Callwell, *Small Wars*. Callwell published extensively, including his "Lessons to be Learnt"; "Notes on the Strategy of Our Small Wars"; and "Notes on the Tactics of Our Small Wars." Callwell, while he was the most cited military theorist and practitioner, was not the first or only author to write about small wars. See, for example, Anglim, "Callwell Versus Graziani." A substantial literature discusses the genealogy of British counterinsurgency strategies and tactics, including Beckett, "British Counter-insurgency"; Thompson, *Defeating Communist Insurgency*; and Kitson, *Low Intensity Operations*.

70. The terms "uncivilised" and "savage" are deployed throughout Callwell's writings.

71. Callwell, *Small Wars*, 102.

72. Other scholars have analyzed Callwell's "moral effect," though have reached differing conclusions regarding the level of British brutality that this ethos engendered. See, for example, Whittingham, "'Savage Warfare,'" 13–29.

73. Callwell, *Small Wars*, 41, 72, 148.

74. Ibid., 72. See also Whittingham, "'Savage Warfare,'" 19.

75. The counterinsurgency expert Ian F. W. Beckett suggests a similar point when he writes, "There was invariably a particular national tradition of how

to go about counter-insurgency stemming from the nineteenth century, if not before." See Beckett, *Modern Insurgencies*, 25, 183.

76. Whittingham, "'Savage Warfare,'" 14.

77. Callwell, *Small Wars*, 40.

78. Pitts, *Boundaries of the International*; and Anghie, "Finding the Peripheries," 1–80.

79. Prior to World War II, the Geneva Conventions (1864) were revised in 1906 and 1929, and the Hague Conventions (1899) in 1907. Sassòli, *International Humanitarian Law*, 6–10; and Mégret, "From 'savages,'" 270–73. Note that there is some historical dispute as to whether Dunant was seeking business concessions in Algeria.

80. Koskenniemi, *Gentle Civilizer of Nations*, passim.

81. Anghie, *Imperialism, Sovereignty*, 13–31; and Koskenniemi, "Empire and International Law," 1–4. For the global circulation of ideas about law and constitutions, see Colley, *The Gun, the Ship*, part three.

82. Koskenniemi, *Gentle Civilizer of Nations*, 127–28.

83. Ibid., 129–31 (quote on 129–30).

84. Ibid., 160. See also Anghie, *Imperialism, Sovereignty*, 32–114; and Lindqvist, *History of Bombing*, 2.

85. Hull, *Absolute Destruction*, 122; and Convention (II) with Respect to the Laws and Customs of War on Land, The Hague, July 29, 1899, Articles 22–28, 47, and 50.

86. Wagner, "Savage Warfare," 225–26, 227; and Mégret, "From 'savages,'" 274–76.

87. Wagner, "Savage Warfare," 224.

88. Bennett et al., "Studying Mars and Clio," 275.

89. As quoted in Khalili, *Time in the Shadows*, 228–29.

90. Hull, *Absolute Destruction*, 192.

91. Auld, "Liberal Pro-Boers," 79.

92. Fitzmaurice, "Liberalism and Empire."

93. An important and robust literature examines the evolution of nineteenth- and twentieth-century international law in the context of liberalism and empire. Here I have drawn primarily on Fitzmaurice, "Liberalism and Empire"; Pagden, "Comment"; Koseknniemi, *Gentle Civilizer*; and Best, *War and Law*.

94. See, for example, Darwin, *Empire Project*, 305–58; and Ashley Jackson, "The British Empire and the First World War," *BBC History Magazine* 9, no. 11 (2008).

95. Darwin, *Empire Project*, 305–58; and Jackson, "British Empire."

96. Mazower, *No Enchanted Palace*, 34–37.

97. Gerth and Mills, *From Max Weber*, 97.

98. Ferguson, *Pity of War*, 212.

99. Walsh, *News from Ireland*, 15.

100. As quoted in Gillingham, "Images of Ireland," 18.

101. See Howe, *Ireland and Empire*; and Smith, *Fighting for Ireland?*

102. See, for example, Curtis, *Apes and Angels*.

103. Engels, *Condition of Working-Class*, 64; and Blake, *Disraeli*, 131.

104. Howe, *Ireland and Empire*, 66, 67.

105. Leadam, *Coercive Measures*, 7. See also Curtis, *Coercion and Conciliation*, 179–210; and Hogan and Walker, *Political Violence*.

106. Simpson, *Human Rights*, 79, 80.

107. Simpson, *Highest Degree Odious*, 4; and Hogan and Walker, *Political Violence*, 12–14.

108. Lino, "Dicey and Constitutional Theory," 763, 774–75.

109. This quote summarizes Simpson's interpretation of Dicey's view of special codes, *Human Rights*, 80–81.

110. Ibid., 81; see also Simpson, *Highest Degree Odious*, 5–7, for a fuller discussion of the Defence of the Realm Acts.

111. Simpson, *Highest Degree Odious*, 6–7.

112. Simpson, *Human Rights*, 82.

113. As quoted in Townshend, *1916*, xviii.

114. Walsh, *News from Ireland*, 50.

115. As quoted in Townshend, *1916*, 147.

116. Ibid., 186.

117. Ibid., 208.

118. Ibid; and Coogan, *1916*, 136.

119. Townshend, *1916*, 208.

120. Townshend, *Easter Rising*, 208–12.

121. Kennedy, *Genesis of the Rising*, 286–87.

122. McGarry, *Rising: Ireland, Easter*, 187.

123. Quoted ibid.

124. Wills, *Dublin 1916*, 51–52.

125. Foley, "'Irish Folly,'" unpublished paper, 8.

126. Ibid.

127. "Continuance of Martial Law," May 11, 1916, vol. 82, cols. 941–42, HC Deb.

128. Walsh, *News from Ireland*, 53, 54.

129. Whitmore, *With the Irish*.

130. McCracken, *Irish Pro-Boers*; and McCracken, *MacBride's Brigade*.

131. Lowry, "'World's No Bigger,'" 280.

132. Elaine Scarry most convincingly draws such connections when linking "the body in pain" with human creativity. See Scarry, *Body in Pain*.

133. William Butler Yeats, "The Rose Tree," https://www.poetryfoundation.org /poems/57315/the-rose-tree.

134. William Butler Yeats, "Easter, 1916," September 15, 1916, https://www.poetry foundation.org/poems/43289/easter-1916.

135. Mazower, *No Enchanted Palace*, 31–37.

136. Ibid., 37. Smuts's evolving thinking, in Mazower's words (20), linked "national-ism" to "broader international affiliations of sentiment, loyalty, and interest."

137. Ibid., 41–43.

138. Pedersen, *Guardians*, 18.

139. Mazower, *No Enchanted Palace*, 21, 44–46, for a discussion of "international trusteeships" in the form of mandates.

140. Wertheim, "League of Nations," 212, 213.

141. Pedersen, *Guardians*, 17, 18.

142. League of Nations, Covenant, Article 22 (emphasis added).

143. Mount, "Parcelled Out," 7–10.

144. Pedersen, *Guardians*. I'm grateful to Susan Pedersen for also highlighting this point to me in correspondence.

145. Mazower, *No Enchanted Palace*, 14.

146. McCarthy, *British People and League of Nations*; and Pedersen's important review, "Triumph of Poshocracy."

147. Pedersen, *Guardians*, 77.

148. Adas, "Contested Hegemony"; and Das, *Race, Empire*.

149. Mazower, *Dark Continent*, 45.

150. Hyam, *Britain's Declining Empire*, 32.

CHAPTER 3: LEGALIZED LAWLESSNESS

1. The account of Jallianwala Bagh, and the general disorder and retributions in the Punjab and beyond in April 1919, draws on a vast and rich literature, including Wagner, *Amritsar 1919*; Collett, *Butcher of Amritsar*; Fein, *Imperial Crime and Punishment*; Sayer, "British Reaction"; Draper, *Amritsar*; Datta, *Jallianwala Bagh*; and Swinson, *Six Minutes to Sunset*.

2. Simpson, *Human Rights*, 82; and Ghosh, *Gentlemanly Terrorists*, 31–32, 42–44.

3. Harper's *Underground Asia* traces the intellectual currents of shared ideas in Asia from 1900 through much of the interwar period, and Gopal's *Insurgent Empire* traces the broader global circulation of people and ideas, as well as the ways in which subject populations actively turned European ideas about liberation against European imperial projects.

4. Heehs, *Bomb in Bengal*; Bose, "Spirit and Form," 129–44; and Hoda, *Alipore Bomb Case*.

5. Adas, "Contested Hegemony," 49–51. I am grateful to Sugata Bose for his raising Tagore's participation in the 1905 movement with me.

6. For the Lucknow Pact of 1916, see, for example, Brown, *Gandhi's Rise*, 31–32. For the emergence of the Indian nationalism and the Indian National Congress, see, for example, Seal, *Emergence of Indian Nationalism*; and Mehrotra, *Emergence of Indian National Congress*.

7. Gandhi, *Affective Communities*; and Hunt, *Gandhi in London*.

8. Brown, *Gandhi's Rise*, 1–33

9. Gandhi, *Gandhi: The Man*, 172.

10. For the Rowlatt Act and its effects, see Brown, *Modern India*, 200–221.

11. Brown, *Gandhi's Rise*, 170–73; and Simpson, *Human Rights*, 64.

12. Sayer, "British Reaction," 136–38; and Ghosh, *Gentlemanly Terrorists*, 42–45. Note that the Rowlatt Act was not enforced on a federal level and was, as Ghosh points out, "repealed quietly in September 1921."

13. As quoted in Simpson, *Human Rights*, 64.

14. *Report on the Committee . . . to Investigate the Disturbances in the Punjab., etc.*, Cmd. 681, xiv–v, 1000–1095.

15. Sayer, "British Reaction," 140.

16. Ibid., 140–42.

17. Ibid., 141.

18. *Report on the Committee ... to Investigate the Disturbances in the Punjab., etc.,* Cmd. 681, 1088.

19. Sayer, "British Reaction," 142. See also Montagu's statement, July 8, 1920, vol. 131, cols. 1707–8, HC Deb.

20. *Report on the Committee ... to Investigate the Disturbances in the Punjab., etc.,* Cmd. 681, 1116, emphasis added.

21. For a more expansive discussion of John Stuart Mill and Rudyard Kipling, see chapter 1. Other scholars have seen the connections between J. S. Mill, Kipling, and the discourse surrounding the Dyer affair. See, for example, Sayer, "British Reaction."

22. Padmore, *History of Pan-African Congress;* Das, *Race, Empire,* 1–32; and James, *George Padmore,* 1–14.

23. Rich, *Race and Empire,* 70–82; and Collett, *Butcher of Amritsar,* 377.

24. Angell, *Fruits of Victory,* 212.

25. Lawrence, "Forging a Peaceable Kingdom," 572–73.

26. For a comprehensive background on Montagu, see Black, "Edwin Montagu," 199–218; and for Montagu's sordid marital life with Venetia Stanley, see Levin, *Politics, Religion, and Love.*

27. *Report on the Committee ... to Investigate the Disturbances in the Punjab., etc.,* Cmd. 681, vii.

28. July 8, 1920, vol. 131, col. 1739, HC Deb.

29. Ibid.

30. Collett, *Butcher of Amritsar;* and Swinson, *Six Minutes to Sunset.*

31. *Report on the Committee ... to Investigate the Disturbances in the Punjab., etc.,* Cmd. 681, 30.

32. As referenced in July 19, 1920, vol. 41, col. 233, HL Deb.

33. The Hunter Committee was also comprised of an Indian minority, including Chimanlal Harilal Setalvad, an eminent barrister. They produced a minority report to accompany the final seven-volume Hunter Committee report. For an excellent discussion of the Hunter Commission and the debates over Dyer in Parliament see Wagner, *Amritsar 1919,* 223–42.

34. Collett, *Butcher of Amritsar,* 337–38.

35. Ibid., 378–79.

36. Ibid., 379.

37. *Daily Mail,* May 4, 1920.

38. *Disturbances in the Punjab: Statement by Brig.-General R.E.H. Dyer, C.B.,* Cmd. 771.

39. July 8, 1920, vol. 131, col. 1707, HC Deb.

40. July 8, 1920, vol. 131, col. 1708, HC Deb.

41. July 8, 1920, vol. 131, cols. 1709–10, HC Deb.

42. Toye, *Churchill's Empire,* 152.

43. July 8, 1920, vol. 131, col. 1725, HC Deb.

44. July 8, 1920, vol. 131, col. 1729, HC Deb.

45. July 8, 1920, vol. 131, cols. 1728–29, HC Deb.

46. Datta, *Jallianwala Bagh*, frontispiece, as cited in Sayer, "British Reaction," 132.
47. July 8, 1920, vol. 131, col 1739, HC Deb.
48. July 8, 1920, vol. 131, col. 1738, HC Deb.
49. July 8, 1920, vol. 131, cols. 1775–76, HC Deb.
50. July 8, 1920, vol. 131, col. 1795, HC Deb.
51. July 19, 1920, vol. 41, col. 307, HC Deb.
52. July 19, 1920, vol. 41, col. 223, HC Deb.
53. Sayer, "British Reaction," 157.
54. Ibid., 158.
55. Collett, *Butcher of Amritsar*, 385.
56. Sayer, "British Reaction," 157.
57. Toye, *Churchill's Empire*, 154–56.
58. Tagore, *Essential Tagore*, 108–9.
59. Brown, *Gandhi's Rise*, 307–42.
60. Rose, *Literary Churchill*, 216.
61. Hyam, *Britain's Declining Empire*, 30–37.
62. Gallagher, "Nationalisms," 362.
63. Ibid., 367.
64. Fahmy, *Ordinary Egyptians*, 136–38; and Jakes, *Egypt's Occupation*, 249–53.
65. Fahmy, *Ordinary Egyptians*, 138.
66. Ibid., 138–39; Schulz, *History of Islamic World*, 54; and Jankowski, *Egypt*, 111–15.
67. As quoted in Gallagher, "Nationalisms," 360.
68. As quoted in Bishku, "British Empire and Egypt's Future" (Ph.D. diss.), 51, 53, 55.
69. Ibid., 58.
70. For the political, strategic, and economic interests at play in Egypt during the interwar period, see, for example, Daly, "British Occupation"; Mak, *British in Egypt*, 214–39; and Darwin, *Britain, Egypt*, 80–137.
71. For a broad assessment of the press during this period, see Koss, *Rise and Fall of Political Press*, 786–821; and Bishku, "British Press," 605.
72. As quoted in Bishku, "British Press," 608.
73. Ibid., 609–10.
74. Blaustein et al., *Independence Documents*, 204.
75. Ibid.
76. The following discussion of the Irish War of Independence draws on Townshend, *British Campaign*; Townshend, *Political Violence*; Bennett, *Black and Tans*; Hart, *I.R.A. at War*; Coogan, *Michael Collins*; Jeffery, *Irish Empire?*; and Hittle, *Michael Collins*.
77. Hopkinson, *Last Days of Dublin Castle*, 64.
78. Holmes, *Little Field Marshal*, 357.
79. Townshend, *British Campaign*, 40–46.
80. See, for example, November 24, 1920, vol. 135, cols. 495–96, HC Deb; February 15, 1921, vol. 138, col. 52, HC Deb; and November 29, 1920, vol. 125, cols. 1083–84, HC Deb.

81. Callwell, *Field-Marshal Sir Wilson*, 2:252.

82. Rast, "Tactics, Politics, and Propaganda" (master's thesis); and Walsh, *News from Ireland.*

83. Kissane, *Politics of Irish Civil War*, 39–98.

84. Lowry, "New Ireland, Old Empire," 173–74.

85. Dwyer, *Squad.*

86. For the origins and nature of the RIC, see Palmer, *Police and Protest;* and Hawkins, "Dublin Castle." For IRA strategy against the RIC, see, for example, Townshend, *British Campaign.*

87. Hart, *I.R.A. and Its Enemies*, 73.

88. Bennett, *Black and Tans*, 24.

89. Leeson, *Black and Tans*, 30.

90. Ibid., 234n94.

91. Bew, *Churchill and Ireland*, 95.

92. Neligan, *Spy in the Castle*, 174.

93. Leeson, *Black and Tans*, 32–33.

94. Simpson, *Highest Degree Odious*, 27–29. For similar early legislation in India, see Ghosh, *Gentlemanly Terrorists*, 34–45.

95. Leeson, *Black and Tans*, 173.

96. Ibid., 170–74.

97. Lawrence, "War, Violence," 577, 584.

98. Hannigan, *Terence MacSwiney*, 54, 56.

99. O'Donovan, *Kevin Barry*, 81, 103; and Golway, *Cause of Liberty*, 257–72.

100. O'Donovan, *Kevin Barry*, 127. Additional accounts include Ainsworth, "Kevin Barry"; and Doherty, "Kevin Barry."

101. O'Donovan, *Kevin Barry*, 213. For additional "Songs, Ballads and Poems," see 212–32.

102. Ryan, "'Drunken Tans,'" 78.

103. Leeson, *Black and Tans*, 51.

104. Ibid., 52.

105. Coogan, *Michael Collins*, 157–60. Note that there is some dispute as to whether or not all fourteen killed were British intelligence agents.

106. Murphy, *Bloody Sunday*, 206.

107. Seedorf, "Lloyd George Government," 60.

108. Townshend, *British Campaign*, 122.

109. Leeson, *Black and Tans*, 33; and Toye, *Churchill's Empire*, 139.

110. Coogan, *Michael Collins*, 156.

111. On January 5, 1921, martial law was extended to the two remaining Munster counties of Clare and Waterford, as well as to Wexford and Kilkenny in Leinster.

112. White and O'Shea, *Burning of Cork*, 111–38.

113. Coogan, *Michael Collins*, 165.

114. As quoted in "A Catholic Review of the Week," *America: The Jesuit Review*, October 23, 1920, 223.

115. "Ireland's Reign of Terror," *Literary Digest* 68, no. 3 (1921): 20.

116. Lawrence, "War, Violence," 577–82.

117. Ibid., 582.

118. This point is made particularly well in ibid.

119. "Military Operations and Inquiries: Disturbances: Military Inquiry into Incendiarism and Looting in Cork," December 1920, WO 35/88A, TNA.

120. Cabinet Meeting Minutes, December 29, 1920, CAB/23/23/341, TNA.

121. See, for example, December 13, 1920, vol. 136, cols. 171–72, 173, 178, and 181–82, HC Deb.

122. December 13, 1920, vol. 136, col. 176, HC Deb.

123. "Ireland in Parliament," *Times*, February 17, 1921, 11.

124. Messenger, *Broken Sword*, 140, 142.

125. Ibid., 145–46.

126. F. P. Crozier, "The R.I.C. and the Auxiliaries: Their Organisation and Discipline," *Manchester Guardian*, March 28, 1921, 7.

127. Messenger, *Broken Sword*, 138, 170; and Leeson, *Black and Tans*, 52.

128. Messenger, *Broken Sword*, 200.

129. Dwyer, *Squad*, 136.

130. Mockaitis, *British Counterinsurgency*, 20.

131. Kalyvas, *Logic of Violence*, 92.

132. Waghelstein, *El Salvador: Observations*, 42, as quoted in Kalyvas, *Logic of Violence*, 54.

133. Toolis, *Rebel Hearts*, 255–56.

134. Ryan, "'Drunken Tans,'" 78–83. Note that sexual assaults, perpetrated by either side of the war, were comparatively rare relative to other British empire wars. I am grateful to Stephen Howe for raising this point with me. See also Clark, "Violence Against Women," 75–90.

135. See, for example, Kautt, *Ground Truths*; Kautt, *Ambushes and Armour*; and Sheehan, *Hard Local War*.

136. Townshend, *British Campaign*, 206.

137. McDonagh, "Losing Ireland."

138. Toye, *Churchill's Empire*, 140.

139. Ibid., 140–41.

140. For a detailed record of the treaty negotiations, the ensuing divisions between De Valera and Collins, and the incipient civil war, see Dwyer, *Big Fellow, Long Fellow*, 192–331. For a complete account of Collins's last days and funeral, see Coogan, *Michael Collins*, 382–432. Note that, given Collins died in an unplanned ambush, it's possible that his killers did not know his identity until after they murdered him.

141. Toye, *Churchill's Empire*, 141.

CHAPTER 4: "I'M MERELY PRO-BRITISH"

1. The impact of Britain's air control policy in the Middle East and the nature of its desert missions have received significant scholarly attention, particularly with regard to its role in incubating later aerial bombing techniques and strategies for the Second World War. For further details on Arthur Harris's missions, see Probert, *Bomber Harris*. The most recent and groundbreaking work on air

control in Iraq is Satia, "Defense of Inhumanity"; and Satia, *Spies in Arabia*, 201–338. See also Omissi, *Air Power*; Townshend, "Civilization and 'Frightfulness'"; and Omissi, "Technology and Repression."

2. Probert, *Bomber Harris*, 23–32.
3. Ibid., 43; Lindqvist, *History of Bombing*, 48.
4. Probert, *Bomber Harris*, 32–43.
5. Corum, "Myth of Air Control," 63–65; Pedersen, *Guardians*, 40–42, 278.
6. Omissi, *Air Power*, 20–21; and Townshend, "Civilization and 'Frightfulness,'" 142–45. For a comprehensive history of the Iraqi Revolt of 1920 and the events leading up to it, see Rutledge, *Enemy on the Euphrates*.
7. Hastings, *Bomber Command*, 5.
8. Miller, *Boom*.
9. As quoted in Gooch, *Airpower*, 92.
10. Satia, "Defense of Inhumanity."
11. Ibid., 19–25; Thomas, *Empires of Intelligence*; and Scott, "Try It on the Natives."
12. Newbury, *Patrons, Clients, and Empire*; and Thomas, *Empires of Intelligence*, 2–4.
13. Bayly, *Empire and Information*, 1–9.
14. Walton, *Empire of Secrets*, 2–5.
15. Bayly, *Empire and Information*, 6–7, 315–37; Thomas, *Empires of Intelligence*, 27; Walton, *Empire of Secrets*, 2; Hyam, *Britain's Declining Empire*, 10; and Kirk-Greene, "'Thin White Line.'"
16. Walton, *Empire of Secrets*, 3–5.
17. Simpson, *Highest Degree Odious*, 37–38; Thomas, *Empires of Intelligence*, 47–50; and Blyth, *Empire of the Raj*, 147–51.
18. Scott, "Try It on the Natives."
19. Westrate, *Arab Bureau*; Blyth, *Empire of the Raj*, 147–51; and Thomas, *Empires of Intelligence*, 49–52.
20. Thomas, *Empires of Intelligence*, 52.
21. Orlans, *T. E. Lawrence*, 120.
22. Mohs, *Military Intelligence*; and Mack, *Prince of Disorder*, 161. For a full biographical account of Lawrence set in the broader Middle Eastern context, see Anderson, *Lawrence of Arabia*.
23. Satia, *Spies in Arabia*.
24. Satia, "Defense of Inhumanity," 40–41.
25. Ibid., 31, 45–47.
26. As quoted in Simpson, *Human Rights*, 72–73.
27. "Forms of Frightfulness" and Enclosure 2.(A), December 16, 1922, AIR 5/264, TNA; and Minute to File, December 28, 1922, AIR 5/264, TNA.
28. Minute to File, December 28, 1922, AIR 5/264, TNA.
29. Catherwood, *Churchill's Folly*, 85, 186.
30. Jonathan Glancey, "Our Last Occupation: Gas, Chemicals, Bombs—Britain Has Used Them All Before in Iraq," *Guardian*, April 19, 2003.
31. Air Marshal Sir J. M. Salmond, "Statement of His Views upon the Principles Govern[ing] the Use of Air Power in Iraq," January 1924, Air Staff Memorandum No. 16 (secret), AIR 5/338, TNA.
32. Ibid. See also Rockel, "Wedding Massacres," 274.

33. Wilson, *After the Victorians*, 219; and Baker, *Human Smoke*, 8.

34. Lindqvist, *History of Bombing*, 48.

35. Rockel, "Wedding Massacres," 274.

36. Ibid.; and Townshend, "Civilization and 'Frightfulness,'" 155.

37. Minute to File, July 10, 1924, AIR 5/338/30A, TNA.

38. Pedersen, *Guardians*, 40.

39. In 1958, Faysal II and several members of his family were executed during a military coup that abolished the 1925 Iraqi constitution, largely a British document that granted the king extraordinary executive power and established the Iraqi Republic. "Constitutional Law of Iraq," *Introduction to the Laws of Kurdistan*, 7–8, Iraq Working Paper Series, Pub. 2013, Iraq Legal Education Initiative, Stanford Law School, https://law.stanford.edu/wp-content/uploads/2018/04/ILEI-Constitutional-Law-2013.pdf.

40. Pedersen, *Guardians*, 263.

41. Ibid., 278.

42. For details on the negotiations over Iraq's emancipation and its admission into the League of nations, see Pedersen, *Guardians*, 263–86. The quote on Iraqi oil being a "lake of petroleum" is on 272.

43. Ibid., quotes on 282, 271.

44. Ibid., quote on 286.

45. Charlton, *Autobiography*, 271.

46. *Note on the Method of Employment of the Air Arm in Iraq*, Cmd. 2217; TNA, AIR 5/338, Bombing policy in Iraq, 1923–24; Townshend, "Civilization and 'Frightfulness,'" 149; Vinogradov, "1920 Revolt Reconsidered," 138; and Lindqvist, *History of Bombing*, 48.

47. Townshend, "Civilization and 'Frightfulness,'" 158.

48. Rabindranath Tagore, "Progress, Hospitality and Humanity: Afghanistan," in Soares, *Lectures and Addresses*.

49. H. Tudor, Diary, 326, Private Papers of Major General Sir HH Tudor, Catalogue 2949, IWMDD.

50. Ibid., 327.

51. Ibid., 326–27; and Jeffery, *Field Marshal Sir Wilson*, 281–86.

52. H. Tudor, Diary, 85–86, 342–48.

53. For the reference to "Arab Khalifate of Islam," see Sherif Husayn of Mecca to Sir Henry McMahon, His Majesty's High Commissioner at Cairo, July 14, 1915, in Pre-State Israel: The Hussein-McMahon Correspondence, July 1915–August 1916, https://www.jewishvirtuallibrary.org/the-hussein-mcmahon-correspondence-july-1915-august-1916#2.

54. Letter from McMahon to Husayn, October 24, 1915, Pre-Israel: The Hussein-McMahon Correspondence, https://www.jewishvirtuallibrary.org/the-hussein-mcmahon-correspondence-july-1915-august-1916#2, accessed November 2, 2020.

55. Lloyd George, *Memoirs*, 2:720.

56. Ibid., 2:721; and Segev, *One Palestine*, 333–56.

57. Weizmann, *Trial and Error*; and Reinharz, *Chaim Weizmann*, 215–20.

58. Fromkin, *Peace to End All Peace*, 274.

59. Zionist Congress: First Zionist Congress & Basel Program, August 29, 1897, https://www.jewishvirtuallibrary.org/first-zionist-congress-and-basel-program -1897.

60. As quoted in Segev, *One Palestine*, 45; and Woodward, *Documents on Foreign Policy*, 4:345.

61. For a useful analysis of the Balfour Declaration, the creation of a "national home for the Jewish people," and its implications, see Shlaim, "Balfour Declaration," 251–70.

62. Friedman, *Question of Palestine*, 268.

63. As quoted in Ingrams, *Palestine Papers*, 48. For a discussion of Lord Curzon and his memorandum "The Future of Palestine," see Hurewitz, *Struggle for Palestine;* and Vereté, "Balfour Declaration."

64. To this end, Nahum Sokolow, secretary general of the Zionist Organization and confidant of Weizmann, crisscrossed Europe collecting declarations of support for Zionism in one capital after the next, even gaining an audience with the pope. With Sokolow's successes, Weizmann leveraged the Foreign Office and also indicated that the German government was poised to issue a statement supporting Zionist demands. Adding credibility to Weizmann's lobbying efforts were the scores of reports that inundated London from an array of foreign officials, suggesting that Zionism and "world Jewry" were virtually synonymous, and that support for the latter was crucial to the war effort.

65. Friedman, *Question of Palestine*, 263–64. Of the considerable volume of literature pertaining to the Balfour Declaration, the first significant analysis is Stein, *Balfour Declaration*. There Mitchell argues a very similar position as here, that Weizmann took the initiative, but imperial and wartime considerations also elided, together with a Christian sense of statesmanship shared by many leaders in London. For the imperial self-interest point of view, see Sanders, *High Walls of Jerusalem*. For the place of World War I and the Balfour Declaration in the rise of Arab nationalism, see Antonius, *Arab Awakening*. For a thorough account of the negotiations, see Friedman, *Question of Palestine*.

66. Many other scholars make a similar point. William Roger Louis states that "using the Balfour Declaration as a historical premise, it was intellectually defensible to develop an argument going in either direction, either for a Jewish state (as opposed to a 'national home') or against it." Louis, *British Empire in Middle East*, 39.

67. I am grateful to Susan Pedersen for her raising these points with me in correspondence. See also Khalidi, *Hundred Years' War*, 23–27.

68. Toynbee, *Study of History*, Volume 10, 554.

69. The following description of Arab Palestine under Ottoman rule, together with patron-client relations, is drawn largely from the following works: Khalidi, *Palestinian Identity*, 1–144; Kayyali, *Palestine*, 22–42; Tamari, *Great War;* Owen, *Middle East;* Swedenburg, "Role of Palestinian Peasantry"; and Swedenburg, *Memories of Revolt*.

70. As quoted in Segev, *One Palestine*, 131.

71. Barr, *Line in the Sand*, 92.

72. Sachar, *History of Israel*, 122–23; Keith-Roach, *Pasha of Jerusalem*, 70–71; and Segev, *One Palestine*, 131–39.

73. As quoted in Huneidi, *Broken Trust*, 35. For Meinertzhagen's complaints and eventual dismissal, see Meinertzhagen, *Middle East Diary*, 81; and Wasserstein, *British in Palestine*, 71. Note that Meinertzhagen's diaries must be treated cautiously as some suspect he may have altered them prior to publication.

74. Kayyali, *Palestine*, 77.

75. As quoted in Segev, *One Palestine*, 9.

76. Ibid., 139.

77. League of Nations, Covenant, Article 22, June 28, 1919; and Palestine Mandate, July 24, 1922, preamble. On August 10, 1922, Britain's Palestine Order in Council, 1922, defined the powers of the high commissioner, the creation and purview of the executive and legislative councils, the regulation of the constitution, and the powers of the Palestine judiciary, among other things. British mandatory rule came into effect in September 1923.

78. White Paper of June 1922, https://avalon.law.yale.edu/20th_century/brwh1922 .asp; and Pedersen, "Impact of Oversight."

79. Kayyali, *Palestine*, 94–95; and Swedenburg, "Role of Palestinian Peasantry," 180–81. For a discussion of the Arab Palestinian political elite, see Al-Hout, "Palestinian Political Elite," 85–111.

80. Horne, *Job Well Done*, 78–84.

81. Fedorowich, "Problems of Disbandment," 98.

82. Ibid., 99.

83. See, for example, Cahill, "'Going Beserk,'" 60.

84. Sinclair, "'Crack Force,'" 51.

85. Duff, *Bailing*, 46.

86. Ibid.

87. Ibid.

88. Lundsten, "Wall Politics," 7.

89. Cahill, "'Going Beserk,'" 64; and Segev, *One Palestine*, 295–97.

90. Lundsten, "Wall Politics," 14n34.

91. Ibid., 14.

92. *Report on the Commission . . . to Determine the Rights and Claims of Moslems and Jews in Connection with the Western or Wailing Wall of Jerusalem*, 36.

93. Ibid., 38.

94. Lundsten, "Wall Politics," 18.

95. Ibid., 21.

96. *Report on the Commission . . . to Determine the Rights and Claims of Moslems and Jews in Connection with the Western or Wailing Wall of Jerusalem*, 7.

97. Winder, "'Western Wall' Riots"; and Swedenburg, "Role of Palestinian Peasantry," 177–84.

98. Winder, "'Western Wall' Riots"; and Segev, *One Palestine*, 316–19.

99. Segev, *One Palestine*, 323.

100. Ibid., 324–26; and Winder, "'Western Wall' Riots," 6.

101. Segev, *One Palestine*, 9, 325

102. Duff, *Bailing*, 168.
103. Cahill, "'Going Beserk,'" 62–64; Segev, *One Palestine*, 296–97, 303, 307, 331; and Duff, *Bailing with a Teaspoon*, 169–73.
104. Segev, *One Palestine*, 307.
105. Anderson, "Petition to Confrontation" (Ph.D. diss.), 498.
106. Pedersen, "Impact of Oversight," 47; and *Report of the Commission on the Palestine Disturbances*, Cmd. 3530.
107. For the authoritative account on this period of the Permanent Mandates Commission and Palestine, see Pedersen, "Impact of Oversight," 39–66, which includes a similar discussion on the PMC's querying Britain on the matters of immigration, coercion, and the like.
108. *Report of the Commission on the Palestine Disturbances*, Cmd. 3530; and *Palestine: Report on Immigration, Land Settlement and Development*, Cmd. 3686.
109. November 17, 1930, vol. 245, col. 78, HC Deb.

CHAPTER 5: IMPERIAL CONVERGENCE

1. Jamaal Husseini, president of Palestine Arab Delegation, to President of Permanent Mandates Commission, June 12, 1939, WO /32/4562, TNA; and Slocombe, *Mirror to Geneva*, 328.
2. League of Nations, Covenant, https://avalon.law.yale.edu/20th_century/leagcov.asp; and Part I, "The Condition of Palestine After the War," July 30, 1921, in League of Nations, *An Interim Report on the Civil Administration of Palestine, During the Period 1st July, 1920–30 June, 1921*, https://unispal.un.org/UNISPAL.NSF/0/349B02280A930813052565E90048ED1C.
3. Pappe, *Rise and Fall*, 275–76.
4. For example, see Archdeacon to chief secretary, June 2, 1936, and J. Hathorn Hall to Stewart, June 3, 1936, both in File 1, Box 61, JEM, GB165-0161, MEC; M. Dixon, government welfare inspector, "Notes on Interview at Secretariat," c. June 13, 1936, File 2, Box 66, JEM, GB165-0161, MEC; B. M. Nasir to Archdeacon Stewart, July 20, 1936, File 1, Box 66, JEM, GB165-0161, MEC; Government welfare inspector to chief secretary, July 13, 1936, File 1, Box 66, JEM, GB165-0161; Archdeacon in Palestine to air vice marshal of Commanding British Forces in Palestine, June 16, 1936, File 1, Box 66, JEM, GB165-0161, MEC; President of Bir Zeit Council (memorandum), c. July 7, 1936, File 1, Box 66, JEM, GB165-0161, MEC; and Eyewitness testimony from colonial police officer beginning in spring 1937, Sydney Burr Private Papers, 88/8/1, Catalogue 3, IWMDD. For an excellent recent book that explores questions of violence during the Arab Revolt (1936–39), see Hughes, *Britain's Pacification*. I shall draw on some of Hughes's earlier articles in this chapter.
5. For example, Arab Ladies of Jerusalem to high commissioner, April 28, 1939, File 1, Box 66, JEM, GB165-0161, MEC; S. O. Richardson to archbishop of Canterbury, November 23, 1938, File 2, Box 66, JEM, GB165-0161, MEC; Bishop of Jerusalem to chief secretary, April 9, 1938, File 2, Box 66, JEM, GB165-0161, MEC; Bishop to High Commissioner MacMichael, August 8,

1938, File 2, Box 66, JEM, GB165-0161, MEC; Archdeacon of Palestine to Chief Secretary Hall, June 2, 1936, File 5, Box 65, JEM, GB165-0161, MEC; Parkinson to Sir Arthur Wauchope, May 18, 1939, CO, 733/413/3, TNA; Minute to file, May 20, 1939 CO 733/413/3, TNA; Dr. Izzat Tannous to Rt. Hon. Malcolm MacDonald, October 28, 1938, CO 733/371/2, TNA; Arab National Bureau to colonial secretary, December 22, 1938, CO 733/371/2, TNA; "Extracts from a Letter Received from an Englishman in Palestine," September 16, 1938, CO 733/371/2, TNA; and R. H. Haining, "Hostile Propaganda in Palestine, its Origin, and Progress in 1938" (memorandum), December 1, 1938, WO 32/4562, TNA.

6. November 24, 1938, vol. 341, col. 1988, HC Deb; "Germany's Hostile Propaganda," *Yorkshire Post*, December 22, 1938; P. Roger, minute to file, October 18, 1938, and J. S. Bennect, October 28, 1938, CO 733/371/2, TNA; Sir G. Ogilvie Forbes (telegram), December 23, 1938, CO 731/371/2, TNA; and under-secretary of state for foreign affairs to under-secretary of state for colonies, "Anti-British Propaganda in Germany," December 2, 1938, CO 733/371/2, TNA.

7. G. D. Roseway to C. G. L. Syers, January 12, 1939, WO 32/4562, TNA.

8. Jamaal Husseini to PMC president, June 12, 1939, WO 32/4562, TNA.

9. Archdeacon to chief secretary, June 2, 1936, File 1, Box 61, JEM, GB165-0161, MEC.

10. Margaret Nixon to chief secretary (memorandum), June 9, 1936, File 2, Box 66, JEM, GB165-0161, MEC; and "Notes on Interview at Secretariat," June 13, 1936, File 2, Box 66, JEM, GB165-0161, MEC.

11. J. Hathorn Hall to [Weston Henry] Stewart, June 3, 1936, File 1, Box 61, JEM, GB165-0161, MEC.

12. "Notes on Interview at Secretariat," June 13, 1936, File 2, Box 66, JEM, GB165-0161, MEC.

13. Weston Henry Stewart to J.G.M., "Disturbances in Palestine" ("strictly confidential" memorandum), June 9, 1936, File 1, Box 61, JEM, GB165-0161, MEC.

14. Pedersen, *Guardians*, 283–84, 374.

15. Kayyali, *Palestine*, 158–59.

16. Mitter, "Financial Life," 289–310; Anderson, "Petition to Confrontation" (Ph.D. diss.), 471–97; Swedenburg, "Role of Palestinian Peasantry," 184–85; and Pedersen, "Impact of Oversight," 54–55.

17. Khalidi, *Palestinian Identity*, 143–75; Kayyali, *Palestine*, 163–71; and Swedenburg, "Role of Palestinian Peasantry," 186–87.

18. Bowden, *Breakdown of Public Security*, 187.

19. Sanagan, *Lightning*, 1–120.

20. *Report of the Commission on the Palestine Disturbance*, Cmd. 3530, 129.

21. Townshend, "Defence of Palestine," 920–21.

22. Anderson, "State Formation," 41–44. See also Winder, "Anticolonial Uprising," 75–95.

23. Simpson, *Human Rights*, 84–85.

24. Ibid., 85–86.

25. Ibid., 86.
26. Hughes, "Banality of Brutality," 318; and Simson, *British Rule, and Rebellion*, 96–103.
27. Simpson, *Human Rights*, 85–86.
28. Gwynn, *Imperial Policing*, 4.
29. War Office, *Manual of Military Law, 1929* (London: HMSO, 1929); Duties in Aid of the Civil Power, WO 279/470, TNA; Notes on Imperial Policing, WO 279/796; and Hughes, "Banality of Brutality," 316–17.
30. Shoul, "Soldiers, Riot Control," 124–26, 132.
31. War Office, *Manual of Military Law*, 103, 255; and Hughes, "Banality of Brutality," 316–17.
32. Kayyali, *Palestine*, 196.
33. Hughes, "From Law and Order," 9–10.
34. Cohen, "Direction of Policy in Palestine," 250.
35. Hughes, "From Law and Order," 10; and Keith-Roach, *Pasha of Jerusalem*, 185.
36. *Palestine Royal Commission Report*, Cmd. 5479, 101.
37. Ibid., 87, 100–101; and Kayyali, *Palestine*, 196. For an excellent biographical account of al-Qawuqji, see Parsons, *The Commander*.
38. *Palestine Royal Commission Report*, Cmd. 5479, 101. The three main insurgent leaders to emerge by the second phase of the Arab Revolt were Abdul Rahim al Haj ('Abd al-Rahim al-Hajj Muhammad), Yousef Abu Dorrah (Yusif Abu Dura), and Aref Abdul Razik (Arif Abd al-Raziq); see Hughes, "Palestinian Collaboration," 298.
39. *Palestine Royal Commission Report*, Cmd. 5479, 87, 373.
40. Ibid., 368.
41. Pedersen, "Impact of Oversight," 59.
42. Permanent Mandates Commission, Minutes, 32nd (Extraordinary) Session, July 30 to August 18, 1937, 39, 44. Widener Library, Harvard University, Cambridge, MA.
43. Pedersen, *Guardians*, 383.
44. Cohen, *Palestine, Retreat from Mandate*, 53; and Pedersen, "Impact of Oversight," 57–59.
45. July 21, 1937, vol. 36, col. 2264, HC Deb.
46. July 21, 1937, vol. 36, col. 2341, HC Deb.
47. For an important analysis of the colonial state, military and administrative complexes, and violence, see Hansen and Stepputat, *States of Imagination*, 1–38; and Young, *African Colonial State*.
48. Pappe, *Rise and Fall*, 280–90.
49. Al-Hout, "Palestinian Political Elite," 85–111; and Hughes, "Palestinian Collaboration," 291–315. Several historians also note that the lines between the Nashashibi and al-Husayni factions were not always clearly drawn. See Anderson, "Petition to Confrontation" (Ph.D. diss.), and Mitter, "Financial Life." I am indebted to Sreemati Mitter for reminding me of this, and for her input on Arab Palestinian nationalism.
50. Porath, *Palestine Arab National Movement*, 255.
51. H. D. Forster, May 1, 1939, 117, Forster Papers, GB-165-0109, MEC.

52. Ibid.

53. Fakhri 'Abd al-Hadi, originally a deputy of al-Qawuqji, became embittered by the rebel cause and turned to the British, who wooed and cultivated him to lead the peace bands.

54. Anderson, "State Formation," 44.

55. Hughes, "Palestinian Collaboration," 295–309.

56. Sydney Burr, letter dated February 2, 1938, Burr Papers, 88/8/1, Catalogue 3, IWMDD.

57. Segev, *One Palestine*, 415, 416.

58. Hoffman, *Anonymous Soldiers*, 72; and Tegart, *Terrorism in India*.

59. For an in-depth analysis of Bengali swadeshi, see Sartori, "Categorical Logic of a Colonial Nationalism"; and Bose, *Nation as Mother*, 1–31, 91–122.

60. For some four decades in Bengal, swadeshi would constitute a political movement unto itself. The Indian National Congress would remain faithful to nonviolence, but at various points the two movements would intertwine organizationally and ideologically. See Sarkar, *Swadeshi Movement*; Bose, "Nation as Mother"; and Chatterjee, "Bombs and Nationalism," 2–4.

61. Sri Aurobindo, "Shall India be Free?" *Bande Mataram* (Calcutta), April 29, 1907.

62. For an authoritative account on Bengali nationalism during this period, see Ghosh, *Gentlemanly Terrorists*.

63. Silvestri, *Ireland and India*; Silvestri, "'Sinn Fein of India'"; Fraser, "Ireland and India"; Davis, "Influence of Irish Revolution"; and Holmes and Holmes, *Ireland and India*.

64. Silvestri, *Ireland and India*, 48.

65. Chatterjee, "Bombs and Nationalism," 11–12; Ghosh, *Gentlemanly Terrorists*, 139–40; and Silvestri, "'Sinn Fein of India,'" 467.

66. Silvestri, "'Sinn Fein of India,'" 469. For a detailed account of hunger striking in Bengal during this period and its impact on local popular sympathy, see Ghosh, *Gentlemanly Terrorists*, 123–26.

67. Chatterjee, "Bombs and Nationalism," 1–33; and Anderson, *Imagined Communities*.

68. Chatterjee, "Bombs and Nationalism," 18; and Ghosh, *Gentlemanly Terrorists*, 71–72.

69. Chatterjee, "Bombs and Nationalism," 15, 18.

70. Ghosh, *Gentlemanly Terrorists*, 139–50; and Silvestri, "'Sinn Fein of India,'" 470.

71. Ibid.

72. Ghosh, *Gentlemanly Terrorists*, 139–60; and Silvestri, "'Sinn Fein of India,'" 461, 463, 466.

73. Silvestri, "'Sinn Fein of India,'" 486; and Silvestri, *Ireland and India*, 73.

74. Cook, "Irish Raj," 507–29; and Sinclair, "'Irish' Policeman," 173, 187.

75. Silvestri, *Ireland and India*, 70.

76. Ghosh, *Gentlemanly Terrorists*, 144, 132.

77. Silvestri, *Ireland and India*, 72–73.

78. Silvestri, "'Sinn Fein of India,'" 483.

79. Hittle, *Michael Collins*, 245.

80. Chatterjee, "Bombs and Nationalism," 24. See also Hittle, *Michael Collins*, 245; and Ghosh, *Gentlemanly Terrorists*, 132, where she discusses Tegart and Anderson's role in creating an "efficient despotism."

81. Griffiths, *To Guard My People*, 409. Also quoted in Silvestri, "'Irishman Is Suited,'" 42.

82. Hittle, *Michael Collins*, 246; Silvestri, "'Irishman Is Suited,'" 41; and Silvestri, "Thrill of 'Dressing Up.'"

83. Tegart, *Terrorism in India*, 11.

84. Ibid.; and Silvestri, "'Irishman Is Suited,'" 43.

85. Silvestri, "'Irishman Is Suited,'" 41; Silvestri, *Ireland and India*, 74; Kevin Connolly, "Charles Tegart and the Forts that Tower over Israel," *BBC Magazine*, September 10, 2012; and Hittle, *Michael Collins*, 246.

86. Murthy, "Cellular Jail," 880.

87. For Tegart's time in Andaman, see Mukherjee, "Colonialism, Surveillance," 70–74. For prisoners' experiences at the Cellular Jail, see, for example, Savarkar, *My Transportation for Life*; Sen, *Disciplining Punishment*; Mathur, *Kala Pani*; Murthy, "Cellular Jail," 879–88; and Cathy Scott-Clark and Adrian Levy, "Survivors of Our Hell," *Guardian*, June 22, 2001.

88. Griffiths, *To Guard My People*, 409; Ghosh, *Gentlemanly Terrorists*, 193–95; and Silvestri, "'Irishman Is Suited,'" 42.

89. Griffiths, *To Guard My People*, 258–61, 409–10; Connolly, "Charles Tegart"; Hittle, *Michael Collins*, 247; and Silvestri, "'Irishman Is Suited,'" 42.

90. Connolly, "Charles Tegart"; and Silvestri "'Irishman Is Suited,'" 42–43. For biographical details on Annie Besant, see Kumar, *Besant's Rise to Power*; and Bevir, "Theosophy and Origins."

91. Ghosh, "Revolutionary Women," 361; Hittle, *Michael Collins*, 246–47; and McMahon, *British Spies and Irish Rebels*, 38–39.

92. Griffiths, *To Guard My People*, 411.

93. In the aftermath of Palestine's 1929 violence, Herbert Dowbiggin had undertaken a full review of the Mandate's police forces, advocating for demilitarization and an integration of British, Arab, and Jewish officers. His appraisal of the Palestine Police Force reflected a misperception of policing in the empire, expressed in the idea that the empire's police forces should be more like those in Britain, where the population was ruled through consent, not through coercion or threats of it. See H. L. Dowbiggin, "Report on the Palestine Police Force," May 6, 1930, CO 935/4/2, TNA; and Kroizer, "Dowbiggin to Tegart," 118–23.

94. Kroizer, "Dowbiggin to Tegart," 132n52.

95. "Tegart Report," January 1938, CO 733/383/1, TNA; and "Summary of the Recommendations Contained in Sir Charles Tegart's Report on the Organisation of the Palestine Police," January 1938, CO 733/383/1, TNA.

96. Hughes, "Palestinian Collaboration," 293–97. See also Cohen, *Army of Shadows*, 95–170.

97. Tegart and Petrie recruited Arthur Giles, a senior officer from the Egyptian police service with close links to the Arab Bureau, to take over Palestine's CID. Better known by the local honorific of "Giles Bey," the ambitious and highly

skilled Middle Eastern specialist with a mastery of Arabic was joined by specially funded reinforcements and by Gerald Foley, another seasoned Palestine officer who had also served in the Royal Irish Constabulary. For additional details and genealogies on empire-tested police officers, many of whom spent time in Ireland, then relocated to the Mandate, see Miles W. Lampson to Harold MacMichael (memorandum), March 8, 1938, CO 733/383/8, TNA; High commissioner of Palestine to colonial secretary (telegram), March 7, 1938, CO 733/383/8, TNA; Harouvi, *Palestine Investigated*, 68; Hoffman, *Anonymous Soldiers*, 73; and "Individuals from ADRIC who Joined Palestine Gendarmerie," http://www.theauxiliaries.com/palestine/individuals.html.

98. Keith-Roach, *Pasha of Jerusalem*, 191; and Segev, *One Palestine*, 428.
99. Frantzman, "Tegart's Shadow," 10–14.
100. Keith-Roach, *Pasha of Jerusalem*, 191; Hoffman, *Anonymous Soldiers*, 73; Segev, *One Palestine*, 416; Kroizer, "From Dowbiggin to Tegart," 126–27; and Frantzman, "Tegart's Shadow," 10–14.
101. Frantzman, "Tegart's Shadow," 13.
102. Desmond Woods, interview, Accession no. 23846, IWMSA; Humphrey Edgar Nicholson Bredin, interview, Accession no. 4550, IWMSA; and Gilbert Alan Shephard, interview, Accession no. 4597, IWMSA.
103. See multiple correspondences in "Police Reorganization: Sir C Tegart's Mission to Palestine," 1938, CO 733/383/1, TNA.
104. As quoted in Porath, *Palestine Arab National Movement*, 238. For the Arab resurgence, particularly in the summer months of 1938, see 237–38.
105. Minute to File, September 13, 1938, CO 733/371/1, TNA.
106. Minute to File, June 5, 1938, CO 733/371/1, TNA; Smith, "Communal Conflict," 70; Segev, *One Palestine*, 428; Frantzman, "Tegart's Shadow," 12; and Kroizer, "From Dowbiggin to Tegart," 128–29.
107. Hoffman, *Anonymous Soldiers*, 87–88.
108. Norris, "Repression and Rebellion," 29; and Smith, "Communal Conflict," 69–70.
109. "Military Lessons of the Arab Rebellion in Palestine, 1936," 166, 169, WO/191/70, TNA.
110. Fred Howbrook, interview, Accession no. 4619, IWMSA.
111. King-Clark, *Free for a Blast*, 158.
112. Ibid.; Humphrey Edgar Nicholson Bredin, interview, Accession no. 4550, IWMSA; Twigger, *Red Nile*, 399; Fred Howbrook, interview, Accession no. 4619, IWMSA; Sir John Evetts, interview, Accession no. 4451, IWMSA; and Tucker, *Great British Eccentrics*, 175.
113. Sykes, *Orde Wingate*, 108–15; and Anglim, *Orde Wingate*, 75.
114. Capt. O. C. Wingate of Force HQ Intelligence at Nazareth, "Appreciation of the Possibilities of Night Movements by Armed Forces of the Crown with the Object of Putting an End to Terrorism in Northern Palestine," June 5, 1938, Private Papers of Maj. Gen. H. E. N. Bredin, Catalogue 4623, IWMDD.
115. Bierman and Smith, *Fire in the Night*, 91.
116. Palestine High Commissioner Wauchope to Dill, December 15, 1936, WO 32/4178, TNA.

117. High Commissioner MacMichael to Rt. Hon. Malcolm MacDonald (secret memorandum), September 17, 1938, CO 733/371/1, TNA. See also S. Burr, letter, March 8, 1939, Burr Papers, 88/8/1, Catalogue 3, IWMDD: "For the last 2 years they have been steadily supplying the Jews out here with all the latest weapons & training them how to use them. Large numbers have joined the regiments here and as far as looks go are the same as the English."

118. Humphrey Edgar Nicholson Bredin, interview, Accession no. 4550, IWMSA; and Bierman and Smith, *Fire in the Night*, 65.

119. Bierman and Smith, *Fire in the Night*, 85. For comments on Wingate, see Bredin interview, IWMSA.

120. Sykes, *Orde Wingate*, 132–33; and Anglim, *Orde Wingate*, 48–53, 72–73.

121. Fred Howbrook, interview, Accession no. 4619, IWMSA.

122. Bierman and Smith, *Fire in the Night*, 115.

123. Ibid., 115–16; and Capt. O. C. Wingate OCSNS, "Report of Operations carried out by Special Night Squads on Night of 11/12 July 1938," GB0099, 11/1936–1938, Capt. Sir Basil Henry Liddell Hart Papers, LHC.

124. Bredin interview, IWMSA; Howbrook interview, IWMSA; and Segev, *One Palestine*, 430.

125. Segev, *One Palestine*, 431. Note that there is considerable debate over whether Wingate was present during some of these incidents, as opposed to whether these instances occurred. The point made here is that the Special Night Squads perpetrated these acts, which continued after Wingate was relieved of his duties in the fall of 1938. For debate on Wingate's presence during some of these instances, see Anglim, *Orde Wingate*, 91–93.

126. Segev, *One Palestine*, 431–32.

127. Sydney Burr, letter c. June 1937, Burr Papers, 88/8/1, Catalogue 3, IWMDD. For use of the term *wogs*, see multiple letters in the file, including July 9, 1937; December 20, 1937; c. March 1938; and c. April 1938.

128. Lord Caradon, interview by Bernard Wasserstein, 1970, (82)14, HI.

129. Probert, *Bomber Harris*, 83.

130. John Stewart Sancroft Grafton, interview, Accession no. 4506, IWMSA; Desmond Woods, interview, Accession no. 23846, IWMSA; Sydney Burr, letters dated c. August 1937, c. December 1937, c. April 1938, Burr Papers, Catalogue 3, IWMDD.

131. Harris to AVM Nichol (memorandum), September 5, 1938, AIR 23/765, TNA.

132. CAB 23/85, CC 56(36), 22, TNA.

133. "Operations Record Book of No. 6 Squadron," September 8, 1936, AIR 27/73, TNA.

134. Probert, *Bomber Harris*, 82; and multiple dated entries in RAF logbook, "Operations Record Book of No. 6 Squadron," AIR 27/73, TNA.

135. H. D. Forster, Diary, entry for December 1, 1938, 97, Forster Papers, GB165-0109, MEC.

136. Ibid., entry for November 18, 1938, 95, Forster Papers, GB165-0109, MEC.

137. Ritchie, *RAF*, 70.

138. "Operations Record Book of No. 6 Squadron," October 19, 1938, and November 6, 1938, AIR 27/73, TNA; "Royal Air Force Operations in Palestine Dur-

ing the Arab Rebellion 1936–39" (lecture notes), 17–18, Harris 3, AVM AT Harris, Sir Arthur Travers Harris Papers, Royal Air Force Museum.

139. Anglim, *Orde Wingate*, 89, 57.

140. Chaim Weizmann to Leon Blum, December 12, 1937, in Weizmann, *Letters and Papers*, 258.

141. Anglim, *Orde Wingate*, 77–78.

142. Ibid., 19–40; and King-Clark, *Free for a Blast*, 177.

143. For the best-documented and most compelling argument regarding Wingate and the balance between his "genius" and military precedents, see Anglim, *Orde Wingate*, from which this passage relies on most heavily for its conclusions. For the quote, see King-Clark, *Free for a Blast*, 178.

144. Bernard Montgomery to Sir Ronald Adam, December 4, 1938, in Hamilton, *Monty, 1887–1942*, 292.

145. Sheehan, *British Voices*, 151.

146. Humphrey Edgar Nicholson Bredin, interview, Accession no. 4550, IWMSA.

147. Segev, *One Palestine*, 432; and Bernard Montgomery to Sir Ronald Adam, January 1, 1939, in Hamilton, *Monty, 1887–1942*, 305.

148. Montgomery to Adam, December 4, 1938, in Hamilton, *Monty, 1887–1942*, 293, 292.

149. Anglim, *Orde Wingate*, 57.

150. Ibid., 94.

151. War Office, *Manual of Military Law*, 255.

152. For punitive raids, see Smiley, *Irregular Regular*, 13–16; Gilbert Alan Shephard, interview, Accession no. 4597; Fred Howbrook, interview, Accession no. 4619; and Desmond Woods, interview, Accession no. 23846, all in IWMSA. For Dr. Forster's recording of looting, see "Personal Impressions of the Night of Friday, 19th August, 1938 and the Morning of Saturday, 20th August, 1938," August 27, 1938, Forster Papers, GB165-0109, MEC.

153. Sydney Burr letter, c. November 1937, Burr Papers, 88/8/1, Catalogue 3, IWMDD.

154. Sydney Burr letters, April 22 and March 1938, ibid.

155. Goodman, "British Press Control," 704, 700, 712; and Bredin interview, IWMSA.

156. John Stewart Sancroft Grafton, interview, Accession no. 4506, IWMSA.

157. For other punitive raids, and the resulting damage to persons and properties see, for example, Complaints from Towns and Villages, A–H, File 1, and Complaints from Towns and Villages, I–Z, File 2, Box 66, JEM, GB165-0161, MEC.

158. Desmond Woods, interview, Accession no. 23846, IWMSA.

159. Arrigonie, *British Colonialism*, 35–36.

160. Goodman, "British Press Control," 708.

161. Woods interview, IWMSA.

162. "Notes: The Bishop's Visit to the Chief Secretary," February 17, 1938, File 1, Box 66, JEM, GB165-0161, MEC. For evidence of physical abuses endured during interrogations, see the extensive documentation in File 5, Box 65; File 1, Box 66; and File 2, Box 66, all in JEM, GB165-0161, MEC.

163. Smiley, *Irregular Regular*, 15.

164. Sydney Burr, letter dated c. September 1937, Burr Papers, 88/8/1, Catalogue 3, IWMDD.

165. Arthur Lane, interview, Accession no. 10295, IWMSA.

166. Ibid.

167. Hughes, "Banality of Brutality," 339–41; and H. D. Forster, Diary, entries for May 13 and 15, 1939, Forster Papers, GB165-0109, MEC.

168. Hughes, "Palestine Collaboration," 310–12.

169. Segev, *One Palestine*, 441.

170. Newton, *Fifty Years*, 275–93.

171. Beers, *Red Ellen*, 377–78.

172. March 23, 1938, vol. 333, col. 1192, HC Deb.

173. Ibid.; and Pedersen, *Guardians*, 388.

174. March 23, 1938, vol. 333, col. 1192, HC Deb.

175. Keith-Roach, *Pasha of Jerusalem*, 195.

176. March 23, 1938, vol. 333, cols. 1192–93, HC Deb; and Bishop in Jerusalem to Rt. Hon. W. G. Ormsby-Gore, M.P., April 6, 1938 and Ormsby-Gore to Right Rev. G. F. Graham Brown, April 25, 1938, File 5, Box 65, JEM, GB165-0161, MEC.

177. R. H. Haining to Archdeacon W. H. Stewart, October 8, 1938, File 5, Box 65, JEM, GB165-0161, MEC.

178. Archdeacon to S. O. Richardson, September 3,1938, File 2, Box 66, JEM, GB165-0161, MEC.

179. Newton, *Fifty Years*, 289–90; and File 5, Box 65, JEM, GB165-0161, MEC. In this file there is extensive documentation of Newton's work once banished from Palestine, including her time in Geneva where she translated and produced multiple documents for Jamal al-Husanyi. See, for example, Newton to Colonial Secretary MacDonald, June 17, 1939, and translated enclosure entitled, "Allegations of Illtreatment of Arabs by British Crown Forces in Palestine"; and Frances E. Newton to Bishop of Jerusalem, June 19, 1939.

180. Permanent Mandates Commission, Minutes, 32nd (Extraordinary) Session, July 30 to August 18, 1937, Annex 4, 211–18.

181. Pedersen, *Guardians*, 386.

182. Ibid., 384.

PART II: EMPIRE AT WAR

1. Anthony Daniel, interview, June 1, 1983, Accession nos. 0277/01 and 0277/02, NAS. For "Fortress Singapore," see Bayly and Harper, *Forgotten Armies*, 106.

2. Bayly and Harper, *Forgotten Armies*, 106–55; Jackson, *British Empire and Second World War*, 405–7; and Farrell and Hunt, *Sixty Years On*, 156–82.

3. Bayly and Harper, *Forgotten Armies*, 116; and Jackson, *British Empire and Second World War*, 407.

4. Bayly and Harper, *Forgotten Armies*, 120–21. See also Leasor, *Singapore*, 208–11.

5. See Headrick, *Bicycle Blitzkrieg*, 10–12; and Bayly and Harper, *Forgotten Armies*, 116.

6. Bayly and Harper, *Forgotten Armies*, 120.

7. Kheng, *Red Star over Malaya;* Farrell and Pratten, *Malaya;* Murfett et al., *Between Two Oceans;* and Bayly and Harper, *Forgotten Armies,* 114–20.
8. Kinvig, *Scapegoat,* 106.
9. Allen, *Singapore,* 195.
10. Callahan, *Worst Disaster,* 19; Bayly and Harper, *Forgotten Armies,* 116; and Jackson, *British Empire and Second World War,* 408.
11. Anthony Daniel, interview, June 1, 1983, Accession no. 0277/01, AVD, NAS.
12. The extensive literature on the fall of Singapore in February 1942 includes Owen, *Fall of Singapore;* Warren, *Singapore, 1942;* Farrell and Hunt, *Sixty Years On;* Callahan, *Worst Disaster;* and Bayly and Harper, *Forgotten Armies,* 106–55.
13. Schofield, *Wavell,* 256.
14. Anthony Daniel, interview, June 1, 1983, Accession nos. 0277/02, 0277/03, and 0277/04, AVD, NAS.

CHAPTER 6: AN IMPERIAL WAR

1. Jackson makes the argument that "until the Second World War, Britain was the world's only superpower." See Jackson, *British Empire and Second World War,* 4–5. John Gallagher suggests that "the period of European civil war to 1941" shifted and after 1941 became a war on a global scale, enveloping the British Empire. See Gallagher, *Decline, Revival and Fall,* 139; and Jeffery, "Second World War," 316–17.
2. May 13, 1940, vol. 360, col. 1502, HC Deb.
3. Morris, *Farewell the Trumpets,* 432.
4. Herman, *Gandhi and Churchill,* 448.
5. Morris, *Farewell the Trumpets,* 432.
6. September 9, 1941, vol. 374, col. 67, HC Deb.
7. Simpson, *Human Rights,* 159.
8. May 13, 1940, vol. 360, col. 1502, HC Deb.
9. Simpson, *Human Rights,* 159–60.
10. Ibid., 161–67.
11. Loughlin, *Public Law,* 14–22, 47–50, 140–68; and Moyn, *Last Utopia,* 112.
12. Simpson, *Human Rights,* 169–70, 171.
13. Franklin Delano Roosevelt, State of the Union address, January 6, 1941, https://www.gilderlehrman.org/sites/default/files/inline-pdfs/Four%20Freedoms%20Speech%201941.pdf, emphasis added.
14. Simpson, *Human Rights,* 174.
15. Moyn makes this point in *Last Utopia* (51) when he states, "the significance of Roosevelt's nonchalant elevation of the phrase ['human rights'] to its wartime career is chiefly that, extending earlier trends, it became an empty vessel that could be filled by a wide variety of different conceptions."
16. Roosevelt, State of the Union address, January 6, 1941.
17. Clarke, *Last Thousand Days,* 8.
18. Roosevelt, *As He Saw It,* 36; Clarke, *Last Thousand Days,* 8; and Louis, *Imperialism at Bay,* 7.
19. Manela, *Wilsonian Moment,* 25.

20. As quoted in Louis, *Imperialism at Bay*, 124.
21. Ibid., 5.
22. Ibid., 4–5.
23. September 9, 1941, vol. 374, col. 67, HC Deb.
24. Atlantic Charter, August 14, 1941, https://avalon.law.yale.edu/wwii/atlantic.asp.
25. Simpson, *Human Rights*, 179.
26. Atlantic Charter, emphasis added.
27. Louis, *Imperialism at Bay*, 125, 149.
28. Ibid., 129.
29. Ibid., 128–29.
30. September 9, 1941, vol. 374, cols. 68–69, HC Deb.
31. Louis, *Imperialism at Bay*, 131.
32. Franklin Delano Roosevelt, address to Congress, December 8, 1941, https://www.loc.gov/resource/afc1986022.afc1986022_ms2201/?r=-0.055,-0.012,1.217,0.75,0.
33. A point well made in Jackson, *British Empire and Second World War*, 8–9.
34. Silvestri, *Ireland and India*, 70 and 236, fn 145; and Silvestri, "'Sinn Fein of India,'" 483. See also Wheeler-Bennett, *John Anderson*, 126.
35. Amery, *War and Peace*, 162–63.
36. Wolpert, *Shameful Flight*, 59.
37. Rose, "Resignation of Eden," 911.
38. Mazower, *No Enchanted Palace*, 57. For a full account of Smuts from the aftermath of World War I until 1950, see Hancock, *Smuts*, Volume II.
39. Florence, *Emissary of the Doomed*, 156.
40. "Daily Express: A Chequered History," *BBC News*, January 25, 2001.
41. Beaverbrook, *Politicians*, 126.
42. Dalton, *Second World War Diary*, 62.
43. Hugh Dalton to Lord Halifax, July 2, 1940, quoted in Foot, *SOE in France*, 8. I am grateful to Priya Satia for pointing out to me Lawrence's influence.
44. See, for example, Rooney, *Mad Mike*; and Bidwell, *Chindit War*.
45. Warren, *World War II*, 239.
46. For Harris's role in World War II bombing and its broader context, see Hastings, *Bomber Command*, 102–29.
47. Goldman, "Defence Regulation 18B," 122.
48. Ibid.; and Simpson, "Detention Without Trial," 230–36.
49. Goldman, "Defence Regulation 18B," 124–26; and Simpson, "Detention Without Trial," 230–31.
50. June 4, 1940, vol. 361, cols. 794–95, HC Deb.
51. Simpson, "Detention Without Trial," 241.
52. Ibid., 247–48; and Simpson, *Highest Degree Odious*, 1–2, 37–50. See also Cotter, "Emergency Detention," 238–86.
53. Simpson, *Highest Degree Odious*, quotes on 61, 79–80, 101.
54. Wheeler-Bennett, *John Anderson*, 316.
55. Simpson, *Highest Degree Odious*, 186.
56. Ibid., 185–91; and Cobain, *Cruel Britannia*, 7–11.

57. For detailed histories on Britain's wartime interrogation centers, see Simpson, *Highest Degree Odious;* Cobain, *Cruel Britannia,* 1–37; and Fry, *London Cage.*

58. Cobain, *Cruel Britannia,* 19.

59. Sir David Petrie, Report on the Security Service (MI5), February 11 to March 1, 1941, CAB 301/25, TNA. For further background on Petrie, see Harper, *Underground Asia,* 199–200, 279–80.

60. Hoare, *Camp 020,* 8; Walton, *Empire of Secrets,* 24–29; and Sillitoe, *Cloak Without Dagger.*

61. Scotland, *London Cage,* 21.

62. "Interference with the Work of C.S.D.I.C. by the Construction of the Aerodrome at Bovingdon: Note for V.C.I.G.S," c. October 1941, WO 208/3456, TNA.

63. Stephens, "Digest of Ham," 41.

64. Ibid.; and Hoare, *Camp 020,* 18.

65. Walton, *Empire of Secrets,* 59–60.

66. Ibid., 60–62.

67. Ibid., 65–67.

68. Simpson, *Highest Degree Odious,* 242.

69. Fry, *London Cage,* 62–75.

70. Cobain, *Cruel Britannia,* 28–33.

71. "The Secrets of the London Cage," *Guardian,* November 11, 2005.

72. Scotland, *London Cage,* 81.

73. Cobain, *Cruel Britannia,* 31–33 (quote on 32); and Streatfeild, *Brainwash,* 365–66.

74. Masterman, *Double Cross System,* 3 (emphasis in the original); and Macintyre, *Double Cross.*

75. West, *Guy Liddell Diaries,* 1:98; Crowdy, *Deceiving Hitler,* 48; and Stephens, "Digest of Ham," 139–40.

76. Simpson, *Highest Degree Odious,* 391, emphasis added.

77. Jackson, *British Empire and Second World War,* 3–4.

78. Ibid., 1–3; Jeffery, "Second World War," 310–18; and Brown, *Modern India,* 319.

79. Jeffery, "Second World War," 316, 318.

80. Mukerjee, *Churchill's Secret War,* 5, 53.

81. Jeffery, "Second World War," 312–13, 324–26; and Brown, *Modern India,* 319.

82. I am grateful to Priya Satia for reminding me of this point. See also von Tunzelmann, *Indian Summer,* 237.

83. August 8, 1941, vol. 364, cols. 402–5, HC Deb.

84. Louis, *Ends of British Imperialism,* 397.

85. Louis, *Imperialism at Bay,* 149–50.

86. Talbot, *Khizr Tiwana,* 134.

87. Bayly and Harper, *Forgotten Armies,* 2–8.

88. Ibid., 122; and Harper, *Underground Asia,* 163–69, 292–97.

89. Bose, *His Majesty's Opponent,* 180–200; Talwar, *Talwars of Pathan Land,* 252; and Bayly and Harper, *Forgotten Armies,* 16–19.

90. Bayly and Harper, *Forgotten Armies*, 247.
91. Ibid., 247–48, 277.
92. Ibid., 278.
93. Tharoor, *Nehru*, 126.
94. Brown, *Prisoner of Hope*, 341.
95. Ibid., 342.
96. Simpson, *Human Rights*, 86–87; Brown, *Modern India*, 317–27; Bayly and Harper, *Forgotten Wars*, 18–19; Brown, *Prisoner of Hope*, 341–43; and Tharoor, *Nehru*, 126–27.
97. Fay, *Forgotten Army*, 75; and Toye, *Springing Tiger*, xiii.
98. Bayly and Harper, *Forgotten Armies*, 277.
99. Subhas Chandra Bose, "Give me blood and I promise you freedom!," July 1944, in Mukherjee, *Great Speeches*, chap. 17.
100. Singh, *Andaman Story*, 247; and Bayly and Harper, *Forgotten Armies*, 323–27.
101. Todman, *Britain's War*, 228.
102. Jeffery, "Second World War," 311.
103. Barker, *Ideas and Ideals*, 168.
104. Rakesh Krishnan Simha, "How India Bailed Out the West in World War II," *India Defence Review*, July 18, 2016, http://www.indiandefencereview.com /spotlights/how-india-bailed-out-the-west-in-world-war-ii/; and Mukerjee, *Churchill's Secret War*, 47–49.

CHAPTER 7: A WAR OF IDEAS

1. George Padmore, "The Second World War and the Dark Races," *Crisis*, November 1939, 327.
2. Numerous colonial subjects imagined and debated the "moral contract" throughout the interwar years. This chapter will focus primarily on the Pan-African movement and Black radicalism, though there were many others from empire, particularly South Asia, participating in these debates and exchanges. See, for example, Gopal, *Insurgent Empire*, chaps. 5 and 6.
3. Nwafor, "Wartime Propaganda," 238–39.
4. The large literature on anticolonial radicalism, transnational and global networks, and the dissemination of ideas through the press and other media includes Gopal, *Insurgent Empire*; Von Eschen, *Race Against Empire*; Pennybacker, *From Scottsboro to Munich*; Schwarz, *West Indian Intellectuals*; and James, *George Padmore*.
5. Azikiwe, *Renascent Africa*, 10, 87, and 174.
6. Williams, *Capitalism and Slavery*; and Kenyatta, *Facing Mount Kenya*. For a definitive study of Lewis's life and contribution to economic theory, see Tignor, *W. Arthur Lewis*.
7. Pyne-Timothy, "Identity, Society," 58.
8. James, *George Padmore*, 17.
9. James, *Beyond a Boundary*, 111, 18.
10. Gopal, *Insurgent Empire*, 331.
11. James, *Beyond a Boundary*, 111.

12. For an in-depth examination of C. L. R. James and his coming to terms with Britishness and the empire, see Howe, "C. L. R. James," 153–74.

13. Ibid., 164–65.

14. Pennybacker, *From Scottsboro to Munich*, 66–77.

15. Ibid., 3; Glynn, "Irish Immigration," 56; and George Padmore, "A Negro Looks at British Imperialism," *Crisis* 45 (1938): 396.

16. Padmore, "Negro Looks at British Imperialism," 396.

17. Du Bois, *Souls of Black Folk*, 2–3.

18. For an enduring analysis of the shifts in Du Bois's thinking, see Lewis, *Du Bois, 1868–1919*, and Lewis, *Du Bois, 1919–1963*.

19. Padmore, *Life and Struggles of Negro Toilers*, 9–27, 55–60.

20. Ibid., 18–19, 23, 65.

21. Ibid., 123–26.

22. Makonnen, *Pan-Africanism from Within*, 102–3. See also James, *George Padmore*, 36–37; and Schwartz, "George Padmore," 136.

23. James, *George Padmore*, passim.

24. For a discussion of Padmore and the Comintern, see Pennybacker, *From Scottsboro to Munich*, 67–87.

25. Ibid., 7; and George Padmore, "Ethiopia and World Politics," *Crisis* 42, no. 5 (1935): 138–39, 156–57, as quoted in Schwartz, "George Padmore," 139.

26. For a discussion of the ILP, its break away from the Labour Party, and its heterogeneous position on colonial affairs, see Pimlott, *Labour and the Left*; Cohen, *Failure of a Dream*; Howe, *Anticolonialism in British Politics*, 67–71; and Gopal, *Insurgent Empire*, 370–73.

27. Howe, *Anticolonialism in British Politics*, passim.

28. Ibid., 98–99.

29. As quoted in Gopal, *Insurgent Empire*, 372.

30. Padmore, *How Britain Rules Africa*, 3.

31. Jomo Kenyatta, "Hitler Could Not Improve on Kenya," *New Leader*, May 21, 1937.

32. James, *George Padmore*, 44.

33. Padmore, *How Britain Rules Africa*, 4, 129, 322, 395.

34. Pennybacker, *From Scottsboro to Munich*, 90.

35. As quoted in Howe, *Anticolonialism in British Politics*, 115.

36. James, *George Padmore*, 57, emphasis added.

37. The IASB's initial journal, which Wallace-Johnson edited, was called *African and the World*. Its name was changed to *African Sentinel*. In the summer of 1938, it was replaced by *International African Opinion*, which James edited initially.

38. Cripps, foreword to Padmore, *Africa and World Peace*, ix.

39. Empire Special Supplement, *New Leader*, April 29, 1938, 1.

40. Ibid.

41. "British Govt. Is Also 'Imperialist Aggressor,' How 100,000 Square Miles Were Added to Empire Last Year, Tribes Terrorised by Aerial Bombing," ibid., iii.

42. "Africa Empire Is Slave Colony: Revolting Workers Shot Down," "Colonial Fascism in the West Indies," and "British Imperialism in Ireland: A Hundred Years of Terror," ibid., iv–vi.

43. Douglas, *Making Black Jacobins*, 18 and chap. 1.

44. James, *Black Jacobins*, 138.

45. Datta, *Jallianwala Bagh*, frontispiece, as cited in Sayer, "British Reaction," 132.

46. Du Bois, *Dusk of Dawn*, 14. See an analysis of this quote and DuBois's relationship to the structures of world systems in James, *George Padmore*, 9.

47. Kelley, "Poetics of Anticolonialism," 20. Note that Kelley is drawing on the arguments of Cedric Robinson. Also referenced in Gopal, *Insurgent Empire*, 359.

48. Kelley, "Poetics of Anticolonialism," 20.

49. Pennybacker, *From Scottsboro to Munich*, 100.

50. Mandle, "British Caribbean Economic History."

51. Ibid.; *Report of the West India Royal Commission*, C. 8665; Marshall, "History of West Indian Migrations"; Kingston, *On the March*; Bolland, *Politics of Labour*; and Fraser, "Twilight of Colonial Rule."

52. Hitler, *Mein Kampf*, 144. For a discussion of Hitler's imperial thought, including the British Empire's influence on it, see Moses, *Problems of Genocide*, 295–309 (which includes a citation on page 295 to a slightly different translation of the quote here).

53. Mazower, *Hitler's Empire*, 581–82. For a discussion of the empire's role in Britain's industrialization and "divergence" from non-Western parts of the world, including China, see Pomeranz, *Great Divergence*. See also Stocking, *Victorian Anthropology*. On the idea of *terra nullius* and deployment of violence, see Lindqvist, *"Exterminate All the Brutes."*

54. As quoted in Mazower, *Hitler's Empire*, 588.

55. Ibid., 587.

56. For Nazi imperial ideology and practices, ibid; and Moses, *Problems of Genocide*, chap. 7. For the military aspects of Nazi imperial ambitions, see Hull, *Absolute Destruction*.

57. Mazower, *Hitler's Empire*, 587.

58. Chatterjee, *Nation and Its Fragments*, 10.

59. Howe, *Anticolonialism in British Politics*, 92–93, 100–103 (quote on 101n62).

60. *West India Royal Commission Report*, Cmd. 6607.

61. Parker, *Brother's Keeper*, 23.

62. Holt, *Problem of Freedom*, 397.

63. Parker, *Brother's Keeper*, 23–24.

64. Lowry, "'World's No Bigger,'" 282; and Smyth, "Britain's African Colonies," 67.

65. Green, "Geoffrey Dawson," 250.

66. Louis, *Ends of British Imperialism*, 969; and May, "Empire Loyalists," 37–56.

67. Green, "Geoffrey Dawson," 251.

68. Ibid., 252; and Howard, "All Souls and the 'Round Table,'" 155–66.

69. Green, "Geoffrey Dawson," 255.

70. Ibid., 255–56; and Louis, *Ends of British Imperialism*, 968. See also Simpson, *Another Life*, 45–50.

71. May, "Empire Loyalists," 40.

72. Louis, *Ends of British Imperialism*, 979.

73. Ibid., 978–79; May, "Empire Loyalists," 39–51.

74. Drayton, "Where Does World Historian Write From?," 676–78. For an excellent analysis of historians' roles in the making of history see Satia, *Time's Monster*.

75. Drayton, "Where Does World Historian Write From?," 676.

76. Egerton, *Wholesale Robbery?*, 4.

77. Ibid., 16.

78. Drayton, "Where Does World Historian Write From?," 677. Note that Harlow held the Rhodes Chair for over ten years until he succeeded Coupland at Oxford in 1959.

79. Smyth, "Britain's African Colonies," 67.

80. See, for example, Mandle, "British Caribbean Economic History"; and Parker, *Brother's Keeper*.

81. As quoted in Howe, *Anticolonialism in British Politics*, 97.

82. Thomas, "Political Economy of Colonial Violence" (unpublished paper), 1–14; Thomas, *Violence and Colonial Order*; Bolland, *Politics of Labour*; and St. Pierre, "1938 Jamaica Disturbances."

83. *Statement of Policy on Colonial Development and Welfare*, Cmd. 6175, 4, 8.

84. Smyth, "Britain's African Colonies," 68.

85. Ibid.

CHAPTER 8: "PARTNERSHIP"

1. Louis, *Imperialism at Bay*, 154–55.

2. Walter Lippmann, "Today and Tomorrow: The Post-Singapore War in the East," *Washington Post*, February 21, 1942; and Smyth, "Britain's African Colonies," 69.

3. James, *George Padmore*, 50. For a broader discussion on wartime regulations and civil liberties, see Stammers, *Civil Liberties in Britain*.

4. Howe, *Anticolonialism in British Politics*, 87–88.

5. James, *George Padmore*, 52.

6. Cunard and Padmore, "White Man's Duty," 130.

7. Ibid., quotes on 156, 151, 148.

8. Margery Perham, "The Colonial Empire, I—The Need For Stocktaking and Review, A Challenge That Can Be Met," *Times*, March 13, 1942, 5.

9. Smith and Bull, *Margery Perham*; and Stockwell, *British End*, 1–141.

10. Perham, "The Colonial Empire, I," 5.

11. Ibid. As William Roger Louis has pointed out to me, it was equality that Perham later emphasized as the fundamental point.

12. William Roger Louis has a similar reading of Perham in *Imperialism at Bay*, 134–46.

13. See Wolton, *Lord Hailey*, 15.

14. "The Colonial Future" (editorial), *Times*, March 14, 1942, 5.

15. May 6, 1942, vol. 122, cols. 896, 928, HL Deb.

16. May 20, 1942, vol. 122, col. 1091, HL Deb.

17. May 6, 1942, vol. 122, cols. 919–20, HL Deb.

18. May 20, 1942, vol. 122, cols. 1091–94, HL Deb.

19. May 20, 1942, vol. 122, col. 1095, HL Deb.

20. May 20, 1942, vol. 122, cols. 1098, 1111, 1118, HL Deb.

21. May 20, 1942, vol. 122, col. 1127, HL Deb.

22. Twaddle, "Margery Perham," 106.

23. Ibid., 103–5.

24. Cunard and Padmore, "White Man's Duty," 155.

25. As quoted in Howe, *Anticolonialism in British Politics*, 136.

26. June 24, 1942, vol. 380, cols. 2041–44, HC Deb.

27. June 24, 1942, vol. 380, col. 2107, HC Deb.

28. Smyth, "Britain's African Colonies," 69–79.

29. Ibid., 74.

30. Furedi, *Colonial Wars*, 67.

31. Hitler, *Mein Kampf*, 430; and Smyth, "Britain's African Colonies," 74, 78. Note different translation from Hitler's original German in Smyth's article.

32. Ibid., 75–76; Chapman, *British at War*; and Woods, "Shaw to Shantaram."

33. As quoted in Rose, *Which People's War?*, 281–82.

34. Harlow was arguably less influential than other Round Table members.

35. Smyth, "Britain's African Colonies," 73.

36. Louis, *Ends of British Imperialism*, 984, 986.

37. Hancock, *Argument of Empire*, 7.

38. Davidson, *Three-Cornered Life*, 202–3.

39. Smyth, "Britain's African Colonies," 72.

40. June 18, 1940, vol. 362, col. 61, HC Deb.

41. Smyth, "Britain's African Colonies," 71.

42. Ibid., 72.

43. White Paper of 1939, https://avalon.law.yale.edu/20th_century/brwh1939.asp.

44. Ben-Gurion, *Memoirs*, 6:200. Note that in addition to the ten thousand annual quota of Jews permitted to immigrate to Palestine, the White Paper of 1939 also stated that "as a contribution towards the solution of the Jewish refugee problem, 25,000 refugees will be admitted as soon as the High Commissioner is satisfied that adequate provision for their maintenance is ensured, special consideration being given to refugee children and dependents."

45. *Revisionism* is a much-debated term. I am using it here to connote its rejection of Zionist political policies, including those of Weizmann and Ben-Gurion. See Zouplna, "Revisionist Zionism"; and Ben-Gurion, *Memoirs*, 6:507.

46. Smyth, "Britain's African Colonies," 68.

47. Jewish Agency for Israel, "The White Paper of 1939," http://archive.jewish agency.org/ben-gurion/content/23436.

48. Bauer, *Diplomacy to Resistance*, 47–48; and Halperin, *Political World*, 220–22. Note that Weizmann hoped there would emerge a close relationship between a new Jewish state and Britain, whereas Ben-Gurion was more determined to create a sovereign state, regardless of whether or not Britain supported it.

49. Bauer, *Diplomacy to Resistance*, 114–18; and Sachar, *History of Israel*, 234–42.

50. For a thorough analysis of the Revisionists, see Bell, *Terror Out of Zion*. For Menachem Begin's ideology and strategies, see Begin, *Revolt*; Haber, *Begin*; and Bell, *On Revolt*, 41–42.

51. Begin, *Revolt*, 42–3.
52. See Brenner, "Stern Gang"; and Heller, *Stern Gang*, 100–108.
53. Hoffman, *Anonymous Soldiers*, 162–64.
54. Bell, *Terror Out of Zion*, 91.
55. Makovsky, *Churchill's Promised Land*, 3.
56. James, *Churchill: Complete Speeches*, 6:6129, 6132–34.
57. Ibid., 6:6035.
58. Grose, "President Versus Diplomats," 35.
59. Wasserstein, "Assassination of Moyne," 81.
60. Hoffman, *Anonymous Soldiers*, 164.
61. Wasserstein, "Assassination of Moyne," 76.
62. Cohen, "Moyne Assassination," 360.
63. Hoffman, *Anonymous Soldiers*, 168–69.
64. Cohen, "Moyne Assassination," 358–62.
65. Wasserstein, "Assassination of Moyne," 76.
66. November 17, 1944, vol. 404, col. 2242, HC Deb.
67. Carruthers, *Hearts and Minds*, quotes on 27, 30.
68. Crossman, *Palestine Mission*, 191, 50.
69. Cohen, *Churchill and Jews*, 255–58; and Cohen, *Palestine to Israel*, chap. 9. For a detailed account of Lord Moyne's assassination, see Frank, *Deed*.
70. Weizmann, *Trial and Error*, 437–38.
71. Segev, *One Palestine*, 471–72.
72. Hoffman, *Anonymous Soldiers*, 174.
73. Ibid., 175.
74. Ibid., quotes on 190, 176, 180.
75. Ibid., 171.
76. Ibid., 194.
77. Ibid., 182.
78. Moore and Fedorowich, *Italian Prisoners of War*, 99–100.
79. Hoffman, *Anonymous Soldiers*, 185–86.
80. Moore and Fedorowich, *Italian Prisoners of War*, 114–29, quotes on 121, 120.
81. Ibid., 114–29.
82. "Report on Security Measures Taken by the British Against the Indian National Army During the War," F. No. 601/12539/H.S, in Sareen, *Indian National Army*, 4:241–47; and "Report on Security Measures," ibid., 4:251–59. See also the writings and papers of former military intelligence officers staffed at Red Fort and other CSDIC locations, including Toye, *Springing Tiger*; and Private Papers of Maj. G. R. Storry, Catalogue 10549, IWMDD.
83. "Report on Security Measures," in Sareen, *Indian National Army*, 4:260–62, 279–83.
84. Ibid., 4:283–87, quote on 4:283.
85. Franklin D. Roosevelt, broadcast to the International Student Assembly, September 3, 1942, https://www.jewishvirtuallibrary.org/president-roosevelt -broadcast-to-international-student-assembly-september-1942.
86. "Declaration by United Nations," January 1, 1942.
87. Franklin D. Roosevelt, "On the Progress of the War," Fireside Chat 20, Feb-

ruary 23, 1942, https://millercenter.org/the-presidency/presidential-speeches/february-23-1942-fireside-chat-20-progress-war.

88. Franklin D. Roosevelt, broadcast to the International Student Assembly, September 3, 1942, https://www.jewishvirtuallibrary.org/president-roosevelt-broadcast-to-international-student-assembly-september-1942.

89. For example, see Bayly, *Recovering Liberties;* and Ibhawoh, *Imperialism and Human Rights.*

90. Fitzmaurice, "Liberalism and Empire," 124. The large literature on universal rights and positivism includes Pagden, "Comment"; Pagden, "Human Rights, Natural Rights"; and Moyn, *Last Utopia*, 28–43.

91. Pagden, "Comment," 144–45.

92. Ibid., 144.

93. Franklin D. Roosevelt, Press Conference, December 22, 1944, https://www.presidency.ucsb.edu/documents/excerpts-from-the-press-conference-21.

94. Mazower, *No Enchanted Palace*, 46–65.

95. Moyn, *Last Utopia*, 56.

96. See Borgwardt, *New Deal for the World*, 180–93. Moyn makes a similar point in *Last Utopia*, passim.

97. Mazower, *No Enchanted Palace*, 61–65.

98. Ibid., 61.

99. Sankey, "Decolonisation," 96.

100. Louis, "Public Enemy Number One," 188. Note that while Poynton's outlook represented the Colonial Office's general views, other British civil servants like Christopher Eastwood proved to be more flexible and realistic, a point raised to me by William Roger Louis.

101. United Nations, Charter, Chapter XI, "Declaration Regarding Non-Self-Governing Territories," Article 73, https://www.un.org/en/sections/un-charter/chapter-xi/index.html.

102. Sankey, "Decolonisation," 96–97.

103. Sherwood, "'There Is No New Deal,'" 90.

104. Moyn, *Last Utopia*, 60.

105. Sherwood, "'There Is No New Deal,'" 72.

106. Sherwood, "'Diplomatic Platitudes,'" 144.

107. Ibid., 146.

108. Getachew, *Worldmaking*, 72.

109. Padmore, *History of Pan-African Congress*, 55.

110. For example, the Manchester delegates resolved that "the principles of the Four Freedoms and the Atlantic Charter be put into practice; and decried the ruthless trampling underfoot of all human rights." Ibid., 5, 57–58.

111. Ibid., 55.

112. Sherwood, "'There Is No New Deal,'" 93.

CHAPTER 9: IMPERIAL RESURGENCE

1. Labour Party, Election Manifesto, 1945, http://www.labour-party.org.uk/manifestos/1945/1945-labour-manifesto.shtml.

2. Ibid.

3. *Social Insurance and Allied Services*, Cmd. 6404.

4. Lough, *No More Champagne*, 316.

5. For an authoritative account of Labour's evolution and embrace of mass media, see Beers, *Your Britain*.

6. The literature on Labour's rise during the interwar years, culminating in the 1945 elections, is large. See, for example, Hutt, *Post-War History*; Miliband, *Parliamentary Socialism*; Savage, *Dynamics of Working-Class Politics*; Rose, *Which People's War?*; and Beers, *Your Britain*.

7. McKibbin, *Ideologies of Class*, chap. 9.

8. Beers, *Your Britain*, introduction and chap. 1.

9. Ibid., chap. 1; and Wring, *Politics of Marketing*, chap. 2.

10. Beers, *Your Britain*, 13.

11. Ibid., 1–2.

12. Labour Party Election Manifesto, 1945.

13. MacKenzie, "Persistence of Empire," 26–27, where he also directly compares postwar Britain and that of the 1890s. For a full account of postwar Britain, see Kynaston, *Austerity Britain*; and for postwar Europe, see Judt, *Postwar*.

14. MacKenzie, *Propaganda and Empire*, 1–12, 253–58.

15. *Report of the Labour Commission to Ireland*, 1.

16. Meyers, *Orwell*, 23.

17. Ibid.

18. Orwell and Angus, *Age Like This*, 394–97.

19. George Orwell, "Rudyard Kipling," *Horizon*, London, February 1942.

20. Orwell, *Lion and Unicorn*, 63.

21. Roberts, *Classic Slum*, 112.

22. MacKenzie, *Propaganda and Empire*, 246. See also Springhall, *Youth, Empire and Society*, 26–31.

23. May, "Empire Loyalists," 37.

24. MacKenzie, *Propaganda and Empire*, 213, 243, 246, 256.

25. The broad literature on Britain's post–World War II culture and empire includes Ward, *British Culture*.

26. Richards, "Imperial Heroes for a Post-Imperial Age," 129–33; MacKenzie, "Persistence of Empire," 26–32; MacKenzie, *Propaganda and Empire*, 255; and Patel, *We're Here*, 51.

27. Judt, *Postwar*, 278–79. For an alternative view on the impact of the empire on British society, see Porter, *Absent-Minded Imperialists*, 1–24.

28. MacKenzie, introduction to *Imperialism and Popular Culture*, 9.

29. Ibid.; and MacKenzie, *Propaganda and Empire*, 254. For an important and trenchant overview of the wide debate over the question of what, if anything, the empire meant to the British public, see Ward, *British Culture*, 1–20.

30. George Orwell, "Boys' Weeklies," in Orwell, *Collection of Essays* (1981 ed.), 305.

31. Bayly and Harper, *Forgotten Armies*, 281.

32. Louis, *British Empire in Middle East*, 381–477.

33. Hyam, *Britain's Declining Empire*, 90–91.

34. July 9, 1946, vol. 425, cols., 238, 342–43, HC Deb, emphasis added.

35. Russell, "'Jolly Old Empire,'" 23.
36. MacDonald, *Labour and Empire*, 103, emphasis original.
37. Howe, "Labour and International Affairs," 128.
38. July 9, 1946, vol. 425, col. 238, HC Deb.
39. Bayly and Harper, *Forgotten Wars*, 96.
40. As quoted in Hyam, *Britain's Declining Empire*, 100.
41. Gilroy, *"There Ain't No Black,"* chap. 2. Estimates are that thirty thousand non-whites were living in Britain in the immediate postwar years. See Hansen, *Citizenship and Immigration*, 3.
42. Rose, *Which People's War?*, 264.
43. Russell, "'Jolly Old Empire,'" 23.
44. Howe, "Labour and International Affairs," 124–25.
45. Ibid., 126.
46. Ibid., 124–26, 130–32.
47. Toye, "Churchill and Britain's Financial Dunkirk," 329.
48. Clarke, *Last Thousand Days*, 366.
49. Pressnell, *External Economic Policy*, 269.
50. Keynes, *How to Pay for the War*.
51. Ferguson, *Empire*, 294–95.
52. "Retrospective Lend-Lease—A New Proposal," *Times*, September 22, 1945, 4.
53. Schenk, "Sterling Area," 772–73.
54. Ibid., 773–78; Krozewski, "Finance and Empire," 48, 54; Alford, "1941–1951," 186–96; and Feinstein, "End of Empire," 224–33.
55. Schenk, "Sterling Area," 771–76.
56. Ibid., 777.
57. Ibid., 776.
58. Clarke, *Last Thousand Days*, 400.
59. Ibid., 399–404.
60. Jeffery, "Second World War," 326.
61. Ibid., 325–26; Fieldhouse, "Metropolitan Economics," 88–113; and Cain and Hopkins, *British Imperialism*, 491–520, 541–64.
62. Baylis, *Diplomacy of Pragmatism*, 50.
63. Louis, *British Empire in Middle East*, 4–11, 120–22, 383–88; Howe, "Labour and International Affairs," 130–32; and Bullock, *Ernest Bevin*, 49–54, 121–25.
64. Russell, "'Jolly Old Empire,'" 23.
65. Howe, *Anticolonialism in British Politics*, 146.
66. For example, Howe, "Labour and International Affairs," 131–32.
67. Bullock, *Ernest Bevin*, 51. For details on Bevin's role in Palestine, which was beyond his remit, see Louis, *British Empire in Middle East*, 383–96.
68. Vickers, *Labour Party and World*, 1:164.
69. For expansion of the Colonial Office and its general lack of transparency, see Ashton, "Keeping Change Within Bounds." The lack of a timetable is a point made several times by Bayly and Harper, as well as by Lynn, *British Empire in 1950s*, 1–15, and various contributors to the volume. It is also made in Mawby, *British Policy in Aden;* Harper, *End of Empire;* Allen, *Burma;* Christie, *Modern History of Southeast Asia;* and Elkins, *Imperial Reckoning*.

70. Gupta, "Imperialism and the Labour Government," 100–1.

71. Murphy, "Britain as a Global Power," 51.

72. Ibid., 54.

73. Clarke, *Last Thousand Days*, 472.

74. Westad, *Global Cold War*, 112–13.

75. Louis, *Ends of British Imperialism*, 460; and Latham, *Right Kind of Revolution*, 28–29.

76. Louis, *Ends of British Imperialism*, 460.

77. Burk, *Old World, New World*, 578.

78. Latham, *Right Kind of Revolution*, 29.

79. Louis, *Ends of British Imperialism*, 460n41.

80. Hyam, *Britain's Declining Empire*, 137–38.

81. Ibid., 136; and Murphy, "Britain as a Global Power," 54.

82. As quoted in Hyam, *Britain's Declining Empire*, 131.

83. Feinstein, "End of Empire," 229.

84. Ibid., 229–30.

85. Bayly and Harper, *Forgotten Wars*, 98.

86. Gupta, "Imperialism and Labour Government," 106–7.

87. Cooper, "Modernizing Colonialism," 64–67; Constantine, *British Colonial Development Policy*; and Hyam, *Britain's Declining Empire*, 132.

88. Fieldhouse, "Metropolitan Economics," 103–13.

89. Ibid., 112–13.

90. Howe, "Labour and International Affairs," 132.

91. Alford, "1945–1951," 190.

92. Cairncross and Eichengreen, *Sterling in Decline*, 111–55.

93. Gupta, "Imperialism and Labour Government," 109.

94. Ibid.

95. Col. D. G. White to Brigadier Sir David Petrie, April 16, 1945, KV 4/327, TNA. See also H. P. Milmo, Minute, October 5, 1944, KV 4/327, TNA; and Richard Butler, Minute, October 4, 1944, KV 4/327, TNA.

96. Stephens, "Digest of Ham," 109.

97. Notes on CSDIC Mediterranean, part 1, CSDIC-Med, "CSDIC (Mediterranean)," Attachment "D," no date, and Appendix I, "Use of 'I' Source in Mediterranean and Middle East Theatres of War between Oct 1940 and May 1945," no date, WO 208/3248, TNA; and "The Interrogation of Prisoners of War," c. May 1943, WO 208/3458, TNA.

98. "Bad Nenndorf Trials (Note on the history leading up to the situation of the 19th June 1948)," c. June 1948, FO 371/70830, TNA; Cobain, *Cruel Britannia*, 24–25; and Simpson, *Highest Degree Odious*, 241–44.

99. Cobain, *Cruel Britannia*, 48; and "Provisional Comments on Detailed Interrogation Centre, Bad Nenndorf," Appendix B, Notes on Galla Case, c. April 1947, and Appendix C, Notes on Bergman Case, c. April 1947, FO 371/70830, TNA.

100. "Provisional Comments on Detailed Interrogation Centre, Bad Nenndorf," Appendix A, Notes on Butler Case, c. April 1947, FO 371/70830, TNA; and, for example, Detailed Interrogation Centre, Bad Nenndorf (Court of Inquiry Reports), FO 1005/1744, TNA; Detailed Interrogation Centre, Court

of Inquiry, FO 1060/735, TNA; Enquiry from Mr. R. Stokes Regarding an Internee detained at Bad Nenndorf, April 28, 1948, 1060/735, TNA; and Major J. Morgan-Jones, witness statement, April 10, 1947, Appendix 12, FO 1005/1744, TNA.

101. Foreign Office to private secretary to Lord President of Privy Council, June 22, 1948, FO 371/70830, TNA; and Foreign Office to private secretary to prime minister, June 22, 1948, FO 371/70830, TNA.

102. "Bad Nenndorf Trials (Note on the history leading up to the situation of 19th June 1948)," no date, FO 371/70830, TNA.

103. Instructions for the Commandant of Bad Nenndorf Detailed Interrogation Centre (top secret), Appendix A, April 17, 1947, FO 371/70830, TNA.

104. Col. R. Stephens, witness statement, Appendix I, and Col. Roland Alfred Frederick Short, witness statement, Appendix II, both April 7, 1947, FO 1005/1744, TNA.

105. "Bad Nenndorf Trials (Note on the history leading up to the situation of 19th June 1948)," no date, FO 371/70830, TNA.

106. Ibid.

107. Cobain, *Cruel Britannia*, 61.

108. Plans and Reports Appertaining to General Conditions at D.I.C, Part II, April 1947, FO 1030/274, TNA; Statement from Prisoners, General, Part III, April 1947, 1030/274, TNA; Statements from Doctors and Camp Commandants at Hospitals and D.I.C.s, April 1947, FO 1030/275, TNA; Statements of Warders, Medical Orderlies, etc., Part V, Appendix A, April 1947, FO 1030/276, TNA; Statements of Prison Control Officers and Interrogators at D.I.C., April 1947, FO 1030/277, TNA; Statement of Colonel Stephens, Statement of Capt. Smith, Notes of Lt. Col. Short, and Statement of Major Mallalieu, April 1947, FO 1030/278, TNA; and Cobain, *Cruel Britannia*, 62–65.

109. Cobain, *Cruel Britannia*, quotes on 67, emphasis added, 68.

110. This theme recurred in the several days of in-camera testimony that Stephens provided in his own defense at his court-martial. See *In the Matter of a Court Martial re: Col. R. W. G. Stephens, O.B.E.*, July 1948, 196–335, WO 71/1176/B, TNA.

111. Ibid., 198.

112. Cobain, *Cruel Britannia*, 74.

113. Ibid., 70.

PART III: TRYSTS WITH DESTINY

1. Constituent Assembly of India, Fifth Session, vol. 5, August 14, 1947, https://www.constitutionofindia.net/constitution_assembly_debates/volume/5/1947-08-14.

2. March 6, 1947, vol. 434, cols. 669, 671, 678, HC Deb.

3. Toye, *Churchill's Empire*, 272.

4. Jalal, *Sole Spokesman*, 9. For an excellent analysis of Jinnah, see Jalal, *Sole Spokesman*, and for a discussion of Gandhi's commitment to a unified and independent India, see Bose, *Nation as Mother*, 127–48.

5. Muhammad Ali Jinnah, First Presidential Address to the Constituent Assembly of Pakistan, August 11, 1947, http://www.columbia.edu/itc/mealac/pritchett/00islamlinks/txt_jinnah_assembly_1947.htm.

6. Dalrymple, "Great Divide," 67.

7. Louis, "Dissolution of British Empire," 329.

8. Aldrich, *Hidden Hand*, 10–12.

9. Simpson, *Human Rights*, 82.

CHAPTER 10: GLASS HOUSES

1. Ghosh, *Glass Palace*, 462.

2. *Jiff* or *JIF* is a term derived from "Japanese-Inspired Fifth Columnist." Its military acronym was JIFC (Japanese-Indian Fifth Column). See Raghavan, *India's War*, 397; and Fay, *Forgotten Army*, 409.

3. Singh, *Testimonies of Indian Soldiers*, 169–70.

4. Ibid., 170–71. Another INA playwright, Purushottam Nagesh Oak, had written *The Rani of Zanshi*. Note that the name of Rani of Jhansi was Lakshmibai and, as it happened, the name of the commander of the Rani of Jhansi regiment of Bose's INA was also Lakshmi (Swaminathan). I am grateful to Sugata Bose for pointing this out to me.

5. "Report on Security Measures Taken by the British Against the Indian National Army During the War," F. No. 601/12539/II.S, in Sareen, *Indian National Army*, 291. This number includes 14,000 INA military and civilian suspects, as well as 4,000 repatriated Western Front suspects and members of the 950th Regiment.

6. For details on Bose's plane crash and death, see Lebra, *Indian National Army*, 194–99; Gordon, *Brothers Against the Raj*, 541; and Bose, *His Majesty's Opponent*, 304–21. Note that Bose's remains were to be kept in the Buddhist temple, Renko-ji.

7. Bose, *His Majesty's Opponent*, 305.

8. Raghavan, *India's War*, 1; and Bayly and Harper, *Forgotten Wars*, 112, 217.

9. Marston, *Indian Army and Raj*, 242–47; and Bayly and Harper, *Forgotten Wars*, 179–81.

10. A term coined by Bayly and Harper in *Forgotten Armies* and *Forgotten Wars*.

11. Bayly and Harper, *Forgotten Wars*, 15.

12. Ibid., 105–10. For quote, see 110.

13. Sen, *Poverty and Famines*, 52–85; and Bose, "Starvation Amidst Plenty," 699–727.

14. Bayly and Harper, *Forgotten Wars*, 287–88.

15. Singh, *INA Trial*, 41–43. The overwhelming number of INA recruits were volunteers, and most of the British allegations about brutal recruitment tactics were never proven. See Fay, *Forgotten Army*, 100–112.

16. Connell, *Auchinleck*, 817–19; Kuracina, "Sentiments and Patriotism," 817–56; and Bayly and Harper, *Forgotten Wars*, 79–80.

17. Bayly and Harper, *Forgotten Wars*, 79–83.

18. For in-depth analyses of the INA trials, see Mukherjee, " 'Right to Wage War,' "

420–43; Kuracina, "Sentiments and Patriotism," 817–56; Alpes, "Congress and INA Trials"; Green, "Indian National Army Trials"; and Singh, *INA Trial*.

19. Raghavan, *India's War*, 447.
20. Ram, *Two Historic Trials*, 153–54. For a full discussion of international law and the INA trial, see Desai, *INA Defence*, 1–172; and Mukherjee, "'Right to Wage War,'" 420–43.
21. Desai, *INA Defence*, 8.
22. Bayly and Harper, *Forgotten Wars*, 88–92.
23. Marston, *Indian Army*, 141.
24. Ibid., 218–19.
25. Spence, "Beyond Talwar," 489–508.
26. Bayly and Harper, *Forgotten Wars*, 221.
27. Weber, "Politics as a Vocation," 78.
28. Bose and Jalal, *Modern South Asia*, 147–80; Metcalf and Metcalf, *Concise History of India*, 206–13; and Brown, *Modern India*, 333–37.
29. Dalrymple, "Great Divide," 67; and Wolpert, *Gandhi's Passion*, 210.
30. Bayly and Harper, *Forgotten Wars*, 244.
31. Brown, *Modern India*, 337–38; Raghavan, *India's War*, 453–54; and Bayly and Harper, *Forgotten Wars*, 242–50, 284.
32. Clarke, *Last Thousand Days*, 475, 476, 478.
33. February 10, 1947, vol. 433, col. 1397, HC Deb.
34. Brecher, *Political Leadership*, 53.
35. Dalrymple, "Great Divide," 68; and Hajari, *Midnight's Furies*, 102.
36. Cohen, *Churchill and Attlee*, 293.
37. Bayly and Harper, *Forgotten Wars*, 287; and "India (Transfer of Power)," June 3, 1947, vol. 438, cols. 35–46, HC Deb.
38. Von Tunzelmann, *Indian Summer*, 188.
39. Wolpert, *Shameful Flight*, 165.
40. Ibid., 171.
41. For a colonial official's observation of the crowd and turmoil that ensued, see, for example, Bayly and Harper, *Forgotten Wars*, 292.
42. A. J. Brown, Office of the UK High Commissioner in the Federation of Malaya, to R. W. Newsham, Commonwealth Relations Office, memorandum (secret), October 17, 1957, 1–3, DO 186/17, TNA.
43. Toye, *Springing Tiger*; and Aldrich, *Intelligence and War Against Japan*, 386–87, and 458n7. See also Hugh Toye, obituary, *Daily Telegraph*, July 17, 2002.
44. Moon, *Wavell*, 347. Wavell's entry was made on September 5, 1946.
45. A. J. Brown, Office of the UK High Commissioner in the Federation of Malaya, to R. W. Newsham, Commonwealth Relations Office, memorandum (secret), October 17, 1957, 2, DO 186/17, TNA.
46. Von Tunzelmann, *Indian Summer*, 6–7, 234–52.
47. For an excellent analysis of Partition's events and its causes, see Jalal, *Sole Spokesman*, 241–93; and Jalal, *Self and Sovereignty*, 472–562. The extensive Partition literature includes Yasmin Khan's epic *Great Partition*; Von Tunzelmann, *Indian Summer*; and Hajari, *Midnight's Furies*.

48. For an important demographic analysis of Partition and its impact, see Hill, et. al., "Demographic Impact of Partition."

49. Hajari, *Midnight's Furies*, xviii–xix; and Dalrymple, "Great Divide."

50. Khan, *Great Partition*, 210.

51. Dalrymple, "Great Divide," 66.

52. Wolpert, *Shameful Flight*, quotes on 177, 173–75, and narrative details, 175–76.

53. Wolpert, *Gandhi's Passion*, 253.

54. Wolpert, *Shameful Flight*, 177.

55. Mishra, *Fundamentals of Gandhism*, 168; and Gandhi, *"Let's Kill Gandhi!,"* 12.

56. Gandhi, *Gandhi The Man*, 657.

57. Chakrabarty, *Politics, Ideology*, 170.

58. Radhakrishnan, *Mahatma Gandhi*, 525.

59. Hancock, *Four Studies*, 83.

60. Ministry of Information, *Homage to Mahatma*, chap. 5.

61. Sir Richard Catling, interview, Accession no. 10392, IWMSA; "Sir Richard Catling: Police Commissioner Who Dealt with Palestine, Malaya and Kenya," *Times*, April 12, 2005, 56; and "Visit to the Middle East" by A. J. Kellar, February 1945, KV 4/384, TNA.

62. Louis, *British Empire in Middle East*, 383.

63. Ibid., 420.

64. Truman, *Memoirs*, 2:144–45.

65. Zweig, *Britain and Palestine*, 112.

66. As quoted in Louis, *British Empire in Middle East*, 388.

67. Ibid., 43.

68. November 13, 1945, vol. 415, col. 1934, HC Deb.

69. Katz, *Days of Fire*, 87; and Cohen, *Palestine and Great Powers*, 69–72.

70. As quoted in Newsinger, *British Counter-Insurgency*, 13.

71. Sachar, *History of Israel*, 245–46.

72. Charters, *British Army*, chap. 3; and Ganin, *Truman, American Jewry*, 4–40, 120–24.

73. Segev, *One Palestine*, 465.

74. Hoffman, *Failure of Military Strategy*, 10. For a more in-depth discussion of the two-front war, see Charters, *British Army*, chap. 3. See also Louis, "Sir Alan Cunningham," 128–47.

75. Charters, *British Army*, 107.

76. Reynolds, *Empire, Emergency*, 92.

77. Hoffman, *Anonymous Soldiers*, 250–52, quote on 252.

78. Begin, *Revolt*, 52.

79. "Palestine. Political. Irgun-Zvai Leumi," c. March 1946, Reference no. 47/154/2, HA.

80. Katz, *Days of Fire*, 110.

81. Begin, *Revolt*, 56. "Logic of the Revolt" is the title of the book's fifth chapter.

82. Ibid., 27.

83. Benjamin Akzin, interview by Bernard Wasserstein, January 7, 1970, (82)3, HI.

84. Bell, *Terror Out of Zion*, 153.

85. Segev, *One Palestine*, 455–56; Horne, *Job Well Done*, 279–80; and "Searches of Jewish Settlements for Arms and Ammunitions," c. November 1943, WO 208/1702, TNA.

86. Hadar to High Commissioner Jerusalem, "Searches of Givat Haim, Shefayim and Hogla Settlements Representation and Protest etc.," November 29, 1945; General Committee Zikhron Yaacov to High Commissioner for Palestine (telegram), November 29, 1945; R. Shreibman to High Commissioner, November 19, 1945; all in POL/29/45, 365/34, Israel State Archives, Jerusalem, Israel; and Hoffman, *Anonymous Soldiers*, 238–39.

87. Hoffman, "Palestine Police Force," 613.

88. Saunders to Tegart, February 23, 1939, File 4, Box 3, Tegart Papers, GB165-0281, MEC; High Commissioner MacMichael to colonial secretary, October 17, 1940, CO 733/416/75015/A, TNA; Kolinsky, *Mandatory Palestine*, 50–51; and Smith, "Communal Conflict," 79.

89. Hoffman, "Palestine Police Force," 614, emphasis original.

90. Sir Charles Wickham, Report, December 2, 1946, CO 537/2269, TNA; Frank Jones, interview, March 16, 2006, GB165-0389, MEC; Martin Duchesne, interview, March 23, 2006, GB165-0390, MEC; John Sankey, interview, September 1988, Accession no. 10300, IWMSA; Hoffman, *Failure of British Strategy*, 123; Horne, *Job Well Done*, 264; Hoffman, *Anonymous Soldiers*, 358–59; and Smith, "Communal Conflict," 81.

91. Hoffman, *Anonymous Soldiers*, 359.

92. Mark Russell, interview, May 16, 2006, GB165-0396, MEC; James Hainge, interview, June 5, 2006, GB165-0402, MEC; Wilson, *Cordon and Search*, 48; and Farran, *Winged Dagger*, 346.

93. Henry Gurney, "Palestine Postscript," 14, GUR 1/ 2, Gurney Papers, GB165-0128, MEC; and Golani, *Diary of Gurney*, 4.

94. Sir Richard Catling, interview, September 1988, Accession no. 10392, IWMSA.

95. Charters, *British Army*, 243n128; and "Avner," *Memoirs of an Assassin*, 12–13, 82–85. For intelligence operations in Palestine, see Charters, "British Intelligence"; Walton, "British Intelligence and Mandate of Palestine"; and Hoffman, "Palestine Police Force."

96. Martin Duchesne, interview, March 23, 2006, GB165-0390, MEC.

97. James Llewelyn Niven, interview, September 1988, Accession no. 10399, IWMSA.

98. Segev, *One Palestine*, 474–75.

99. Wilson, *Cordon and Search*, 48.

100. Heller, "Anglo-American Commission." For a unique American perspective from someone who served as secretary on the committee, see Wilson, *Decision on Palestine*.

101. Montgomery, *Memoirs*, 387–88.

102. Peter Lawrence de Carteret Martin, interview, November 12, 1992, Accession no. 12778, IWMSA.

103. Bell, *Terror Out of Zion*, 169–73; Hoffman, *Anonymous Soldiers*, 290–312; and Segev, *One Palestine*, 7–8.

104. Catling interview, IWMSA; and Hoffman, *Anonymous Soldiers*, 290–302.

105. Ernest de Val, interview, September 1988, Accession no. 12592, IWMSA.
106. Catling interview, IWMSA.
107. Montgomery to Dempsey, July 24, 1946. WO 216/194, TNA.
108. Catling interview, IWMSA.
109. Bell, *Terror Out of Zion*, 173.
110. Begin, *Revolt*, 231.
111. Shindler, *Land Beyond Promise*, 28.
112. Hoffman, *Anonymous Soldiers*, 364–65.
113. Carruthers, *Hearts and Minds*, 34.
114. Bell, *Terror Out of Zion*, 174.
115. Segev, *One Palestine*, 480.
116. Ibid.
117. Mark Russell, interview, May 16, 2006, GB165-0396, MEC; and Frank Jones, interview, March 16, 2006, GB165-0389, MEC.
118. John Sankey, interview, September 1988, Accession no. 10300, IWMSA.
119. Montgomery, *Memoirs*, 428–29.
120. Hamilton, *Monty, 1944–1976*, 665–67.
121. Maj.-Gen. Harold Pyman to Hobart, January 1947, Pyman Diaries, 6/1/2, Private Papers, LHC.
122. James, *Churchill: Complete Speeches*, 7:7422.
123. "Use of Armed Forces, Part I: War Office View," December 19, 1946, CO 537/1731, TNA.
124. Montgomery to Pyman, January 2, 1947, Pyman Diaries, 6/1/2, Private Papers, LHC.
125. "Annex, Directive to the High Commissioner, Note on Conference at the Colonial Office," January 3, 1947, FO 371/61762, TNA.
126. Colonial secretary, "Use of Armed Forces" (memorandum), January 7, 1947, CP (47)3, CAB 129/16, TNA. Also Churchill, *Memoirs*, 469. Note that even when Jerusalem and Tel Aviv were "put under martial law" for fifteen days in March 1947, it was statutory martial law that was in place. The chiefs of staff had argued against martial law, noting it was no more severe than statutory martial law, which brought the added benefit that it could not be challenged in court. Some historians, however, do not "distinguish martial law proper from statutory martial law." See Simpson, *Human Rights*, 88–89, 89n127.

CHAPTER 11: EXIT PALESTINE, ENTER MALAYA

1. "Politics and the English Language," in Orwell, *Collection of Essays*.
2. Bastian, "Down and Almost Out," 95.
3. Ibid., 95–97.
4. Orwell, *1984*, 214.
5. Bastian, "Down and Almost Out," 97. Some say that Orwell's twisting of 1948 to create *1984* is a myth. The book was also partly intended to serve as a warning to the Labour government.
6. Orwell, "Politics and the English Language."
7. Orwell, *1984*, 214.

8. Ibid., 289–90, emphasis original.

9. Kynaston, *Austerity Britain*, 185–205.

10. Clarke, *Last Thousand Days*, 476.

11. Crossman, *Palestine Mission*, 46, emphasis original.

12. Clarke, *Last Thousand Days*, 408–9; and for statistics, Ibid., 407, 416.

13. Ibid., 408–9, quote on 416.

14. Louis, *British Empire in Middle East*, 434–35. Note that Louis here suggests that the Morrison-Grady plan was a sensible one given the historical context in which it was written.

15. Ibid., 436.

16. Clarke, *Last Thousand Days*, 480–81; and Rose, *Baffy*, 242–47.

17. Jasse, "Great Britain and Palestine," 560.

18. Ibid., 565, 568.

19. February 18, 1947, vol. 433, cols. 988–89, HC Deb.

20. Clarke, *Last Thousand Days*, 481.

21. February 18, 1947, vol. 433, col. 989, HC Deb.

22. Ibid.

23. Cesarani, *Major Farran's Hat*, 28–29; Aldrich, *Hidden Hand*, 260; and Horne, *Job Well Done*, 523–25, 563–64.

24. Sinclair, *End of the Line*, 109.

25. Cesarani, *Major Farran's Hat*, 30.

26. Ibid., 30–31.

27. Townshend, *Britain's Civil Wars*, 118–19.

28. Secondment of Army Officers to Palestine Police, c. February 1947, CO 537/2279, TNA.

29. Cesarani, "War on Terror," 652; and Cesarani, *Major Farran's Hat*, 63–83.

30. Secondment of Army Officers to Palestine Police, c. February 1947, CO 537/2279, TNA.

31. Farran, *Winged Dagger*, 348.

32. Smith, "Communal Conflict," 77; and Catling interview, IWMSA.

33. Walton, "British Intelligence and Mandate of Palestine," 435–37.

34. Ibid., 435–37, 454–55; Walton, *Empire of Secrets*, 91–101; and Cesarani, *Major Farran's Hat*, 45–46.

35. Cesarani, *Major Farran's Hat*, 44.

36. Walton, *Empire of Secrets*, xix–xx, 97–99.

37. Haber, *Begin*, 182–87.

38. Hoffman, *Anonymous Soldiers*, 412. Of the forty-one prisoners selected for liberation, only twenty-three survived. More than two hundred Arab prisoners were unintentionally freed, including nine who had been serving sentences for alleged crimes committed during the Arab Revolt (1936–39).

39. Grunor, *Let My People Go*, 187.

40. "Report on the Alleged Abduction and Murder of Alexander Rubovitz, and Subsequent Police Investigation," June 19, 1947, 2, CO 537/2302, TNA; and Cesarani, "War on Terror," 650–51.

41. "Report on the Alleged Abduction and Murder of Alexander Rubovitz, and Subsequent Police Investigation," June 19, 1947, 2, CO 537/2302, TNA.

42. "Strong Guard at Trial," *Palestine Post*, October 2, 1947, 3; Jewish Telegraphic Agency, "Farran's Gang Still at Work?," June 27, 1947, CO 537/2302, TNA; "Purge of Palestine Police Ordered," June 23, 1947, CO 537/2302, TNA; and Cesarani, "War on Terror," 659–62.

43. Cesarani, "War on Terror," 662; Cesarani, *Major Farran's Hat*, chaps. 4 and 5; "Farran in Liverpool," *Palestine Post*, October 14, 1947, 1; "Yard Keeping Watch on Farran," *Daily Herald*, October 31, 1947, CO 537/2302, TNA; and "Death Threat to Farran—By Post," *Daily Sketch*, October 31, 1947, CO 537/2302, TNA.

44. Begin, *Revolt*, 284.

45. Haber, *Begin*, 185–91; Bell, *Terror Out of Zion*, 227–28; Bethel, *Palestine Triangle*, 323–24; Hoffman, *Anonymous Soldiers*, 453–58; "Death in a Eucalyptus Grove—30 July 1947," Kent Collection, GB165-0453, MEC; and "Report on the Murder of Sgt Paice and Sgt Martin from 1st Guards Brigade," August 1, 1947, Papers of Palestine Police Old Comrades' Association, GB165-0224, MEC. Note that Weinberg begged not to be chloroformed because of his asthma so the Irgun operatives blindfolded and gagged him instead.

46. Haber, *Begin*, 185–91; Bell, *Terror Out of Zion*, 227–28; Bethel, *Palestine Triangle*, 323–24; Hoffman, *Anonymous Soldiers*, 453–58; "Death in a Eucalyptus Grove—30 July 1947," Kent Collection, GB165-0453, MEC; and "Report on the Murder of Sgt Paice and Sgt Martin from 1st Guards Brigade," August 1, 1947, Papers of Palestine Police Old Comrades' Association, GB165-0224, MEC.

47. Wilson, *Cordon and Search*, 132.

48. Peter Lawrence de Carteret Martin, interview, December 11, 1992, Accession no. 12778, IWMSA; James Llewelyn Niven, interview, September 1988, Accession no. 10399, IWMSA; John Sankey, interview, September 1988, Accession no. 10300, IWMSA; Frank Jones, interview, March 16, 2006, GB165-0389, MEC; and Martin Duchesne, interview, March 23, 2006, GB165-0390, MEC.

49. Bagon, "Impact of Jewish Underground" (M.Phil. thesis), 126–29.

50. Carruthers, *Hearts and Minds*, quotes on 51, 53, and narrative details, 54–59.

51. Ibid., 61–63.

52. "Back to Partition," *Economist*, August 9, 1947, 227.

53. Ibid., 228.

54. Hoffman, *Anonymous Soldiers*, 461.

55. August 12, 1949, vol. 441, cols. 2340–44, HC Deb.

56. August 1, 1946, vol. 426, cols. 1256–57, HC Deb.

57. Jeffery, *MI6*, 691–95; and Walton, *Empire of Secrets*, 106–7.

58. Bethell, *Palestine Triangle*, 316–43.

59. Weizmann, *Letters and Papers*, 22:72.

60. UN General Assembly Resolution 181 (Partition Plan), November 29, 1947, https://www.mfa.gov.il/mfa/foreignpolicy/peace/guide/pages/un%20general%20assembly%20resolution%20181.aspx.

61. Louis, *British Empire in Middle East*, 487–93.

62. Jasse, "Great Britain and Palestine," 573.

63. Hoffman, *Anonymous Soldiers*, 469.

64. Ibid., 470.
65. United Nations, "U.K. Accepts UNSCOP General Recommendations," September 26, 1947, Summary Press Release GA/PAL/2, https://unispal.un.org /unispal.nsf/9a798adbf322aff38525617b006d88d7/ecb5eae2e1d29ed08525686 d00529256?OpenDocument.
66. J. H. H. Pollock, interview by Bernard Wasserstein, March 2, 1970, (82)11, HI.
67. Stankey interview, IWMSA.
68. Brendon, *Decline and Fall*, 484.
69. Ibid., 486; and Jasse, "Great Britain and Palestine," 558.
70. Pappe, *Ethnic Cleansing*; Gelber, *Palestine 1948*; Morris, *1948*; and Rogan and Shlaim, *War for Palestine.*
71. Pappe, *Ethnic Cleansing*, xiii.
72. Horne, *Job Well Done*, 581.
73. Brendon, *Decline and Fall*, 484–86.
74. Chindit Memorial, Victoria Embankment Gardens, London, unveiled October 16, 1990.
75. Hillel Kuttler, "75 Years After His Death, Why Orde Wingate Remains a Hero in Israel," *Times of Israel*, March 23, 2019.
76. Sinclair, "'Crack Force,'" 56–60.
77. Horne, *Job Well Done*, epigraph.
78. Catling interview, IWMSA.
79. Heller, *Behind Prison Walls*, 5; and Gurney Diary, 28, 53, GUR 1/2, Gurney Papers, MEC.
80. Haber, *Begin*, 191.
81. Quote in Andrew, *Defence of the Realm*, 451. See also Rathbone, "Political Intelligence and Policing," 84–104; and Sinclair, "'Crack Force,'" 56–60.
82. Andrew, *Defence of the Realm*, 452.
83. The high commissioner extended the state of emergency to the entire colony two days later.
84. Catling interview, IWMSA.
85. Ho, *Tainted Glory*, 254–55. Note that Bayly and Harper also discuss Ho in *Forgotten Wars*, 41, 129–30.
86. Ibid., 255–56.
87. Ibid., 252.
88. Ibid., 21, 260.
89. Ibid., 29.
90. Ibid., 38–67.
91. Walton, *Empire of Secrets*, 168.
92. Chapman, *Jungle Is Neutral*, 31, 157.
93. Blackburn, "Collective Memory," 74–75.
94. Sandhu, "Saga of the 'Squatter,'" 147.
95. Kheng, "Aspects of the Interregnum," 52–53; and Bayly and Harper, *Forgotten Wars*, 31.
96. Bayly and Harper, *Forgotten Wars*, 37–48.
97. Ibid., 203.
98. For a comprehensive discussion of the Malayan Union and citizenship, see Lau,

"Malayan Union Citizenship." For the complicated responses to the Malayan Union, which transcended rigidly imposed ethnic categories, see Harper, *End of Empire*, 84–148.

99. The combined total in the government's 1947 census of Malays includes "Malays" and "Other Malaysians." For a summary of the Federation of Malaya's 1947 census data, see del Tufo, *Report on the 1947 Census*, 40.

100. Harper, *End of Empire*, 133.

101. Bayly and Harper, *Forgotten Wars*, 210.

102. White, *Business, Government, and End of Empire*, 12; and Stockwell, "British Imperial Policy," 78.

103. Carnell, "Malayan Citizenship Legislation," 504–18; and Hack, "Detention, Deportation," 612–13.

104. Fong, "Labor Laws."

105. MacDonald would later take up the position of commissioner-general for Southeast Asia. For details on MacDonald, see Leebaert, *Grand Improvisation*, 127–29, 241–49, and 290–96; and Bayly and Harper, *Forgotten Wars*, 276–77.

106. John D. Dalley, "Internal Security, Malaya," June 14, 1948, CO 537/6006, TNA.

107. Hack, "Detention, Deportation," 611–12.

108. James Llewelyn Niven, interview, September 1988, Accession no. 10399, IWMSA.

109. Hurst, *Colonel Gray*, 9, 7.

110. E. W. A. Scarlett, memorandum (private and confidential), February 19, 1950, CO 717/194/5, TNA.

111. Stockwell, "Policing During Malayan Emergency," 110; Bennett, "'Very Salutary Effect,'" 422; and Tan, "Oral History," 217.

112. Sinclair, "'Sharp End,'" 473; and Walton, *Empire of Secrets*, 174–75.

113. *Report of the Police Mission to Malaya, March 1950* (Kuala Lumpur: Government Printer, 1950), CO 537/5417, TNA.

114. Hurst, *Colonel Gray*, 7.

115. "Report of the Police Mission," March 16, 1950, CO 717/194/6, TNA; and secretary of the Association of British Malaya to colonial secretary, June 27, 1950, CO 717/194/6, TNA.

116. Barber, *War of Running Dogs*, 30.

117. Bayly and Harper, *Forgotten Wars*, 439–40.

118. The MNLA, originally constituted as the Malayan Peoples' Anti-British Army, changed its name to the Malayan National Liberation Army in 1949. British officials mistakenly translated "National" as "Races," often referring to the MNLA as the Malayan Races Liberation Army.

119. Min Yuen was an abbreviation for Min Chung Yuen Tung, or "People's Movement."

120. "Law and Order," CID report, July 15, 1948, CO 717/171/3, TNA.

121. J. B. Williams, Minute to file, August 19, 1948, CO 537/3746, TNA.

122. This pattern of recirculating colonial officials, despite their previous failures, to other parts of the empire is one that stretches back to at least the nineteenth century, when British officials in India were appointed to posts elsewhere in the empire after the 1857 mutiny. My gratitude to Priya Satia for pointing this out.

123. Simpson, *Human Rights*, 82.

124. Federation of Malaya, "Detention and Deportation During the Emergency in the Federation of Malaya," White Paper no. 24 of 1953, CO 1022/132, TNA; and Dhu Renick, "Emergency Regulations."

125. Editorial, "Sir Henry Gurney," *Straits Times*, September 6, 1948.

126. Walton, *Empire of Secrets*, 172.

127. Andrew, *Defence of the Realm*, 448.

128. Stockwell, "Policing During Malayan Emergency," 110; Walton, *Empire of Secrets*, 197; and Bayly and Harper, *Forgotten Wars*, 437–39.

129. White, *Business, Government, and End of Empire*, 30, 116–17.

130. Carruthers, *Hearts and Minds*, 124n176; Harper, *End of Empire*, 151; and Gurney to colonial secretary (telegram), October 8, 1948, CO 537/3758, TNA.

131. Carruthers, *Hearts and Minds*, 77.

132. High Commissioner Gurney to colonial secretary (telegram), December 2, 1948, CO 537/4240, TNA.

133. High Commissioner Gurney, Minute to file, May 31, 1949, CO 537/4751, TNA.

134. Lau, "Malayan Union Citizenship," 217; and Harper, *End of Empire*, 22–23, 35–44.

135. J. P. Morton, "The Problems We Faced in Malaya and How They Were Solved," July 1954, 11, KV 4/408, TNA; and "The Colonial Empire Today: Summary of Our Main Problems and Policies," May 1950, CO 537/5698, TNA.

136. Carruthers, *Hearts and Minds*, 88.

137. Stenson, *Communist Revolt in Malaya*; and Walton, *Empire of Secrets*, 177.

138. Carruthers, *Hearts and Minds*, 88–89.

139. Barber, *War of Running Dogs*, 42.

140. Short, *Communist Insurrection* 120, 136–37.

141. "Mine Murder, 2 of Gang Held," *Straits Times*, September 1, 1948; "Threats on Estate Alleged," *Straits Times*, September 1, 1948; "Murder of Federal Councillor, Shot Dead by Unknown Gunman," *Straits Times*, September 2, 1948; "Details of the War Damage Plan," *Straits Times*, September 3, 1948; "Bandits Raid Estate, Burn Factory," *Straits Times*, September 8, 1948; "Bandits Shoot Another Chief," *Straits Times*, October 4, 1948; and "Terrorists Kill Ten Gurkhas, Lorry Ambushed on Perak Road," *Straits Times*, October 7, 1948.

142. "Malaya's Security Forces Are Not Enough," *Straits Times*, October 12, 1948.

143. July 8, 1948, vol. 453, cols. 699–700, HC Deb.

144. Barber, *War of Running Dogs*, 24.

145. Ibid., 41.

146. "Sir Henry Gurney's Words of Hope: End of Terror Only Matter of Time," *Straits Times*, October 7, 1948.

147. Department of Information, *Communist Banditry in Malaya*, 36.

148. "Malayan Emergency, II—Discontents in a Plural Society," *Times*, August 12, 1952, 5.

149. Ibid.; and "Malaya Emergency, I—Four Phases of an Unfinished Campaign," *Times*, August 11, 1952, 7.

CHAPTER 12: SMALL PLACES, CLOSE TO HOME

1. Arthur Hugh Peter Humphrey, interview, Reel 5, Accession no. 0995, AVD, NAS.

2. Eleanor Roosevelt, "Adoption of the Declaration of Human Rights," speech to the UN General Assembly, December 9, 1948, https://awpc.cattcenter.iastate .edu/2017/03/21/adoption-of-the-declaration-of-human-rights-dec-9-1948/.

3. Monteiro, *Ethics and Human Rights*, 434.

4. February 26, 1948, vol. 447, cols. 2263–65, HC Deb.

5. Simpson, *Human Rights*, 456.

6. Ibid., 457.

7. Klose, " 'Source of Embarrassment,' " 242.

8. Simpson, *Human Rights*, 458.

9. Ibid., 460.

10. Koskenniemi, *Gentle Civilizer of Nations*, 400.

11. For a detailed account of Lauterpacht's life, see Sands, *East West Street*, 66–117; and Vrdoljak, "Human Rights and Genocide," 1163–94.

12. Cairns, "Spinoza's Theory of Law"; and Vrdoljak, "Human Rights and Genocide," 1180.

13. Koskenniemi, *Gentle Civilizer of Nations*, 359–60.

14. Ibid., 376–77.

15. Pennybacker, *From Scottsboro to Munich*, 7; and George Padmore, "Ethiopia and World Politics," *Crisis* 42, no. 5 (1935): 138–39, 156–57, as quoted in Schwartz, "George Padmore," 139.

16. Buergenthal, "Evolving International," 783.

17. Van Dijk, "Human Rights in War," 561–63.

18. Ibid., 562–66.

19. For a trenchant critique of the UDHR, liberalism, and the evolution of human rights norms prior to World War II, see Mutua, *Human Rights*, 39–49. For non-Western human rights discourse, see Mutua, *Human Rights*, chap. 3, and Sikkink, *Evidence for Hope*, chap. 3.

20. Castrén, *Civil War*, 66, as cited in Bicknell, "Penumbra of War" (Ph.D. diss.), 226. For a discussion of the drafting of Common Article 3, see Elder, "Historical Background," 37–69.

21. Van Dijk, "Human Rights in War," 568.

22. Pictet, *Geneva Convention*, 12; and Van Dijk, "Human Rights in War," 571.

23. Van Dijk, "Human Rights in War," 574.

24. Interdepartmental Committee on the Review of the Geneva Convention, "Partisans (Memorandum by the Chairman for consideration by the Committee at their second meeting to be held on Wednesday, 17th September, 1947)," WO 32/12526, TNA.

25. Pictet, *Geneva Convention*, 25. Note that for decades, combatants and noncombatants were seen as dichotomous, and international humanitarian law largely protected the former. Responding to the civilian horrors of the Second World War, the Fourth Geneva Convention ensured this was no longer the case.

26. Chetail, "Contribution of International Court," 240.

27. Van Dijk, "Human Rights in War," 555n13.

28. Best, *War and Law*, 165. For a discussion of prosecutions and extraditions for "grave breaches" of the Geneva Conventions, together with questions of amnesty and necessity, see, for example, Ratner, "New Democracies, Old Atrocities," 712–26; and Roht-Arriaza, "State Responsibility to Investigate," 451–513.

29. Best, *War and Law*, 177.

30. Congress of Europe in the Hague, European Court of Human Rights, May 7–10, 1948, https://www.cvce.eu/en/recherche/unit-content/-/unit/o4bfa 990-86bc-402f-a633-11f39c9247c4/aadf5a4c-2972-41e8-9d44-9d5d4edb 8dd1.

31. Reynolds, *Empire, Emergency*, 118.

32. Simpson, *Human Rights*, 808–9.

33. Significant negotiation and discussion occurred within the British government's ranks as the ECHR effected its domestic jurisdiction. In particular, Britain wanted to retain the right to enforce future laws that could be brought into effect under DORAs, including detention without trial. Without individual petition, British officials believed they had solved this issue. See Moravcsik, "Origins of Human Rights Regimes," 238–43.

34. Simpson, *Human Rights*, 813.

35. Ibid., 825.

36. Simpson, "Usual Suspects," 685. Simpson also details the language in the ECHR whereby "until 1966, only interstate applications to the Commission were possible. Under article 25(1) of the Convention, the Commission was empowered to receive individual petitions from persons claiming to be the victims of violations, but only if the relevant state agreed. The acceptance of the jurisdiction of the European Court, established on April 20, 1959, was also optional. By December 31, 1959, nine contracting parties, including the Republic of Ireland, had accepted a right of individual petition, but not the United Kingdom."

37. Reynolds, *Empire, Emergency*, 119.

38. European Convention on Human Rights, Article 3, "Prohibition on Torture," 7, https://www.echr.coe.int/Documents/Convention_ENG.pdf.

39. "Revision of Geneva Conventions," Minutes of a Meeting of Ministers, December 2, 1949, CAB 130/46/281, TNA.

40. "Law and Order in the Federation," January 28, 1949, Annexure A to Minute of BDDC(FE), CO 537/4773, TNA.

41. High Commissioner Gurney to colonial secretary (telegram), December 19, 1948, CO 537/3758, TNA.

42. "Law and Order in the Federation," January 28, 1949, Annexure A to Minute of BDCC(FE), CO 537/4473, TNA.

43. High Commissioner Gurney to colonial secretary, Federation of Malaya Dispatch No. 5, May 30, 1949, 2, CO 537/5068, TNA.

44. Ibid., 6.

45. Khalili, *Time in the Shadows*, 199; High Commissioner Gurney to colonial sec-

retary, May 30, 1949, Federation of Malaya Dispatch No. 5, 6, CO 537/5068, TNA; and Short, *Communist Insurrection*, 142–43.

46. Sir Henry Gurney to colonial secretary (telegram), October 25, 1948, File 9, Box 29, Papers of Arthur Creech Jones, Mss. Brit. Emp. s. 332, BL.

47. Federation of Malaya, "Detention and Deportation During the Emergency in the Federation of Malaya," 3, White Paper no. 24 of 1953, CO 1022/132, TNA.

48. Extract from Special Meeting of Conference of Rulers, Malay States, December 4, 1951, Appendix A, CO 1022/163, TNA.

49. At this time, in the early years of the war, the Federation government was equipped to handle only 7,250 detainees, not the thousands of suspects slated to flow into and out of the camps.

50. Hale, *Massacre in Malaya*, 285.

51. High Commissioner Gurney to colonial secretary, Federation of Malaya Dispatch No. 5, May 30, 1949, 3, CO 537/5068, TNA.

52. "80 Houses Burned by Police," *Straits Times*, September 24, 1948. For parliamentary discussion on collective punishments, see, for example, April 2, 1952, vol. 498, cols. 1668–70, HC Deb; and November 19, 1952, vol. 507, col. 1870, HC Deb.

53. Hale, *Massacre in Malaya*, 286; and Bayly and Harper, *Forgotten Wars*, 450.

54. Hale, *Massacre in Malaya*, 285.

55. Bayly and Harper, *Forgotten Wars*, 449.

56. Hack, "Everyone Lived in Fear," 682.

57. Officer administering the government (OAG), Federation of Malaya, to colonial secretary (telegram), November 21, 1950, CO 717/197/5, TNA.

58. Bayly and Harper, *Forgotten Wars*, 480; Khoo, *Life as River Flows*, 186–87; and Ramakrishna, *Emergency Propaganda*, 54–86.

59. Sandhu, "Saga of the 'Squatter,'" 153.

60. Harper, *End of Empire*, 169; and Bayly and Harper, *Forgotten Wars*, 488–89.

61. Short, *Communist Insurrection*, 164.

62. Hack, "Detention, Deportation," 617–18.

63. High Commissioner Gurney to colonial secretary (telegram), April 2, 1949, CO 717/191, TNA.

64. Hack, "Detention, Deportation," 625.

65. "Undesirables Must Go," *Straits Times*, September 20, 1948.

66. Hack, "Detention, Deportation," 626.

67. Sir Henry Gurney to colonial secretary (telegram), October 25, 1948, File 9, Box 29, Mss. Brit. Emp. 332, BL; and Federation of Malaya, "Detention and Deportation During the Emergency in the Federation of Malaya," 7, White Paper no. 24 of 1953, CO 1022/132, TNA. See pages 7–10 for a full description of Emergency Regulations empowering the deportation, as well as detention, of those "foreign" to the territory.

68. According to Federation of Malaya official policy, "Emergency Regulation 17D, which was made on the 10th of January, 1949, empowers the High Commissioner to order the detention and the High Commissioner in Council the subsequent deportation of all or any of the inhabitants, other than Federal citi-

zens and British subjects, of any area who have aided and abetted the terrorists or suppressed or failed to provide information to the responsible authorities of the activities or presence in their area of terrorists." Emergency Regulation 17C was amended on January 22, 1949, "so that the dependents of a person who had been required to leave the Federation were also required to leave." See Federation of Malaya, "Detention and Deportation During the Emergency in the Federation of Malaya," 8, White Paper no. 24 of 1953, CO 1022/132, TNA.

69. Sir Henry Gurney to colonial secretary (telegram), October 25, 1948, File 9, Box 29, Mss. Brit. Emp. s. 332, BL; Low, "Repatriation of Chinese," 368; Tan, "Oral History," 86; Hack, "Detention, Deportation," 627; and Bayly and Harper, *Forgotten Wars*, 481.

70. Hack, "Detention, Deportation," 638n67.

71. "Deportation of British Subjects in the Federation of Malaya," March 26, 1953, CO 1022/137/22, TNA.

72. Low, "Repatriation of Chinese," 363–92.

73. Federation of Malaya OAG to colonial secretary, October 16, 1950, Savingram no. 1349, CO 717/199/1, TNA; and Hack, "Detention, Deportation," 620. In 1953 the Federation government reported to London that between December 1949 and March 1953, it had repatriated 24,036 "persons who are not citizens of the Federation or locally born British subjects." In 1955, this official number would reach 31,245. Of those deported by spring 1953, a little more than ten thousand repatriates and their dependents were shipped back before October 1950, and the remainder after that date. See Federation of Malaya, "Detention and Deportation During the Emergency in the Federation of Malaya," 8, 18, White Paper no. 24 of 1953, CO 1022/132, TNA; and French, *British Way*, 110.

74. Federation of Malaya OAG to colonial secretary, Savingram no. 1349, October 16, 1950, CO 717/199/1, TNA.

75. Short, *Communist Insurrection*, 190–91.

76. D. C. Watherston to A. T. Lennox-Boyd, October 6, 1950, CO 717/199/1, TNA; and Federation of Malaya OAG to colonial secretary, Savingram no. 1349, October 16, 1950, CO 717/199/1, TNA.

77. French, *British Way*, 110.

78. D. C. Watherston to A. T. Lennox-Boyd, October 6, 1950, CO 717/199/1, TNA.

79. "Extract from Minutes of Malaya Committee Meeting Held at the House of Commons," June 19, 1950, CO 717/199/1, TNA.

80. Arthur Hugh Peter Humphrey, interview, no date, 527/9/2, *End of Empire, Malaya*, Mss. Brit. Emp. s. 527, BL.

81. Arthur Hugh Peter Humphrey, interview, Accession no. 0995, AVD, NAS.

82. T. G. Askwith, "Detention and Rehabilitation," report submitted to Henry Potter, August 27, 1953, MAA 8/154/2 and AB 4/133/11, KNA; Federation of Malaya, "Detention and Deportation During the Emergency in the Federation of Malaya," White Paper no. 24 of 1953, CO 1022/132, TNA; "Malaya—Detention, Repatriation and Resettlement of Chinese," c. December 1950, CO

717/199/2, TNA; and *Federation of Malayan Government Gazette*, Supplement, July 23, 1948, no. 13, vol. 1, federal notification no. 2032. Also note that the police special branch replaced the Malayan Security Service in August 1948. For an excellent analysis of Malaya's detention camp system, see Hack, "Detention, Deportation."

83. James Marshall Patrick, interview, September 30, 1985, Accession no. 9141, IWMSA.

84. Taiping was for Chinese men, whereas the rehabilitation centers at Morib and Majeedi were for Malay men and women of all "races," respectively. There was also a separate camp for children known as Henry Gurney Approved School at Telok Mas, Malacca. See Federation of Malaya, "Detention and Deportation During the Emergency in the Federation of Malaya," White Paper no. 24 of 1953, 6, CO 1022/132, TNA; and Sandhu, "Saga of the 'Squatter,'" 167.

85. Tom Driberg, "In Detention," *Reynolds News*, November 12, 1950.

86. "Extract from Record of Meeting with B.D.C.C. and to Secretaries of State on 4th June" Annex II, CO 717/199/1, TNA; and James Marshall Patrick, interview, September 30, 1985, Accession no. 9141, IWMSA. See also Jack Morton, "The Problems We Faced in Malaya and How We Solved Them," July 1954, 16, KV 4/408, TNA, in which he states, "The tragedy was the thorough ignorance or lack of good information in the first place, many of these prisoners were innocent but were now being converted into embittered communists."

87. "Gang Forced Camp Strike," *Straits Times*, July 20, 1950; and Short, *Communist Insurrection*, 193.

88. The PRC established the Overseas Chinese Relief Committee under the auspices of the People's Relief Administration of China, the Red Cross Society of China, and the Returned Overseas Chinese Society.

89. Enclosure to Canton P/L dispatch S/O 15 (10/17-1/51) of 23.5.51 to Far Eastern Dept., Foreign Office, CO 717/199/3, TNA.

90. Ibid.

91. Peking to Foreign Office, telegram no. 483, March 9, 1951, CO 717/199/2, TNA.

92. Ibid.; and Peking to Foreign Office, telegram no. 484, March 9, 1951, CO 717/199/2, TNA.

93. "Peking Bluff Over Malaya 'Persecution,'" *Observer*, March 11, 1951; and "Red 'Investigators' Ask Entry in Malaya," *New York Times*, March 10, 1951.

94. Peking to Foreign Office, telegram no. 483, March 9, 1951, CO 717/199/2, TNA.

95. Chin, "Repatriation of Chinese," 385.

96. Sir Henry Gurney to colonial secretary (telegram), February 3, 1951, CO 717/199/2, TNA.

97. Geneva Convention Relative to the Treatment of Prisoners of War, August 12, 1949, Article 3, 91–92, https://www.un.org/en/genocideprevention/documents/atrocity-crimes/Doc.32_GC-III-EN.pdf; and commissioner-general in Southeast Asia to colonial secretary (telegram), March 24, 1951, CO 717/199/2, TNA.

98. Foreign Office, telegram no. 66 Intel, March 22, 1951, CO 717/199/2, TNA.

99. Foreign Office to Peking, telegram no. 442, March 17, 1951, CO 717/199/2, TNA.

100. Henry Gurney to Malcolm MacDonald (top secret), February 15, 1950, enclosure, "The Armed Communist Situation in Malaya," 1, CO 537/5974, TNA.

101. Henry Gurney to Malcolm MacDonald (top secret), February 15, 1950, 1, CO 537/5974, TNA. The government's focus on the "squatter problem" as the linchpin to winning the war is discussed in Sandhu, "Saga of the 'Squatter.'" Other historians later addressed and expanded on this analysis, including Karl Hack in various articles.

102. Henry Gurney to Malcolm MacDonald (top secret), February 15, 1950, 1, CO 537/5974, TNA.

103. Short, *Communist Insurrection*, 234–35.

104. Monteiro, *Ethics and Human Rights*, 434.

105. Tan, "Oral History," 98.

106. Bayly and Harper, *Forgotten Wars*, 489–90.

107. Tan, "Oral History," 97–99; and Hack, "Detention, Deportation," 632–33.

108. Henry Gurney to Malcolm MacDonald (top secret), February 15, 1950, 2, CO 537/5974, TNA.

109. Malaya Committee, "Various Matters Discussed with the Authorities in Malaya," July 14, 1950, CAB 21/1681, TNA.

110. "Top Secret—Outline of Future Anti-Bandit Policy in Malaya," c. May 1950, 2, CO 537/5975, TNA.

111. Ibid., 1–2.

112. Sandhu, "Saga of the 'Squatter,'" 159, 164; and "Resettlement in Malaya," no date, CO 1022/29, TNA. Labor lines on the rubber estates were comprised of some 50 percent Indians, 30 percent Chinese, and 16 percent Malays; on the mines, nearly all the laborers were Chinese.

113. "Extract from Record of Meeting with B.D.C.C. and the Secretaries of State on 4th June," Annex II, CO 717/199/1, TNA.

114. Ibid.

115. Federation of Malaya, "Detention and Deportation During the Emergency in the Federation of Malaya," 3, White Paper no. 24 of 1953, CO 1022/132, TNA.

116. See various documents in CO 717/199/1, TNA, and exchanges between Malaya and London on the question of detention and the committees of review.

117. Federation of Malaya OAG to colonial secretary (telegram), November 21, 1950, CO 717/197/5, TNA, emphasis added.

118. John Davis, interview, Accession no. 1652, AVD, NAS.

119. Tan, "Oral History," 101.

120. Sandhu, "Saga of the 'Squatter,'" 161; and Tan, "Like a Concentration Camp," 222–23.

121. Strauch, "Chinese New Villages," 130; and Tan, "Like a Concentration Camp," 222.

122. For example, Tan, "Like a Concentration Camp," 223.

123. "$11 Million Spent on Squatters," *Straits Times*, November 22, 1950.

124. Han, *House Has Two Doors*, 66, 131–32.

125. Sandhu, "Saga of the 'Squatter,'" 160; and Han, *Rain My Drink*, 143–44.

126. "770 Tons Barbed Wire Needed," *Straits Times*, September 28, 1950.

127. Tan, "Like a Concentration Camp," 222–25; and Sandhu, "Saga of the 'Squatter,'" 163, 175–76.
128. Sandhu, "Saga of the 'Squatter,'" 163; and Tan, "Like a Concentration Camp," 221. The analogy of "concentration camp" was used by other villagers. For example, Luo Lan testified, "These so-called New Villages were, in fact, concentration camps to keep the sympathizers of the Communists away from the guerilla army." Khoo, *Life as River Flows*, 123.
129. Colonial Secretary, "Review of Police and Security Forces in Relation to Communist Activities: Special Constables," 1949, CO 573/4404, TNA.
130. Colonial Office to Maj. Gen. C. D. Packard (memorandum), September 10, 1949, CO 717/172/3, TNA.
131. O. H. Morris to Lt. Col. J. V. B. Jervis Read (memorandum), August 31, 1948, CO 717/172/3, TNA.
132. G. F. Seel to A. H. Clough (memorandum), August 3, 1949, CO 717/172/4, TNA.
133. "Provision of Interpreters and Interrogators for Operations in the Federation of Malaya," July 25, 1949, CO 717/172/4, TNA; and Gray to Morris, "Interrogation Center" (telegram), August 9, 1949, CO 717/172/4, TNA.
134. O. H. Morris to Lt. Col. J. V. B. Jervis Read, August 31, 1948, CO 717/172/3, TNA; and J. D. Higham to Maj. Gen. C. D. Packard, September 10, 1948, CO 717/172/3, TNA.
135. Maguire, "Interrogation," 138.
136. Comber, *Malaya's Secret Police*, 86.
137. Ibid., x.
138. Ibid., 111.
139. J. C. Morgan, "Preparation by Malayan Government of a Paper Setting Out Experiences Gained in Malayan Operations As Affecting Internal Security Arrangements," February 7, 1949, CO 537/5068, TNA; and High Commissioner Gurney to Colonial Secretary Creech Jones, Federation of Malaya top secret dispatch no. 5, May 30, 1949, CO 537/5068, TNA.
140. Maguire, "Interrogation," 12–14.
141. Andrew, *Defence of the Realm*, 450.
142. Joint Service Pamphlet, "Interrogation in War," 1955, 18, WO 33/2335, TNA.
143. As quoted in Cobain, *Cruel Britannia*, 70.
144. French, *British Way*, 159; and Walton, *Empire of Secrets*, 192–93.
145. Guy Madoc, interview, August 1981, *End of Empire*, Mss. Brit. Emp. s. 527, BL.
146. John Sankey, interview, September 1988, Accession no. 10300, IWMSA.
147. French, *British Way*, 162.
148. Jeremy Hespeler-Boultbee, interview by author, November 12, 2013.
149. Walton, *Empire of Secrets*, 190.
150. Comber, *Malaya's Secret Police*, 83.
151. Miller, *Communist Menace*, 89.
152. Robinson, *Transformation in Malaya*, 79.
153. Tan, "Like a Concentration Camp," 225; and Khoo, *Life as River Flows*, 284.
154. Khoo, *Life as River Flows*, 123. Han Suyin also refers to a British security force member as a "red-haired great man" in *Rain My Drink*, 133.

155. Khoo, *Life as River Flows*, 283–84.

156. Bayly and Harper, *Forgotten Wars*, 513.

157. High commissioner to colonial secretary, "MCP's October Resolutions" (enclosure), December 31, 1952, CO 1022/187, TNA; Hack, "Everyone Lived in Fear," 684–85; and Hack, "Malayan Emergency," 397–401.

158. Tan, "Like a Concentration Camp," 226.

159. Short, *Communist Insurrection*, 303–5; and Guy Madoc, interview, August 1981, *End of Empire*, Mss. Brit. Emp. s. 527, BL.

160. Peng, *My Side of History*, 287–89; and Short, *Communist Insurrection*, 303–6.

161. Peter Lawrence de Carteret Martin, interview, December 11, 1992, Accession no. 12778, IWMSA.

162. Sir Richard Catling, interview, September 1988, Accession no. 10392, IWMSA.

163. Guy Madoc, interview, August 1981, *End of Empire*, Mss. Brit. Emp. s. 527, BL.

CHAPTER 13: SYSTEMATIZED VIOLENCE

1. Attlee, *As It Happened*, 291.

2. Labour Party Election Manifesto, 1951, http://www.labour-party.org.uk /manifestos/1951/1951-labour-manifesto.shtml.

3. "Social Survey: Study of Public Knowledge of Colonial Affairs Conducted by Central Office," 1951, CO 875/2/3, TNA; and French, *British Way*, 222.

4. Conservative Party, General Election Manifesto, 1951, http://www.conservative manifesto.com/1951/1951-conservative-manifesto.shtml.

5. Ibid.

6. "Prorogation," October 30, 1952, vol. 505, col. 2160, HC Deb.

7. Document 260, "Success in Malaya," note by Field Marshal Lord Montgomery (M/222, January 2, 1952), enclosed with Appointment of Templer, letter from Field Marshal Lord Montgomery to Mr. Churchill, PREM 11/169, January 2, 1952, in Stockwell, *Malaya: Communist Insurrection*. See also Cloake, *Templer*, 201.

8. Document 260, "Success in Malaya," note by Field Marshal Lord Montgomery (M/222, January 2, 1952), enclosed with Appointment of Templer, letter from Field Marshal Lord Montgomery to Mr. Churchill, PREM 11/169, January 2, 1952, in Stockwell, *Malaya: Communist Insurrection*; Lyttleton to Churchill, January 4, 1952, Telegram No. T6/52, Document 259, PREM 11/639, in Stockwell, *Malaya: Communist Insurrection*.

9. Cloake, *Templer*, 59.

10. "Sir Gerald Templer Is Dead at 81; Repressed Red Rebels in Malaya," *New York Times*, October 27, 1979, 24; and Jack Morton, "The Problems We Faced in Malaya and How They Were Solved," July 1954, 14, KV 4/408, TNA.

11. Cloake, *Templer*, chaps. 9 and 10.

12. Short, *Communist Insurrection*, 334.

13. Komer, *Malayan Emergency*, 47; Short, *Communist Insurrection*, 326; and Bayly and Harper, *Forgotten Wars*, 522.

14. Short, *Communist Insurrection*, 326–29; and Bayly and Harper, *Forgotten Wars*, 521–22.

15. Walton, *Empire of Secrets*, 174; and Sinclair, "'Sharp End,'" 473.

16. C (51) 59, "Malaya," December 21, 1951, in Stockwell, *Malaya: Communist Insurrection*, 344–45.

17. Secretary of Defence, "Official Designation of Communist Forces" (memorandum), May 20, 1952, CO 1022/48, TNA.

18. Aldrich, *Hidden Hand*, 513.

19. E. N. Pierce on behalf of secretary for defence, Kuala Lumpur, appendix: Instructions for the use of "GUARD," December 16, 1953, FCO 141/7497, TNA; and colonial secretary, Savingram and Circular on "GUARD" procedure, December 28, 1954, FCO 141/7497, TNA.

20. Cloake, *Templer*, 260.

21. Ibid., 227.

22. Walton, *Empire of Secrets*, 180.

23. Comber, *Malaya's Secret Police*, 17.

24. Aldrich, *Hidden Hand*, 506–7.

25. John William Noble, interview, March 24, 1997, Accession no. 1733, IWMSA; and Bayly and Harper, *Forgotten Wars*, 470.

26. Aldrich, *Hidden Hand*, 505–6.

27. "Monthly Political Intelligence Report for Period Ending 20th June 1953." FCO 141/7377, TNA.

28. Secretary for defence, "Perimeter Fences" (memorandum), April 28, 1952, CO 1022/30, TNA; and "Perimeter Lighting in New Villages," c. September 1952, CO 1022/30, TNA.

29. C (51) 59, "Malaya," December 21, 1951, in Stockwell, *Malaya: Communist Insurrection*, 344.

30. Aldrich, *Hidden Hand*, 511.

31. Barber, *War of Running Dogs*, 89.

32. Peng, *My Side of History*, 324; Andrew, *Defence of the Realm*, 450; Aldrich, *Hidden Hand*, 509–10; and Komer, *Malayan Emergency*, 52.

33. Extract from Malayan Weekly Intelligence Summary, no. 26, "Effect of Sodium Arsenate on Bandits Crops," November 2, 1950, CO 717/197/5, TNA; Judith Perera and Andy Thomas, "This Horrible Natural Experiment," *New Scientist*, April 18, 1985; and Hay et al., "Poison Cloud," 632.

34. C. G. Eastwood to Geoffrey Blackman, November 20, 1951, CO 1022/26, TNA.

35. Institute of Medical Research, Kuala Lumpur, "Precautions to Be Taken During the Handling of Sodium Trichloroacetate (STCA)," May 1952, CO 1022/26, TNA.

36. Ibid.; Perera and Thomas, "This Horrible Natural Experiment," 34–36; and G. E. Blackman to C. Eastwood, November 27, 1951, CO 1022/26, TNA.

37. T. C. Jerrom (memorandum), April 8, 1953, in Doug Weir, "The U.K.'s Use of Agent Orange in Malaya," November 12, 2014, https://www.toxicremnantsof war.info/uk-agent-orange-malaysia/.

38. November 19, 1952, vol. 507, col. 1867, HC Deb.

39. "Templer of Malaya," *Time*, December 15, 1952, vol. 60, issue 24, 26–33.

40. "Heroic Village," *Daily Worker*, August 26, 1952; "Village to Be Destroyed—

Malayans Punished," *Manchester Guardian*, August 26, 1952; and "A Village Vanishes," *Daily Herald*, August 19, 1952.

41. Linstrum, "Facts About Atrocity," 121.

42. Ibid., 108–127.

43. April 3, 1952, vol. 498, col. 1915, HC Deb; and November 19, 1952, vol. 507, col. 1870, HC Deb.

44. December 3, 1952, vol. 508, col. 1557, HC Deb.

45. J. M. Gullick to M. J. Hayward, May 7, 1956, FCO 141/7357, TNA.

46. Barber, *War of Running Dogs*, 96; and "Batang Kali Shooting," *Straits Times*, December 24, 1948. Note that press reports at the time put the number of insurgents killed at twenty-six, whereas later reports put the number at twenty-four and twenty-five.

47. "82 Terrorists Killed, Seized in 3 Weeks," *Straits Times*, December 18, 1948.

48. Written Answer 104, "Incident, Selangor," January 26, 1949, vol. 460, col. 138, HC Deb.

49. Bayly and Harper, *Forgotten Wars*, 453.

50. Ibid., 454; and Walton, *Empire of Secrets*, 196.

51. March 4, 1953, vol. 512, col. 382, HC Deb. For the extension of citizenship rights to villagers, see Short, *Communist Insurrection*, 341–42.

52. Robinson, *Transformation in Malaya*, 79.

53. A. W. D. James (memorandum), November 8, 1955, FCO 141/7307, TNA.

54. Dwight D. Eisenhower to Gen. Sir Gerald Templer, October 5, 1953, FCO 141/7498, TNA.

55. Stubbs, "Counter-Insurgency," 51.

56. Department of Information, *Communist Banditry in Malaya*, 36.

57. Stubbs, "Counter-Insurgency"; and Bayly and Harper, *Forgotten Wars*, 527–28.

58. Draft Development Plan of the Federation of Malaya, 1950, 3, NAM.

59. Report of the Director of Audit on the Accounts of the Federation of Malaya, 1950, NAM; and Stubbs, "Counter-Insurgency."

60. Report of the Director of Audit on the Accounts of the Federation of Malaya, 1949 and 1951, NAM; and Rudner, "Draft Development Plan," 67.

61. Legislative Council Proceedings, Fifth Session, 1953, 11.

62. Commissioner-general in South-East Asia to Rt. Hon. Oliver Lyttleton, July 23, 1953, FO 371/106984, TNA.

63. Acting British Advisor Pahang to OAG (memorandum), Kuala Lumpur, February 3, 1956, FCO 141/7356, TNA.

64. Bayly and Harper, *Forgotten Wars*, 528.

65. Aldrich, *Hidden Hand*, 515–17.

66. Lapping, *End of Empire*, 180–81; and Bayly and Harper, *Forgotten Wars*, 530.

67. Harper, *End of Empire*, 322.

68. Bayly and Harper, *Forgotten Wars*, 532.

69. Ibid., 532–33.

70. Ibid., 532.

71. Political History of Singapore 1945–1965, David Saul Marshall, interview, September 24, 1984, Accession no. 0156, AVD, NAS.

72. Andrew, *Defence of the Realm*, 451; Walton, *Empire of Secrets*, 200–1; Bayly and Harper, *Forgotten Wars*, 533–35; and Lapping, *End of Empire*, 182–84.

73. Bayly and Harper, *Forgotten Wars*, 534.

74. Ibid., 535.

75. Brendon, *Decline and Fall*, 465.

76. Sutton, "British Imperialism," 476–77.

77. Ibid., 479.

78. Ibid., 477–80; and White, "Beginnings of Crony Capitalism."

79. Malaya: Defence Agreement between UK and Federation of Malaya; Working Party on the Agreement on External Defence and Mutual Assistance, January 1, 1956, to December 31, 1956, FCO 141/7234, TNA.

80. Sutton, "British Imperialism," 483.

81. A. J. Brown to R. W. Newsham, October 17, 1957, DO 186/17, TNA; M. L. McCaul, security liaison officer, "Destruction of Records in the Federation of Malaya," September 9, 1957, DO 186/17, TNA; W. M. Young, "Records of the British Military Administration in Malaya," August 8, 1957, FCO 141/7524, TNA; Secretary for internal defence and security, "Records of the British Military Administration in Malaya," August 2, 1957, FCO 141/7524, TNA; "Records of the British Military Administration in Malaya," July 12, 1957, FCO 141/7524, TNA; Private secretary to high commissioner (memorandum), July 5, 1956, FCO 141/7524, TNA; W. J. Watts, various memoranda re: strong room, and appendices, July 1956, FCO 141/7524, TNA; and M. L. McCaul, "Destruction of Records in the Federation of Malaya," September 9, 1957, DO 186/17, TNA.

82. M. L. McCaul, "Destruction of Records in the Federation of Malaya," September 9, 1957, DO 186/17, TNA.

83. Mathieson to Gorell Barnes, Minute, July 23, 1955, CO 822/888, TNA.

84. Council of Ministers, Resettlement Committee, seventeenth meeting, April 27, 1956, Minutes, CO 822/1229/1, TNA.

85. Brief for colonial secretary for visit to Kenya, "The Continuation of the Emergency," 1957, CO 822/1229/1, TNA.

86. Berman, *Control and Crisis*, 150–51; and Leo, *Land and Class in Kenya*, chap. 1.

87. Berman, *Control and Crisis*, 168–70, 267–68.

88. For a history of squatters in Kenya, see Kanogo, *Squatters and Roots*. Note that Kenyatta returned from Kenya in September 1946, taking over as president of the Kenya African Union in June 1947.

89. Jomo Kenyatta, "Hitler Could Not Improve on Kenya," *New Leader*, May 21, 1937; Murray-Brown, *Kenyatta*; and Lonsdale and Berman, "Labors of *Muigwithania*."

90. Andrew, *Defence of the Realm*, 454–56.

91. For the most comprehensive accounts of the emergence and spread of Mau Mau and the socioeconomic roots of the movement, see Kanogo, *Squatters and Mau Mau*; Throup, *Origins of Mau Mau*; and Furedi, *Mau Mau War*.

92. Annual Report, 1950, 2, African Affairs Department, KNA.

93. Nelson Macharia Gathigi, interview by author, February 20, 1999.

94. Elkins, *Imperial Reckoning*, 26–28.

95. Gathigi, interview by author, February 20, 1999; and Lucy Ngima Mugwe, interview by author, March 10, 2002.

96. Bruce, Minute, November 25, 1955, CO 822/794, TNA.

97. Roberts, foreword to *Mau Mau in Kenya*, 7–9. Such adjectives are found throughout official files in Britain's and Kenya's government archives.

98. For accounts of early forms of settler rough justice, see *Correspondence Relating to the Flogging of Natives by Certain Europeans in Nairobi*, Cd. 3256; *Report on the Native Labour Commission, 1912–13*; Kennedy, *Islands of White*, 142–44; and Anderson, "Master and Servant in Colonial Kenya."

99. Frederick Crawford to E. B. Davis, memorandum (secret), March 16, 1953, CO 822/489/20, TNA; and *End of Empire, Kenya*, vols. 1 and 2, Mss. Brit. Emp. S. 527/528, BL.

100. Lyttleton, *Memoirs of Lord Chandos*, 370.

101. "A Small-Scale African Hitler," *Daily Telegraph*, November 1, 1952.

102. Elkins, *Imperial Reckoning*, 44–46.

103. Clayton, *Counter-insurgency in Kenya*, 51.

104. Blundell to Harding, April 18, 1953, Cameron to Redman (VCIGS), April 30, 1953, WO 216/851, TNA; Report on the Commander-in-Chief, Middle East Land Forces, Visit to Kenya, May 11–16, 1953, WO 216/852, TNA; Lyttleton to Churchill, May 27, 1953, PREM 11/472, TNA; and "Top Secret Directive to C-in-C East Africa," June 3, 1953, 75/134/1, Erskine Papers, IWM.

105. Clayton, *Counter-insurgency in Kenya*, 11n21.

106. Anderson, *Histories of the Hanged*, 230–31, 248–50.

107. In debates over the movement of Kikuyu between late 1952 and January 1953, members of Kenya's legislative council used the phrase "trickle became a stream" repeatedly, indicating the rise in volume of Kikuyu repatriates from the Rift Valley to the Kikuyu reserves. See Kenya Legislative Council Debates, February 19, 1953, vol. 54, 128–85; Kenya Legislative Council Debates, May 7, 1953, vol. 55, 74–117; and "Advisory Committee on Kikuyu Movement," MAA 8/163, KNA.

108. "Outline Plan for Operation ANVIL," February 1954, CO 822/796 and WO 276/214, TNA; and Gen. Sir George Erskine, "The Kenya Emergency," April 25, 1955, WO 236/18, TNA.

109. Evans, *Law and Order*, 270; T. G. Askwith, interview by author, June 9, 1998; and acting governor to colonial secretary (telegram), May 9, 1954, CO 822/796/32, TNA.

110. Andrews, *Defence of the Realm*, 447, 456–59; Walton, *Empire of Secrets*, 125–26; and Elkins, "Archives, Intelligence and Secrecy," 267–68.

111. Heather, "Of Men and Plans," 23; and Walton, *Empire of Secrets*, 245.

112. Government's Policy for Rehabilitating Mau Mau, c. 1954, AA 45/22/2, HD; and Summary of Central Province Emergency Committee (South) Plan in Response to War Council Directive No. 11, September 10, 1956, AA 45/79/7A, HD.

113. Osborne, "Introduction," 19–35.

114. Henderson and Goodhart, *Hunt for Kimathi*.

115. For details on General China, Henderson, Kimathi, and the Land and Freedom Army, see Anderson, *Histories of the Hanged*, 230–50, 273–77, 288–90; and Itote, *"Mau Mau" General*; and Itote, *Mau Mau in Action*.

116. "Canon T. F. C. Bewes, African Secretary of the CMS on his Special Mission to the 'Mau Mau' Area of Kenya," February 9, 1953, CO 822/471/5, TNA; Granville Roberts to Potter (cable), February 10, 1953, CO 822/471/7, TNA; and T. F. C. Bewes to Governor Baring (private and confidential), January 28, 1953, CO 822/471/6, TNA.

117. Elkins, *Imperial Reckoning*, chap. 3; "Mau Mau" files, Box 2, Christian Council of Kenya, "The Forces of Law and Order," c. January 1954, Records of the Anglican Church, Imani House, Nairobi.

118. Anonymous, interview by author, Naivasha, Kenya, January 14, 1999.

119. Governor Baring to colonial secretary, July 17, 1953, CO 822/692/3, TNA.

120. "Rehabilitation," January 6, 1954, CO 822/794/1, TNA; and Federation of Malaya, "Detention and Deportation During the Emergency in the Federation of Malaya," 15, White Paper no. 24 of 1953, CO 1022/132, TNA.

121. *South Asian* refers to a large swath of different ethnic groups coming from British colonial India. "Coolies" were from Sindh, Punjab, and other areas in close proximity to Karachi. Skilled workers were drawn largely from Bombay; Goans engaged in railway and administrative work. For the migration and presence of South Asians and Middle Easterners in East Africa, see Mangat, *Asians in East Africa*; Adam, *Indian Africa*; and Middleton, *World of Swahili*.

122. Fitz de Souza, interview by author, August 11, 2003. See also Fitz de Souza, *End of Empire, Kenya*, vol. 1, Mss. Brit. Emp. s. 527/528, BL.

123. Anderson, *Histories of the Hanged*, 7.

124. Elkins, *Imperial Reckoning*, 131–32.

125. Ibid., chap. 5.

126. Hugh Fraser, MP, "Report of Visit to Kenya," October 6, 1953, CO 822/479/3, TNA.

127. Bruce, Minutes, November 25, 1955, CO 822/794, TNA.

128. T. G. Askwith, "Address Given to the African Affairs Sub-Committee of the Electors Union on November 16, 1953," 1 (courtesy of Mr. Askwith).

129. Askwith, interview by author, June 9, 1998. For further details on Askwith, oathing, and rehabilitation, see T. G. Askwith, "Detention and Rehabilitation," report submitted to Henry Potter, August 27, 1953, MAA 8/154/2 and AB 4/133/11, KNA.

130. T. G. Askwith, *Memoirs of Kenya, 1936–61*, 1:55, Thomas Askwith Papers, Mss. Afr. 1770, BL; "Rehabilitation," January 6, 1954, 2, CO 822/794/1, TNA; Carothers, "Psychology of Mau Mau"; and Leakey, *Defeating Mau Mau*, 85–86.

131. Ronald Sherbrooke-Walker, "Visitor to Mau Mau Kenya," March 1953, File 6, 1–4, Box 6, Sir Arthur Young Papers, Mss. Afr. s. 486, BL.

132. Minister for finance and development on the cost of the emergency (memorandum), November 16, 1954, EMER 45/70A, HD.

133. Villagization took place throughout the Kiambu, Fort Hall, Nyeri, and Embu districts. The Kenya government did not pursue a wide-scale policy in Meru District, largely because the district commissioner argued against it. In Meru,

because of the sparser population density, the district commissioner believed that it was a security benefit not to concentrate the population into villages. In total, fifty villages were officially created in Meru. See District commissioner, Meru, "Villagisation" (memorandum), November 6, 1954, OP/EST 1/986/21/1, KNA. Villagization had been introduced, as initially in Malaya, as an ad hoc measure in various locations throughout the Kikuyu reserves beginning in March 1953, though it was not until the War Council's decision in June 1954 that it became a full-scale policy. See "Memorandum on the Aggregation of the Population into Villages in Rural Areas," April 12, 1954, AB 2/53/1, KNA; Press Office, handout no. 28, March 19, 1953, CO 822/481/1, TNA; and Central Province, Annual Report, 1956, VQ 16/103, KNA.

134. Elkins, *Imperial Reckoning*, 199.
135. Mrs. Beecher, "Resolution" (memorandum), March 4, 1955, OP/EST 1/688/2, KNA.
136. Elkins, *Imperial Reckoning*, 429n1.
137. Ruth Wanjugu Ndegwa, interview by author, March 22, 1999.
138. Chief secretary, War Council minutes, September 10, 1954, vol. 2, 40A, WAR/C/MIN.45, HD.
139. Bennett, *Fighting the Mau Mau*, 222.
140. Secretary of local government, health, and housing to Askwith, "Emergency Work Among Women—Central Province" (memorandum), June 6, 1955, AB 2/51/34, KNA. Missionary perspectives are partly drawn from Archdeacon Peter Bostock, interview by author, March 20, 1998; and Reverend Alan Page, interview by author, June 14, 1999.
141. Provincial medical officer, Central Province, to the director of medical services, "Commentary on Work of Red Cross Team in Nyeri" (memorandum), July 8, 1954, AB 17/11/46, KNA.
142. Klose, "Colonial Testing Ground," 112.
143. Ibid., 111–12.
144. Central Province Emergency Committee Meeting Held on Friday 17th February 1956, vol. 2, AA 45/23/1/3A, HD.
145. War Office, *Imperial Policing and Duties in Aid of the Civil Power* (London: HMSO, 1949), 5.
146. Emphasis in the original. For further discussion, see Bennett, *Fighting the Mau Mau*, 88–89; and Trafford Smith to C. G. Kemball, June 25, 1949, LCO 2/4309, TNA. For the broader discussion over the applicability of the Geneva Conventions, see Geneva Convention Rules of War: Minutes of Meetings, 1949–1951, LCO, 2/4309, TNA.
147. Bicknell, "Penumbra of War" (Ph.D. diss.), 286.
148. Bennett, *Fighting the Mau Mau*, 88, emphasis added.
149. Ibid., 75.
150. Ibid., 89.
151. War Office, *Imperial Policing and Duties*, 35.
152. "Appreciation by the Commander-in-Chief of the Operational Situation in Kenya in June 1955," vol. 1, AA 45/66A, HD.
153. Committee of Enquiry into Thumaita Village to Baring, January 5, 1956,

E19/12492A, HD. For "punitive" policy, see Central Province Emergency Committee, January 8, 1954, vol. 2, EMER 45/23/1/3A, HD.

154. "Communal Labor," January 24, 1956, vol. 2, AA 45/51A, HD; and Elkins, *Imperial Reckoning*, chap. 8.

155. Elkins, *Imperial Reckoning*, chap. 8; and "Kenya: White Terror," *BBC Correspondent*, November 11, 2002.

156. "Food Denial Measures—Draft Press Announcement," September 30, 1955, vol. 1, AA 45/51A, HD.

157. J. A. Rutherford, *History of the Kikuyu Guard*, 178–79, Mss. Afr. s. 424, BL.

158. Caroline Macy Elkins, witness statement, May 25, 2012, paragraph 141, 54, *Ndiku Mutua and 4 Others and FCO*, Royal Courts of Justice.

159. Christina Wambui, interview, *End of Empire*, Mss. Brit. Emp. s. 527/28, BL.

160. K. P. Hadingham, assistant commissioner of police, "The Situation in South Nyeri Reserve with Particular Reference to Mathira," December 14, 1954, AA 45/55/2/21, HD.

161. "Finding of R. A. Wilkinson, 1st Class Magistrate at Embu who was in charge of enquiring into the death of Elijah Gideon Njeru at Embu on the 29th of January, 1953," CO 822/471, TNA.

162. "Telegram no. 282 to Secretary of State," March 9, 1953; and "Africans Death after Beating—Two Europeans Fined," *Times*, October 1, 1953, both in CO 822/471/12, TNA.

163. "Record of Meeting Between the Solicitor General and Mr. Hughes, of the British Council, and Two Africans, 26 May, 1953," vol. 1, AA 45/26/2A, HD.

164. Erskine to secretary of state for war, December 12, 1953, WO 32/15834, TNA.

165. Clayton, *Counter-insurgency in Kenya*, 38–39.

166. Lyttleton to Baring (telegram), March 12, 1953, CO 822/728/31, TNA.

167. Ibid.

168. Cusack to Tatton-Brown, Minute, November 20, 1954, AH 9/36/59, KNA, emphasis original.

169. Arthur Young, "Introduction to Sir Arthur Young," no date, 18, File 1, Box 5, Sir Arthur Young Papers, Mss. Afr. s. 486, BL.

170. Ibid., 14.

171. Governor Baring to Gorell Barnes (memorandum), November 6, 1954, CO 822/1037/7, TNA.

172. Arthur Young, "Introduction to Sir Arthur Young," no date, 13, File 1, Box 5, Sir Arthur Young Papers, Mss. Afr. s. 486, BL.

173. Boyd, "Opening Address," 5; and Heinlein, *British Government Policy*, passim.

174. Assistant commissioner of police Nyeri to Young (memorandum), November 22, 1954, 1, File 6, Box 5, Sir Arthur Young Papers, Mss. Afr. s. 486, BL.

175. Ibid., 29–30.

176. Colonel Young, official statement of resignation, February 1955, CO 822/1293/1, TNA; and Colonel Young (Resignation), Written Answers, February 2, 1955, vol. 536, col. 119, HC Deb.

177. *Report to the Secretary of State for the Colonies by the Parliamentary Delegation to Kenya, 1954*, Cmd. 9081.

178. Colonel Young, official statement of resignation, February 1955, CO

822/1293/1, TNA; and Colonel Young (Resignation), Written Answers, February 2, 1955, vol. 536, col. 119, HC Deb.

179. Sir Richard Catling, interview, September 1988, reels 7 and 8, Accession no. 10392, IWMSA.

180. Minister of African Affairs, memorandum, September 2, 1954, vol. 1, CAB 19/4, HD.

181. Minute 1, January 13, 1955, CC (55), 3, CAB 128/28, TNA; and CC (55), 4, January 13, 1955, CAB 128/28, TNA.

182. Kenya Colony and Protectorate, public relations officer, "Governor's Speech at Nyeri," January 19, 1955, CO 822/1075/14, TNA. Colonial officials made numerous public statements about their plan for the future exile of the Mau Mau hard-core. See, for example, Reuters report, "Exile," July 1955, CO 801/822/51, TNA.

183. J. H. Lewis to minister of defence, "Prisons Department Emergency Expenditure Sanitation Mackinnon Road and Manyani" (memorandum), May 21, 1954, AH 9/5/16, KNA; and War Council, "Number of Detainees" (brief), October 15, 1954, CO 822/801/35, TNA.

184. Elkins, *Imperial Reckoning*, chap. 7.

185. J. H. Lewis, "Welfare—Warder Staff and European Officers below the Rank of Assistant Superintendent" (memorandum), February 19, 1955, JZ 4/51, KNA; and "Re: Exemption Certificates for KEM Special Tax," April 1, 1955, AB 1/90/23, KNA.

186. Resettlement Committee, "Long Term Absorption of Displaced Kikuyu—Absorption in the Kikuyu Districts," February 15, 1955, CO 822/797/8, TNA, emphasis original.

187. Ibid.

188. Kenya's deputy governor to colonial secretary (telegram), August 23, 1957, CO 822/802, TNA.

189. Colonial secretary to Governor Baring (telegram), August 28, 1956, CO 822/802, TNA.

190. "Classification of Detainees," March 4, 1955, JZ 4/20, KNA; and Resettlement Committee, "Releases from Custody and Rate of Absorption of Landless K.E.M," April 25, 1956, CO 822/798/32, TNA. The detainees, once reclassified, would move up and down the Pipeline to camps that corresponded with their new classification. Johnston also designated certain camps as "special rehabilitation camps," where prison and rehabilitation staff were supposed to convince the newly segregated "Y1s"—or lesser hard-cores—of the benefits of confession. For a reconstruction of this system, see A. B. Simpson, "Classification" (memorandum), October 9, 1956, JZ 2/17, KNA; "Movement of Detainees," October 20, 1956, AB 1/84/2, KNA; Ministry of Community Development, Community Development Conference, January 14–17, 1957, JZ 6/26/50A, KNA; and "Minutes of the 18th Meeting of the Rehabilitation Advisory Committee," November 12, 1956, JZ 6/26/48, KNA. See also Elkins, *Imperial Reckoning*, 369.

191. John Cowan, "The Mwea Camps and Hola," no date (courtesy of Mr. Cowan); J. Cowan to J. H. Lewis, "Transfer of Detainees Ex Manyani," December 7,

1956, AH 9/21/215, KNA; Cusack, "Detention Camps—Progress Report No. 34" (memorandum), December 12, 1956, CO 822/802/128, TNA; "Minutes of the Nineteenth Meeting of the Rehabilitation Advisory Committee," March 11, 1957, JZ 6/26/51, KNA; Annual Report 1956—Aguthi Works Camp, January 20, 1957, JZ 18/7/41A, KNA; E. C. V. Kelsall, officer in charge, Gatundu Works Camps, Annual Report, January 25, 1957, JZ 18/7/54A, KNA; and R. J. Rowe, officer in charge, "Subject: Annual Report: 1956," January 7, 1957, JZ 18/7/39A, KNA.

192. Governor Baring to colonial secretary, February 5, 1957, telegram no. 104, CO 822/1249/1, TNA.

193. Governor Baring to colonial secretary, February 16, 1957, telegram no. 144, CO 822/1249/3, TNA.

194. Small batches of Manyani detainees were loaded onto railcars for dispatchment to Mwea, where systematized violence awaited them. Gavaghan, *Of Lions and Dung Beetles*, 226–27. Gavaghan described this scene to the author on numerous occasions. For a "kind of rape," see Terence Gavaghan, interview, "Kenya: White Terror."

195. Permanent Secretary for Community Development, "Rehabilitation—Mwea Camps," July 12, 1957, vol. 1, Bates 004637-39, AA 57A, HD.

196. Secretary for community development, memorandum, "War Council, Rehabilitation of Category 'Z' Detainees," March 8, 1957, War Council Memoranda, vol. 12, Bates 013769-70, HD.

197. Governor Baring to Colonial Secretary Lennox-Boyd (secret), June 25, 1957, CO 822/1251/1, TNA.

198. Eric Griffith-Jones, " 'Dilution' Detention Camps—Use of Force in Enforcing Discipline" (memorandum), June 1957, CO 822/1251/E/1, TNA.

199. "Detention Camps and Movement of Detainees," September 5, 1957, vol. 1, Bates 004582-85, AA 57A, HD.

200. Eric Griffith-Jones, " 'Dilution' Detention Camps—Use of Force in Enforcing Discipline" (memorandum), June 1957, CO 822/1251/E/1, TNA.

201. Lewis to Cusack, "Intake of 'Z' Detainees, July 27, 1957, vol. 1, Bates 004621, AA 57A, HD.

202. Eric Griffith-Jones, " 'Dilution' Detention Camps—Use of Force in Enforcing Discipline" (memorandum), June 1957, CO 822/1251/E/1, TNA; colonial secretary to Governor Baring, July 16, 1957, telegram no 53, CO 822/1251/7, TNA; and Governor Baring to colonial secretary, July 17, 1957, telegram no. 597, CO 822/1251/8, TNA.

203. Elkins, *Imperial Reckoning*, 322.

204. T. G. Askwith to chief secretary, "Rehabilitation," December 16, 1957 (courtesy of Askwith).

205. John Cowan, interview by author, London, July 24, 1998.

CHAPTER 14: OPERATION LEGACY

1. Barbara Castle, "Foley's Fight," *New Statesman*, January 5, 1962.

2. Grob-Fitzgibbon, *Imperial Endgame*, 294.

3. Louis, "Dissolution of British Empire," 340.

4. Shuckburgh, *Descent to Suez*, 173, 112.

5. Winston Churchill, *The Nobel Prize in Literature 1953*, https://www.nobelprize .org/prizes/literature/1953/summary/.

6. Louis and Robinson, "Imperialism of Decolonization," 464.

7. Reynolds, *Empire, Emergency*, 130.

8. Ibid., 129, 131.

9. Ibid., passim. For a discussion of France and the European Convention on Human Rights, see Simpson, *Human Rights*, 2–9.

10. Edmund S. Morgan's "that potent fiction" when referring to "rule of law" as quoted in Hussain, *Jurisprudence of Emergency*, 8.

11. The concept of a "through-line" in history is drawn from McCurry, *Women's War*, 129–30.

12. The challenges of Labour's economic recovery included devaluation, the convertibility crisis, and the massive trade deficit, as well as continued high unemployment rates, rationing, and defense expenditure.

13. Alford, "1945–1951," 186–89; and Feinstein, "End of Empire," 212–16.

14. Hyam, *Britain's Imperial Century*, 52.

15. T. B. Macaulay, Minute, February 2, 1835, http://www.columbia.edu/itc /mealac/pritchett/oogenerallinks/macaulay/txt_minute_education_1835.html.

16. Newsome, *Victorian World Picture*, 131.

17. Hyan, *Britain's Imperial Century*, 280.

18. General Act of the Berlin Conference on West Africa, February 26, 1885.

19. Hobson, *Imperialism*; Hunt and Lautzenheiser, *History of Economic Thought*, 350–55; and Richmond, "John A. Hobson," 283–94.

20. Strachey, *End of Empire*, 146; and Feinstein, "End of Empire," 222.

21. Feinstein, "End of Empire," 217n11.

22. Pakenham, *Boer War*, 119–20.

23. Orwell, *Wigan Pier*, 98.

24. Ibid.

25. Hopkins, "Rethinking Decolonisation," 212. Australia and New Zealand did not accept the statute until 1942 and 1947, respectively; moreover, as Hopkins and others point out, the Statute of Westminster (1931) was, in itself, an "ambiguous document."

26. Brockway, *Why Mau Mau?*, 14, Item 10, File 4, Box 117, Fabian Colonial Bureau Papers, Mss. Brit. Emp. s. 365, BL.

27. Hopkins, "Rethinking Decolonisation," 221–24.

28. "Milner's Credo," *Times*, July 27, 1925.

29. May, "Empire Loyalists," 39–40.

30. Hopkins, "Rethinking Decolonisation," 221.

31. Krozewski, "Finance and Empire," 48.

32. Ibid., 49.

33. Schenk, "Sterling Area," 771–90; Feinstein, "End of Empire," 224–33; and Hopkins, "Macmillan's Audit."

34. For Bevin's role in NATO and Europe more broadly, see Adonis, *Ernest Bevin*.

35. Alford, "1945–1951," 190.

36. Feinstein, "End of Empire," 229–30; and Strachey, *End of Empire*, 182–86.
37. Alford, "1945–1951," 209.
38. Goldsworthy, *Colonial Issues*, 170–71.
39. Alford, "1945–1951," 186.
40. Feinstein, "End of Empire," 227–29.
41. Drayton, "Anglo-American 'Liberal' Imperialism," 326, 328.
42. Ibid., 329–39.
43. Louis and Robinson, "Imperialism of Decolonization," 468–69.
44. Ibid., 477.
45. Louis, *British Empire in Middle East*, 747.
46. Louis, "Tragedy of Anglo-Egyptian Settlement," 43–72; Louis, *British Empire in Middle East*, 229–30; and Hyam, *Britain's Declining Empire*, 221–26.
47. Hyam, *Britain's Declining Empire*, 227.
48. Westad, *Global Cold War*, 125.
49. Shuckburgh, *Descent to Suez*, 341.
50. Ibid., 281.
51. Kunz, "Importance of Having Money," 215.
52. Westad, *Global Cold War*, 125.
53. Louis and Robinson, "Imperialism of Decolonization," 479–80.
54. Ibid., 480.
55. Louis, "Dissolution of British Empire," 343.
56. Louis and Robinson, "Imperialism of Decolonization," 481.
57. Macmillan, "Future Constitutional Development in the Colonies," Minute to Lord Salisbury, January 28, 1957, CPC(57)6, CAB 134/1555, in Hyman and Louis, *Conservative Government*, 1. For a trenchant account of Macmillan's audit of empire, see Hopkins, "Macmillan's Audit."
58. McIntyre, "Admission of Small States," 260.
59. Moore, *Margaret Thatcher*, vol. 1.
60. McIntyre, "Admission of Small States," 260.
61. "Future Constitutional Development in the Colonies': Memorandum for Cabinet Colonial Policy Committee," September 6, 1957, CPC (57)30, CAB 134/1556, in Hyman and Louis, *Conservative Government*, 34–35.
62. Ibid., 31–35.
63. *Defence: Outline of Future Policy*, Cmnd. 124 (London: HMSO, 1957), 3.
64. Ibid., 8–10.
65. Hopkins, "Macmillan's Audit," 254–58.
66. Ibid., 255–56.
67. Robinson and Gallagher, "Imperialism of Free Trade," 1–15.
68. "Future Constitutional Development in the Colonies," May 27, 1957, CPC (57), CAB 134/1551, in Hyman and Louis, *Conservative Government*, 4–28.
69. "Future Constitutional Development in the Colonies: Memorandum for Cabinet Colonial Policy Committee," September 6, 1957, CPC (57)30, CAB 134/1556, ibid., 36–37.
70. Aldrich, *Hidden Hand*, 567–70; and Walton, *Empire of Secrets*, 304–5.
71. The following account of Cyprus is drawn from Holland, *Britain and Revolt in Cyprus*; French, *Fighting EOKA*; Drohan, *Brutality*; Crawshaw, *Cyprus Revolt*;

Foley, *Island in Revolt;* Foley, *Memoirs of Grivas;* Anderson, "Policing and Communal Conflict"; and Robbins, "British Counter-insurgency in Cyprus."

72. French, *Fighting EOKA,* 51–52.

73. Aldrich, *Hidden Hand,* 574.

74. Brendon, *Decline and Fall,* 622–23.

75. Walton, *Empire of Secrets,* 307–9.

76. War Office, *Imperial Policing and Duties in Aid of the Civil Power* (London: HMSO, 1949); "Report on the Cyprus Emergency," July 31, 1959, Annex "T," Emergency Legislation, 91–98, WO 106/6020, TNA; and Emergency Powers (Public Officer's Protection) Regulation, 1956, November 24, 1956, CO 926/561, TNA.

77. Andrew, *Defence of the Realm,* 463.

78. Cyprus governor to secretary of state, November 14, 1958, FCO 141/4502, TNA.

79. Cyprus governor to Colonial Office, December 16, 1958, FCO 141/4502, TNA.

80. For informers during the Cyprus insurgency, see French, "Toads and Informers."

81. Secretary of state to Cyprus governor,"Sickening Gas," October 28, 1955, FCO 141/4308, TNA; Cyprus governor to Colonial Office, June 1, 1956, FCO 141/4308, TNA; Chief of staff to Cyprus governor to Force Nairobi, August 24, 1956, FCO 141/4308, TNA; and Holland, *Britain and Revolt in Cyprus,* 108.

82. "GB" [Geoffrey Baker] to "Y.E." [Governor Harding], "An Appreciation of the Security Situation as at end September 1956" (secret), FCO 141/4308, TNA.

83. Harding to Baker and Baker to Harding, "Interrogation," April 4, 1956, FCO 141/4314, TNA.

84. For quote, see governor to secretary of state (telegram), February 22, 1957, FCO 141/4310, TNA. For evidence of the above-referenced tortures, see the complete files of FCO 141/4310, TNA; Alleged ill-treatment of prisoners and detainees (1956–57); Complaints against Security Forces (1956–57), FCO 141/4390, TNA; Complaints against the Security Forces in Nicosia and Kyrenia (1956–59), FCO 141/4686, TNA; Reports of alleged ill-treatment of prisoners and detainees (1957–58), FCO 141/4674, TNA; and Complaints of ill-treatment of Greek Cypriots by the Security Forces, FCO 141; and Memorandum of evidence from Bar Council (1957). For details on individual torturers and torture techniques, see Spanou, *EOKA.* See also Newsinger, *British Counter-Insurgency,* 100–107; Foley, *Island in Revolt,* 131; and Drohan, *Brutality,* chaps. 1 and 2. In addition, I interviewed former EOKA detainees and Greek Cypriot civilians: Petros Petrides, North Finchley, England, August 15, 2013; Daphnis Panagides, Limassol, Cyprus, August 17, 2013; Vassos Giargallas, Zygi, Cyprus, August 20, 2013; Avghi Georgiandou-Karyda, Lanarka, Cyprus, August 20, 2013; Frixos Demetriades, Limassol, Cyprus, August 21, 2013; Esychios Sophocleaous, Nicosia, Cyprus, August 21, 2013; and Giannis Spanos, Nicosia, Cyprus, August 22, 2013.

85. Simpson, *Human Rights,* 910.

86. Draft Letter to Colonial Office, Clerides to Benenson, Annexure I, Decem-

ber 17, 1956, FCO 141/4361, TNA. For examples of the Cyprus Bar Council's documentation, see "Note by the Attorney-General on matters raised by the Bar Council of Cyprus," August 1956, FCO 141/4361, TNA; and "Memorandum of Evidence Prepared by the Bar of Cyprus," August 1956.

87. "Allegations About Ill-Treatment of Villagers of Phrenaros by Troops," April 3, 1956, FCO, 141/4390, TNA.

88. "Allegations in the Press Against Security Forces," August 2, 1956, FCO 141/4390, TNA.

89. For the most thoroughgoing examination of the ECHR case in Cyprus, see Simpson, *Human Rights*, 924–1052. For a more recent examination, see Drohan, *Brutality*, chaps. 1 and 2.

90. A point well made by Drohan, *Brutality*, 42–46.

91. Ibid., 44.

92. L. Papastratis, M. N. Pissas, C. Loizou, S. Ellinas, and Y. Matsis to chairman of the Human Rights Committee of UNO, October 31, 1956, FCO 141/4390, TNA.

93. Howe, *Anticolonialism in British Politics*, 231–37. See also Goldsworthy, *Colonial Issues*, 324–30; and Owen, "Four Straws in the Wind," 122–26.

94. Governor Baring to secretary of state (telegram), March 9, 1953, CO 822/471/12, TNA.

95. Kenneth Grubb, Church Missionary Society president, H. S. Mance, chairman of executive committee, and II. B. Thomas, chairman of African committee, letter to the editor, *Times*, January 22, 1955.

96. Church Missionary Society, "Kenya—Time for Action," January 28, 1955.

97. February 10, 1955, vol. 190, col. 1139, HL Deb.

98. Castle, *Fighting*, 263–64.

99. Barbara Castle, interview, 116, *End of Empire, Kenya*, vol. 1, Mss. Brit. Emp. s. 527/528, BL.

100. Castle, *Fighting*, 264.

101. Barbara Castle, interview, 117, *End of Empire, Kenya*, vol. 1, Mss. Brit. Emp. s. 527/528, BL.

102. "The Truth About the Secret Police," *Daily Mirror*, December 9, 1955; and "Justice in Kenya," *New Statesman and Nation*, December 17, 1955.

103. December 14, 1955, vol. 547, col. 1177, HC Deb.

104. Perkins, *Red Queen*, 140.

105. B. W. Hemsley for commissioner of prisons, "Security of Information" (memorandum), October 4, 1954, JZ 8/8/86, KNA; and J. Lewis, "Photographs" (memorandum), May 11, 1956, AB 2/49/30, KNA.

106. Drohan, *Brutality*, 37.

107. February 27, 1957, vol. 202, cols. 99–100, HL Deb.

108. Cyprus governor to secretary of state (telegram), March 2, 1957, FCO, 141/4310, TNA.

109. Drohan, *Brutality*, 54.

110. Ibid., 57–58; and Simpson, *Human Rights*, 1018–19, 1049.

111. Cyprus governor to Colonial Office (telegram), September 1, 1958, FCO 141/4423, TNA.

112. Perkins, *Red Queen*, 155.

113. Drohan, *Brutality*, 59–64, quote on 64.

114. Ibid., 157.

115. Ibid.

116. French, *British Way*, 224–25. Note that Julian Amery, son of Leo Amery, was a leading Conservative politician protesting accelerated decolonization.

117. November 6, 1958, vol. 594, col. 1131, HC Deb.

118. N. Stylianakis, chief registrar Supreme Court, to John Martin, Colonial Office, February 19, 1958, FCO 141/4423, TNA; and Simpson, *Human Rights*, 1049.

119. N. Stylianakis to John Martin, February 19, 1958, FCO 141/4423, TNA.

120. Macmillan, *Riding the Storm*, 699.

121. Simpson, *Human Rights*, 1052.

122. For detainee letters, see entire files in JZ/7/4 and AH 9/17, KNA, together with those held in the Murumbi Papers, also in KNA. The multiple widely published accounts of abuses in Kenya's detention camps and screening centers include those from Eileen Fletcher and Captain Philip Meldon. See "Kenya's Concentration Camps—An Eyewitness Account," *Peace News—The International Pacifist Weekly*, May 4, 11, and 18, 1956; *Report on My Period of Employment in the Community Development Department of the Kenya Government*, July 1956, CO 822/1239, TNA; Memorandum on Allegations Published by Miss Eileen Fletcher on Conditions in Prisons and Camps, no date, CO 822/1239, TNA; *Peace News—The International Pacifist Weekly*, January 11, 1957; Philip Meldon, "I Saw Men Tortured," *Reynolds News*, January 13, 1957; and Philip Meldon to Allan Lennox-Boyd, February 4, 1957, CO 822/1237/30, TNA. For additional details, see Elkins, *Imperial Reckoning*, chap. 10. The *Observer* article is "No More Whitewash," *Observer*, June 17, 1956.

123. Parliamentary questions, February 12, 1959; and "Kenya Inquiry Refused," *Daily Telegraph*, February 25, 1959, CO 912/21/20, TNA.

124. "No Inquiry in Kenya," *New Statesman and Nation*, February 28, 1959; and "Fair Play for Mau Mau," *Economist*, February 28, 1959.

125. Press Office, "Death of Ten Detainees at Hola," March 4, 1959, Handout no. 142, MSS 115/51, KNA.

126. See the colonial secretary's explanation to the editor of the *Observer*: Alan Lennox-Boyd to David Astor, July 14, 1958, CO 822/1705/12, TNA.

127. Colonial Office, *Documents Relating to the Deaths of Eleven Mau Mau Detainees at Hola Camp in Kenya*, Cmnd. 778 (London: HMSO, 1959), 4, 14.

128. Horne, *Macmillan*, 174.

129. Gorell Barnes, Minute to file, June 4, 1959, CO 822/1261, TNA.

130. Horne, *Macmillan*, 175.

131. Simpson, "Devlin Commission," 21.

132. "African Leaders' Charges," *Times*, August 25, 1959, 6.

133. *Report of the Nyasaland Commission of Inquiry*, Cmnd. 814; and Walton, *Empire of Secrets*, 281.

134. Castle, *Fighting*, 288.

135. July 27, 1959, vol. 610, col. 234, HC Deb.

136. July 8, 1920, vol. 131, col. 1725, HC Deb; and July 27, 1959, vol. 610, col. 234, HC Deb.

137. July 27, 1959, vol. 610, cols. 235–36, HC Deb.

138. July 27, 1959, vol. 610, col. 237, HC Deb.

139. Macmillan, *Riding the Storm*, 735–36.

140. Ibid., 738.

141. For biographical details on Henri Junod and the Junod family, see Morier-Genoud, "Missions and Institutions."

142. Governor Baring to Lennox-Boyd (secret), June 25, 1957, CO 822/1251/1, TNA.

143. Gavaghan, *Of Lions and Dung Beetles*, 235.

144. Klose, "Colonial Testing Ground," 113–14.

145. Governor Baring to colonial secretary, April 29, 1959, CO 822/1269, TNA.

146. Klose, *Human Rights*, 131–32.

147. "Second Mission of the ICRC to Kenya, 1959," CO 822/1258, TNA.

148. Klose, *Human Rights*, 132.

149. "Conservative Manifesto 1959," in Craig, *British General Election Manifestos*, 215.

150. Ibid., 220.

151. Hopkins, "Rethinking Decolonisation," 237–47.

152. Macleod to Renison, November 10, 1959, CO 822/1230, TNA.

153. Colonial secretary, "Disposal of Classified Record and Accountable Documents," May 3, 1961, FCO 141/9657, TNA.

154. W. J. Marquand, "Operation Legacy," March 3, 1961, FCO 141/6957, TNA. Of the documentation, "Operation Legacy" is found in the Uganda correspondence, though the Kenya system, with its "Watch" and "Legacy" categories, suggests a similar "Operation Legacy."

155. Ellerton, "The Designation of Watch" (memorandum), May 13, 1961, Bates 024225-231, 1943/17/B, HD; and Ministry of Defence to various departmental heads, provincial commissioners, and permanent secretaries, May 13, 1961, Bates 013042, I&S.137/O2(S), HD.

156. Colonial Office, "Protection and Disposal of Classified and Accountable Documents and Records Generally," September 1962, Bates 024198-200, 1943/17/B, HD; governor to colonial secretary, "Intel and Guidance Papers from Foreign Office" (telegram), November 23, 1963, Bates 024193, 1943/17B, HD; and secretary of state to governor, "Disposal of Records" (telegram), May 10, 1963, Bates 0241935, 1943/17B, HD.

157. Kenya Intelligence Committee, "Down Grading and Destruction of Classified Materials," October 6, 1958, Bates 013173-75, CS 10/2/4, HD; "Destruction of Classified Waste," September 24, 1959, Bates 013178, CS 10/2/4, HD; "Method of Destroyed Classified Documents," September 24, 1959, Bates 013179, CS 10/2/4, HD; and "Routine Destruction." Within the Hanslope Disclosure, the entire Rec. #488, 1943/17/B, "Security of Instructions for Handling Classified Documents, released with Hanslope Disclosure," Bates 0131782-83, CS 10/2/4, HD; and Rec. #487, CS 10/2, vol. 2, "Security of Documents Including Those in Transit to and from Government House," provide

further details of summary of removal/destruction of documents in Kenya. See also the "Migrated Archives" at TNA, such as "Kenya: Security of Official Correspondence," March 1960–January 1962, FCO 141/6957, TNA; and "Kenya: Security of Official Correspondence," March 1962–April 1963, FCO 141/6958, TNA.

158. Colonial Office, "Protection and Disposal of Classified and Accountable Documents and Records Generally," September 1962, Bates 024198-200, 1943/17/B, HD.

159. For example, T. J. F. Gavaghan, "Transfer of Functions to the Governor's Office," March 2, 1962, Bates 024217-20, AA 1943/17/B, HD. See also Gavaghan, "Protective Security in Headquarters Offices in Nairobi," March 6, 1962, FCO 141/6958, TNA.

160. For discussion of document destruction and removal in other parts of empire, see Elkins, witness statement, May 25, 2012, 54–61; Cobain, *History Thieves;* and Sato, "'Operation Legacy.'"

161. Harold Macmillan, address to Members of both Houses of the Parliament of the Union of South Africa, Cape Town, February 3, 1960, https://web-archives.univ-pau.fr/english/TD2doc1.pdf.

162. United Nations, Official Records of the General Assembly, Fifteenth Session, Supplement No. 2 (A/4494), 1514 (V), "Declaration on the Granting of Independence to Colonial Countries and Peoples," 947th plenary meeting, December 14, 1960, 66–67, www.un.org/a15-emergency_special_sess-4_1(1).pdf.

163. Blundell, *So Rough a Wind*, 266.

164. Murray-Brown, *Kenyatta*, 300–1.

165. Corfield, *Historical Survey of Origins and Growth of Mau Mau*.

166. Lord Howick (Sir Evelyn Baring) and Dame Margery Perham, interview, November 19, 1969, 20–21, Mss. Afr. s. 1574, BL.

167. Lonsdale, "Kenyatta's Trials," 235–36.

168. Murray-Brown, *Kenyatta*, 304–5.

169. Hunja Njuki, interview by author, January 23, 1999.

170. Elkins, *Imperial Reckoning*, 359–60.

171. Kenyatta, *Harambee!*, 2.

172. Kenyatta, *Suffering Without Bitterness*, 189.

173. Edgerton, *Mau Mau*, 217.

174. Department for International Development Annual Report & Resource Accounts—International Development Committee Contents, *Written Evidence Submitted by the Jubilee Debt Campaign*, February 3, 2011, https://publications.parliament.uk/pa/cm201011/cmselect/cmintdev/605/605vw12.htm; and The Future of CDC—International Development Committee Contents, *Written Evidence Submitted by Richard Brooks, Private Eye*, March 3, 2011, https://publications.parliament.uk/pa/cm201011/cmselect/cmintdev/607/607we03.htm.

175. John Cowan, interview by author, July 24, 1998; Jamie Merrill, "Government Refuses to Release Details of Relationship with Authoritarian Bahrain," *Independent*, March 10, 2015; and Glenn Greenwald, "In the Same Week, the U.S.

and U.K. Hide Their War Crimes by Invoking 'National Security,'" *Intercept*, May 21, 2015.

176. Gavaghan, *Of Lions and Dung Beetles*, 286.

177. John Lonsdale, foreword, ibid., 7–8, 10–11.

178. Drayton, "Where Does the World Historian Write From?," 677–78.

179. Hopkins, "Macmillan's Audit," 258.

180. "Sir Robert Thompson," *Times*, May 20, 1992.

181. Thompson, *Defeating Communist Insurgency*, 142, 146.

182. Beckett, "Robert Thompson," 41, 54–55.

183. Ibid., 56.

184. For Thompson's critique of U.S. military operations in Vietnam, see Thompson, *No Exit from Vietnam*.

185. Beckett, "Robert Thompson," 58.

186. "Malaya: The Myth of Hearts and Minds," *Small Wars Journal*, April 16, 2012, https://smallwarsjournal.com/jrnl/art/malaya-the-myth-of-hearts-and-minds; and Andrew J. Bacevich, "The Petraeus Doctrine," *Atlantic*, October 2008.

187. Drohan, *Brutality*, 79–80, 159–60.

188. "Sir John Prendergast," *Times*, October 4, 1993, 19.

189. Ibid.; and Drohan, *Brutality*, 102–50. For details on Aden and torture in Fort Morbut Interrogation Center, in particular, see "Allegation of Torture of Detainees in Aden: Amnesty International Report; Report of Investigation by Roderic Bowen QC," PREM 13/1294; "Allegations by Detainees of Torture Whilst in Detention," FCO 8/165; and "Monthly Returns on Complaints from Detainees," FCO 8/164. For a trenchant overview of investigations into abuses in Aden, see Bennett, "'Detainees Are Always.'"

190. "Northern Ireland Police Cover Up RUC Report by 'Racist' Officer," *Irish Times*, October 9, 2017.

191. Ibid.; and Phil Miller, "MI5 Report on RUC Special Branch to Remain Secret," *Irish Times*, May 13, 2019.

192. Miller, "MI5 Report on RUC Special Branch."

193. McCoy, *Question of Torture*, 8–12, 33–35.

194. Ibid., 5–20; Geraghty, *Irish War*, 46–51; Cobain, *Cruel Britannia*, 140–41, 158–59; and *Ireland v. United Kingdom*, judgment, January 18, 1978, Strasbourg, https://www.law.umich.edu/facultyhome/drwcasebook/Documents/Documents/Republic%20of%20Ireland%20v.%20United%20Kingdom.pdf.

195. McGuffin, *Guinea Pigs*; and "British Ministers Sanctioned Torture of NI internees," *Irish Times*, June 5, 2014.

196. Rodley and Pollard, *Treatment of Prisoners*, 101.

197. *Ireland v. United Kingdom*, judgment, January 18, 1978, Strasbourg, https://www.law.umich.edu/facultyhome/drwcasebook/Documents/Documents/Republic%20of%20Ireland%20v.%20United%20Kingdom.pdf.

198. Geraghty, *Irish War*, 137.

199. Morgan, "Northern Ireland and Minimum Force."

200. Kitson, *Low Intensity Operations*.

201. For critiques of British counterinsurgency precedent as a model for contempo-

rary wars, see Ucko and Egnell, *Counterinsurgency in Crisis;* and Porch, *Counter-insurgency.*

202. William Borders, "Lord Mountbatten Is Killed as His Fishing Boat Explodes; I.R.A. Faction Says It Set Bomb," *New York Times,* August 28, 1979.

203. Lesley Kennedy, "The IRA Assassination of Lord Moyne: Facts and Fallout," History.com, https://www.history.com/news/mountbatten-assassination-ira-thatcher.

204. Borders, "Mountbatten Is Killed."

205. Oppenheimer, *IRA, Bombs and Bullets,* 113.

206. Dimbleby, *Prince of Wales,* 267.

207. Caroline Davies, "Prince Charles to Visit Scene of 1979 Mountbatten Murder," *Guardian,* May 20, 2015.

208. Epstein, "Stuart Hall, Familiar Stranger," 193.

209. Kariuki, *"Mau Mau" Detainee;* and wa Thiong'o, *Weep Not, Child.*

210. Fanon, *Wretched of the Earth,* 92.

211. For an excellent discussion of Soyinka and the Royal Court Theatre in the context of Enoch Powell, see Schofield, *Enoch Powell,* 133–34.

212. Soyinka, "Past Must Address Its Present," Nobel Lecture.

213. Chimdi Maduagwu, "Soyinka's 1960 Play: Leave the dead some room to dance . . . ," *Vanguard,* October 3, 2015, https://www.vanguardngr.com/2015/10/soyinkas-1960-play-leave-the-dead-some-room-to-dance/.

214. Davidson, *Black Man's Burden.*

215. Hussain, *Jurisprudence of Emergency,* 1–3, 137–39.

216. Ibid., 139–40; and Simpson, "Usual Suspects," 658.

217. Chatterjee, *Empire and Nation;* and Simpson, "Usual Suspects," 633, 657–58.

EPILOGUE: EMPIRE COMES HOME

1. Elkins, "Looking Beyond Mau Mau," fig. 1, 855. Five claimants initially filed suit, but Ndiku Mutua later withdrew his claim, and Susan Ngondi passed away before the first strike-out hearing, thus leaving three claimants.

2. "Claim Form," June 23, 2009, High Court of Justice, Queen's Bench Division, Royal Courts of Justice; and "Particulars of Claim," October 22, 2009, ibid.

3. Hon. Mr. Justice McCombe, approved judgment, July 21, 2011, paragraph 13, *Ndiku Mutua and 4 Others and FCO,* Royal Courts of Justice.

4. Nietzsche, *Use and Abuse of History,* 7.

5. Kwasi Kwarteng, "Britain's Imperial Landmarks: The Empire on Our Doorsteps," *History Extra: BBC History Magazine,* October 4, 2018, https://www.historyextra.com/period/georgian/british-empire-landmarks-doorsteps-kwasi-kwarteng-mp-cities-britain.

6. "Case Study: *Donoghue v. Stevenson* (1932)," https://lawgovpol.com/case-study-donoghue-v-stevenson-1932/; and "*Caparo v. Dickman* Case Summary," https://www.lawteacher.net/cases/caparo-industries-v-dickman.php. I am indebted to Liora Lazarus and Daniel Leader for their comments on my analysis of the Mau Mau High Court case.

7. For two files of detainee letters, see JZ/7/4 and AH 9/17, KNA; see also Elkins, *Imperial Reckoning*, 205–16.

8. Lennox-Boyd to Baring, telegram no. 53, July 16, 1957, CO 822/1251/7, TNA. Three other documents substantively outline the "dilution technique" and demonstrate further that the Colonial Office knew of and approved its deployment in Kenya's Mwea camps: Baring to Lennox-Boyd (telegram), July 17, 1957, CO 822/1251/8, TNA; Baring to Lennox-Boyd (secret), June 25, 1957, CO 822/1251/1, TNA; and Eric Griffith-Jones, "'Dilution' Detention Camps—Use of Force in Enforcing Discipline" (memorandum), June 1957, CO 822/1251/E/1, TNA.

9. The Royal Courts of Justice, commonly referred to as the Law Courts, comprise the High Court and Court of Appeal of England and Wales.

10. Earlier in the case, the court defined the legal limitations of our work for the claimants when Justice McCombe referred to my role in producing evidence stating, "She [Elkins] had written one of the seminal texts in 2005. [The court] accepted that her evidence was relevant in identifying documents or other material, but should not be admitted as expert evidence (that is evidence of opinion) as to what was to be inferred from those documents taken as a whole. Because of her familiarity with documents, she is thus able to identify documents which are likely to be of greatest interest in the arguments of the respective parties." These same restrictions would apply to Anderson and Bennett when they joined the case. See Hon. Mr. Justice McCombe, approved judgment, July 21, 2011, paragraph 35, *Ndiku Mutua and 4 Others and FCO*, Royal Courts of Justice.

11. Caroline Macy Elkins, witness statement, February 20, 2011, ibid.

12. Hon. Mr. Justice McCombe, approved judgment, July 21, 2011, paragraph 128, ibid.

13. Ibid., paragraphs 153–54.

14. "Archive at 'Spook Central' Had Secret Mau Mau Files," *Times*, April 8, 2011.

15. "Mau Mau Case Casts Light on Colonial Records," *Financial Times*, April 6, 2011.

16. Lord Howell of Guildford, Minister of State, FCO, statement, Public Records: Colonial Documents, April 5, 2011, HL Deb.

17. "Hague Lifts the Lid on Britain's Secret Past: Foreign Secretary Responds to *Times* Campaign," *Times*, April 9, 2011.

18. Anthony Cary, "The Migrated Archives: What Went Wrong and What Lessons Should We Draw?" Foreign and Commonwealth Office, February 24, 2011; and Lord Howell of Guildford, Minister of State, FCO, statement, Public Records: Colonial Documents, May 5, 2011, HL Deb.

19. Lord Howell of Guildford, Minister of State, FCO, statement, Public Records: Colonial Documents, June 30, 2011, HL Deb.

20. For example, Ben Macintyre, "Secret Colonial Files May Show More Blood on British Hands," *Times*, April 7, 2011. The full media spectrum was caught up in this moment of transparency, though later *The Guardian* published more in-depth coverage questioning the British government's release of files. Ian

Cobain and Richard Norton-Taylor, "Files That May Shed Light on Colonial Crimes Still Kept Secret by UK," *Guardian*, April 23, 2013. See also Cobain's later *History Thieves*.

21. The FCO had a separate section of its website dedicated to the migrated archives, their review, and schedule of release that offered various news releases and documents, such as the Cary Report. This section of the FCO's website has since been taken down.

22. "Britain Destroyed Records of Colonial Crimes," *Guardian*, April 17, 2012; and Badger, "Historians," 803, 806.

23. Badger, "Historians," 803.

24. Andrew, *Defence of the Realm*; and Walton, *Empire of Secrets*.

25. Aldrich, *Hidden Hand*, quotes on 1, 6, 7–8.

26. Caroline Macy Elkins, witness statement, May 25, 2012, with Exhibits CE1–CE5, *Ndiku Mutua and 4 Others and FCO*, Royal Courts of Justice; David McBeath Anderson, witness statement, June 18, 2012, with Exhibit 3, ibid.; and Huw Charles Bennett, witness statement, May 25, 2012, with Exhibit 1, ibid.

27. Jane Muthoni Mara, witness statement, November 4, 2010, paragraph 32, 12, ibid.

28. "UKIP Nigel Farage—Channel 4 News, Speaking on Torture in 1950s Kenya," https://www.youtube.com/watch?v=jtS-32dW1bE.

29. June 6, 2013, vol. 563, col. 1692, HC Deb.

30. June 6, 2013, vol. 563, cols. 1692–93, HC Deb.

31. High Commission Nairobi, "Launch of Memorial to Victims of Torture and Ill-Treatment During the Colonial Period in Kenya," September 12, 2015, https://www.gov.uk/government/news/launch-of-memorial-to-victims-of-torture-and-ill-treatment.

32. Wambugu wa Nyingi, witness statement, November 4, 2010, paragraph 90, 29, *Ndiku Mutua and 4 Others and FCO*, Royal Courts of Justice.

33. "An Imperial History Lesson for Mr Brown," *Independent*, March 16, 2005.

34. Roberts, *History of English Speaking Peoples*, quotes on 648, 2.

35. Andrew Roberts, "Why We Need Empires," *Telegraph*, January 19, 2005.

36. Warwick Mansell, "Michael Gove Redrafts New History Curriculum After Outcry," *Guardian*, June 21, 2013.

37. Sally Weale, "Michael Gove's Claims About History Teaching Are False, Says Research," *Guardian*, September 12, 2016.

38. "UK Government Pays £1m to Cyprus 'Torture Victims,'" *BBC News*, January 24, 2019.

39. Ian Cobain, "Ministry of Defence Holds 66,000 Files in Breach of 30-Year Rule," *Guardian*, October 6, 2013; and "Foreign Office Hoarding 1m Historic Files in Secret Archive," *Guardian*, October 18, 2013.

40. The opinion polls and accompanying statistics are drawn throughout from Richard J. Evans, "The History Wars," *New Statesman*, June 17, 2020.

41. "UKIP Nigel Farage—Channel 4 News, Speaking on Torture in 1950s Kenya."

42. Enoch Powell, "Rivers of Blood," speech to the Conservative Association meeting, April 20, 1968, https://anth1001.files.wordpress.com/2014/04/enoch-powell_speech.pdf.

43. George Padmore, "A Negro Looks at British Imperialism," *Crisis* 45 (December 1938): 396.

44. While sometimes seen as a "moment of origin" in the history of migration from the empire to Britain, the arrival of *Windrush* was not, as we have seen with the migration of individuals like Padmore and James, a moment of origin. Instead it dates back to at least the seventeenth century, a point made by Patel in his excellent recent account, *We're Here*, 1–2, passim.

45. Ibid., 4. Note that, as Patel points out, there can be much confusion about what citizenship and subjecthood meant. He notes how "Commonwealth citizen" and "British subject" were synonymous under the 1948 Act. Moreover, as he states: "The 1948 Act took the idea of the Commonwealth and used it as the underlying foundation of British nationality, despite the fact that independent Commonwealth states had their own independent legislatures. . . . If, for example, you were an Indian or Canadian citizen, your status in the eyes of British law was nonetheless as a non-alien Commonwealth citizen within British nationality in a wider imperial sense. Equally, a British citizen, a 'citizen of the United Kingdom and Colonies,' was in a wider imperial sense a 'Commonwealth citizen' attached to the Commonwealth empire. This conceptual recognition of Commonwealth citizenship occurred despite the fact that the British parliament could not legislate in independent Commonwealth states." Also note that for a large number of people living in the empire's protectorates, the 1948 British Nationality Act did not apply. They were not Commonwealth citizens, but instead had the status of "British Protected Persons." Ibid., 56–58.

46. Ibid., 55.

47. Tomlinson, "Enoch Powell," 4. The extensive literature on empire, immigration, race, and national identity includes Gilroy, *There Ain't No Black*; Gilroy, *After Empire*; Clarke, *Growing Up Stupid*; Kinkaid, *Small Place*; Hall, "Thinking the Diaspora"; Mead, "Empire Windrush"; Cummings, "Ain't No Black"; and Murdoch, "Enoch Powell, Stuart Hall."

48. Coleman, "U.K. Statistics on Immigration," 1148.

49. Tomlinson, "Enoch Powell," 4–5; and Cummings, "Ain't No Black," 598 99.

50. James, "Migration, Racism and Identity Formation," 254. For population statistics, see Patel, *We're Here*, 72. He also notes that from 1958, the number of South Asian migrants rose dramatically.

51. Favell, *Philosophies of Integration*, 105.

52. Schofield and Jones, "'Whatever Community Is,'" 151.

53. Alan Travis, "After 44 Years Secret Papers Reveal Truth About Five Nights of Violence in Notting Hill," *Guardian*, August 24, 2002.

54. Richard J. Evans, "The History Wars," *New Statesman*, June 17, 2020.

55. David Hendy, "The Black and White Minstrel Show," *History of the BBC*, https://www.bbc.com/historyofthebbc/100-voices/people-nation-empire/make-yourself-at-home/the-black-and-white-minstrel-show.

56. Patel, *We're Here*, 11, passim.

57. Tomlinson, "Enoch Powell," 5.

58. Spencer, *British Immigration*, 117–19; and Patel, *We're Here*, 75.

59. Gilroy, *Small Acts*, 57.

60. Dorian Lynskey, "Enoch Was Wrong: The Attempted Rehabilitation of a Racist," *New Statesman*, June 18, 2012.

61. Enoch Powell, Speech to a Dinner of the Royal Society of St. George in London on St. George's Day, April 23, 1961, www.churchill-society-london.org.uk/StGeorg*.html.

62. Patel, *We're Here*, 86–90, 182–85.

63. Bunce and Field, "Obi B. Egbuna"; and Angelo, "Black Panthers."

64. Race Relations Act 1965, https://www.legislation.gov.uk/ukpga/1965/73/contents/enacted; and, for legislation pertaining to boardinghouses and shops, see Race Relations Act 1968, https://www.legislation.gov.uk/ukpga/1968/71/enacted. See also, Hepple, "British Race Relations," 248–57.

65. Gus John, "A Walk Down a Long Road with Ian Macdonald QC," *Garden Court North Chambers*, November 19, 2019, https://www.gcnchambers.co.uk/walk-down-long-road/.

66. Bryan Knight, "Black Britannia: Today's Anti-Racist Movement Must Remember Britain's Black Radical History," *Novara Media*, June 18, 2020, https://novaramedia.com/2020/06/18/todays-anti-racist-movement-must-remember-britains-black-radical-history/; and Robin Bunce and Paul Field, "Landmark Court Case Against Police Racism," *Diverse Magazine*, December 1, 2010, https://web.archive.org/web/20180429025134/http://diversemag.co.uk/landmark-court-case-against-police-racism.

67. Ife Thompson, "Black Lives Matter UK: For Lasting Change, We Need 'Movement Lawyers,'" *Each Other*, August 3, 2020.

68. Aamna Mohdin, "The Brixton Riots 40 Years On: 'A Watershed Moment for Race Relations,'" *Guardian*, April 11, 2021.

69. Thatcher, Grenada TV interview, January 30, 1978, https://www.margaretthatcher.org/document/103485, accessed June 20, 2021, emphasis added.

70. Scarman, *Scarman Report*, quotes on 209–10, 201–7.

71. Patel, *We're Here*, 8. Note that there were other types of British citizenship, qualified with terms such as "dependant" and "overseas," though they were distinct from "British citizenship."

72. Sir William MacPherson of Cluny, *The Stephen Lawrence Inquiry*, Report presented to Parliament by the home secretary, February 1999. For statement on the *Scarman Report*, see, for example, paragraph 2.20; for "institutional racism," see paragraph 6.39; and for the seventy recommendations, see chap. 47, "Recommendations."

73. Leroy Logan, "I'm an Ex-Officer. The Met Police Today Looks and Feels as Racist as It Was Before Macpherson," *Guardian*, October 20, 2020; and Peter Walker, Aamna Mohdin, and Alexandra Topping, "Downing Street Suggests UK Should Be Seen As Model of Racial Equity," *Guardian*, March 31, 2021.

74. Institute of Race Relations, "Ethnicity and Religion Statistics," https://irr.org.uk/research/statistics/ethnicity-and-religion/. The institute's nationwide statistics are from data collected in 2014, and its London statistics are from 2011.

75. Biggar, *Between Kin and Cosmopolis*, 91.

76. Craig Simpson, "Sadiq Khan Unveils London Statue Review Panel Branded 'Unelected Activists,'" *Telegraph*, February 9, 2021.

77. I am grateful to Maya Jasanoff for making this important point in conversations as well as in her recent essay, "Misremembering the British Empire," *New Yorker*, October 26, 2020.

78. Home Office, "Windrush Lessons Learned Review," March 19, 2020, 7, https://www.gov.uk/government/publications/windrush-lessons-learned-review.

79. Patrick Freyne, "Harry and Meghan: The Union of Two Great Houses, the Windsors and the Celebrities, Is Complete," *Irish Times*, March 8, 2021.

80. Commission on Race and Ethnic Disparities, *Report*, March 31, 2021, 8–9, https://www.gov.uk/government/publications/the-report-of-the-commission-on-race-and-ethnic-disparities; and Walker et al., "Downing Street," *Guardian*, March 31, 2021.

81. Commission on Race and Ethnic Disparities, *Report*, 7, 11; and Walker et al., "Downing Street," *Guardian*, March 31, 2021.

82. Commission on Race and Ethnic Disparities, *Report*, 8.

83. Robert Cooper, "The New Liberal Imperialism," *Guardian*, April 7, 2002.

84. Ibid.

85. Strong, *Public Opinion, Legitimacy*, 123.

86. Bosco, "From Empire to Atlantic 'System.'"

87. Parmar, "'I'm Proud of the British Empire,'" 225.

88. Stuart Ward and Astrid Rasch, "Introduction: Greater Britain, Global Britain," in Ward and Rasch, *Embers of Empire*, 1–14; and Kennedy, "Ongoing Imperial History Wars."

89. "A British Illusion of Commonwealth Trade After Brexit," *Financial Times*, April 18, 2018.

Bibliography

LIST OF ABBREVIATIONS

AIR	Air Ministry
AVD	Audio-Visual Department
BL	Bodleian Library, Oxford University
C.	Command Paper (1870–1899)
Cd.	Command Paper (1900–1918)
Cmd.	Command Paper (1919–1956)
Cmnd.	Command Paper (1956–1986)
CAB	Cabinet Office
CO	Colonial Office
DO	Dominions Office
FO	Foreign Office
FCO	Foreign and Commonwealth Office
HA	Haganah Historical Archives
HC Deb	House of Commons Debates
HL Deb	House of Lords Debates
HD	Hanslope Disclosure, Royal Courts of Justice, London
HI	Harman Institute of Contemporary Jewry, Oral History Division, Hebrew University, Jerusalem
HMSO	Her Majesty's Stationery Office, London
IWM	Imperial War Museum, London
IWMDD	Imperial War Museum Department of Documents, London
IWMSA	Imperial War Museum Sound Archive, London
JEM	Jerusalem and East Mission
KNA	Kenya National Archives, Nairobi
KV	Security Service
LCO	Lord Chancellor's Office
LHC	Liddell Hart Centre for Military Archives, King's College, London
MEC	Middle East Centre, St. Anthony's College, Oxford University
Mss. Afr. s.	Manuscript Africa Series

Mss. Brit. Emp. s.   Manuscript British Empire Series
NAM   National Archives of Malaysia (Arkib Negara Malaysia), Kuala
                  Lumpur
NAS   National Archives of Singapore
PREM   Prime Minister's Office
TNA   The National Archives, Kew, Richmond
WO   War Office

ROYAL COURTS OF JUSTICE, LONDON

In case No. HQ09X02666, documentary evidence, referred to by the court as the "Hanslope Disclosure," was made available to me as an expert witness in the case. These documents are cited by the abbreviation HD, and reference to the original files series and/or Bates stamp numbers. The British government later deposited many of these papers, reclassified in the Foreign and Commonwealth Office (FCO) Series 141, using new file reference numbers. In addition, the approved judgments and a subset of the case's pleadings and witness statements were consulted.

The court case at the Royal Courts of Justice was *Ndiku Mutua, Paulo Nzili, Wambugu wa Nyingi, Jane Muthoni Mara, Susan Ngondi and the Foreign and Commonwealth Office*, Claim No: HQ09X02666, common to all the documents cited below.

Anderson, David McBeath. Witness statement, June 18, 2012, with Exhibit 3.
Bennett, Huw Charles. Witness statement, May 25, 2012, with Exhibit 1.
"Claim Form," June 23, 2009, High Court of Justice, Queen's Bench Division.
Elkins, Caroline Macy. Witness statement, February 20, 2011, with Exhibits CE1–CE2.
Elkins, Caroline Macy. Witness statement, May 25, 2012, with Exhibits CE1–CE5.
Mara, Jane Muthoni. Witness statement, November 4, 2010.
Mara, Jane Muthoni. Witness statement, May 25, 2012.
McCombe, Hon. Mr. Justice. Approved judgment, July 21, 2011.
Nyingi, Wambugu wa. Witness statement, November 4, 2010.
Nyingi, Wambugu wa. Witness statement, May 25, 2012.
Nzili, Paulo Muoka. Witness statement, May 25, 2012.
Nzili, Paulo Muoka. Witness statement, November 3, 2010.
"Particulars of Claim," October 22, 2009, High Court of Justice, Queen's Bench Division.

BRITISH GOVERNMENT DOCUMENTS AND REPORTS

Commission on Race and Ethnic Disparities. *Report*, March 31, 2021, https://www.gov.uk/government/publications/the-report-of-the-commission-on-race-and-ethnic-disparities.
Correspondence Relating to the Flogging of Natives by Certain Europeans in Nairobi. Cd. 3256. London: HMSO, 1907.
Defence: Outline of Future Policy. Cmnd. 124. London: HMSO, 1957.
Department of Information. *Communist Banditry in Malaya: The Emergency with an*

Important Chronology of Events, June 1948–June 1951. Kuala Lumpur: Standard Engravers and Art Printers, 1951.

Department for International Development Annual Report and Resource Accounts—International Development Committee Contents. *Written Evidence Submitted by the Jubilee Debt Campaign,* February 3, 2011, https://publications.parliament.uk /pa/cm201011/cmselect/cmintdev/605/605vw12.htm.

Disturbances in the Punjab: Statement by Brig.-General R.E.H. Dyer, C.B. Cmd. 771. London: HMSO, 1920.

Documents on British Foreign Policy, 1919–1939. London: HMSO, 1952.

Documents Relating to the Deaths of Eleven Mau Mau Detainees at Hola Camp in Kenya. Cmnd. 778. London: HMSO, 1959.

External Economic Policy Since the War: The Post-War Financial Settlement vol. 1. London: HMSO, 1986.

Foreign and Commonwealth Office. *Cary Report on Release of the Colonial Administration Files,* February 24, 2011, https://www.gov.uk/government/publications/cary -report-on-release-of-the-colonial-administration-files.

Future of CDC—International Development Committee Contents. *Written Evidence Submitted by Richard Brooks, Private Eye,* February 3, 2011, https://publications .parliament.uk/pa/cm201011/cmselect/cmintdev/607/607we03.htm.

High Commission Nairobi. "Launch of Memorial to Victims of Torture and Ill-Treatment During the Colonial Period in Kenya," September 12, 2015, https:// www.gov.uk/government/news/launch-of-memorial-to-victims-of-torture-and -ill-treatment.

Historical Survey of the Origins and Growth of Mau Mau. Cmnd. 1030. London: HMSO, 1960.

Home Office. "Windrush Lessons Learned Review," March 19, 2020, https://www .gov.uk/government/publications/windrush-lessons-learned-review.

Imperial Policing and Duties in Aid of the Civil Power. London: HMSO, 1949.

Note on the Method of Employment of the Air Arm in Iraq. Cmd. 2217. London: HMSO, 1924.

Palestine: Report on Immigration, Land Settlement and Development. Cmd. 3686. London: HMSO, 1930.

Palestine Royal Commission Report. Cmd. 5479. London: HMSO, 1937.

Pre-State Israel: The Hussein-McMahon Correspondence, July 1915–August 1916, https://www.jewishvirtuallibrary.org/the-hussein-mcmahon-correspondence -july-1915-august-1916#2.

Report on the commission appointed by His Majesty's government in the United Kingdom of Great Britain and Northern Ireland, with the approval of the Council of the League of Nations, to determine the rights and claims of Moslems and Jews in connection with the Western or Wailing Wall at Jerusalem, December 1930. London: HMSO, 1931.

Report of the Commission on the Palestine Disturbances of August, 1929. Cmd. 3530. London: HMSO, 1930.

Report on the Committee Appointed by the Government of India to Investigate the Disturbances in the Punjab, etc. Cmd. 681. London: HMSO, 1920.

Report on the Committee Appointed by the Government of India to Investigate the Disturbances in the Punjab. Cmd. 1088. London: HMSO, 1920.

Report on the Concentration Camps in South Africa, by the Committee of Ladies Appointed by the Secretary of State for War. Cd. 893. London: HMSO, 1902.

Report of the Jamaica Royal Commission. 15573. London: Her Majesty's Stationary Office, 1866.

Report of the Labour Commission to Ireland. London: Caledonian Press Ltd., 1921.

Report of the Native Labour Commission. 1912–13. Nairobi: Government Printer, 1914.

Report of the Nyasaland Commission of Inquiry. Cmnd. 814. London: HMSO, 1959.

Report to the Secretary of State for the Colonies by the Parliamentary Delegation to Kenya, 1954. Cmd. 9081. London: HMSO, 1954.

Report of the West India Royal Commission. C. 8655. London: HMSO, 1897.

Royal Commission on the War in South Africa, Minutes of Evidence Taken Before the Royal Commission on the War in South Africa. Cd. 1789. London: HMSO, 1903.

Social Insurance and Allied Services, Report by Sir William Beveridge. Cmd. 6404. London: HMSO, 1942.

Statement of Policy on Colonial Development and Welfare. Cmd. 6175. London: HMSO, 1940.

War Office. *Imperial Policing and Duties in Aid of the Civil Power.* London: HMSO, 1949.

———. *King's Regulations for the Army and the Royal Army Reserve.* London: HMSO, 1940.

———. *Manual of Military Law, 1929.* London: HMSO, 1929.

———. *Queen's Regulations for the Army.* London: HMSO, 1955.

West India Royal Commission Report. Cmd. 6607. London: HMSO, 1945.

White Paper of 1939, https://avalon.law.yale.edu/20th_century/brwh1939.asp.

White Paper of June 1922, https://avalon.law.yale.edu/20th_century/brwh1922.asp.

INTERNATIONAL DOCUMENTS

Atlantic Charter, August 14, 1941, https://avalon.law.yale.edu/wwii/atlantic.asp.

Congress of Europe in the Hague, European Court of Human Rights, https://www.cvce.eu/en/recherche/unit-content/-/unit/04bfa990-86bc-402f-a633-11f39c9247c4/aadf5a4c-2972-41e8-9d44-9d5d4edb8dd1.

Convention (II) with Respect to the Laws and Customs of War on Land, The Hague, July 29, 1899, https://ihl-databases.icrc.org/ihl/INTRO/150.

European Convention on Human Rights, https://www.echr.coe.int/Documents/Convention_ENG.pdf.

General Act of the Berlin Conference on West Africa, February 26, 1885, https://loveman.sdsu.edu/docs/1885GeneralActBerlinConference.pdf.

Geneva Convention Relative to the Treatment of Prisoners of War, August 12, 1949, https://www.un.org/en/genocideprevention/documents/atrocity-crimes/Doc.32_GC-III-EN.pdf.

Ireland v. United Kingdom. Judgment, January 18, 1978, Strasbourg, https://www.law.umich.edu/facultyhome/drwcasebook/Documents/Documents/Republic%20of%20Ireland%20v.%20United%20Kingdom.pdf.

League of Nations. Covenant. http://avalon.law.yale.edu/20th_century/leagcov.asp#art22.

League of Nations. *An Interim Report on the Civil Administration of Palestine, During the Period 1st July, 1920–30 June, 1921*, https://unispal.un.org/UNISPAL.NSF/0/34 9B02280A930813052565E90048ED1C.

League of Nations. "The Palestine Mandate," July 24, 1922, https://avalon.law.yale .edu/20th_century/palmanda.asp.

United Kingdom Public General Acts. 1965, c. 73. "Race Relations Act 1965," https:// www.legislation.gov.uk/ukpga/1965/73/contents/enacted.

United Kingdom Public General Acts. 1968, c. 71. "Race Relations Act 1968," https:// www.legislation.gov.uk/ukpga/1968/71/contents/enacted.

United Nations. Charter. Chapter XI, "Declaration Regarding Non-Self-Governing Territories," https://www.un.org/en/sections/un-charter/chapter-xi/index.html.

United Nations. Declaration, January 1, 1942, https://www.unmultimedia.org/search ers/yearbook/page.jsp?volume=1946-47&page=36&searchType=advanced.

United Nations. Official Records of the General Assembly. Fifteenth Session, Supplement No. 2 (A/4494), 1514 (V), "Declaration on the Granting of Independence to Colonial Countries and Peoples," 947th plenary meeting, December 14, 1960, www.un.org/a15-emergency_special_sess-4_1(1).pdf.

United Nations. Statute of the International Court of Justice, https://www.un.org/en /sections/un-charter/chapter-xi/index.html.

United Nations. Resolution 181 (II). Future government of Palestine, November 29, 1947, https://unispal.un.org/DPA/DPR/unispal.nsf/0/7F0AF2BD897689B7852 56C330061D253.

United Nations. "U.K. Accepts UNSCOP General Recommendations," September 26, 1947, Summary Press Release GA/PAL/2, https://unispal.un.org/unispal.nsf/9a7 98adbf322aff38525617b006d88d7/ecb5eae2e1d29ed08525686d00529256.

Zionist Congress. First Zionist Congress & Basel Program, August 1897, https:// www.jewishvirtuallibrary.org/first-zionist-congress-and-basel-program-1897.

SPEECHES, STATEMENTS, AND MANIFESTOS

Churchill, Winston. "Never Give In, Never, Never, Never," October 29, 1941, https:// www.nationalchurchillmuseum.org/never-give-in-never-never-never.html/.

———. *The Nobel Prize in Literature 1953*, https://www.nobelprize.org/prizes /literature/1953/summary/.

———. Primrose League Speech, July 26, 1897, http://www.churchillarchive.com /explore/page?id=CHAR%202%2F21%2F1#image=0.

Conservative Party. General Election Manifesto, 1951, http://www.conservativemani festo.com/1951/1951-conservative-manifesto.shtml.

Disraeli, Benjamin. *Speech at the Banquet of the National Union of Conservative and Constitutional Associations at the Crystal Palace, June 24, 1872*. London: R.J. Mitchell and Sons, 1872.

Elizabeth II. "A Speech by the Queen on her 21st Birthday, 1947," April 21, 1947, https://www.royal.uk/21st-birthday-speech-21-april-1947.

Jinnah, Muhammad Ali. First Presidential Address to the Constituent Assembly of Pakistan, August 11, 1947, http://www.columbia.edu/itc/mealac/pritchett /00islamlinks/txt_jinnah_assembly_1947.html.

Labour Party. Election Manifesto, 1945, http://www.labour-party.org.uk/manifestos /1945/1945-labour-manifesto.shtml.

———. Election Manifesto, 1951, http://www.labour-party.org.uk/manifestos/1951 /1951-labour-manifesto.shtml.

Macmillan, Harold. Address to Members of both Houses of the Parliament of the Union of South Africa, February 3, 1960, https://web-archives.univ-pau.fr /english/TD2doc1.pdf.

Oriel College, Oxford University. "Cecil John Rhodes (1853–1902)," https://www .oriel.ox.ac.uk/cecil-john-rhodes-1853-1902#:~:text=By%20the%201890s%20 Rhodes%20was,in%20his%20will%20%5B7%5D.

Powell, Enoch. "Rivers of Blood." Speech to the Conservative Association meeting, April 20, 1968, https://anth1001.Ailes.wordpress.com/2014/04/enoch-powell _speech.pdf.

———. Speech to a Dinner of the Royal Society of St George in London on St. George's Day, April 23, 1961, www.churchill-society-london.org.uk/StGeorg*html.

Roosevelt, Eleanor. "Adoption of the Declaration of Human Rights." Speech to the UN General Assembly, December 9, 1948, https://awpc.cattcenter.iastate .edu/2017/03/21/adoption-of-the-declaration-of-human-rights-dec-9-1948/.

Roosevelt, Franklin Delano. State of the Union Address, January 6, 1941, https:// www.gilderlehrman.org/sites/default/files/inline-pdfs/Four%20Freedoms%20 Speech%201941.pdf.

———. Address to Congress, December 8, 1941, https://www.loc.gov/resource/afc 1986022.afc1986022_ms2201/?r=-0.317,-0.115,1.653,0.75,0.

———. "On the Progress of the War," Fireside Chat 20, February 23, 1942, https:// millercenter.org/the-presidency/presidential-speeches/february-23-1942 -fireside-chat-20-progress-war.

———. Address to the International Student Assembly, September 3, 1942, http:// www.fdrlibrary.marist.edu/_resources/images/msf/msfb0043.

———. Press Conference, December 22, 1944, https://www.presidency.ucsb.edu /documents/excerpts-from-the-press-conference-21.

Soyinka, Wole. "This Past Must Address Its Present." Nobel Prize in Literature, December 8, 1986, https://www.nobelprize.org/prizes/literature/1986/1053ecolon /lecture.

Thatcher, Margaret. Grenada TV interview, January 30, 1978, https://margaret thatcher.org/document/103485.

UNPUBLISHED PAPERS AND THESES

Anderson, Charles W. "From Petition to Confrontation: The Palestinian National Movement and the Rise of Mass Politics, 1929–1939." Ph.D. diss., New York University, 2013.

Bagon, Paul. "The Impact of the Jewish Underground Upon Anglo Jewry: 1945–1947." M.Phil. thesis, University of Oxford, 2003.

Bicknell, David. "A Penumbra of War: The Use of Lethal Force in British Military Operations in Internal Armed Conflicts." Ph.D. diss., King's College London, 2021.

Bishku, Michael Barry. "The British Empire and the Question of Egypt's Future, 1919–1922." Ph.D. diss., New York University, 1981.

Chatterjee, Partha. "Bombs and Nationalism in Bengal." Paper presented at "Empire and Terror" conference, Columbia University, New York, 2004, http://sarr .emory.edu/subalterndocs/Chatterjee.pdf.

Foley, Michael. "'The Irish Folly': The Easter Rising: the Press; the People; the Politics." Paper presented at Reflecting the Rising, Dublin Institute of Technology, March 28, 2016, https://arrow.tudublin.ie/aaconmuscon/19/.

Griffin, Brittany. "Tales of Empire: Orientalism and Nineteenth-Century Children's Literature." Ph.D. diss., University of South Florida, 2012.

May, Alexander. "The Round Table, 1910–66." Ph.D. diss., University of Oxford, 1995.

Rast, Mike. "Tactics, Politics, and Propaganda in the Irish War of Independence, 1917–1921." Master's thesis, Georgia State University, 2011, https://scholar works.gsu.edu/history_theses/46/.

Stubbs, Richard. "Counter-Insurgency and the Economic Factor: The Impact of the Korean War Boom on the Malayan Emergency." Occasional Paper No. 19, Institute of Southeast Asian Studies, Singapore, 1974.

Thomas, Martin. "The Political Economy of Colonial Violence in Interwar Jamaica." Paper presented at the "Terror and the Making of Modern Europe" Conference, Stanford University, April 2008, http://stanford.edu/dept/1055ecolo-stanford /Conferences/Terror/Thomas.pdf.

BOOKS AND ARTICLES

Abrams, Philip. *Historical Sociology*. Ithaca, NY: Cornell University Press, 1983.

Adam, Michel. *Indian Africa: Minorities of Indian-Pakistani Origin in Eastern Africa*. Dar es Salaam: Mkuki na Nyota Publishers, 2015.

Adas, Michael. "Contested Hegemony: The Great War and the Afro-Asian Assault on the Civilizing Mission Ideology." *Journal of World History* 15, no. 1 (2004): 31–63.

Adonis, Andrew. *Ernest Bevin: Labour's Churchill*. London: Biteback Publishing, 2020.

Agamben, Giorgio. *State of Exception*. Translated by Kevin Attell. Chicago: University of Chicago Press, 2005.

Ainsworth, John. "Kevin Barry, the Incident at Monk's Bakery and the Making of an Irish Republican Legend." *History* 87 (2002): 372–87.

Al-Hout, Bayan Nuweihid. "The Palestinian Political Elite During the Mandate Period." *Journal of Palestine Studies* 9, no. 1 (1979): 85–111.

Aldrich, Richard J. "Britain's Intelligence Service in Asia During the Second World War." *Modern Asian Studies* 32, no. 1 (1998): 179–217.

———. *The Hidden Hand: Britain, America, and Cold War Secret Intelligence*. Woodstock, NY: Overlook Press, 2002.

———. *Intelligence and the War against Japan: Britain, America and the Politics of Secret Service*. Cambridge: Cambridge University Press, 2000.

Aldrich, Robert. *Greater France: A History of French Overseas Expansion*. New York: St. Martin's Press, 1996.

Alford, Bernard. "1945–1951: Years of Recovery or a Stage in Economic Decline?" In *Understanding Decline: Perceptions and Realities of British Economic Performance*, ed. Peter Clarke and Clive Trebilcock, 186–211. Cambridge: Cambridge University Press, 1997.

Allen, Louis. *Burma: The Longest War, 1941–45*. London: J.M. Dent, 1984.

———. *Singapore, 1941–42*. Abingdon: Frank Cass, 1993.

Alpes, Maybritt Jill. "The Congress and the INA Trials, 1945–50: A Contest over the Perception of 'Nationalist' Politics." *Studies in History* 23, no. 1 (2007): 135–58.

Amery, L. S. *War and Peace 1914–1929*. Vol. 2 of *My Political Life*. London: Hutchinson, 1953.

Anderson, Benedict. *Imagined Communities: Reflections on the Origin and Spread of Nationalism*. London: Verso, 1983.

Anderson, Charles W. "State Formation from Below and the Great Revolt in Palestine." *Journal of Palestine Studies* 47, no. 1 (2017): 39–55.

Anderson, Clare. "The Politics of Convict Space: Indian Penal Settlements and the Andaman Islands." In *Isolation: Places and Practices of Exclusion*, ed. Alison Bashford and Carolyn Strange, 37–52. New York: Routledge, 2003.

Anderson, David M. *Histories of the Hanged: The Dirty War in Kenya and the End of Empire*. New York: Norton, 2005.

———. "Master and Servant in Colonial Kenya, 1895–1939." *Journal of African History* 41, no. 3 (2000): 459–85.

———. "Policing and Communal Conflict: The Cyprus Emergency, 1954–60." In *Policing and Decolonisation: Politics, Nationalism and the Police, 1917–1965*, ed. David M. Anderson and David Killingray, 187–217. Manchester: Manchester University Press, 1992.

Anderson, Perry. *Lineages of the Absolutist State*. 1974; reprint New York: Verso, 2013.

Anderson, Scott. *Lawrence in Arabia: War, Deceit, Imperial Folly and the Making of the Modern Middle East*. New York: Anchor Books, 2013.

Andrew, Christopher M. *Secret Service: The Making of the British Intelligence Community*. London: Heinemann, 1985.

———. *The Defence of the Realm: The Authorized History of MI5*. London: Penguin Books, 2010.

Andrew, Christopher, and Simona Tobia, eds. *Interrogation in War and Conflict: A Comparative and Interdisciplinary Analysis*. London: Routledge, 2014.

Angell, Norman. *The Fruits of Victory, A Sequel to "The Great Illusion."* London: W. Collins & Sons, 1921.

Angelo, Anne-Marie. "The Black Panthers in London, 1967–1972: A Diasporic Struggle Navigates the Black Atlantic." *Radical History Review* 103 (2009): 17–35.

Anghie, Anthony. "Finding the Peripheries: Sovereignty and Colonialism in Nineteenth-Century International Law." *Harvard International Law Journal* 40, no. 1 (1999), 1–80.

———. *Imperialism, Sovereignty and the Making of International Law*. Cambridge: Cambridge University Press, 2005.

Anglim, Simon. "Callwell Versus Graziani: How the British Army Applied 'Small Wars' Techniques in Major Operations in Africa and the Middle East, 1940–41." *Small Wars and Insurgencies* 19, no. 4 (2008): 588–608.

———. *Orde Wingate and the British Army, 1922–1944.* London: Pickering & Chatto, 2010.

Antonius, George. *The Arab Awakening.* London: Hamish Hamilton, 1938.

Araujo, Ana Lucia. *Slavery in the Age of Memory: Engaging the Past.* London: Bloomsbury, 2021.

Arendt, Hannah. *The Origins of Totalitarianism.* 1951; reprint New York: Harcourt, 1976.

Armitage, David. "The Fifty Years' Rift: Intellectual History and International Relations." *Modern Intellectual History* 1, no. 1 (2004): 97–109.

———. "Greater Britain: A Useful Category of Analysis?" *American Historical Review* 104, no. 2 (1999): 427–45.

———. *The Ideological Origins of the British Empire.* Cambridge: Cambridge University Press, 2000.

———. "The International Turn in Intellectual History." In *Rethinking Modern European Intellectual History,* ed. Darrin M. McMahon and Samuel Moyn, 232–52. New York: Oxford University Press, 2014.

———. "John Locke, Carolina, and the Two Treatises of Government." *Political Theory* 32, no. 5 (2004): 602–27.

———. "John Locke: Theorist of Empire?" In *Empire and Modern Political Thought,* ed. Sankur Muthu (Cambridge: Cambridge University Press, 2012), 84–111.

Arneil, Barbara. *John Locke and America: The Defence of English Colonialism.* Oxford: Oxford University Press, 1996.

Arrigonie, Harry. *British Colonialism: Thirty Years Serving Democracy or Hypocrisy?* Devon: Edward Gaskell, 1998.

Ashton, S. R. "Keeping Change Within Bounds: A Whitehall Reassessment." In *The British Empire in the 1950s: Retreat or Revival?,* ed. Martin Lynn, 32–52. Basingstoke: Palgrave Macmillan, 2006.

Attlee, C. R. *As It Happened.* London: Viking Press, 1954.

Auld, John W. "The Liberal Pro-Boers." *Journal of British Studies* 14, no. 2 (1975): 78–101.

"Avner." *Memoirs of an Assassin.* Translated by Burgo Partridge. New York: Yoseloff, 1959.

Azikiwe, Nnamdi. *Renascent Africa.* New York: Negro Universities Press, 1937.

Badger, Anthony. "Historians, a Legacy of Suspicion and the 'Migrated Archives.'" *Small Wars and Insurgencies* 23, no. 4–5 (2012): 799–807.

Baker, Nicholson. *Human Smoke: The Beginnings of World War II, the End of Civilization.* New York: Simon & Schuster, 2008.

Barber, Noel. *The Black Hole of Calcutta: A Reconstruction.* 1965; reprint Pleasantville, NY: Akadine Press, 2000.

———. *The War of the Running Dogs: How Malaya Defeated the Communist Guerrillas, 1948–1960.* 1971: reprint London: Cassell, 2004.

Barker, Sir Ernest. *Ideas and Ideals of the British Empire.* 2d ed. Cambridge: Cambridge University Press, 1951.

Barr, James. *A Line in the Sand: The Anglo-French Struggle for the Middle East, 1914–1948.* New York: Norton, 2013.

Bastian, Hilda. "Down and Almost Out in Scotland: George Orwell, Tuberculosis and

Getting Streptomycin in 1948." *Journal of the Royal Society of Medicine* 99, no. 2 (2006): 95–98.

Bauer, Yehuda. *From Diplomacy to Resistance: A History of Jewish Palestine, 1939–1945.* New York: Atheneum, 1970.

Baylis, John. *The Diplomacy of Pragmatism: Britain and the Formation of NATO, 1942–49.* Kent, Ohio: The Kent State University Press, 1993.

Bayly, Christopher A. *Empire and Information: Intelligence Gathering and Social Communication in India, 1780–1870.* Cambridge: Cambridge University Press, 1996.

———. *Recovering Liberties: Indian Thought in the Age of Liberalism and Empire.* Cambridge: Cambridge University Press, 2011.

Bayly, Christopher A., and Tim Harper, eds. *Forgotten Armies: The Fall of British Asia, 1941–1945.* Cambridge, MA: Harvard University Press, 2005.

———. *Forgotten Wars: The End of Britain's Asian Empire.* London: Allen Lane, 2007.

Beaverbrook, Baron Max Aitken (Lord Beaverbrook). *Politicians and the War, 1914–1916.* London: Thornton Butterworth, 1928.

Beckett, Ian F. W. "British Counter-insurgency: A Historiographical Reflection." In *British Ways of Counter-insurgency: A Historical Perspective,* ed. Matthew Hughes, 209–26. London: Routledge, 2013.

———. *Modern Insurgencies and Counter-Insurgencies: Guerrillas and their Opponents since 1750.* London: Routledge, 2001.

———. "Robert Thompson and the British Advisory Mission to South Vietnam, 1961–65." *Small Wars and Insurgencies* 8, no. 3 (1997): 41–63.

Beers, Laura. *Red Ellen: The Life of Ellen Wilkinson, Socialist, Feminist, Internationalist.* Cambridge, MA: Harvard University Press, 2016.

———. *Your Britain: Media and the Making of the Labour Party.* Cambridge, MA: Harvard University Press, 2010.

Begin, Menachem. *The Revolt: Story of the Irgun.* London: W.H. Allen, 1951.

Bell, Duncan. *The Idea of Greater Britain: Empire and the Future of World Order, 1860–1900.* Princeton: Princeton University Press, 2007.

———. *Reordering the World: Essays on Liberalism and Empire.* Princeton: Princeton University Press, 2016.

Bell, J. Bowyer. *On Revolt: Strategies of National Liberation.* Cambridge, MA: Harvard University Press, 1976.

———. *Terror Out of Zion: Irgun Zvai Leumi, LEHI, and the Palestine Underground, 1929–1949.* New York: St. Martin's Press, 1977.

Ben-Gurion, David. *Memoirs.* New York: World, 1970.

Benjamin, Walter. *Walter Benjamin: Essays, Aphorisms, Autobiographical Writings,* ed. Peter Demetz. New York: Harcourt Brace Jovanovich, 1978.

Bennett, Huw. "'Detainees Are Always One's Achilles Heel': The Struggle over the Scrutiny of Detention and Interrogation in Aden, 1963–1967." *War in History* 23, no. 4 (2016): 457–88.

———. *Fighting the Mau Mau: The British Army and Counter-Insurgency in the Kenya Emergency.* Cambridge: Cambridge University Press, 2012.

———. "'A Very Salutary Effect': The Counter-Terror Strategy in the Early Malayan Emergency, June 1948 to December 1949." *Journal of Strategic Studies* 32, no. 3 (2009): 415–44.

Bennett, Huw, et al. "Studying Mars and Clio: Or How Not to Write About the Ethics of Military Conduct and Military History." *History Workshop Journal* 88 (2019): 274–80.

Bennett, Richard. *The Black and Tans.* Barnsley, South Yorkshire: Pen & Sword Military, 2010.

Benton, Lauren A. *A Search for Sovereignty: Law and Geography in European Empires, 1400–1900.* Cambridge: Cambridge University Press, 2010.

———. *Law and Colonial Cultures: Legal Regimes in World History, 1400–1900.* Cambridge: Cambridge University Press, 2002.

Berman, Bruce. *Control and Crisis in Colonial Kenya: The Dialectic of Domination.* London: James Currey, 1990.

———. "The Perils of Bula Matari: Constraint and Power in the Colonial State." *Canadian Journal of African Studies* 31, no. 3 (1997): 555–70.

Berry, Sara. "Hegemony on a Shoestring: Indirect Rule and Access to Agricultural Land." *Africa* 62, no. 3 (1992): 327–55.

Besant, Walter. *The Queen's Reign and its Commemoration: A Literary and Pictorial Review of the Period.* London: Werner, 1897.

Best, Geoffrey. *War and Law Since 1945.* Oxford: Clarendon Press, 1994.

Bethell, Nicholas. *The Palestine Triangle: The Struggle for the Holy Land, 1935–48.* New York: G.P. Putnam's Sons, 1979.

Bevir, Mark. "Theosophy and the Origins of the Indian National Congress." *International Journal of Hindu Studies* 7 (2003): 99–115.

Bew, Paul. *Churchill and Ireland.* Oxford: Oxford University Press, 2016.

Bhabha, Homi K. "Foreword: Framing Fanon." Preface to Fanon, *Wretched of the Earth,* vii–xli.

———. "Of Mimicry and Man: The Ambivalence of Colonial Discourse." In Cooper and Stoler, *Tensions of Empire,* 152–60.

Bidwell, Shelford. *The Chindit War: The Campaign in Burma, 1944.* London: Hodder & Stoughton, 1979.

Bierman, John, and Colin Smith. *Fire in the Night: Wingate of Burma, Ethiopia, and Zion.* New York: Random House, 1999.

Biggar, Nigel. *Between Kin and Cosmopolis: An Ethic of the Nation.* Eugene, OR: Cascade Books, 2014.

Bishku, Michael B. "The British Press and the Future of Egypt, 1919–1922." *International History Review* 8, no. 4 (1986): 604–12.

Bivona, Daniel. *British Imperial Literature, 1870–1940: Writing and the Administration of Empire.* Cambridge: Cambridge University Press, 1998.

Black, Eugene. "Edwin Montagu." *Jewish Historical Studies* 30 (1987–1988): 199–218.

Blackburn, Kevin. "The Collective Memory of the Sook Ching Massacre and the Creation of the Civilian War Memorial of Singapore." *Journal of the Malaysian Branch of the Royal Asiatic Society* 73, no. 2 (2000): 71–90.

Blake, Robert. *Disraeli.* London: Prion Books, 1998.

Blaustein, Albert Paul, et al., eds. *Independence Documents of the World.* Dobbs Ferry, NY: Oceanic, 1977.

Blundell, Michael. *So Rough a Wind.* London: Weidenfeld & Nicolson, 1964.

Blyth, Robert J. *The Empire of the Raj: India, Eastern Africa and the Middle East, 1858–1947*. New York: Palgrave Macmillan, 2003.

Bolland, O. Nigel. *The Politics of Labour in the British Caribbean*. Kingston: Ian Randle, 2001.

Borgwardt, Elizabeth. *A New Deal for the World: America's Vision for Human Rights*. Cambridge, MA: Harvard University Press, 2005.

Bosco, Andrea. "From Empire to Atlantic 'System': The Round Table, Chatham House and the Emergence of a New Paradigm in Anglo-American Relations." *Journal of Transatlantic Studies* 16, no. 3 (2018): 222–46.

Bose, Sugata. *His Majesty's Opponent: Subhas Chandra Bose and India's Struggle against Empire*. Cambridge, MA: Belknap Press, 2011.

———. "Nation as Mother: Representations and Contestations of 'India' in Bengali Literature and Culture." In *Nationalism, Democracy and Development: State and Politics in India*, ed. Sugata Bose and Ayesha Jalal, 50–75. New York: Oxford University Press, 1997.

———. *Peasant Labour and Colonial Capital: Rural Bengal Since 1770*. Cambridge: Cambridge University Press, 1993.

———. "The Spirit and Form of an Ethical Polity: A Meditation on Aurobindo's Thoughts." *Modern Intellectual History* 4, no. 1 (2007): 129–44.

———. "Starvation Amidst Plenty: The Making of Famine in Bengal, Honan and Tonkin, 1942–45." *Modern Asian Studies* 24, no. 4 (1990): 699–727.

Bose, Sugata, and Ayesha Jalal. *Modern South Asia: History, Culture, Political Economy*. Fourth Edition. London: Routledge, 2018.

Bourke, Richard. *Empire and Revolution: The Political Life of Edmund Burke*. Princeton: Princeton University Press, 2015.

Bowden, Tom. *The Breakdown of Public Security: The Case of Ireland 1916–1921 and Palestine 1936–1939*. London: Sage, 1977.

Boyd, Viscount [Allan Lennox-Boyd]. "Opening Address." In *The Transfer of Power: The Colonial Administrator in the Age of Decolonisation*, ed. Anthony Kirk-Greene, 2–9. Oxford: Committee for African Studies, 1979.

Brecher, Michael. *Political Leadership and Charisma, Nehru, Ben-Gurion and Other Twentieth-Century Political Leaders: Intellectual Odyssey I*. New York: Palgrave Macmillan, 2016.

Brendon, Piers. *The Decline and Fall of the British Empire, 1781–1997*. New York: Knopf, 2008.

Brenner, Y. S. "The Stern Gang, 1940–48." *Middle Eastern Studies* 2, no. 1 (1965): 2–30.

Brighton, Paul, and Dennis Foy. *News Values*. London: Sage, 2007.

Brockway, Fenner. *Why Mau Mau? An Analysis and Remedy*. London: Congress of Peoples Against Imperialism, 1953.

Brown, Christopher Leslie. "Empire Without Slaves: British Concepts of Emancipation in the Age of the American Revolution." *William and Mary Quarterly* 56, no. 2 (1999): 273–306.

———. *Moral Capital: Foundations of British Abolitionism*. Chapel Hill: The University of North Carolina Press, 2006.

Brown, Judith M. *Gandhi: Prisoner of Hope*. New Haven, CT: Yale University Press, 1989.

———. *Gandhi's Rise to Power: Indian Politics, 1915–1922*. Cambridge: Cambridge University Press, 1972.

———. *Modern India: The Origins of an Asian Democracy*. Oxford: Oxford University Press, 1994.

Brown, Stephen R. *Merchant Kings: When Companies Ruled the World, 1600–1900*. New York: St. Martin's Press, 2009.

Brown, Vincent. *The Reaper's Garden: Death and Power in the World of Atlantic Slavery*. Cambridge: Harvard University Press, 2008.

Bryant, Joshua. *Account of an Insurrection of the Negro Slaves in the Colony of Demerara*. Demarara: A. Stevenson, 1824.

Buergenthal, Thomas. "The Evolving International Human Rights System." *American Journal of International Law* 100, no. 4 (2006): 783–807.

Bullock, Alan. *Ernest Bevin Foreign Secretary, 1945–1951*. New York: Norton, 1983.

Bunce, R. E. R., and Paul Field. "Obi B. Egbuna, C. L. R. James and the Birth of Black Power in Britain: Black Radicalism in Britain 1967–72." *Twentieth Century British History* 22, no. 3 (2011): 391–414.

Burk, Kathleen. *Old World, New World: Great Britain and America from the Beginning*. New York: Atlantic Monthly Press, 2008.

Burke, Edmund. *The Speeches of the Right Honourable Edmund Burke on the Impeachment of Warren Hastings*. Vol. I. London: Henry G. Bohn, 1857.

Cahill, Richard Andrew. "'Going Beserk': 'Black and Tans' in Palestine." *Jerusalem Quarterly* 38 (2009): 59–68.

Cain, Peter J., and Anthony G. Hopkins. *British Imperialism: Crisis and Deconstruction, 1914–1990*. London: Longman, 1993.

———. "Gentlemanly Capitalism and British Overseas Expansion." *Economic History Review* 39, no. 4 (1986): 501–25, and 40, no. 1 (1987): 1–26.

Cairncross, Sir Alec, and Barry Eichengreen. *Sterling in Decline: The Devaluations of 1931, 1949 and 1967*. London: Palgrave Macmillan, 2003.

Cairns, Huntington. "Spinoza's Theory of Law." *Columbia Law Review* 48, no. 7 (1948): 1032–48.

Callahan, Raymond A. *The Worst Disaster: The Fall of Singapore*. London: Associated University Press, 1977.

Callwell, Colonel C. E. *Field-Marshal Sir Henry Wilson: His Life and Diaries*. London: Cassell, 1927.

———. "Lessons to Be Learnt from the Campaigns in Which British Forces Have Been Employed Since the Year 1865." *Journal of the Royal United Service Institution* 31, no. 139 (1887): 357–412.

———. "Notes on the Strategy of Our Small Wars." *Minutes of Proceedings of the Royal Artillery Institution* 12 (1884): 531–52, and 13 (1885): 403–20.

———. *Small Wars: Their Principles and Practices*. 1906; reprint, Lincoln: University of Nebraska Press, 1996.

Cannadine, David. "The Context, Performance and Meaning of Ritual: The British Monarchy and the 'Invention of Tradition.'" In *The Invention of Tradition*, ed.

Eric Hobsbawm and Terence Ranger, 101–64. Cambridge: Cambridge University Press, 1992.

Carlyle, Thomas. "Occasional Discourse on the Negro Question." In *Fraser's Magazine for Town and Country* 40 (1849): 670–79.

Carnell, F. G. "Malayan Citizenship Legislation." *International and Comparative Law Quarterly* 1, no. 4 (1952): 504–18.

Carothers, J. C. "The Psychology of Mau Mau." Nairobi: Government Printer, 1954.

Carrington, Charles. *Rudyard Kipling: His Life and Work.* New York: Penguin, 1970.

Carroll, Lewis. *Alice's Adventures in Wonderland & Through the Looking-Glass.* New York: Bantam Classics, 1984.

Carruthers, Susan L. *Winning Hearts and Minds: British Governments, the Media and Colonial Counter-Insurgency, 1944–1960.* London: Leicester University Press, 1995.

Castle, Barbara. *Fighting All the Way.* London: Macmillan, 1993.

Castle, Kathryn. *Britannia's Children: Reading Colonialism Through Children's Books and Magazines.* Manchester: Manchester University Press, 1996.

Castrén, Erik. *Civil War.* Helsinki: Suomalainen Tiedeakatemia, 1966.

Catherwood, Christopher. *Churchill's Folly: How Winston Churchill Created Modern Iraq.* New York: Basic Books, 2005.

Césaire, Aimé. *Discourse on Colonialism.* Translated by Joan Pinkham. New York: Monthly Review Press, 1955 [1950].

Cesarani, David. *Major Farran's Hat: The Untold Story of the Struggle to Establish the Jewish State, 1945–1948.* London: William Heinemann, 2009.

———. "The War on Terror That Failed: British Counter-Insurgency in Palestine 1945–1947 and the 'Farran Affair.'" *Small Wars and Insurgencies* 23, no. 4–5 (2012): 648–70.

Chakrabarty, Bidyut. *Politics, Ideology and Nationalism: Jinnah, Savarkar and Ambedkar Versus Gandhi.* New Delhi: Sage, 2020.

Chakravarty, Gautam. *The Indian Mutiny and the British Imagination.* Cambridge: Cambridge University Press, 2005.

Chanock, Martin. *Law, Custom, and Social Order: The Colonial Experience in Malawi and Zambia.* Cambridge: Cambridge University Press, 1985.

Chapman, F. Spencer. *The Jungle Is Neutral.* New York: Norton, 1949.

Chapman, James. *The British at War: Cinema, State and Propaganda, 1939–1945.* London: I.B. Tauris, 1998.

Charlton, L. E. O. *Charlton: An Autobiography.* London: Faber & Faber, 1931.

Charters, David A. *The British Army and Jewish Insurgency in Palestine, 1945–47.* London: Macmillan, 1989.

———. "British Intelligence in the Palestine Campaign, 1945–47." *Intelligence and National Security* 6, no. 1 (1991): 115–40.

Chatterjee, Partha. *The Black Hole of Empire: History of a Global Practice of Power.* Princeton: Princeton University Press, 2012.

———. *Empire and Nation: Essential Writings 1985–2005.* London: Orient Black Swan, 2010.

———. *The Nation and Its Fragments: Colonial and Postcolonial Histories.* Princeton: Princeton University Press, 1993.

Chaudhuri, Nirad C. *The Autobiography of an Unknown Indian.* 1951; reprint, Berkeley: University of California Press, 1968.

Chetail, Vincent. "The Contribution of the International Court of Justice to International Humanity Law." *International Review of the Red Cross* 85, no. 4 (2003): 235–68.

Christie, Clive J. *A Modern History of Southeast Asia: Decolonisation, Nationalism, and Separatism.* New York: I.B. Tauris, 1996.

Churchill, Winston. *Memoirs of the Second World War.* London: Houghton Mifflin Harcourt, 1990.

———. *My Early Life.* 1930; reprint, London: Eland, 2000.

———. *The Story of the Malakand Field Force: An Episode of Frontier War.* London: Longmans, Green, 1898.

Church Missionary Society. "Kenya—Time for Action!," January 28, 1955.

Clark, Gemma. "Violence Against Women in the Irish Civil War, 1922–3: Gender-Based Harm in Global Perspective." *Irish Historical Studies* 44, no. 165 (2020): 75–90.

Clarke, Austin. *Growing Up Stupid Under the Union Jack.* Toronto: Thomas Allen, 1980.

Clarke, Peter. *The Last Thousand Days of the British Empire: Churchill, Roosevelt, and the Birth of Pax Americana.* New York: Bloomsbury, 2008.

Clayton, Anthony. *Counter-insurgency in Kenya: A Study of Military Operations Against Mau Mau.* Nairobi: Transafrica, 1976.

Cloake, John. *Templer: Tiger of Malaya, the Life of Field Marshal Sir Gerald Templer.* London: Harrap, 1985.

Cobain, Ian. *Cruel Britannia: A Secret History of Torture.* London: Portobello Books, 2012.

———. *The History Thieves: Secrets, Lies and the Shaping of a Modern Nation.* London: Portobello Books, 2016.

Cohen, David. *Churchill and Attlee: The Unlikely Allies Who Won the War.* London: Biteback Publishing, 2018.

Cohen, Gidon. *The Failure of a Dream: The Independent Labour Party from Disaffiliation to World War II.* London: I.B. Tauris, 2007.

Cohen, Hillel. *Army of Shadows: Palestinian Collaboration with Zionism, 1917–1948.* Berkeley: University of California Press, 2008.

Cohen, Michael J. *Churchill and the Jews.* London: Frank Cass, 1985.

———. "Direction of Policy in Palestine, 1936–45." *Middle Eastern Studies* 11, no. 3 (1975): 237–61.

———. "The Moyne Assassination, November 1944: A Political Analysis." *Middle Eastern Studies* 15, no. 3 (1979): 358–73.

———. *Palestine and the Great Powers, 1945–1948.* Princeton: Princeton University Press, 1982.

———. *Palestine, Retreat from the Mandate: A Study of British Policy, 1936–45.* New York: Holmes & Meier, 1978.

———. *Palestine to Israel: From Mandate to Independence.* London: Frank Cass, 1988.

Coleman, David A. "U.K. Statistics on Immigration: Development and Limitations." *International Migration Review* 21, no. 4 (1987): 1138–69.

Collett, Nigel. *The Butcher of Amritsar: General Reginald Dyer.* London: Hambledon, 2005.

Colley, Linda. *The Gun, the Ship, and the Pen: Warfare, Constitutions, and the Making of the Modern World.* New York: Liveright, 2021.

Comaroff, Jean, and John L. Comaroff. *The Truth About Crime: Sovereignty, Knowledge, Social Order.* Chicago: University of Chicago Press, 2016.

Comaroff, John L. "Colonialism, Culture, and the Law: A Foreword." *Law and Social Inquiry* 26, no. 2 (2001): 305–14.

———. "Images of Empire, Contests of Conscience: Models of Colonial Domination in South Africa." In Cooper and Stoler, *Tensions of Empire,* 163–97.

Comber, Leon. *Malaya's Secret Police Force 1945–60: The Role of the Special Branch in the Malayan Emergency.* Singapore: Institute of Southeast Asian Studies, 2008.

Conklin, Alice. *A Mission to Civilize: The Republican Idea of Empire in France and West Africa, 1895–1930.* Palo Alto, CA: Stanford University Press, 1997.

Connell, John. *Auchinleck: A Biography of Field-Marshal Sir Claude Auchinleck.* London: Cassell & Company, 1959.

Constantine, Stephen. *The Making of British Colonial Development Policy, 1914–40.* London: Frank Cass, 1984.

Coogan, Tim Pat. *Michael Collins: The Man Who Made Ireland.* New York: Palgrave, 2002.

———. *1916: The Easter Rising.* London: Weidenfeld & Nicolson, 2005.

Cook, Scott B. "The Irish Raj: Social Origins and Careers of Irishmen in the Indian Civil Service, 1855–1914." *Journal of Social History* 20, no. 3 (1987): 507–29.

Cooper, Frederick. "Modernizing Colonialism and the Limits of Empire." In *Lessons of Empire: Imperial Histories and American Power,* ed. Craig Calhoun, Frederick Cooper, and Kevin W. Moore, 63–72. New York: New Press, 2006.

Cooper, Frederick, and Ann Laura Stoler. *Tensions of Empire: Colonial Cultures in a Bourgeois World.* Berkeley: University of California Press, 1997.

Corum, James S. "The Myth of Air Control: Reassessing History." *Aerospace Power Journal* 14, no. 4 (2000): 61–77.

Cotter, Cornelius P. "Emergency Detention in Wartime: The British Experience." *Stanford Law Review* 6, no. 2 (1954): 238–86.

Craig, F. W. S., ed. *British General Election Manifestos, 1900–1974.* London: Macmillan, 1975.

Crawshaw, Nancy. *The Cyprus Revolt: An Account of the Struggle for Union with Greece.* London: George Allen & Irwin, 1978.

Cripps, Stafford. Foreword to George Padmore, *Africa and World Peace.* London: Secker & Warburg, 1937.

Crossman, Richard. *Palestine Mission: A Personal Record.* New York: Harper & Brothers, 1947.

Crowdy, Terry. *Deceiving Hitler: Double-Cross and Deception in World War II.* London: Osprey, 2008.

Cudjoe, Selwyn R., and William E. Cain, eds. *C. L. R. James: His Intellectual Legacies.* Amherst: University of Massachusetts Press, 1995.

Cummings, Ronald. "Ain't No Black in the (Brexit) Union Jack? Race and Empire in the Era of Brexit and the *Windrush* Scandal." *Journal of Postcolonial Writing* 56, no. 5 (2020): 593–606.

Cunard, Nancy, and George Padmore. "The White Man's Duty: An Analysis of the Colonial Question in Light of the Atlantic Charter." In *Essays on Race and Empire,* ed. Nancy Cunard and Maureen Moynagh, 127–78. Petersborough, Canada: Broadview Press, 2002.

Curtis, Lewis Perry, Jr. *Apes and Angels: The Irishman in Victorian Caricature.* Washington, DC: Smithsonian Institution Press, 1971.

———. *Coercion and Conciliation in Ireland, 1880–1892.* Oxford: Oxford University Press, 1963.

Dalrymple, William. "The Great Divide: The Violent Legacy of Indian Partition." *New Yorker,* June 29, 2015.

———. *The Last Mughul: The Fall of a Dynasty, Delhi, 1857.* London: Bloomsbury, 2006.

Dalton, Hugh. *The Second World War Diary of Hugh Dalton 1940–45,* ed. Ben Pimlott. London: Jonathan Cape, 1986.

Daly, M. W. "The British Occupation, 1882–1922." In *Modern Egypt, from 1517 to the End of the Twentieth Century,* ed. M. W. Daly, 239–51. Vol. 2 of *The Cambridge History of Egypt.* New York: Cambridge University Press, 1998.

Darwin, John. *Britain, Egypt and the Middle East, 1918–1922.* London: St. Martin's Press, 1981.

———. *The Empire Project: The Rise and Fall of the British World-System, 1830–1970.* Cambridge: Cambridge University Press, 2009.

Das, Santanu, ed. *Race, Empire and First World War Writing.* Cambridge: Cambridge University Press, 2011.

Datta, Vishwa Nath. *Jallianwala Bagh.* Ludhiana: Kurukshetra Lyall Book Depot, 1969.

Davidson, Basil. *The Black Man's Burden: Africa and the Curse of the Nation-State.* London: James Currey, 1992.

Davidson, Jim. *The Three-Cornered Life: The Historian WK Hancock.* Sydney: University of New South Wales Press, 2010.

Davis, Clarence B., Kenneth E. Wilburn, and Ronald F. Robinson, eds. *Railway Imperialism.* New York: Praeger, 1991.

Davis, Richard P. "The Influence of the Irish Revolution on Indian Nationalism: The Evidence of the Indian Press, 1916–192." *South Asia* 9, no. 2 (1986): 55–68.

Del Tufo, M. V. *A Report on the 1947 Census of Population.* London: Crown Agents for the Colonies, 1949.

Denoon, Donald. "Participation in the 'Boer War': People's War, People's Non-War, or Non-People's War?" In *War and Society in Africa,* ed. Bethwell A. Ogot, 109–22. London: Frank Cass, 1972.

Desai, Bhulabhi. *INA Defence.* Delhi: INA Defence Committee, 1954.

Dhu Renick, Rhoderick, Jr. "The Emergency Regulations of Malaya Causes and Effect." *Journal of Southeast Asian History* 6, no. 2 (1965): 1–39.

Dicey, Albert Venn. *England's Case against Home Rule.* London: John Murray, 1886.

———. *Introduction to the Study of the Law of the Constitution,* 9th ed., 1885; reprint, London: Macmillan, 1952.

Dimbleby, Jonathan. *The Prince of Wales: A Biography*. Toronto: Doubleday Canada, 1994.

Dirks, Nicholas. *The Scandal of Empire: India and the Creation of Imperial Britain*. Cambridge, MA: Harvard University Press, 2006.

Doherty, M. A. "Kevin Barry and the Anglo-Irish Propaganda War." *Irish Historical Studies* 32, no. 126 (2000): 217–31.

Douglas, Rachel. *Making the Black Jacobins: C. L. R. James and the Drama of History*. Durham, NC: Duke University Press, 2019.

Douglas, R. M. *The Labour Party, Nationalism and Internationalism, 1939–1951*. London: Routledge, 2004.

Douglas, Roy. *Liberals: The History of the Liberal and Liberal Democrat Parties*. New York: Palgrave Macmillan, 2005.

Draper, Alfred. *Amritsar: The Massacre That Ended the Raj*. London: Littlehampton Book Services, 1981.

Drayton, Richard. "Anglo-American 'Liberal' Imperialism, British Guiana, 1953–64, and the World Since September 11." In *Yet More Adventures in Britannia: Personalities, Politics and Culture in Britain*, ed. William Roger Louis, 321–42. London: I.B. Tauris, 2005.

———. "Biggar vs Little Britain: God, War, Union, Brexit and Empire in Twenty-first Century Conservative Ideology." In *Embers of Empire in Brexit Britain*, ed. Stuart Ward and Astrid Rasch, 143–55. London: Bloomsbury Academic, 2019.

———. "Science, Medicine, and the British Empire." In *Historiography*, ed. Robin W. Winks and Alaine Low, 264–76. Oxford: Oxford University Press, 1999.

———. "Where Does the World Historian Write From? Objectivity, Moral Conscience and the Past and Present of Imperialism." *Journal of Contemporary History* 46, no. 3 (2011): 671–85.

Drohan, Brian. *Brutality in an Age of Human Rights: Activism and Counterinsurgency at the End of the British Empire*. Ithaca, NY: Cornell University Press, 2017.

Du Bois, W. E. B. *Dusk of Dawn: An Essay Toward an Autobiography of a Concept of Race*. 1940; reprint, New York: Oxford University Press, 2007.

———. *The Souls of Black Folk*. New York: Dover, 1903.

Duff, Douglas V. *Bailing with a Teaspoon*. London: John Long, 1953.

Dwyer, Philip, and Amanda Nettelbeck. "'Savage Wars of Peace': Violence, Colonialism and Empire in the Modern World." In *Violence, Colonialism and Empire in the Modern World*, ed. Philip Dwyer and Amanda Nettelbeck, 1–22. London: Palgrave Macmillan, 2018.

Dwyer, T. Ryle. *Big Fellow, Long Fellow: A Joint Biography of Collins and De Valera*. New York: St. Martin's Press, 1998.

———. *The Squad and the Intelligence Operations of Michael Collins*. Cork: Mercier Press, 2005.

Edgerton, Robert B. *Mau Mau: An African Crucible*. London: I.B. Tauris, 1990.

Egerton, H. E. *Is the British Empire the Result of Wholesale Robbery?* Oxford: Oxford University Press, 1914.

Eisenstadt, Shmuel N. *The Political Systems of Empires*. New York: Free Press, 1963.

Elder, David A. "The Historical Background of Common Article 3 of the Geneva Convention of 1949." *Case Western Reserve Journal of International Law* 11, no. 1: 37–69.

Elkins, Caroline. "Archives, Intelligence and Secrecy: The Cold War and the End of the British Empire." In *Decolonization and the Cold War: Negotiating Independence*, ed. Leslie James and Elisabeth Leake, 257–84. London: Bloomsbury, 2015.

———. *Imperial Reckoning: The Untold Story of Britain's Gulag in Kenya*. New York: Henry Holt, 2005.

———. "Looking Beyond Mau Mau: Archiving Violence in the Era of Decolonization." *American Historical Review* 120, no. 3 (2015): 852–68.

———. "The 'Moral Effect' of Legalized Lawlessness: Violence in Britain's Twentieth-Century Empire." *Historical Reflections* 44, no. 1 (2018). 78–90.

Ellis, John. *The Social History of the Machine Gun*. Baltimore: Johns Hopkins University Press, 1986.

Engels, Friedrich. *The Condition of the Working-Class in England in 1844*. Translated by Florence Kelley Wischnewetzky. 1887; reprint, Las Vegas: Benediction Classics, 2012.

Epstein, James. "Stuart Hall, Familiar Stranger: A Life Between Two Islands." *American Historical Review* 124, no. 1 (2019): 193–96.

Evans, Peter. *Law and Disorder: Scenes of Life in Kenya*. London: Secker & Warburg, 1956.

Fahmy, Ziad. *Ordinary Egyptians: Creating the Modern Nation Through Popular Culture*. Stanford, CA: Stanford University Press, 2011.

Fanon, Franz. *Wretched of the Earth* (1961). Translated by Richard Philcox. New York. Grove Press, 2004.

Farran, Roy. *Winged Dagger: Adventures on Special Service*. London: Collins, 1948.

Farrell, Brian, and Garth Pratten. *Malaya: 1941–42*. Sydney: Big Sky Publishing, 2009.

Farrell, Brian, and Sandy Hunts, eds. *Sixty Years On: The Fall of Singapore Revisited*. Singapore: Marshall Cavendish Academic, 2003.

Farwell, Bryon. *Queen Victoria's Little Wars*. New York: Harper & Row, 1972.

Favell, Adrian. *Philosophies of Integration: Immigration and the Idea of Citizenship in France and Britain*. New York: St. Martin's Press, 1998.

Fay, Peter Ward. *The Forgotten Army: India's Armed Struggle for Independence, 1942–1945*. Ann Arbor: University of Michigan Press, 1993.

Fedorowich, Kent. "The Problems of Disbandment: The Royal Irish Constabulary and Imperial Migration, 1919–29." *Irish Historical Studies* 30, no. 117 (1996): 88–110.

Fein, Helen. *Imperial Crime and Punishment: The Massacre at Jallianwala Bagh and British Judgment, 1919–1920*. Honolulu: University of Hawaii Press, 1977.

Feinstein, Charles H. "The End of Empire and the Golden Age." In *Understanding Decline: Perceptions and Realities of British Economic Performance*, ed. Peter Clarke and Clive Trebilcock, 212–33. Cambridge: Cambridge University Press, 1997.

Ferguson, Niall. *Empire: How Britain Made the Modern World*. London: Allen Lane, 2003.

———. *The Pity of War: Explaining World War I*. New York: Basic Books, 2000.

Field, John. *Working Men's Bodies: Work Camps in Britain, 1880–1940*. Manchester: Manchester University Press, 2013.

Fieldhouse, D. K. "The Metropolitan Economics of Empire." In *The Twentieth Century*, ed. Judith M. Brown and William Roger Louis, 88–113. Vol. 4 of *The Oxford History of the British Empire*. Oxford: Oxford University Press, 1999.

Fischer, Sibylle. *Modernity Disavowed: Haiti and the Cultures of Slavery in the Age of Revolution.* Durham, NC: Duke University Press, 2004.

Fitzmaurice, Andrew. "Liberalism and Empire in Nineteenth-Century Law." *American Historical Review* 117, no. 1 (2012): 122–40.

Florence, Ronald. *Emissary of the Doomed: Bargaining for Lives in the Holocaust.* New York: Viking, 2010.

Foley, Charles. *Island in Revolt.* London: Longmans, 1962.

———, ed. *The Memoirs of General Grivas.* New York: Praeger, 1965.

Fong, Leong Yee. "Labor Laws and the Development of Trade Unionism in Peninsular Malaysia, 1945–1960." *Journal of the Malaysian Branch of the Royal Asiatic Society* 69, no. 2 (1996): 23–38.

Foot, M. R. D. *SOE in France: An Account of the Work of the British Special Operations Executive in France, 1940–1944.* London: Routledge, 2004.

Forth, Aidan. *Barbed-Wire Imperialism: Britain's Empire of Camps, 1876–1903.* Berkeley: University of California Press, 2017.

———. "Britain's Archipelago of Camps: Labor and Detention in a Liberal Empire, 1871–1903." *Kritika: Explorations in Russian and Eurasian History* 16, no. 3 (2015): 651–80.

Forth, Aidan, and Jonas Kreienbaum. "A Shared Malady: Concentration Camps in the British, Spanish, American and German Empires." *Journal of Modern European History* 14, no. 2 (2016): 245–67.

Foucault, Michel. *Discipline and Punish: The Birth of the Prison.* Translated by Alan Sheridan. London: Routledge, 1995.

Frank, Gerold. *The Deed.* New York: Simon & Schuster, 1963.

Frantzman, Seth J. "Tegart's Shadow." *Jerusalem Post Magazine*, October 21, 2011, 10–14.

Fraser, Cary. "The Twilight of Colonial Rule in the British West Indies: Nationalist Assertion vs Imperial Hubris in the 1930s." *Journal of Caribbean History* 30, no. 1 (1996): 1–27.

Fraser, T. G. "Ireland and India." In *An Irish Empire? Aspects of Ireland and the British Empire*, ed. Keith Jeffery, 77–93. Manchester: Manchester University Press, 1996.

French, David. *The British Way in Counter-Insurgency, 1945–1967.* Oxford: Oxford University Press, 2011.

———. *Fighting EOKA: The British Counter-Insurgency Campaign on Cyprus, 1955–1959.* Oxford: Oxford University Press, 2015.

———. "Toads and Informers: How the British Treated Their Collaborators During the Cyprus Emergency, 1955–59." *International History Review* 39, no.1 (2017): 71–88.

Friedman, Isaiah. *The Question of Palestine: British-Jewish-Arab Relations, 1914–1918.* London: Routledge, 1973.

Fromkin, David. *A Peace to End All Peace: Creating the Modern Middle East, 1914–1922.* New York: Henry Holt, 1989.

Fry, Helen. *The London Cage: The Secret History of Britain's World War II Interrogation Centres.* New Haven, CT: Yale University Press, 2017.

Furedi, Frank. *Colonial Wars and the Politics of Third World Nationalism.* London: I.B. Tauris, 1994.

————. *The Mau Mau War in Perspective.* London: James Currey, 1989.

Gallagher, Catherine, and Stephen Greenblatt. *Practicing New Historicism.* Chicago: University of Chicago Press, 2000.

Gallagher, John. *The Decline, Revival and Fall of the British Empire.* Cambridge: Cambridge University Press, 1982.

————. "Nationalisms and the Crisis of Empire, 1919–1922." *Modern Asian Studies* 15, no. 3 (1981): 355–68.

Gallagher, John, and Ronald Robinson. "The Imperialism of Free Trade." *Economic History Review* 6, no. 1 (1953): 1–15.

Gandhi, Leela. *Affective Communities: Anticolonial Thought, Fin-de-Siècle Radicalism, and the Politics of Friendship.* Durham, NC: Duke University Press, 2006

Gandhi, Rajmohan. *Gandhi: The Man, His People, the Empire.* Berkeley: University of California Press, 2007.

Gandhi, Tushar A. *"Let's Kill Gandhi!": A Chronicle of His Last Days, the Conspiracy, Murder, Investigation, and Trial.* New Delhi: Rupa & Co., 2007.

Ganin, Zvi. *Truman, American Jewry, and Israel, 1945–1948.* New York: Holmes & Meier, 1979.

Gavaghan, Terence. *Of Lions and Dung Beetles: A "Man in the Middle" of Colonial Administration in Kenya.* Devon: Arthur H. Stockwell, 1999.

Gelber, Yoav. *Palestine 1948: War, Escape and the Emergency of the Palestinian Refugee Problem.* Brighton: Sussex Academic Press, 2001.

Geraghty, Tony. *The Irish War: The Hidden Conflict between the IRA and British Intelligence.* London: HarperCollins, 1998.

Gerth, H. H., and C. Wright Mills, eds. *From Max Weber: Essays in Sociology.* 1919; reprint, New York: Oxford University Press, 1946.

Getachew, Adom. *Worldmaking After Empire: The Rise and Fall of Self-Determination.* Princeton: Princeton University Press, 2019.

Ghachem, Malick W. *The Old Regime and the Haitian Revolution.* Cambridge: Cambridge University Press, 2012.

Ghosh, Amitav. *The Glass Palace: A Novel.* New York: Random House, 2001.

Ghosh, Durba. *Gentlemanly Terrorists: Political Violence and the Colonial State in India, 1919–1947.* Cambridge: Cambridge University Press, 2017.

————. "Revolutionary Women and Nationalist Heroes in Bengal, 1930 to the 1980s." *Gender & History* 25, no. 2 (2013): 355–75.

Gillingham, John. "Images of Ireland, 1170–1600: The Origins of English Imperialism." *History Today* 37, no. 2 (1987): 16–22.

Gilroy, Paul. *After Empire: Melancholia or Convivial Culture.* Abingdon: Routledge, 2004.

————. *Small Acts: Thoughts on the Politics of Black Cultures.* London: Serpent's Tail, 1993.

————. *"There Ain't No Black in Union Jack": The Cultural Politics of Race and Nation.* Chicago: University of Chicago Press, 1987.

Glynn, Sean. "Irish Immigration to Britain, 1911–1951: Patterns and Policy." *Irish Economic and Social History* 8, (1981): 50–69.

Golani, Motti. *The End of the British Mandate for Palestine, 1948: The Diary of Sir Henry Gurney.* London: Palgrave Macmillan, 2009.

Goldman, Aaron L. "Defence Regulation 18B: Emergency Internment of Aliens and Political Dissenters in Great Britain During World War II." *Journal of British Studies* 12, no. 2 (1973): 120–36.

Goldsworthy, David. *Colonial Issues in British Politics 1945–1961.* Oxford: Clarendon Press, 1971.

Gollin, A. M. *Proconsul in Politics: A Study of Lord Milner in Opposition and in Power.* New York: Macmillan, 1964.

Golway, Terry. *For the Cause of Liberty: A Thousand Years of Ireland's Heroes.* New York: Simon & Schuster, 2012.

Gooch, John, ed. *Airpower: Theory and Practice.* Milton Park: Routledge, 1995.

Goodman, Giora. "British Press Control in Palestine During the Arab Revolt, 1936–39." *Journal of Imperial and Commonwealth History* 43, no. 4 (2015): 699–720.

Gopal, Priyamvada. *Insurgent Empire: Anticolonial Resistance and British Dissent.* London: Verso, 2019.

Gordon, Leonard A. *Brothers Against the Raj: A Biography of Indian Nationalists Sara and Subhas Chandra Bose.* New York: Columbia University Press, 1990.

Gorrie, John. *Jamaica Papers, No. 6. Illustrations of Martial Law in Jamaica.* London: J. Kenny, 1866.

Gott, Richard. *Britain's Empire: Resistance, Repression and Revolt.* London: Verso, 2011.

Green, L. C. "The Indian National Army Trials." *Modern Law Review* 11, no. 1 (1948): 47–69.

Green, S. J. D. "Geoffrey Dawson, All Souls College and the 'Unofficial Committee for the Destinies of the British Empire,' c. 1919–1931." In *The Tory World: Deep History and the Tory Theme in British Foreign Policy, 1679–2014,* ed. Jeremy Black, 243–64. Abingdon: Routledge, 2016.

Griffiths, Sir Percival. *To Guard My People: The History of the Indian Police.* London: Ernest Benn, 1971.

Grob-Fitzgibbon, Benjamin. *Imperial Endgame: Britain's Dirty Wars and the End of Empire.* New York: Palgrave Macmillan, 2011.

Grose, Peter. "The President Versus the Diplomats." In *The End of the Palestine Mandate,* ed. William Roger Louis and Robert W. Stookey, 32–60. Austin: University of Texas Press, 1986.

Grundlingh, Albert. "The War in Twentieth-Century Afrikaner Consciousness." In *Impact of South African War,* ed. David Omissi and Andrew Thompson, 23–37. New York: Palgrave, 2002.

Grunor, Jerry A. *Let My People Go.* New York: iUniverse, 2005.

Gupta, Brijen K. *Sirajjuddaullah and the East India Company, 1756–1757: Background to the Foundation of British Power in India.* Leiden: E.J. Brill, 1962.

Gupta, Partha Sarathi. "Imperialism and the Labour Government of 1945–1951." In *The Working Class in Modern British History: Essays in Honor of Henry Pelling,* ed. Jay Winter, 99–124. Cambridge: Cambridge University Press, 1983.

Gwynn, Charles W. *Imperial Policing.* London: Macmillan, 1934.

Haber, Eitan. *Menachem Begin: The Legend and the Man.* New York: Delacorte Press, 1978.

Hack, Karl. "Detention, Deportation and Resettlement: British Counterinsurgency and Malaya's Rural Chinese, 1948–60." *Journal of Imperial and Commonwealth History* 43, no. 4 (2015): 611–40.

———. "Everyone Lived in Fear: Malaya and the British Way of Counter-Insurgency." *Small Wars and Insurgencies* 23, no. 4–5 (2012): 671–99.

———. "The Malayan Emergency as Counter-Insurgency Paradigm." *Journal of Strategic Studies* 32, no. 3 (2009): 383–414.

Hajari, Nisid. *Midnight's Furies: The Deadly Legacy of India's Partition.* New York: Houghton Mifflin Harcourt, 2015.

Hale, Christopher. *Massacre in Malaya: Exposing Britain's My Lai.* Stroud: History Press, 2013.

Hall, Catherine. *Civilising Subjects: Metropole and Colony in the English Imagination 1830–1867.* Chicago: University of Chicago Press, 2002.

———. *Macaulay and Son: Architects of Imperial Britain.* New Haven, Yale University Press, 2012.

Hall, Stuart. "Thinking the Diaspora: Home-Thoughts from Abroad." *Small Axe* 6, no. 9 (1999): 1–18.

Halperin, Samuel. *The Political World of American Zionism.* Detroit: Wayne State University Press, 1961.

Hamilton, Nigel. *Monty: The Field-Marshall, 1944–1976.* London: Hamish Hamilton, 1986.

———. *Monty: The Making of a General, 1887–1942.* New York: McGraw-Hill, 1981.

Han Suyin. *. . . And the Rain My Drink.* London: Jonathan Cape, 1959.

———. *My House Has Two Doors.* London: Jonathan Cape, 1980.

Hancock, W. K. *Argument of Empire.* Harmondsworth: Penguin Books, 1943.

———. *Four Studies of War and Peace in This Century.* Cambridge: Cambridge University Press, 1961.

———. *Smuts. Fields of Force, 1919–1950.* Cambridge: Cambridge University Press, 1968.

———. *Smuts. The Sanguine Years, 1870–1919.* Cambridge: Cambridge University Press, 1962.

Hannigan, Dave. *Terence MacSwiney: The Hunger Strike That Rocked an Empire.* Dublin: O'Brien Press, 2010.

Hansen, Randall. *Citizenship and Immigration in Post-war Britain: The Institutional Origins of a Multicultural Nation.* Oxford: Oxford University Press, 2000.

Hansen, Thomas Blom, and Finn Stepputat, eds. *States of Imagination: Ethnographic Explorations of the Postcolonial State.* Durham, NC: Duke University Press, 2001.

Harouvi, Eldad. *Palestine Investigated: The Criminal Investigation Department of the Palestine Police Force, 1920–1948.* Eastbourne: Sussex Academic Press, 2016.

Harper, Timothy. *The End of Empire and the Making of Malaya.* Cambridge: Cambridge University Press, 1999.

———. *Underground Asia: Global Revolutionaries and the Assault on Empire.* Cambridge: Belknap Press, 2021.

Hart, Peter. *The I.R.A. and Its Enemies: Violence and Communities in Cork, 1916–1923.* Oxford: Oxford University Press, 1998.

———. *The I.R.A. at War, 1916–1923.* Oxford: Oxford University Press, 2003.

Hastings, Max. *Bomber Command.* New York: Dial Press, 1979.

Hastings, Warren. *The History of the Trial of Warren Hastings.* London: J. Debrett & Vernon & Hood, 1796.

Hawkins, Richard. "Dublin Castle and the Royal Irish Constabulary (1916–1922)." In *The Irish Struggle, 1916–1926,* ed. Desmond Williams, 167–83. Toronto: Toronto University Press, 1966.

Hay, Alastair, et al. "The Poison Cloud Hanging Over Europe." *New Scientist* 93, no. 1296 (1982): 630–35.

Headrick, Alan C. *Bicycle Blitzkrieg: The Malayan Campaign and the Fall of Singapore.* Chicago: Verdun Press, 2014.

Heather, Randall W. "Of Men and Plans: the Kenya Campaign as Part of the British Counterinsurgency Experience." *Journal of Conflict Studies* 13, no. 1 (1993): 17–26.

Heehs, Peter. *The Bomb in Bengal: The Rise of Revolutionary Terrorism in India, 1900–1910.* Oxford: Oxford University Press, 1993.

Heinlein, Frank. *British Government Policy and Decolonisation, 1945–1963: Scrutinising the Official Mind.* London: Frank Cass, 2002.

Heller, Joseph. "The Anglo-American Commission of Inquiry on Palestine (1945–46): The Zionist Reaction Reconsidered." In *Zionism and Arabism in Palestine and Israel,* ed. Elie Kedourie and Sylvia G. Haim, 139–71. London: Frank Cass, 1982.

———. *The Stern Gang: Ideology, Politics and Terror, 1940–1949.* London: Frank Cass, 1995.

Heller, Tzila Amidror. *Behind Prison Walls: A Jewish Woman Freedom Fighter for Israel's Independence.* Hoboken, NJ: KTAV, 1999.

Henderson, Ian, and Philip Goodhart. *The Hunt for Kimathi.* London: Hamish Hamilton, 1958.

Hensley, Nathan K. *Forms of Empire: The Poetics of Victorian Sovereignty.* Oxford: Oxford University Press, 2016.

Hepple, B. A. "The British Race Relations Acts, 1965 and 1968." *The University of Toronto Law Journal* 19, no. 2 (1969): 248–59.

Herbert, Christopher. *War of No Pity: The Indian Mutiny and Victorian Trauma.* Princeton: Princeton University Press, 2007.

Herman, Arthur. *Gandhi and Churchill: The Epic Rivalry That Destroyed an Empire and Forged Our Age.* New York: Bantam Dell, 2008.

Hill, K., W. Seltzer, J. Leaning, S. J. Malik and S. S. Russell. "The demographic impact of Partition in the Punjab in 1947." *Population Studies* 62, no. 2 (2008): 155–70.

Hitler, Adolf. *Mein Kampf.* 1925, 1927; reprint, New York: Houghton Mifflin, 2001.

Hittle, J. B. E. *Michael Collins and the Anglo-Irish War: Britain's Counterinsurgency Failure.* Dulles, VA: Potomac Books, 2011.

Ho, Thean Fook. *Tainted Glory.* Kuala Lumpur: University of Malaya Press, 2000.

Hoare, Oliver. *Camp 020: MI5 and the Nazi Spies.* Richmond: Public Record Office, 2000.

Hobbes, Thomas, *Leviathan* (1651), ed. A. P. Martinich and Brian Battiste. Peterborough, Ont.: Broadview Literary Texts, 2002.

Hobhouse, Emily. *Report of a Visit to the Camps of Women and Children in the Cape and Orange River Colonies.* London: Friars, 1901.

Hobsbawm, Eric. *Industry and Empire: The Birth of the Industrial Revolution*. New York: New Press, 1999.

———. "Mass-Producing Traditions: Europe, 1870–1914." In *The Invention of Tradition*, ed. Eric Hobsbawm and Terence Ranger, 263–307. Cambridge: Cambridge University Press, 1983.

Hobson, J. A. *Imperialism: A Study*. New York: James Pott & Co., 1902.

Hochschild, Adam. *Bury the Chains: Prophets and Rebels in the Fight to Free the Empire's Slaves*. New York: Mariner Books, 2006.

———. *King Leopold's Ghost: A Story of Greed, Terror, and Heroism in Colonial Africa*. New York: Houghton Mifflin, 1999.

Hoda, Noorul. *The Alipore Bomb Case: A Historic Pre-Independence Trial*. New Delhi: Niyogi Books, 2008.

Hoffman, Bruce. *Anonymous Soldiers: The Struggle for Israel, 1917–1947*. New York: Knopf, 2015.

———. *The Failure of British Military Strategy Within Palestine, 1939–1947*. Ramat Gan: Bar Ilan University, 1983.

———. "The Palestine Police Force and the Challenges of Gathering Counterterrorism Intelligence, 1939–1947." *Small Wars and Insurgencies* 24, no. 4 (2013): 609–47.

Hogan, Gerald, and Clive Walker. *Political Violence and the Law in Ireland*. Manchester: Manchester University Press, 1990.

Holland, Robert. *Britain and the Revolt in Cyprus 1954–1959*. Oxford: Clarendon Press, 1998.

Holmes, Michael, and Denis Holmes, eds. *Ireland and India: Connections, Comparisons, Contrasts*. Dublin: Folens, 1997.

Holmes, Richard. *The Little Field Marshal Sir John French*. London: Jonathan Cape, 1981.

———. *Sahib: The British Soldier in India, 1750–1914*. New York: Harper Perennial, 2006.

Holt, Thomas C. *The Problem of Freedom: Race, Labor and Politics in Jamaica and Britain, 1832–1938*. Baltimore: Johns Hopkins University Press, 1992.

Holwell, John Zephaniah. *India Tracts*. London: T. Becket & P. A. de Hondt, 1764.

Hopkins, A. G. "Macmillan's Audit of Empire, 1957." In *Understanding Decline: Perceptions and Realities—Essays in Honour of Barry Supple*, ed. Peter Clarke and Clive Trebilcock, 234–60. Cambridge: Cambridge University Press, 1997.

———. "Rethinking Decolonisation." *Past and Present* 200, no.1 (2008): 211–47.

Hopkinson, Michael, ed. *The Last Days of Dublin Castle: The Mark Sturgis Diaries*. Dublin: Irish Academic Press, 1999.

Horne, Alistair. *Macmillan, 1957–1986*. London: Macmillan, 1989.

Horne, Edward. *A Job Well Done: A History of the Palestine Police Force, 1920–48*. Tiptree: Anchor Press, 1982.

Howard, Michael. "All Souls and the 'Round Table.'" In *All Souls and the Wider World*, ed. S. J. D. Green and Peregrine Horden, 155–66. Oxford: Oxford University Press, 2012.

Howe, Stephen. *Anticolonialism in British Politics: The Left and the End of Empire 1918–1964*. Oxford: Oxford University Press, 1993.

———. "C. L. R. James: Visons of History, Visons of Britain." In *West Indian Intellectuals in Britain*, ed. Bill Schwarz, 153–74. Manchester: Manchester University Press, 2003.

———. "Colonising and Exterminating? Memories of Imperial Violence in Britain and France." *Histoire@Politique, Politique, culture, société* 11 (2010): 1–18.

———. *Ireland and Empire: Colonial Legacies in Irish History and Culture*. Oxford: Oxford University Press, 2000.

———. "Labour and International Affairs." In *Labour's First Century*, ed. Duncan Tanner, Pat Thane, and Nick Tiratsoo, 119–50. Cambridge: Cambridge University Press, 2000.

Hudson, William Henry, ed. *Macaulay's Essays on Lord Clive*. London: George G. Harrap & Co., 1910.

Hughes, Matthew. "The Banality of Brutality: British Armed Forces and the Repression of the Arab Revolt in Palestine, 1936–39." *English Historical Review* 124, no. 507 (2009): 313–54.

———. *Britain's Pacification of Palestine: The British Army, the Colonial State, and the Arab Revolt, 1936–1939*. Cambridge: Cambridge University Press, 2019.

———. "From Law and Order to Pacification: Britain's Suppression of the Arab Revolt in Palestine, 1936–39." *Journal of Palestine Studies* 39, no. 2 (2010): 6–22.

———. "Palestinian Collaboration with the British: The Peace Bands and the Arab Revolt in Palestine, 1936–39." *Journal of Contemporary History* 51, no. 2 (2015): 291–315.

Hull, Isabel V. *Absolute Destruction: Military Culture and the Practices of War in Imperial Germany*. Ithaca, NY: Cornell University Press, 2005.

Huneidi, Sahar. *A Broken Trust: Herbert Samuel, Zionism and the Palestinians, 1920–1925*. London: I.B. Taurus, 2001.

Hunt, E. K., and Mark Lautzenheiser. *History of Economic Thought*, 3rd ed. Armonk, NY: M.E. Sharpe, 2011.

Hunt, James D. *Gandhi in London*. New Delhi: Promilla & Co., 1978.

Hurewitz, J. C. *The Struggle for Palestine*. New York: Norton, 1950.

Hurst, Steve. *Colonel Gray and the Armoured Cars: The Malayan Police, 1948–1952*. Clayton, Australia: Monash University Press, 2003.

Hussain, Nasser. *The Jurisprudence of Emergency: Colonialism and the Rule of Law*. Ann Arbor: University of Michigan Press, 2003.

———. "Towards a Jurisprudence of Emergency: Colonialism and the Rule of Law." *Law and Critique* 10, no. 2 (1999): 93–115.

Hutt, Allen. *The Post-War History of the British Working Class*. London: V. Gollancz, 1937.

Hyam, Ronald. *Britain's Declining Empire: The Road to Decolonisation, 1918–1968*. Cambridge: Cambridge University Press, 2006.

———. *Britain's Imperial Century 1815–1914: A Study of Empire and Expansion*. London: Palgrave Macmillan, 2002.

Hyam, Ronald, and William Roger Louis, eds. *The Conservative Government and the End of Empire, 1957–1964, Part I, High Policy, Political and Constitutional Change*. London: Stationery Office Books, 2000.

Ibhawoh, Bonny. *Imperialism and Human Rights: Colonial Discourses of Rights and Liberties in African History*. Albany: State University of New York Press, 2007.

Ingrams, Doreen. *Palestine Papers, 1917–1922: Seeds of Conflict*. London: Eland, 2009.

Itote, Waruhiu. *Mau Mau in Action*. Nairobi: Transafrica, 1979.

———. *"Mau Mau" General*. Nairobi: East African Publishing House, 1967.

Jablonsky, David. *Churchill, the Great Game and Total War*. New York: Routledge, 1991.

Jackson, Ashley. *The British Empire and the Second World War*. London: Hambledon Continuum, 2006.

Jalal, Ayesha. *Self and Sovereignty: Individual and Community in South Asian Islam Since 1850*. London: Routledge, 2000.

———. *The Sole Spokesman: Jinnah, the Muslim League and the Demand for Pakistan*. Cambridge: Cambridge University Press, 1985.

Jamaica Committee. *Jamaica Papers, No. 1. Facts and Documents Relating to the Alleged Rebellion in Jamaica and the Measures of Repression*. London: J. Kenny, 1866.

James, C. L. R. *Beyond a Boundary*. Durham, NC: Duke University Press, 1993.

———. *The Black Jacobins: Toussaint L'Ouverture and the San Domingo Revolution*. 1938; reprint, New York: Vintage Books, 1989.

James, Leslie. *George Padmore and Decolonization from Below: Pan-Africanism, the Cold War, and the End of Empire*. London: Palgrave Macmillan, 2015.

James, Robert Rhodes, ed. *Winston S. Churchill: His Complete Speeches, 1897–1963*. New York: Chelsea House, 1974.

James, Winston. "Migration, Racism and Identity Formation: The Caribbean Experience in Britain." In *Inside Babylon: The Caribbean Diaspora in Britain*, ed. Winston James and Clive Harris, 231–87. London: Verso, 1993.

Jankowski, James. *Egypt: A Short History*. Oxford: Oneworld Publications, 2000.

Jasse, Richard L. "Great Britain and Palestine Towards the United Nations." *Middle Eastern Studies* 30, no. 3 (1994): 558–78.

Jeffery, Keith. *Field Marshal Sir Henry Wilson: A Political Soldier*. Oxford: Oxford University Press, 2006.

———. *MI6: The History of the Secret Intelligence Service 1909–1949*. London: Bloomsbury, 2010.

———. "The Second World War." In *The Twentieth Century*, ed. Judith M. Brown and William Roger Louis, 306–28. Oxford: Oxford University Press, 1999.

———, ed. *An Irish Empire?: Aspects of Ireland and the British Empire*. Manchester: Manchester University Press, 1996.

Jenkins, Roy. *Churchill: A Biography*. New York: Farrar, Straus and Giroux, 2001.

Jha, Saumitra, and Steven Wilkinson. "Does Combat Experience Foster Organizational Skill? Evidence from Ethnic Cleansing During the Partition of South Asia." *American Political Science Review* 106, no. 4 (2012): 883–907.

Johnson, Richard R. "Empire." In *A Companion to Colonial America*, ed. Daniel Vickers, 99–117. Oxford: Blackwell, 2003.

Judd, Denis. *The Lion and the Tiger: The Rise and Fall of the British Raj, 1600–1947*. Oxford: Oxford University Press, 2004.

Judt, Tony. *Postwar: A History of Europe Since 1945*. New York: Penguin Books, 2005.

Kalyvas, Stathis N. *The Logic of Violence in Civil War*. Cambridge: Cambridge University Press, 2006.

Kanogo, Tabitha. *Squatters and the Roots of Mau Mau*. London: James Currey, 1987.

Kariuki, Josiah Mwangi. *"Mau Mau" Detainee*. Oxford: Oxford University Press, 1963.

Katz, Samuel. *Days of Fire: The Secret Story of the Making of Israel.* London: W.H. Allen, 1968.

Kautt, W. H. *Ambushes and Armour: The Irish Rebellion 1919–1921.* Dublin: Irish Academic Press, 2010.

———. *Ground Truths: British Army Operations in the Irish War of Independence.* Kildare: Irish Academic Press, 2014.

Kayyali, ʿAbd a-Wahhāb. *Palestine: A Modern History.* London: Routledge, 1978.

Keith-Roach, Edward. *Pasha of Jerusalem: Memoirs of a District Commissioner Under the British Mandate.* London: Radcliffe Press, 1994.

Kelley, Donald R. *Frontiers of History: Historical Inquiry in the Twentieth Century.* New Haven, CT: Yale University Press, 2006.

Kelley, Robin D. G. "A Poetics of Anticolonialism." In *Discourse on Colonialism,* by Aimé Césaire. 7–28. New York: Monthly Review Press, 2000.

Kennedy, Christopher M. *Genesis of the Rising, 1912–1916: A Transformation of Nationalist Opinion.* New York: Peter Lang, 2010.

Kennedy, Dane. *The Imperial History Wars: Debating the British Empire.* London: Bloomsbury, 2018.

———. *Islands of White: Settler Society and Culture in Kenya and Southern Rhodesia, 1890–1939.* Durham, NC: Duke University Press, 1987.

———. "The Ongoing Imperial History Wars." In *Embers of Empire in Brexit Britain,* ed. Stuart Ward and Astrid Rasch, 169–74. London: Bloomsbury Academic, 2019.

Kenyatta, Jomo. *Facing Mount Kenya.* London: Secker & Warburg, 1938.

———. *Harambee! The Prime Minister of Kenya's Speeches 1963–1964.* Oxford: Oxford University Press, 1964.

———. *Suffering Without Bitterness: The Founding of the Kenya Nation.* Nairobi: East African Publishing House, 1968.

Keynes, John Maynard. *How to Pay for the War: A Radical Plan for the Chancellor of the Exchequer.* London: Macmillan, 1940.

Khalidi, Rashid. *The Hundred Years' War on Palestine: A History of Settler Colonialism and Resistance, 1917–2017.* New York: Metropolitan Books, 2020.

———. *Palestinian Identity: The Construction of Modern National Consciousness.* New York: Columbia University Press, 1997.

Khalili, Laleh. *Time in the Shadows: Confinement in Counterinsurgencies.* Stanford, CA: Stanford University Press, 2013.

Khan, Yasmin. *The Great Partition: The Making of India and Pakistan.* 2007; reprint, New Haven, CT: Yale University Press, 2017.

Kheng, Cheah Boon. *Red Star over Malaya: Resistance and Social Conflict During and After the Japanese Occupation of Malaya, 1941–46.* Singapore: NUS Press, 2012.

———. "Some Aspects of the Interregnum in Malaya (14 August–3 September 1945)." *Journal of Southeast Asian Studies* 8, no. 1 (1977), 48–74.

Khoo, Agnes. *Life as the River Flows: Women in the Malayan Anti-colonial Struggle.* Monmouth, Wales: Merlin Press, 2005.

Kincaid, Jamaica. *A Small Place.* New York: Penguin, 1988.

King, Richard H., and Dan Stone, eds. *Hannah Arendt and the Uses of History: Imperialism, Nation, Race, and Genocide.* New York: Berghahn Books, 2007.

King-Clark, R. *Free for a Blast.* London: Grenville, 1988.

Kingston, O. Nigel. *On the March: Labour Rebellions in the British Caribbean, 1934–39.* London: James Currey, 1995.

Kinvig, Clifford. *Scapegoat: General Percival of Singapore.* London: Brassey's, 1996.

Kipling, Rudyard. *Absent-Minded Beggar.* 1899; reprint, New York: HardPress, 2013.

———. *A Diversity of Creatures.* London: Macmillan, 1917.

Kirk-Greene, A. H. M. "The Thin White Line: The Size of the British Colonial Service in Africa." *African Affairs* 79, no. 314 (1980): 25–44.

———, ed. *The Transfer of Power: The Colonial Administrator in the Age of Decolonisation.* Oxford: Committee for African Studies, 1979.

Kissane, Bill. *The Politics of the Irish Civil War.* Oxford: Oxford University Press, 2005.

Kitson, Frank. *Low Intensity Operations: Subversion, Insurgency, Peace-keeping.* London: Faber & Faber, 1971.

Klose, Fabian. "The Colonial Testing Ground: The International Committee of the Red Cross and the Violent End of Empire." *Humanity: An International Journal of Human Rights, Humanitarianism, and Development* 2, no. 1 (2011): 107–26.

———. *Human Rights in the Shadow of Colonial Violence: The Wars of Independence in Kenya and Algeria.* Translated by Dona Geyer. Philadelphia: University of Pennsylvania Press, 2013.

———. "'Source of Embarrassment': Human Rights, State of Emergency, and the Wars of Decolonization." In *Human Rights in the Twentieth Century,* ed. Stefan-Ludwig Hoffman, 237–57. Cambridge: Cambridge University Press, 2011.

Knochlein, Fritz. *The London Cage: The Experiences of Fritz Knochlein.* Canterbury: Steven Book, 2005.

Kolinsky, Martin. *Law, Order and Riots in Mandatory Palestine, 1928–1935.* Basingstoke: Palgrave Macmillan, 1993.

Kolsky, Elizabeth. *Colonial Justice in British India: White Violence and the Rule of Law.* Cambridge: Cambridge University Press, 2010.

Komer, R. W. *The Malayan Emergency in Retrospect: Organization of a Successful Counterinsurgency Effort.* Santa Monica, CA: Rand Corporation, 1972.

Koseknniemi, Martti. "Empire and International Law: The Real Spanish Contribution." *University of Toronto Law Journal* 61, no. 1 (2011): 1–36.

———. *The Gentle Civilizer of Nations: The Rise and Fall of International Law, 1870–1960.* Cambridge: Cambridge University Press, 2001.

Koss, Stephen. *The Rise and Fall of the Political Press in Britain.* London: Fontana Press, 1990.

Kroizer, Gad. "From Dowbiggin to Tegart: Revolutionary Change in the Colonial Police in Palestine During the 1930s." *Journal of Imperial and Commonwealth History* 32, no. 2 (2004): 115–33.

Krozewski, Gerold. "Finance and Empire: The Dilemma Facing Great Britain in the 1950s." *International History Review* 18, no. 1 (1996): 48–68.

Kumar, Raj. *Annie Besant's Rise to Power in Indian Politics, 1914–1917.* New Delhi: Concept Publishing, 1981.

Kunz, Diane B. "The Importance of Having Money: The Economic Diplomacy of the Suez Crisis." In *Suez 1956: The Crisis and its Consequences,* ed. William Roger Louis and Roger Owen, 215–32. Oxford: Clarendon Press, 1989.

Kuracina, William F. "Sentiments and Patriotism: The Indian National Army, General Elections and the Congress's Appropriation of the INA Legacy." *Modern Asian Studies* 44, no. 4 (2010): 817–56.

Kynaston, David. *Austerity Britain, 1945–51*. London: Bloomsbury, 2007.

Lapping, Brian. *End of Empire*. New York: St. Martin's Press, 1985.

Latham, Michael E. *The Right Kind of Revolution: Modernization, Development, and U.S. Foreign Policy from the Cold War to the Present*. Ithaca, NY: Cornell University Press, 2011.

Lau, Arthur. "Malayan Union Citizenship: Constitutional Change and Controversy in Malaya, 1942–48." *Journal of Southeast Asian History* 20, no. 2 (1989): 216–43.

Lawrence, Jon. "Forging a Peaceable Kingdom: War, Violence, and Fear of Brutalization in Post–First World War Britain." *Journal of Modern History* 75, no. 3 (2003): 557–89.

Leadam, I. S. *Coercive Measures in Ireland, 1830–1880*. London: National Press Agency, 1880.

Leakey, L. S. B. *Defeating Mau Mau*. London: Methuen, 1954.

Leasor, James. *Singapore: The Battle That Changed the World*. Cornwall: House of Stratus, 1968.

Lebra, Joyce Chapman. *The Indian National Army and Japan*. Singapore: Institute of Southeast Asian Studies, 1971.

Leebaert, Derek. *Grand Improvisation: America Confronts the British Superpower, 1945–1957*. New York: Farrar, Straus and Giroux, 2018.

Leeson, D. M. *The Black and Tans: British Police and Auxiliaries in the Irish War of Independence, 1920–1921*. Oxford: Oxford University Press, 2011.

Lenin, Vladimir. *Imperialism, The Highest Stage of Capitalism*. 1917; reprint, Chippendale: Resistance Books, 1999.

Leo, Christopher. *Land and Class in Kenya*. Toronto: University of Toronto Press, 1984.

Levin, Naomi. *Politics, Religion, and Love: The Story of H. H. Asquith, Venetia Stanley, and Edwin Montagu*. New York: New York University Press, 1991.

Lewis, David Levering. *W. E. B. Du Bois, 1868–1919: Biography of a Race*. New York: Henry Holt, 1994.

———. *W. E. B. Du Bois, 1919–1963: The Fight for Equality and the American Century*. New York: Henry Holt, 2000.

Lindqvist, Sven. *A History of Bombing*. Translated by Linda Haverty Rugg. New York: New Press, 2001.

———. *"Exterminate All the Brutes": One Man's Odyssey into the Heart of Darkness and the Origins of European Genocide*. Translated by Joan Tate. New York: New Press, 1997.

Lino, Dylan. "Albert Venn Dicey and the Constitutional Theory of Empire." *Oxford Journal of Legal Studies* 36, no. 4 (2016): 751–80.

———. "The Rule of Law and the Rule of Empire: A. V. Dicey in Imperial Context." *The Modern Law Review* 81, no. 5 (2018): 739–64.

Linstrum, Erik. "Facts About Atrocity: Reporting Colonial Violence in Postwar Britain." *History Journal Workshop* 84 (2018): 108–27.

Lloyd George, David. *Memoirs of the Peace Conference*. New Haven, CT: Yale University Press, 1993.

Locke, John. *Two Treatises of Government*. 1689; reprint, New York: Franklin Classic, 2018.

Lonsdale, John. "Kenyatta's Trials: Breaking and Making an African Nationalist." In *The Moral World of Law*, ed. Peter Coss, 196–239. Cambridge: Cambridge University Press, 2000.

Lonsdale, John M., and Bruce J. Berman. "The Labors of *Muigwithania*: Jomo Kenyatta as Author, 1928–45." *Research in African Literatures* 29, no. 1 (1998): 16–42.

Losurdo, Domenico. *Liberalism: A Counter-History*. Translated by Gregory Elliot. London: Verso, 2011.

Lough, David. *No More Champagne: Churchill and His Money*. New York: Picador, 2015.

Loughlin, Martin. *Public Law and Political Theory*. Oxford: Clarendon Press, 1992.

Louis, William Roger. *The British Empire in the Middle East, 1945–1951: Arab Nationalism, the United States, and Postwar Imperialism*. Oxford: Oxford University Press, 1984.

———. "The Dissolution of the British Empire." In *The Twentieth Century*, ed. Judith M. Brown and William Roger Louis, 329–56. Vol. 4 of *The Oxford History of the British Empire*. Oxford: Oxford University Press, 1999.

———. *Ends of British Imperialism: The Scramble for Empire, Suez, and Decolonization*. London: I.B. Tauris, 2006.

———. *Imperialism at Bay: The United States and the Decolonization of the British Empire, 1941–1945*. Oxford: Oxford University Press, 1987.

———. "Public Enemy Number One: The British Empire in the Dock at the United Nations, 1957–71." In *The British Empire in the 1950s, Retreat or Revival?*, ed. Martin Lynn, 186–213. Basingstoke: Palgrave Macmillan, 2006.

———. "Sir Alan Cunningham and the End of British Rule in Palestine." *Journal of Imperial and Commonwealth History* 16, no. 3 (1988): 128–47.

———. "The Tragedy of the Anglo-Egyptian Settlement of 1954." In *Suez 1956: The Crisis and its Consequences*, ed. William Roger Louis and Roger Owen, 43–72. Oxford: Clarendon Press, 1989.

Louis, William Roger, and Ronald Robinson. "The Imperialism of Decolonization." *Journal of Imperial and Commonwealth History* 22, no. 3 (1994): 462–511.

Low, Choo Chin, "The Repatriation of the Chinese as a Counter-insurgency Policy During the Malayan Emergency." *Journal of Southeast Asian Studies* 45, no. 3 (2014): 363–92.

Lowry, Donald. "New Ireland, Old Empire and the Outside World, 1922–49: The Strange Evolution of a 'Dictionary Republic.'" In *Ireland: the Politics of Independence, 1922–1949*, ed. Mike Cronin and John Regan, 164–216. London: Macmillan, 2000.

———. "'The World's No Bigger Than a Kraal': The South African War and International Opinion in the First Age of 'Globalization.'" In *The Impact of the South African War*, ed. David Omissi and Andrew Thompson, 268–88. New York: Palgrave, 2002.

Lundsten, Mary Ellen. "Wall Politics: Zionist and Palestinian Strategies in Jerusalem, 1928." *Journal of Palestine Studies* 8, no. 1 (1978): 3–27.

Luxemburg, Rosa. *The Accumulation of Capital*. Translated by Agnes Schwarzschild. 1951; reprint, Mansfield Center, CT: Martino Publishing, 2015.

Lynn, Martin. *The British Empire in the 1950s, Retreat or Revival?* Basingstoke: Palgrave Macmillan, 2006.

Lyttleton, Oliver. *The Memoirs of Lord Chandos.* London: Bodley Head, 1962.

MacDonald, Ramsey. *Labour and the Empire.* London: George Allen, 1907.

Macintyre, Ben. *Double Cross: The True Story of the D-Day Spies.* New York: Crown, 2012.

Mack, John E. *A Prince of Our Disorder: The Life of T. E. Lawrence.* Cambridge, MA: Harvard University Press, 1998.

MacKenzie, John M. "The Persistence of Empire in Metropolitan Culture." In *British Culture and the End of Empire*, ed. Stuart Ward, 21–36. Manchester: Manchester University Press, 2001.

———. "The Popular Culture of Empire in Britain." In *The Twentieth Century*, ed. Judith M. Brown and William Roger Louis, 212–31. Oxford: Oxford University Press, 1999.

———. *Propaganda and Empire: The Manipulation of British Public Opinion, 1880–1960.* Manchester: Manchester University Press, 1984.

———, ed. *Imperialism and Popular Culture.* Manchester: Manchester University Press, 1986.

Macmillan, Harold. *Riding the Storm 1956–1959.* New York: Harper & Row, 1971.

Maguire, Thomas J. "Interrogation and 'Psychological Intelligence': The Construction of Propaganda During the Malayan Emergency, 1948–1958." In *Interrogation in War and Conflict: A Comparative and Interdisciplinary Analysis*, ed. Christopher Andrew and Simona Tobia, 132–52. London: Routledge, 2014.

Mak, Lanver. *The British in Egypt: Community Crime and Crises, 1882–1922.* London: I.B. Tauris, 2012.

Makonnen, Ras. *Pan-Africanism from Within.* London: Oxford University Press, 1973.

Makovsky, Michael. *Churchill's Promised Land: Zionism and Statecraft.* New Haven, CT: Yale University Press, 2007.

Mandle, Jay R. "British Caribbean Economic History: An Interpretation." In *The Modern Caribbean*, ed. Franklin W. Knight and Colin A. Palmer, 229–58. Chapel Hill: University of North Carolina Press, 1989.

Manela, Erez. *The Wilsonian Moment: Self-Determination and the International Origins of Anticolonial Nationalism.* Oxford: Oxford University Press, 2007.

Mangat, J. S. *A History of the Asians in East Africa, c. 1886 to 1945.* Oxford: Clarendon Press, 1969.

Mantena, Karuna. *Alibis of Empire: Henry Maine and the Ends of Liberal Imperialism.* Princeton: Princeton University Press, 2010.

Marks, Shula, and Stanley Trapido. "Lord Milner and the South African State." *History Workshop* 8, no. 1 (1979): 50–81.

Marshall, Dawn. "History of West Indian Migrations: Overseas Opportunities and 'Safety-Valve' Policies." In *The Caribbean Exodus*, ed. Barry B. Levin, 15–31. Westport, CT: Praeger, 1987.

Marshall, Peter J. *The Impeachment of Warren Hastings.* Oxford: Oxford University Press, 1965.

———. "The Making of an Imperial Icon: The Case of Warren Hastings." *Journal of Imperial and Commonwealth History* 27, no. 3 (1999): 1–16.

————, ed. *The Writings and Speeches of Edmund Burke*. Oxford: Clarendon Press, 1981–2000.

Marston, Daniel. *The Indian Army and the End of the Raj*. Cambridge: Cambridge University Press, 2014.

Masterman, J. C. *The Double Cross System: The Incredible True Story of How Nazi Spies Were Turned into Double Agents*. Guildford: Lyons Press, 2000.

Mathur, L. P. *Kala Pani: History of Andaman and Nicobar Islands with a Study of India's Freedom Struggle*. Delhi: Eastern Book Corporation, 1985.

Matikkala, Mira. *Empire and Imperial Ambition: Liberty, Englishness and Anti-Imperialism in Late Victorian Britain*. London: I.B. Tauris, 2011.

Matthew, H. C. G. *Gladstone, 1809–1898*. Oxford: Oxford University Press, 1997.

Mawby, Spencer. *British Policy in Aden and the Protectorate 1955–67*. London: Routledge, 2005.

May, Alex. "Empire Loyalists and 'Commonwealth Men': The Round Table and the End of Empire." In *British Culture and the End of Empire*, ed. Stuart Ward, 37–56. Manchester: Manchester University Press, 2001.

Mayhew, Thomas. *London Labour and the London Poor*. 1851; reprint, New York: Penguin Classics, 1985.

Mazower, Mark. *Dark Continent: Europe's Twentieth Century*. London: Allen Lane, 1998.

————. *Hitler's Empire: How the Nazis Ruled Europe*. New York: Penguin Books, 2008.

————. *No Enchanted Palace: The End of Empire and the Ideological Origins of the United Nations*. Princeton: Princeton University Press, 2009.

————. "The Strange Triumph of Human Rights, 1933–1950." *Historical Journal* 47, no. 2 (2004): 379–98.

McCarthy, Helen. *The British People and the League of Nations: Democracy, Citizenship and Internationalism, c. 1918–45*. Manchester: Manchester University Press, 2011.

McCoy, Alfred W. *A Question of Torture: CIA Interrogation, from the Cold War to the War on Terror*. New York: Henry Holt, 2006.

McCracken, Donald P. *The Irish Pro-Boers, 1877–1902*. Johannesburg: Perskor, 1989.

————. *MacBride's Brigade: Irish Commandos in the Anglo-Boer War*. Johannesburg: Four Courts Press, 1999.

McCurry, Stephanie. *Women's War: Fighting and Surviving the American Civil War*. Cambridge, MA: Belknap Press, 2019.

McDonagh, Luke. "Losing Ireland, Losing the Empire: Dominion Status and the Irish Constitutions of 1922 and 1937." *International Journal of Constitutional Law* 17, no. 4 (2019): 1192–212.

McGarry, Fearghal. *The Rising: Ireland, Easter 1916*. Oxford: Oxford University Press, 2010.

McGuffin, John. *The Guinea Pigs*. New York: Penguin Books, 1974.

McIntyre, W. David. "The Admission of Small States to the Commonwealth." *Journal of Imperial and Commonwealth History* 24, no. 2 (1996): 244–77.

McKibbin, Ross. *The Ideologies of Class: Social Relations in Britain, 1880–1950*. Oxford: Clarendon Press, 1990.

McMahon, Paul. *British Spies and Irish Rebels: British Intelligence and Ireland, 1916–1945*. Woodbridge, Suffolk: Boydell Press, 2008.

Mead, Matthew. "Empire Windrush: The Cultural Memory of an Imaginary Arrival." *Journal of Postcolonial Writing* 45, no. 2 (2009): 137–49.

Mégret, Frédéric. "From 'Savages' to 'Unlawful Combatant': A Postcolonial Look at International Humanitarian Law's 'Other.'" In *International Law and Its Others*, ed. Anne Orford, 265–317. Cambridge: Cambridge University Press, 2006.

Mehrotra, S. R. *The Emergence of the Indian National Congress*. New Delhi: Rupa, 1971.

Mehta, Uday Singh. *Liberalism and Empire: A Study in Nineteenth-Century British Liberal Thought*. Chicago: University of Chicago Press, 1999.

Meinertzhagen, Richard. *Middle East Diary, 1917–1956*. New York: Thomas Yosellof, 1960.

Messenger, Charles. *Broken Sword: The Tumultuous Life of General Crozier, 1879–1937*. Barnsley, South Yorkshire: Pen & Sword Praetorian Press, 2013.

Metcalf, Barbara D., and Thomas R. Metcalf. *A Concise History of India*. Cambridge: Cambridge University Press, 2002.

Metcalf, Thomas R. *Ideologies of the Raj*. Cambridge: Cambridge University Press, 1994.

———. *An Imperial Vision: Indian Architecture and Britain's Raj*. Berkeley: University of California Press, 1989.

———. *Early Nineteenth Century Architecture in South Africa: A Study of the Interaction of Two Cultures, 1795–1837*. Cape Town: A. A. Balkema, 1963.

Meyers, Jeffrey. *Orwell: Life and Art*. Urbana: University of Illinois Press, 2010.

Middleton, John. *The World of the Swahili: An African Mercantile Civilization*. New Haven, CT: Yale University Press, 1992.

Miliband, Ralph. *Parliamentary Socialism: A Study in the Politics of Labour*. London: George Allen & Unwin, 1961.

Mill, James. *The History of British India*. London: James Madden, 1817.

Mill, John Stuart. *The Collected Works of John Stuart Mill*, ed. J. M. Robson and Alexander Brady. Toronto: University of Toronto Press, 1977.

———. *Dissertations and Discussions: Political, Philosophical, and Historical*. Boston: William V. Spencer, 1867.

———. *Essays on Politics and Society by John Stuart Mill*, ed. J. M. Robson and Alexander Brady. Toronto: University of Toronto Press, 1977.

———. *The Later Letters of John Stuart Mill, 1846–1873*, ed. Francis E. Mineka and Dwight N. Lindley. Toronto: University of Toronto Press, 1972.

———. *Public and Parliamentary Speeches by John Stuart Mill, November 1850–November 1868*, ed. John M. Robson and Bruce L. Kinzer. Toronto: University of Toronto Press, 1988.

Miller, Harry. *The Communist Menace in Malaya*. London: Praeger, 1954.

Miller, Russell. *Boom: The Life of Viscount Trenchard, Father of the Royal Air Force*. London: Weidenfeld & Nicolson, 2016.

Miller, Sergio. "Malaya: The Myth of Hearts and Minds." *Small Wars Journal*, April 16, 2012, https://smallwarsjournal.com/jrnl/art/malaya-the-myth-of-hearts-and-minds.

Milner, Alfred. *England in Egypt*. London: Edward Arnold, 1894.

Ministry of Information and Broadcasting, Government of India. *Homage to the Mahatma*. New Delhi: Publication Division, 2005.

Mishra, Anil Dutta. *Fundamentals of Gandhism*. New Delhi: Mittal, 1995.

Mitter, Sreemati. "Bankrupt: Financial Life in Late Mandate Palestine." *International Journal of Middle East Studies* 52, no. 2 (2020): 289–310.

Mockaitis, Thomas R. *British Counterinsurgency, 1919–60*. London: Macmillan, 1990.

Mohs, Polly A. *Military Intelligence and the Arab Revolt: The First Modern Intelligence War*. New York: Routledge, 2008.

Monteiro, A. Reis. *Ethics and Human Rights*. New York: Springer, 2014.

Montgomery, Bernard Law. *The Memoirs of Field-Marshal the Viscount Montgomery of Alamein*. Cleveland, OH: World Publishing Company, 1958.

Moon, Penderel, ed. *Wavell: The Viceroy's Journal*. London: Oxford University Press, 1973.

Moore, Barrington. *Social Origins of Dictatorship and Democracy: Lord and Peasant in the Making of the Modern World*. Boston: Beacon Press, 1966.

Moore, Bob, and Kent Fedorowich. *The British Empire and Its Italian Prisoners of War, 1940–1947*. New York: Palgrave Macmillan, 2002.

Moore, Charles. *Margaret Thatcher: The Authorized Biography*. London: Allen Lane, 2013.

Moravcsik, Andrew. "The Origins of Human Rights Regimes: Democratic Delegation in Postwar Europe." *International Organization* 54, no. 2 (2000): 217–52.

Morgan, B. W. "Northern Ireland and Minimum Force: The Refutation of a Concept?" *Small Wars and Insurgencies* 27, no. 1 (2016): 81–105.

Morier-Genoud, Eric. "Missions and Institutions: Henri-Philippe Junod, Anthropology, Human Rights and Academia Between Africa and Switzerland, 1921–1966," *Schweizerische Zeitschrift für Religions- und Kulturgeschichte* 105 (2011): 193–219.

Morris, Benny. *1948: The First Arab-Israeli War*. New Haven, CT: Yale University Press, 2009.

Morris, James. *Farewell the Trumpets: An Imperial Retreat*. New York: Harcourt Brace, 1978.

Moses, A. Dirk. *The Problems of Genocide: Permanent Security and the Language of Transgression*. Cambridge: Cambridge University Press, 2021.

Mount, Ferdinand. "Parcelled Out." *London Review of Books* 37, no. 20 (2015): 7–10.

Moyn, Samuel. *The Last Utopia: Human Rights in History*. Cambridge, MA: Belknap Press, 2010.

Mukerjee, Madhusree. *Churchill's Secret War: The British Empire and the Ravaging of India During World War II*. New York: Basic Books, 2010.

Mukherjee, Mithi. "The 'Right to Wage War' Against Empire: Anticolonialism and the Challenge to International Law in the Indian National Army Trial of 1945." *Law & Social Inquiry* 44, no. 2 (2019): 420–43.

Mukherjee, Rudrangshu, ed. *The Great Speeches of Modern India*. London: Random House, 2011.

Mukherjee, Tutun. "Colonialism, Surveillance and Memoirs of Travel: Tegart's Diaries and the Andaman Cellular Jail." In *Travel Writing and Empire*, ed. Schidananda Mohanty, 63–83. New Delhi: Katha, 2003.

Murdoch, H. Adlai. "Enoch Powell, Stuart Hall, and Post-Windrush Caribbean Identity in Britain." *Small Axe: sx Salon* 29 (2018), http://smallaxe.net/sxsalon

/discussions/enoch-powell-stuart-hall-and-post-windrush-caribbean-identity
-britain.

Murfett, Malcolm H., et al., eds. *Between Two Oceans: A Military History of Singapore from First Settlement to Final British Withdrawal*. Singapore: Cavendish Square, 2004.

Murphy, Joseph. *Bloody Sunday: The Story of the 1920 Irish Rebellion*. Bloomington, IN: Xlibris, 2006.

Murphy, Phillip. "Britain as a Global Power in the Twentieth Century." In *Britain's Experience of Empire in the Twentieth Century*, ed. Andrew Thompson, 33–75. Oxford: Oxford University Press, 2012.

Murray-Brown, Jeremy. *Kenyatta*. London: George Allen & Unwin, 1972.

Murthy, R. V. R. "Cellular Jail: A Century of Sacrifices." *Indian Journal of Political Science* 67, no. 4 (2006): 879–88.

Mutua, Makau. *Human Rights: A Political & Cultural Critique*. Philadelphia: University of Pennsylvania Press, 2011.

Nairn, Tom. *The Break-Up of Britain: Crisis and Neo-Nationalism*. New York: Verso, 1981.

Nasson, Bill. *The South African War, 1899–1902*. London: Arnold, 1999.

Neligan, David. *The Spy in the Castle*. London: Prendeville, 1999.

Newbury, Colin. *Patrons, Clients, and Empire: Chieftaincy and Over-rule in Asia, Africa, and the Pacific*. Oxford: Oxford University Press, 2003.

Newsinger, John. *British Counter-Insurgency: From Palestine to Northern Ireland*. New York: Palgrave Macmillan, 2002.

Newsome, David. *The Victorian World Picture: Perceptions and Introspections in an Age of Change*. New Brunswick, NJ: Rutgers University Press, 1997.

Newton, Frances E. *Fifty Years in Palestine*. Wrotham, UK: Coldharbour Press, 1948.

Nicolson, Harold. *Curzon: The Last Phase 1919–1925: A Study in Post-War Diplomacy*. New York: Harcourt, Brace & Howe, 1939.

Nicolson, Nigel, ed. *Diaries & Letters of Harold Nicolson: The Later Years, 1945–1962*. New York: Atheneum, 1968.

Nietzsche, Friedrich. *The Use and Abuse of History*. Translated by Adrian Collins. 2nd ed. New York: Macmillan, 1957.

Norris, Jacob. "Repression and Rebellion: Britain's Response to the Arab Revolt in Palestine of 1936–1939." *Journal of Imperial and Commonwealth History* 36, no. 1 (2008): 25–45.

Novick, Peter. *That Noble Dream: the "Objectivity" Question and the American Historical Profession*. Cambridge: Cambridge University Press, 1988.

Nwafor, Emmanuel. "Wartime Propaganda, Devious Officialdom, and the Challenge of Nationalism During the Second World War in Nigeria." *Nordic Journal of African Studies* 18, no. 3 (2009): 235–57.

O'Brien, Terence Henry. *Milner: Viscount Milner of St. James's and Cape Town, 1854–1925*. London: Constable, 1979.

O'Donovan, Donal. *Kevin Barry and His Time*. Dublin: Glendale, 1989.

Oliver, Peter C. *The Constitution of Independence: The Development of Constitutional Theory in Australia, Canada, and New Zealand*. Oxford: Oxford University Press, 2005.

Omissi, David E. *Air Power and Colonial Control: The Royal Air Force, 1919–1939*. Manchester: Manchester University Press, 1990.

———. "Technology and Repression: Air Control in Palestine, 1922–36." *Journal of Strategic Studies* 13, no. 4 (1990): 41–63.

Omissi, David, and Andrew Thompson, eds. *The Impact of the South African War*. London: Palgrave, 2002.

Oppenheimer, A. R. *IRA, the Bombs and the Bullets: A History of Deadly Ingenuity*. Sallins: Irish Academic Press, 2008.

Orlans, Harold. *T. E. Lawrence: Biography of a Broken Hero*. Jefferson, NC: McFarland, 2002.

Orwell, George. *1984*. New York: Signet Classics, 1961 [1949].

———. *A Collection of Essays*. 1954; reprint, New York: Houghton Mifflin, 1981.

———. *The Lion and the Unicorn: Socialism and the English Genius*. 1941; reprint, New York: Penguin Books, 1982.

———. *The Road to Wigan Pier*. Oxford: Benediction Classics, 2007 [1937].

Orwell, Sonia, and Ian Angus. *An Age Like This, 1920–1940*. New York: Harcourt, Brace & World, 1968.

Osborne, Myles. "Introduction." In *The Life and Times of General China: Mau Mau and the End of Empire in Kenya*, ed. Myles Osborne, 1–39. Princeton: Markus Wiener Publisher, 2015.

Owen, Frank. *The Fall of Singapore*. New York: Penguin Books, 2001.

Owen, Nicholas. "Four Straws in the Wind: Metropolitan Anti-Imperialism, January–February 1960." In *The Wind of Change: Harold Macmillan and British Decolonization*, ed. L. J. Butler and Sarah Stockwell, 116–39. Basingstoke: Palgrave Macmillan, 2013.

Owen, Roger. *The Middle East and the World Economy, 1800–1914*. London: I.B. Tauris, 1993 [1981].

Padmore, George. *Africa and World Peace*. London: Secker & Warburg, 1937.

———. *How Britain Rules Africa*. London: Wishart Books, 1936.

———. *The Life and Struggles of Negro Toilers*. London: Tonbridge, 1931.

———, ed. *History of the Pan-African Congress*. 1947; reprint, London: Hammersmith Bookshop, 1963.

Pagden, Anthony. "Comment: Empire and Its Anxieties." *American Historical Review* 117, no. 1 (2012): 141–48.

———. "Human Rights, Natural Rights, and Europe's Imperial Legacy." *Political Theory* 31, no. 2 (2003): 171–99.

Pakenham, Thomas. *The Boer War*. New York: Random House, 1979.

Palmer, Stanley H. *Police and Protest in England & Ireland, 1780–1850*. Cambridge: Cambridge University Press, 1988.

Pappe, Ilan. *The Ethnic Cleansing of Palestine*. Oxford: Oneworld, 2006.

———. *The Rise and Fall of a Palestinian Dynasty: The Husaynis, 1700–1948*. Berkeley: University of California Press, 2011.

Parker, Jason C. *Brother's Keeper: The United States, Race, and Empire in the British Caribbean, 1937–1962*. Oxford: Oxford University Press, 2008.

Parmar, Inderjeet. "'I'm Proud of the British Empire,' Why Tony Blair Backs George W. Bush." *Political Quarterly* 76, no. 2 (2005): 218–31.

Parsons, Laila. *The Commander: Fawzi al-Qawuqji and the Fight for Arab Independence, 1914–1948*. New York: Hill and Wang, 2016.

Patel, Ian Sanjay. *We're Here Because You Were There: Immigration and the End of Empire*. London: Verso, 2021.

Pedersen, Susan. *The Guardians: The League of Nations and the Crisis of Empire*. Oxford: Oxford University Press, 2015.

———. "The Impact of League Oversight on British Policy in Palestine." In *Britain, Palestine and Empire: The Mandate Years*, ed. Rory Miller, 39–66. Farnham, UK: Ashgate, 2010.

———. "Triumph of Poshocracy." *London Review of Books* 35, no. 15 (2013): 18–20.

Peng, Chin. *My Side of History*. Singapore: Media Masters, 2003.

Pennybacker, Susan D. *From Scottsboro to Munich: Race and Political Culture in 1930s Britain*. Princeton: Princeton University Press, 2009.

Perkins, Anne. *Red Queen: The Authorized Biography of Barbara Castle*. London: Macmillan, 2003.

Perry, John. *Winston Churchill*. Nashville, TN: Thomas Nelson, 2010.

Pictet, John S., ed. *Geneva Convention Relative to the Protection of Civilian Persons in Time of War*. Geneva: International Committee of the Red Cross, 1958.

Pimlott, Ben. *Labour and the Left in the 1930s*. Cambridge: Cambridge University Press, 2008.

Pitts, Jennifer. *A Turn to Empire: The Rise of Imperial Liberalism in Britain and France*. Princeton: Princeton University Press, 2005.

———. *Boundaries of the International: Law and Empire*. Cambridge: Harvard University Press, 2018.

———. "Political Theory of Empire and Imperialism." *Annual Review of Political Science* 13 (2010): 211–35.

Pomeranz, Kenneth. *Great Divergence: China, Europe, and the Making of the Modern World Economy*. Princeton: Princeton University Press, 2000.

Poole, Thomas. *Reason of State: Law, Prerogative and Empire*. Cambridge: Cambridge University Press, 2015.

Porath, Yehoshua. *The Palestine Arab National Movement: From Riots to Rebellion*. London: Frank Cass, 1977.

Porch, Douglas. *Counterinsurgency: Exposing the Myths of the New Way of War*. Cambridge: Cambridge University Press, 2013.

Porter, Bernard. *The Absent-Minded Imperialists: Empire, Society, and Culture in Britain*. Oxford: Oxford University Press, 2004.

———. *Critical of Empire: British Radicals and the Imperial Challenge*. London: I.B. Tauris, 2007.

Pressnell, L. S. *External Economic Policy Since the War*, vol. 1, *The Post-War Financial Settlement*. London: HMSO, 1986.

Probert, Henry. *Bomber Harris: His Life and Times, the Biography of Marshal of the Royal Air Force, Sir Arthur Harris, the Wartime Chief of Bomber Command*. London: Greenhill Books, 2001.

Pyne-Timothy, Helen. "Identity, Society, and Meaning: A Study of the Early Stories of C. L. R. James." In *C. L. R. James: His Intellectual Legacies*, ed. Selwyn R. Cudjoe and William E. Cain, 51–60. Amherst: University of Massachusetts Press, 1995.

Radhakrishnan, Sarvepalli. *Mahatma Gandhi: Essays and Reflections on His Life and Work, Presented to Him on His Seventieth Birthday, October 2nd, 1939.* London: G. Allen & Unwin, 1939.

Raghavan, Srinath. *India's War: World War II and the Making of Modern South Asia.* New York: Basic Books, 2016.

Ram, Moti. *Two Historic Trials in Red Fort.* New Delhi: Moti Ram, 1946.

Ramakrishna, Kumar. *Emergency Propaganda: The Winning of Malayan Hearts and Minds 1948–1958.* Richmond, Surrey: Curzon, 2002.

Rathbone, Richard. "Political Intelligence and Policing in Ghana in the Late 1940s and 1950s." In *Policing and Decolonisation: Politics, Nationalism and the Police, 1917–1965,* ed. David M. Anderson and David Killingray, 84–104. Manchester: Manchester University Press, 1992.

Ratner, Steven R. "New Democracies, Old Atrocities: An Inquiry in International Law." *Georgetown Law Review* 87, no. 3 (1999): 707–48.

Reinharz, Jehuda. *Chaim Weizmann: The Making of a Modern Statesman.* New York: Oxford University Press, 1993.

Renan, Ernest. *Qu'est-ce qu'une nation?* Translated by Ethan Rundell. Paris: Presses-Pocket, 1992.

Rex v. Pinney, Esq. (1832). In *Reports of Cases Argued and Determined in the English Courts of Common Law,* vol. 24. Philadelphia: T. & J.W. Johnson, 1853.

Reynolds, John. *Empire, Emergency, and International Law.* Cambridge: Cambridge University Press, 2017.

Rice, Edward. *Captain Sir Richard Francis Burton: A Biography.* New York: Da Capo Press, 2001.

Rich, Paul B. *Race and Empire in British Politics.* Cambridge: Cambridge University Press, 1986.

Richards, Jeffrey M. "Imperial Heroes for a Post-Imperial Age: Films and the End of Empire." In *British Culture and the End of Empire,* ed. Stuart Ward, 128–44. Manchester: Manchester University Press, 2001.

———, ed. *Imperialism and Juvenile Literature.* Manchester: Manchester University Press, 1989.

Richmond, W. H. "John A. Hobson: Economic Heretic." *American Journal of Economics and Sociology* 37, no. 3 (1978): 283–94.

Ritchie, Sebastian. *The RAF, Small Wars and Insurgencies in the Middle East, 1919–1939.* Shrivenham: Air Media Center, 2011.

Robbins, Simon. "The British Counter-insurgency in Cyprus." *Small Wars and Insurgencies* 23, no. 4–5 (2012): 720–43.

Roberts, Andrew. *A History of the English-Speaking Peoples Since 1900.* New York: HarperCollins, 2007.

Roberts, Granville. Foreword to *The Mau Mau in Kenya.* London: Hutchinson, 1954.

Roberts, Robert. *The Classic Slum: Salford Life in the First Quarter of the Century.* Manchester: Manchester University Press, 1971.

Robinson, Cedric J. *Black Marxism: The Making of the Black Radical Tradition.* 1983; reprint, Chapel Hill: University of North Carolina Press, 2000.

Robinson, John Broadstreet Perry. *Transformation in Malaya.* London: Secker & Warburg, 1956.

Rockel, Stephen J. "Wedding Massacres and the War in Afghanistan." In *Theatres of Violence: Massacre, Mass Killing, and Atrocity Throughout History*, ed. Philip G. Dwyer and Lyndall Ryan, 271–84. New York: Berghahn, 2012.

Rodley, Nigel S., and Matt Pollard. *The Treatment of Prisoners Under International Law*, 3rd ed. Oxford: Oxford University Press, 2009.

Rodney, Walter. *How Europe Underdeveloped Africa*. 1972; reprint, London: Verso, 2018.

Rogan, Eugene, and Avi Shlaim, eds. *The War for Palestine: Rewriting the History of 1948*. Cambridge: Cambridge University Press, 2001.

Roht-Arriaza, Naomi. "State Responsibility to Investigate and Prosecute Grave Human Rights Violations in International Law." *California Law Review* 78, no. 2 (1990): 449–513.

Rooney, David. *Mad Mike: A Life of Michael Calvert*. London: Leo Cooper, 1997.

Roosevelt, Elliot. *As He Saw It*. New York: Duell, Sloan, Pearce, 1946.

Rose, Jonathan. *The Literary Churchill: Author, Reader, Actor*. New Haven, CT: Yale University Press, 2014.

Rose, Norman, ed. *Baffy: The Diaries of Blanche Dugdale 1936–1947*. London: Vallentine Mitchell, 1973.

———. "The Resignation of Anthony Eden." *Historical Journal* 25, no. 4 (1982): 911–31.

Rose, Sonya O. *Which People's War?: National Identity and Citizenship in Wartime Britain, 1939–1945*. Oxford: Oxford University Press, 2003.

Rudner, Martin. "The Draft Development Plan of the Federation of Malaysia, 1950–1955." *Journal of Southeast Asian Studies* 3, no. 1 (1972): 63–96.

Rugemer, Edward B. *Slave Law and the Politics of Resistance in the Early Atlantic World*. Cambridge, MA: Harvard University Press, 2018.

Russell, David. "'The Jolly Old Empire': Labour, the Commonwealth and Europe, 1945–51." In *Britain, the Commonwealth and Europe: The Commonwealth and Britain's Applications to Join European Communities*, ed. Alex May, 9–29. New York: Palgrave, 2001.

Rutledge, Ian. *Enemy on the Euphrates: The Battle for Iraq, 1914–1921*. London: Saqi Books, 2014.

Ryan, Louise. "'Drunken Tans': Representations of Sex and Violence in the Anglo-Irish War (1919–21)." *Feminist Review* 66 (2000): 73–94.

Sachar, Howard M. *A History of Israel from the Rise of Zionism to Our Time*, 3rd ed. New York: Knopf, 2007.

Said, Edward W. *Orientalism*. New York: Vintage Books, 1979.

Sanagan, Mark. *Lightning Through the Clouds: 'Izz al-Din al-Qassam and the Making of the Modern Middle East*. Austin: University of Texas Press, 2020.

Sanders, Ronald. *The High Walls of Jerusalem: A History of the Balfour Declaration and the Birth of the British Mandate for Palestine*. New York: Henry Holt, 1984.

Sandhu, Kernial Singh. "The Saga of the 'Squatter' in Malaya: A Preliminary Survey of the Causes, Characteristics and Consequences of the Resettlement of Rural Dwellers During the Emergency between 1948 and 1960." *Journal of Southeast Asian History* 5, no. 1 (1964): 143–77.

Sands, Philippe. *East West Street: On the Origins of "Genocide" and "Crimes Against Humanity."* New York: Vintage Books, 2016.

Sankey, John. "Decolonisation: Cooperation and Confrontation at the United Nations." In *The United Kingdom—The United Nations*, ed. Erik Jensen and Thomas Fisher, 90–119. London: Macmillan, 1990.

Sareen, T. R., ed. *Indian National Army: A Study*. New Delhi: Gyan Publishing, 2004.

Sarkar, Sumit. *The Swadeshi Movement in Bengal, 1903–1908*. New Delhi: People's Publishing House, 1973.

Sartori, Andrew. "The British Empire and Its Liberal Mission." *Journal of Modern History* 78, no. 3 (2006): 623–42.

———. "The Categorical Logic of a Colonial Nationalism: Swadeshi Bengal, 1904–1908." *Comparative Studies of South Asia, Africa and the Middle East* 23, nos. 1–2 (2003): 271–85.

———. *Liberalism in Empire: An Alternative History*. Berkeley: University of California Press, 2014.

Sartre, Jean-Paul. Preface to Fanon, *The Wretched of the Earth*. Translated by Richard Philcox. 1961; reprint, New York: Grove Press, 2004.

Sassòli, Marco. *International Humanitarian Law: Rules, Controversies, and Solutions to Problems Arising in Warfare*. Cheltenham: Edward Elgar, 2019.

Satia, Priya. "The Defense of Inhumanity: Air Control and the British Idea of Arabia." *American Historical Review* 111, no. 1 (2006): 16–51.

———. *Spies in Arabia: the Great War and the Cultural Foundations of Britain's Covert Empire in the Middle East*. Oxford: Oxford University Press, 2008.

———. *Time's Monster: How History Makes History*. Cambridge: Belknap Press, 2020.

Sato, Shohei. "'Operation Legacy': Britain's Destruction and Concealment of Colonial Records Worldwide." *Journal of Imperial and Commonwealth History* 45, no. 4 (2017): 697–719.

Savage, Michael. *The Dynamics of Working-Class Politics: The Labour Movement in Preston, 1880–1940*. Cambridge: Cambridge University Press, 1987.

Savarkar, Vinayak Damodar. *The Story of My Transportation for Life*. Bombay: Sadbhakti, 1984.

Sayer, Derek. "British Reaction to the Amritsar Massacre 1919–1920." *Past and Present* 131, no. 1 (May 1991): 130–64.

Scarman, Leslie George. *The Scarman Report*. 1981; reprint, New York: Penguin Books, 1982.

Scarry, Elaine. *Body in Pain: The Making and Unmaking of the World*. Oxford: Oxford University Press, 1987.

Schenk, Catherine. "The Sterling Area 1945–1972." In *Handbook of the History of Money and Currency*, ed. Stefano Battilossi, Youssef Cassis, and Kazuhiko Yago, 771–90. Singapore: Springer, 2020.

Schofield, Camilla. *Enoch Powell and the Making of Postcolonial Britain*. Cambridge: Cambridge University Press, 2013.

Schofield, Camilla, and Ben Jones. "'Whatever Community Is, This Is Not It': Notting Hill and the Reconstruction of 'Race' in Britain after 1958." *Journal of British Studies* 58, no. 1 (2019): 142–73.

Schofield, Victoria. *Wavell: Soldier and Statesman.* London: John Murray, 2006.

Schmitt, Carl. *Political Theology* (1922). Translated by George Schwab. Cambridge, MA: MIT Press, 1985.

Schulze, Reinbard. *A Modern History of the Islamic World.* London: I.B. Tauris, 2002.

Schwarz, Bill, ed. *West Indian Intellectuals in Britain.* Manchester: Manchester University Press, 2003.

Scotland, Alexander P. *The London Cage.* London: Evan Brothers, 1957.

Scott, James C. "Try It on the Natives." *London Review of Books* 30, no. 19 (2008): 29–30.

Seal, Anil. *The Emergence of Indian Nationalism: Competition and Collaboration in the Later Nineteenth Century.* Cambridge: Cambridge University Press, 1968.

Seedorf, Martin Frederick. "The Lloyd George Government and the Strickland Report on the Burning of Cork, 1920." *Albion* 4, no. 2 (1972): 59–66.

Seeley, John Robert. *The Expansion of England: Two Courses of Lectures.* 1884; reprint, New York: Wentworth Press, 2019.

Segev, Tom. *One Palestine, Complete: Jews and Arabs Under the British Mandate.* New York: Henry Holt, 2000.

Seibold, Birgit Susanne. *Emily Hobhouse and the Reports on the Concentration Camps During the Boer War, 1899–1902: Two Different Perspectives.* Stuttgart: Ibidem Press, 2011.

Sen, Amartya. *Poverty and Famines: An Essay on Entitlement and Deprivation.* Oxford: Oxford University Press, 2013 [1981].

Sen, Satadru. *Disciplining Punishment: Colonialism and Convict Society in the Andaman Islands.* Oxford: Oxford University Press, 2000.

Sheehan, William. *British Voices from the Irish War of Independence 1918–1921: The Words of British Servicemen Who Were There.* West Link Park, Ireland: Collins Press, 2005.

———. *A Hard Local War: The British Army and the Guerrilla War in Cork, 1919–1921.* Stroud, Gloucestershire: History Press, 2011.

Sherwood, Marika. "'Diplomatic Platitudes': The Atlantic Charter, the United Nations and Colonial Independence." *Immigrants and Minorities* 15, no. 2 (1996): 135–50.

———. "'There Is No New Deal for the Blackman in San Francisco': African Attempts to Influence the Founding Conference in the United Nations, April–July 1945." *International Journal of African Historical Studies* 29, no. 1 (1996): 71–94.

Shindler, Colin. *The Land Beyond Promise: Israel, Likud and the Zionist Dream.* London: I.B. Tauris, 2002.

Shklar, Judith. "Torturers." *London Review of Books* 8, no. 17 (1986): 26–27.

Shlaim, Avi. "The Balfour Declaration." In *Yet More Adventures in Britannia: Personalities, Politics and Culture in Britain,* ed. William Roger Louis, 251–70. London: I.B. Tauris, 2005.

Short, Anthony. *The Communist Insurrection in Malaya, 1948–1960.* London: Frederick Muller, 1975.

Shoul, Simeon. "Soldiers, Riot Control and Aid to the Civil Power in India, Egypt and Palestine, 1919–1939." *Journal of the Society for Army Historical Research* 86, no. 346 (2008): 120–39.

Shuckburgh, Evelyn. *Descent to Suez: Diaries, 1951–1956*. London: Weidenfeld & Nicolson, 1986.

Sikkink, Kathryn. *Evidence for Hope: Making Human Rights Work in the 21st Century*. Princeton: Princeton University Press, 2017.

Sillitoe, Percy. *Cloak Without Dagger*. London: Cassell, 1955.

Silvestri, Michael. *Ireland and India: Nationalism, Empire and Memory*. New York: Palgrave Macmillan, 2009.

———. "'An Irishman Is Specially Suited to Be a Policeman': Sir Charles Tegart and Revolutionary Terrorism in Bengal." *History Ireland* 8, no. 4 (2000): 40–44.

———. "'The Sinn Féin of India': Irish Nationalism and the Policing of Revolutionary Terrorism in Bengal." *Journal of British Studies* 39, no. 4 (2000): 454–86.

———. "The Thrill of 'Simply Dressing Up': The Indian Police, Disguise, and Intelligence Work in Colonial India." *Journal of Colonialism and Colonial History* 2, no. 2 (2001).

Simpson, A. W. Brian. "Detention Without Trial in the Second World War: Comparing the British and American Experiences." *Florida State Law Review* 16, no. 2 (1988): 225–67.

———. "The Devlin Commission (1959): Colonialism, Emergencies, and the Rule of Law." *Oxford Journal of Legal Studies* 22, no. 1 (2002): 17–52.

———. *Human Rights and the End of Empire: Britain and the Genesis of the European Convention*. Oxford: Oxford University Press, 2001.

———. *In the Highest Degree Odious: Detention Without Trial in Wartime Britain*. Oxford: Clarendon Press, 1992.

———. "Round Up the Usual Suspects: The Legacy of British Colonialism and the European Convention on Human Rights." *Loyola Law Review* 41, no. 4 (1996): 629–711.

Simpson, Andrew R. B. *Another Life: Lawrence After Arabia*. Gloucestershire: Spellmount, 2008.

Simpson, Sir John Hope. *Palestine: Report on Immigration, Land Settlement and Development*. Cmnd. 3686. London: HMSO, 1930.

Simson, H. J. *British Rule, and Rebellion*. London: W. Blackwood & Sons, 1937.

Sinclair, Georgina. *At the End of the Line: Colonial Policing and the Imperial Endgame 1945–80*. Manchester: Manchester University Press, 2006.

———. "'Get into a Crack Force and Earn £20 a Month and All Found . . .': The Influence of the Palestine Police upon Colonial Policing, 1922–1948." *European Review of History* 13, no. 1 (2006): 49–65.

———. "The 'Irish' Policeman and the Empire: Influencing the Policing of the British Empire-Commonwealth." *Irish Historical Studies* 36, no. 142 (2008): 173–87.

———. "'The Sharp End of the Intelligence Machine': The Rise of the Malayan Police Special Branch 1948–1955." *Intelligence and National Security* 26, no. 4 (2011): 460–77.

Singh, Gajendra. *The Testimonies of Indian Soldiers and the Two World Wars*. London: Bloomsbury, 2014.

Singh, Harkirat. *The INA Trial and the Raj*. Delhi: Atlantic, 2003.

Singh, N. Iqbal. *The Andaman Story*. New Delhi: Vikas, 1978.

Slocombe, George. *A Mirror to Geneva: Its Growth, Grandeur and Decay.* New York: Henry Holt, 1938.

Smiley, David. *Irregular Regular.* Norwich, UK: Michael Russell, 1994.

Smith, Alison, and Mary Bull, eds. *Margery Perham and British Rule in Africa.* New York: Routledge, 2013.

Smith, Charles. "Communal Conflict and Insurrection in Palestine, 1936–48." In *Policing and Decolonisation: Politics, Nationalism and the Police, 1917–1965,* ed. David M. Anderson and David Killingray, 62–83. Manchester: Manchester University Press, 1992.

Smith, M. L. R. *Fighting for Ireland?: The Military Strategy of the Irish Republican Movement.* London: Routledge, 1997.

Smuts, J. C. *Jan Christian Smuts.* London: Cassell, 1952.

Smyth, Rosaleen. "Britain's African Colonies and British Propaganda During the Second World War." *Journal of Imperial and Commonwealth History* 14, no. 1 (1985): 65–82.

Soares, Anthony Xavier, ed. *Lectures and Addresses by Rabindranath Tagore.* New York: Macmillan, 1980.

Soyinka, Wole. "A Dance of the Forests." In *Collected Plays* 1:1–78. Oxford: Oxford University Press, 1973.

Spanou, Giannis Chr. *EOKA: That's How Greeks Fight.* Translated by Domniki Georgopoloulou. Nicosia: Andreas I. Spanos, 1997.

Spence, David Owen. "Beyond Talwar: A Cultural Reappraisal of the 1946 Royal Indian Navy Mutiny." *Journal of Imperial and Commonwealth History* 43, no. 3 (2015): 489–508.

Spencer, Ian R. G. *British Immigration Policy Since 1939: The Making of Multi-Racial Britain.* London: Routledge, 1997.

Spies, S. B. *Methods of Barbarism?: Roberts and Kitchener and Civilians in the Boer Republics, January 1900–May 1902.* Cape Town: Human & Rousseau, 1977.

Spies, S. B., and Gail Nattrass, eds. *Jan Smuts: Memoirs of the Boer War.* Johannesburg: Jonathan Ball, 1994.

Springhall, John. *Youth, Empire and Society: British Youth Movements, 1883–1942.* London: Croom Helm, 1977.

Stammers, Neil. *Civil Liberties in Britain During the Second World War: A Political Study.* London: Croom Helm, 1983.

Stedman Jones, Gareth. *Outcast London: A Study in the Relationship Between Classes in Victorian Society.* 1971; reprint, London: Verso, 2014.

Stein, Leonard. *The Balfour Declaration.* London: Valentine-Mitchell, 1961.

Stenson, Michael. *The 1948 Communist Revolt in Malaya.* Singapore: Institute of Southeast Asian Studies, 1971.

Stephen, James Fitzjames. *Horae Sabbaticae, Reprint of Articles Contributed to "The Saturday Review."* London: Macmillan, 1892.

———. *Liberty, Equality, Fraternity* (1873). Ed. R. J. White. Cambridge: Cambridge University Press, 1967.

Stephen, Leslie. *The Life of Sir James Fitzjames Stephen.* London: Elder & Co., 1895.

Stephens, R. W. G. "A Digest of Ham." In *Camp 020: MI5 and the Nazi Spies,* by Oliver Hoare. Richmond: Public Record Office, 2000.

Stevenson, Robert Louis. *The Strange Case of Dr. Jekyll and Mr. Hyde*, in *Dr. Jekyll and Mr. Hyde with The Merry Men & Other Tales and Fables*. Hertfordshire: Wordsworth Editions, 1993 [1886].

Stocking, George W., Jr. *Victorian Anthropology*. London: Free Press, 1991.

———, ed. *Race, Culture, and Evolution: Essays in the History of Anthropology*. Chicago: University of Chicago Press, 1982.

Stockwell, A. J. "British Imperial Policy and Decolonization in Malaya 1942–52." *Journal of Imperial and Commonwealth History* 13, no. 1 (1984): 68–87.

———. *Malaya: The Communist Insurrection 1948–1953*. London: HMSO, 1995.

———. "Policing During the Malayan Emergency, 1948–60: Communism, Communalism and Decolonisation." In *Policing and Decolonisation: Politics, Nationalism and the Police, 1917–1965*, ed. David M. Anderson and David Killingray, 105–26. Manchester: Manchester University Press, 1992.

Stockwell, Sarah. *The British End of the British Empire*. Cambridge: Cambridge University Press, 2018.

Stokes, Eric. *The English Utilitarians in India*. Oxford: Oxford University Press, 1959.

———. "Milnerism." *Historical Journal* 5, no. 1 (1962): 47–60.

———. *The Peasant and the Raj: Studies in Agrarian Society and Peasant Rebellion in Colonial India*. Cambridge: Cambridge University Press, 1980.

Stoler, Ann Laura. *Imperial Debris: On Ruins and Ruination*. Durham, NC: Duke University Press, 2013.

———. "Perceptions of Protest: Defining the Dangerous in Colonial Sumatra," *American Ethnologist* 12, no. 4 (1985): 642–58.

———. *Race and the Education of Desire: Foucault's History of Sexuality and the Colonial Order of Things*. Durham, NC: Duke University Press, 1995.

Stoler, Ann Laura, and Frederick Cooper. "Between Metropole and Colony: Rethinking a Research Agenda." In Cooper and Stoler, *Tensions of Empire*, 1–56.

Stora, Benjamin. *Histoire de l'Algérie coloniale, 1830–1954*. Paris: La Découverte, 1999.

St. Pierre, Maurice. "The 1938 Jamaica Disturbances. A Portrait of Mass Reaction Against Colonialism." *Social and Economic Studies* 27, no. 2 (1978): 171–96.

Strachey, John. *The End of Empire*. New York: Random House, 1959.

Strauch, Judith. "Chinese New Villages of the Malayan Emergency, a Generation Later: A Case Study." *Contemporary Southeast Asia* 3, no. 2 (1981): 126–39.

Streatfeild, Dominic. *Brainwash: The Secret History of Mind Control*. London: Thomas Dunne Books, 2007.

Strong, James. *Public Opinion, Legitimacy and Tony Blair's War in Iraq*. New York: Routledge, 2017.

Sullivan, Eileen P. "Liberalism and Imperialism: J. S. Mill's Defense of the British Empire." *Journal of the History of Ideas* 44, no. 4 (1983): 599–617.

Sutton, Alex. "British Imperialism and the Political Economy of Malayan Independence." *Journal of Imperial and Commonwealth History* 44, no. 3 (2016): 470–91.

Swedenburg, Ted. *Memories of Revolt: The 1936–1939 Rebellion and the Palestinian National Past*. Fayetteville: University of Arkansas Press, 2003.

———. "The Role of the Palestinian Peasantry in the Great Revolt (1936–1939)." In *Islam, Politics, and Social Movements*, eds. Edmund Burke and Ira Lapidus, 169–203. Berkeley: University of California Press, 1988.

Swinson, Arthur. *Six Minutes to Sunset: The Story of General Dyer and the Amritsar Affair.* London: P. Davies, 1964.

Sykes, Christopher. *Orde Wingate: A Biography.* Cleveland, OH: World Publishing Company, 1959.

Symonds, Richard. *Oxford and Empire: The Last Lost Cause?* Oxford: Oxford University Press, 1993.

Tagore, Rabindranath. *The Essential Tagore*, ed. Fakrul Alam and Radha Chakravarty. Cambridge, MA: Belknap Press, 2011.

Talbot, Ian. *Khizr Tiwana: The Punjab Unionist Party and the Partition of India.* Richmond, Surrey: Curzon Press, 1996.

Talwar, Bhagat Ram. *The Talwars of Pathan Land and Subhas Chandra's Great Escape.* New Delhi: People's Publishing House, 1976.

Tamari, Salim. *The Great War and the Remaking of Palestine.* Oakland: University of California Press, 2017.

Tan, Teng Phee. "'Like a Concentration Camp, Iah': Chinese Grassroots Experience of the Emergency and New Villages in British Colonial Malaya." *Chinese Southern Diaspora Studies* 3 (2009): 216–28.

———. "Oral History and People's Memory of the Malayan Emergency (1948–60): The Case of Pulai." *Sojourn: Journal of Social Issues in Southeast Asia* 27, no. 1 (2012): 84–119.

Tegart, Sir Charles. *Terrorism in India.* Calcutta: New Age, 1983.

Tharoor, Shashi. *Nehru: The Invention of India.* New York: Arcade Press, 2003.

Thiong'o, Ngũgĩ wa. *Weep Not, Child.* London: Heinemann, 1964.

Thomas, Martin. *Empires of Intelligence: Security Service and Colonial Disorder After 1914.* Berkeley: University of California Press, 2008.

———. *Violence and Colonial Order: Police, Workers, and Protest in the European Colonial Empires, 1918–40.* Cambridge: Cambridge University Press, 2012.

Thompson, Andrew. "Publicity, Philanthropy and Commemoration: British Society and the War." In *Impact of South African War*, ed. David Omissi and Andrew Thompson, 99–123. New York: Palgrave, 2002.

———. *The Empire Strikes Back? The Impact of Imperialism on Britain from the Mid-Nineteenth Century.* London: Harlow, 2005.

Thompson, Andrew, and Meaghan Kowalsky. "Social Life and Cultural Representation: Empire in the Public Imagination." In *Britain's Experience of Empire in the Twentieth Century*, ed. Andrew Thompson, 251–97. Oxford: Oxford University Press, 2012.

Thompson, J. Lee. *A Life of Alfred, Viscount Milner of St. James's and Cape Town, 1854–1925.* Vancouver: Fairleigh Dickinson University Press, 2007.

———. *A Wider Patriotism: Alfred Milner and the British Empire.* London: Pickering & Chatto, 2007.

Thompson, Sir Robert. *Defeating Communist Insurgency: The Lessons of Malaya and Vietnam.* New York: Frederick A. Praeger, 1966.

———. *No Exit from Vietnam.* New York: David McKay, 1970.

Throup, David. *Economic and Social Origins of Mau Mau.* London: James Currey, 1987.

Tignor, Robert L. *W. Arthur Lewis and the Birth of Development Economics.* Princeton: Princeton University Press, 2005.

Todman, Daniel. *Britain's War: Into Battle, 1937–1941.* Oxford: Oxford University Press, 2016.

Tomkins, Stephen. *David Livingstone: The Unexplored Story.* London: Lion Books, 2013.

Tomlinson, Sally. "Enoch Powell, Empires, Immigrants and Education." *Race Ethnicity and Education* 21, no. 1 (2018): 1–14.

Toolis, Kevin. *Rebel Hearts: Journeys within the IRA's Soul.* New York: St. Martin's Griffin, 1997.

Townshend, Charles. *Britain's Civil Wars: Counterinsurgency in the Twentieth Century.* London: Faber & Faber, 1986.

———. *The British Campaign in Ireland, 1919–1921: The Development of Political and Military Policies.* Oxford: Oxford University Press, 1975.

———. "Civilization and 'Frightfulness': Air Control in the Middle East Between the Wars." In *Warfare, Diplomacy and Politics,* ed. Chris Wrigley, 142–62. London: Hamish Hamilton, 1986.

———. "The Defence of Palestine: Insurrection and Public Security, 1936–1939." *English Historical Review* 103, no. 409 (1988): 917–49.

———. *Easter 1916: The Irish Rebellion.* Chicago: Ivan R. Dee, 2005.

———. *Political Violence in Ireland: Government and Resistance since 1848.* Oxford: Oxford University Press, 1983.

Toye, Hugh. *The Springing Tiger: A Study of the Indian National Army and of Netaji.* 1959; reprint, New Delhi: Allied, 2009.

Toye, Richard. "Churchill and Britain's Financial Dunkirk." *Twentieth Century Britain* 15, no. 4 (2004): 329–60.

———. *Churchill's Empire: The World That Made Him and the World He Made.* New York: St. Martin's Griffin, 2010.

Toynbee, Arnold. *A Study of History.* London: Oxford University Press, 1948.

Trapido, Stanley. "Liberalism in the Cape in the 19th and 20th Centuries." *Collected Seminar Papers. Institute of Commonwealth Studies* 17 (1974): 53–66.

Travers, Robert. *Ideology and Empire in Eighteenth-Century India: The British in Bengal.* Cambridge: Cambridge University Press, 2007.

Truman, Harry S. *Memoirs: Years of Trial and Hope.* New York: Doubleday, 1956.

Tucker, S. D. *Great British Eccentrics.* London: Amberley, 2015.

Tucker, Samuel L., ed. *Macaulay's Essay on Warren Hastings.* New York: Longmans, Green, 1910.

Twaddle, Michael. "Margery Perham and Africans and British Rule: A Wartime Publication." *Journal of Imperial and Commonwealth History* 19, no. 3 (1991): 100–111.

Twigger, Robert. *Red Nile: A Biography of the World's Greatest River.* New York: St. Martin's Press, 2013.

Ucko, David H., and Robert Egnell. *Counterinsurgency in Crisis: Britain and the Challenges of Modern Warfare.* New York: Columbia University Press, 2013.

Urbinati, Nadia. "The Many Heads of the Hydra: J. S. Mill on Despotism." In *J. S. Mill's Political Thought: A Bicentennial Reassessment,* ed. Nadia Urbinati and Alex Zakaras, 66–97. Cambridge: Cambridge University Press, 2007.

Van Dijk, Boyd. "Human Rights in War: On the Entangled Foundations of the 1949 Geneva Conventions." *American Journal of International Law* 112, no. 4 (2018): 553–82.

Van Heyningen, Elizabeth. *The Concentration Camp of the Anglo-Boer War: A Social History*. Auckland Park: Jacana Media, 2013.

Vereté, Mayir. "The Balfour Declaration and Its Makers." *Middle Eastern Studies* 6, no. 1 (1970): 48–76.

Vickers, Rhiannon. *The Labour Party and the World*, vol. 1, *The Evolution of Labour's Foreign Policy, 1900–1951*. Manchester: Manchester University Press, 2003.

Vinogradov, Amal. "The 1920 Revolt in Iraq Reconsidered: The Role of Tribes in National Politics." *International Journal of Middle Eastern Studies* 3, no. 2 (1972): 123–39.

Viotti da Costa, Emilia. *Crown of Glory, Tears of Blood: The Demerara Slave Rebellion of 1823*. New York: Oxford University Press, 1994.

Von Eschen, Penny M. *Race Against Empire: Black Americans and Anticolonialism, 1937–1957*. Ithaca, NY: Cornell University Press, 1997.

Von Tunzelmann, Alex. *Indian Summer: The Secret History of the End of an Empire*. New York: Picador, 2007.

Vrdoljak, Ana Filipa. "Human Rights and Genocide: The Work of Lauterpacht and Lemkin in Modern International Law." *The European Journal of International Law* 20, no. 4 (2009): 1163–94.

Waghelstein, John D. *El Salvador: Observations and Experiences in Counterinsurgency*. Carlisle Barracks, PA: U.S. Army War College, 1984.

Wagner, Kim A. *Amritsar 1919: An Empire of Fear and the Making of a Massacre*. New Haven, CT: Yale University Press, 2019.

———. "Savage Warfare: Violence and the Rule of Colonial Difference in Early British Counterinsurgency." *History Workshop Journal* 85 (2018): 217–37.

Walsh, Maurice. *The News from Ireland: Foreign Correspondents and the Irish Revolution*. London: I.B. Tauris, 2008.

Walton, Calder. "British Intelligence and the Mandate of Palestine: Threats to British National Security Immediately After the Second World War." *Intelligence and National Security* 23, no. 4 (2008): 435–62.

———. *Empire of Secrets: British Intelligence, the Cold War and the Twilight of Empire*. London: Harper Press, 2013.

Ward, Alan J. "Lloyd George and the 1918 Conscription Crisis." *The Historical Journal* 17, no. 1 (1974): 107–29.

Ward, Stuart, ed. *British Culture and the End of Empire*. Manchester: Manchester University Press, 2001.

Ward, Stuart, and Astrid Rasch. *Embers of Empire in Brexit Britain*. London: Bloomsbury Academic, 2019.

Warren, Alan. *Singapore, 1942: Britain's Greatest Defeat*. London: Hambledon & London, 2003.

———. *World War II: A Military History*. Stroud, Gloucestershire: History Press, 2008.

Wasserstein, Bernard. "The Assassination of Lord Moyne." *Transactions and Miscellanies (Jewish Historical Society of England)* 27 (1978–80): 72–83.

———. *The British in Palestine: The Mandatory Government and the Arab-Jewish Conflict, 1917–1929*. Oxford: Blackwell, 1991.

Weber, Max. "Politics as a Vocation." In *From Max Weber: Essays in Sociology*. Edited and translated by H. H. Gerth and C. Wright Mills, 77–128. 1919; reprint, New York: Oxford University Press, 1946.

Weizmann, Chaim. *The Letters and Papers of Chaim Weizmann*, vol. 18, *January 1937–December 1938*, ed. Barnet Litvinoff and Aaron Klieman. London: Jerusalem: Transaction, 1979.

———. *Trial and Error: The Autobiography of Chaim Weizmann*. London: Hamish Hamilton, 1949.

Wertheim, Stephen. "The League of Nations: A Retreat From International Law?" *Journal of Global History* 7, no. 2 (2012): 210–32.

West, Nigel. *The Guy Liddell Diaries*. 2 vols. London: Routledge, 2005.

Westad, Odd Arne. *The Global Cold War: Third World Interventions and the Making of Our Times*. Cambridge: Cambridge University Press, 2005.

Westrate, Bruce. *The Arab Bureau: British Police in the Middle East, 1916–1920*. University Park: Pennsylvania State University Press, 1992.

Wheeler-Bennett, John W. *John Anderson, Viscount Waverley*. London: Palgrave Macmillan, 1962.

White, Gerry, and Brendan O'Shea. *The Burning of Cork*. Cork: Mercier Press, 2006.

White, Nicholas J. "The Beginnings of Crony Capitalism: Business, Politics and Economic Development in Malaysia, c. 1955–70." *Modern Asia Studies* 38, no. 2 (2004): 389–417.

———. *Business, Government, and the End of Empire: Malaya, 1942–1957*. Oxford: Oxford University Press, 1996.

Whitmore, W. J. Brennan. *With the Irish in Frongoch*. Cork: Mercier Press, 2013.

Whittingham, Daniel. "'Savage Warfare': C. E. Callwell, the Roots of Counter-Insurgency, and the Nineteenth Century Context." In *British Ways of Counter-insurgency: A Historical Perspective*, ed. Matthew Hughes, 13–30. London: Routledge, 2013.

Williams, Eric. *Capitalism and Slavery*. Chapel Hill: University of North Carolina Press, 1994.

Wills, Clair. *Dublin 1916: The Siege of the GPO*. London: Profile Books, 2010.

Wilson, A. N. *After the Victorians: The Decline of Britain in the World*. New York: Picador, 2005.

Wilson, Evan M. *Decision on Palestine: How the U.S. Came to Recognize Israel*. Stanford, CA: Stanford University Press, 1979.

Wilson, Jon. *The Chaos of Empire: The British Raj and the Conquest of India*. New York: Public Affairs, 2016.

Wilson, R. Dare. *Cordon and Search with the Sixth Airborne Division in Palestine*. Nashville, TN: Battery Press, 1989.

Winder, Alex. "Anticolonial Uprising and Communal Justice in Twentieth-Century Palestine." *Radical History Review* 2020, no. 137 (2020): 75–95.

———. "The 'Western Wall' Riots of 1929: Religious Boundaries and Communal Violence." *Journal of Palestine Studies* 42, no. 1 (2012): 6–23.

Winks, Robin W., and Alaine Low, eds. *Historiography*, vol. 5 of *The Oxford History of the British Empire*. Oxford: Oxford University Press, 1999.

Wolpert, Stanley. *Gandhi's Passion: The Life and Legacy of Mahatma Gandhi*. Oxford: Oxford University Press, 2001.

————. *Shameful Flight: The Last Years of the British Empire in India.* Oxford: Oxford University Press, 2006.

Wolton, Suke. *Lord Hailey, the Colonial Office and the Politics of Race and Empire in the Second World War: The Loss of White Prestige.* New York: St. Martin's Press, 2000.

Woods, Philip. "From Shaw to Shantaram: The Film Advisory Board and the Making of British Propaganda Films in India, 1940–43." *Historical Journal of Film, Radio and Television* 21, no. 3 (2001): 293–308.

Woodward, E. L., ed. *Documents on British Foreign Policy, 1919–1939.* London: HMSO, 1952.

Wring, Dominic. *The Politics of Marketing the Labour Party.* New York: Palgrave Macmillan, 2005.

Young, Crawford. *The African Colonial State in Comparative Perspective.* New Haven, CT: Yale University Press, 1994.

Zouplna, Jan. "Revisionist Zionism: Image, Reality and the Quest for Historical Narrative." *Middle Eastern Studies* 44, no. 1 (2008); 3–27.

Zweig, Ronald. *Britain and Palestine During the Second World War.* Woodbridge: Boydell Press, 1986.

Index

Page numbers in *italics* refer to captions.

ILLUSTRATION CREDITS

532 Picture Post/Getty Images
544 Popperfoto/Getty Images
551 Popperfoto/Getty Images
555 Map by Mapping Specialists
558 Popperfoto/Getty Images
559 Popperfoto/Getty Images
562 Estate of Alistair Mathieson
592 Trinity Mirror/Mirrorpix/Alamy Stock Photo
594 Keystone Press/Alamy Stock Photo
600 Map by Mapping Specialists
606 Heritage Image Partnership Ltd/Alamy Stock Photo
608 Picture Post/Getty Images
610 Corbis Historical/Getty Images
612 Associated Press
613 Associated Press
619 Pictorial Press Ltd/Alamy Stock Photo
621 Everett Collection Historical/Alamy Stock Photo
623 Keystone Press/Alamy Stock Photo
631 PA Images/Alamy Stock Photo
632 Keystone Press/Alamy Stock Photo
634 Trinity Mirror/Mirrorpix /Alamy Stock Photo
636 roger tillberg/Alamy Stock Photo
642 Dominic Lipinski/Associated Press
644 Arcaid Images/Alamy Stock Photo
646 Ian Mcilgorm
657 REUTERS/Alamy Stock Photo
662 Trinity Mirror/Mirrorpix/Alamy Stock Photo
663 Contraband Collection/Alamy Stock Photo
665 Allan Cash Picture Library/Alamy Stock Photo
667 Trinity Mirror/Mirrorpix /Alamy Stock Photo
670 FLHC Maps 15/Alamy Stock Photo
674 Janine Wiedel Photolibrary/Alamy Stock Photo

A NOTE ABOUT THE AUTHOR

Caroline Elkins is professor of history and of African and African American studies at Harvard University, with appointments at Harvard Business School and Harvard Law School. She is the author of *Imperial Reckoning: The Untold Story of Britain's Gulag in Kenya*, which won the Pulitzer Prize for General Nonfiction in 2006, was selected as one of *The Economist*'s best history books of the year, and was an editor's choice for *The New York Times*. She has co-edited volumes on settler colonialism and reparations and written numerous articles and book chapters. She lives in Watertown and Marion, Massachusetts, with her wife and two sons.

A NOTE ON THE TYPE

This book was set in Janson, a typeface long thought to have been made by the Dutchman Anton Janson, who was a practicing typefounder in Leipzig during the years 1668–1687. However, it has been conclusively demonstrated that these types are actually the work of Nicholas Kis (1650–1702), a Hungarian, who most probably learned his trade from the master Dutch typefounder Dirk Voskens. The type is an excellent example of the influential and sturdy Dutch types that prevailed in England up to the time William Caslon (1692–1766) developed his own incomparable designs from them.

Composed by North Market Street Graphics,
Lancaster, Pennsylvania

Printed and bound by Lakeside Book Company,
Harrisonburg, Virginia